McGRAW-HILL

Microsoft Office 97 Professional

McGRAW-HILL

Microsoft Office 97 Professional

Timothy J. O'Leary
Arizona State University

Linda I. O'Leary

Irwin McGraw-Hill

Boston, Massachusetts Burr Ridge, Illinois Dubuque, Iowa
Madison, Wisconsin New York, New York San Francisco, California St. Louis, Missouri

Irwin/McGraw-Hill

A Division of The ***McGraw-Hill*** *Companies*

Microsoft Office Professional 97

This book is printed on acid-free paper.

domestic 5 6 7 8 9 0 BAN BAN 9 0 0 9
international 5 6 7 8 9 0 BAN BAN 9 0 0 9

ISBN 0-07-561041-8

The Sponsoring Editor was Rhonda Sands.
The Developmental Editor was Kristin Hepburn.
The Editorial Assistant was Kyle Thomes.
The Marketing Manager was James Rogers.
The Production Supervisor was Richard DeVitto.
The cover was designed by Lorna Lo.
Project management was by Elaine Brett, Fritz/Brett Associates.
Composition was by Pat Rogondino, Rogondino & Associates.
The typeface was ITC Clearface.
Banta Co. was the printer and binder.

Library of Congress Cataloging Card Number 97-72183

International Edition

When ordering this title, use ISBN 0-07-115475-2

http://www.mhhe.com

Contents

Preface

No matter what career you choose, information technology will affect your life. Knowledge of information technology and the effective use of information technology can make the difference between whether those effects are positive or negative. Our goal is to give students a basic understanding of computing concepts and to build the skills necessary to ensure that information technology is an advantage in whatever path they choose in life.

A Unique Visual Orientation

Because we believe that students learn better and retain more when concepts are reinforced visually, we feature a unique visual orientation. Accordingly, each lab balances text with more full-color graphics early on, when students need more help, and less later in the labs as students develop skills and confidence. Our visual Concept Summaries at the end of each lab capture "in a nutshell" the key concepts covered in that lab. Adopters have long held that the visual orientation enhances their students' interest and comprehension.

Distinguishing Features

The lab modules follow the "learn by doing" approach by combining conceptual coverage with detailed software instructions. A realistic case study based on real-world use of software in a business situation runs throughout each module and leads the student step by step from *problem* to *solution*.

Each lab module includes:

- **Concept Boxes**—provide an overview of the concepts covered in each lab (chapter).
- **Competencies**—clearly state the desired outcome of each lesson.
- **Visual Summaries**—exciting graphics that reinforce key concepts of each lesson.
- **Case Study**—students follow one business through the use of word processing, spreadsheet, database, and presentation software to address realistic situations that arise in everyday business.

- **Numerous Screen Displays** throughout keep the student on track.
- **Summaries of Key Terms and Commands**.
- **Lab Reviews**—matching and fill-in-the-blank questions.
- **Hands-On Practice Exercises**.
- **Case Project**—provides students with an opportunity to integrate knowledge gained in preceding lessons, and reinforces conceptual understanding of integrating applications to solve more complex problems.
- **Glossary of Key Terms**.
- **Summary of Commands**.
- **Index**.

The Support Package Comprehensive Teaching Material Sets are available. Each set includes:

- **Instructor's Manual**—contains objectives, sample schedules, procedural requirements, teaching tips, answers to end-of-chapter problems, solutions to case project, command summary, answers to practice exercises, a printed test bank, and student data files.
- **PowerPoint Presentations**—present key figures from the text in an interactive and customizable format.

Also available:

- A Windows-based computerized test bank makes it easy to pick and choose from our text-specific test items or to add your own. You choose whether to print your test, or to post it to a LAN or even a Web page!

For information on how to obtain any of the supplements described, please contact your McGraw-Hill representative.

Acknowledgments

We are, as always, deeply indebted to our reviewers: Said Fares, Valdosta State University; Gail Gemberling, University of Texas at Austin; Seth Hock, Columbus State Community College, Mike Michealson, Palomar College; and Bruce White, Dakota State University.

We are also very appreciative of all the efforts of the Irwin/McGraw-Hill staff and others who worked on this book: Mike Junior, Garrett Glanz, and Kyle Thomes for their support of this edition; Kristin Hepburn for her developmental support; Richard DeVitto for production supervision; and Jim Rogers and Barbara Arvia for their marketing support. Most importantly, we would like to thank our editor, Rhonda Sands, for her skill, patience, and creativity in bringing this edition to press.

We are also grateful for the contributions of those outside Irwin/McGraw-Hill: Colleen Hayes for her creativity, hard work, and continued dedication to the project; Carol Dean for her creative practice exercises and ongoing contributions to the project; Marianne Virgili of Glenwood Springs Chamber of Commerce and Jim Price of the Sports Authority for their contributions toward the development of case materials; GTS for prepress work; Lorna Lo for her innovative cover design; Elaine Brett for production supervision; Pat Rogondino, Detta Penna, and Beth Bevans for design and page makeup; Susan Defosset, Catherine Linberg, and Karla Maree for their continued excellent editorial and proofreading support.

Windows® 95

Timothy J. O'Leary
Linda I. O'Leary

0 BAN BAN 9 0 9

ISBN 0-07-049054-6

Library of Congress Catalog Card Number 95-77491

Credits: Page WN2, Figure 1 courtesy of Gateway 2000; page WN5, Figure 3 courtesy of Microsoft Corp.; page WN5, Figure 4 courtesy of Intel; page WN10, Figure 7 (inset) courtesy of Hewlett-Packard.

Contents

Introduction to the Windows 95 Labs

Each lab module in the *McGraw-Hill Microcomputing* series consists of a sequence of labs that each require about one hour to complete. They are designed to provide you with practical skills in using the following kinds of software, which are the most widely used in business and industry:

- Windows 95
- Word processor
- Spreadsheet
- Database
- Graphics presentation

The labs describe not only the most important commands and concepts, but also explain why and under what circumstances you will use them. By presenting an ongoing case study based on input from actual business managers, we show how such software is used in a real business setting.

Organization of the Lab Modules

The Lab Modules Are Organized in the Following Categories: Overview, Labs, Case Project, Glossary of Key Terms, Functional Summary of Selected Commands, Windows 95 Review, and Index.

Overview The overview, which appears at the beginning of each module, describes (1) what the program can do for you, (2) what the program is, (3) the generic terms that this and all similar programs use (for example, all word processing programs, regardless of brand name), and (4) the case study to be presented in the module for that program. The overview also includes a Before You Begin section that presents information for both students and instructors about hardware and software settings and other items of importance to be considered before beginning the labs.

Labs The labs consist of both concept coverage and detailed, step-by-step directions for completing the problem presented in the case. The concepts appear in folder-like boxes preceding the step-by-step directions on how to apply the concept. Your progress through the labs is reinforced by the use of carefully placed figures that represent how your screen should appear after you complete a procedure. Labs should be followed in sequence, because each succeeding lab builds on the one preceding it. In addition, as you progress through the labs, the number of screen displays decreases and directions become less specific. This feature allows you to think about what you have learned, avoids simple rote learning, and reinforces earlier concepts and commands, helping you to gain confidence.

In case there is not enough lab time to complete the entire lab, the labs are often divided into two parts. When needed, instructions about how to end Part 1 and begin Part 2 appear at the end of Part 1.

Case Project Many lab modules include a complex project that allows you to apply and integrate the concepts you have learned throughout the labs.

Glossary of Key Terms The glossary, which appears at the end of each lab module, defines all the key terms that appear in bold in the overview and throughout the labs.

Functional Summary of Selected Commands Each lab module includes a quick-reference source for selected commands. The commands are listed in the order in which they appear in the application's menu.

Windows 95 Review A brief review of Windows 95 features and concepts is included as an appendix to assist students who need help with basic Windows 95 features.

Index Each lab module contains an index for quick reference to specific items within that module.

Organization of the Labs

The Labs Consist of the Following Parts: Competencies, Concept Overview, Case Study, Lab Review, Hands-On Practice Exercises, and Concept Summary.

Competencies The competencies list appears at the beginning of each lab. It lists the concepts and commands to be learned in that particular lab.

Concept Overview Throughout the labs, the major concepts appear in folder-like boxes. The concept overview at the beginning of each lab provides a brief introduction to those concepts. They are in numbered order as presented in the lab.

Case Study The ongoing case study shows how to solve real-world business problems using the application covered by that particular module. The ongoing case study was written with the help of real-world experience contributed by industry managers. The specific case study used in each lab module is explained in the overview section for the module. The reader follows the instructions in the labs to solve the case problems.

Lab Review The Lab Review includes a summary of terms and commands, as well as a variety of exercises designed to reinforce concepts and procedures presented in the lab. The review exercises do not require the use of a computer. The Lab Review consists of the following elements:

- *Key Terms* Terms that are defined in the labs appear in **boldface** type. They are also listed at the end of each lab in alphabetical order. The number of the page on which the term is introduced follows the term.
- *Command Summary* All commands that are used in the lab and the actions they perform are listed at the end of each lab in the order in which they appear on menus. The Command Summary also includes keyboard and toolbar shortcuts.
- *Matching* A variety of different types of matching problems is presented. The matching problems emphasize both concepts and procedures through the use of traditional matching and identification exercises and action/result–type matching exercises.
- *Fill-In Questions* The ten fill-in questions are designed to reinforce concepts presented in the lab.

Hands-On Practice Exercises Each lab also includes a Hands-On Practice Exercises section that requires the use of a computer to complete. This section is divided into two areas: Step by Step and On Your Own. The Step by Step exercises lead the student through the steps needed to complete the problem. The On Your Own exercises provide limited directions. Each exercise is marked with stars that indicate the difficulty level of the problem. The star rating system is: *Easy, **Moderate, ***Difficult. Each section includes problems having a variety of levels of difficulty.

Concept Summary The final item that appears at the end of each lab is the Concept Summary. This two-page spread presents a visual summary of the concepts presented in the lab.

Procedural Conventions

Commands and Directions Are Expressed Through Certain Standard Conventions.

We have followed certain conventions in the labs for indicating keys, key combinations, commands, command sequences, and other directions.

Keys Computer keys are expressed in abbreviated form, as follows:

Computer Keys	Display in Text
Alternate	Alt
Backspace	←Backspace
Caps Lock (Capital Lock)	Caps Lock
Ctrl (Control)	Ctrl
Del (Delete)	Del
End	End
ESC (Escape)	Esc
(Enter/Return)	↵Enter
Home	Home
Ins (Insert)	Ins
Num Lock (Number Lock)	Num Lock
Pg Dn (Page Down)	Page Down
Pg Up (Page Up)	Page Up
Prt Sc (Print Screen)	Prt Sc
Scroll Lock	Scroll Lock
Shift	⇧Shift
Tab	Tab ⇆
Function Keys	
F1 through F12	F1 through F12
Cursor Movement	
↑ (Up)	↑
↓ (Down)	↓
← (Left)	←
→ (Right)	→

Key Combinations Many programs require that you use a combination of keys for a particular command (for example, the pair of keys Ctrl and F4). You should press them in the order in which they appear, from left to right, holding down the first key while pressing the second. In the labs, commands that are used in this manner are separated by a plus—for example, Ctrl + F4.

Directions The principal directions in the labs are "Press," "Move to," "Type," "Choose," "Select," and "Click." These directions appear on a separate line beginning at the left margin, as follows:

- *Press:* This means you should strike a key. Usually a command key will follow the direction (such as [Delete] for "Delete"). For example:

  Press: [Delete]

- *Move to:* This means you should move the insertion point or highlight to the location indicated. For example, the direction to move to cell A5 would appear as:

  Move to: A5

- *Type:* This means you should type or key in certain letters or numbers, just as you would on a typewriter keyboard. Whatever is to be typed will appear in bright blue type. For example:

  Type: **January**

- *Choose and Select:* A sequence of selections from a menu or dialog box is often required to complete a command. The selections are made using the mouse or keyboard. The command sequences will follow the word "Choose." If a letter of a command appears with an underline and in **boldface**, you can select that command by typing the letter. The command sequence that is to be typed will appear in bright blue.

  "Select" is used to indicate selecting or marking an item from a list of available options. "Select" does not begin an action as "Choose" does. Selecting may be part of a command sequence and will usually appear when procedures are initially introduced. In the beginning these commands are introduced separately. For example:

  Choose: **F**ile
  Select: **O**pen
  Select: MEMBERS.DOC
  Choose: OK

  Later, as you become more familiar with the program, the commands are combined on a single line. Each command may be separated by a /. For example,

  Choose: **F**ile/**O**pen/MEMBERS.DOC/OK

- *Click:* If a command procedure has a mouse shortcut, the mouse shortcut is preceded with the word "Click." (The menu equivalent or keyboard shortcut appears as a marginal note.) For example:

Click: **B** **Bold**

Additional directions may appear as bright blue text embedded within the main text. They appear like this only after the procedure to perform the directions is very familiar to the student. Follow the directions using the appropriate procedure.

Marginal Notes Throughout the labs notes appear in the margins. These notes may be reminders of how to perform a procedure, clarifications or alternate methods, or brief side notes that expand upon a concept. The marginal notes symbols have different meanings as illustrated below:

A standard informational note:

> The menu equivalent is Format/Font/Bold and the keyboard shortcut is Ctrl + B.

An informational note for mouse users:

> "Double-click" means to click the left mouse button twice in rapid succession without moving the mouse.

A note for keyboard users:

> Tab will make the next area active and ⇧Shift + Tab will make the previous area active.

A note that refers the reader to information in the Overview:

> See the Overview for more information about memory and drives.

A note that refers readers to information in the Windows 95 Review:

> Refer to the File Name section of the Windows 95 Review for more information on this feature.

A warning note:

> **WARNING!**
>
> To avoid damaging files, always shut down Windows before you turn off your computer.

General System Requirements

To complete the labs, the following hardware and software are needed:

- An IBM or IBM-compatible computer system with a hard disk and one or two floppy disk drives. The amount of RAM memory your computer must have varies with the application software program you will be using. If you are using a networked system, your instructor will provide additional instructions as needed.
- A mouse. Mouse use is assumed, although keyboard directions are provided as marginal notes.
- A printer.
- Windows 95 and the application software programs selected by your instructor and installed on your computer.
- Student data disk containing the files needed to perform the labs and to complete the hands-on practice exercises; these files are supplied by your instructor.

Special Assumptions Any special directions or hardware and software assumptions that have been made in the preparation of these lab modules are described at the end of the overview for that particular software application module under the heading "Before You Begin."

Supplements

Each Lab Module Is Accompanied by the Following Supplements:

- **Teaching Materials** The Instructors Manual provides lecture notes and guidelines for the instructor on the concepts and procedures presented in each lab. It also includes the answers to all lab review problems and hands-on practice exercises, as well as for the case project. In addition, a copy of the test bank questions and the test answer key is supplied.
- **Transparency Masters** Illustrations and screen shots that can be used to demonstrate concepts and procedures are provided as transparency masters.

- **Electronic Transparencies** The illustrations and screen shots that are included as transparency masters are also available in electronic form as PowerPoint slides.
- **Computerized Test Bank** A minimum of 40 true/false and multiple choice–type questions is supplied for each lab. With the MicroTest III Computerized Test Bank, instructors can network a test in the lab, give students a test on disk, and prepare traditional pencil-and-paper tests. It also allows full editing of individual test items.
- **Data Disk** The files that are required to complete the labs and hands-on practice exercises are provided on the data disk that is supplied with the teaching materials. Answers to all lab exercises are also included.

Windows 95 Overview

GETTING STARTED WITH YOUR MICROCOMPUTER

A microcomputer system is composed of five essential parts: people, procedures, software, hardware, and data. The end users (people) need to know how to operate the computer hardware and use the software programs to input and analyze data or information. To learn how to operate or use the software, hardware, and data, the end users follow procedures. Procedures consist of rules or guidelines to follow that are described in manuals. This overview will focus briefly on the hardware and software aspects of your computer system.

Computer Hardware

The physical part of the computer system, called **hardware**, consists of four parts: input devices, the system unit, secondary storage devices, and output devices.

The **input devices** take data and programs and put them into a form the computer can process. The most common input devices are a keyboard and a mouse. The **system unit** is the electronic circuitry housed within the computer cabinet. It holds the computer's **memory** and the **central processing unit** (CPU). The system unit executes programs, performs calculations, and temporarily stores data and programs. The most common form of **secondary storage** is a disk. It provides a place to permanently store information or data that is input into the computer. **Output devices** are pieces of equipment that translate the processed information from the CPU into a form that you can understand. A computer screen or monitor is the most common output device. It displays your work while you are using the computer. A printer is used to create printed output. In addition, speakers are becoming common sound output devices on many systems. A typical computer system is shown in Figure 1.

Figure 1

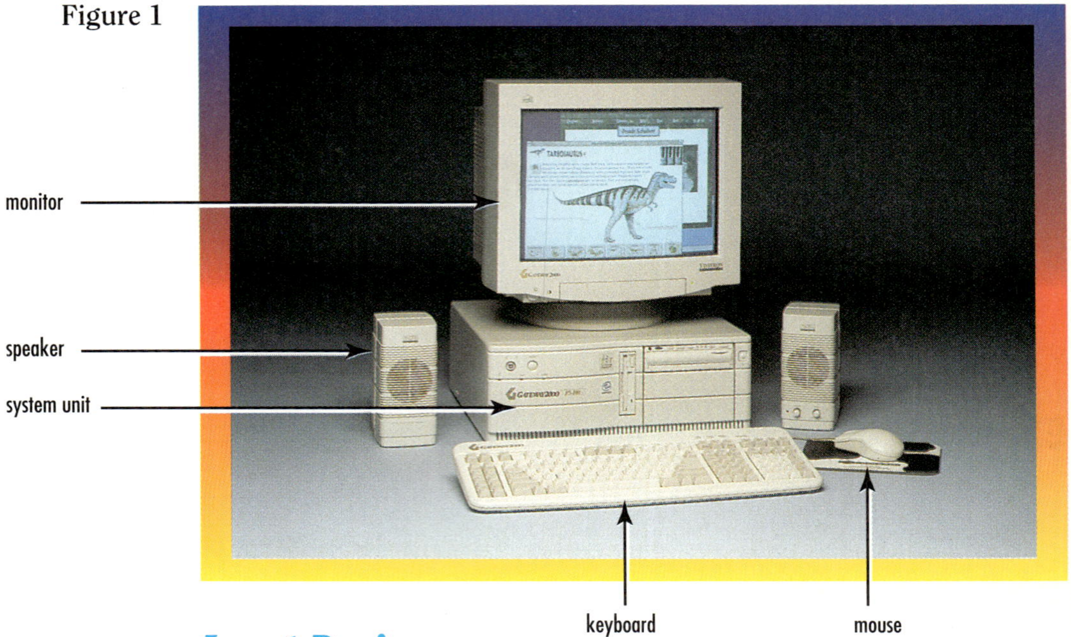

Input Devices

Keyboard The **keyboard** is the most common type of input device. It allows you to communicate with the computer. It consists of four main areas: the function keys, the typewriter keys, the numeric keypad, and special-purpose keys. Two styles of keyboards are commonly found: the standard keyboard and the enhanced keyboard. Figure 2 shows a standard and an enhanced IBM keyboard.

Figure 2

Enhanced Keyboard

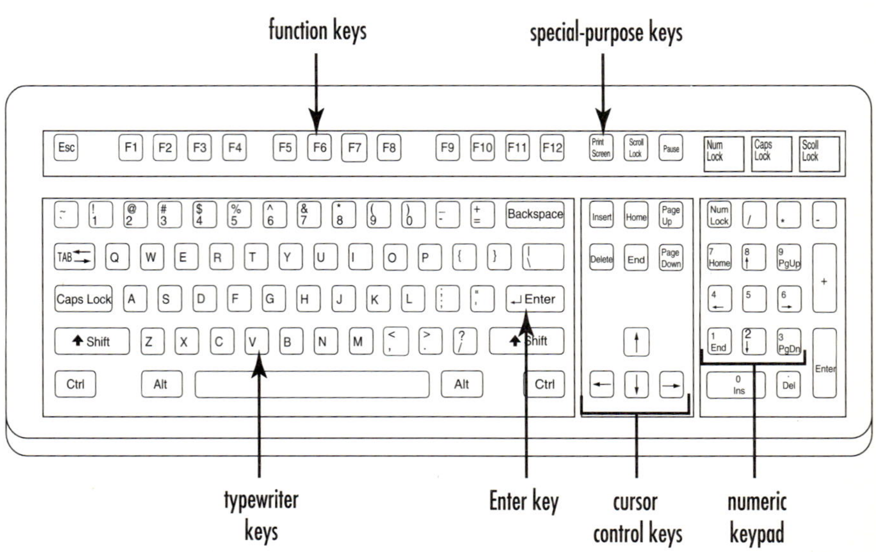

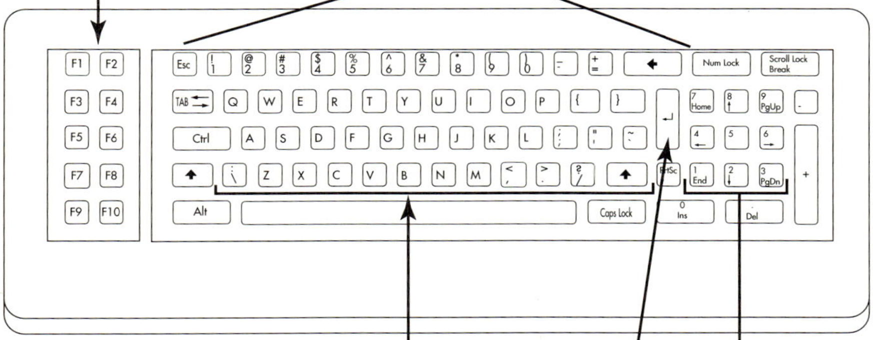

Standard Keyboard

The central area of the keyboard contains the standard typing keys and the spacebar. The standard keys consist of letters, numbers, and special characters such as the semicolon and the dollar sign, as they appear on a standard typewriter. You use these keys just like you would a normal typewriter. As you type, the characters appear on the computer screen rather than on paper. The **cursor**, also called the **insertion point**, is a flashing bar that identifies your location on the screen.

The other typing keys and their uses are described below.

Key	Action
⇧Shift + letter	Types uppercase letter
⇧Shift + number	Types symbol shown above number on that key
Caps Lock	Allows entry of all uppercase alphabetic characters without using ⇧Shift
Tab ↹	Moves insertion point preset number of spaces to the right
⇧Shift + Tab ↹	Moves insertion point preset number of spaces to the left
←Enter	Moves the insertion point to the next line (same as a typewriter); allows the user to enter data or command sequences

At the right side of the keyboard is the numeric keypad. It consists of nine keys with arrows and numbers on them. These keys can be used to enter numbers or to direct the movement of the insertion point on the screen. To use the numeric keypad to enter numbers, the Num Lock key must be on. To turn on Num Lock, press the Num Lock key. When Num Lock is on, the indicator light on an enhanced keyboard is lighted. When [Num Lock] is off, use of the keys in the numeric keypad moves the insertion point in the direction of the arrow. The [Num Lock] key acts like a toggle switch to switch control of the numeric keypad between numeric entry and insertion point movement. On the enhanced keyboard there is a separate directional keypad consisting of four arrow keys that are used exclusively to move the insertion point.

There are also some keys in the numeric keypad with words on them: [Home], [End], [Page Up], and [Page Down]. These keys will have different meanings depending on the software program you are using. You can use these keys to quickly move around information on your screen.

Function keys are located across the top on the enhanced keyboard or on the left side of standard keyboards. They are labeled [F1], [F2], etc. They are used to send instructions to the software being used. Therefore, their use varies with the software program you are using. Frequently, function keys are shortcuts for a long command. For example, instead of having to press several keys to perform a command, all you need to do is press one function key.

Scattered throughout the keyboard are special-purpose keys. The uses of these keys change with the type of work you are doing. Generally they have the following uses:

Key	Action
[Esc] (escape)	Quits or goes back one step in a program command; erases existing command
[Ctrl] (control)	Used in combination with another key to perform a special task
[Alt] (alternate)	Assigns another function to a given key
[Print Screen]	Prints a hard copy of whatever is on the screen (on standard keyboards you must hold down [⇧Shift] in conjunction with [Print Screen]).
[Scroll Lock]	When on, using the [↑] and [↓] keys moves document up or down on the screen, and insertion point does not move
[Pause]	May let you stop a program for a short time
[Break]	Stops a command from completing execution
[Insert] and [Ins]	Allows you to insert characters between other characters
[Delete] and [Del]	Erases character insertion point is on
[Backspace]	Moves insertion point to left and erases character (this key may also appear as a left-facing arrow [←]).
[End],[Home], [Page Up], [Page Down]	Same effect as their equivalents on numeric keypad

Mouse The mouse is an input device that is used in addition to the keyboard. It is a hand-held device that controls a pointer on the screen. When you move the mouse around the desktop, the rubber-coated ball on the bottom of the mouse moves. The ball's movement is translated into signals that tell the computer how to move the onscreen pointer. On top of the mouse are two buttons that are used to make selections from items on the screen.

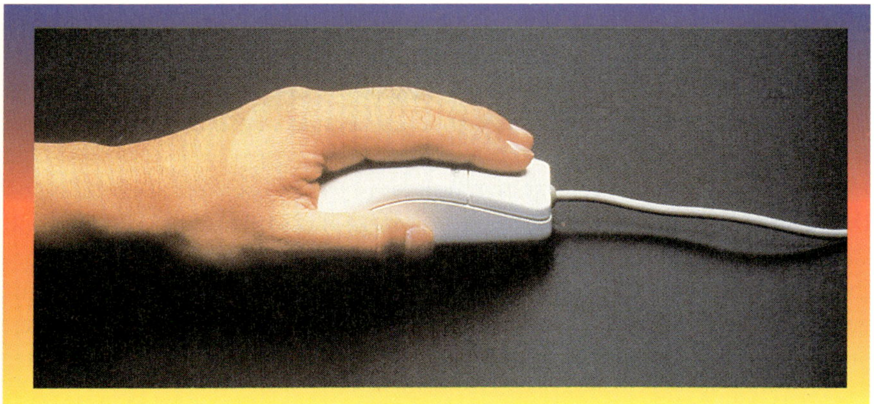

Figure 3

The System Unit

The system unit contains the central processing unit (CPU) and memory. Figure 4 displays the parts of a system unit.

Figure 4

The **central processing unit (CPU)** is the part of the computer system that does the actual computing. It contains the electronic circuitry through which data is processed and instructions are executed. In a microcomputer, the CPU consists of a single silicon chip, called a **microprocessor**, such as the model shown in Figure 4 made by Intel Corporation.

Memory, also called **primary storage**, is where data and instructions are stored during processing by the microprocessor. There are two types of memory, **read-only memory (ROM)** and **random-access memory (RAM)** (see Figure 4). The ROM chips contain programs that are built into the chips and direct the operations of the computer. ROM is not accessible to the user. The other type of memory, RAM, is accessible to the user. It is the computer's workplace. The RAM chips hold the software programs and data that the CPU is currently processing. RAM is also referred to as **temporary memory** because whatever is in RAM is lost if the power is turned off.

Memory is located in the system unit on tiny memory chips. Depending on the amount of memory your computer system has, the number of chips will vary. The amount of memory is measured in **bytes**. A byte is a single memory location. Usually a byte stores one character. A **kilobyte (KB)** equals 1024 (or approximately 1000) bytes. A **megabyte (MB)** holds approximately 1 million bytes, and a **gigabyte (GB)** holds approximately 1 billion bytes. Most microcomputer systems sold today have a memory capacity of 8MB or more.

Secondary Storage

Secondary storage devices provide a means of permanently storing the information contained in temporary memory. There are several types of secondary storage devices. The most common type of secondary storage is a **disk**. The disk is the permanent storage medium for either data (for example, a business letter) or a software program (for example, a word processor to edit that letter). The data and program information are stored on circular metal or plastic disks as a series of electromagnetic spots. The disk can be an internal **hard disk** that is housed within the system unit, or an external **floppy disk**. In addition, the **CD-ROM disk** is another type of secondary storage device commonly found in computer systems sold today. This type of disk is an optical disk that uses a laser beam to alter the surface of the disk to store data

The amount of data a disk can hold is called **disk capacity**. Disk capacity, like memory, is measured in kilobytes, megabytes, and gigabytes.

Hard Disk The hard disk is a permanent fixture containing one or more circular metallic disks that are used to store data files and software programs. The internal hard disk is sealed in a container to prevent any foreign matter from getting inside. Most microcomputer systems sold today have a hard disk capacity of at least 540MB.

The **hard-disk drive** in the system unit provides the means for you to retrieve and save your data and programs onto the hard disk. This disk drive contains an access arm and read-write heads for writing data to and reading data from the disk. It is usually referred to as the C drive.

The main advantages of a hard disk are that more information can be stored on it, and it is more quickly accessed than the information from a floppy disk.

Floppy Disk The second main type of secondary storage is the floppy disk. Floppy disks store data on a flexible plastic disk. It allows the user to load instructions into the computer from disks containing software programs and to save data onto and retrieve data from disks that contain information you create. The main advantage of floppy disks is that they are transportable.

Floppy disks come in several sizes. The most common sizes are 5.25 inches and 3.5 inches. The 3.5-inch disk is the most common disk used today. The type of disk you use will depend on your computer hardware requirements. Figure 5 shows the 3.5-inch disk.

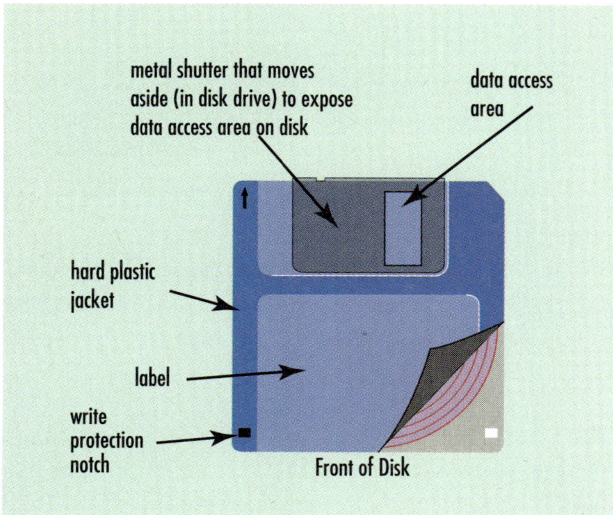

Figure 5

The 3.5-inch disks are contained within a hard plastic jacket that protects the disk. Inside the hard jacket is the soft plastic disk that is used to store the data. The write-protect notch is covered by a sliding shutter. When the shutter is open, the write-protect hole is exposed, preventing information from being changed on the disk.

A **floppy-disk drive** is used to read information from the floppy-disk to RAM and write information from RAM to the disk. The floppy disk drive also has an access arm and read-write heads. All microcomputers have at least one floppy-disk drive.

The floppy-disk drive is housed in the front of the computer as shown in Figure 5. A slot allows you to insert a floppy disk into the drive. The data is read from or written to the disk by the read-write head mechanism inside each drive.

If there are two disk drives, they are referred to as the A drive and the B drive. If the drives are positioned side by side, generally the A drive is on the left. If your drives are located one above the other, the A drive is the one on top.

The capacity of floppy disks varies with the type of disk, from 360KB up to 2.88MB. Several factors control how much data can be stored on a floppy disk. If the disk is a single-sided disk, data can be stored on one side of the disk only. Double-sided disks store data on both sides of the disk. Most disks are double-sided disks. Another factor that affects the amount of data that can be stored on a disk is whether the disk is a single-density, double-density, or high-density disk. Density refers to the number of bytes that can be recorded on the disk in a specified space. The higher density the disk is, the more data that can be stored. The chart below summarizes the different types and capacities of floppy disks.

Diameter (inches)	Description (bytes)	Capacity
5.25	Double-sided, high-density	1.25MB
3.5	Double-sided, double-density	720KB
3.5	Double-sided, high-density	1.44MB

It is important to be aware of the density of disks because the disk drive on your computer must be able to support the disk capacity of the disk, or it will be unable to use the disk. A higher density drive can read from and write to a lower density disk, but a lower density drive cannot read from or write to a higher density disk.

Floppy Disk Care Since floppy disks contain a permanent copy of your work or program files that you use frequently, it is very important that this data not be lost or destroyed. If it is, you could lose a lot of time and effort. To help preserve your disks, there are some things you should know about their care and handling:

1. Excessive heat can melt or warp the disk. Do not, for example, expose your disk to excessive sunlight through the window of your car or to excessive heat by placing it on your heater.
2. Disks use magnetism to store your data. Do not expose the disk to magnetic fields such as your telephone receiver, a loudspeaker, or a television. The magnetic fields from these machines can alter the data on your disk.
3. Do not touch the surface of the plastic disk. Always handle the case only. The oils from your skin can damage the surface of the disk.

In addition, if you are using 5.25-inch disks, the following precautions should be taken:

1. Store your disks standing up or in a vertical position. This way they will not bend or warp. Always place the 5.25-disk in its protective envelope.
2. Do not bend disks or place heavy objects on them.
3. Do not write on a 5.25-inch disk with a ball-point pen. The pressure from the pen can crease the disk and damage it. If you must write on your disk, use a felt-tip pen. It is best, however, to write on the label before you place it on the disk.

CD-ROM Disks The third main type of secondary storage is the **CD-ROM disk**. CD-ROM stands for compact disk-read-only memory. Like compact disks you buy at a music store, a CD-ROM disk is a read-only disc. This means that it cannot be written on or erased by the user. Thus, you only have access to the information imprinted on the disk by the publisher. Figure 6 shows a CD-ROM and CD-ROM drive.

Figure 6

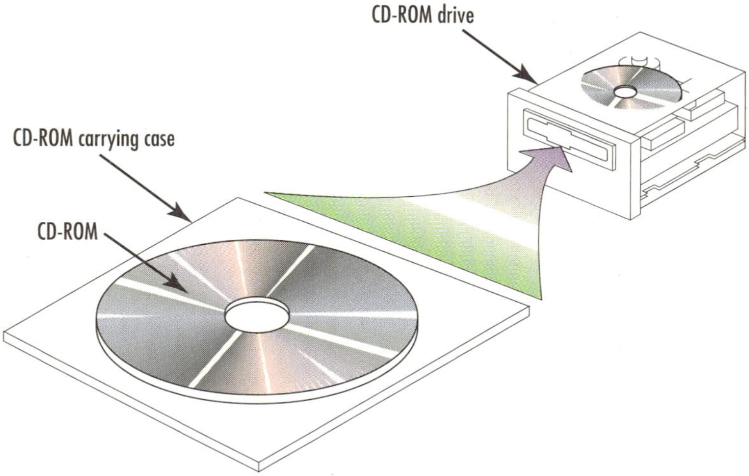

A CD-ROM disk is created using a laser beam, which alters the surface of the disk, creating flat and bumpy areas called "pits" on the bottom of the disk. These areas represent data. A **CD-ROM drive** uses a laser that projects a tiny beam of light onto the disk to read the data.

A typical CD-ROM disk is 5.25 inches in diameter and can store 650MB of data, the equivalent of 147 floppy disks. Because of their large storage capacity, they are commonly used to distribute large databases and references, such as an encyclopedia. In addition, they are used to distribute large software programs and computer games.

Output Devices

The Computer Screen The computer screen, or **monitor**, is how the computer communicates with you. The monitor displays instructions you send to the computer and the information and results from the computer back to you. It relays program messages or instructions called prompts and displays results of calculations, graphs, and text input.

The computer screen can be either a monochrome screen display or a color screen display. A monochrome screen uses only one color—usually white, green, amber, or black—to display text on a contrasting background. Color screens commonly display 256 colors at once from a selection of over 256,000 choices.

The Printer Along with the computer screen, a **printer** serves as a way for the computer to tell you what you have input and what it has done. The difference is that the printer generates a permanent hard copy of your work on paper.

Some printers can print both text and graphics (pictures). Others can print only text. If you have a printer that prints only text, you would need a device called a **plotter** to print graphs. Printers can produce hard copy that is either near letter (draft) quality or letter quality. Draft-quality print is formed by a series of dots and consequently may not appear solid. Letter-quality print is solid, like that produced by a typewriter. Many printers can also produce color output.

Dot-matrix printers are often used to create draft-quality output. They produce letters by a series of pins that press on a printer ribbon to produce dots in the form of the letter. These printers are fast and economical, but noisy. Letter-quality print is commonly produced by ink-jet and laser printers. The ink-jet printer sprays ink in the pattern of the character. Ink-jet printers have recently become the most widely used type of printer. The laser printer creates characters by means of an electronic charge. The laser printer is a high-resolution printer that produces typeset-quality text and graphics. Figure 7 shows a laser printer and how it creates letter-quality text.

Although most printers can also print graphs, you may want to use a plotter to draw pictures and graphs. Most plotters use several pens of different colors to

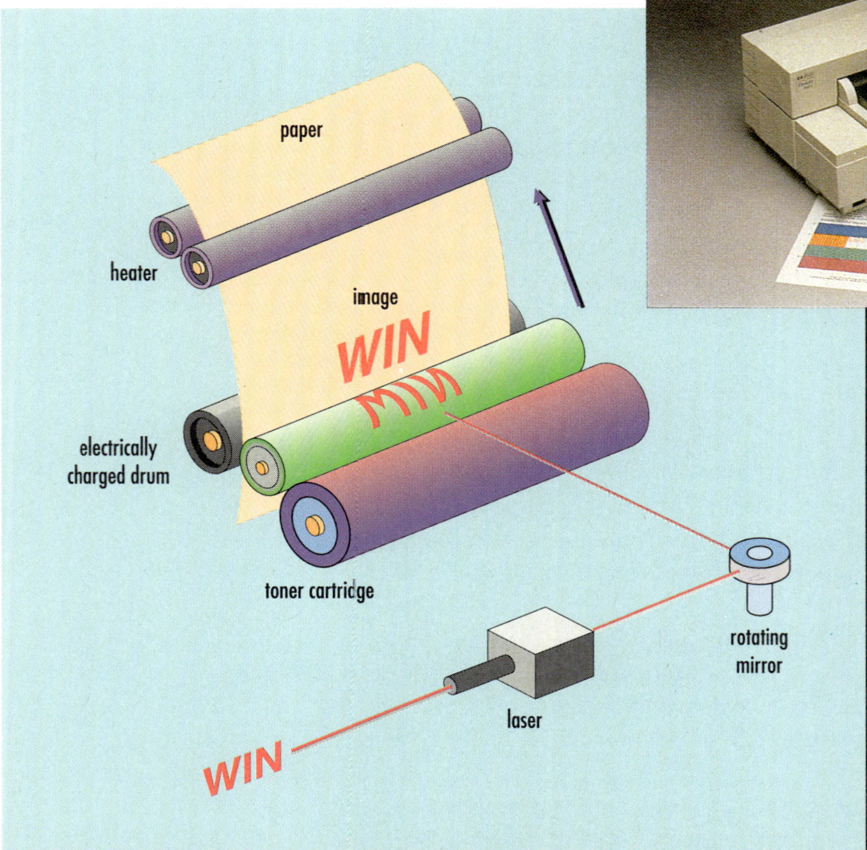

produce a multicolor drawing. The graphs and drawings produced by a plotter have much better line resolution and precision than graphs produced by a dot-matrix printer. A plotter produces professional presentation-quality graphs.

Computer Software

Software is the set of instructions that directs the computer to process information. These instructions are called **programs**. Without software, the computer cannot work. A commonly used analogy is that the computer hardware is the engine, while the software is the fuel that allows the engine to operate. Without software the hardware would be useless. There are two types of software available for computers: system software and application software.

System Software **System software** programs coordinate the operation of the various hardware components of the computer. The system software or operating system program helps the user to actually operate the computer system. They are an interface between the user and the computer.

The operating system oversees the processing of the application programs and all input and output of the system. Without the operating system, you cannot use the applications software programs provided with this book. The operating system controls computer system resources and coordinates the flow of data to and from the microprocessor and to and from input and output devices such as the keyboard and the monitor.

System software is usually provided by the computer manufacturer. The various types of computers require different types of system software programs in order to operate. Some of the most popular are DOS, Macintosh operating system, OS/2, Windows 95, and UNIX.

Application Software **Application software** is a set of programs designed for specific uses or "applications," such as word processing, graphics, or spreadsheet analysis. Application software can be custom-written but is usually purchased ready-made.

Normally, to use an application program like Excel 7.0, you load the program into the computer's memory; execute (run) the program; and then create, edit, or update a file. When you have finished, you need to save the work you have done on a disk. If you do not save your work and you turn off the computer, it is erased from memory and everything you have done will be lost.

The operating system acts as a communications link between the hardware and the application program. It is responsible for loading the application software into memory and then starting the program. It also retrieves data files and saves them to disk when directed. When you have finished using the application software you are returned to the operating system.

Before You Begin

We suggest that schools use the default Windows settings stored in the initial.ini file, and that this .ini file is copied over the .ini file that is saved on exiting

Windows. This way student changes will not be saved, and the same layout will be in effect each time Windows 95 is started.

Command sequences appear following the word "Choose." Multiple menu selections are separated with a /. If available, keyboard shortcuts will be presented in marginal notes. Alternative toolbar shortcuts for the command will appear following the word "Click." Any one of these methods can be used to enter the command.

We have also made the following assumptions:

- Data files are in separate folders for the different applications that will be used (Word 7.0, Excel 7.0, Windows 95, etc.) under the Student Data File folder on the hard drive.
- The Windows 95 supplemental applications Clipboard Viewer and Quick View have also been installed. To install these, use Add/Remove Programs from the Control Panel.

Windows 95 Basic Skills

1

Learning to use a computer is like any other skill. You start by learning the basic concepts and skills. Then you build upon these basics as you apply and expand your knowledge.

COMPETENCIES

In this lab you will learn how to:

1. **Start your computer system and Windows 95.**
2. **Use a mouse.**
3. **Use menus.**
4. **Use Help.**
5. **Use dialog boxes.**
6. **Move and size windows.**
7. **Format a disk.**
8. **View disk properties.**
9. **Quit Windows 95.**

This lab marks the beginning in your pursuit of computer competency by introducing you to many of the basic features and concepts that are common to all Windows applications. At the same time you will learn about the Windows 95 operating system and how to use it to perform tasks you will need to use on a daily basis. This includes the ability to identify and use the parts of the desktop and a window. In addition, you will learn about other features such as using a mouse, moving and sizing windows, using menus and dialog boxes, accessing and using Help, and formatting a disk. These concepts are basic to all Windows applications and provide you with the skills you will need while learning to use all other Windows applications.

Concept Overview

The following concepts will be introduced in this lab:

1. What's Windows 95?	Windows 95 is an operating system program that uses a graphical interface to control all the parts of your computer.
2. The Desktop	The Windows 95 screen is called the desktop. It displays icons that represent various tools and features.
3. The Mouse	The mouse is a hand-held hardware device that is attached to your computer. It controls an arrow called a pointer that appears on your screen.
4. Menus	A menu is one of many methods used to tell a program what you want it to do. When opened, a menu displays a list of commands.
5. Help	The Windows Help facility is a quick source of information about commands or features.
6. Dialog Box	A dialog box is how Windows programs provide and request information from you in order to complete a task.
7. Scroll Bar	A scroll bar is used with a mouse to bring additional lines of information into view in a window or list box.
8. Window	A window is a rectangular section of the screen that is dedicated to a specific activity or application.
9. Moving Windows	Moving a window displays the window at another location on the desktop, making it easier to view other items.
10. Sizing Windows	A window can be changed to just about any size you want, making it easier to see more or less information in the window.
11. Formatting a Disk	Before a new disk can be used, you must format or convert it from a generic state into a format that can be used by your computer.
12. Status Bar	A status bar at the bottom of the window displays information about program settings you are using and the task being performed.
13. Properties	All items on the screen have settings and attributes, called properties, associated with them.

Part 1

Starting Windows 95

The **operating system** program controls computer system resources and coordinates the flow of data to and from the system unit and to and from input and output devices like the keyboard and the display screen. It allows you to create and manage files and run applications software programs. This series of labs will introduce you to the newest operating system, Windows 95.

Concept 1: What's Windows 95?

Windows 95 is an operating system program that controls all the parts of your computer. It uses a **graphical user interface** (GUI, pronounced "gooey"). This kind of interface displays graphical objects called **icons**, which represent the items you use. The icons are buttons that when "pushed" activate the item.

All programs that use the Windows operating system have a **common user interface** that makes it easy to learn and use different programs that run under Windows. A common user interface means that programs have common features, such as the same menu commands. For example, you will find the command to open a file is the same command in all Windows 95 applications.

The Windows operating system gets its name from its use of rectangular boxes called **windows** that are used to display information and other programs. Multiple windows can be open at the same time, making it easy to move from one task to another. This is how people work. More than likely you have several projects you are working on during the day, and need to be able to switch easily from one to the other.

How you proceed depends on whether your computer is on or off. Your computer is on if you can hear the fan running and, on many machines, lights are lit on the front. Otherwise, your computer is off.

Refer to the Overview for information about memory and drives.

If your computer is off, turning it on performs a memory check to determine whether all the memory locations are able to receive and store data correctly and initializes the equipment for use by accessing the disk drives and printer. This is called a **cold start**.

If your computer is on, you can restart the computer without turning the power switch off and on again. This is called a **warm start**. A warm start does not perform a memory check, but it does initialize the equipment for use.

Following either a cold or warm start, the Windows 95 files are automatically loaded into the main memory of your computer.

If your computer is off, follow the steps below:

1. **Turn on the power switch.** The power switch is commonly located on the back or right side of your computer. It may also be a button that you push on the front of your computer.
2. **If necessary, turn your monitor on and adjust the contrast and brightness.** Generally, the button to turn on the monitor is located on the front of the monitor. Use the dials (generally located in the panel on the front of the monitor) to adjust the monitor.
3. **Continue the lab below the box on page 17.**

If your computer is on, follow the steps below:

1. **If necessary, turn your monitor on and adjust the contrast and brightness.** Generally, the button to turn on the monitor is located on the front of the monitor. Use the dials (generally located in the panel on the front of the monitor) to adjust the monitor.
2. **If your screen looks like Figure 1-3 on page 20, Windows 95 is already started. Skip to the section "Exploring the Desktop" on page 19.**
3. **If your screen looks like Figure 1-2 on page 18, Windows 95 is already started. Skip to below Figure 1-2 to continue.**
4. **If your screen displays the box shown in Figure 1-1, you need to restart your computer following the directions below.**

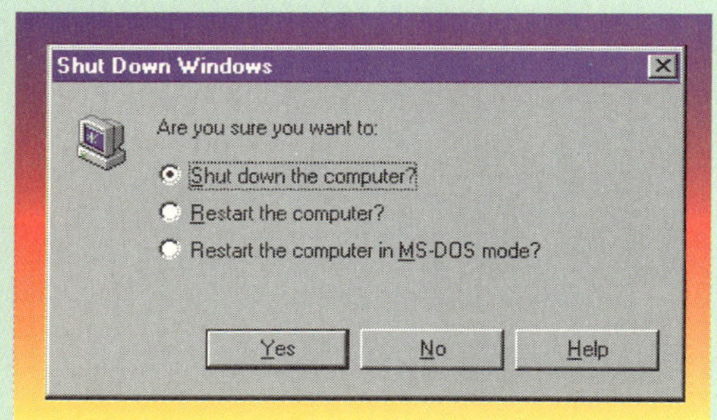

Figure 1-1

The box on your screen (shown in Figure 1-1) displays 3 (or 4 if your system is networked) choices or options. To select the option to restart the computer,

Type: R

A dot appears in the circle before this option, indicating that it is selected.

Then, to confirm your selection, you need to choose "Yes." To do this,

Press: ←Enter

After a few moments, the Windows opening screen is displayed. This screen is quickly followed by the Windows 95 screen and a Welcome to Windows 95 box as shown in Figure 1-2.

If your screen does not display the Welcome box, this feature has been turned off. If this is the case, skip to the section "Exploring the Desktop on page 19."

The Welcome box displays a "Did you know" message that provides different short informational tips about Windows 95 each time the program is started.

Read the "Did you know" message.

You can type lowercase or uppercase letters.

If you know how to use a mouse already, you can click on the Restart the Computer option to select it.

If you know how to use a mouse already, you can click on Yes to select it.

If a log-on prompt appears, type in your user name and password in the appropriate spaces and then press ←Enter (or click OK).

Figure 1-2

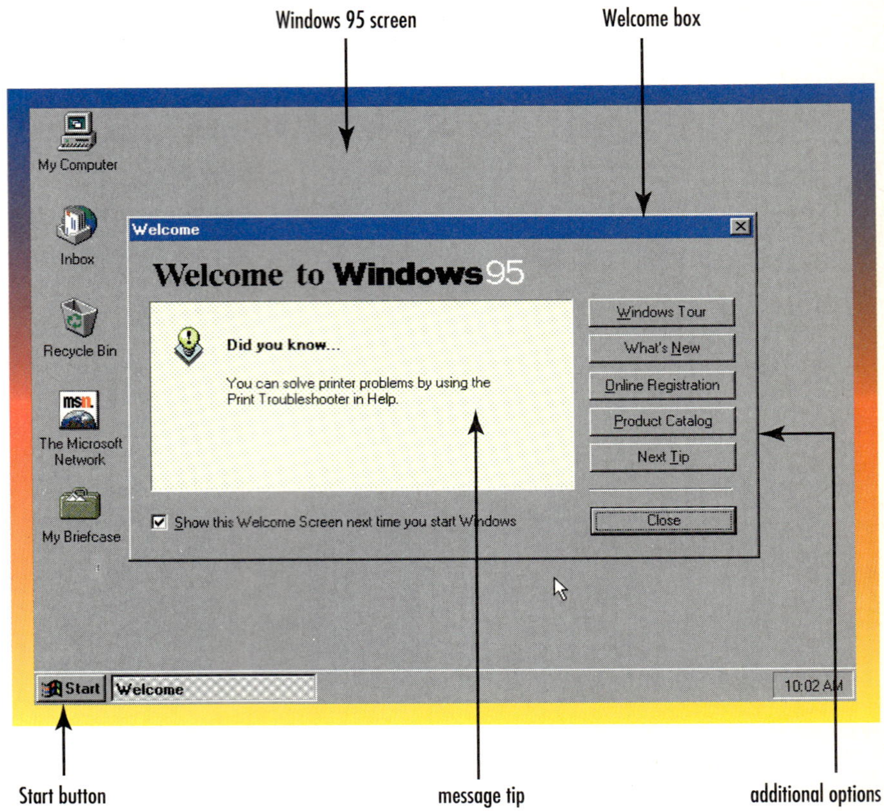

In addition, the Welcome box includes several options that when selected access information about different features, such as the Windows Tour and a discussion of What's New in Windows 95. You will learn how to use this type of box later in the lab. For now, to close the box,

If you already know how to use a mouse, you can click Close.

Press: Esc

The Welcome box is closed, and your screen should be similar to Figure 1-3 on the page 20.

Exploring the Desktop

The screen displays the Windows desktop. It is called a desktop because it is similar to the way you might organize the work on your desk — a different place or pile of paper for each tool or related group of materials.

Concept 2: The Desktop

The Windows 95 screen is called a **desktop**. It displays icons that represent various tools and features. Like your own desk at home or work, you can add and remove items from the desktop, rearrange items, or get rid of them by throwing them into the "trash." You can also open items and, much like a drawer in your desk, find other tools or materials you have stored. You can place these items on the desktop, or take items off the desktop and place them in the "drawer." Just like your own desk, your most frequently used items should be on the desktop so you can quickly begin work while those items that you use less frequently should be put away for easy access as needed, just as you might put papers in a drawer or on a nearby shelf.

Note: If your screen is different, it is because your school may have modified the default Windows 95 layout.

The default desktop, shown in Figure 1-3 on the following page, is very simple and contains only a few essential items that are needed to get started using Windows 95. Your desktop may have been customized to include other items.

Read the information in "Parts of the Windows 95 Desktop" on the following page.

Parts of the Windows 95 Desktop

Figure 1-3

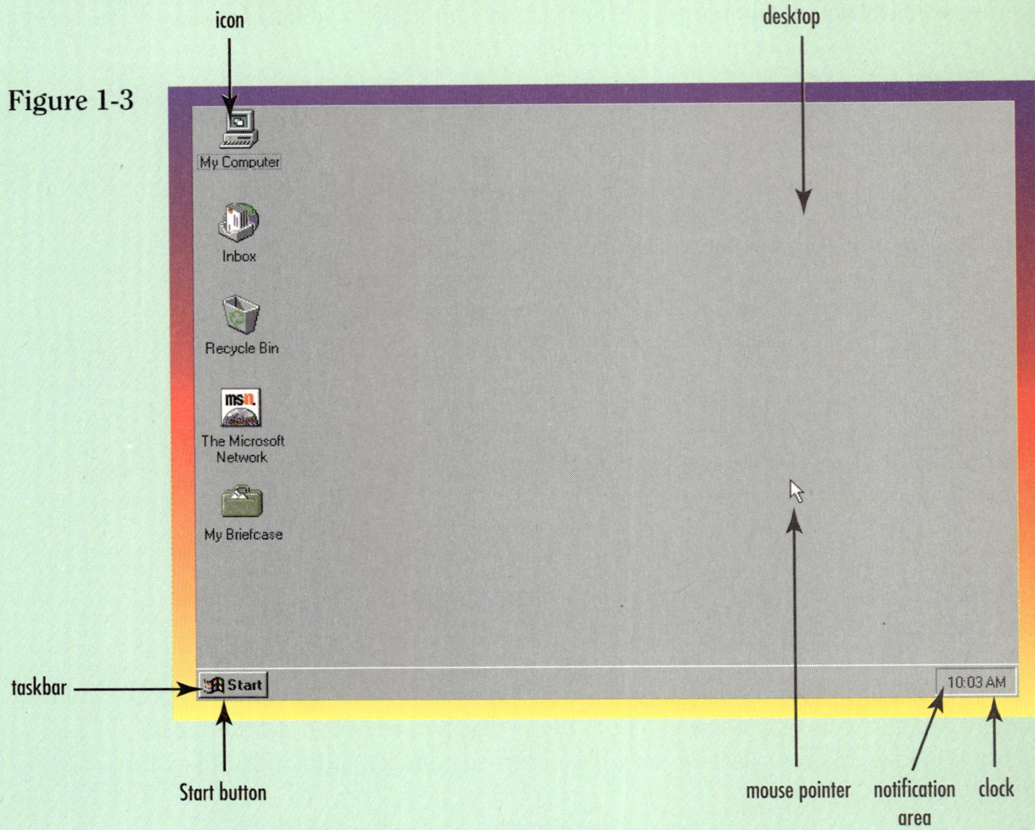

If your computer is part of a network, the Network Neighborhood icon will appear.

The initial Windows 95 screen displays icons such as My Computer and Recycle Bin. The icon picture generally represents the item.

At the bottom of the screen is the **taskbar.** It displays the **Start button** on the left end of the bar. The Start button is used to start a program, open a document, get help, find files, and change system settings. The center of the taskbar is currently blank. It will display buttons representing currently active tasks as you use Windows, making switching between tasks easy. The clock on the right end of the taskbar displays the time as maintained by your computer. To the left of the clock, is the **notification area**. The notification area will display indicators, such as a printer when printing is in progress or a speaker if your system includes audio hardware.

Using the Mouse

The mouse that is attached to your computer displays an arrow-shaped symbol  on your screen.

Concept 3: The Mouse

The **mouse** is a hand-held hardware device that is attached to your computer. It controls the **mouse pointer** that currently appears on your screen as an arrow. The pointer is controlled by the rubber-coated ball on the bottom of the mouse. This ball must move within its socket for the pointer to move on the screen. The ball moves when the mouse is moved along a flat surface. The ball's movement is translated into signals that tell the computer how to move the onscreen pointer. The direction the ball moves controls the direction the pointer moves on the screen.

Moving the mouse across your desktop moves the pointer in the direction you are moving the mouse. If you pick up the mouse and move it to another location on your work surface, the pointer will not move on the screen. Some computers use a track ball to move the mouse pointer. You move this ball with your fingertips in the direction you want the onscreen pointer to move.

The mouse pointer changes shape on the screen depending on what it is pointing to. Some of the most common shapes are shown in the table below.

Pointer Shape	Meaning
	Select
	Insert text
	Busy
	Area is not available
	Displays Help on selected item
	Horizontal resize
	Diagonal resize
	Move

On top of the mouse are two buttons. These buttons are used to choose items on the screen. The mouse actions and descriptions are shown in the table below.

Action	Description
Point	Move the mouse so the mouse pointer is positioned on the item you want to use
Click	Press and release a mouse button
Double-click	Quickly press and release a mouse button twice
Drag	Move the mouse while holding down a mouse button

Your computer may use a track ball to move the mouse pointer.

This text assumes mouse use. Keyboard tips or alternative ways of doing things will be provided in marginal notes.

Moving the mouse over your work surface moves the mouse pointer on your screen.

Move the mouse in any direction.

The pointer on the screen moved in the direction you moved the mouse.

Move the mouse in all directions (up, down, left, and right) and note the movement and shape of the mouse pointer.

Displaying the Start Menu

As you learn about Windows 95, you will find there are many ways to perform the same task. However, using the Start button is one of the best places to learn how to use Windows 95. It provides quick and easy access to most features you will use frequently.

Move the mouse pointer so that it is on the Start button.

This is called **pointing**. When you hold the mouse pointer over the Start button a box containing the message "Click here to begin" is briefly displayed.

While pointing to the Start button, click the left mouse button.

Your screen should be similar to Figure 1-4.

Figure 1-4

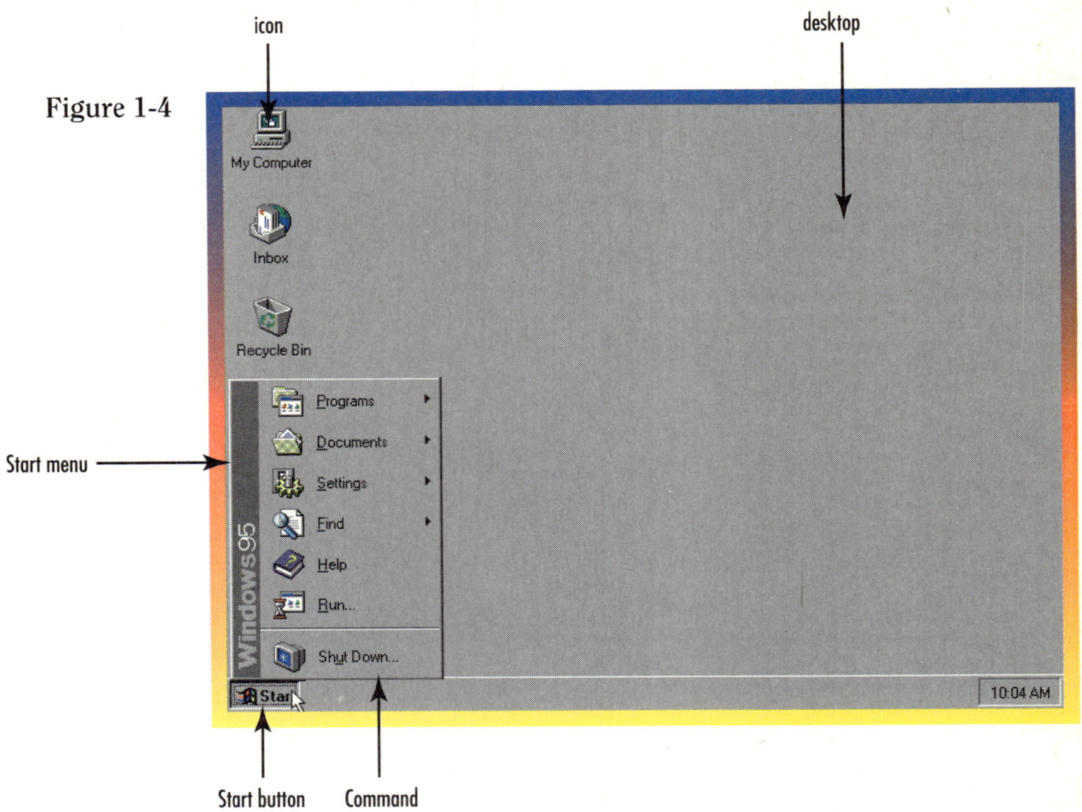

You can also display the Start menu by pressing Ctrl + Esc.

Clicking on the Start button displays the Start menu. The Start menu is a special Windows 95 menu that is used to access and begin all activities you want to perform on the computer. It is one of many menus you will see in Windows 95.

Concept 4: Menus

A **menu** is one of many methods you can use to tell a program what you want it to do. When opened, a menu displays a list of commands. Most menus can simply be opened by clicking on the menu name, as you did the Start menu.

Many menus appear in a **menu bar** rather than as a button. When chosen, a menu bar command displays a **pull-down menu** of additional commands from which you can select. Other menus pop up when you right-click (click the right mouse button) on an area of the desktop. This type of menu is called a **shortcut menu**. Menus are everywhere in Windows 95, but they all operate in the same way.

Once a menu is open, you can select and choose commands from the menu. **Selecting** a command moves a colored highlight bar, called the **selection cursor**, to the command. Simply pointing to the command moves the selection cursor to it. When a command is selected, this indicates the command will be activated when chosen. You **choose** the selected command by clicking on the command, or by typing the underlined command letter, or by pressing ←Enter. When the command is chosen, the associated action is performed.

Menus may include the following features, (not all menus include all features):

Feature	Meaning
Ellipses (...)	Indicates a dialog box will be displayed
▸	Indicates a cascading menu will be displayed
Dimmed command	Indicates the command is not available for selection until certain other conditions are met
Shortcut key	A key or key combination that can be used to execute a command without using the menu
Checkmark (✔)	Indicates a toggle type of command. Selecting it turns the feature on or off. A checkmark indicates the feature is on
Bullet (•)	Indicates that the commands in that group are mutually exclusive: only one can be selected. The bullet indicates the currently selected feature.

If your system has Microsoft Office 95 installed, your Start menu will include the New Office Document and Open Office Document commands.

Selecting Commands

The basic Start menu consists of a list of seven commands from which you can select. The icons to the left of each command are graphic representations of the command. The commands and what they are used for are described briefly in the table below.

Command	Used to
Programs	Start programs
Documents	Open files and related programs
Settings	Change or view the computer system settings
Find	Locate files
Help	Obtain direct access to the Help feature
Run	Start a program using DOS command-line type functionality
Shut Down	Shut down, restart, and log off the computer

You can also move the selection cursor using the ↑ and ↓ keys.

To select a command, point to Shut Down.

The selection cursor is displayed, indicating the currently selected command.

Point to the Run command and then the Help command.

The selection cursor moves to each command as you point to it. To the right of the Find command, an arrowhead ▶ symbol is displayed, indicating that selecting it will display a submenu of commands. To see the submenu for the Find command,

Point to: Find

Your screen should be similar to Figure 1-5.

Figure 1-5

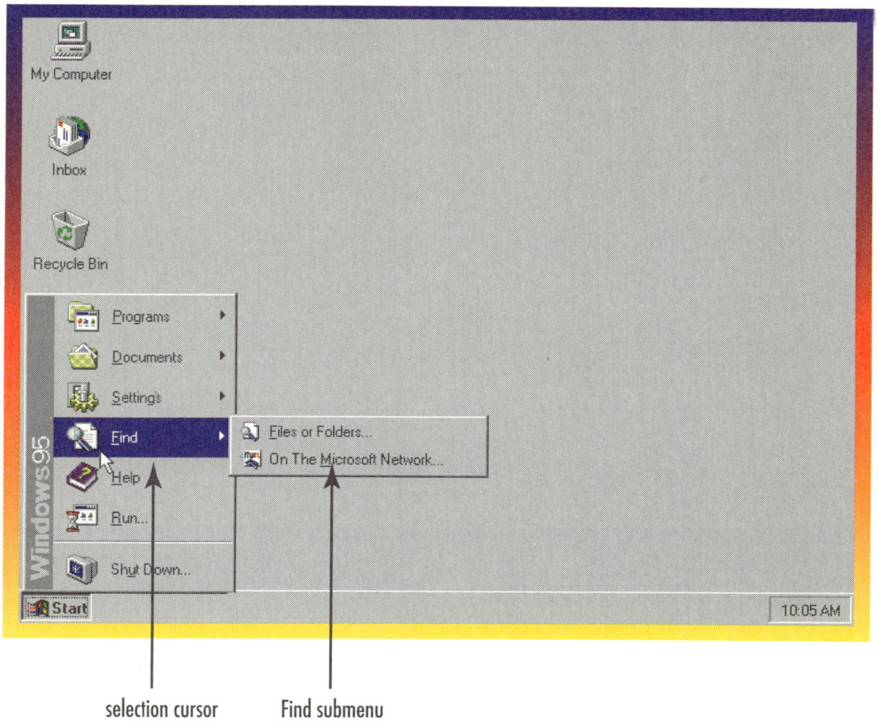

The submenu displays two options that can be selected to search for files.

Point to the Settings, Documents, and Programs commands to see the submenu associated with each.

After opening a menu, you may decide you do not want to select a command. To close or cancel the Start menu you can click the Start button again or click anywhere outside the menu box.

Pressing Esc also cancels menu selections, one menu level at a time.

Cancel the Start menu.

Developing the skill for moving the mouse and correctly positioning the pointer takes some time. If you accidentally find yourself in the wrong location or in a command that you did not intend to select, cancel the selected menu as you did above and try again.

Choosing Commands

Now that you have learned how to move the mouse pointer and select commands, you are ready to choose a command from the menu. As you learned in Concept 4: Menus, the process of *selecting* a command simply moves the selection cursor to the item, whereas *choosing* performs the action associated with the command. To see how this works, you will choose the Help command from the Start menu. The Help command starts the Help program.

Concept 5: Help

Windows **Help** is a quick way to find out information about commands or features. It is a separate application that is loaded when you choose the Help command and specify a topic that you want help information on. Help is available in all Windows applications and operates in the same way as Windows Help.

You can also type the underlined letter of a command to choose it. Command letters to type will appear underlined.

Open the Start menu again.

To choose a command, point to the command and click the left button.

Choose: **Help**

Your screen should be similar to Figure 1-6.

Figure 1-6

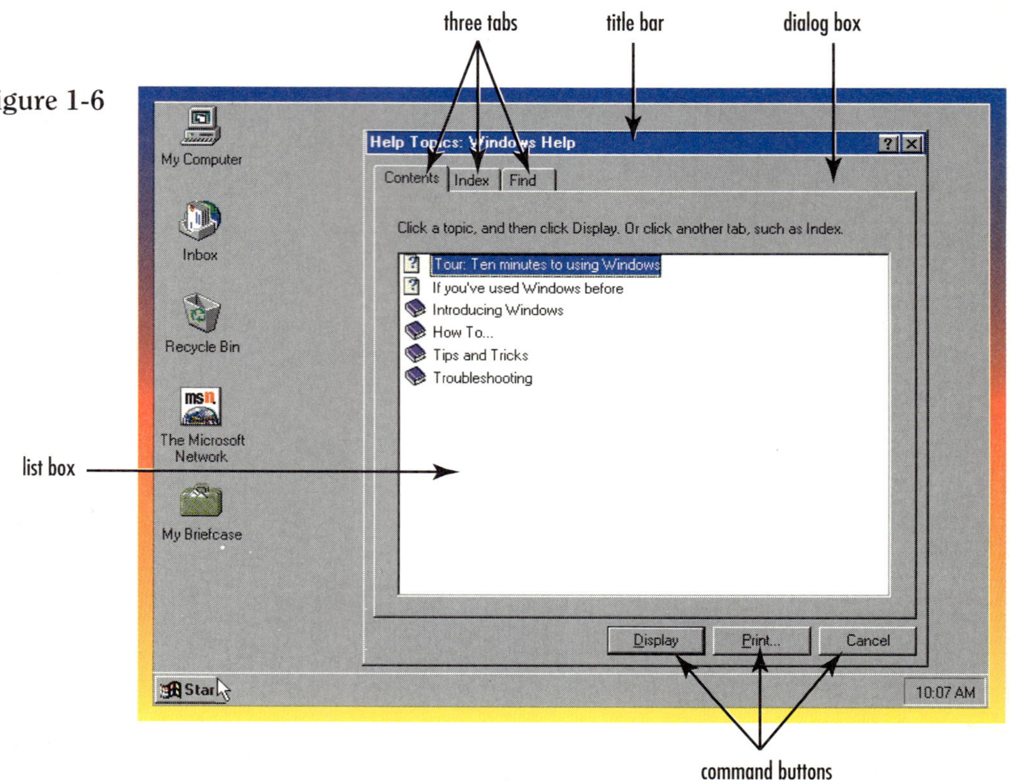

Do not be concerned if your Help dialog box displays different information.

You have executed the Help command, the Start menu is cleared from the screen, and the Help Topics dialog box is displayed.

Using a Dialog Box

A dialog box is a common feature that is displayed whenever the program requires additional information to complete a command.

Concept 6: Dialog Box

A **dialog box** is how Windows programs provide and request information from you in order to complete a task. All dialog boxes have a **title bar** at the top of the box, which displays a name identifying the contents of the dialog box and buttons. Inside the dialog box are areas to select or specify the needed information, and command buttons. The features shown in the table below may be found in dialog boxes; however, not all features are found in every dialog box.

Feature	**Meaning**
Close Button	Used to close a dialog box.
What's This	Displays Help on dialog box options.
Text box	An area where you type in the requested information.
Option button	An option preceded with a circle. The selected option displays a black dot. Only one option can be selected from a list of option buttons.
List box	A box displaying a list of information from which you can select.
Drop-down list box	A text box that displays the currently selected item and a ▾ button. Clicking the ▾ button displays a drop-down list of items from which you can select, or you can type the information in the text box.
Check box	An option preceded with a square. The selected option displays ✔. You can select more than one check box option.
Sliding control	Dragging the lever in the control increases or decreases the related setting, such as volume.
Command button	Instructs Windows to carry out the instructions on the button. The two most common command buttons are OK and Cancel. Other buttons you will see are Close, Help, Options, Setup, Display, and Settings.

Many dialog boxes also include folder-like tabs across the top of the dialog box that open to display related options. This type of dialog box is called a **tab dialog box**. The tab names identify the content of the tab. The active tab appears in front of the other tabs and displays the available options for the feature.

The Help topics tab dialog box displays the dialog box name "Help Topics: Windows Help" in the title bar. It also contains three tabs—Contents, Index, and Find—that are used to access the three different means of getting Help information. To select and open a tab, click on it with the mouse. To see the contents of the three tab areas,

You can also press Ctrl + Tab to select the tab to the right or Ctrl + Shift + Tab to select the tab to the left.

Click: **Find**

The Find tab is open and displays three numbered areas. Area 1 displays a drop-down list box where you enter a word or phrase you want to locate. Areas 2 and 3 are list boxes. The list boxes display a list of words or topics from which you can select. You will learn shortly how these features work when you use the Index tab.

Click: **Contents**

The Contents tab (shown in Figure 1-6) is open and displays six items. Double-clicking on an item preceded with a ◆ opens a book and displays additional books or specific Help topics.

"Double-click" means to click the left mouse button twice in rapid succession without moving the mouse.

Double-click: ◆ **Introducing Windows**

The Introducing Windows book icon appears as an open book and two new book icons appear indented below it.

Double-click: ◆ **Welcome**

Three items appear under the Welcome book.

Topics preceded with a ? display a Help window of information on that topic when chosen. You will open a Help window from the Index tab next. The Index tab is the area you will probably use the most often.

Click: **Index**

Your screen should be similar to Figure 1-7.

Figure 1-7

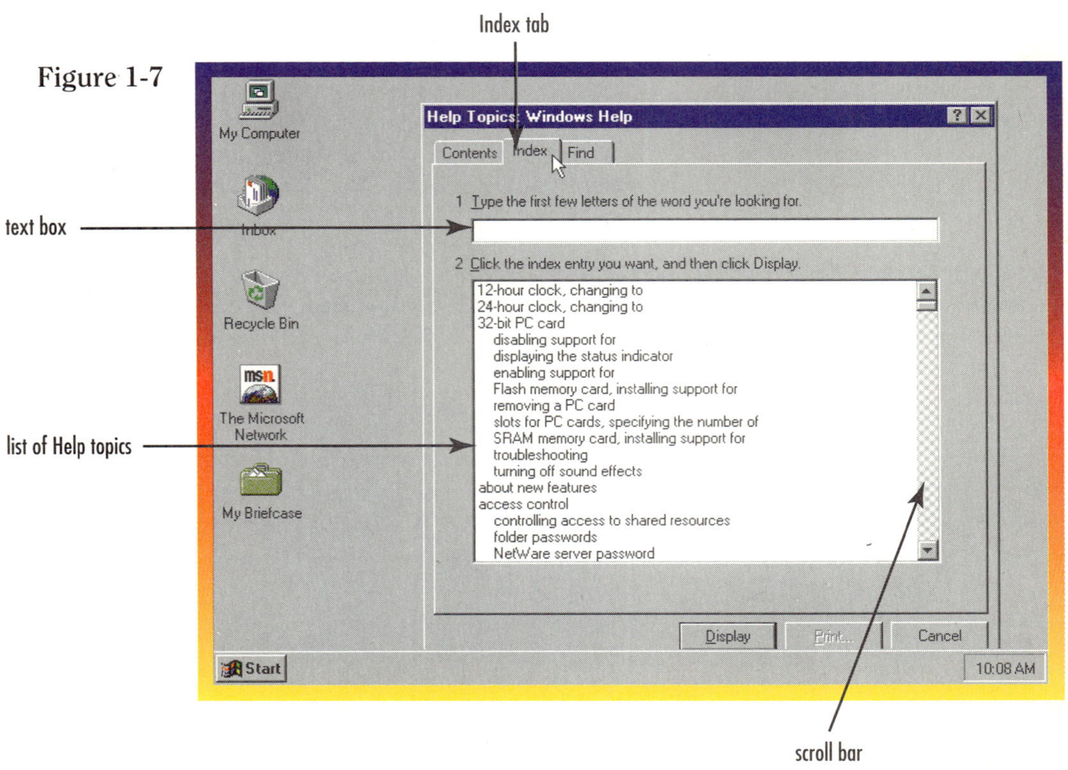

The Index tab has two numbered areas. Area 1 consists of a text box where you can type a word or phrase that best describes the topic you want to locate. Area 2 is a list box displaying a complete list of Help topics in alphabetical order.

Using Scroll Bars

The topic list box contains many more topics than can be displayed at one time in the box. Whenever there is more information than can be displayed in a window or list box, a scroll bar is displayed.

Concept 7: Scroll Bar

vertical scroll bar

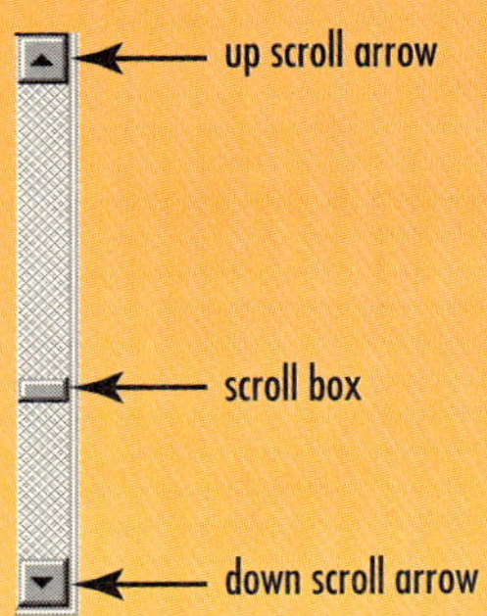

horizontal scroll bar

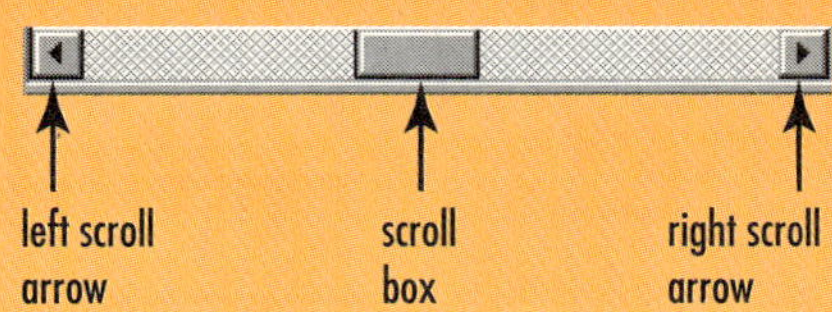

A **scroll bar** is used with a mouse to bring additional lines of information into view in a window or list box. Scroll bars can run vertically along the right side or horizontally along the bottom of a window or list box. The vertical scroll bar is used to move vertically and the horizontal scroll bar moves horizontally in the space. The scroll bar consists of **scroll arrows** and a **scroll box**. Clicking the arrows moves the information in the direction of the arrows, allowing new topics to be displayed in the space.

You can also move to a general location within the area by dragging the scroll box up or down the scroll bar. The location of the scroll box on the scroll bar indicates your relative position within the area of available information. In many scroll bars, the size of the scroll box also indicates the relative amount of the information that is available. For example, a small box indicates that only a small amount of the total available information is displayed, whereas a large box indicates that almost all or a large portion of the total amount of available information is displayed.

To bring more topics into view, you will scroll the list using the scroll bar.

Point to the down scroll arrow in the list box and click the left mouse button five times.

The list of topics has moved up line by line, allowing new topics to be displayed at the bottom of the box.

To continuously scroll the list, point to the down scroll arrow and hold down the left mouse button for a few seconds.

The list has moved down continuously, line by line.

Point to the up scroll arrow and click several times.

Press Tab to move from one area in a dialog box to another, and use the ↓ or ↑ directional keys to scroll a list line by line.

The list scrolled up several lines. Did you notice the movement of the scroll box as you scrolled the list? It moves up or down along the scroll bar to show your relative location within the list.

Click on the scroll bar below the scroll box several times.

Clicking above or below the scroll box moves the list up or down a boxful of topics at a time.

> Press [Page Up] and [Page Down] to move a boxful at a time.

Click above the scroll box.

Dragging the scroll box moves to a general location within the list.

Drag the scroll box to the lower third of the scroll bar.

Your screen should be similar to Figure 1-8.

Figure 1-8

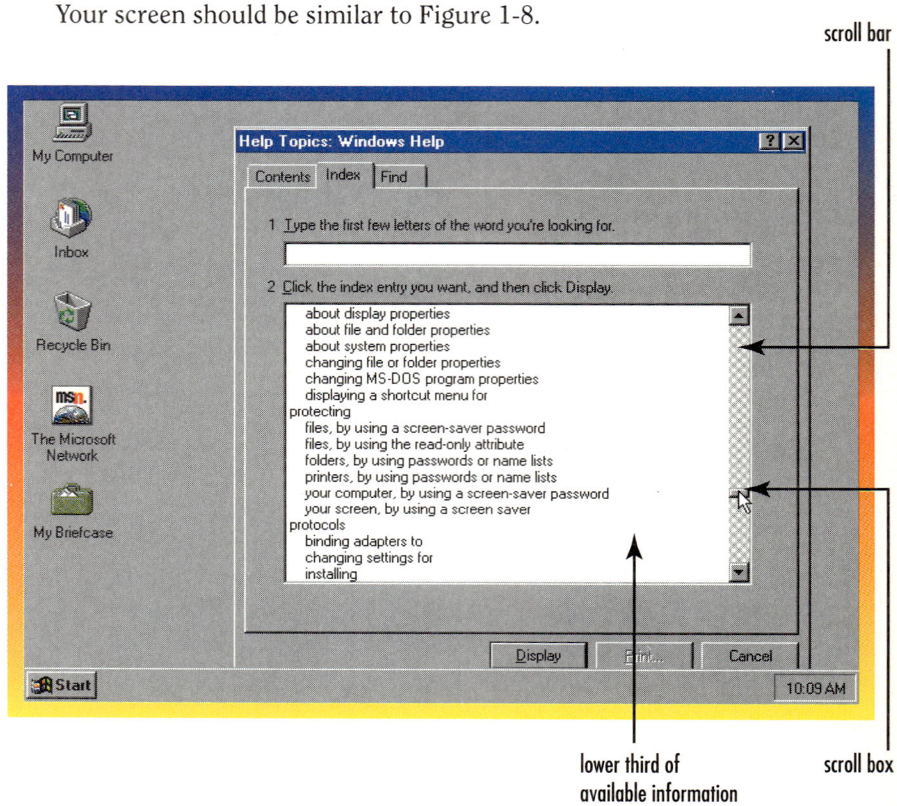

The location of the scroll box in the lower third of the bar indicates the information you see in the list is in the lower third of available information.

> Press [Ctrl] + [Home] to move to the top of the list and [Ctrl] + [End] to move to the end.

Drag the scroll box to the top of the scroll bar.

The features you have learned to scroll a list in this dialog box can be used to scroll whenever a scroll bar appears.

When the topic you want help on appears, click on it to select it.

Click on any topic in the list.

The selection cursor highlights the selected topic and the topic appears in the text box.

Getting Help on a Topic

Refer to Concept 6: Dialog Box for information on text boxes.

An easier way to locate a topic is to type the first few letters of the topic in the text box. To see how this works, you will locate Help on formatting a disk.

To quickly move to the formatting topic in the list box, you will type the word "format" in the text box. The text box must be active before you can type information in it. When active, a blinking vertical bar called the **insertion point** is displayed or the information in the text box is highlighted. To activate the text box,

Press Tab or Ctrl + Tab to move to and activate different areas of the dialog box. Buttons and list boxes display a dotted box when active, and text boxes highlight existing entries and display the insertion point.

Click on: the text box

The insertion point appears in the text box. Because the box displays a topic, the insertion point is positioned in the topic text wherever you were pointing when you clicked the mouse. The mouse pointer appears as an I-beam in the text box. It is used to position the insertion point.

Before you can type the new text, you need to clear the current entry. To do this, you could use ←Backspace or Del to remove each character one character at a time. Another way is to select or highlight the entry and then type the new entry. To select text displayed in a text box, you drag the mouse pointer from one end of the entry to the other.

"Drag" means to hold down the left mouse button while moving the mouse.

Select the text in the text box.

The entire entry should appear highlighted, indicating that it is selected.

Now, as soon as you begin typing, the existing entry will be cleared and replaced by the text you are typing.

Type: f

Your screen should be similar to Figure 1-9.

Figure 1-9

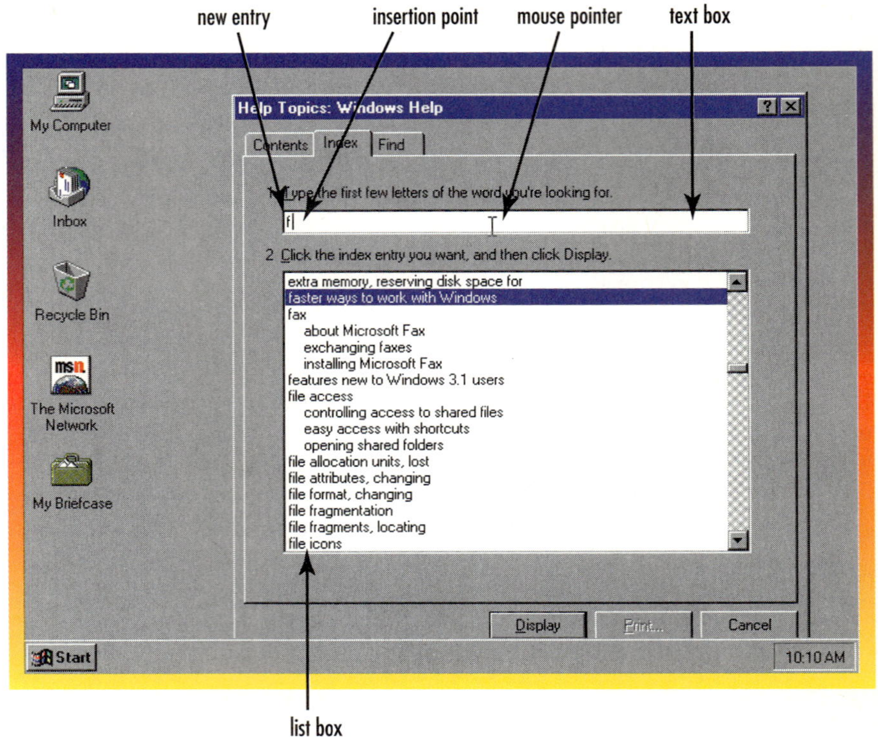

The selection cursor jumps to the first word in the topic list beginning with the letter "f." If you scrolled this list, you would eventually locate the word "format." To narrow the list even more, you will type the next letter of the word.

Type: o

The selection cursor now jumps to the first topic beginning with "fo." To continue to narrow the list,

If you make a typing error, use ←Backspace to erase characters to the left of the insertion point and retype the entry correctly.

Type: r

The selection cursor now highlights the first word beginning with "for" and the formatting topic is now visible in the list. The "disks" subhead under the formatting topic is the topic you want help on.

Select: disks

Your screen should be similar to Figure 1-10.

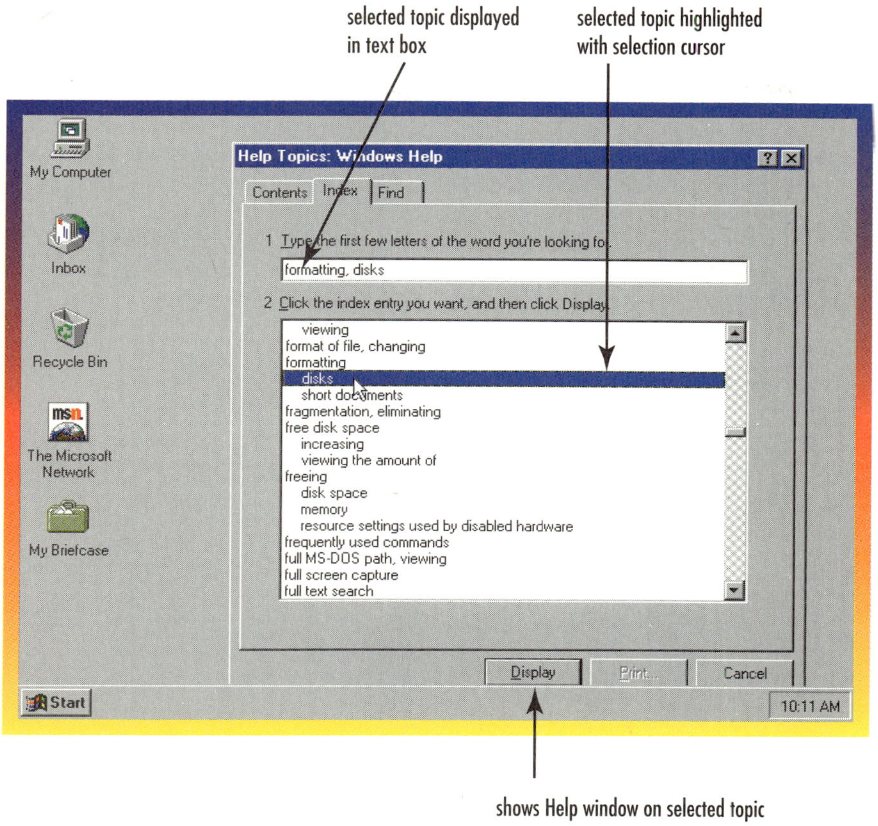

Figure 1-10

The selection cursor should be highlighting the word "disks" and the complete topic, "formatting, disks," appears in the text box.

The bottom of the dialog box displays three command buttons. As the name in the button indicates, Display is used to display the selected topic, Print is used to print the selected topic, and Cancel is used to close the Help dialog box. To display the Help information on the selected topic,

Choose: **Display**

Command buttons that appear dimmed are not currently available for selection.

You can also double-click on the topic in the list box to both select it and to choose Display.

To choose command buttons, type the underlined letter or select the button and press ←Enter.

Your screen should be similar to Figure 1-11.

Figure 1-11

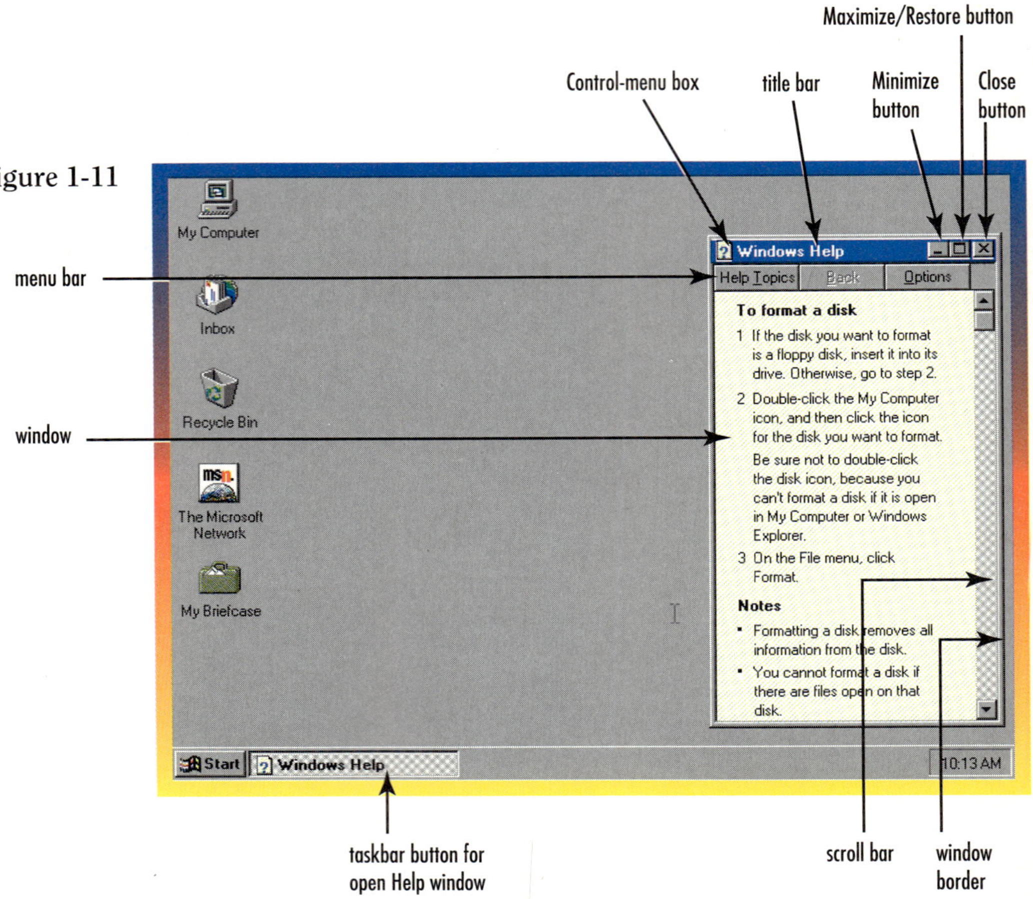

A Help window of information on how to format a disk is displayed. The title bar displays the application name, Windows Help. The menu bar displays three menu buttons that are used to access Help features.

Concept 8: Window

As you learned in Concept 1: What's Windows 95?, a window is a rectangular section of the screen that is dedicated to a specific activity or application. The **window border** outlines the window. All windows have the basic parts described below:

Feature	Meaning
Title bar	A bar located at the top of the window that displays the application name and buttons.
Control-menu box	An icon located on the left end of the title bar that when opened, displays the Control menu. This consists of a list of commands that are used to move, size, and otherwise control the window.
Minimize button	Used to reduce a window to a its smallest size.
Maximize/Restore button /	Used to enlarge a window to its maximum size. Changes to when maximized to allow you to return the window to its previous size.
Close button	Used to exit the application running in the window and to close the window.
Menu bar	A bar located below the title bar, containing a list of menus that can be used with the application displayed in the window.

A scroll bar also appears in many windows whenever the window cannot fully display the information. Some windows also have additional features such as a toolbar and status bar, which will be described later in these labs.

All applications that you open are displayed in their own window. In addition, the taskbar displays a button for each open window. The button appears depressed, indicating the window is the **active window** or the window that is currently in use. Multiple windows can be open on the desktop at once, but only one window is active at a time.

Do not confuse a window and a dialog box. A window always includes a menu bar and does not display command buttons.

Moving Windows

Sometimes, when a window is displayed, it overlaps other information on the desktop. To see the area under the window, you can easily move it.

A dialog box can be moved just like a window.

Concept 9: Moving Windows

When a window opens, it can appear anywhere on your desktop. Sometimes the location of the window is inconvenient. Moving a window simply displays the window at another location on the desktop. It does not change the size of the window.

A window is moved by pointing to the title bar and dragging an outline of the window to the new location on the desktop.

Open the Control menu (press Alt + Spacebar) and select Move. Then use the directional keys to specify the direction to move. Press ←Enter when done.

With the pointer anywhere within the Help title bar, click and drag the mouse. Do not release the mouse button.

An outline of the window is displayed as you drag it across the desktop. When you release the button, the window moves to the new location.

Move the Help window to the center of the desktop and release the mouse button.

Your screen should be similar to Figure 1-12.

Figure 1-12

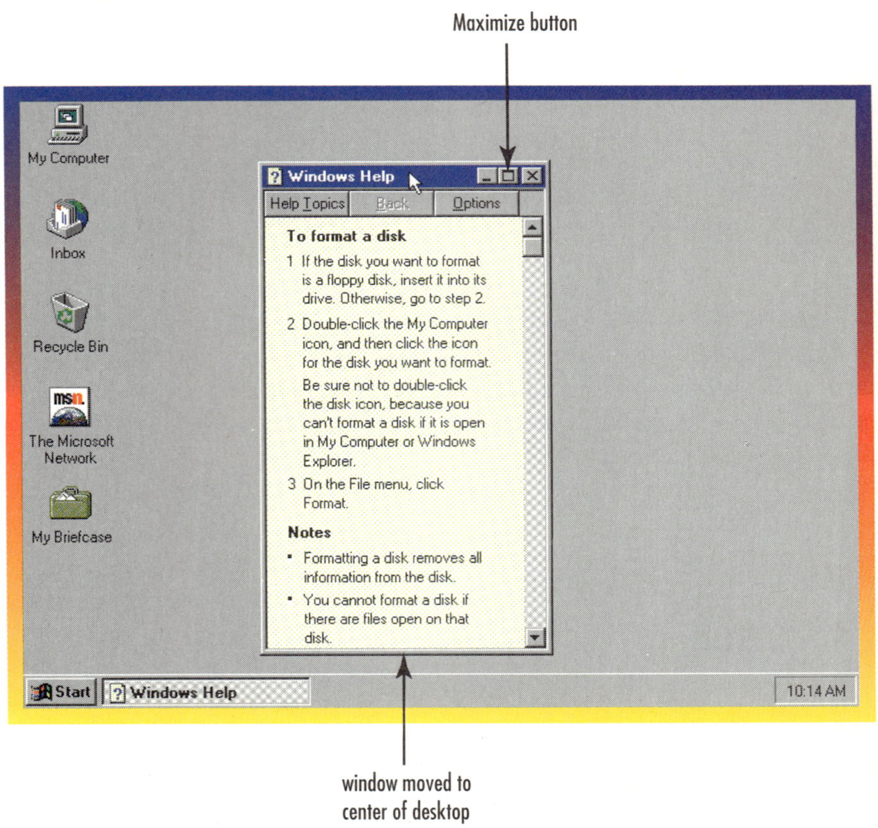

Sizing Windows

Windows appear on the desktop in different sizes, and sometimes the current size is too small or too large. The size of a window can easily be changed.

Concept 10: Sizing Windows

The size of a window can be changed to just about any size you want. A window can be **minimized** to its smallest size using the Minimize button, or **maximized** to its largest size using the Maximize button. A maximized window can then be **restored** to its previous size using the Restore button. In addition, a window can be custom sized by pointing to the window border and dragging the border in the direction you want to go. Dragging inward decreases the size and dragging outward increases the size. Dragging a corner increases or decreases the size, of the two adjoining borders at the same time.

A dialog box cannot be sized.

Notice that a scroll bar appears along the edge of the window. This indicates there is more information that cannot be displayed in the window space. To enlarge the window to its maximum size,

Click: Maximize

Open the Control menu (Alt + Spacebar) and select Maximize.

The Help window now occupies the entire desktop. Because all the information can be displayed in the window, the scroll bar is not displayed.

Read the information about formatting a disk.

Notice that the Maximize button has changed to . This is the Restore button. Restoring a window returns it to its previous size and location.

Click: Restore

Select Restore from the Control menu.

You can also custom size and shape a window by adjusting the window borders. When you point to a border or corner, the mouse pointer changes to a two-headed arrow ↔. The directions in which the arrowheads point indicate the directions you can drag the border or corner.

Point to the lower right corner of the Help window. (The pointer is correctly positioned when the pointer changes to a two-headed diagonal arrow ↘.)

As you drag the mouse, an outline of the window will appear showing you the new size.

Reduce the window size to about a 2-inch square and then release the button.

Select Size from the Control menu and then use the directional keys to position the ✥ and to specify the direction to size. Press ←Enter when done.

Your screen should be similar to Figure 1-13.

Figure 1-13

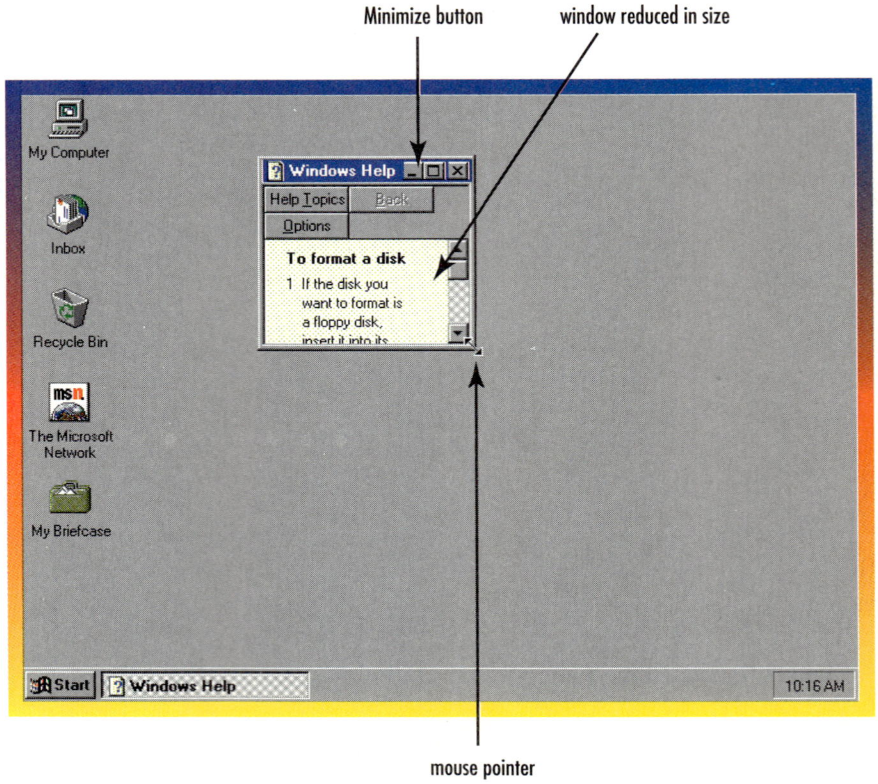

As much of the Help information as possible is displayed in the window. To view the rest of the information, you would need to scroll the window.

Once a window has been custom sized, the only way to return it to the original size is by dragging the borders again.

Enlarge the Help window to its original size (see Figure 1-12).

Often you will want to keep a window open for future reference, but you do not want it to occupy space on the desktop. To do this, you can minimize the window.

Select Minimize from the Control menu.

Click: Minimize

Your screen should be similar to Figure 1-14.

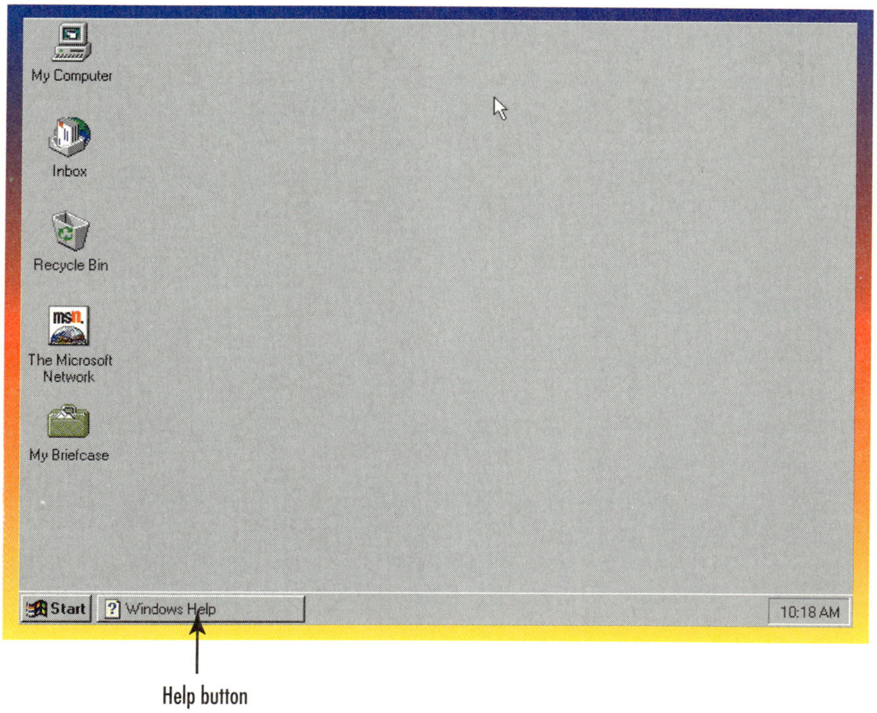

Figure 1-14

The Help window is minimized. Notice that the Windows Help button in the taskbar is still displayed. This indicates the window is still open, but minimized. To redisplay the Help window, simply click on its taskbar button.

Click: [?] Windows Help

The window is redisplayed on the screen. Now, you can either close the Help window or return to the Help topics dialog box. Returning to the dialog box is often useful if the topic you selected does not provide the information you need. To return,

Choose: **Help Topics**

The last topic selected is still highlighted. Now you could use the Help dialog box to display information on other Help topics in the Help window. However, the information the Help window currently displays is appropriate. To close the dialog box,

Choose: **Cancel**

or

Click: [X]

The [X] button is located at the right end of the title bar.

The dialog box is closed, but the Help window that was under the dialog box is still open and is now visible.

Note: If you are running short on lab time, you can quite before beginning Part 2. To do this, close the Help window, then follow the directions to quit Windows 95 on page WN49. When you begin Part 2, display the Help window on formatting a disk.

Part 2

Formatting a Disk

You would like to keep the Help on how to format a disk open so you can refer to the directions while you are formatting a disk next.

To see more of the desktop, move the Help window back to the right edge of the desktop (as in Figure 1-11).

You will format a new disk so you can copy the data files needed to complete the next two labs to the new disk.

Concept 11: Formatting a Disk

Before a new disk can be used, you must **format** or convert it from a generic state into a format that can be used by your computer. Many disks are shipped from the manufacturer in a blank (**unformatted**) form so they can be used by a variety of computers. Others are preformatted and do not need to be formatted before use.

Formatting prepares a new disk to accept information and files. Specifically, it sets up and labels the **tracks** (concentric rings where data is stored on the disk) and **sectors** (divisions of the tracks) to accept information. It checks the tracks for any bad spots that are unable to store information and marks off these areas so they cannot be used. It also sets up the area on the disk where the directory of files will be maintained.

Any disk, old or new, can be formatted. However, if you format a used disk, any files or information on it will be erased during formatting. Be careful only to format disks that do not contain information that you may want. Be especially careful when formatting that you do not accidentally format the hard disk, as all your programs and files will be erased. If you attempt to format the hard disk, Windows displays a warning message.

Even if your disk is preformatted, you can complete the directions below and format it again.

Following the directions in Step 1 of the Help window, place a blank floppy disk in the appropriate drive.

Next, following the directions in Step 2,

A single click on an icon selects (highlights) it, and a double-click opens it.

Double-click:  My Computer

Your screen should be similar to Figure 1-15.

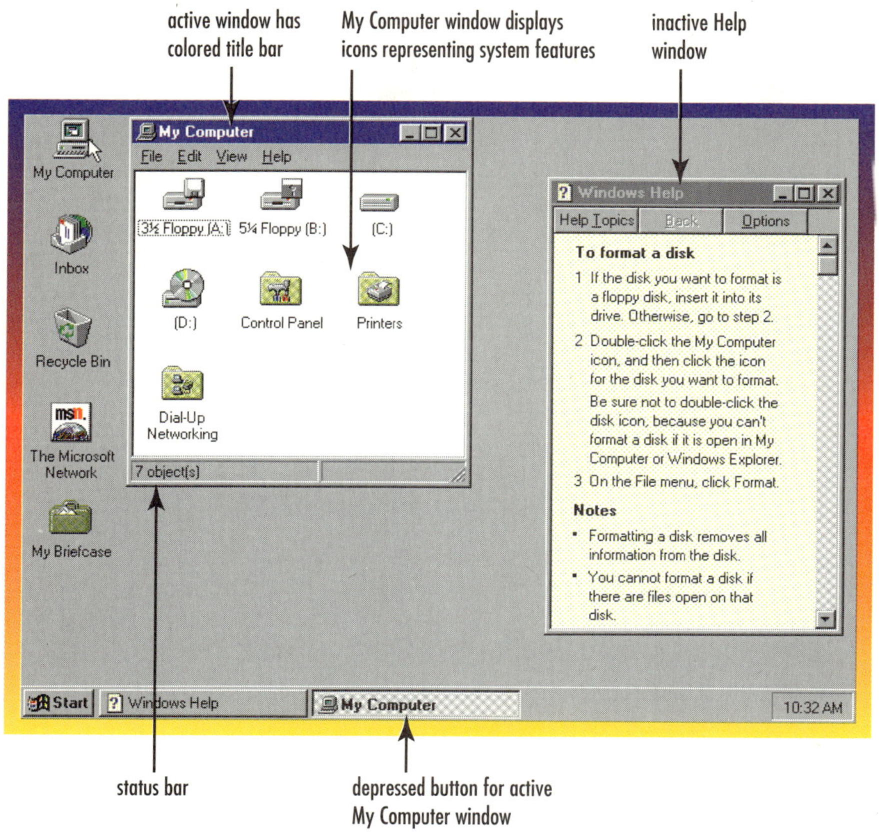

Figure 1-15

A second window is open on the desktop, and the taskbar displays a new button for this open window. The My Computer window is the active window. You can tell it is the active window because the taskbar button is depressed and the window title bar is colored. The My Computer window is used to view the information on your computer. It displays icons representing various features associated with your computer. Some or all of the items shown in the table below may be displayed in your My Computer window.

Icon	Representation
 3½ Floppy (A:)	3.5-inch floppy-disk drive
 5¼ Floppy (B:)	5.25-inch floppy-disk drive
 (C:)	Hard-disk drive
	Network drive
 (D:)	CD-ROM drive

If the status bar is not displayed, after formatting your disk, you can turn it on by choosing Status Bar from the View menu.

In addition, at the bottom of the window a status bar is displayed.

Concept 12: Status Bar

Many windows display a **status bar** at the bottom of the window. The information displayed in the status bar varies with the program you are using and the task being performed. The purpose of the status bar is to advise you of the status of different program conditions and features as you use the program.

Currently the status bar tells you the number of items, called objects, in the window.

Still following the directions in Step 2, to select the drive that contains the disk to be formatted.

Do not double-click the disk icon, because this opens the disk and you cannot format a disk if it is open in My Computer.

Click: 

(or the appropriate drive for your station)

The drive icon is highlighted, indicating it is selected. Also notice that the status bar indicates that one object is selected.

Finally, to begin formatting the disk, following the instructions in Step 3, you use the Format command on the File menu. To open the File menu,

Press Alt and the underlined letter of the menu to open the menu.

Click: **File**

Refer to Concept 4: Menus to review menu features.

If the status bar is covered by the pull-down menu, make the My Computer window larger.

A pull-down menu of File commands is displayed. Pull-down menus operate just like the Start menu. They include the same features as the Start menu, except they do not display icons. Horizontal lines within many menus divide the commands into related groups. Also notice that the status bar displays a brief description of what the selected File menu command does.

To select the Format command,

Point to: **Format**

The Format command is selected and now the status bar displays a description for the selected command. Notice that the Format command displays ellipses. This indicates that a dialog box will appear when the command is chosen. To choose the Format command,

Click: **Format**

Your screen should be similar to Figure 1-16.

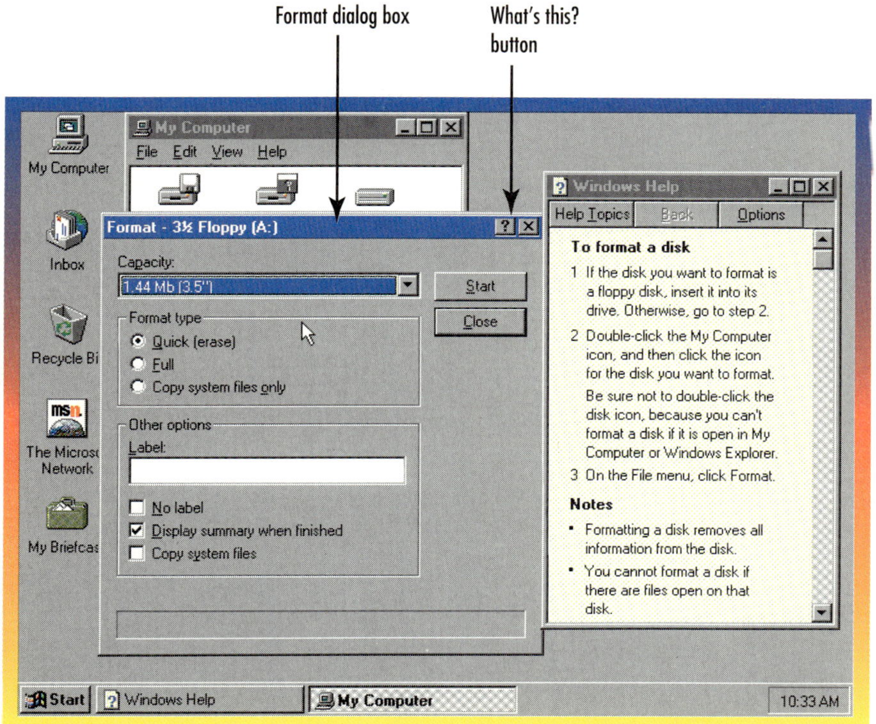

Figure 1-16

The Format dialog box is displayed. Another feature frequently found in dialog boxes is the [?] "What's this" button located at the right end of the title bar. It is used to get Help on the dialog box options. To do this,

> If necessary, move the dialog box to see the [?] button.

Click: [?] **What's this?**

The mouse pointer changes to a ↖?, indicating it will provide brief Help information about any item in the dialog box that you click on. The first dialog box option is used to specify the capacity of the disk. **Capacity** refers to the maximum number of bytes the disk can hold. To get help on this option,

> Not all dialog boxes have a [?] button. To get Help on using these boxes, use the Help command button if available or try pressing F1.

Click: **Capacity**

Your screen should be similar to Figure 1-17.

Figure 1-17

definition of "capacity" in pop-up window

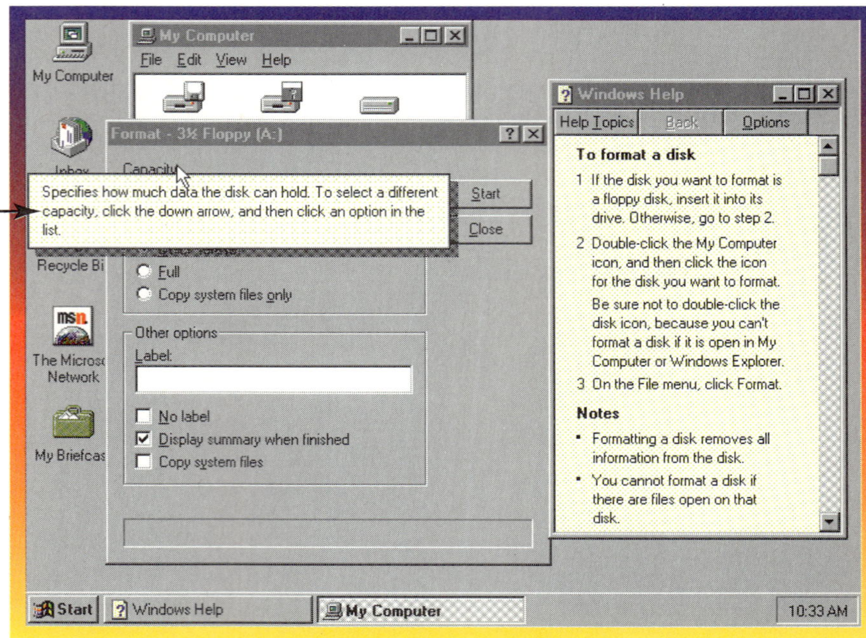

A pop-up window containing an explanation of what the Capacity option does is displayed.

> You can also press (Esc) to close the pop-up window.

Read the information provided in the window. Then, to close the pop-up window, click inside the box.

Windows assumes that you want to format the disk with the maximum capacity for the drive. Not all types of floppy disks are compatible with all types of floppy-disk drives. Generally, a disk can be formatted at a capacity less than or equal to the capacity of the disk drive. For example, to format a disk at 720K in a disk drive that has a maximum capacity of 1.44MB, you would change the capacity to 720K in the capacity list box. If you are unsure of the size of the drive or disk, check with your instructor.

> To display the drop-down list of Capacity options, click ▾ or press (↓).

If necessary, change the capacity to the size of the disk you are formatting.

The Format Type section of the dialog box displays three options: Quick (erase), Full, and Copy System Files Only. Quick format is used only on previously formatted disks that you know are in good condition. It does not check for bad spots on the disk. Full performs a complete format and is always used on new disks. The Copy System Files Only option will copy system files to a formatted disk without removing any existing files.

Use ? What's this? to get more information about the format types.

The Format Type options are preceded with option buttons, indicating only one can be selected. The best format option for your purpose is Full. To select Full,

Click: Full

Press Tab to move to different areas of the dialog box.

The last area in the dialog box contains several additional check box options. Any number of these options can be selected.

Use What's this? to read information on each option.

You want to include a label on the disk that will display your name. This is an electronic label that is recorded during the formatting process. If the No Label check box is selected (that is, if it displays a ✔), you will need to clear the selection first.

If necessary, clear the checkmark from the No label option.

Then, to specify the label to include on your disk, click in the Label text box.

Type: **your first initial and as much of your last name as possible**

The disk label can contain up to 11 characters including spaces.

You want Windows to display the summary information when formatting is done and you do not want the system files copied to your disk.

If necessary, select the Display Summary When Finished option and deselect the Copy System Files option.

Your screen should be similar to Figure 1-18.

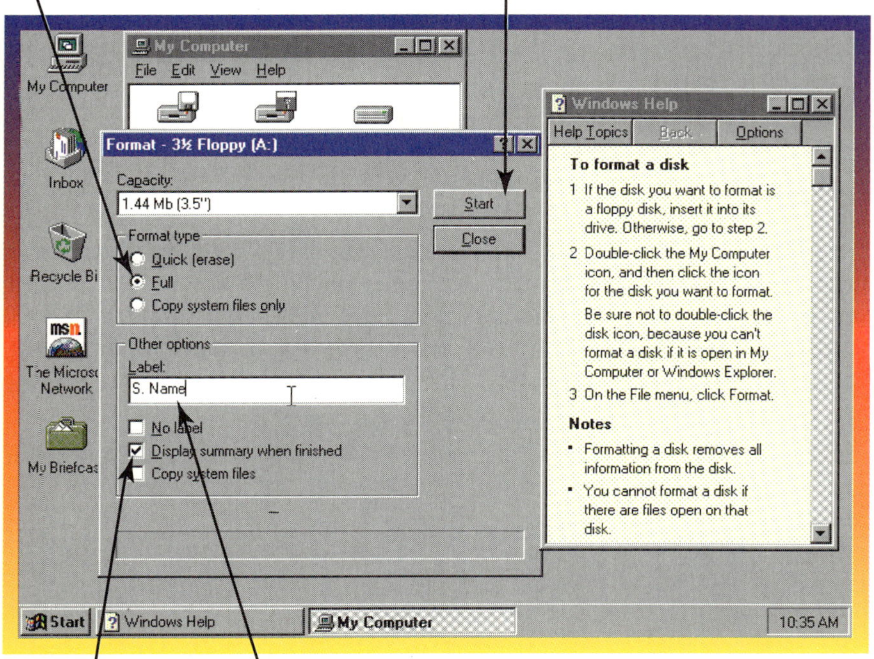

Figure 1-18

To carry out the command to format the disk in the drive specified using the settings you have selected in the dialog box,

> If an informational dialog box appears indicating there is no disk in the drive, follow the directions in the box and choose Retry.

Click: Start

Notice the Formatting progress bar at the bottom of the dialog box. It indicates how much of the formatting task is completed. When formatting is complete, your screen should be similar to Figure 1-19.

Figure 1-19

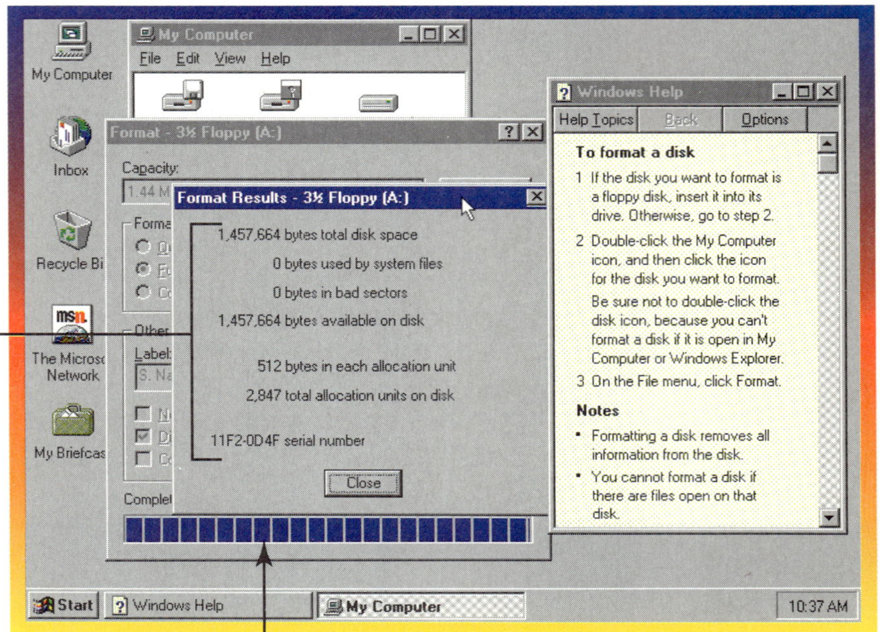

The Format Results dialog box is displayed. It shows the total number of bytes on the disk and bytes available for use. If any bad sectors were located, Windows tells you the number of bytes in bad sectors. The number of bytes available in each allocation unit, how many allocation units were created (indicates how Windows has divided the disk for file storage into groups or sectors), and the serial number are also displayed.

You have formatted your disk, and it is now ready to be used. To close the Format Results dialog box,

Choose: Close

> You could also click ☒ to close the dialog box.

The Format dialog box is still open, allowing you to format another disk. To close the Format dialog box,

Choose: Close

> If you need to format additional disks, repeat the procedure.

The My Computer window is active again.

Now that you know how to use menus, if necessary, turn on the display of the status bar (View/Status Bar).

Viewing Disk Properties

Next, you would like to see the properties associated with the newly formatted disk.

Concept 13: Properties

Properties are the settings and attributes associated with an object on the screen such as an icon. Just about all the objects on the desktop have properties associated with them. The desktop itself is an object that has properties. The properties can be viewed and changed if necessary to suit your needs.

To view the properties associated with the disk in your floppy drive,

Right-click: 

(or other appropriate drive)

Your screen should be similar to Figure 1-20.

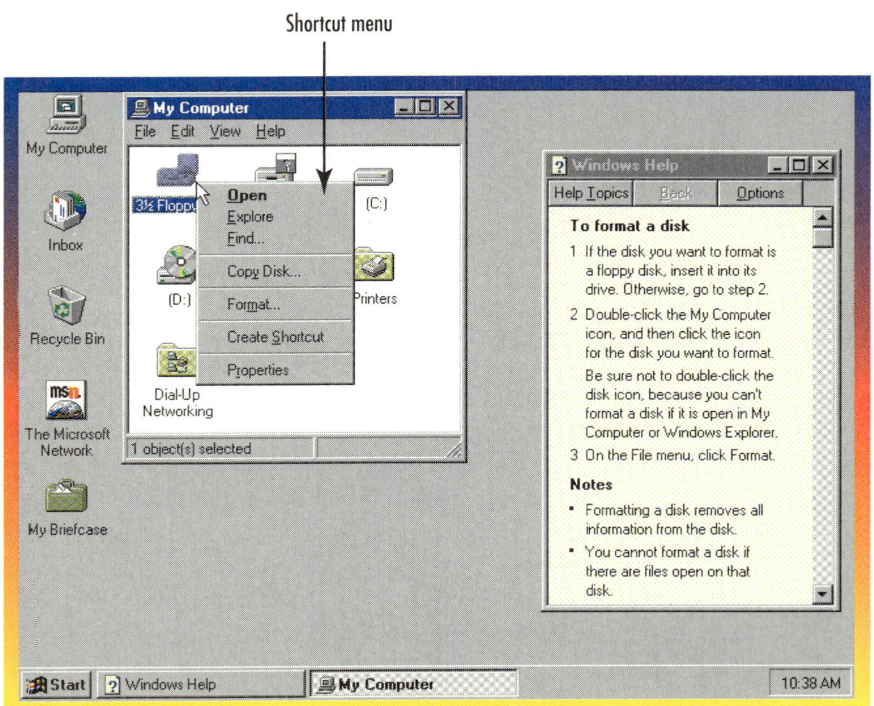

Figure 1-20

A shortcut menu of options appears. Shortcut menus appear whenever you right-click an item on the desktop. The options in the shortcut menu vary with the item that is clicked on.

The Properties command can also be selected from the File menu.

Choose: **Properties**

The Properties tab dialog box is displayed. It includes two tabs that access different options associated with Disk properties.

If necessary, select the General tab.

Your screen should be similar to Figure 1-21.

Figure 1-21

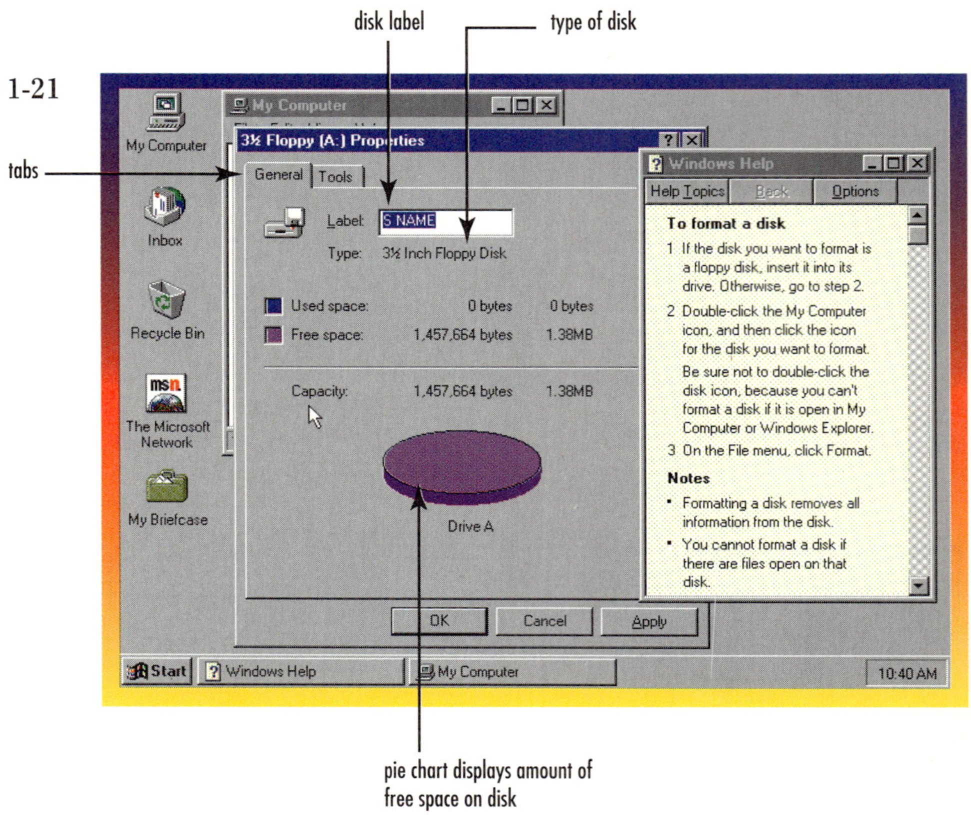

The Label text box displays the disk label you entered during formatting. If needed, you can change the label on a disk using this text box. Below the Label text box, the type of disk is identified.

The General tab also displays information on the amount of used and free space on the disk. Since this disk is newly formatted, it does not contain any data. The capacity value indicates the total capacity available on the disk. This value should equal the amount of free and used space. Finally, a pie chart visually displays the amount of free and used space. Again, because this disk is newly formatted, the chart shows that the disk is 100 percent unused.

Close the Properties dialog box.

Choose Cancel or click ☒.

Remove the newly formatted disk from the drive. To show that this disk has been formatted, put a paper label on it. Include your name and other identifying information such as the class, and the words "Windows 95 DATA DISK" on the label.

If you are using 5.25-inch disks and you need to write on a label that is already on a disk, use a felt-tip pen only.

Now that your disk has been formatted, it is ready to be used to store information. You will use this disk to hold a copy of the files you will need to complete the next two Windows 95 labs. You will learn how to copy files to the disk in Lab 2.

With formatting finished, you can close the My Computer and Help windows. To close the My Computer window,

You could also choose Close from the File menu to close a window.

Click: ☒

The My Computer button is also removed from the taskbar.

In a similar manner, close the Help window.

Choose Close from the Control menu or press Alt + F4 to close the Help window.

Quitting Windows 95

WARNING!

To avoid damaging files, always follow the procedure below to shut down Windows 95 before you turn off your computer.

When you want to stop working with Windows 95 and turn off your computer, always use the Shut Down command in the Start menu.

Click: Start
Choose: Shut Down

The Shut Down Windows dialog box is displayed. It contains options for turning off your computer. These options have the following effects:

Your Shut Down dialog box may not include all options listed.

Option	Effect
Shut down the computer?	Saves any settings you have changed in Windows 95 and prepares the computer to be turned off
Restart the computer?	Saves any settings you have changed in Windows 95 and restarts computer
Restart the computer in MS-DOS mode?	Saves any settings you have changed in Windows 95 and restarts computer in MS-DOS mode. This mode is needed to run DOS programs that will not run under Windows 95.
Close all programs and log-on as a different user?	If your computer is connected to a network, this option is displayed. It disconnects you from a network and prepares the computer to be used by someone else.

Choosing No cancels the Shut Down Windows dialog box and returns you to your Windows 95 session.

Select the option as directed by your instructor.

Choose: **Yes**

WARNING!

If you choose Shut Down the Computer, *do not* turn off your computer until you see the message indicating it is safe to do so.

LAB REVIEW

Key Terms

active window WN35
capacity WN43
choose WN23
cold start WN16
common user interface WN16
desktop WN19
dialog box WN27
format WN40
graphical user interface WN16
Help WN26
icon WN16
insertion point WN31
maximize WN37
menu WN23
menu bar WN23
minimize WN37
mouse WN21
mouse pointer WN21
notification area WN20
operating system WN15
pointing WN22
properties WN47
pull-down menu WN23
restore WN37
scroll arrow WN29
scroll bar WN29
scroll box WN29
sectors WN40
select WN23
selection cursor WN23
shortcut menu WN23
Start button WN20
status bar WN42
tab dialog box WN27
taskbar WN20
title bar WN27
track WN40
unformatted WN40
warm start WN16
window WN16
window border WN35

Command Summary

Command	**Action**
Start Menu	
Help	Opens Windows Help program
Shut Down	@Afely shuts downs your computer before you turn the power off
My Computer	
File/Format	Sets up a disk for use
View/Status Bar	Turns on/off display of status bar

Matching

1. Match the following with the correct definition or function.

1. 	_____	**a.**	button that restores a maximized window
2. scroll bar	_____	**b.**	a mouse pointer
3. window border	_____	**c.**	where you point to change the size of a window
4. formatting	_____	**d.**	used to provide information to complete a command
5. dialog box	_____	**e.**	icon for a hard-disk drive
6. 	_____	**f.**	settings associated with an object
7. properties	_____	**g.**	used to bring additional information into a window
8. 	_____	**h.**	rectangular section dedicated to a specific activity or application
9. window	_____	**i.**	prepares a disk for use
10. 	_____	**j.**	closes a window

2. Use the figure below to match each action with its result.

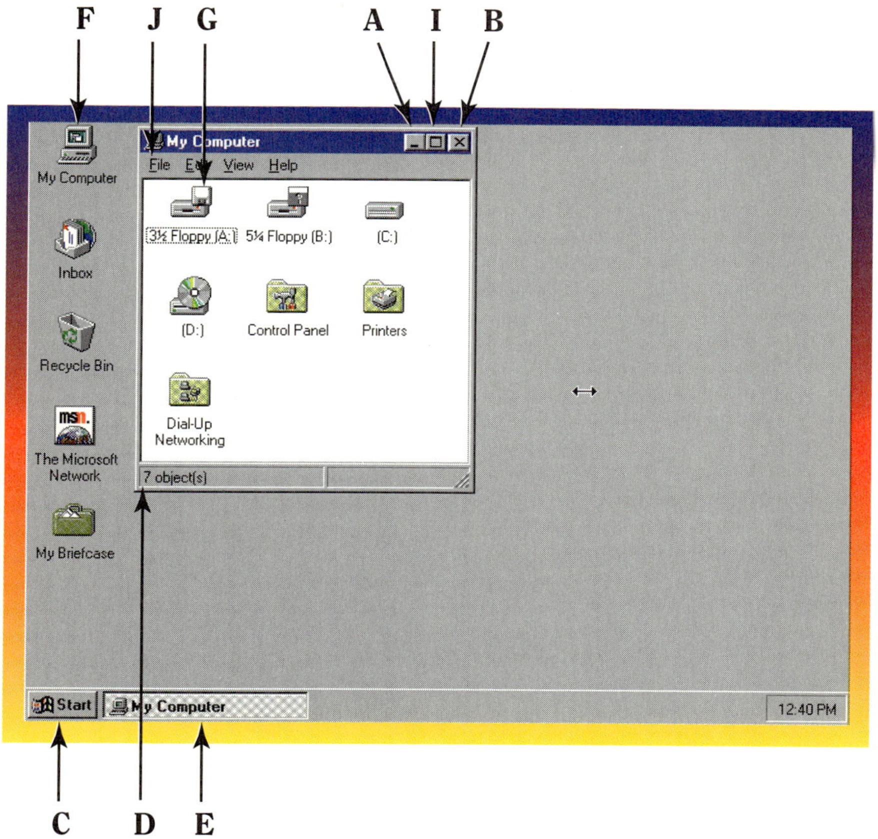

Action	**Result**	
1. click E	_____	**a.** displays properties of disk in A drive
2. right-click G	_____	**b.** selects the A drive icon
3. click I	_____	**c.** sizes the window
4. click G	_____	**d.** minimizes the window
5. click C	_____	**e.** maximizes the window
6. click B	_____	**f.** closes the window
7. double-click F	_____	**g.** opens the Start menu
8. click I	_____	**h.** displays File drop-down menu
9. drag D	_____	**i.** restores a minimized window
10. click A	_____	**j.** opens the My Computer window

3. In the following Windows 95 screen, several items are identified by letters. Enter the correct term for each item in the space provided.

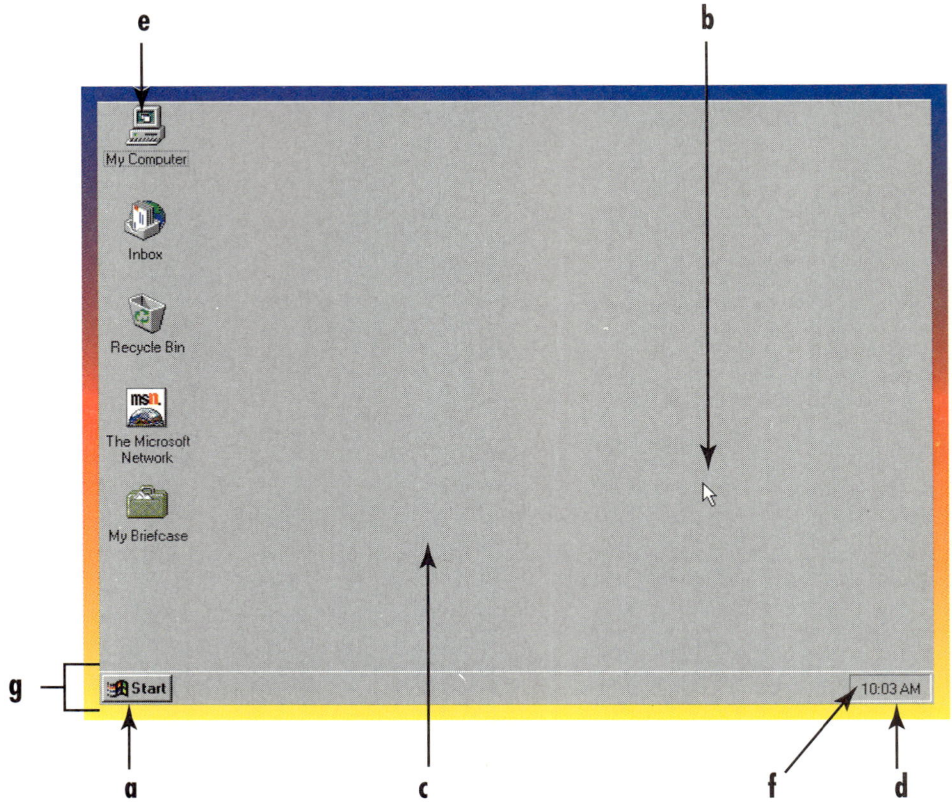

a. ______________________

b. ______________________

c. ______________________

d. ______________________

e. ______________________

f. ______________________

g. ______________________

4. In the following window, several items are identified by letters. Enter the correct term for each item in the space provided.

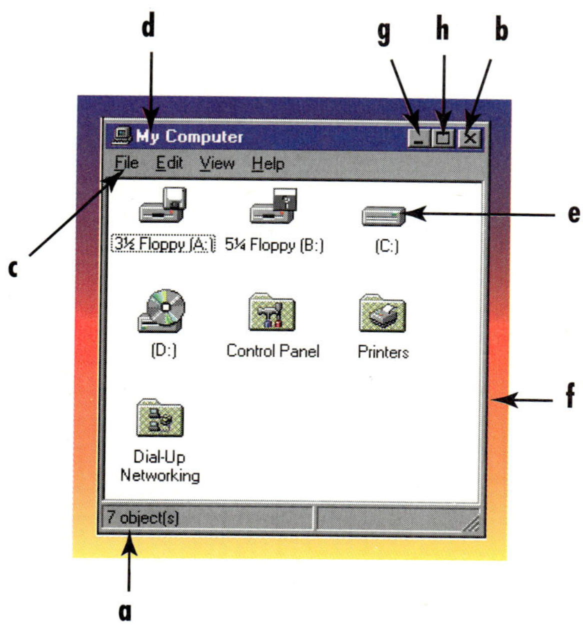

a. ______________________________

b. ______________________________

c. ______________________________

d. ______________________________

e. ______________________________

f. ______________________________

g. ______________________________

h. ______________________________

5. Identify the parts of a dialog box by entering the correct term for each item in the space provided.

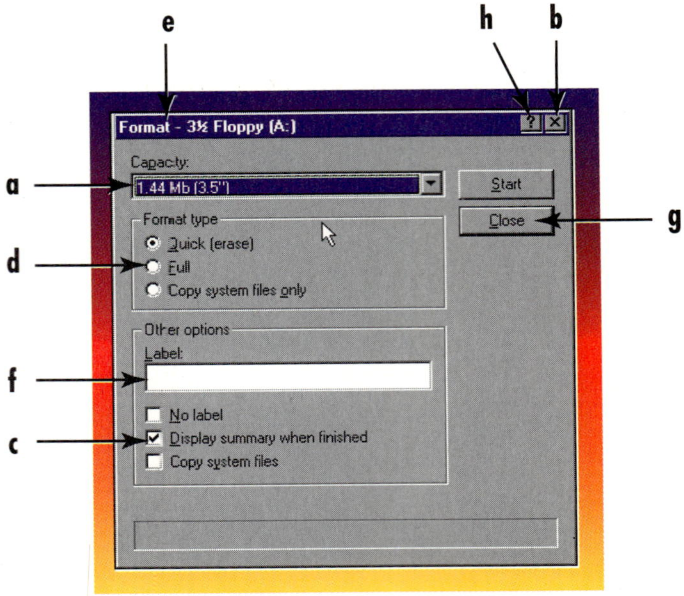

a. ______________________________

b. ______________________________

c. ______________________________

d. ______________________________

e. ______________________________

f. ______________________________

g. ______________________________

h. ______________________________

6. Answer the following with respect to the floppy-disk properties shown below.

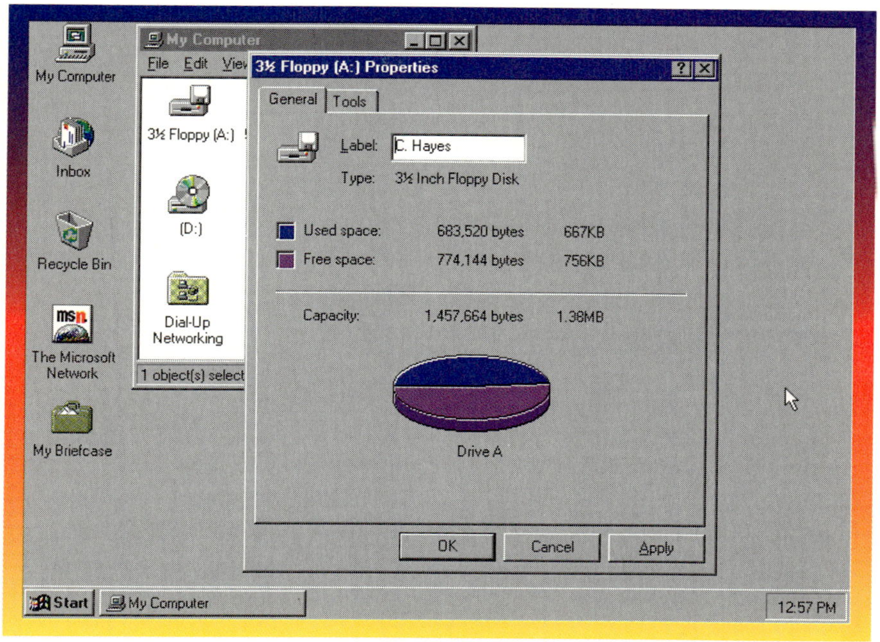

a. What is the total used disk space? ______________________

b. What is the total unused disk space? ______________________

c. What is the total number of available bytes? ______________

d. What is the disk label? ______________________________

e. What is the type of disk? ____________________________

Fill-In Questions

1. Complete the following statements by filling in the blanks with the correct terms.

a. The ______________________ program controls computer system resources and coordinates the flow of data to input and output devices.

b. If your computer is not on, turning on the computer and starting Windows 95 is called a ____________________.

c. The ______________ button is used to start a program, open a document, get help, find files, and change system settings.

d. Quickly pressing and releasing the mouse button twice is called ________________________.

e. The ______________________ is a colored highlight that indicates the currently selected command.

f. The ________________ is used with a mouse to bring additional lines of information into view.

g. When the taskbar button appears depressed this indicates the window is the _______________ window.

h. Before a new disk can be used, it must be _______________ from its generic state into a form that can be used by your computer.

i. ________________ are settings and attributes associated with an object.

j. To avoid damaging files, always use the ___________________________ commands before you turn off your computer.

HANDS-ON PRACTICE EXERCISES

Step by Step

Rating System
☆ Easy
☆☆ Moderate
☆☆☆ Difficult

☆

You need the Windows 95 CD, or the Tour must be loaded on your system before you can complete this problem. Your instructor will provide you with instructions for loading the Tour of Windows 95.

1. The Windows 95 program includes a Tour of Windows 95 that introduces and explains many of the basic Windows features. This problem will use the Tour of Windows 95 to reinforce many of the features presented in this lab.

a. Load the Tour of Windows 95.

b. Choose Using Help from the Welcome to Windows 95 Tour menu.

c. As you read and work through the Using Help tour, answer the following questions:

1) What feature do you get help on? ___________________

2) How did you display the Help topic?___________________

3) What type of button did you use to see the properties dialog box?_________________

4) How did you display a definition in the dialog box?________________

d. Exit the Tour by clicking Exit and the Exit Tour.

☆

2. In this problem you will expand your knowledge of Windows 95 by using Help to find out about and open the Calculator accessory.

a. Open Help and use the Index tab to learn how to start the Calculator.

b. Use the shortcut button in the Help window to start the Calculator application.

c. Use the Calculator Help menu to open Calculator Help and to learn more about the Calculator application. Briefly explain the Calculator accessory features.

d. Using Help as a guide, use the Calculator in standard and scientific views to perform the following calculations; write the answers in the spaces provided.

1. 6 + 18 + 34 = ________________

2. 8432 × 4324328 = ________________

3. 939 ÷ 83 = ____________________

4. Average of 34, 84, 283, 231, 423 = ____________

5. Square root of 343 = __________________

e. Close Calculator Help. Close the Calculator window.

★★

3. In the lab you learned to use the Index tab of Help. In this problem, you will use the Help Contents and Find tabs to learn more about using Help, to print Help topics, and to locate information about changing the mouse properties.

a. Start Help and display the Contents tab. The Tips and Tricks book contains many hints about how to best use Windows 95.

b. Open the Tips and Tricks book and then the Tips of the Day book.

c. Read the Help information on Using Help.

d. The Options menu in the Help menu bar contains a Print Topic command that will print a copy of the contents of the displayed Help window. Use this command to print the Using Help window of information.

Before printing, make sure your printer is on and is ready to print.

Next, you will use the Help Find tab to locate information about mouse properties.

e. Return to the Help Topics dialog box and display the Find tab. The Find tab operates much like the Index tab.

f. Enter a word or words in the text box to search for information on changing the speed of your mouse pointer. Then display the Help window on this topic.

g. This Help window includes a shortcut button. Click on this button to open the mouse properties dialog box. Look through all the tabs in the dialog box and use the ? Help button in the dialog box to find out about areas or settings you may not understand. What are some of the mouse property settings and why would you want to change these settings? Cancel the dialog box when you are done.

h. In the motion tab, adjust the pointer speed and turn on the show pointer trails options. Move the mouse to see the results of your selections.

i. Close the Help window.

☆☆

4. The character or font size of information in the Help windows can be changed by making it larger so it is easier to read, or smaller so more information is displayed in the window.

a. Use the Help Index tab to learn how to change the font size of a Help topic.

b. Try out the different size options.

c. Print the Help topic with the font size of small.

d. Return the font size to normal.

e. Close all open windows.

☆☆

5. As you learned in the lab, windows can be both sized and moved. This is an important skill to develop because many times windows will cover other information you want to see or may be an inappropriate size when they are opened. To develop this skill you will open, move, and size several windows.

a. Open the My Computer window.

b. Display a Help window on changing the clock.

c. Move the Help window to the lower right corner of the screen.

d. Move the My Computer window to the upper left corner of the screen.

e. Size the My Computer window until it covers the left half of the desktop.

f. Size the Help window until it covers the right half of the desktop.

g. Return the windows to their approximate original size.

h. Minimize the My Computer window. Redisplay the window, maximize it, then restore it.

i. Close all open windows.

On Your Own

☆

6. Every item on the desktop has properties associated with it that can be changed to suit your needs. Display the properties associated with the desktop. Try changing several of the property settings and preview how they would look in the sample area of the tab. Write down the settings that you changed and the effect the changes would have on the desktop. Cancel the dialog box.

☆

7. In the lab you displayed the properties associated with the floppy disk. Display the properties associated with the hard disk and answer the following questions:

- How much free space is on the disk?
- How much space is used on the disk?
- How many megabytes can the drive hold?

☆☆

8. Read several articles about Windows 95. Identify and describe five new features of the program, for example, Plug-and-play and 32-bit architecture.

☆☆☆

9. If you were the operations manager of a large company and had to decide whether to upgrade to Windows 95, what factors would you need to take into consideration? For example, what are the minimum hardware requirements to use Windows 95 effectively, and will the current hardware at your company need to be upgraded? At what cost? With what benefits?

Concept Summary

Windows 95: Basic Skills

1

What's Windows 95?

Windows 95 is a graphical operating system program that controls all parts of a computer.

The Mouse

The mouse is a hand-held hardware device that controls an arrow, called a pointer, on the screen.

The Desktop

The Windows 95 screen, called the desktop, displays icons that represent various tools and features.

Concepts

What's Windows 95?
The Desktop
The Mouse

Help
Dialog Box
Scroll Bar

Window
Moving Windows
Sizing Windows

Formatting

Menus
Status Bar
Properties

Window

A window is a rectangular section of the screen that is dedicated to a specific activity or application.

Sizing Windows

Sizing a window makes it larger or smaller, allowing more or less information to appear in the window.

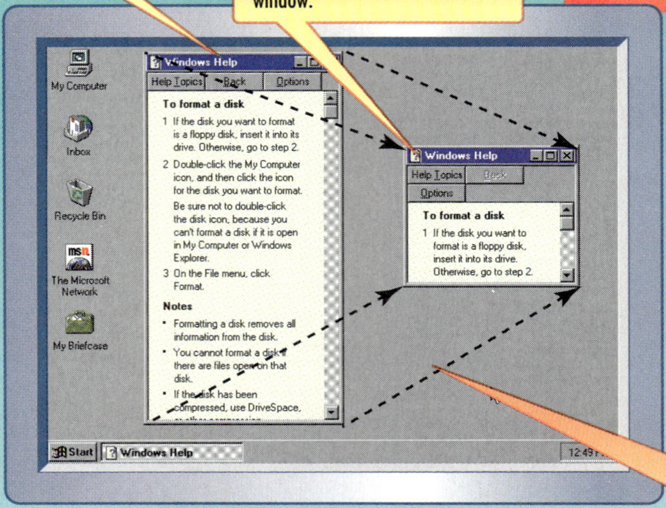

Moving Windows

Moving a window displays the window at another location on the desktop.

Help

The Help facility displays on-screen information about a program's features.

Dialog Box

A dialog box is used to enter information needed to complete a task.

Scroll Bar

A scroll bar is used with a mouse to bring additional lines of information into view in a window or list box.

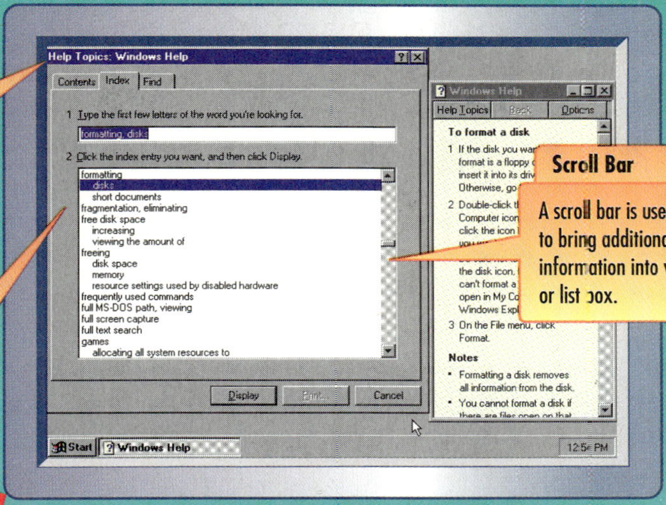

Formatting a Disk

Formatting converts a new disk from a generic state into a format your computer can use.

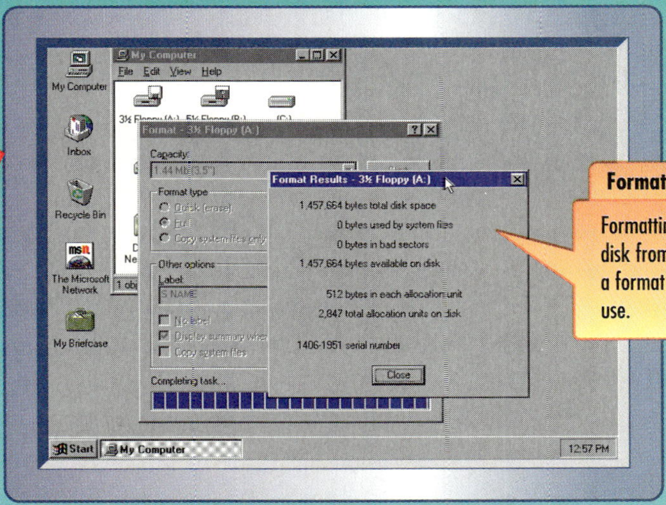

Menus

You enter instructions for the computer by choosing commands from menus.

Status Bar

The status bar displays information about current program settings and the task being performed.

Properties

All items on the screen have settings and attributes, called properties, associated with them.

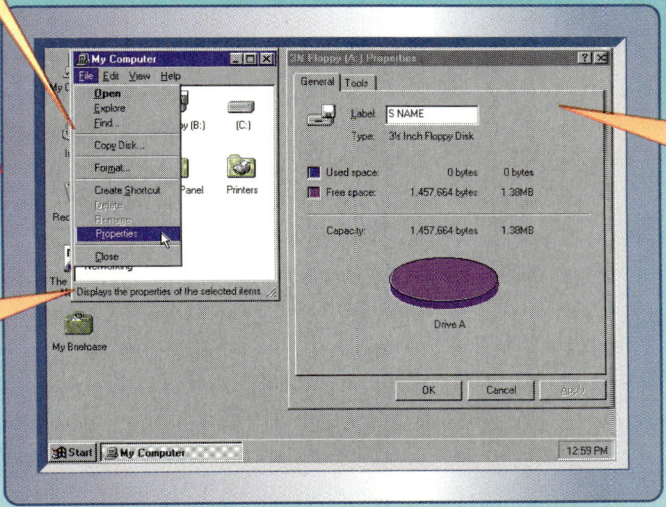

Windows 95 Disk Organization

2

Organizational skills are very important skills in any profession. When you are disorganized, it takes much longer to complete tasks accurately. Many Windows 95 features are aimed at making it easier for you to work effectively by helping you organize your work.

COMPETENCIES

In this lab you will learn how to:

1. Use My Computer to view files and folders.
2. Change the window view.
3. Arrange icons and windows.
4. Close minimized windows.
5. Use Explorer.
6. Copy and delete files.
7. Create and delete folders.
8. Move and rename files.
9. Select multiple files.

In this lab you will learn about many of Windows 95's organizational features. You will organize files into related categories, and display files in many different ways, making it easy to quickly locate files. You will arrange windows on the desktop to make it easier to view and work with information. In addition, many other file management features and shortcuts that will improve your efficiency will be introduced.

Concept Overview

The following concepts will be introduced in this lab:

1. Files and Folders	The information on your computer is stored as files. Folders contain files that are related.
2. Toolbar	The toolbar contains buttons that are shortcuts for many of the most common menu commands.
3. Arranging Windows	Windows can be arranged in two ways on the desktop, Cascade and Tile.
4. Undo	The Undo feature allows you to reverse your last action or command.
5. Hierarchy of Folders	The organization of folders, subfolders, and files on your disk is called a hierarchy or tree.
6. Cut, Copy, and Paste	All Windows applications include features that allow you to remove (cut), duplicate (copy), and insert (paste) information from one location to another.
7. File and Folder Names	Both files and folders are assigned names that are descriptive of the contents of the file or folder.
8. Drag and Drop	Common to all Windows applications is the ability to copy or move selections by dragging and dropping.

Part 1

Using My Computer to View Files and Folders

Turn on the computer. If necessary, close the Welcome window.

Information is stored as files on the computer's hard disk or on a floppy disk. A disk can hold many files of different types. To make it easy to locate files, you can store related files in folders. The My Computer window is used to view the files, folders, and other items that are on your computer.

Concept 1: Files and Folders

The information your computer uses is stored in a variety of different types of **files**. Two of the most common are program and data files. Instructions to run a program are stored in program files. For example, the word processing program on your computer consists of many files that contain the program statements required to use the program. The information you create while using a program is stored in data files. For example, if you write a letter to a friend using the word processing program, the contents of the letter are stored as a data file.

In addition, you can create **folders** and **subfolders** in which you store files that are related. Storing related files in folders keeps the disk organized and makes it much easier to locate files. Both files and folders are identified by names that are descriptive of the contents of the file or folder.

In many operating systems, folders are called directories.

Open the My Computer window.

Your screen should be similar to Figure 2-1.

Figure 2-1

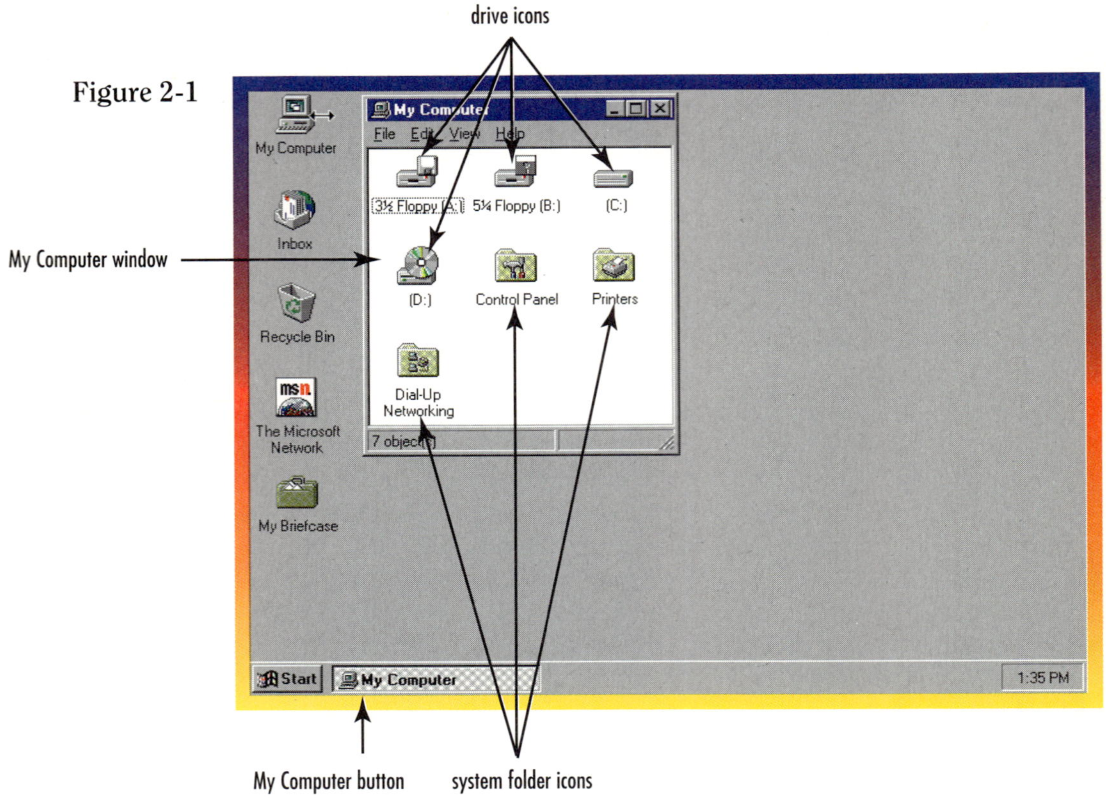

The My Computer window is open, and the taskbar displays the button for the window. The window size and placement on your desktop may be different than in Figure 2-1. This is because Windows 95 displays the window as it appeared when last used.

Do not be concerned if the icons in your My Computer window are displayed differently than in Figure 2-1. You will learn about how to change the icon display shortly.

The My Computer window displays icons that reflect the setup of your computer system. The drive icons represent the drives on your computer system. In addition, the window displays system folder icons. The  Control Panel folder contains additional icons that are used to modify Windows 95 settings, and the  Printers folder contains icons that are used to modify the printer settings.

Selecting a drive icon displays the contents of the disk in that drive. To see the contents of your computer's hard drive,

Double-click: 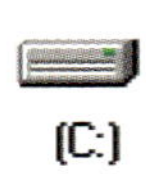 **(or the appropriate hard drive for your system)**

A second window is open, and the taskbar displays the button for this window. The window displays file folder icons , which represent the folders on the hard disk. The folder name appears to the right of each folder icon. The folders are displayed in alphabetical order.

You may need to scroll the window to see the Windows folder.

Locate the Windows folder.

To see the contents of this folder,

Double-click: Windows folder

Your screen should be similar to Figure 2-2.

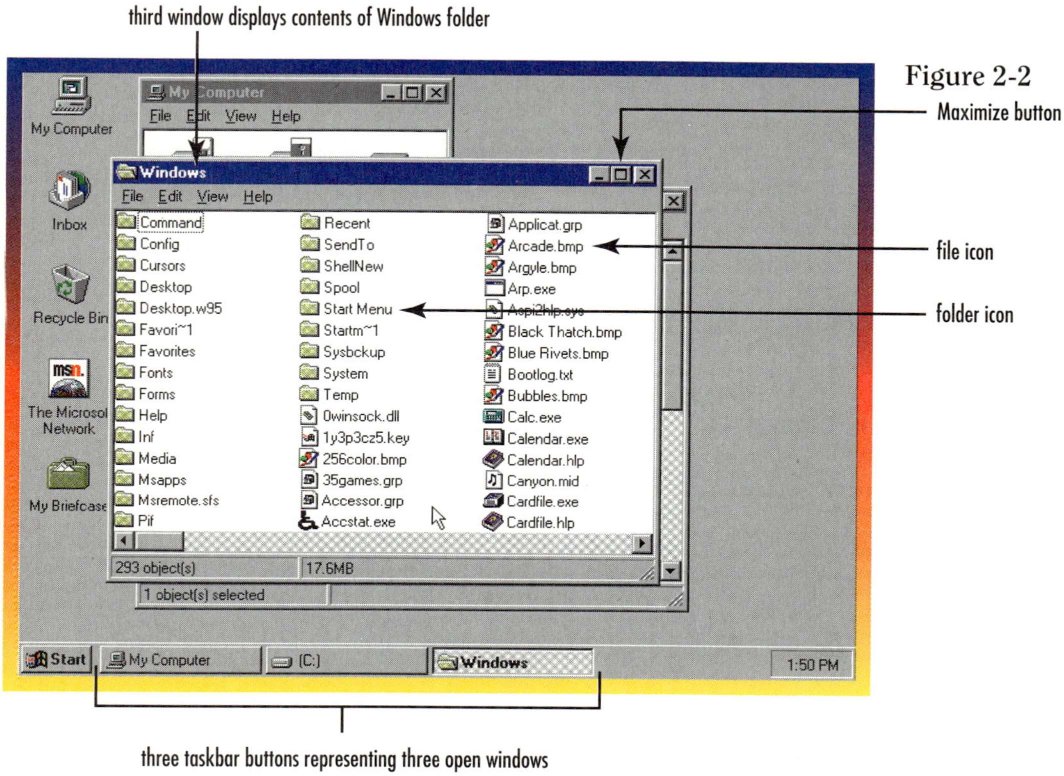

Figure 2-2

A third window appears, and a third button is displayed in the taskbar. Each time you open an item while in My Computer, the contents of the item appear in a new window and a new button appears in the taskbar.

The Windows folder window contains many other folders. Again, do not be concerned if the display of the icons in this window is different than in Figure 2-2. You will learn how to change the appearance of the window next.

Maximize the Windows folder window.

In addition, you will see many other kinds of icons that represent files on your disk. Files follow folders in the list and also appear in alphabetical order by name. The different file icons represent different types of files. The various file icons help you distinguish the type of file: a program file, an associated file, or another type of file (generally a nonassociated document file). An **associated file** is a file that has a specific application program attached to it that will open when the file is opened. The table below describes several of the file icons.

Icon	Kind of File
	Represents program (executable) files and batch files
	Represents a Microsoft Word document file
	Represents a Lotus 1-2-3 worksheet file
	Represents a bitmap file
	Represents a Help file
	Represents document files that are not associated with an application

Changing the Window View

Items in a window can be viewed or displayed in four different ways. These views change the icon size, display order, and the amount of information about the files and folders. Depending upon what you are doing, one view may be more helpful than another.

The View menu contains the commands to change views. In addition, many of these commands have toolbar button shortcuts that can be used instead of selecting from the menu.

Concept 2: Toolbar

The **toolbar** is a bar of buttons that is commonly displayed below the menu bar. The buttons are shortcuts for many of the most common menu commands. The picture in the button is a graphic representation of the task the button activates. The buttons that appear in the toolbar vary with the application that is open in the window. All of the My Computer windows display the toolbar shown below.

If the toolbar is not displayed, you need to turn it on. To do this,

Choose: View

The View menu commands are used to customize the appearance of the window. To turn on the display of the toolbar,

A ✔ checkmark or a ● bullet next to a command indicates the feature is on.

Choose: Toolbar

If necessary, in a similar manner, display the status bar.

Your screen should be similar to Figure 2-3.

Figure 2-3

Although the toolbar button icons represent specific features, it is often difficult to know what each button does. To find out the function of a button, you can display the button name. To do this, rest the mouse pointer over the button, and a **Tooltip** displaying a description of the button will appear.

Point to each toolbar button and read the related Tooltip.

Next you will change the window to display the information in several different views. To set the view to display the icons as large icons,

Click:  **Large Icons**

The menu equivalent is View/Large Icons.

Your screen should be similar to Figure 2-4.

Figure 2-4

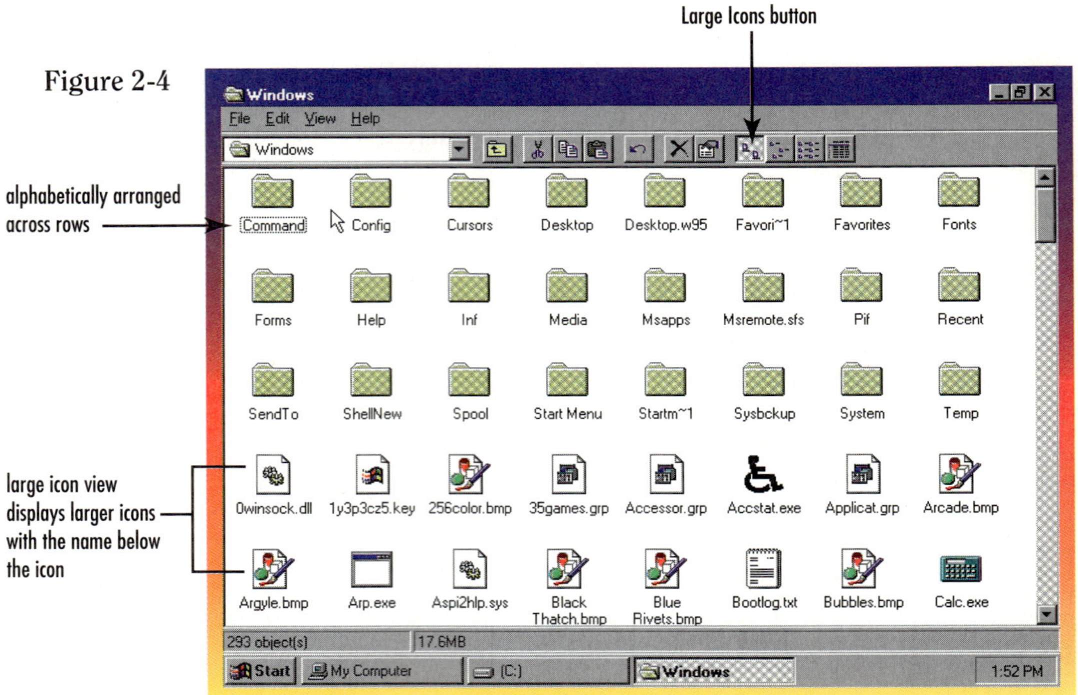

The icons are large, with the icon name displayed below the icon. They appear in alphabetical order from left to right across the window. Notice that the Large Icons toolbar button appears depressed. This indicates the current view.

Another view is Small Icons. To see how this changes the display,

> The menu equivalent is View/Small Icons.

Click: Small Icons

Your screen should be similar to Figure 2-5.

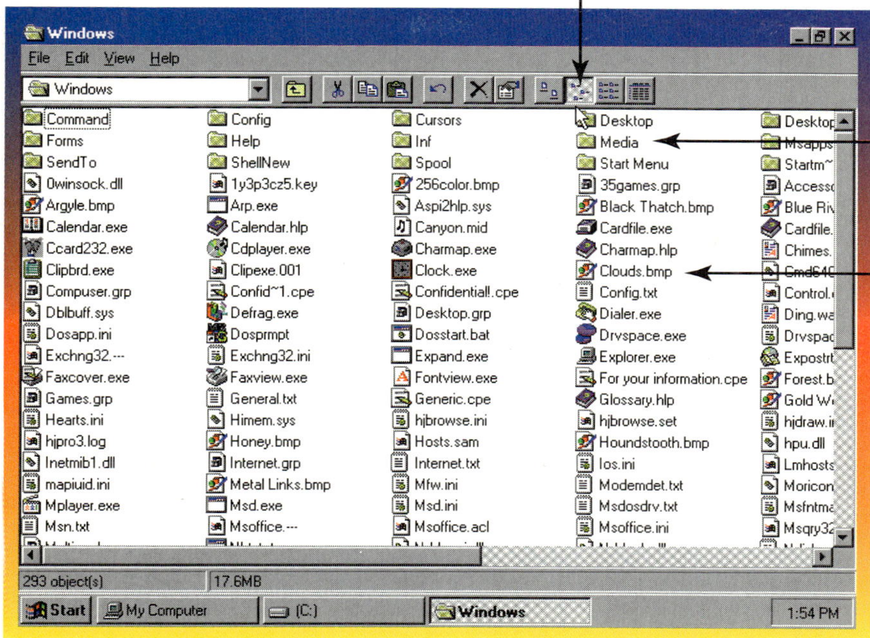

Figure 2-5

The information is displayed in the same order, but many more folders and files can be displayed because the icon size is much smaller. The icon name appears to the right of the icon.

The next view, List, is similar to the Small Icons view.

Click: **List**

The menu equivalent is View/List.

The icons are the same size as in Small Icon view, but they are arranged alphabetically down columns rather than across rows in the window.

The last view setting displays the file details, such as total file size, type, and date and time of creation. To see this view,

Click: **Details**

The menu equivalent is View/Details.

Your screen should be similar to Figure 2-6.

Figure 2-6

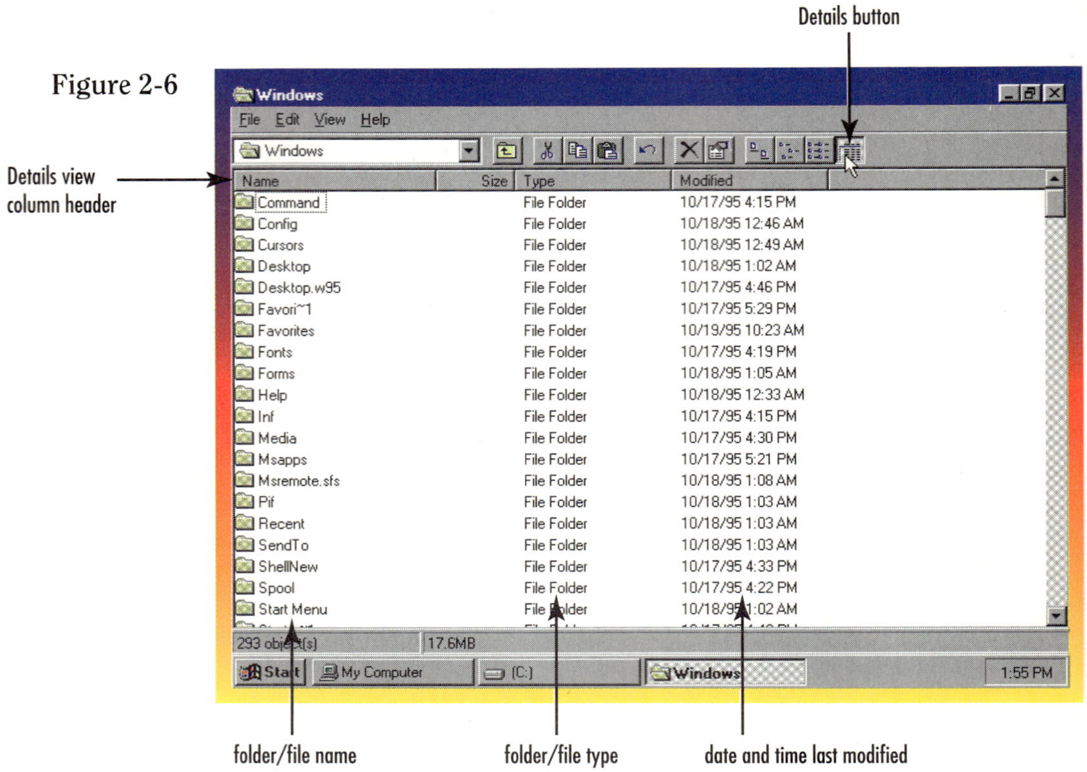

The names of the folders and files appear in a single column down the window, with the additional file information displayed in columns to the right. The columns are labeled with a column header. The columns display the file or folder name, the file size (in bytes), type of file, and date and time the file was last modified.

If necessary, scroll the window to see the file icons.

This additional information takes up a lot of space in the window, making it necessary to scroll the window to locate a file or folder that is not visible. Rather than use this view to see the file's details, you can display the details for an individual file by viewing the file's properties. To see how this works, you will change the view back to List. Another way to change the view is to select the command from the folder shortcut menu. This method is useful if the toolbar is not displayed.

> Right-click on the window background, not a folder or file, to display the folder shortcut menu.

Using the folder window shortcut menu, return the view to List.

Now, to view the properties of a file, select any file from the list.

> The menu equivalent is File/Properties or Properties from the file's shortcut menu. You can also hold down Alt while double-clicking the filename to display the Properties box.

Click: Properties

Depending upon the type of file you selected, the Properties tab dialog box may display the General tab and the Version tab. The Version tab only appears if the file type is a program file.

If necessary, open the General tab.

Your screen should be similar to Figure 2-7.

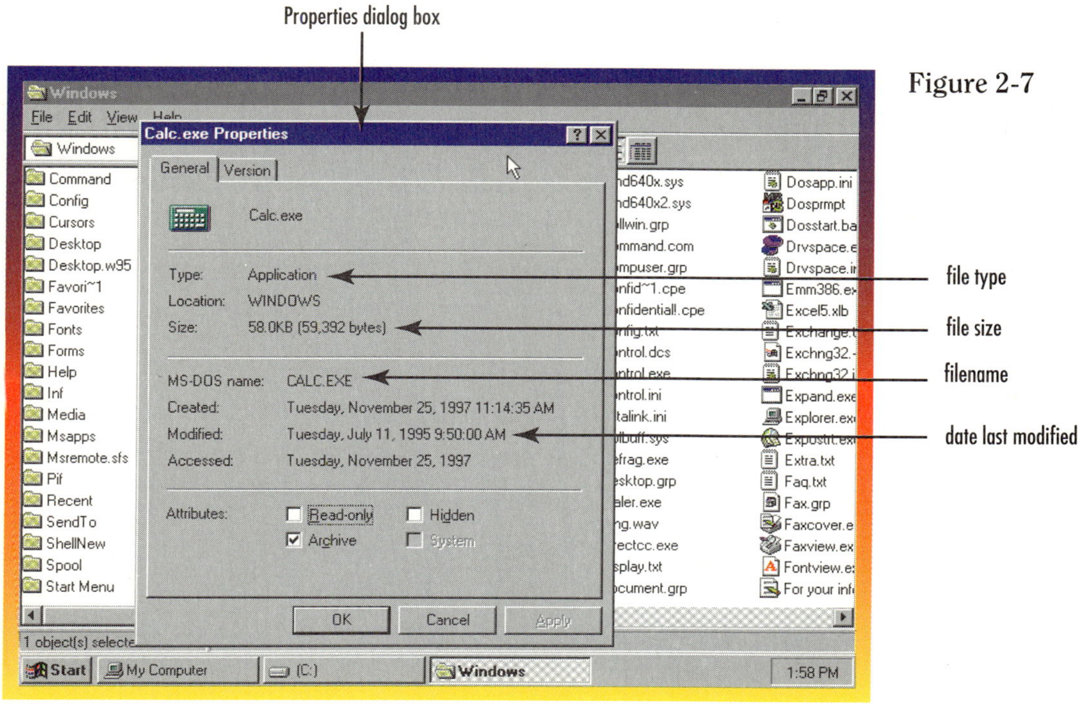

Figure 2-7

The General tab displays the same information as in Details view, such as file size and date for the selected file, plus some additional information.

After looking at the property information, close the dialog box.

Arranging Icons

Regardless of the view you are using, folders always appear first as a group, followed by files. Typically, folders and files are displayed in alphabetical order by name. Sometimes, however, this order is not convenient. For example, you may be unable to remember the name of the file, but you can remember the date you last modified it. The Arrange Icons command in the View menu lets you select an arrangement that may be more convenient for the task you are performing.

To arrange the files by size rather than name,

Choose: **View/Arrange Icons/by Size**

To verify that the files are in ascending order by file size, change the view to Details and scroll the window, looking at the Size column of information.

Your screen should be similar to Figure 2-8.

Figure 2-8

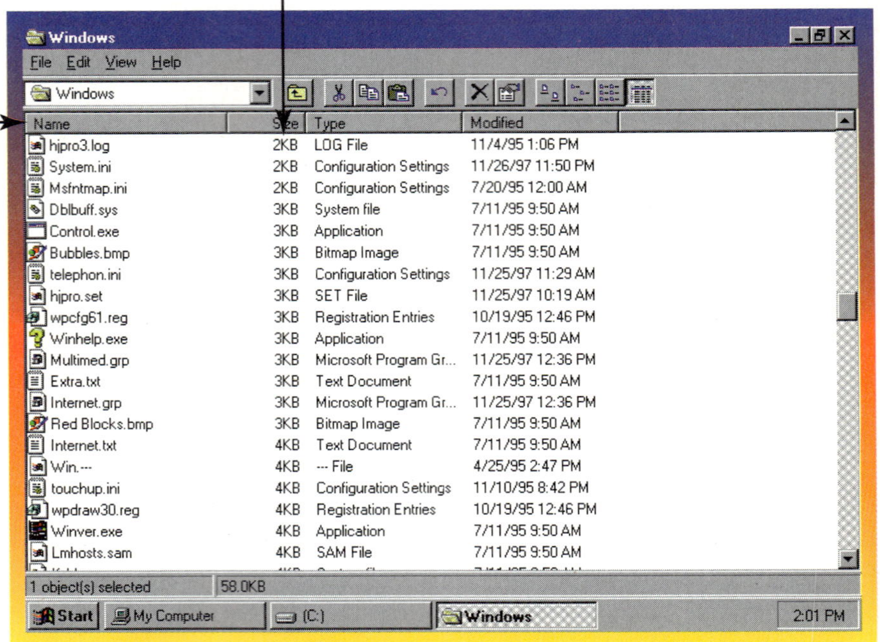

> Because folders do not include a size, they remain at the top of the list in alphabetical order.

The order can also be changed to display by date or by file type (according to the file extension). Usually, the most useful view is by name.

Another way to change the display order when using Details view is to click the column heads. For example, clicking the Name column head changes the display order back to ascending alphabetical order by filename. Clicking the column head of a selected order switches between ascending and descending order. To change the order back to display the files by filename,

> The menu equivalent is View/Arrange Icons/ by Name.

Click: Name

Return the view to List view.

Switching Between Windows

Next you would like to see the contents of your newly formatted data disk.

Put the disk you formatted in Lab 1 in the appropriate drive.

To view the disk's contents, you need to return to the My Computer window to select the drive icon that contains your disk. However, you cannot see the window on your desktop because it is covered by the Windows folder window. To bring the My Computer window to the forefront,

> My Computer is in the taskbar.

Click: My Computer

The My Computer window becomes the active window and it appears on top of the other windows. It is easy to tell which window on the screen is active. Active windows are displayed on top, have colored title bars, and their buttons are depressed in the taskbar.

> Drive A will be used throughout the text. If you are using another drive, select the appropriate drive for your system.

Double-click: 

(or the drive containing your formatted disk)

Your screen should be similar to Figure 2-9.

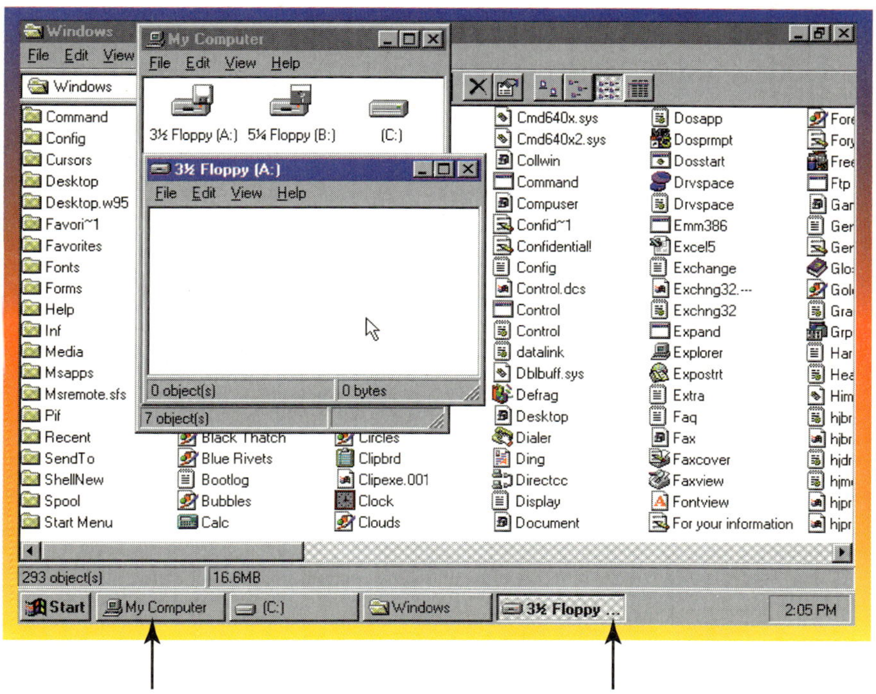

Figure 2-9

The drive window is open and displayed on top of the other windows. It is the active window. Because the disk is newly formatted, the window does not display any files or folder objects.

There are now four buttons displayed in the taskbar along with four windows open on the desktop. You can switch to any window you can see on the desktop simply by clicking on it.

Click on the Windows folder window to make it active, restore the window to its original size, then minimize the window.

Now there are three displayed windows on the desktop. However, there are still four buttons in the taskbar. Notice that as more windows are opened on the desktop, the taskbar buttons get smaller to allow all buttons to be displayed on the taskbar. This shortens the amount of text in the button and makes it difficult to know which button is which. Ellipses following the button name indicate the name has been shortened. Pointing to the button will display the complete window name in a Tooltip box.

Point to the floppy-disk button to see the Tooltip.

> The taskbar can also be moved just like a window.

Another way to see more of the button identification is to make the taskbar larger, just like you would a window.

Drag the upper border of the taskbar upward.

Your screen should be similar to Figure 2-10.

Figure 2-10

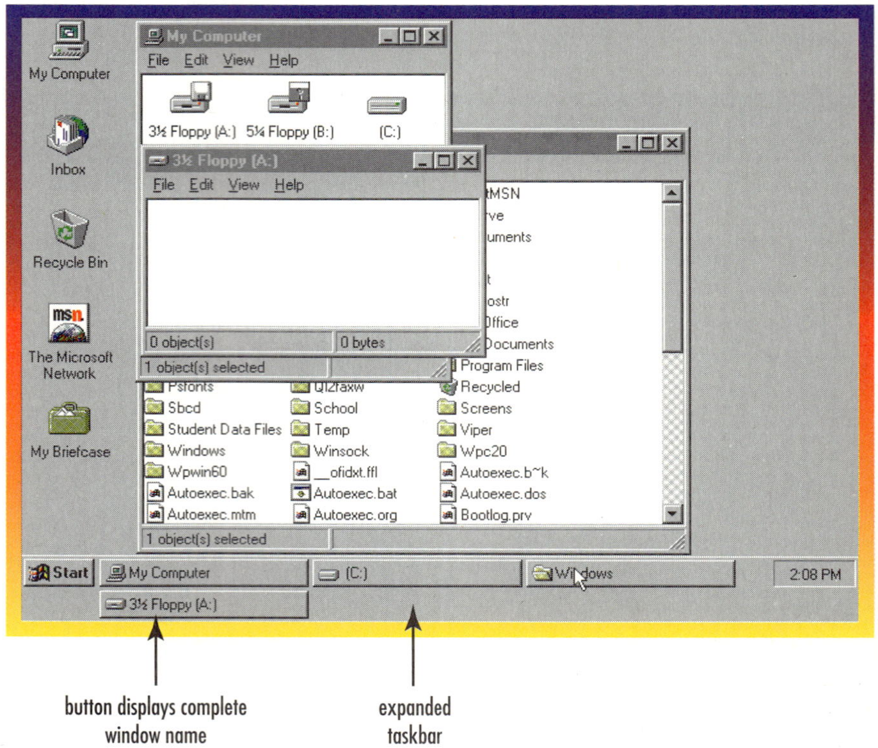

The taskbar now displays two lines, allowing more space for the buttons, and the window name is fully displayed.

Arranging Windows

As you can see, as more windows are open on the desktop, it is harder to see the information in the windows. To make viewing of multiple windows easier, you could move and size windows as you learned to do in Lab 1. Another way is to use built-in windows arranging features.

Concept 3: Arranging Windows

There are two ways to arrange windows on the desktop: Cascade and Tile.

Cascade Layers open windows, displaying the active window fully and only the title bars of all other open windows behind it

Tile Resizes each open window and arranges the windows vertically or horizontally on the desktop

Cascading windows is useful if you want to work primarily in one window but you want to see the titles of other open windows. Tiling is most useful when you want to work in several applications simultaneously, because it allows you to quickly see the contents of all open windows and move between them. However, the more windows that are open, the smaller is the space available to display the tiled window contents.

The taskbar shortcut menu displays options that allow you to arrange windows.

Right-click on any blank area of the taskbar to display its shortcut menu.

To cascade the three open windows,

Choose: Cascade

Your screen should be similar to Figure 2-11.

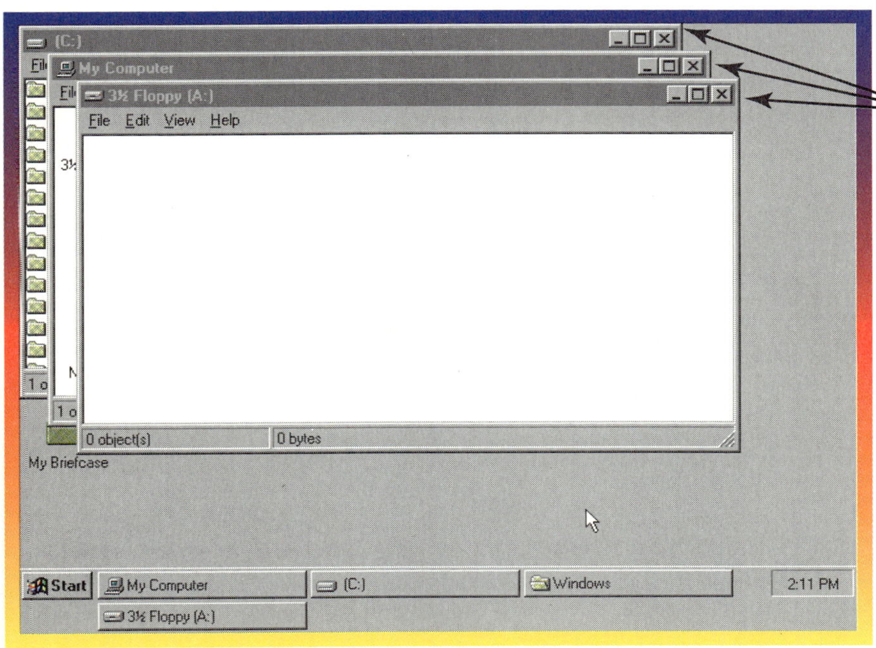

Figure 2-11

The windows are resized and overlap with the title bars visible. Only open windows that are not minimized are arranged.

You can click on any visible part of the window to make it active.

Make the My Computer window active.

The My Computer window is now active. It is pulled to the front of the stack and covers the other cascaded windows. Depending on how the windows overlap, you may need to use the taskbar buttons to make a window that is no longer visible active, or use the Cascade command again to rearrange the windows in cascade order.

As you switch between windows, it becomes more difficult to see the title bars. To restore the window size and arrangement as it was prior to cascading the windows, you can use the Undo command.

Concept 4: Undo

The Undo feature allows you to reverse your last action or command. However, some actions you perform in Windows cannot be undone. If the Undo command is unavailable, it appears dimmed and you cannot cancel your last action. Some programs allow you to undo multiple actions, up to a certain limit. This command is found on the Edit menu. The shortcut key is Ctrl + Z and the toolbar button is [Undo button]. It is also on many Shortcut menus. Undo is selected from the menu or toolbar in the window in which the action you want to undo was performed.

Display the Taskbar shortcut menu.

Notice that the shortcut menu now displays an Undo Cascade command. The Undo option appears only after windows have been arranged. Because the commands to arrange windows are in the taskbar shortcut menu, this is also the location of the command to undo window arrangement. From the taskbar shortcut menu,

Choose: **Undo Cascade**

The windows are arranged and sized again as they were before using the Cascade command. If you do not undo the arrangement before switching to another arrangement, the windows remain in the size and position set by the second arrangement and cannot be returned to their original size without custom sizing and moving the windows.

To arrange the three windows on the desktop without overlapping, from the taskbar shortcut menu,

Choose: **Tile Vertically**

The three windows are vertically arranged on the desktop, each taking up one third of the vertical space. The minimized window is not included in the arrangement.

Check the taskbar button to display the window.

Display the Windows folder window.

Your screen should be similar to Figure 2-12.

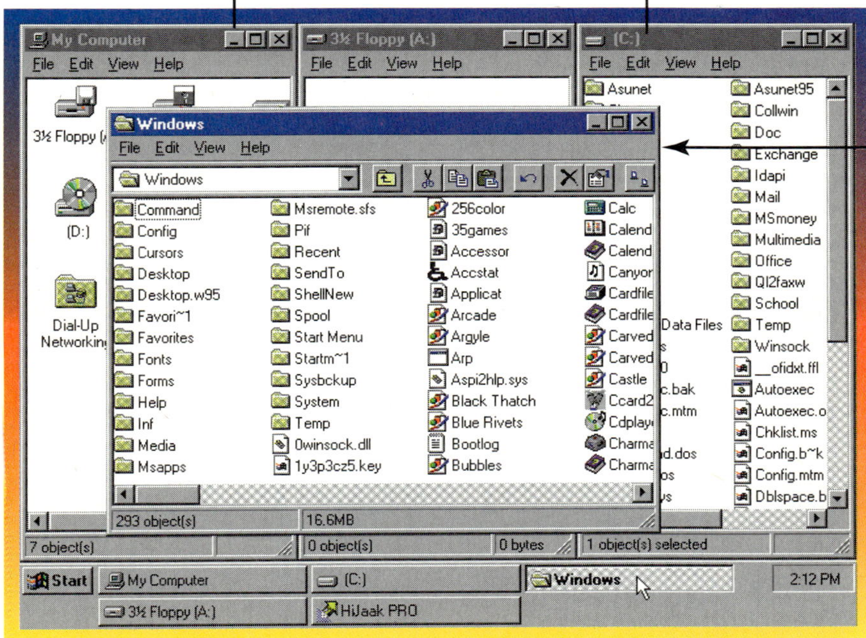

Figure 2-12

The window is opened on top of the three arranged windows. The program does not automatically arrange new windows as they are opened on the desktop.

Minimize the Windows folder window again.

Again, the tile arrangement can be reversed using the Undo command. From the taskbar shortcut menu,

Choose: **Undo tile**

Then, to tile the open windows horizontally, from the taskbar shortcut menu,

Choose: **Tile Horizontally**

Your screen should be similar to Figure 2-13.

Figure 2-13

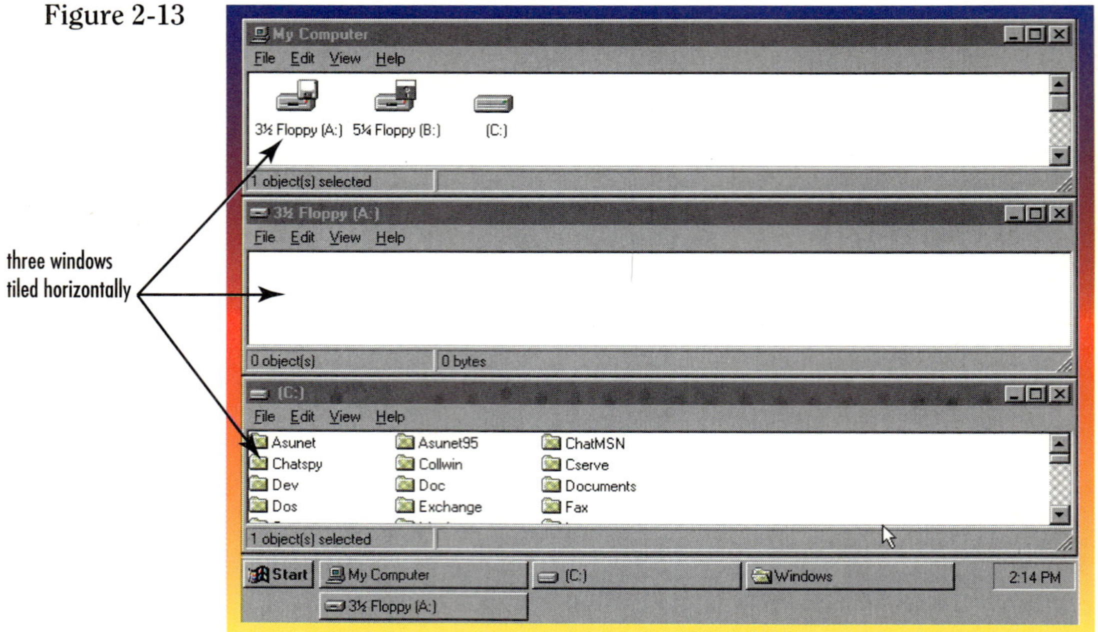

Undo this arrangement.

Finally, the taskbar shortcut menu also allows you to quickly minimize all open windows. From the taskbar shortcut menu,

Choose: **Minimize All Windows**

The desktop is cleared of all open windows. This is much quicker than minimizing each window individually.

Closing Minimized Windows

When a window is minimized, it can be closed by using the Close command on the button's shortcut menu. First you will close the Windows folder window.

Display the shortcut menu for the Windows folder taskbar button.

Right-click on the taskbar button to display the button's shortcut menu.

Choose: Close

The window is closed, and the button no longer appears in the taskbar. The shortcut to close the active windows is Alt + F4. However, when all windows are minimized, using this shortcut quits the Windows 95 program, closing all open windows for you.

Since you do not want to quit yet, close the other three open windows using the Close command.

Resize the taskbar to its original size by dragging the top border down.

If you drag too far, move the mouse pointer to the bottom of the screen and drag the taskbar back onto the desktop.

Note: If you are ending your lab session now, quit Windows 95.

Part 2

Using Explorer

Windows **Explorer** is another application included in Windows 95 that helps you view and organize the files on your disk. You can start the Windows Explorer application in many different ways. One way is to select the command from the File menu in the My Computer window. The shortcut for this is to use the My Computer shortcut menu, eliminating the need to open the My Computer window first.

Display the My Computer shortcut menu.

The My Computer shortcut menu displays the commonly used commands in the My Computer window. To open the Windows Explorer,

Choose: Explore

The Exploring window is displayed.

If necessary, maximize the window, use the View menu to turn on the toolbar and status bar, and change the view to Large Icons.

Your screen should be similar to Figure 2-14 on the following page. The title bar displays the name of the application, and the menu bar displays five menus. The menus contain many of the same commands as in My Computer. In addition, the toolbar displays the same buttons.

Read the information in the Parts of the Exploring Window box on the next page for a description of this window.

Parts of the Exploring Window

Figure 2-14

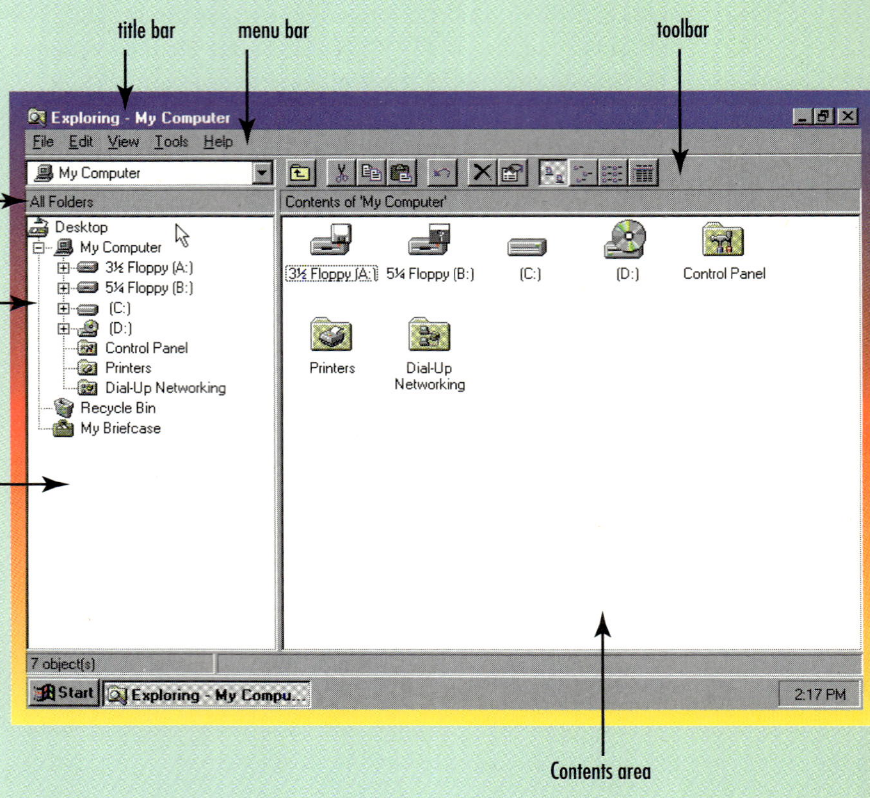

The Exploring window on your screen may display different folders and icons than those in Figure 2-14.

You can change the size of either area by dragging the bar that separates the two areas.

The Exploring window is divided into two areas. The **description bar** above each area identifies the area content. The left area is the **All Folders area**, which shows a graphic representation of the organization of the major parts of your computer.

The right area, called the **Contents area**, displays the contents of the selected item in the All Folders area. In this case, because you opened Windows Explorer from the My Computer shortcut menu, the Contents area shows icons for the drives on your computer and the same folders as in the My Computer window. The description bar identifies the contents that are currently displayed in the area.

The graphic representation of the organization of the disk displayed in the All Folders area is called a hierarchy or tree.

Concept 5: Hierarchy of Folders

The organization of folders, subfolders, and files on your disk is displayed as a **hierarchy** or **tree**. The top-level folder of a disk is the **main folder**. On the hard disk, the main folder is represented by the Desktop icon (see Figure 2-15). On a floppy disk, the main folder is represented by the drive icon. This folder is created when the disk is formatted. The leftmost vertical line is the main tree line. On the hard disk it includes all items that appear on the desktop (under the Desktop icon). All folders are branches from the main folder. Subfolders are branches under a folder. Files can be stored in the main folder, a folder, or a subfolder.

Selecting a different item in the All Folders area displays the contents of the selected item in the Contents area. To see the contents of the hard drive,

Selections can also be made by using the ↑ or ↓ keys and pressing ←Enter.

Click: (C:) (or the appropriate drive for your system)

Your screen should be similar to Figure 2-15.

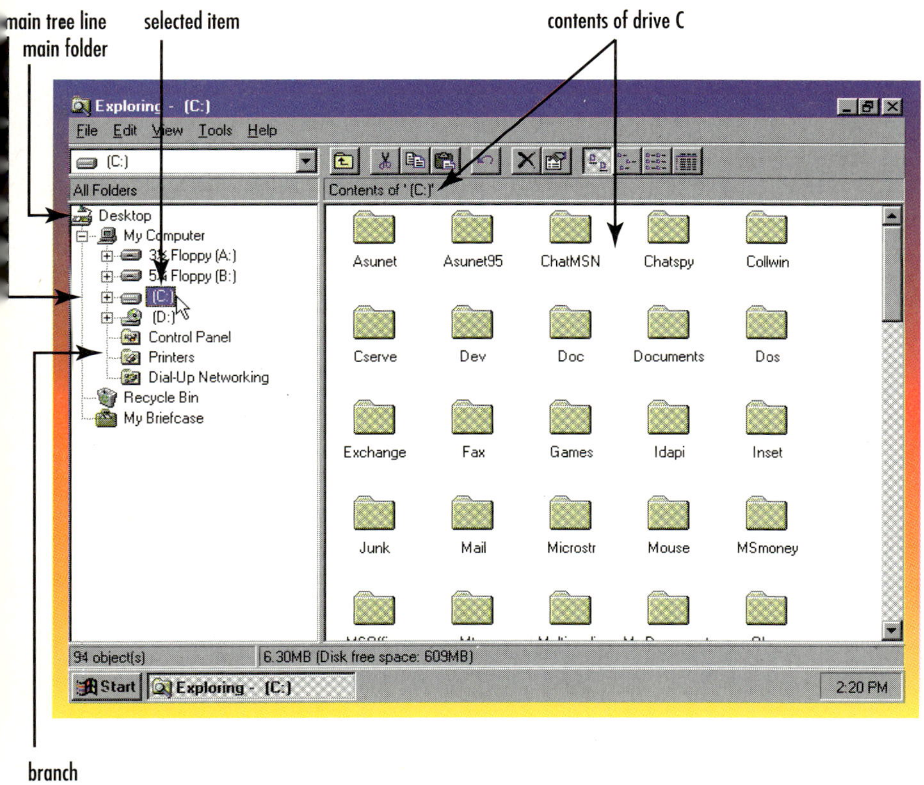

Figure 2-15

The selection cursor (the dotted blue rectangle surrounding the text) appears over the selected item in the All Folders area.

The Contents area on your screen will reflect the folders and files on your computer's hard drive.

The Contents area displays the contents of the selected item. The Contents area description bar indicates the area is displaying the contents of the C drive. If the drive contains folders, they are displayed first, in alphabetical order, followed by the files.

You can also display the folders in the All Folders area of the window. To do this, you click the [+] sign that is displayed to the left of the drive icon to expand the hierarchy. To display the folders on your hard drive,

Click: [+] **beside your hard drive icon**

Your screen should be similar to Figure 2-16.

Figure 2-16

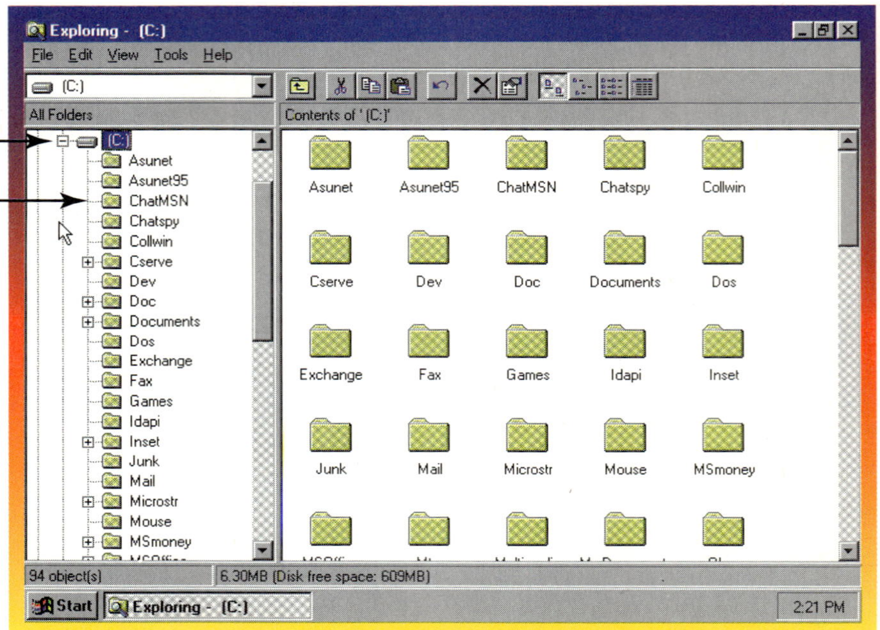

The All Folders area displays the folders on your hard drive as a third branch on the hierarchy. Notice that the [+] changed to a [-], which shows that the drive icon is fully open or expanded.

Clicking the [-] sign or double-clicking an expanded folder hides the folders again in the All Folders area.

You can also expand a folder that contains subfolders. The [+] appears next to a folder only if it contains subfolders. Another way to expand the hierarchy display is by double-clicking the folder or drive icon. To expand the Windows folder,

You may need to scroll the All Folders area to see the Windows folder icon.

Double-click: **Windows**

The selection cursor highlights the folder name, the Windows folder icon appears open, indicating the folder is open, and the [-] symbol indicates it is expanded. The folders in the Windows folder appear as a fourth branch on the hierarchy. As you select items in the All Folders area, the Contents area displays the folders and files in the selected item.

The same information you viewed by opening multiple windows using My Computer is displayed in one window using Explorer. Fewer windows makes it much easier to view and manage the information, and as you will see, it makes it very easy to copy and move folders and files from one disk or folder to another.

Copying Files

Now that you know how to browse your computer to locate folders and files, you will copy the files needed to complete this lab (and others your instructor may be using) to your newly formatted data disk.

Concept 6: Cut, Copy, and Paste

All Windows applications include features that allow you to remove (**cut**), duplicate (**copy**), and insert (**paste**) information from one location to another. The commands to perform these tasks are found in the Edit menu and on the toolbar. The information must be selected before it is copied or cut. The location that contains the information you want to cut or copy is called the **source**. Then the command to cut or copy the selection is used, and the selection is stored in a temporary storage area in memory called the **Clipboard**. Finally, you select the location, called the **destination**, where you want to insert a copy of the information stored in the Clipboard, and then you use the Paste command.

You will learn more about the Clipboard in Lab 3.

The files you will copy should be in a folder on your hard disk. First you need to open the folder containing the data files.

This text assumes the files are in a folder named "Student Data Files" on your hard drive. If your school uses a different folder name or your computer is on a network and the data files are in a folder on another system disk, your instructor will provide additional instructions.

Open the Student Data Files folder (or the folder containing your data files).

The subfolders contained in your Student Data Files folder are displayed in the Contents area.

Expand the Student Data Files folder.

The folders should now appear in the hierarchy in the All Folders area.

Open the Windows 95 folder.

The data files you will need to complete the Windows 95 lab are displayed in alphabetical order by filename in the Contents area (see Figure 2-17 on the next page).

Next you will select the files you want to copy to your floppy disk. When you copy a file from one location to another, you first need to select the file you want to copy from the Contents area.

Click: **anywhere in the Contents area**

Your screen should be similar to Figure 2-17.

Figure 2-17

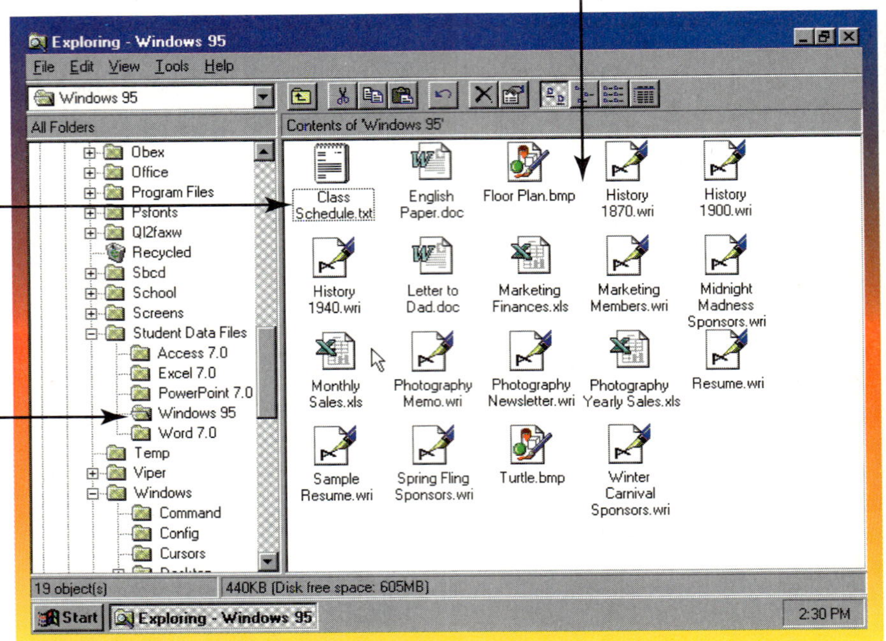

Shift + Tab will make the previous area active, and Tab will make the next area active.

If you clicked on a file, the file icon is selected (highlighted). If you clicked on an open area, a dotted box appears around the name of the first file in the list. The highlight no longer appears in the All Folders area. Whichever area contains the dotted box or highlight is the **active area**, or the area that will be affected by the next action you perform. Clicking anywhere in either area makes it the active area.

First you will copy the file named Class Schedule. To select this file,

Click:  **Class Schedule.txt**

Your screen should be similar to Figure 2-18.

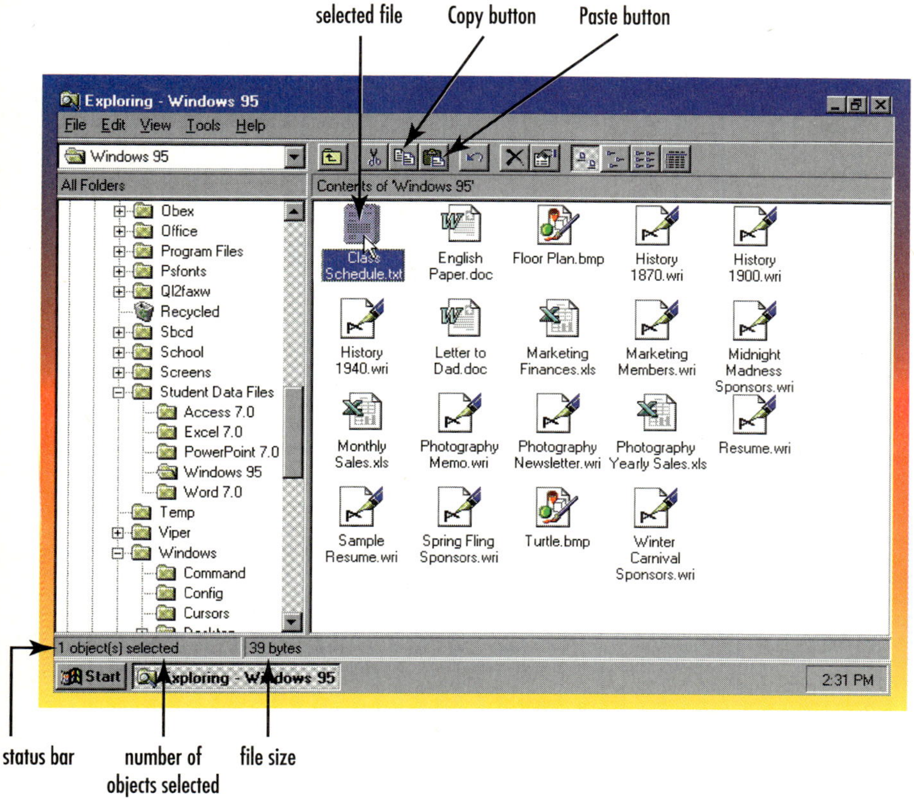

Figure 2-18

The selection cursor appears over the selected file icon. The status bar indicates one object is selected and its size. To copy the file,

Click: Copy

The menu equivalent is Edit/Copy and the shortcut key is Ctrl + C. Copy is also on the selected objects shortcut menu.

When you use the Copy command, a copy of the selected item, in this case the file, is stored in the Clipboard. Now you need to tell Windows 95 where you want the file copied to by specifying the destination. Your destination will be the disk in the floppy drive. To select the destination, you need to make the All Folders area active and select the drive containing your data disk.

Make the All Folders area active.

You may need to scroll the All Folders area to see the floppy drive icon.

Select: 3½ Floppy (A:)

The Contents area is empty because there are no files or folders on this disk yet. The Paste command is used to insert the copy of the information, which is stored in the Clipboard, in the selected destination.

You can also use the Edit/Paste command, the shortcut key Ctrl + V, or Paste on the Exploring Window shortcut menu.

Click: Paste

A Copying message box is displayed as the file is copied.

Your screen should be similar to Figure 2-19.

Figure 2-19

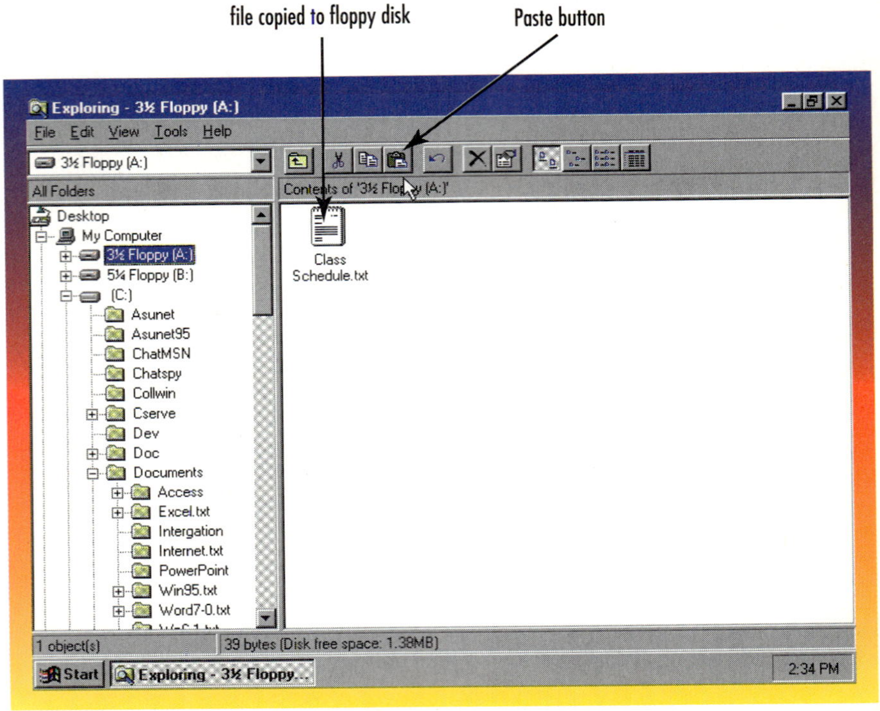

The Contents area is updated, and the Class Schedule file icon is displayed. The file was copied to the main folder of the floppy disk (this folder was created when the disk was formatted). You are now ready to copy the rest of the files to your data disk.

Select the Windows 95 folder in the All Folders area again.

Notice that the Class Schedule file is still displayed in the Windows 95 Contents area. Because you copied the file, it is now in both the Windows 95 folder and on your data disk.

Using Send To

Next you need to copy the other Windows 95 data files to the main folder of your data disk. Instead of using copy and paste, you can use the Send To command on the File menu. This command makes the process easier by allowing you to copy files directly to the main folder of a destination disk without having to select it first.

Rather than select and copy each file individually, you will select all the files in the folder and copy them at the same time.

Make the Contents area active.

The shortcut for this command is Ctrl + A.

Choose: **Edit/Select All**

All the file icons in the folder are selected. To quickly copy the files to the disk in the floppy drive,

Choose: File/Send To

> The Send To command is also on the selected objects shortcut menu.

A submenu listing the drives you can copy the files to is displayed. To select the drive where you want the copied files sent,

Select: 3½ Floppy (A:)

The Copying message box is displayed as the files are copied. In addition, because the Class Schedule file is already on the disk in drive A, a Confirm File Replace dialog box appears. Windows 95 displays this message so you do not accidentally overwrite one file with another of the same name.

Your screen should be similar to Figure 2-20.

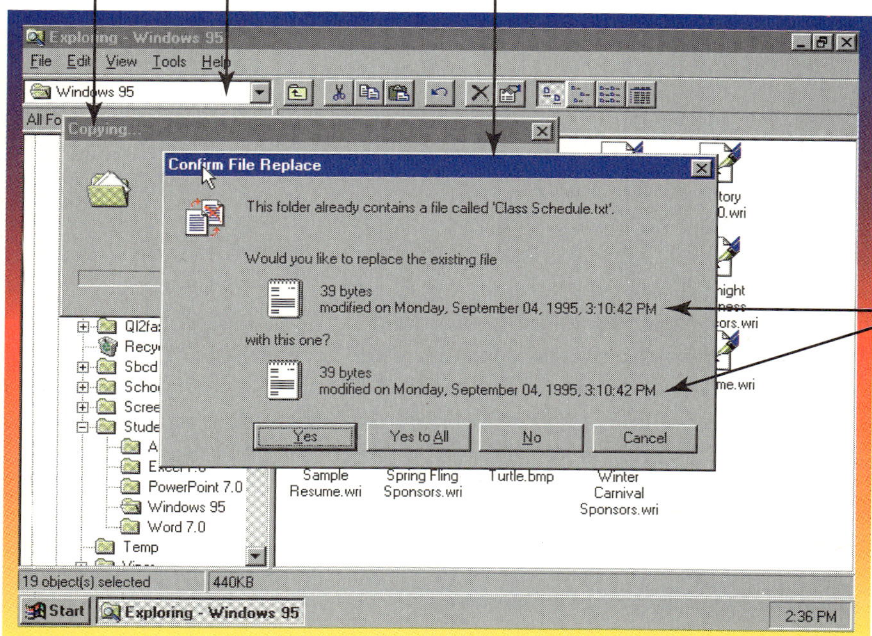

Figure 2-20

The dialog box shows the size of the duplicate files and date and time the files were last modified. Because you just copied the Class Schedule file, you can overwrite it without changing its contents, or you can choose No to bypass this operation and continue. To bypass copying this file again,

Choose: No

There are no other duplicate files, and all the files have been copied to the main folder of your data disk.

To view the contents of your data disk, you could select the drive icon from the All Folders area as you did previously. However, when the disk contains a large number of folders, this requires scrolling the area. A quicker way to change locations is to use the Go to a Different Folder button on the toolbar, shown in Figure 2-20 on the previous page. This type of button is called a drop-down list button. It consists of two parts: a text box that displays the current selection, in this case the selected folder, and a ▾ button. Clicking the button displays a drop-down list of options.

Click: ▾

A brief version of the disk hierarchy is displayed. To switch to the drive containing your data disk,

Select: 3½ Floppy (A:)

The Contents area displays the 19 files that were copied from the source to your data disk.

Creating Folders

Now that you have learned how Windows organizes folders and files, you will learn how to create folders to organize the files on your disk. As you add more files to the main folder of a disk, it gets very crowded and disorganized. This is especially true of hard disks, which can hold large amounts of data. To help organize files into like categories, you can create folders. For example, you may want to store software programs and the files you create using these programs by the program type. Alternatively, you might want to store your programs and information by project. You can create further divisions within each folder by creating additional subfolders.

Currently the files on your disk are simply alphabetically arranged by name in the main folder on the disk. You will create folders for the related files to help organize your disk. The folders and subfolder hierarchy you will create is shown in Figure 2-21.

Figure 2-21

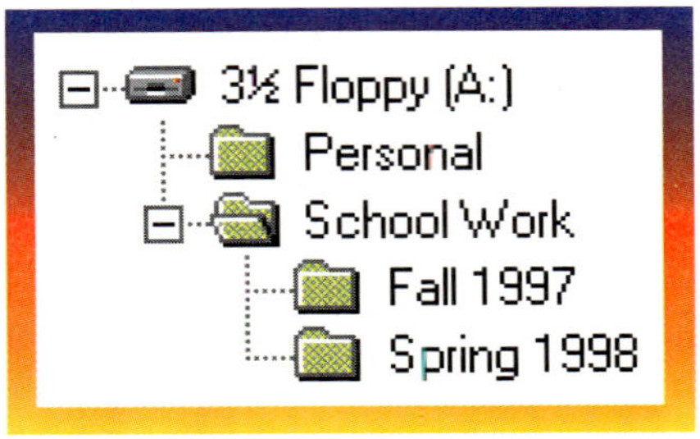

The first folder you will create on your data disk will be used to hold school-related documents. The command to create a folder is New on the File menu. To indicate where you want the folder created, the destination location must be selected first. Since the drive containing your data disk is already selected, you are ready to create the folder.

Choose: **File/New/Folder**

Your screen should be similar to Figure 2-22.

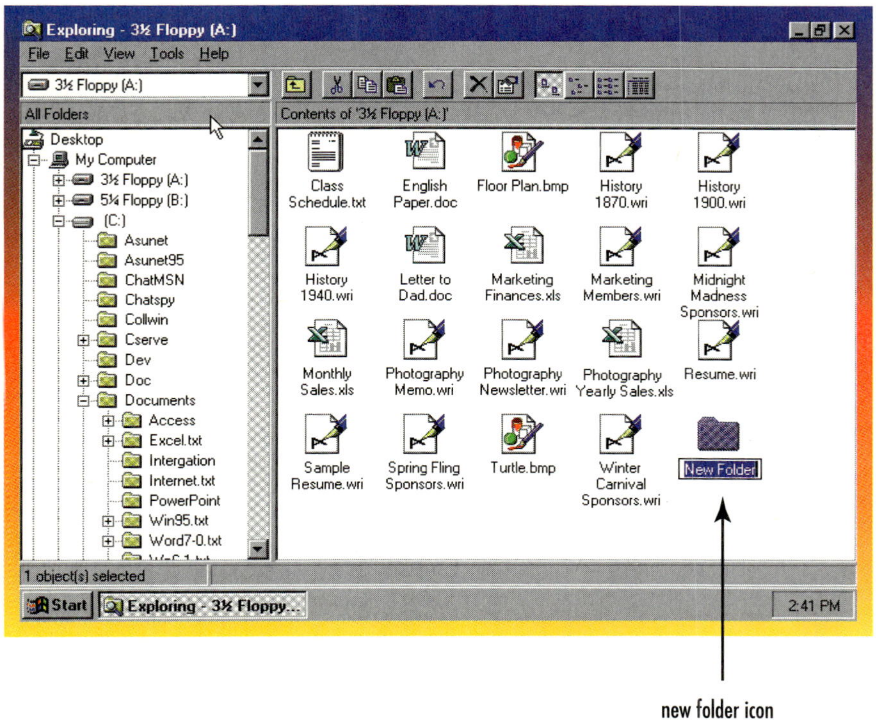

Figure 2-22

A folder icon is displayed in the Contents area, with the temporary folder name of New Folder highlighted. Notice the insertion point displayed at the end of the folder name. This indicates that Windows 95 is waiting for you to replace the default name with a descriptive name for the folder you are creating.

Concept 7: File and Folder Names

File and folder names are used to identify the contents of a file or folder. The name you assign a folder or file must be unique for the folder it is in. For example, if you give a new file the same name as an existing file in the same folder, the contents of the original file will be replaced by the contents of the new file. Many software programs have safeguards to prevent accidentally overwriting one file with another. Folder names must also be unique.

In addition to a filename, a **filename extension** can be added. A filename extension is up to three characters and is separated from the filename by a period. Generally a filename extension is used to identify the type of file. It is not always necessary to enter a filename extension because most application programs automatically add an identifying filename extension to any files created using the program. For instance, Word 7.0 files have a filename extension of "doc." A folder extension is not generally used and is never supplied by the operating system.

The parts of a filename are shown below.

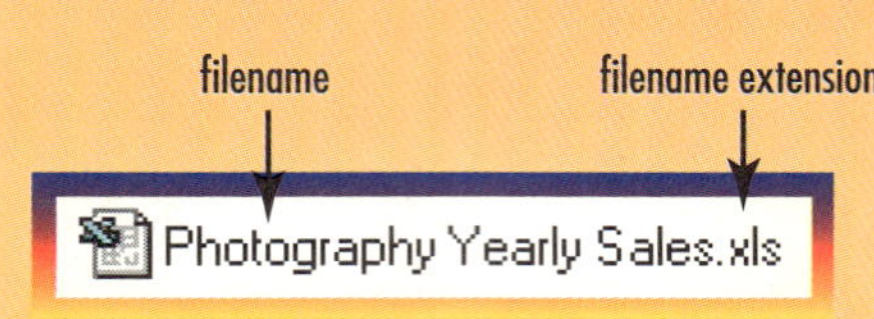

Windows 95 and programs that are designed to operate under Windows 95 allow you to use long folder and **filenames** of up to 255 characters. They can contain the letters A to Z, the numbers 0 to 9, and any of the following special characters: underscore (_), caret (^), dollar sign ($), tilde (~), exclamation point (!), number sign (#), percent sign (%), ampersand (&), hyphen (-), braces ({}), parentheses (), "at" sign (@), apostrophe ('), and the grave accent (`). Spaces are allowed in names, but the following characters are not allowed: \ / : * ? " < > |.

The restrictions regarding characters also apply to filename extensions.

Because this folder will be used to hold files related to your school work, you will name the new folder School Work. With the text "New Folder" highlighted,

> If you make a typing error, use the ←Backspace key to delete the characters to the left of the insertion point.

Type: School Work

To complete the entry,

Press: ←Enter

The folder name appears exactly as you typed it (including case). The insertion point is no longer displayed, but the folder is still selected.

Next you want to create another folder named Personal to hold your personal files. You also want this folder in the main folder.

Select the A drive icon in the All Folders area. Create a new folder named Personal.

Now that the disk in the drive contains folders, the drive icon in the All Folders area is preceded with a [+] .

Expand the A Floppy drive icon to display the folders in the All Folders area.

Your screen should be similar to Figure 2-23.

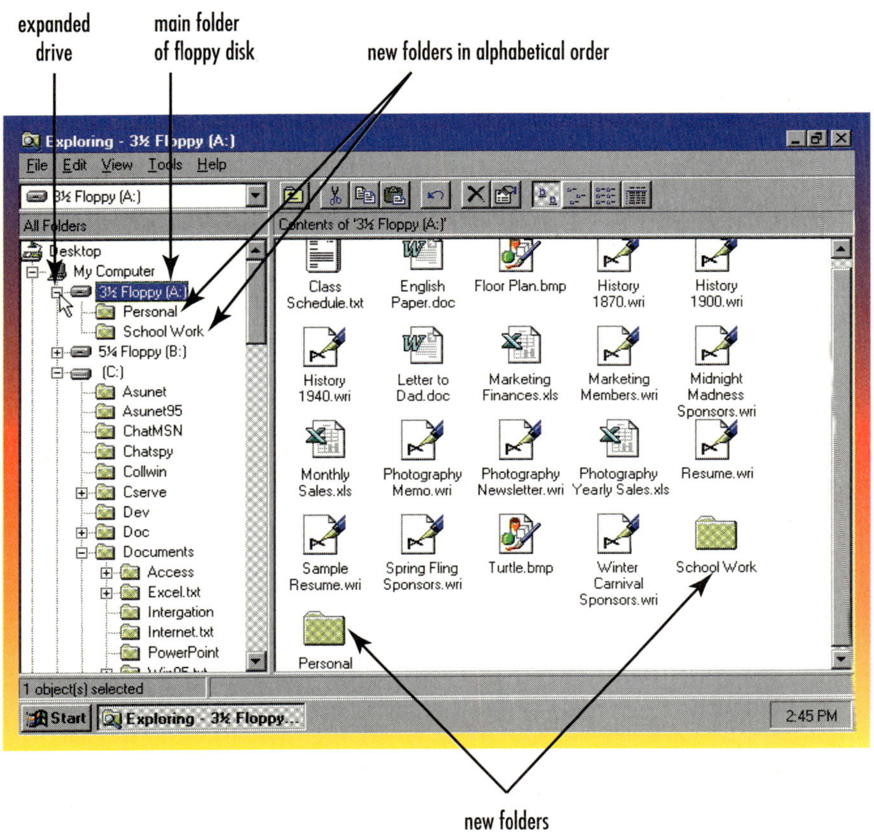

Figure 2-23

The two folders you created appear in alphabetical order in the All Folders area. However, the two new folders are not yet displayed in alphabetical order in the Contents area. To update the order of display of icons in the Contents area,

Choose: View/Arrange Icons/by Name

The folders now appear first in the Contents area and in alphabetical order.

Next you would like to further subdivide your files in the School Work folder by semesters: Fall 1997 and Spring 1998. To create a subfolder under the School folder, you must first select the School folder. When a folder is selected, it is the **current folder** or the folder you can work on. Only one folder can be current at a time.

Select the School Work folder in the All Folders area.

Notice that the Contents area is now blank. This is because there are no files or folders in the selected folder. The description bar displays "Contents of School Work."

Create a folder named Fall 1997.

The new folder is displayed in the School Contents area, and a [+] appears next to the School Work folder in the All Folders area to show that the folder contains a subfolder.

Next create the Spring 1998 subfolder in the School Work folder. (Make sure the School folder is selected first.)

The folder appears in the Contents area.

Then, to display the folders in the All Folders area, expand the School Work folder.

Your screen should be similar to Figure 2-24.

Figure 2-24

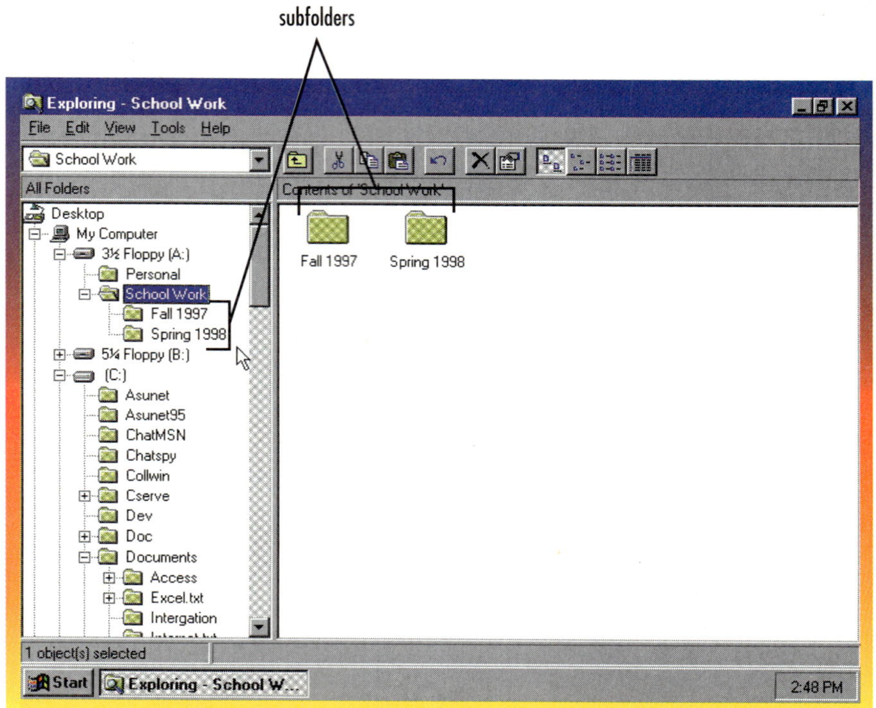

The two new folders are displayed under the School folder.

Copying a File to a Folder

Next you will copy a file from the main folder of your data disk into one of the folders you just created. You will copy the file Class Schedule into the School Work folder.

To select the file you want to copy, select the A drive icon in the All Folders area.

Select the Class Schedule icon in the Contents area.

Rather than using the Copy and Paste commands, you can use the drag and drop feature to copy a file.

Concept 8: Drag and Drop

Common to all Windows applications is the ability to copy or move selections using the **drag and drop** feature. After selecting the item to be copied or moved, pointing to it and dragging displays the drag and drop insertion point. The insertion point displays a + when copying will take place. Then dragging the mouse moves or copies the selection to the new location specified when you release the mouse button. The location you want to drag and drop to should be visible in the window.

If you drag a file to a folder on the same disk, it will be moved. If you drag a file to a folder on another disk, it will be copied. You can hold down ⇧Shift while dragging to always move a file, or Ctrl to copy a file. If you drag holding down the right mouse button, a shortcut menu appears with options to either copy or move the selection.

You will drag and drop the selected file icon from the Contents area to the School folder in the All Folders area.

With the mouse pointer on the selected file icon, hold down Ctrl and drag to the School Work folder in either area.

The mouse pointer appears as while copying the file using drag and drop. When the pointer is positioned over the School Work folder and the folder is selected, release the mouse button and Ctrl.

A circle/slash symbol ⃠ is displayed when the mouse pointer is in an area where the file cannot be copied or moved.

The Copying message box appears while copying occurs. As you can see from the Contents area, the original file remains in the main folder. To verify that the file was copied,

Double-click: **School Work (in the Contents area)**

Your screen should be similar to Figure 2-25.

Figure 2-25

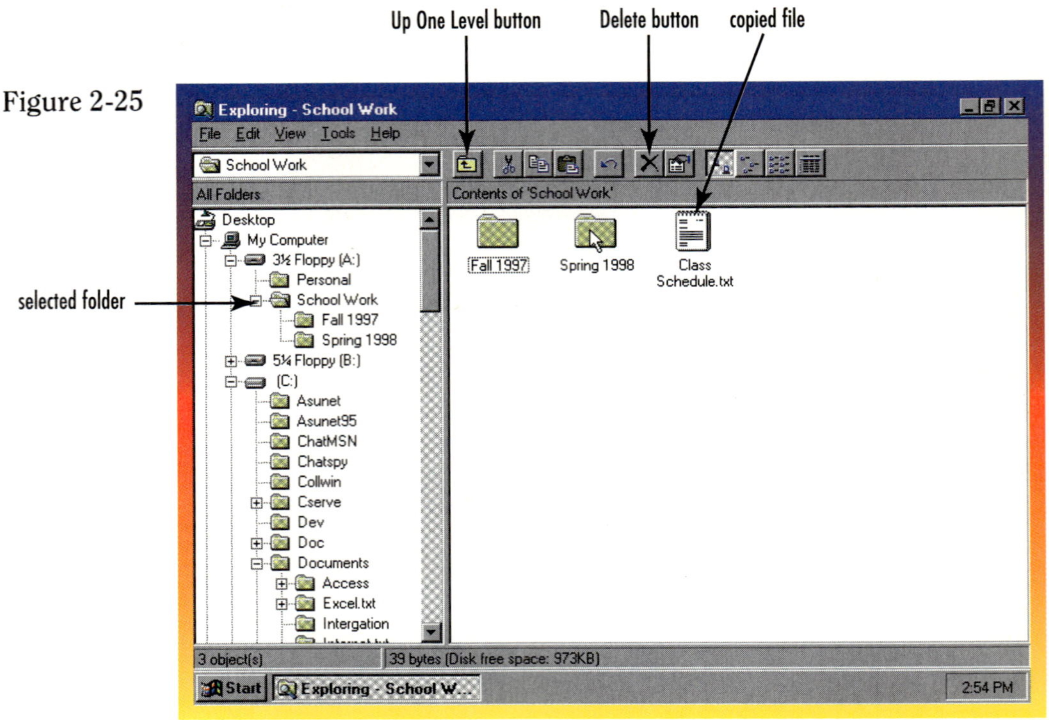

The Contents area displays a file icon for the copied file.

Deleting Files

At some point, some of the files you have on your disk may no longer be needed and you will want to remove them from your disk to save space.

You will delete the Class Schedule file from the main folder now that you have a copy of it in the School Work folder. To quickly move up one level of the hierarchy to the main folder,

You can also press ←Backspace to move back one level.

Click: Up One Level

Select the Class Schedule file icon in the Contents area.

To delete this file,

You can also use the Delete command on the File or shortcut menus or the shortcut key Delete to delete a file or folder.

Click: Delete

The Confirm File Delete message box appears in which you must confirm that you want to remove the file. This is especially important when deleting files from a floppy disk, because they are permanently deleted. Files and folders that are deleted from the hard disk are not permanently deleted, but are placed in the Recycle Bin where they are held until they are permanently deleted from that location.

You will learn about the Recycle Bin in Lab 3.

If you changed your mind, choosing No would cancel the procedure. To continue,

Choose: Yes

> You cannot use Undo to reverse the action of deleting a file from a floppy disk.

Your screen should be similar to Figure 2-26.

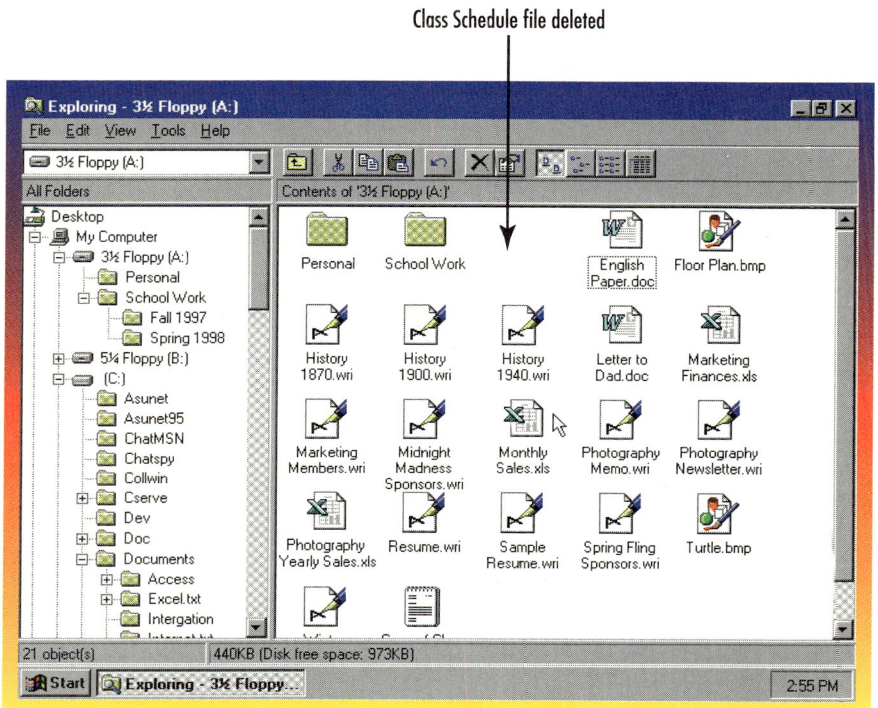

Figure 2-26

The file is removed from the main folder of the disk, and its icon is no longer displayed in the Contents area.

Moving Files

Rather than copying and deleting files, you can **move** them from one location to another. First you would like to move the file English Paper to the School Work folder.

Select the English Paper file icon from the main folder of your data disk.

Files can be moved from one folder on a disk to another by using drag and drop.

Drag the English Paper file to the School Work folder in either area.

> You can also use the Cut and Paste commands on the Edit or shortcut menus or the toolbar buttons and to move a file.

As the file is moved, the Moving message box is displayed. When the move is complete, the English Paper file icon is no longer displayed in the Contents area.

To see the file icon in the School Work folder, open the School Work folder.

The English Paper file icon is displayed in the folder. However, you decide you want this file to be in one of the subfolders of the School folder. It should really be in the Fall 1997 folder. To undo the move,

The menu equivalent is Edit/Undo. The action that will be undone appears after the command name in the menu and Tooltip.

Click: Undo

The Moving dialog box is displayed again and the move is reversed. The English Paper file is removed from the School Work folder and placed back in the main folder.

Return to the main folder and move the English Paper file to the Fall 1997 folder. Open the Fall 1997 folder to verify that the file was moved to the correct location.

Extending a Selection

You can also select several files to copy or move at the same time. This is called **extending a selection**. You can quickly select several files that are scattered throughout the list, or several adjacent files. You can also select multiple groups of files from the list.

Reminder: You can click to move up a level.

Open the main folder of your data disk.

First you will move two nonadjacent files, Letter to Dad and Resume, to the Personal folder.

Select the Letter to Dad file icon.

The next file you will select is Resume.

If necessary, scroll the window until it is displayed.

To select a second file, you hold down Ctrl while clicking the file icon.

Hold down Ctrl.

Now, when you click on any other files, they will be selected (highlighted).

Select the Resume file icon.

To deselect a file (remove the highlight), click on it again while holding down Ctrl.

If necessary, deselect any other files that you may have selected accidentally. Release Ctrl.

Your screen should be similar to Figure 2-27.

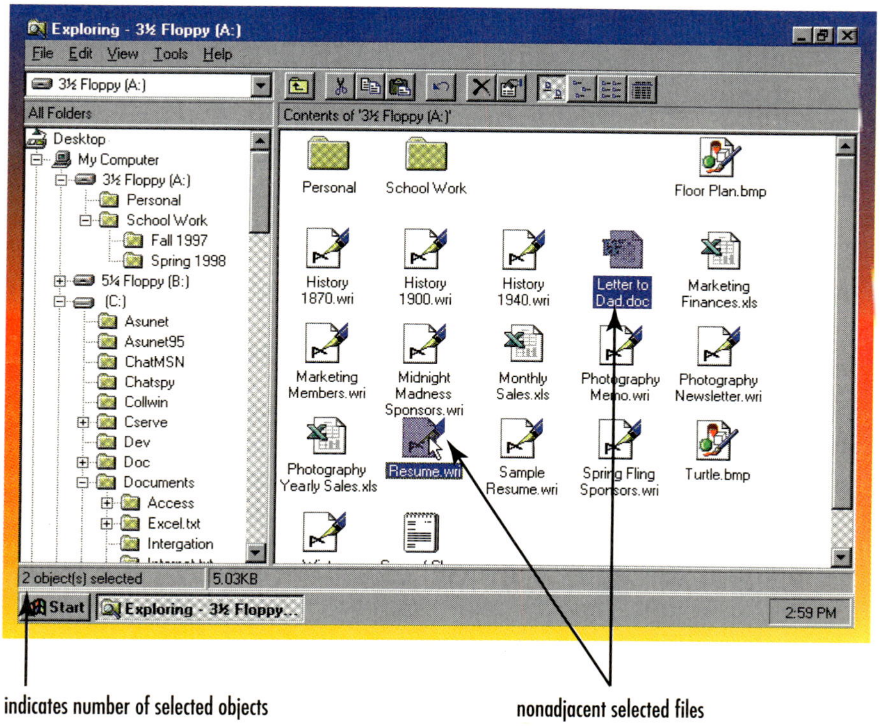

Figure 2-27

The two files are highlighted and the status bar indicates that two objects are selected.

Move the files to the Personal folder.

To verify that the files were moved, open the Personal folder.

You can also use drag and drop with multiple files.

Next you will select and copy a series of adjacent files from the main folder to the Fall 1997 folder of the School folder. The three files you want to copy are the three History files.

Open the main folder of your data disk.

You will select the three adjacent files, History 1870 , History 1900, and History 1940. To do this you can hold down the mouse button and drag to create a box around the files. If a file you do not want selected is included in the box, holding down Ctrl while clicking the file deselects it, leaving all others selected. Likewise, you can add other files to the selection by holding down Ctrl while selecting them.

Select the History 1870, History 1900, and History 1940 files by dragging a box around the file icons and adding or clearing selections as needed.

Do not point to a file icon while dragging to create a box.

Notice that the status bar indicates three objects are selected.

Move the selected files to the Fall 1997 folder under the School Work folder.

To verify that the files were moved to the destination folder, open the Fall 1997 folder.

4) How did you find the Letter to Robert file?

d. Exit the Tour of Windows 95.

☆☆

2. You are working on a project for your computer class that requires you to create multiple documents on a subject of your choice using several different applications. You have created your documents on the topic of photography. After creating several documents and storing them on your disk in the main folder, you have decided to organize the documents into folders to make them easier to locate.

a. Create a new folder named Computer Project on your data disk to store your files for this project.

b. Create subfolders for the different sections of the project, including folders for word processing documents, graphics, and financial documents.

c. Move the files Photography Memo and Photography Newsletter to the word processing folder.

d. Move the file Monthly Sales to the graphics folder.

e. Copy the file Photography Yearly Sales to the financial folder.

f. Confirm that all the files have been moved or copied to the correct folders.

☆☆

3. You have been elected to the position of Recording Secretary for the Marketing Association club at your school. The association keeps records on finances, members, and sponsors. You would like to set up a disk to keep track of the files you create for the association.

a. Using Windows Explorer, create two new folders on your data disk. Name one Finances, and name the other People. Under the People folder create two subfolders, one for Members and the other for Sponsors.

b. Make the main folder active.

c. Move the file Marketing Finances to the Finance folder.

d. Copy the Marketing Members file to the Members subfolder.

e. Delete the Marketing Members file from the main folder.

f. Copy the three sponsor files from the main folder to the Sponsors subfolder.

g. Confirm that all the files have been copied or moved to the folders.

h. Close the Exploring window.

★★

4. In this lab you used many, but not all, of the taskbar features. In this problem you will learn about other features of the taskbar. Use the taskbar and answer the following questions.

a. Double-click on the time in the taskbar. What happened?

b. Use What's This? Help for information on the Date/Time Properties dialog box. Describe the date and time properties that can be changed. Close the dialog box.

c. Select Properties from the taskbar shortcut menu. Turn on the Auto Hide property. Choose OK. What happened to the taskbar?

d. To redisplay the taskbar, move the mouse pointer to the bottom of the window. Then open the taskbar Properties dialog box and turn off the Auto Hide taskbar property.

e. The taskbar can be moved along any border of the screen. Move it to each border and describe what happens to the desktop and the taskbar. Return the taskbar to the bottom of the window.

On Your Own

★★

5. The Find command on the Start menu can be used to locate files on your system disk or data disk.

a. Use Help to learn how to use this feature. Which search type do you think would take longest and why?

b. Use Find to locate all the files on your hard disk (C) that contain the word "Window" in the name.

c. Locate all files that were modified during the last month on your hard disk. How may files did you find?

d. Locate all files containing the text "Sponsors" on your data disk. How many files did you find?

e. Close Find.

★★★

6. You are the manager of 12 employees, all of whom are going to share files on a file server. Describe how you plan to allocate a private folder for each employee and how you plan to set up folders for the accounting, research, and cost management projects your employees will be working on.

Concept Summary

2 Windows 95: Disk Organization

File and Folder Names

Both files and folders are assigned names that are used to identify contents of the file or folder.

Hierachy of Folders

The organization of folders, subfolders, and files on your disk is called a hierachy or tree.

Files and Folders

The information on your computer is stored as files. Folders contain files that are related.

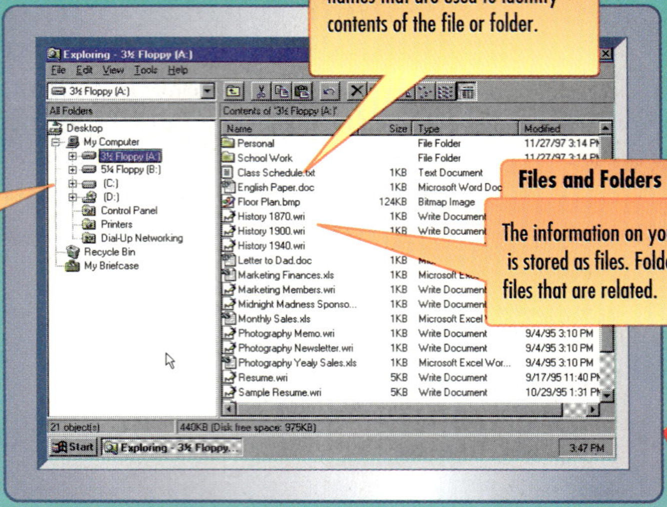

Arranging Windows

Windows can be arranged on the desktop: cascaded, tiled horizontally, or tiled vertically.

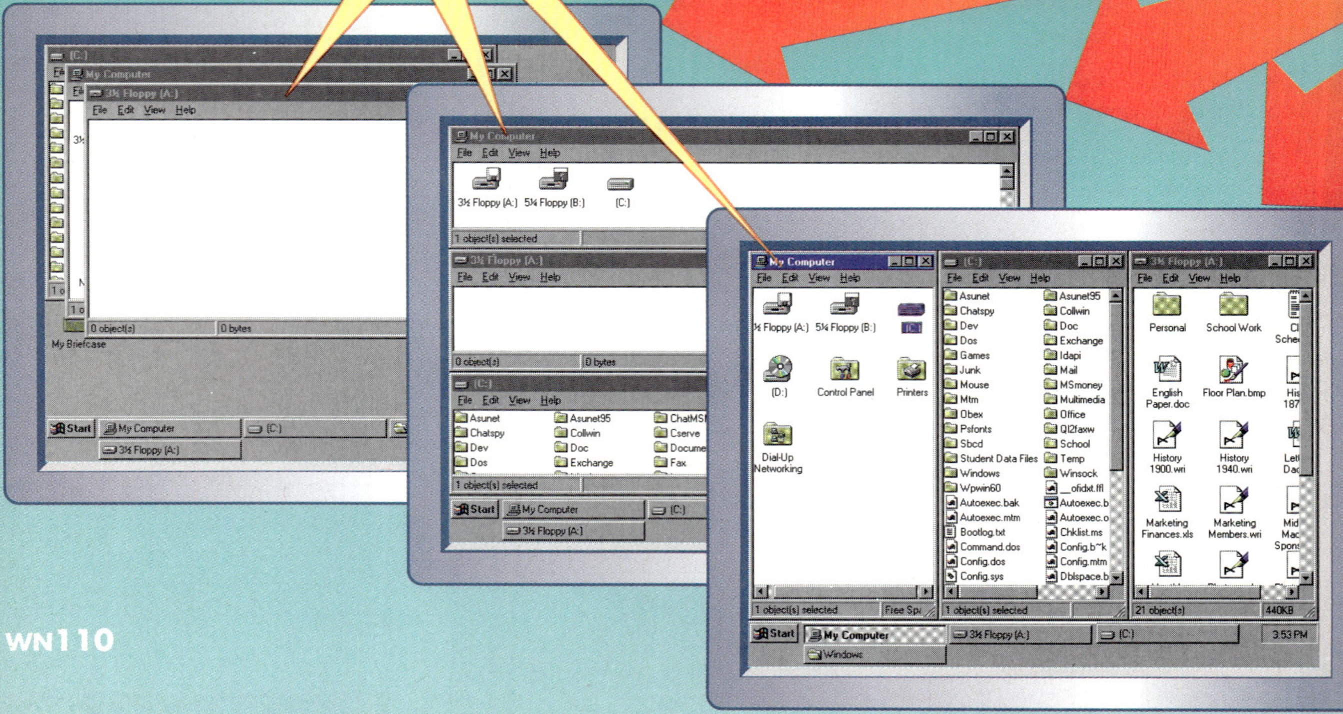

Undo

The Undo feature allows you to reverse your last action or command.

Toolbar

The toolbar contains buttons that are shortcuts for many of the most common menu commands.

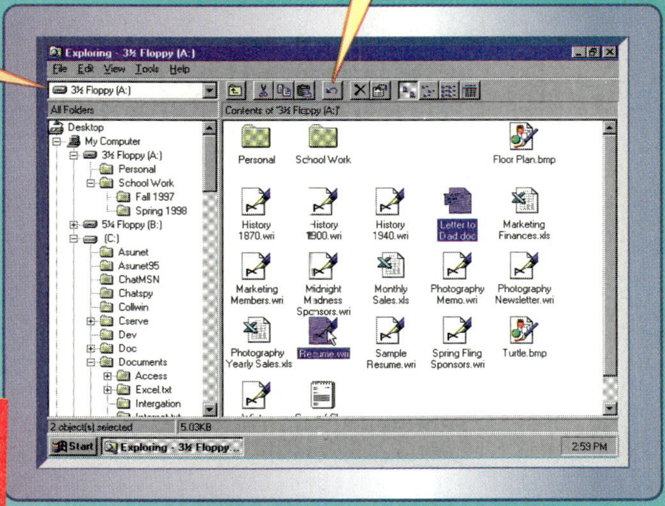

Concepts

Files and Folders
File and Folder Names
Hierarchy of Folders

Arranging Windows

Toolbar
Undo

Cut, Copy, and Paste
Drag and Drop

Cut, Copy, and Paste

All Windows applications include features that allow you to remove (cut), duplicate (copy), and insert (paste) information from one location to another.

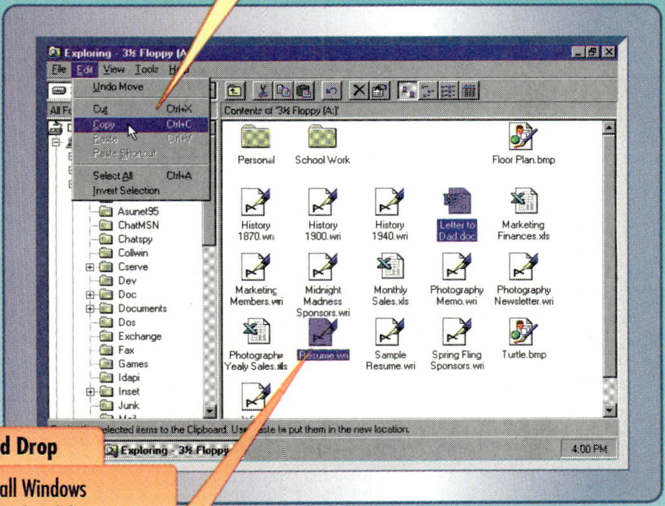

Drag and Drop

Common to all Windows applications is the ability to copy or move selections by dragging and dropping.

Using Windows 95 Applications

3

COMPETENCIES

In this lab you will learn how to:

1. Use WordPad.
2. Select and align text.
3. Change type size and color.
4. Save and print a document.
5. Use Paint.
6. View Clipboard contents.
7. Copy between applications.
8. Create a shortcut icon.
9. Use the Recycle Bin.
10. Use QuickView.
11. Create scraps.

Not long ago, trained specialists were required to perform many day-to-day operations. Secretaries used typewriters to produce typed correspondence. Accountants used pens and paper ledgers to record and analyze data. Artists used pen and paper to produce graphic artwork. Now with the development of specialized applications software, you can easily do many of these jobs yourself.

There are applications software programs that help you create written correspondence, drawings and artwork, or financial statements and budgets. Others help you maintain records and produce informational reports. And still others help you connect and communicate with other computers.

In this lab you will learn to use two application software programs that are included with Windows 95: WordPad and Paint. Learning how to use these programs builds upon the skills you acquired while learning about the operating system. In addition, you will learn about features that are common to other applications that run under Windows 95. This will make it easier for you to learn to use new applications in the future.

Concept Overview

The following concepts will be introduced in this lab:

1. Word Processor	Word processing applications are designed to help you create, edit, and print documents.
2. Editing	The process of correcting or changing existing text is called editing.
3. Selecting Text	Selecting highlights the text that will be affected by your next action.
4. Font Size	Font size refers to the height of printed characters.
5. Saving Files	Saving creates a permanent copy of your onscreen document in a file on a disk.
6. Drawing Programs	Drawing programs are used to create illustrations.
7. Objects	An object is any set of information created in one application, then inserted or stored in a document that was created using a different application.
8. Linking and Embedding	When objects are copied from one application to another, they can be inserted into the receiving document as a pasted object, a linked object, or an embedded object.
9. Shortcut Icons	Shortcut icons provide quick access to the associated feature.

Part 1

Using WordPad

In addition to the programs that run as part of Windows 95, such as Windows Explorer, Windows 95 includes several small programs that are designed to help you with your work, or amuse you while passing time. Some, but not all, are installed automatically on the hard disk of the computer when Windows 95 is installed. Others must be added individually. The table below lists and briefly describes many of these programs.

Refer to Help for information on adding programs.

Application	Description
Briefcase	Quickly transfers files between a laptop and desktop computer
CD Player	Plays music from CDs using the CD disk drive
Calculator	Performs calculations
Character Map	Inserts symbols/characters in documents
Clipboard Viewer	Displays contents of Windows Clipboard
Desktop Wallpaper	Background images for desktop
Document Templates	Creates new document for most common programs
DriveSpace	Disk compression program
Games	Solitaire, Minesweeper, Hearts, and Free Cell
(continued)	

Application	Description
HyperTerminal	Connects via modem to a remote computer, sends/receives files
Microsoft Network	Standard on-line service offering electronic mail, bulletin boards, newsgroups, etc.
Microsoft Exchange	Electronic mailbox
Media Player	Plays audio, video, and animation files
Mouse Pointers	Variety of easy-to-see pointers
Net Watcher	Monitors network server and connections
Online User's Guide	Online version of user guide
Paint	Used to create, modify, or view pictures
Phone Dialer	Dials phone numbers in your personal phone book
Quick View	Previews document without opening it
ScanDisk	Checks disks for errors
Screen Savers	Displays moving images when computer is idle
Sound Recorder	Records and plays sounds
System Monitor	Monitors system performance
System Resource Meter	Views system resource levels
Window 95 Tour	Teaches a few basics on Windows 95
WordPad	Word processor for short memos and documents

Many of these additional programs are in the Accessories section of the Programs menu. To display the accessories on your system,

Choose: Start/Programs/Accessories

All the accessory programs that are available on your system are displayed. One of the most useful programs is WordPad, a word processing program designed to produce day-to-day business and personal documents.

Concept 1: Word Processor

Word processing applications are designed to help you create, edit, and print documents. **Documents** are any kind of text material such as memos, letters, and research papers. Word processors have replaced the typewriter, and moreover have greatly enhanced what a typewriter could do. The biggest advantage of a word processor is that it displays the text as you type it on your computer screen rather than on paper. This makes it easy to make changes and corrections onscreen before the document is printed on paper. Word processors are probably the most used of all software programs and are credited with producing the highest gains in user productivity.

You are planning a party to celebrate a friend's 21st birthday. You decide to use WordPad to create and print an invitation. The completed invitation will look like that shown in Figure 3-1 below.

Figure 3-1

To open WordPad,

Click: WordPad

If necessary, maximize the window.

Your screen should be similar to Figure 3-2 shown in the box on the next page.

The WordPad application is opened in its own window, and the taskbar displays a button for the open application. The parts of the WordPad window are described on the next page.

Parts of the WordPad Window

Figure 3-2

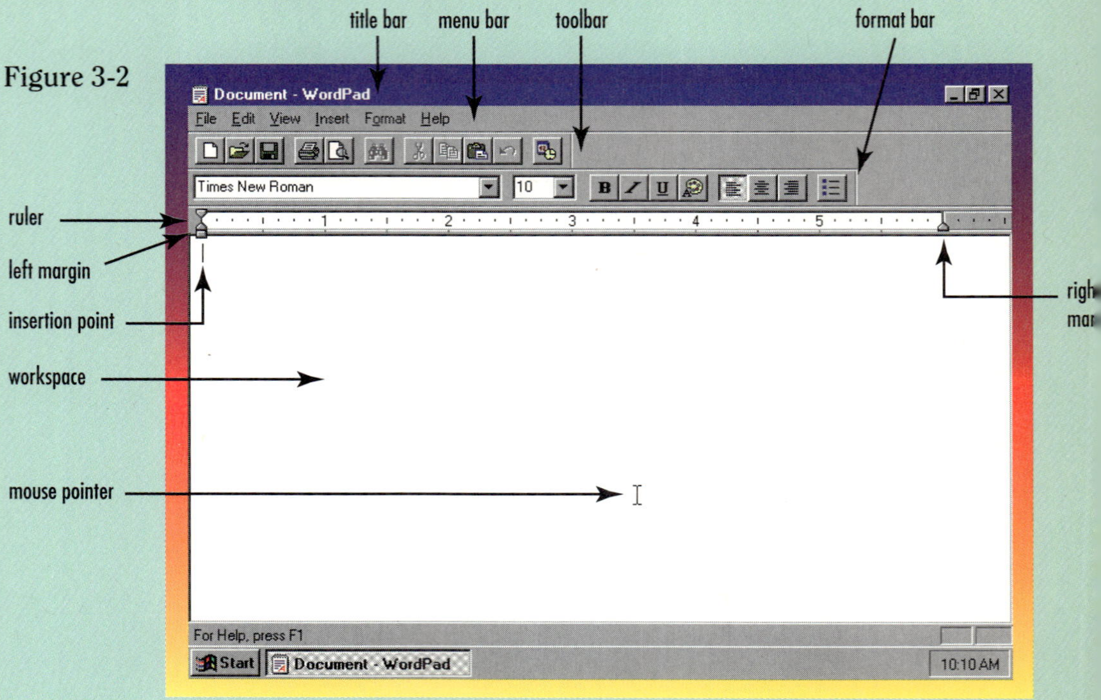

The title bar displays the temporary filename, Document, followed by the name of the program. The temporary filename is displayed until you save the file and give it a more descriptive name. Below the title bar is a menu bar displaying six menus: File, Edit, View, Insert, Format, and Help. The toolbar contains button shortcuts for many of the most frequently used menu commands. Displayed below the toolbar is the **format bar**. The format bar contains buttons representing the most frequently used text-editing and text-layout features.

The **ruler** is displayed below the format bar. The ruler shows the line length in inches. The zero position on the ruler marks the location of the left margin. The ⌂ symbol on the right end of the ruler at the 6-inch position marks the right margin. The ruler is used to set tab stops and indents for selected paragraphs. The ruler can also be used to change the page margins and to help place items on the page.

The large blank area below the ruler is the **workspace**. This is where your work is displayed. The insertion point is positioned in the upper left corner of the workspace, ready for you to begin typing. When the mouse pointer is positioned in the workspace, it appears as an I-beam, just as it does in a text box of a dialog box.

If any of the WordPad window features are not displayed, use the View menu to select the appropriate option to turn on the feature.

You would like to enter the text for the invitation next. To enter text in WordPad, simply begin typing. As you are typing, the insertion point moves to show you where the next character will appear. The character after the insertion point is the **active character**. This is the character that will be affected by your next action.

While typing, you will certainly make typing errors or you will want to change what you have typed. The process of correcting or changing existing text is called **editing**.

Concept 2: Editing

A word processor excels in its ability to change or edit a document. You can quickly delete a character, word, sentence, or paragraph and replace it with new text. There are many methods you can use to edit text. The two most common are to use the ←Backspace key to delete unwanted characters to the left of the insertion point, or the Delete key to remove the active character. Then you can retype the text correctly.

The directional keys or the mouse are used to move the insertion point back within the text. To move the insertion point with the mouse, position the I-beam at the location in the text where you want the insertion point to be and click the left mouse button.

Make sure the pointer is an I-beam before clicking to move the insertion point.

To begin the invitation,

Type: **Party, Party, Party -- Get Ready to Party!**
Press: ←Enter

Pressing ←Enter ends a line and moves the insertion point to the beginning of the next line. To create a blank line,

Press: ←Enter

When the insertion point is at the beginning of a line and ←Enter is pressed, a blank line is created.

To continue the invitation, enter the following text without pressing the ←Enter key,

Type: **We're having a pool party and barbecue to celebrate Dan's 21st birthday! Bring your suit and a smile, we will provide the rest.**

Notice that as you type, the text automatically moves to the next line when it reaches the right margin defined by the 6-inch mark on the ruler. This feature of word processors is called **word wrap**.

Press: ←Enter **(2 times)**

To continue the invitation, type the text shown below. Press ↵Enter at the end of each line and follow each colon with two spaces.

When: Friday August 7
Time: 7:00 p.m.
Where: [Your Name]

Press: ↵Enter

Your screen should be similar to Figure 3-3.

Figure 3-3

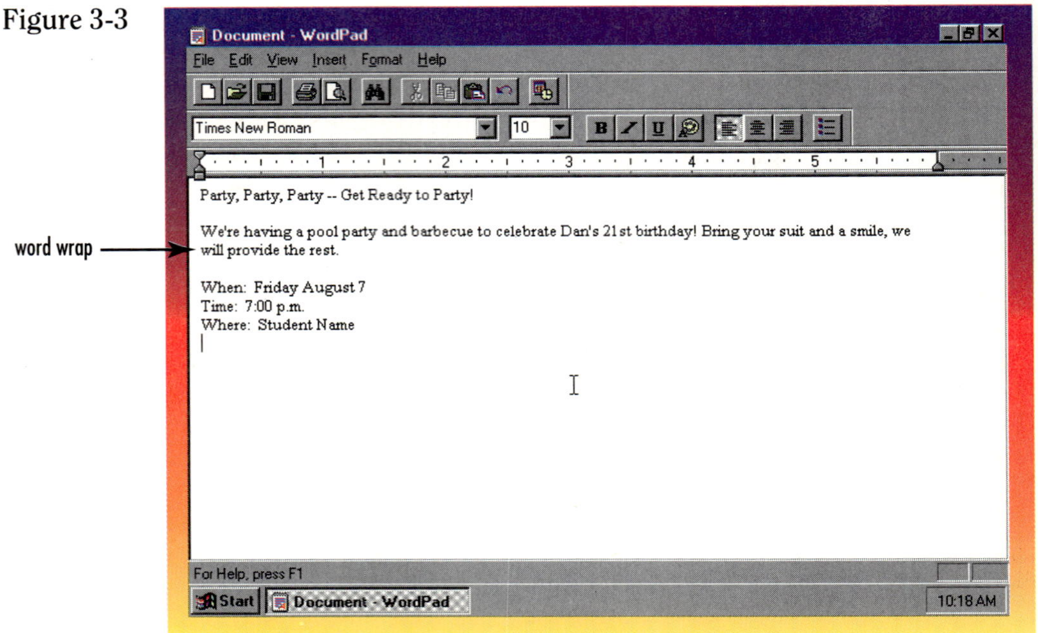

Check your typing for any errors. If you see any errors, correct them using the editing features discussed in Concept 2: Editing.

Centering Text

After entering the text of the invitation, you would like to improve its appearance by centering all the lines of the invitation between the margins and increasing the type size of the characters. Enhancing the appearance of a document is called **formatting**.

Before you can apply the formatting effects, you first need to select the text you want to format.

Concept 3: Selecting Text

Selecting text highlights the text that will be affected by your next action, much like selecting files or folders before copying or moving. There are many methods you can use to select an area of text.

The most common method is to drag the mouse to select an area of text, just as in a text box. You can drag in any direction in the document to extend the highlight. You can drag diagonally across text to extend the highlight from the character the insertion point is on to the last character in the selection. You can also drag in the opposite direction to deselect text. The keyboard can be used to select text by holding down ⇧Shift while pressing a directional key. Either method requires that you move the insertion point to the beginning or end of the area to be selected before you select it. You can also select the entire document using the Select All command on the Edit menu in all Windows 95 applications.

A selection is cleared by clicking anywhere outside the selection or by pressing a direction key.

To select the entire document,

Choose: Edit/Select All

The keyboard shortcut is Ctrl + A.

All the text in the invitation is highlighted, indicating it is selected.

The format bar buttons are used to format text in the document. The [Align Left], [Center], and [Align Right] buttons are used to align text with the left margin, center it between the margins, and align it with the right margin. To center the text,

Click: [Center] Center

The menu equivalent is Format/Paragraph/Alignment/Center.

Your screen should be similar to Figure 3-4.

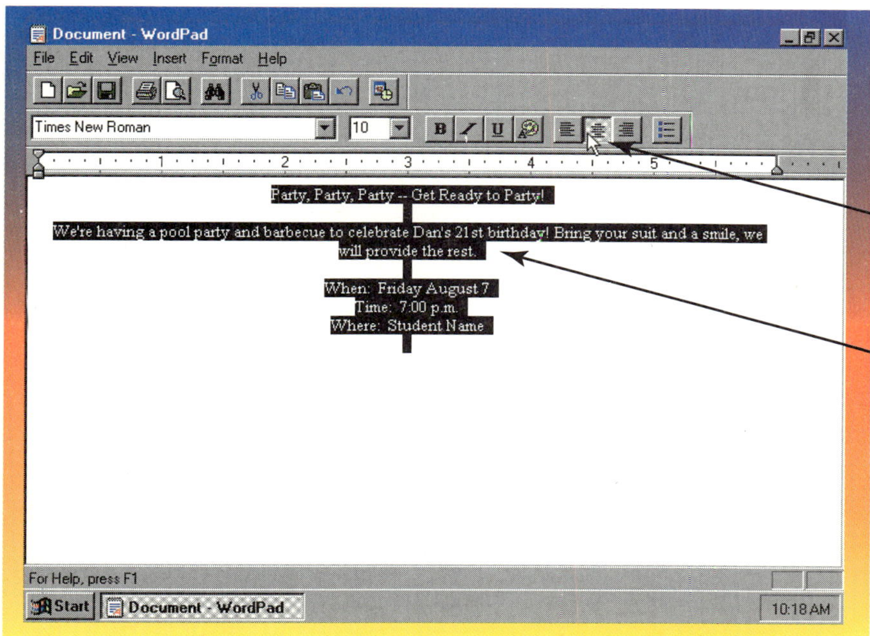

Figure 3-4

The selected lines of text are centered between the margins.

Changing Type Size

To further enhance the appearance of the invitation, you would like to increase the font size of the currently selected text.

Concept 4: Font Size

Font size, also commonly called type size or point size, refers to the height and width of printed characters. Font size is measured in **points**, which refers to the height of the character, with each point about 1/72 inch. Most documents use a type size of 10 or 12 points. The larger the number of points, the larger the size of the characters.

> The menu equivalent to size text is Format/Font/Size.

The Font Size drop-down list button in the format bar is used to change font size. The text box shows the font size of characters in the selection. If the selection included mixed font sizes, the text box would be blank. Because the font size is the same for all characters in this selection, it displays 10. To change the size, you can type the new font size in the text box and press ↵Enter. Alternatively, you can select from a list of font sizes that is displayed when you open the drop-down list. You will increase the size to 16 points by selecting the size from the drop-down list. To do this,

> Click ▾ to display the drop-down list.

Click: 10 ▾ Font Size

The drop-down list of font size options is displayed.

Select: 16

> Click outside the selection to clear it.

Clear the highlight and, if necessary, move to the top of the document.

Your screen should be similar to Figure 3-5.

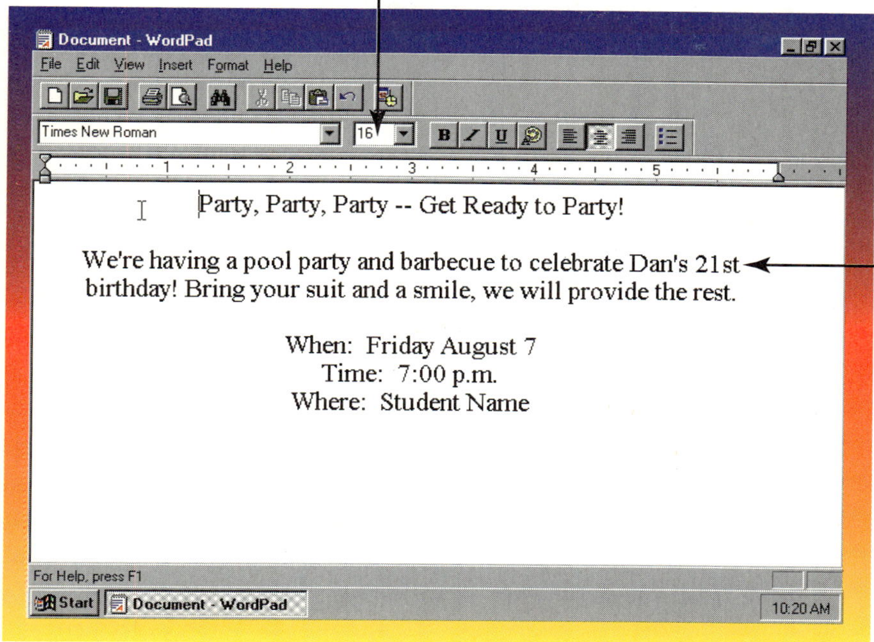

Figure 3-5

The text appears on the screen in 16-point font size, as it will appear when printed.

Next you would like to make the invitation title line an even larger font size than the rest of the text.

Using either selection method presented in Concept 3: Selecting Text, select the invitation title only.

The entire line is selected.

Increase the title to 24 points.

Adding Color to Text

While the title is still selected, you would also like to apply a color to the title text. The Color button on the format bar can be used to change the color of the text.

Click: Color

> The menu equivalent is Format/Font/Color.

A drop-down list of 16 colors is displayed.

To select a color, click on a color of your choice. Then clear the highlight.

Your screen should be similar to Figure 3-6.

Figure 3-6

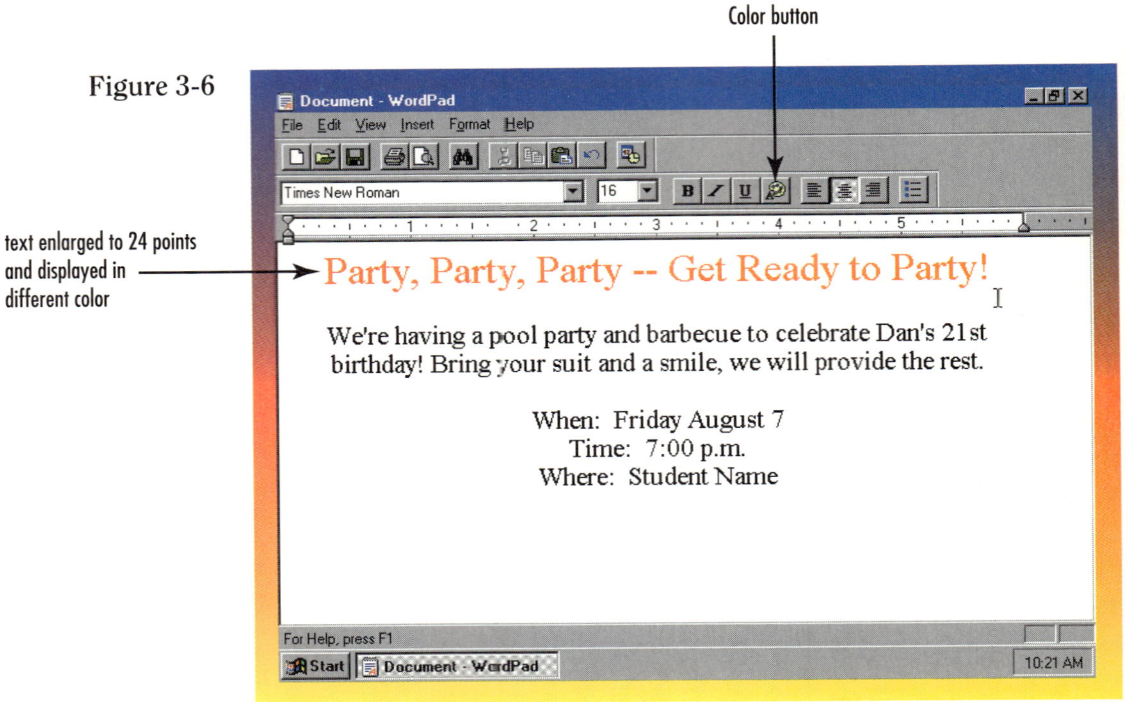

Saving a File

Now that the text of the invitation is how you want it to appear, you will save your work to a file. If you do not save your work, the document will no longer exist when you exit WordPad.

Concept 5: Saving Files

While working on a document, your changes are stored temporarily in the computer's memory. Not until you **save** the document as a file on a disk are you safe from losing your work due to a power failure or other mishap.

Two commands found on the File menu of all Windows programs can be used to save a file: Save and Save As. The Save command saves a document using the same path and filename as the existing disk file, by replacing the contents of the file with the changes you have made. The Save As command allows you to select a different path and/or provide a different filename. This command lets you save both an original version of a document and a revised document as two separate files.

When you save a file for the first time, either command can be used. Although many programs create automatic backup files if your work is accidentally interrupted, it is still a good idea to save your work frequently.

The [Save icon] Save button on the toolbar can be used to save a file.

> The menu and keyboard equivalents are File/Save and Ctrl + S.

Click: Save

Your screen should be similar to Figure 3-7.

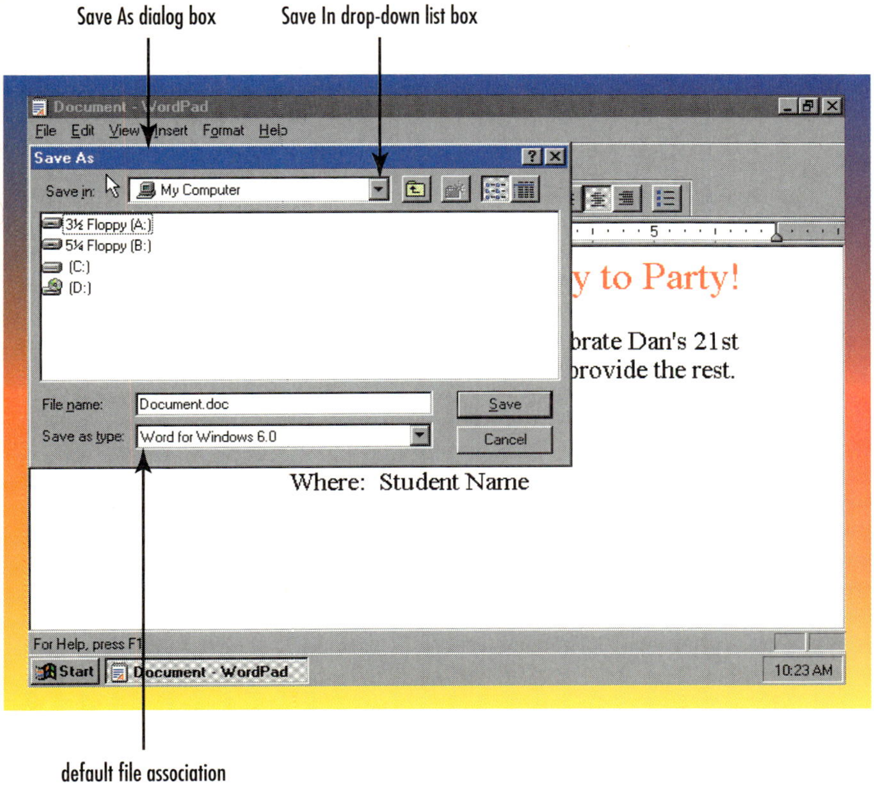

Figure 3-7

> Your dialog box may display different folders or files.

Whenever you save a file for the first time, the Save As dialog box is displayed so you can specify where you want the file saved and the filename. You want to save the file to your data disk.

Open the Save In drop-down list box.

Select: **A: (or the drive containing your data disk)**

The selected location is displayed in the Save In text box.

The Save As Type drop-down list box displays the name of the application that will be associated with the saved file. If you do not specify a file extension when naming a file, the extension associated with the selected application will automatically be added to the filename. You can also select a different application from the drop-down list box to change the association, or include a specific file extension when naming the file to override the selection. In Figure 3-7 the default associates the file with the Word for Windows 6.0 application.

You are now ready to name the file.

Select the existing default filename, Document.doc, in the File Name text box.

> Refer to Lab 2 for information about associated files and file naming rules.

> Your computer may associate the file with another word processor or with WordPad.

> Drag or double-click on the word to select it.

As soon as you begin typing, the existing filename will be erased. You will name the file Invitation and include the WordPad file extension, .wri. To name the file,

The filename can be entered in either uppercase or lowercase letters.

Type: Invitation.wri
Choose: Save

The document is saved to the disk using the specified filename. The new filename now appears in the title bar and in the taskbar button.

Next you want to add a picture of balloons to the invitation using the Paint application program, which is also included with Windows 95. Because you will use WordPad again shortly, you will not exit the application before opening Paint.

Minimize the WordPad window.

Using Paint

The Paint application is a drawing program that is used to create graphic images.

Concept 6: Drawing Programs

Drawing programs are used to create illustrations. They allow you to create attractive, sophisticated line art by combining lines, arcs, circles, and other shapes. These programs are commonly used by professional illustrators to produce artwork used in publications such as books and magazines.

When you opened the WordPad application, you used the Programs command in the Start menu. Another way to open a program and create a new document is to use the desktop shortcut menu.

Right-click the desktop background.

Display the desktop shortcut menu.

The New command is used to create new documents.

Select: New

Next you need to specify the type of file you want to create. The Paint program creates graphics that consist of many small dots on the screen called a **bitmap**. These files are saved as bitmap files.

Bitmap files have a file extension of .bmp.

Choose: Bitmap Image

Your screen should be similar to Figure 3-8.

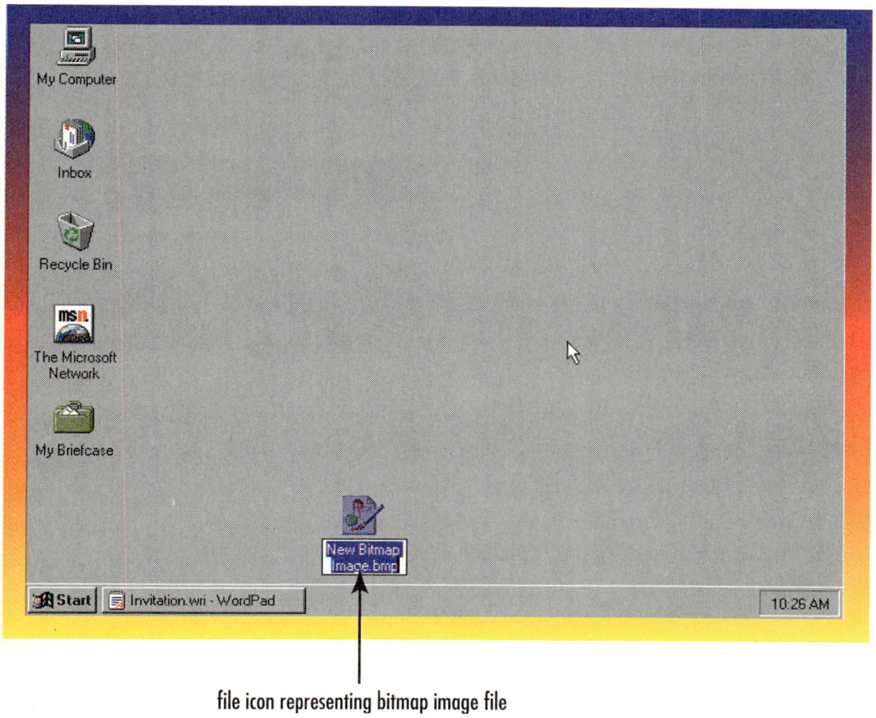

Figure 3-8

A file icon representing an application that is associated with bitmap images is displayed on the desktop. The text under the icon displays the default button name "New Bitmap Image.bmp." You will replace the default name with the filename you will use to name the balloon file, just as you did when naming a new folder. To do this,

Type: **Balloons.bmp**
Press: ↵Enter

Then, to open the Balloons file and the associated application, Paint,

Double-click: 

If necessary, maximize the Paint window so that more workspace is displayed to create the drawing.

Your screen should be similar to Figure 3-9 on the next page.

The Paint program is loaded with the Balloons file open. You now have two programs open and running as indicated by the two buttons in the taskbar. The parts of the Paint window are described below.

Parts of the Paint Window

Figure 3-9

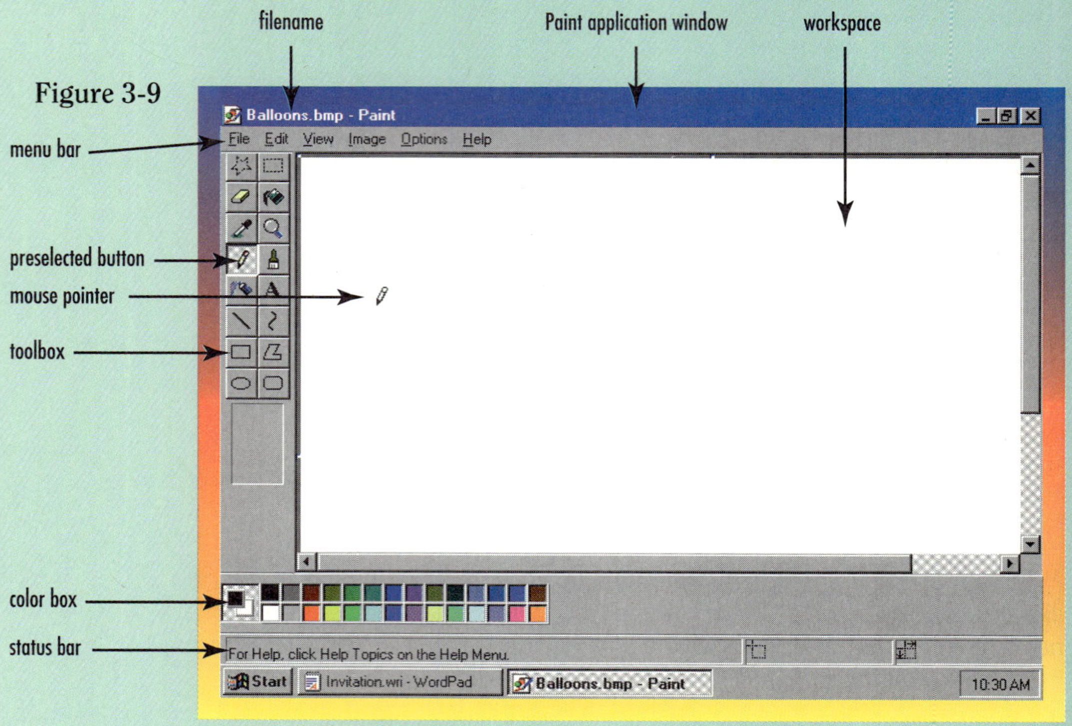

The Paint program has some of the same features as the WordPad program, including a workspace, a menu bar, and a toolbar, called a **toolbox** in Paint. By default the toolbox is displayed on the left edge of the window. Displayed at the bottom of the window is the color box and status bar.

If these features are not displayed, use the View menu to turn them on.

You would like to draw a picture of three balloons that you can copy into the invitation you created using WordPad. The toolbox buttons are used to draw shapes, fill shapes with colors, edit the drawing, and so on.

You can also use Help to learn more about the Paint program.

Read the Tooltip and the description in the status bar for each of the toolbox buttons to find out what they do.

The preselected button is the Pencil button. You can tell it is selected because it appears depressed. The mouse pointer appears as a ✎ when this button is selected, indicating that when it is used a free-form line will be created.

Creating Shapes

First you will draw a balloon in the center of the window. The button creates an ellipse or circular shape. To use this button to draw the balloon,

Click: **Ellipse**

Your screen should be similar to Figure 3-10.

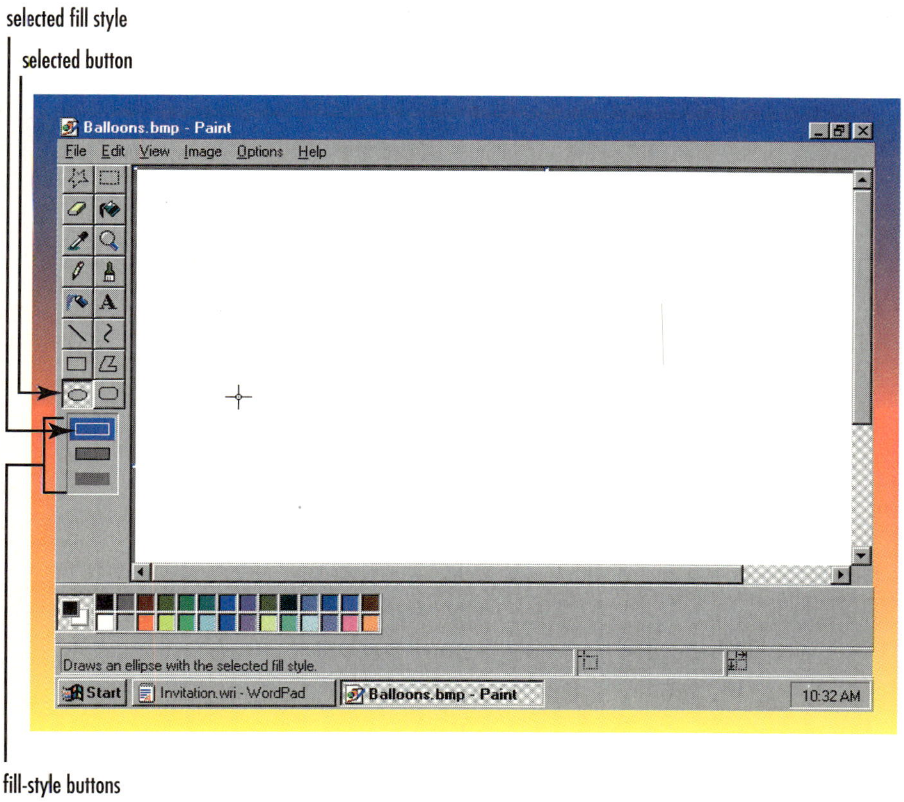

Figure 3-10

The button appears depressed in the toolbox, indicating it is selected. Whichever tool is selected will be drawn when you drag or click in the workspace. Notice that there are now three additional buttons, called fill-style buttons, displayed at the bottom of the toolbox. The first button will draw an ellipse with an outline border in the selected fill color without filling the object. The second button will draw an outline border and also fill the object with the selected fill color. The last fill style will create an object without a border using the selected fill color. The default style of a border with no fill is acceptable for this drawing.

> The selected fill style button appears highlighted.

When you move the mouse pointer into the workspace, it changes to a +. To begin drawing, move the mouse pointer to where you want the circle to begin.

Point to: **top center of the workspace**

> Dragging diagonally creates an ellipse. Hold [⇧Shift] while dragging to create a perfect circle.

A circle or ellipse is created by dragging the mouse until the shape is displayed on the screen as you want it to look. When the shape is how you want it to appear, release the mouse button.

Drag the mouse to create a balloon of a shape and size of your choice.

Your screen should be similar to Figure 3-11.

Figure 3-11

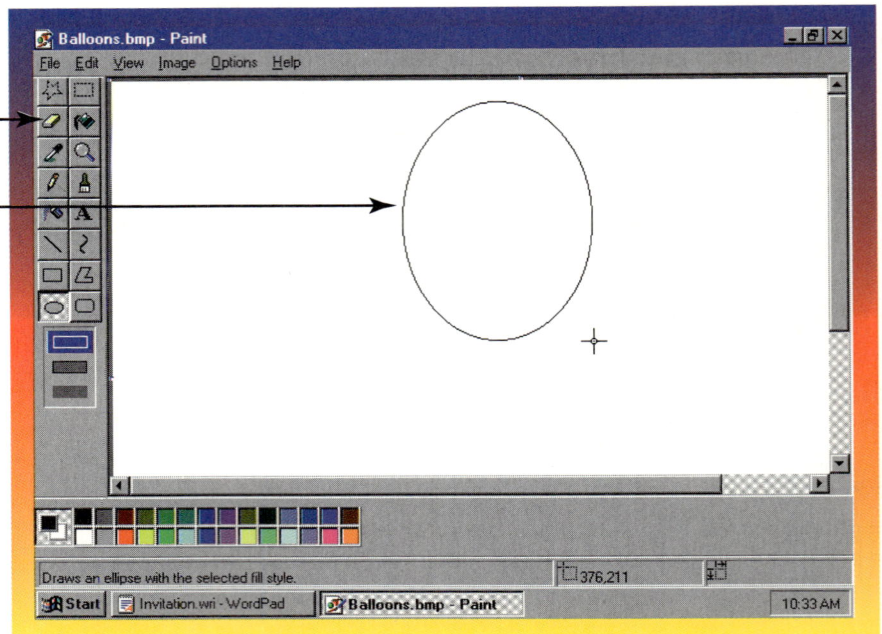

The mouse pointer is still a +, indicating it is ready to create another ellipse. Not until you select another tool button will the ellipse shape be turned off.

If you do not like the shape, you can use Edit/Undo to delete the shape and try again.

> Undo can be used to undelete your last three actions in Paint. The Undo command shortcut is [Ctrl] + Z. There is no Undo button.

In a similar manner, draw two more balloons, one on either side of the first (make one of them overlap another).

To clean up the drawing, you can use the Eraser button to delete the part of the outline on the overlapping balloon that is in the foreground. To do this,

Click: **Eraser**

The mouse pointer changes to a □, indicating that any line you drag it over will be erased.

Drag the mouse over the line you want to erase. If you make a mistake, use Undo to restore the line and try again.

Next you would like to add bottoms (ties) to the balloons (see Figure 3-12 for reference as to how the ties should appear). Since there is no tool that will create this particular shape, you will use the Polygon tool to draw the shapes you need.

Click: **Polygon tool**

To use the [Polygon button] Polygon tool, point to the location where you want the shape to start and then drag and click on the corner locations. Double-click when the shape is complete. If the shape is not a closed shape, the program will close it for you by adding a final line.

Draw bottoms on all three balloons.

To complete the drawing, you would like to add strings at the bottoms of the balloons. You can use the [Line button] Line tool button to draw the strings.

Click: [Line button] **Line**

To use the [Line button] Line tool, point to where you want the line to start and drag to the location where you want the line to end. When you release the mouse button, the line is created.

Draw three lines from the balloons to a point below the balloons.

Your screen should be similar to Figure 3-12.

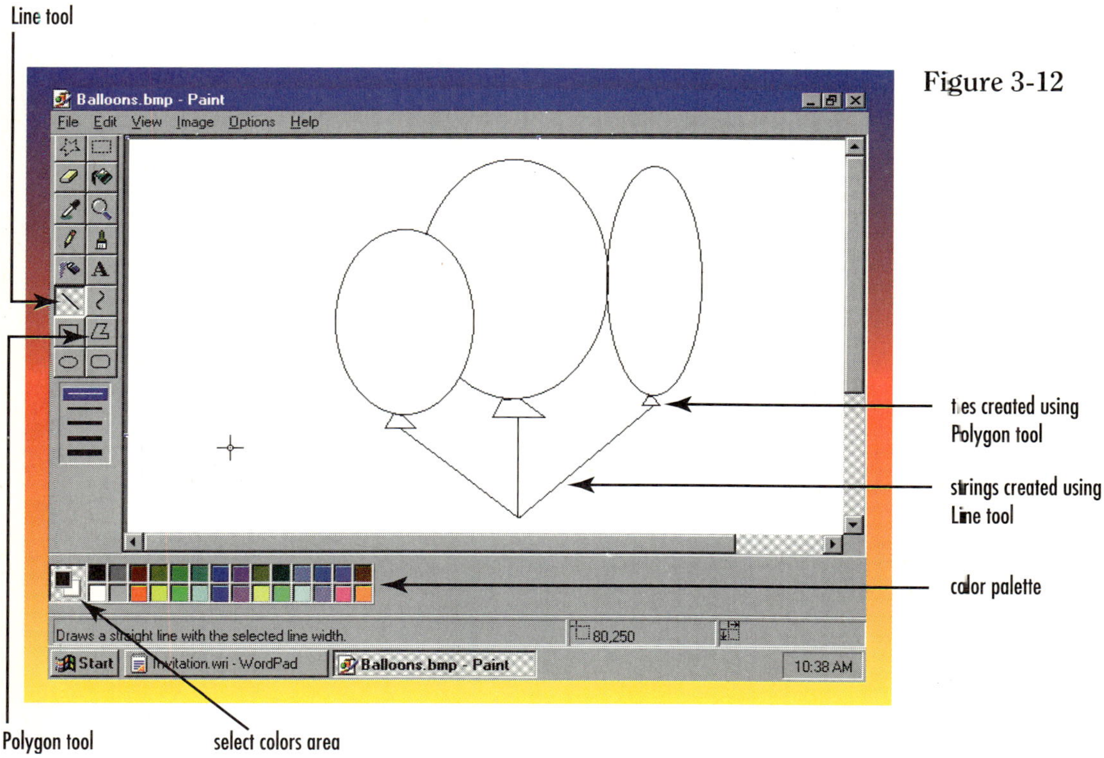

Figure 3-12

Adding Colors

Next you would like to add colors to the balloons. You do this by selecting colors from the color box. The color box consists of two areas: the select colors area and the color palette. The select colors area displays the currently selected foreground and background colors. The box in the foreground shows the currently selected foreground color, and the box in the background shows the background color. By default the foreground color is black while the background color is white.

The background color is selected by right-clicking on a color in the palette, and the foreground color is selected by left-clicking on a color. If you select colors before creating a shape, the shape's outline is created using the foreground color while the inside of the shape is filled with the background color. You can also fill an existing shape with color.

You would like to fill the balloons with different colors.

Select colors from the palette for the foreground and background.

You can fill a shape with a different color after it is created using the Fill with Color tool.

Click: **Fill with Color**

The mouse pointer changes to a , indicating it can be used to fill an object. To use the tool, point to the area you want to fill and click the left mouse button to fill the shape with the foreground color, or click the right mouse button to fill the shape with the background color.

Fill a balloon with one of the colors you selected.

If the shape being filled has any breaks in its border, the filling color leaks through to the rest of the drawing area.

If the color leaks to another balloon or area, Undo the fill and fix the edge of the balloon using the Line tool. Then fill the shape again.

Next you will fill the tie. If you drew small ties, they may be difficult to fill. Carefully place the end of the paint stream inside the object before clicking the mouse button.

> If the color appears in the wrong space, use Undo and try again.

Fill the balloon tie with the same color.

Your screen should be similar to Figure 3-13.

Figure 3-13

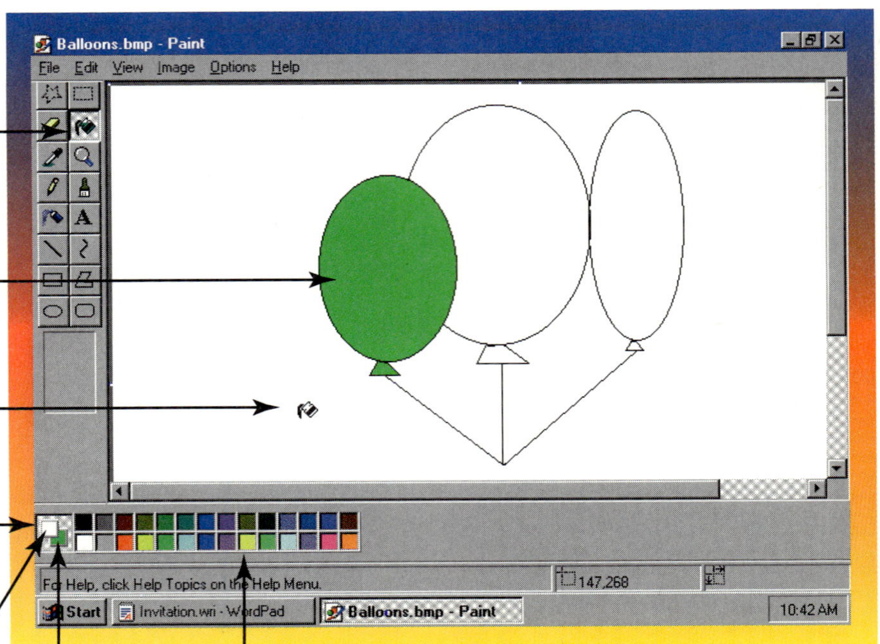

In a similar manner, fill the other two balloons and their ties with color.

Now that you have completed the drawing, you are ready to paste a copy of it into the invitation. First you will save the changes you have made to the Balloon file.

Choose: **File/Save**

The Save command saves the document as it appears onscreen to the same filename, automatically replacing the original contents with the new contents.

Note: If you are ending your lab session now, close both the applications. Move the file icon Balloons.bmp to your data disk and quit Windows 95. When you begin Part 2, start WordPad and use File/Open to open the Invitation.wri document. Then start Paint and open the Balloons.bmp file. Copy Balloons.bmp from your data disk to the desktop.

Part 2

Copying the Graphic

To insert the picture of the balloons into the invitation, you will make a copy of the graphic and store it in the Clipboard. You can copy the entire workspace or any part of the screen by selecting an area. Since the drawing is much smaller than the entire screen, you will select just the drawing.

To select the drawing, you can use the Free-Form Select or Select tool. The Free-Form Select tool allows you to draw an irregular shape around the part of the object you want to select, while the Select tool allows you to select a rectangular area.

Click: **Select**

The mouse pointer changes to a +. To use the selection tool, you drag the mouse to create a box around the area you want to copy. This is similar to selecting multiple files by creating a box around the file icons.

If necessary, first scroll the workspace to position the drawing in the workspace so it is entirely visible.

Click above the top-left corner of the drawing and drag the mouse pointer to the opposite corner to select the entire picture. If the box does not enclose the entire drawing, click anywhere outside the selection to clear the box and try again.

Your screen should be similar to Figure 3-14.

Figure 3-14

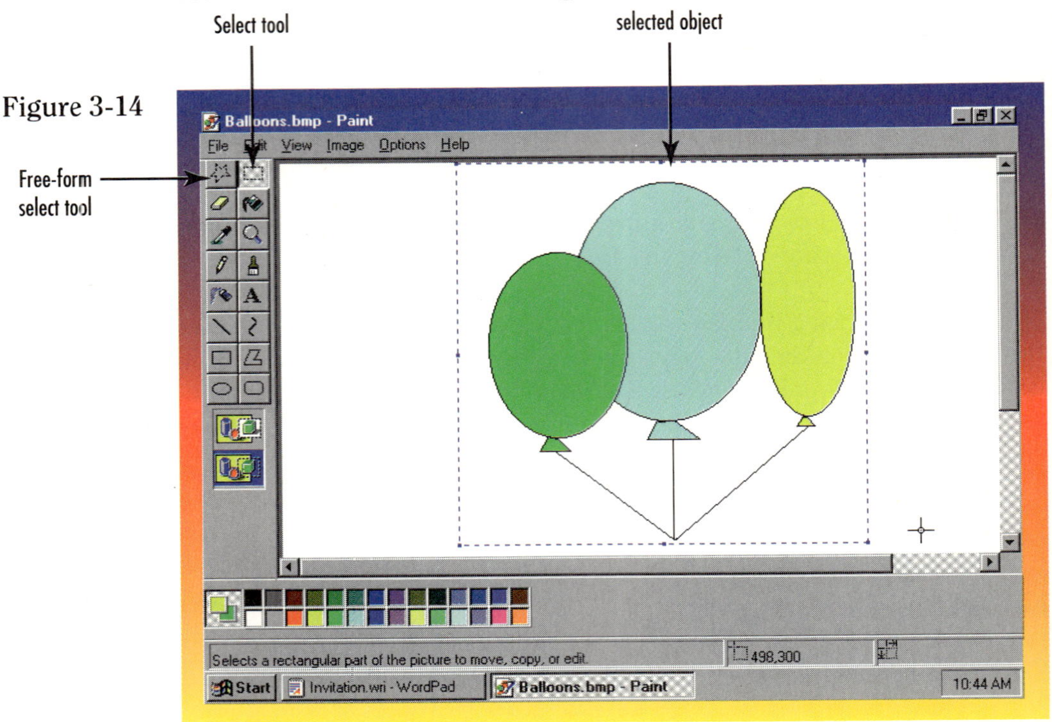

Then, to copy the selection to the Clipboard,

> The keyboard shortcut equivalent is Ctrl + C. Copy is also an option on the shortcut menu.

Choose: Edit/Copy

The contents of the selected area are copied to the Clipboard.

Viewing Clipboard Contents

You can view the contents of the Clipboard to verify that the selected graphic is stored in it using the Clipboard Viewer program. Clipboard Viewer is another application that is in the Accessories menu. To open the Clipboard Viewer,

> The Clipboard Viewer needs to be installed separately. See your instructor or skip this section if this option is not available.

Choose: Start/Programs/Accessories/Clipboard Viewer

Your screen should be similar to Figure 3-15.

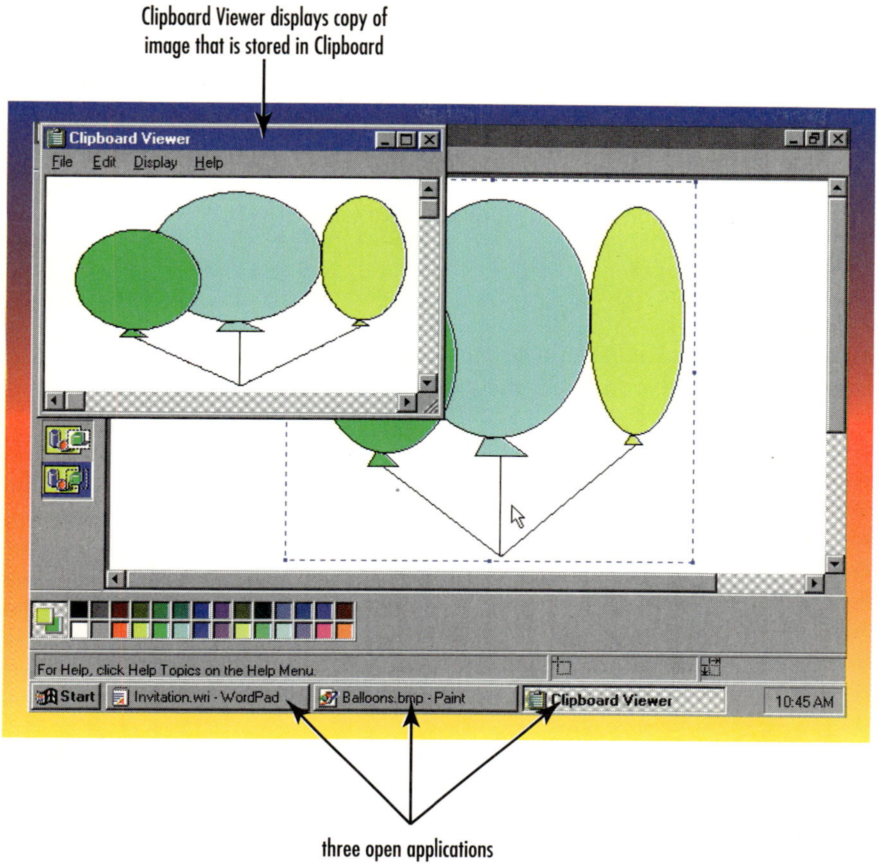

Figure 3-15

The Clipboard Viewer is opened and displays a copy of the balloons graphic. The Viewer is displayed in a window on top of the Paint program window; it has some of the same features as other applications, including a title bar and a menu bar. You now have three applications running at the same time as you can see from the taskbar.

You can leave the Clipboard Viewer open or close it. Since you opened the Viewer only to verify its contents, to close the application,

Click: ☒ **Close**

The command equivalent is File/Exit.

Copying to Another Application

You are now ready to paste the picture into the WordPad document. To redisplay the WordPad window,

Click: invitation.wri - WordPad **(on the taskbar)**

You would like to paste the picture that is stored in the Clipboard into the top left corner of the invitation.

If necessary, move the insertion point to the top of the document.

To insert two blank lines above the text in the invitation and move to it,

Press: ↵Enter 2 times
Press: ↑ 2 times

The insertion point appears at the center of the blank line because the Center feature was in effect for the line the insertion point was on when the two new lines were created. To return the alignment to left,

Click: Left

The insertion point is positioned on the left margin. The information that is stored in Clipboard is an object that you want to copy to another application.

Concept 7: Objects

An **object** is any set of information created using a Windows application, and that is inserted and stored in a document created using a different application. The object can be text, graphics, or any other element created in the source application, called the **server**. The file containing the original object is the **source file**. The file receiving the copy of the object is the **destination document**. This document is also commonly referred to as a **compound document** because it is made up of objects from multiple applications.

An object can be copied from one application to another as a pasted object, an embedded object, or a linked object.

Concept 8: Linking and Embedding

Pasting an object simply places an image of the object in the compound document. If possible, the object is converted into a format that the destination document can edit. If this is not possible, the image cannot be updated or edited.

An object that is **linked** also displays only a graphic representation of the object; however, it also stores the location of the object's source file, creating a connection between the source and the destination document. Any changes made to the object in the source file are automatically made to the image in the destination document.

When an object is **embedded**, it is stored in the compound document. Because the entire object, along with a reference to the source application, is included in the compound document, it can be edited from within the compound document by opening the server application it references if it is loaded on the computer you are using. Any editing changes are made to the embedded object only, while the original source file is not changed.

DDE (Dynamic Data Exchange) and **OLE** (Object Linking and Embedding) are the processes that allow the linking and embedding of information between applications. DDE creates linked objects and OLE creates embedded objects. Not all applications support object linking and embedding.

The Paste and Paste Special commands are used to insert a copy from the Clipboard into a document. Generally, the Paste command or [Paste button] button simply inserts a copy of the Clipboard contents into a document without linking or embedding it. The Paste Special command allows you to create a link or to embed the Clipboard contents. To embed the Balloons object,

Choose: Edit/Paste Special

Your screen should be similar to Figure 3-16.

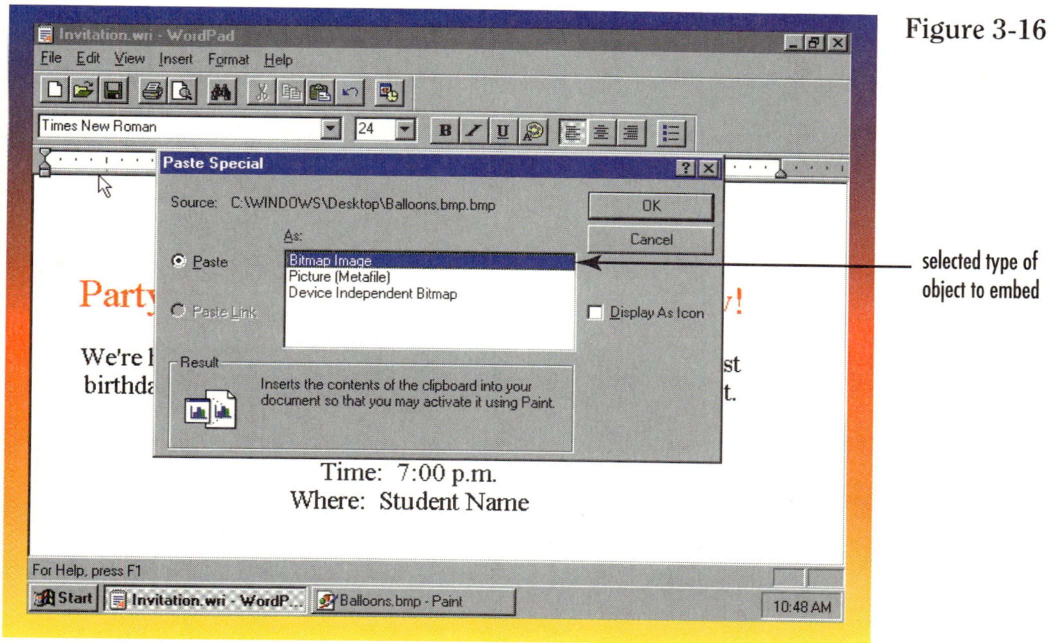

Figure 3-16

The Paste Special dialog box is displayed. The Paste option creates an embedded object. If necessary,

Select: Paste

The As list box lists three object types that can be selected. The type controls how the object will be inserted into the document. Because the object was created as a bitmap, this is the default selected type. In addition, the result area indicates that selecting this option will let you edit the image using Paint. If necessary,

Select: Bitmap Image
Choose: OK

Your screen should be similar to Figure 3-17.

Figure 3-17

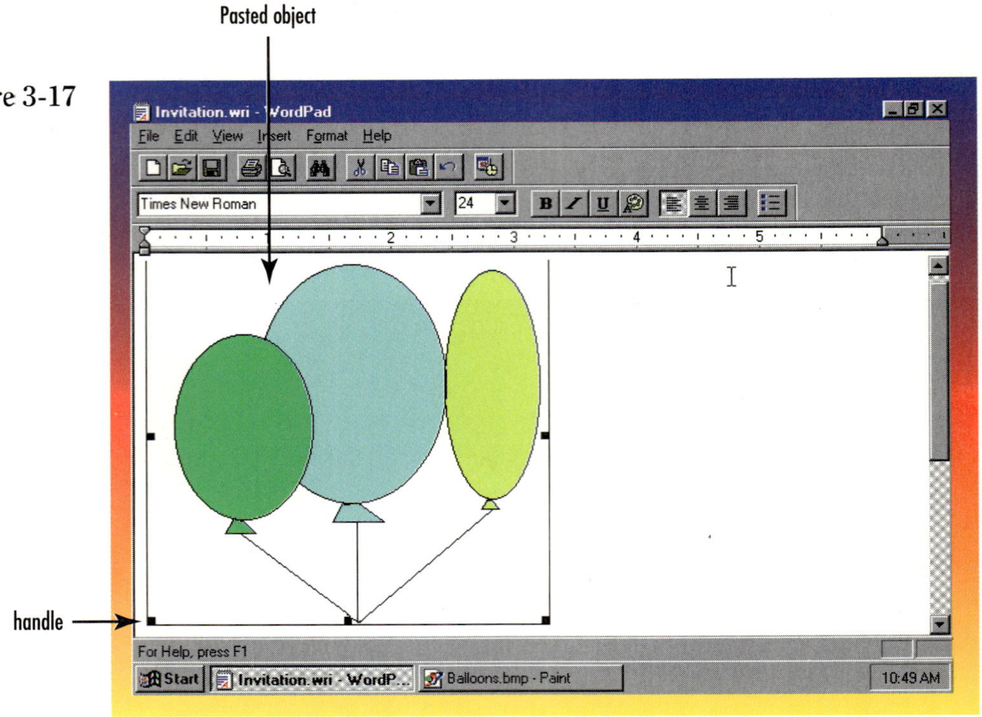

The graphic of balloons that was stored in the Clipboard is pasted into the document. It is surrounded by a box and eight solid squares called **handles**. These indicate the object is selected and can be manipulated. You can adjust the size of any selected object by dragging the handles in the same manner as sizing windows.

Use the ruler as a guide for sizing the object.

Point to the handle in the lower right corner and drag the box outline until it is approximately a 1.5-inch square.

Deselect the graphic by clicking outside the image.

Your screen should be similar to Figure 3-18.

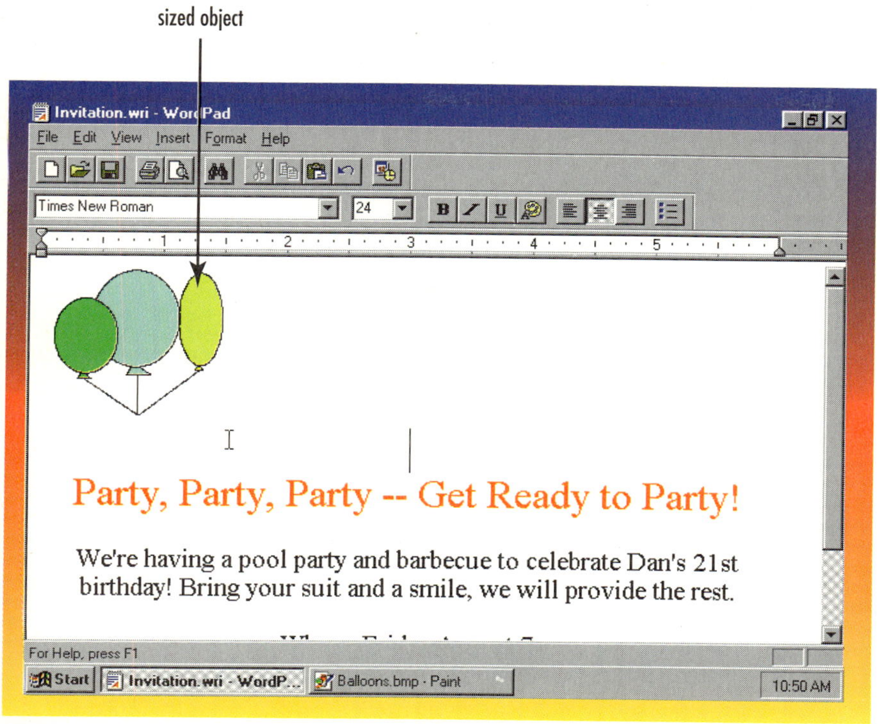

Figure 3-18

Next you want to copy another picture of the balloons into the invitation. To quickly move to the bottom of the document,

Press: Page Down

The insertion point is positioned at the end of the document. To make room for the second graphic, you need to insert a blank line.

Press: ←Enter

The insertion point should be displayed in the center of the line. You want the graphic centered, so there is no need to change the alignment.

If it is not centered, click [center button].

The copy of the balloons graphic is still in the Clipboard. Anything you select and copy is stored in Clipboard until it is replaced by another copied item or you quit Windows. To insert the same picture,

Choose: Edit/Paste Special/OK

A second graphic of the balloons is added to the invitation.

Editing an Embedded Object

After looking at the inserted graphic, you decide you want to add some text inside the balloons. To edit an embedded object, you open the object server. This allows you to edit the embedded graphic from within WordPad.

The menu equivalent is Edit/Bitmap Image Object/Edit.

Double-click: the bottom graphic

Your screen should be similar to Figure 3-19.

Figure 3-19

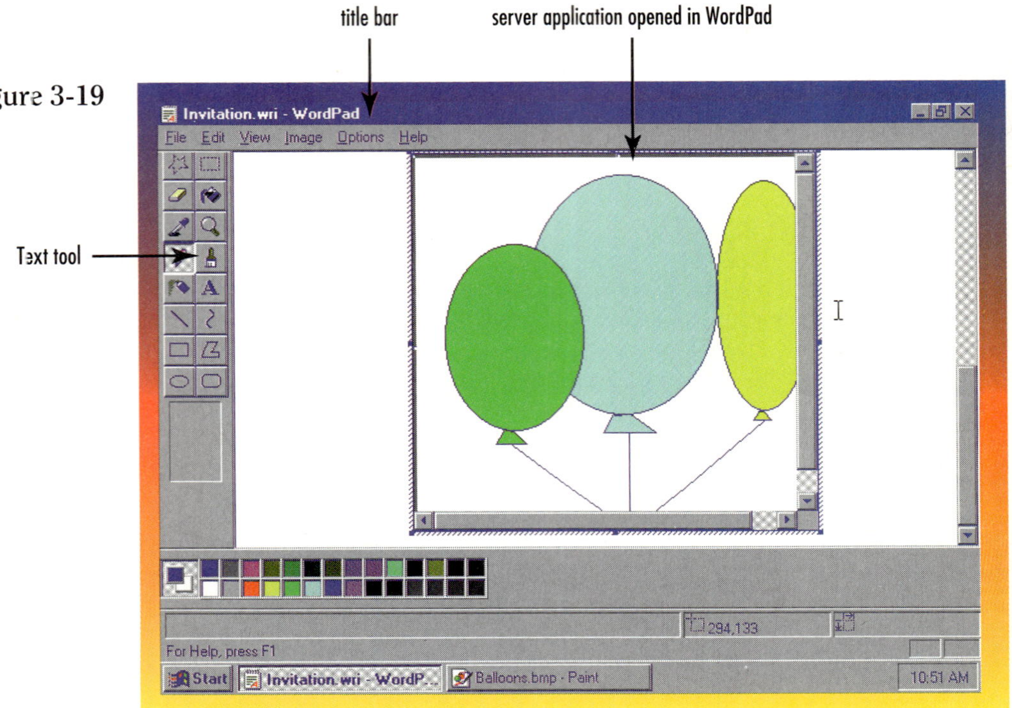

Paint (the server application) is opened within WordPad and the graphic appears in its own editing window. Notice that there is still only one Paint application button in the taskbar. This indicates that the Paint program has not been opened a second time in its own application window. Also notice that the title bar still displays "WordPad," and if you scroll up, the text of the invitation is still displayed. You now have access to the Paint menus and toolbar so you can edit the object while you are still in the WordPad document.

The Text tool [A] is used to add text to a paint object. To add text to a balloon,

Click: [A] Text

The mouse pointer changes to a ┼ when in the server editing window. When adding text, you first create a box, called a **text box**, then type the text inside it.

Drag to create a box inside the leftmost balloon.

The text box displays an insertion point and the Fonts dialog box is displayed. It shows the default type style and size that will be used when you type the text entry. These settings are acceptable.

Before typing the text, you can choose a color for the text. The color that will be applied to the text is the foreground color.

Select the foreground color of your choice.

To enter text in the balloon,

Click on the color button with the left mouse button to select a foreground color.

Type: **Happy**

To close the text box,

Click: **anywhere outside the box within the server editing window**

Create another text box in the middle balloon, select a text color, and enter the text "21st." In the third balloon, display the word "Dan." Deselect the text box.

Your screen should be similar to Figure 3-20.

You may need to adjust the size of the text box to accommodate the text.

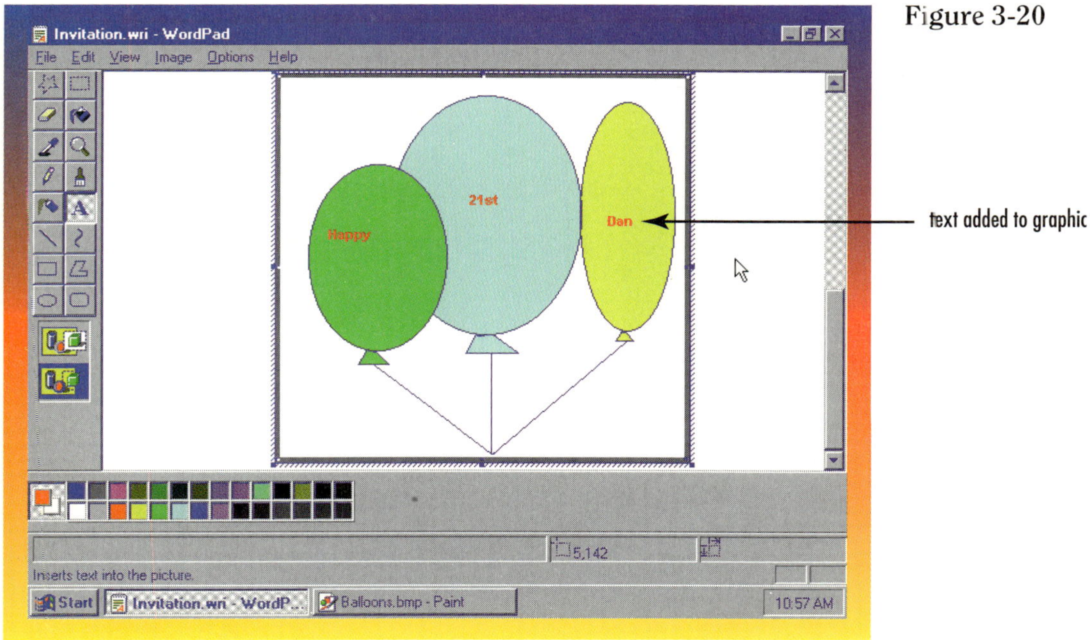

Figure 3-20

To close the Paint program that is opened within WordPad, click anywhere outside the object.

To verify that the original picture file in Paint has not changed, switch to the Paint application window.

The text does not appear in the balloons.

Exit the Paint application.

A single click selects the object.

Since no changes were made to the file, you are not prompted to save the file before the program is closed.

WordPad is displayed again, because it was the last used application.

Select the bottom graphic object and make it slightly larger.

Previewing and Printing the Document

The menu equivalent is File/Print Preview.

To see how the invitation will look when it is printed, you can preview the document.

Click: Print Preview

Your screen should be similar to Figure 3-21.

Figure 3-21

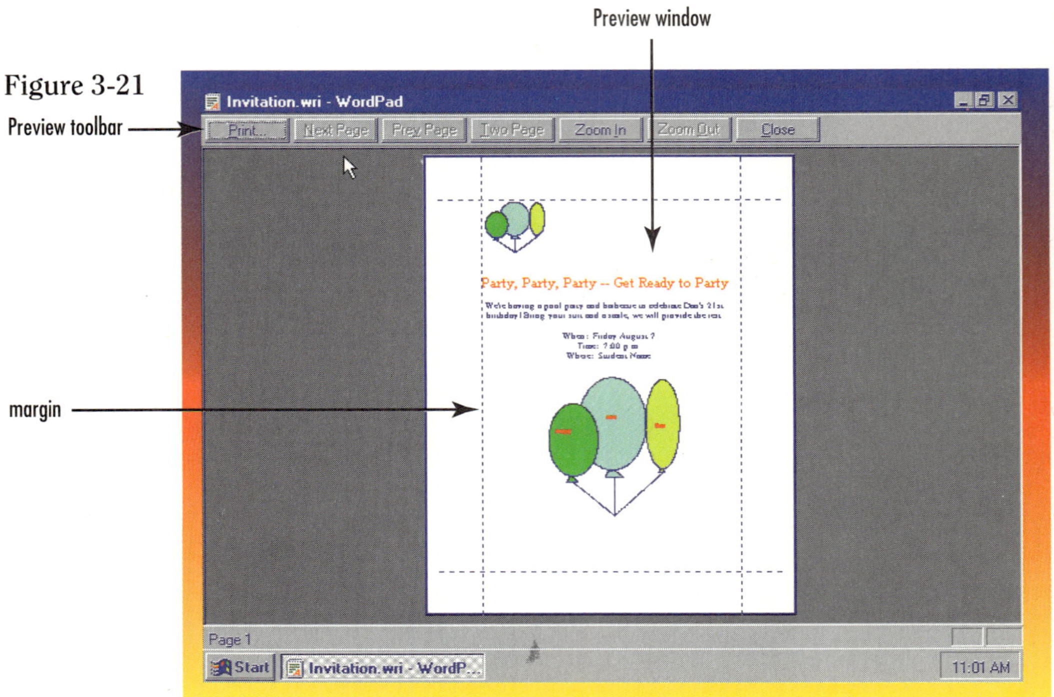

If you want to adjust the pictures on the invitation, choose Close. Then when you are done, select the Print Preview command again.

Preview displays the full page as it will appear when printed. The dotted lines indicate the margin areas. The Preview window has its own set of toolbar buttons. Some are dimmed because they are not available.

You like how the invitation looks and want to print the document.

Please consult your instructor for printing procedures that may differ from the directions provided.

Click: Print...

You can also print using File/Print or without previewing the document.

The Print dialog box is displayed. The active printer name is displayed at the top of the dialog box. The Print Range area of the dialog box lets you specify how much of the document you want printed. All is the default setting. You can also select to print individual pages or text that is selected in a document. The Copies area lets you specify the number of copies.

Now you are ready to instruct WordPad to print the document.

First turn on the printer and make any necessary adjustment to prepare the printer to print.

To print,

If you need to select a different printer, your instructor will provide the printer to select.

Choose: OK

The printer indicator icon is displayed in the notification area of the taskbar while printing is in progress. If you double-click on the indicator, the Printer dialog box is displayed so you can see the printer status and settings and cancel a print job if needed.

The type of printer you use will determine how the balloons will be printed. Most black-and-white printers will print the balloons in shades of gray.

Now that the invitation is complete, you are ready to close the WordPad program.

Before closing the window, restore it to its original size. Close WordPad.

Click or choose File/Exit to close WordPad.

Because you modified the document since last saving it, you are prompted to save it. To do this,

Choose: Yes

Creating a Shortcut Icon

Next you want to copy the Balloons file to your data disk in drive A. You could do this using the file icons shortcut menu and choosing the appropriate command. However, because you will frequently be using the A drive to access files, you decide to create a shortcut to the drive.

Concept 9: Shortcut Icons

A **shortcut icon** can be created for any programs, files, or other Windows features that you use frequently. If the shortcut is to a program, double-clicking the shortcut icon loads the program. If it is to a file, the shortcut loads the application the file was created in and opens the file at the same time. If it is to a feature, such as Windows Explorer, the icon shortcut displays the Explorer window. The shortcut saves you from having to select from menus or other icons in order to access the item. The shortcut icon contains a link to the appropriate application.

You will use the My Computer window to create this shortcut.

Open the My Computer window.

Select: 

Choose: File/Create Shortcut

A Shortcut dialog box appears, indicating a shortcut cannot be created in the My Computer window, and will be created on the desktop for you. Generally, shortcuts are created in the active window. If you wanted the shortcut icon in another location, you could simply drag it to where you wanted it to appear. However, you cannot add a shortcut to the My Computer window. Since you do want the shortcut on the desktop,

Choose: Yes

Your screen should be similar to Figure 3-22.

Figure 3-22

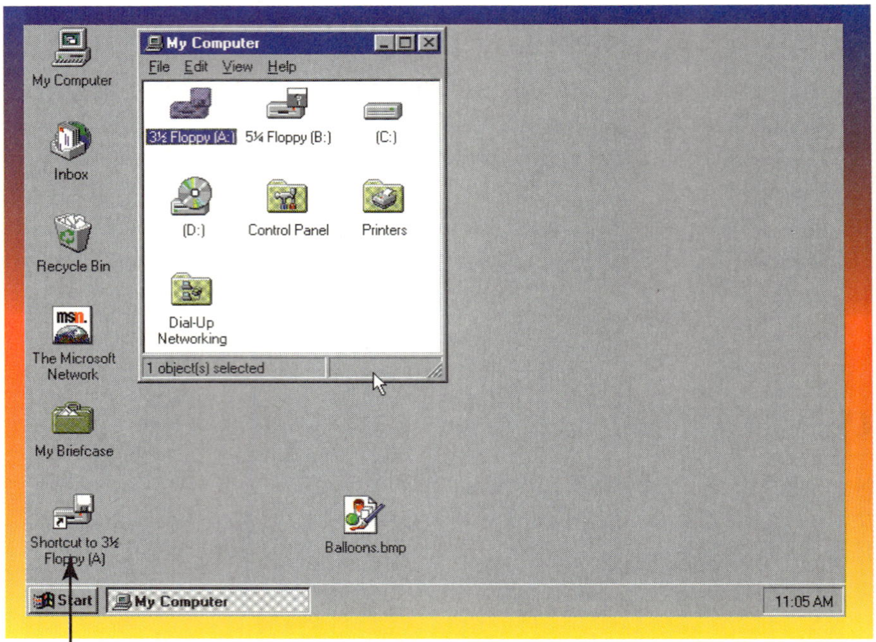

shortcut for drive A

> If you do not see the shortcut icon, it may be under the My Computer window. Move the window to see it.

> Click on the shortcut icon text box to rename the icon.

The shortcut icon is added to the desktop.

Select the shortcut icon and rename it "A Drive."

To see how the shortcut works,

Double-click:

The contents of your data disk are displayed in the A Drive window. This is the same as if you had selected the A drive icon from the My Computer window.

Close the window.

Now you can quickly copy the Balloons file to the disk in the A drive by dragging the file icon to the shortcut.

Drag the Balloons file icon to the A Drive shortcut icon. The file is copied to your data disk.

Open the A Drive window and verify the file was copied to the disk in the drive. Close the A Drive window. Close the My Computer window.

Using the Recycle Bin

The Balloons file icon is still on the desktop. Since you have a copy of it on your data disk, you do not need the file on the desktop anymore.

Select: **balloons.bmp**

To delete it from the desktop, you can use the (Delete) key, or you can drag the icon to the Recycle Bin icon.

Drag the Balloons icon to the Recycle Bin icon.

When a folder, file, or shortcut is deleted from the hard disk, it is moved to the Recycle Bin, where it is stored until you permanently delete it. This protects you from accidentally deleting files or folders that you might want later. When the Recycle Bin contains files, it appears full ; otherwise it appears empty .

To see the files that are in the Recycle Bin,

Double-click: **Recycle Bin**

Your screen should be similar to Figure 3-23.

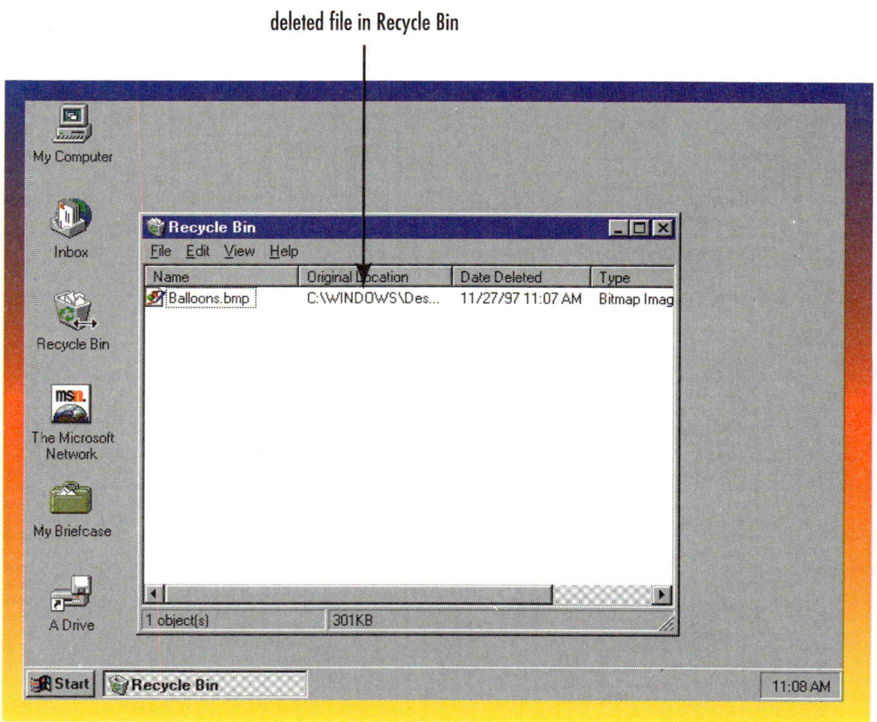

Figure 3-23

The Recycle Bin window is opened, and a button appears in the taskbar. To remove a file from the Recycle Bin, you would select the filename and press (Delete) or choose File/Delete. If you wanted to remove all the files from the Recycle Bin, you would use the File/Empty Recycle Bin command. You can also retrieve files from the Recycle Bin by dragging them back to the desktop or using File/Restore to return a file to its original location.

To remove the Balloons file,

> The shortcut key is [Delete].

Select: **Balloons.bmp**
Choose: **File/Delete**

The Confirm Delete dialog box is displayed. This is another precaution against the accidental deletion of files you may want to keep.

Choose: **Yes**

The Balloons file is removed from the list. If you delete a shortcut icon, the shortcut is deleted, but the object to which it is linked is not deleted.

Close the Recycle Bin window.

Anything that is deleted from the hard disk appears in the Recycle Bin. The number of items the Recycle Bin can hold is determined by the size of the bin. This size is set to 10 percent of your hard disk space by default. When the bin is full, the oldest items in it are removed to make space for new items.

Using Quick View

After you have created a number of files and saved them to your disk, you may be unsure, with all the filenames which file you want to use. Instead of loading the program and opening the file, you can use the Quick View command on the File menu to check the contents of the file before launching the program.

You would like to find the file on your data disk that contains a resume, so that you can use some of the text as a guide to create a brief resume to send to a prospective employer.

Open the A Drive window (use the shortcut) and display the files on your floppy disk.

To view the file named Sample Resume before opening it,

> The Quick View option must be installed separately. See your instructor if this option is not available.

> If Quick View is not available, double-click Sample Resume to open the file.

Select: **Sample Resume.wri**
Choose: **File/Quick View**

The contents of a file containing a resume for Colleen T. Hayes is displayed in a View window. You can scroll through the document to determine if it is the file you want to open. This is the file you want to use. To open the document from the Quick View window,

> The menu equivalent is File/Open File for Editing.

Click: **Open File for Editing**

Your screen should be similar to Figure 3-24.

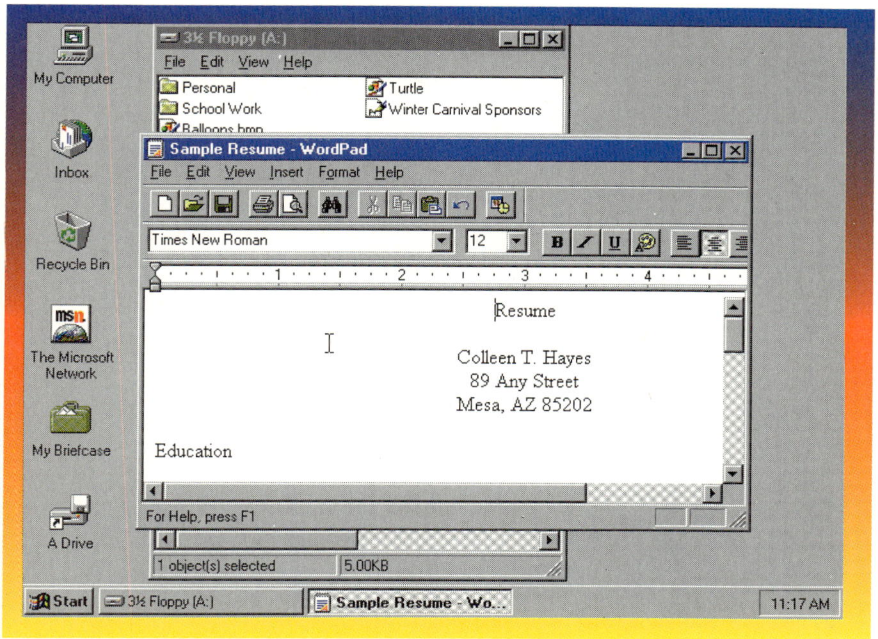

Figure 3-24

The Quick View window is closed, and the document is opened in WordPad.

Creating Scraps

You want to create a brief resume that will include some of the information in this file. The first sections you want to include in the brief resume are the resume header and the education section.

Select the text in the resume header and the entire education section.

You want to copy the selected text into another document. However, WordPad only allows you to have one document file open at a time. Rather than closing and opening WordPad documents, you will use the Windows 95 **scrap** feature. This feature copies selected text and places the copy in a separate "scrap" file on the desktop. The desktop must be visible when using this feature.

If necessary, restore or size the WordPad window so the desktop is visible.

Drag the selected text to the desktop.

Your screen should be similar to Figure 3-25.

Figure 3-25

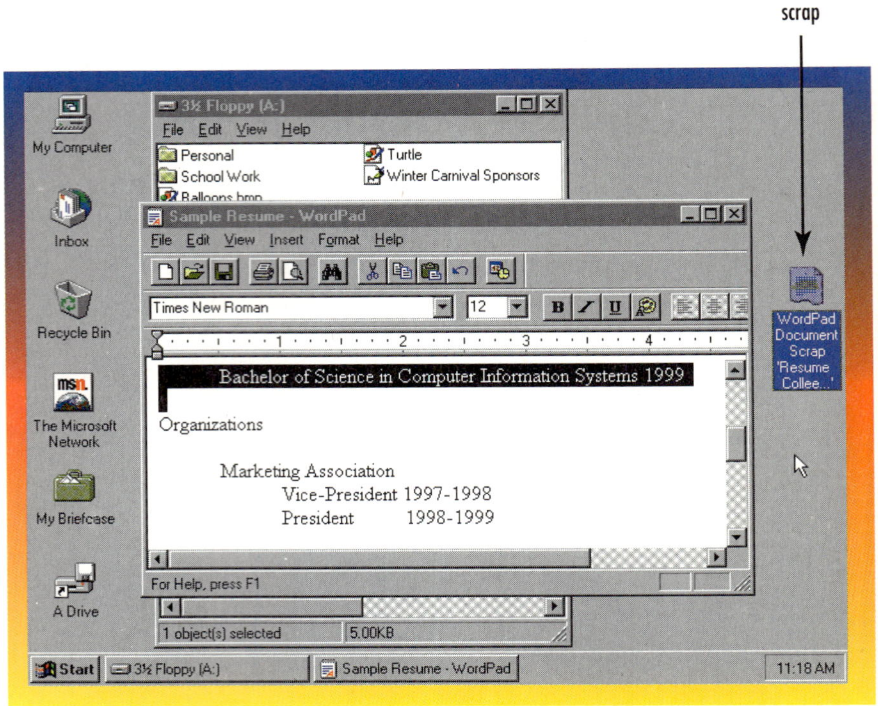

You can use the scrap feature only if your program supports drag-and-drop functions.

A WordPad document scrap is created. The default scrap name includes the application name and the first few words of the selected text in the document. A scrap can then be dragged to another document, where the contents are then pasted.

Next you would like to copy the information in the employment section of the resume to another scrap file.

Select the employment section and scrap it to the desktop.

You now have two scrap files on the desktop that you want to copy into the new document for the brief resume. To close the Sample Resume file and open a new blank document,

The command equivalent is File/New.

Click: New

In the New dialog box, you are asked to specify the type of document to create and the name of the program to associate it with. The word processing program on your system is selected by default. To associate the file with the word processing program on your system,

Your instructor will provide you with the file extension if the file should be associated with a different program.

Choose: OK

A blank WordPad document is displayed. First you want to copy the contents of the scrap containing the resume header and education text into the document. To insert a scrap, you drag it to the document workspace where it will be inserted at the location of the insertion point.

Drag the [Resume...] scrap icon to the new document. If necessary, scroll to the top of the document.

Your screen should be similar to Figure 3-26.

scrap copied to new document

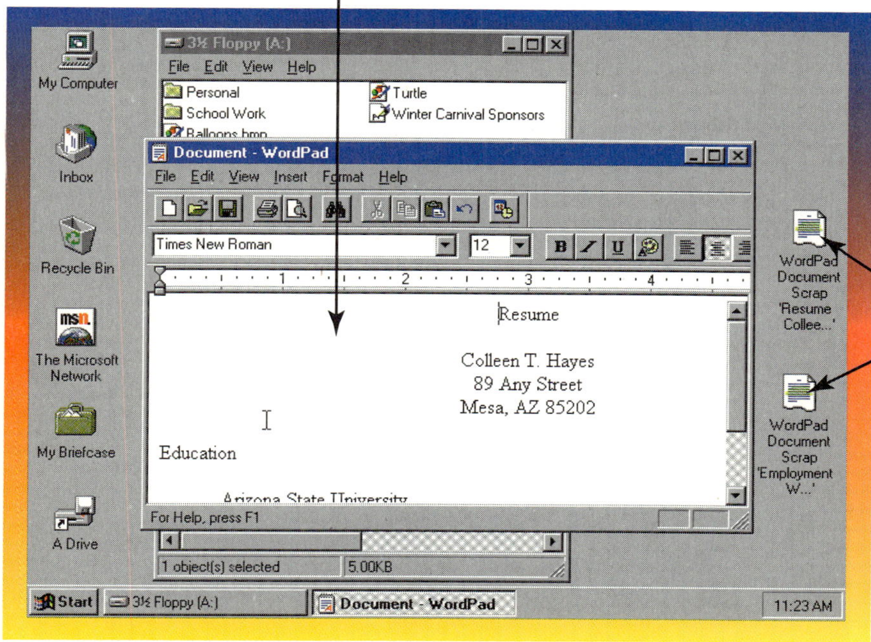

two scrap files

Figure 3-26

The text contained in the scrap file is copied into the new document. Notice that the formatting, in this case centered lines, is also included in the copy. Next, you want to copy the Employment scrap into the document. You want it to be placed above the Education section.

Move the insertion point to the blank line above the Education section. In a similar manner, copy the Employment scrap file into the new document above the Education section.

The document now contains the two sections from the original resume document.

Save the file with the name Brief Resume in the Spring 1998 folder of your data disk. Close WordPad. Close all the open windows.

You are returned to the desktop. Notice that the scraps are still displayed on the desktop. You can leave the scraps there, move them to a folder, or place them in the Recycle Bin.

Drag the scraps to the Recycle Bin. Drag the A drive shortcut to the Recycle Bin. Open the Recycle Bin and delete the two scrap files and the A drive shortcut.

Follow the procedure at your school to quit working in Windows 95.

Select multiple files by holding down Ctrl while clicking each item.

LAB REVIEW

Key Terms

active character WN117
bitmap WN124
compound document WN134
DDE WN134
destination document WN134
document WN114
drawing program WN124
editing WN117
embedded object WN134
font size WN120
format bar WN116
formatting WN118
handles WN136
linked object WN134
object WN134
OLE WN134
points WN120
ruler WN116
save WN122
scrap WN145
server WN134
shortcut icon WN141
source file WN134
text box WN138
toolbox WN126
word processing WN114
word wrap WN117
workspace WN116

Command Summary

Command	Shortcut Key	Button	Action
Start Menu			
Programs			Displays folders and programs on your system
Programs/Accessories			Displays accessory programs on your system
My Computer			
File/Create Shortcut			Creates a shortcut icon
File/Quick View			Displays a preview of an unopened document
WordPad			
File/Save	Ctrl + S		Saves a file with same name
File/Save As			Saves a file with a new name
File/ Print	Ctrl + P		Prints the document
File/Print Preview			Displays document onscreen as it will appear when printed
File/Exit			Closes an application
Edit/Paste	Ctrl + V		Inserts Clipboard contents
Edit/Paste Special			Inserts Clipboard contents as linked or embedded object
Edit/Select All	Ctrl + A		Selects all text in a document
Edit/Object			Activates linked or embedded object
Format/Font/Size		10	Changes height of characters
Format/Font/Color			Changes color of text characters
Format/Paragraph/Alignment			Aligns text within margins

Command	Shortcut Key	Button	Action
Paint			
			Selects a free-form-shaped object
			Selects an object
			Erases part of drawing
			Fills an area with color
			Adds text to a drawing
			Creates a line
			Creates a polygon
			Creates an ellipse
File/Exit			Closes an application
Edit/Copy	Ctrl + C		Copies a selected object
Edit/Paste	Ctrl + V		Inserts contents of Clipboard
Recycle Bin			
File/Empty Recycle Bin			Empties Recycle Bin of all files
File/Delete	Delete		Deletes selected item from Recycle Bin
File/Restore			Returns a selected item to its original location
Quick View			
File/Open File for Editing			Opens viewed files in associated application

Matching

1. Match the following with the correct definition or function.

1) 	____	**a.** adds a color to selected text
2) scrap	____	**b.** word-processing application
3) word wrap	____	**c.** displays a preview of document before it is opened
4) WordPad	____	**d.** undoes last action
5) 	____	**e.** a drawing application
6) 	____	**f.** centers text on a line
7) Paint	____	**g.** a file that is created when you drag part of a document to the desktop
8) 	____	**h.** displays how document will appear when printed
9) Print Preview	____	**i.** moves text to next line when margin setting is reached
10) Quick View	____	**j.** adds text to a Paint document

OPERATING SYSTEM

e. A ________________ can be created on the desktop for any program, file, or window feature that you use frequently.

f. The temporary storage area called the ____________________ holds cut or copied information until it is pasted or replaced.

g. ____________________ can be used to see the information that is stored in the Clipboard.

h. A graphic object that is selected and can be manipulated is surrounded by a box and eight solid squares called ____________________.

i. When a folder, file, or shortcut is deleted from the hard disk, it is moved to the ______________________.

j. A ______________ file is created when you drag a selection from a document and place it on the desktop.

HANDS-ON PRACTICE EXERCISES

Step by Step

Rating System ☆ Easy ☆☆ Moderate ☆☆☆ Difficult

You need the Windows 95 CD, or the Tour must be loaded on your system before you can complete this problem. Your instructor will provide you with instructions for loading the Tour of Windows 95.

☆

1. You will use the Tour of Windows 95 to complete this problem.

a. Load the Tour of Windows 95.

b. Choose Starting a Program from the Welcome to Windows 95 Tour.

c. As you read and work through the tour, answer the following questions:

1) What option on the Start menu is used to find a list of programs?

2) What can WordPad be used for?

d. Next, read and work through the Switching Windows tour until you can answer the following questions:

1) How can you switch to another open window?

2) How can you temporarily clear a window from the screen?

e. Exit the tour.

Your instructor will provide you with the location of the file if you did not complete the previous lab.

☆☆

2. While doing research for a history paper, you created the document History 1870. This file should be in the Fall 1997 subfolder in the School Work folder if you completed Lab 2.

a. Open the History 1870 document.

b. Select the text and increase the font size to 12 points.

c. Add the title "Rockefeller Controls Refining." Increase the font size of the title to 14 points and select a color of your choice. Center the title on the line.

d. Enter two blank lines below the title.

e. Enter your name below the paragraph.

f. Preview and print the document.

g. Save the document using the same filename.

☆☆

3. As part of a graphic design workshop, you started to create a floor plan for a kitchen.

a. Open the file Floor Plan on your data disk.

b. Use the features you learned in the lab to modify the floor plan as shown below. Enter your name somewhere in the drawing.

Use Image/Flip to rotate the text.

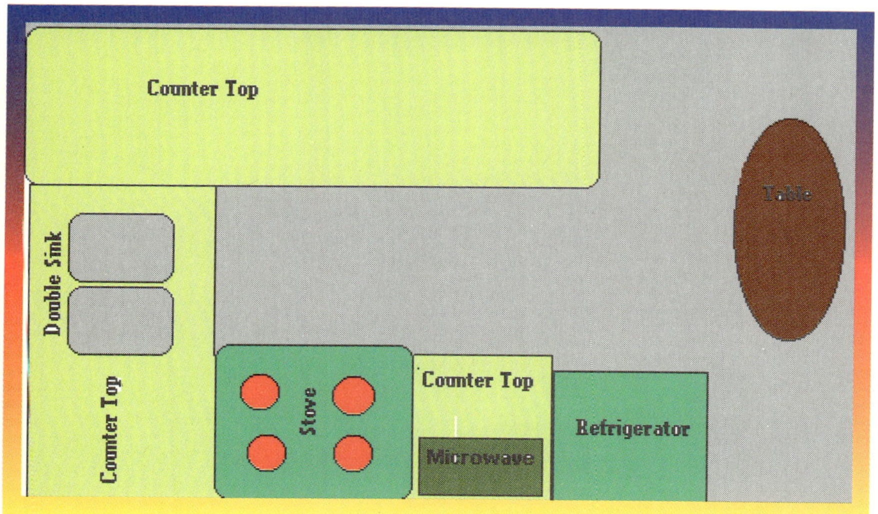

c. Save your new floor plan using the same filename.

d. Print the completed floor plan.

☆☆☆

4. You are planning a children's birthday party and want to use Paint and WordPad to create a card for the party. To make a card that can be folded, you must place the picture upside down in the upper left portion of the page and the text in the lower right portion of the page.

a. Open Paint and WordPad.

b. Switch to the Paint application. Open the file Turtle.bmp on your data disk. Modify the colors of the turtle. Add any text that might be appropriate for the front of the card. Make the text 14 points.

c. Flip the turtle graphic vertically. Rotate the text 180 degrees.

d. Select the turtle graphic and text. Copy the selection to the Clipboard.

e. Embed the bitmap object into the WordPad document. Size the object until it is in the top left quarter of the page. Use Print Preview to check your layout.

f. Edit the embedded object to include a color box around the text.

g. Enter some blank lines below the graphic.

h. Below the graphic add appropriate text that would appear on the inside of the card. Include your name somewhere in the text. Size the text to 16 points. Righ-align all the lines of text.

i. Use Print Preview and adjust the layout of the document. (See the sample below for layout guidance.)

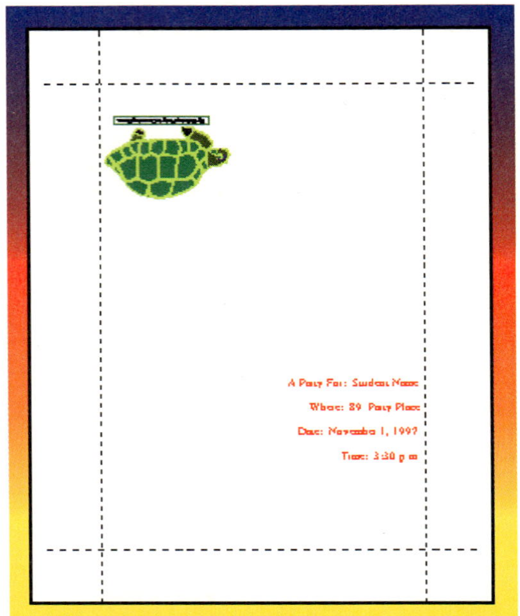

j. Save the document as Party Card. Print the card.

k. Fold the card so that the picture is on the front.

On Your Own

☆☆

5. As the manager of Flowers and Bows floral shop, you would like to create a company logo. Use Paint to create a logo for the company. Copy the logo to a WordPad document and insert your name and the date into the file. Save the document as Flowers Logo. Preview and print the document.

☆☆

6. Use Help to learn more about the Briefcase. Then answer the following questions:

a. If you want to work on files on your main computer and also on a portable computer, the Briefcase will ______________________________.

b. To use Briefcase, you can ______________________ from shared folders on your main computer to the Briefcase icon on your portable computer.

c. When you are copying files from your main computer into Briefcase, the two computers must be connected, by a ______________________ or ______________.

d. To automatically replace the unmodified files on your main computer with the modified files in your Briefcase, you would need to ______________________________.

☆☆

7. You can copy the contents of the active window or the entire screen using Windows 95.

a. For information about this feature, look up Screen Capture in Help.

b. Complete Practice Exercise 2 in Lab 2. Expand all the folders.

c. Capture an image of the entire screen. The screen is stored in the Clipboard.

d. View the Clipboard contents.

e. Paste the image in a blank WordPad document.

f. Size the object.

g. Capture a second image of the active window only and add it to the WordPad document. Size the image.

h. Enter your name and the current date in the document.

i. Save the document as Screen Capture. Print the document.

☆☆

8. Disk cleanup: Do not complete this problem unless it is assigned to you by your instructor. You will not need any of the files or folders you used to complete this text. To clean up your data disk, remove all the folders from your data disk. You can now use the disk to hold other files you may need for the rest of this class.

Concept Summary

3 Windows 95: Applications

Word Processor

Word processing applications are designed to help you create, edit, and print documents.

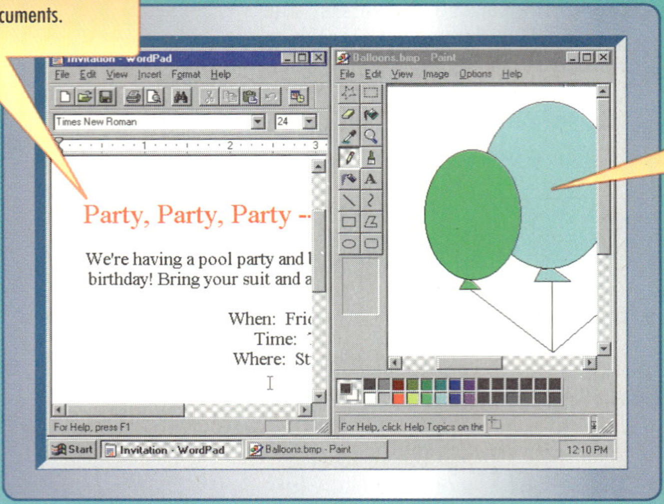

Drawing Programs

Drawing programs are used to create illustrations.

Concepts

- Word Processor
- Drawing Programs
- Objects
- Linking and Embedding
- Editing
- Selecting Text
- Font Size
- Saving Files
- Shortcut Icons

Objects

An object is any set of information created in one application, then inserted or stored in a document that was created using a different application.

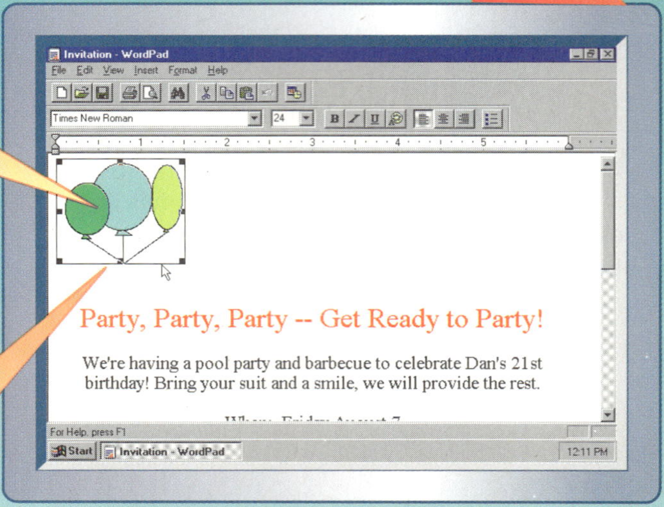

Linking and Embedding

When objects are copied from one application to another, they can be inserted into the receiving document as a pasted object, linked object, or an embedded object.

Font Size

Font size refers to the height of printed characters.

Selecting Text

Selecting highlights the text that will be affected by your next action.

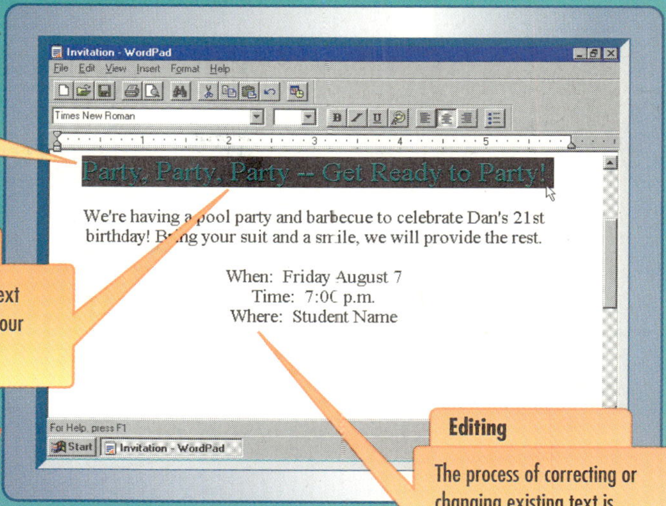

Editing

The process of correcting or changing existing text is called editing.

Saving Files

Saving creates a permanent copy of your onscreen document in a file on a disk.

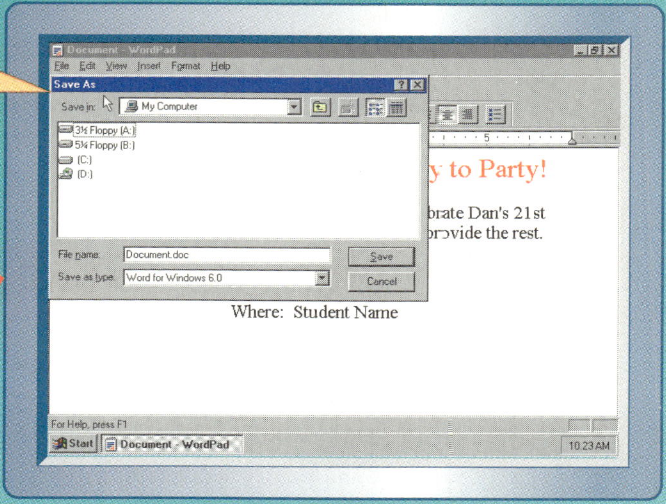

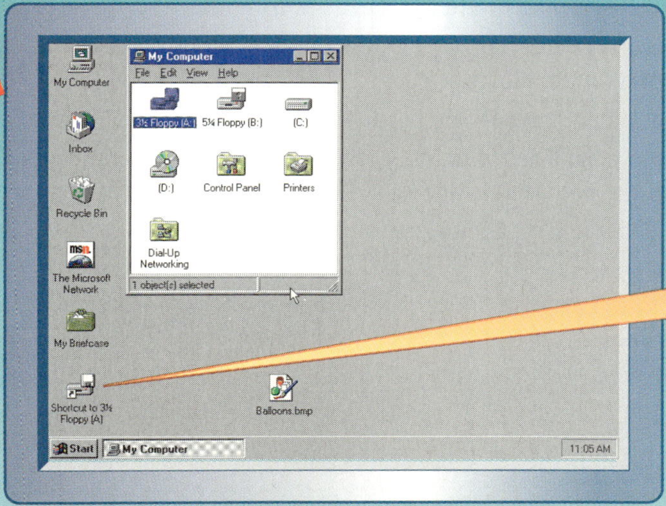

Shortcut Icons

Shortcut icons provide quick access to the associated feature.

Summary: Windows 95

Glossary of Key Terms

Active area: The area of the Exploring window that is affected by any action you perform.

Active character: The character after the insertion point.

Active window: The window you can work in. It is displayed in the foreground and the title bar is a different color or intensity to distinguish it from other open windows.

All Folders area: The left area of the Exploring window, which shows a graphic representation of the organization of the disk.

Associated file: A file that has a specific application program attached to it that will open when the file is opened.

Bitmap: Graphics that consist of arrangements of small dots.

Capacity: Refers to the maximum number of bytes a disk can hold.

Cascade: A window arrangement that layers open windows, displaying the active window fully and only the title bars of all other open windows behind it.

Choose: To select a command so that the associated action is performed.

Clipboard: An area of memory that temporarily stores and if necessary translates information to be copied or moved within or between files and applications.

Cold start: Turning on the power to the computer and starting Windows 95.

Common user interface: Programs that have common features, such as menu commands and toolbars.

Compound document: The document in which an object is inserted.

Contents area: The right area of the Explorer window, which displays the contents of the item that is selected in the All Folders area.

Copy: Feature that allows you to duplicate information from one location to another.

Current folder: The folder that your are working in and that is affected by commands.

Cut: To remove a selection and store it temporarily in the Clipboard.

DDE: Dynamic Data Exchange. The process that allows the linking of information between applications.

Description bar: The bar above each Explorer area that identifies the area's content.

Desktop: The opening Windows 95 screen used to display items on your screen in a similar way you might organize the work on your desk.

Destination: The location where you want to place a copy of the information stored in the Clipboard.

Destination document: The document in which an object is inserted.

Dialog box: A window that requests or provides information needed to complete a command.

Document: Any kind of text material such as memos, letters, and research papers.

Drag and drop: To copy or move a selected item by dragging it with the mouse to the new location.

Drawing program: An application software program used to create illustrations from line art.

Editing: The process of correcting or changing existing text.

Embedded object: An object that is stored in the destination document and can be edited using the server application.

Explorer: A Windows 95 application that helps you view and organize the files on your disk.

Extend a selection: To select more than one file at the same time.

File: The method of storing information on a disk. A disk can hold many files of different types.

Filename: A name assigned to a file. It can be up to 255 characters in length.

Filename extension: An extension of the filename. It can be up to three characters and is separated from the file name by a period. Generally, a file extension is used to identify the type of file.

Folder: A named division of the disk used to hold related files.

Font size: The height and width of printed characters.

Format: To convert a disk from its generic state into a format that can be used by your computer.

Format bar: The toolbar in WordPad that contains buttons representing the most frequently used text-editing and text-layout features.

Formatting: Enhancing the appearance of a document.

Graphical user interface: The capability to communicate with a computer by selecting graphic objects on the screen.

Handles: Eight solid squares displayed around a selected object, used to move and size the object.

Help: An application that provides information about commands and features.

Hierarchy: The tree-like representation of the organization of folders and files on a disk.

Icon: A graphic object that represents Windows elements, such as a program that can be run or a document that can be opened.

Insertion point: A solid blinking vertical line that is displayed in areas where you enter text. It shows you where the next character you type will appear.

Linked object: An object that is inserted into the destination document as a graphic representation of the data and is connected to the source document. Editing the source document changes the linked object.

Main folder: The top level of the hierarchy.

Maximize: To increase a window to its largest possible size.

Menu bar: The second line of a window, which displays the menu names that can be selected.

Minimize: To decrease a window to its smallest possible size.

Mouse: A hand-held hardware device that is attached to your computer. It controls an arrow, called a pointer, that appears on your screen.

Mouse pointer: An arrow-shaped symbol that appears on your screen if you have a mouse device installed. It is used to indicate items you want to select with the mouse. The pointer may change shape, depending on the task being performed.

Move: To remove information from its original location and insert it in a new location.

Notification area: Area in the taskbar to the left of the clock used to display indicators, such as a printer when printing is in progress or a speaker if the system includes audio hardware.

Object: An item in a window, or any set of information created in one application and inserted or stored in another application.

OLE: Object Linking and Embedding. The process that allows the creation of an embedded object.

Operating system: Program that controls computer system resources and coordinates the flow of data to and from the system unit and to and from input and output devices like the keyboard and the display screen. It allows you to create and manage files and run applications software programs.

Paste: To insert a copy the contents of the Clipboard into another location.

Pointing: To move the mouse pointer until the tip of the pointer rests on the item you want to choose.

Points: Font size measurement, with each point about $^{1}/_{72}$ inch. The larger the number of points, the larger the size of the characters.

Properties: Settings and attributes associated with an object. Most objects on the desktop have properties associated with them.

Pull-down menu: A menu bar command that displays a list of additional commands from which you can select.

Restore: To return a window to its previous size.

Ruler: A ruler, located above the document workspace in WordPad, that shows the line length in inches and the location of the margins and tabs.

Save: To store the work you have created using an application as a file on a disk.

Scrap: A file that is created when you drag selected text from a document and place it on the desktop.

Scroll arrows: Arrows in the scroll bar that move information in the direction of the arrows, allowing new information to be displayed in the space.

Scroll bar: A window element located on the right or bottom window border that lets you display text that is not currently visible in the window. It contains scroll arrows and a scroll box.

Scroll box: A box in the scroll bar that indicates your relative position within the area of available information. The box can be moved to a general location within the area of information by dragging it up or down the scroll bar.

Sector: A division of a disk track.

Select: To highlight a menu option or pick an item from a dialog box.

Selection cursor: The highlight bar in a menu.

Server: The application that created the embedded document.

Shortcut icon: An icon that provides a shortcut to any program, file, or other Windows feature that is used frequently.

Shortcut menu: A menu that appears when you right-click an item. It displays common commands associated with the selected item.

Source: The location that contains the information you want to cut or copy.

Source file: The document an object was created in.

Start button: A button in the taskbar that displays a menu of commands that are used to start a program, open a document, get help, find files, and change system settings.

Status bar: A bar of information displayed at the bottom of many windows. It advises you of the status of different program conditions and features as you use the program.

Subfolder: A folder that is created under another folder.

Tab dialog box: A dialog box that includes folder-like tabs that open to display related options. The tab names appear across the top of the dialog box and indicate the different categories of tabs.

Taskbar: A Windows 95 desktop element that contains the Start button, buttons representing active applications, the clock, and other indicators.

Text box: In a dialog box, an area where you type information needed. In a word processor, a user-created box that contains an insertion point and typed text.

Tile: A window arrangement that resizes open windows and arranges the windows vertically or horizontally on the desktop.

Title bar: The top line of a window or dialog box. It displays a name identifying the contents of the window or dialog box.

Toolbar: A bar of buttons commonly displayed below the menu bar that are shortcuts for many of the most common menu commands.

Toolbox: In Paint, the toolbar of buttons provided for many of the most common drawing commands.

Tooltip: A description that is displayed when you point to a toolbar or taskbar button.

Tracks: Concentric rings where data is stored on the disk.

Tree: The hierarchical organization of folders on the disk.

Unformatted: Disks that are shipped from the manufacturer in a blank form so that they can be used by a variety of computers.

Warm start: Restarting the computer without turning the power switch off and on again.

Window: A rectangular box that displays information in a dialog box and application programs on the Windows desktop.

Window border: The outside edge of a window.

Word processor: An application software program used to create text documents.

Word wrap: Word processing feature that wraps text to the beginning of a new line when the end of the line reaches the right margin.

Workspace: The large blank area in an application window where your work is displayed.

Summary of Selected Windows 95 Commands

Command	Shortcut Key	Button	Action
Start Menu			
Programs			Displays folders and programs on your system
Documents			Opens files and related programs
Settings			Changes or views the computer system settings
Find			Locate files
Help			Opens Windows Help program
Run			Starts a program using DOS command-line type functionality
Shut Down			Safely shuts downs your computer before you turn the power off
My Computer			
File/New/Folder			Creates a new folder
File/Format			Sets up a disk for use
File/Create Shortcut			Creates a shortcut icon
File/Delete			Deletes selected item
File/Rename			Changes name of a folder or file
File/Properties			Displays properties associated with selected object
File/Quick View			Displays a preview of an unopened document.

Command	Shortcut Key	Button	Action
File/Send to			Copies selected folder and/or files directly to a disk
File/Close			Closes active window
Edit/Cut	Ctrl + X		Removes selected object and copies it to Clipboard
Edit/Copy	Ctrl + C		Copies selected object to Clipboard
Edit/Paste	Ctrl + V		Pastes selected object to new location
Edit/Select All	Ctrl + A		Selects all folders and/or files in active window
My Computer			
View/Toolbar			Turns on display of toolbar
View/Status Bar			Turns on/off display of status bar
View/Large Icons			Displays folders and files as large icons
View/Small Icons			Displays folders and files as small icons
View/List			Displays folders and files as a list
View/Details			Displays all folder and file details
View/Arrange Icons/by Name		Name	Organizes icons alphabetically by name
View/Arrange Icons/by Type		Type	Organizes icons by type of files
View/Arrange Icons/by Size		Size	Organizes icons by size of files
View/Arrange Icons/by Date		Modified	Organizes icons by last modification date of files
WordPad			
File/Save	Ctrl + S		Saves a file with same name
File/Save As			Saves a file with a new name
File/ Print	Ctrl + S		Prints the document
File/Print Preview			Displays document onscreen as it will appear when printed
File/Exit			Closes an application
Edit/Paste	Ctrl + V		Inserts Clipboard contents
Edit/Paste Special			Inserts Clipboard contents as linked or embedded object
Edit/Select All	Ctrl + A		Selects all text in a document

Command	Shortcut Key	Button	Action
Edit/Object			Activates linked or embedded object
Format/Font/Size			Changes height of characters
Format/Font/Color			Changes color of text characters
Format/Paragraph/Alignment			Aligns text within margins
Paint			
			Creates an ellipse
			Erases part of drawing
			Fills an area with color
			Selects an object
			Adds text to a drawing
			Creates a polygon
			Creates a line
File/Print Preview			Displays document onscreen as it will appear when printed
File/Close			Closes a window
File/Exit			Closes an application
Edit/Copy	Ctrl + C		Copies a selected object
Edit/Paste	Ctrl + V		Inserts contents of Clipboard
Recycle Bin			
File/Empty Recycle Bin			Empties Recycle Bin of all files
File/Delete			Deletes selected item from Recycle Bin
File/Restore			Returns a selected item to its original location
Quick View			
File/Open File for Editing			Opens viewed files in associated application

INDEX

McGRAW-HILL

Microsoft Word 97

Timothy J. O'Leary
Arizona State University

Linda I. O'Leary

Irwin
McGraw-Hill

Boston, Massachusetts Burr Ridge, Illinois Dubuque, Iowa
Madison, Wisconsin New York, New York San Francisco, California St. Louis, Missouri

Irwin/McGraw-Hill

A Division of The **McGraw-Hill** *Companies*

Microsoft Word 97

This book is printed on acid-free paper.

domestic 4 5 6 7 8 9 0 BAN BAN 9 0 0 9
international 2 3 4 5 6 7 8 9 0 BAN BAN 9 0 0 9 8

ISBN 0-07-228253-3

The Sponsoring Editor was Rhonda Sands.
The Developmental Editor was Kristin Hepburn.
The Editorial Assistant was Kyle Thomes.
The Marketing Manager was James Rogers.
The Production Supervisor was Richard DeVitto.
The cover was designed by Lorna Lo.
Project management was by Elaine Brett, Fritz/Brett Associates.
Composition was by Pat Rogondino, Rogondino & Associates.
The typeface was ITC Clearface.
Banta Co. was the printer and binder.

Library of Congress Cataloging Card Number 97-72182

When ordering this title, use ISBN 0-07-115477-9.

http://www.mhhe.com

Contents

Word Processing Overview

One of the most widely used software applications is a word processor. Putting your thoughts in writing, from the simplest note to the most complex book, is a time-consuming process. Even more time-consuming is the task of editing and retyping the document to make it better. With the introduction of word processing, errors should be nearly nonexistent—not because they are not made, but because they are easy to correct. Word processors let you throw away the correction fluid, scissors, paste, and erasers. Now, with a few keystrokes, you can easily correct errors, move paragraphs, and reprint your document.

Definition of Word Processing

Word processing software is a program that helps you create any type of written communication. A word processor can be used to manipulate text data to produce a letter, a report, a memo, or any other type of correspondence. Text data is any letter, number, or symbol that you can type on a keyboard. The grouping of the text data to form words, sentences, paragraphs, and pages of text results in the creation of a document. Through a word processor you can create, modify, store, retrieve, and print part or all of a document.

Advantages of Using a Word Processor

The speed of entering text data into the computer depends on the skill of the user. If you cannot type fast, a word processor will not improve your typing speed. However, a word processor will make it easier to correct and change your document. Consequently, your completed document will take less time to create.

Another time saver is word wrap. As you enter text you do not need to decide where to end each line, as you do on a typewriter. When a line is full, the program automatically wraps the text down to the next line.

A word processor excels in its ability to change, or edit, a document. Editing involves correcting spelling, grammar, and sentence-structure errors. As you enter characters using the keyboard, they are displayed on the screen and stored electronically in the computer's main memory. As you find errors, you can electronically delete or correct them. Once the document is the way you want it to appear, it can be permanently saved on a disk and printed on paper. Good-bye, correction fluid!

In addition to editing a document, you can easily revise or update it by inserting or deleting text. For example, a price list can easily be updated to reflect new prices. A document that details procedures can be revised by deleting old procedures and inserting new ones. This is especially helpful when a document is used repeatedly. Rather than recreating the whole document, you change only the parts that need to be revised.

Revision also includes the rearrangement of selected areas of text. For example, while writing a report you may decide to change the location of a single word or several paragraphs or pages of text. You can do it easily by "cutting" or removing selected text from one location, then "pasting" or placing the selected text in another location. The selection can also be duplicated or copied from one location to another.

Combining text in another file with text in your document is another advantage of word processors. An example of this is a group term paper where each section of the paper is written by a different person. Before printing the document, the text for all sections, which is stored in different files, is combined to create the complete paper. The opposite is also true: text that may not be appropriate in your document can easily be put in another file for later use.

Many word processors include additional support features to help you produce a perfect document. A spelling checker checks the spelling in a document by comparing each word to those in a dictionary stored in memory. If an error is found, the program suggests the correct spelling. A grammar checker electronically checks grammar, phrasing, capitalization, and other types of grammar errors. A thesaurus displays alternative words that have a meaning similar or opposite to the word you entered.

You can also easily control the appearance or format of the document. Formatting includes such operations as changing the line spacing and margin widths, adding page numbers, and displaying page headers and footers. You can also quickly change how your text is aligned with the left or right margin. For example, text can be centered between the margins, or justified—evenly aligned on both the left and right margins—as are these pages. Perhaps the most noticeable formatting feature is the ability to apply different fonts (type styles and sizes) and text appearance changes such as bold, italics, and color to all or selected portions of the document. Most word processing programs also have the ability to produce and display graphic lines and boxes. Graphic boxes can then be used to hold text or graphic images that you place into the document.

Word Processing Terminology

The following terms and definitions are generic in nature and are associated with most word processing programs.

Bold: Produces dark or heavy print.

Center: To center a line of text evenly between the margins.

Edit: To change or modify the content of the document.

Font: Type style and size.

Format: Defines how the printed document will appear; includes settings for underline, boldface, print size, margin settings, line spacing, and so on.

Grammar checker: A support feature that checks grammar, phrasing, capitalization, and other types of syntax errors.

Justified: Text that is evenly aligned on both the left and right margins.

Spelling checker: A support feature that checks words or the entire document for correct spelling.

Text data: Any number, letter, or symbol you can type on a keyboard.

Thesaurus: A support feature that displays synonyms and antonyms for words in your document.

Word wrap: The automatic adjustment of the number of characters or words on a line that eliminates the need to press the ←Enter (or ←Return) key at the end of each line.

Case Study for Labs 1–5

As a recent college graduate, you have accepted your first job as a management trainee for The Sports Company. The Sports Company is a chain of discount sporting goods shops located in large metropolitan areas throughout the United States. The program emphasis is on computer applications in the area of retail management and requires that you work in several areas of the company.

In this series of labs, you are working in the Southwest Regional office and are responsible for setting up the credit card enrollment program and for assisting with the monthly newsletter.

In Labs 1 and 2 you will create a letter to be sent to all new credit card recipients. You will learn how to use the Word 97 to create, edit, format, and print the letter.

In Lab 3 the regional office has decided to send a monthly newsletter to credit card customers. You have been asked to prepare several articles for inclusion in the newsletter and create a sample newsletter design using the articles.

In Lab 4 you will prepare a table that summarizes gross sales for the regional stores. You will also personalize the credit card letter by creating a form letter and merging the recipients' personal information such as name and address into the form letter.

Lab 5 demonstrates how to use Word 97 to create a home page for The Sports Company to use on their new World Wide Web site.

Before You Begin

To the Student

The following assumptions have been made:

- Microsoft Word 97 has been properly installed on the hard disk of your computer system.
- The data disk contains the data files needed to complete the series of Word 97 labs and practice exercises. These files are supplied by your instructor.
- You have completed the McGraw-Hill Windows 95 lab module or you are already familiar with how to use Windows 95 and a mouse.

To the Instructor

Please be aware that the following settings are assumed to be in effect for the Word 97 program. These assumptions are necessary so that the screens and directions in the manual are accurate.

- Language is set to English [US]. (Use Tools/Language/Set Language and set English (United States) as default.)
- Navigation keys for WordPerfect users and Help for WordPerfect users are off. (Use Tools/Options/General.)
- The ScreenTips feature is active (use Tools/Options/View).
- Toolbar ScreenTips are displayed (use Tools/Customize/Options).
- The Office Assistant is on.
- The Normal view is on. Zoom is 100 percent. (Use View/Normal; View/Zoom/100%.)
- The Wrap to Window setting is off. (Use Tools/Options/View.)
- All default settings for a normal template document are in effect.
- In addition, all figures in the manual reflect the use of a standard VGA display setting (640 x 480) and an Epson AP5000 printer. If another monitor type is used, there may be more lines of text displayed in the windows than in the figures. This setting can be changed using Windows setup. The selected printer also affects how text appears onscreen. If possible, select a printer and monitor type that will match the figures in the manual.

Microsoft Office Shortcut Bar

The Microsoft Office Shortcut Bar (shown below) may be displayed automatically on the Windows 95 desktop. Commonly, it appears in the upper right section of the desktop; however, it may appear in other locations, depending upon your setup. Because the Shortcut Bar can be customized, it may display different buttons than shown below.

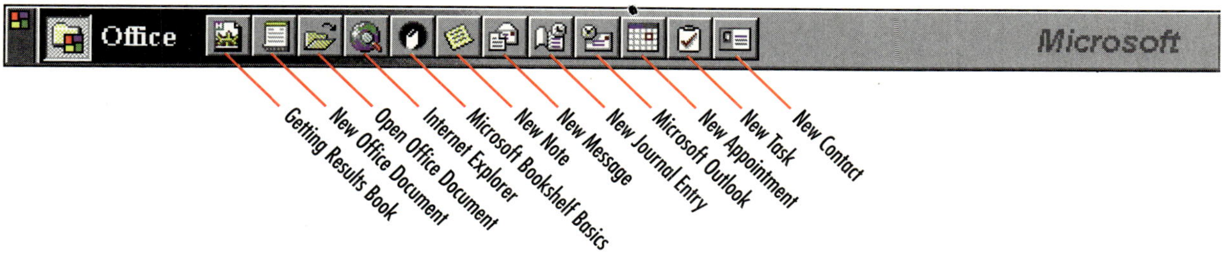

The Office Shortcut Bar makes it easy to open existing documents or to create new documents using one of the Microsoft Office applications. It can also be used to send e-mail, add a task to a to-do list, schedule appointments using Outlook, or add contacts or notes.

Instructional Conventions

This text uses the following instructional conventions:

- Steps that you are to perform are preceded with a bullet (■) and are in blue type.
- Command sequences you are to issue appear following the word "Choose." Each menu command selection is separated by a /. If the command can be selected by typing a letter of the command, the letter will appear bold and underlined.
- Commands that can be initiated using a button and the mouse appear following the word "Click." The menu equivalent and keyboard shortcut appear in a margin note when the action is first introduced.
- Anything you are to type appears in bold text.

1 Creating and Editing a Document

COMPETENCIES

After completing this lab, you will know how to:

1. **Load Word 97.**
2. **Use the Office Assistant.**
3. **Create a new document.**
4. **Enter and edit text.**
5. **Insert and delete blank lines.**
6. **Move around the document window.**
7. **Open, close, and save files.**
8. **Move through a document.**
9. **Insert and delete text.**
10. **Display special characters.**
11. **Select text.**
12. **Undo editing changes.**
13. **Document a file.**
14. **Preview and print a document.**
15. **Exit Word 97.**

CASE STUDY

As a recent college graduate, you have accepted a job in a management training program for The Sports Company, a chain of warehouse-oriented sporting goods stores. The training program emphasis is on computer applications in the area of retail management. Your current assignment is in the Southwest Regional Office, where you are responsible for setting up the new credit card program and for assisting with the monthly newsletter.

The software tool you will use while on this assignment is the word processing application Word 97. Its purpose is to help you create text documents such as letters, reports, and research papers. Specifically, you will learn about entering, editing, previewing, and printing a document while you create the first draft of a letter to be sent to all new credit card recipients. This letter is shown on the right.

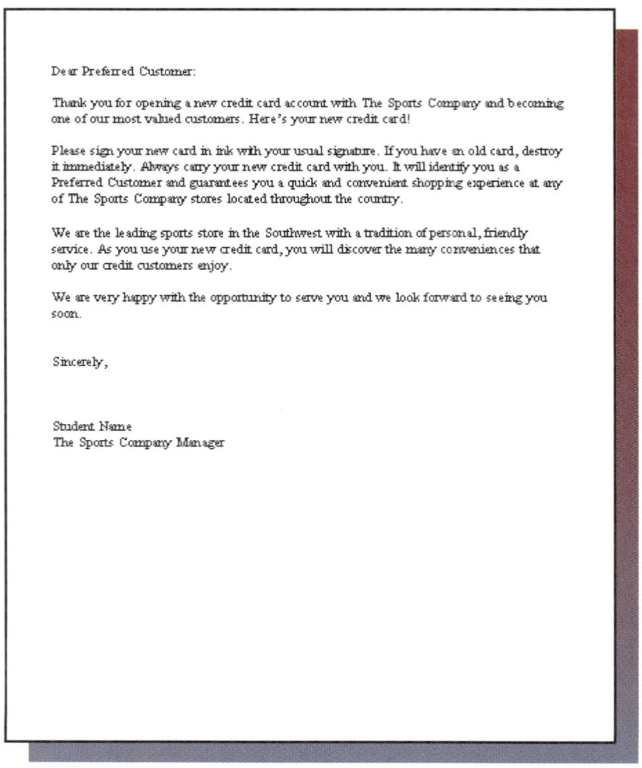

Dear Preferred Customer:

Thank you for opening a new credit card account with The Sports Company and becoming one of our most valued customers. Here's your new credit card!

Please sign your new card in ink with your usual signature. If you have an old card, destroy it immediately. Always carry your new credit card with you. It will identify you as a Preferred Customer and guarantees you a quick and convenient shopping experience at any of The Sports Company stores located throughout the country.

We are the leading sports store in the Southwest with a tradition of personal, friendly service. As you use your new credit card, you will discover the many conveniences that only our credit customers enjoy.

We are very happy with the opportunity to serve you and we look forward to seeing you soon.

Sincerely,

Student Name
The Sports Company Manager

Concept Overview

The following concepts will be introduced in this lab:

1. Document Development	The development of a document follows several steps: plan, enter, edit, format, and preview and print.
2. Document Template	A document template is a document file that includes predefined settings that can be used as a pattern to create many common types of documents.
3. AutoCorrect	The AutoCorrect feature makes some basic assumptions about the text you are typing and, based on these assumptions, automatically identifies and/or corrects the entry as you type.
4. Spelling and Grammar Checkers	Word includes a Spelling Checker and a Grammar Checker that automatically advise you of misspelled words or incorrect grammar as you create and edit a document.
5. Word Wrap	The word wrap feature automatically decides where to end a line and wrap text to the next line based on the margin settings.
6. Document Preview	The Print Preview feature displays each page of your document in reduced size so you can see its layout.

Part 1

Loading Word 97

You will use Word 97 to create your letter to new credit card customers.

- If necessary, turn on your computer and put your data disk in drive A (or the appropriate drive for your system).
- Click Start.
- Choose Programs/Microsoft Word.

If a shortcut to Word button Microsoft Word is displayed on your desktop, you can double-click on the button to start the program.

If the Microsoft Office Suite is on your system and the Office Shortcut Bar is displayed, you can load Word by clicking the New Office Document button and selecting Blank Document.

After a few moments, the Word application window is displayed. Your screen should be similar to Figure 1-1.

FIGURE 1-1

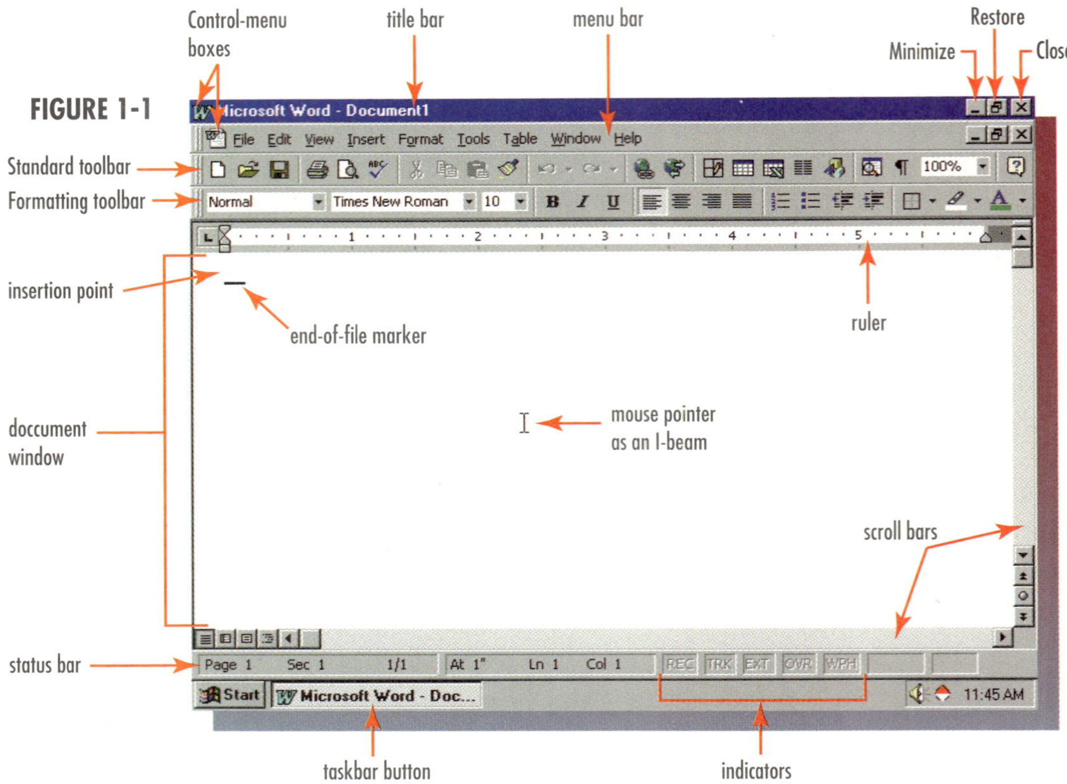

If necessary, maximize the Word application window.

As you can see, many of the features in the Word window are the same as in other Windows 95 applications. Among those features are a title bar, a menu bar, toolbars, a document window, scroll bars, and mouse compatibility. You can move and size Word windows, select commands, use Help, and switch between files and programs, just as you can in Windows. The common user interface makes learning and using new applications much easier.

The mouse pointer may appear as an I-beam or an arrow, depending on its location in the window.

The Word window title bar displays the program name, Microsoft Word, followed by the file name Document1, the default name of the file displayed in the window. The left end of the title bar contains the Word application window Control-menu icon, and the right end displays the Minimize, Restore, and Close buttons. They perform the same functions and operate in the same way as in Windows 95.

If the title bar does not display the file name, maximize the document window.

The menu bar below the title bar displays the Word program menu, which consists of nine menus. The left end of the menu bar displays the document window Control-menu icon, and the right end displays the document window Minimize, Restore, and Close buttons.

There are 13 different toolbars in Word.

The two toolbars below the menu bar contain buttons that are mouse shortcuts for many of the menu items. The upper toolbar is the **Standard toolbar**. It contains buttons that are used to complete the most frequently used menu commands. The bottom is the **Formatting toolbar**. It contains buttons that are used to change the appearance or format of the document.

- To quickly identify the toolbar buttons, point to each button in both toolbars to display the button name in the ScreenTip.

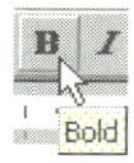

The left end of both the menu and toolbar displays a move handle that when dragged moves the menu or toolbar to another location. Both menu and toolbars can be docked (as they are now) or floating. When **docked** they are fixed to an edge of the window and display the move handle. When **floating** they appear in a separate window that can be moved by dragging the title bar.

If the ruler is not displayed, choose Ruler from the View menu.

The **ruler** is displayed below the Formatting toolbar. The ruler shows the line length in inches and is used to set margins, tab stops, and indents.

The large center area of the Word application window is where documents are displayed in open windows. Currently there is one open document window, which is maximized and occupies the entire text area. The **insertion point**, also called the **cursor**, is the blinking vertical bar that marks your current location in the document. The solid horizontal line is the **end-of-file marker**. Because there is nothing in this document, the end-of-file marker appears at the first character space on the first line.

The **status bar** at the bottom of the Word window displays information about the location of the insertion point and the status of different settings as they are used.

Using Office Assistant

The Office Assistant should also be displayed on your screen. The **Office Assistant** automatically suggests help topics as you work. It anticipates what you are going to do and then makes suggestions on how to perform a task. In addition, you can activate the Assistant at any time to get help on features in the Office application you are using. To activate the Office Assistant,

If your Office Assistant is not displayed, click [?] or press F1.

The Office Assistant feature is common to all Office 97 programs.

- Click  Office Assistant.

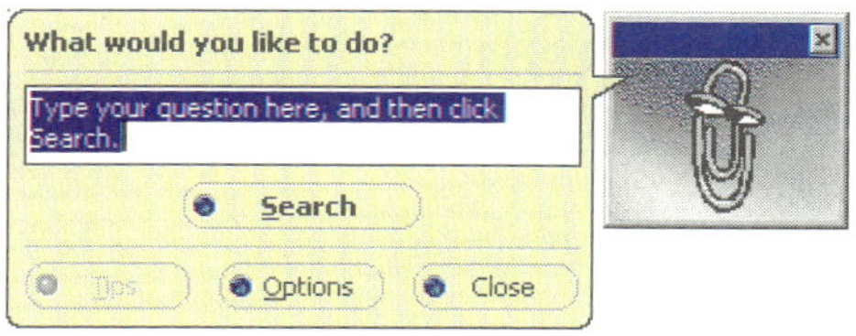

The Office Assistant balloon displays a prompt and a text box in which you can type the topic you want help on. Then you click the Search button to display a list of related topics from which you can select. The Tips Options button displays the most recent tip and lets you scroll through tips that the Office Assistant has recently displayed. The Options button is used to change Office Assistant so it provides different levels of help.

- Click: Options.

The dialog box on your screen should be similar to Figure 1-2.

FIGURE 1-2

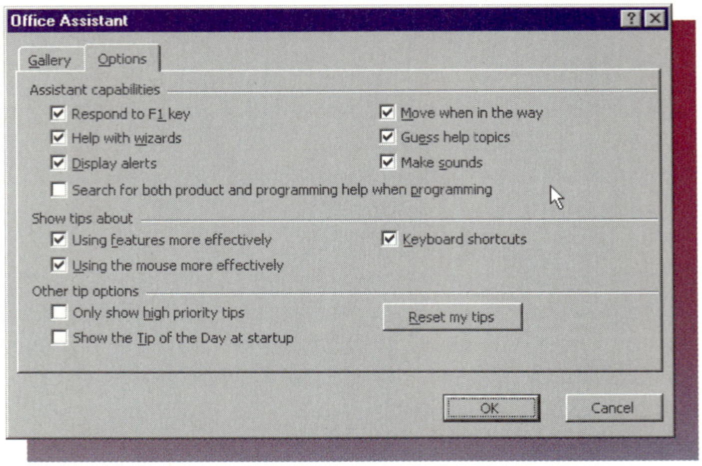

Changes you make to these options affect the Assistant in all the Office programs.

The Options tab of the Office Assistant dialog box displays the settings. The options that appear checked are on. As you work in Word, you may want to turn on or off some of these options.

- If necessary, turn on/off the Assistant options to reflect the same settings as in Figure 1-2.

You also want to reset the tips so that tips already seen can appear again.

- Click Reset my tips.
- Click OK.

Now you will ask the Office Assistant to provide help on the toolbars. While using Word, you will see that many of the toolbars open automatically as different tasks are performed. However, you can also open toolbars whenever you want. To find out how to open and close toolbars, you will use the Office Assistant.

- Click Office Assistant.
- Type **display toolbars**.
- Click Search.
- Click Show or hide a toolbar.

Office Assistant displays topics related to your request.

The Help window appears, explaining how to show or hide a toolbar.

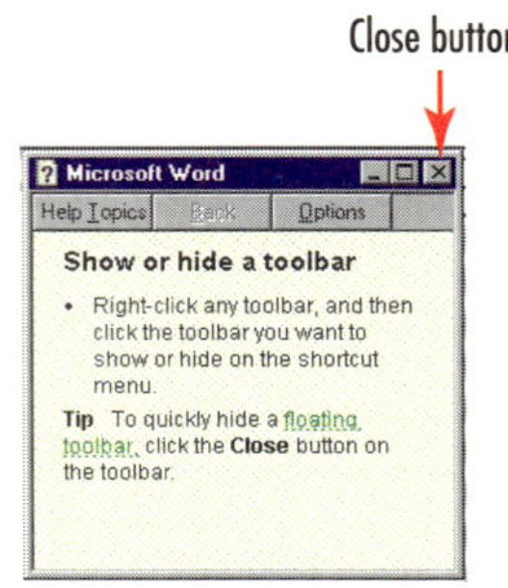

- Click anywhere outside the Help window.
- Right-click on any toolbar.

The menu equivalent is View/Toolbars.

The Shortcut menu displays a list of 13 toolbar names. Those that are currently displayed are checked. Clicking on a toolbar from the list will display it onscreen. Likewise, clicking on a checked toolbar will hide the toolbar.

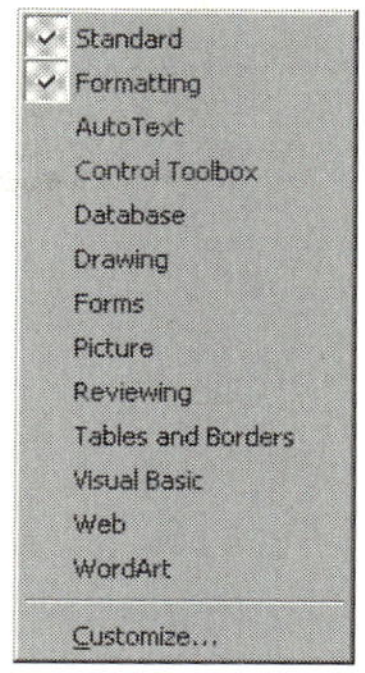

- Clear the Shortcut menu by clicking anywhere outside the menu.
- Click to close the Help window.

Developing a Document

Your first project with The Sports Company is to create a letter to be sent to all new credit card holders.

Concept 1: Document Development

The development of a document follows several steps: plan, enter, edit, format, and preview and print.

Plan — The first step in the development of a document is to understand the purpose of the document and to plan what your document should say.

Enter — After planning the document, you can begin entering the content of the document by typing the text using the word processor.

Edit — Making changes to your document is called **editing**. While typing, you are bound to make typing and spelling errors that need to be corrected. This is one type of editing. Another is to revise the content of what you have entered to make it clearer, or to add or delete information.

Format — Enhancing the appearance of the document to make it more readable or attractive is called **formatting**. This step is usually performed when the document is near completion. It includes many features such as boldfaced text, italics, and bulleted lists.

Preview and Print — The last step is to preview and print the document. Previewing displays the document onscreen as it will appear when printed, allowing you to check the document's overall appearance and make any final changes before printing.

You will find that you will generally follow these steps in order for your first draft of a document. However, you will probably retrace steps such as editing and formatting as the final document is developed.

During the planning phase, you have spoken with the regional manager regarding the purpose of the letter and the content in general. The purpose of the letter is to thank the customer for opening a new charge account with The Sports Company. The content of the letter should include instructions to the customer about how to use the card and the benefits associated with being a charge card holder.

Entering and Editing Text

Now that you understand the purpose of the letter and have a general idea of the content, you are ready to enter the text. A new Word document is like a blank piece of paper that already has many predefined settings. These settings are generally the most commonly used settings. They are called **default** settings and are stored as a document template.

Concept 2: Document Template

Every Word document is based on a document template. A document **template** is a document file that includes predefined settings that can be used as a pattern to create many common types of documents. The default document settings are stored in the Blank document template. Whenever you create a new document using this template, the same default settings are used.

There are many other template styles you can use that are designed to help you create professional-looking documents. They include templates that create different styles of memos, letters, and reports.

The Blank document template sets the top and bottom margins to 1 inch and the left and right margins to 1.25 inches. Other default settings include a standard paper-size setting of 8½ by 11 inches, tab settings at every half inch, and single-line spacing.

To verify several of the default settings, you can look at the information displayed in the status bar.

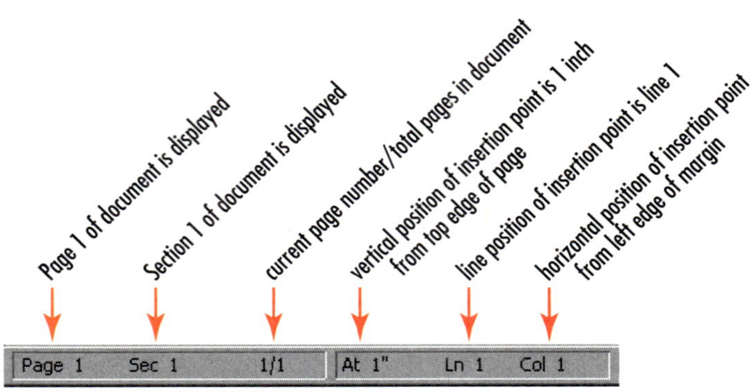

The indicators on the status bar show both the location of the text that is displayed in the document window as well as the location of the insertion point in a document. The numbers following the indicators specify the exact location in the document.

You can also look at the ruler to verify several default settings.

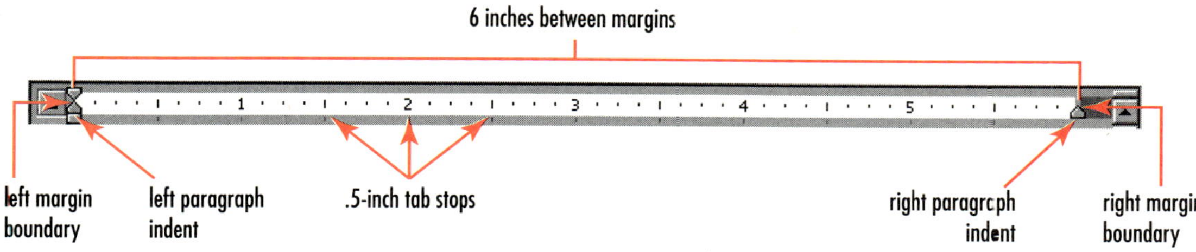

The margin boundaries on both ends of the ruler show the location of the left and right margins. The symbol ⧗ at the zero position on the ruler marks the location of the left paragraph indent and the △ symbol on the right end of the ruler line at the 6-inch position marks the right paragraph indent. The default paragraph indent locations are the same as the margin settings. The ruler shows that the distance between the left and right margins is 6 inches. Knowing that the default page size is 8.5 inches wide, this leaves 2.5 inches for margins: 1.25 inches for equal-sized left and right margins. The ruler also displays dimmed tab marks below each half-inch position along the ruler, indicating a default tab setting of every half inch.

To create a new document, simply begin typing the text. On the first line of the letter you will enter the salutation "Dear Preferred Customer:". As you enter the text, it will include several intentional errors. Type the entries exactly as they appear.

- Type **dear**

Notice that as you type, the character appears to the left of the insertion point. The location of the insertion point shows where the next character will appear as you type. Also, the status bar reflects the new horizontal position of the insertion point on the line. It shows the insertion point is currently positioned on column 5 of line 1.

The Office Assistant moves around the screen and changes size as you work to keep out of your way.

- Press Spacebar.

Your screen should be similar to Figure 1-3.

automatically capitalized word

FIGURE 1-3

As soon as you complete a word, the program checks the word for accuracy. In this case, notice that Word automatically capitalized the first letter of the word. This is part of the automatic correcting feature of Word.

Concept 3: AutoCorrect

Word includes a feature called **AutoCorrect**, which makes some basic assumptions about the text you are typing and, based on these assumptions, automatically identifies and/or corrects the entry. The AutoCorrect feature automatically inserts proper capitalization at the beginning of sentences and the names of days of the week. It will also change to lowercase letters any words that were incorrectly capitalized due to the accidental use of the Caps Lock key. In addition, it also corrects common spelling errors automatically.

The program automatically corrects by looking for certain types of errors. This is part of Office 97's IntelliSense feature, which automatically gives you assistance while you work. For example, if two capital letters appear at the beginning of a word, Word changes the second capital letter to a lowercase letter. If a lowercase letter appears at the beginning of a sentence, Word capitalizes the first letter of the first word. If the name of a day begins with a lowercase letter, Word capitalizes the first letter.

In some cases, you may want to exclude an abbreviation or capitalized item from automatic correction. You can do this by adding the word to an exception list. Alternatively, you can add words to the list of words you want to be automatically corrected. For example, if you commonly misspell a word, you can add the word to the list and it will be automatically corrected as you type.

Word also includes **AutoText** entries, which are commonly used phrases. If Word detects you are typing one of the AutoText phrases, it automatically suggests the remainder of the phrase. You can choose to accept the suggestion or continue typing. You can also add your own entries to the AutoText list.

To continue entering the salutation,

- Type **Prefered**
- Press Spacebar.

Your screen should be similar to Figure 1-4.

FIGURE 1-4

red wavy line indicates misspelled word

This time Word has identified the word as misspelled by underlining it with a wavy red line.

Concept 4: Spelling and Grammar Checkers

Word includes a Spelling Checker and a Grammar Checker that automatically advise you of misspelled words or incorrect grammar as you create and edit a document.

The Spelling Checker compares the word you type to a **main dictionary** of words supplied with the program. If the word does not appear in the main dictionary, it checks the **custom dictionary**, a dictionary that you can create to hold words you commonly use but that are not included in the main dictionary. If the word does not appear in either dictionary, the program identifies it as misspelled by displaying a red wavy line below the word. You can then correct the misspelled word by editing it. Alternatively, you can display a list of suggested spelling corrections for that word and select the correct spelling from the list to replace the misspelled word in the document.

Word also checks the grammar of your sentences. If Word detects grammatical errors in subject-verb agreements, verb forms, capitalization, or commonly confused words, to name a few, they are identified with a wavy green line. You can correct the grammatical error by editing it or you can display a suggested correction. Not all grammatical errors identified by Word are actual errors. Use discretion when correcting the errors.

The Spelling and Grammar status bar icon  changes to  when a document contains errors. Double-clicking the icon moves to the next spelling or grammar error and opens the Shortcut menu.

Because you have discovered this error very soon after typing it, and you know that the correct spelling of this word is "preferred," you can quickly correct it using ←Backspace. The ←Backspace key removes the character or space to the left of the insertion point; therefore, it is particularly useful when you are moving from right to left (backward) along a line of text. To correct this word,

- Press ←Backspace 3 times.

The space and the letters d and e are removed. Notice the wavy underline is also cleared. This is because the word "Prefer" is spelled correctly. However, this is not the word you want to use. To complete the word and enter the last word of the salutation,

- Type **red**
- Press Spacebar twice.
- Type **Custommer**
- Press Spacebar.

Again, the word is identified as misspelled. Also notice that the Office Assistant displays a light bulb, indicating there is a tip available.

- Click the light bulb and read the tip.

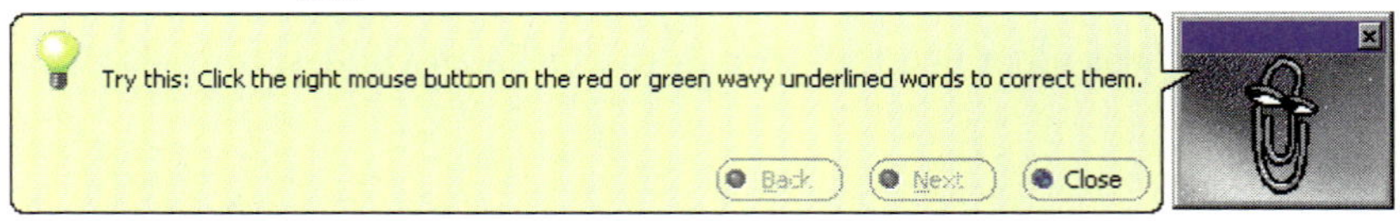

- Click Close.

As suggested in the tip, another way to quickly correct a misspelled word is to select the correct spelling from a list of suggested spelling corrections displayed on the Spelling Shortcut menu.

- Right-click on Custommer to display the Spelling Shortcut menu.

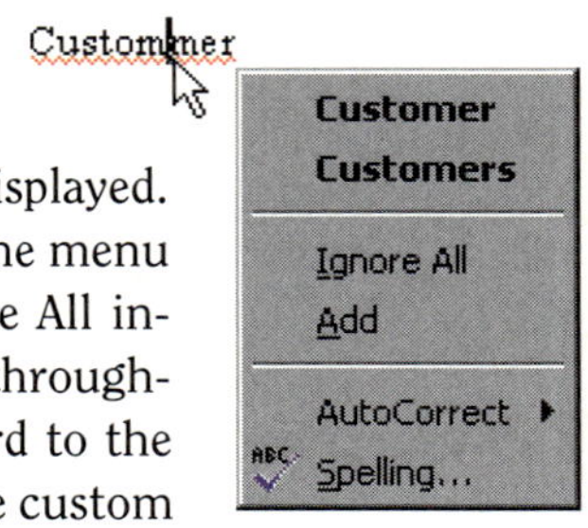

A Shortcut menu of suggested correct spellings is displayed. In this case, two correct spellings are suggested. The menu also includes several related menu options. Ignore All instructs Word to ignore the misspelling of this word throughout the rest of this session, and Add adds the word to the custom dictionary list. When a word is added to the custom dictionary, Word will always accept that spelling as correct. The AutoCorrect option adds the word to the AutoCorrect list so Word can correct misspellings of it automatically as you type. The last option, Spelling, starts the spell-checking program to check the entire document. You will learn about this feature in Lab 2.

Notice that the suggested replacements reflect the same capitalization as used in the document. Sometimes there are no suggested replacements because Word cannot locate any words in its dictionary that are similar in spelling or the suggestions are not correct. If this happens, you need to edit the word manually. The first suggestion is correct. To select it and complete the salutation,

- Click Customer.
- Type **:**

Inserting and Deleting Blank Lines

Next you will enter the first paragraph of the letter. The ←Enter key is used to insert a blank line into text or to end a short line.

- Press ←Enter.

Your screen should be similar to Figure 1-5.

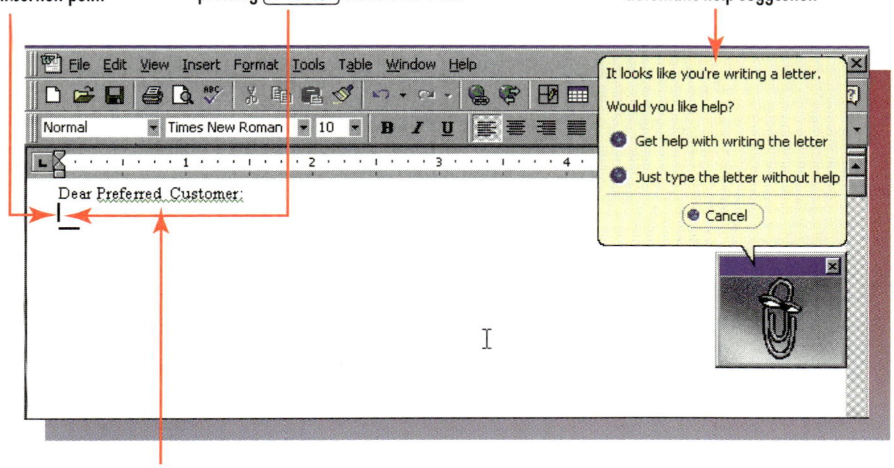

FIGURE 1-5

The insertion point moves to the beginning of the next line. The status bar shows that the insertion point is positioned on line 2, column 1 of the page. Office Assistant detects that you may be typing a letter and offers help. You won't use the help to create the letter.

- Click Just type the letter without help.

Also notice that there is a green wavy line under "Preferred Customer" indicating that there is a grammatical error.

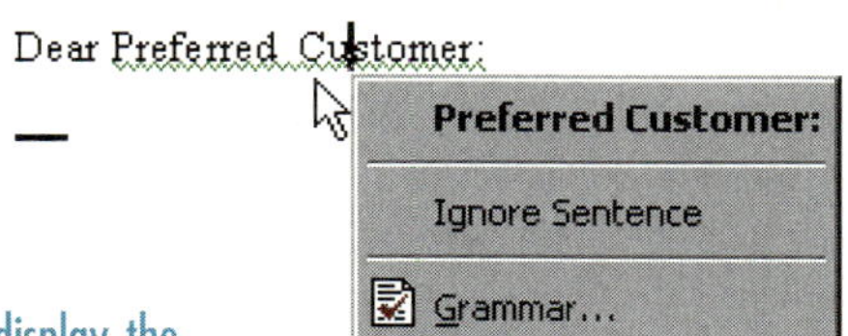

- Right-click on Preferred Customer to display the Grammar Shortcut menu.

The Grammar Checker is very labor intensive on your computer, so the wavy green lines may not show up as quickly as the Spelling Checker.

A Shortcut menu showing a suggested correction is displayed. The second option, Ignore Sentence, instructs Word to ignore the grammatical error in this sentence. The last option, Grammar, provides an explanation of the error.

- Choose Grammar.

Your screen should be similar to Figure 1-6.

FIGURE 1-6

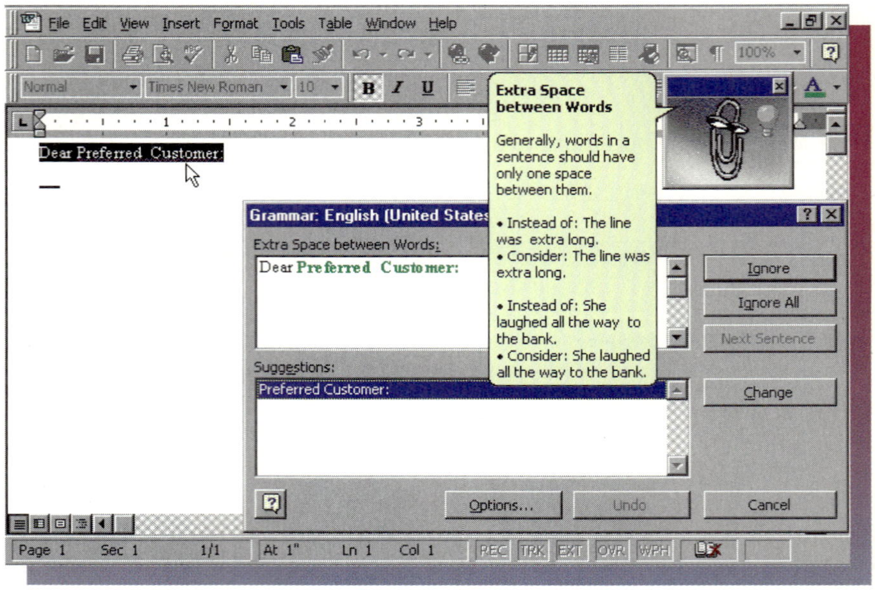

The Grammar dialog box is open and the Assistant tells you that the grammatical error is an extra space between words, in this case between the words "Preferred" and "Customer." The suggested correction is correct. To select it,

- Click Change.

You want to separate the salutation from the first paragraph with a blank line. To do this,

- Press ↓.
- Press ←Enter.

When ←Enter is pressed at the beginning of a line, a blank line is inserted into the document. If the insertion point is in the middle of a line of text and you press ←Enter, all the text to the right of the insertion point moves to the beginning of the next line. Now you can type the text for the first paragraph of the letter. Do not worry about making typing errors as you enter the text; you will learn how to correct them next.

- Type **Thank**
- Press Spacebar.

The Office Assistant has anticipated what you are typing by displaying the AutoText "Thank you" above your text. Also notice that the Office Assistant displays a light bulb again, indicating there is another tip available.

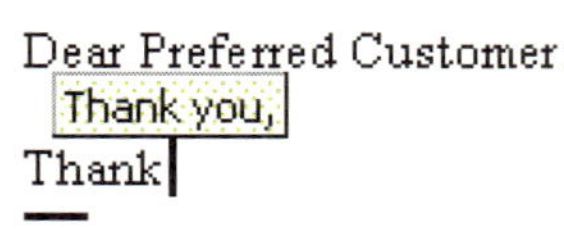

- Click the and read the tip.

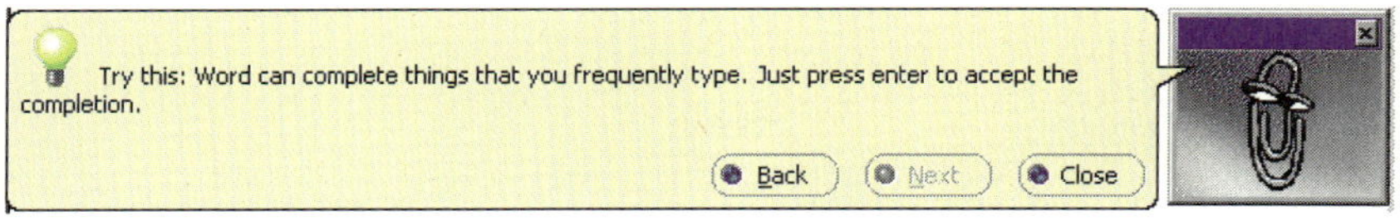

> If the Office Assistant were not displayed, the light bulb would appear in the on the toolbar.

- Click Close.

If you wanted to accept the AutoText suggestion, pressing ←Enter would enter the text for you. However, you do not want to accept the suggested text because it includes a comma. If you keep typing, the AutoText suggestion will disappear.

- Type **you for opening a new credit card account with The Sports Company and becoming one of our**

The line of text is very near the right margin. As you continue to type, when the text reaches the right margin, Word will automatically wrap the text to the next line.

Concept 5: Word Wrap

The **word wrap** feature automatically decides where to end a line and wrap text to the next line based on the margin settings. This saves time when entering text, as you do not need to press ←Enter at the end of a full line to begin a new line. The only time you need to press ←Enter is to end a paragraph, to insert blank lines, or to create a short line such as the salutation. In addition, if you change the margins or insert or delete text on a line, the program automatically readjusts the text on the line to fit within the margin settings. Word wrap is common to all word processors.

- Press Spacebar.
- Type **most valued customers.**

Your screen should be similar to Figure 1-7.

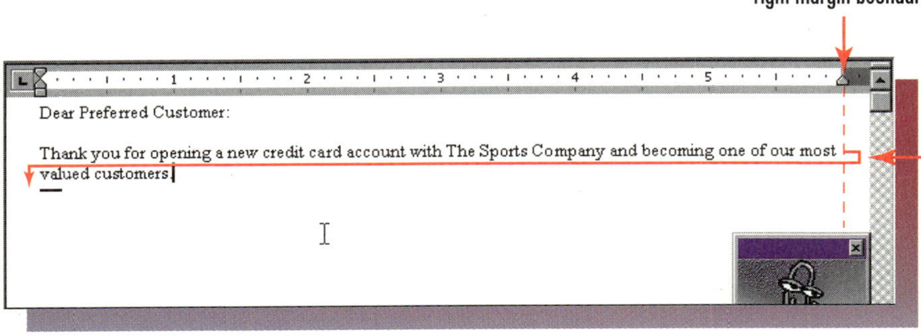

FIGURE 1-7

> Do not be concerned if the text on your screen wraps differently from that in Figure 1-7.

The program has wrapped the text that would overlap the right margin to the beginning of the next line. To continue the paragraph by entering a second sentence,

> Generally, when using a word processor, separate sentences with a single space rather than a double space, which was common when using typewriters.

- Press Spacebar.
- Type **Here's your new credit card!**

Once text is entered into a document, it is important to know how to move around within the text to correct errors or make changes. As soon as you learn about moving through a document, you will correct any errors you have made.

Moving Around the Document Window

Either the mouse or the keyboard can be used to move through the text in the document window. Depending on what you are doing, the mouse is not always the quickest means of moving. For example, if your hands are already on the keyboard as you are entering text, it may be quicker to use the keyboard rather than take your hands off to use the mouse. Therefore, you will learn how to move through the document using both methods.

You use the mouse to move the insertion point to a specific location in a document. When you can use the mouse to move the insertion point, it is shaped as an I-beam. However, when the mouse pointer is positioned in the unmarked area to the left of a line (the left margin), it changes to an arrow ⇗. This area is called the **selection bar** (see Figure 1-8). When the mouse is in this area, it can be used to highlight text.

> You will learn about selecting text using this feature shortly.

- Move the mouse pointer into the selection bar. Move it back to the document text.

To move the insertion point, position the I-beam at the location in the text where you want it to be, then click the left mouse button.

- Click on the y of "you" (first line of first paragraph).
- Move the mouse pointer out of the way so you can see the insertion point better.

Your screen should be similar to Figure 1-8.

FIGURE 1-8

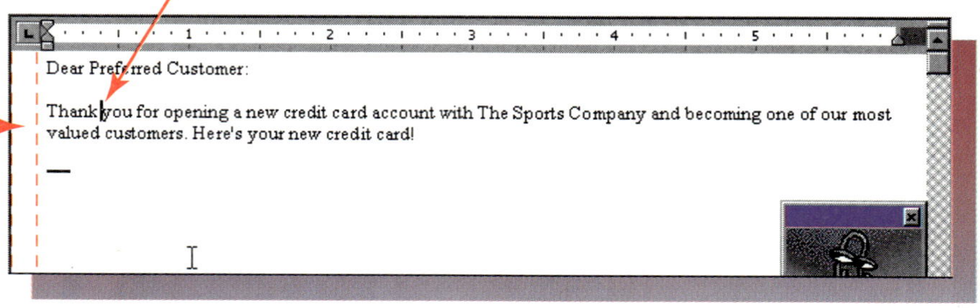

The insertion point should now be positioned on one side or the other of the y, with the status bar showing the new location of the insertion point.

If it is positioned to the left of the y, this means that the I-beam was positioned more to the left side of the character when you pressed the mouse button. The letter to the right of the insertion point is the selected character, in this case the y. If it is positioned to the right of the y, this means the I-beam was positioned more to the right side of the character when you clicked the mouse button. The letter to the right of the insertion point is the selected character, in this case the o.

Throughout these labs, you will be instructed to move to a specific letter in the text. This means to move the insertion point to the *left* side of the character so the character to the right is selected.

To practice using the mouse to move the insertion point to the left side of a character,

- Move to S in Sports.
- Move to P in Preferred.

Make sure the pointer is an I-beam before clicking to move the insertion point. If text appears highlighted, click anywhere in the document where the mouse pointer is an I-beam to clear the highlighting.

The insertion point can also be moved around the window using the arrow keys located on the numeric keypad or the directional keypad. The arrow keys move the insertion point one character space in the direction indicated by the arrow.

- Press → (10 times).
- Press ↓ (2 times).

If you are using the arrows on the numeric keypad, be sure the Num Lock key is off.

The insertion point first moved 10 character spaces to the right, then down two lines to the o in "opening." It moved to that position because it was last located in a line containing text at that position. The insertion point will attempt to maintain its position in a line of text as you move up or down through the document.

When you hold down either → or ←, the insertion point moves quickly, character by character, along the line.

- To see how this works, hold down → until the insertion point is positioned on the C in "Company."

If you moved too far to the right along the line of text, use ← to move back to the correct position.

This saves multiple presses of the arrow key. Many of the Word insertion point movement keys can be held down to execute multiple moves.

To move word by word along a line,

- Press Ctrl + → (2 times).
- Press Ctrl + ← (3 times).

The insertion point moved two words to the right, then back three words to the left along the line.

The Home and End keys can also be used to quickly move the insertion point to the beginning or end, respectively, of a line of text.

- Press End.
- Press Home.

You can use ←Backspace to delete characters to the left of the insertion point or Delete to delete characters to the right of the insertion point.

- Now that you know how to move within text on the window, move to any errors you may have made while entering the paragraph and correct them.

You can also correct misspellings and grammar errors using the Shortcut menus.

Closing and Saving Files

The rest of the letter has been entered for you and saved in a file named Credit Card Letter on your data disk. Before opening this file, you will close the current document file using the Close command on the File menu.

- Choose File.

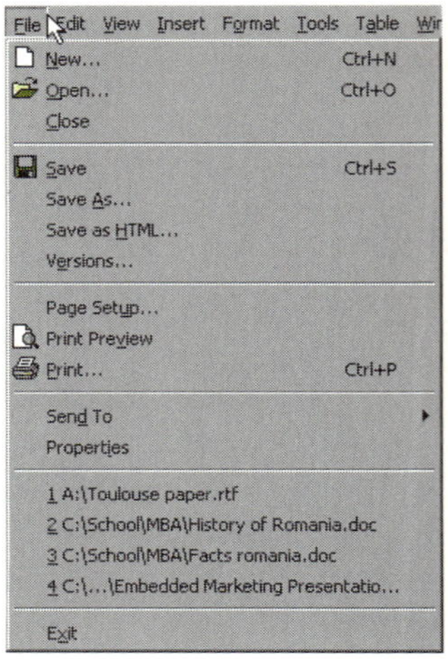

Up to nine recently used documents may be displayed.

The File drop-down menu consisting of 13 commands is displayed. In addition to the commands you would expect to see in the File menu, such as Save and Exit, there are several commands that are specific to Word. At the bottom of the File menu, a list of the names of the most recently used Word document files may be displayed. Clicking on a file name opens the file.

To close the document,

You could also click the document window's ☒ button to close the document file.

- Choose Close.

As a precaution against losing your work, the Office Assistant displays an advisory balloon asking if you want to save the contents of the current document to disk. As you create a new document or edit an existing document, the changes you make are immediately displayed onscreen and are stored in your computer's memory. To create a permanent copy of your document, it must be saved as a file on a disk. Selecting Yes saves the document as a file on a disk, No closes the document without saving, and Cancel returns you to the document. To save the document you have created to a file on your data disk,

If the Office Assistant is closed, Word displays the same message in a dialog box.

- Click Yes.

The Save As dialog box on your screen should be similar to Figure 1-9.

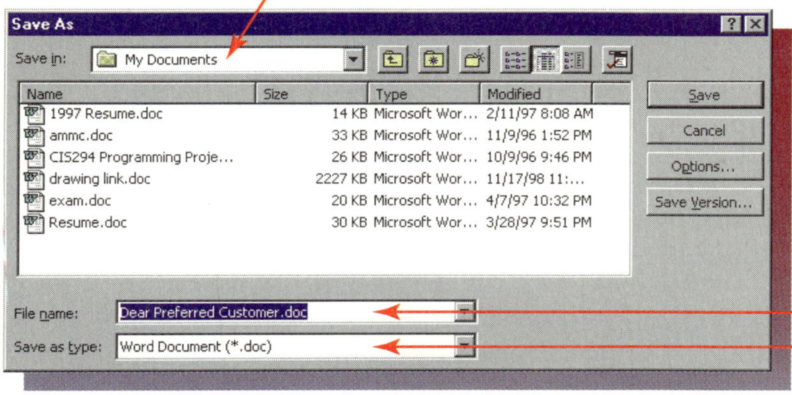

FIGURE 1-9

This dialog box is used to specify the location to save the file and the file name. The Save In drop-down list box displays the default folder as the location where the file will be saved, and the File Name text box displays the proposed file name. First you need to change the location where the file will be saved to the drive containing your data disk.

Place your data disk in drive A (or the appropriate drive for your system).

- Select Save In.
- Select A: (or the drive containing your data disk).

Now the large list box displays the names of all Word files on your data disk. Only Word document files are displayed because the Save As Type list box shows that the currently selected file type is Word Document. Word document files are identified by the file extension .doc, which is automatically added to the file name when the file is saved.

If a system error message appears, check that your disk is properly inserted in the drive.

Next you need to enter a file name. The File Name list box displays the default file name, consisting of the first few words from the document. You will change the name to Letter Lab 1.

A Word file name can be up to 255 characters and follows standard file-naming rules.

- Triple-click the default file name in the File Name text box.
- Type **Letter Lab 1**
- Click Save.

The file name can be entered in either uppercase or lowercase letters and will appear exactly as you type it.

The document is saved on disk and the document window is closed. Now the Word window displays an empty text area, and the status bar indicators are blank because there are no open documents.

Opening a File

You are now ready to open the file named Credit Card Letter. As in all Windows 95 applications, the Open command on the File menu is used to open files. In addition, the toolbar shortcut Open can be used instead of the menu command.

The File/New command or the New button opens a blank new document.

The keyboard shortcut is Ctrl + O.

- Click Open.

The Open dialog box on your screen should be similar to Figure 1-10.

FIGURE 1-10

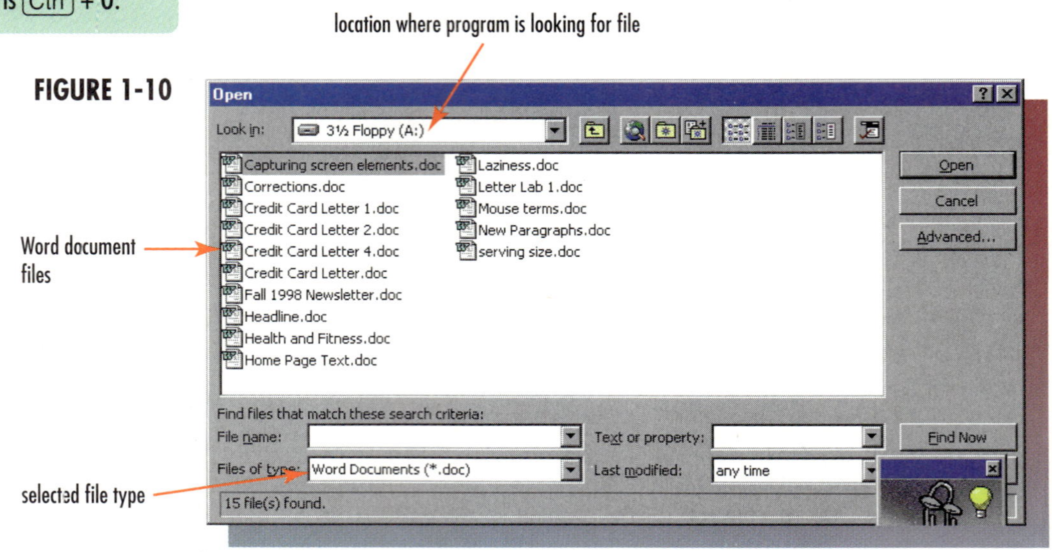

In the Open dialog box, you specify the location and name of the file you want to open. The Look In drop-down list box displays the drive you specified when saving as the location where the program will look for files. The location should be the drive containing your data disk. The large list box displays the names of all Word files on your data disk. Again, only Word document files are displayed because the currently selected type is Word Documents.

If the Look In location is not correct, select the appropriate location from the Look In drop-down list box.

If necessary, scroll the list box until the file name Credit Card Letter is visible. If the file name is not displayed, ask your instructor for help.

- Select Credit Card Letter.
- Click Open.

You could also double-click the file name to both select it and choose Open.

Your screen should be similar to Figure 1-11.

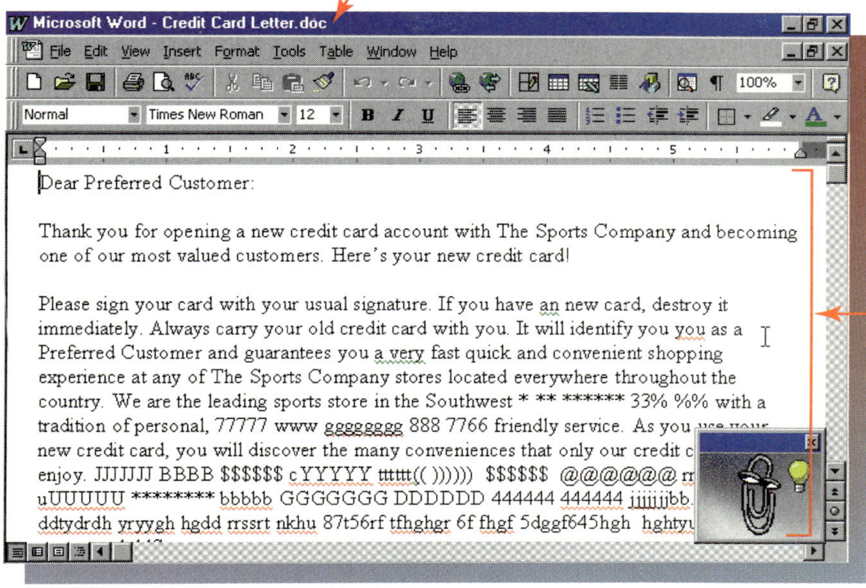

FIGURE 1-11

The file is loaded and displayed in the document window. This file contains the rest of the first draft of the letter to new credit card customers. It contains many errors that need to be edited.

Note: If you end your lab session now, close the file and follow the instructions on page WP42 to exit the program. When you continue the lab at Part 2, load Word and open the Credit Card Letter file.

Part 2

Moving Through a Document

As you can see, the text area is not large enough to display the entire document. To bring additional text into view in the window, you can scroll the text using either the scroll bars or the keyboard. Again, both methods are useful, depending on what you are doing.

- Click the ▼ in the vertical scroll bar to scroll the document until the closing is displayed in the window.

Your screen should be similar to Figure 1-12.

FIGURE 1-12

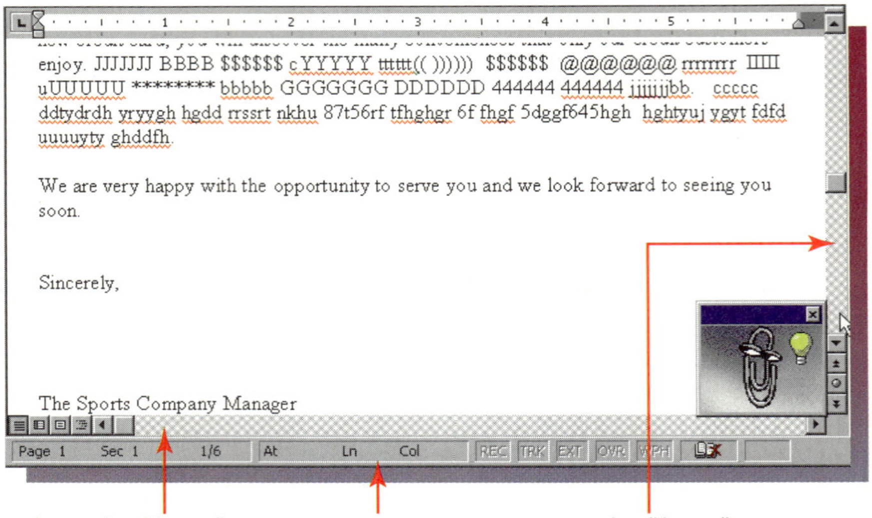

The text at the beginning of the letter has scrolled off the window, and the bottom of the letter is now displayed. Notice that the insertion point is no longer visible in the window, and the insertion point location information in the status bar is blank. To actually move the insertion point, you must click in a location in the window.

- Move to T in The Sports Company Manager.

You can also scroll the document using the keyboard. While scrolling using the keyboard, the insertion point also moves. To return to the top of the letter,

- Hold down ↑ for several seconds until the insertion point is on the D in Dear.

You can move quickly through a document in large jumps by moving a window or a page at a time, moving to a specific page, or moving to the end or beginning of the document.

- Press Page Down (2 times).

Clicking above or below the scroll box in the vertical scroll bar also moves window by window through the document.

The insertion point moved to the bottom line of the current window and then to the bottom line of the next full window of text. You are still viewing page 1 of the document. The Previous Page and Next Page Navigator buttons located at the bottom of the vertical scroll bar move page by page through a document. To move to the top of the next page,

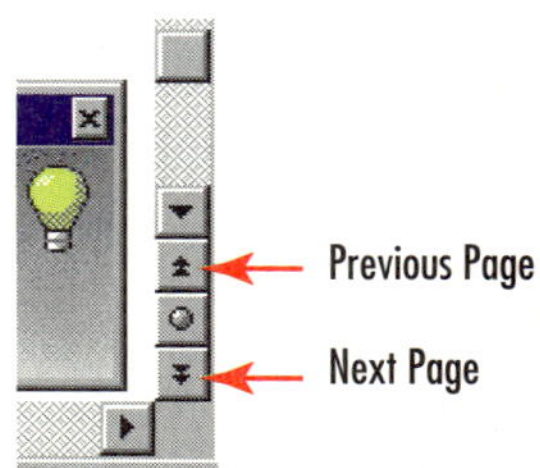

- Click Next Page.

The insertion point is positioned on the first line of page 2. Notice that the status bar displays "Page 2." To show where one page ends and another begins, Word displays a dotted line to mark the page break. To see this line,

- Press [↑].

Your screen should be similar to Figure 1-13.

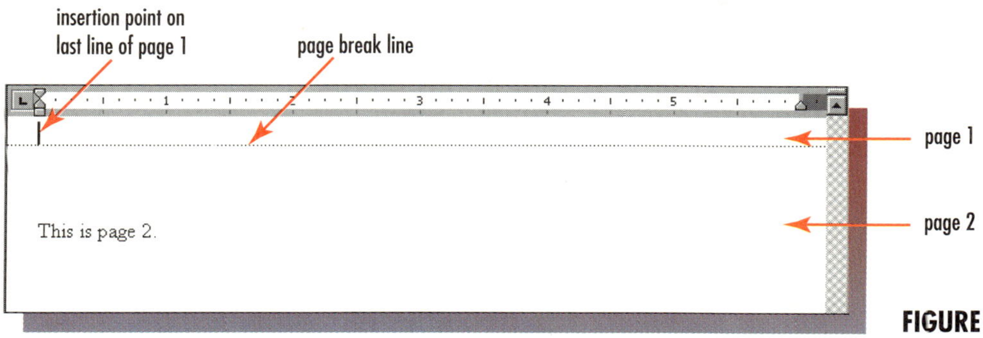

FIGURE 1-13

The insertion point is positioned on the last line of page 1, and the status bar displays "Page 1." Word automatically enters a page break line in a document when the preceding page is full to show where a new page of text begins.

Dragging the scroll box moves multiple windows forward or backward through the document. The location of the scroll box in the vertical scroll bar reflects your position in a document. When the scroll box is midway on the scroll bar, the displayed text is approximately in the middle of the document. As you drag the scroll box, a ScrollTip tells you the page that will be displayed in the window.

- Drag the scroll box down the vertical scroll bar and release it when the ScrollTip displays "Page: 3."

You can also use the Select Browse Object button to select the way you want to browse through the document. The method you choose changes how the and buttons work. Because the default is by page, using these buttons moves by page through the document,

- Click Select Browse Object.

From the browser box you select the element by which you want to navigate, such as by tables or by headings instead of by page.

- Point to each button in the browser to see the option name.

You can also move directly to a specific location in the document using the Go To option.

> The menu equivalent is Edit/Go To, and the keyboard shortcut is [Ctrl] + G.

- Click Go To.

The Find and Replace dialog box on your screen should be similar to Figure 1-14.

FIGURE 1-14

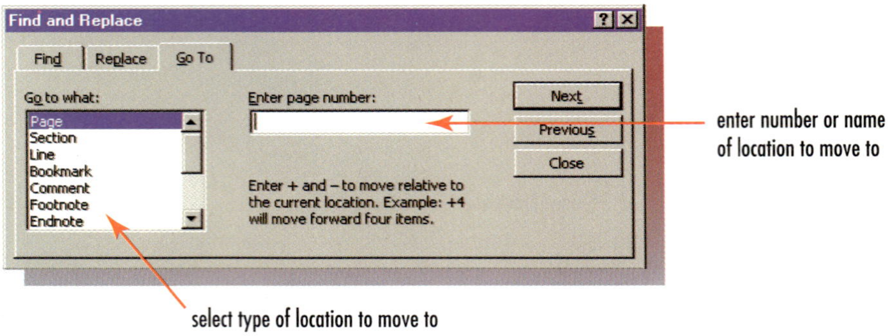

Office Assistant continues to offer tips as you work. You can choose to read the tips or ignore them.

Page is the default type of location to move to. To specify a specific page to move to, in the Enter Page Number text box,

- Type 5
- Click [Go To].

Reminder: You can press [←Enter] to choose the Go To command button.

The insertion point moves directly to the first line of page 5.

To close the dialog box,

- Click [Close].

You could also click [X] to close the dialog box.

The biggest jump the insertion point can make is to move to the beginning or end of a document. To move to the end of this document,

- Press [Ctrl] + [End].

Your screen should be similar to Figure 1-15.

FIGURE 1-15

The insertion point should be positioned on a blank line on page 6 of this document. The status bar displayss "6/6," indicating that you are viewing the sixth page of a six-page document. In addition, the end-of-file marker is displayed. This is the last line in the file.

To move quickly back to the beginning of the document,

- Press Ctrl + Home.

To review, the following features can be used to move through a document:

You can also drag the scroll box to the bottom or top of the scroll bar to quickly move to the end or beginning of the document.

Mouse	Action
Click new location	Positions insertion point.
Click scroll arrow	Scrolls line by line or character by character in the direction of the scroll arrow.
Click above/below scroll box	Scrolls the document window by window.
Drag scroll box	Moves multiple windows up/down.
Click	Select object to browse by.
Click	Go to previous page.
Click	Go to next page.

Key	Action
→	One character to right.
←	One character to left.
↑	One line up.
↓	One line down.
Ctrl + →	One word to right.
Ctrl + ←	One word to left.
Home	Left end of line.
End	Right end of line.
Page Up	Top of window.
Page Down	Bottom of window.
Ctrl + Home	Beginning of document.
Ctrl + End	End of document.
Edit/Go To	Moves to specified location.

Inserting Characters

After entering the text of a document, you should proofread it for accuracy and completeness and modify or edit the document as needed. As you check the document, you see that the first sentence of the second paragraph is incorrect. It should read: "Please sign your new card in ink with your usual signature." The sentence is missing three words, "new," "in," and "ink." These words can easily be entered into the sentence without retyping it using either Insert or Overtype mode.

The default setting for Word is Insert mode.

In **Insert mode** new characters are inserted into the existing text by moving the existing text to the right to make space for the new characters. To insert the word "new" before the word "card" in the first sentence,

- Move to c in card.
- Type **new**
- Press Spacebar.

Your screen should be similar to Figure 1-16.

FIGURE 1-16

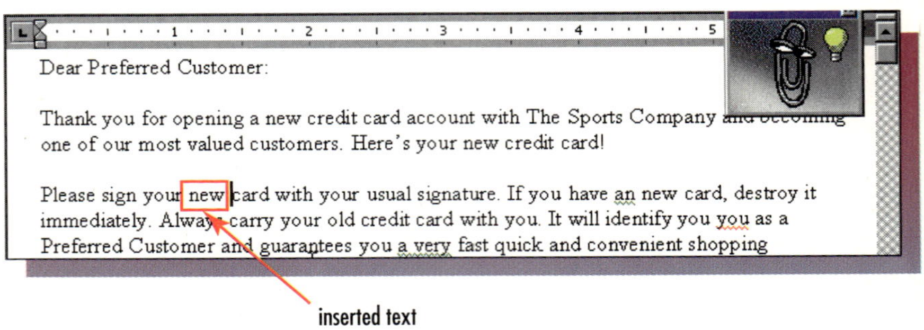

- Continue to correct the sentence by entering the words "in ink" before the word "with."

In the second sentence, you notice that the word "new" should be "old."

- Move to n of new.

You could delete this word and type in the new word, or you can use the Overtype mode to enter text in a document. When you use **Overtype mode**, new text types over the existing characters. To switch to this mode,

The OVR button is in the status bar.

- Double-click OVR.

Notice the OVR status indicator button letters appear bright. This indicates the Overtype mode is on. To change the word "new" to "old,"

- Type **old**

Your screen should be similar to Figure 1-17.

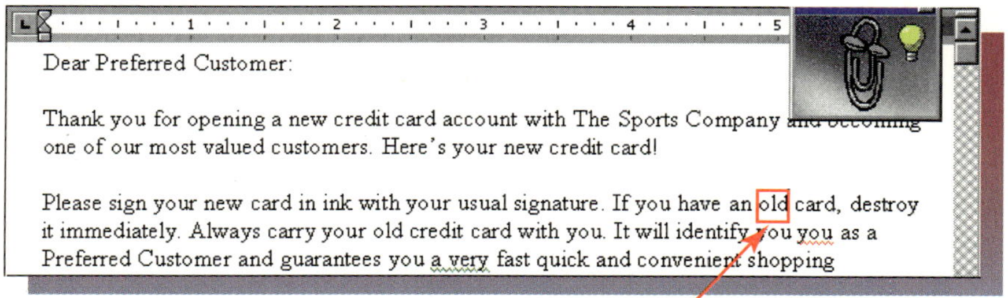

FIGURE 1-17

As each character was typed, the selected character (or space) was replaced with the character being typed.

- Next replace the word "old" in the third sentence of the paragraph with "new."
- Double-click OVR.

The OVR status indicator button letters are dimmed again, indicating the Overtype feature is off.

Deleting Words

As you continue to read, you find that the fourth sentence of the second paragraph contains a repeated word and several unnecessary words. The repeated word "you" has been identified by the automatic spell-checking feature.

- To quickly delete a repeated word, display the Spelling Shortcut menu for the identified word "you" and select the Delete Repeated Word option.

Not all words you may want to delete, however, are repeated words. Other words may be unnecessary to the content. In the same sentence, the word "fast" is not needed because the following word "quick" conveys the same information. To delete the word "fast,"

- Move to f in fast.
- Press Ctrl + Delete.

Your screen should be similar to Figure 1-18.

FIGURE 1-18

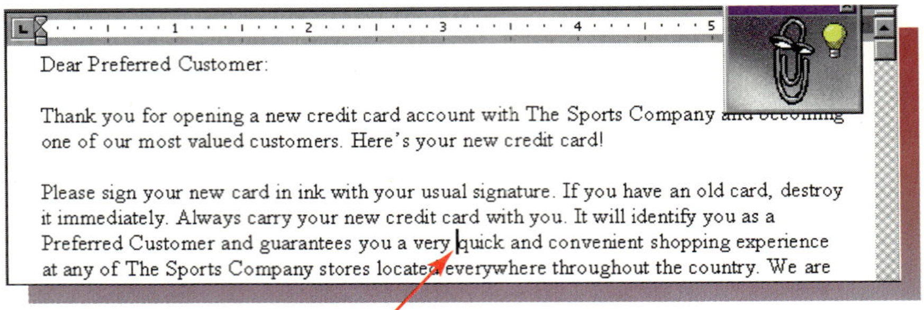

word "fast" was deleted

When the insertion point is positioned on the beginning or end of a word, the entire word is deleted.

The characters to the right of the insertion point are deleted, including the blank space following the word. As you read the revised sentence, you also decide the word "very" is unnecessary. You can delete the character and space to the left of the insertion point using the Ctrl + ←Backspace key combination.

- Press Ctrl + ←Backspace.
- In the same sentence, use either method to delete the word "everywhere."

Displaying Special Characters

As you continue to proof the letter, you decide that the second paragraph is too long and should be divided into two separate paragraphs.

- Move to W in We (fourth line of second paragraph).
- Press ←Enter (2 times).

Each time you press ←Enter, Word inserts a special character called a **paragraph mark** at that location in the document. Word does not display these special characters because they clutter the screen, nor does it print them. However, there are times when you need to delete a special character, so you need to be able to see where it is.

The menu equivalent is Tools/Options/View/Spaces/Paragraph Marks.

- Click ¶ Show/Hide.

Your screen should be similar to 1-19.

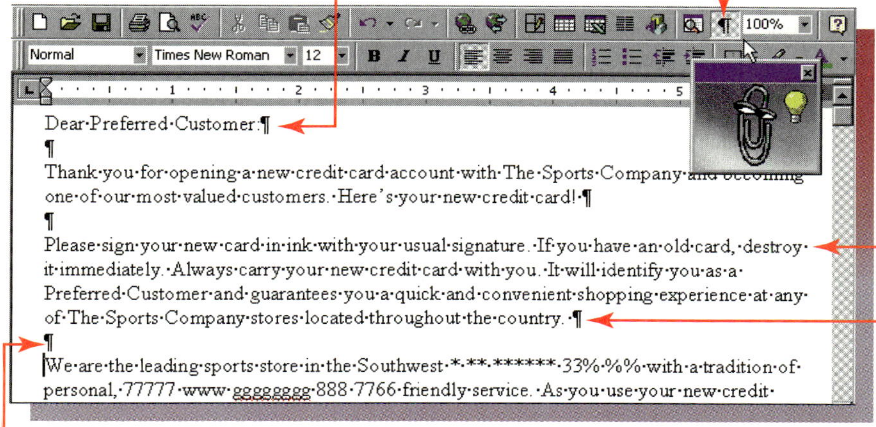

FIGURE 1-19

The document now displays the special characters. A paragraph mark character ¶ is displayed wherever the ←Enter key was pressed. Between each word, a dot shows where the Spacebar was pressed. The ¶ character on the line above the insertion point represents the pressing of ←Enter that created the blank line between the second and third paragraphs. The ¶ character at the end of the line above that represents the pressing of ←Enter that ended the paragraph and moved the insertion point to the beginning of the next line.

To delete a special character, position the insertion point on the character and press Delete, or position the insertion point to the right of the character and press ←Backspace. This works the same way as if you were deleting text in the document. To delete the two ¶ characters that you just inserted,

- Press ←Backspace (2 times).

The blank line is removed, the text moves up to fill in the blank space at the end of the previous line, and the two paragraphs return to a single paragraph. To separate the text into two paragraphs again,

- Press ←Enter (2 times).

In many editing situations, it is necessary to display the special characters; however, this is not needed for simple text deletions. For normal entry of text, you will probably not want the characters displayed. To hide the characters,

- Click ¶ Show/Hide.

The screen returns to normal display. Now that you know how to turn this feature on and off, you can use it whenever you want when entering and editing text.

Selecting Text

As you continue proofreading the letter, you see that the third paragraph contains several large areas of junk characters. To remove these characters, you could use [Delete] and [←Backspace] to delete each character individually or [Ctrl] + [Delete] or [Ctrl] + [←Backspace] to delete each word. However, this is very slow. Several characters, words, or lines of text can be deleted at once by first **selecting** the text and then pressing [Delete]. Text is selected by highlighting it. To select text, first move the insertion point to the beginning or end of the text to be selected. Then select the text by dragging the mouse. You can select as little as a single letter or as much as the entire document.

> You can also select text with the keyboard by holding down [⇧Shift] while using the direction keys to expand the highlight in the direction indicated. Holding down [Ctrl] + [⇧Shift] while using the [→] or [←] keys selects word by word.

The first area of characters to be removed follows the word "Southwest" in the first line of the third paragraph. To position the insertion point on the first character of the text to be selected,

- Move to * (first line of third paragraph).
- Drag the mouse until the junk text is highlighted (including the space before the word "with").

The junk text is selected. Text that is selected can then be modified using many different Word features. In this case, you want to remove the selected text. To do this,

- Press [Delete].
- In a similar manner, select and delete the next set of junk characters following the word "personal" in this sentence.
- Scroll the window to view the entire third paragraph.

> You can also select an area of text by clicking on the beginning of the text area and then holding down [⇧Shift] while clicking on the end of the text area.

The last two sentences of the paragraph consist entirely of junk characters. You can also quickly select a standard block of text. A standard block consists of a sentence, paragraph, page, tabular column, rectangular portion of text, or the entire document. The following table summarizes the techniques used to select standard blocks.

To select a:	Procedure:
Word	Double-click in the word.
Sentence	Press [Ctrl] and click within the sentence.
Line	Click in the selection bar next to the line.
Multiple lines	Drag in the selection bar next to the lines.
Paragraph	Triple-click on the paragraph or double-click in the selection bar next to the paragraph.
Multiple paragraphs	Drag in the selection bar next to the paragraphs.
Document	Triple-click in the selection bar or press [Ctrl] and click in the selection bar.

You will select and delete the first sentence of nonsense characters in this paragraph. To do so,

- Press Ctrl and click anywhere in third sentence of third paragraph.

Your screen should be similar to Figure 1-20.

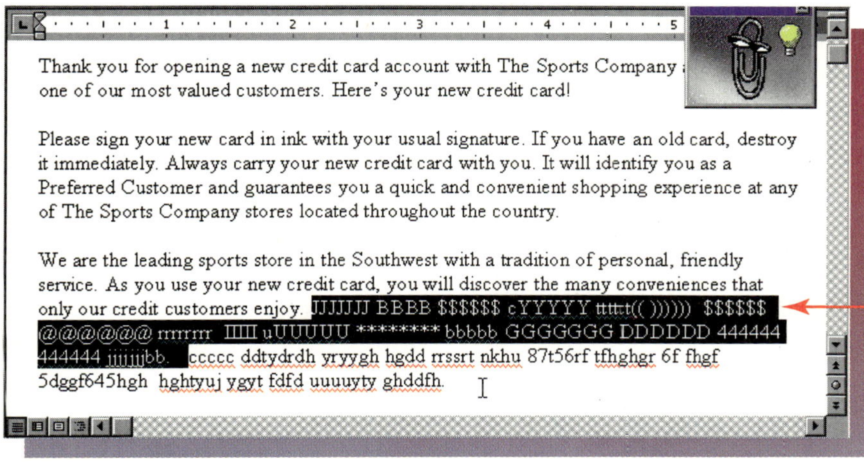

FIGURE 1-20

- Press Delete.
- In a similar manner, delete the second sentence of junk characters.

Undoing Editing Changes

Finally, you are not too pleased with the last sentence of the letter and are considering removing it.

- Double-click in the selection bar next to the last sentence of the letter to select it.
- Delete the selection.

After thinking about this change, you decide the last sentence may not be so bad after all. To quickly restore this sentence, you can use Undo to reverse your last action or command.

- Click Undo.

The menu equivalent is **E**dit/**U**ndo or Ctrl + Z.

Undo returns your last deletion and restores it to its original location in the text, regardless of the current insertion point location. Notice that the Undo button includes a drop-down list button. Clicking this button displays a list of your most recent actions. When you select an action from the drop-down list, you also undo all actions above it in the list. Immediately after you Undo an action, the Redo button is available so you can restore the action you just undid.

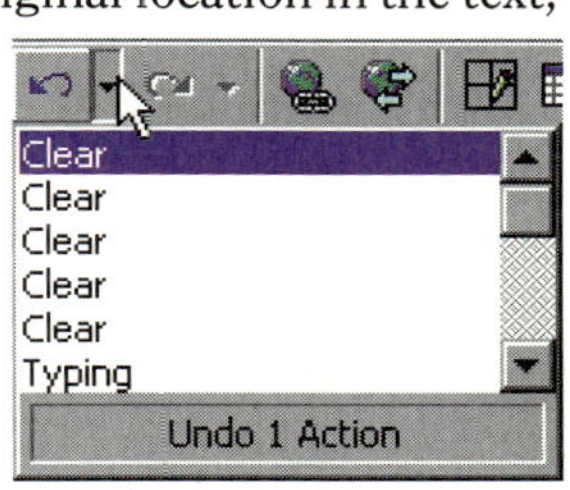

The Undo and Redo toolbar ScreenTips include the name of the feature that will be affected by their use.

The menu equivalent is **E**dit/**R**edo or Ctrl + Y.

- Click Redo.

The sentence is removed again. To reverse this action again,

If an action cannot be reversed, Can't Undo is displayed in the Edit menu.

- Click Undo.
- Enter your name in the closing on the line above "The Sports Company Manager."

Finally, you also do not need the extra pages that were included in this document to demonstrate how to move around a document. To select and delete the text from the insertion point to the end of the file,

You could also scroll to the end of the file and hold ⇧Shift while clicking to select all text between the current insertion point location and the end location.

- Move the insertion point to the line below the closing, "The Sports Company Manager."
- Press ⇧Shift + Ctrl + End.
- Press Delete.

The status bar now shows that the insertion point is positioned on page 1 of a one-page document.

Word keeps track of the last three locations where you entered or edited text. To quickly return to a previous editing location, press ⇧Shift + F5.

To review, the following editing keys have been covered:

Key	Button	Action
←Backspace		Deletes character to left of insertion point.
Delete		Deletes character to right of insertion point.
Ctrl + ←Backspace		Deletes word to left of insertion point.
Ctrl + Delete		Deletes word to right of insertion point.
↵Enter		Ends a line and moves insertion point to next line or inserts a blank line.
Edit/**U**ndo		Reverses your last action or command.
Edit/**R**edo		Reverses the effects of the Undo.

Documenting a File

Next you will add your own documentation to the file properties. To see the information associated with this file,

- Choose File/Properties.
- If necessary, open the General tab.

The Properties dialog box on your screen should be similar to Figure 1-21.

FIGURE 1-21

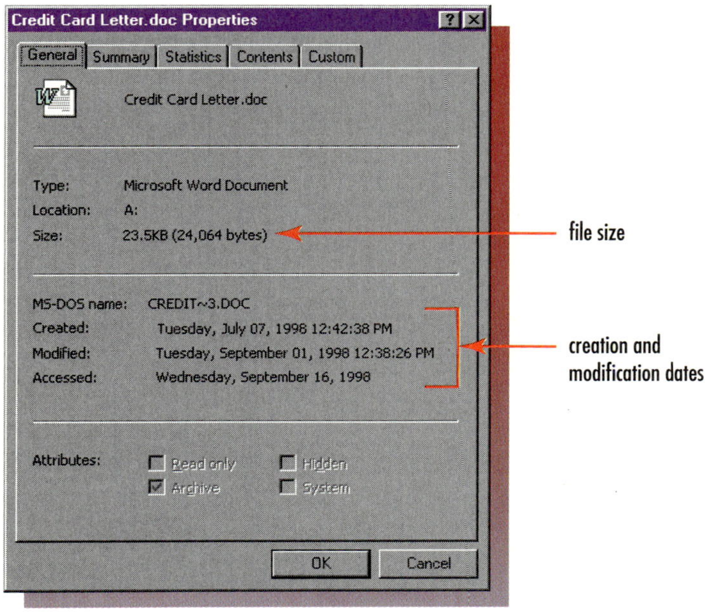

Each tab displays information about the document. The General tab displays basic information such as when the file was created and last modified, and the size of the file in bytes.

- Select each tab and look at the recorded information.

To make it easier to find files, you can add your own properties to the file using the Summary tab.

- Open the Summary tab.

The Summary Tab on your screen should be similar to Figure 1-22.

FIGURE 1-22

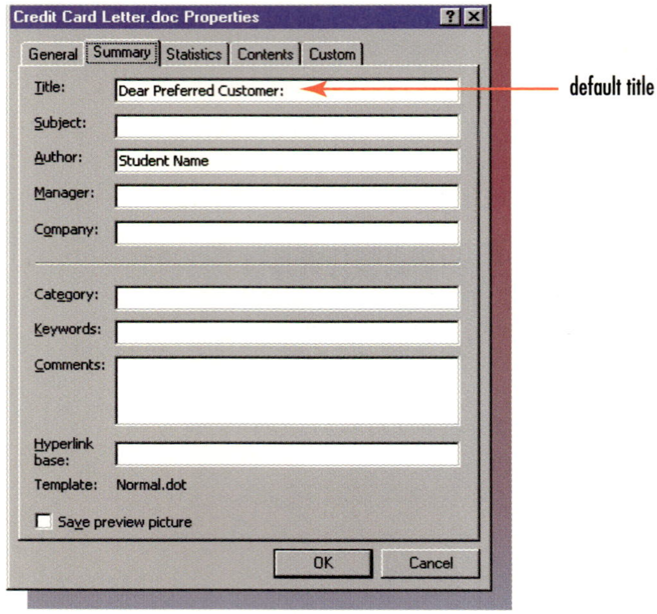

The Summary tab contains text boxes that allow you to enter a title, subject, author, keywords, and comments about the file. This information helps you locate the file you want to use as well as provides information about the objectives and use of the document. First you will enter a descriptive title for the document. By default, Word displays the first few words from the document as the default title. To replace the default title with your own title,

The title can be different from the actual file name.

- Select Dear Preferred Customer:
- Type **Credit Card Letter**
- Enter the following information in the text boxes indicated:

Use Tab both to move and to select the entry in a text box.

Subject:	**Letter to all new credit card holders**
Author:	**[your name]**
Company:	**The Sports Company**
Comments:	**First draft - [current date]**

The Author text box may be blank or show your school or some other name. Clear the existing contents first if necessary.

- Click OK.

Now you are ready to save the changes you have made to the file on your data disk using the Save or Save As commands on the File menu. The Save command or the Save button will save the document using the same file name. The Save As command allows you to save the current file using a new file name. Because you may want to redo this lab and use the Credit Card Letter file again, you will save your edited version using a new file name.

The keyboard shortcut for File/Save is Ctrl + S.

- Choose File/Save As.

The file name of the file you opened, Credit Card Letter, is displayed in the File Name text box of the Save As dialog box. To save the document as Credit Card Letter 1, you can type the new file name entirely, or you can edit the existing name. In this case, it is easier to edit the file name by adding the number 1 to the end of the name.

If you do not clear the highlight, the selected file name will be cleared and replaced with the new text as it is typed.

- Click at the end of the file name (before the file extension) to both clear the highlight and place the insertion point at the end of the name.
- Press Spacebar.
- Type **1**
- Click Save.

The new file name, Credit Card Letter 1, is displayed in the window title bar. The original document file is unchanged on your data disk.

Previewing and Printing a Document

Although you still plan to make several formatting changes to the document, you want to give a copy of the letter to the regional manager to get feedback regarding the content of the letter. Before printing, it is helpful to preview how the document will look when it is printed.

Concept 6: Document Preview

To save time and unnecessary printing and paper waste, it is always a good idea to preview onscreen how your document will appear when printed. The Print Preview feature displays each page of your document in a reduced size so you can see the layout. You can also make last-minute editing and formatting changes while previewing and then print directly from the Preview screen.

The menu equivalent is **F**ile/Print Pre**v**iew.

To preview the letter,

- Click Print Preview.

Your screen should be similar to Figure 1-23.

FIGURE 1-23

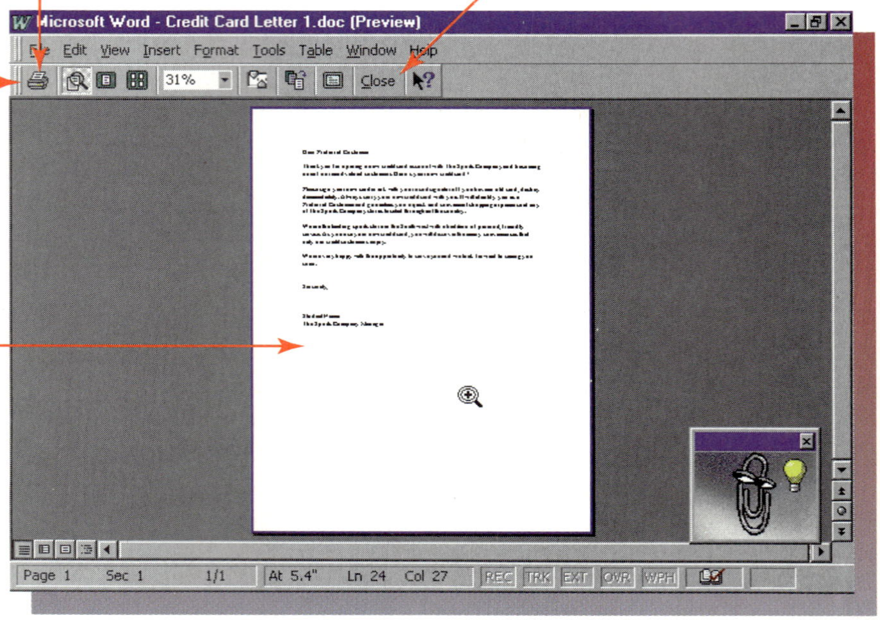

The Print Preview window displays a reduced view of how the current page will appear when printed. This view allows you to check your page layout before printing. The letter appears balanced within the left and right margins and does not appear to need any further modifications immediately.

This window also includes its own toolbar. You can print the letter directly from the Preview window using the Print button; however, this sends the document directly to the printer. Before printing, you need to check the print settings. To close the Print Preview window,

- Click Close.

The Print button on the Standard toolbar will also send the document directly to the printer. To check the print settings, you need to use the Print command on the File menu.

Please consult your instructor for printing procedures that may differ from the following directions.

- If necessary, make sure your printer is on and ready to print.
- Choose File/Print.

The keyboard shortcut for the Print command is Ctrl + P.

The Print dialog box on your screen should be similar to Figure 1-24.

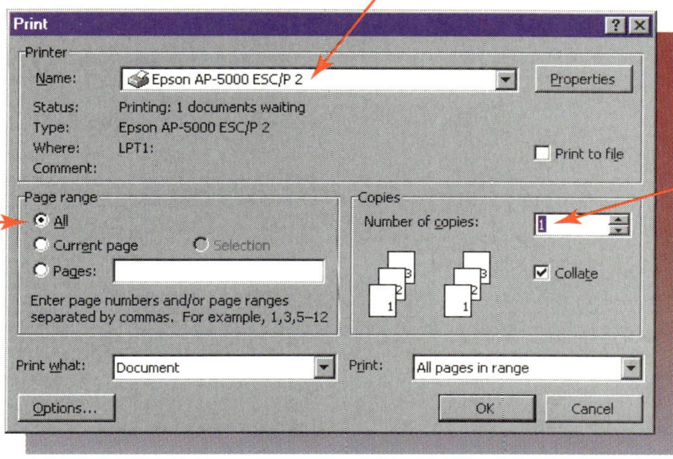

FIGURE 1-24

From the Print dialog box, you need to specify the printer you will be using and the document settings. The printer that is currently selected is displayed in the Name drop-down list box in the Printer section of the dialog box.

- If you need to change the selected printer to another printer, open the Name drop-down list box and select the appropriate printer (your instructor will tell you which printer to select).

The Page Range area of the Print dialog box lets you specify how much of the document you want printed. The range options are described in the following table:

Option	Action
All	Prints the entire document.
Current page	Prints selected page or the page the insertion point is on.
Pages	Prints pages you specify by typing page numbers in the text box.
Selection	Prints selected text only.

The default range setting, All, is the correct setting. In the Copies section, the default setting of one copy of the document is acceptable. To begin printing using the settings in the Print dialog box,

- Click OK.

Your printer should be printing out the current page of the document file. The printed copy of the credit card letter should be similar to the one shown at the beginning of the lab on page WP6.

Note: Your printed copy may not match exactly if the printer you selected uses a different font size from the one used to display the document on the screen. You will learn about fonts in the next lab.

Exiting Word

The keyboard shortcut for the Exit command is Alt + F4.

The Exit command on the File menu is used to quit the Word program. Alternatively, you can click the ☒ Close button in the application window title bar.

- Click ☒ Close.

The Windows 95 desktop is visible again.

WARNING!

To avoid losing data, always exit Word 97 using the Exit command or the ☒ Close button.

LAB REVIEW

Key Terms

AutoCorrect (WP14)
AutoText (WP14)
cursor (WP9)
custom dictionary (WP15)
default (WP12)
docked (WP9)
edit (WP11)
end-of-file marker (WP9)
floating (WP9)
format (WP11)
Formatting toolbar (WP9)
Insert mode (WP30)
insertion point (WP9)
main dictionary (WP15)
Office Assistant (WP9)
Overtype mode (WP30)
paragraph mark (WP32)
ruler (WP9)
select (WP34)
selection bar (WP20)
Standard toolbar (WP8)
status bar (WP9)
template (WP12)
word wrap (WP19)

Command Summary

Command	Shortcut Key	Button	Action
File/New	Ctrl + N		Opens new file
File/Open	Ctrl + O		Opens selected file
File/Close			Closes file
File/Save	Ctrl + S		Saves file using same file name
File/Save As			Saves file using a new file name
File/Properties			Shows properties of active document
File/Print Preview			Displays document as it will appear when printed
File/Print	Ctrl + P		Prints file using selected print settings
File/Exit	Alt + F4		Exits Word program
Edit/Undo	Ctrl + Z		Restores last editing change
Edit/Redo or Repeat	Ctrl + Y		Restores last Undo or repeats last command or action
Edit/Go To	Ctrl + G		Moves insertion point to specified location in document
View/Toolbars			Displays or hides selected toolbars
Tools/Customize/Options			Changes display options
Tools/Options/View/Spaces/Paragraph Marks		¶	Displays or hides special characters
Help/Microsoft Word Help	F1		Displays Office Assistant

Matching

1.  ______ **a.** new text writes over existing text
2. document template ______ **b.** deletes word to the right of the insertion point
3. Overtype ______ **c.** moves to the top of the document
4. Ctrl + ←Backspace ______ **d.** constant adjustment of text to fill in extra space in a line without exceeding the margin setting
5. .doc ______ **e.** displays help and tips to improve your efficiency as you work
6. Ctrl + Home ______ **f.** displays the Print Preview window
7. Office Assistant ______ **g.** a predesigned document that is used as a pattern to create many common types of documents
8.  ______ **h.** deletes word to the left of the insertion point
9. word wrap ______ **i.** Word document file extension
10. Ctrl + Delete ______ **j.** saves a document using the same file name

Fill-In Questions

1. Complete the following statements by filling in the blanks with the correct terms.

a. A(n) ______________________________ indicates a potential grammar error.

b. A(n) __________________________ is a predesigned document.

c. Name the first three steps in developing a document: _________________________, _________________________, and ___________________________.

d. Text can be entered in a document in either the _______________ or ________________ mode.

e. The ______________ key erases the character to the right of the insertion point.

f. The automatic ______________________ feature makes entering text in a document faster than typing on a typewriter.

g. The Word document file name extension is ______________________.

h. The ________________________ displays a tip about a more efficient or alternative method directly related to the procedure you are trying to perform.

i. Word inserts hidden ________________ into a document to control the display of text.

j. The _______________ feature automatically identifies and corrects certain types of errors.

2. In the following Word screen, letters identify important elements. Enter the correct term for each screen element in the space provided.

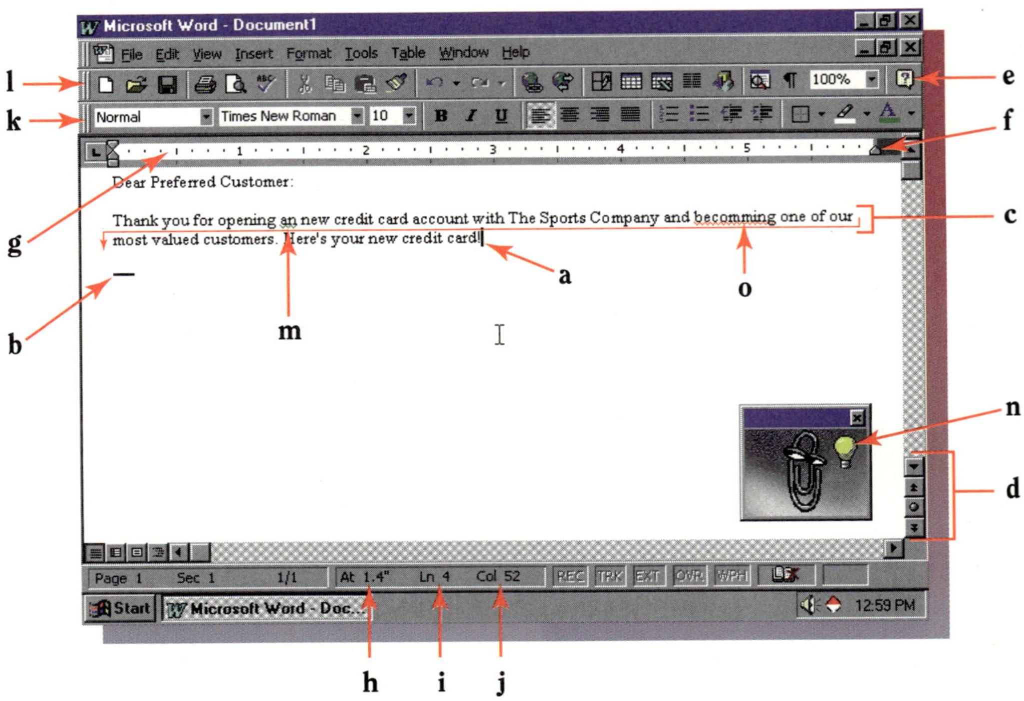

a. ______________________

b. ______________________

c. ______________________

d. ______________________

e. ______________________

f. ______________________

g. ______________________

h. ______________________

i. ______________________

j. ______________________

k. ______________________

l. ______________________

m. ______________________

n. ______________________

o. ______________________

3. The following screen identifies several errors and changes that need to be made to a document. From the list below, match the letter to the procedure that will make the change.

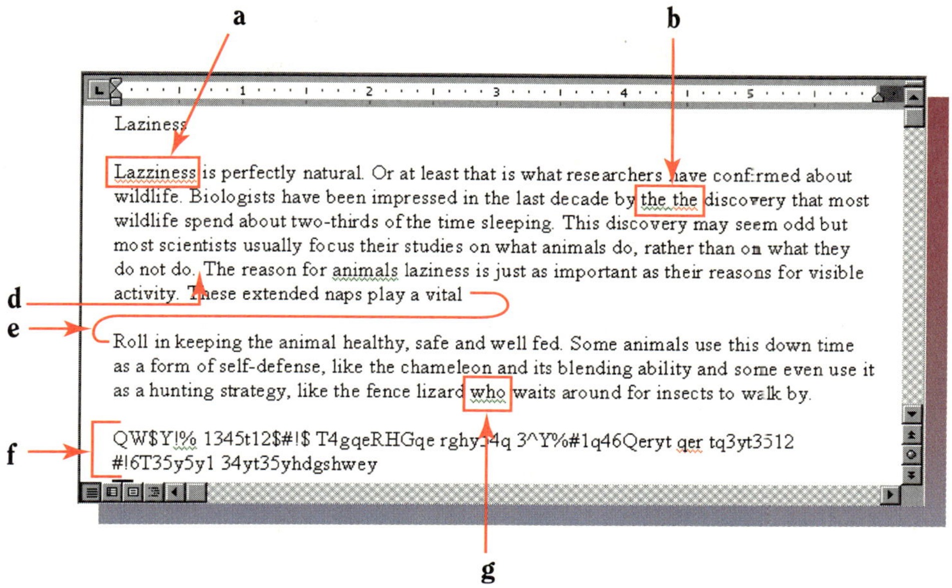

a. fix spelling	_______	Display the Grammar Shortcut menu and make necessary correction.
b. remove second "the"	_______	Display the Spelling Shortcut menu and select the correct spelling.
c. fix grammar	_______	Move to the letter "T" and press ←Enter twice.
d. begin new paragraph	_______	Display the Spelling Shortcut menu and select a better word.
e. combine with previous paragraph	_______	Display the Spelling Shortcut menu and select Delete Repeated Word.
f. delete paragraph	_______	Move to the letter r and press ←Backspace three times.
g. fix grammar	_______	Triple-click in the selection bar and press Delete.

Discussion Questions

1. Discuss several uses you may have for a word processor. Then explain the steps you would follow to create a document.

2. Discuss how the AutoCorrect and Spelling and Grammar Checker features help you as you type. What types of corrections does the AutoCorrect feature make?

3. Discuss how word wrap works. What happens when text is added? What happens when text is removed?

4. Discuss three ways you can select text. Discuss when it would be appropriate to use the different methods.

5. Describe how the Undo and Redo features work. What are some advantages of these features?

Hands-On Practice Exercises

Step by Step

Rating System
☆ Easy
☆☆ Moderate
☆☆☆ Difficult

☆

1. In this problem you will use the commands and features you learned in the lab to correct a document.

a. Open the file Corrections on your data disk. Follow the directions to edit the file, and reveal a saying found on the wall of a fix-it shop.

b. When you are finished, enter your name and the current date below the document. Save the file with the same name. Preview and print the document.

c. Delete the lines of instructions to reveal only the lines of the saying, your name, and the date. Combine the first four lines to form one paragraph.

d. Document the file by adding appropriate information to the Summary tab of the Properties dialog box. Save the document as Three Kinds of Jobs on your data disk. Preview and print the saying.

☆

2. The mouse is a standard hardware device that makes performing many tasks much quicker. In this problem you will edit a document about using a mouse.

a. Open the file Mouse Terms on your data disk. Use the editing techniques you learned in Lab 1 to correct the errors in the document.

b. Insert your name and current date below the document.

c. Document the file by adding appropriate information to the Summary tab of the Properties dialog box. Save the document as Mouse Terms 1. Preview and print the document.

You will continue this exercise as Practice Exercise 1 in Lab 2.

☆

3. Universal Industries has banned smoking in all buildings. Mr. Biggs, the CEO, has sent a memo informing employees of this policy.

a. Create the memo shown below. Press Tab after you type colons (:) in the To, From, Date, and RE lines. This will cause information following colons to line up evenly.

To: [Your Name]
From: Mr. Biggs
Date: [Current Date]
RE: No Smoking Policy

Effective next Monday, smoking will be banned in all buildings. Ashtrays will be placed outside each door, and smoking material must be extinguished before you enter.

Thank you for your cooperation in this matter.

JBB/xxx

b. Document the file by adding appropriate information to the Summary tab of the Properties dialog box. Save the document as No Smoking Memo on your data disk. Preview then print the memo.

You will complete this exercise as Practice Exercise 1 in Lab 3.

☆☆

4. You are in the process of compiling your grandmother's cookie recipes. You are going to pass the recipes on to several family members and friends who have requested them over the years. Following is a letter that you will enclose with the recipes.

a. Enter the letter as shown below, only pressing [←Enter] at the end of the paragraphs.

[Your Name]
[Street Address]
[City, State, Zip Code]
[Current Date]

Dear Friends and Family:

Enclosed, as promised, is a copy of Grandma Gertie's famous cookie recipes. We have all enjoyed them over the years, and it has been my pleasure to compile the recipes so you can continue to enjoy them for years to come.

For my next project, I would like to compile recipes from our own generation and pass them along, so we can pass them down. If you have any recipes that you would like to share with the rest of us, please send them to me at the above address.

Sincerely,

[Your Name]

b. Document the file by adding appropriate information to the Summary tab of the Properties dialog box. Save the document as Cookie Letter on your data disk. Preview then print the letter.

You will continue this exercise as Practice Exercise 3 in Lab 4.

☆☆

5. Here is the first of the cookie recipes that will be included in the collection referred to in the previous exercise.

a. Enter the recipe for potato chip cookies shown below.

Potato Chip Cookies

Potato chips give these cookies a crunchy texture and eliminate the need for baking soda.

Ingredients:
2 sticks of butter (softened)
½ c. dark brown sugar (firmly packed)
½ c. crushed potato chips
1 tsp. vanilla extract
½ c. sifted flour
confectioner's sugar

Directions:
Cream the butter and brown sugar together.
Add vanilla, chips, and nuts.
Gradually add the flour. Mix thoroughly.
Cover and chill the dough for at least 1 hour.
Roll dough into 1" balls, and roll in confectioner's sugar.
Place 1" apart on greased cookie sheet.
Bake in 350 degree oven for 12–15 minutes.
This recipe makes about 3-½ dozen cookies.

b. Insert a blank line between the crushed potato chips and the vanilla extract in the Ingredients section. Add "½ c. chopped pecans" to the list of ingredients.

c. Enter your name and the current date below the recipe.

d. Document the file by adding appropriate information to the Summary tab of the Properties dialog box. Save the document as Potato Chip Cookies on your data disk. Preview and then print the recipe.

You will continue to add more recipes to your collection in Practice Exercise 3 in Lab 2.

On Your Own

☆☆

6. You are about to open a bed and breakfast inn in the Pocono Mountains. You are going to advertise the B&B in a local travel guide. Type the following information to create the first draft of the ad.

> **Pocono Mountain Retreat**
> **124 Mountain Laurel Trail**
> **Pocono Manor, PA 18349**
>
> **Phone: 1-717-839-5555**
> **Host: [Your Name]**
>
> **Number of Rooms: 4**
> **Number of private baths: 1**
> **Maximum number sharing baths: 4**
> **Double rate for shared bath: $85.00**
> **Double rate for private bath: $95.00**
> **Single rate for shared bath: $65.00**
> **Single rate for private bath: $75.00**
> **Open: All year**
> **Breakfast: Continental**
> **Children: Welcome, over 12**
> **Smoking: No**
> **Social Drinking: Permitted**
>
> **Located in the heart of the Poconos is this rustic country inn where you can choose to indulge yourself in the quiet beauty of the immediate surroundings or take advantage of the numerous activities at nearby resorts, lakes, and parks.**
>
> **In the winter, shuttle buses will transport you to the Jack Frost and Big Boulder ski resorts. We have trails for cross-country skiing right on the property, and we will take you for a ride in our horse-drawn sleigh. In the summer, you can be whisked away to beautiful Lake Wallenpaupack for swimming and boating. The fall foliage is beyond compare, and you can hike our nature trails and take in the breathtaking scenery at this, or any time of year.**
>
> **In the evenings, you can relax in front of a cozy fire or take advantage of the swinging nightlife in the Poconos. The choice is yours!**
>
> **We have literature concerning all areas of interest in the Poconos. You can design your own custom tour, and Ed, our resident guide, will provide the transportation.**
>
> **Be sure to call well in advance for reservations during the winter and summer months.**

Insert the text "Pets: No" above "Children: Welcome, over 12." Enter the current date below the ad. Document the file by adding appropriate information to the Summary tab of the Properties dialog box. Save the document as B&B Ad on your data disk. Print the ad.

You will continue this exercise as Practice Exercise 4 in Lab 2.

☆☆☆

7. Toward the end of each set of Practice Exercises in each lab, you can complete a problem that will help you prepare for a job interview. This lab's exercise helps you create a cover letter. In Lab 2 you can create a list of tips on how to prepare for an interview. In Lab 3 you can create a document that tells what should be included in a resume and cover letter. In Lab 4 you merge the cover letter and create the resume.

Much of the information contained in these exercises was extracted from *The Work Book* by Barbara N. Price, Ph.D., Director of Career Planning and Placement, Luzerne County Community College, Nanticoke, PA.

Use the format on the next page as a guide to creating a cover letter.

[Your Street Address]
[City, State, Zip Code]

[Date of Writing]

Mr. John Doe
[Job Title]
[Company]
[Street Address]
[City, State, Zip Code]

Dear Mr. Doe:

Tell why you are writing; name the position, field, or general occupational area that you are asking about; if you know of a specific job opening, mention it. When responding to an advertisement, be sure to include the name and date of the publication in which it was placed. If referred by a contact person, mention that fact and include the person's name in your opening sentence.

Mention one or two qualifications you think would be of greatest interest to the employer, slanting your remarks to his/her point of view. Tell why you are particularly interested in his/her company, location, or type of work. If you have had related experience or specialized training, be sure to point it out.

Refer the reader to the enclosed resume, application, or the medium that gives information concerning your qualifications. Close by making a specific request for an interview. Make sure your closing is not vague, but makes a specific action from the reader likely.

Sincerely,

[Your handwritten signature]

[Your Name]

ENCL.

Document the file by adding appropriate information to the Summary tab of the Properties dialog box. Save the document as Cover Letter on your data disk. Print the document.

You will continue this exercise as Practice Exercise 8 in Lab 4.

1 Creating and Editing a Document

Document Development

The development of a document follows several steps: plan, enter, edit, format, and preview and print.

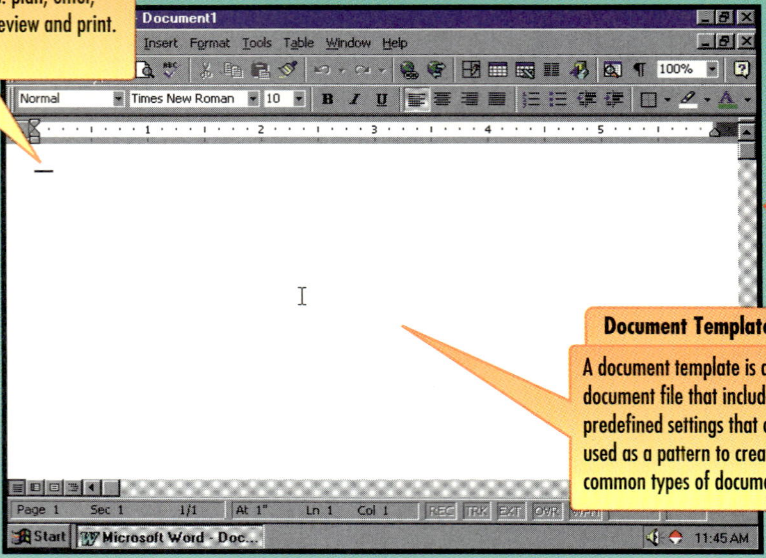

Document Template

A document template is a document file that includes predefined settings that can be used as a pattern to create many common types of documents.

AutoCorrect

The AutoCorrect feature makes some basic assumptions about the text you are typing and, based on these assumptions, automatically identifies and/or corrects the entry as you type.

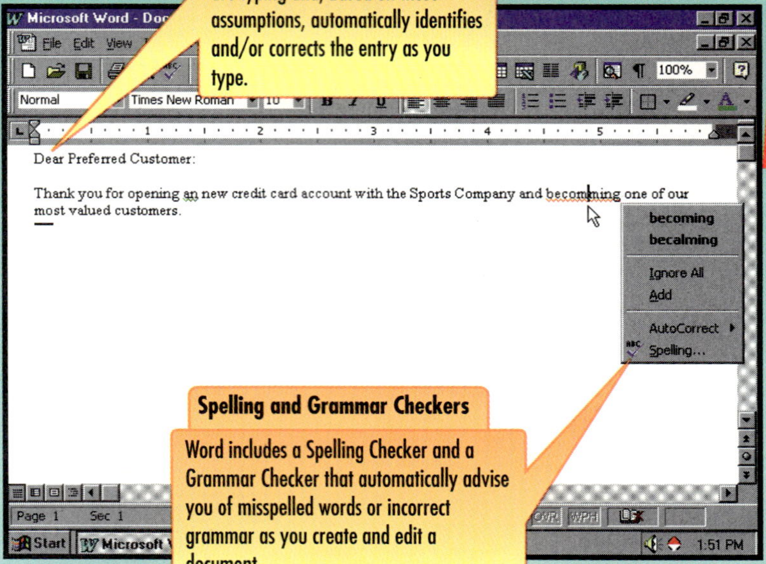

Spelling and Grammar Checkers

Word includes a Spelling Checker and a Grammar Checker that automatically advise you of misspelled words or incorrect grammar as you create and edit a document.

Concepts

- Document Development
- Document Template
- AutoCorrect
- Spelling and Grammar Checkers
- WordWrap
- Document Preview

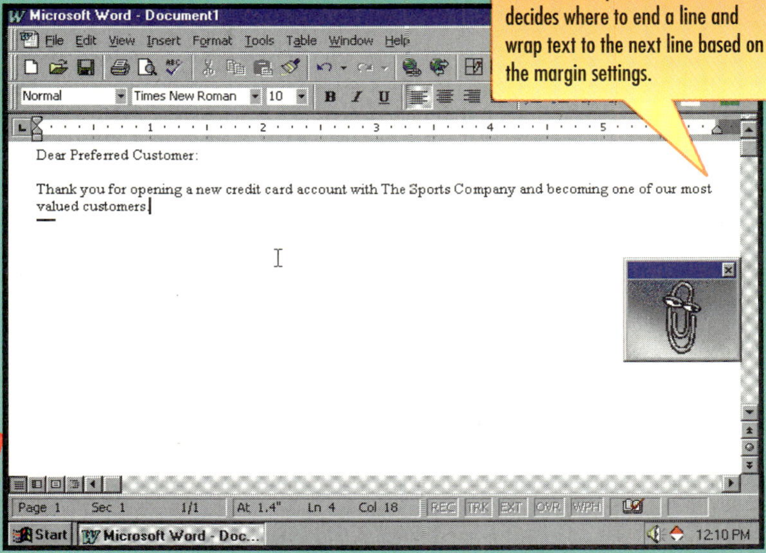

Word Wrap

The word wrap feature automatically decides where to end a line and wrap text to the next line based on the margin settings.

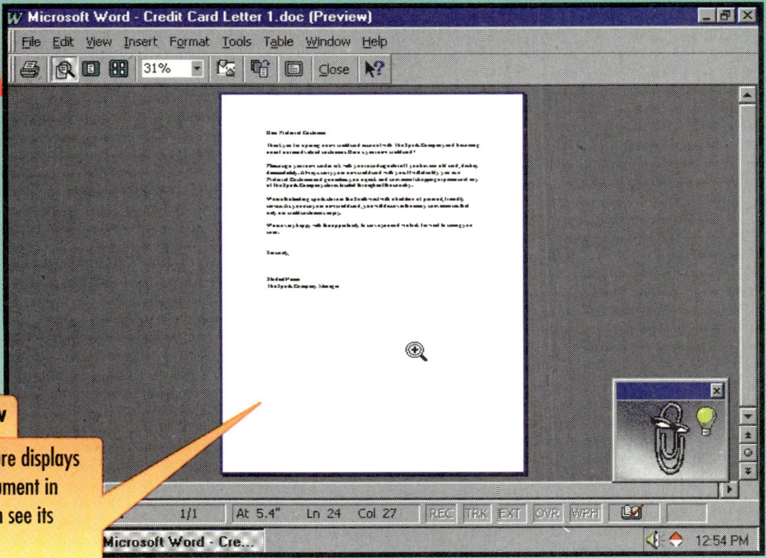

Document Preview

The Print Preview feature displays each page of your document in reduced size so you can see its layout.

2 Formatting a Document

COMPETENCIES

After completing this lab, you will know how to:

1. Check spelling and grammar.
2. Move selected text.
3. Replace selected text.
4. Use the Find and Replace feature.
5. Use drag and drop.
6. Use the Thesaurus.
7. Use the Date and Time command.
8. Set margins.
9. Change document views.
10. Indent paragraphs.
11. Create an itemized list.
12. Change the character formatting.
13. Set paragraph alignment.
14. Edit in Print Preview.

CASE STUDY

After editing the rough draft of the credit card letter, you showed it to The Sports Company regional manager. The manager wants the letter to include information about The Sports Company newsletter and a first-purchase discount when customers use their new credit card. In addition, the manager has made several suggestions on how to improve the letter's style and appearance.

You will use many of the formatting features included in Word 97 to add style and interest to the credit card letter. You will see how using these features greatly improves the appearance and design of the letter. The result is that the letter not only looks better — it also conveys the message more clearly. The completed letter to new credit card customers is shown here.

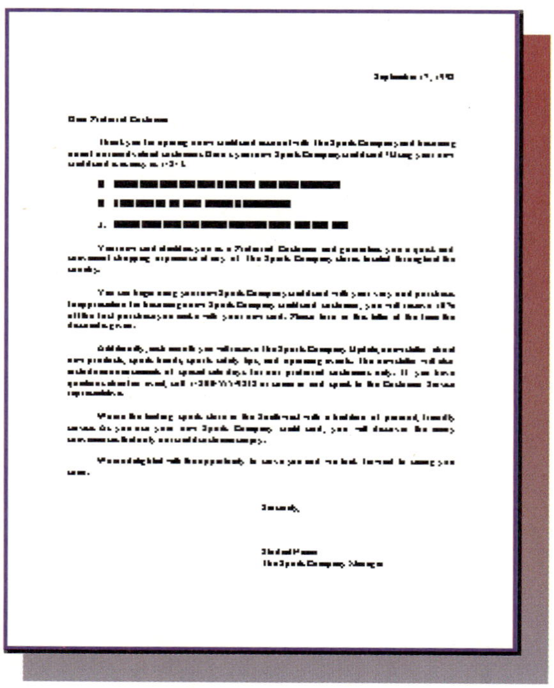

Concept Overview

The following concepts will be introduced in this lab:

1. Move and Copy	Selections can be moved or copied to new locations in a document, saving you time by not having to retype the same information.
2. Find and Replace	To make editing easier, you can use the Find and Replace feature to find text in a document and automatically replace it with other text.
3. Thesaurus	Word's Thesaurus is a reference tool that provides synonyms, antonyms, and related words for a selected word or phrase.
4. Fields	A field is a placeholder that instructs Word to insert information into a document.
5. Margins	The margin is the distance from the text to the edge of the paper. Standard single-sided documents have four margins: top, bottom, left, and right.
6. Document Views	You can view a Word document in eight different ways. Each view offers different features for working with your documents.
7. Indents	To help your reader find information quickly, you can indent paragraphs from the margins. Indenting paragraphs sets them off from the rest of the document.
8. Bulleted and Numbered Lists	Whenever possible, use bulleted or numbered lists to organize information and make your writing clear and easy to read.
9. Fonts	A font, also commonly referred to as a typeface, is a set of characters with a specific design.
10. Character Effects	Different character effects can be applied to selections to add emphasis or interest to a document.
11. Paragraph Alignment	Alignment is how text is positioned on a line between the margins or indents. There are four types of paragraph alignment: left, center, right, and justified.

Part 1

Checking Spelling and Grammar

The regional manager noted changes to be made to the credit card letter (shown in the marked-up copy on the next page) and suggested the content for the two paragraphs about the newsletter and discount to be incorporated into the credit card letter. You hastily added the two new paragraphs to the letter.

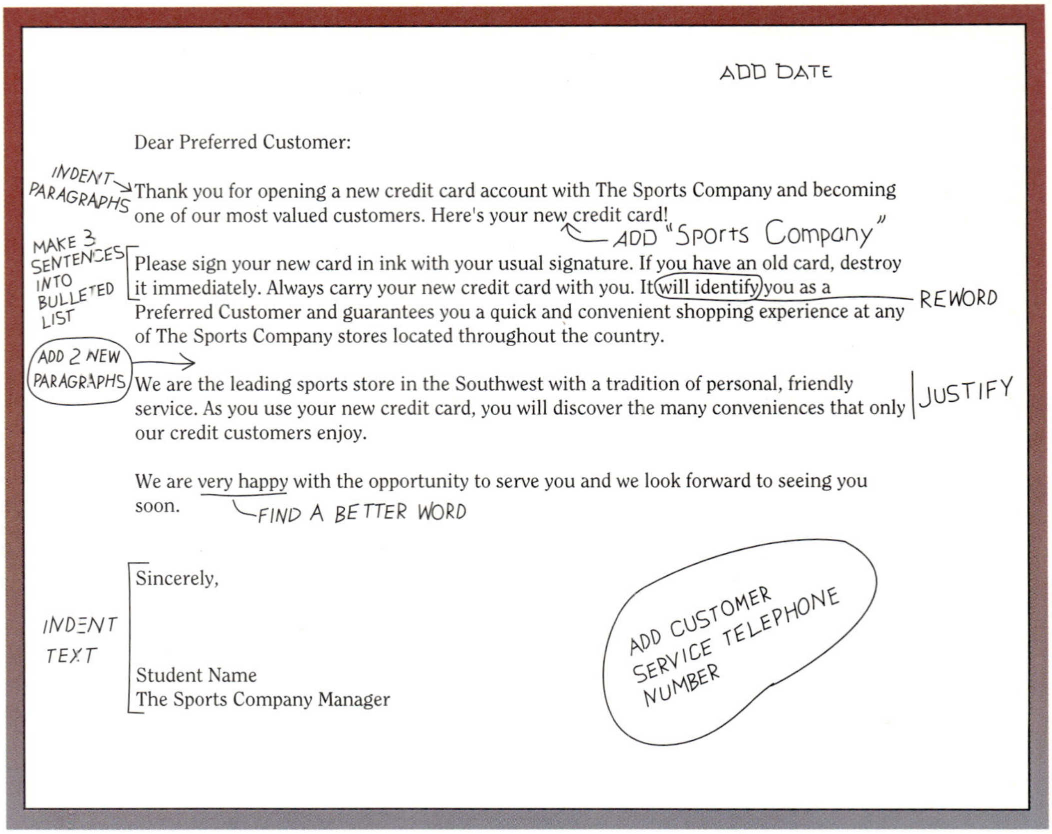

Dear Preferred Customer:

Thank you for opening a new credit card account with The Sports Company and becoming one of our most valued customers. Here's your new credit card!

Please sign your new card in ink with your usual signature. If you have an old card, destroy it immediately. Always carry your new credit card with you. It will identify you as a Preferred Customer and guarantees you a quick and convenient shopping experience at any of The Sports Company stores located throughout the country.

We are the leading sports store in the Southwest with a tradition of personal, friendly service. As you use your new credit card, you will discover the many conveniences that only our credit customers enjoy.

We are very happy with the opportunity to serve you and we look forward to seeing you soon.

Sincerely,

Student Name
The Sports Company Manager

- Load Word 97. Put your data disk in drive A (or the appropriate drive for your system).
- Open the file Revised Credit Card Letter.

> The text will not display the Office Assistant throughout the remaining labs.

As you are reading the document, you see that Word has identified several typing and grammar errors in the new paragraphs. To correct the misspelled words and grammatical errors, you can use the Shortcut menu to correct each individual word or error, as you learned in Lab 1. However, in many cases you may find it more efficient to wait until you are finished writing before you correct any spelling or grammatical errors. Rather than continually breaking your train of thought to correct errors as you type, you can use the Spelling and Grammar tool to check and correct all the words in the document at once.

> The menu equivalent is Tools/Spelling and Grammar, and the keyboard shortcut is F7.

- Click Spelling and Grammar.

Your screen should be similar to Figure 2-1.

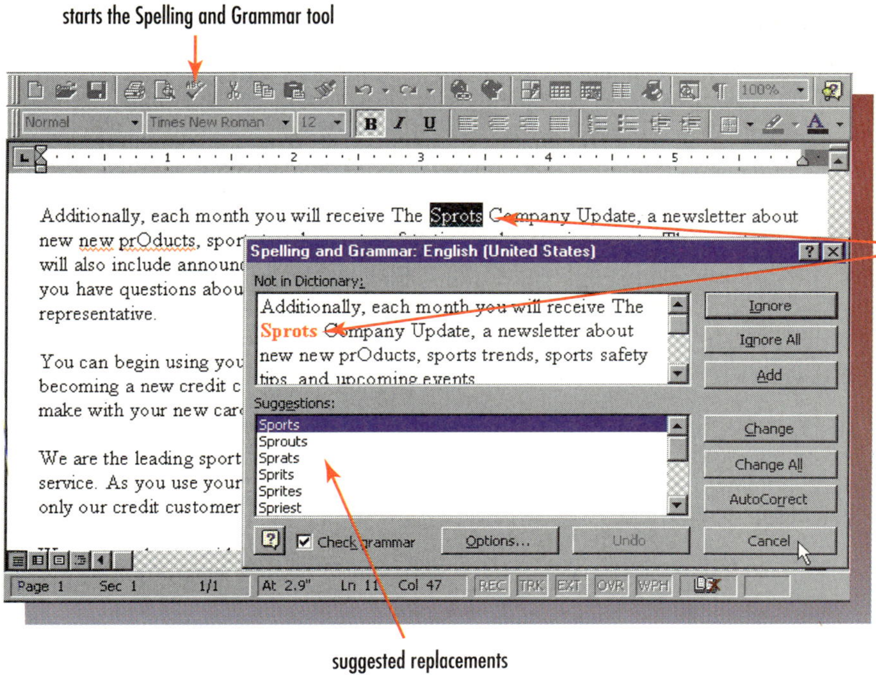

FIGURE 2-1

The Spelling and Grammar dialog box is displayed, and the Spelling and Grammar tool has immediately located the first word that may be misspelled. It displays the sentence with the misspelled word "Sprots" in red in the Not in Dictionary text box and highlights it in the document.

The Suggestions list box displays the words the Spelling tool has located in the dictionary that most closely match the misspelled word. The first word is highlighted. Sometimes the Spelling tool does not display any suggested replacements because it cannot locate any words in its dictionary that are similar in spelling. If there are no suggestions, the Not in Dictionary text box simply displays the word that is highlighted in the text.

To tell the Spelling tool what to do, you need to choose from the six option buttons. They have the following effects:

Button	Effect
Ignore	Accepts word as correct for this occurrence only.
Ignore All	Accepts word as correct throughout the spell checking of the document.
Add	Adds word to the custom dictionary. The Spelling tool will always accept an added word as correct.
Change	Replaces word with the selected word in the suggestions box.
Change All	Replaces same word throughout the document with the word in the suggestions text box.
AutoCorrect	Adds word to the AutoCorrect list so Word can correct misspellings of it automatically as you type.

The Check Grammar check box is used to turn the grammar-check feature on or off. If it is not checked,

- Select Check grammar.

To change the spelling of the word to one of the suggested spellings, highlight the correct word in the list and then choose Change. If there were no suggested replacements, and you did not want to use any of the option buttons, you could edit the word yourself by typing the correction in the Not in Dictionary box. Because "Sports" is already highlighted and is the correct replacement,

You can also press ↵Enter or double-click on the correctly spelled word in the Suggestions list to both select it and choose Change.

- Click Change.

The Spelling Checker replaces the misspelled word with the selected suggested replacement and moves on to locate the next error.

- Continue to respond to the Spelling and Grammar checker by selecting the action shown below in response to the identified error:

Identified Error	Cause	Action	Result
new	Repeated word	Delete	Duplicate word "new" is deleted
prOducts	Inconsistent capitalization	Change	products
a event	Grammatical error	Change	an
received	Incorrect verb form	Change	receive
discount are	Subject-verb disagreement	Change	discount is

There should be no other misspelled words or grammatical errors. However, if the Spelling and Grammar tool encounters others in your file, correct them as needed. When no others are located, a message appears telling you that the spelling and grammar check is complete.

If the Office Assistant displays the message, it disappears automatically.

- Click OK.

Moving Selected Text

After looking over the credit card letter, you decide to change the order of the paragraphs. You want the paragraph about the 10 percent discount (fourth paragraph) to follow the second paragraph. To do this, you will move the paragraph from its current location to the new location.

Concept 1: Move and Copy

Selections can be moved or copied to new locations in a document, saving you time by not having to retype the same information. A selection that is moved is deleted (cut) from its original location, called the **source**, and inserted (pasted) in a new location, called the **destination**, in the document. Selections that are copied are duplicated (copied) and pasted. When you cut or copy selections, the contents are stored in the Clipboard. Then when they are pasted to the new location, the Clipboard contents are copied to the location of the insertion point in the document. You can move and copy within or between document files.

The Clipboard is a temporary storage area in Windows 95.

There are several methods you can use to move and copy selections. One method is to use the Cut, Copy, and Paste commands on the Edit menu. You will use the Shortcut menu to select the Cut command. This menu displays options related to the current selection.

The Cut shortcuts are [Cut button] or Ctrl + X, the Copy shortcuts are [Copy button] or Ctrl + C, and the Paste shortcuts are [Paste button] or Ctrl + V.

- Select the paragraph beginning with "You can . . ."
- Display the Shortcut menu for the selected paragraph.
- Select [Cut button] Cut.
- Delete the extra blank line.

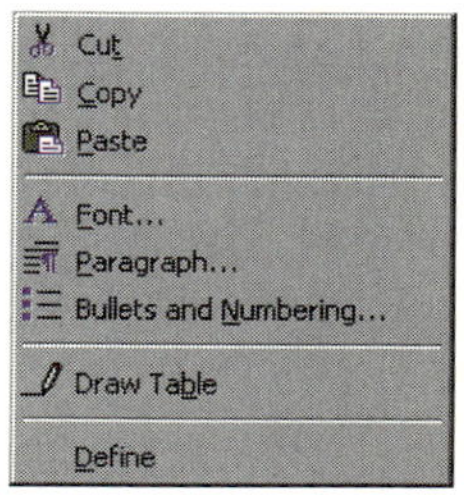

Reminder: Drag or double-click in the selection bar next to the paragraph to select it.

Reminder: Point to the selected text while right-clicking or press Shift + F10 to display the Shortcut menu.

The selected paragraph is removed from the document and copied to the Clipboard. Next you need to move the insertion point to the destination location where the text will be inserted and paste the text into the document from the Clipboard.

- Move to the A in "Additionally" (first sentence, third paragraph).
- Click [Paste button] Paste.
- Insert a blank line between the paragraphs.

You can also choose Paste from the Shortcut menu.

Your screen should be similar to Figure 2-2.

FIGURE 2-2

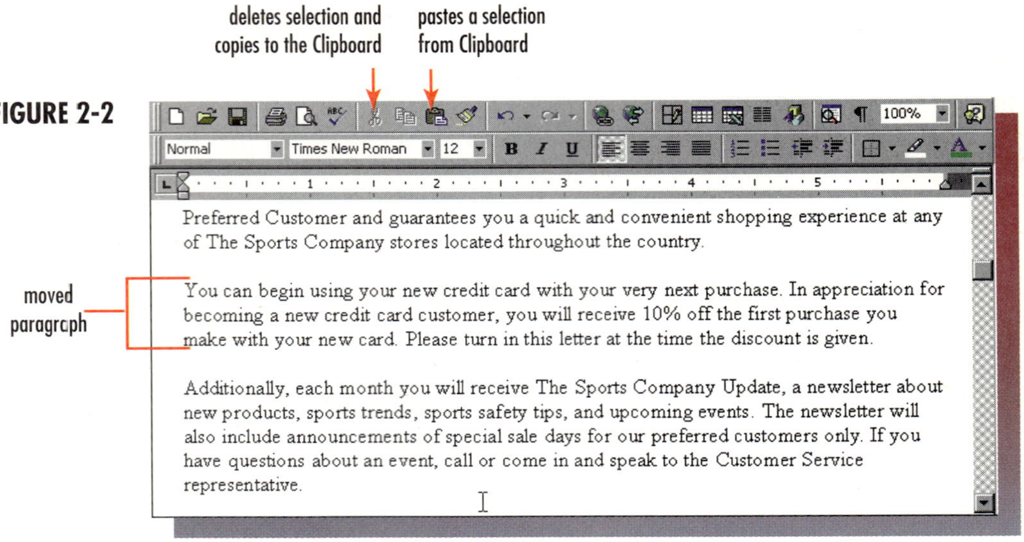

The deleted paragraph is reentered into the document at the insertion point location. That was a lot quicker than retyping the whole paragraph!

Replacing Selected Text

As you continue checking the letter, you want to make several text changes suggested by the regional manager. First you will reword the last sentence of the second paragraph. Instead of "It will identify you as a . . ." you would like it to say, "Your new credit card identifies you as a . . . ." Because the part you want to replace is shorter than the new text, Overtype mode will cut off some of the text you want to keep. By first selecting the text you want to remove and then typing in the new text, the part you want to keep will not be affected.

- Select "It will identify" (second paragraph, fourth sentence).
- Type **Your new card identifies**

The selected text was deleted as soon as you began to type the new text.

Using the Find and Replace Feature

The next item you want to change is to replace all occurrences of the words "new credit card" in the letter with "new Sports Company credit card" where appropriate. This process is very quick and easy using the Find and Replace feature.

Concept 2: Find and Replace

To make editing easier, you can use the Find and Replace feature to find text in a document and automatically replace it with other text. For example, suppose you created a lengthy document describing the type of clothing and equipment you need to set up a world-class home gym. You decide to change "sneakers" to "athletic shoes." Instead of deleting every occurrence of "sneakers" and typing "athletic shoes," you can use the Find and Replace feature to perform the task automatically. You can also find occurrences of special formatting, such as replacing bold text with italicized text, and special characters. This feature is fast and accurate; however, use care when replacing so that you do not replace unintended matches.

The Edit/Find command or Ctrl + F simply locates but does not replace specified text.

The Replace command on the Edit menu is used to find and replace text. Word will search for all occurrences of words beginning at the insertion point. If the search does not begin at the top of the document, when Word reaches the end of the document it asks if you want to continue searching from the beginning of the document. You can also highlight text to restrict the search to the selection.

To start the search at the beginning of the letter,

- Press Ctrl + Home.
- Choose Edit/Replace.
- Click More.

The keyboard shortcut for the Replace command is Ctrl + H.

The More button displays the advanced search and replace criteria.

You also could click [button], then select [button] to open the Find and Replace dialog box.

The Replace tab of the Find and Replace dialog box on your screen should be similar to Figure 2-3.

FIGURE 2-3

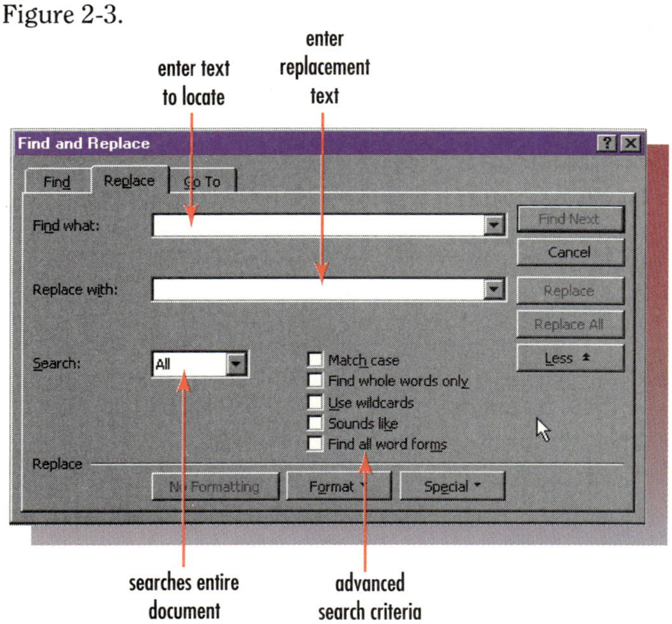

In the Find What text box, you enter the text you want to locate. In addition, you can use the options shown below to refine the search. These options can be combined in many ways to help you find and replace text in documents.

Option	Effect on Text
Match case	Replaces words and retains the capitalization.
Find whole words only	For example, finds "cat" only and not "catastrophe" too.
Use wildcards	Fine-tunes a search; for example, c?t finds "cat" and "cot," while c*t finds "cat" and "catastrophe."
Sounds like	Finds words that sound like the word you type; very helpful if you do not know the correct spelling of the word you want to find.
Find all word forms	Finds and replaces all forms of a word; for example, "buy" will replace "purchase" and "bought" will replace "purchased."

> Word may display the last text entered in the text boxes. In addition, the four most recent text entries can be displayed by opening the drop-down lists. If the existing entry is already correct, you do not need to retype it.

> After entering the text to find, do not press [←Enter] or this will choose [Find Next] and the search will begin.

When you enter the text to find, you can type everything lowercase, because the Match Case option is not selected. If Match Case is not selected, the search will not be **case sensitive**. This means that lowercase letters will match both upper- and lowercase letters in the text. The text you want to replace is entered in the Replace With text box. The replacement text must be entered exactly as you want it to appear in your document.

- Type **new credit card** (do not press [←Enter]).
- Press [Tab].
- Type **new Sports Company credit card**

The default search selection is All, which means Word will search the entire document, including headers and footers. You can also choose to search up and down the document, which excludes the headers and footers. Because you want to search the entire document, All is the appropriate setting. To hide the display of the advanced criteria and begin the search,

> The [Less] button hides the advanced search criteria.

- Click [Less].
- Click [Find Next].

Immediately the insertion point moves to the first occurrence of text in the document that matches the Find text and highlights it.

Your screen should be similar to Figure 2-4.

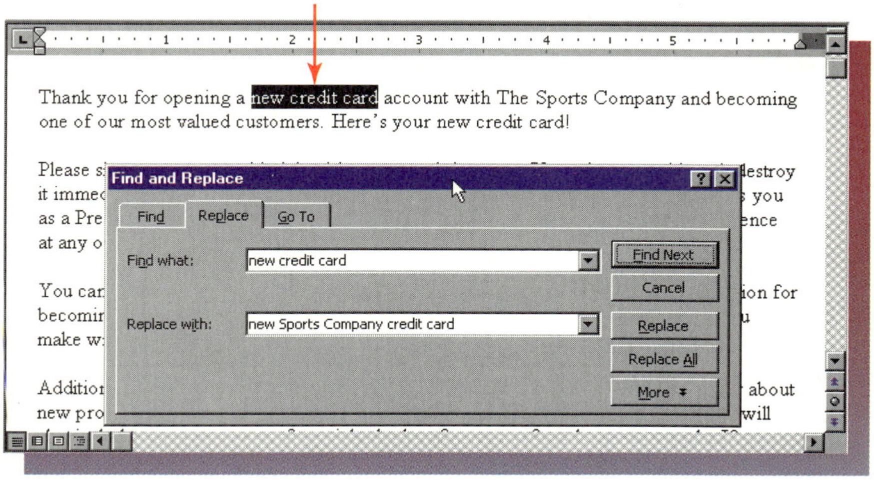

FIGURE 2-4

> If necessary, move the dialog box so you can see the located text.

You do not, however, want to replace this text, because the company name would appear twice in the same sentence. To tell the program to continue the search without replacing the highlighted text,

- Click Find Next.

Word immediately locates a second occurrence of the Find text. To replace this text with the replacement text,

- Click Replace.

- In the same manner, replace the rest of the located occurrences.

> Do not use Replace All, because it will replace all occurrences including the one you skipped.

If you are changing all the occurrences, it is much faster to use Replace All. Exercise care when using Replace All, however, because the search text you specify might be part of another word and you may accidentally replace text you want to keep. When Word has completed the search, a message is displayed advising you that Word has finished searching the document.

> When using the Find command, you can close the dialog box and use the and buttons to find the previous or next occurrence of the text.

- If necessary, close the message box, then close the Find and Replace dialog box.

> If the Office Assistant displays the message, it disappears automatically.

Using Drag and Drop

Next you want to add the telephone number of the Customer Service Department to the letter. You want it to follow the reference to the Customer Service representative in the last sentence of the fourth paragraph.

- Enter **(1-800-555-9838)** before the period of the last sentence in the fourth paragraph.

After looking at the sentence, you decide you would like to move the telephone number to follow the word "call" in the same sentence. Word also includes a

To use drag and drop to copy a selection, hold down Ctrl while dragging. The pointer shape is .

drag and drop editing feature that can be used to move or copy selections. It is most useful for copying or moving short distances in a document. To use drag and drop to move a selection, point to the selection and drag the pointer to the location where you want the selection inserted. The I-beam attached to the pointer shows you where the text will be placed.

- Select the telephone number, excluding the parentheses.
- Drag the selection to the space after "call" in the same sentence.
- Correct the spacing as necessary around the telephone number and delete the parentheses at the end of the sentence.

Your screen should be similar to Figure 2-5.

FIGURE 2-5

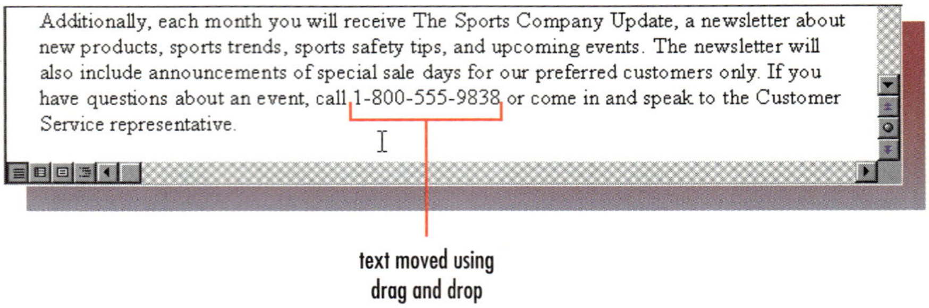

Using the Thesaurus

The next text change you want to make is to find a better word for "happy" in the last sentence of the letter. To help find a similar word, you will use the Thesaurus tool.

Concept 3: Thesaurus

Word's **Thesaurus** is a reference tool that provides synonyms, antonyms, and related words for a selected word or phrase. Synonyms are words with a similar meaning, such as "cheerful" and "happy." Antonyms are words with an opposite meaning, such as "cheerful" and "sad." Related words are words that are variations of the same word, such as "cheerful" and "cheer." The Word Thesaurus can help to liven up your documents by adding interest and variety to your text.

The keyboard shortcut is ⇧Shift + F7.

To identify the word you want looked up and to use the Thesaurus,

- Move to anywhere in the word "happy" (last paragraph).
- Choose Tools/Language/Thesaurus.

Your screen should be similar to Figure 2-6.

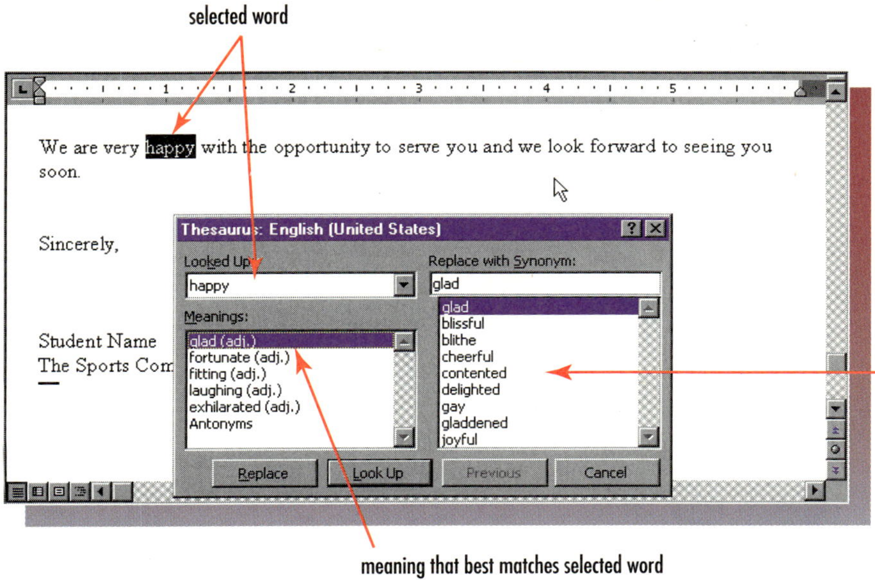

FIGURE 2-6

The Thesaurus dialog box displays a list of possible meanings for the looked-up word. From this list you can select the most appropriate meaning for the word. The highlighted word "glad" is appropriate for this sentence. The words in the Replace with Synonym box are synonyms for the word "happy" with a meaning of "glad." The best choice from this list is "delighted." To replace "happy" with "delighted,"

If a synonym, antonym, or related word is not found, the Thesaurus displays an alphabetical list of entries that are similar in spelling to the selected word.

- Select delighted.
- Click Replace.
- Remove the word "very" from the sentence.

Using the Date Command

The last text change you need to make is to add the date to the letter. You want to enter the date on the first line of the letter four lines above the salutation. The Date and Time command on the Insert menu inserts into your document the current date as maintained by your computer system.

Reminder: Use Ctrl + Home to quickly move to the top of a document.

- Move to the D in "Dear" at the top of the letter.
- Insert four blank lines and move to the first blank line.
- Choose Insert/Date and Time.

The Date and Time dialog box on your screen should be similar to Figure 2-7.

FIGURE 2-7

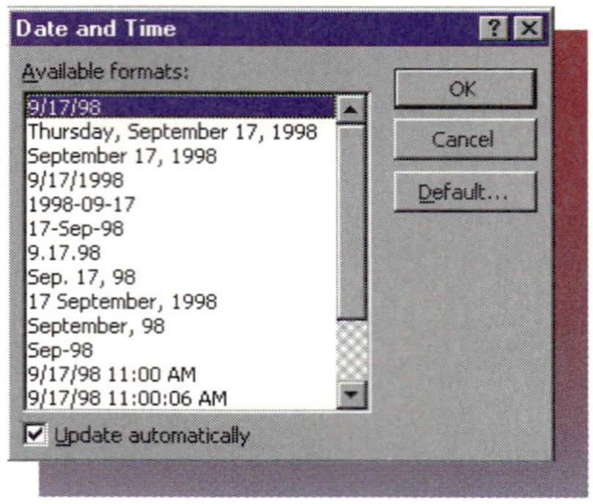

The Available Formats list box displays the format styles for the current date and time. You want to display the date in the format Month XX, 199X. This format is the third setting in the list.

You also want the date to be updated automatically whenever the letter is sent to a new credit card customer. The Update Automatically option is used to do this by entering the date as a field.

Concept 4: Fields

A **field** is a placeholder that instructs Word to insert information into a document. The **field code** contains the directions that tell Word what type of information to insert. The information that is displayed as a result of the field code is called the **field result**. Many field codes are automatically inserted when you use certain commands. Others you can create and insert yourself. Many fields update automatically when the document changes. Using fields makes it easier and faster to perform many common or repetitive tasks.

Alt + Shift + D will insert the current date as a field in the format MM/DD/YY.

- Select the third format setting.
- If necessary, select Update Automatically.
- Click OK.

Although the date appears as text, it is a field. To see this,

- Press ←.

Your screen should be similar to Figure 2-8.

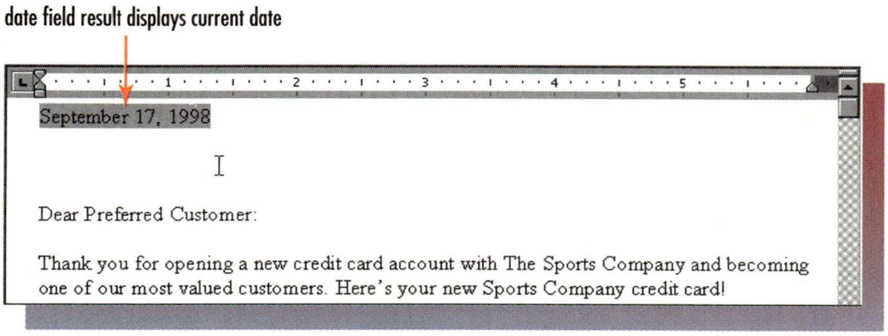

FIGURE 2-8

The date in Figure 2-8 will be different from the date that appears on your screen.

The entire date is shaded, indicating that the insertion point is positioned on a field entry. Whenever this file is printed, Word will print the current system date using this format.

The field code can be viewed by displaying the field's Shortcut menu and choosing Toggle Field Codes.

Note: If you are ending your session now, replace Student Name with your name in the closing and save the file as Revised Credit Card Letter 2. Print the letter. When you begin Part 2, open this file.

Part 2

Setting Margins

Next the regional manager has suggested that you make several formatting changes to improve the appearance of the letter. The first change you will make is to reduce the size of the margins.

Concept 5: Margins

The **margin** is the distance from the text to the edge of the paper. Standard single-sided documents have four margins: top, bottom, left, and right. Double-sided documents also have four margins: top, bottom, inside, and outside.

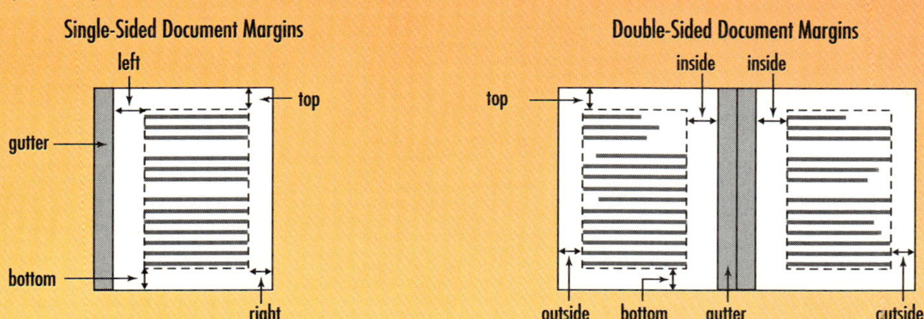

You can also set a gutter margin that reserves space in the left or inside margin to accommodate binding. There are also special margin settings for headers and footers. You will learn about these features in Lab 3. The default left and right margins are set at 1.25 inches and the top and bottom margins at 1 inch. You can set different margin widths to alter the appearance of the document.

You would like to see how the letter would look if you changed the right and left margin widths to 1 inch. The Page Setup command on the File menu is used to change settings associated with entire pages.

- Choose File/Page Setup.
- If necessary, open the Margins tab.

The Page Setup dialog box on your screen should be similar to Figure 2-9.

FIGURE 2-9

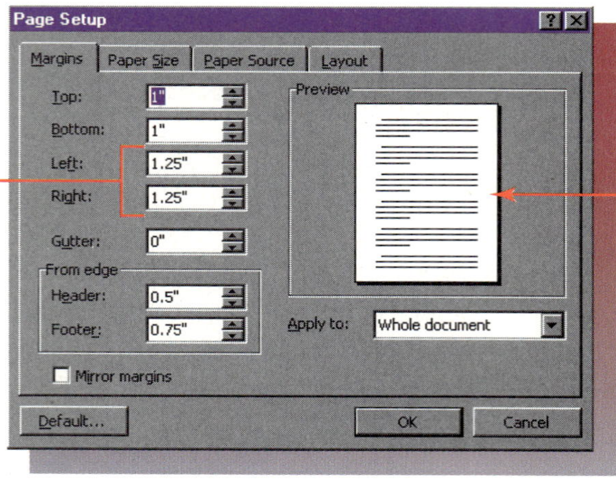

The Margins tab displays the default margin settings for a single-sided document. The Preview box shows how the current margin settings will appear on a page. New margin settings can be entered by typing the value in the text box, or by clicking the ▲ and ▼ buttons or pressing the ↑ or ↓ keys to increase or decrease the setting by tenths of an inch.

> To set margins for double-sided documents, choose Mirror Margins.

- Using any of these methods, set the left and right margins to 1 inch.
- Click OK.

Your screen should be similar to Figure 2-10.

FIGURE 2-10

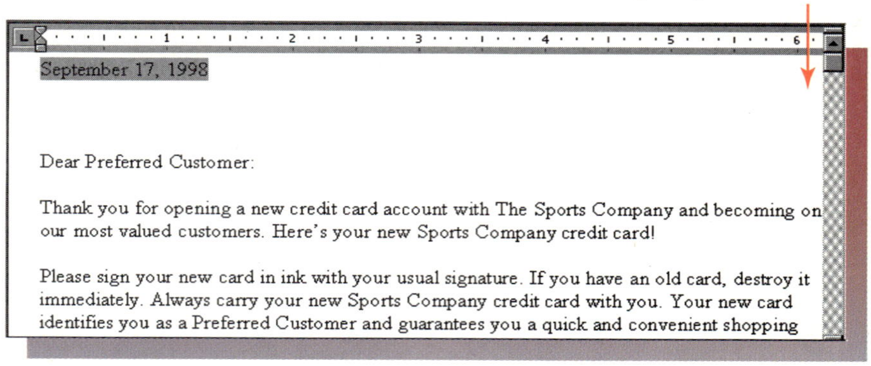

> Depending on your monitor settings, the entire line length may still be visible.

The letter has been reformatted to fit within the new margin settings. Because the margins are smaller, more text can be displayed on a line. However, now the line is too long to fit within the window.

■ Scroll the window to the right to view the end of the line.

The ruler's right margin boundary shows that the text space has increased from 6 inches to 6.5 inches.

Dragging the margin boundaries on the ruler can also be used to change margin settings.

Changing Document Views

Because you have to scroll the window, it is difficult to see how the margins have changed the layout of the document. To make it easier to see how the document lays out on the page, you will change the document view.

Concept 6: Document Views

You can view a Word document in eight different ways. Each view offers different features for creating and editing your documents. It's best to start your document in Normal view. Then, to add finishing touches like headers, footers, and graphics, switch to Page Layout view. Finally, use Print Preview to check the document before you print.

Document View	Command	Button	Effect on Text
Normal View	View/Normal		Shows text formatting but not the layout of the page. This is the best view to use when typing, editing, or formatting text.
Online Layout View	View/Online Layout		Shows the document in the best format for online reading. Also turns on the Document Map feature, which helps you move around the document easily.
Page Layout View	View/Page Layout		Shows how the text and objects are positioned on the printed page. This is the view to use when adjusting margins, working in columns, drawing objects, and placing graphics.
Outline View	View/Outline		Shows the structure of the document. This is the view to use to move, copy, and reorganize text in a document.
Master Document	View/Master Document		Shows several documents organized into a master document. This is the view to use to organize and maintain a long document that is divided into several documents.
Document Map	View/Document Map		Shows the document headings in a vertical pane along the left side of the document. Click the heading to go to that location in the document.
Full Screen	View/Full Screen		Shows the document without Word's toolbars, menus, scroll bars, and other screen elements.
Print Preview	File/Print Preview		Shows multiple pages of a document in a reduced size. This is the view to use to check the layout of a document and make editing and format changes before you print.

Four of the View buttons are located on the left edge of the horizontal scroll bar.

To display the document in Page Layout view,

■ Click Page Layout View.

Your screen should be similar to Figure 2-11.

FIGURE 2-11

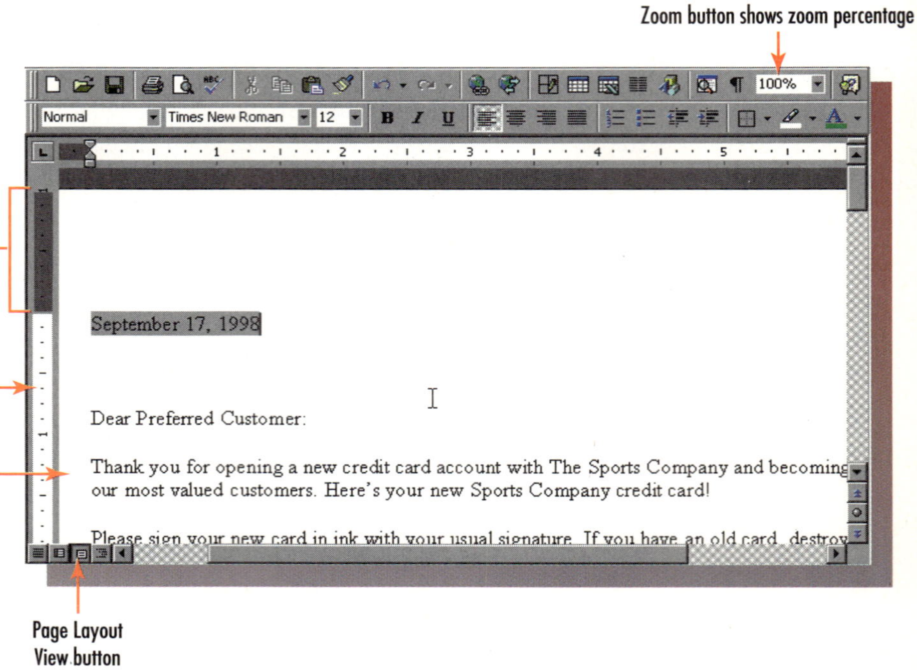

Your screen may display more or less text than is shown in Figure 2-11. This is because your zoom setting may be different. You will learn about this feature next.

This view displays the current page of your document as it will appear when printed. The text still extends off the window space to the right. In addition, the screen now displays a vertical ruler that shows the vertical position of text. Notice that the date will be printed 1 inch from the top of the paper (the default top margin setting).

To see more of the text in the window at one time, you can decrease the onscreen character size using the Zoom command.

The menu equivalent is View/Zoom.

■ Click 100% Zoom.

The default display, 100%, shows the characters the same size as they will be when printed. You can increase the character size up to five times normal display (500%) or reduce the character size to 10%.

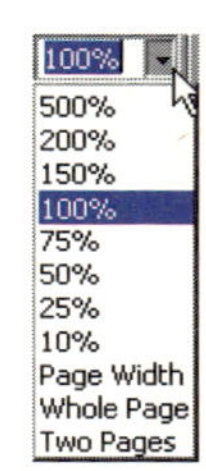

Your zoom percentage may be different than 100%. Word uses the zoom percentage that was in use when you last exited the file or program.

■ Click 50%.

Your screen should be similar to Figure 2-12.

zoom set at 50%

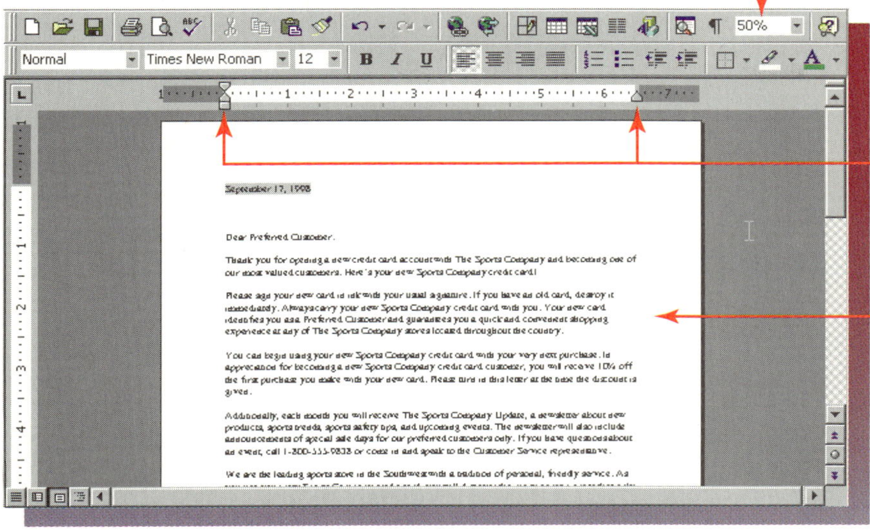

FIGURE 2-12

new left and right margin settings

3 sides of page visible

The text is fully displayed across the width of the window, and you also can see three sides of paper. You can now easily see how the change in margin width has affected the document. You would like to see what the whole page looks like.

- Click 50% Zoom.
- Click Whole Page.

The menu equivalent is View/Zoom/Whole Page.

Your screen should be similar to Figure 2-13.

whole-page zoom

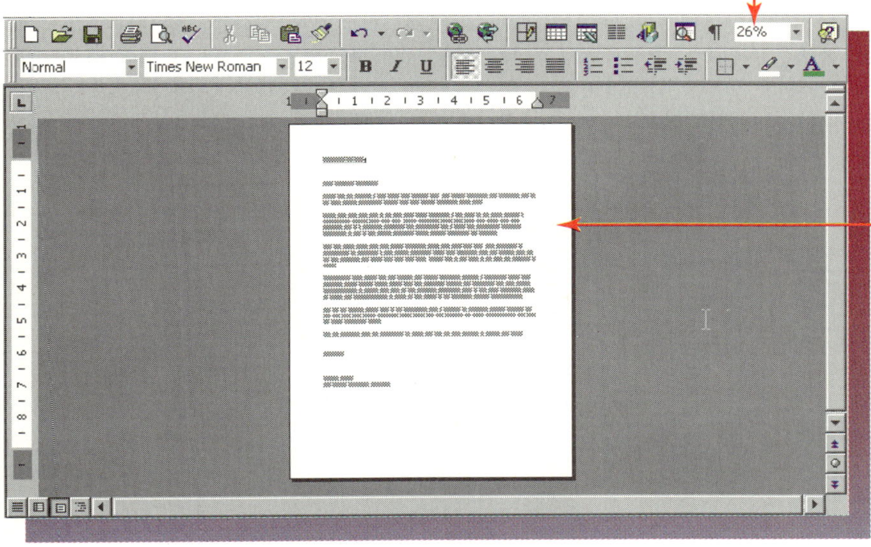

FIGURE 2-13

displays entire page

Your zoom percentage may be slightly higher.

This view is similar to Print Preview. The zoom percentage is 26% (displayed in the Zoom button). The Whole Page option automatically sets the percent value to display the entire page on the screen. Now the text is too small to read.

- Return the zoom percentage to 100%.

You can also change the zoom in Normal view.

- Click Normal View.
- Click 100% Zoom.
- Click Page Width.

Indenting Paragraphs

Next you want to change the letter style from the block paragraph style to an indented paragraph style.

Concept 7: Indents

To help your reader find information quickly, you can indent paragraphs from the margins. Indenting paragraphs sets them off from the rest of the document. There are four types of indents you can use to stylize your documents.

Indent		Effect on Text
Left		Indents the entire paragraph from the left margin. To extend the paragraph into the left margin, use a negative value for the left indent.
Right	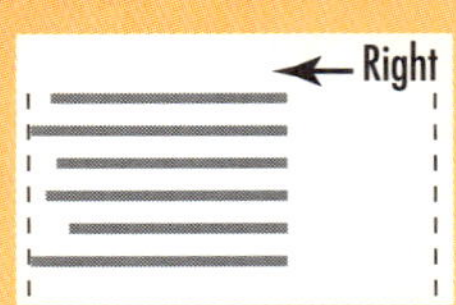	Indents the entire paragraph from the right margin. To extend the paragraph into the right margin, use a negative value for the right indent.
First Line	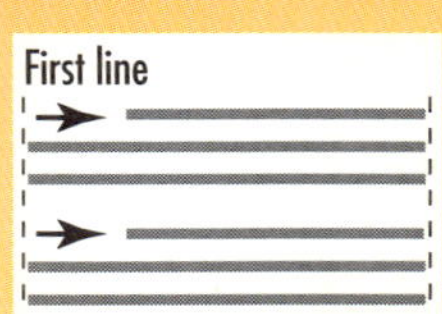	Indents the first line of the paragraph. All following lines are aligned with the left margin.
Hanging		Indents all lines after the first line of the paragraph. The first line is aligned with the left margin. A hanging indent typically is used for bulleted and numbered lists.

To indent the first line of the first paragraph,

- Move to the T in "Thank" (first sentence, first paragraph).
- Choose Format/Paragraph/Indents and Spacing.

The Paragraph dialog box on your screen should be similar to Figure 2-14.

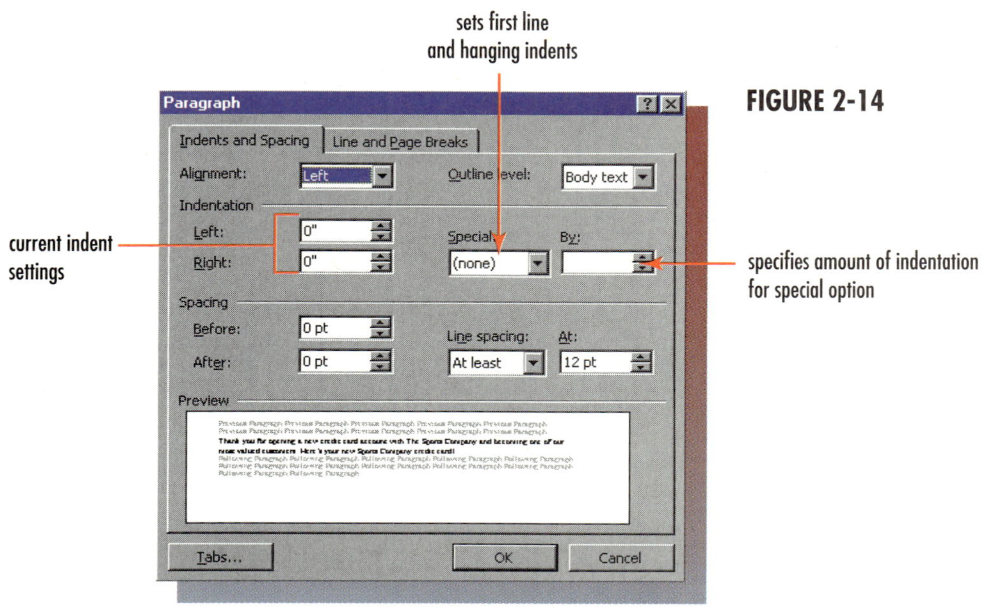

FIGURE 2-14

The Indents and Spacing tab shows that the left and right indentation settings for the current paragraph are 0. This setting aligns each line of the paragraph with the margin setting. Specifying an indent value would indent each line of the paragraph the specified amount from the margin. To indent the first line only,

- Choose Special/First Line.

The default first line indent setting of .5" displayed in the By text box is acceptable.

- Click OK.

Your screen should be similar to Figure 2-15.

FIGURE 2-15

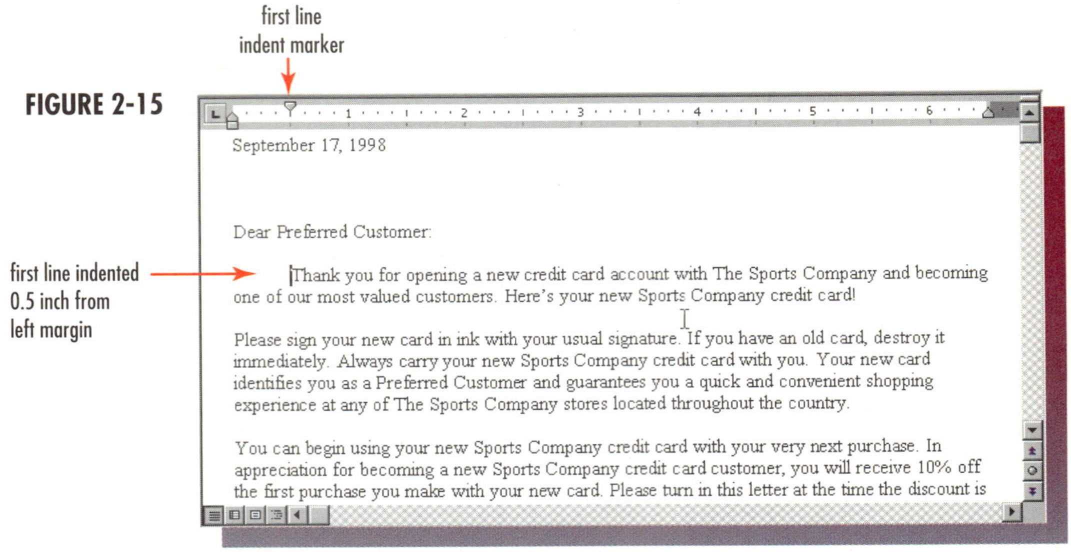

The first line of the paragraph indents 0.5 inch from the left margin to the first tab setting. The text in the paragraph wraps as needed. The text on the following line begins at the left margin. Notice that the upper indent marker on the ruler moved to the 0.5-inch position. This marker controls the location of the first line of text in the paragraph.

You will learn about setting custom tab stops in Lab 3.

A much quicker way to indent the first line of a paragraph is to press Tab at the beginning of the paragraph. Pressing Tab indents the first line of the paragraph to the first tab stop from the left margin.

- Move to the P in "Please."
- Press Tab.

You can indent the remaining four paragraphs individually, or you can select the paragraphs and indent them simultaneously by either using the Format menu or dragging the upper indent marker on the ruler.

A dotted vertical line is displayed as you drag to show where the indent will appear in the text.

The lower indent marker controls the indent for all lines in a paragraph after the first line.

- Select the remaining four paragraphs.
- Drag the upper indent marker on the ruler to the 0.5-inch position.
- In the same manner, select the closing lines and indent them to the 3.25-inch position on the ruler.
- Move to the top of the document.

Creating an Itemized List

Now you want to display the first three sentences in the second paragraph as a list and add a new sentence to the first paragraph to tell the reader what the list is about. The completed paragraph adjustment is shown below.

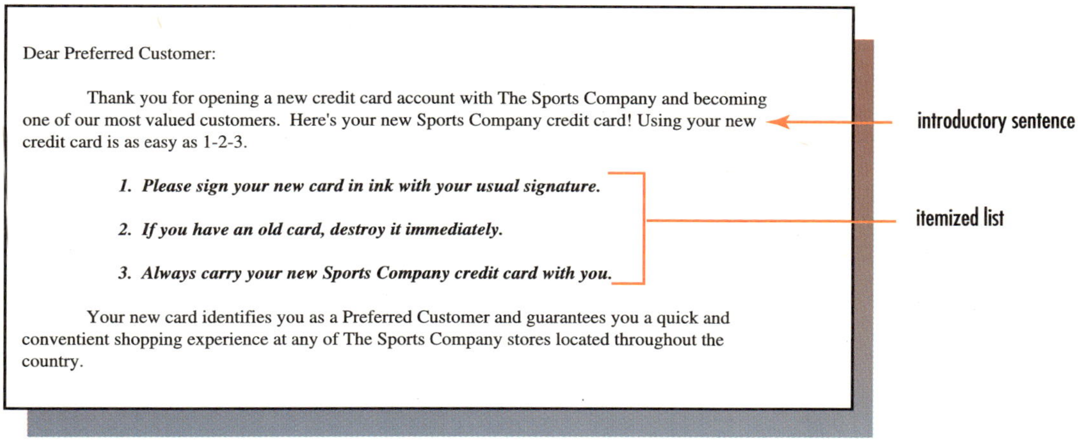
Dear Preferred Customer:

Thank you for opening a new credit card account with The Sports Company and becoming one of our most valued customers. Here's your new Sports Company credit card! Using your new credit card is as easy as 1-2-3.

1. ***Please sign your new card in ink with your usual signature.***
2. ***If you have an old card, destroy it immediately.***
3. ***Always carry your new Sports Company credit card with you.***

Your new card identifies you as a Preferred Customer and guarantees you a quick and conventient shopping experience at any of The Sports Company stores located throughout the country.

■ Add the following introductory sentence to the end of the first paragraph: **Using your new credit card is as easy as 1-2-3.**

Next you will create the itemized list using the first three sentences of the second paragraph.

Concept 8: Bulleted and Numbered Lists

Whenever possible, use bulleted or numbered lists to organize information and to make your writing clear and easy to read. A list can be used whenever you present three or more related pieces of information.

Use a bulleted list when you have several items that logically fall out from a paragraph into a list. A bulleted list displays one of several styles of bullets before each item in the list. You can select from several types of symbols to use as bullets and you can change the color, size, and position of the bullet.

Use a numbered list when you want to convey a sequence of events, such as a procedure that has steps to follow in a certain order. A numbered list displays numbers or letters before the text. Word automatically increments the number or letter as you start a new paragraph. You can select from several different numbering schemes to create your numbered lists.

> **You can also drag the upper indent marker to the 0 position on the ruler or press [←Backspace] to clear the indent.**

First you need to remove the indent at the beginning of the second paragraph and then place each sentence that you want to be itemized in the list on a separate line. To do this,

- Move to the P in "Please."
- Press [⇧Shift] + [Tab].
- Move to the I in "If" (second sentence, second paragraph).
- Press [↵Enter] (2 times).
- In a similar manner, place the next sentence on a separate line.
- Make the last sentence, beginning with "Your new . . .", a new paragraph. (Remember to indent the first line of the paragraph.)

Your screen should be similar to Figure 2-16.

FIGURE 2-16

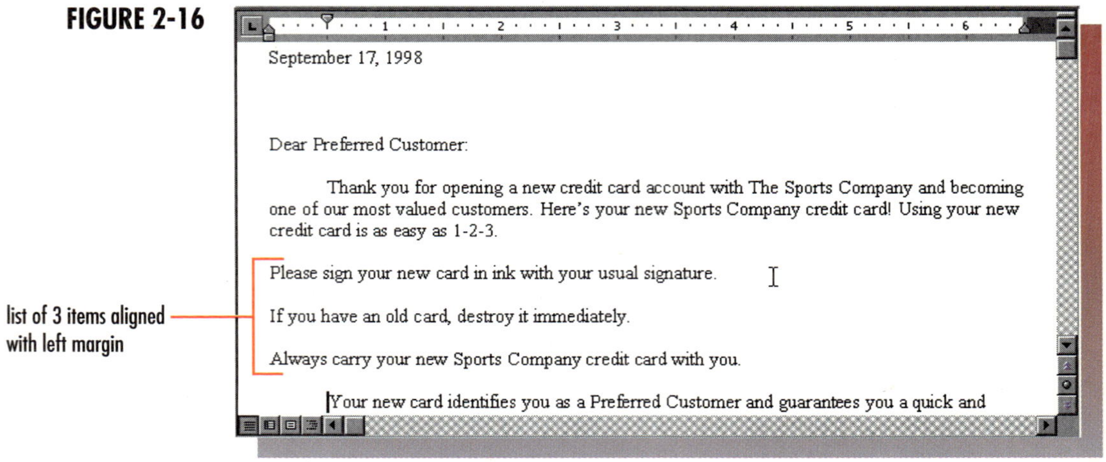

You should now have a list of three items, each separated with a blank line. Leaving a blank line between items in a list makes the list easier to read. Next you will add a number before each of the items.

- Select the three items.
- Choose Format/Bullets and Numbering.
- Open the Numbered tab.

The Bullets and Numbering dialog box on your screen should be similar to Figure 2-17.

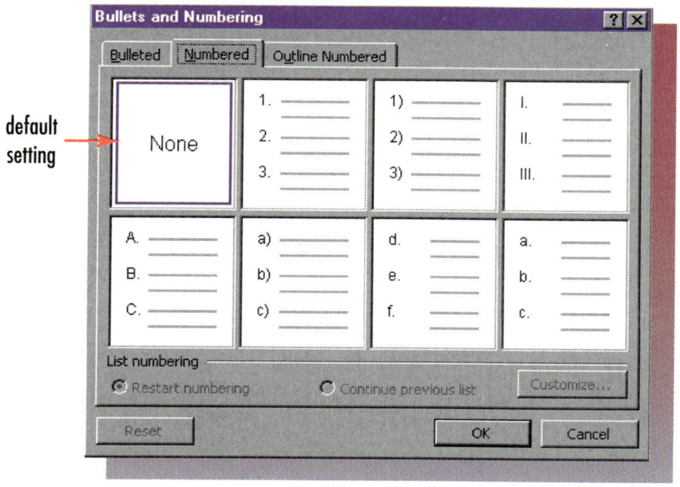

FIGURE 2-17

Seven numbered list styles are available. The document default is None. The first style to the right of None is the style you will use.

- Select the first numbered list style.
- Click OK.

Your screen should be similar to Figure 2-18.

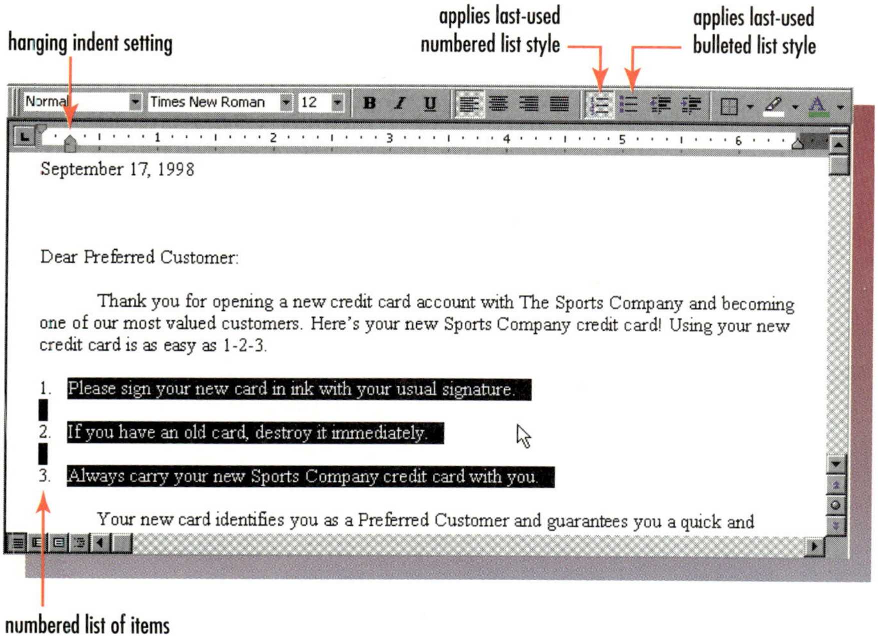

FIGURE 2-18

A number is inserted at the left margin before each sentence, and the text following the number is indented to the 0.25-inch position. The ruler displays the lower indent marker at the 0.25-inch position to show the hanging indent setting for text in the selection. If the text following each bullet were longer than a line, the text on the following lines would also be indented to the 0.25-inch position.

> To remove bullets or numbers, choose Format/Bullets and Numbering/Remove, then select the None option or click the [button] or [button] button again.

You can also create bulleted and numbered lists as you type. To create a bulleted list, type an asterisk (*), press Tab, and then type the text. To create a numbered list, type a number, type a period, press Tab, and then type the text. When you press ←Enter, Word automatically creates a list and numbers or bullets the next line. To turn off the list, press ←Enter twice.

Finally, you want to change the indent for the three items so that the number aligns with the 0.75-inch position. The three items should still be highlighted.

- If necessary, select the 3 numbered items.
- Press Tab (2 times).

Your screen should be similar to Figure 2-19.

FIGURE 2-19

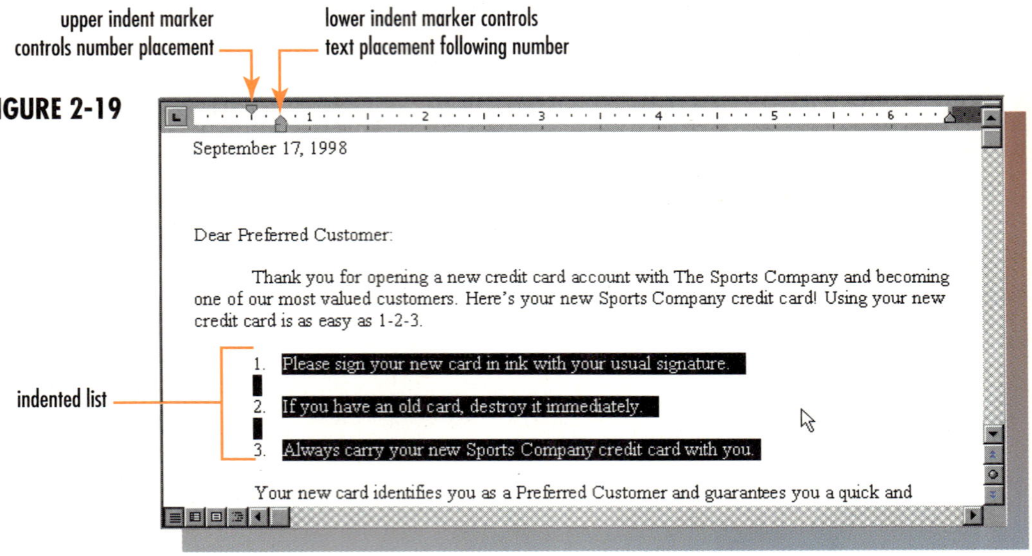

The numbers align with the 0.5-inch position and the text with the 1-inch position in the document. In an itemized list, the upper indent marker on the ruler controls the position of the number or bullet, and the lower indent marker controls the position of the item following the number or bullet.

Changing the Character Formatting

To make the numbered list stand out even more from the rest of the document, you will change the character format by selecting a different font and font size.

Concept 9: Fonts

A **font**, also commonly referred to as a **typeface**, is a set of characters with a specific design. The designs have names such as Times New Roman and Courier. Using fonts as a design element can add interest to your document and give readers visual cues to help them find information quickly.

There are two basic types of fonts, serif and sans serif. **Serif fonts** have a flair at the base of each letter that visually leads the reader to the next letter. Two common serif fonts are Roman and Times New Roman. Serif fonts generally are used in paragraphs. **Sans serif fonts** do not have a flair at the base of each letter. Arial and Helvetica are two common sans serif fonts. Because sans serif fonts have a clean look, they are often used for headings in documents. It is good practice to use only two types of fonts in a document, one for text and one for headers. Too many styles can make your document look cluttered and unprofessional.

Each font has one or more sizes. Size is the height and width of the character and is commonly measured in **points**, abbreviated "pt". One point equals about 1/72 inch, and text in most documents is 10 pt or 12 pt.

Several common fonts in different sizes are shown in the following table.

Font Name	Font Type	Font Size	Font Style (Bold)
Arial	Sans serif	This is 10 pt. This is 16 pt.	**Bold 10 pt.** **Bold 16 pt.**
Courier New	Serif	This is 10 pt. This is 16 pt.	**Bold 10 pt.** **Bold 16 pt.**
Times New Roman	Serif	This is 10 pt. This is 16 pt.	**Bold 10 pt.** **Bold 16 pt.**

You would like the numbered list to be in a different font and type size than the rest of the text in the letter. To change a font setting for existing text, select the text you want to change and then use the command.

To change the font before typing the text, use the command and then type. All text will appear in the specified font setting until another font setting is selected.

- If necessary, select the 3 numbered items.
- Choose Format/Font.
- If necessary, open the Font tab.

The Font dialog box on your screen should be similar to Figure 2-20.

FIGURE 2-20

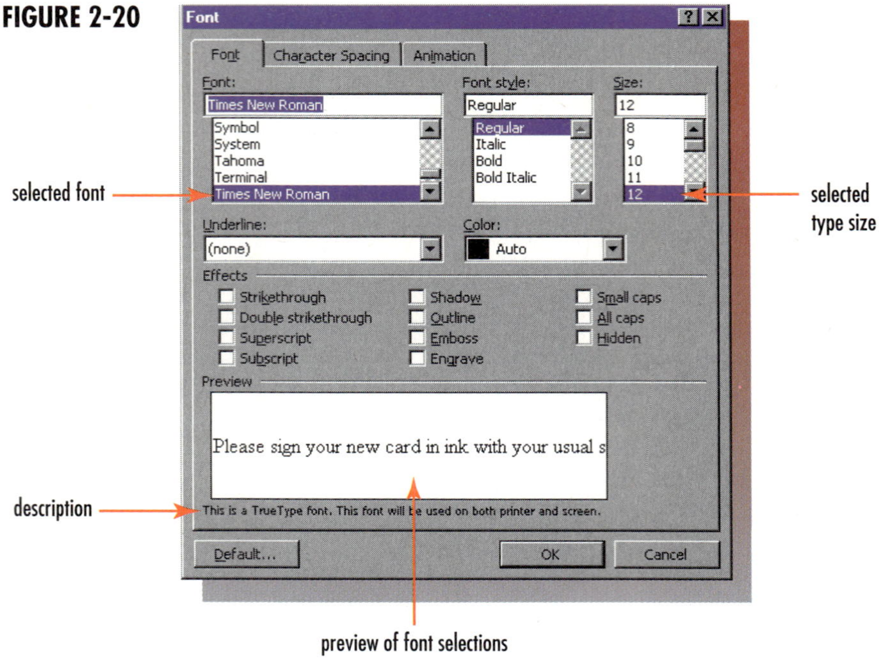

The Font list box displays the fonts supported by your active printer in alphabetical order. The Word default font, Times New Roman, is the currently selected font.

Notice the description of the font below the Preview box. It states that the selected font is a TrueType font. TrueType fonts are fonts that are automatically installed when you install Windows. They appear onscreen exactly as they will appear when printed. Some fonts are printer fonts, which are available only on your printer, and may look different onscreen than when printed. Courier is an example of a printer font.

You will change the font to Arial and the point size to 10. As you make the selections, the Preview box displays how your selections will appear.

> You also can select the font from the Font drop-down list and the font size from the Font Size drop-down list in the Formatting toolbar.

- Select Arial.
- Select 10.
- Click OK.
- Clear the highlight.

Your screen should be similar to Figure 2-21.

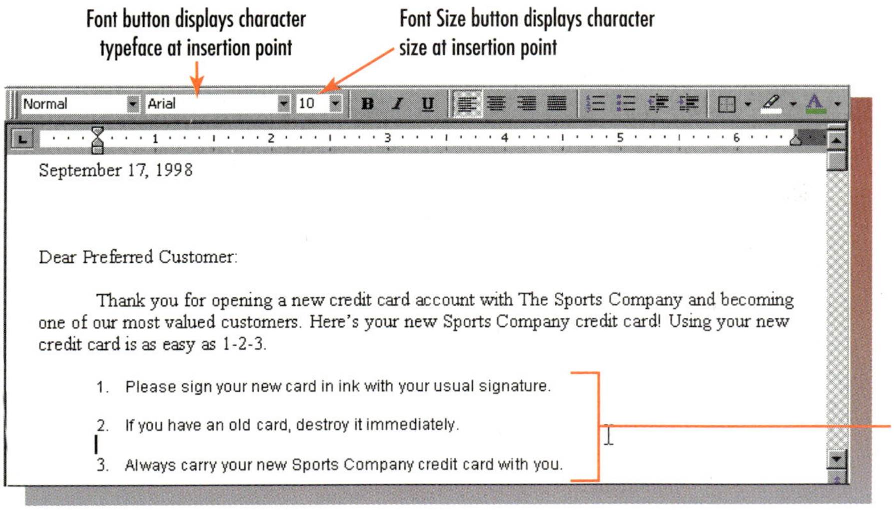

FIGURE 2-21

The Font and Font Size buttons in the Formatting toolbar display the current font and size setting for the text at the location of the insertion point.

In addition to changing font and font size, you can apply different character effects to enhance the appearance of text.

Concept 10: Character Effects

Different character effects can be applied to selections to add emphasis or interest to a document. The table below describes some of the effects and their uses.

Format	Example	Use
Bold, italic	**Bold** *Italic*	Adds emphasis
Underline	Underline	Adds emphasis
Strikethrough	~~Strikethrough~~	Indicates words to be deleted
Double strikethrough	~~Double Strikethrough~~	Indicates words to be deleted
Superscript	"To be or not to be."[1]	Used in footnotes and formulas
Subscript	H_2O	Used in formulas
Shadow	Shadow	Adds distinction to titles and headings
Outline	Outline	Adds distinction to titles and headings
Small caps	SMALL CAPS	Adds emphasis when case is not important
All caps	ALL CAPS	Adds emphasis when case is not important
Hidden	Displays, but does not print	Notes or comments you do not want printed
Color	Color Color Color	Adds interest

The menu equivalent is Format/Font/Font Style/Bold/Italic, and the keyboard shortcuts are Ctrl + B for bold and Ctrl + I for italic.

You would like to change the itemized list to display as both bold and italic.

- Select the three numbered items.
- Click **B** Bold.
- Click *I* Italic.
- Clear the highlight.

Your screen should be similar to Figure 2-22.

FIGURE 2-22

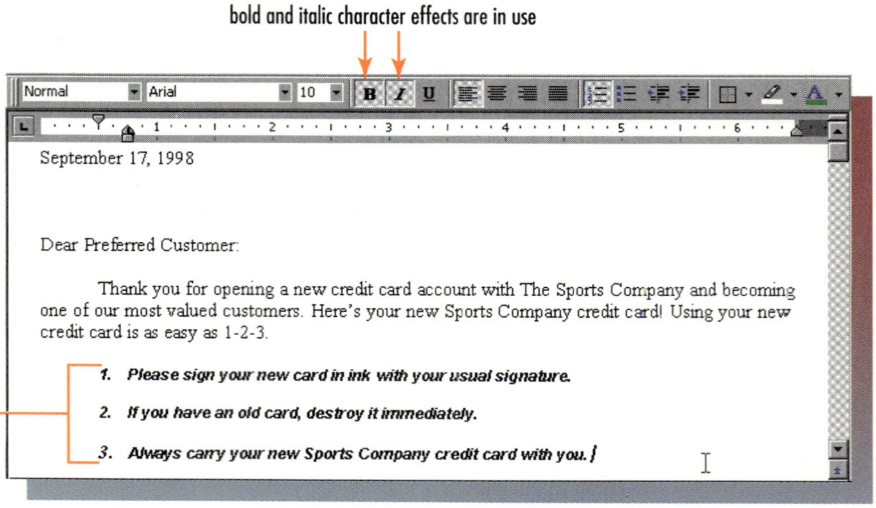

Now you want to emphasize the information in the third paragraph about the 10 percent discount by underlining it.

The menu equivalent is Format/Font/Underline/Single, and the keyboard shortcut is Ctrl + U.

- Select the text "10% off the first purchase."
- Click U Underline.
- Clear the highlight.

You could also click Undo.

The selected text appears underlined. However, you do not like how the underline format looks. To clear any of the appearance settings, reselect the exact area of text and use the command again.

- Remove the underline from the text.

Setting Paragraph Alignment

The final formatting change you want to make is to change the paragraph alignment.

Concept 11: Paragraph Alignment

Alignment is how text is positioned on a line between the margins or indents. There are four types of paragraph alignment: left, center, right, and justified.

Alignment	Effect on Text
Left 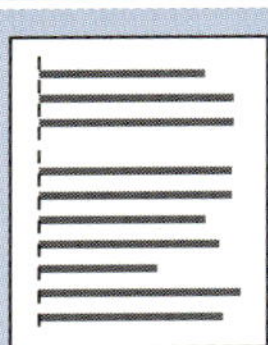	Aligns text against the left margin of the page, leaving the right margin ragged. This is the most commonly used paragraph alignment type and therefore the default setting in all word processing software packages.
Center 	Centers each line of text between the left and right margins. Center alignment is used mostly for headings or centering graphics on a page.
Right 	Aligns text against the right margin, leaving the left margin ragged. Use right alignment when you want text to line up on the outside of a page, such as a chapter title or a header.
Justified 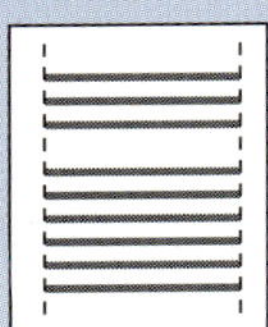	Aligns text against the right and left margins and evenly spaces out the words. Newspapers commonly use justified alignment so the columns of text are even.

The commands to change paragraph alignment are under the Format/Paragraph menu. However, it is much faster to use the shortcuts shown below.

Alignment	Keyboard Shortcuts	Button
Left	Ctrl + L	
Center	Ctrl + E	
Right	Ctrl + R	
Justified	Ctrl + J	

The keyboard shortcut is Ctrl + A.

The menu equivalent is Format/Paragraph/Indents and Spacing/Alignment/Justified.

You want to change the alignment of all paragraphs in the letter from the default of left-aligned to justified.

- Choose Edit/Select All.
- Click Justify.
- Clear the highlight and scroll through the letter to see the changes in the alignment of text on the right margin.
- Return to the top of the document.

Your screen should be similar to Figure 2-23.

FIGURE 2-23

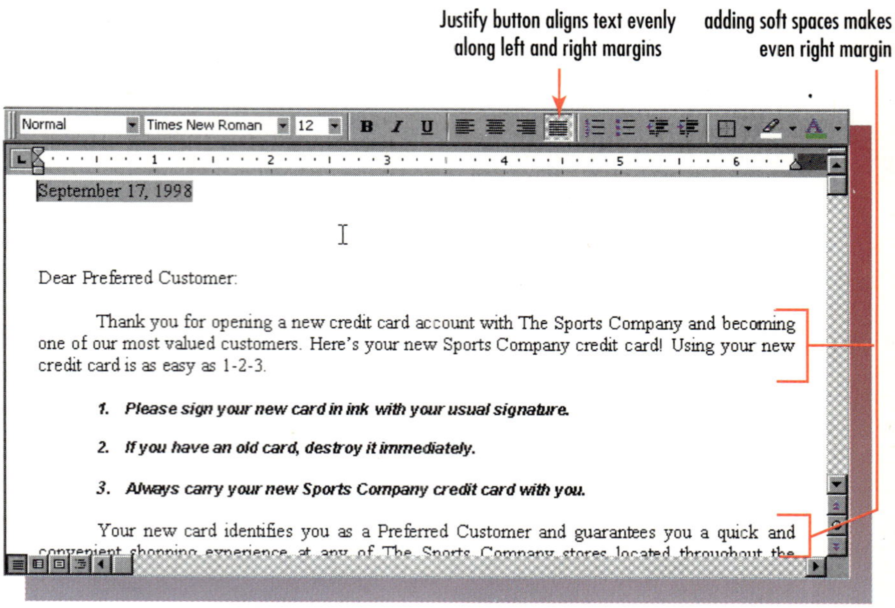

All full lines now end even with the right margin. To do this, Word inserts extra spaces between words to push the text to the right margins. These are called **soft spaces** and are adjusted automatically whenever additions and deletions are made to the text.

Next you want the date to be aligned flush against the right margin.

- Move to the date field.
- Click Align Right.

Your screen should be similar to Figure 2-24.

> The alignment settings can also be specified before typing in new text. As you type, it is aligned according to your selection until the alignment setting is changed to another setting.

> The menu equivalent is Format/Paragraph/Indents and Spacing/Alignment/Right.

Align Right button aligns text even with right margin

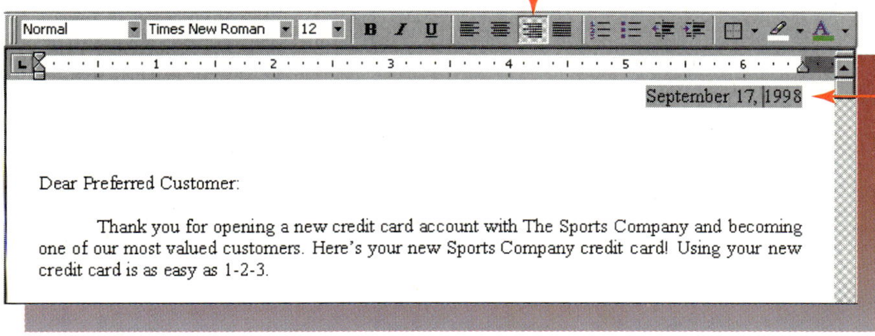

date right aligned

FIGURE 2-24

- Return the zoom percentage to 100%.
- Replace Student Name with your name in the closing.

Editing in Print Preview

You would like to save the edited version of the credit card letter as Revised Credit Card Letter 2. This will allow the original file, Revised Credit Card Letter, to remain unchanged in case you want to repeat the lab for practice.

- Use the Save As command to save the file on your data disk as Revised Credit Card Letter 2.
- Preview the letter.

Your screen should be similar to Figure 2-25.

FIGURE 2-25

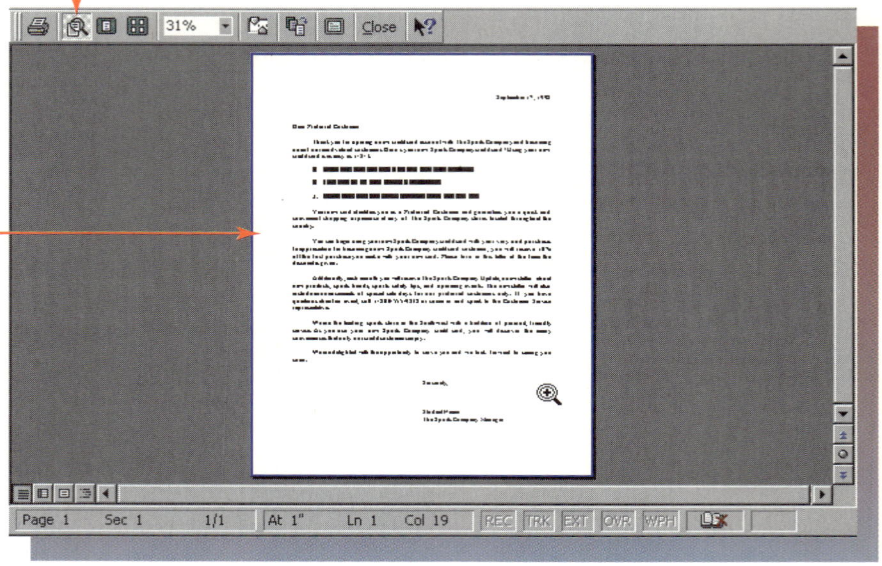

Now that you can see the entire letter, you decide that the date would look better at the 3.25-inch tab position. While in Print Preview, you can edit and format text. Notice that the mouse pointer is a magnifying glass when it is positioned on text in the window. This indicates that when you click on a document, the screen will toggle between the whole page view you currently see and 100% magnification.

- To edit the date in the Print Preview window, point to the date and click the mouse button.

The text is displayed in the size it will appear when printed (100% zoom). Then, to switch between zooming the document and editing it,

- Click Magnifier.

When positioned near text, the mouse pointer changes to an I-beam and the insertion point is displayed. Now you can edit the document as in Normal view. First you need to return the date to left-aligned. Because the Formatting toolbar is not displayed, you will use the keyboard shortcut, Ctrl + L, to left-align the date. Then you will indent the date to the 3.25-inch position.

- If necessary, move the insertion point to the date.
- Press Ctrl + L.
- Click View Ruler.
- Move the upper indent marker to the 3.25-inch position.

Pointing to the top or left edge of the window will also temporarily display the ruler.

Your screen should be similar to Figure 2-26.

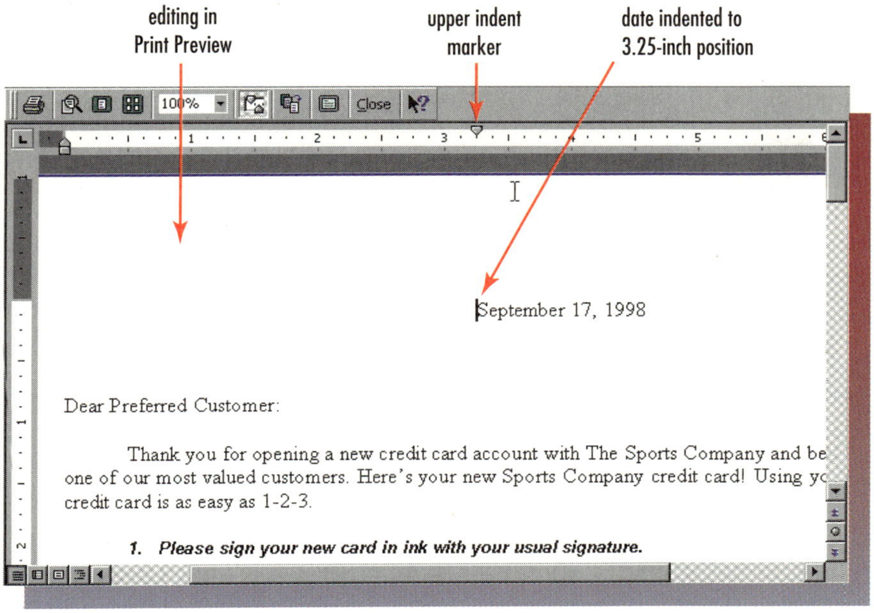

FIGURE 2-26

To switch back to zooming the document and restore it to the original preview size,

- Click Magnifier.
- Click the document.
- Click View Ruler.

Next, you will print a copy of the letter from the Print Preview window using the default print settings.

- Click Print.
- Close the Print Preview window.
- If necessary, change the view to Normal and the zoom percentage to 100%.
- Choose File/Exit.
- Click Yes.

The Zoom button can also be used to specify the magnification.

Make sure your printer is on and ready to print.

If you need to specify a different printer, you will need to close Print Preview and use the Print command on the File menu.

LAB REVIEW

Key Terms

alignment (WP83)
case sensitive (WP62)
destination (WP59)
drag and drop (WP64)
field (WP66)
field code (WP66)
field result (WP66)
font (WP79)
margin (WP67)
point (WP79)
sans serif font (WP79)
serif font (WP79)
soft space (WP85)
source (WP59)
Thesaurus (WP64)
typeface (WP79)

Command Summary

Command	Shortcut Keys	Button	Action
File/Page Setup			Changes layout of page including margins, paper size, and paper source
Edit/Cut	Ctrl + X		Cuts selected text and copies it to Clipboard
Edit/Copy	Ctrl + C		Copies selected text to Clipboard
Edit/Paste	Ctrl + V		Pastes text from Clipboard
Edit/Find	Ctrl + F		Locates specified text
Edit/Replace	Ctrl + H		Locates and replaces specified text
View/Normal			Displays document in Normal view
View/Online Layout			Displays document best for onscreen reading
View/Page Layout			Displays document as it will appear when printed
View/Outline			Displays structure of document as an outline
View/Master Document			Shows several documents organized into a master document
View/Document Map			Shows document headings along left side of document
View/Full Screen			Shows document without Word's toolbars, menus, scroll bars, and other screen elements
View/Zoom		100%	Changes onscreen character size
View/Zoom/Whole Page			Displays entire page onscreen
Insert/Date and Time			Inserts current date or time, maintained by computer system, in selected format

Command	Shortcut Keys	Button	Action
Format/Font			Changes appearance of characters
Format/Font/Font Style/Italic	Ctrl + I		Makes selected text italic
Format/Font/Font Style/Bold	Ctrl + B		Makes selected text bold
Format/Font/Underline/Single	Ctrl + U		Underlines selected text
Format/Paragraph/Indents and Spacing/ Special/First Line			Indents first line of paragraph from right margin
Format/Paragraph/Indents and Spacing/ Alignment/Left	Ctrl + L		Aligns text to left margin
Format/Paragraph/Indents and Spacing/ Alignment/Centered	Ctrl + E		Centers text between left and right margins
Format/Paragraph/Indents and Spacing/ Alignment/Right	Ctrl + R		Aligns text to right margin
Format/Paragraph/Indents and Spacing/ Alignment/Justified	Ctrl + J		Aligns text equally between left and right margins
Format/Bullets and Numbering			Creates a bulleted or numbered list
Tools/Spelling and Grammar	F7		Starts Spelling and Grammar tool
Tools/Language/Thesaurus	Shift + F7		Starts Thesaurus tool

Matching

1. justified ______ **a.** suggests synonyms and antonyms
2. date field ______ **b.** allows you to select the entire document
3. Edit/Select All ______ **c.** shortcut for bold command
4. margins ______ **d.** used to copy or move a selection
5. Ctrl + B ______ **e.** text that has even left and right margins
6. ______ **f.** white space between printed text and edge of paper
7. drag and drop ______ **g.** removes text from the document and stores it in the Clipboard
8. Thesaurus ______ **h.** quickly locates specified text
9. ______ **i.** creates bulleted list
10. Find ______ **j.** a code that instructs Word to insert the current date in the document using the selected format whenever the document is printed

Fill-In Questions

1. Complete the following statements by filling in the blanks with the correct terms.

a. The white space between the text and the edge of the paper is the ________________ .

b. Use a(n) ______________________ list to convey a sequence of events.

c. The __________________ text format is used to indicate words to be deleted.

d. The _____________ and __________________ views show how text will appear on the printed page.

e. Use the ____________________ to find synonyms for common words.

f. When text aligns evenly against the right and left margins, it is ____________________ .

Discussion Questions

1. What is the purpose of formatting a document? What criteria would you suggest for a professional document?

2. Discuss the differences between serif and sans serif fonts. When would it be appropriate to combine font styles? How does a font's point size affect the display of characters?

3. Discuss the different ways information can be moved within a document. When would it be appropriate to use either method?

4. Discuss the different document views. When would it be appropriate to switch to a different view?

5. Discuss the problems that can be associated with finding and replacing text. What can you do to avoid some of these problems?

Hands-On Practice Exercises

Step by Step

Rating System
☆ Easy
☆☆ Moderate
☆☆☆ Difficult

☆

1. To complete this exercise, you must have first completed Practice Exercise 2 in Lab 1. Open the file Mouse Terms 1 on your data disk. *(Note*: You can only complete step a if you have Wingdings in your font collection. If you do not have Wingdings, select and change the title to Arial 16 pt, and go to step b.)

a. Wingdings are a set of icons that can be used to add fun and flair to your documents. A "Wingding" 7 is a keyboard; a "Wingding" 8 is a mouse. In this portion of the exercise, you will replace the word "Mouse" with a picture of a mouse. Replace the word "mouse" in the title with the number 8. Select the number 8, and change the font to Wingdings 18 pt. Change the font of the word "Terms" in the title to Arial 16 pt.

b. Bold and italicize the terms ("Point," "Click," "Double-click," etc.).

c. Find all occurrences of the word "thing" and replace them with the word "object."

d. Use the Thesaurus to find synonyms for the words "often" and "several" in the last sentence of the Click paragraph. Then use the Thesaurus to find a synonym for "location" in the Drag and Drop paragraph.

e. Set the paragraph alignment to justified, and center and bold the title. Change all margins to 1.5 inches.

f. Bullet the five terms and their definitions.

g. Save the document as MOUSE TERMS 2. Print the document.

☆☆

2. You have been accepted at Metropolitan Community College, and have received a letter from the Director of Admissions informing you of the orientation that you will be required to attend. You will create that letter in this exercise.

a. Before you type the letter (shown below), change all margins to 1.5 inches, and set the alignment to justified. Type the letter as shown except use the Date and Time command to insert the date as a field, and substitute information that pertains to you in the bracketed areas. *(Note:* only press ←Enter at the end of heading text or to end paragraphs.)

Metropolitan Community College
123 Metropolitan Blvd.
Anytown, USA

[Current Date]

[Your Name]
[Street Address]
[City, State Zip Code]

Dear [Your Name]:

Congratulations on your acceptance into the [Your Major] program at Metropolitan Community College.

Orientation for new students will be held next Friday morning from 9:00 - Noon. It is imperative that you attend this session prior to your enrollment at Metropolitan Community College.

Student leaders from the [Your Major] program will be there to give you a guided tour of the Metropolitan Community College campus with an emphasis on your course of study.

We will initially meet in the Student Center, where you will be introduced to the [Your Major] program coordinator. Light refreshments will be served at this time while you become acquainted with others in your major field as well as faculty members in attendance.

After the orientation ends at 12:00, you are encouraged to join us for a luncheon in the cafeteria.

Once again, [Your Name], congratulations on your acceptance, and we hope to see you next Friday.

If you are unable to attend, please call me at 1-800-555-1622.

Sincerely,

Joseph K. College
Director of Admissions

JKC/xxx

b. Add documentation to the file. Save the document as Acceptance Letter. Print the letter.

c. Search for all occurrences of Metropolitan Community College. Replace all but the first occurrence (in the address) with M.C.C.

d. Italicize and bold the word "imperative" in the second paragraph. Then use the Thesaurus to replace the word with an appropriate synonym.

e. Reverse the order of the third and fourth paragraphs.

f. Center and bold the return address. Right-align the date.

g. Indent the three closing lines to the 3-inch position on the ruler.

h. Save the document again with the same name. Print the letter.

You will complete this exercise as Practice Exercise 4 in Lab 4.

☆☆☆

3. In this problem you will continue creating Grandma Gertie's cookie recipes cookbook. To complete this exercise, you must have completed Practice Exercise 5 in Lab 1. Open the file Potato Chip Cookies from your data disk.

- **a.** Bold the name of the cookie at the top of the document. Bold and italicize the headings Ingredients: and Directions:.
- **b.** Indent the instructions from "2 sticks of butter" to "Confectioner's sugar" 0.5 inch from the left. Bullet the directions from "Cream the butter. . ." to "Bake in 350 degree oven. . . ." Indent the bulleted directions 0.5 inch from the left.
- **c.** Copy the entire file to the Clipboard. Save the file using the same name. Close the document.
- **d.** Open the file More Recipes on your data disk. Paste the Potato Chip Cookies file from the Clipboard to the end of the More Recipes file.
- **e.** Center and bold the title at the top of the document. Italicize the note at the top of the document, and justify that paragraph only.
- **f.** The Cut-Out Sugar Cookies have their Ingredients and Directions sections mixed up. Reverse the order of these two sections. "Makes about 5 dozen 2" cookies" should be the last line in the recipe.
- **g.** Change the font to Times New Roman 12 pt for the entire document. Then change the title to a 14 pt font of your choice.
- **h.** Bold the names of the first two cookies. Bold and italicize the headings Ingredients: and Directions: for the first two cookies.
- **i.** Indent the instructions for the first two cookies 0.5 inch from the left. Bullet the directions for the first two cookies, and indent the bulleted directions 0.5 inch from the left.
- **j.** Document the file. Save the document as Updated Cookie Recipes. Print the document.

You will complete this exercise as Practice Exercise 5 in Lab 3.

☆☆☆

4. To complete this exercise, you must have completed Practice Exercise 6 in Lab 1. Open the file B&B Ad from your data disk.

- **a.** Bold and center the first three lines. Italicize the two lines that contain the host's phone number and name.
- **b.** Bullet the lines from "Number of Rooms" to "Social Drinking" and indent them to the 1-inch position on the ruler.
- **c.** Reverse the order of the third and fourth paragraphs.
- **d.** Set the alignment of the five paragraphs to justified, and change all margins to 1.3 inches.
- **e.** Search for all occurrences of "Poconos" and replace them with "Pocono Mountains."
- **f.** Use the Thesaurus to find synonyms for "rustic" and "numerous" in the first paragraph and "breathtaking" in the second paragraph.
- **g.** Select the five paragraphs below the indented items, and increase the font size to 11 pt.
- **h.** Save the document as B&B Ad Part 2. Print the ad.

You will complete this exercise as Practice Exercise 4 in Lab 3.

On Your Own

☆☆

5. Many people create lists of things they need to do each day or each week. In this problem you will create a list of things you need to do for the week.

Create a numbered "to do" list of all the things you have to do this week (or all the things you would like to do this week) either in order of importance or in chronological order.

Add a title that includes your name and the current date. Use the formatting techniques you have learned to improve the appearance of the list.

Document the file. Save the document as To Do List. Print the document.

☆☆

6. In this exercise you will modify a document containing tips on how to prepare for a job interview.

Open the file Preparing for the Interview on your data disk. Center and bold the title and change the font to Arial 16 pt. Bold the heading Helpful Tips.

Bullet the four Helpful Tips from "Know the exact place and time of the interview" to "Dress for success." Indent the bulleted list to the 0.5-inch position.

Italicize and bold the first sentence in each of the four tips. In the second tip, emphasize the sentence "Failure to do homework can be the kiss of death." In the last tip, emphasize the text "only one" in the seventh sentence. In the same section, emphasize the last sentence, "Call attention to what you say, not what you wear." Italicize the reference "CPC Annual 1990-91 Edition" below the list of tips.

Justify all lines below the title. Increase the margins to 1.5 inches all around.

Insert your name and the current date below the document. Document the file. Save the document as Interview Tips. Print the document.

☆☆☆

7. In this exercise you will format a document that tells how to redisplay screen elements that have, for one reason or another, disappeared!

Open the file Capturing Screen Elements on your data disk. This document tells how to hide and display toolbars and how to return the document from full-screen view to the last view you used. Spell- and grammar-check the document.

Enter the following text above the Toolbars section:

> **The Ruler**
>
> **The ruler is usually displayed below the toolbars. You can use the ruler to conveniently set margins or tabs with a click of the mouse. If the ruler is not displayed, here's how to get it back.**
>
> **Open the View menu. The Ruler command is just below Toolbars. Clicking a checked Ruler turns it off, and clicking an unchecked Ruler turns it on.**

Add appropriate text formatting to emphasize the title, Capturing Screen Elements At Large, and the headings The Ruler, Toolbars, and Help! All I Have Is This Big White Screen! In the line Choose: View/Toolbars, bold and underline the V in View and the T in Toolbars.

Move The Ruler section below the Toolbars section. Adjust spacing as needed.

Change the alignment to justified for the document, and center the title.

Locate all occurrences of Ruler Bar and replace them with Ruler.

Adjust margins until the document just fits on one page. What settings did you use?

Indent the three lines of instruction (Choose: View/Toolbars, Choose: OK when you are finished, and Press: Esc!) to the 0.5-inch mark on the ruler.

Document the file and save it as Capturing Screen Elements 2. Print the document.

2 Formatting a Document

Move and Copy

Selections can be moved or copied to new locations in a document, saving you time by not having to retype the same information.

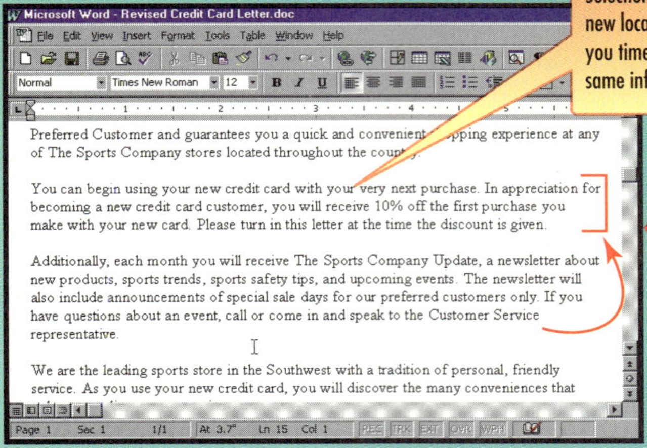

Concepts

- Move and Copy
- Find and Replace
- Thesaurus
- Fields
  Margins
  Indents
- Document Views
- Bulleted and Numbered Lists
  Fonts
  Character Effects
  Paragraph Alignment

Thesaurus

Word's Thesaurus is a reference tool that provides synonyms, antonyms, and related words for a selected word or phrase.

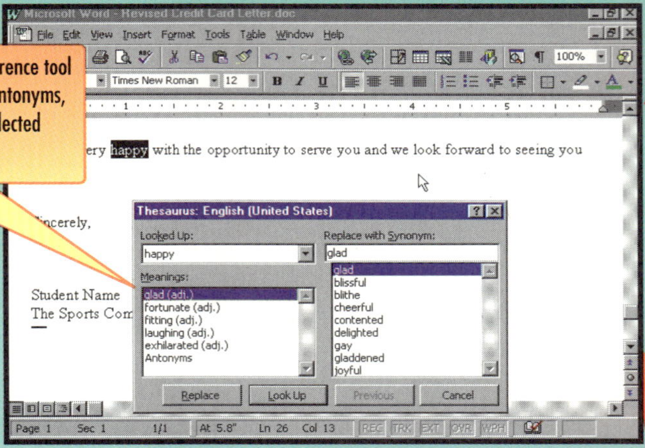

Document Views

You can view a Word document in eight different ways. Each view offers different features for working with your documents.

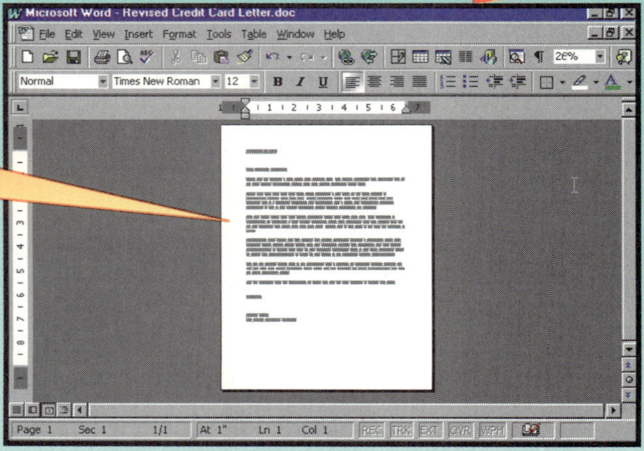

Find and Replace

To make editing easier, you can use the Find and Replace feature to find text in a document and automatically replace it with other text.

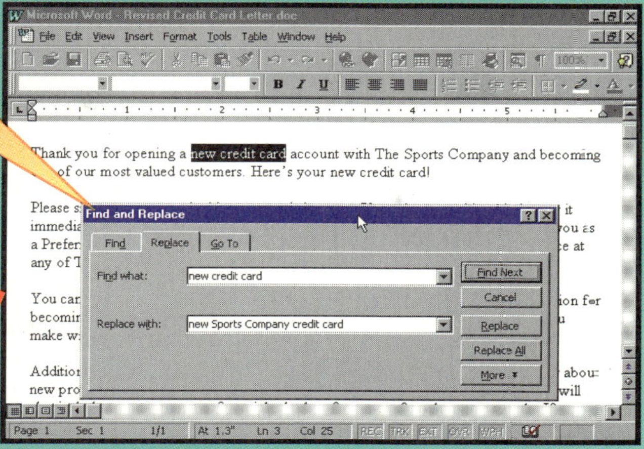

Fields

A field is a placeholder that instructs Word to insert information into a document.

Margins

The margin is the distance from the text to the edge of the paper. Standard single-sided documents have four margins: top, bottom, left, and right.

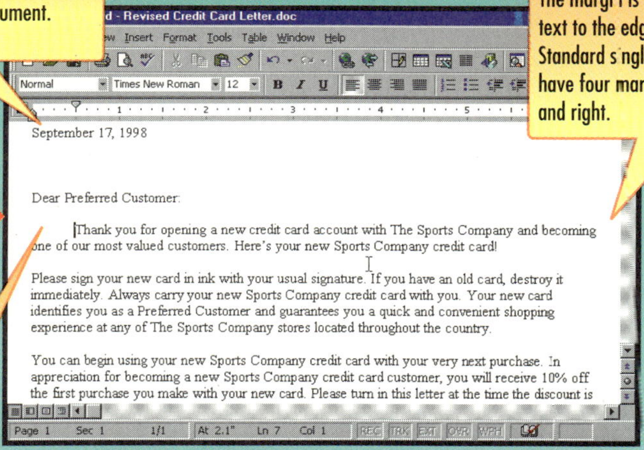

Indents

To help your reader find information quickly, you can indent paragraphs from the margins. Indenting paragraphs sets them off from the rest of the document.

Fonts

A font, also commonly referred to as a typeface, is a set of characters with a specific design.

Bulleted and Numbered Lists

Whenever possible, use bulleted or numbered lists to organize information and make your writing clear and easy to read.

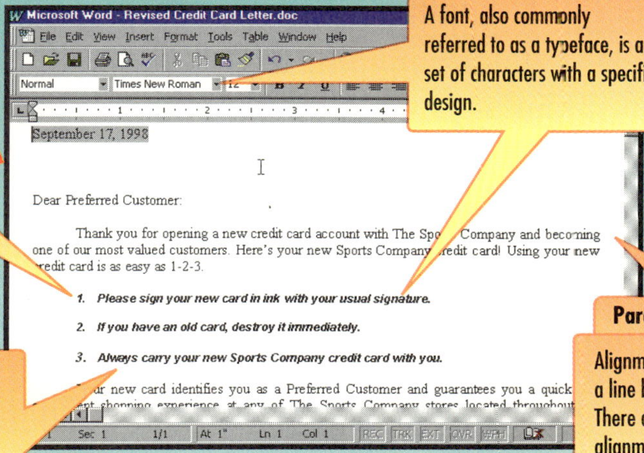

Character Effects

Different character effects can be applied to selections to add emphasis or interest to a document.

Paragraph Alignment

Alignment is how text is positioned on a line between the margins or indents. There are four types of paragraph alignment: left, center, right, and justified.

3 Creating a Report and a Newsletter

COMPETENCIES

After completing this lab, you will know how to:

1. **Create a page break.**
2. **Format headings.**
3. **Use the Document Map.**
4. **Create and update a table of contents.**
5. **Center a page vertically.**
6. **Add footnotes.**
7. **Set tab stops.**
8. **Insert and size graphic objects.**
9. **Add captions and cross-references.**
10. **Add headers and footers.**
11. **Create and enhance a WordArt object.**
12. **Create horizontal rules.**
13. **Create newspaper columns.**
14. **Use hyphenation.**
15. **Insert text boxes.**
16. **Add a drop cap.**

CASE STUDY

The Southwest regional manager is very pleased with your work so far, and has asked you to help with the development of the first monthly newsletter.

You have been asked to develop several topics to be used as articles in the newsletter. In this lab you will use many features of Word 97 that make it easy to create a well-organized and attractive report. The first two pages of your report are shown here.

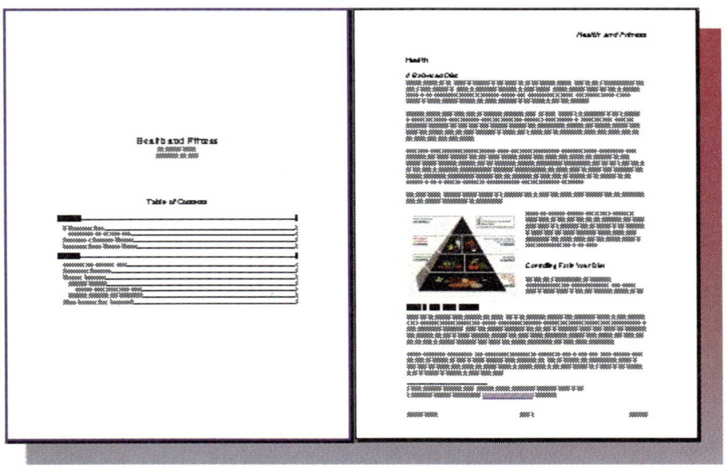

In addition you are to create a sample newsletter design using several of the topics from your report. In a newsletter, information must be easy to read and, most importantly, be visually appealing. In this lab you will use some of the desktop publishing tools in Word 97 to create a newsletter. The first page of the newsletter is shown here.

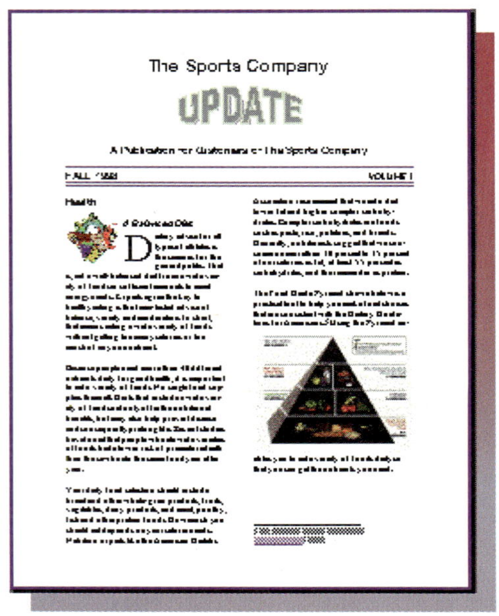

Concept Overview

The following concepts will be introduced in this lab:

1. Document Breaks	There are three types of breaks that can be inserted into a document: page, column, and section.
2. Styles	A style is a set of formats that is assigned a name.
3. Footnotes and Endnotes	Footnotes are source references or text offering additional explanation that are placed at the bottom of a page. Endnotes are also source references or long comments that typically appear at the end of a document.
4. Tab Stops	A tab stop is a stopping point along a line to which text will indent when you press Tab ⭾.
5. Graphics	A graphic is a non-text element or object, such as a picture or drawing, that can be added to a document.
6. Captions and Cross-References	A caption is a title or explanation for a table, picture, or graph. A cross-reference is a reference from one part of your document to related information in another part.
7. Headers and Footers	A header is a line or several lines of text at the top of each page just below the top margin. A footer is text at the bottom of every page just above the bottom margin.
8. WordArt	The WordArt feature is used to enhance your documents by changing the shape of text, adding 3-D effects, and changing the alignment of text on a line.
9. Special Effects	Word 97 includes many commands that add special effects, such as shadows and 3-D effects, to enhance drawing objects, including WordArt.
10. Hyphenation	The hyphenation feature inserts a hyphen in long words that fall at the end of a line to split the word between lines.

Part 1

Creating a Page Break

You have just attended the first planning session for the newsletter, during which it was decided that the purpose of the newsletter would be two-fold: to promote The Sports Company and to provide information related to a healthy, active lifestyle.

After several days of research, you have organized your notes and written a brief report on topics related to nutrition and fitness using information from many sources including books, magazine articles, and the World Wide Web.

- To see the report, load Word 97 and open the file Newsletter Research from your data disk.
- If necessary, maximize the document window and switch to Normal view.

Your screen should be similar to Figure 3-1.

FIGURE 3-1

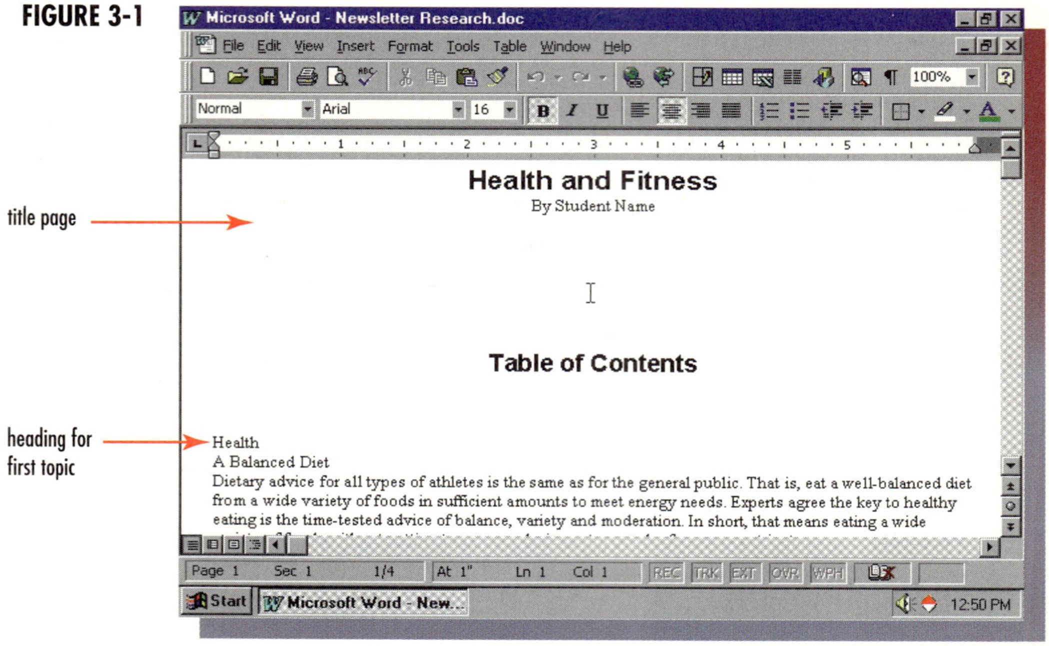

The first page of the report is the title page. This page commonly includes information such as the report title, the name of the author, and the date. In addition, you have decided to include a brief table of contents on this page.

- Replace Student Name with your name.
- Enter the current date below your name.

Notice that the text for the first topic currently begins on the same page as the title. You want the title page to print on a page by itself. To force a new page to begin at a specified location, you need to insert a page break. A page break is one of several types of document breaks.

- Move to the H in "Health."

Concept 1: Document Breaks

There are three types of breaks that can be inserted into documents: page, column, and section. Page and column breaks start a new page or column beginning with the next line. Normally Word inserts "soft" page and column breaks automatically into a document whenever the text fills the page or column. Entering a **manual** (or "hard") **page break** or column break instructs Word to begin a new page or column regardless of the amount of text on the previous page or column.

Section breaks divide a document into sections that can be formatted differently. The section break stores the format settings associated with that section of the document. The type of section break selected controls whether the following text begins on the next page, on the next even or odd page, or continues on the same page.

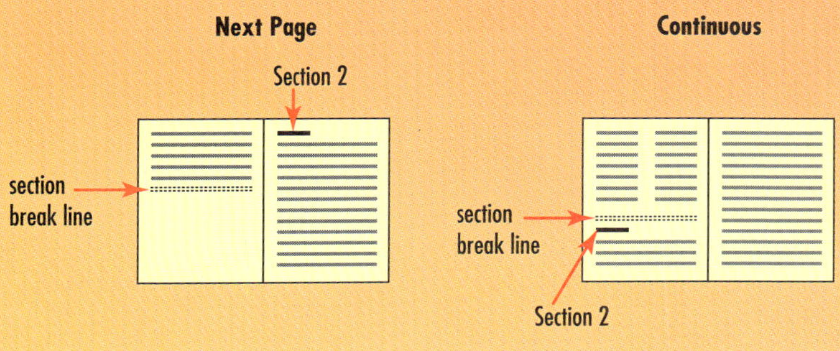

Word automatically inserts section breaks for you if you change the formatting of selected text, such as inserting columns or centering selected text vertically on a page.

- Choose Insert/Break.
- If necessary, select Page Break.
- Click OK.

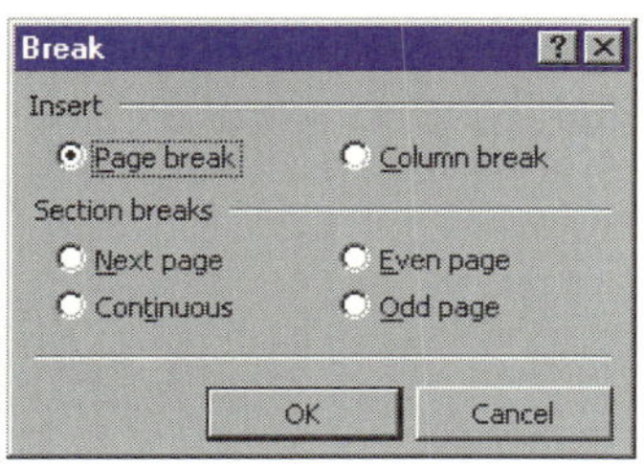

The keyboard shortcut is Ctrl + ←Enter.

Your screen should be similar to Figure 3-2.

FIGURE 3-2

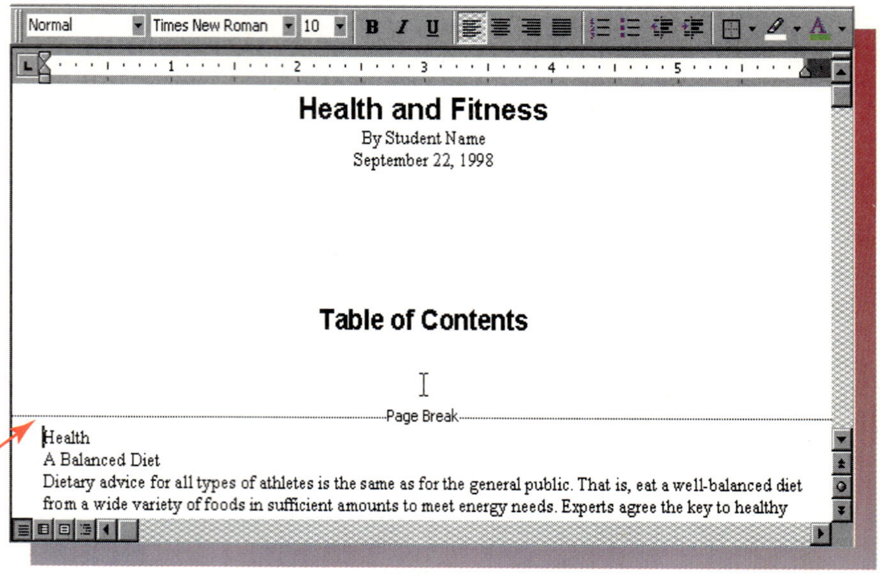

manual page break line

A dotted Page Break line appears above the heading indicating that a manual page break was entered at that position. All soft page breaks following the insertion of a manual page break are immediately adjusted.

Formatting Headings

Next you would like to improve the appearance of the document by adding formatting to the headings. Although you could apply different fonts, sizes, and character effects to each heading, it is easier to use Word's built-in formatting styles.

Concept 2: Styles

A **style** is a set of formats that is assigned a name. Word includes 75 predefined styles, or you can create your own custom styles. Many styles are automatically applied when certain features, such as footnotes, are used. Others must be applied manually to selected text.

Styles can be applied to characters or paragraphs. **Character styles** consist of a combination of any character formats in the Fonts dialog box that affect selected text. **Paragraph styles** are a combination of any character formats and paragraph formats that affect all text in a paragraph. A paragraph style can include all the font settings that apply to characters as well as tab settings, indents, and line settings that apply to paragraphs. The default paragraph style is Normal, and it includes character settings of Times New Roman 10 pt and paragraph settings of left indent to 0, single line spacing, and left alignment. The Styles drop-down list box in the Formatting toolbar displays the style of the current selection.

In addition, many paragraph styles are designed to affect specific text elements such as headings, captions, and footnotes. One of the most commonly used styles is a **heading style**, which is designed to identify different levels of headings in a document. Heading styles include combinations of fonts, type sizes, bold, and italics. The first four heading styles and the formats associated with each are shown below:

Heading Level	Appearance
Heading 1	**Arial 14 pt bold**
Heading 2	***Arial 12 pt bold, italic***
Heading 3	Arial 12 pt
Heading 4	**Arial 12 pt bold**

The most important heading in a document should be assigned a Heading 1 style. This style is the largest and most prominent. The next most important heading should be assigned the Heading 2 style, and so on. Headings give your reader another visual cue about how the information is grouped in your document.

This document contains four levels of headings that you would like to identify with different heading styles. The two main headings are Health at the beginning of page 2 and Fitness on page 4. You will apply a Heading 1 style to these headings.

- If necessary, move to anywhere in the Health heading on page 2.
- Choose Format/Style.
- If necessary, select All Styles from the List drop-down list box.

The Style dialog box on your screen should be similar to Figure 3-3.

FIGURE 3-3

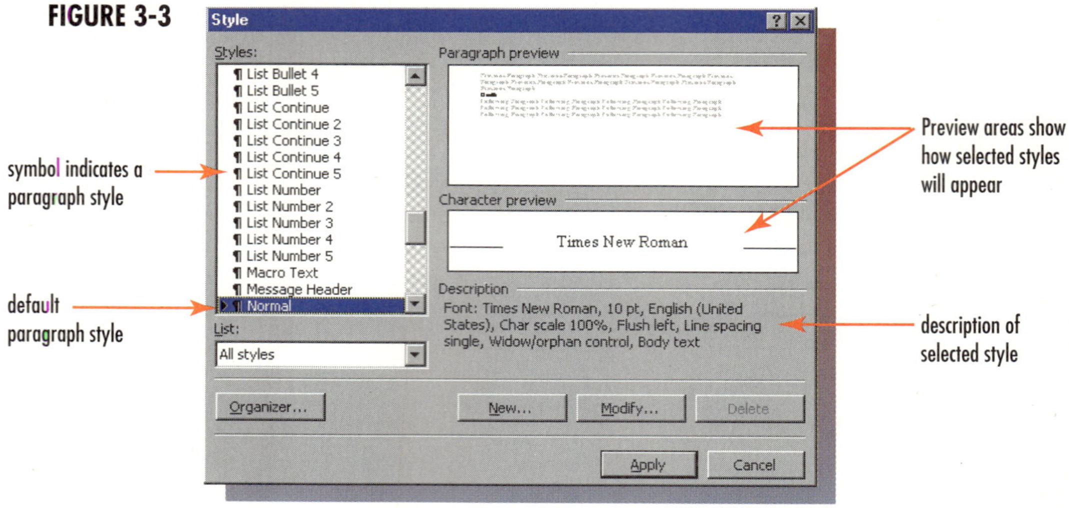

> A character style is preceded with the letter a.

The Styles list box displays the names of all the preset styles that are included in the Word program in alphabetical order. The default style, Normal, is highlighted. Notice the ¶ symbol preceding the style. This indicates it is a paragraph style. The format settings included in the currently selected style of Normal are displayed in the Description box, and the Preview areas show how text formatted in this style will appear. To apply the Heading 1 style to the text,

- Select Heading 1.
- Click Apply.

Your screen should be similar to Figure 3-4.

FIGURE 3-4

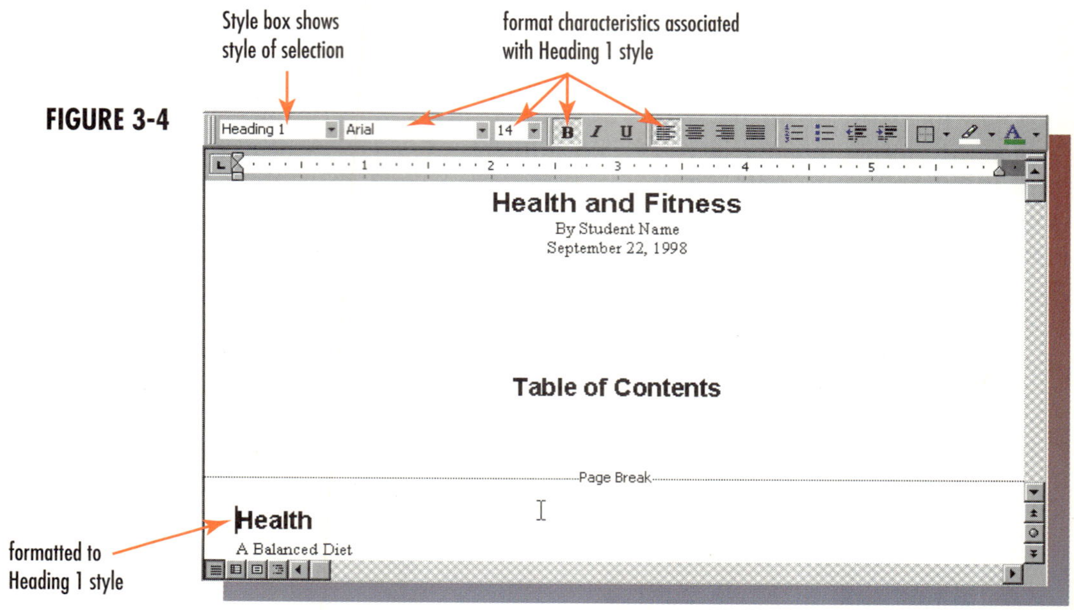

Notice that the entire heading appears in the selected style. This is because a Heading 1 style is a paragraph style and it affects the entire paragraph that the insertion point is on. Also notice that the Styles drop-down list box in the Formatting toolbar now displays Heading 1 as the style applied to the selected paragraph.

Word 97 will apply the Heading 1 style automatically to text as you type if you end a sentence without punctuation and press ←Enter twice.

Using the Document Map

Next you want to apply the same heading style to the second main topic heading, Fitness, located on page 4. To help you locate and move through the document, you can use Online Layout view. This view is designed for reading online.

- Click Online Layout View.

The menu equivalent is View/Online Layout.

Your screen should be similar to Figure 3-5.

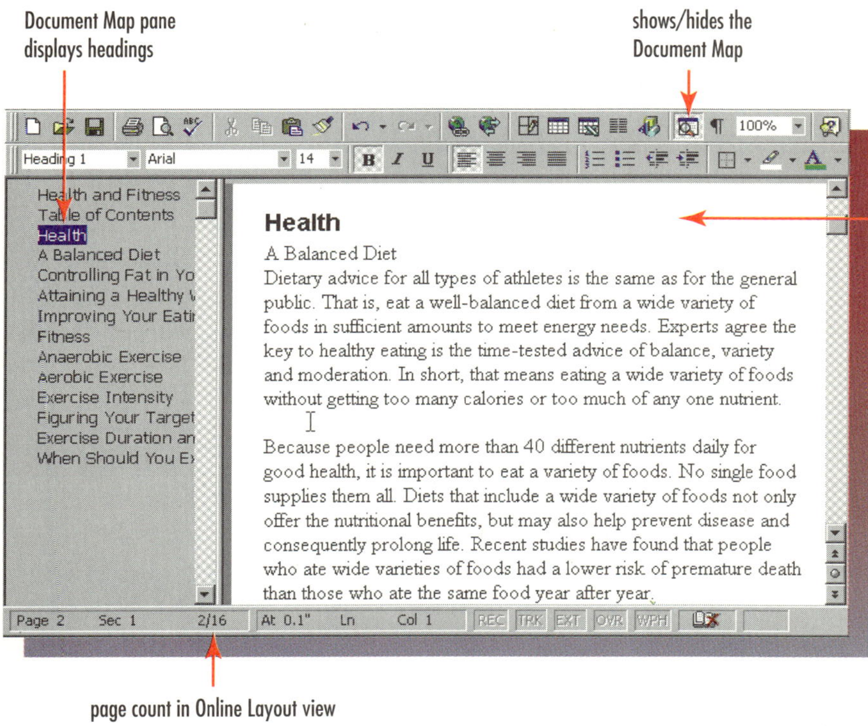

FIGURE 3-5

Do not be concerned if your screen does not display all the headings. They will appear as you apply heading styles.

The workspace is divided vertically into two sections or **panes**. The **document pane** on the right displays the document in Online Layout view. In this view the character size is displayed at 12 pt to make the text easier to read, and the text automatically wraps to fit the window space, rather than the way it would actually print. This causes the page numbering shown in the status bar to adjust based on the new size and length of the document.

Both panes can be scrolled independently and can be resized.

The **Document Map pane** on the left displays the headings in your document. All text that is formatted with a heading style is displayed in this pane. When your document does not contain any headings formatted with heading styles, the program automatically searches the document for paragraphs that

If the Document Map is not displayed on your screen, click or choose View/Document Map to display it.

> If your Document Map does not display the headings, scroll to page 9 and move the insertion point to the Fitness heading.

look like headings (for example, short lines with a larger font size) and displays them in the Document Map. If it cannot find any such headings, the Document Map is blank. The highlighted heading shows your location in the document. Clicking on a heading in the Document Map quickly jumps to that location in the document.

- Click Fitness (in the Document Map).

> The Repeat command displays the last action performed following the command. If you cannot repeat the last action, the Repeat command displays "Can't Repeat."

Rather than reselecting the same style from the menu again, you can quickly repeat your last action. To do this,

- Choose Edit/Repeat Style.

> The keyboard shortcut is Ctrl + Y.

The Fitness heading is formatted to the Heading 1 style. The next heading to be formatted is the title of the first article in the Health section of the report. To quickly move back to the Health section heading,

- Click Health (in the Document Map).

The insertion point moves to the beginning of the Health heading. The article title is a subheading below the main topic heading. Because it is one level lower than the heading above it, the Heading 2 style will be used. Another way to select a style is from the Style button.

> The Styles list displays the most commonly used styles.

> The menu equivalent is Format/Style/Styles/Heading 2/Apply.

- Move the insertion point to anywhere in the heading "A Balanced Diet" on page 2.
- Open the Style drop-down list box.
- Choose Heading 2.

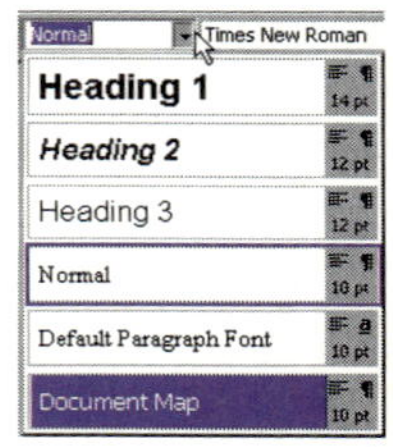

Your screen should be similar to Figure 3-6.

FIGURE 3-6

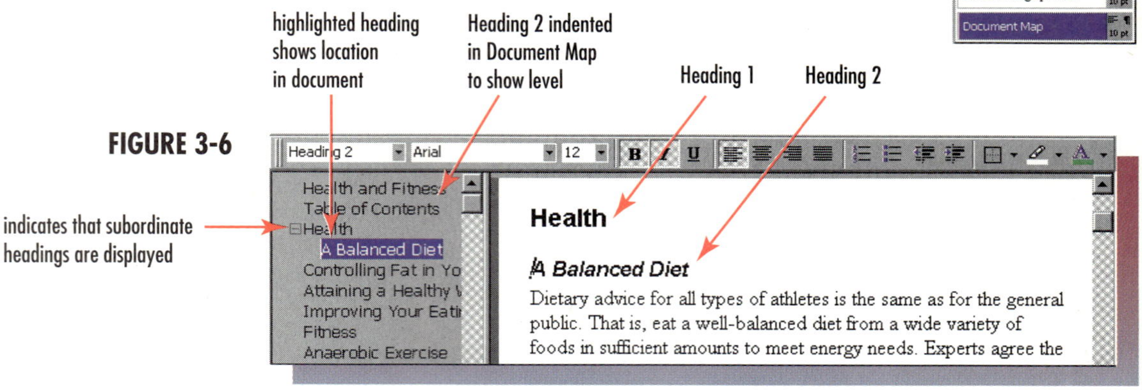

Notice the ⊟ symbol to the left of the Health heading in the Document Map; this indicates that all subordinate headings are displayed. A ⊞ symbol would indicate that subordinate headings are not displayed.

- Apply the heading styles in the table below to the remaining headings in the document:

Page #	Heading	Style
4	Controlling Fat in Your Diet	Heading 3
6	Attaining a Healthy Weight	Heading 2
7	Improving Your Eating Habits	Heading 2
9	Exercise and Weight Loss	Heading 2
10	Anaerobic Exercise	Heading 2
11	Aerobic Exercise	Heading 2
12	Exercise Intensity	Heading 3
13	Figuring Your Target Heart Rate	Heading 4
14	Exercise Duration and Frequency	Heading 3
16	When Should You Exercise?	Heading 2

- When you are done, use the Document Map to quickly return to the top of the document.
- Return to Normal view.

To display the Heading 4 style in the Styles drop-down list, hold down ⇧Shift while clicking to open the list. All available styles are displayed.

If you accidentally apply the wrong heading style, reselect the text and select the correct style. To return the style to the default, select Normal.

Creating a Table of Contents

Now you are ready to create the table of contents to appear on the title page. A table of contents is a listing of the topics that appear in a document and their associated page references. It shows the reader at a glance what topics are included in the document and makes it easier for the reader to locate information. A table of contents can be generated automatically by Word once you have applied heading styles to the document headings.

You want the table of contents listing to be displayed several lines below the heading Table of Contents on the title page. To create the table of contents,

- Move to the second blank line below the Table of Contents heading (page 1).
- Choose Insert/Index and Tables.
- If necessary, open the Table of Contents tab.

The Index and Tables dialog box on your screen should be similar to Figure 3-7.

FIGURE 3-7

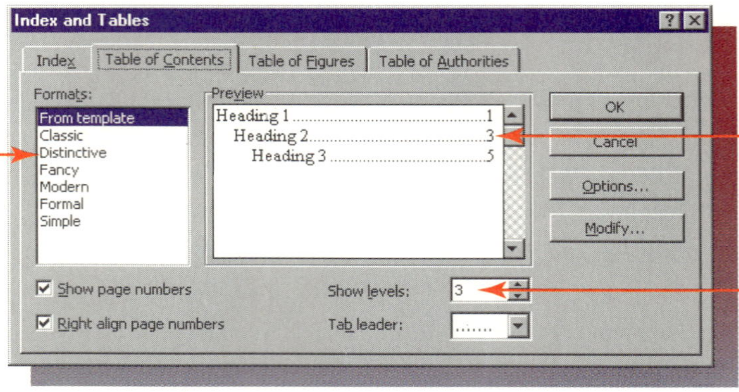

First you need to select the format or design of the table of contents. The Formats list box displays the names of the available formats, and the Preview box displays an example of the selected format, From Template. This format option is used to design your own table of contents and save it as a template by modifying the existing format.

- Highlight each format option to preview the different table of contents formats.
- Select the Formal format.

This style will display the page numbers flush with the right margin, and with a series of dots called **tab leaders** between the heading and the page number. The Show Levels text box shows that Word will create a table of contents for three levels of headings. Your document has four levels of headings.

- Change the Show Levels to 4.
- Click OK.

Your screen should be similar to Figure 3-8.

FIGURE 3-8

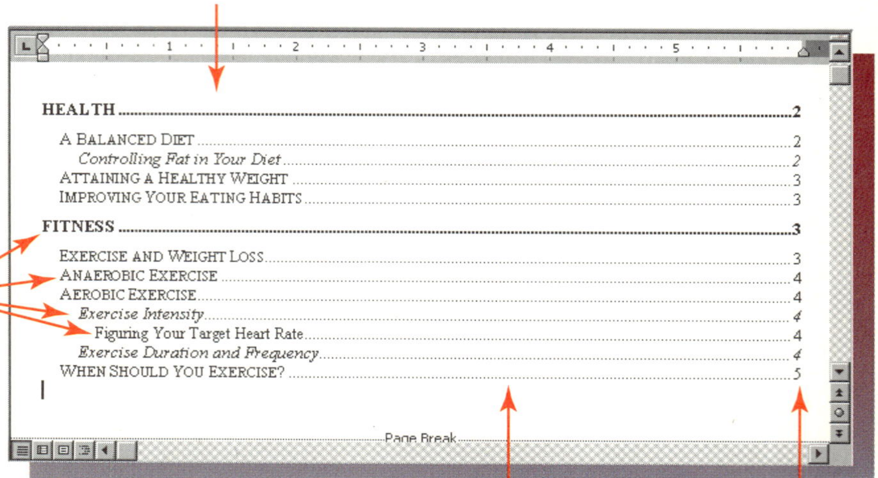

Word searches for headings with the specified styles, sorts them by heading level, references their page numbers, and displays the table of contents in the document. The headings that were assigned a Heading 1 style are aligned with the left margin, and subordinate heading levels are indented as appropriate.

- Click anywhere within the table of contents.

Notice that the text in the table of contents is shaded, indicating it is a field. This means it can be updated to reflect changes you may make at a later time in your document. Also notice that the Styles box displays "TOC" followed by a number. Each line in the table of contents is formatted using the appropriate table of contents style.

Centering a Page Vertically

Finally, you want the information on the title page to be centered vertically. To do this,

- Select all text on the title page.
- Choose File/Page Setup.
- If necessary, open the Layout tab.

The Page Setup dialog box on your screen should be similar to Figure 3-9.

FIGURE 3-9

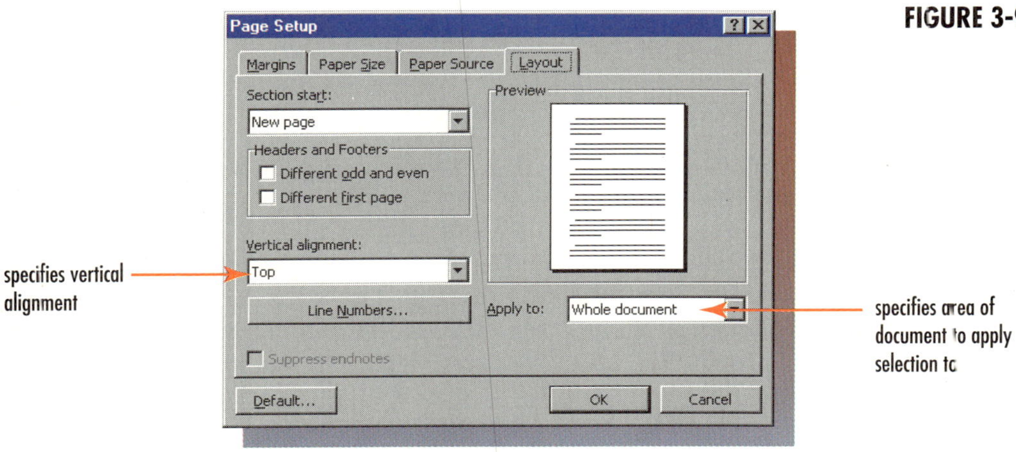

From the Vertical Alignment list box you specify how the text is to be aligned on the page vertically. In addition, in the Apply To list box you need to specify what part of the text you want to be aligned to the new setting. To center the selected text vertically on the page,

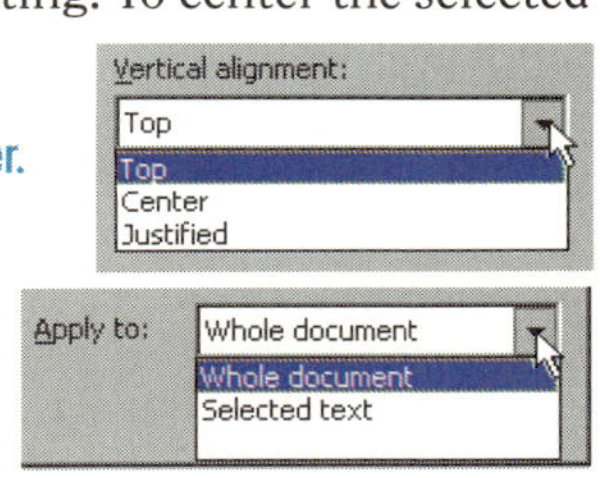

- From the Vertical Alignment drop-down list, select Center.
- From the Apply To drop down-list, select Selected Text.
- Click OK.

- Clear the selection.
- Switch to Page Layout view and set the zoom to Whole Page.

Your screen should be similar to Figure 3-10.

FIGURE 3-10

text centered vertically on page

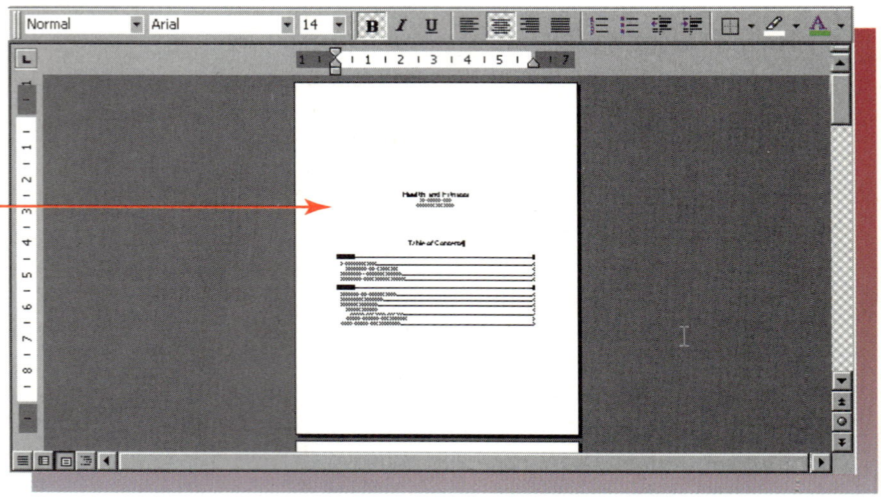

Now you can see the text on the title page is centered vertically between the top and bottom margin.

- Return to Normal view and scroll to the bottom of page 1.

Notice that, in addition to the page break line, a section break line is displayed. Word automatically inserts a section break whenever different page formats are used within the same document. In this case, a section break was inserted because the title page now has a different vertical alignment than the rest of the document. This type of section break starts the next page of the document on a new page. Therefore the page break you added earlier, if left in the document, would cause a blank page to be printed.

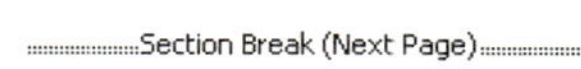

To remove a manual page break, select the page break line and press Delete.

- Delete the manual page break.
- If necessary, delete any blank lines above the Health heading.

Adding Footnotes

Next you need to add several footnotes to the document.

Concept 3: Footnotes and Endnotes

Footnotes are source references or text offering additional explanation that are placed at the bottom of a page. **Endnotes** are also source references or long comments that typically appear at the end of a document. You can have both footnotes and endnotes in the same document.

Footnotes and endnotes consist of two parts, the note reference mark and the note text. The **note reference mark** is commonly a superscript number appearing in the document at the end of the material being referenced (for example text[1]). It can also be a character or combination of characters. The **note text** for a footnote appears at the bottom of the page on which the reference mark appears. The footnote text is separated from the document text by a horizontal line called the **note separator**. Endnote text appears as a listing at the end of the document.

The Footnote command on the Insert menu will automatically number and place footnotes and endnotes in a document. The first reference that needs to be footnoted is the text in the second paragraph on page 2. Before using the Footnote command, the insertion point must be positioned where the footnote number is to be displayed. To quickly move to that location in the document, you can use the Document Map.

- Click Document Map.

Document Map can be displayed in all views.

Notice that the text in the right window is not adjusted in size as it is when in Online Layout view, and the text does not wrap to fit the window.

- Click A Balanced Diet (in the Document Map).
- Move to the end of the second paragraph after the word "year."
- Choose Insert/Footnote.

The keyboard shortcut to insert a footnote using the default setting is Alt + Ctrl + F.

In the Footnote and Endnote dialog box, you specify whether you want to create footnotes or endnotes and the type of reference mark you want to appear in the document: a numbered mark or a custom mark. A custom mark can be any nonnumeric character, such as an asterisk, that you enter in the text box. You want to create numbered footnotes, so the default settings of Footnote and AutoNumber are acceptable.

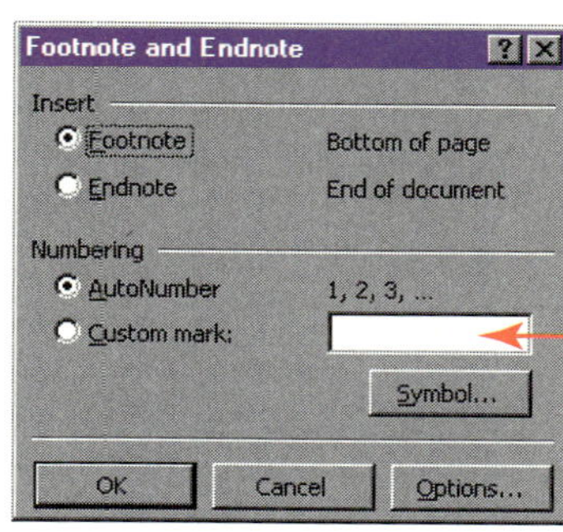

use to specify a custom mark

- Click OK.

Your screen should be similar to Figure 3-11.

FIGURE 3-11

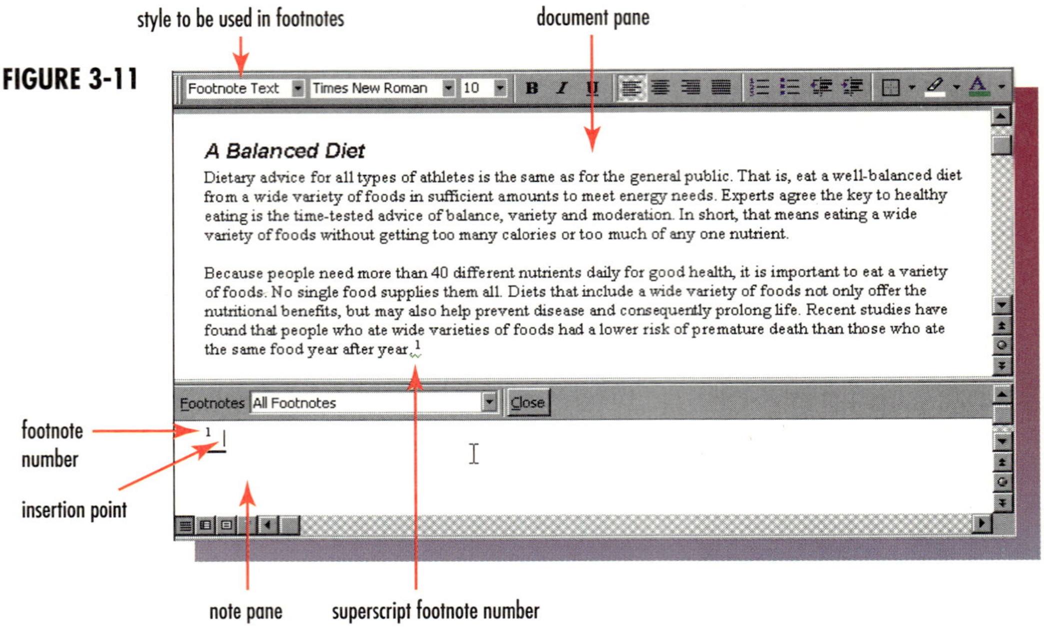

The Document Map is cleared, and the workspace is now horizontally divided into an upper document pane and a lower **note pane**. The footnote number, 1, appears as a superscript in the document at the location of the insertion point. The note pane displays the footnote number 1 and the insertion point. This is where you enter the text for the footnote. When you enter a footnote, you can use the same menus, commands, and features as you would in the document window. Any commands that are not available are dimmed.

If necessary, choose Ignore All for all names that are identified as misspelled words as they occur when you enter the note text.

- Type **Sally Squires, "Expand Your Palate."** ***Weight Watchers,*** **Nov/Dec 1996, p. 16.** (Do not press ←Enter.)

The note pane on your screen should be similar to Figure 3-12.

FIGURE 3-12

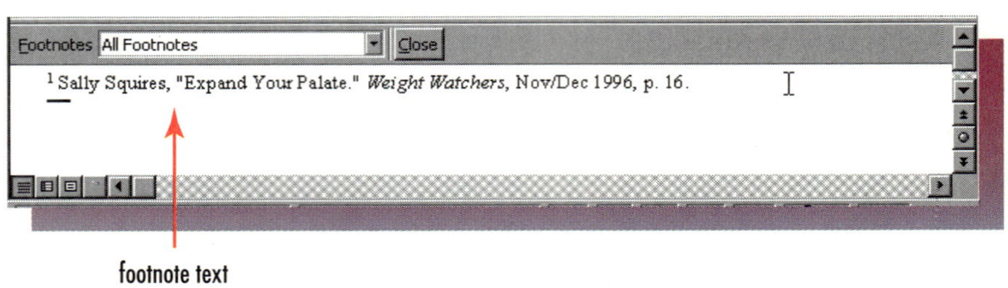

The second footnote will provide the source for information located on page 3. To move to this location and insert a second footnote,

- Click Document Map.
- Click Attaining a Healthy Weight.
- Move to after the sentence ending "woman 22%."
- Choose Insert/Footnote/ OK .

The footnote number 2 is entered at the insertion point location. The note pane is active again, so you can enter the text for the second footnote.

- Type **Covert Bailey, *The New Fit or Fat* (Boston: Houghton Mifflin Company), p. 18.**

To delete a footnote or endnote, highlight the reference mark and press Delete. The reference mark and associated note text are removed, and the following footnotes are renumbered.

Now you realize that you forgot to enter a footnote earlier in the text, on page 2.

- Display the Document Map and click A Balanced Diet.
- Set the zoom to Page Width.
- Move to the end of the first line of paragraph 5 on page 2 (following the word "need").
- Insert a footnote at this location.

You may need to scroll the window to see the end of the sentence.

A footnote or endnote can be copied or moved by selecting the marker and using cut or copy and paste. You also can use drag and drop to copy or move a note.

The note pane on your screen should be similar to Figure 3-13.

footnote inserted between existing footnotes

FIGURE 3-13

Notice that this footnote is now number 2 in the document, and a blank footnote line has been entered in the note pane for the footnote text. Word automatically adjusted the footnote numbers when the new footnote was inserted. This footnote reference is to a site on the World Wide Web. It will include the URL to the site. A **URL** (**Uniform Resource Locator**) is the address that indicates the location of a document on the World Wide Web.

- Type **American Dietetic Association. http://www.eatright.org (9/16/98).**

If you click on a URL hyperlink, Word tries to start the program on your system that accesses the Internet and the World Wide Web.

You'll learn more about URLs and the Word Wide Web in a later lab.

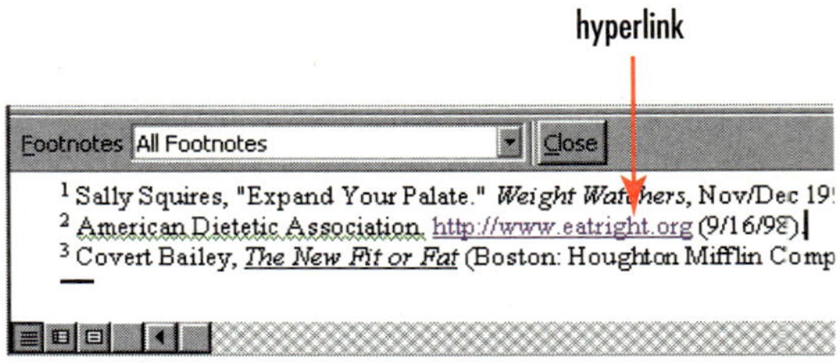

The text of the URL appears in blue and underlined. This indicates Word has changed the text to a hyperlink. A **hyperlink** is a connection to a location in the current document, another document, or to a WWW site. It allows the reader to jump to the referenced location by clicking on the hyperlink when reading the document on the screen.

- Add the following two footnotes to the document:

Section	Paragraph	Following	Footnote
Improving Your Eating Habits	2nd	"frustrating"	**Squires, p. 20.**
Anaerobic Exercise	2nd	"long"	**Daryn Eller, "The Energy Edge." *Health*, Nov/Dec 1996, p. 93.**

Additional footnotes will be added to the report as a practice exercise.

Now that you are finished entering footnotes, to close the note pane, move to the first article and turn off the Document Map.

- Click Close.
- Click Health (in the Document Map).
- Click Document Map.

You can also hide and display the footnote pane any time by using the View/Footnotes command or by double-clicking on a footnote reference mark.

In Normal view you can see the footnote associated with a note reference mark by pointing to the reference mark. The footnote will be displayed as a Screen Tip.

If your Screen Tip does not display, use Tools/Options/View/Screen Tips to turn on this feature.

- Point to note reference mark 1 in the document.

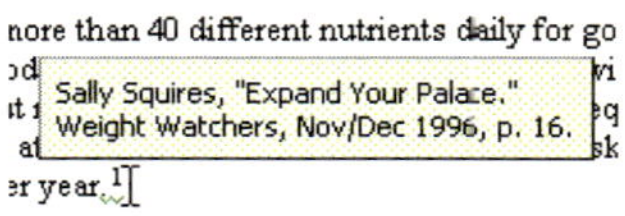

Finally, you want to see how the footnotes will actually appear when the document is printed.

If the zoom percentage is too small, the footnote numbers will not display correctly.

- Switch to Page Layout view and set the zoom percentage to 75 percent.
- Scroll to the bottom of page 2 to see the footnotes.

Your screen should be similar to Figure 3-14.

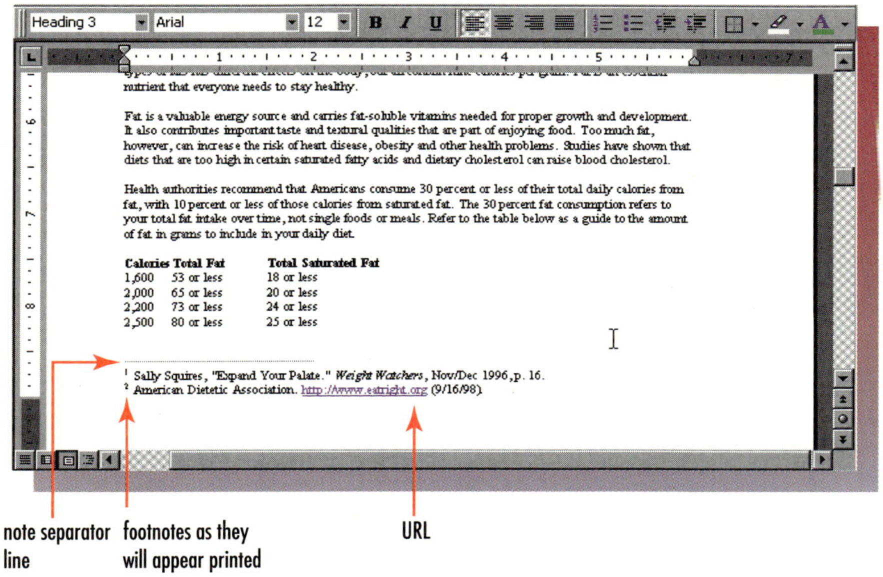

FIGURE 3-14

The footnotes are displayed immediately above the bottom margin separated from the text by the note separator line.

- Scroll to the bottom of the next page to see the third and fourth footnotes.

While looking at the third footnote, you see that you forgot to include the publication date. While in Page Layout view, you can edit and format footnotes just like any other text.

- Insert a comma and the year 1991 after the word "Company" in footnote 3.
- Check the other footnotes. If you see any other errors, correct them.

Setting Tab Stops

Next you want to improve the appearance of the calorie data on the bottom of page 2.

- Move to the information on calories located near the bottom of page 2.

The first column of data is aligned with the left margin. The second and third columns of data have been indented to tab stops. However, because the default tab stops are set at every 0.5 inch, the columns are not evenly spaced. To improve the appearance of the data, you will create custom tab stops that will align the data in evenly spaced columns.

Concept 4: Tab Stops

A **tab stop** is a stopping point along a line to which text will indent when you press Tab. The default tab stops of every 0.5 inch are visible on the ruler as light vertical lines below the numbers. As with other default settings, you can change the location of tab stops in the document. You can also select from five different types of tab stops that control how characters are positioned or aligned with the tab stop. The five tab types, the alignment tab mark that appears on the ruler, and the effects on the text are explained in the following table.

default tab stop markers

Alignment	Tab Mark	How It Affects Text	Example
Left	∟	Extends text to right from tab stop	left
Center	⊥	Aligns text centered on tab	center
Right	┘	Extends text to left from tab stop	right
Decimal	⊥.	Aligns text with decimal point	35.78
Bar	|	Draws a vertical line through text at the tab stop	text

When setting new tab stops, the new settings affect the current paragraph or selected paragraphs. When you insert custom tab stops, all default tab stops to the left of the custom tab stop are deleted. You can quickly specify custom tab stop locations and types using the ruler. To select a tab stop type, click the **tab alignment selector box** on the left end of the ruler to cycle through the types. Then, to specify where to place the selected tab stop type, click on the location in the ruler.

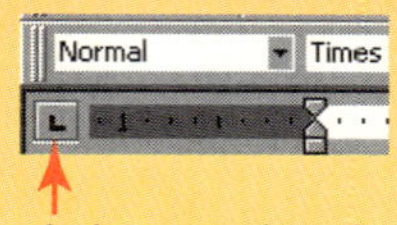

tab alignment selector box

Setting different types of tab stops is helpful for aligning text or numeric data vertically in columns. Using tab stops ensures that the text will indent to the same set location. Setting custom tab stops instead of pressing Tab or Spacebar repeatedly is a more professional way to format a document, as well as faster and more accurate. It also makes editing easier because you can change the tab stop settings for several paragraphs at once.

To align the calorie data, you will place two left tab stops at the 1-inch and 2.25-inch positions on the ruler.

> The menu equivalent is Format/Tabs/1.0/2.25/Left.

- Select the table heading line and the four lines of data.
- If necessary, click the tab alignment selector box until the left tab icon ∟ appears.
- Click the 1-inch position on the ruler.
- Click the 2.25-inch position on the ruler.

Your screen should be similar to Figure 3-15.

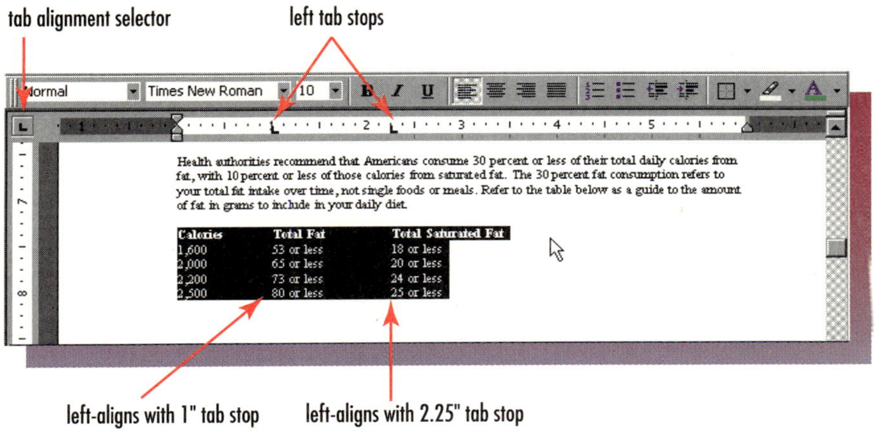

FIGURE 3-15

The two tabbed columns appropriately align with the new tab stops. All default tabs to the left of the new tab stops are cleared. After looking at the columns, you decide the third column heading would look better centered over the column of data. To make this change,

- Move to anywhere in the heading line.
- Drag the 2.25 tab stop mark off the ruler.
- Click the tab alignment selector box until the center tab icon appears.
- Set a center tab stop at the 2.5-inch position.

The menu equivalent is Format/Tabs/2.5/Center.

Your screen should be similar to Figure 3-16.

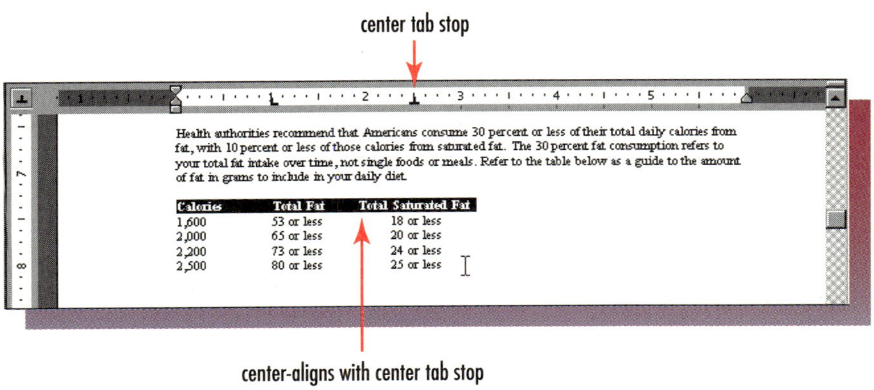

FIGURE 3-16

Inserting and Sizing Graphics

Next you want to add a picture of the Food Guide Pyramid to the report that will complement the subject of the first article. A picture is one of several different graphic objects that can be added to a Word document.

Graphic files commonly have file extensions such as .wmf, .bmp, .tif, .pcx, .wpg, .pic, and .cgm.

The only places you cannot place a graphic object are into a footnote, endnote, or caption.

If you "lose" an object in a stack, you can press Tab to cycle forward (or Shift + Tab to cycle backward) through the objects until the one you want is selected.

Concept 5: Graphics

A **graphic** is a non-text element or object, such as a drawing or picture, that can be added to a document. An **object** is an item that can be sized, moved, and manipulated. A graphic can be a simple **drawing object** consisting of shapes such as lines and boxes that can be created using the Drawing toolbar. A **picture** is an illustration such as a scanned photograph.

Each graphic object is surrounded by a **frame**, which is an invisible box or container. The frame keeps the items it contains together and lets you place the graphic object anywhere on the page, including in the margins or on top of or below other objects, including text.

When you insert or draw a graphic object, it is attached or **anchored** to a paragraph. However, sometimes the graphic and the paragraph may not appear on the same page. To keep the graphic and paragraph together on a page, you can **lock** the anchor. The text in the paragraph may wrap around the object in different ways. The five wrapping styles are shown below.

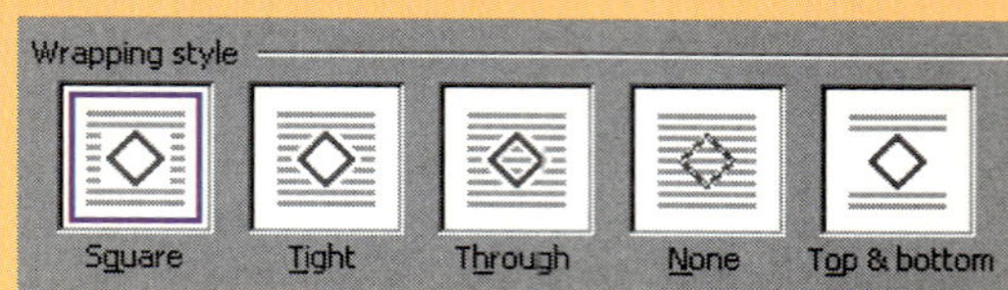

A graphic object can be manipulated in many ways. You can change its size, add captions, borders or shading, or move it to another location. In most cases you can simply drag a graphic to move it. If you have several graphics that you would like to manipulate as one unit, you can **group** them together as if they were a single object. You can then format and manipulate all the objects of a group at the same time. One way to group text and graphics is to include them inside a text box. A text box is a mini-document that acts as an object in that it is surrounded by a frame.

As objects are added to a document, they stack in layers and may overlap. You can move objects up or down within a stack.

Triangle is on top of stack | Triangle is sent to the back | Square is brought to the front

Add graphics to your documents to help the reader understand concepts, to add interest, and to make your document stand out from others.

You would like the picture of the Food Guide Pyramid to appear after the fourth paragraph on page 2.

- Move to the beginning of the fifth paragraph on page 2, which begins, "Using the Pyramid. . . ."

- Choose Insert/Picture/From File.
- Change the Look In location to the drive containing your data disk.
- Select Pyramid.pcx.
- Click Insert.

The Preview box displays the selected picture. If the Preview box is not displayed, click Preview in the toolbar.

The picture of the Food Guide Pyramid is inserted in the document at the insertion point (see Figure 3-17). However, the graphic is very large and you would like to reduce its size. To do this you must first select the object.

Graphic objects are not displayed in Normal view. If you insert a graphic in Normal view, Word automatically changes the view to Page Layout.

- Click on the pyramid picture.

Your screen should be similar to Figure 3-17.

FIGURE 3-17

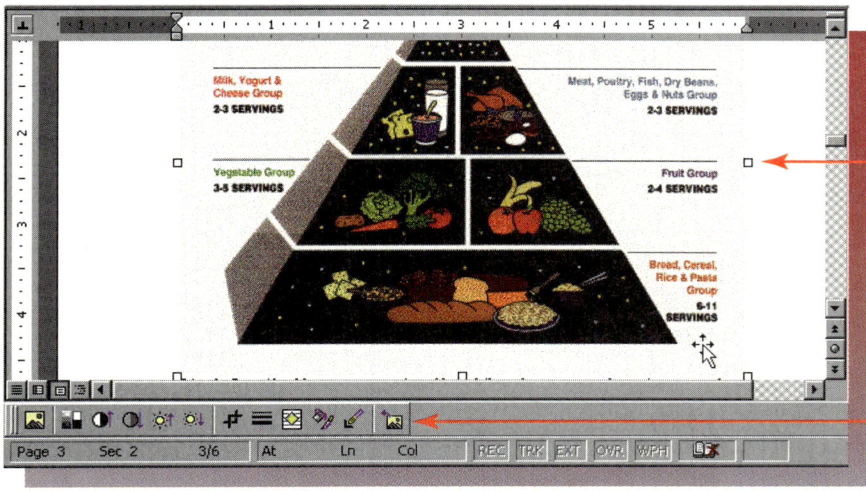

handles surround selected object

Picture toolbar

The picture is surrounded by eight boxes, called **handles**, indicating it is a selected object and can now be sized and moved anywhere in the document. The Picture toolbar is also automatically displayed. Its buttons (identified below) are used to modify the selected picture object. Your Picture toolbar may be floating or docked along an edge of the window, depending on where it was when last used.

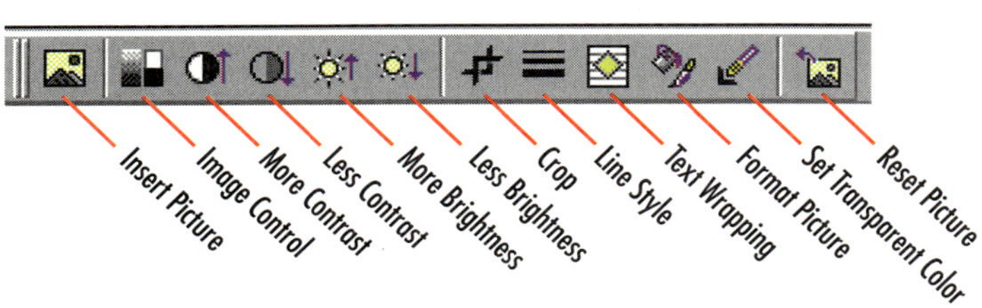

Refer to Toolbars in Lab 1 for information on this feature.

- If necessary, move the Picture toolbar to the left end of the status bar as in Figure 3-17.

> The mouse pointer changes to ⤡, just as it does when resizing a window.

> Use the rulers as a guide and refer to Figure 3-18 for size reference.

> Dragging a corner handle maintains the original proportions of the picture.

> The menu equivalent is F<u>o</u>rmat/P<u>i</u>cture/Wrapping/S<u>q</u>uare.

The handles are used to size the object, much as you would size a window. You want to reduce the image to approximately 3 inches wide by 2.25 inches high.

- Point to the lower right corner handle.
- Drag the mouse to reduce the size of the picture to approximately 3 x 2.25 inches.

Now that the picture is much smaller, you decide to have the text wrap around the graphic object.

- Click Text Wrapping.
- Choose Square.
- Resize the picture until the text wraps around it as in Figure 3-18.
- Clear the selection by clicking anywhere outside the graphic object.

Your screen should be similar to Figure 3-18.

FIGURE 3-18

picture object reduced in size

text wraps around object

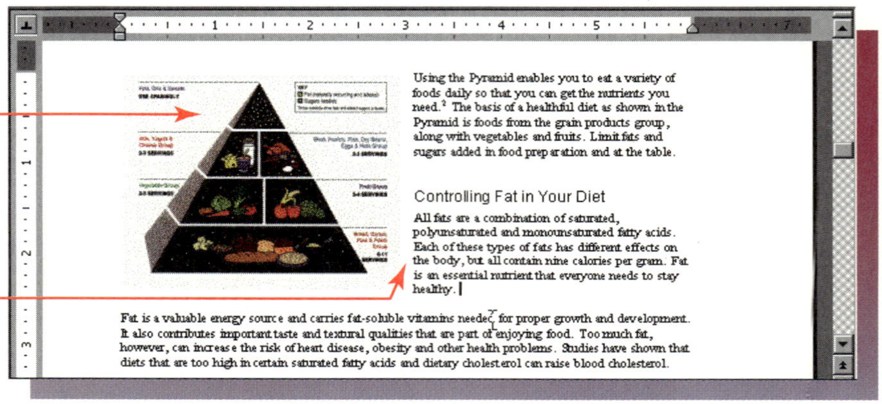

Because the picture object is aligned with the left margin, the text wraps to the right side of the object. If the object were centered between the margins, the text would wrap around the object on both sides.

Adding Captions and Cross-References

Next you want to add a caption to the pyramid figure, and a cross-reference to the figure in another part of the document.

Concept 6: Captions and Cross-References

A **caption** is a title or explanation for a table, picture, or graph. Captions aid the reader in quickly finding information in a document. Word can automatically add captions to graphic objects as they are inserted, or you can add them manually. The caption can be changed to reflect the type of object to which it refers, such as a table, chart, or figure. In addition, Word automatically numbers graphic objects and adjusts numbering when objects of the same type are added or deleted.

Once you have captions you can also include cross-references. A **cross-reference** is a reference from one part of your document to related information in another part. For example, if you have a graph in one part of the document that you would like to refer to in another section, you can add a cross-reference that tells the reader what page the graph is on. A cross-reference can also be inserted as a hyperlink, allowing you to jump to another location in the same document or in another document.

First you will add a caption below the Food Guide Pyramid picture.

- Move to the blank line below the Food Guide Pyramid picture.
- Choose Insert/Caption.

The Caption dialog box on your screen should be similar to Figure 3-19.

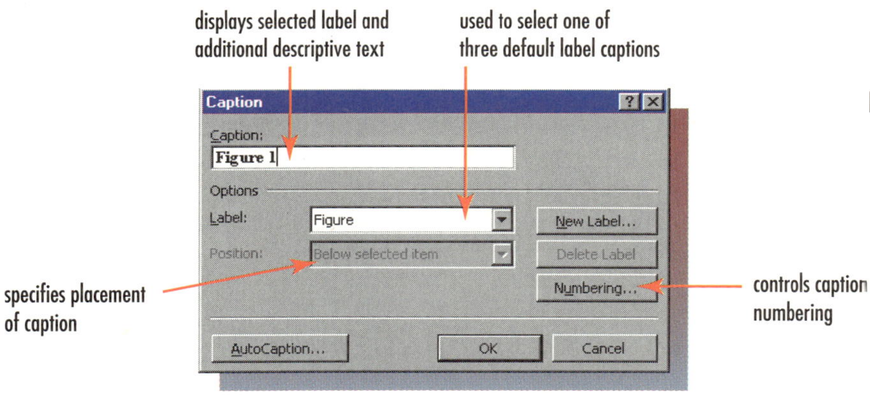

FIGURE 3-19

The options in this box are described below.

Option	Description
Label	Select from one of three default captions: Table, Figure, or Equation.
Position	Specify the location of the caption, either above or below a selected item. When an item is selected, the Position option is available.
New Label	Create your own captions.
Numbering	Specify the numbering format and starting number for your caption.
AutoCaption	Turns on the automatic insertion of a caption (label and number only) when you insert selected items into your document.

The most recently selected caption label and number appear in the Caption text box. You want the caption to be Figure 1, and you want to add additional descriptive text.

- If necessary, select Figure from the Label drop-down list.
- In the Caption text box, type **: Food Guide Pyramid** following "Figure 1."
- Click OK.

Your screen should be similar to Figure 3-20.

FIGURE 3-20

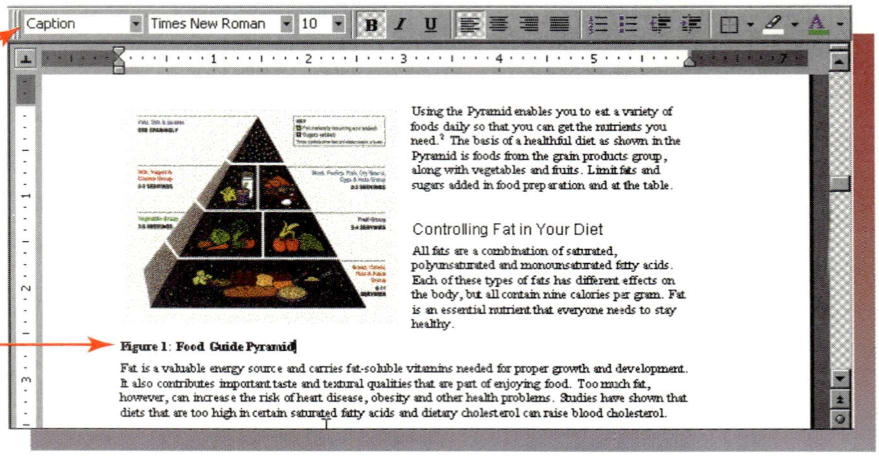

style used

caption added below figure

Later in the report, you have included a reference to information provided in the Food Guide Pyramid. To clarify this reference, you will use the cross-reference feature.

- Move to page 4, to the space following "recommended number of servings" in the first paragraph below the heading Improving Your Eating Habits.
- Type **in**
- Press Spacebar.
- Choose Insert/Cross-reference.

The Cross-reference dialog box on your screen should be similar to Figure 3-21.

FIGURE 3-21

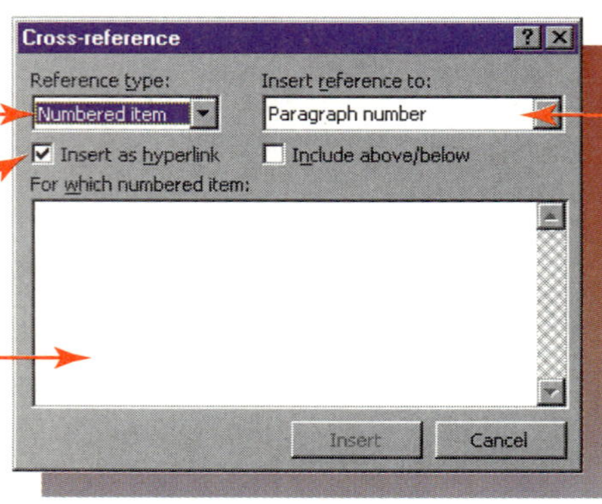

specifies type of item to be referenced

creates hyperlink cross-reference

displays list of selected reference types

specifies information to include in the cross-reference

You need to specify the type of item you are referencing and how you want the reference to appear. You want to reference the Food Guide Pyramid figure, and you only want the label "Figure 1" entered in the document.

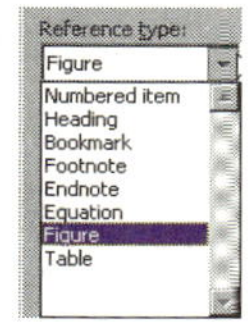

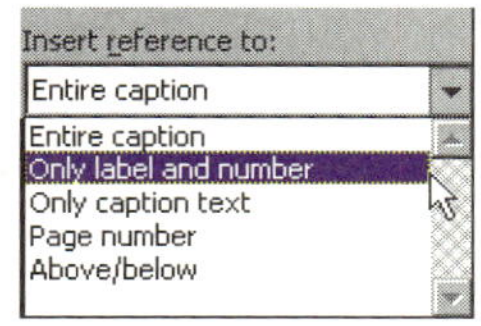

- From the Reference Type drop-down list box, select Figure.
- From the Insert Reference To list box, select Only label and number.

Because there is only one figure in this document, the Refers To list box correctly selects the figure to refer to. If there were multiple figures in the document, you would need to select the appropriate figure. Notice that the Insert as Hyperlink option is selected by default. This option creates a hyperlink between the cross-reference and the caption. The default setting is appropriate.

- Click Insert.
- Click Close.
- Press Spacebar.

Your screen should be similar to Figure 3-22.

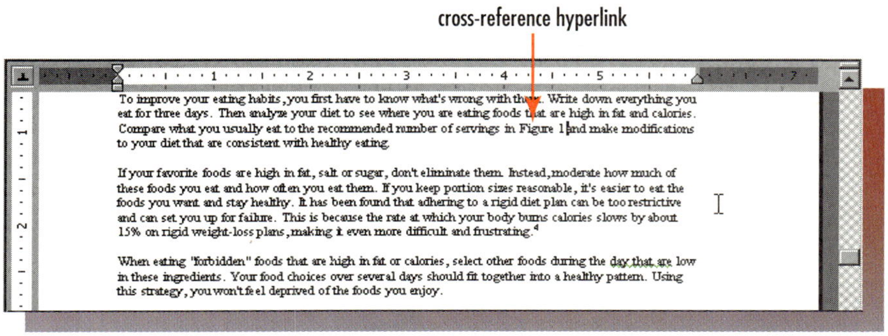

FIGURE 3-22

A cross-reference is entered into the document as a field. Therefore, if you insert another picture, the captions and cross-references will renumber automatically. When you are working on a long document with several figures, tables, and graphs, this feature is very helpful.

To use a cross-reference hyperlink to jump to the source it references, simply click on it.

- Click on the Figure 1 cross-reference.

> The mouse pointer shape changes to a 👆 when pointing to a hyperlink to show that the cross-reference is a hyperlink.

The document automatically jumps to the caption beneath the Food Guide Pyramid. The Web toolbar is automatically displayed because many hyperlinks are to items on the World Wide Web.

- Close the Web toolbar.

Adding Headers and Footers

Next you want to add a header to the report.

Concept 7: Headers and Footers

A **header** is a line or several lines of text at the top of each page just below the top margin. The header usually contains the title and the section of the document. A **footer** is a line or several lines of text at the bottom of every page just above the bottom margin. The footer usually contains the page number and perhaps the date. Headers and footers help the reader locate information in a document.

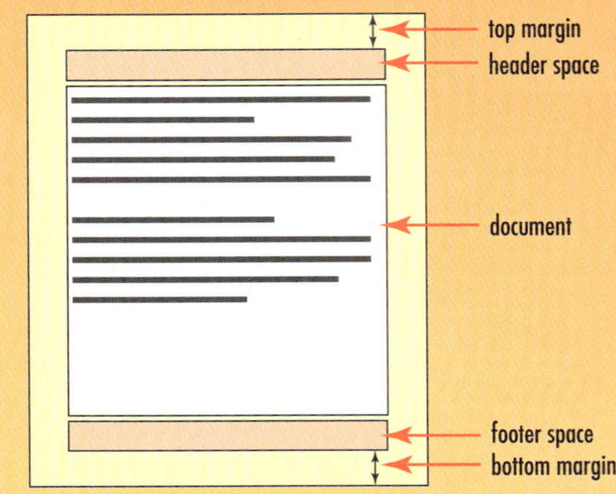

You want to add the title of your document to the header. To do this,

- Choose View/Header and Footer.

Your screen should be similar to Figure 3-23.

FIGURE 3-23

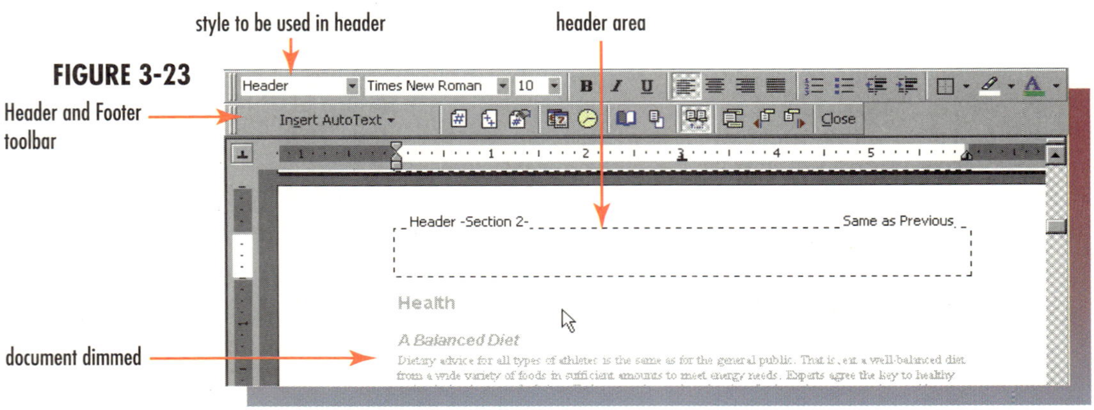

The document dims, the header area becomes active, and the Header and Footer toolbar is displayed. Its buttons are identified below.

> You could also double-click in the header or footer area to activate it.

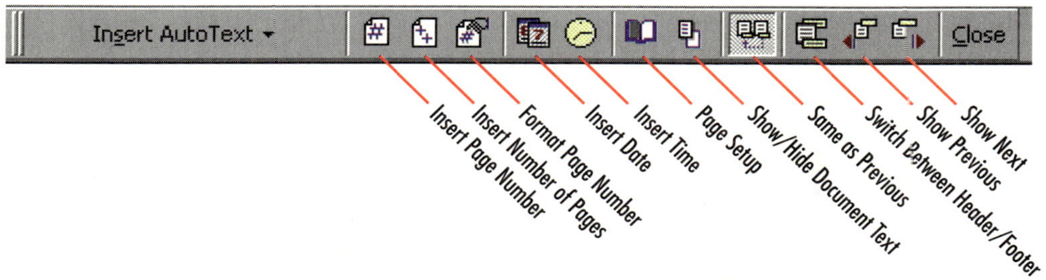

- If necessary, dock the Header and Footer toolbar below the Formatting toolbar.

Notice that you are in the header for Section 2. Section 1 is the title page. In the upper right corner is the message, "Same as Previous." This means that the Section 2 header will be the same as Section 1. Since the title page does not have a header, you need to turn off the Same as Previous option.

> If Same as Previous is on, the header in the sections before and after the section in which you are entering a header will have the same header.

- Click Same as Previous.

You type in the header as if it were a mini-document. The header and footer text can be formatted just like any other text. In addition, you can control the placement of the header and footer text by specifying where it should appear: left-aligned, centered, or right-aligned in the header or footer space.

- Set the format to Arial 14 pt, bold, italic, and right-aligned.
- Type **Health and Fitness**

Next you will insert your name, a page number, and today's date in the footer. To quickly add this information, you will use an AutoText entry. These are common entries that are stored in Word that can be selected and used multiple times.

> You can create your own AutoText entries using Insert/AutoText.

- Click Switch between Header and Footer.
- Turn off the Same as Previous option.
- Click Insert AutoText.

- Choose Author, Page#, Date.

AutoText entry

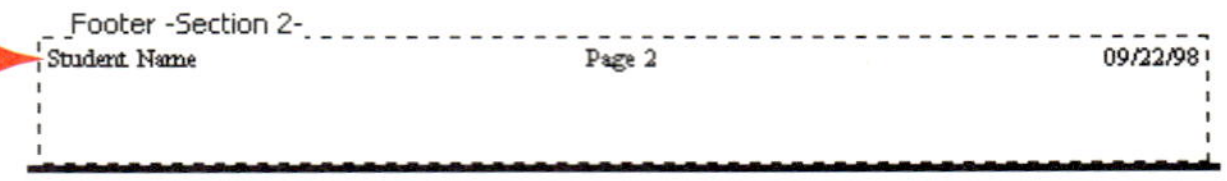

- Replace Student Name with your name in the footer.

The page number displayed in the footer is the current page, 2. The title page is counted as page 1 of the document. You want to begin page numbers with the first page of Section 2. To make this change,

You can also add and format page numbers using Insert/Page Numbers.

- Click Format Page Number.

The Page Number Format dialog box on your screen should be similar to Figure 3-24.

FIGURE 3-24

changes the starting page number

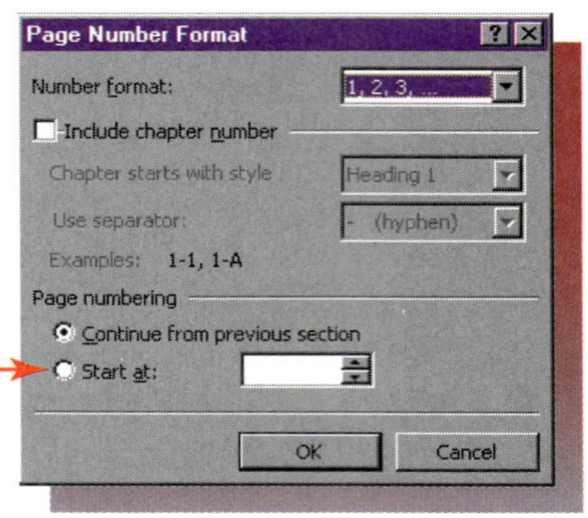

This dialog box is used to change the format of page numbers, include chapter numbers, and to change the page numbering sequence. The default page numbering setting continues the numbering from the first section. To reset the page number sequence to begin Section 2 with page 1,

The default starts the current section (2) with page 1. You could enter any number as the starting number for a section.

- Choose Start At.
- Click OK.

The footer now displays page 1 as the current page.

- Close the Header and Footer toolbar.
- Scroll down to see the top of page 2 and the bottom of page 1.

Your screen should be similar to Figure 3-25.

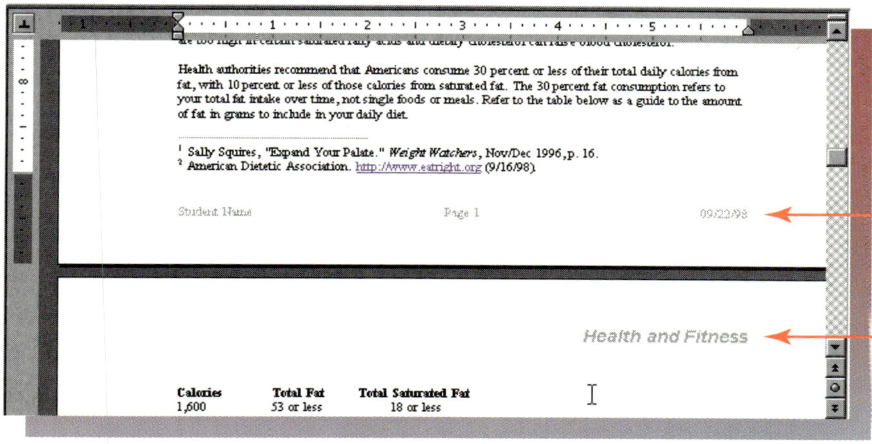

FIGURE 3-25

The document area is active again, and the header and footer text appears dimmed.

Updating the Table of Contents

You have made many modifications to the report since generating the table of contents, so you want to update the page references in the listing. Because the table of contents is a field, if you add or remove headings, rearrange topics, or make other changes that affect the table of contents listing, you can quickly update the table of contents using the Update Field command on the Shortcut menu.

The keyboard shortcut to the Update Field command is F9.

Right-click the table of contents to display the Shortcut menu.

- Move to anywhere in the table of contents and display the Shortcut menu.
- Choose Update Field.

From the Update Table of Contents dialog box, you specify the part of the table of contents that needs updating. You need to update the page references.

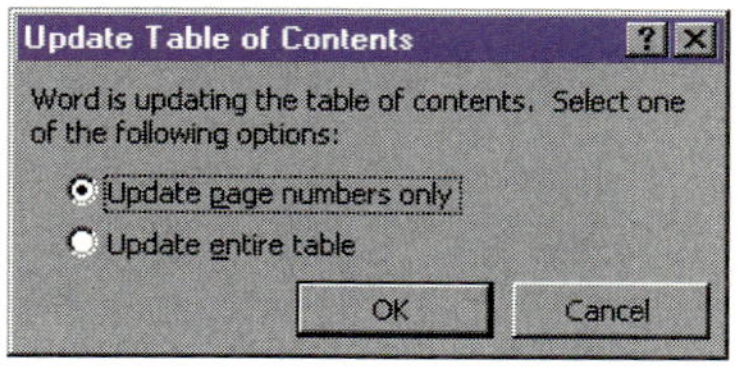

- If necessary, choose Update Page Numbers Only.
- Click OK.

Your screen should be similar to Figure 3-26.

FIGURE 3-26

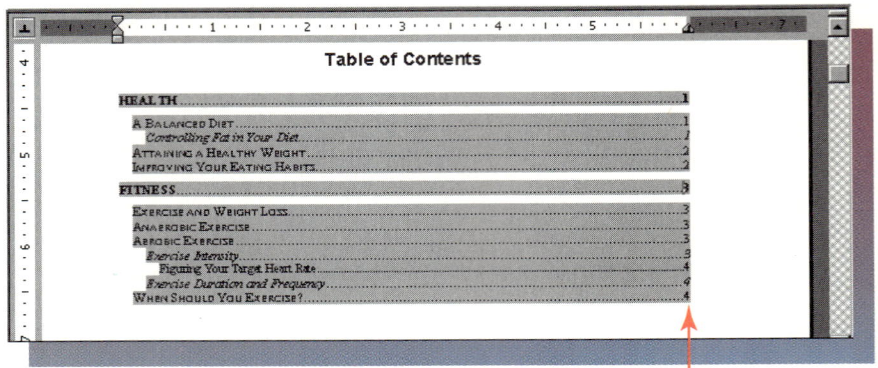

page numbers updated to reflect new locations of headings in document and page numbering

You can click a table of contents page number to quickly move to that page in a document.

You are now ready to print the complete report.

- Preview, then print the entire document.
- Save the edited document as Newsletter Topics and close the file.

Note: If you are ending your lab session now, exit Word. To begin Part 2, load Word.

Part 2

Using WordArt

The topics in your report were well received by your manager. Now you will create a sample newsletter design using several of the topics from your report.

A newsletter commonly consists of two basic parts: the headline and the body. (See the figure on the next page.) The headline, also called the nameplate or banner, is the top portion of the newsletter that generally contains the name, issue identification, and publication date. It may also include a company logo, a line that announces the main subject or article included in the newsletter and a brief table of contents. The body, which is the text of the newsletter, is commonly displayed in two- or three-column format. Article headings often include subheadings that help organize the newsletter topics. The headline is often visually separated from the body by horizontal lines, called rules. The sample newsletter you will create will include many of these features.

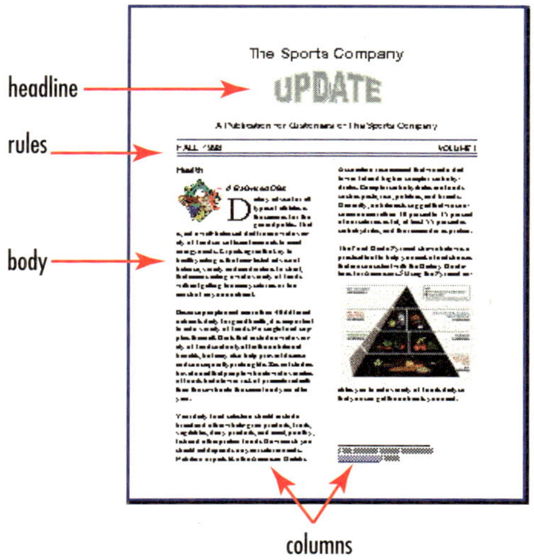

The first thing you want to do is to create a headline for the newsletter. The headline will display the name of the newsletter, The Sports Company Update, and issue identification information that includes the date of publication and volume number. The headline you will create is shown here.

The text for the headline has already been entered for you.

- To see the headline text, open the file Headline from your data disk.

Your screen should be similar to Figure 3-27.

FIGURE 3-27

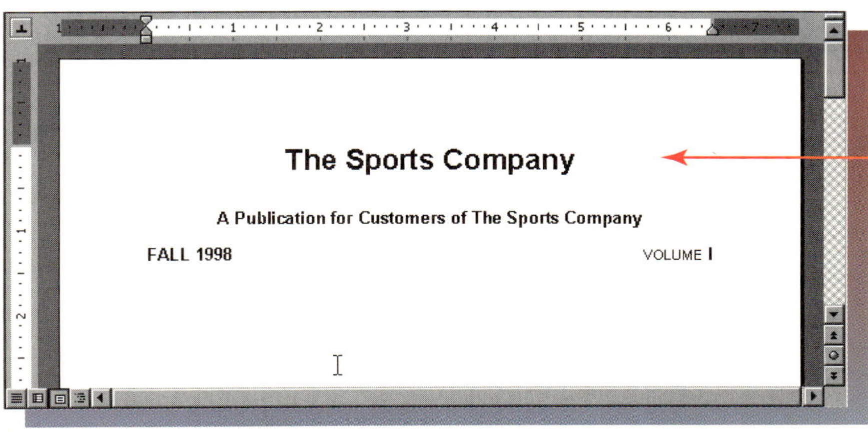

text for the newsletter headline

The Edit WordArt Text dialog box on your screen should be similar to Figure 3-29.

FIGURE 3-29

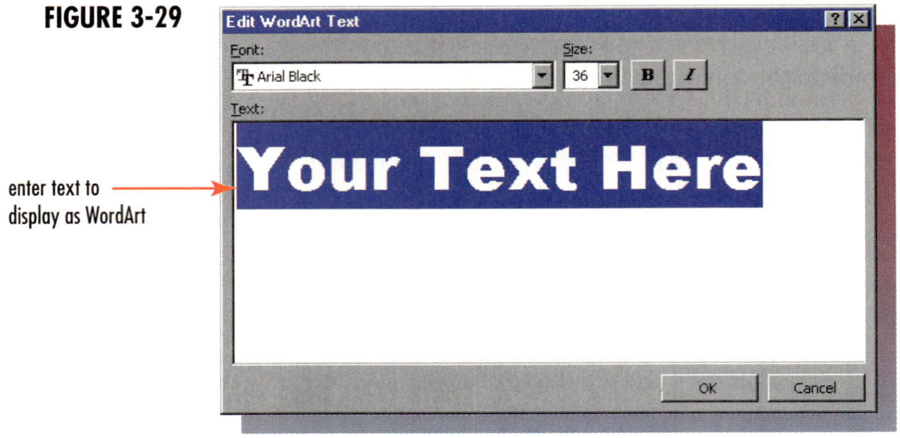

Next you need to enter the text you want displayed using the selected WordArt design.

- Type **UPDATE**.
- Click OK.

Your screen should be similar to Figure 3-30.

FIGURE 3-30

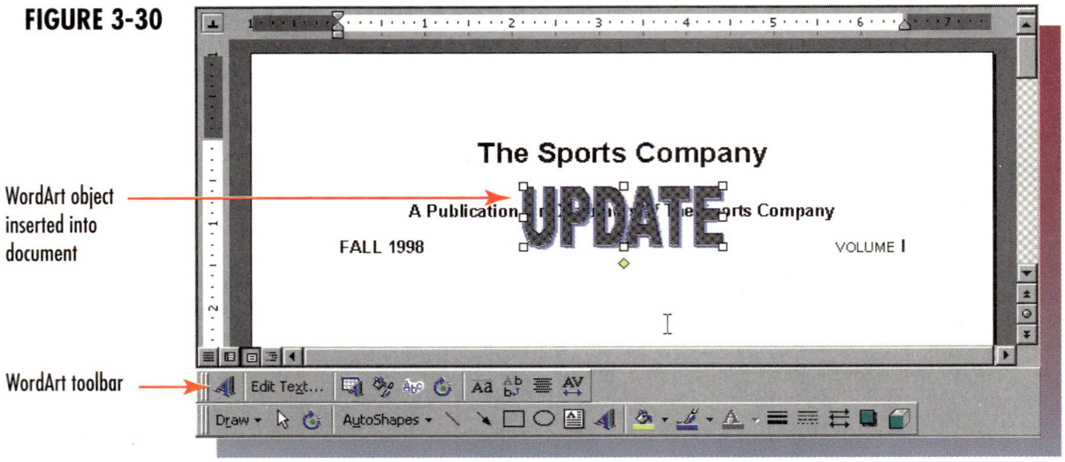

Refer to Concept 5: Graphics to review these features.

Now the word you entered is displayed in the selected WordArt style in the document. When a WordArt object is first inserted in the document, it is displayed at the location of the insertion point. The object is centered because the paragraph alignment to which it is associated is centered. It also floats over the text on the page. This is because the default wrapping style for WordArt objects is None.

The handles surrounding the WordArt object indicate that it is selected. Whenever a WordArt object is selected, the WordArt toolbar is displayed. The WordArt toolbar buttons (identified below) are used to modify the WordArt.

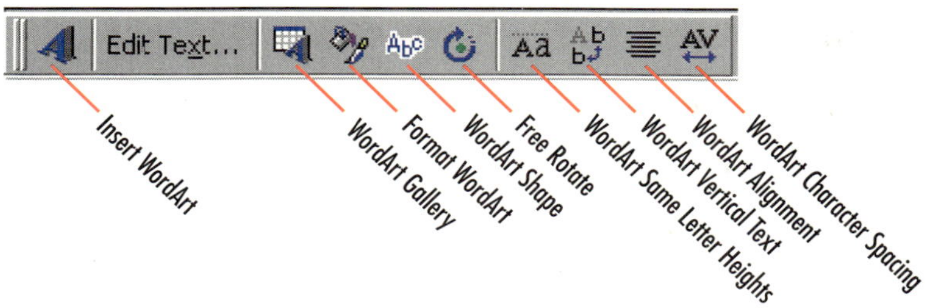

- If necessary, move and dock the WordArt toolbar above the Drawing toolbar (see Figure 3-30).

You want to change the wrapping style of the object so the text appears above and below it.

- Click Format WordArt.
- Open the Wrapping tab if necessary.

The Format WordArt dialog box on your screen should be similar to Figure 3-31.

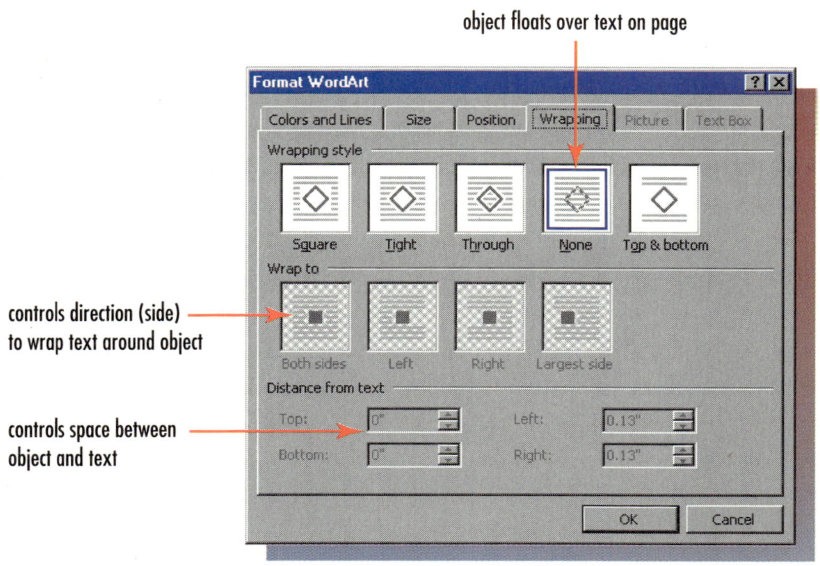

FIGURE 3-31

Depending on the wrapping style you select, you can also specify the space between the object and the text by entering values in the Distance from Text option boxes. The default of 0 places the object as close to the text above and below it as possible. You want text in the headline to wrap above and below the WordArt object. To make this change,

- Click Top & bottom.
- Click OK.

Your screen should be similar to Figure 3-32.

FIGURE 3-32

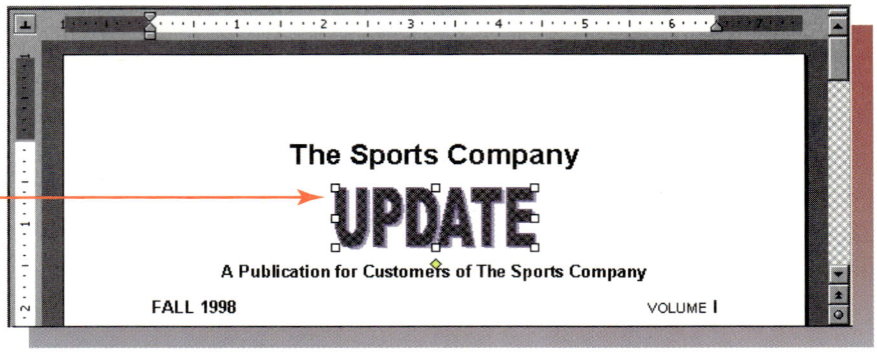

text wraps above and below WordArt object

The object can still be moved anywhere on the page, but text will always appear above and below the object, not to the sides or underneath it.

Changing the WordArt Shape

Now you want to change the appearance of the WordArt object to have a curved top. You select shapes from the WordArt palette.

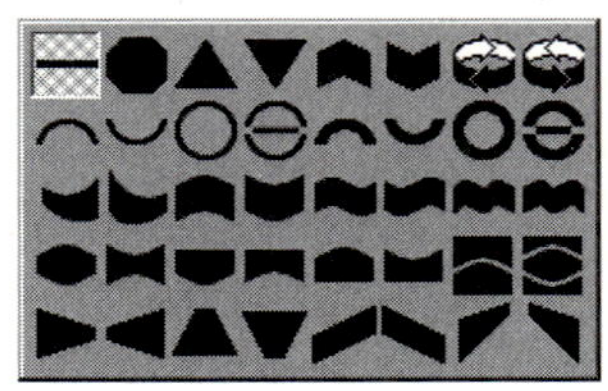

- Click WordArt Shape.
- Choose Inflate Top (fifth column, fourth row).

Your screen should be similar to Figure 3-33.

FIGURE 3-33

Inflate Top object shape

Changing the Fill and Line Color

Next you want to change the color of the WordArt characters to reflect the corporate colors used in the company logo. You can easily do this using many of the special effects options that can be applied to graphic objects.

Concept 9: Special Effects

Word 97 includes many commands that add special effects, such as shadows and 3-D effects, to enhance drawing objects, including WordArt. When you draw an object, a border is drawn around the object automatically. You can change the thickness and color of the border. You also can fill a drawing object with a solid color, gradient color, texture, or a picture. Adding shadows or 3-D effects gives depth to an object.

Fill and line colors

Shadows

Patterns and textures

3-D effects

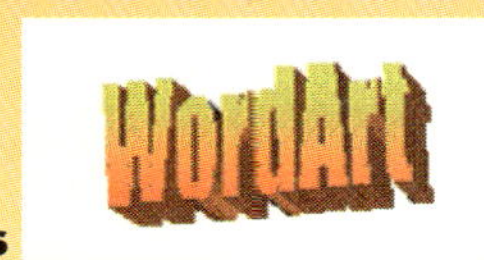

Use these effects in moderation. You want to capture the reader's interest with your graphics, not detract from your message.

- Click Format WordArt.
- Open the Colors and Lines tab.

The Format WordArt dialog box on your screen should be similar to Figure 3-34.

FIGURE 3-34

applies fill color to selected object

applies color to line surrounding WordArt shape

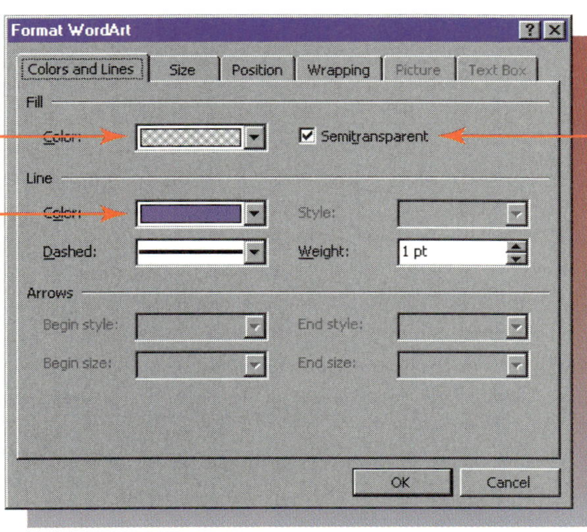

makes fil color partially transparent

The color and line settings for the selected WordArt design style is a light gray semitransparent fill color with a blue line. The Semitransparent option when selected makes the selected fill color partially transparent, allowing the shadow color to bleed through. When not selected, the color is solid or opaque. You want to use the corporate colors of light green and medium blue in your newsletter. You also do not want the background shadow color of gray to bleed through the letters, so you will turn off the semitransparent selection. To make these changes,

> The fill color is used to fill the object, and the line color is applied to the outline surrounding the UPDATE shape.

- Open the Fill Color drop-down list box.
- Select Light Green (fourth column, fifth color).
- Clear the Semitransparent check box.
- Click OK.

Creating Horizontal Rules

Next you want the issue identification information to be displayed between two horizontal rules. Rules can be added to any side of a paragraph or object using the Borders toolbar. The paragraph or object must be selected first.

- Move to anywhere within the issue identification text.
- Choose Format/Borders and Shading/Borders.

The Borders and Shading dialog box on your screen should be similar to Figure 3-35.

FIGURE 3-35

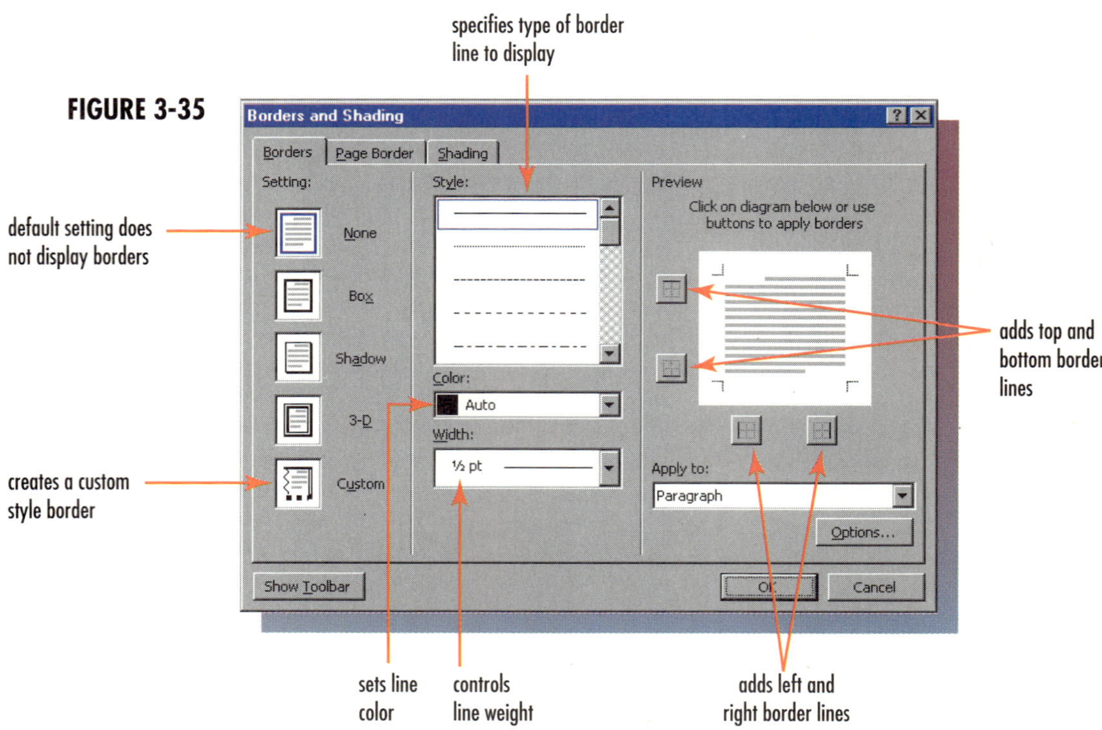

You want to add a $1^{1}/_{2}$ pt single-line border in blue above the text and a 3 pt double-line border in blue below the text. As you specify the border line settings, the Preview area will reflect your selections.

- Click Custom.
- From the Width drop-down list box, select $1^{1}/_{2}$ pt.
- From the Color drop-down list box, select Blue.
- Click Top Border.
- From the Line Style drop-down list, select .
- From the Width drop-down list, select 3 pt.
- From the Color drop-down list, select Blue.
- Click Bottom Border.

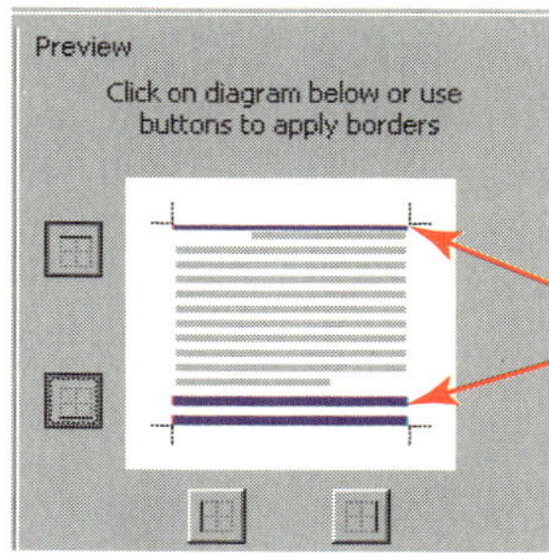

previews how your border selection will appear

The Preview area of the dialog box shows how your selections will appear.

- Click OK.

Your screen should be similar to Figure 3-36.

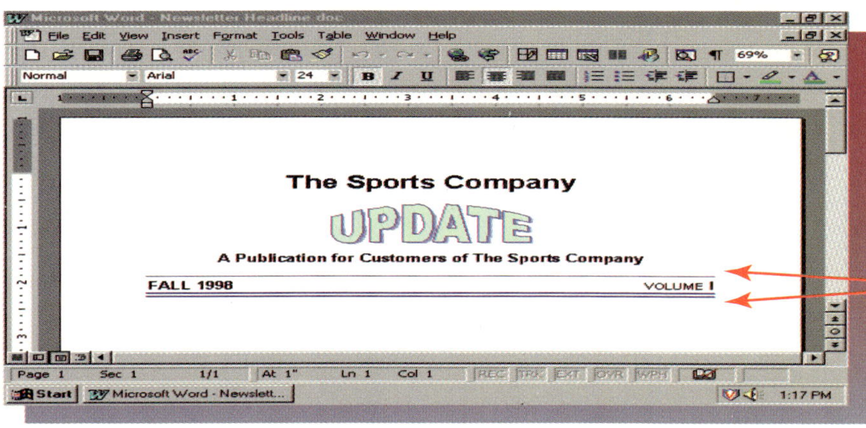

FIGURE 3-36

top and bottom border lines create headline rules

The horizontal border lines extend between the margins above and below the text in the color, style, and point size you specified. The newsletter headline is now complete and can be used with any newsletter.

- Save the headline as Newsletter Headline.

> You also can create border lines automatically as you type. To create a single line, press [-] three times and press [←Enter]. To create a double line, press [=] three times and press [←Enter].

Now you are ready to copy the headline for the newsletter into the file containing the newsletter text. Following your manager's suggestions, you shortened the topic coverage and divided the topics into several short articles on the same theme that could be continued to the next newsletter. In addition, you revised the text so that footnote references were not needed. The only footnote you kept was to the figure of the Food Guide Pyramid. To see the revised document,

- Open the file Newsletter Articles.
- Scroll through the text to view the contents of the two articles you selected for the sample newsletter. When you are done, return to the top of the document.

You now have two document files open in two separate document windows. Although you can have multiple document windows open at one time, only one can be active. The **active window** is the window you can work in and that is affected by any commands you use. To make a window active, you switch to the window of your choice from the Window menu.

You can also press Ctrl + F6 to cycle forward through all open documents, or Ctrl + ⇧Shift + F6 to cycle backward.

- Switch to the Newsletter Headline window and use the Select All command on the Edit menu to select the entire file.
- Copy the selection text to the Clipboard.
- Make the Newsletter Articles window active. If necessary, move the insertion point to the top of the file (Ctrl + Home).
- Paste the selection from the Clipboard to this location in the file.

Your screen should be similar to Figure 3-37.

FIGURE 3-37

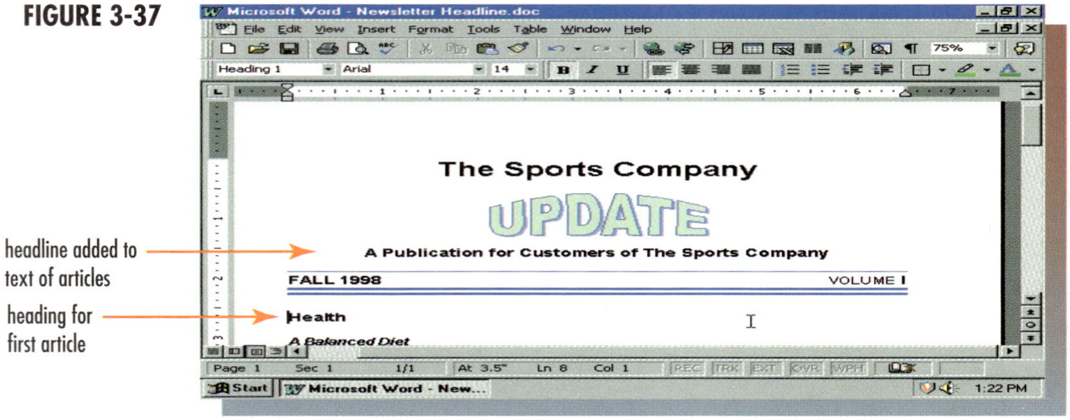

The newsletter headline is displayed at the top of the document. The Health heading should be separated from the bottom border line by one blank line.

- If necessary, insert or delete blank lines above it to position it there.

Creating Newspaper Columns

You want the articles in the newsletter to be displayed in newspaper style columns. **Newspaper columns** display text so that it flows from the bottom of one column to the top of the next. The Normal template has one column the full width of the margins, so the text appears to flow continuously from one page to the next. On occasion, the layout for your document may call for two or more columns on a page. A common application for this is a newsletter.

The optimum column width for reading comfort is 4.5 inches. In a newsletter, narrower columns help the reader read the articles more quickly, and you as the writer can fit more information on a page in a visually pleasing arrangement. It is not wise to use more than four columns on an 8½ by 11-inch page. The columns will be too narrow and the page will look messy.

The Columns command on the Format menu is used to set the text format of a document to columns. When using the column feature, the text in the entire document is changed to the new format. To affect only a portion of a document, the document must be divided into sections. Because you do not want the headline to appear in column format, you will create a section break below the headline.

- Move to the blank line under the bottom border line.
- Choose Insert/Break/Continuous/ OK .

Although section break lines do not display in Page Layout view, the status bar shows that the insertion point is positioned in Section 2. The new section continues to the end of the document unless another section break is inserted. To change the Section 2 format to newspaper columns,

- Choose Format/Columns.

The Columns dialog box on your screen should be similar to Figure 3-38.

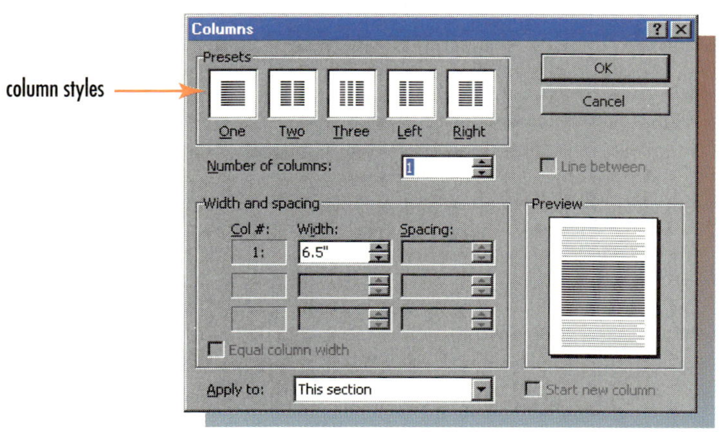

FIGURE 3-38

The Presets area displays five preset column styles and shows the default style is one column the full width of the page. Using the Presets area you can select up to three evenly spaced columns or two unevenly spaced column formats. If none of the preset styles is appropriate, you can enter a number in the Number of Columns text box to create up to 13 columns. You want the newsletter to have two columns of text on the first page. From the Presets area,

- Select Two.

The Number of Columns text box now displays 2. Based on the number of columns you specify and your document's left and right margin settings, Word automatically calculates the size of columns and the spacing between columns. Using the default setting, the two columns will be 3 inches wide, separated by 0.5 inch. The Preview box shows how text will appear on the page using the specified column settings.

- Click OK.
- If necessary, set the zoom to 75 percent. Scroll the window to display more of the first article in the two-column format.

Your screen should be similar to Figure 3-39.

FIGURE 3-39

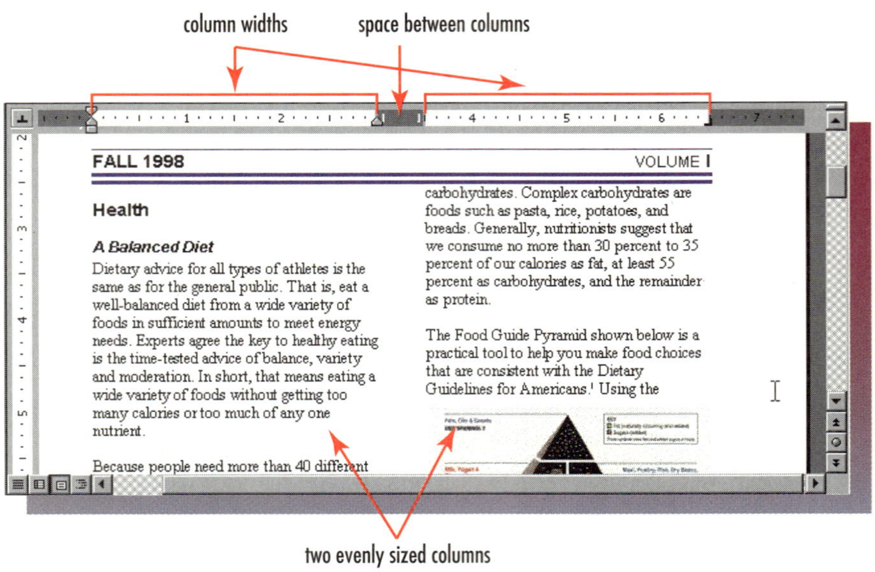

Do not be concerned if the text in your columns wraps differently than in Figure 3-39. This is a function of the selected printer on your system.

The text is displayed as two evenly sized newspaper columns, with 0.5 inch of space between. The text at the bottom of the first column continues at the top of the second column. The column markers on the horizontal ruler show the size and spacing of each column.

You would like the second page of the newsletter to be in three-column format. Rather than inserting a section break first, you can select the area of the text to be affected before setting the format to columns and Word will automatically insert the section break at the beginning (and end if necessary) of your selection. Another way to specify columns is to use the Columns button on the Standard toolbar. It allows you to specify up to six columns using the default column definitions.

- Select the text from the Fitness heading to the end of the document.
- Click Columns.
- Click on the third column.
- Move to the Fitness heading at the beginning of the three-column section.

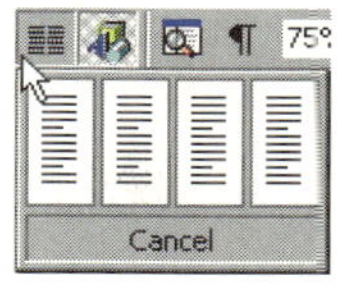

The menu equivalent is Format/Columns/Number of Columns/3.

Your screen should be similar to Figure 3-40.

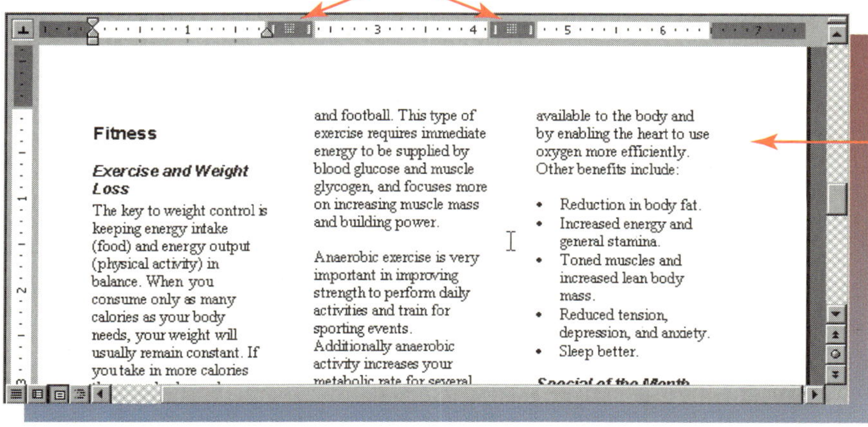

FIGURE 3-40

The default width of 0.5 inch between the columns was appropriate for two columns, but seems too wide for three columns. To reduce the space between columns to 0.3 inch and maintain equal column widths,

- Choose Format/Columns.
- In the Width and Spacing section of the dialog box, set the spacing to 0.3 for Column 1.
- Select Equal Column Width.
- Click OK.

You can also drag the column marker in the ruler to adjust the column size and spacing between columns.

Using Hyphenation

Now that the layout is in columns, you notice that many of the lines have very uneven right margins, especially in the three-column layout. On lines of text where there are several short words, the wrapping of text to the next line is not a problem. However, on lines that contain long words, the long word is wrapped to the next line, leaving a large gap on the previous line. To help solve this problem you will use the hyphenation feature.

Concept 10: Hyphenation

The **hyphenation** feature inserts a hyphen in long words that fall at the end of a line to split the word between lines. Because word processors automatically wrap long words that fall at the end of a line to the beginning of the next line, uneven right margins or large gaps of white space commonly occur in a document. Using hyphenation reduces the amount of white space and makes line lengths more even to improve the appearance of a document. The program inserts **optional hyphens**, which only break the word if it appears at the end of a line. Then, as you edit the document, the hyphenation is adjusted appropriately.

To hyphenate the document,

- Choose Tools/Language/Hyphenation.

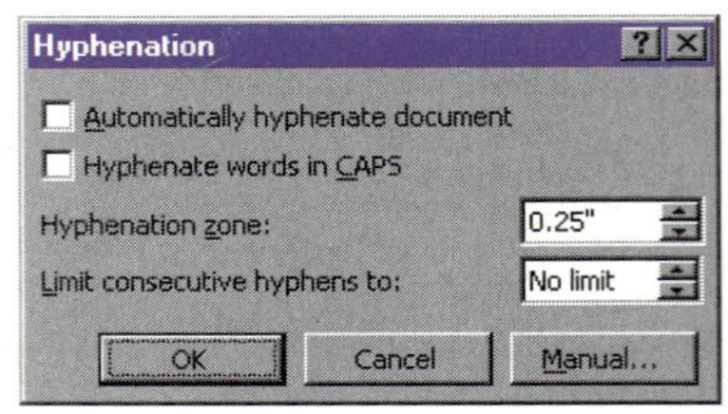

The Hyphenation dialog box is displayed. The Automatically Hyphenate Document option lets Word set hyphenation for the entire document. You can also specify the size of the **hyphenation zone**, an unmarked space along the right margin that controls the amount of white space in addition to the margin that Word will allow at the end of a line. Making the hyphenation zone narrower (a smaller number) reduces the unevenness of lines by hyphenating more words, while making the zone wider (a larger number) hyphenates fewer words.

Word generally proposes accurate hyphenation. If you do not agree with how a word is hyphenated after it has been done, you can select the word and hyphenate it manually.

Use the Manual command button only if you want to be able to accept, reject, or change the proposed hyphenation of each word that Word is considering hyphenating.

- Select Automatically Hyphenate Document.
- If necessary, specify a hyphenation zone setting of 0.25".
- Click OK.

Your screen should be similar to Figure 3-41.

FIGURE 3-41

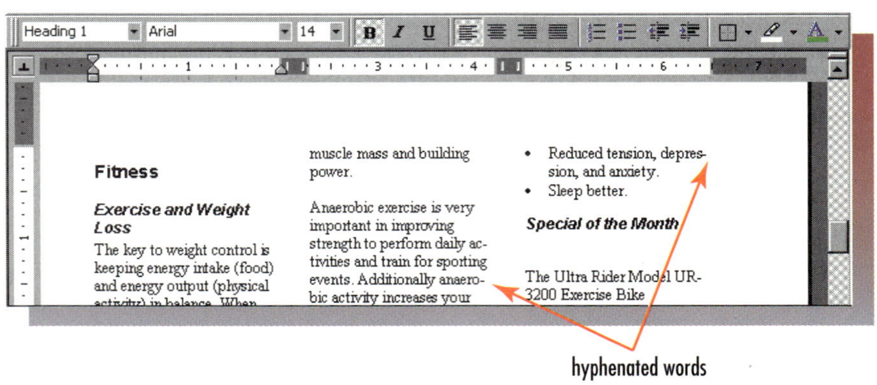

Depending on your printer, different words may be hyphenated.

Word has examined each line and determined where it is possible to hyphenate a word. Hyphenating the newsletter has made the column margins much less uneven.

- To save the changes you have made to the document to this point, save the document as Fall 1998 Newsletter.

If the text in three-column format now begins at the bottom of page 1, insert a continusous section break before the Fitness heading.

Inserting Text Boxes

To make certain elements in your newsletter stand out, you decide to put them into text boxes. **Text boxes** are graphic objects, so you can place them on the page as you would a picture or WordArt. You can also add drawing features to text boxes to enhance their appearance. You want to create a text box for the information about the special of the month and include a picture of the item from the catalog.

- Select the text located at the end of column 3 on page 2 beginning with the heading Special of the Month and ending with "description."
- Click Text Box.

The menu equivalent is Insert/Text Box.

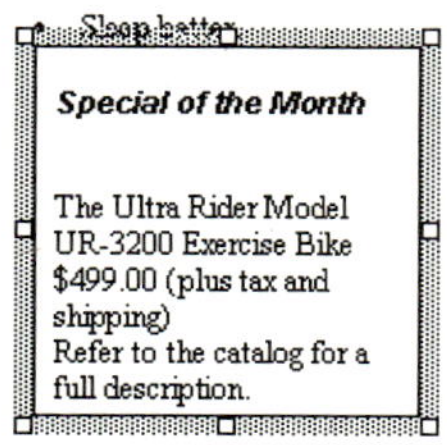

The selected text is placed in a text box, and the Text Box toolbar is displayed. Its buttons (identified below) are used to link text boxes together so text flows from one to the next. You can use this feature to place text into a newsletter and have it automatically flow from one page to another page later in the newsletter.

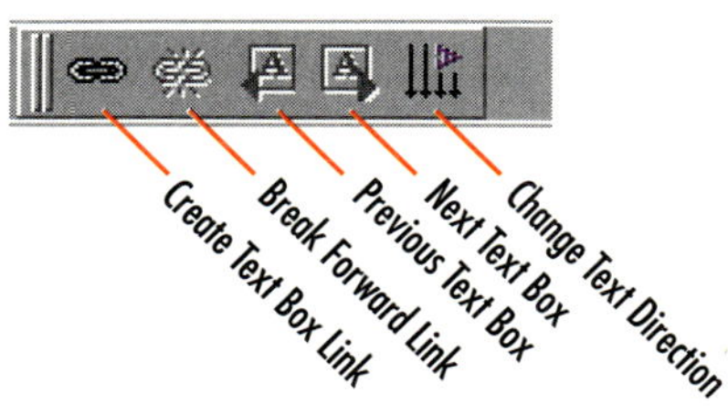

- If necessary, adjust the size of the text box so it is the same width as the column.
- Fill the text box with the Light Green color.
- Change the line color to Blue.

Use the Drawing toolbar buttons to make these changes.

Next you want to add a picture of the exercise bike to the text box.

- Move to the blank line beneath the heading Special of the Month.
- Choose Insert/Picture/From File.
- Change the Look In location to the drive containing your data disk.

- Select Exercise Bike.jpg.
- Click Insert.
- Increase the length of the text box to fully display the text.
- Select the Exercise Bike object and increase the size of the object to nearly the full width of the text box as in Figure 3-42.
- Add a blue border around the exercise bike graphic.
- Move the text box down the column slightly to separate it from the end of the text in the column.

Use the button to draw a border, then use to apply the color.

Reminder: Drag the corner handle when resizing to maintain proportions.

When you are done, your screen should be similar to Figure 3-42.

FIGURE 3-42

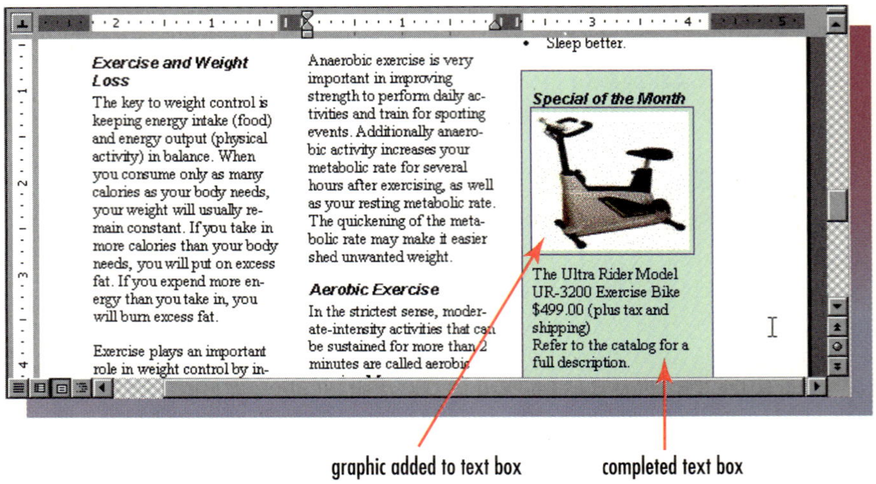

Notice that when you moved the text box, all the objects inside the text box moved too. This is because the text box is a grouped object and is considered one graphic element. However, you can still format the text and size the graphic as separate items.

You also want to add two more pictures to the newsletter. The first will be a picture that will complement the Health topic area and the second the Fitness topic area.

- Move to the heading A Balanced Diet on page 1.
- Insert the picture file Foodgrps.wmf from your data disk.
- Select the picture and reduce its size to about a 1-inch square (see Figure 3-43).
- Change the wrapping style to Tight and the direction to wrap to Right.

Office 97 comes with many clip art images that are located in the Clip Gallery.

You can also purchase clip art packages to add to your collection.

The text in the paragraph now wraps tightly around the object to the right. The food groups object is a clip art image. **Clip art** is a term used to describe a collection of graphics that usually is bundled with a software application.

- Add the picture Jogger.wmf from your data disk to the first paragraph below Fitness on page 2. Size the graphic to approximately 1 x 3 inches.
- Set the wrapping to Tight Both Sides.
- Move the graphic to the location shown in Figure 3-43.

Now you need to check the newsletter layout and move text and graphic elements around on the page until the newsletter has an orderly yet interesting appearance.

- Set the zoom to Two Pages.
- Position all the graphic elements in the newsletter so they are similar to those shown in Figure 3-43.

Your screen should be similar to Figure 3-43.

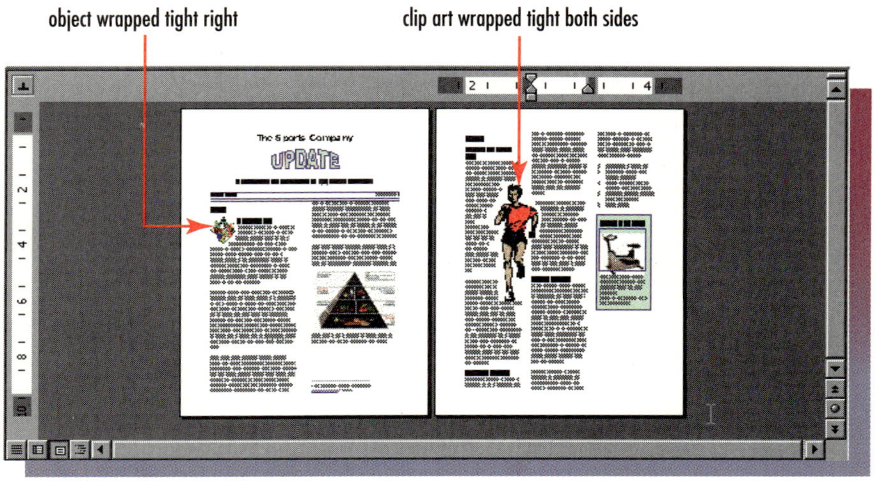

FIGURE 3-43

Adding a Drop Cap

Finally, you would like to make the first letter of the first paragraph of the newsletter a drop cap. A **drop cap**, used most often with the first character in a paragraph, appears as a large, uppercase character with the top part of the letter even with the line and the rest of the letter extending into the paragraph below it. The character is changed to a graphic object in a frame and the text wraps to the side of the object. To create a drop cap,

- Change the zoom to Page Width.
- Select the D in "Dietary" (first letter on the first page where the columns start).
- Choose Format/Drop Cap/Dropped/2/ OK .

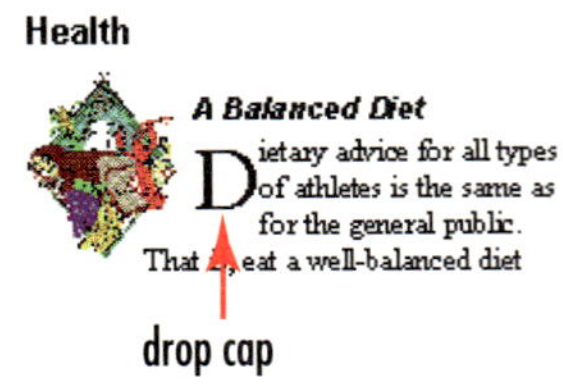

- Move the graphic object to the right of the picture as shown here.
- Deselect the object.
- Insert a blank line above the second column to separate the text from the bottom headline rule.

The drop cap effect emphasizes the beginning of the paragraph and makes the columns appear more like those in a magazine.

- Add the same style and size drop cap to the T of "The" at the beginning of the first article under Fitness.
- Preview the newsletter. Set the Print Preview window to display two pages by selecting View/Zoom/Many Pages or by clicking Multiple Pages and then selecting 1x2 pages.

Your screen should be similar to Figure 3-44.

FIGURE 3-44

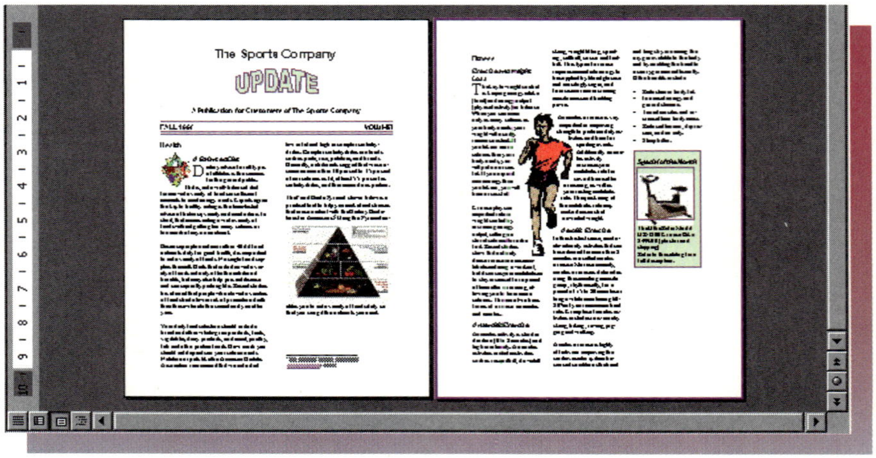

- Close the Preview window.
- Add your name at the bottom of page 2 only.
- Save the formatted newsletter.
- If necessary, select the appropriate printer for your computer system.
    - Because the text is reformatted to the font and graphic capabilities of your printer, scroll through the document to see the changes that were made.
    - Adjust the text wherever necessary to produce a newsletter as similar as possible to the one you created in this lab.
    - Preview your changes, then resave the document.

You may need to insert a blank line or two below the last column of text to add space to enter your name.

- Print the newsletter.
- Set the Page Layout view zoom back to 100 percent, set the view back to Normal, and turn off the Drawing toolbar.
- Close all the open files and Exit Word.

To close all open documents at the same time, hold down ⇧Shift while you select File, then choose Close All.

LAB REVIEW

Key Terms

active window (WP136)
anchor (WP116)
caption (WP119)
character style (WP101)
clip art (WP142)
cross-reference (WP119)
Document Map pane (WP103)
document pane (WP103)
drawing object (WP116)
drop cap (WP143)
endnote (WP109)
footer (WP122)
footnote (WP109)
frame (WP116)
graphic (WP116)
group (WP116)
handle (WP117)
header (WP122)
heading style (WP101)
hyperlink (WP112)
hyphenation (WP140)
hyphenation zone (WP140)
lock (WP116)
manual page break (WP99)
newspaper column (WP137)
note pane (WP110)
note reference mark (WP109)
note separator (WP109)
note text (WP109)
object (WP116)
optional hyphen (WP140)
pane (WP103)
paragraph style (WP101)
picture (WP116)
style (WP101)
tab alignment selection box (WP114)
tab leaders (WP106)
tab stop (WP114)
text box (WP141)
URL (Uniform Resource Locator) (WP111)
WordArt (WP128)

Command Summary

Command	Shortcut	Button	Action
File/Page Setup/Layout/ Vertical Alignment			Aligns text vertically on a page
View/Header and Footer			Displays header and footer areas
View/Footnotes			Hides or displays note pane
Insert/Break/Page Break	Ctrl + ←Enter		Inserts manual page break
Insert/Break/Continuous			Starts next section on same page as current section
Insert/Page Numbers			Specifies page number location
Insert /Footnote	Alt + Ctrl + F		Inserts footnote reference at insertion point
Insert/Caption			Inserts caption at insertion point
Insert/Cross-reference			Inserts cross-reference at insertion point
Insert/Index and Tables			Inserts index or table, such as table of contents
Insert/Picture/From File			Inserts picture from file
Insert/Text Box			Inserts text box
Format/Borders and Shading			Adds borders and shadings to selection
			Adds top border
			Adds bottom border
Format/Columns			Specifies number, spacing, and size of columns
Format/Tabs			Inserts tab stops
Format/Drop Cap/Dropped			Changes character to drop cap
Format/Style			Applies, creates, or modifies styles
Format/Picture			Changes picture scaling, size, wrapping, position, and cropping information
Tools/Language/Hyphenation			Specifies hyphenation settings

Matching

1. note pane	_____	**a.**	text that appears at the bottom of each page above the bottom margin
2. tab leaders	_____	**b.**	dots that separate table of contents headings from page numbers
3. footer	_____	**c.**	source reference displayed at the bottom of a page
4. caption	_____	**d.**	lower section of workspace that displays footnote text
5. footnote	_____	**e.**	instructs Word to begin a new page at that location regardless of the amount of text on the previous page
6. manual page break	_____	**f.**	a title or explanation for a table, picture, or graph
7. tight wrap	_____	**g.**	a graphic object that contains text or other graphic objects
8. text box	_____	**h.**	text closely follows contours around a graphic
9. WordArt	_____	**i.**	non-text element that adds visual interest to a document
10. graphic	_____	**j.**	applies shapes and special effects to text

Discussion Questions

1. Discuss the differences between footnotes and endnotes. Why is it necessary to add notes to a document?

2. Discuss how you can move and place graphic objects in a document. Use Help to learn more about anchors and locked anchors. Discuss the different wrapping options.

3. How can newspaper columns enhance the look of a document? What types of documents are columns best suited for? How can the adjustment of widths, spacing, and hyphenation affect the layout?

Fill-In Questions

1. Complete the following statements by filling in the blanks with the correct terms.

a. A(n)_______________ is a named group of formats.

b. _______________ are useful for aligning text or numeric data vertically in columns.

c. The _______________ displays the headings in your document, making it easier to navigate.

d. A(n) _______________ can be displayed below a graphic to identify the object.

e. A(n) _______________ can be placed within a document to refer back to a figure or other reference in the document.

f. A(n) _______________ allows you to jump to another location in a document, another document, or the WWW.

g. A(n) _______________ is used to apply different formats to different parts of a document.

h. The _______________ feature changes the shape of text.

i. _______________ divides words to allow more text to be displayed on each line.

j. Non-text elements such as drawings and pictures are called _______________.

Hands-On Practice Exercises

Step by Step

Rating System
☆ Easy
☆☆ Moderate
☆☆☆ Difficult

☆

1. To complete this exercise, you must have completed Practice Exercise 3 in Lab 1. Open the file No Smoking Memo on your data disk.

   a. Change the font to Arial 12 pt. Set a left-aligned tab at 0.75 inch, and set the alignment to Justified. Change all margins to 1.5 inches.

   b. Enter the current date following "Date."

   c. Go to the beginning of the first paragraph and insert the picture Nosmoke.wmf from your data disk. Size the picture and wrap the text until it fits perfectly to the left of the two paragraphs.

   d. Save the file as Revised No Smoking Memo. Print the memo.

☆☆

2. In this exercise you will create a letterhead for yourself using a WordArt image for your name.

   a. Enter your name as a WordArt object. Apply a shape and a shadow to the image.

   b. Size the object appropriately and center it between the margins.

   c. Enter your address, centered, below your name. Change the font and size of the address.

   d. Place the object 0.5 inch from the top of the page. Two lines below the address, enter a date that will update automatically when the letter is printed. Right-align the date, and change its font to Times New Roman 12 pt.

   e. Use the AutoShapes button to add a drawing object to the left of the address. It should display the text "New Address!". (Use Help for information on this feature.)

   f. Document the file. Save the letterhead as Letterhead. Print the letterhead.

☆☆

3. To complete this problem, you must have completed the Newsletter Topics document in Lab 3. Open the Newsletter Topics document from your data disk.

   a. Turn on the Document Map and add the following footnotes to the document:

Section	Paragraph	Following Word	Footnote
Aerobic Exercise	1st	"rate"	Lisa Balbach, "What is Aerobic Exercise and Why Should I do it?" http://k2.kirkland.cc.mi.us/~balbach/fitness.htm#Aerobics (current date)
Exercise Intensity	1st	"maximum"	Bailey, p. 161.
Exercise Duration and Frequency	1st	"week"	Nordictrac, "Too Much. . . Too Little. . . How Do I Know How Much is Enough?" *Designing an Aerobic Exercise Program.* http://www.nordictrack.com/aerobic_program.html (current date)
Exercise Duration and Frequency	3rd	"days"	"Physical Activity and Health: A Report of the Surgeon General." http://www.cdc.gov/needphp/sqr/ataglan.htm (current date)

   b. You want to add another illustration to the document. Move to the blank line after the fourth paragraph in the Controlling Fat in Your Diet section. Insert another blank line. Insert the picture file Nutrition Label.bmp.

   c. Size the picture to 3 x 2.5 inches.

   d. Add the figure caption, "Figure 2: Nutrition Label."

   e. Save the file as Newsletter Topics Revised. Print the document.

☆☆

4. To complete this exercise, you must have completed Practice Exercise 4 in Lab 2. Open the file B&B Ad Part 2.

a. Change the name of the inn (Pocono Mountain Retreat) to a WordArt object. Use a shape of your choice. Explore and use several additional special effects such as shadows, 3-D, and colors to enhance your WordArt object.

b. Select the five paragraphs below the indented items, and enclose them in a text box. Apply a color line and fill to the text box.

c. Surround the page in a colored border. (Use Help for information on page borders.)

d. Update the documentation to indicate that this is the final ad. Save the file as Camera Ready B&B Ad. Print the ad.

☆☆☆

5. To complete this problem, you must have completed Practice Exercise 3 in Lab 2. Open the file Updated Cookie Recipes from your data disk.

a. Enter your name on the line below the title and the current date on the next line. Make sure they are 12 pt and centered.

b. Insert the picture Cookie from your data disk centered above the title. Size the picture appropriately.

c. Enter the heading Table of Contents three lines below the date. The heading should be 16 pt and centered. Insert a section break below the note on this page.

d. Insert a hard page break between each cookie recipe so that each page will contain just one recipe. Insert page numbers that will print at the bottom center of each page, beginning with the first cookie recipe page.

e. Apply the Heading 1 style to the names of the cookies at the top of each recipe. Use the Formal format to create a table of contents of the cookie recipes on the second blank line below the Table of Contents heading. Increase the font size of the table of contents to 12 pt. Make sure there are two or three blank lines between the table of contents and the note. Center the table of contents on the page.

f. Next you will insert three footnotes to add information to some of the recipes.

- Go to the Cut-Out Sugar Cookies recipe on page 1. Move to the end of the line that displays the ingredient "1 1/2 tsp. vanilla extract." Insert the following footnote: **You can substitute pure anise extract for vanilla.**
- Go to the Cut-Out Gingerbread People recipe on page 2. Move to the end of the line that displays the ingredient "1 tsp. allspice." Insert the following footnote: **Add a bit more of each spice to give the cookies an extra kick.**
- Go to the Peanut Butter Surprise recipe on page 4. Move to the end of the line that reads "Double Peanut Butter Cookie recipe . . ." Insert the following footnote: **Use smooth peanut butter for this recipe.**

g. Remove your name and date from below the Potato Chip Cookie recipe. Save the file as Completed Cookie Recipes. Print the document.

h. Optional: Open the file Updated Cookie Recipes and modify the document using layouts of your own choice. Save the file with a new name, and print the document.

☆☆☆

6. You have written an article for your travel newsletter on scenic drives in your state. You want to enhance the appearance of the article. Open the file Top 10 Scenic Drives from your data disk.

a. Insert six blank lines at the top of the document. Create a centered WordArt report title that displays "Top 10 Scenic Drives" on the first line. Center your name and the current date on lines 2 and 3 below the title. Add a section break below the date. Center the page vertically.

b. Zoom the title page to full page and drag the WordArt title so that it is centered just above your name.

c. On page 2, insert a picture of a car (from the Clip Gallery or your data disk). Display the picture to the left of the first paragraph and size the picture appropriately.

d. Create a drop cap as the first character in the first paragraph. Justify the first three paragraphs only. Bold each of the numbered locations.

e. Add the following footnote at the end of the first sentence of the third paragraph: **This top 10 list was obtained from the Weissmann Travel Reports in the America Online Traveler's Corner.**

f. Change the format to two columns for the 10 locations. Change the spacing between columns to 0.6 inch. Make the columns evenly sized and check the Line Between box to draw a line between the columns of text. Hyphenate the document.

g. Insert the picture of a 1st place award (from the Clip Gallery or your data disk) at the beginning of the Rocky Mountains paragraph. Size it to fit to the left of the first five lines of the paragraph.

h. Number the pages, excluding the cover page.

i. Check the layout of your document and make adjustments to the text as necessary.

j. Document the file. Save the document as Scenic Drives Newsletter. Print the document.

k. Optional: Open the file Top 10 Scenic Drives and modify the document using layouts of your own choice. Save the file with a new name, and print the document.

On Your Own

☆☆

7. Create a flier to announce an event (party, garage sale, bake sale, auction, and so on) or advertise something you have for sale (used car, used books, and so on), a service you are offering, or a service you need (babysitting, tutoring, car pool, dog walking, and so on).

Integrate any or all of the following features into the flier:

Borders, shading, colors

Bullets and/or numbering

Indents

Different fonts in different sizes, colors, and styles

WordArt

Pictures (you can use the images from the Clip Gallery or you can create your own with the Paint program)

Different alignment options

Anything else you can think of!

Document and save the file. Print the flier.

☆☆☆

8. Prepare a brief research paper (or use a paper you have written in the past) on a topic of interest to you. The paper must include the following features:

- A title page that displays the report title, your name, the current date (using the Date and Time command), and a table of contents.
- The body of the paper should include at least two levels of headings and a minimum of three footnotes.
- The report layout should include page numbers on the top right corner of every page (excluding the title page). The title page should be vertically aligned.
- Include at least one graphic object with a caption.

☆☆☆

9. The Career Services department is presenting a series of discussions on how to find a job. You have prepared a document for distribution to participants on how to write an effective resume and cover letter. You want to make a few enhancements to the document. Open the file How to Write a Resume on your data disk.

- Justify the entire document. Center the report title, and apply a font and font size of your choice. Center the name and date lines below the title. Enter the heading "Table of Contents" below the date. Center the heading and increase the point size. Insert a page break at the beginning of The Resume title line on page 1.
- Apply the Heading 1 style to the Overview of Resumes and Overview of Cover Letters headings. Apply the Heading 2 style to the Basic Principles of Resume Construction and Organizing Your Resume headings.
- Create a table of contents on the title page. Use any format you wish. Adjust the spacing and overall layout of the title page any way you wish.
- In the Overview of Resumes section, bullet and indent the five lines from "Who you are" to "What kind of job you would like." In the Overview of Cover Letters section, bullet and indent the four measures that are needed for the cover letter. Number the eight Basic Principles of Resume Construction in the resume section and the four "abilities you have developed in school" at the end of the cover letter section.
- Arrange the paragraphs so they are in the following order: Name, Address, and Phone Number, Career Objective, Education, Work Experience, Activities, Honors and Awards, Special Skills, and References.
- Below the first sentence of the Overview of Resumes on page 1, insert the following footnote: **This information was obtained from *The Work Book* by Barbara N. Price, Ph.D., Director of Career Planning and Placement, Luzerne County Community College, Nanticoke, PA.**
- Insert page numbers in any position, excluding the title page.
- Adjust the layout of the document so that the pages contain the following information:

  Page 0: The report title, your name, the current date, and the table of contents.

  Page 1: The Overview, all eight Basic Principles of Resume Construction, and the footnote.

  Page 2: All of the Organizing Your Resume information.

  Page 3: All of The Cover Letter information.
- Document the file. Save the file as Resume Tips. Print the document.

Optional: Open the file How to Write a Resume and modify the document using layouts of your own choice. Save the file with a new name, and print the document.

Concept Summary

Creating a Report and a Newsletter

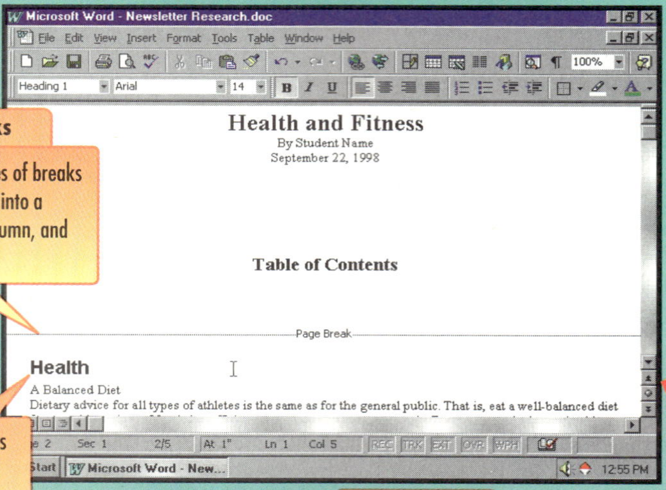

Document Breaks

There are three types of breaks that can be inserted into a document: page, column, and section.

Styles

A style is a set of formats that is assigned a name.

Tab Stops

A tab stop is a stopping point along a line to which text will indent when you press Tab.

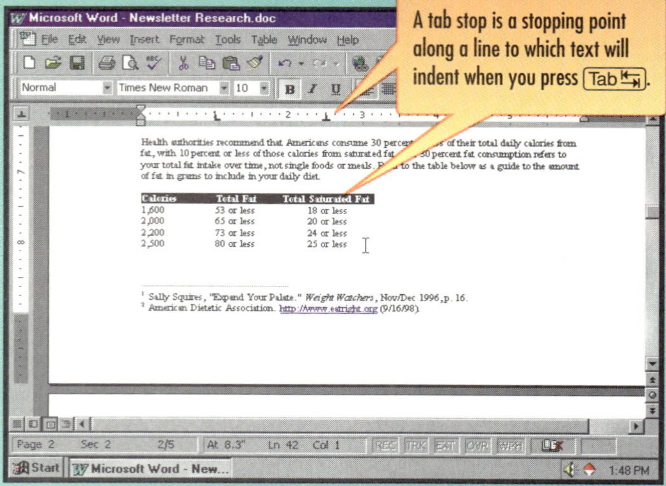

Concepts

- Document Breaks
  Styles
- Footnotes and Endnotes
- Tab Stops
- Graphics
  Captions and Cross-References
- Headers and Footers
- WordArt
  Special Effects
  Hyphenation

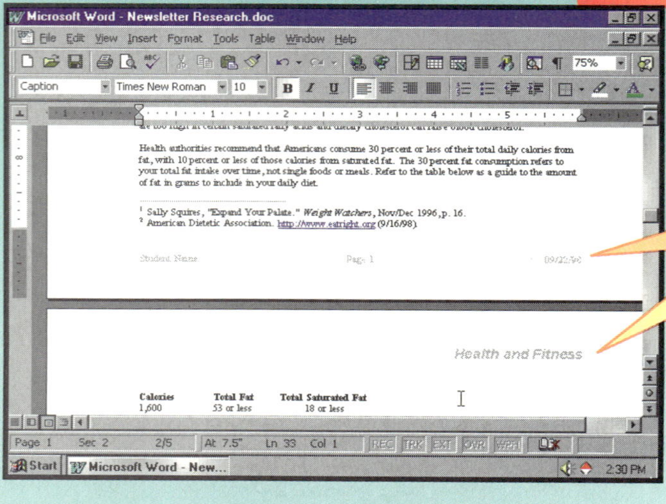

Headers and Footers

A header is a line or several lines of text at the top of each page just below the top margin. A footer is text at the bottom of every page just above the bottom margin.

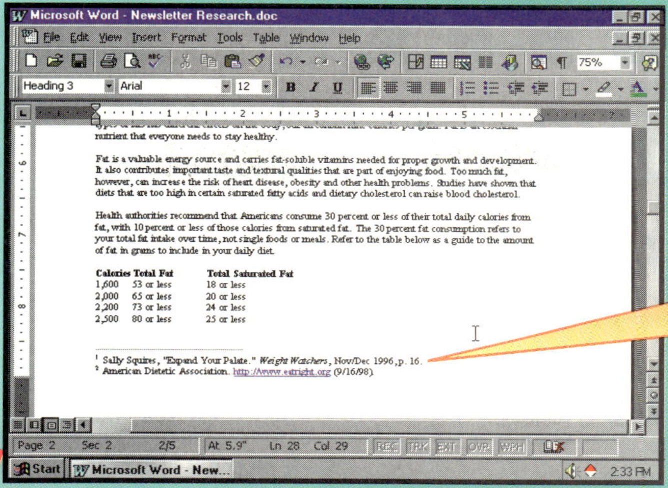

Footnotes and Endnotes

Footnotes are source references or text offering additional explanation that are placed at the bottom of a page. Endnotes are also source references or long comments that typically appear at the end of a document.

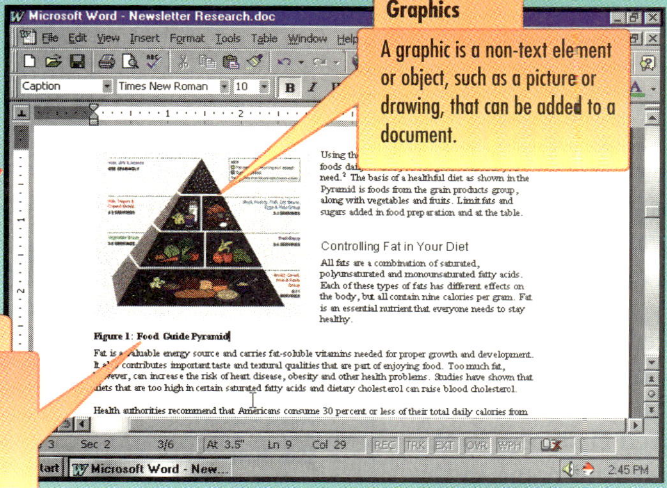

Graphics

A graphic is a non-text element or object, such as a picture or drawing, that can be added to a document.

Captions and Cross-References

A caption is a title or explanation for a table, picture, or graph. A cross-reference is a reference from one part of your document to related information in another part.

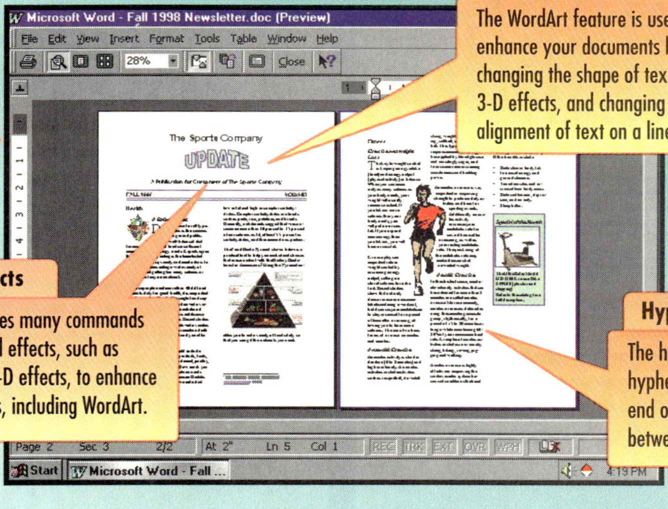

WordArt

The WordArt feature is used to enhance your documents by changing the shape of text, adding 3-D effects, and changing the alignment of text on a line.

Special Effects

Word 97 includes many commands that add special effects, such as shadows and 3-D effects, to enhance drawing objects, including WordArt.

Hyphenation

The hyphenation feature inserts a hyphen in long words that fall at the end of a line to split the word between lines.

The New dialog box on your screen should be similar to Figure 4-1.

FIGURE 4-1

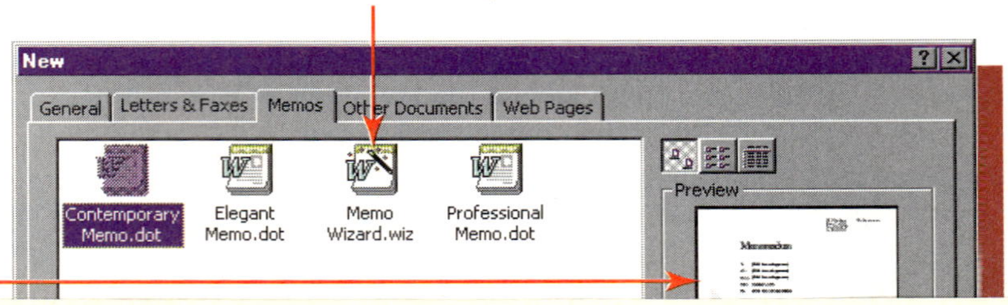

Your screen should be similar to Figure 4-3.

FIGURE 4-3

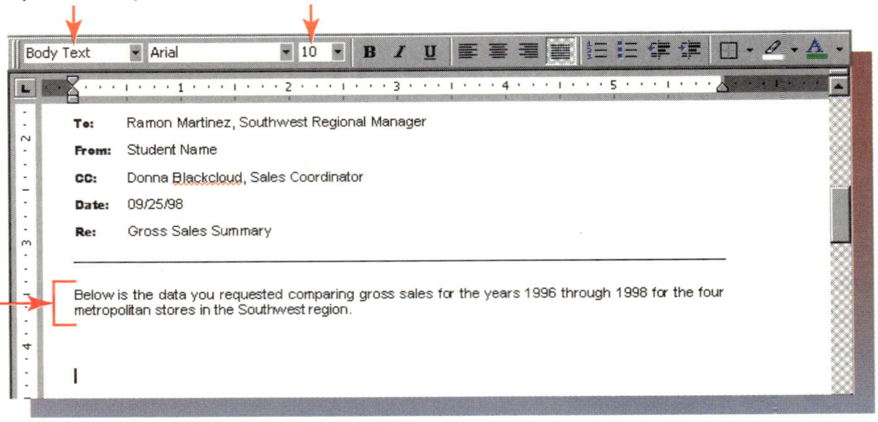

Notice that the Style button now shows the style as Body Text and the font as Arial 10 pt.

Creating a Table

Next you want to enter the sales data as a table.

Concept 1: Tables

A **table** is used to organize information into an easy-to-read format. A table displays information in horizontal **rows** and vertical **columns**. The insertion of a row and column creates a **cell** in which you can enter data or other information.

Cells in a table are identified first by a letter and number, called a **table reference**. Columns are identified from left to right beginning with the letter A, and rows are numbered from top to bottom beginning with the number 1. The table reference of the top leftmost cell is A1 because it is in the first column (A) and first row (1) fo the table. The second column is cell B2. The fourth cell in column 3 is C4.

column B

row 3

	A	B	C	D
1	Cell A1			
2		Cell B2		Cell D2
3				
4			Cell C4	
5				
6				

Tables are a very effective method for presenting information. The table layout organizes the information for the reader and greatly reduces the number of words they have to read to interpret the data. Use tables whenever you can to make your documents easier to read.

The table you want to create will display the data for the three years in the columns. The rows will display the data for the four stores and a total. Your completed table will be similar to the one shown below.

ANNUAL SALES				
		1996	**1997**	**1998**
Store	#48 -- Metro Center Mall	$719,590	$761,000	$782,205
	#55 -- Superstition Springs Mall	544,900	589,800	592,800
	#57 -- Fiesta Mall	620,700	633,800	631,700
	#62 -- Park Central Mall	578,900	569,400	565,300
	TOTAL	$2,464,090	$2,554,000	$2,572,005

Word includes several different methods you can use to create tables. One method (Table/Convert Text to Table) will quickly convert existing text that is separated into columns using separators such as tabs into a table. Another method uses the Table/Insert Table command or the button to create a simple table consisting of the same number of rows and columns. The last method, called Draw Table, is used to create any type of table, but is most useful for creating complex tables that contain cells of different heights or a varying number of columns per row. You will use the Draw Table feature to create this table.

- Click Tables and Borders.

The menu equivalent is Table/Draw Table.

The Tables and Borders toolbar appears, and the mouse pointer changes to a pen when positioned in the text area. The Tables and Borders toolbar buttons (identified below) are used to modify table settings.

If the Assistant is on, directions on how to draw a table are displayed.

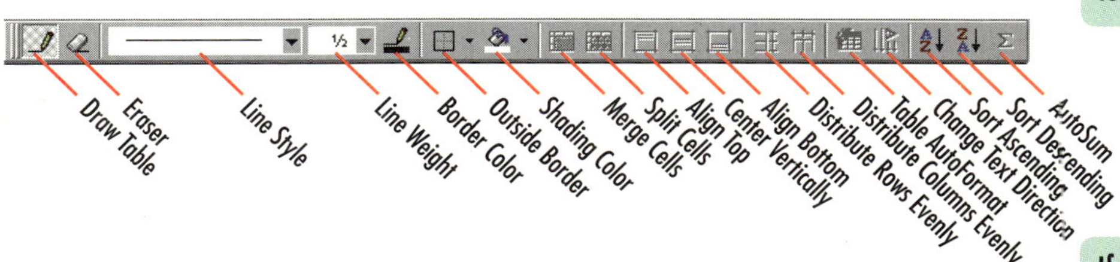

If necessary, move and dock the Tables and Borders toolbar below the Formatting toolbar.

Using Draw Table to create a table is similar to the way you would use a pen to draw a table. First you define the outer table boundaries, then you draw the column and row lines. A dotted line appears to show the boundary or lines you are creating as you drag. When creating row or column lines, drag from the beginning boundary to the end to extend the line the distance you want.

- Drag downward and to the right to create an outer table boundary of approximately 2 inches by 6 inches (refer to Figure 4-4).
- Add four vertical column lines at positions 0.5, 2.25, 3.5, and 4.5 on the ruler (see Figure 4-4 on the next page).
- Then draw five horizontal lines to create the rows as shown in Figure 4-4. Lines 2, 3, and 4 begin at the first column.

If you make an error, click or click Eraser and drag over the line.

Your screen should be similar to Figure 4-4.

FIGURE 4-4

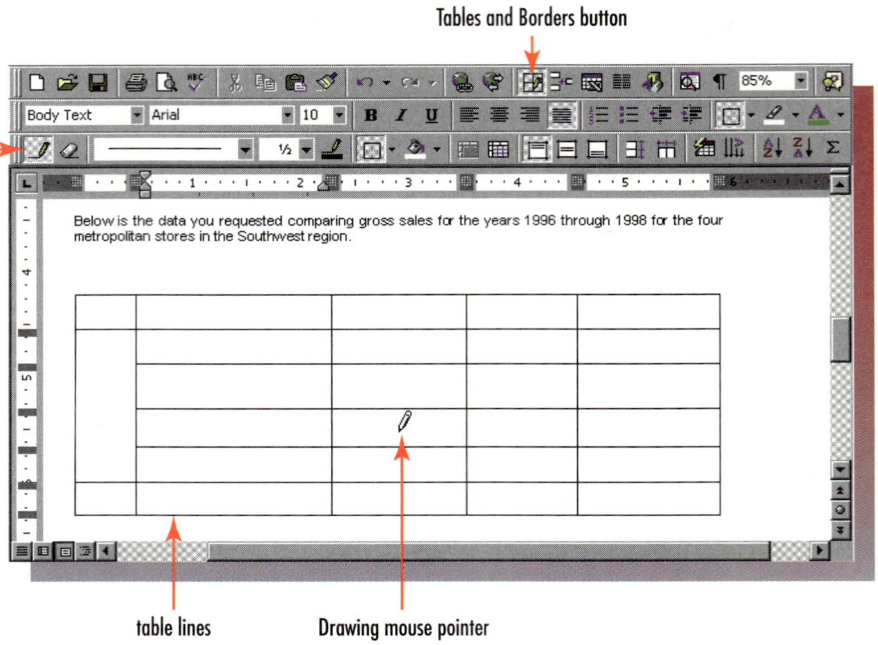

Do not be concerned if your table is not exactly like Figure 4-4. You will learn all about adjusting table lines shortly.

Entering Data in a Table

Now you are ready to enter information in the table. Each cell contains a single line space where you can enter data. You can move from one cell to another by using the arrow keys or by clicking on the cell. In addition, you can use the keys in the table below to move around a table.

To move to:	Press:
Next cell in a row	Tab
Previous cell in row	⇧Shift + Tab
First cell in row	Alt + Home
Last cell in row	Alt + End
First cell in column	Alt + Page Up
Last cell in column	Alt + Page Down
Previous row	↑
Next row	↓

The mouse pointer may also appear as an arrow when positioned in the table. When it is an arrow and you click on a cell, the entire cell is highlighted, indicating that it is selected. You will learn more about this feature shortly.

You will begin by entering the year column headings 1996 through 1998 in cells C1 through E1. Typing in any cell will turn off the Draw Table feature and allows you to type in the cell as you would anywhere in a normal document.

You can also click at any time to turn on or off the Draw Table feature.

- Click C1.
- Type **1996**
- Press Tab.
- In the same manner, continue entering the years 1997 and 1998 in cells D1 and E1.

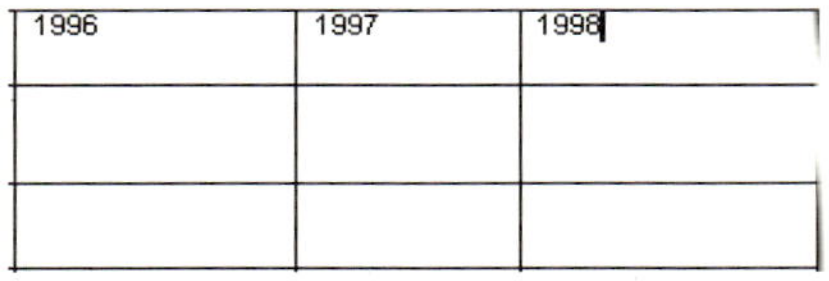

By default, entries in cells are left-aligned horizontally and top-aligned vertically in the cell space.

- Next enter the store names and a Total label as row headings and the sales data as shown below.

	Col B	Col C	Col D	Col E
Row 2	#48 – Metro Center Mall	$719,590	$761,000	$782,205
Row 3	#55 – Superstition Springs Mall	544,900	589,800	592,800
Row 4	#57 – Fiesta Mall	620,700	633,800	631,700
Row 5	#62 – Park Central Mall	578,900	569,400	565,300
Row 6	TOTAL			

Include the currency symbol as shown in row 2.

Your screen should be similar to Figure 4-5.

FIGURE 4-5

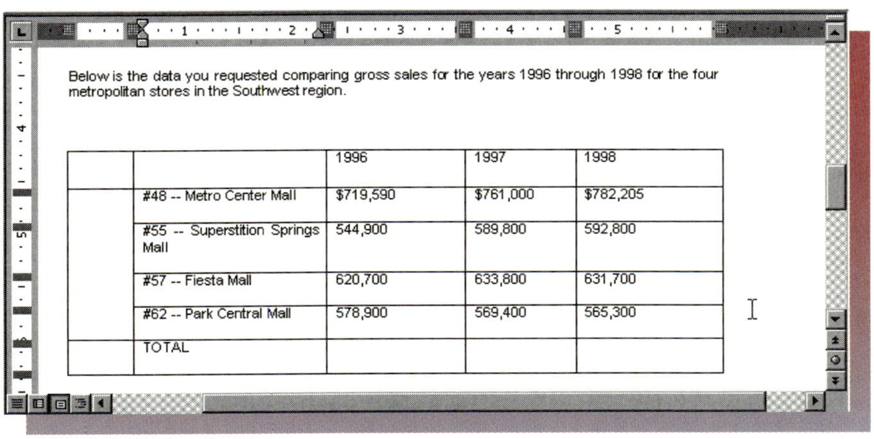

Entering a Formula

Now you are ready to enter the data for the totals. Rather than adding the values for each column of data and entering them in the Total row, you can enter a formula to make this calculation for you.

Concept 2: Formulas and Functions

Formulas and functions are used to perform calculations. A **formula** is a expression that contains any combination of numbers, fields resulting in numbers, table references, and operators. Operators are used to specify the type of calculation to perform. The most common operators are + (add), – (subtract), * (multiply), and / (divide).

To use the operators, follow the common arithmetic laws: multiply and divide before adding and subtracting, and calculate whatever is in parentheses first. For example, the formula, 125 + D3 * D5 will multiply the value in cell D3 by the value in cell D5 and then add 125. If you want to add 125 to D3 and then multiply the result by D5, put 125 and D3 in parentheses: (125 + D3) * D5.

A **function** is a prewritten formula. One function you may use frequently is the SUM function. SUM adds the numbers directly above the current cell. Other functions include:

Function	Description
AVERAGE	Calculates the average of a column of numbers.
COUNT	Totals the number of cells in the column.
MAX	Displays the maximum value in the column.
MIN	Displays the minimum value in the column.

To reference cells in formulas and functions, use a comma to separate references to individual cells and a colon to separate the first and last cells in a block. For example C1, C5 references the values in cells C1 and C5, whereas C1:C5 references the values in cells C1, C2, C3, through C5.

Formulas and functions are entered as fields in the table. The calculated result is displayed in the cell containing the formula or function. Because Word inserts the result of the calculation as a field, if you change the data in the referenced cells in the formula or function, you can update the calculation by selecting the field and then pressing F9.

The formulas and functions in Word let you create simple tables and spreadsheets for your documents. For larger, more complex spreadsheets, use Excel and then paste the spreadsheet into your document.

Refer to Concept 4: Fields in Lab 2 for information on this feature.

To enter the formula to sum the values in the 1996 column of data,

- Move to cell C6.
- Click Σ AutoSum.

Your screen should be similar to Figure 4-6.

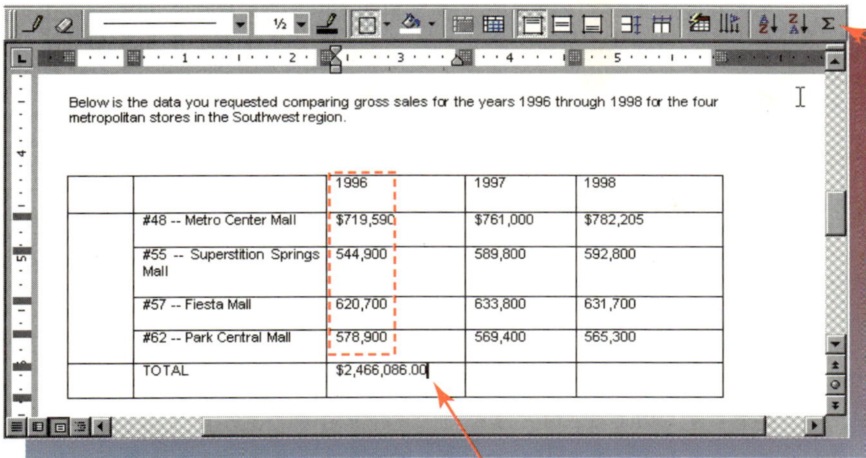

FIGURE 4-6

AutoSum calculates a total of a column or row of numbers

calculated result includes year value of 1996

The calculated value of $2,466,086.00 is diaplayed in cell C6. The calculated value for this column is incorrect. It should be $2,464,090. To see the formula used to make the calculation,

> If your Total does not display currency symbols, precede the entry in cell C2 with a $, then press F9 in cell C6 to update the display.

- Choose Table/Formula.

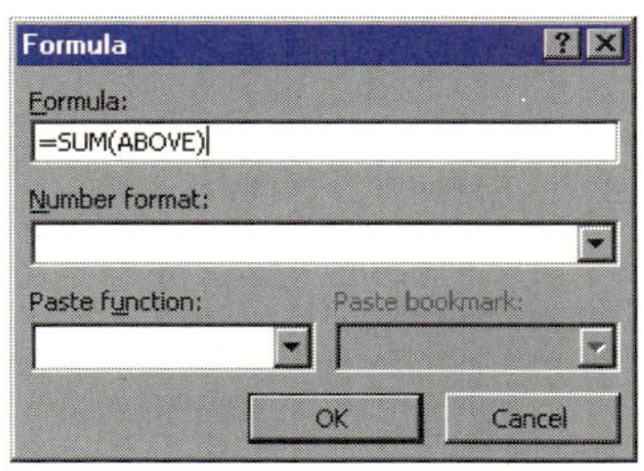

In the Formula text box of the Formula dialog box, the function =SUM(ABOVE) is displayed. Using the Σ AutoSum button enters a function that calculates the sum of all the numbers above the current cell. Because it includes the number in cell C1, the year 1996, the calculated total is incorrect. To correct this you need to replace "ABOVE" with the specific table cell references.

- In place of the word "ABOVE" in the parentheses, enter **C2:C5**
- Click OK.

> Double-click the word "ABOVE" to quickly select it.

The formula correctly calculates the result of $2,464,090.00 using the values in the specified cells of the table. Notice that the value is displayed with a dollar sign. This is because Word used the same format as the value in cell C2. It also includes two decimal places by default because most currency entries may include decimals. You decide you do not want the decimal places displayed.

- Select the result and delete the .00 from the entry.
- Enter the functions to calculate the totals for the other two years in cells D6 and E6. Delete the two decimal places from both results.

> Because the result is a field, the entire entry is shaded.

The Table/Insert Columns command is used to add a column to the left of the current column.

The Insert Cells button on the Standard toolbar can also be used to insert columns and rows.

The menu equivalent is Table/Merge Cells.

Inserting a Row

After looking at the table, you decide to add a row above the years to display a table heading. Because the row will display a table heading centered over all columns of the table, you will also combine the cells in the row to create a single cell.

- Move to cell A1.
- Choose Table/Insert Rows.
- Click Merge Cells.
- Click in the cell to clear the highlight.

Your screen should be similar to Figure 4-7.

FIGURE 4-7

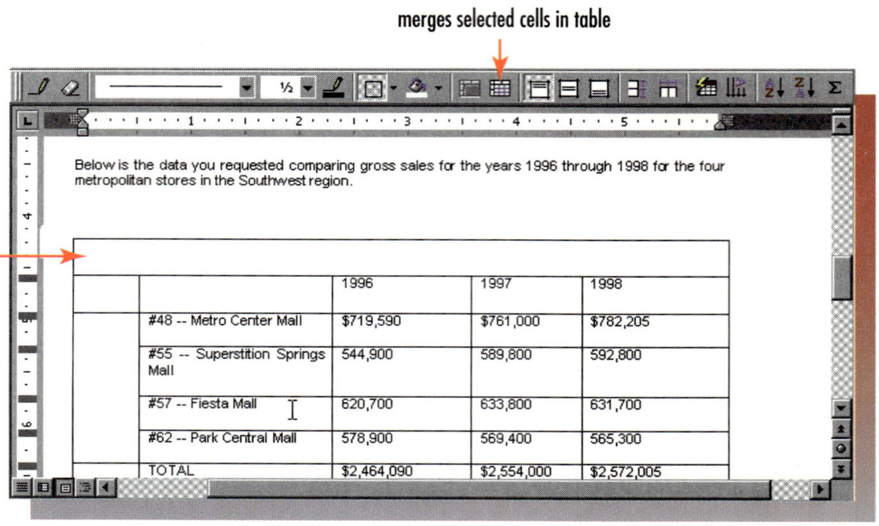

The three column dividers are eliminated, and the top row is one cell. Now you are ready to add the text for the heading and to center it within the cell space. You also want to enter the heading "Store" in cell A3 and align it vertically within the cell space.

- Type **ANNUAL SALES**
- Click Center.
- Enter **Store** in cell A3.
- Click Change Text Direction (twice).
- Click Center.

Your screen should be similar to Figure 4-8.

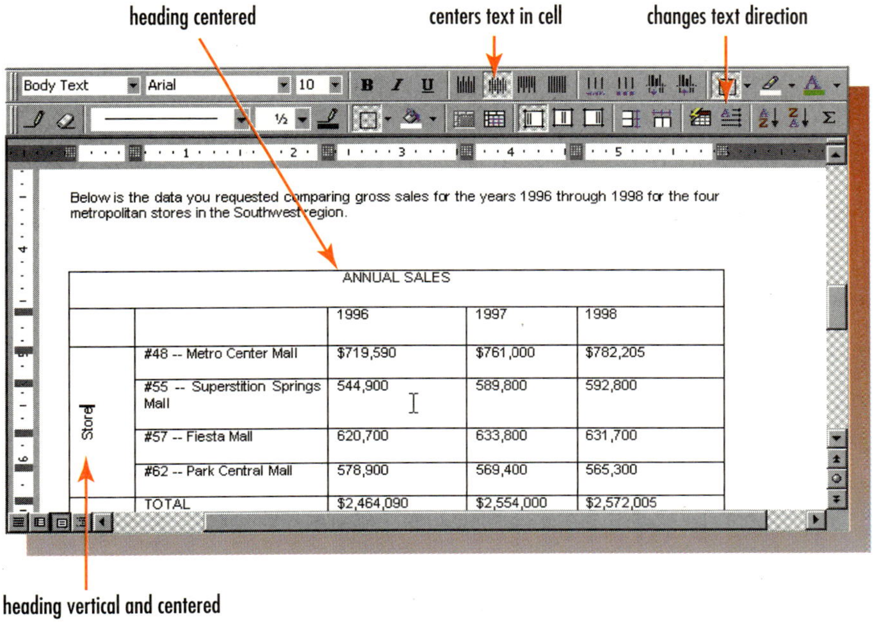

FIGURE 4-8

Changing Column Width

The table is really taking shape. However, it can still be improved by adjusting the size of the columns. You want to increase the width of column B so that the store names are displayed on a single line. To change the width of a column, point to the column divider line and drag it to the right or left to increase or decrease the column width. A temporary dotted line appears to show your new setting.

- Point to the right border of column B. The mouse pointer should be displayed as ⟺.
- Drag to the right to increase the column width to fully display all store names on a single line (approximately 2.5-inch position on the ruler).

You also want to adjust the widths of columns C through E to be equally sized. As you continue to modify the table, many cells can be selected and changed at the same time. The table on page 166 describes how to select different areas of a table.

You can also increase or decrease the height of a row by dragging the row divider line.

The menu equivalent is Table/Cell Height and Width.

The menu equivalent to select a row is Table/Select Row, and for a column is Table/Select Column.

The menu equivalent is Table/Select Table.

Area to Select	Procedure
Cell	Click the left edge of the cell when the pointer is ↗.
Row	Click to the left of the row when the pointer is ↗.
Column	Click the top of the column when the pointer is ⬇.
Multiple cells, rows, or columns	Drag through the cells, rows, or columns, or select the first cell, row, or column, and hold down ⇧Shift while clicking on another cell, row, or column.
Contents of next cell	Press Tab.
Contents of previous cell	Press ⇧Shift + Tab.
Entire table	Press Alt + 5 (on the numeric keypad with NumLock off).

- Select cells C2 through E7.
- Click Distribute Columns Evenly.

Your screen should be similar to Figure 4-9.

FIGURE 4-9

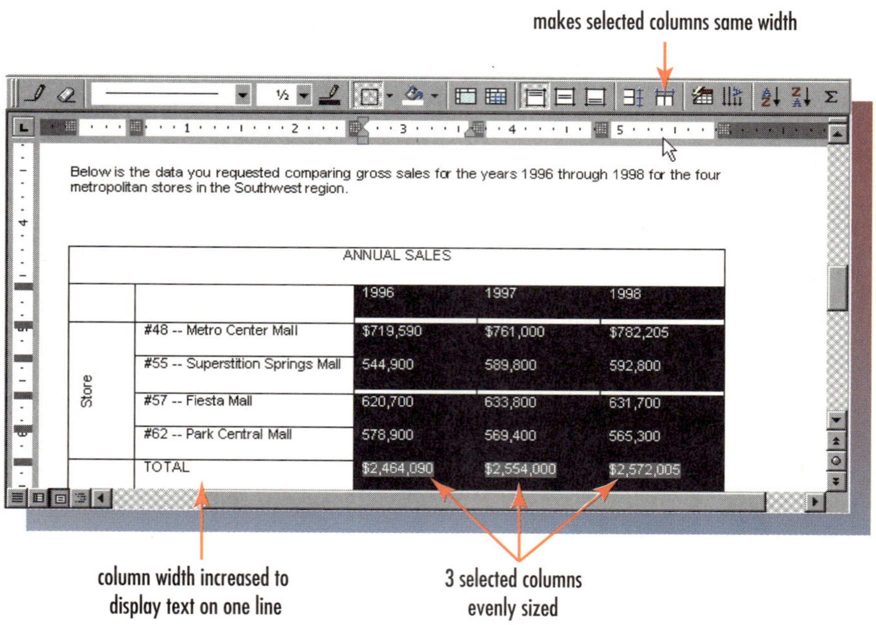

Formatting the Table

To enhance the appearance of the table, you can apply many different formats to the cells. This is similar to adding formatting to a document except the formatting affects the selected cells only.

You want the entries in the currently selected range, C2 through E7, to be right-aligned in their cell spaces. You also want the year headings to be centered, 12 pt, and bold, and the table title and the Store heading to be in a different font, larger, and bold. To make these changes,

- Click Align Right.
- Select cells C2 through E2.
- Change the font to 12 pt and bold.
- Click Center.
- Change the table title font (cell A1) to Times New Roman, 14 pt, and bold.
- Change the Store heading (cell A3) to Times New Roman, 12 pt, and bold.

To change the format settings of all text within a cell, simply move to the cell and apply the formats.

Finally, you want to add color shading behind the table title.

- Move to cell A1.
- Open the Shading Color drop-down list and select a color of your choice from the color palette.
- Clear the highlight.

You can also use Table/Table AutoFormat or to apply a predesigned table design and layout to an entire table.

Your screen should be similar to Figure 4-10.

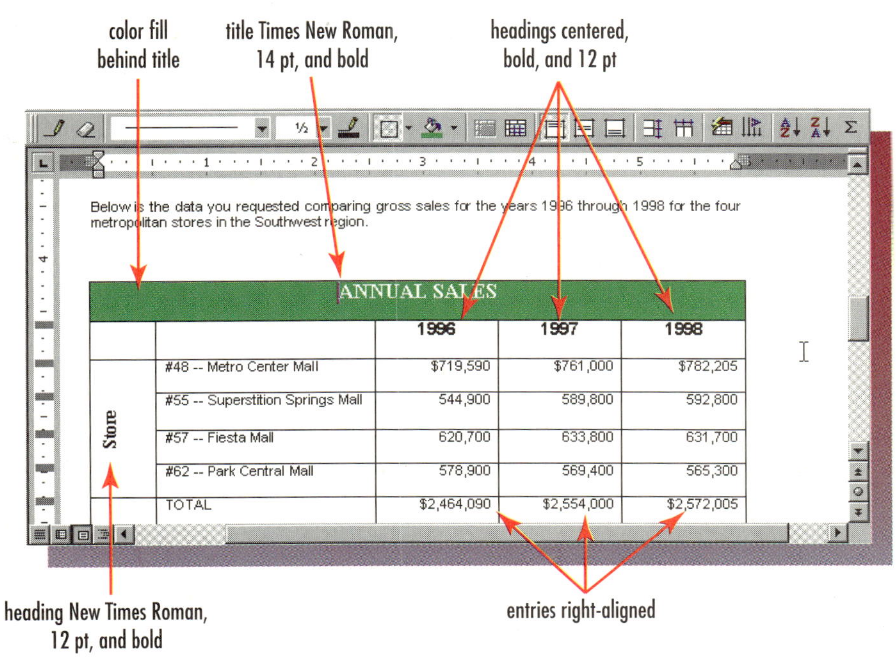

FIGURE 4-10

- Apply any additional formatting you wish, such as shadings, different border line weights, text and line colors, and so on, to the table.
- When you are done, close the Tables and Borders toolbar.

The memo is now complete.

- Save the document as Sales Summary Memo.
- Preview, then print the memo (select the appropriate printer).
- Close the file.

Part 2

The Mail Merge Feature

Next you will change the letter sent to new credit card customers to a form letter.

- Open the file Credit Card Letter 4. If necessary, maximize the document window and switch to Normal view.
- If necessary, set the zoom to Page Width so that the entire document width is visible.

This letter is similar to the credit card letter you saved as Revised Credit Card Letter 2 in Lab 2. Notice that the date in the letter on your screen is the same date the file was saved. When this letter is printed, the date will automatically be updated to print the current system date. This is because you entered a date field in the document. To manually update the date displayed on your screen,

- Move to the date field.
- Select Update Field from the Shortcut menu.

To create the personalized form letter to be sent to all new credit card recipients, you will use the Mail Merge feature of Word.

Concept 3: Mail Merge

The **Mail Merge** feature combines a list of data (typically a file of names and addresses) with a document (commonly a form letter) to create a new document. The names and addresses are entered (merged) into the form letter in the blank spaces provided. The result is a personalized form letter.

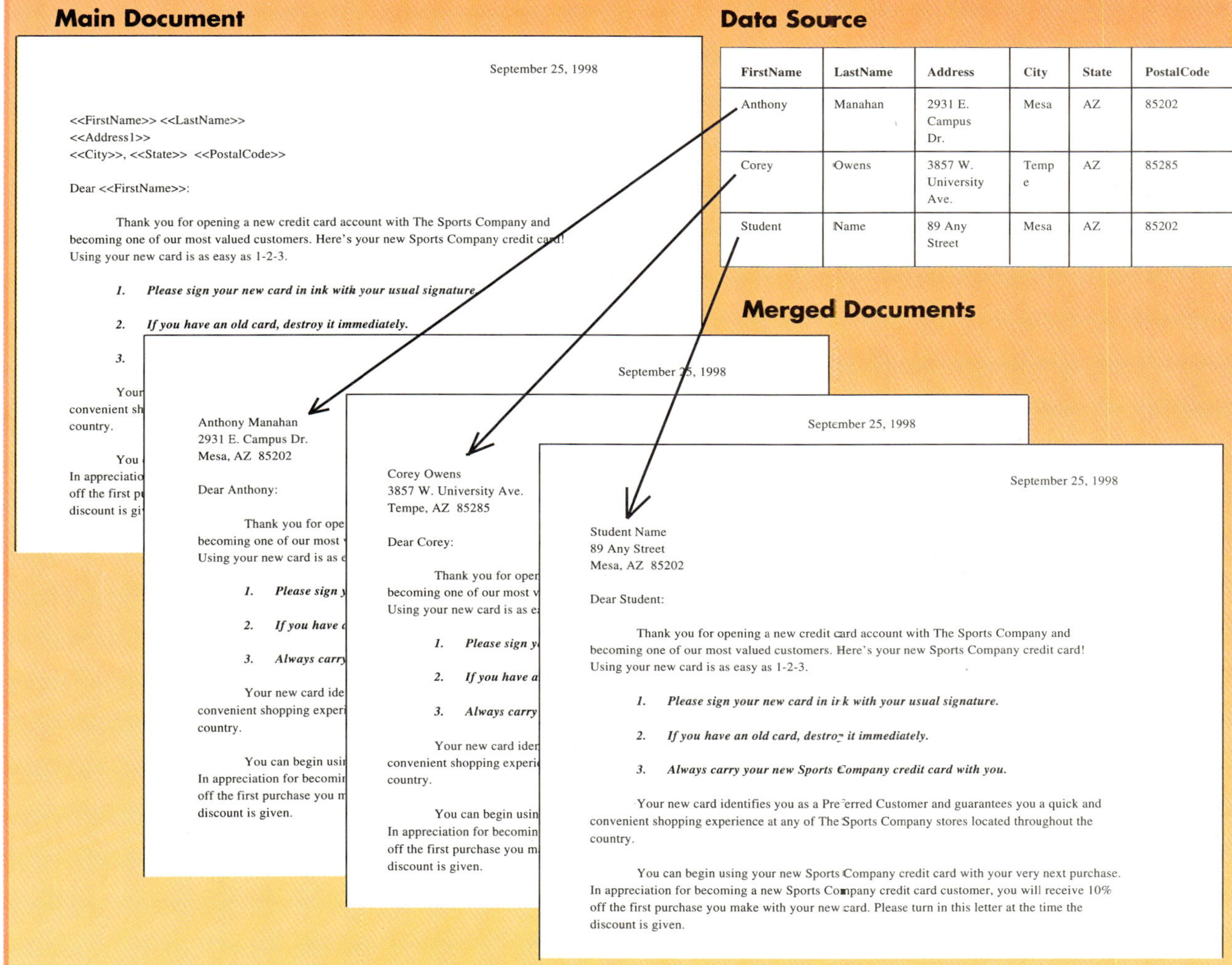

FirstName	LastName	Address	City	State	PostalCode
Anthony	Manahan	2931 E. Campus Dr.	Mesa	AZ	85202
Corey	Owens	3857 W. University Ave.	Tempe	AZ	85285
Student	Name	89 Any Street	Mesa	AZ	85202

Mail Merge usually requires the use of two files: a main document and a data source. The **main document** contains the basic form letter. It directs the merge process through the use of merge fields. A **merge field** is a field code that controls what information is used from the data source and where it is entered in the main document. The **data source** contains the information needed to complete the letter in the main document. It can also be called an **address file** because it commonly contains name and address data. Each category of information in the data source is called a **data field**. For example, the customer's first name is a data field, the last name is a data field, the street address is another data field, the city a fourth data field, and so on. All the data fields that are needed to complete the information for one person (or other entity) are called a **record**. Commonly, a database file created using a database application is used as the data source. However, the data source can also be created using Word.

Creating the Main Document

To start the Mail Merge feature,

- Choose Tools/Mail Merge.

The Mail Merge Helper dialog box on your screen should be similar to Figure 4-11.

FIGURE 4-11

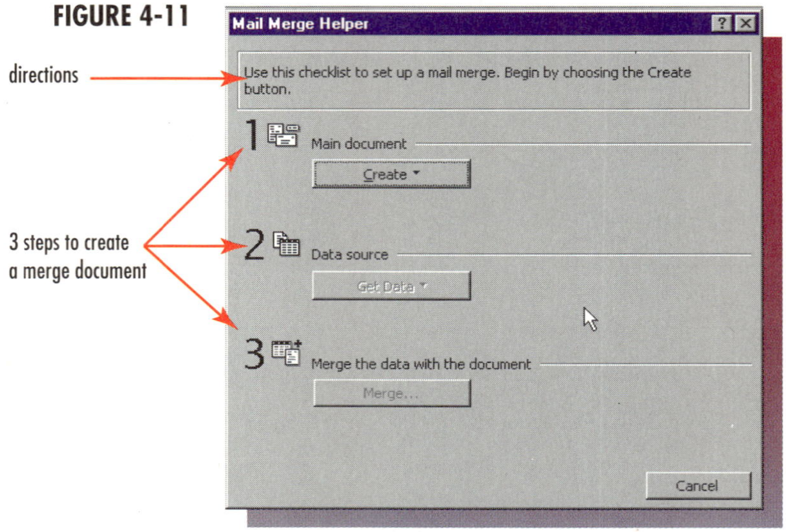

This dialog box is designed to take you step by step through the process of creating a merge. The three steps are:

1. Create a main document.
2. Create a data source.
3. Perform the merge.

The credit card letter will be modified to be the main document. Then you will create the data source of customers' names and addresses using Word. When you perform the merge, Word takes the data field information from the data source and combines or merges it into the main document. The merge fields in the main document control what data fields are used from the data source and where they are entered in the main document.

To create the main document form letter from the credit letter in the active window,

- Choose Create /Form Letters/ Active Window .

Mail Merge can also be used to create mailing labels, envelopes, or catalogs.

The dialog box now shows the type of merge (Form Letters) and name of the file (Credit Card Letter 4) that will be used as the main document, along with a second button, Edit , which is used to edit your main document.

Creating the Data Source

The dialog box also now indicates that the next step is to create the data source file. This file will contain the customers' names and addresses, which will be merged with the main document. To create this file,

- Select [Get Data]/Create Data Source.

The Create Data Source dialog box on your screen should be similar to Figure 4-12.

FIGURE 4-12

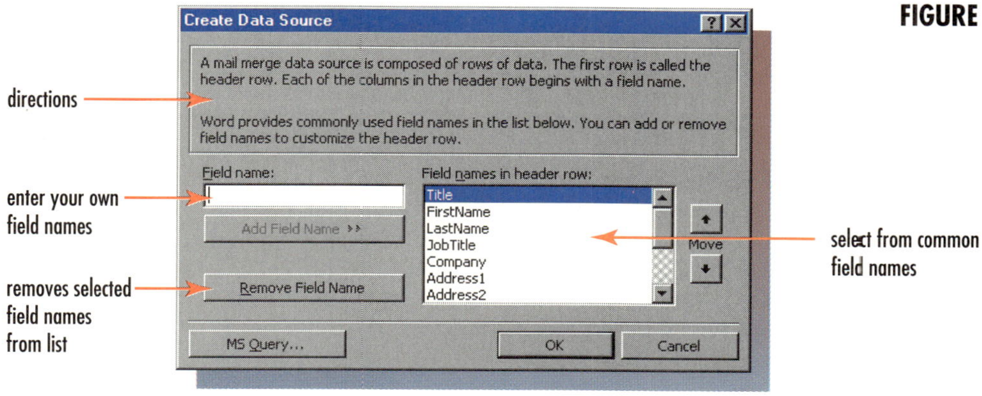

In this dialog box you specify the field names for the data that will be entered in the data source file.

Concept 4: Field Names

Field names are used to label each data field in the data source. A field name can contain only letters, numbers, or the underline character. It can be a maximum of 40 characters and cannot contain spaces. The first character of a field name must be a letter. Field names should be descriptive of the contents of the data field.

Commonly used form letter field names are displayed in the Field Names in Header Row list box. You can remove from the list field names that you do not need in your letter, or you can add additional field names to the list by typing them in the Field Name text box. In this case, you will remove field names that you do not want to use in the credit card letter. The first field you do not need is Title. To remove it,

The Move buttons to the right of the list let you rearrange the order of fields.

- Click [Remove Field Name].
- In the same manner select and remove the following field names: JobTitle, Company, Address2, Country, HomePhone, and WorkPhone.

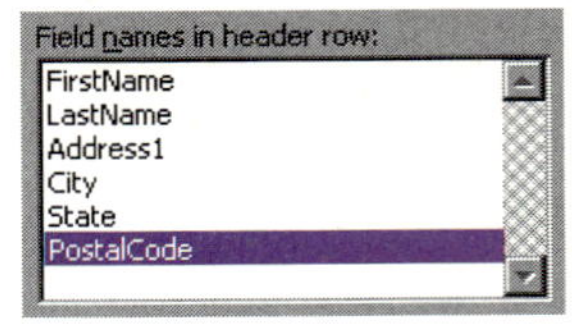

The list now reflects only those fields you will include in the data source.

- Click OK.
- Save the file as Credit Data Source on your data disk.

The informational dialog box displayed on your screen advises you that you need to add the record information to the data source file and edit the main document to include the merge fields. You will add data to the data source file first.

adds date to data source file

- Click Edit Data Source.

The Data Form dialog box on your screen should be similar to Figure 4-13.

field names

fill in the information for each field to create a record

FIGURE 4-13

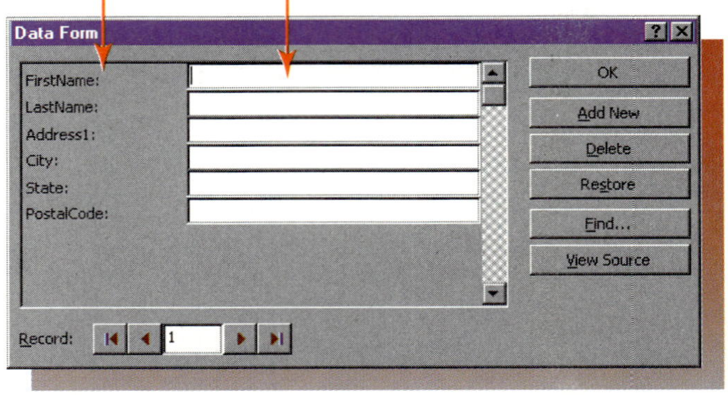

This dialog box displays the field names and a text box to be used to enter the data for each record. The data must be entered exactly as you want it to appear in the letter. If you do not have the information needed to complete a field, you can leave it blank. To enter the data for the first field of the first record, the customer's first name,

- Type **Anthony**
- Press Tab or ←Enter.
- Enter the information for the remaining fields for this record using the following information:

  LastName: **Manahan**

  Address1: **2931 E. Campus Dr.**

  City: **Mesa**

  State: **AZ**

  PostalCode: **85202**

- If you see any errors in the field data, move back to the entry and edit it.

The dialog box on your screen should be similar to Figure 4-14.

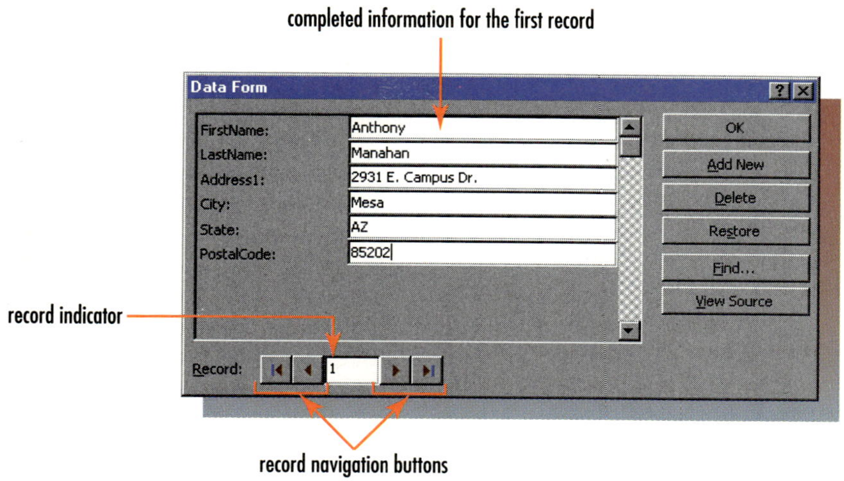

FIGURE 4-14

To add this record to the data source file and display a new blank data form,

- Click Add New.

Notice that the record indicator shows that the current data form will be used to hold the data for the second record.

- Enter the field data for the second record using the following information:

  FirstName: **Corey**

  LastName: **Owens**

  Address1: **3857 W. University Ave.**

  City: **Tempe**

  State: **AZ**

  PostalCode: **85285**

- Enter your name and address as the third record in the data source.
- Move to each of the records and verify the data you entered. If necessary, correct any errors.

You can also view multiple records at once in the window. To see the three records,

- Choose View Source.

The record navigation buttons can be used to quickly move between records.

The number of records you enter into the data source is limited only by your disk space. At any time, you can add more records using the Data Form as you just did.

Your screen should be similar to Figure 4-15.

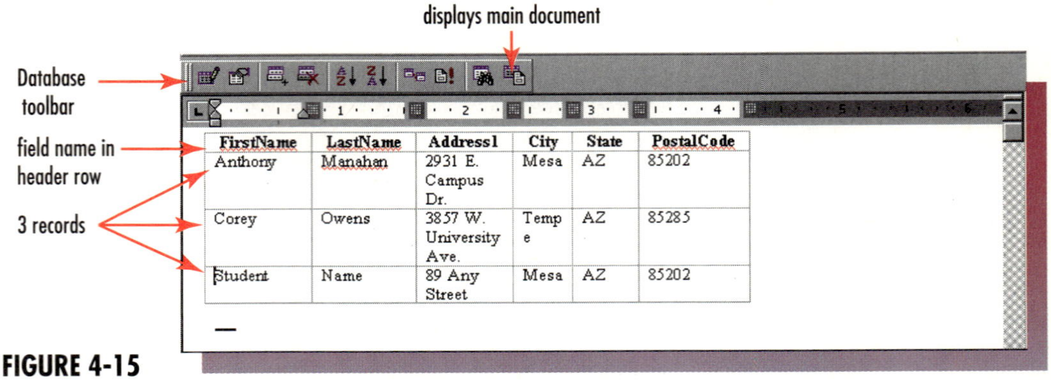

FIGURE 4-15

The data source is displayed in a document window in table form. The field names are displayed as the top row of the table, and each record is displayed as a row. In addition, the Database toolbar shown below is displayed.

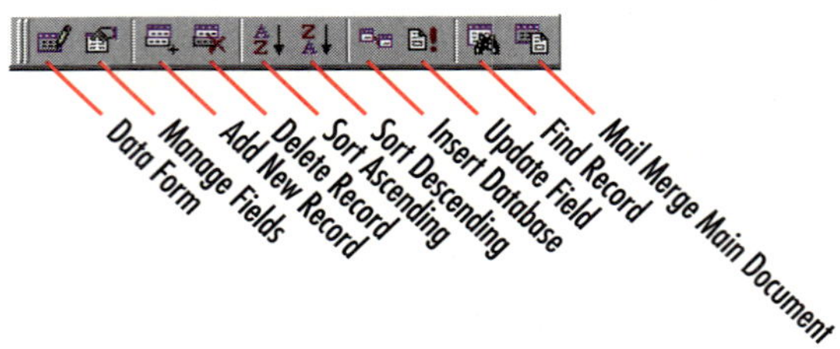

- If necessary, move the Database toolbar below the Formatting toolbar.
- Now that the data source contains records, save the file again.
- Click Mail Merge Main Document.

The main document is displayed in the window along with the Mail Merge toolbar shown below.

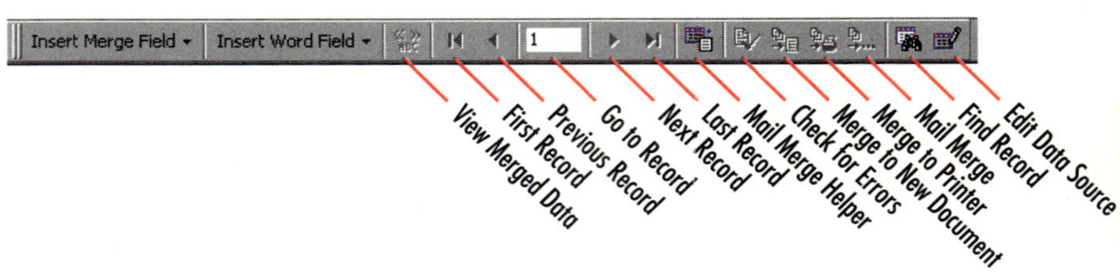

Entering Merge Fields in the Main Document

How will Word know where to enter the customer's name and other source data in the main document? Word uses merge fields to do this. Merge fields direct the program to accept information from the data source at the specified location in the main document. To prepare the credit card letter to accept the fields of information from the data source, you need to add merge fields to the letter.

The credit card letter needs to be modified to allow entry of the name and address information for each preferred customer from the data source. The inside address will hold the following three lines of information:

FirstName LastName
Address1
City, State PostalCode

The first line of the inside address, which will hold the preferred customer's full name, will be entered as line 5 of the credit card letter.

A merge field needs to be entered in the main document for each field of data you want copied from the data source. The location of the merge field indicates where to enter the field data. To position the insertion point on the line where the preferred customer's name will appear as the first line of the inside address, and to enter the fields into the main document,

- Move to the blank line above the salutation.
- Click Insert Merge Field ▾.

A drop-down list of field names from the data source file is displayed. To insert the FirstName merge field at the location of the insertion point,

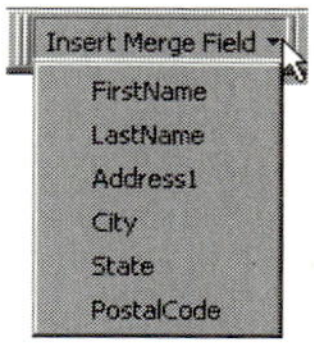

- Select FirstName.

Your screen should be similar to Figure 4-16.

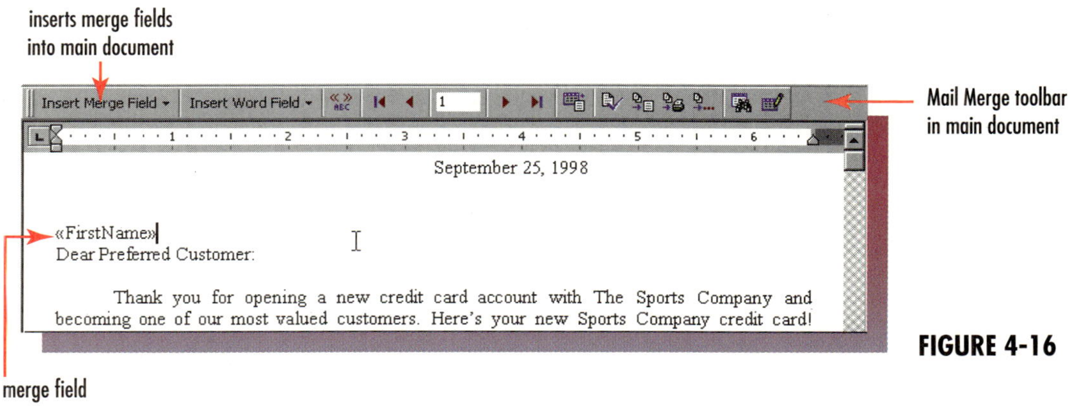

FIGURE 4-16

The merge field <<FirstName>> is displayed at the insertion point location in the main document. It is a field code that instructs Word to insert the information from the first name data field (from the data source) at this location in the main document when the merge is performed.

The next merge field that needs to be entered is the preferred customer's last name.

- Press Spacebar.
- Enter the LastName merge field.
- Press ←Enter.
- Enter the remaining merge fields in the inside address using the punctuation as shown in Figure 4-17.
- Enter a blank line between the inside address and the salutation.
- Then select and replace the words "Preferred Customer" in the salutation with the FirstName merge field.

The same merge field can be used more than once in the main document.

Your screen should be similar to Figure 4-17.

FIGURE 4-17

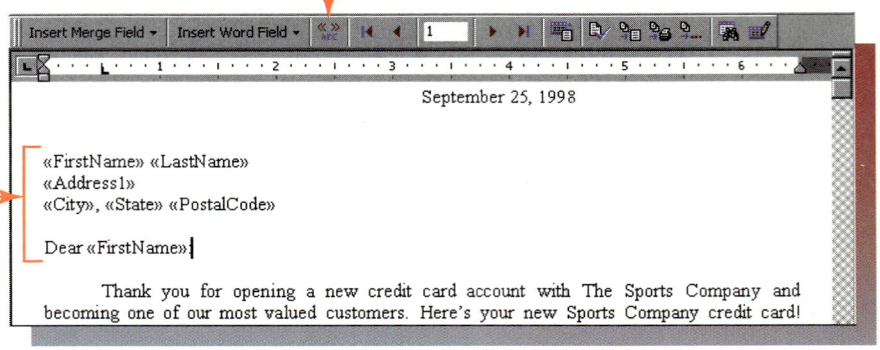

To see how the form letter will appear with the merged data,

- Click View Merged Data.

Your screen should be similar to Figure 4-18.

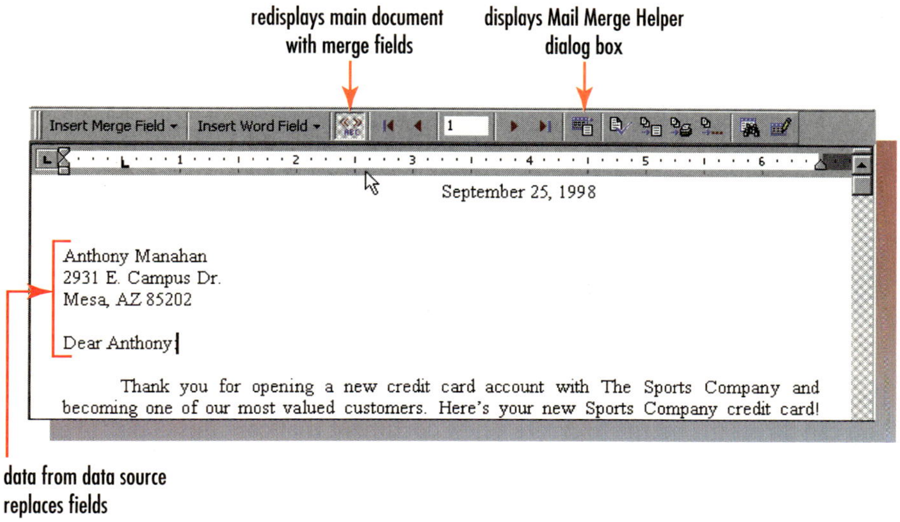

FIGURE 4-18

The data in the first record of the data source is displayed in place of the merge fields. To redisplay the merge fields and check that the entire letter still fits on a single page,

- Click View Merged Data.
- Preview the letter.

If your letter is longer than one page,

- Click Shrink to Fit.
- Close the Print Preview window.
- Save the main document as Credit Main Document.

Performing the Merge

Now that you have created the main document and data source document, you are ready to combine them to create the new personalized credit card letter. During this process a third file is created. The original main document and data source file are not altered or affected in any way. The third file is the result of merging the main document with the data source file.

- Click Mail Merge Helper.
- Click Merge... .

	Date	Time In	Time Out	Regular Hours	Overtime Hours	Total Hours
Monday	1/6/97	8:00	5:00	8	0	8
Tuesday	1/7/97	8:00	5:00	8	0	8
Wednesday	1/8/97	8:00	5:00	8	0	8
Thursday	1/9/97	7:00	6:00	8	3	11
Friday	1/10/97	7:00	6:00	8	3	11
Total Hours						**46**

b. Select and delete the Company Name Here box in the upper right corner.

c. Create the sample time sheet (as shown above) below the memo using the Draw Table feature.

d. Apply a table autoformat of your choice to the table.

e. Use a formula to calculate the Total Hours column. Make sure all numbers are right-aligned.

f. Enter and format a row to display a table title.

g. Adjust the column widths appropriately and make additional formatting changes to improve the appearance of the table as needed.

h. Document the file and save it as Time Sheet Memo. Print the document.

☆☆

2. As the owner of Susie's Sundries, you are replenishing your stock of some very popular items: widgets, gadgets, smidgens, and do-dads. In this exercise you will create an order form.

Item	Vendor	Quantity	Unit Cost	Total Cost
Widgets	Wonder Widgets	100	.50	
Gadgets	Gadgets Galore	100	2.00	
Smidgens	Smidgen Sensations	50	12.00	
Do-Dads	Do-Dad Delights	250	10.00	
Grand Total				

a. Use Draw Table to create the table shown above.

b. Enter the formula =c2*d2 to calculate a total for widgets. While you are in the Formula dialog box, use the Number Format drop-down list to apply the second format (#,###.00) to the value. Using this logic, calculate totals and apply the same number format to all values representing total amounts for gadgets, smidgens, and do-dads.

c. Calculate a grand total at the bottom of the Total Cost column. Format the grand total amount to display a dollar sign (third Number Format option). Bold the grand total value. Merge this row to a single cell.

d. Select the entire table and use the AutoFit option located in the Column tab of the Cell Height and Width dialog box to accommodate the widest entry in each column.

e. Insert a row at the top of the table and merge the cells. Enter the title "Order Form" in a different font that is larger than the text in the rest of the table. Center this title.

f. Left-align all entries in the first two columns, and right-align all number entries (and their column headings) in subsequent columns.

g. Insert your name and the current date in a header.

h. Document the file and save it as Order Form Table. Print the form.

☆☆

3. To complete this exercise, you must have completed Practice Exercise 4 in Lab 1. In this exercise, you will create a form letter to be sent to the friends and relatives who want a copy of Grandma Gertie's cookie recipes.

a. Open the file Cookie Letter from your data disk.

b. Follow the procedures you learned in this lab to define the document in the active window as the main document, and create the data source. Assign the file name Cookie Data Source. Enter the following records and at least three more of your own choice:

Susan
Wagner
463 E. Tioga Ave.
Forty Fort
PA
18704

George
Peterson
832 Colonial Dr.
Wellesley
MA
02181

c. When you are finished entering the records, view the data source file. Save the data source file again.

d. In the Cookie Letter document, create an inside address by inserting data source merge fields above the salutation. In the salutation replace "Friends and Family" with the FirstName merge field.

e. Insert the current date as a field above the inside address and right-align it.

f. Increase the font size for the letter to 12 pt. Justify the letter. Center your return address. When you are finished, document the file and save the letter as Cookie Main Document.

g. Merge the data source and main document files. Document the merge file and save the merged letters as Cookie Merge Document. Print the letters.

☆☆

4. To complete this exercise, you must have completed Practice Exercise 2 in Lab 2. In this exercise, you will modify the document Acceptance Letter to be a form letter.

a. Open the file Acceptance Letter from your data disk. Define Acceptance Letter as the main document, and create a data source named Student Data Source consisting of the following fields. (Hint: After you have removed all unnecessary fields, enter the field name Major in the Field Name text box. Then click the Add Field Name button.)

Title
FirstName
LastName
Address1
City
State
PostalCode
Major

b. Enter information that pertains to you as record 1 of the data source, and then enter records for three of your friends. When you have finished entering records, view the data source. Document the file and resave it.

c. Modify the Acceptance Letter to contain appropriate merge fields where your name, address, or major appears throughout the letter. Insert the current date as a field. You might have to right-align the date again. Increase the font size to 12 pt for the entire letter. Use the Shrink to Fit command if the entire letter does not fit on one page. Document and save the modified main document as Student Main Document.

d. Merge the letters. Document and save the file as Student Merge Document. Print the letters.

☆☆☆

5. Murphy's Department Store is holding a private sale for its preferred customers. As CEO, you are sending a "personal" letter to each of these customers inviting them to the sale.

a. Open the file Preferred Customer from your data disk. Cut the first line ("murphy's") to the Clipboard, and paste it (Ctrl + V) into the WordArt Enter Your Text Here dialog box. Create a title using the WordArt features you learned in Lab 3. Center the title, and enter another blank line below it.

b. Go to the line of text below the title. Set a centered tab at the 3-inch position, and a right-aligned tab at 6 inches. Move the street address to the centered tab, and move the city, state, and postal code information to the right tab. Draw a box around this line.

c. Use Find and Replace to locate and replace "preferred customer" with "Special Preferred Customer" in the first and third paragraphs only. Bold and italicize those two occurrences of "Special Preferred Customer." Italicize the text "Any day this month" at the beginning of the second paragraph.

d. Use the Insert Date and Time command to replace [Current Date] at the top of the document.

e. Use the active document to create a form letter. Create a data source named Customer Data Source that contains the following fields:

Title
FirstName
LastName
Address1
City
State
PostalCode

f. Enter the following records:

Mr. Joel Allen
316 River St.
Wilkes-Barre, PA 18702

Ms. Ronnie Lee
452 Valley View Dr.
Shavertown, PA 18706

Mr. Dean Walter
409 Laurel Rd.
Mountain Top, PA 18707

g. When you are finished entering records, view the data source. Document the file and resave it.

h. In the main document, insert fields representing the customers' names and addresses above the salutation line. Remove "Preferred Customer" from the salutation, and replace it with the customer's FirstName merge field. Remove [Customer's First Name] from the third paragraph, and replace it with the appropriate merge field code. Insert your name as the CEO in the closing.

i. Document the file and save the main document as Customer Main Document. Merge the main document and the data source. Document the merged letter file and save it as Customer Merge Document. Print the letters.

On Your Own

★

6. Use Draw Table to create a schedule of your classes for the semester. The column headings should display the days of the week, and the row headings should display hours. The cells below the column headings should display the classes you have on those days. Include a merged cell to display a table title. Appropriately format the table to improve its appearance. Document and save the file as Schedule. Print the document.

★★★

7. In this exercise you will use the Draw Table feature to create a resume.

Create a table with two columns and sixteen rows.

Apply the Grid 1-AutoFormat and clear the Borders check box under Formats to Apply so that no borders will print.

Note: When the table is displayed, dotted grid lines will be displayed for you to use as a guide. These lines will not print, however.

Career Objective	Type your objective(s) here.
Education	
Date: [Enter Date Here]	Institution City Degree Courses included:
Work Experience (most recent first)	
Date: [Enter Date Here]	Your Job Title Name of Company Duties Included:
Activities	List Activities
Honors and Awards	List Honors and Awards (Dean's List, Who's Who)
Special Skills	List skills that would enhance your job performance
References	List References or "Available upon request from..."

Enter the resume headings in column A as displayed in the table above.

Enter resume information into column B. Cells follow the same formatting rules as a paragraph. If you right-align a cell, all entries in the cell will be right-aligned. When listing information that exceeds the width of a cell, overflow information will wrap to the next line. You can press ←Enter to add multiple lines (for example, the date, job title, company, and duties) to a cell. If you had more than one job or graduated from more than one school, you can enter additional information below the first set of information in the same cell.

When you are finished, increase the font size to 12 pt.

Create a centered return address above the table. The return address should contain your name, address, city, state, postal code, and phone number(s). It can be slightly larger than the resume text, and you can use a different font to attract attention. Just don't get too carried away! Remember . . . keep it conservative.

If the document does not fit on one page, reduce the margins to 1 inch all around. If the document still does not fit, use the Shrink to Fit command.

When you are finished, document and save the file as Resume. Print the resume.

☆☆☆

8. To complete this exercise, you must have completed Practice Exercise 7 in Lab 1. Open the file Cover Letter from your data disk. In this exercise you will create a data source and convert the Cover Letter to a main document file.

Create the data source containing at least three prospective employers, using information of your own choice. Use the fields that are described in the return address of the Lab 1 exercise. Save the file as Cover Data Source.

Insert the data source fields into the appropriate locations of the Cover Letter to create a main document. Increase the font size of the letter to 12 pt and change the font.

Hint: Use a font for the cover letter and resume that is conservative and easy to read. When in doubt, use Times New Roman and/or Arial. Fancy fonts (script, for example) can be difficult to read, and Courier looks as though you just "cranked it out" on a typewriter. You're better than that!

Save the file as Cover Main Document.

Merge the two files. Document the merged letter file and save it as Cover Merge Document. Print the letters.

Concept Summary

4 Creating a Table and Merging Documents

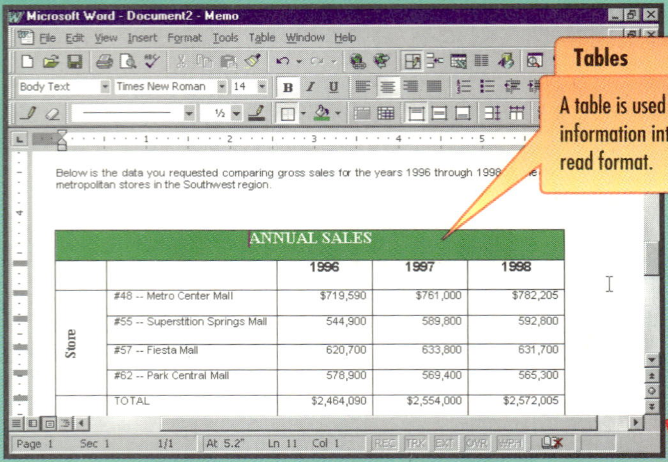

Tables

A table is used to organize information into an easy-to-read format.

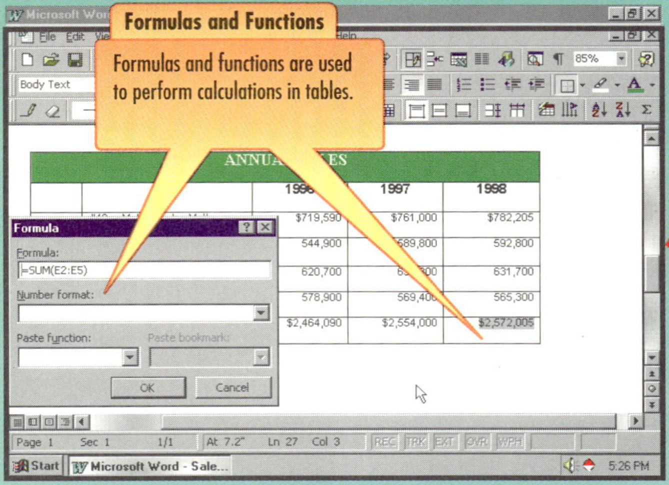

Formulas and Functions

Formulas and functions are used to perform calculations in tables.

Concepts

- Tables
- Formulas and Functions
- Mail Merge
- Field Names

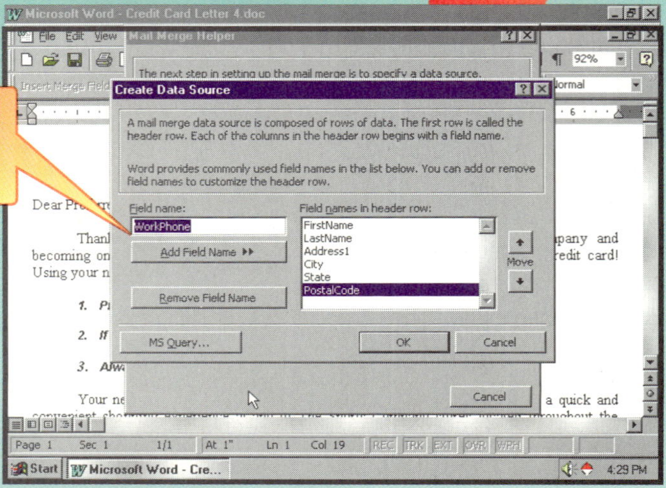

Field Names

Field names are used to label each data field in the data source.

Main Document

September 25, 1998

<<FirstName>> <<LastName>>
<<Address1>>
<<City>>, <<State>> <<PostalCode>>

Dear <<FirstName>>:

Thank you for opening a new credit card account with The Sports Company and becoming one of our most valued customers. Here's your new Sports Company credit card! Using your new card is as easy as 1-2-3.

1. ***Please sign your new card in ink with your usual signature.***
2. ***If you have an old card, destroy it immediately.***
3. ***Always carry your new Sports Company credit card with you.***

Your new card identifies you as a Preferred Customer and guarantees you a quick and convenient shopping experience at any of The Sports Company stores located throughout the country.

You can begin using your new Sports Company credit card with your very next purchase. In appreciation for becoming a new Sports Company credit card customer, you will receive 10% off the first purchase you make with your new card. Please turn in this letter at the time the discount is given.

Additionally, each month you will receive The Sports Company Update, a newsletter about new products, sports trends, sports safety tips, and upcoming events. The newsletter will also include announcements of special sale days for our preferred customers only. If you have questions about an event, call 1-800-555-9839 or come in and speak to the Customer Service representative.

We are the leading sports store in the Southwest with a tradition of personal, friendly service. As you use your new Sports Company credit card, you will discover the many conveniences that only our credit customers enjoy.

We are delighted with the opportunity to serve you and we look forward to seeing you soon.

Sincerely,

The Sports Company Manager

Data Source

FirstName	LastName	Address	City	State	PostalCode
Anthony	Manahan	2931 E. Campus Dr.	Mesa	AZ	85202
Corey	Owens	3857 W. University Ave.	Temp e	AZ	85285
Student	Name	89 Any Street	Mesa	AZ	85202

Merged Documents

September 25, 1998

Anthony Manahan
2931 E. Campus Dr.
Mesa, AZ 85202

Dear Anthony:

Thank you for opening a new credit car
becoming one of our most valued customers. Here's
Using your new card is as easy as 1-2-3.

1. ***Please sign your new card in ink***
2. ***If you have an old card, destroy i***
3. ***Always carry your new Sports Co***

Your new card identifies you as a Prefer
convenient shopping experience at any of The Sport
country.

Se

Corey Owens
3857 W. University Ave.
Tempe, AZ 85285

Dear Corey:

Thank you for opening a new
becoming one of our most valued custom
Using your new card is as easy as 1-2-3.

1. ***Please sign your new c***
2. ***If you have an old car***
3. ***Always carry your new***

Your new card identifies you
convenient shopping experience at any of
country.

September 25, 1998

Student Name
89 Any Street
Mesa, AZ 85202

Dear Student:

Thank you for opening a new credit card account with The Sports Company and becoming one of our most valued customers. Here's your new Sports Company credit card! Using your new card is as easy as 1-2-3.

1. ***Please sign your new card in ink with your usual signature.***
2. ***If you have an old card, destroy it immediately.***
3. ***Always carry your new Sports Company credit card with you.***

Your new card identifies you as a Preferred Customer and guarantees you a quick and convenient shopping experience at any of The Sports Company stores located throughout the country.

Mail Merge

The Mail Merge feature combines a list of data (typically a file of names and addresses) with a document (commonly a form letter) to create a new document.

5 Creating a Web Page

COMPETENCIES

After completing this lab, you will know how to:

1. **Design a Web page.**
2. **Create an HTML document.**
3. **Insert inline images.**
4. **Create hyperlinks.**
5. **Make a Web page public.**

CASE STUDY

The Sports Company has decided to join the Internet by creating a World Wide Web site for the company. They hope to be able to promote their products through the Web site and broaden the audience of customers. In addition to the obvious marketing and sales potential, they want to provide an avenue for interaction between themselves and the customer to improve their customer service. They also want the Web site to provide articles of interest to the customers. The articles would include topics such as nutrition and fitness and would change on a monthly basis as an added incentive for readers to return to the site.

You have been asked to develop an overall design and layout for the Web site. Your completed Web page will look like that shown below.

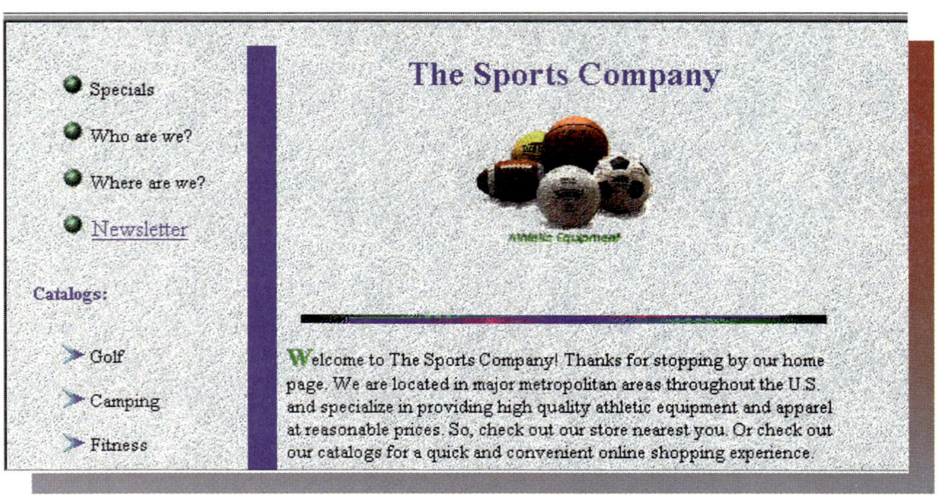

Concept Overview

The following concepts will be introduced in this lab:

1. Web Sites and Home Pages	The World Wide Web is a massive collection of Web sites. The top-level or opening page of a Web site is called the home page.
2. Web Page Design	You can add many elements to a Web page, such as graphic objects, images, art, and color, to make it attractive and easy to use.
3. Hypertext Markup Language	All pages on the WWW are written using a programming language called HTML (Hypertext Markup Language).
4. Inline Images	Word inserts graphics in Web pages as inline images, which are positioned directly in the text at the insertion point.
5. Hyperlinks	Hyperlinks provide a way to quickly jump to other documents, objects, or Web pages.

Designing Your Web Page

The Sports Company's plans for the Web site include a home page that will link to additional Web pages such as a catalog, order form, newsletter, and customer service. You have been asked to develop an overall plan for the Web site and to design the home page for the site.

Concept 1: Web Sites and Home Pages

The **World Wide Web** (WWW or Web for short) is a massive collection of Web sites. Web **sites** are locations on computers called **servers** that store the documents contained at the site. The basic document of the WWW is a **page**. Each site usually consists of many pages. Some large servers support multiple sites.

The top-level or opening page of a site is called the **home page.** It is displayed by default when a user visits your Web site. A site may even have many home pages if it is very large. The home page usually contains an introduction to the site along with connections that allow you to jump to another location on the same page, to another page in the same site, or to another page on a different site altogether. These connections may also be to a multimedia file such as a video or audio clip or even to a program.

When creating or **authoring** a Web page, you want to make the page both attractive and informative. You also want it to be easy to use and you want it to work right. It is important therefore to plan the design of the Web site and the pages it will include.

Concept 2: Web Page Design

You can add many elements to a Web page to make it attractive and easy to use. Graphic objects, images, art, and color are perhaps the most important features of Web pages. They entice the user to continue to explore the Web site.

You can also use forms to make your Web page interactive. **Forms** are collections of fields that you can use to get information or feedback from users. When the user submits a completed form, it is sent to a form handler where it is processed.

Other elements, such as animations, scrolling banners, blinking text, audio, and video can be added to a Web page to make it even more dynamic. With all these elements available, it is easy to add too many to a page and end up with a cluttered and distracting mess. Keep the following design tips in mind when authoring your own Web pages.

- Text should be readable against the background. Check for proper spelling and grammar.
- Background colors and patterns add interest and pizazz to a page, but be careful that they do not make the page hard to read. Additionally, keep in mind that more complex patterns take longer to download. Since many users have 256-color monitors, higher-resolution colors will be lost and may not look good on their monitors.
- Adding graphics and animations to a page make it more interesting, but keep them simple to speed up downloading, and avoid busy animations and blinking text. A good suggestion is to keep images less than 100K in file size. Smaller is even better.
- At the bottom of each page, include navigation links back to the home page and other major site pages so users will not get lost. Also include text links for users who have turned off graphics loading in their browsers to improve their speed.
- Page dimensions should be the same as the browser window size. Because many users have their screen resolution set to 640 x 480 pixels, designing a page for 600 x 800 pixels will be too large for their screens.
- Get permission before using text, sounds, and images that are copyrighted. Copyright laws and infringement fines apply to pages posted on the Internet.

You and the marketing manager have discussed the features that The Sports Company wants to include in their Web site pages. For example, the manager suggested that the site use the company colors of blue and green, and wanted to include a graphic image on the home page to make the site more interesting to view. After considering these features, you drew a sample page layout that you feel may be both interesting and easy to use.

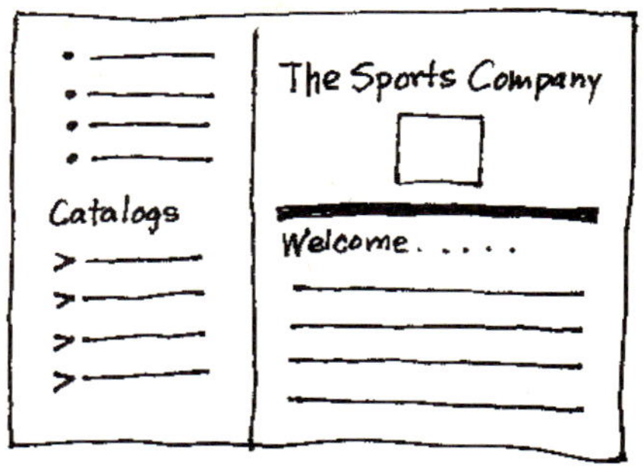

You have already entered in a Word document the text that will be displayed on the home page.

- If necessary, turn on your computer and load Word.
- Open the file Home Page Text from your data disk.

Your screen should be similar to Figure 5-1.

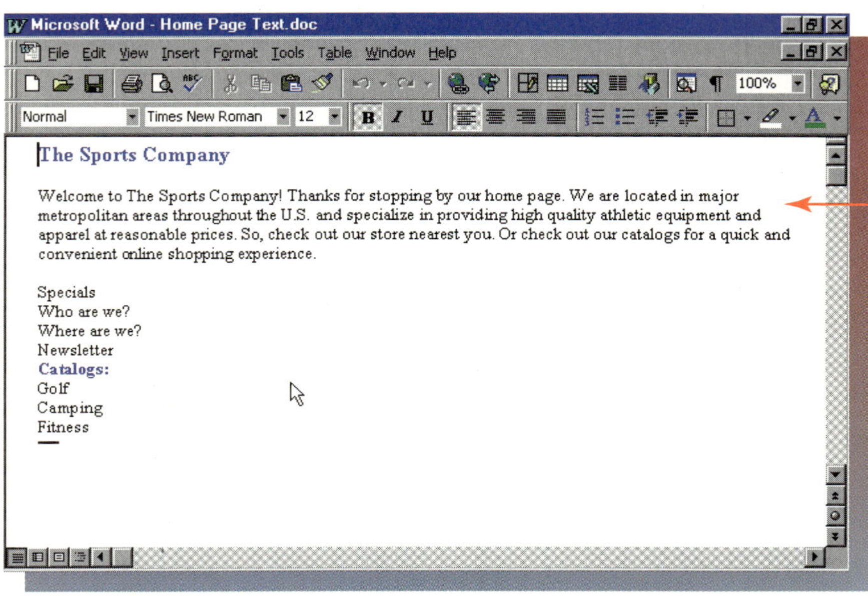

FIGURE 5-1

text for home page

As you can see, this is a simple text document. The only enhancements you have made to this document are a few text formats.

Creating an HTML Document

Your next step is to change this document into an HTML (Hypertext Markup Language) document that can be used on the WWW, and to add the design elements to the page.

Concept 3: Hypertext Markup Language

All pages on the WWW are written using a programming language called **HTML (Hypertext Markup Language)**. HTML commands control how the information on a page is displayed, such as font colors and size, and how an item, such as a form, will be processed. HTML also allows users to click on highlighted text or images and jump to other locations on the same page, other pages in the same site, or to other sites and locations on the WWW altogether.

HTML commands are interpreted by the browser software program you are using to access the WWW. The **browser** is a program that connects you to the remote computers and displays the pages you request. The server stores the pages and sends them to a browser when requested.

Every item on a Web page has properties associated with it that are encoded in HTML **tags**, which are embedded codes that supply information about the page's structure, appearance, and contents. They tell your browser where the title, heading, paragraphs, images, and other information are to appear on the page. In addition, they designate links to other Web pages. Examples of some simple tags and their effects are shown below.

Tags do not show when you load the HTML page on your browser.

Tagged text	Effect
<B> Hello </B>	**Hello** (makes it bold)
<P> text </P>	Marks the beginning and end of paragraph
<TITLE>The Sports Company</TITLE>	Displays text as a title for the page

All Web pages commonly include a title, different levels of headings, and text design elements such as horizontal rules. Each of these elements has its own tag.

This document needs to be changed to HTML format. Word includes an authoring tool that lets you create a Web page without needing to know the HTML codes. It generates the HTML tags automatically while you are using many of the same features that you would use to create a text document, such as spelling and grammar checking, AutoText, and tables. You can apply bold, italic, underline, strikethrough, superscript, and subscript formats to selected text. Some features, such as graphical bullets and lines, are customized for use in pages to make Web authoring easier.

Features that are not supported by HTML or other Web browsers are not available when you author Web pages. This includes the emboss, shadow, and engrave character formatting effects, line spacing, margins, and spacing before and after paragraphs. Tabs are not available because they are displayed as spaces by many Web browsers. Instead, to shift the first line of text to the right, you can use an indent.

Word offers three ways to create Web pages. You can use the Web Page Wizard to help you quickly create a Web page. The Web Page Wizard provides dialog boxes from which you select a layout and graphical designs. The Web Page Wizard creates a sample Web page based on your selections, which you then can modify to your own needs. The second method is to convert an existing Word document to HTML. Finally, you can start with a blank Web page.

You will convert the simple text document to an HTML document. Word converts the file by adding the HTML tags to the document and then by saving it to a new file with an .html file extension.

- Choose File/Save as HTML.
- Save the file as Sports Company Home Page on your data disk.
- Click Save.

Your screen should be similar to Figure 5-2.

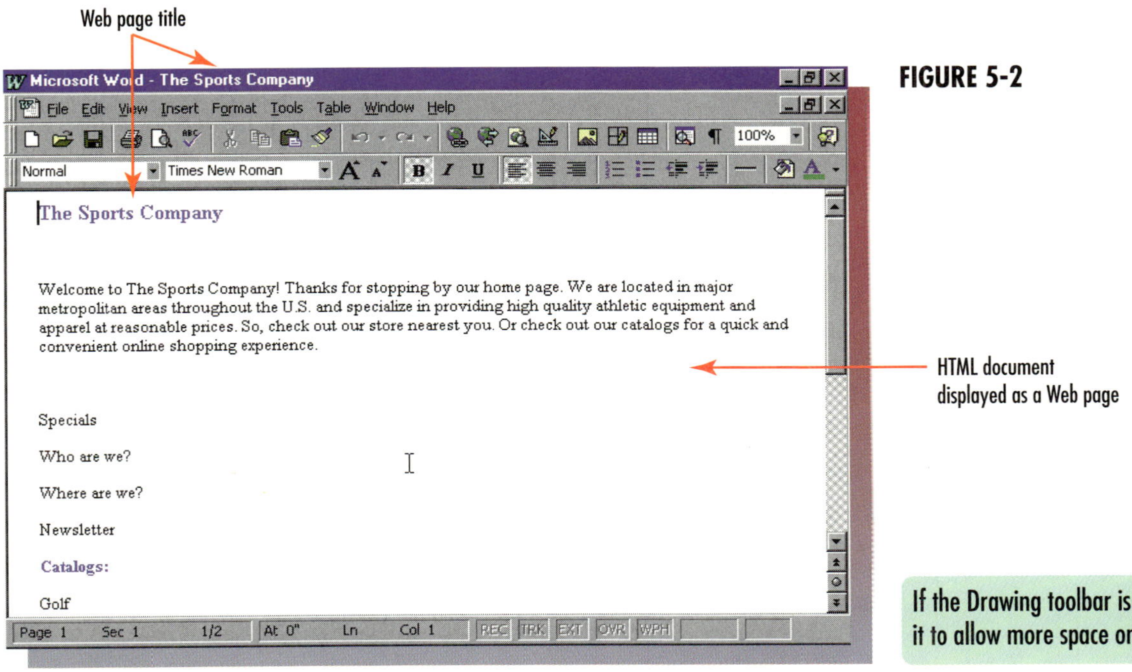

FIGURE 5-2

If the Drawing toolbar is displayed, close it to allow more space on the screen.

The Web page title, rather than the file name, is displayed in the title bar.

Word displays the HTML document as a Web page in a format that is similar to how it will appear in a Web browser. The formatting and features that are supported by HTML, in this case the text size and color attributes, have been converted to HTML format. To see the HTML code,

- Choose View/HTML Source.

Your screen should be similar to Figure 5-3.

FIGURE 5-3

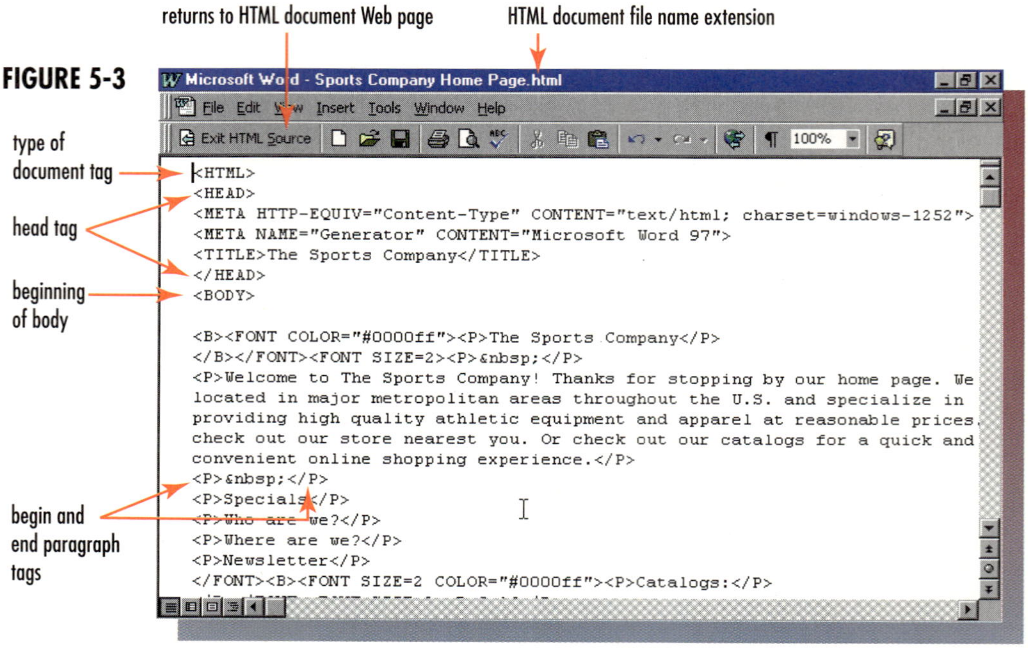

All HTML document files begin with the <HTML> tag, which tells the browser that the document it is reading is an HTML document. They also contain a <HEAD> tag, which includes basic information needed by the browser, and a <TITLE> tag identifying the text to be used as the title of the page, which is usually displayed in the browser window title bar. The <BODY> tag indicates the area where the body of the page will appear. Each paragraph begins and ends with a paragraph tag (<P> </P>). Converting this document to HTML format using Word was a lot easier than learning to enter the code yourself. To return to the Web page,

- Click Exit HTML Source.

Inserting Inline Images

Below the company name on the Web page, you want to display a picture. Pictures and other types of graphic objects are one of the most important features of Web pages. Authors use images to provide information or decoration, or to communicate their personal or organizational style. They are also commonly used to display graphic artwork or pictures of products for sale. Graphic objects that appear when a Web page is loaded are called inline images.

Concept 4: Inline Images

Graphics cannot be embedded in Web pages as they can in Word documents. Therefore Word inserts graphics as inline images. **Inline images** are inserted directly in the text at the insertion point, as opposed to graphics, which are inserted in layers that stack. Thus you can position inline images precisely on the page or in front of or behind text or other objects.

Each graphic you insert in an HTML file is stored in a separate file that is accessed and loaded by the browser when the page is loaded. Word creates a link, which includes the location and file name, to the object's file in the HTML file. When graphic files are added to a page, they are copied to the same folder location as the page. They must always reside in the same location as the HTML document file in which they are used.

Graphic objects are commonly inserted into HTML documents in GIF and JPEG file formats. If you insert an image that is not in either of these formats, the image will be saved in the GIF format when the file is saved.

JPEG files use the file name extension .jpg.

You can also add drawing objects, such as shapes created using the Drawing toolbar and WordArt, to a Web page. When the HTML file is closed, however, and they have been converted to GIF file format, they can no longer be edited in Word when you reopen the HTML file. In these cases, it is a good idea to also save the Word file as a regular document in case you want to edit these objects at a later date. Then you can insert the edited object in place of the original object in the HTML page.

You want to add to the Web page a picture that is representative of some of the items The Sports Company sells, along with a colored and textured background.

- Move to the blank space below the company name.
- Click Insert Picture.
- Change the location to your data disk and select the picture file Balls.gif.
- Click Insert.
- Select the picture and reduce the size to be similar to that in Figure 5-4. Deselect the picture.

Drag the corner handle to maintain picture proportions.

- Click Background.

The menu equivalent is Format/Background.

- Select Fill Effects.
- From the Texture palette, select Blue Tissue Paper.
- Click OK.

Your screen should be similar to Figure 5-4.

FIGURE 5-4

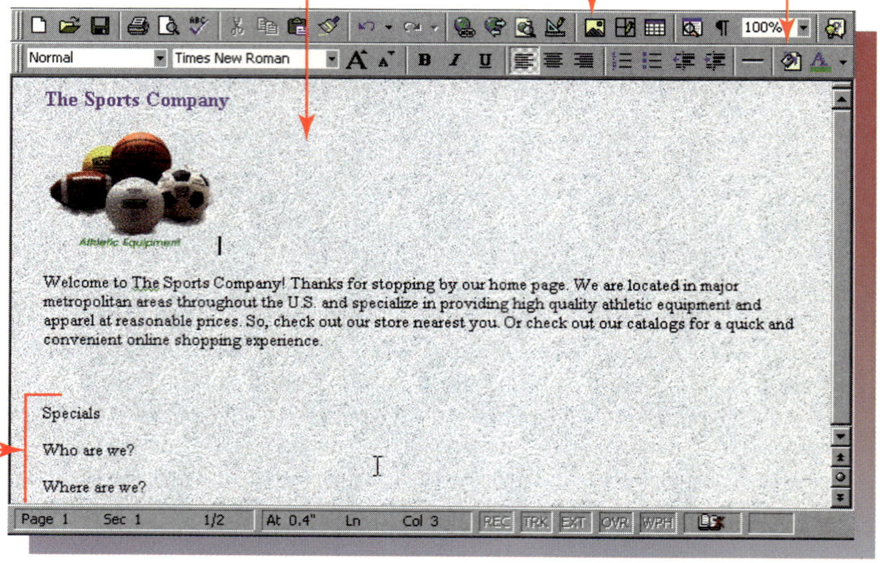

So far your page is very plain and contains a lot of blank space. In addition you want the entire list to be visible without scrolling the page. You will continue to make several changes to improve the appearance of the page. First you will change the layout of the page so that the list of items will appear to the left of the company name and welcome text, making it unnecessary to scroll the page. Unlike a regular document where you could use columns to display text side by side, in a Web page you need to use a table to control the page layout. The table allows you to place items in different locations on the Web page. You want to create a table the full width of the text on the page (6 inches) and approximately 2 inches deep with three vertical cells.

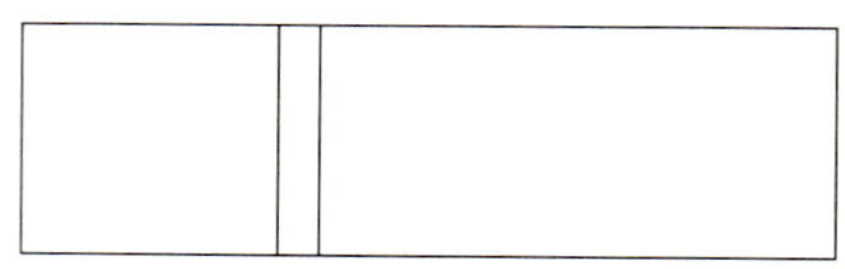

- Click Tables and Borders.

The mouse pointer changes to a pen so you can draw a table.

- Drag to create the outside boundary of the table (approximately 6 inches wide by 2 inches high) starting at the very top of the page above the company name.

Display the ruler by pointing to the top boundary of the window. The ruler will temporarily display so you can check the table size and line locations.

- Draw a vertical column line at the 2-inch position and another about 0.25 inch to the right of the first (refer to Figure 5-5).
- Click Tables and Borders.

Your screen should be similar to Figure 5-5.

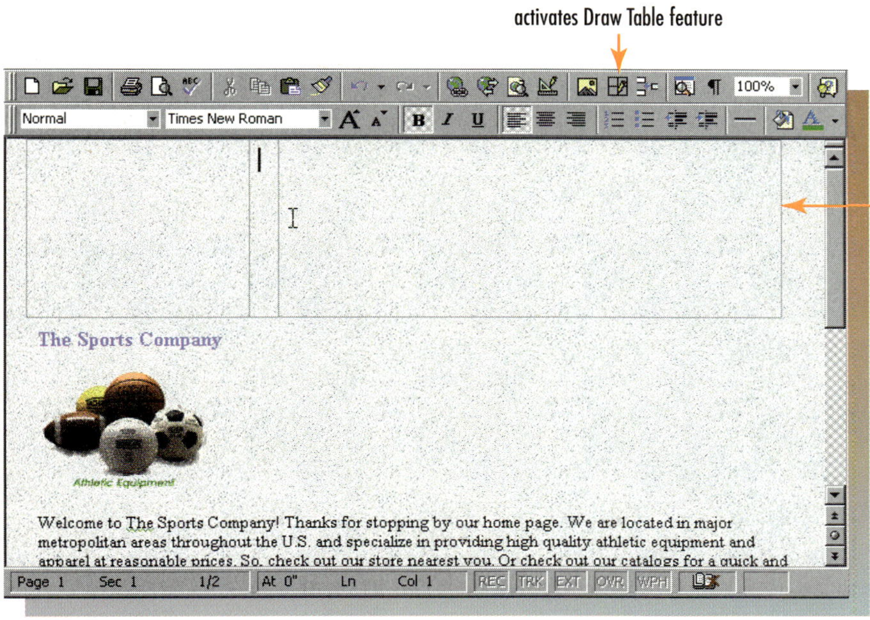

FIGURE 5-5

Next you need to move the text and picture into the appropriate cells of table.

- Select the title, picture, and welcome paragraph. Cut and paste (or drag) this selection into the rightmost cell of table. Clear the highlight.
- Select the list of items. Cut and paste (or drag) this selection into the leftmost cell of the table. Clear the highlight.

Your screen should be similar to Figure 5-6.

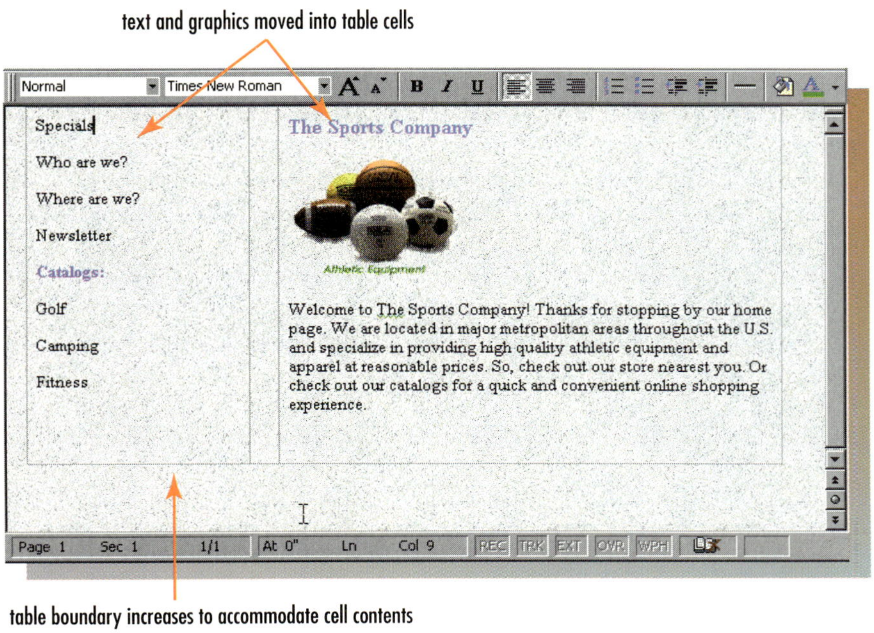

FIGURE 5-6

As you moved the selections into the table cells, the table boundary increased to accommodate the cell contents. It expands the table to the maximum size that can be displayed in the window. If additional space were needed, a new cell would be created to hold the overflow.

To see how your page will look when displayed by your browser, you can preview it.

> The menu equivalent is File/Web Page Preview.

- Click Web Page Preview.

You are prompted to save the changes you have made to the HTML file before previewing the page. This is necessary so that the links to the inline image graphic files are correctly saved, and so the browser can load and display the most up-to-date version of your page.

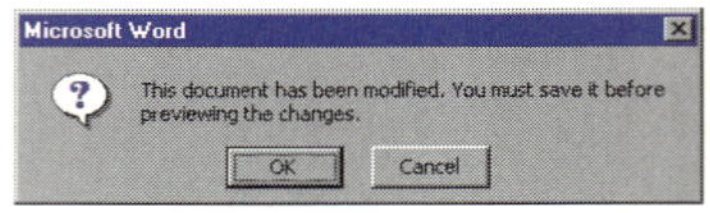

- Click OK.

Your screen should be similar to Figure 5-7.

FIGURE 5-7

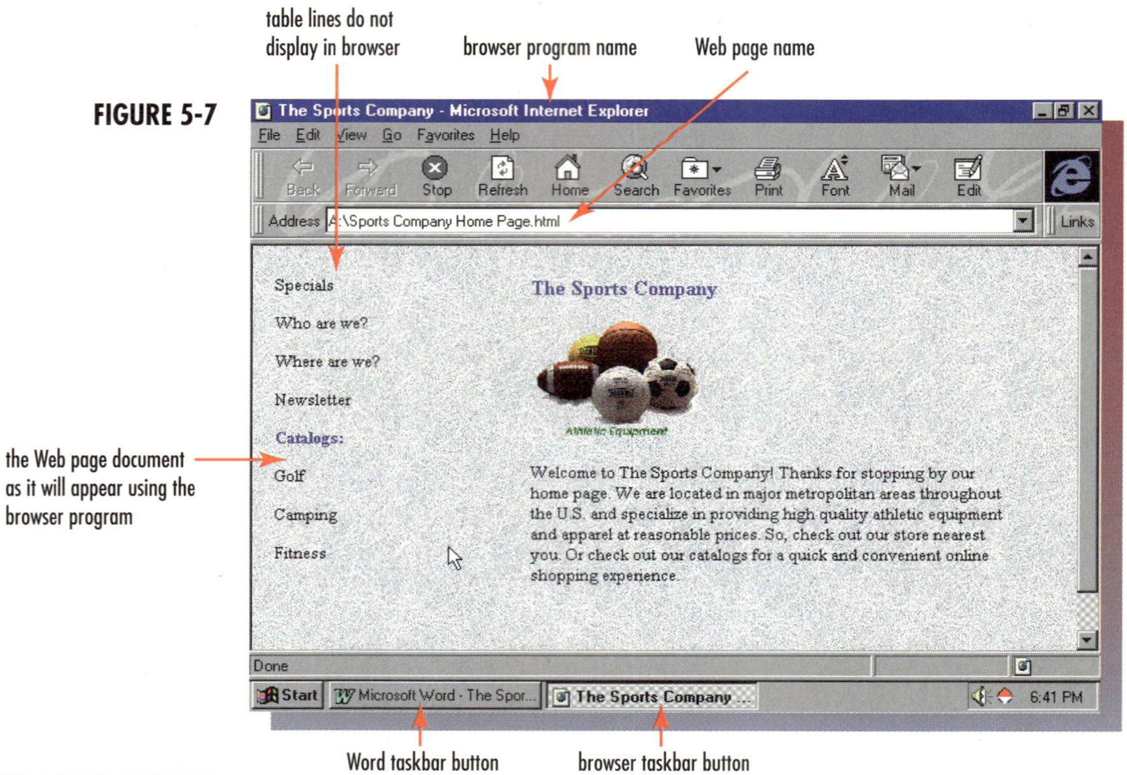

> Your screen will display the Web page in the browser that is on your computer system.

> Offline means the browser program is not connected to the Internet.

The browser on your system is loaded offline, and the page you are working on is displayed in the browser window.

All the information you want is visible in the browser window, but it is still not very visually appealing. You want to add formatting, lines, bullets, and other enhancements to improve its appearance. To return to the Word document,

- Click Microsoft Word - The Spor... in the taskbar.

First you will increase the size of the title and center it. In HTML documents, font sizes are not measured in points, but in a range from 1 to 7. When a file is converted to HTML, point sizes are converted to the closest HTML size.

- Select the company name.
- Click Increase Font Size (2 times).
- Click Center.
- Select and center the picture.

Your screen should be similar to Figure 5-8.

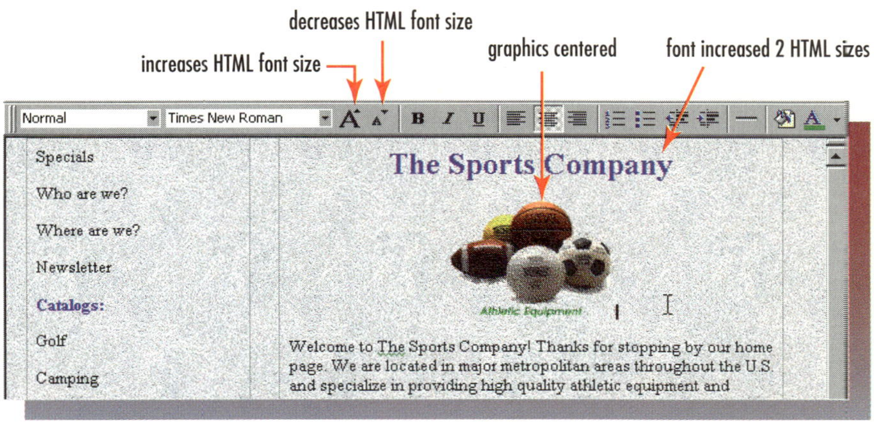

FIGURE 5-8

Next you want to separate the headline area from the welcome paragraph with a horizontal line. Word includes special graphic horizontal lines that can only be used in Web pages.

- Move to the beginning of the paragraph.
- Select Insert/Horizontal line.
- Select the fifth line style (rainbow).
- Click OK.

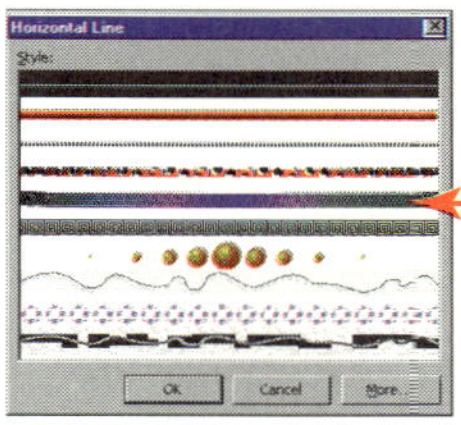

5th line style is a rainbow

Clicking inserts the last-used horizontal line style.

With the addition of the horizontal line, the text in the paragraph may have overlapped below the cell space.

- If this happened, reduce the size of the picture to allow the entire paragraph to display in the cell space.

You also want to add emphasis to the paragraph by increasing the font size of the first letter of the word Welcome and adding color to it.

- Select W.
- Click [A] Increase Font Size (2 times).
- Change the format to bold and the text color to green.
- Clear the highlight.

Your screen should be similar to Figure 5-9.

FIGURE 5-9

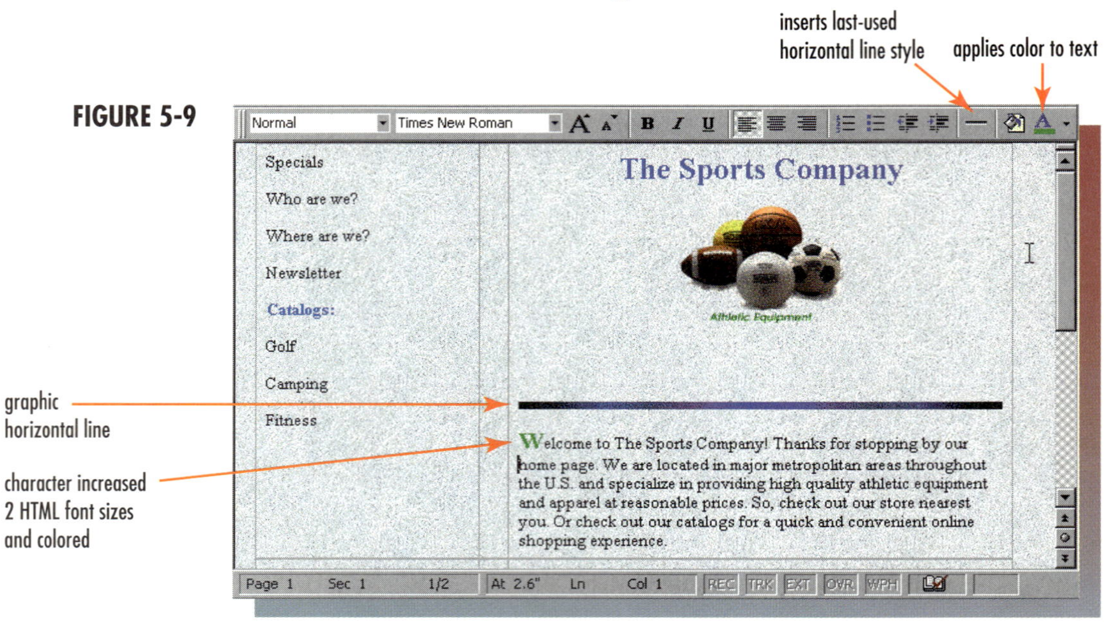

Next you want to add bullets to the items in the list. Like the special graphic horizontal lines, Word includes special graphic bullets that can be used on Web pages.

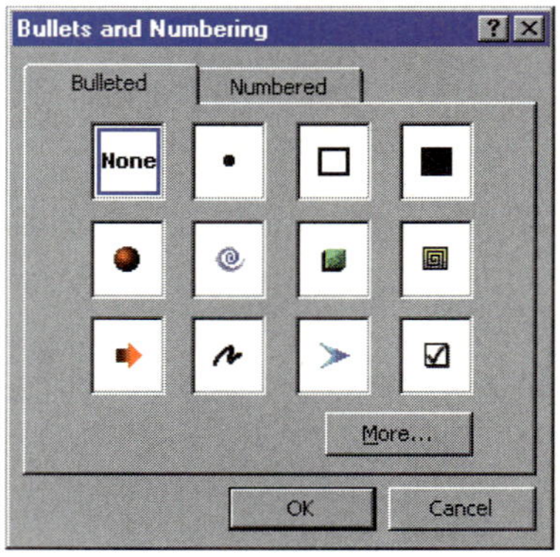

- Select the top four items in the list.
- Choose Format/Bullets and Numbering/Bulleted/[More...]/Green Ball.gif/[Insert].
- Select the bottom three items and add the [➤] bullet style.

Like regular bullets, these bulleted items are also automatically indented.

You would like again to see how your changes look. Each time you want to preview how your changes will look in the browser, you need to save the Web page file. In addition, because the browser is already open, you can simply switch to the window.

- Click Save.
- Switch to the browser window.

Click the browser's taskbar button.

The browser still displays the original page. To see the changes you have made,

- Click Refresh.

On some browsers, the button is Reload.

Your screen should be similar to Figure 5-10.

graphic bullets

reloads file and updates image display

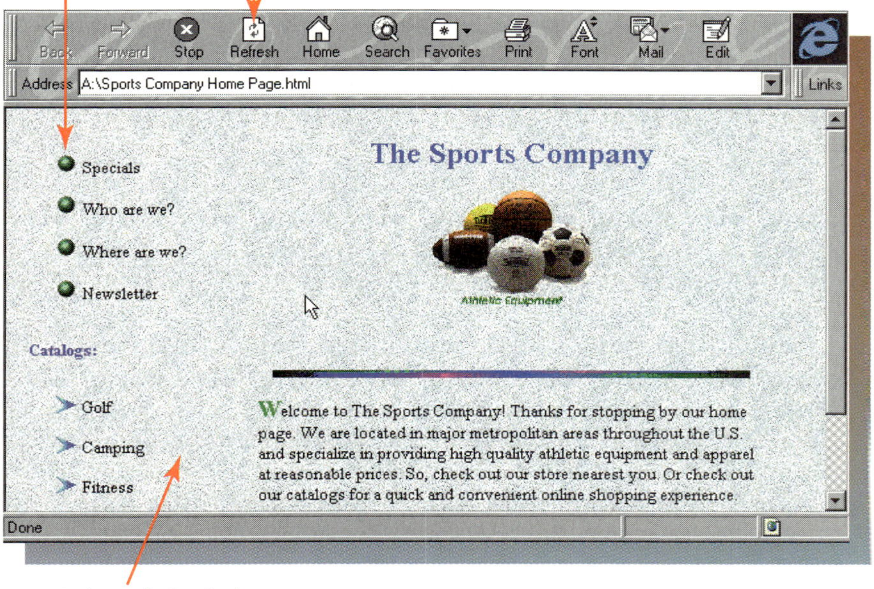

Web page displayed in browser

FIGURE 5-10

The Web page is almost done. The last improvements you want to make are to add a vertical color bar to visually separate the list of items from the welcome text, and to add a hyperlink to the newsletter page. First you will add color to the narrow vertical cell separating the two areas of the table.

- Switch back to Word.
- Move to the narrow vertical cell to the right of the bulleted list.
- Choose Table/Cell Properties/Background/Blue/OK.

Your screen should be similar to Figure 5-11.

FIGURE 5-11

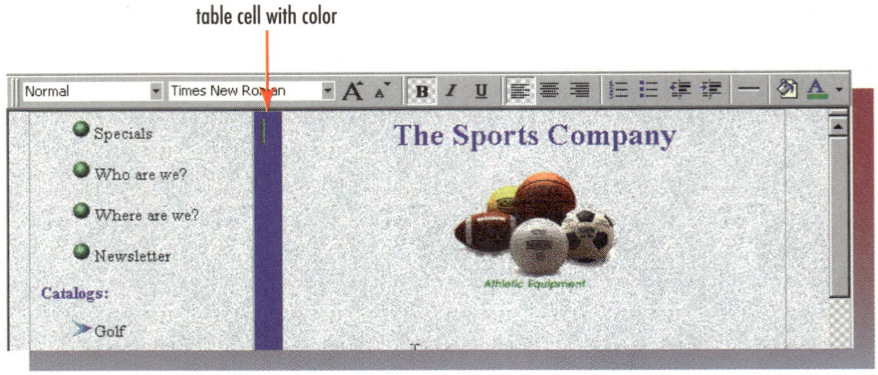

Creating Hyperlinks

Next you want to create a hyperlink to the newsletter.

Concept 5: Hyperlinks

As you have learned, **hyperlinks** provide a quick way to jump to other documents, objects, or Web pages. Hyperlinks are the real power of the WWW. You can jump to sites on your own system and network as well as to sites on the Internet and WWW. A hyperlink can also be to an object within a Word document, such as a cross-reference.

When you create a hyperlink in a document, you can make the path to the destination of the hyperlink an absolute link or a relative link. An **absolute link**, also called a **fixed link**, identifies the file location of the destination by its full address, such as c:\Word Data File\Sales.doc. Fixed links are usually only used if you are sure the location of the object will not change. A **relative link** identifies the destination location in relation to the location of the HTML file. A relative link is based on a path you specify in which the first part of the path is shared by both the file that contains the hyperlink and the destination file.

Hyperlinks to other Web sites should typically use a fixed file location that includes the full path to the location or address of the page called the Uniform Resource Locator (URL). All URL's have at least two basic parts. The first part presents the protocol used to connect to the resource. The **protocol** is the set of rules that control how software and hardware on a network communicate. The protocol http (Hypertext Transfer Protocol), shown in the example below, is by far the most common. The protocol is always followed by a colon (:). The second part presents the name of the server where the resource is located (www.eatright.org). This is always preceded by two forward slashes (//) and each part of the path is separated by a single forward slash (/).

http://www.eatright.org

- Select the word "Newsletter."
- Click Insert Hyperlink.
- Click Browse... .
- Select the file Fall 1998 Newsletter from your data disk.
- Click OK .

Your screen should be similar to Figure 5-12.

> The menu equivalent is Insert/Hyperlink, and the keyboard shortcut is Ctrl + k.

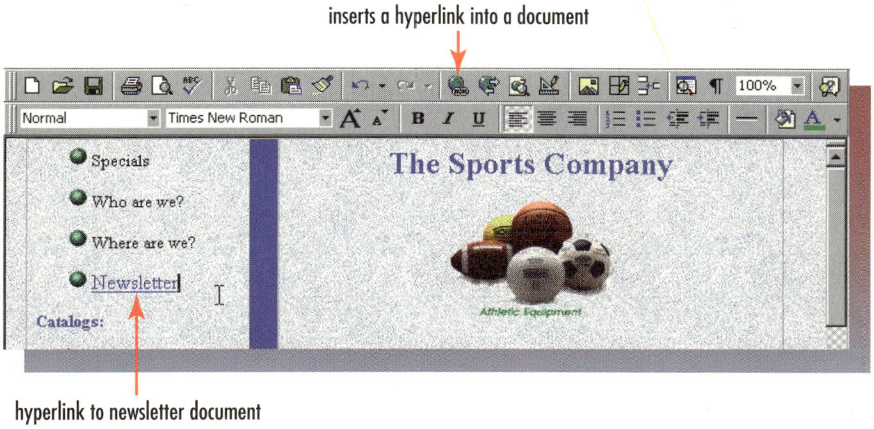

FIGURE 5-12

Typically a text hyperlink appears in a document underlined and in blue.

- Save the page and then preview your changes in the browser.

> The hyperlink color may vary from one browser to another.

> Images that are hyperlinked are not identified in any particular way.

Clicking on a hyperlink to a page directs the browser to get the page from the server and display it. Clicking on a hyperlink to a file directs the browser to get the file from the server and to open it using the appropriate program, such as an audio program to play an audio file.

To see if your link works correctly,

- Click Newsletter.

> The pointer changes to a hand over a hyperlink, and the URL appears in the status bar.

The browser locates the file, loads it, and displays it in the browser window.

Your screen should be similar to Figure 5-13.

newsletter document loaded and displayed in browser

FIGURE 5-13

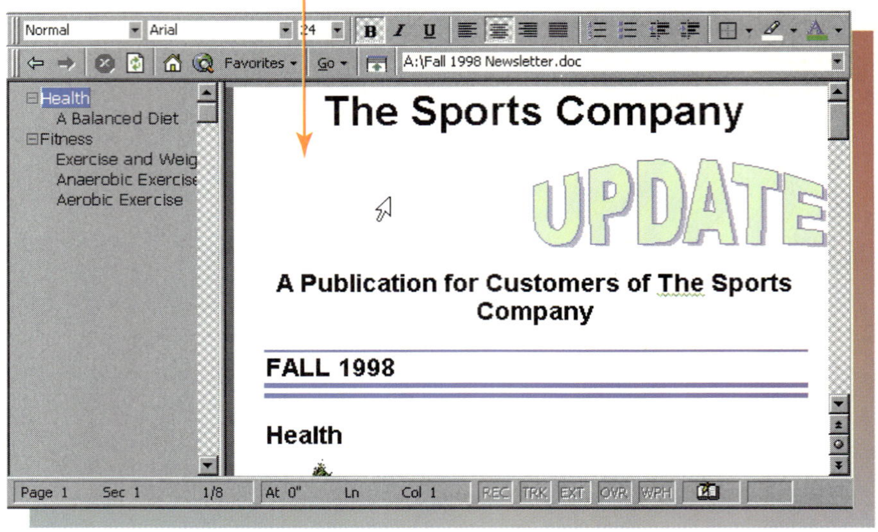

> Users who do not have Word can use the Word Viewer to display Word documents. Word Viewer is a separate application this is available for free by downloading it from the WWW.

> If this file had already been converted to an HTML document, the browser would display it as an HTML document.

> If you are using Netscape as your Web browser, your computer may launch another browser window.

The newsletter file is displayed in Online Layout view.

- Change to Page Layout view.
- Scroll the window to see the entire newsletter document.

Next you will try out the link to the American Dietetic Association on the first page of the newsletter. If your system is not connected to the Internet, skip the next three steps.

- Click www.eatright.org.
- If your computer displays the screen to access your Internet provider, enter the requested user identification.

Your screen should be similar to Figure 5-14.

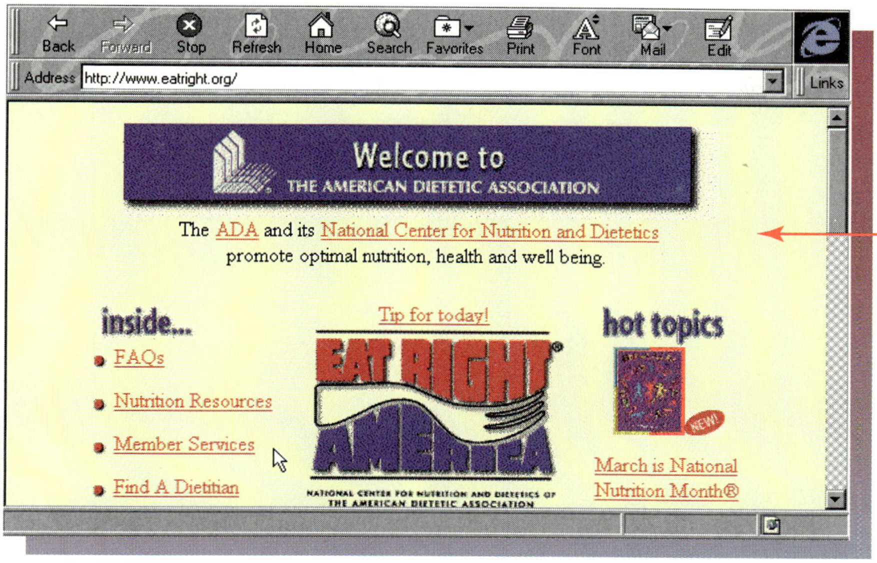

FIGURE 5-14

clicking link in newsletter connects to the Internet and displays associated Web page

To return to The Sports Company home page,

- Click Back (2 times).
- Click ☒ to exit the browser program.
- If necessary, follow the procedure to disconnect from the Internet.
- Exit Word.

When you return to a Web page after following a hyperlink, the hyperlink text color changes to purple.

Making a Web Page Public

Before making your Web page available for others to see, you should test that all links work correctly. In addition, because all browsers do not display the HTML tags the same way, it is a good idea to preview your page using different browsers. Many of the differences in how browsers display a page are appearance differences, not structural.

The steps that you take to make your pages public depend on how you want to share them. There are two main avenues: on your local network or intranet for limited access by people within an organization, or on the Internet for access by anyone using the WWW. To make pages available to other people on your network, save your Web pages and related files, such as pictures, to a network location. To make your Web pages available on the WWW, you need to either install Web server software on your computer or locate an Internet service provider that allocates space for Web pages.

LAB REVIEW

Key Terms

absolute link (WP202)
authoring (WP190)
browser (WP192)
fixed link (WP202)
form (WP190)
home page (WP189)
hyperlink (WP202)
Hypertext Markup Language (HTML) (WP192)
inline image (WP195)
page (WP189)
protocol (WP202)
relative link (WP202)
server (WP189)
site (WP189)
tag (WP192)
World Wide Web (WP189)

Command Summary

Command	Shortcut Key	Button	Action
File/Save as HTML			Converts file to HTML format
File/Web Page Preview			Previews Web page in browser
View/HTML Source			Displays HTML codes
Insert/Horizontal Line			Adds graphic horizontal line to Web page
Insert/Hyperlink	Ctrl + K		Inserts a hyperlink in Web page
Format/Background			Applies background color to selection
Table/Cell Properties/Background			Changes background of selected cell

Matching

1. home page	______	**a.** link that allows user to jump to other documents
2. URL	______	**b.** creates a hyperlink in Web page
3. hyperlink	______	**c.** identifies the location of a hyperlink by its full address
4. 	______	**d.** address of the page
5. tags	______	**e.** basic document of the World Wide Web
6. browser	______	**f.** embedded codes that supply information about a page
7. 	______	**g.** software program used to access WWW
8. absolute link	______	**h.** creating a Web page
9. authoring	______	**i.** previews Web page in browser
10. page	______	**j.** top-level page

Fill-In Questions

1. Complete the following statements by filling in the blanks with the correct terms.

a. Web sites are locations on computers called ______________ that store the documents contained at the site.

b. HTML ______________ are embedded codes in a Web page.

c. The top-level or opening page of a site is called the ______________.

d. HTML commands are interpreted by the ______________ software program used to access the WWW.

e. __________ and __________ are the two graphic file formats commonly used in HTML documents.

f. Web sites use a fixed file location that includes the full path to the location or address of the page called the ______________ .

g. ______________ give the ability to quickly jump from one location to another with a simple click.

Discussion Questions

1. Discuss three attributes of a well-designed Web page.

2. Discuss how inline images are saved in an HTML document.

3. Discuss how hyperlinks work.

4. Discuss how to get your Web page on the Internet.

Hands-On Practice Exercises

Step by Step

Rating System
☆ Easy
☆☆ Moderate
☆☆☆ Difficult

☆

1. In this problem you will create a personal home page.

- **a.** Plan the design of your home page. You may want to visit other personal home pages on the Web to get an idea of what you like and do not like for your page.
- **b.** Develop a Word document that contains the text of your home page.
- **c.** Convert the Word document into an HTML document.
- **d.** Create columns and rows as necessary to align your text.
- **e.** Add a background.
- **f.** Add clip art, pictures, and animation to your home page.
- **g.** Create a list of links to other pages that are of interest to you.
- **h.** If possible, load your home page to a server so others can enjoy your work.
- **i.** Print your home page.

☆☆

2. Andrew Beinbrink has just accepted a job with the Call Animation Studio. He has been asked to create a new Web page to promote the company.

- **a.** Use the Web Page Wizard to create a two-column layout. Apply the visual style Festive.
- **b.** Replace the headline with the name of the company.
- **c.** Replace the paragraph text with the following information about the Call Animation Studio.

  Call Animation Studio specializes in a variety of media services for your corporate, broadcast, and film projects. Check out:

- **d.** Change the sample text in the list to:

  3D Graphics Animation

  3D Computer Animation

  3D Modeling

- **e.** Create three new pages for 3D Graphics Animation, 3D Computer Animation, and 3D Modeling. Link the three pages to the list on the home page.
- **f.** Add clip art pictures of animation characters to the pages to add interest.
- **g.** Print the four pages.

☆☆

3. Sarah Harvey has accepted a position with one of her university professors. Her professor has already created a class Web page but would like to include a calendar for the upcoming month. The calendar should include all classroom hours, the professor's office hours, and assignments due.

- **a.** Use the Web Page Wizard to create a calendar for next month.
- **b.** Choose the visual style of your choice.
- **c.** Insert a course title as the main heading and the month and year as the subheading.
- **d.** Write a short introduction above the calendar to explain its contents.
- **e.** Add text to the days of the week to represent the information the professor requested.

f. Enhance the calendar by using lines, borders, and pictures as appropriate. Print the Web page.

g. If possible at your school, follow the procedure to load the page to a server so others can enjoy your work.

On Your Own

☆☆☆

4. To complete this problem, you must have completed Practice Exercise 1 on page 208. After designing your home page, you would like to know how others feel about what you added to your page. A good way of asking for input is to use a feedback form. With this form you can ask visitors to respond to questions. Use the Web Page Wizard to create a feedback form in the same visual style as your home page. Enhance the page using lines, borders, and pictures as appropriate. Link the feedback form to your home page. Print the page. If possible at your school, follow the procedure to load your new page to a server.

☆☆

5. To complete this problem, you must have completed the Web page from this lab. You would like to add an order form page linked to The Sports Company home page. Refer to the help topic on Web forms for information on forms. Create an order form for The Sports Company that will allow the user to order information about products available from The Sports Company. Enhance the page using the features discussed in the lab. Link the order form to The Sports Company home page.

Case Project

Introduction

This project is designed to reinforce your knowledge of the word processing features used in the five Microsoft Word 97 labs. You will also be expected to use the Office Assistant to learn more about advanced features available in Word 97.

Case

Marianne Virgili is the Director of the Glenwood Springs Chamber Resort Association. Semiannually the chamber produces a newsletter called *Trends,* which reviews the latest economic indicators for Garfield county. It is sent to all chamber members. Marianne has compiled much of the data to be included in the next issue and has asked you to work on several of the articles.

Part I

a. Open the file Trends from your data disk. This file contains some of the text that will be used in the newsletter.

b. The first paragraph contains many errors. Use the editing techniques you learned in the labs to correct the paragraph.

c. Spell-check the document. Check that the document has a single space between words and following a period at the end of a sentence.

d. Search for the word "TRENDS" throughout the document and change it to be displayed in italics. Locate all occurrences of incorrect capitalization for Glenwood Springs and replace them with the correct capitalization.

e. Delete the paragraph about school attendance in the Population, Housing, and Construction section. In the same section, use the Document Map to move the paragraph about commercial construction below the paragraph on residential construction.

f. Bold the section headings throughout the document. Change the font type, bold, and enlarge the main heading "Trend Indicators."

g. Save and replace your document. Print the document.

Part II

This issue of *Trends* will contain two tables. The first table will provide employment information for 1996 to 1997 for Garfield county. The second table will provide information on gross sales.

a. The employment information is shown below. Use the Draw Table feature to create a table from this data in a new document. Use the List 8 table AutoFormat.

Job Category	1996	1997	% Change
Agr., For., Fish.	141	174	23.4
Mining	705	813	15.3
Construction	856	1,171	36.8
Manufacturing	284	327	15.1
Trans., Comm., Util.	443	504	13.8
Wholesale Trade	338	410	21.3
Retail Trade	2,580	2,859	10.9
Fin., Ins., Real Est.	522	601	15.1
Services	2,679	2,767	3.3
Government	2,234	2,328	4.2
TOTAL			

b. Right-align the entries in the three data columns, including the column heads. Left-align the row heads. Bold and underline the column heads.

c. Enter functions to sum the 1996 and 1997 columns of data, and average the % Change column. (Hint: You will need to exclude the cells containing the date column headings from being included in the calculated total.) Bold the Total row.

d. Insert a new row above the table. Remove the column dividers. Add the title "JOBS IN GARFIELD COUNTY." Center and bold the title.

e. Enhance the appearance of the table by appropriately sizing the columns and making the gridlines thicker.

f. Save the table. Print the table.

The second table will display the percent of gross sales for the first half of 1998 for the five major cities in the county.

g. Open a new document file. Use the Draw Table feature to create a table from the following data. Select a table AutoFormat of your choice.

City	Sales	% of Total
Glenwood Springs	165.7	61.0
Parachute	2.3	0.8
Silt	3.4	1.3
Carbondale	19.3	7.1
Rifle	34.7	12.8
Remainder of County	46.1	17.0
TOTAL 1st Half		

h. Enter formulas to total the two columns of data.

i. Insert a new row above the table. Clear the column dividers. Enter the title "TOTAL GROSS SALES" on the first line, "JANUARY-JUNE 1998" on the second line, and "(In millions of dollars)" on the third line. Center the title lines.

j. Right-align the data columns. Left-align the City column.

k. Enhance the appearance of the table by adding bold and making other format changes as you like. Appropriately size the table columns.

l. Save the table. Print the table.

Part III

You need to create the newsletter headline next.

a. The headline should display the following information:

Newsletter name:	TRENDS
Subheadings:	A Semiannual Review of Economic Indicators
	Glenwood Springs Chamber Resort Association
[Your Name]	
[Current Date]	

b. Use the following features when designing the headline:

- centered text
- font and type sizes of your choice
- italics
- bold
- borders with different line weights
- WordArt

c. Save the headline as a separate document file.

Part IV

Now you are ready to create the newsletter.

a. Copy the headline to the top of the text file, Trends. Change the newsletter text to display two columns. Make the page margins 0.5 inch. Make the space between columns 0.25 inch.

b. Copy each table into the newsletter near the reference to the table in the text. Add a caption below the tables in the document. Size the tables to fit within the column widths.

c. Hyphenate the newsletter.

d. Display the last paragraph of text in a shaded text box.

e. Save the newsletter. If necessary, select another printer and adjust the newsletter layout (you may need to change font and type sizes, adjust columns, or change the placement of the tables). Print the newsletter.

Part V

The final document you need to create is a cover memo to the Director to accompany a sample copy of the newsletter.

a. Open a memo template of your choice.

b. Enter the information that is needed to complete the template. (Use your name following "FROM:".)

c. Enter the body of the memo. The memo should introduce the newsletter and indicate that you can revise the newsletter as needed.

d. Save the memo. Print the memo.

Glossary of Key Terms

Absolute link: A link that identifies the file location of the destination by its full address. Also called a fixed link.

Active window: The window you can work in. It is identified by a highlighted title bar, the insertion point, and scroll bars.

Address file: The data source file used in a merge; it typically contains name and address data to be combined with the main document.

Alignment: Positioning of text on a line, such as flush left, centered, flush right, or justified.

Anchor: To attach a graphic object to a paragraph.

Authoring: Creating a Web page.

AutoCorrect: A Word feature that makes basic assumptions about the text you are typing and automatically corrects the entry.

AutoText: Commonly used words or phrases that are recognized by the program and can be automatically completed for you.

Browser: Software program used to access the World Wide Web.

Caption: A title or explanation for a table, picture, or graph.

Case sensitive: Capable of distinguishing between uppercase and lowercase characters.

Cell: The space created by the intersection of a vertical column and a horizontal row.

Character style: A combination of any character formats that affect selected text.

Click and type: A feature found in many templates that lets you click on the placeholder and replace it with the text you type.

Clip art: A collection of graphics that is usually bundled with a software application.

Column: A vertical block of cells one cell wide in a table.

Cross-reference: A reference in one part of a document to related information in another part.

Cursor: The blinking vertical bar that shows you where the next character you type will appear. Also called the insertion point.

Custom dictionary: A dictionary of terms you have entered that are not in the main dictionary of the Spelling Checker.

Data field: Each category of information in the data source.

Data source: The file that supplies the data in a mail merge.

Default: Initial Word settings that can be changed to customize documents.

Destination: The location to which text is moved or copied.

Docked: Menus and toolbars that are fixed to the edge of the window.

Document pane: When footnotes are created, the upper portion of the window that displays the document; in Online Layout view, the pane that displays the document text.

Drag and drop: A mouse procedure that moves or copies a selection to a new location.

Drawing object: A simple object consisting of shapes such as lines and boxes.

Drop cap: A large, uppercase character with the top part of the letter even with the line and the rest of the letter extending into the paragraph below it.

Edit: The process of changing and correcting existing text in a document.

Endnote: A reference note displayed at the end of the document.

End-of-file marker: The horizontal line that marks the end of a file.

Field: A placeholder code that instructs Word to insert information in a document.

Field code: The code containing the instructions about the type of information to insert in the document.

Field name: A name used to label each data field in the data source.

Field result: The results displayed in a field according to the instructions in the field code.

Fixed link: A link that identifies the file location of the destination by its full address. Also called an absolute link.

Floating: Menus and toolbars that appear in separate windows.

Font: A set of characters with a specific design. Also called a typeface.

Footer: The line or several lines of text at the bottom of every page just above the bottom margin.

Footnote: A reference note displayed at the bottom of the page where the reference occurs.

Form: Collection of fields on a Web page that you can use to get information or feedback from users.

Formatting: Features that enhance the appearance of the document to make it more readable or attractive.

Formatting toolbar: The toolbar, displayed below the Standard toolbar, that contains buttons representing the most frequently used text-editing and text-layout features.

Formula: Table entry that does arithmetic calculations.

Frame: An invisible box containing text, a table, a graphic, or another object that you can move freely on a page.

Function: A prewritten formula that performs a calculation automatically.

Graphic: Non-text element in a document.

Group: A set of objects that can be minipulated as a single unit.

Handles: Small boxes surrounding a selected object that allow you to manipulate its size and placement.

Header: The line or several lines of text at the top of each page just below the top margin.

Heading style: A style that is designed to identify different levels of headings in a document.

Home page: The top-level or opening page to a site.

Hyperlink: Special type of link that provides a quick way to jump to other documents, objects, or Web pages.

Hypertext Markup Language (HTML): Programming language used to create Web pages.

Hyphenation: Feature that inserts a hyphen in long words that fall at the end of a line to split the word between lines.

Hyphenation zone: An unmarked space along the right margin that controls the amount of white space in addition to the margin that Word will allow at the end of a line.

Inline image: A graphic object that appears on a Web page when the page is loaded.

Insert mode: Method of text entry in which new characters are inserted into existing text, which moves to the right to make space for the new characters; the text on the line is reformatted as necessary.

Insertion point: The blinking vertical bar that shows you where the next character you type will appear on the line. Also called the cursor.

Lock: To keep a graphic and a paragraph together on a page.

Mail Merge: A feature that combines a text document with a data document or file containing names and addresses to produce a merged document or form letter.

Main dictionary: The dictionary of terms that comes with Word 97.

Main document: Document that contains the basic form letter in a merge operation.

Manual page break: Begins a new page regardless of the amount of text on the previous page.

Margin: The distance from the text to the edge of the paper.

Merge field: A field code that controls what information is used from the data source and where it is entered in the main document.

Newpaper columns: Display text so that it flows from the bottom of one column to the top of the next column.

Note pane: Lower portion of the window that displays footnotes.

Note reference mark: A superscript number or character appearing in the document at the end of the material being referenced.

Note separator: The horizontal line separating footnote text from main document text.

Note text: The text in a footnote.

Object: An item that can be sized, moved, and manipulated.

Office Assistant: A feature that automatically suggests help topics as you work.

Optional hyphen: Hyphen inserted by Word when a word is broken between two lines because the full word did not fit.

Overtype mode: Method of text entry in which new text types over the existing characters.

Page: The basic document of a World Wide Web site.

Pane: A division of the workspace.

Paragraph mark: Special hidden character that indicates the end of a paragraph.

Paragraph style: A combination of any character formats and paragraph formats that affects all text in a paragraph.

Picture: An illustration such as a scanned photograph.

Placeholder: Text in a template that marks the space and provides instructions for the text that should be entered at that location.

Point: Measure used for height of type; one point equals 1/72 inch.

Protocol: The rules that control how hardware and software on a network communicate.

Record: All the fields of data that are needed to complete the main document for one entity in a merge operation.

Relative link: Identifies the destination location in relation to the location of the HTML file.

Row: A horizontal block of cells in a table.

Ruler: The ruler located below the Formatting toolbar that shows the line length in inches.

Sans serif font: A font, such as Arial or Helvetica, that does not have a flair at the base of each letter.

Select: To highlight text.

Selection bar: The unmarked area to the left of the document area where the mouse can be used to highlight text lines.

Serif font: A font, such as Times New Roman, that has a flair at the base of each letter.

Server: A computer that stores the documents contained in a Web site.

Site: Web location on a computer.

Soft space: A space automatically entered by Word to align the text properly on a single line.

Standard toolbar: The toolbar, displayed below the menu bar, that gives quick access to editing features.

Status bar: The line of information at the bottom of the screen.

Style: A set of formats that is assigned a name.

Tab alignment selection box: A box on the left end of the ruler from which you select tab alignment types.

Tab leaders: Series of dots between a heading and the page number in the table of contents.

Tab stop: A stopping point along the ruler that marks the locations of a tab.

Table: A grid of horizontal rows and vertical columns; the intersection of rows and columns creates cells in which you can enter data.

Table reference: The column letter and row number that identifies a cell in a table.

Tag: An embedded code that supplies information about a Web page's structure, appearance, and contents.

Template: A prewritten blank worksheet that is used repeatedly to enter text.

Text box: A mini-document that acts as a graphic object in that it is surrounded by a frame.

Thesaurus: The file of synonyms and antonyms provided with Word.

Typeface: A set of characters with a specific design. Also called a font.

Uniform Resource Locator (URL): The address that indicates the location of a document on the World Wide Web.

WordArt: A supplementary application included with the Word program that is used to enhance a document by changing the shape of text, adding 3-D effects, and changing the alignment of text on a line.

Word wrap: Feature that automatically determines where to begin the next line of text; the user does not press ←Enter at the end of a line unless it is the end of a paragraph or to insert a blank line.

World Wide Web: A massive collection of sites.

Command Summary

Command	Shortcut Key	Button	Action
File/New	Ctrl + N		Opens new file
File/Open	Ctrl + O		Opens selected file
File/Close			Closes file
File/Save	Ctrl + S		Saves file using same file name
File/Save As			Saves file using a new file name
File/Save as HTML			Converts file to HTML format
File/Web Page Preview			Previews Web page in browser
File/Page Setup			Changes layout of page including margins, paper size, and paper source
File/Page Setup/Layout/Vertical Alignment			Aligns text vertically on a page
File/Print Preview			Displays document as it will appear when printed
File/Print	Ctrl + P		Prints file using selected print settings
File/Properties			Shows properties of active document
File/Exit	Alt + F4		Exits Word program
Edit/Undo	Ctrl + Z		Restores last editing change
Edit/Redo or Repeat	Ctrl + Y		Restores last Undo or repeats last command or action
Edit/Cut	Ctrl + X		Cuts selected text and copies it to Clipboard
Edit/Copy	Ctrl + C		Copies selected text to Clipboard
Edit/Paste	Ctrl + V		Pastes text from Clipboard
Edit/Find	Ctrl + F		Locates specified text

Command	Shortcut Key	Button	Action
Edit/Replace	Ctrl + H		Locates and replaces specified text
Edit/Go To	Ctrl + G		Moves insertion point to specified location in document
View/Normal			Displays document in Normal view
View/Online Layout			Displays document best for onscreen reading
View/Page Layout			Displays document as it will appear when printed
View/Outline			Displays structure of document as an outline
View/Master Document			Shows several documents organized into a master document
View/Toolbars			Displays or hides selected toolbars
View/Document Map			Shows document headings along left side of document
View/Header and Footer			Displays header and footer areas
View/Footnotes			Hides or displays note pane
View/Full Screen			Shows document without Word's toolbars, menus, scroll bars, and other screen elements
View/Zoom		100%	Changes onscreen character size
View/Zoom/Whole Page			Displays entire page onscreen
View/HTML Source			Displays HTML codes
Insert/Break/Page Break	Ctrl + ↵Enter		Inserts manual page break
Insert/Break/Continuous			Starts next section on same page as current section
Insert/Page Numbers			Specifies page number location
Insert/Date and Time			Inserts current date or time, maintained by computer system, in selected format
Insert /Footnote	Alt + Ctrl + F		Inserts a footnote reference at insertion point
Insert/Caption			Inserts a caption at insertion point
Insert/Cross-reference			Inserts a cross-reference at insertion point
Insert/Index and Tables			Inserts an index or table, such as a table of contents
Insert/Picture/From File			Inserts a picture from a file
Insert/Text Box			Inserts text box
Insert/Horizontal Line			Adds graphic horizontal line to Web page
Insert/Hyperlink	Ctrl + K		Inserts a hyperlink in Web page

Command	Shortcut Key	Button	Action
Format/Font			Changes appearance of characters
Format/Font/Size			Increases HTML character size
Format/Font/Font Style/Italic	Ctrl + I		Makes selected text italic
Format/Font/Font Style/Bold	Ctrl + B		Makes selected text bold
Format/Font/Underline/Single	Ctrl + U		Underlines selected text
Format/Paragraph/Indents and Spacing/Special/First Line			Indents first line of paragraph from right margin
Format/Paragraph/Indents and Spacing/Alignment/Left	Ctrl + L		Aligns text to left margin
Format/Paragraph/Indents and Spacing/Alignment/Centered	Ctrl + E		Centers text between left and right margins
Format/Paragraph/Indents and Spacing/Alignment/Right	Ctrl + R		Aligns text to right margin
Format/Paragraph/Indents and Spacing/Alignment/Justified	Ctrl + J		Aligns text equally between left and right margins
Format/Bullets and Numbering			Creates a bulleted or numbered list
Format/Borders and Shading			Adds borders and shadings to selection
			Adds top border
			Adds bottom border
Format/Columns			Specifies number, spacing, and size of columns
Format/Tabs			Inserts tab stops
Format/Drop Cap/Dropped			Changes character to a drop cap
Format/Style			Applies, creates, or modifies styles
Format/Background			Applies background color to selection
Format/Picture			Changes picture scaling, size, wrapping, position, and cropping information
Tools/Spelling and Grammar	F7		Starts Spelling and Grammar tool
Tools/Language/Thesaurus	⇧Shift + F7		Starts Thesaurus tool
Tools/Language/Hyphenation			Specifies hyphenation settings
Tools/Mail Merge			Starts Mail Merge feature
Tools/Customize/Options			Changes display options

Command	Shortcut Key	Button	Action
Tools/Options/View/Spaces/ Paragraph Marks			Displays or hides special characters
Table/Draw Table			Creates a table using the Draw Table feature
Table/Insert Table			Inserts a table where you drag in document
Table/Insert Columns			Inserts new columns in a table
Table/Insert Rows			Inserts new rows in a table
Table/Merge Cells			Merges cells in a table
Table/Cell Properties/Background			Changes background of selected cell
Table/Formula			Inserts a formula into a table
Table/Table AutoFormat			Applies predesigned table layouts to table
Table/Distribute Columns Evenly		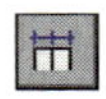	Evenly sizes selected columns
Table/Convert Text to Table			Converts existing text separated into columns to a table
Help/Microsoft Word Help	F1		Displays Office Assistant

Index

Notes

WP236 Notes

Appendix A

Additional Microsoft Word 97 User Specialist Certification Topics

- Create and Modify an Outline
- Create a Folder
- Use Alternate Headers and Footers
- Use Tabs with Leaders
- Adjust Line Spacing
- Use Underline Styles
- Edit Styles
- Key and Edit Text in Columns
- Create and Modify 3-D Shapes
- Create and Modify Lines
- Prepare and Print Envelopes and Labels

Create and Modify an Outline

When creating a new document, one of the hardest parts is getting started. Often the best way to start is by creating an outline of the main topics using Outline view. Outline view shows the hierarchy of topics in a document by displaying the different heading levels of a document indented to represent their level in the document's structure. Headings that are level 1 appear as the top level of the outline, level two headings appear indented below level 1 headings and so forth. The

Heading 1
  Heading 2
  Heading 3
    Heading 3
  Heading 2
    Heading 3
    Heading 3
    Heading 3

arrangement of headings in a hierarchy of importance quickly shows the relationship between topics.

You can use Outline view to help you create a new document or to view and reorganize the topics in an existing document. In a new document, Word automatically applies the built-in heading styles as you enter and rearrange the topic headings and subheadings. In an existing document, you need to apply the heading style levels before viewing the document in Outline view.

First you will create a new document using Outline view. As you enter each heading, it is initially formatted with a Heading 1 style. Then as you construct the outline, different heading levels are applied based upon the position of the topic within the outline hierarchy.

Use View/Outline or click [Outline View button] to switch to Outline View.

- Start Word and switch to Outline view.
- Close the Document Map.
- Type the following headings pressing Enter after each.

The Outline toolbar contains buttons that make it easy to modify the outline.

Health and Fitness
Health
A Balanced Diet
Controlling Fat in Your Diet
Improving Your Eating Habits
Attaining a Healthy Weight

Your screen should be similar to Figure A-1.

FIGURE A-1

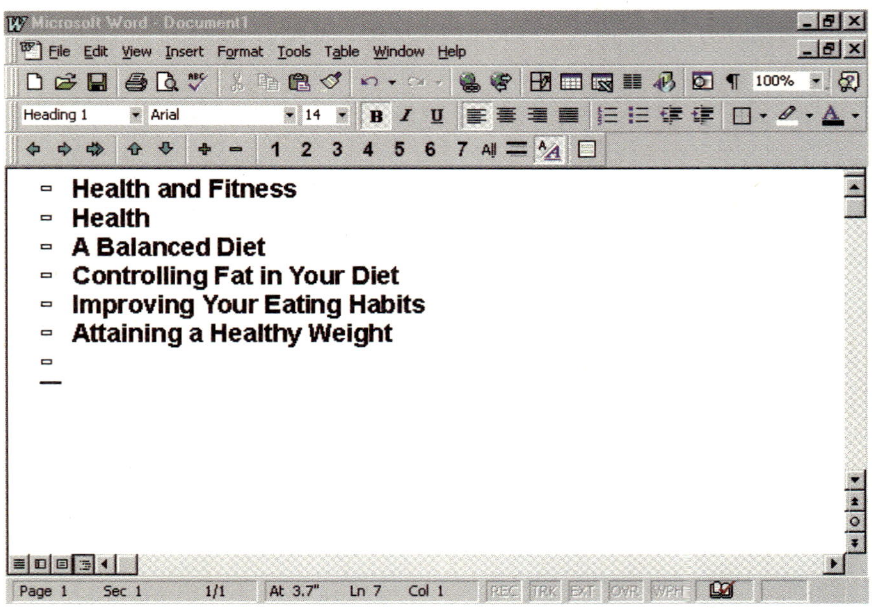

Next, you need to arrange the headings by outline levels. The outline symbols (▭ and ✥) to the left of the headings are used to select and move the heading to a new location or level within the document. To demote a heading to a lower level, drag the symbol to the right and to promote a heading to a higher level, drag the symbol to the left. You need to demote the Health heading so that is is a subtopic below the main heading.

> You can also click [⇦] to promote levels and [⇨] to demote levels.

- Drag the ▭ of the Health heading to the right one level.
- Demote the heading A Balanced Diet two levels.

> The mouse pointer changes to ⟷ indicating dragging it will move the heading.

Your screen should be similar to Figure A-2.

FIGURE A-2

The Health heading has changed to a Heading 2 style and the heading is indented one level to show it is subordinate to the heading above it. The A Balanced Diet heading is a Heading 3 style and is indented two levels in the outline. The ✥ outline symbol indicates the topic heading includes subtopics.

- Demote the 3 remaining topics to the heading levels shown below.

Controlling Fat in Your Diet	Level 3
Improving Your Eating Habits	Level 2
Attaining a Healthy Weight	Level 2

Next you want to change the order of topics. To move a heading to a different location, drag the outline symbol up or down. A horizontal line shows where the heading will be placed when you release the mouse button.

> You can also click [⇧] and [⇩] to move a topic.

- Drag the Attaining a Healthy Weight heading up above the Improving Your Eating Habits heading.

Your screen should be similar to Figure A-3.

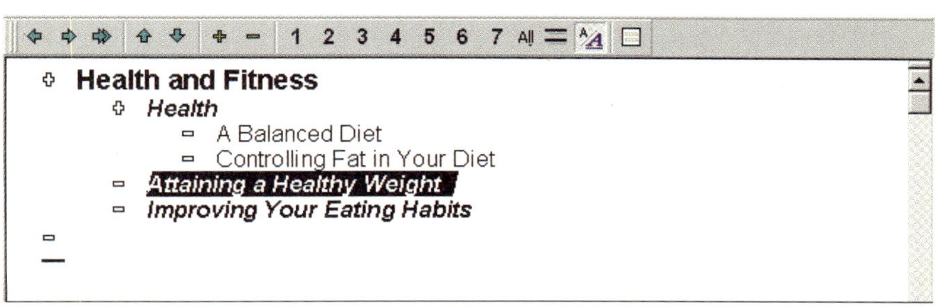

FIGURE A-3

When you are satisfied with the organization of your outline you can switch to normal view or page layout view to add detailed body text and graphics.

- Switch to Normal view.
- Add your name and date as a header.

Create a New Folder

Next you will save the outline you have created in a folder on your data disk that you will use to hold files related to the newsletter. You can create a new folder at the same time you save a file.

- Choose File/Save As.
- Change the Save In location to the drive containing your data disk.
- Click Create New Folder.

The New Folder dialog box displays the path of the active directory. The new folder will be created as a subfolder in the active directory.

- Enter the folder name **Newsletter** in the Name text box.
- Click OK.
- Change the active directory to the new folder, Newsletter.
- Enter the file name **Outline.**
- Click Save.
- Print the document.
- Close the file.

Checking an Existing Document in Outline View

Next you will open an existing document that is already formatted with heading styles and check its organization using Outline view.

This file was saved at the end of Part 1 in Lab 3.

- Open the file Newsletter Topics from your data disk.
- Switch to Outline view and close the Document Map.
- Scroll the window to view the entire document outline. Return to the top of the second section.

Your screen should be similar to Figure A-4.

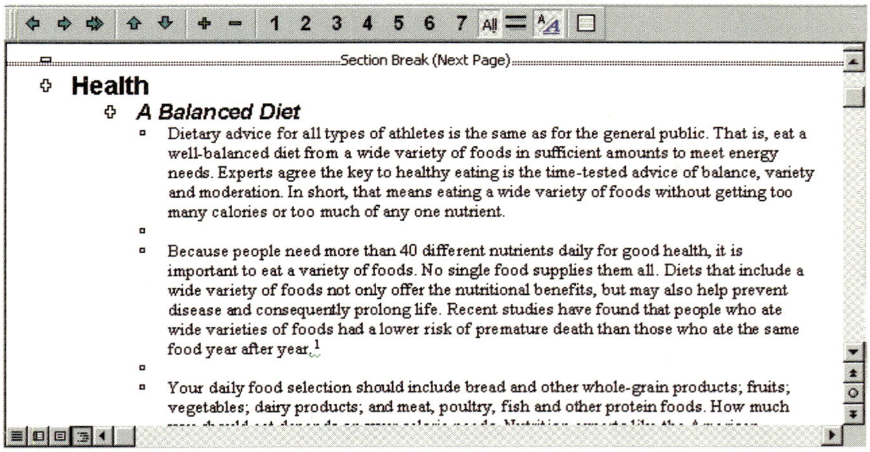

FIGURE A-4

The document is displayed as an outline with the topic headings indented appropriately. In Outline view you can display as much or little of the document text as you want. To make it easier to view and reorganize the document's structure, you can collapse the document to show just the headings you want. Alternatively, you can display part of the body text below each heading or the entire body text. The body text is any part of the document that is not formatted with a heading style. You can then easily move the headings around until the order is logical. The body text will follow the heading. The following tables show how you can expand and collapse the amount of text displayed in Outline view.

To expand	Do this
All headings and body text	Click All
All collapsed subheadings and body text under a heading	Double-click ✥ next to the heading.
Collapsed text under a heading, one level at a time	Click the heading text, then Click ✚ Expand

To collapse	Do this
Text below a specific heading level	Click the numbered button for the lowest heading you want to display.
All subheadings and body text under a heading	Double-click next to the heading.
Text under a heading, one level at a time	Click the heading text, and then click
Text below all headings to show only the first line of body text	Click Show First Line Only
All body text	Click All

- Double-click of the A Balanced Diet heading.

Your screen should be similar to Figure A-5.

FIGURE A-5

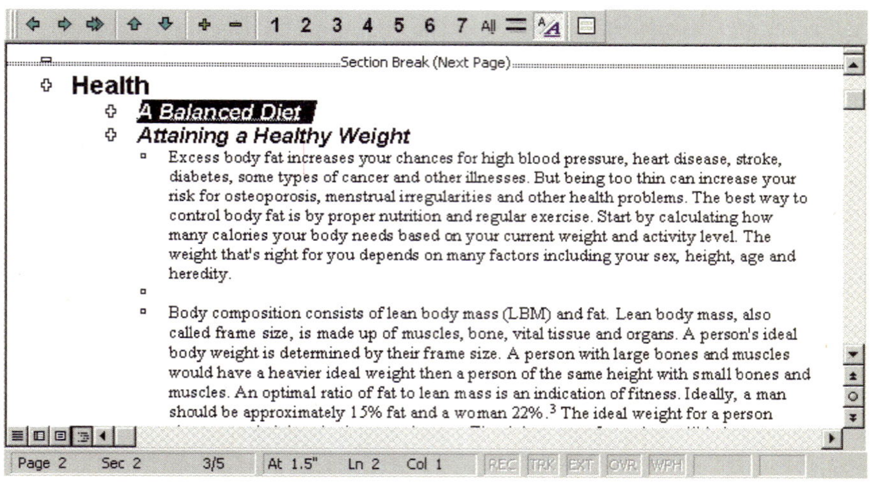

All the body text below this heading is hidden. You would like to see only the 4 heading levels of the document, not the body text so you can quickly check its organization.

- Click 4 Show Heading 4.

Your screen should be similar to Figure A-6.

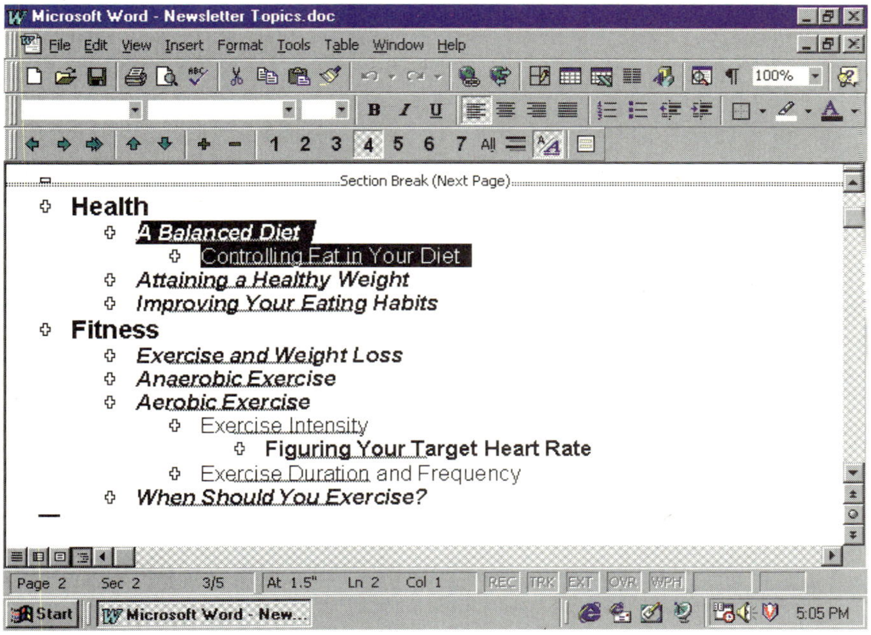

FIGURE A-6

Now you decide the discussion of controlling fat in your diet should appear as a subtopic in the Attaining a Healthy Weight topic.

- Move the heading Controlling Fat in Your Diet as a subtopic below Attaining a Healthy Weight.

Your screen should be similar to Figure A-7.

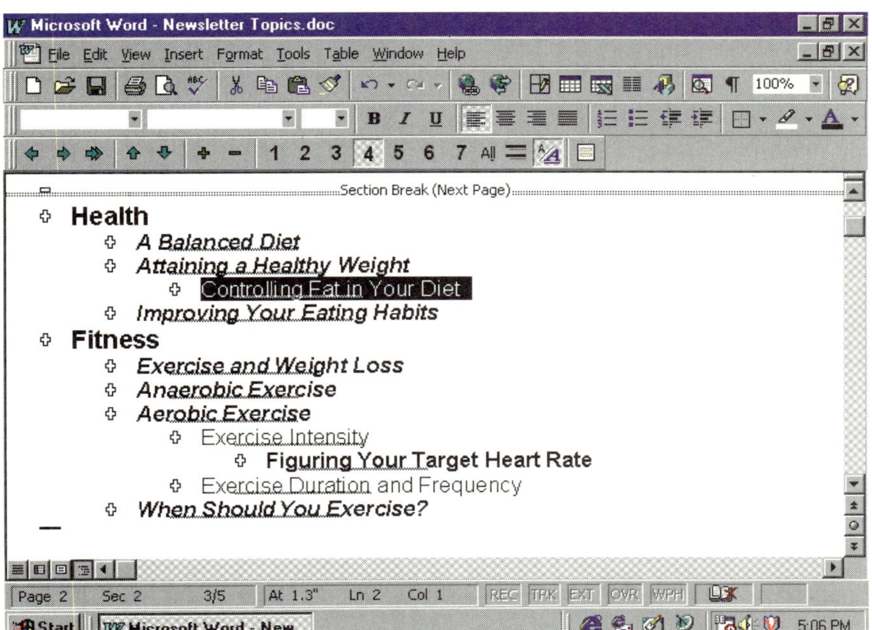

FIGURE A-7

When you move or change the level of a heading that includes collapsed subordinate text, the collapsed text is also selected and any changes you make to the heading such as moving, copying, or deleting it also affect the collapsed text. To verify this, you will display all body text again.

- Click [All] Show All Headings.

The body text appears below the heading you moved.

Use Alternate Headers and Footers

You can also design the headers and footers in a document to have different content displayed on odd and even numbered pages.

- Change to Page Layout view.
- Move to the top of page 2.

You will change the headers and footers in section 2 of this document to display different information on odd and even-numbered pages.

- Choose View/Header and Footer.
- Click  Page Setup.
- If necessary, open the Layout tab.
- Select Different odd and even.
- Click [OK].

You will leave the header on the odd page the same as it is and will change the footer to display the date.

- Switch to the odd page footer.
- Clear the existing footer information.
- Click [Insert AutoText ▾].
- Choose -PAGE-.

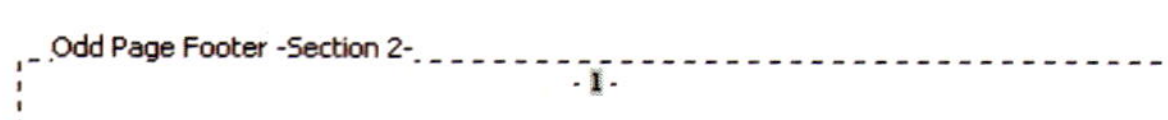

You will make the even page footer the same as the odd page footer.

- Click 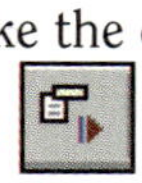 Next.
- Click [Insert AutoText ▾].
- Choose -PAGE-.

Next you will change the even page header to display your name and the date.

- Click  Switch.
- Type your name in the header text box.
- Press Tab twice. 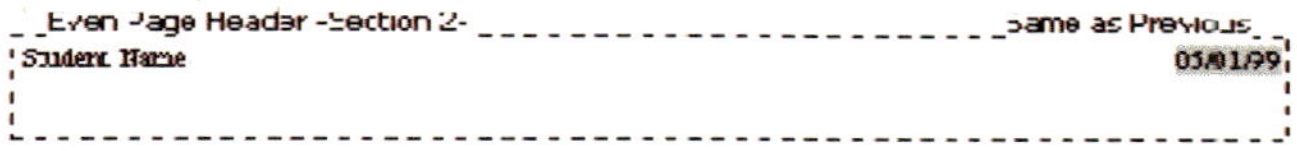

- Click .
- Click Close.
- Change the zoom to Two Pages and scroll the document to check the header and footer text on the odd and even pages of section 2.

Your screen should be similar to Figure A-8.

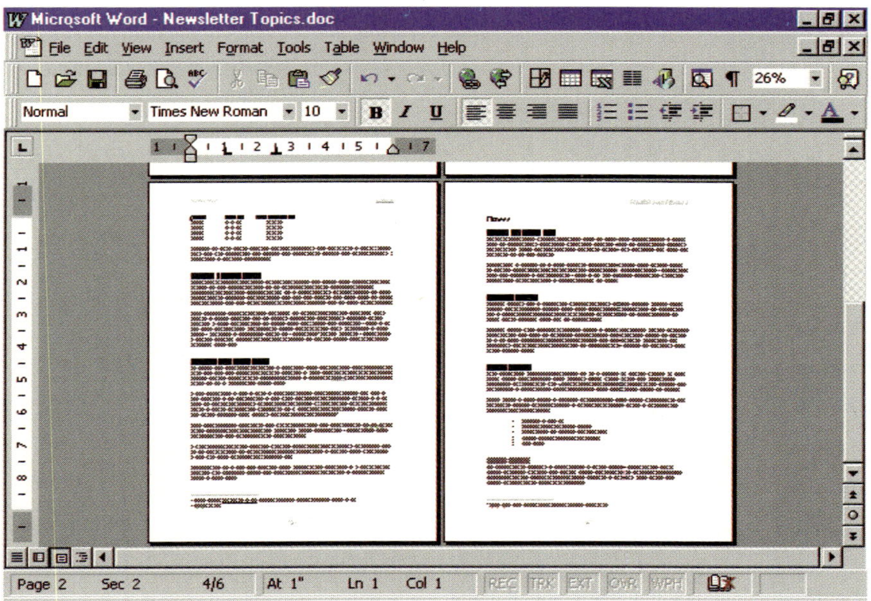

FIGURE A-8

- Return the zoom to Page Width.

Use Tabs with Leaders

To make the fat grams table of data even easier to read you will add tab leaders to the two tab stops you specified for the table.

- Select the fat gram table on page 2 of Section 2, excluding the heading line.

- Choose Format/Tabs

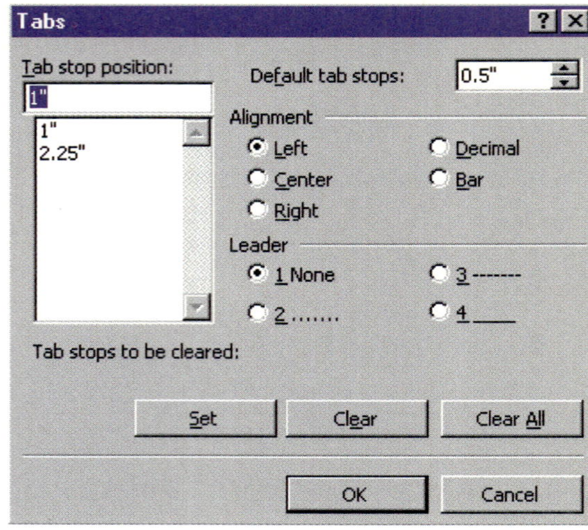

The current tab leader setting is set to none for the 1 inch tab stop position. There are three styles of tab leaders you can select. You will use the style three tab leader for both tab stop settings.

- Select 3 ------ .
- Click Set .
- Select the 2.25 inch tab stop setting from the Tab Stop Position list box.
- Select 3 ------.
- Click Set .
- Click OK .

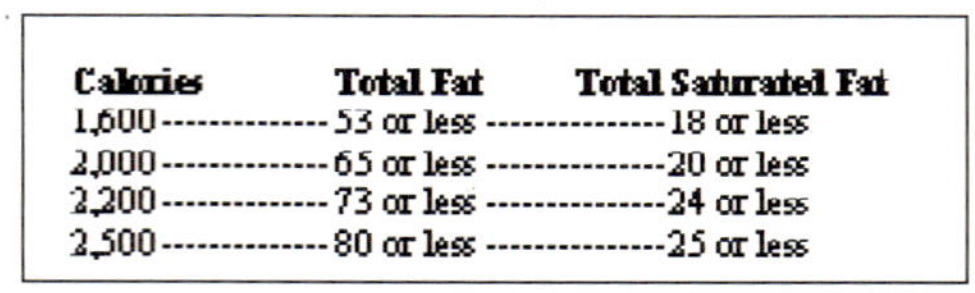

Calories	Total Fat	Total Saturated Fat
1,600 -------------	53 or less --------------	18 or less
2,000 -------------	65 or less --------------	20 or less
2,200 -------------	73 or less --------------	24 or less
2,500 -------------	80 or less --------------	25 or less

Adjust Line Spacing

You will also change the line spacing for the table. Line spacing is the vertical space between lines of text. The default setting of single line spacing accommodates the largest font in that line, plus a small amount of extra space. The other line spacing options are described below.

Spacing	Effect
1.5 Lines	Spacing is one-and-one-half times that of single line spacing.
Double	Spacing is twice that of single line spacing.
At Least	Uses the point value in the At text box as the minimum line spacing amount that can be used to accommodate larger font sizes or graphics that would not otherwise fit within the specified spacing.
Exactly	Uses the point value in the At text box as a fixed line spacing amount that is not changed making all lines evenly spaced.
Multiple	Uses the percentage value in the At text box as the amount to increase or decrease line spacing. For example, a 1.3 multiple line spacing setting will increase the space by 33 percent.

Line spacing is a paragraph format setting, therefore it effects the selected paragraph or selection.

- Select the fat grams table including the heading line.
- Choose Format/Paragraph.
- If necessary, open the Indents and Spacing tab.
- Choose 1.5 lines from the Line Spacing drop-down list.
- Click OK.

Calories	Total Fat	Total Saturated Fat
1,600 -------------	53 or less --------------	18 or less
2,000 -------------	65 or less --------------	20 or less
2,200 -------------	73 or less --------------	24 or less
2,500 -------------	80 or less --------------	25 or less

Use Underline Styles

Finally, you will add underlines to the fat gram table heading. In addition to the default single underline style, there are eight other types of underlines.

- Select the heading line of the table.
- Choose Format/Font.
- Open the Underline drop-down list box and select each underline type and look at how it appears in the Preview box.
- Select a type of your choice.
- Click OK.

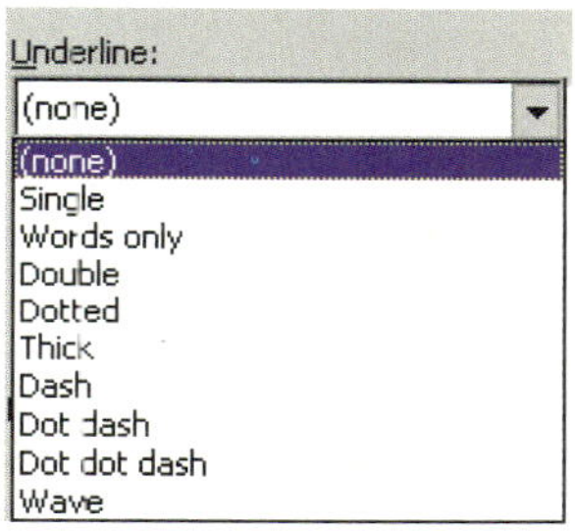

<u>Calories</u>	<u>Total Fat</u>	<u>Total Saturated Fat</u>
1,600 -------------	53 or less --------------	18 or less
2,000 -------------	65 or less --------------	20 or less
2,200 -------------	73 or less --------------	24 or less
2,500 -------------	80 or less --------------	25 or less

Edit Styles

You would also like to improve the appearance of the title page by applying a style to the title. Currently, the title has been formatted individually, however, you want to see if there is a predefined style that you can use to quickly improve the title.

- Move to the title line on the title page.
- Choose Format/Style.
- Select Title from the Styles list box.

The Title style settings are very similar to the settings that were applied individually to the title; Arial, 16 pt, bold and centered. Using this style will not change the appearance of the title, so you decide to create your own special style. You can do this by modifying an existing style or by creating a new style that you name. You will create a new style that you will name Fancy Title.

If the Fancy Title style is listed in the Styles text box, select it and press [Delete].

- Click [New...].
- Type **Fancy Title** in the Name text box.
- Click [Format].
- Choose Font.
- Select a font of Times New Roman, size of 20 and the Shadow effect.
- Click [OK] twice.
- Click [Apply].

Your screen should be similar to Figure A-9.

FIGURE A-9

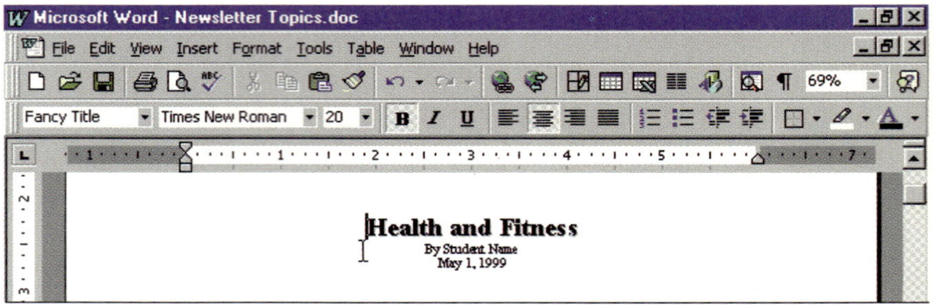

The style you designed is applied to the title. The name also appears in the Style button. You can also create styles by selecting text that contains the formatting you want included in the style and then naming the style in the Style button.

- Save the file as Newsletter Topics2 in the Newsletter folder.
- Print pages 2-3 of the report.
- Close the file.

The style you created is saved with the document. If you want to use the style in other documents you can copy it to the Normal.dot template or another document using the Organizer option in the Style dialog box.

Enter and Edit Text in Columns

You still have a few changes you want to make to the text of the newsletter. Although it is easier to enter and edit text when a document is in single column format, it is sometimes necessary to make changes when the document is formatted with multiple columns. As in a single column document, the text is automatically reformatted on a line when insertions and deletions are made. Using the [→] and [←] keys moves the insertion right or left along a line in a column. When it reaches the margin of the column it moves up or down to the next line in the column. Using the [↑] and [↓] keys moves the insertion point up or down line by line in a column. When it reaches the beginning or end of the column it moves to the bottom or top of the next column in the direction you are moving. Similarly, if you are dragging to select text, it highlights down then across columns. You want to add a paragraph to the end of the second article.

- Open the file Fall 1998 Newsletter on your data disk.

This file was saved at the end of Lab 3.

- If necessary, change to Page Layout view.
- Move to the end of the third column on page 2.
- Move the Special of the Month box to the bottom of the column.
- Type the following paragraph below the list of bulleted items.

  Two important factors of an aerobic workout are intensity and duration. Intensity is measured by checking your heart rate. A heart rate between 65 and 80 percent of its maximum is needed for the greatest cardiovascular improvement and most efficient fat burning. The duration recommended ranges from 12 to 60 minutes. Generally, 30 minutes of moderate-intensity physical activity on most days of the week is needed to maintain and improve weight.

- Delete the words "maintain and" from the last sentence of the paragraph.

Your screen should be similar to Figure A-10.

FIGURE A-10

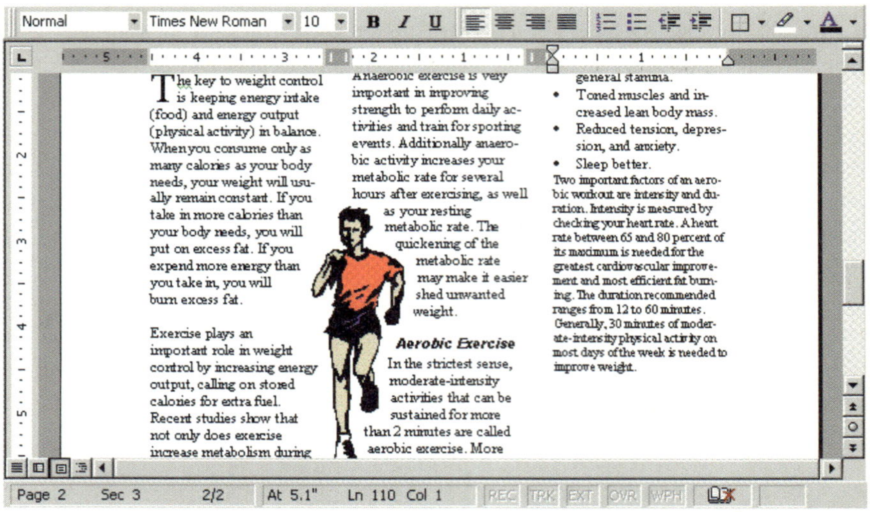

After reading over the section on aerobic exercise, you decide to move the paragraph above the preceding paragraph.

- Select the paragraph.
- Drag it to the beginning of the paragraph above it.
- Insert a blank line between the paragraphs.

Create and Modify 3-D Shapes and Lines

Since this is the first issue of the company newsletter, you want to add a special graphic to the headline to catch the reader's attention.

- Move to the top of the newsletter.
- Display the Drawing toolbar.
- Click AutoShapes.
- Click Stars and Banners.
- Click Explosion 1.

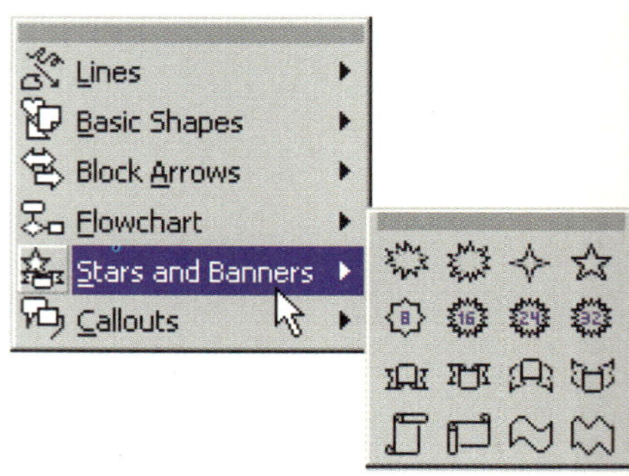

- In the upper left-hand corner of the headline, click and drag to draw a shape similar to that shown in Figure A-11.
- Fill the drawing with the Light Green color.

Click Fill Color and then select Light Green.

The AutoShape object should be similar to Figure A-11.

FIGURE A-11

Next you will add text to the drawing.

- Right-click on the shape to open the Shortcut menu.
- Click Add Text.
- Change the font to Arial, size 12, bold, italic and center.
- Type **Premiere**
- Press Enter.
- Type **Issue!**

Next you will add depth to the object.

- Click .
- Select any shape from the 3-D pop-up menu.

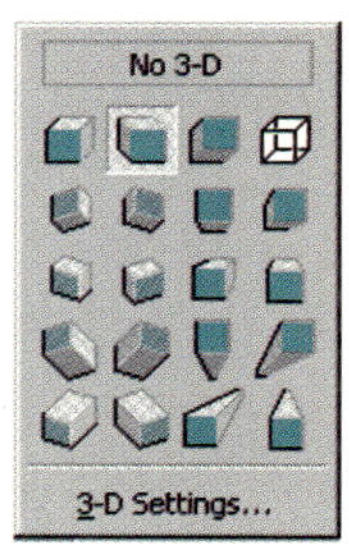

Your screen should be similar to Figure A-12.

FIGURE A-12

- Select several other 3-D shapes to see how they look when applied to the object.

In addition, you can modify the 3-D settings using the 3-D Settings toolbar. To open this toolbar,

- Click and choose 3-D Settings.

The buttons in this toolbar are used to modify the depth (the extrusion) of the object and its color, rotation, angle, direction of lighting, and surface texture.

- Use each of the 3-D settings to modify your shape.
- Select a 3-D design that you think looks good.
- Click anywhere outside the graphic.
- Close the 3-D Settings toolbar.

The object should be similar to Figure A-13.

FIGURE A-13

Finally, you want to add a line after the Health and Fitness heads to further distinguish the sections of the newsletter. You will create a straight graphic line consisting of a series of colored boxes.

The other Lines options can be used to quickly create many common line types as well as create non-straight lines.

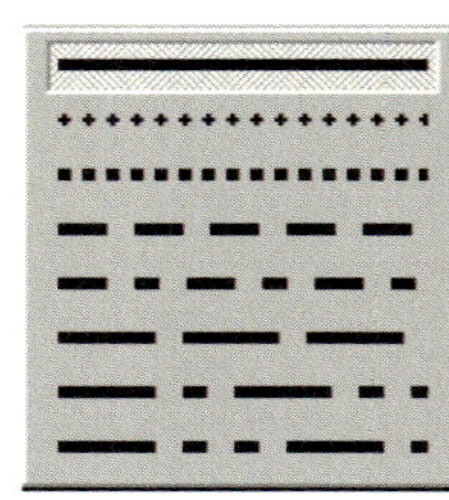

- Move to the end of the word Health.
- Click AutoShapes.
- Select Lines.
- Click .
- Drag to create a straight line that extends from the end of the word Health to the right column margin.
- Click Dash Style and choose from the menu.
- Click Line Color and choose the Sea Green color.

Clicking on the Drawing toolbar is the same as choosing it from the Autoshapes menu.

Your screen should be similar to Figure A-14.

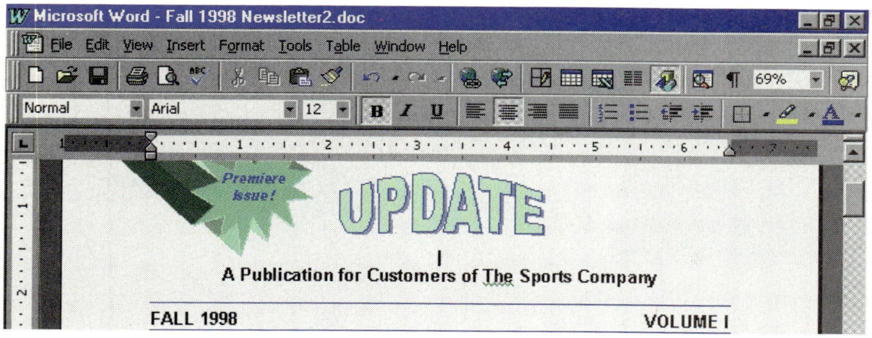

FIGURE A-14

- Copy the line object and paste it to the right of the Fitness heading on page 2.
- Size the line appropriately.
- Save the revised newsletter as Fall 1998 Newsletter2 in the Newsletter folder.
- Close the file.

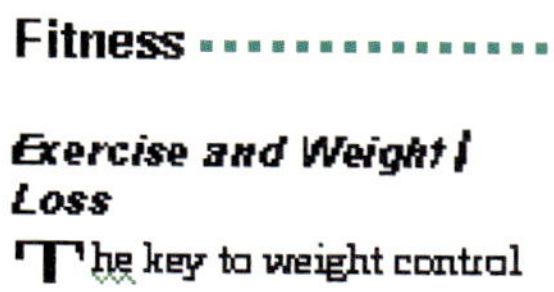

Prepare and Print Envelopes

Word 97 helps you easily create and print address information directly on an envelope on mailing labels that are applied to envelopes. You will address an envelope for the credit card letter.

- Open the file Credit Card Letter 4 from your data disk.
- Add your name and address above the salutation as the inside address.
- Choose Tools/Envelopes and Labels.
- If necessary, open the Envelopes tab.

The Labels tab is used to create labels rather than to print the address directly on the envelope.

The dialog box on your screen should be similar to Figure A-15.

FIGURE A-15

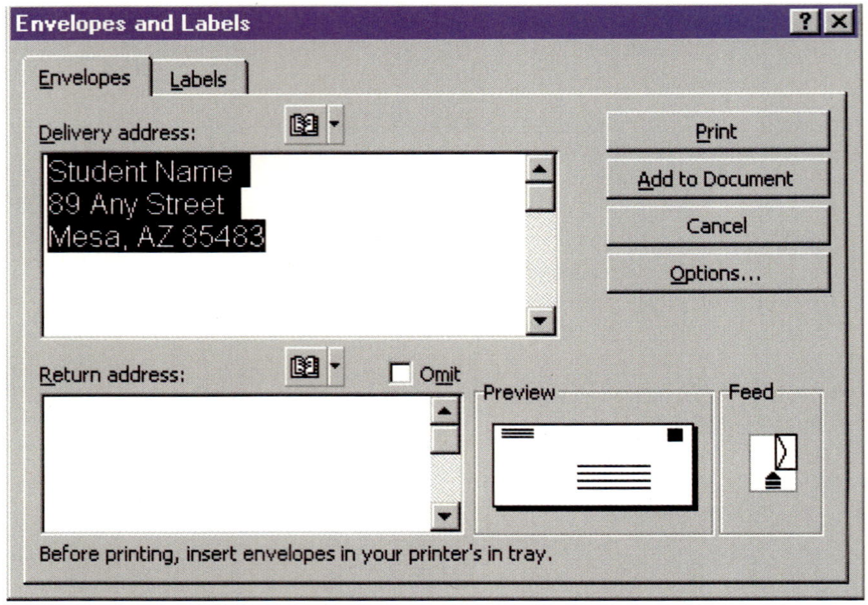

You can also type an address directly in the Delivery Address text box.

Word automatically copies the inside address from the letter into the Delivery Address text box. To complete the information for the envelope, you need to add the return address. Then you will check the options for printing and formatting the envelope.

- Enter your school's address in the Return Address text box.
- Click Options... .
- If necessary open the Envelope Options tab.

The dialog box on your screen should be similar to Figure A-16.

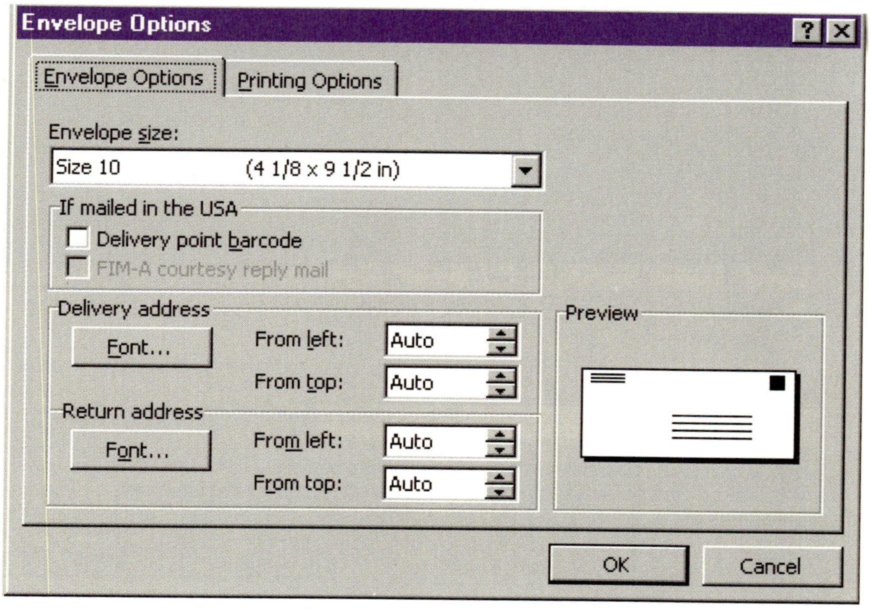

FIGURE A-16

Using this dialog box you can change the envelope size and the font and placement of the delivery and return addresses. The Preview area shows how the envelope will appear when printed using the current settings. To see the envelope size options,

- Open the Envelope Size drop-down list.

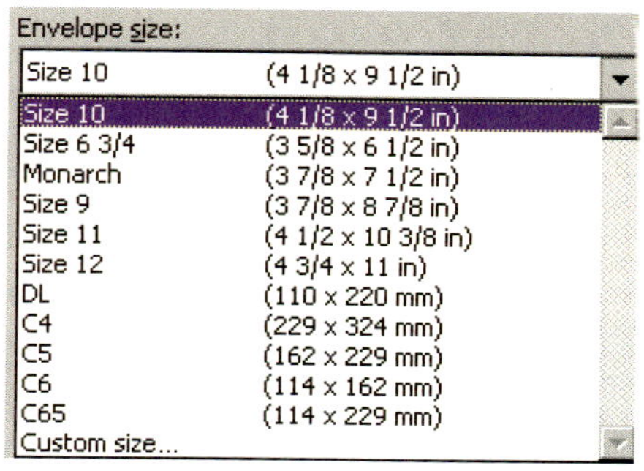

The default envelope size of 10 is for a standard 8 1/2 x 11 inch letter paper size. This is the appropriate size for the letter. Next you will check the print options.

- Open the Printing Options tab.

- If necessary, select Avery standard from the Label Products drop-down list.
- Select 5160 - Address from the Product number list.
- Click OK.

Word remembers and displays the last selected label type.

The dialog box on your screen should be similar to Figure A-17.

FIGURE A-17

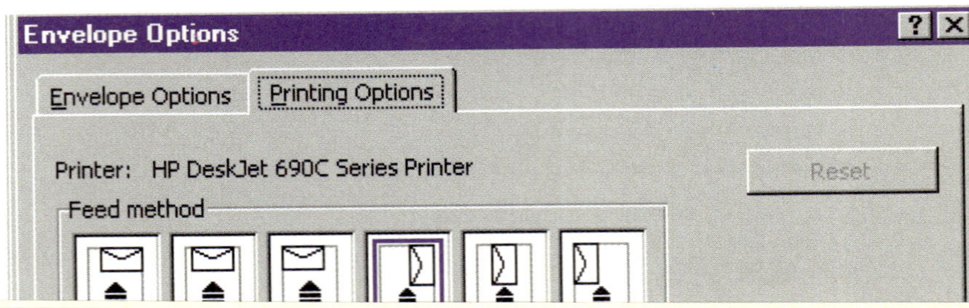

Practice Exercises

1. Open the Cookie Merge Document you created in problem 3 of Lab 4. Follow the procedures you learned in this appendix to add envelopes to the file in front of the letters. Add your address as the return address. Print the first two letters with envelopes (you can print the envelopes on regular paper). Save the document to your data disk.
2. Open the Scenic Drives Newsletter you created in problem 6 of lab 3. Delete the WordArt on the title page and replace it with an AutoShapes banner that contains the same words. Add 3-D effects to the banner. Print the title page. Save the document as Scenic Drives Newsletter Revised on your data disk.
3. Open the Camera Ready B&B Ad you created in problem 4 of Lab 3. Insert a Tab after each item in the bulleted list. Add tab leaders to the table. Delete the WordArt and replace it with an AutoShape of your choice that contains the same words. Add 3-D effects to the shape. Print the document. Save the document at B&B revised on your data disk.
4. Open the Customer Main Document you created in problem 5 of lab 4. Format the paragraphs with 1.5 line spacing. Merge the document again. Create envelopes that contain your address as the return address adds the envelopes to the file. Print the first two letters and envelopes. Save the document as Revised Customer Merge.
5. Open the file How to Create a Resume. Create and apply a style of your own to the title and another style to the name and date lines below the title. Add Heading 1 styles to all topic heads then view the document in Outline view. Adjust the heading levels appropriately. In the Overview of Resumes section, arrange the paragraphs in the following order: Name, Address, and Phone Number, Career Objectives, Education, Work Experience, Activities, Honors and Awards, Special Skills, and References. Change to Page Layout view and indent the five items to include in a resume and precede each item in the list with dot leaders of your choice. Set the line spacing for the list to 1.5. Bullet the list of basic principles of resume construction. Add a different underline style to each of the eight paragraph topic headings in the Organizing Your Resume section. Add a header and alternate footer of your own choosing. Save the document with a new file name to a new folder named Resume on your data disk. Print the document.

- Open a new document window.
- Choose Tools/Mail Merge
- Click Create ▾.
- Choose Mailing Labels
- Click Active Window.
- Click Get Data ▾ to specify the data source
- Choose Open Data Source....
- Change the location to the drive containing your data disk and select the Credit Data Source file.
- Click Open.
- Click Set Up Main Document.

This file was created in Part 2 of Lab 4.

The dialog box on your screen should be similar to Figure A-18.

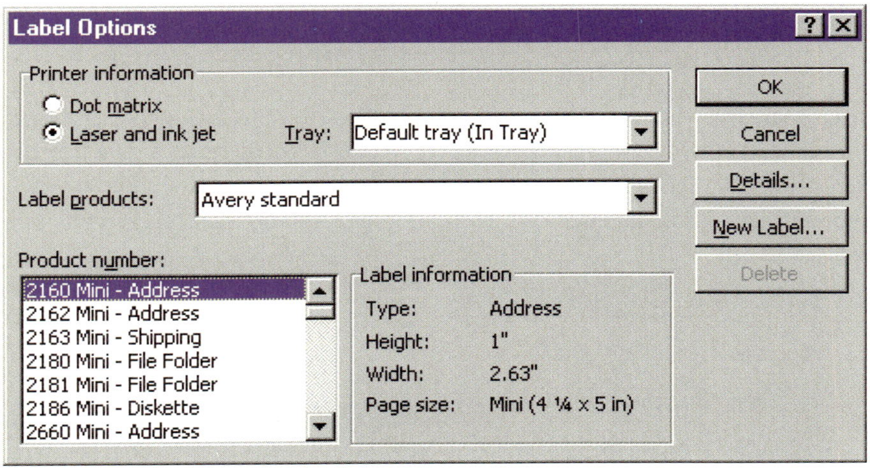

FIGURE A-18

In this dialog box you specify the printer and label product information. You can either use a predefined label or create a custom label. You will use a standard mailing label made by Avery. These labels appear three across the width of the paper.

- If necessary, select Avery standard from the Label Products drop-down list.
- Select 5160 - Address from the Product number list.
- Click OK.

Word remembers and displays the last selected label type.

The dialog box on your screen should be similar to Figure A-19.

FIGURE A-19

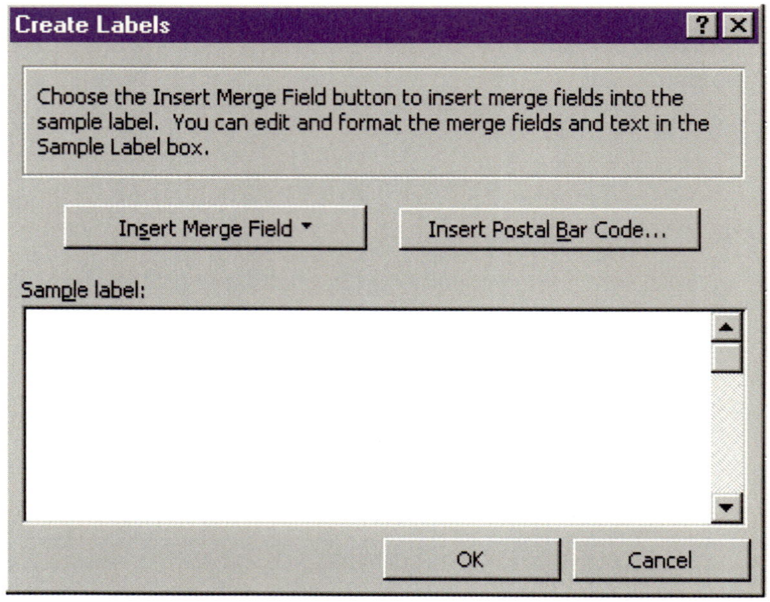

Just as you did when you entered the merge fields into the letter, you select the merge fields from the data source to include in the labels. As you select the fields you also design the label layout in the Sample Label text box. You may type any additional text, such as punctuation or a holiday message, directly into the text box.

- Click [Insert Merge Field].
- Choose the FirstName field.
- Press [Spacebar].
- Add the LastName field to the sample label.
- Press [Enter].
- To complete the rest of the label, add the Address, City, State, and PostalCode fields to the sample label box using the punctuation and spacing shown here.
- Click [OK].

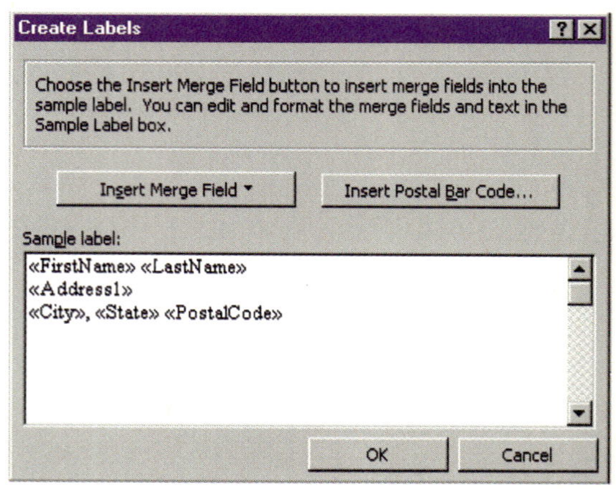

Your merge label settings are complete and the Merge Helper dialog box is displayed. The open document behind the dialog box shows how the active document has been formatted with the merge codes and labels. You are now ready to perform the merge.

- Click Merge.

The dialog box on your screen should be similar to Figure A-20.

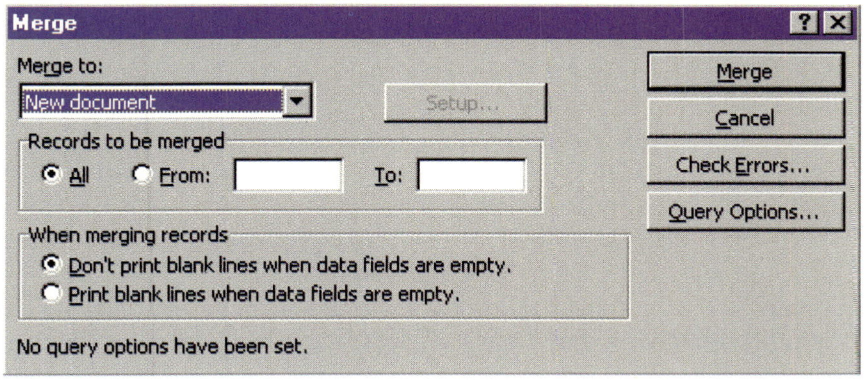

FIGURE A-20

You can merge to a new document or directly to the printer. It is safest to merge to a document so that you can check your output before printing the labels. This is the default setting.

- Click Merge.

Your screen should be similar to Figure A-21.

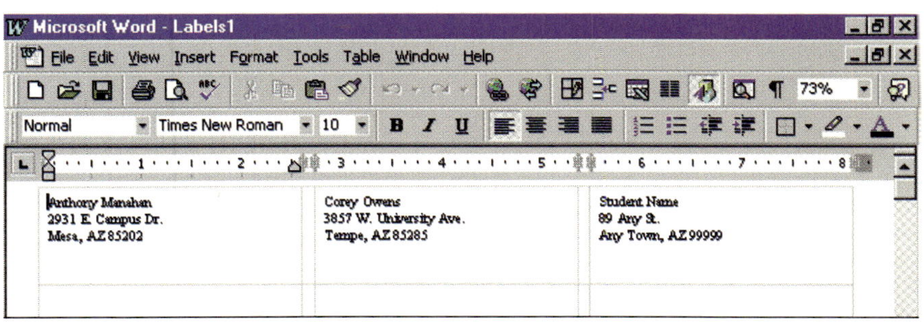

FIGURE A-21

Three mailing labels appear across the width of the page. The placement of the labels on the page corresponds to the 5160 Avery labels you selected. Before printing the actual labels, you would need to insert the correct label paper in the printer. However, you will simply print it on a sheet of paper.

- Print the document.
- Close all open documents without saving.

Practice Exercises

1. Open the Cookie Merge Document you created in problem 3 of Lab 4. Follow the procedures you learned in this appendix to add envelopes to the file in front of the letters. Add your address as the return address. Print the first two letters with envelopes (you can print the envelopes on regular paper). Save the document to your data disk.
2. Open the Scenic Drives Newsletter you created in problem 6 of lab 3. Delete the WordArt on the title page and replace it with an AutoShapes banner that contains the same words. Add 3-D effects to the banner. Print the title page. Save the document as Scenic Drives Newsletter Revised on your data disk.
3. Open the Camera Ready B&B Ad you created in problem 4 of Lab 3. Insert a Tab after each item in the bulleted list. Add tab leaders to the table. Delete the WordArt and replace it with an AutoShape of your choice that contains the same words. Add 3-D effects to the shape. Print the document. Save the document at B&B revised on your data disk.
4. Open the Customer Main Document you created in problem 5 of lab 4. Format the paragraphs with 1.5 line spacing. Merge the document again. Create envelopes that contain your address as the return address adds the envelopes to the file. Print the first two letters and envelopes. Save the document as Revised Customer Merge.
5. Open the file How to Create a Resume. Create and apply a style of your own to the title and another style to the name and date lines below the title. Add Heading 1 styles to all topic heads then view the document in Outline view. Adjust the heading levels appropriately. In the Overview of Resumes section, arrange the paragraphs in the following order: Name, Address, and Phone Number, Career Objectives, Education, Work Experience, Activities, Honors and Awards, Special Skills, and References. Change to Page Layout view and indent the five items to include in a resume and precede each item in the list with dot leaders of your choice. Set the line spacing for the list to 1.5. Bullet the list of basic principles of resume construction. Add a different underline style to each of the eight paragraph topic headings in the Organizing Your Resume section. Add a header and alternate footer of your own choosing. Save the document with a new file name to a new folder named Resume on your data disk. Print the document.

McGRAW-HILL

Microsoft Excel 97

Timothy J. O'Leary
Arizona State University

Linda I. O'Leary

Irwin McGraw-Hill

Boston, Massachusetts Burr Ridge, Illinois Dubuque, Iowa
Madison, Wisconsin New York, New York San Francisco, California St. Louis, Missouri

Spreadsheet Overview

In contrast to a word processor, which manipulates text, an electronic spreadsheet manipulates numerical data. The first electronic spreadsheet software program, VisiCalc, was offered on the market in 1979. Since then the electronic spreadsheet program has evolved into a powerful business tool that has revolutionized the business world.

Definition of Electronic Spreadsheets

The electronic spreadsheet, or worksheet, is an automated version of the accountant's ledger. Like the accountant's ledger, it consists of rows and columns of numerical data. Unlike the accountant's ledger, which is created on paper using a pencil and a calculator, the electronic spreadsheet is created using a computer system and an electronic spreadsheet application software program.

The electronic spreadsheet eliminates the paper, pencil, and eraser. With a few keystrokes, the user can quickly change, correct, and update the data. Even more impressive is the spreadsheet's ability to perform calculations from very simple sums to the most complex financial and mathematical formulas. The calculator is replaced by the electronic spreadsheet. Analysis of data in the spreadsheet has become a routine business procedure. Once requiring hours of labor and/or costly accountants' fees, data analysis is now available almost instantly using electronic spreadsheets.

Nearly any job that uses rows and columns of numbers can be performed using an electronic spreadsheet. Typical uses of electronic spreadsheets are for budgets and financial planning in both business and personal situations.

Advantages of Using an Electronic Spreadsheet

An electronic spreadsheet application helps you create well-designed spreadsheets that produce accurate results. The application not only makes it faster to create the spreadsheet, but produces a professional-appearing result. The advantages are in the ability of the spreadsheet program to quickly edit and format data, perform calculations, create graphs, and print the spreadsheet.

The data entered in an electronic spreadsheet can be edited and revised using the program commands. Numeric or text data is entered into the worksheet in a location called a cell. These entries can then be erased, moved, copied, or edited. Formulas can be entered that perform calculations using data contained in specified cells. The results of the calculations

Creating a Worksheet: Part 1

COMPETENCIES

After completing this lab, you will know how to:

1. Load Excel 97.
2. Use toolbars.
3. Use the Office Assistant.
4. Move around the worksheet.
5. Design a worksheet.
6. Enter data.
7. Delete and edit cell entries.
8. Open and close workbooks.
9. Copy data.
10. Enter formulas.
11. Recalculate a worksheet.
12. Change cell alignment.
13. Document, save, and print a workbook.
14. Exit Excel.

CASE STUDY

The Sports Company is a chain of sporting goods shops located in large metropolitan areas across the United States. The stores are warehouse oriented, discounting the retail price of most items 15 percent. They stock sporting goods products for the major sports: team sports, racquet sports, aerobics, golf, and winter sports.

As a recent college graduate, you have accepted your first job in a management training program for The Sports Company. The training program emphasis is on computer applications in the area of retail man-

S. Name							
10/10/98		1999 First Half Budget					
	JAN	FEB	MAR	APR	MAY	JUN	TOTAL
SALES							
Clothing	140000	135000	175000	210000	185000	185000	1030000
Hard Goc	94000	89000	120000	145000	125000	125000	
Total Sales							
EXPENSES							
Advertising							
Cost of Goods							
Salary	30000	30000	30000	30000	30000	30000	
Lease	19000	19000	19000	19000	19000	19000	
Miscellar	16000	16000	16000	16000	16000	16000	
Overheac	22000	22000	22000	22000	22000	22000	
Total Expenses							
INCOME							

agement. The program requires that you work in several areas of the company, beginning in a retail store as an assistant to the store manager.

The software tool you will learn about in this series of labs is the spreadsheet application, Microsoft Excel 97. Its purpose is to store, manipulate, and display numeric data. During the next six labs, you will use Excel to create several spreadsheets for The Sports Company that will help with budget projections and sales analysis.

In this lab you will learn how to enter and edit descriptive row and column headings, enter numbers and formulas, copy data, and align entries as you create a six-month budget for the store, as shown on the previous page.

Concept Overview

The following concepts will be introduced in this lab:

1. Worksheet Design	A well-designed worksheet produces accurate results, and is clearly understood, adaptable, and efficient.
2. Types of Entries	The information or data you enter in a cell can be text, numbers, or formulas.
3. Copy and Move Cell Contents	The contents of worksheet cells can be copied or moved to new locations in the worksheet.
4. Range	A selection consisting of two or more cells on a worksheet is a range.
5. Formulas	A formula is an entry that performs a calculation.
6. Automatic Recalculation	Excel automatically recalculates formulas whenever a change occurs in a referenced cell.
7. Format	Formats control how information is displayed in a cell and are used to improve the appearance of the worksheet data.
8. Alignment	Alignment settings allow you to change the horizontal and vertical placement and the orientation of an entry in a cell.
9. Dates	Excel automatically recognizes certain types of data input, such as dates and times, and formats the entry as appropriate.

Part 1

Loading Excel 97

You will use Excel 97 to create the budget for The Sports Company for the first six months of 1999. To start Excel 97,

- If necessary, turn on your computer.
- Click Start.
- Choose Programs Microsoft Excel.

If a Shortcut to Excel button Microsoft Excel is displayed on your desktop, you can double-click on the button to start the program.

If the Microsoft Office suite is on your system and the Office Shortcut Bar is displayed, you can load Excel by clicking the New Office Document button and selecting Blank Workbook.

After a few moments the Excel application window is displayed. Your screen should be similar to Figure 1-1.

FIGURE 1-1

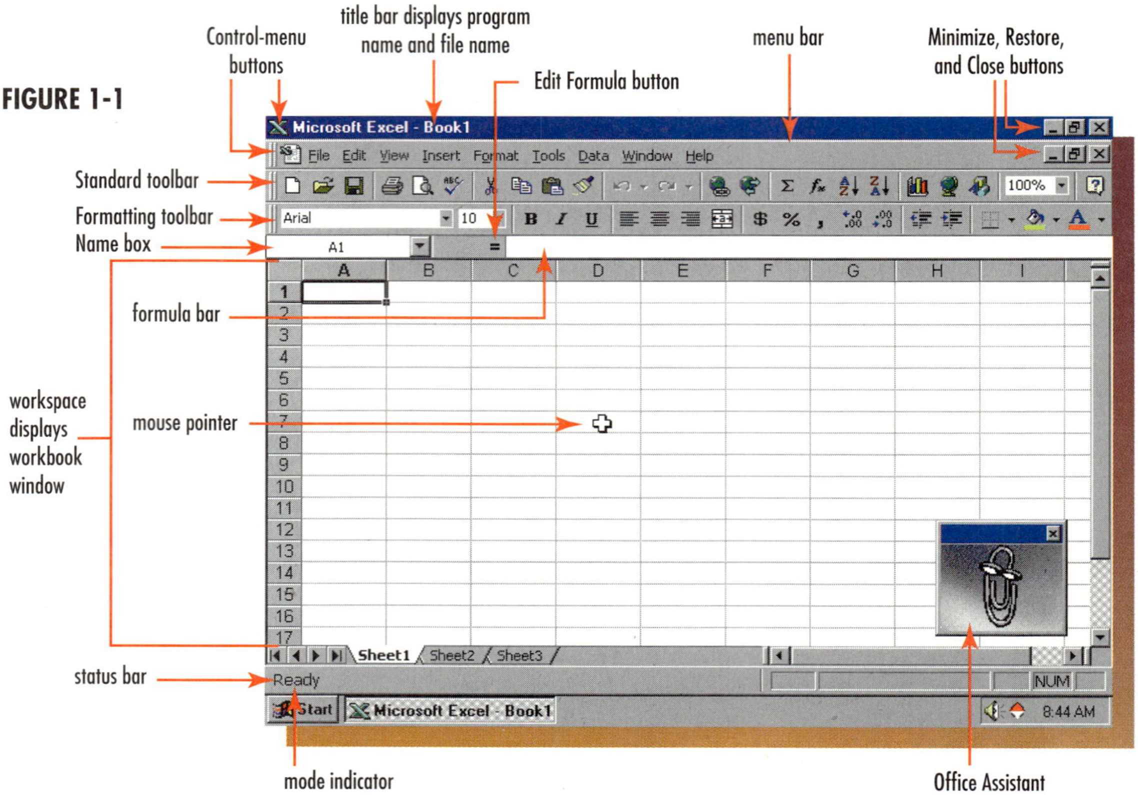

If necessary, maximize the Excel application window.

If the title bar does not display the file name, the workbook window is not maximized. Maximize the workbook window by clicking on the workbook window Maximize button.

As you can see, many of the features in the Excel application window are common to the Windows 95 environment. Among those features are a title bar, menu bar, control menus, Minimize and Restore buttons, toolbars, scroll bars, document windows, and mouse compatibility. You can move and size Excel windows, select commands, use Help, and switch between files and programs just as in Windows and other Windows-based applications. Your knowledge of how to use Windows makes using Excel much easier. The Excel window includes all these features, plus some additional features that are specific to Excel.

The Excel window title bar displays the program name, Microsoft Excel, followed by the file name Book1, the default name of the file displayed in the workbook window. The left end of the title bar contains the Excel application window Control-menu icon, and the right end displays the Minimize, Restore, and Close buttons. They perform the same functions and operate in the same way as in Windows 95.

The menu bar below the title bar displays the Excel program menu. The left end of the menu bar displays the workbook window Control-menu icon, and the right end displays the workbook window Minimize, Restore, and Close buttons.

The two toolbars below the menu bar contain buttons that are mouse shortcuts for many of the menu items. The upper toolbar is the **Standard toolbar**, and the bottom is the **Formatting toolbar**. There are 13 different toolbars in Excel, and they operate just like Windows 95 toolbars. You will learn more about Excel toolbars shortly.

Below the toolbars is the formula bar. The **formula bar** displays entries as they are made and edited in the workbook window. The **Name box**, located at the left end of the formula bar, provides information about the selected item. The Edit Formula button is used to create or edit a cell formula.

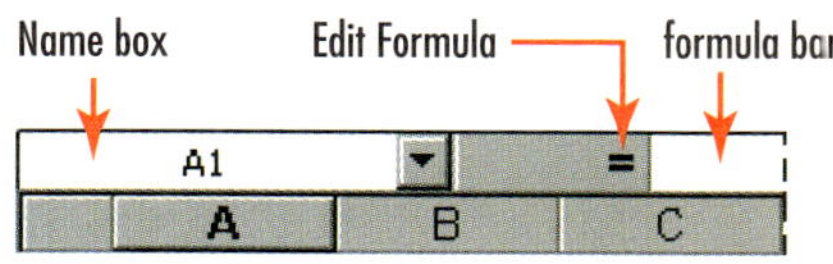

The largest area of the Excel window is the **workspace**. The workspace is where different windows are displayed. Currently there is only one window open, and it occupies the entire workspace. The window displays a workbook. A **workbook** is an Excel file that stores the information you enter using the program. Excel calls a window that displays a workbook file a **workbook window**. You can have several workbook files open at once, each displayed in their own workbook window in the workspace. You will learn about the different parts of the workbook window shortly.

The status bar at the bottom of the Excel window displays information about various Excel settings. The left side of the status bar displays the current mode or state the Excel program is in. The current mode is Ready. When "Ready" is displayed, you can move around the workbook, enter data, use the function keys, or choose a command. As you are using the program, the status bar will display the current mode. The modes will be discussed as they appear throughout the labs.

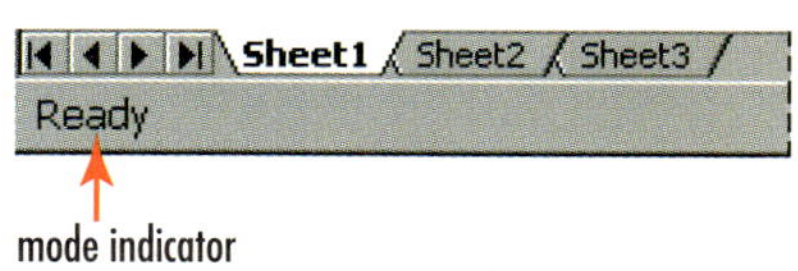

The mouse pointer probably appears as a or on your screen. As in Windows 95, the mouse pointer changes shape depending upon the task you are performing or where the pointer is located on the window.

Finally, your screen may display the Office Assistant. You will learn about this feature shortly.

The Workbook Window

The workbook window displays a new blank workbook file containing three blank sheets. A sheet is used to display different types of information, such as financial data or charts. Whenever you open a new workbook, it displays a worksheet.

The default workbook opens with three worksheets. The number of sheets in a workbook is limited only by the available memory on your computer.

A **worksheet,** also commonly referred to as a **spreadsheet,** is a rectangular grid of **rows** and **columns** used to enter data. It is always part of a workbook and is the primary type of sheet you will use in Excel. The parts of the worksheet are shown in Figure 1-2, below.

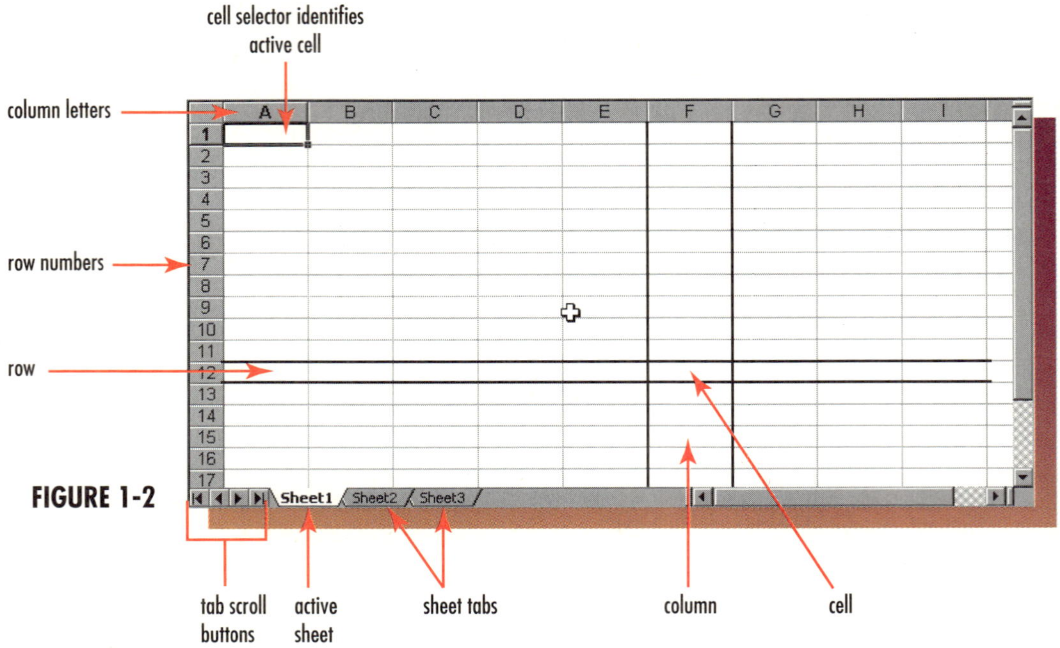

FIGURE 1-2

> Do not be concerned if your workbook window displays more column letters and row numbers than in Figure 1-2. This is a function of your computer monitor.

The **row numbers** along the left side and the **column letters** across the top of the workbook window identify each worksheet row and column. The intersection of a row and column creates a **cell**. Notice the heavy border, called the **cell selector**, surrounding the cell located at the intersection of column A and row 1. The cell selector identifies the **active cell**, which is the cell your next entry or procedure affects. In addition, the row number and column letter appear bold to further identify the location of the active cell. Finally, the Name box displays the **reference**, consisting of the column letter and row number of the active cell. The reference of the active cell is A1.

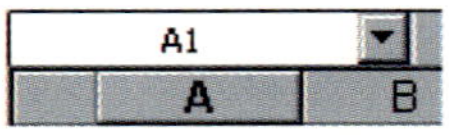

Each sheet in a workbook is named. The default names are Sheet1, Sheet2, and so on, displayed on **sheet tabs** at the bottom of the workbook window. The name of the **active sheet**, which is the sheet you can work in, appears bold. The currently displayed worksheet in the workspace, Sheet1, is the active sheet.

The sheet tab area also contains **tab scroll buttons**, which are used to scroll tabs right or left when there are more worksheet tabs than there is available space. You will learn about these features throughout the labs.

Using Toolbars

By default the Standard toolbar and the Formatting toolbar, shown below, are automatically displayed.

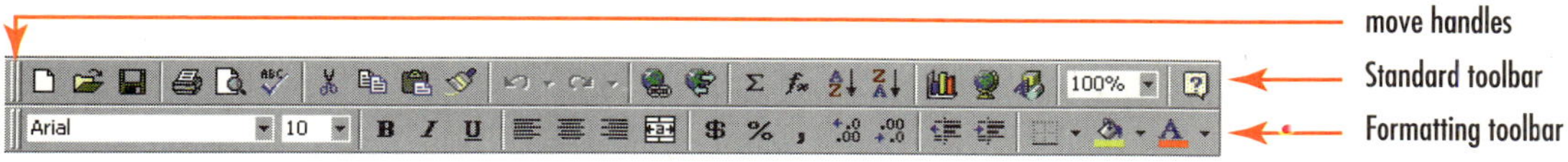

The Standard toolbar contains buttons that are used to complete the most frequently used menu commands. The buttons in the Formatting toolbar are used to change the format or design of the worksheet. Many of the buttons are the same as those you have seen in toolbars in other Windows 95 applications. Many, however, are specific to the Excel 97 application. Any buttons that are dimmed indicate they are not available for use.

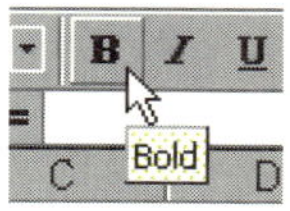

- To quickly identify the toolbar buttons, point to each button in both toolbars to display the button name in the Screen Tip.

Although many of the toolbars open automatically as different tasks are performed, you can also open toolbars whenever you want using the toolbar Shortcut menu. Clicking on a toolbar from the menu will display it onscreen. Likewise, clicking on a checked toolbar will remove the toolbar from the screen.

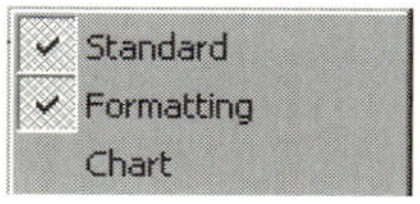

- To open the toolbar Shortcut menu, right-click on the toolbar.
- Press Esc to clear the Shortcut menu.

The menu equivalent is View/Toolbars.

You can also click outside the Shortcut menu to clear it.

Using the Office Assistant

Note: If you are already familiar with this feature, skip this section.

The **Office Assistant** is used to get Help on features that are specific to the Office application you are using. The Assistant can display tips that point out how to more effectively use the features or keyboard shortcuts in the program. A tip is available when a yellow light bulb appears in the Assistant; click the light bulb to see the tip. It can also automatically display Help suggestions based on your actions. In addition, you can activate the Assistant at any time to ask for Help on any topic. To activate it,

- Click Office Assistant.

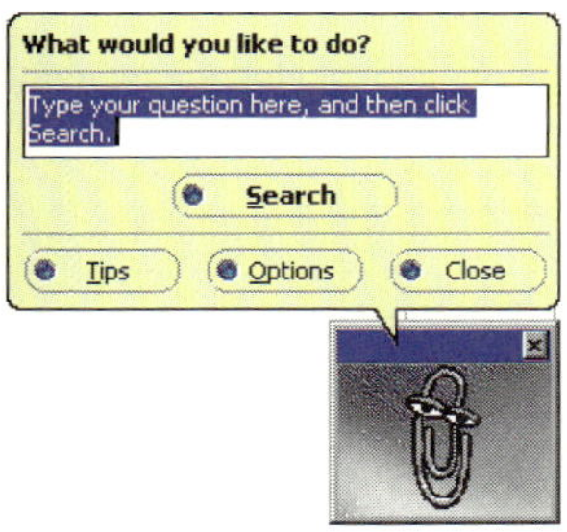

A yellow balloon displays a prompt and a text box in which you can type the topic on which you want help. Then you click the Search button to display a topic list related to your question. In addition, the Tips option button displays the most recent tip and lets you scroll through tips that the Office Assis-

If your Office Assistant is not displayed, click or press F1.

The Office Assistant feature is common to all Office 97 programs.

Your Assistant may be different than the one displayed in this text.

You can also access Help using the Help menu.

tant has recently displayed. The Options button is used to configure the Office Assistant to provide different levels of help or display a different Assistant.

- Click [Tips] and read the tip that appears in the box.

Your tip may be different than shown here.

- To clear the tip, click [Close].

You can leave the Office Assistant open or you can close it and activate it when needed. This text will not display the Assistant open.

- If you want to hide the Assistant, click [X] in the Assistant's window.

Moving Around the Worksheet

You can use the directional keys in the numeric keypad or, if you have an extended keyboard, you can use the separate directional keypad area.

If you are using the numeric keypad area, make sure the Num Lock feature is off. "NUM" is displayed in the status bar when it is on.

Either the mouse or the keyboard can be used to move the cell selector from one cell to another in the worksheet. To move using a mouse, simply point to the cell you want to move to and click the mouse button. Depending upon what you are doing, using the mouse to move may not be as convenient as using the keyboard, in which case the directional keys can be used. To use the mouse, then the keyboard to move the cell selector,

- Click cell B3.
- Press [→] (3 times).
- Press [↓] (4 times).

Your worksheet should be similar to Figure 1-3.

FIGURE 1-3

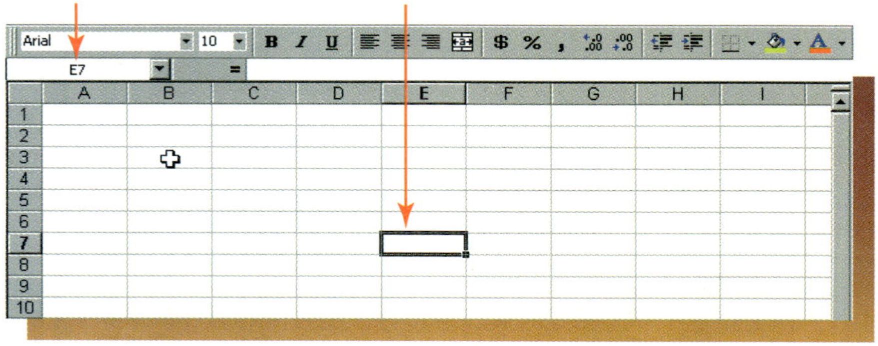

The cell selector is now in cell E7, making this cell the active cell. To return quickly to the upper left corner, cell A1, of the worksheet,

- Press Ctrl + Home.

The column letter and row number containing the cell selector appear raised.

Scrolling the Worksheet

The worksheet is much larger than the part you are viewing in the window. The worksheet actually extends many columns to the right and many rows down. An Excel worksheet has 256 columns and 65,536 rows. For example, to see the rows immediately below row 17,

- Press Page Down.

Page Up moves up a window on the worksheet.

Your worksheet should be similar to Figure 1-4.

FIGURE 1-4

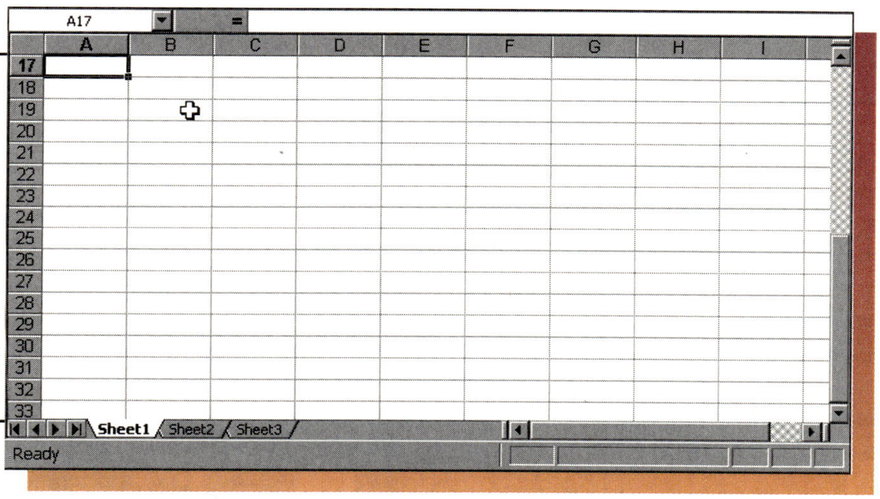

pressing Page Down displays next full window down in worksheet

The worksheet has scrolled upward in the window and is positioned over rows 17 through 33 of the worksheet. Columns A through I have remained the same.

Either the keyboard or the mouse can be used to quickly scroll a worksheet to see an area that is not currently in view. Again, both methods are useful depending upon what you are doing. The keys and mouse procedures shown in the table that follows can be used to move around the worksheet. In addition, if you hold down the arrow keys, the Alt + Page Down or Alt + Page Up keys, or the Page Up or Page Down keys, you can quickly scroll through the worksheet. As you scroll the worksheet using the keyboard, the cell selector moves to the new location. When you use the mouse and the scroll bar, however, the cell selector does not move until you click on a cell that is visible in the window.

Entering Data

As you can see, the budget contains both descriptive text entries and numeric data. These are the two types of entries you can make in a worksheet.

Concept 2: Types of Entries

The information or data you enter in a cell can be text, numbers, or formulas. **Text** entries can contain any combination of letters, numbers, spaces, and any other special characters. **Number** entries can include only the digits 0 to 9, and any of the special characters, + – ( ) , . / $ % E e. Number entries are used in calculations. An entry that begins with an equal sign (=) is a **formula**. Formula entries perform calculations using numbers or data contained in other cells. The resulting value is a **variable** value because it can change if the data it depends on changes. In contrast, a number entry is a **constant** value. It does not begin with an equal sign and does not change unless you change it directly by typing in another entry.

First you will enter the worksheet headings. Row and column **headings** are entries that are used to create the structure of the worksheet and describe other worksheet entries. Generally, headings are text entries. The column headings in this worksheet consist of the six months (January through June) and a total (sum of entries over six months) located in columns B through H. To enter data in a worksheet, you must first select the cell where you want the entry displayed. The column heading for January will be entered in cell B2.

- Move to B2.
- Type J.

Your worksheet should be similar to Figure 1-5.

FIGURE 1-5

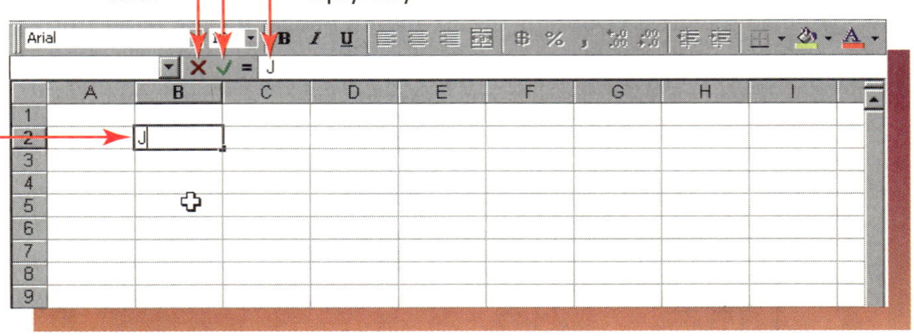

Several changes have occurred in the window. As you type, the entry is displayed both in the active cell and in the formula bar. An insertion point appears in the active cell and marks your location in the entry. Two new buttons, Cancel and Enter, appear in the formula bar. They can be used by the mouse to complete your entry or cancel it.

Notice also that the mode displayed in the status bar has changed from "Ready" to "Enter." This notifies you that the current mode of operation in the worksheet is entering data. To continue entering the heading,

- Type **anuary**.

If you made an error while typing the entry, use Backspace to erase the characters back to the error. Then retype the entry correctly.

Although the entry is displayed in both the active cell and the formula bar, you need to press the ←Enter key or click ✓ to complete your entry. If you press Esc or click ✗, the entry is cleared and nothing appears in the cell. Since your hands are already on the keyboard, it is quicker to press ←Enter than it is to use the mouse to click ✓.

- Press ←Enter.

Your worksheet should be similar to Figure 1-6.

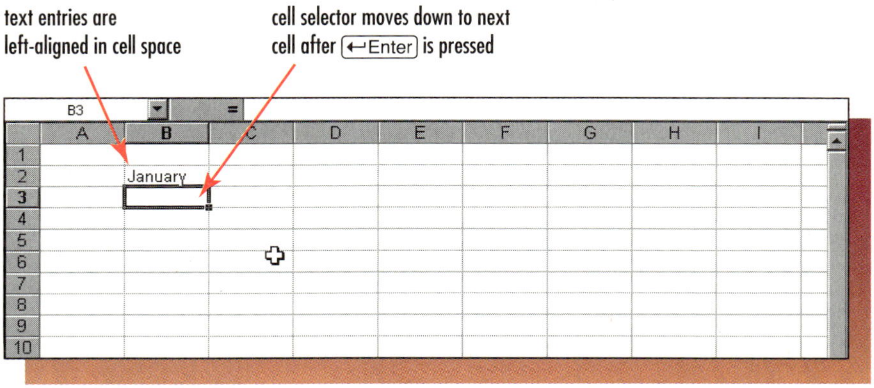

FIGURE 1-6

The entry "January" is displayed in cell B2, and the mode has returned to Ready. Notice that the entry is positioned to the left side of the cell space. The positioning of cell entries in the cell space is called alignment. By default text entries are displayed left-aligned. You will learn more about this feature later in the lab.

Pressing ←Enter also moves the cell selector down one cell.

Pressing ⇧Shift + ←Enter to complete an entry moves the cell selector up a cell, and Ctrl + ←Enter completes the entry without moving the cell selector.

Clearing an Entry

After looking at the entry, you decide you want the column headings to be in row 3 rather than in row 2. This will leave more space above the column headings for a worksheet title.

The Delete key can be used to clear the contents from a cell. To remove the entry from cell B2 and enter it in cell B3,

The menu equivalent is Edit/Clear/Contents. Clear Contents is also an option on the Shortcut menu.

- Move to B2.
- Press Delete.
- Move to B3.
- Type **January**.
- Click ✓.

The cell selector remains in the active cell when you use ✓ to complete an entry. Also notice, because the cell selector is positioned on a cell containing an entry, the contents of the cell are displayed in the formula bar.

Editing an Entry

You would like to change the heading from January to JAN. An entry in a cell can be entirely changed in the Ready mode or partially changed or edited in the Edit mode. To use the Ready mode, you move the cell selector to the cell you want to change and retype the entry the way you want it to appear. As soon as a new character is entered, the existing entry is cleared.

Pressing the F2 key will also change to Edit mode.

Generally, however, if you need to change only a part of an entry, it is quicker to use the Edit mode. To change to Edit mode, double-click on the cell whose contents you want to edit.

The mouse pointer must be ✣ when you double-click on the cell.

■ Double-click B3.

Your worksheet should be similar to Figure 1-7.

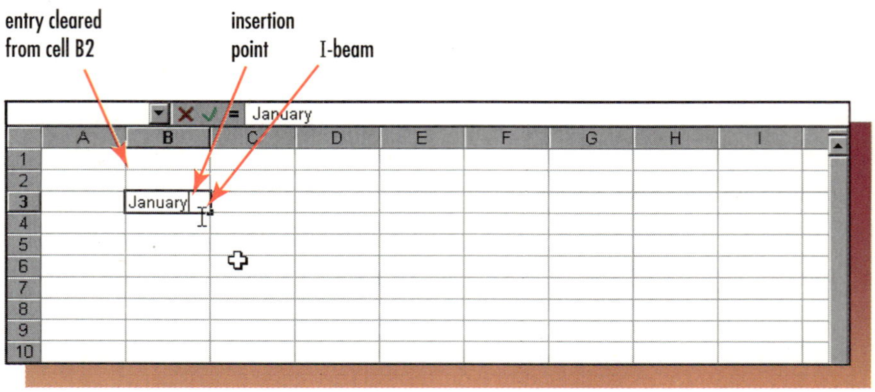

FIGURE 1-7

Excel automatically corrects common spelling errors as you type.

The status bar shows the new mode of operation is Edit. The insertion point appears in the entry, and the mouse pointer changes to an I-beam I when positioned on the cell. The mouse pointer can now be used to move the insertion point in the entry by positioning the I-beam and clicking.

In addition, in the Edit mode, the following keys can be used to move the insertion point:

Key	Action
Home	Moves insertion point to beginning of entry
End	Moves insertion point to end of entry
→	Moves insertion point one character right
←	Moves insertion point one character left

Once the insertion point is appropriately positioned, you can edit the entry by removing the incorrect characters and typing the correct characters. The Delete key erases characters at the insertion point, and the ←Backspace key erases characters to the left of the insertion point. To change this entry to JAN,

- If necessary, move the insertion point to the end of the entry.
- Press ←Backspace (4 times).
- Press Home.
- Press Caps Lock.
- Press →.
- Press Insert.
- Type **AN**.
- Press ←Enter.
- Press Caps Lock.

the insertion point is a highlight when overwrite is on

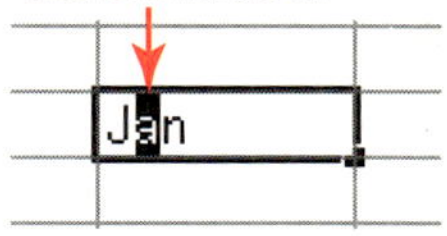

The new heading JAN is entered into cell B3, replacing January. As you can see, editing will be particularly useful with long or complicated entries.

Next you will enter the month heading for February in cell C3. You can also complete an entry by moving to any other worksheet cell. To try this,

- Move to C3.
- Type **February**.
- Press → or click D3.
- Using Edit mode, change February to FEB.
- Complete the column headings by entering MAR, APR, MAY, JUN, and TOTAL in cells D3 through H3.
- When you are done, turn off Caps Lock.

Above the column headings, in row 2, you want to enter a title for the worksheet.

- Move to C2.
- Type **1999 First Half Budget**.
- Press ←Enter.

Ctrl + Delete will delete everything to the right of the insertion point.

The Caps Lock key produces uppercase characters when on.

The Insert key acts as a toggle to switch between inserting and overwriting text.

Overwrite is automatically turned off when you leave Edit mode or if you press Insert again.

Your worksheet should be similar to Figure 1-8.

FIGURE 1-8

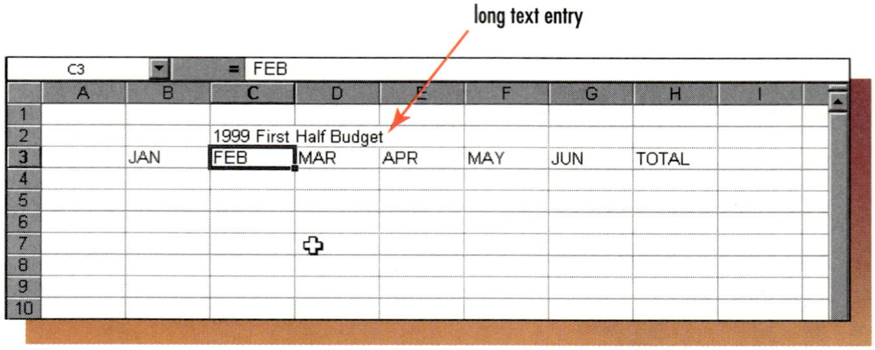

When a text entry is longer than the cell's column width, Excel will display as much of the entry as it can. If the cell to the right is empty, the whole entry will be displayed. If the cell to the right contains an entry, the overlapping part of the entry is not displayed.

Next the row headings need to be entered into column A of the worksheet. The row headings and what they represent are shown below:

Heading	Represents
SALES	Category head for all items that are a result of sales
Clothing	Income from clothing sales
Hard Goods	Income from equipment, machines, and miscellaneous sales
Total Sales	Sum of clothing and hard goods sales
EXPENSES	Category head for all items that are a result of expenses
Advertising	Monthly advertising costs (4 percent of total sales)
Cost of Goods	Cost of items sold (58 percent of total sales)
Salary	Personnel expenses
Lease	Monthly lease expense
Miscellaneous	Monthly expenses for phone, electricity, water, trash removal, and so on
Overhead	Monthly payment to corporate headquarters
Total Expenses	Sum of advertising, cost of goods, salary, lease, miscellaneous, and overhead expenses
INCOME	Total Sales minus Total Expenses

- Complete the row headings for the SALES portion of the worksheet by entering the following headings in the indicated cells:

Cell	Heading
A4	**SALES**
A5	**Clothing**
A6	**Hard Goods**
A7	**Total Sales**

> Remember to press ←Enter or an arrow key to complete the last entry.

Your worksheet should be similar to Figure 1-9.

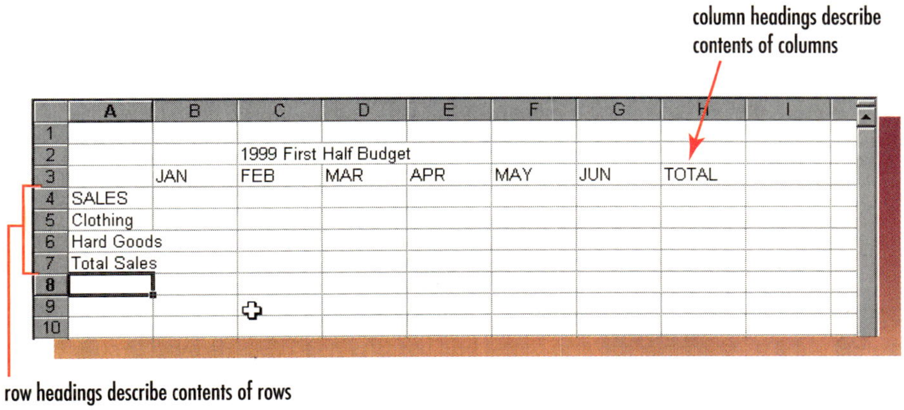

FIGURE 1-9

Entering Numbers

Next you will enter the expected clothing sales numbers for January through June into cells B5 through G5. As you learned earlier, number entries can include the digits 0 to 9 and any of these special characters: + – ( ), . / $ % E e. When entering numbers, it is not necessary to type the comma to separate thousands or the currency ($) symbol. You will learn about adding these symbols later.

To enter the expected clothing sales for January,

> Refer to Concept 2: Types of Entries.

- Move to B5.
- Type **140000**.
- Press →.

> You can use the number keys above the alphabetic keys or the numeric keypad area to enter numbers. If you use the numeric keypad, the Num Lock key must be on.

The Open dialog box on your screen should be similar to Figure 1-12.

FIGURE 1-12

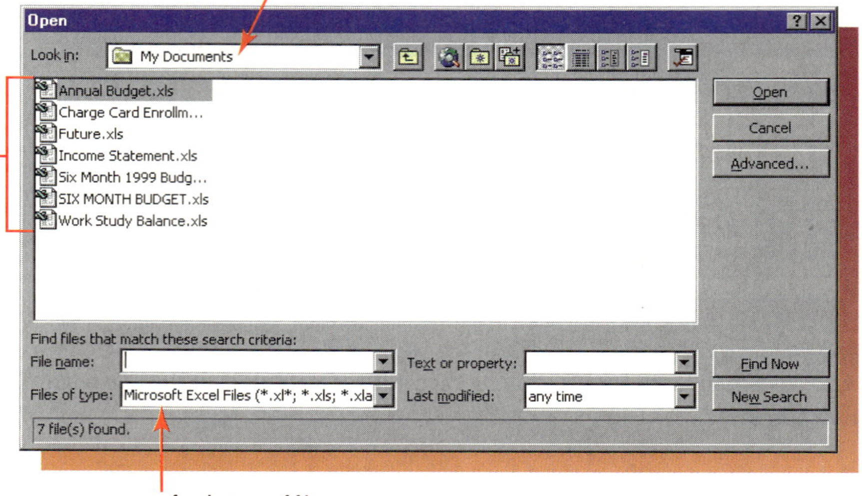

This dialog box is used to specify the name and location of the file to open. You may need to change the location shown in the Look In drop-down list box to the drive containing your data disk. If necessary,

> If your drive is already correctly specified in the Look In list box, skip this step.

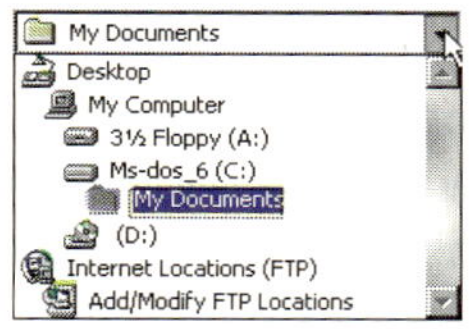

- Select Look in.
- Select 3½ Floppy (A:) (or the drive containing your data disk).

> If an error message is displayed, check that your disk is properly inserted in the drive.

Now the file list area of the dialog box displays the names of the Excel files on your data disk. The file you want to open is January Data. The file name extension .xls identifies this file as an Excel workbook file. If there are other types of files on your data disk, they are not listed. This is because the Files of Type list box shows the currently selected type is Excel files.

> If your screen does not display file extensions, your Windows 95 program has this option deactivated.

> If necessary, scroll the list box until the file name January Data is visible. If the file name is not displayed, ask your instructor for help.

- Select January Data.
- Click Open.

> You can double-click on the file name to both select it and choose Open.

The new workbook file is loaded and displayed in the workbook window.

- Move to A18.

Your screen should be similar to Figure 1-13.

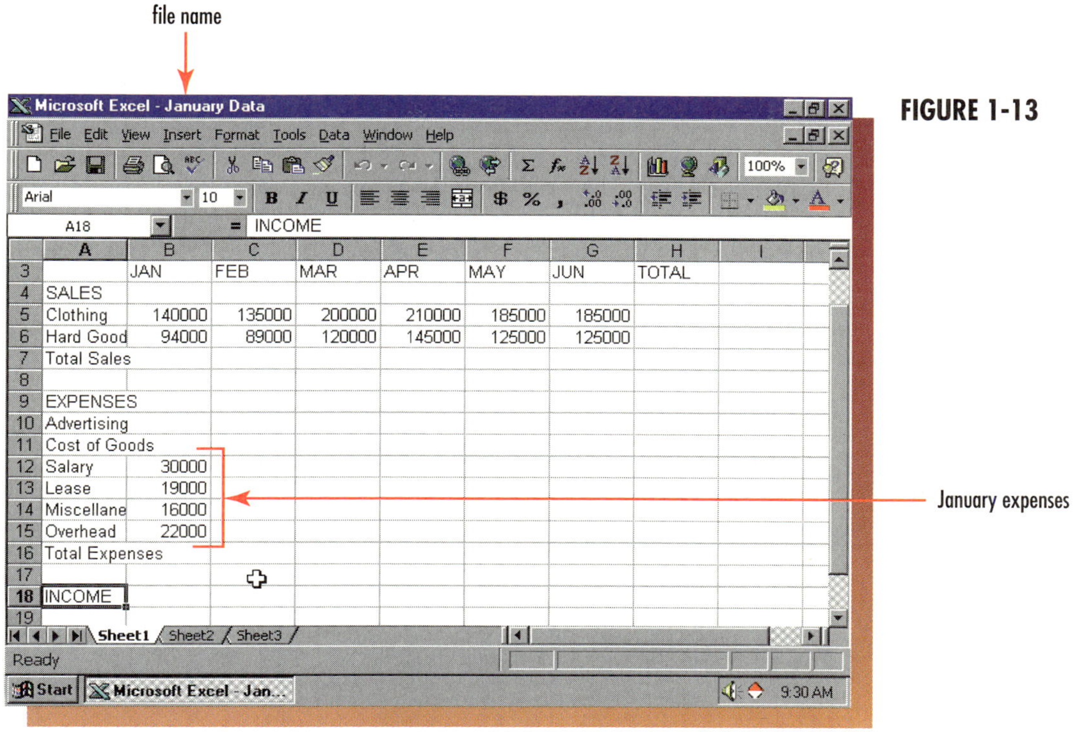

FIGURE 1-13

The opened workbook, January Data, contains the expense row headings and numbers for salary, lease, miscellaneous, and overhead for the month of January.

Note: If you are stopping at the end of Part 1, follow the instructions on page SS40 to exit the program. When you begin Part 2, load Excel and open the January Data file.

Part 2

Copying Data

Next you want to enter the estimated expenses for salary, lease, miscellaneous, and overhead for February through June. They are the same as the January expense numbers.

When you entered the sales numbers for January through June, you entered them individually into each cell because the numbers changed from month to month. However, the number in cell B12 is the same number that needs to be entered in cells C12 through G12. You could type the same amount into each month, or you can copy the number in B12 into the other cells.

Concept 3: Copy and Move Cell Contents

The contents of worksheet cells can be moved by cutting them and then pasting them in a new location in the worksheet. They can also be duplicated (copied) and pasted. When you cut or copy cell contents, the contents are stored in the Clipboard. Then when they are pasted to the new location, the Clipboard contents are copied into the selected cells. Be careful when pasting to the new location because any existing entries will be replaced.

The Clipboard is a temporary storage area in your computer's memory.

There are several methods you can use to copy entries in a worksheet. One method is to use the Copy and Paste commands on the Edit menu or their toolbar shortcuts. To use the Copy command, you first must select the cell or cells containing the data to be copied. This is called the **copy area** or **source**.

To copy the value in cell B12,

The menu equivalent is Edit/Copy and the shortcut key is Ctrl + C. Copy is also an option on the Shortcut menu.

- Move to B12.
- Click Copy.

Your screen should be similar to Figure 1-14.

FIGURE 1-14

Copy button

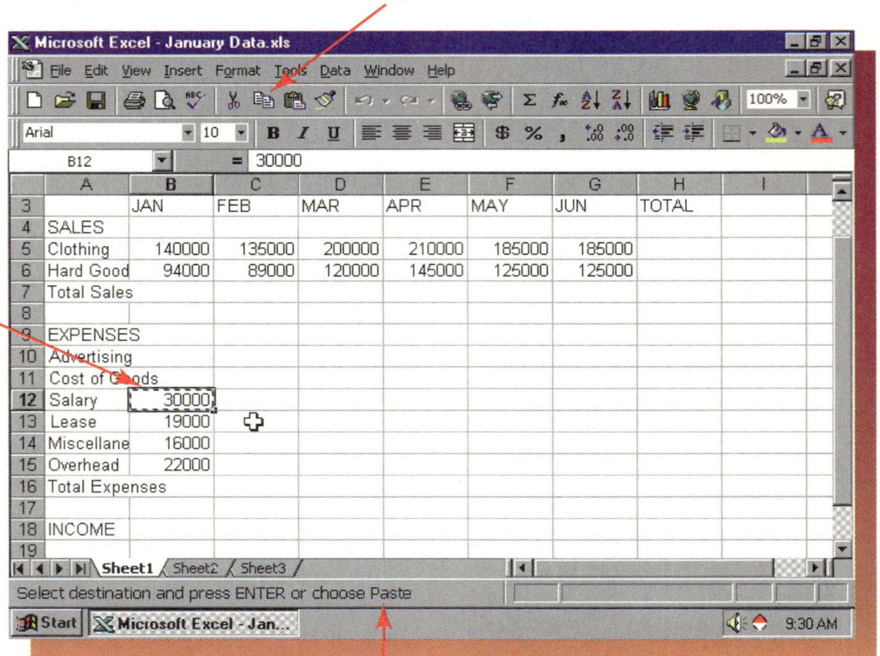

The moving border indicates the source has been copied to the Clipboard

Status bar displays instructions on how to complete the command

The instructions displayed in the status bar tell you to select a **destination**, also called the **paste area**, where you want the contents copied. To specify cell C12 as the destination,

- Move to C12.
- Click [Paste button] Paste.

> While the moving border is still displayed, you can also simply press ←Enter to paste. However, because using this method clears the contents of the Clipboard immediately, it can only be used once. You can cancel the moving border by pressing Esc.

> The menu equivalent is Edit/Paste and the shortcut key is Ctrl + V. Paste is also an option on the Shortcut menu.

Your worksheet should be similar to Figure 1-15.

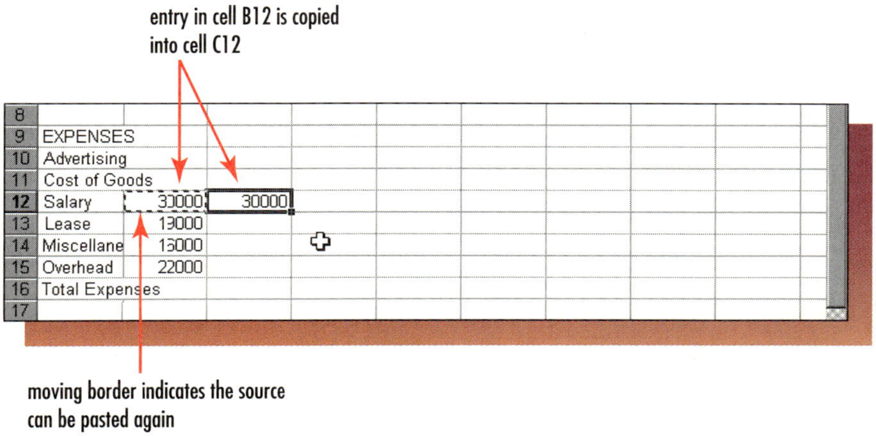

FIGURE 1-15

To complete the data for the Salary row, you could continue to paste the contents of Clipboard into the cells one after another. Instead, it is much faster to select a paste area that consists of multiple cells, called a range, and paste the contents to all cells in the selection at once.

Concept 4: Range

A selection consisting of two or more cells is a **range**. The cells in a range can be adjacent or nonadjacent. An **adjacent range** is a rectangular block of adjoining cells. In the example shown below, the shaded areas show examples of valid and invalid adjacent ranges. A **nonadjacent range** is two or more selected cells or ranges that are not adjoining. If all the valid ranges in the example were selected at the same time, they would be a non-adjacent range.

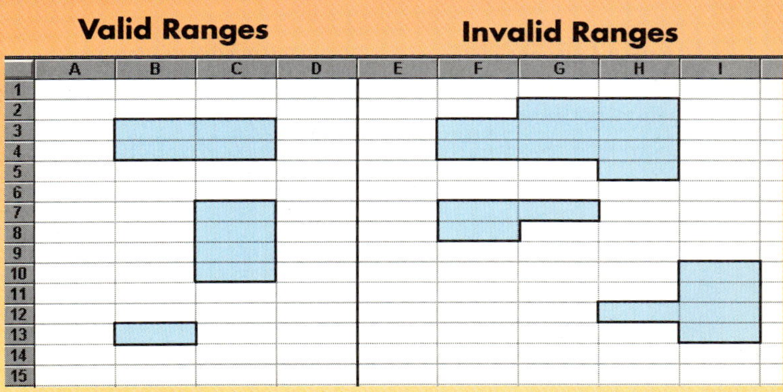

You can also hold down ⇧Shift and use the directional keys to select a range.

The paste area does not have to be adjacent to the copy area.

To complete the data for the Salary row, you want to copy the Clipboard contents to the range of cells D12 through G12. To select a range, drag the mouse from one corner of the range to the other.

- Select cells D12 to G12.
- Click Paste.

Your worksheet should be similar to Figure 1-16.

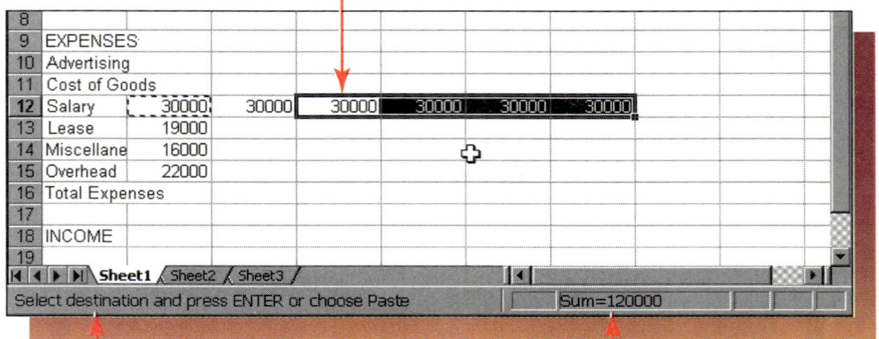

FIGURE 1-16

You can display the average or count of numbers in a selection by choosing from the AutoCalculate button's Shortcut menu.

The paste area range selection will clear as soon as you select another cell.

Ctrl + R is the keyboard shortcut to fill to the right, and Ctrl + D to fill down.

If a range is not selected, the contents of the cell to the left or above are copied into the active cell.

Next you will copy the January lease expense to cells C13 through G13. Another way to copy is to use the Fill command on the Edit menu. This command requires that the destination range be adjacent to the source and that the entire range is selected before the command is used. You then specify the direction to fill from the Fill Command submenu. You will fill to the right.

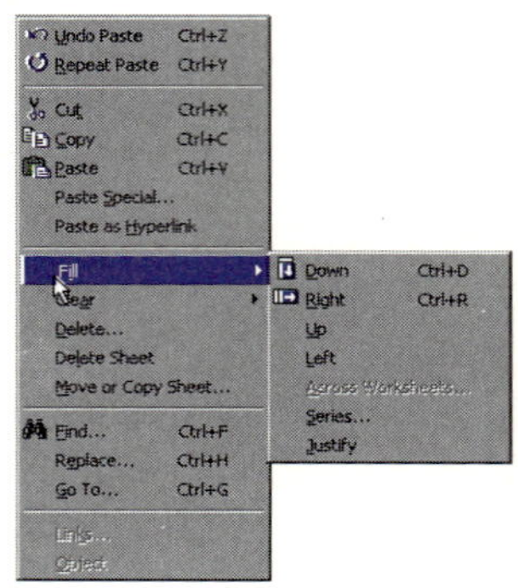

- Select cells B13 through G13.
- Choose Edit/Fill/Right.

The selected range of cells to the right of the active cell is filled with the same value as in the active cell. The Fill command does not copy the source to the Clipboard; therefore, you cannot paste the source multiple times.

Finally, the numbers for the miscellaneous and overhead expenses (cells B14 and B15) need to be copied to February through June (C14 through G15). A shortcut for the Fill command is to drag the **fill handle**, the black box in the lower right corner of the selection.

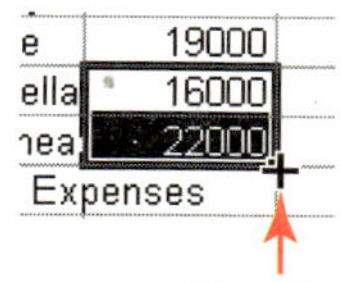

- Select the source range B14 through B15.
- Point to the fill handle, and when the mouse pointer is a +, drag the mouse to extend the selection to cells B14 through G15.
- Release the mouse button.

Your worksheet should be similar to Figure 1-17.

FIGURE 1-17

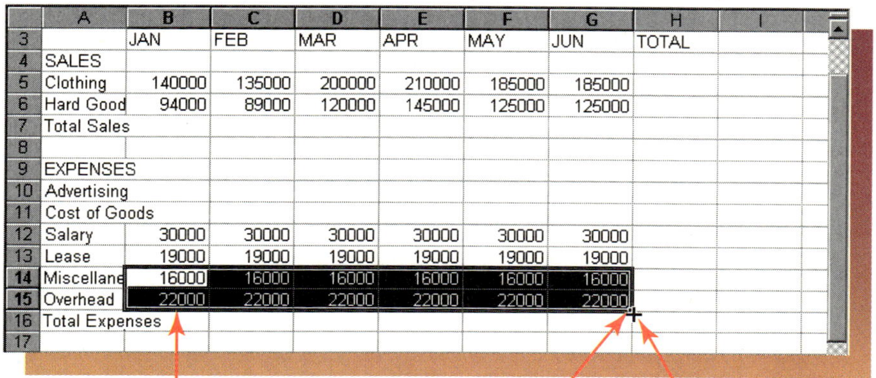

Review of Copying Methods

To review, you have learned two methods to copy an entry:

1. Use the Copy and Paste commands: Edit/Copy (Ctrl + C) or [Copy button] and Edit/Paste (Ctrl + V) or [Paste button].
2. Use the Edit/Fill command: Right, Left, Up, or Down or drag the fill handle.

When you use the Copy command, the contents are copied to the Clipboard and can be copied to any location in the worksheet, another workbook, or another application. When you use Edit/Fill or drag the fill handle, the destination must be in the same row or column as the source, and the source is not copied to the Clipboard.

Entering Formulas

The remaining entries that need to be made in the worksheet are formula entries.

Concept 5: Formulas

A formula is an entry that performs a calculation. The result of the calculation is displayed in the cell containing the formula. A formula always begins with an equal sign (=), which defines it as a numeric entry. Formulas use the following arithmetic operators to specify the type of numeric operation to perform:

+	for addition
–	for subtraction
/	for division
*	for multiplication
^	for exponentiation

In a formula that contains more than one operator, Excel performs the calculation in a specific order of precedence. First exponentiations are performed, then multiplications and divisions, and finally additions and subtractions. This order can be overridden by enclosing the operation you want performed first in parentheses. Excel evaluates operations in parentheses working from the innermost set of parentheses out.

For example, in the formula =5*4–3, Excel first multiplies 5 times 4 to get 20, and then subtracts 3, for a total of 17. If you enter the formula as =5*(4–3), Excel first subtracts 3 from 4 because the operation is enclosed in parentheses. Then Excel multiplies the result, 1, by 5, for a final result of 5. If two or more operators have the same order of precedence, calculations are performed in order from left to right.

The values on which a numeric formula performs a calculation are called **operands**. Numbers or cell references can be operands in a formula. Usually cell references are used, and when the numeric entries in the referenced cell(s) change, the result of the formula is automatically recalculated. You can also use single-word row and column headings in place of cell references and formulas.

The first formula you will enter will calculate the total clothing sales for January through June by summing the numbers in cells B5 through G5. You will use cell references in the formula as the operands and the + arithmetic operator to specify addition. A formula is entered in the cell where you want the calculated value to be displayed. To enter the formula in cell H5 to sum the numbers in these cells,

Cell references can be typed in either uppercase or lowercase letters. Spaces between parts of the formula are optional.

If you enter a formula incorrectly, Excel displays an error in the cell or a message box proposing a correction.

- Move to H5.
- Type =.
- Type **B5+C5+D5+E5+F5+G5**.
- Press ←Enter.
- Move to H5.

Your worksheet should be similar to Figure 1-18.

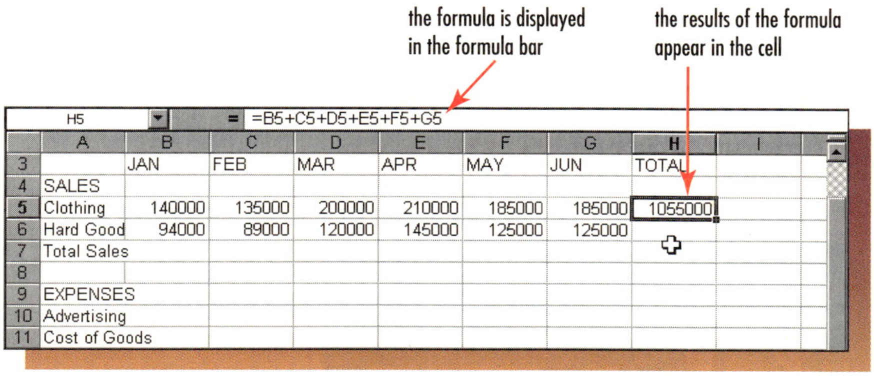

FIGURE 1-18

You will learn more about formula entries in the next lab, when you will complete the worksheet by entering the formulas to calculate the cost of goods, total sales, total expenses, and income in the worksheet.

Recalculating the Worksheet

After considering the sales estimates for the six months, you decide that the estimated clothing sales for March are too high, and you want to reduce this number from 200000 to 175000.

- Change the entry in cell D5 to 175000.

The total in cell H5 has been automatically recalculated, and the number displayed is now 1030000.

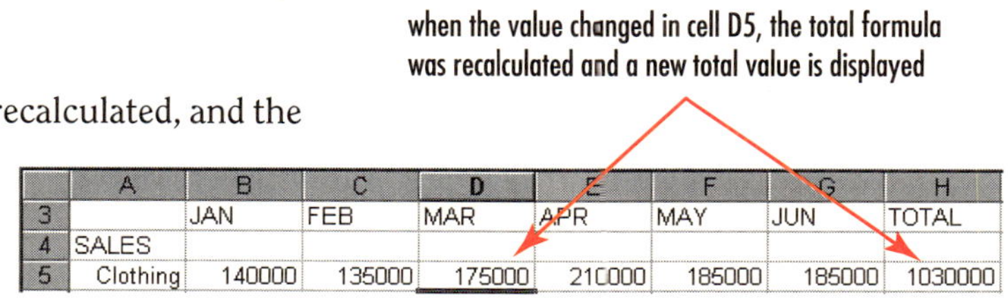

Concept 6: Automatic Recalculation

The **automatic recalculation** of a formula whenever a number in a referenced cell in the formula changes is one of the most powerful features of electronic worksheets. Only those formulas directly affected by a change in the data are recalculated. This is called **minimal recalculation**. Without this feature, in large worksheets it could take several minutes to recalculate all formulas each time a number was changed in the worksheet. The minimal recalculation feature decreases the recalculation time by only recalculating dependent formulas.

The dialog box on your screen should be similar to Figure 1-22.

FIGURE 1-22

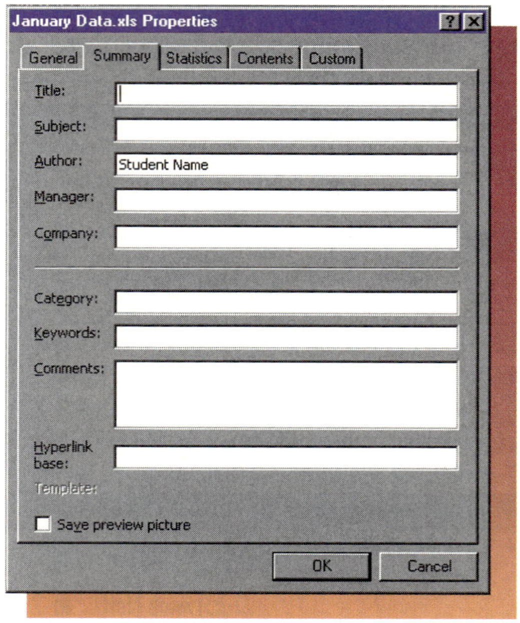

The Summary tab is used to specify information you want associated with the file such as a title, subject, author, keywords, and comments about the workbook file. This information helps you locate the workbook file you want to use as well as indicates the objectives and use of the workbook.

> The Author text box may be blank or show your school or some other name. Clear the existing contents first if necessary.

> You could also add more detailed information about the workbook in the Comments text box.

- Enter the following information in the appropriate text boxes:

  Title: **The Sports Company 1999 Budget**

  Subject: **First Half**

  Author: **[your name]**

- Click OK.

Saving a Workbook

> The button is the shortcut for File/Save.

You are now ready to save the active workbook in a file on your data disk.

While working on a document, your changes are stored in memory. Not until you **save** the document as a file on a disk are you safe from losing your work due to a power failure or other mishap. Two commands found on the File menu of all Windows programs can be used to save a file: Save and Save As. The Save command saves a document using the same path and file name by replacing the contents of the existing disk file with the changes you have made. The Save As command allows you to select the path and provide a different file name. This command lets you save both an original version of a document and a revised document as two separate files. When you save a file for the first time, either command can be used. Although most programs create automatic backup files if your work is accidentally interrupted, it is still a good idea to save your work frequently.

You will use the Save As command and save the changes you have made to the January Data file using a different file name.

- Choose File/Save As.

The dialog box on your screen should be similar to Figure 1-23.

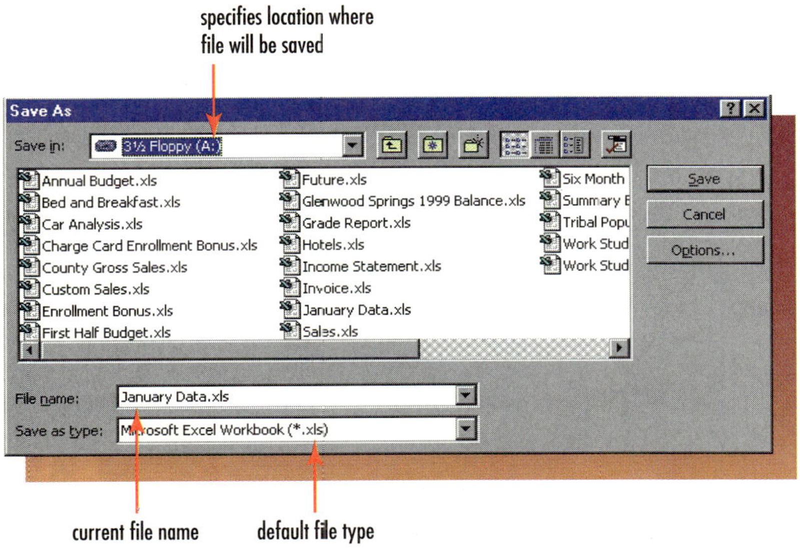

FIGURE 1-23

The Save As dialog box is used to specify the location to save the file to and the file name. The Save In list box displays the location of the current file as the location where the new file will be saved.

The file name of the file you opened, January Data, is displayed in the File Name text box. An Excel file name follows the same file name rules as other Windows 95 products. It is automatically saved with the file name extension .xls, which identifies it as a workbook file. You will save the file using a new file name.

- If the Save In location is not correct, select the appropriate location from the drop-down list.
- Replace the existing file name in the file name text box with **Six Month Budget**.
- Click Save.

The new file name is displayed in the worksheet window title bar. The worksheet data that was on your screen and in the computer's memory is now saved on your data disk in a new file called Six Month Budget.

Always save your active workbook before closing a file or leaving the Excel program. As a safeguard against losing your work if you forget to save the workbook changes, Excel will remind you to save before closing the file or exiting the program.

Previewing and Printing a Workbook

If you have printer capability, you can print a copy of the worksheet.

The shortcut key is Ctrl + P.

- If necessary, turn the printer on and check to see that it is on-line. If your printer uses continuous form-feed paper, adjust the paper so that the perforation is just above the printer scale (behind the ribbon).
- Choose File/Print.

The dialog box on your screen should be similar to Figure 1-24.

FIGURE 1-24

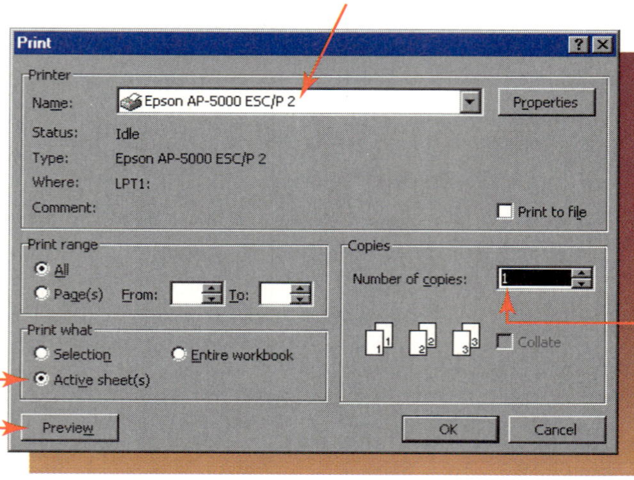

The Print dialog box is used to specify your print settings. The default print settings will print one copy of the entire worksheet. These settings are satisfactory for now. The name of the printer displayed in the Printer information area of the dialog box should be your printer.

- If you need to select a different printer, open the Name drop-down list in the Printer section and select the appropriate printer.

Before printing, you may want to preview how the worksheet will appear on the printed page. To do this,

File/Print Preview or the button will also preview the worksheet.

- Click Preview.

Your screen should be similar to Figure 1-25.

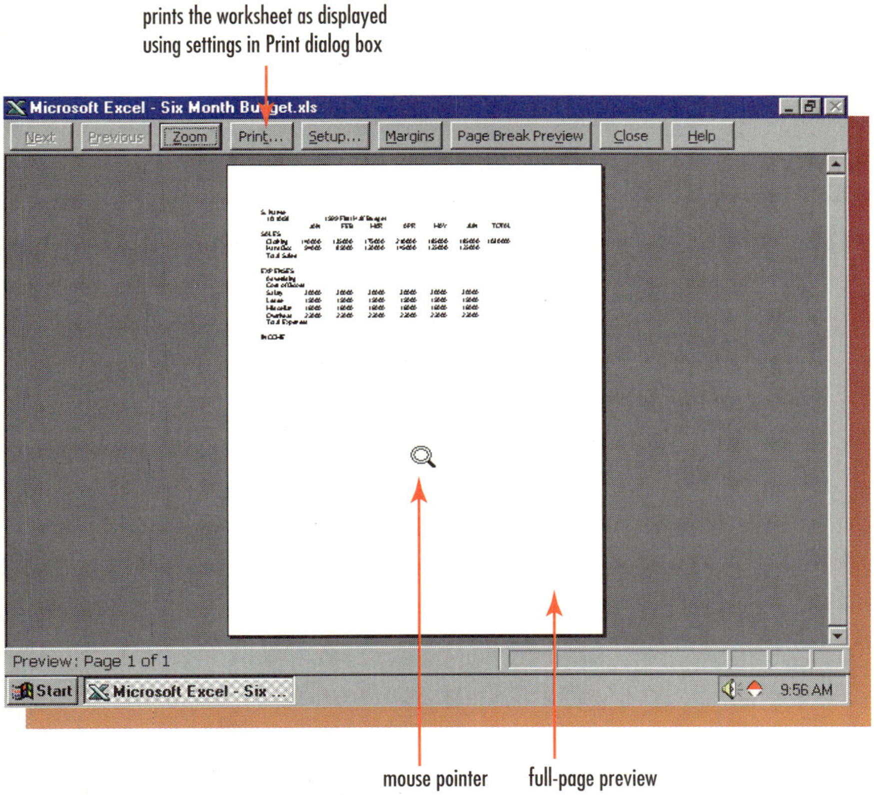

FIGURE 1-25

The Print Preview dialog box window displays the worksheet as it will appear on the printed page. This is called the full-page view, but it is difficult to read. While previewing a worksheet, you can enlarge the display to a magnified view.

- If necessary, move the mouse pointer onto the preview page.

The mouse pointer appears as a 🔍, indicating that you can switch between a full-page view and a magnified view.

- Click the worksheet title.

The area you click on is the area that will be displayed in the Preview window.

The worksheet is displayed in the actual size it will appear when printed. Notice that the row and column lines are not displayed and will not print.

To display the worksheet again in the full-page view, and then print the sheet,

- Click the worksheet.
- Click Print... .

If you do not need to change the default print settings, you can click 🖨 to print the worksheet.

Your printer should be printing out the worksheet, and your printed output should look like the figure shown in the Case Study at the beginning of the lab.

Exiting Excel

The menu equivalent is File/Exit.

If you want to quit or exit the Excel program at this time,

- Click ☒.

You have exited from the Excel program, and the Windows 95 desktop is displayed.

LAB REVIEW

Key Terms

active cell (SS10)
active sheet (SS10)
adjacent range (SS27)
alignment (SS32)
automatic recalculation (SS31)
cell (SS10)
cell selector (SS10)
column (SS9)
column letter (SS10)
constant (SS16)
copy area (SS26)
date number (SS35)
destination (SS27)
fill handle (SS29)
format (SS32)
Formatting toolbar (SS9)
formula (SS16)
formula bar (SS9)
heading (SS16)
minimal recalculation (SS31)
Name box (SS9)
nonadjacent range (SS27)
number (SS16)
Office Assistant (SS11)
operand (SS30)
paste area (SS27)
range (SS27)
reference (SS10)
row (SS9)
row number (SS10)
save (SS36)
sheet tab (SS10)
source (SS26)
spreadsheet (SS9)
Standard toolbar (SS9)
tab scroll button (SS10)
text (SS16)
variable (SS16)
workbook (SS9)
workbook window (SS9)
worksheet (SS9)
workspace (SS9)

Command Summary

Command	Shortcut	Toolbar	Action
File/Open <file name>	Ctrl + O		Opens an existing workbook file
File/Close			Closes open workbook file
File/Save <file name>	Ctrl + S		Saves current file on disk using same file name
File/Save As <file name>			Saves current file on disk using a new file name
File/Properties			Displays information about a file
File/Print Preview			Displays worksheet as it will appear when printed
File/Print	Ctrl + P		Prints a worksheet
File/Exit			Exits Excel
Edit/Copy	Ctrl + C		Copies selected data to Clipboard
Edit/Paste	Ctrl + V		Pastes selections stored in Clipboard
Edit/Fill			Fills selected cells with contents of source cell
Edit/Clear/Contents	Delete		Clears cell contents
View/Toolbars			Displays/hides selected toolbars
Format/Cells/Alignment/Horizontal/Left (Indent)			Left-aligns entry in cell space
Format/Cells/Alignment/Horizontal/Center			Center-aligns entry in cell space
Format/Cells/Alignment/Horizontal/Right			Right-aligns entry in cell space
Format/Cells/Horizontal/Left (Indent)/1			Left-aligns and indents cell entry one space

Matching

1. source ________ **a.** right-aligns cell entry
2. * ________ **b.** moves cell selector to upper left corner of worksheet
3. ________ **c.** the cell you copy from
4. Ctrl + Home ________ **d.** two or more worksheet cells
5. .xls ________ **e.** a cell reference
6. F2 ________ **f.** displays current cell entry
7. =C19+A21 ________ **g.** an arithmetic operator
8. range ________ **h.** accesses Edit mode
9. D11 ________ **i.** a formula summing two cells
10. formula bar ________ **j.** Excel workbook file name extension

Fill-In Questions

1. In the following worksheet, several items are identified by letters. Enter the correct term for each item in the spaces that follow.

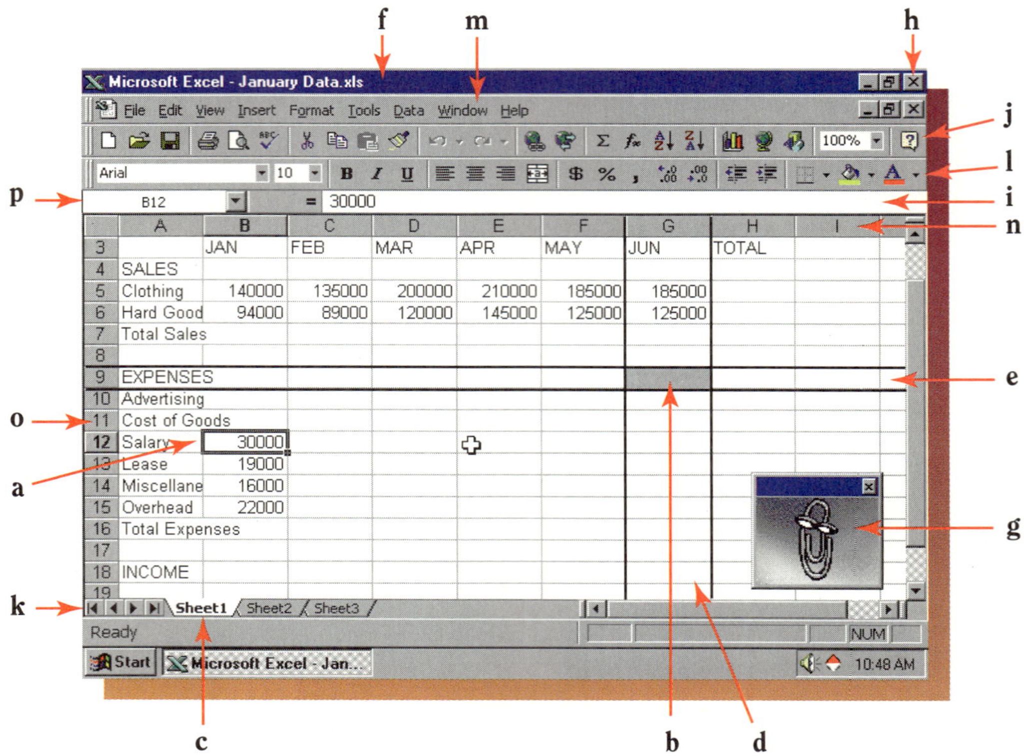

a. ______________________

b. ______________________

c. ______________________

d. ______________________

e. ______________________

f. ______________________

g. ______________________

h. ______________________

i. ______________________

j. ______________________

k. ______________________

l. ______________________

m. ______________________

n. ______________________

o. ______________________

p. ______________________

2. Complete the following statements by filling in the blanks with the correct terms.

a. The ____________________ occupies the center of the Excel window and can display multiple windows.

b. The worksheet displays a rectangular grid of _______ and ______________.

c. A(n) ____________________ consists of two or more worksheet cells.

d. The intersection of a row and column creates a(n)________________.

e. _________ are text entries that are used to create the structure of the worksheet.

f. By default, text entries are ______________ -aligned and number entries are ____________ -aligned.

g. A(n) ____________________ consists of the column letter and row number used to identify a cell.

h. A(n) ______________ is an entry that performs a calculation.

i. ____________________ is the recalculation of only those formulas in the worksheet that are directly affected by a change of data.

j. ___________________ control how information is displayed in a cell.

Discussion Questions

1. Discuss why it is important to design a worksheet before you begin entering actual data into it.

2. What types of entries are used in worksheets? Discuss the uses of each type of entry.

3. Discuss how formulas are created. Why are they the power behind worksheets?

4. Discuss the formatting features presented in the lab. Why are they important to the look of the worksheet?

Hands-On Practice Exercises

For all exercises, go to cell A1 before you save the workbook. That way, the next time you open the workbook, the cell selector will be at the top of the worksheet.

Step by Step

Rating System
☆ Easy
☆☆ Moderate
☆☆☆ Difficult

☆

1. Open the workbook file Bed and Breakfast on your data disk. Scott and Toni have researched several bed and breakfast inns for a family trip to New England. This worksheet lists the inns they are considering and occupancy rates for single and double rooms with private or shared baths. Follow the directions below to modify the worksheet.

a. Change the first word in the title to uppercase.

b. Correct the names of the inns so that only the first letter of each word is in uppercase. Similarly, correct the names of the cities and make sure they are all left-aligned.

c. Center cells E3 through H3 and cell E4, and make sure all worksheet numbers are right-aligned. Indent the names of the bed and breakfast inns in column A.

d. Copy the state abbreviation "Conn" in cell D5 to cells D6 through D8. Copy the word "Bath" from cell E4 to the three adjacent cells (F4 through H4) to the right. What else was copied with the text?

e. Enter the state name "Maine" in cell D14. What happened after you typed the first three letters? Use the Office Assistant to obtain information on this feature by asking about repeated entries. Then, from the Help topic "Enter data in worksheet cells," read the information on the topic, "Quickly fill in repeated entries in a column."

Your corrected worksheet will look like the worksheet below.

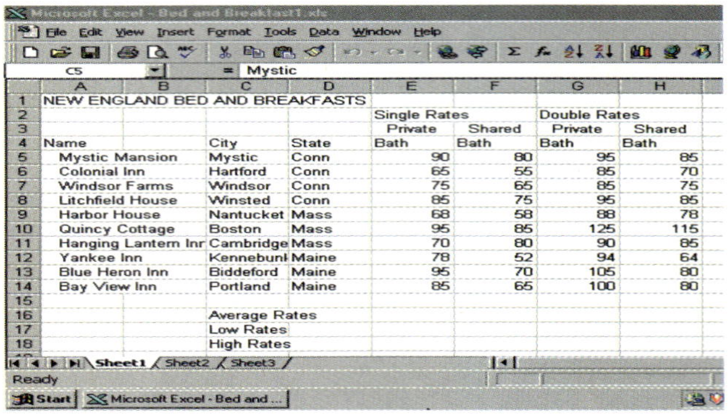

	A	B	C	D	E	F	G	H
1	NEW ENGLAND BED AND BREAKFASTS							
2					Single Rates		Double Rates	
3					Private	Shared	Private	Shared
4	Name		City	State	Bath	Bath	Bath	Bath
5	Mystic Mansion		Mystic	Conn	90	80	95	85
6	Colonial Inn		Hartford	Conn	65	55	85	70
7	Windsor Farms		Windsor	Conn	75	65	85	75
8	Litchfield House		Winsted	Conn	85	75	95	85
9	Harbor House		Nantucket	Mass	68	58	88	78
10	Quincy Cottage		Boston	Mass	95	85	125	115
11	Hanging Lantern Inr		Cambridge	Mass	70	80	90	85
12	Yankee Inn		Kennebunl	Maine	78	52	94	64
13	Blue Heron Inn		Biddeford	Maine	95	70	105	80
14	Bay View Inn		Portland	Maine	85	65	100	80
15								
16			Average Rates					
17			Low Rates					
18			High Rates					

f. Enter your name and the current date on separate rows below the worksheet.

g. Move to cell A1. Use the Properties dialog box to document the workbook. Save and replace the workbook file Bed and Breakfast. Preview and print the worksheet.

You will complete this exercise as Practice Exercise 1 in Lab 2.

☆☆

2. You are the owner of The Cookie Jar, a shop that sells gourmet cookies by the pound. You are interested in tracking first quarter sales for each type of cookie.

a. Create the worksheet as shown below.

	A	B	C	D	E	F	G
1	The Cookie Jar						
2							
3	Type			Jan	Feb	Mar	Total
4	Chocolate Chip			1800	1825	1835	
5	Chocolate Chip w/ Nuts			1430	1425	1390	
6	White Chocolate Macadamia			1220	1250	1295	
7	Butterscotch			750	775	800	
8	Peanut Butter			1000	1050	975	
9	Oatmeal Raisin			450	375	415	
10	Gingerbread			530	535	500	
11	Total						
12							

b. Right-align the month and total headings in row 3. Indent the types of cookies in column A.

c. Calculate a total for chocolate chip cookies only.

d. Enter your name and the current date on separate rows below the worksheet.

e. Move to A1. Use the Properties dialog box to document the workbook. Save the workbook as Cookie Jar. Preview and print the worksheet.

You will complete this exercise as Practice Exercise 2 in Lab 2.

☆☆

3. Laura is changing her eating habits to include foods that obtain no more than 30 percent of their calories from fat. She has listed several of her favorite "diet" snack foods and decides to calculate the percent of fat for each one. Complete the following steps to help Laura with her task.

a. Create the worksheet as shown below.

	A	B	C	D	E	F	G
1	Food			Fat Grams	Calories	% Fat	
2	Bagel			1	240		
3	Lite Cream Cheese			5	60		
4	Peanut Butter (25% Less Fat)			13	190		
5	Saltine Crackers			1.5	60		
6	Lite Pop Corn			2	40		
7	Cholesterol Free Potato Chips			6	130		
8	Lite Frozen Fudge Pops			1.2	35		
9	Pretzels			1	110		
10							

Next you want to enter a formula to calculate the percent of fat. Each gram of fat contains nine calories. To calculate the percent of fat, multiply fat grams by nine and divide that product by the number of calories.

b. In cell F2, enter the formula =D2*9/E2 to calculate the percent of fat for bagels. Then calculate the percent of fat for lite cream cheese. Are bagels and lite cream cheese a good snack for Laura?

c. Right-align the headings in columns E and F. Indent the foods in column A.

d. Enter your name and the current date on separate rows below the worksheet.

e. Move to A1. Use the Properties dialog box to document the workbook. Save the workbook as Fat Grams. Preview and print the worksheet.

You will continue this exercise as Practice Exercise 3 in Lab 2.

☆☆

4. Open the workbook file Invoice on your data disk. You are an employee of The Office Center, a discount office super store. You recently sold computer equipment to a new computer training facility. Follow the directions below to complete the transaction with the customer.

a. Replace The Office Center address with your address information, and enter the current date in the appropriate cell.

b. Make changes you feel are necessary to improve the appearance of the invoice.

c. Enter a formula to calculate a total for the Pentium computers only.

d. Enter your name below the worksheet.

Your modified worksheet will look similar to the worksheet below.

	A	B	C	D	E	F	G	H	I
1	The Office Center						Invoice #	11001	
2	Street Address						Date:	[Current Date]	
3	City, State, and Zip Code								
4									
5	Customer:	Lionel Computer Training							
6		123 Main St.							
7		Greenwich, CT 06830							
8									
9	Qty	Description			Price	Total			
10	15	Pentium-75 MHz Computers			1975	29625			
11	15	Ergonomic Mice			34.95				
12	15	Mouse Pads			4.75				
13	3	Laser Printers			850				
14	5	Power Strips			30				
15	15	Desk Chairs			95.99				
16	6	Tables			300				
17					Subtotal:				
18					State Tax:				
19					Total:				

e. Move to cell A1. Use the Properties dialog box to document the workbook. Save and replace the workbook file Invoice. Preview and print the worksheet.

You will continue this exercise as Practice Exercise 4 in Lab 2.

On Your Own

☆☆☆

5. Open the file Income Statement on your data disk. Custom Manufacturing Company is drawing up a budgeted income statement for the next year. Sales amounts reflect past trends. Cost of goods sold is traditionally 60 percent of sales, variable costs are 15 percent of sales, and fixed costs are budgeted at $1,500 a month for the first half of the year. Other calculations are performed as follows:

Gross Profit = Sales – Cost of Goods Sold
Contribution Margin = Gross Profit – Variable Costs
Income = Contribution Margin – Fixed Costs
Income Tax Expense = 40% of Income Before Taxes
Net Income = Income Before Taxes – Income Tax Expense

Use the above information to calculate net income for the month of January only. Appropriately align the month and total headings in row 5. Enter your name and the current date on separate rows below the worksheet. Document the worksheet and save it as Income Statement. Preview and print the worksheet. Your modified worksheet will look similar to the worksheet below.

	A	B	C	D	E	F	G	H
1	Custom Manufacturing Company							
2	Budgeted Income Statement							
3	For the Year Ending December 31, 1997							
4								
5			Jan	Feb	Mar	Apr	May	
6	Sales		80000	65000	80000	100000	120000	125
7	Cost of Goods Sold		48000					
8	Gross Profit		32000					
9	Variable Costs		12000					
10	Contribution Margin		20000					
11	Fixed Costs		1500					
12	Income Before Taxes		18500					
13	Income Tax Expense		7400					
14	Net Income		11100					
15								

You will continue this exercise as Practice Exercise 5 in Lab 2.

☆☆☆

6. Obtain an IRS Form 1040EZ. Use Excel to create a worksheet for an IRS Form 1040EZ. Enter formulas to perform the necessary calculations. Change the values you entered to see how the refund or amount you owe is affected by increases and decreases to total wages and other amounts you adjust. Move to A1. Use the Properties dialog box to document the workbook. Save the workbook file as IRS Form 1040EZ, and preview and print the worksheet.

Concept Summary

Creating a Worksheet: Part 1

Worksheet Design

A well-designed worksheet produces accurate results, and is clearly understood, adaptable, and efficient.

Types of Entries

The information or data you enter in a cell can be text, numbers, or formulas.

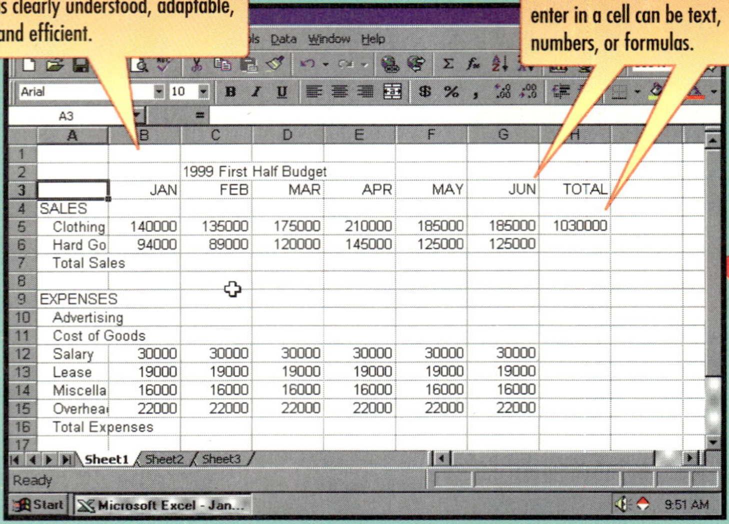

Concepts

- Worksheet Design
- Types of Entries

- Copy and Move Cell Contents
- Range

- Formulas
- Automatic Recalculation

- Format
- Alignment
- Dates

Formulas

A formula is an entry that performs a calculation.

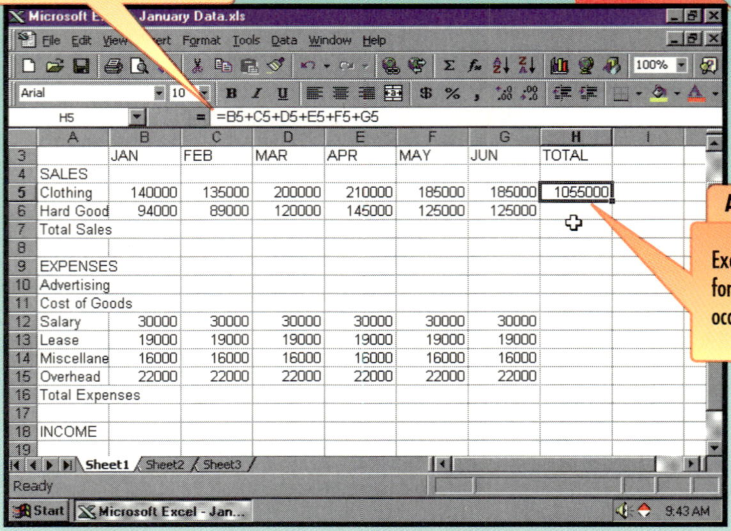

Automatic Recalculation

Excel automatically recalculates formulas whenever a change occurs in a referenced cell.

Copy and Move Cell Contents

The contents of worksheet cells can be copied or moved to new locations in the worksheet.

Range

A selection consisting of two or more cells on a worksheet is a range.

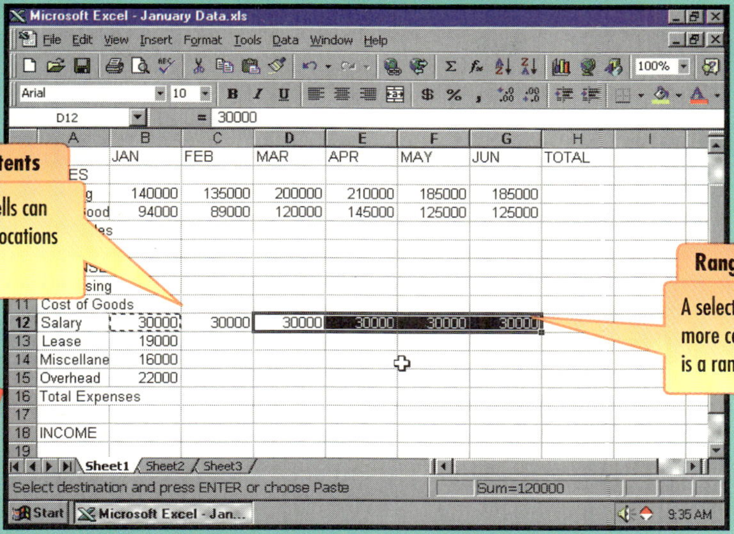

Dates

Excel automatically recognizes certain types of data input, such as dates and times, and formats the entry as appropriate.

Alignment

Alignment settings allow you to change the horizontal and vertical placement and the orientation of an entry in a cell.

Format

Formats control how information is displayed in a cell and are used to improve the appearance of the worksheet data.

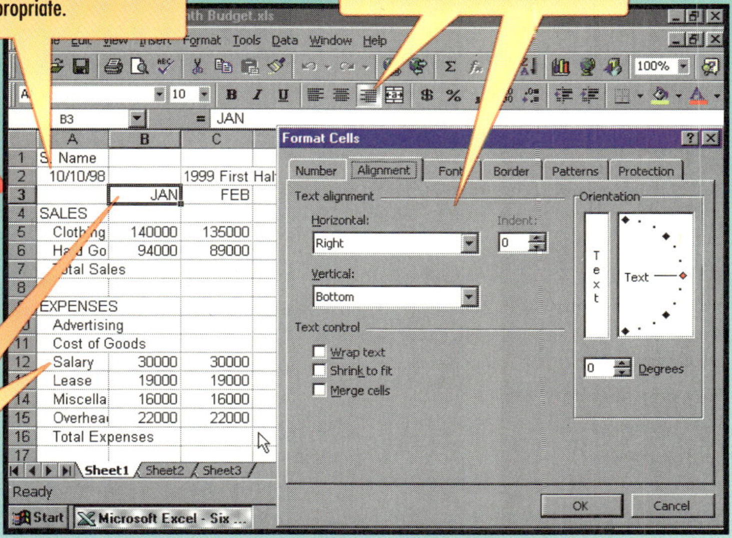

2 Creating a Worksheet: Part 2

COMPETENCIES

After completing this lab, you will know how to:

1. Enter formulas using Point mode.
2. Copy formulas.
3. Enter functions.
4. Use the Paste Function feature.
5. Use absolute references.
6. Add cell comments.
7. Adjust column widths.
8. Use Undo.
9. Zoom the worksheet.
10. Format numbers.
11. Apply styles.
12. Insert and delete rows and columns.
13. Move and center cell contents.
14. Change fonts and font styles.
15. Add predefined headers and footers.
16. Change page orientation.

CASE STUDY

You have created the basic structure for The Sports Company budget worksheet by entering the row and column headings, the expected sales figures, and many of the expected expenses. You also entered a formula to calculate the total clothing sales for six months. You will complete the worksheet by entering the remaining formulas and functions. You will also improve the physical appearance of the worksheet by using many additional formatting features. These features also help to clarify the meaning of the information in the worksheet. The complete budget worksheet is shown below.

In this lab, as you continue to build the budget worksheet, you will learn about many features in Excel that make life easier. As you learn about these features, think what it would be like to do the same task by hand. How long would it take? Would it be as accurate or as attractive? Your appreciation of the application grows as you learn more about what it can do for you.

1999 First Half Budget

	JAN	FEB	MAR	APR	MAY	JUN	TOTAL	AVG	
SALES									
Clothing	$ 140,000	$ 135,000	$ 175,000	$ 210,000	$ 185,000	$ 185,000	$ 1,030,000	$ 171,667	59.61%
Hard Goods	$ 94,000	$ 89,000	$ 120,000	$ 145,000	$ 125,000	$ 125,000	$ 698,000	$ 116,333	40.39%
Total Sales	$ 234,000	$ 224,000	$ 295,000	$ 355,000	$ 310,000	$ 310,000	$ 1,728,000	$ 288,000	
EXPENSES									
Advertising	$ 9,360	$ 8,960	$ 11,800	$ 14,200	$ 12,400	$ 12,400	$ 69,120	$ 11,520	
Cost of Goods	$ 135,720	$ 129,920	$ 171,100	$ 205,900	$ 179,800	$ 179,800	$ 1,002,240	$ 167,040	
Salary	$ 30,000	$ 30,000	$ 30,000	$ 30,000	$ 30,000	$ 30,000	$ 180,000	$ 30,000	
Lease	$ 19,000	$ 19,000	$ 19,000	$ 19,000	$ 19,000	$ 19,000	$ 114,000	$ 19,000	
Miscellaneous	$ 16,000	$ 16,000	$ 16,000	$ 16,000	$ 16,000	$ 16,000	$ 96,000	$ 16,000	
Overhead	$ 22,000	$ 22,000	$ 22,000	$ 22,000	$ 22,000	$ 22,000	$ 132,000	$ 22,000	
Total Expenses	$ 232,080	$ 225,880	$ 269,900	$ 307,100	$ 279,200	$ 279,200	$ 1,593,360	$ 265,560	
INCOME	$ 1,920	$ (1,880)	$ 25,100	$ 47,900	$ 30,800	$ 30,800	$ 134,640	$ 22,440	
						Profit Margin	7.79%		

Concept Overview

The following concepts will be introduced in this lab:

1. Relative Reference	A relative reference is a cell or range reference in a formula whose location is interpreted by Excel in relation to the position of the cell that contains the formula.
2. Functions	Functions are prewritten formulas that perform certain types of calculations automatically.
3. Absolute Reference	An absolute reference is a cell or range reference in a formula whose location does not change when the formula is copied.
4. Column Width	The size or width of a column controls how much information can be displayed in a cell.
5. Number Formats	Number formats affect how numbers look onscreen and when printed.
6. Styles	A style consists of a combination of formats that have been named and that can be quickly applied to a selection.
7. Insert and Delete Cells, Rows, and Columns	Individual cells or entire rows or columns can be inserted and deleted from a worksheet.
8. Fonts	Fonts consist of typefaces, point size, and styles that can be applied to characters to improve their appearance.
9. Headers and Footers	Lines of text displayed below the top margin or above the bottom margin of each page are called headers and footers.

Part 1

Entering Formulas Using Point Mode

You will continue to build the budget worksheet by entering the remaining formulas.

- Load Excel 97.
- Put your data disk in drive A (or the appropriate drive for your system).
- Open the workbook file First Half Budget on your data disk.
- If necessary, maximize the workbook window.

Your screen should be similar to Figure 2-1.

FIGURE 2-1

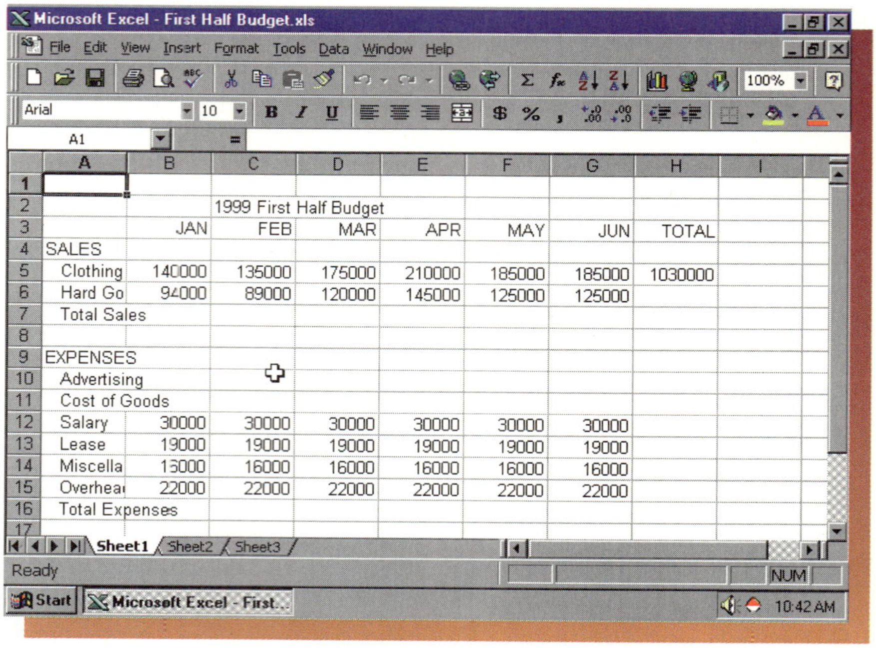

First you will enter the formula to calculate total sales. This formula will sum the numbers for clothing and hard goods sales in cells B5 and B6. Rather than typing the cell references into the formula, you will enter them by selecting the worksheet cells.

You can also use the directional keys to move to the cell.

- Move to B7.
- Type =.
- Click B5.

Your worksheet should be similar to Figure 2-2.

FIGURE 2-2

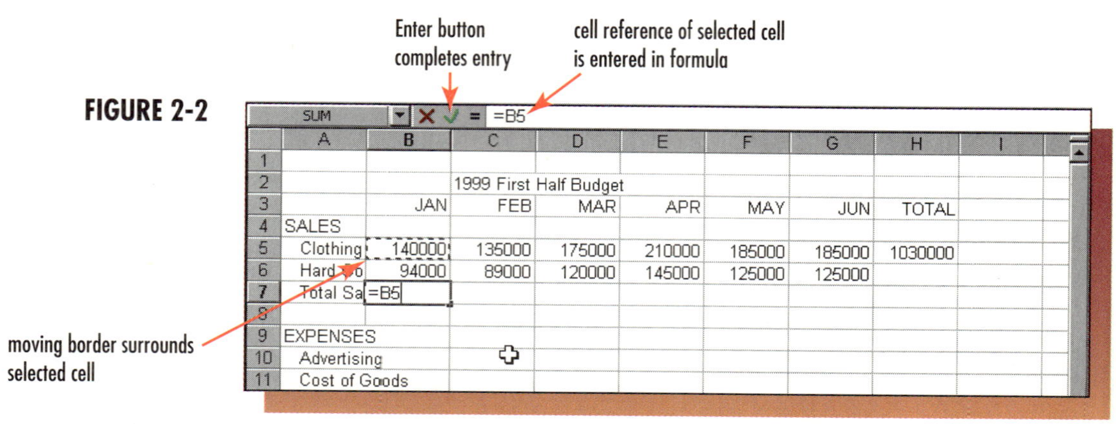

Notice that the status bar displays the current mode as Point. This tells you the program is allowing you to select cells by highlighting them. The cell reference, B5, is entered following the = sign. To continue the formula and enter the reference for the cell containing the January hard goods sales, B6,

- Type +.
- Click B6.
- Click ✓.

The formula entry in cell B7 is =B5+B6 and the calculated value is 234000.

Copying Formulas

The formulas to calculate the February through June total sales (C7 through G7) can be entered next. Just like text and numeric entries, you can copy formulas from one cell to another.

- Copy the formula in cell B7 to cells C7 through G7.
- Move to C7.

Refer to the Review of Copying Methods box on page SS29 to review how to copy.

Your worksheet should be similar to Figure 2-3.

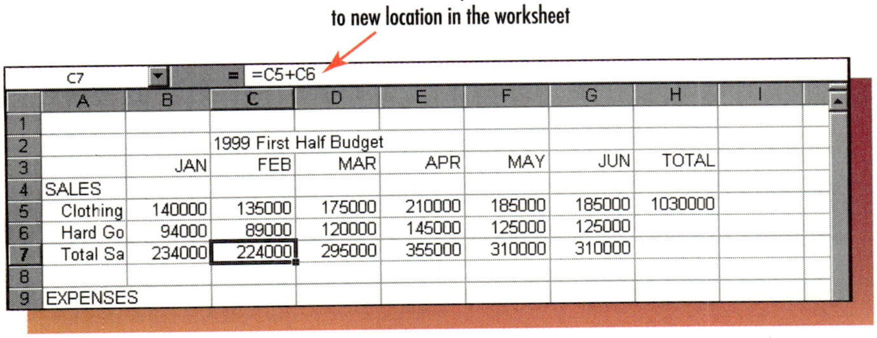

	A	B	C	D	E	F	G	H	I
1									
2			1999 First Half Budget						
3		JAN	FEB	MAR	APR	MAY	JUN	TOTAL	
4	SALES								
5	Clothing	140000	135000	175000	210000	185000	185000	1030000	
6	Hard Go	94000	89000	120000	145000	125000	125000		
7	Total Sa	234000	224000	295000	355000	310000	310000		
8									
9	EXPENSES								

FIGURE 2-3

The number 224000 is displayed in the cell. The formula displayed in the formula bar is =C5+C6. The formula to calculate the February total sales is not an exact duplicate of the formula used to calculate the January total sales (=B5+B6). Instead the cells referenced in the formula have been changed to reflect the new location of the formula in column C. This is because the references in the formula are relative references.

Concept 1: Relative Reference

A **relative reference** is a cell or range reference in a formula whose location is interpreted by Excel in relation to the position of the cell that contains the formula. For example in the formula to calculate total sales in cell C7, the cell reference to C5 tells Excel to use the contents of the cell two cells above the cell containing the formula. When a formula is copied, the referenced cells in the formula automatically adjust to reflect the new worksheet location. The relative relationship between the referenced cell and the new location is maintained. Because relative references automatically adjust for the new location, the relative references in a copied formula refer to different cells than the references in the original formula. The relationship between cells in both the copied and pasted formula is the same although the cell references are different.

- Move to D7.

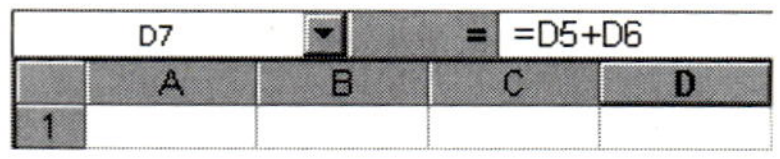

This formula has also changed to reflect the new column location, and appropriately calculates the total based on the March sales.

Next you will enter the formulas to calculate the advertising and cost of goods sold. These numbers are estimated by using a formula to calculate the number as a percent of total sales. As a general rule, The Sports Company calculates advertising expenses at 4 percent of sales and cost of goods expenses at 58 percent of sales. The formula to make these calculations for January takes the number in cell B7 and multiplies it by the percentage.

To make the process of entering and copying entries even easier, you can enter data into the first cell of a range and have it copied to all other cells in the range at the same time by using Ctrl + ←Enter to complete the entry. You will use this feature to enter the formulas to calculate the advertising expenses for January through June.

Even when a range is selected, you can still point to specify cells in the formula.

- Select cells B10 through G10.
- Type **=B7*4%**.
- Press Ctrl + ←Enter.

The formula to calculate the January advertising expenses was entered in cell B10 and copied to all cells of the selected range.

- In the same manner, select the range B11 through G11 and enter the formula =B7*58% in cell B11 to calculate the cost of goods sold for January through June.

Your worksheet should be similar to Figure 2-4.

FIGURE 2-4

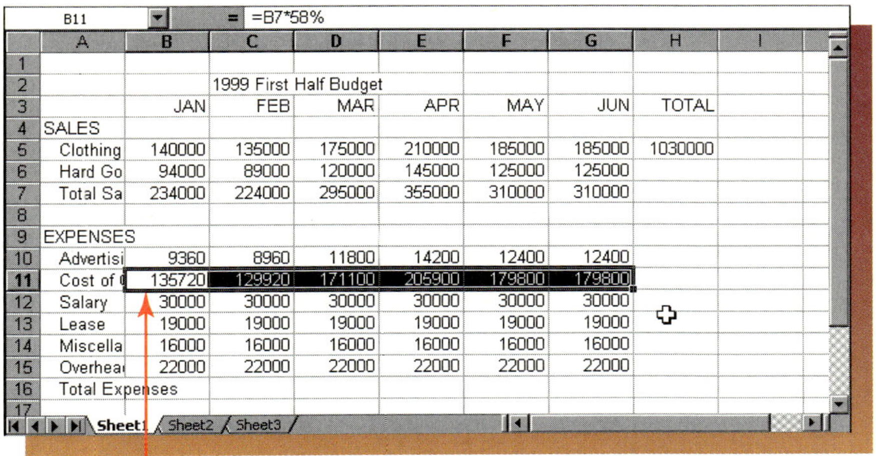

formula entered and copied in one step using Ctrl + ←Enter

Entering Functions

Now that all the expenses have been entered into the worksheet, the total expenses can be calculated. The formula to calculate the total expenses for January needs to be entered in cell B16 and copied across the row through June. You could use a formula similar to the formula used to calculate the total sales (B7). The formula would be =B10+B11+B12+B13+B14+B15. However, it is faster and more accurate to use a function.

Concept 2: Functions

Functions are prewritten formulas that perform certain types of calculations automatically. The **syntax** or rules of structure for entering all functions is:

Function name (argument1, argument2,...)

The function name identifies the type of calculation to be performed. Most functions require that you enter one or more arguments following the function name. An **argument** is the data the function uses to perform the calculation. The type of data the function requires depends upon the type of calculation being performed. Most commonly the argument consists of numbers or references to cells that contain numbers. The argument is enclosed in parentheses, and multiple arguments are separated by commas. If a function starts the formula, enter an equals sign before the function name (=SUM(D5:F5)/25).

Excel includes several hundred functions* divided into 9 categories. Some common functions and the results they calculate are shown below.

Category	Function	Calculates
Financial	PMT	Calculates the payment for a loan based on constant payments and a constant interest rate.
	PV	Returns the present value of an investment: the total amount that a series of future payments is worth now.
Time & Date	TODAY	Returns the serial number that represents today's date.
	DATE	Returns the serial number of a particular date.
	NOW	Returns the serial number of the current date and time.
Math & Trig	SUM	Adds all the numbers in a range of cells.
	ABS	Returns the absolute value of a number, a number without its sign.
Statistical	AVERAGE	Returns the average (arithmetic mean) of its arguments.
	MAX	Returns the largest value in a set of values. Ignores logical values and text.
Lookup & Reference	COLUMNS	Returns the number of columns in an array or reference.
	CHOOSE	Chooses a value or action to perform from a list of values, based on an index number.
Database	DSUM	Adds the numbers in the field (column) or records in the database that match the conditions you specify.
	DAVERAGE	Averages the values in a column in a list or database that match conditions you specify.
Text	DOLLAR	Converts a number to text, using currency format.
	UPPER	Converts text to uppercase.
Logical	IF	Returns one value if a condition you specify evaluates to True and another value if it evaluates to False.
	AND	Returns True if all its arguments are True; returns False if any arguments is False.
Information	ISLOGICAL	Returns True if value is a logical value, either True or False.
	ISREF	Returns True if value is a reference.

**Use Help for detailed explanations of every function.*

You will use the SUM function to calculate the total expenses for January. Because the SUM function is the most commonly used function, it has its own toolbar button.

- Move to B16.
- Click [Σ] AutoSum.

Pressing [Alt] + = is the keyboard shortcut for AutoSum.

Your worksheet should be similar to Figure 2-5.

FIGURE 2-5

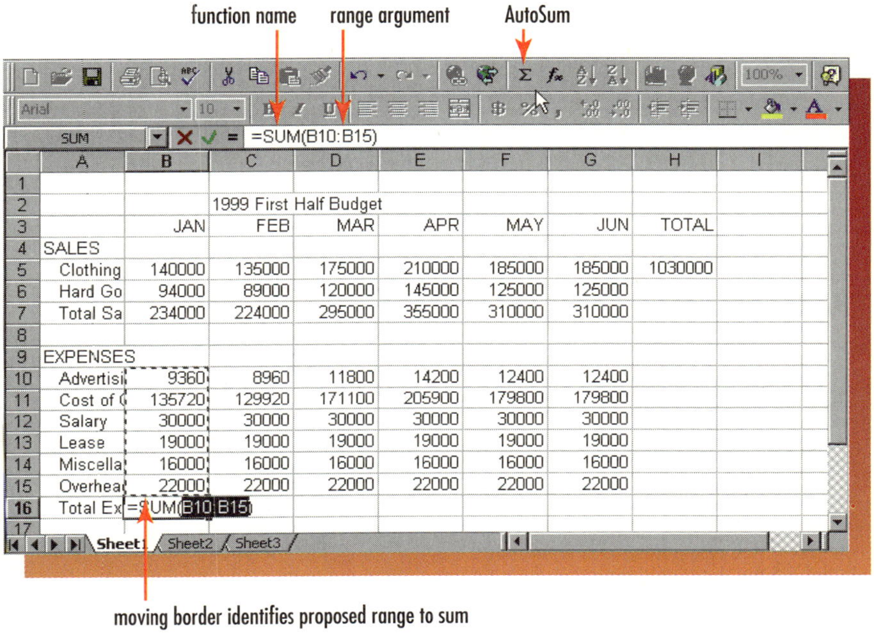

Excel automatically proposes a range based upon the data above or to the left of the active cell. The name of the function followed by the range argument enclosed in parentheses is displayed in the formula bar. Excel displays a range reference as the leftmost cell and rightmost cell in the range separated by a colon (B10:B15). To accept the proposed range and enter the function,

- Click [✓] Enter.

If you used the [←Enter] key, move to B16.

The result, 232080, calculated by the SUM function is displayed in cell B16.

Next you need to calculate the total expenses for February through June.

- Copy the function from cell B16 to cells C16 through G16.
- Move to C16.

The result calculated by the function, 225880, is displayed in cell C16, and the copied function is displayed in the formula bar. The range reference in the function adjusted relative to its new cell location because it is a relative reference.

> You can point to specify the cell references in the formula.

Now that the total expenses are calculated, the formula to calculate income can be entered. This number is the difference between sales and total expenses.

- Select the range B18 through G18.
- Enter the formula =B7–B16 in cell B18.
- Press Ctrl + ↵Enter.

The calculated income numbers are displayed in cells B18 through G18. The income number for February shows a loss, while January and March through June show positive numbers. You are not concerned that the February income number is negative, because this is a projected budget to help the store manager make adjustments for the actual budget.

Finally, the total over the six months needs to be entered down column H.

- Move to H6.
- Click Σ AutoSum.

> The AutoSum button can also calculate a grand total if your worksheet contains subtotals. Select a cell below or the right of a cell that contains a subtotal and then click AutoSum.

Your worksheet should be similar to Figure 2-6.

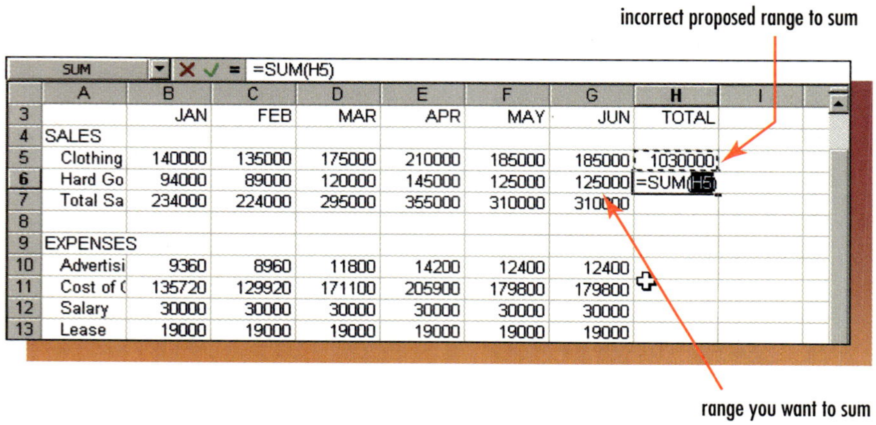

FIGURE 2-6

Notice that the moving border is around cell H5 and not the row. AutoSum first checks for values above and then to the left of the active cell. If the values above are not the range you want to sum, you can edit the function by selecting another range.

> As you drag, the mouse pointer displays the number of rows (R) and the number of columns (C) selected ([1R x 6C]).
>
> 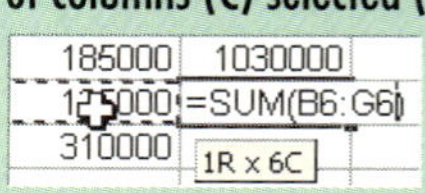
>

- Select B6 through G6.
- Press ↵Enter.
- Copy the function down the column to cell H18.
- Move to H8.

Your screen should be similar to Figure 2-7.

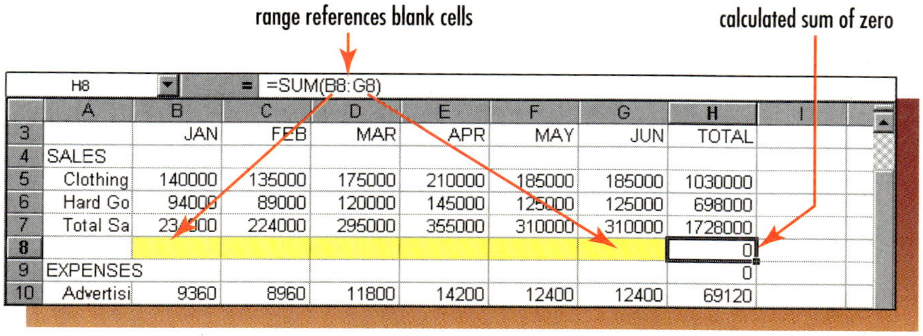

FIGURE 2-7

This cell displays a zero because the formula was copied into a cell that references empty cells. Cells H9 and H17 also display zeros for the same reason. You will clear the formulas from these cells using the fill handle.

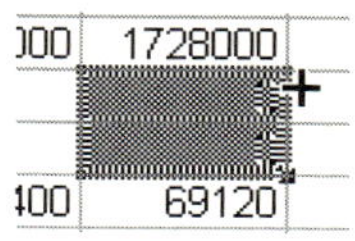

- Select H8 through H9.
- Point to the fill handle of the selected range, and when the mouse pointer changes to +, drag the mouse up until the entire selection is gray.
- Release the mouse button.
- In the same manner, delete the formula from cell H17.

Using the Paste Function Feature

Next you decide you want to add a new column showing the average values for the six months.

Refer to Changing Cell Alignment on page SS32 in Lab 1 to review this feature.

- Enter and right-align the heading AVG in cell I3.
- Move to I5.

Another way to enter a function is to use the Paste Function feature. This feature simplifies entering functions by prompting you to select a function from a list and then helps you to enter the arguments correctly.

- Click *fx* Paste Function.

The menu equivalent is Insert/Function and the shortcut key is ⇧Shift + F3.

The Paste Function dialog box on your screen should be similar to Figure 2-8.

FIGURE 2-8

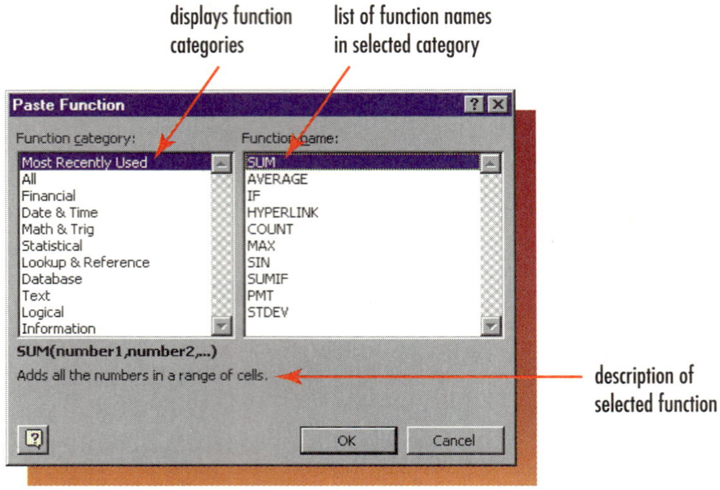

The Most Recently Used function category initially displays 10 of the most common functions.

First, you select the type of function you want to use. The Function Category list box displays the names of the function categories, and the Function Name list box displays the names of the functions in the selected category. The currently selected category is Most Recently Used. This category displays the names of the last 10 functions used.

If AVERAGE is not displayed in the list box, select it from the Statistical category.

- Select AVERAGE from in the Function Name list box.
- Click OK.

Your screen should be similar to Figure 2-9.

FIGURE 2-9

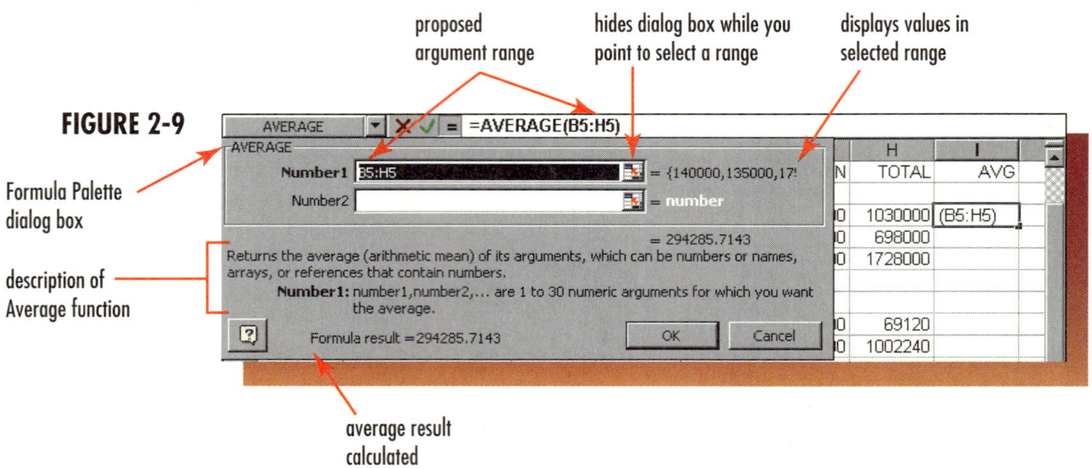

Next, the Formula Palette dialog box is displayed to help you enter the arguments required for the selected function. The upper section displays the proposed argument range in the Number 1 text box. Also notice the actual numbers in the selected range are displayed to the right of the textbox. The lower section describes the Average function and what the function requires for arguments.

Because the proposed argument range is incorrect (it includes the total value in cell H5) you need to specify the correct range (B5:G5) in the Number1 text box. The numbers or the cell references containing the numbers can be entered in the text box directly, or can be entered by selecting the cell or range from the worksheet. Selecting the range is usually faster, and it avoids the accidental entry of incorrect references. To select the range B5 through G5 from the worksheet,

You can also display the Formula Palette by clicking Edit Formula in the Formula bar.

Keyboard users must type the range B5:G5 in the text box.

- Click

Your worksheet should be similar to Figure 2-10.

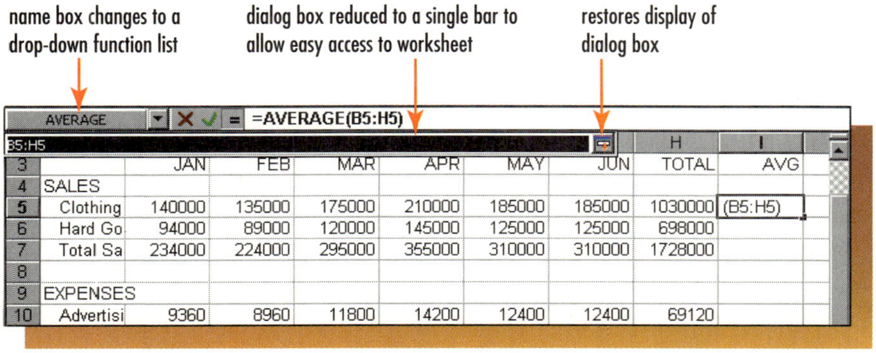

FIGURE 2-10

When the Formula Palette is open, the name box changes to a drop-down function list.

- Select B5 through G5.

The new range appears in the formula bar and the cell, as well as in the dialog box bar. To redisplay the dialog box and complete the function,

- Click .
- Click OK.

The average of the clothing sales for the six months, 171666.7, is calculated and displayed in cell I5. By default numbers are displayed with as many decimal places as cell space allows and are rounded appropriately.

- Copy the function down column I through row 18.

Your worksheet should be similar to Figure 2-11.

FIGURE 2-11

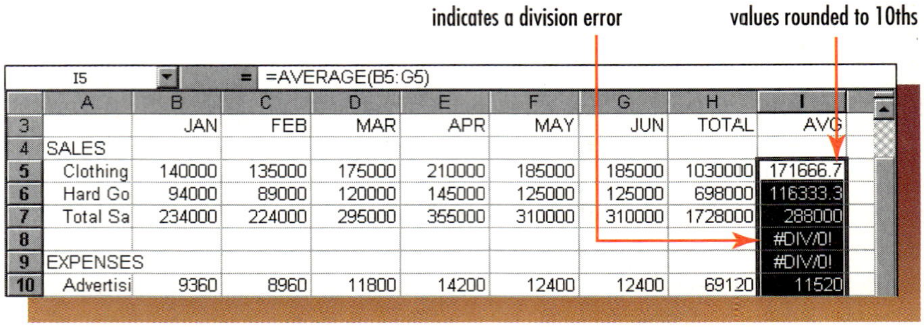

The average value has been correctly calculated for each row. Notice three cells display #DIV/0!. This indicates a division error occurred because the formula divides by zero.

- Clear the function from the three cells that display #DIV/0!.

Using Absolute References

Next you decide to enter a formula to calculate what proportion the total clothing sales and total hardware sales for six months are of the total sales. You will display the proportion in the column to the right of the Average column. The formula to calculate the proportion for clothing is Total Clothing Sales/Total Sales.

- Move to J5
- Enter the formula =H5/H7 in cell J5.

The value 0.596065 is displayed in cell J5. This shows that the clothing sales are approximately 60 percent of total sales.

Next, to calculate the proportion that hardware sales are of total sales, you will copy the formula from J5 to J6. Another quick way to copy cell contents is to drag the cell border while holding down Ctrl. This method is most useful when the distance between cells is short and they are both visible in the window. It cannot be used if you are copying to a larger range than the source range.

> **The mouse pointer appears as ↖+ to show that it will copy the cell contents.**

- Point to the border of cell J5 and when the mouse pointer shape is ↖, hold down Ctrl, and drag the mouse pointer to cell J6.

Your worksheet should be similar to Figure 2-12.

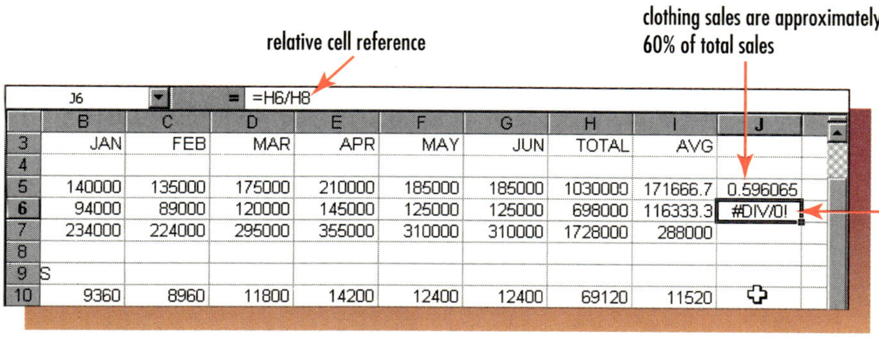

FIGURE 2-12

A #DIV/0! error occurred because the reference to cell H7 changed to cell H8, a blank cell, when the formula was copied. The formula in J5 needs to be entered so that the row of the referenced cell, row 7, does not change to row 8 when it is copied. To do this you need to make the cell reference absolute.

Concept 3: Absolute Reference

An **absolute reference** is a cell or range reference in a formula whose location does not change when the formula is copied.

To stop the relative adjustment of cell references, enter a $ (dollar sign) character before the column letter and row number. This changes the cell reference to absolute. When a formula containing an absolute cell reference is copied to another row and column location in the worksheet, the cell reference does not change. It is an exact duplicate of the cell reference in the original formula.

A cell reference can also be a **mixed reference**. In this type of reference, either the column letter or the row number is preceded with the $. This makes only the row or column absolute. When a formula containing a mixed cell reference is pasted to another location in the worksheet, only the part of the cell reference that is not absolute changes relative to its new location in the worksheet.

The table below shows examples of relative and absolute references and the results when a reference in cell C10 to cell B28 is copied to cell E13.

Cell Contents of C10	Copied to Cell E13	Type of Reference
B28	B28	Absolute reference
B$28	D$28	Mixed reference
$B28	$B31	Mixed reference
B28	D31	Relative reference

You can change a cell reference to absolute or mixed by typing in the dollar sign directly or by using the ABS (Absolute) key, F4. To use the ABS key, the program must be in the Edit mode.

■ Move to cell J5 and turn on the Edit mode.

Press F2 or double-click cell J5.

Your worksheet should be similar to Figure 2-13.

FIGURE 2-13

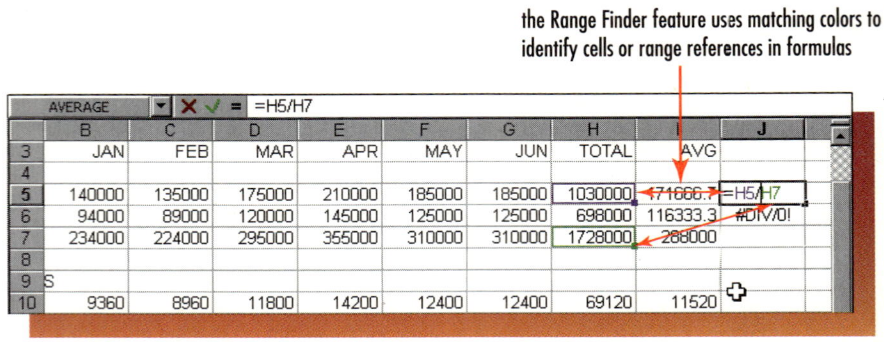

Notice that the cell references in the formula are color coded to match the borders Excel displays around the referenced worksheet cells. This is Excel's Range Finder feature. It is designed to provide visual cues to the relationships between the cells that provide values to the formulas or the cells that depend on the formulas.

You need to change the H7 cell reference to absolute. When using the ABS key, first position the insertion point on or immediately to the right of the cell reference that you want to change.

- If necessary, move the insertion point to the cell reference H7.
- Press F4.

The cell reference now displays $ characters before the column letter and row number, making this cell reference absolute. If you continue to press F4, the cell reference will cycle through all possible combinations of cell reference types. Leaving the cell reference absolute, as it is now, will stop the relative adjustment of the cell reference when you copy it again.

- Click Enter.
- Copy the revised formula to cell J6.
- Move to J6.

A mixed reference of H$7 would also have solved the problem.

Your worksheet should be similar to Figure 2-14.

FIGURE 2-14

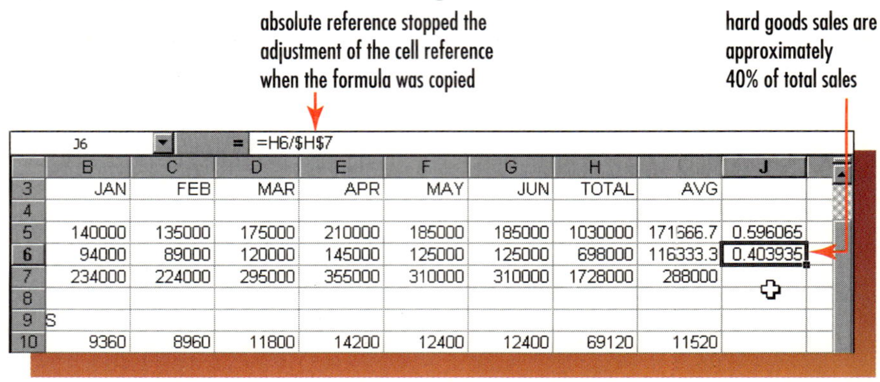

Adding Cell Comments

To clarify the meaning of the two proportion values, you decide to add cell comments. Cell comments are notes that are attached to a cell and that automatically appear whenever the mouse pointer rests on the cell. To add a comment to clarify the hard goods proportion value,

- Choose Insert/Comment.

Your worksheet should be similar to Figure 2-15.

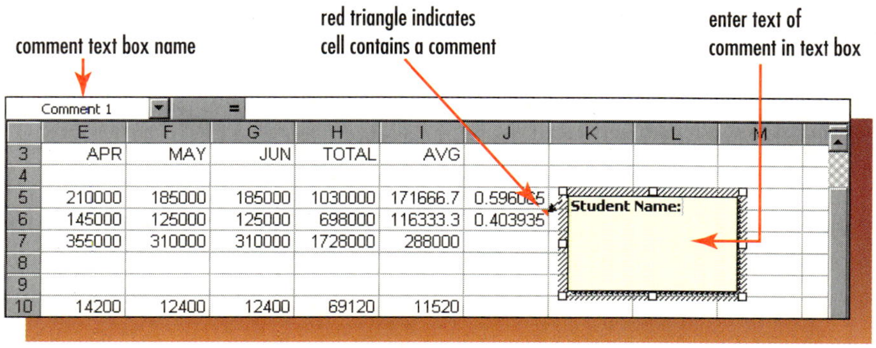

FIGURE 2-15

Notice the cell displays a red triangle in the upper right corner. This indicates the cell contains a comment. In the comment text box you enter the text you want to appear in the comment.

- Select the name and type your name.
- Press ↵Enter.
- Type **Total hard goods sales as a percent of total sales.**
- To close the comment, click anywhere outside the comment box.
- To display the comment, point to cell J6.

Your worksheet should be similar to Figure 2-16.

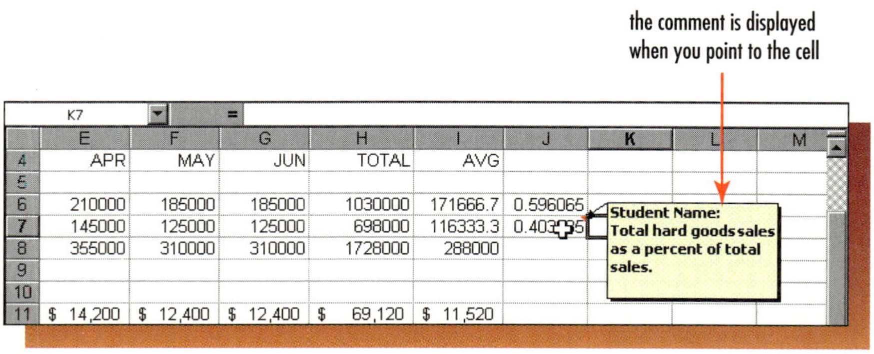

FIGURE 2-16

The comment text box displays the user name assigned to the program by default.

The text wraps within the comment text box as you type.

The cell does not need to be active to display the cell comment.

You can copy the text from the comment text box of cell J6 and edit it in the comment text box for cell J5.

To delete a comment, use Edit/Clear/Comment.

As long as the cells to the left are blank, when you right-align an entry, it will overlap into the cell to the left.

Reminder: Use Ctrl + Home to quickly move to cell A1.

- Add the comment, "Total clothing sales as a percent of total sales," to cell J5.
- Close the comment text box and display the comment.

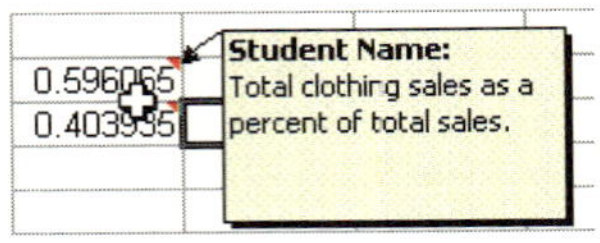

The last formula you need to add to the worksheet is to calculate the total profit margin for the first six months. You will enter the formula in cell H20 and a descriptive text entry in cell G20.

- In cell G20 enter and right-align the entry, Profit Margin.
- In cell H20 enter the formula =H18/H7.

The profit margin for the first half of the year is approximately 8 percent (0.077917).

- Move to A1.

Note: If you are stopping at the end of Part 1, enter your name in cell A1, save the workbook file as 1999 First Half Budget, print the worksheet, and exit Excel. When you begin Part 2, open the file 1999 First Half Budget.

Part 2

Adjusting Column Widths

Now that the worksheet data is complete, you want to improve its appearance by adjusting column widths, using underlining, and setting different number format styles.

After entering the numbers for January in column B, any long headings in column A were cut off or interrupted. To allow the long text entries in column A to be fully displayed, you can increase the column's width.

column A contains many interrupted headings

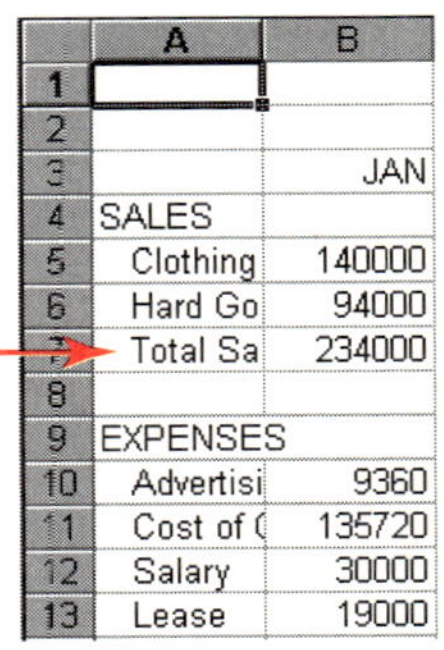

Concept 4: Column Width

The size or width of a column controls how much information can be displayed in a cell. A text entry that is larger than the column width will be fully displayed only if the cells to the right are blank. If the cells to the right contain data, the text is interrupted. On the other hand, when numbers are entered in a cell, the column width is automatically increased to fully display the entry.

The default column width setting in Excel is 8.43. The number represents the average number of digits that can be displayed in a cell using the standard font. The column width can be any number from 1 to 255.

When the worksheet is printed, it appears as it does currently on the screen. Therefore, you want to increase the column width to display the largest entry. Likewise, you can decrease the column width when the entries in a column are small.

The column width can be quickly adjusted by dragging the column divider line located to the right of the column letter. Dragging it to the left decreases the column width, while dragging it to the right increases the width. As you drag, a temporary column reference line shows where the new column will appear, and the mouse pointer displays the width of the column.

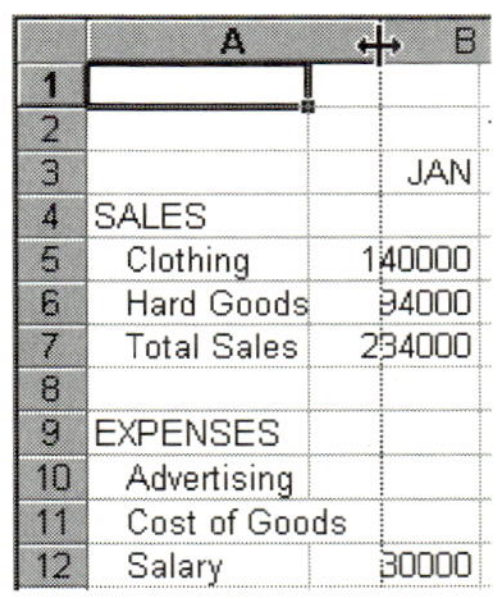

- Point to the column divider line to the right of the column letter A and drag the mouse pointer to the right.
- When the mouse pointer displays 15.00, release the mouse button.

The menu equivalent is Format/Column/Width.

The mouse pointer changes to ↔ when you can size a column.

You can also adjust the height of a row by dragging the row divider line.

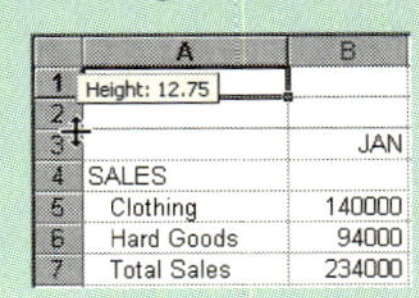

Your worksheet should be similar to Figure 2-17.

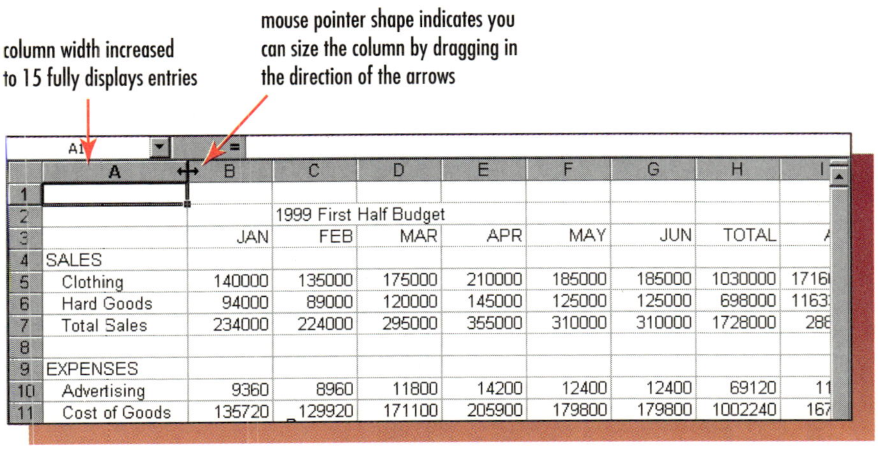

	A	B	C	D	E	F	G	H	I
1									
2			1999 First Half Budget						
3		JAN	FEB	MAR	APR	MAY	JUN	TOTAL	A
4	SALES								
5	Clothing	140000	135000	175000	210000	185000	185000	1030000	1716
6	Hard Goods	94000	89000	120000	145000	125000	125000	698000	1163
7	Total Sales	234000	224000	295000	355000	310000	310000	1728000	288
8									
9	EXPENSES								
10	Advertising	9360	8960	11800	14200	12400	12400	69120	11
11	Cost of Goods	135720	129920	171100	205900	179800	179800	1002240	167

FIGURE 2-17

Next you want to see how the worksheet would look if you decreased the column widths of all the other columns in the worksheet. You can decrease the width of each column individually, but it would be faster to change the width of all the columns at once. First you need to select the columns you want to change.

When you drag beyond the visible window, the window will scroll in the same direction.

- Click on the column letter B.
- Drag the mouse to the right until columns B through J are selected.

Clicking the column letter selects the entire column to the last worksheet row. Next you want to reduce the column width of all selected columns to 5.

- Drag the right border of any column in the selected range to the left until the mouse pointer displays 5.00.
- Release the mouse button.
- Move to cell A1.

Your screen should be similar to Figure 2-18.

FIGURE 2-18

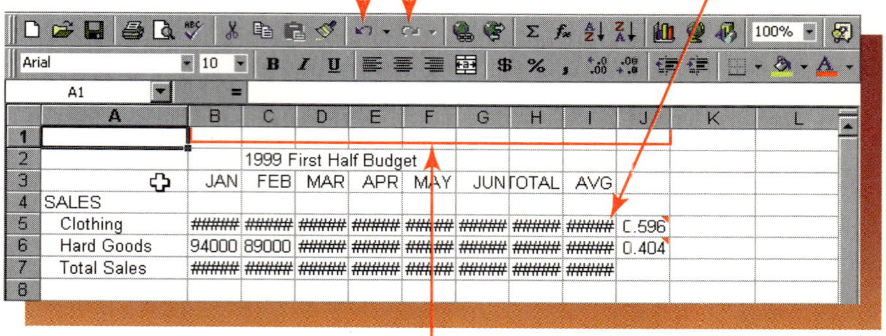

All the cells in the selected columns have changed to five character spaces. Notice that a series of number signs (#####) appears in most of the worksheet cells. Whenever the width of a cell is too small to display the entire number, number signs are displayed.

Using Undo

As you can see, this new column width is much too small. To cancel the most recent operation and restore the worksheet to how it was prior to your change,

The menu equivalent is Edit/Undo Column Width, and the shortcut key is Ctrl + Z.

- Click [Undo button] Undo.

The effects of the column width setting are reversed and the columns are restored to the prior column width setting. The previously selected range is highlighted again.

The Undo feature is primarily used to undo errors and is an important safeguard against mistakes that may take a lot of time to fix. Clicking Undo reverses the effects of the most recent command performed or deletes the last entry you typed. If the action cannot be undone, the button appears dimmed.

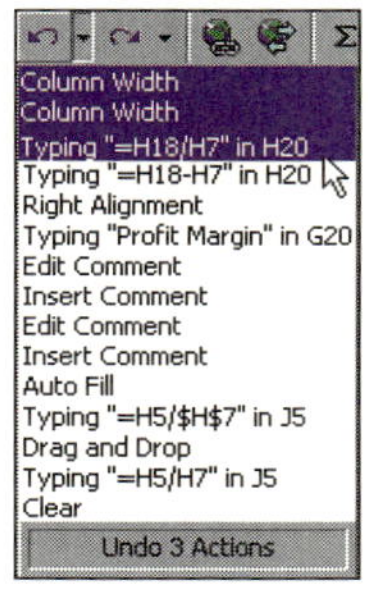

To Undo several actions at once, open the Undo drop-down list and select the actions you want to reverse. All actions above the selected action are also reversed.

- Move to cell A1 to clear the selection.

Immediately after you undo an action, the command changes to Redo and the Redo button is available to allow you to restore the action(s) you just undid.

Zooming the Worksheet

Before adjusting the column widths any more, you want to improve the appearance of the numbers in columns B through J. This range, however, is not entirely visible in the window. You can change how much information is displayed in the window to make it easier to navigate, view, and select the worksheet data by adjusting the zoom percentage. The 100% Zoom button at the right end of the Standard toolbar shows the current zoom percentage is 100 percent. This is the default display percent setting, and it displays data onscreen as it will appear on the printed page. You can reduce or enlarge the amount of information displayed onscreen by changing the magnification from between 10 to 400 percent. You want to decrease the zoom percent to display more information in the window.

The Zoom feature is common to all Office 97 programs.

The menu equivalent is View/Zoom.

- Open the 100% Zoom drop-down menu.
- Select 75%.

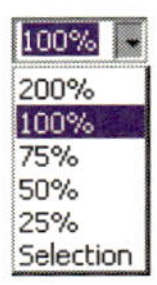

The Selection option adjusts the percentage to fit the selected range in the current window size.

Your screen should be similar to Figure 2-19.

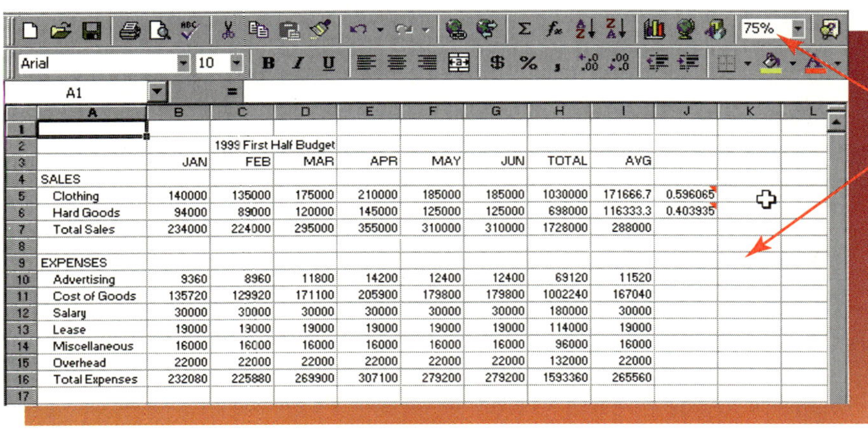

reducing the zoom percentage displays more information in the window

FIGURE 2-19

Formatting Numbers

Now you can more easily select the range to change. You want to improve the appearance of the numbers in the worksheet by changing their format.

Concept 5: Number Formats

Number formats affect how numbers look onscreen and when printed. They do not affect the way Excel stores or uses the values in calculations. The default format setting that controls how numbers are displayed in the worksheet is General. The General format setting automatically sets the number format to a Date, Time, Comma, Currency, Percent, or Scientific number format setting depending on the symbols you used when entering the data.

The table below shows samples of how Excel automatically formats a number based on how it appears when you enter it.

Entry	Format
10,000	Comma
$102.20	Currency with two decimal places
90%	Percent with zero decimal places
10/30/98	Date
9:10	Time

If no symbol is used, Excel leaves the number unformatted. Unformatted numbers are displayed without a thousands separator such as a comma, with negative values preceded by a – (minus sign), and with as many decimal place settings as cell space allows.

First you will change the number format of cells B5 through I18 to display dollar signs, commas, and decimal places.

A quick way to select a range is to click on the first cell of the range and then hold down ⇧Shift while clicking on the last cell of the range. This method is particularly useful when the range is large or if it is not entirely visible in the window.

The keyboard shortcut is Ctrl + 1. Format Cells is also an option on the Shortcut menu.

- Use this method to select the range B5 through I18.
- Choose Format/Cells.
- If necessary, open the Number tab.
- Select Currency.

The dialog box on your screen should be similar to Figure 2-20.

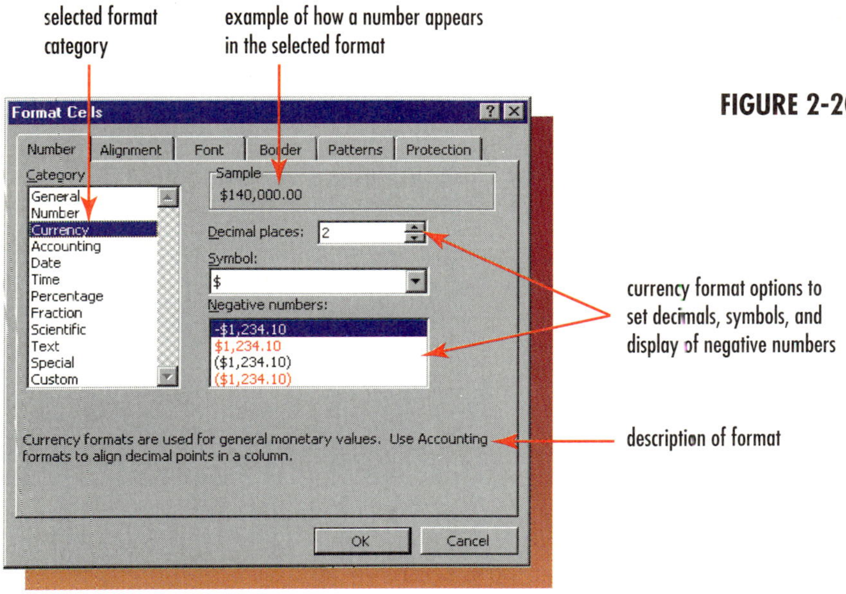

FIGURE 2-20

The Currency category includes options that allow you to specify the number of decimal places, how negative numbers will appear, and whether a currency symbol such as a dollar sign will be displayed.

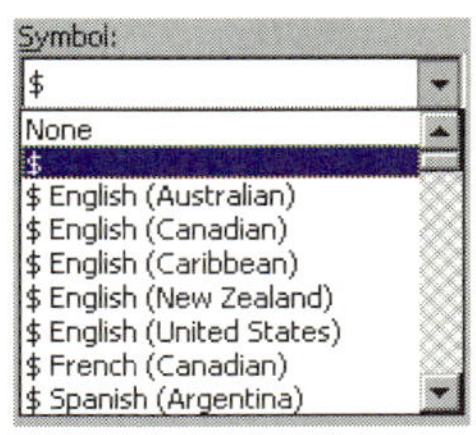

- If a dollar sign is not displayed in the Symbol drop-down list box, turn it on by selecting $English (United States) from the drop-down list.
- Click OK.

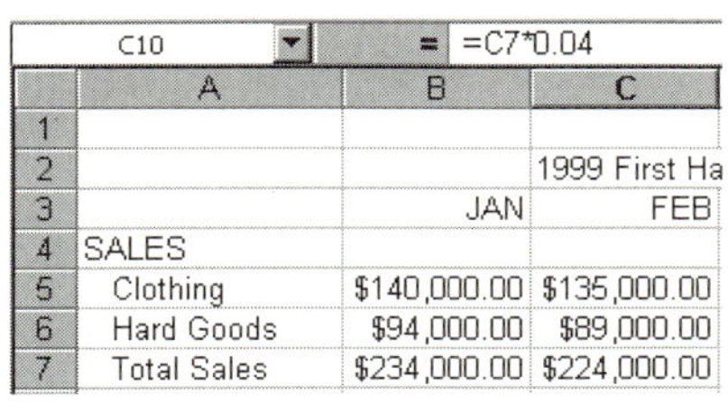

The number entries in the selected range appear with a currency symbol, comma, and two decimal places. The column widths for most columns increased automatically to fully display the formatted values.

A second format category that displays numbers as currency is Accounting.

- Click $.

Your screen should be similar to Figure 2-21.

FIGURE 2-21

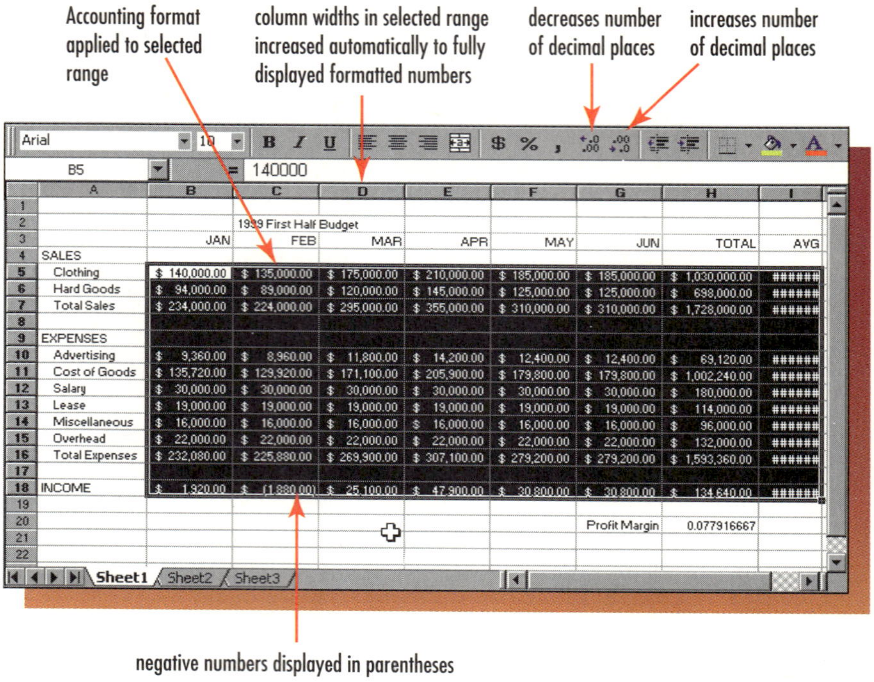

The numbers now appear in Accounting format. The primary difference between the Accounting and the Currency formats is that the Accounting format aligns numbers at the decimal place and places the dollar sign in a column at the left edge of the cell space. In addition, it does not allow you to select different ways of displaying negative numbers, but displays them in black in parentheses. You feel the Accounting format will make it easier to read the numbers in a column.

> The menu equivalent is Format/Cells/Accounting.

> The button increases the number of decimal places.

As you look at the numbers, you decide it is not necessary to display the decimal places since most of the values are whole numbers. To do this,

- Click Decrease decimal (2 times).

Now that the numbers are displayed with zero decimal places, the column widths are larger than they need to be. Because Excel does not automatically reduce column widths, you need to make this change yourself. You will do this using the AutoFit feature. This feature automatically sets the column widths to the minimum necessary to display the contents of the selected cells.

- Choose Format/Column/AutoFit Selection.

Your screen should be similar to Figure 2-22.

the AutoFit feature automatically adjusts column widths to the minimum width to display the contents of cells within the selection

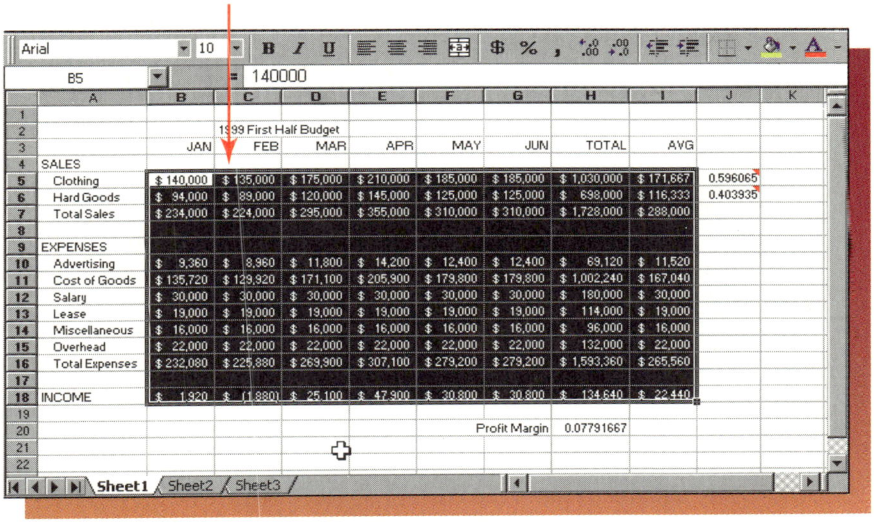

FIGURE 2-22

The width of columns B through I automatically decreased to the minimum column width needed to fully display the numbers. The width of column A remained the same because it was not included in the selection.

Applying Styles

Next you want to format the two proportion values in cells J5 and J6 and the profit margin to display as a percent. You could apply the Percent format using the Format/Cells menu command as you just did. Another way, however, is to select a predefined format style.

Concept 6: Styles

A **style** consists of a combination of formats that have been named and that can be quickly applied to a selection. Normal is the default style. It sets the number format to General and controls other format settings that are applied to all entries.

Examples of the six predefined styles are shown on the right. Notice the two Currency styles. They will display dollar signs, commas, and two or zero decimal places, just as if you had selected these formats from the Format Cells dialog box.

Style	Examples
Normal	89522
Comma	89.522.00
Comma[0]	89,522
Currency	$89,522.00
Currency[0]	$ 89,522
Percent	89.52200%

- Select J5 and J6.
- Choose Format/Style.

The dialog box on your screen should be similar to Figure 2-23.

FIGURE 2-23

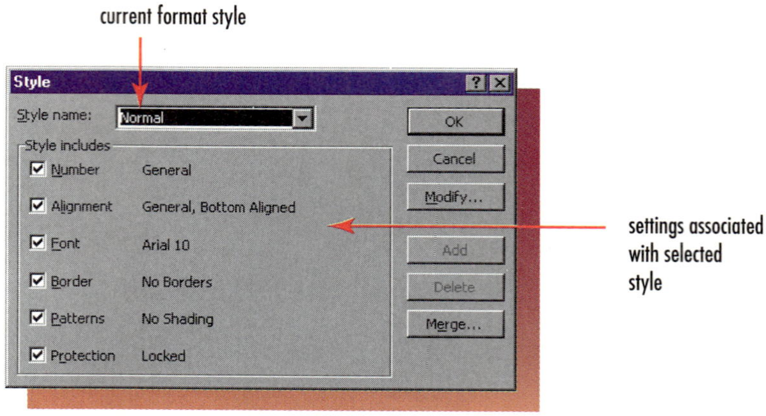

The Style Name list box displays the current style, Normal. The check boxes in the Style Includes area of the dialog box show the options that are included in this style and a description or sample. You want to use the Percent style.

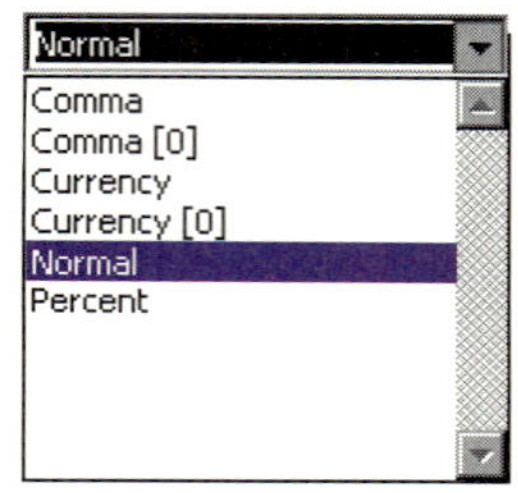

- Open the Style Name drop-down list box.
- Select Percent.
- Click OK.

Your worksheet should be similar to Figure 2-24.

FIGURE 2-24

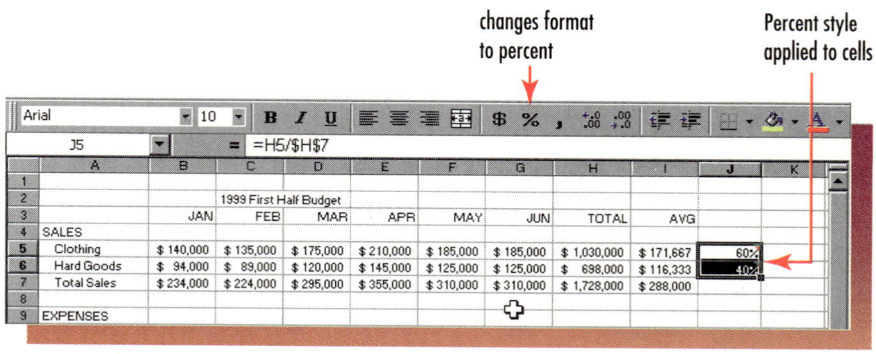

Setting the cell format to Percent takes the value in the cell and multiplies it by 100. The decimal value is converted to a percent by moving the decimal point two places to the right and rounding the value to the nearest whole.

- To make the percentage more accurate, increase the decimal place setting to 2.

Next you need to change the profit margin number to display as a percent with two decimal places. To quickly change the value to percent, you can also use the [%] button on the formatting toolbar.

- Move to H20.
- Click [%] Percent.
- Format the profit margin percent to display two decimal places.
- Press Ctrl + Home.

Inserting Rows

The appearance of the worksheet is greatly improved already. However, it looks crowded and could be further improved by inserting a blank row below the worksheet title as row 3.

Concept 7: Insert and Delete Cells, Rows, and Columns

Individual cells or entire rows or columns can be inserted and deleted from a worksheet. A cell is inserted by moving the contents of the active cell down or to the right. When inserting a row, the new row is added at the cell selector position, moving the current row and all others down. When a column is added, the current column and all other columns move to the right. The formats associated with surrounding cells are applied to the newly inserted cell, row, or column.

You can also delete individual cells as well as entire columns and rows. When you delete the cell, column, or row, the surrounding cells, columns, and rows shift to fill the space. Deleting cells is different from clearing cells. When you clear a cell, the cell contents, formats, or comments are erased, leaving a blank cell on the worksheet. Be very careful when you delete, however, because any information in the cell, column, or row will be erased.

When you insert or delete cells, rows, or columns, all cell references in formulas and functions are automatically adjusted to their new locations. This keeps your formulas up to date. However, a worksheet formula containing a reference to a deleted cell displays a #REF! error message.

To insert a blank row into the worksheet, begin by moving the cell selector to the row where the new blank row will be inserted.

- Move to A3.
- Choose Insert/Rows.

To delete a cell, row, or column, select it and choose Edit/Delete/Entire Row or Entire Column.

To insert a column, choose Insert/Columns.

Insert and Delete are also on the Shortcut menu.

Your worksheet should be similar to Figure 2-25.

FIGURE 2-25

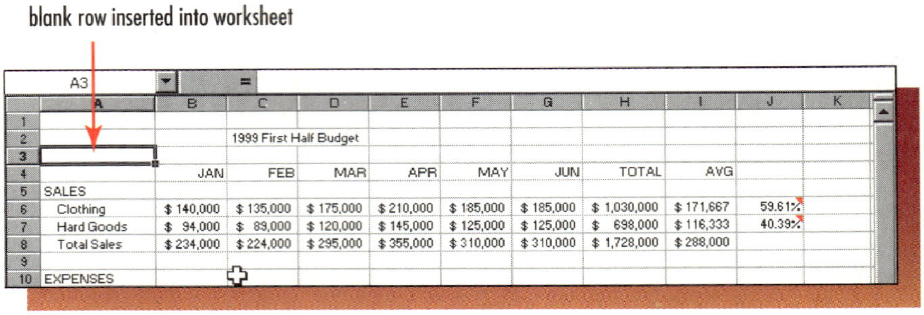

A blank row has been inserted into the worksheet at the cell selector location by moving everything below row 3 down one row.

Moving Cell Contents

Next you want the worksheet title centered in the range A2 through I2 so it appears centered over the worksheet data. To center-align across a selection, the text you want aligned must be in the leftmost cell of the range. To move the worksheet title in cell C2 to cell A2, you could cut and paste the contents, or you can drag the cell border to move the cell contents. This is similar to copying by dragging. Dragging is quickest and most useful when the distance between cells is short and they are visible within the window, whereas Cut and Paste are best for long-distance moves.

As you drag, an outline of the cell appears and the mouse pointer displays the cell reference to show its new location in the worksheet.

If you move cells containing formulas, the formulas are not adjusted relative to their new worksheet locations.

- Move to C2.
- Point to the border of the cell and when the mouse pointer shape is ↖, drag the mouse pointer to cell A2 and release the mouse button.

The contents of cell C2 are copied into cell A2 and cleared from the original cell.

Centering Across a Selection

Now you are ready to center the worksheet title. The text will be centered across cells A2 through I2.

- Select A2 through I2.
- Click Merge and Center.

The menu equivalent is Format/Cells/Alignment/Horizontal/Center Across Selection.

Your worksheet should be similar to Figure 2-26.

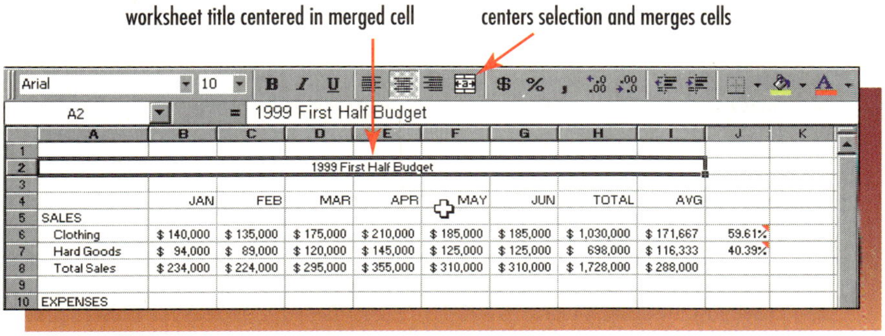

FIGURE 2-26

Combining all cells in the selected range into one has created a **merged cell**. The cell reference for the merged cell is the upper left cell in the range. The contents of the leftmost cell of the range are centered within the merged cell space.

Changing Fonts and Font Styles

Finally, you want to improve the worksheet appearance by enhancing the appearance of the title. To do this you can change the font settings.

The Font settings are common to all Office 97 programs.

Concept 8: Fonts

Fonts consist of typefaces, size, and style. The **typeface** is the appearance and shape of characters. Two common typefaces are Times New Roman and Courier. Size refers to the size of the printed characters and is commonly measured in points, abbreviated pt. A point is about 1/72 inch in height. A common point size for text is 12 pt. This means the printed character is about 12/72 inch in height. Arial 10 pt is the default font for a worksheet. Additionally, you can change the font style, such as bold, italics, and underlines, associated with a cell entry. The box below shows several examples of the same text in various typefaces, sizes, and styles.

Typeface	Font Size (12 pt/18 pt)	Font Style (Bold)
Arial	This is 12 pt. This is 18 pt.	**Bold 18 pt**
Courier New	This is 12 pt. This is 18 pt.	**Bold 18 pt**
Times New Roman	This is 12 pt. This is 18 pt.	**Bold 18 pt**

The fonts on your computer system will be either printer or true-type fonts. True-type fonts appear onscreen as they will appear when printed. They are installed when Windows is installed. Printer fonts are supported by your printer and are displayed as close as possible to how they will appear onscreen, but may not match exactly when printed.

The Arial Font and 10 Font Size drop-down list boxes on the Formatting toolbar show the typeface and point size associated with the current cell. First you will change the typeface.

> The menu equivalent is Format/Cells/Font.

- Open the Arial Font drop-down list box.

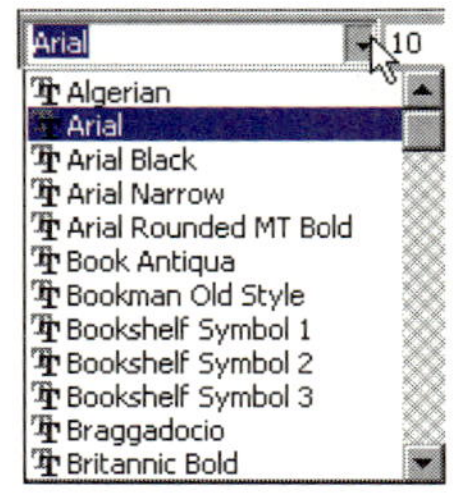

The Font drop-down menu displays the available typefaces in alphabetical order. If a font name is preceded with a printer icon, this means it is a font associated with your printer. Those preceded with TT are true-type fonts.

- Select TT Times New Roman.

The title appears in the selected typeface. Next you will increase the font size to 14 and change the font style to bold.

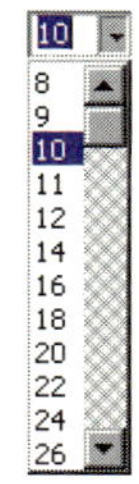

- Open the 10 Font Size drop-down list box.
- Select 14.
- Click B Bold.

Your worksheet should be similar to Figure 2-27.

FIGURE 2-27

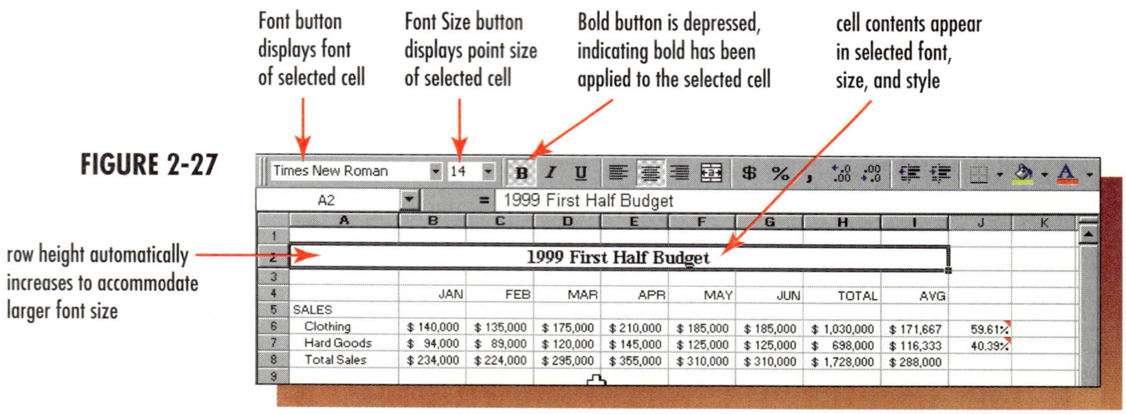

The title is in the typeface, size, and style you specified. Notice that the height of the row has increased to accommodate the larger character size of the heading in that row.

You also want to add bold, italics, and underlines to several other worksheet entries.

- Format the row headings in cells A8 and A17 to bold.

Next you would like to change the row headings in cells A5, A10, and A19 to bold and italic.

> The keyboard shortcut for bold is Ctrl + B, and for italic is Ctrl + I.

- Move to A5.
- Click B Bold, I Italic.

You could repeat the same sequence for cells A10 and A19, but a quicker method is to copy the format from one cell to another using Format Painter on the Standard toolbar. To copy the format of the active cell to the other cells,

- Double-click Format Painter.
- Click A10.
- Click A19.
- Click Format Painter.

A single click on Format Painter allows you to copy formats to a single cell.

The formatting was quickly added to each cell as it was selected, and the feature is off.

Finally, you want to bold and underline the column headings.

- Select B4 through I4.
- Click **B** Bold, U Underline.
- Move to A4.

The keyboard shortcut for underline is Ctrl + U.

The last formatting change you would like to make to the worksheet is to adjust the width of column A to fully display the row headings again. You will use the AutoFit shortcut to make this change.

- Double-click the right column boundary of column A.

The mouse pointer displays as a ✛.

Your screen should be similar to Figure 2-28.

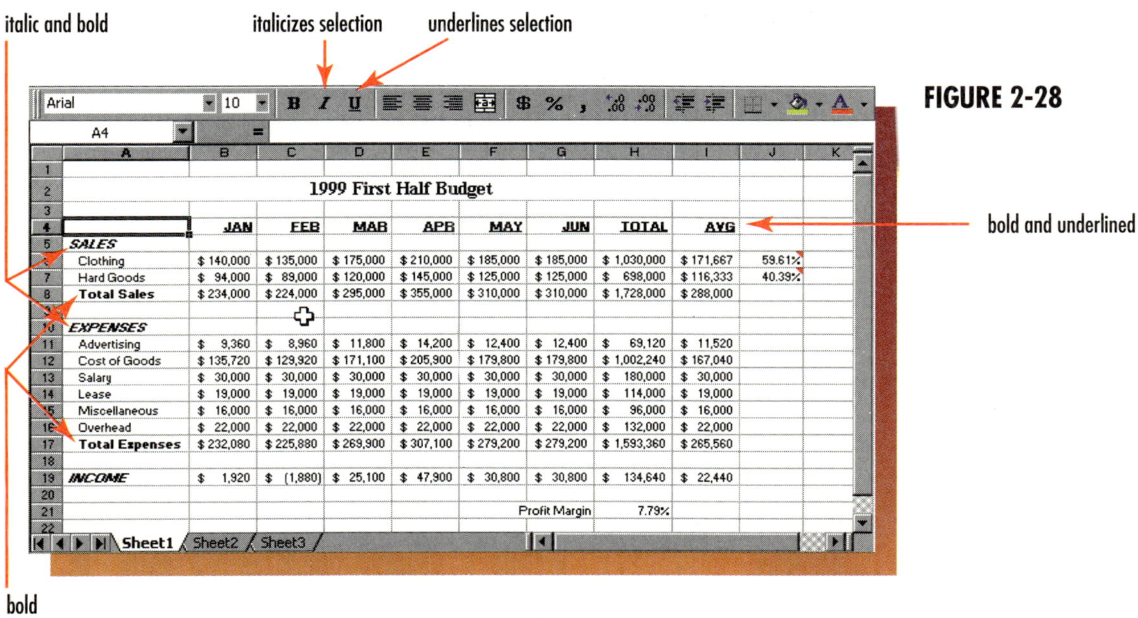

FIGURE 2-28

The six-month budget is now complete.

Use File/Properties/Summary to update the documentation.

- Return the zoom percentage to 100%.
- Update the workbook documentation to include your name.
- Save the changes you have made to the workbook file as 1999 First Half Budget.

Adding Predefined Headers and Footers

You would like to include your name and the date in a header.

Concept 9: Headers and Footers

A **header** is a line or several lines of text that appears at the top of each page just below the top margin. A **footer** is a line or several lines of text that appears at the bottom of each page just above the bottom margin. The text can be formatted like any other text. In addition, you can control the placement of the header and footer text by specifying where it should appear: left-aligned, centered, or right-aligned in the header or footer space. Information that is commonly placed in a header or footer is the date and page number.

To add a header,

Click Print Preview to preview the worksheet.

- Preview the worksheet.
- Click Setup... .
- Open the Header/Footer tab.

The dialog box on your screen should be similar to Figure 2-29.

The File/Page Setup command can also be used to modify page layout settings.

FIGURE 2-29

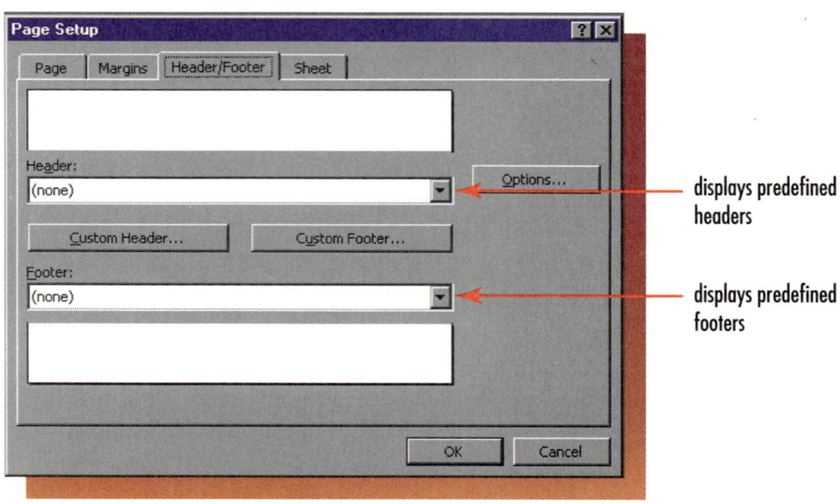

The Header drop-down list box contains a list of predefined headers that you select to appear in the header.

- Open the Header drop-down list box and select the Prepared By **[your name] [date]**, Page 1 option.

The selected header is displayed in the header area of the dialog box.

- Click OK.

Your screen should be similar to Figure 2-30.

Footers are entered in the same way as headers.

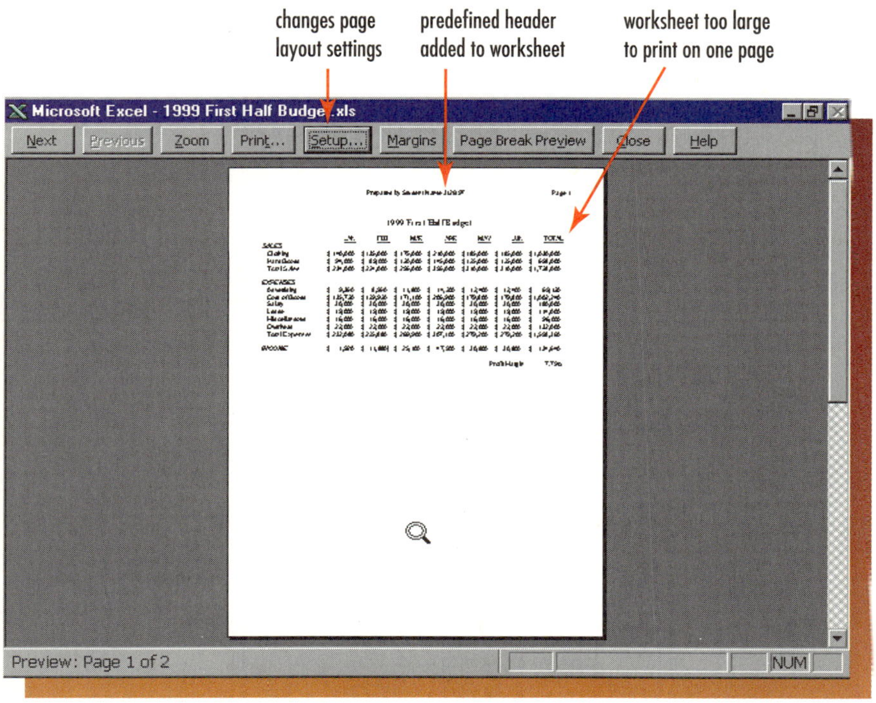

FIGURE 2-30

Changing Page Orientation

Notice that the entire sheet does not fit across the width of the page. To see the second page,

- Click Next.

The sheet requires two pages to print using the default settings. To print the entire sheet on a single page, you can change the orientation (layout of the printed worksheet on the paper) so that the worksheet prints across the length of the paper. This type of layout is called **landscape** style. You also feel the worksheet may be easier to read if the row and column lines were printed. To change the orientation of the worksheet on the page from **portrait** (prints across the width of the page) to landscape and to print the gridlines,

> Not all printers can print landscape style. If your printer does not have this capability, skip the instructions on changing the orientation.

- Click Previous.
- Click Setup....
- From the Page tab select Landscape.
- From the Sheet tab select Gridlines.
- Click OK.

Your screen should be similar to Figure 2-31.

FIGURE 2-31

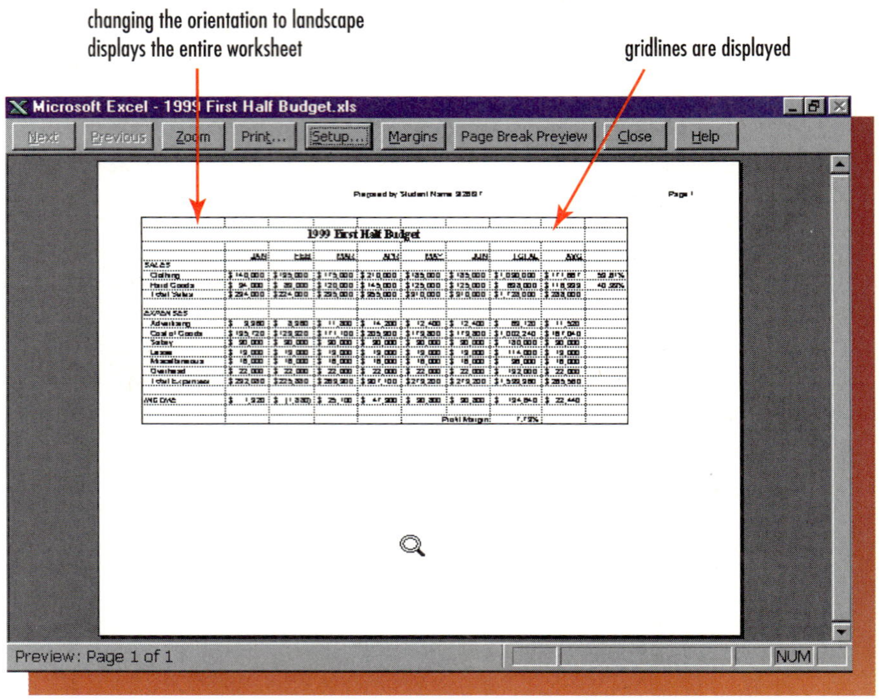

The Preview screen is recreated showing how the sheet will appear in landscape orientation and with gridlines. To print the workbook,

- Click Print....
- If necessary, select the appropriate printer for your system.
- Click OK.
- When you are ready, exit Excel, saving the workbook file using the same file name.

LAB REVIEW

Key Terms

absolute reference (SS61)
argument (SS54)
font (SS75)
footer (SS78)
function (SS54)
header (SS78)
landscape (SS79)
merged cell (SS75)
mixed reference (SS61)
portrait (SS80)
relative reference (SS52)
style (SS71)
syntax (SS54)
typeface (SS75)

Command Summary

Command	Shortcut	Toolbar	Action
File/Page Setup/Header/Footer			Adds header and/or footer
File/Page Setup/Landscape			Prints worksheet across length of paper
Edit/Undo	Ctrl + Z		Undoes last editing or formatting change
Edit/Clear/Comment			Removes comment from cell
Edit/Delete/Entire Row			Deletes selected rows
Edit/Delete/Entire Column			Deletes selected columns
View/Zoom		100%	Changes magnification of window
Insert/Rows			Inserts a blank row
Insert/Columns			Inserts a blank column
Insert/Function	Shift + F3		Inserts a function
Insert/Comment			Inserts a comment to a cell
Format/Cells/Number/Currency			Applies Currency format to selection
Format/Cells/Number/Accounting			Applies Accounting format to selection
Format/Cells/Alignment/Center Across Selection			Centers cell contents across selected cells
Format/Cells/Font			Changes font and attributes of cell contents
Format/Column/Width			Changes width of columns
Format/Column/Autofit Selection			Changes column width to match widest cell entry
Format/Style			Applies selected style to selection

Matching

1. General	______	**a.**	function to add a series of numbers
2. F4	______	**b.**	prints across length of paper
3. point	______	**c.**	an absolute cell reference
4. B4	______	**d.**	indicates insufficient cell width to display numbers
5. footer	______	**e.**	method of entering a cell range or reference in a formula
6. style	______	**f.**	a line of text that appears at the bottom of each page
7. SUM	______	**g.**	centers across selection
8. landscape	______	**h.**	a named group of format settings
9. ######	______	**i.**	in Edit mode, the ABS key
10. 	______	**j.**	default cell format

Fill-In Questions

1. Complete the following statements by filling in the blanks with the correct terms.

a. ________________ are predefined formulas that perform certain types of calculations automatically.

b. To display more characters in a cell, you would increase the ____________________.

c. When a formula is copied, and a cell reference does not adjust to the new location, the reference is __________________.

d. To print a worksheet across the length of the page, you would change the orientation to ____________________________.

e. A(n) ______________ is a named group of formats.

f. When column widths are adjusted based on their contents, the ________________ command is used.

g. _______________ appear when a cell width is too small to display the entire number in that cell.

h. A(n) _______________ character is used to make a reference absolute.

i. A(n) ____________________ is the data the function uses to perform the calculation.

j. _____________________ consist of typefaces and size.

Discussion Questions

1. How is the formula F6+F7+F8 changed when it is copied from cell F10 to cell B16? How would the formula change if all the cell references were made absolute? How would the formula change if all the cell references were mixed references with the row number fixed?

2. Discuss the differences between relative, mixed, and absolute cell references.

3. What are the advantages of using a function instead of a formula to calculate a value?

4. Discuss the differences between the way numbers are displayed when the following formats are used: Currency, Accounting, Percent, and Date.

Hands-On Practice Exercises

Step by Step

Rating System
☆ Easy
☆☆ Moderate
☆☆☆ Difficult

☆

1. To complete this problem, you must have completed Practice Exercise 1 in Lab 1. Open the workbook file Bed and Breakfast on your data disk. In this exercise you will continue to modify the worksheet comparing prices of bed and breakfast inns in New England.

a. Delete column B. Size column A to fully display the names of the inns. Change the width of columns B, and C to accommodate the widest entries. Center the title across columns A to G. Increase the title font and bold it.

b. Format the numbers in columns D through G to display dollar signs and two decimals.

c. Insert a row at row 2 and row 6.

d. Bold the contents of cells A1 through G5, and underline the row 5 headings.

e. Center the heading Single Rates across columns D and E, and center Double Rates across columns F and G. Increase the font size of those two headings by two points.

f. In cell D18, enter the formula =AVERAGE(D7:D16) to calculate the average rate for a single room with a private bath. Copy the formula to the three adjacent cells to the right. Use the Office Assistant to look up the MIN and MAX functions, and calculate the low and high rates for the four occupancy categories.

g. Italicize the row headings Average Rates, Low Rates, and High Rates.

h. Clear your name and the date from the worksheet.

i. Save and replace the workbook file Bed and Breakfast. Preview the worksheet. Add a predefined header that displays your name and the date, then print the worksheet with gridlines.

☆☆

2. To complete this problem, you must have completed Practice Exercise 2 in Lab 1. Open the workbook file Cookie Jar on your data disk. In this exercise you will continue to modify the quarterly sales worksheet for the gourmet cookie shop, The Cookie Jar.

a. Delete columns B and C and widen column A appropriately.

b. Format the sales numbers to display commas without dollar signs and with two decimals.

c. Delete the formula that you used to calculate a total for chocolate chip cookies. Replace it with a SUM function, and copy the function down the column. Calculate totals for the three months, and sum the Total column. List three different ways you can total a column. Which do you think is the most efficient?

d. Make the necessary changes to column widths.

e. Center the worksheet title across the columns. Bold the title. Select a different font and increase the size to 14 pt.

f. Bold and underline the column headings. Insert a blank row between the column headings and the chocolate chip cookie information.

g. Italicize the names of the cookies. Bold, italicize, and right-align the row heading Total.

h. Clear your name and the date from the worksheet.

i. Preview the worksheet. Add a predefined header that displays your name and the date. Print the worksheet. Save and replace the workbook file Cookie Jar.

You will complete this exercise as Practice Exercise 5 in Lab 3.

☆☆

3. To complete this problem, you must have completed Practice Exercise 3 in Lab 1. Open the workbook file Fat Grams on your data disk. In this exercise you will continue to modify the fat analysis worksheet.

a. Eliminate columns B and C, and change the width of column A to accommodate the widest entry.

b. Bold and underline the column headings and make any necessary adjustments to column width.

c. Enter a title centered above the worksheet. Insert a blank row below the title.

d. Insert a blank row between the column headings and the bagel information.

e. By law, all prepared foods must contain nutrition facts, including calories and fat grams per serving. Go to the kitchen and look up the nutrition facts on some of your favorite snacks. Insert a few rows below the Pretzels row and use this information to add your snacks to the list. Copy the lite cream cheese fat formula down the column. What foods should Laura eliminate? What foods, if any, should you eliminate?

f. Display one decimal place for all numbers in the Fat Grams column. Format the % Fat column to display a percent sign and two decimals.

g. Add the following cell comments:
   Cell D5: **Warning: "Lite" cream cheese is VERY high in fat!**
   Cell D6: **Stay away from the peanut butter!**

h. Delete the date and your name from the worksheet.

i. Save and replace the workbook file Fat Grams. Preview the worksheet. Add a predefined header that displays your name and the date then print the worksheet with gridlines.

You will complete this exercise as Practice Exercise 1 in Lab 3.

☆☆☆

4. To complete this problem, you must have completed Practice Exercise 4 in Lab 1. Open the workbook file Invoice on your data disk. In this exercise you will continue to modify the invoice worksheet of computer equipment you sold to a new computer training facility.

a. Use the formatting techniques you learned to improve the appearance of the invoice.

b. Copy the total for the Pentium computers down the column and calculate a subtotal.

c. Calculate the tax based on the tax rate in your state, and then calculate the total amount due.

d. Format numbers using settings of your choice.

e. As you are ringing up the total for a customer, he decides he needs some diskettes. Insert a row between Tables and the Subtotal. Enter the following information:

Qty	Description	Price
1	Formatted 2HD Diskettes100 Pk	49.95

f. Calculate a total for the diskettes and edit the subtotal formula.

g. Clear the date and your name from the worksheet. Make any last-minute formatting changes you wish.

h. Save and replace the workbook file Invoice. Preview the worksheet. Add a predefined header that displays your name and the date, then print the worksheet.

You will complete this exercise as Practice Exercise 2 in Lab 5.

On Your Own

☆☆☆

5. To complete this problem, you must have completed Practice Exercise 5 in Lab 1. Open the workbook file Income Statement on your data disk. In this exercise you will continue to modify the budget income worksheet for the Custom Manufacturing Company.

Copy the January formulas and the fixed cost entries to the months February through June. Calculate totals in column I.

Format the Sales and Net Income numbers to display dollar signs, commas, and two decimals. Change all other numbers to display commas and two decimals.

Make changes you feel are necessary to improve the appearance of the invoice, such as font size, type and style changes, and centering the worksheet title.

You are interested in seeing how each month's net income compares to the total net income for the six months. Below the Net Income row, calculate the percent of total net income for each month. Format the new calculated values appropriately and add a row heading.

Delete your name and date from the worksheet. Add a predefined header that displays your name and the date, then print the worksheet on one page. Save and replace the workbook file.

You will continue this exercise as Practice Exercise 2 in Lab 3.

☆☆☆

6. While attending college at night, Ilsa has a full-time day job. To better keep track of her weekly hours, she uses the time sheet shown below. Now that she has a computer, Ilsa will maintain her time sheet information using Excel. Follow the example below to create a time sheet.

	A	B	C	D	E
1	Time Sheet Of:	[Student's Name]			
2	Week Of:	[Starting Date]			
3		**Total**	**Regular**	**Overtime**	**Adjusted**
4	**Day**	**Hours**	**Hours**	**Hours**	**Total Hours**
5	Monday	10	8		
6	Tuesday	11	8		
7	Wednesday	8	8		
8	Thursday	9	8		
9	Friday	7	7		
10			Weekly Total:		
11					
12					

Enter the formulas to calculate Overtime Hours and Adjusted Total Hours. Overtime Hours is the difference between Regular Hours and Total Hours multiplied by 1.5. The Adjusted Total Hours is the sum of Regular and Overtime Hours. Sum the Adjusted Total Hours to calculate a Weekly Total. (The Weekly Total should be equal to 48.) Enter last Monday's date as the Starting Date in B2. Use the formatting techniques you learned to improve the appearance of the time sheet.

Document and save the workbook file as Time Sheets. Add a predefined header that displays your name and the date, then print the worksheet changing the page setup as needed.

You will complete this exercise as Practice Exercise 6 in Lab 3.

Creating a Worksheet: Part 2

Relative Reference

A relative reference is a cell or range reference in a formula whose location is interpreted by Excel in relation to the position of the cell that contains the formula.

Absolute Reference

An absolute reference is a cell or range reference in a formula whose location does not change when the formula is copied.

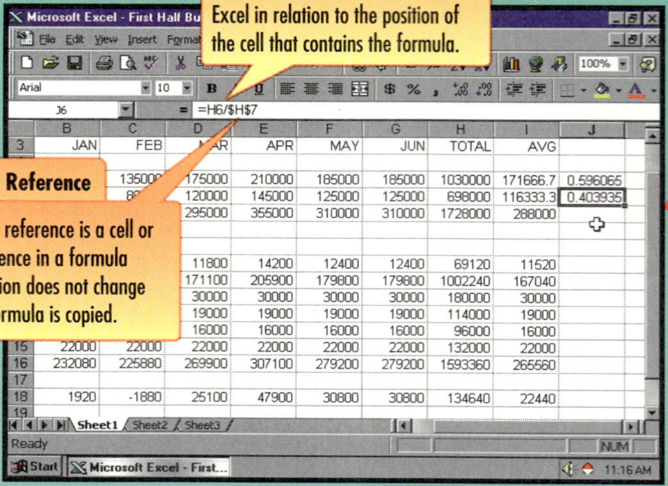

Concepts

- Relative Reference
  Absolute Reference
- Functions
- Column Width
  Inserte and Delete
  Cells, Rows, and Columns
- Number Formats
  Fonts
  Styles
- Headers and Footers

Insert and Delete Cells, Rows, and Columns

Individual cells or entire rows or columns can be inserted and deleted from a worksheet.

Column Width

The size or width of a column controls how much information can be displayed in a cell.

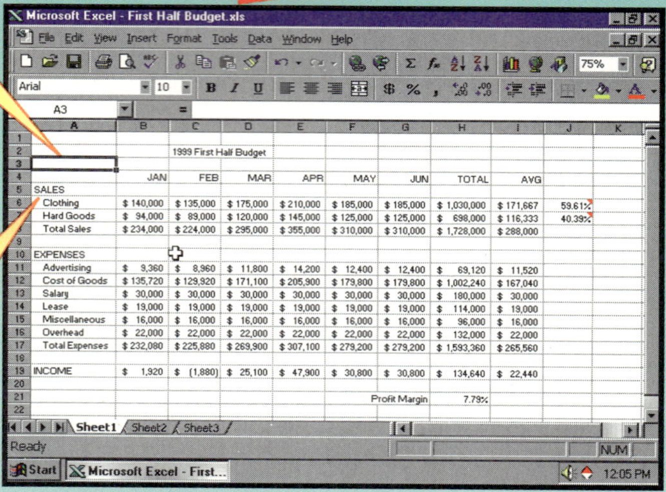

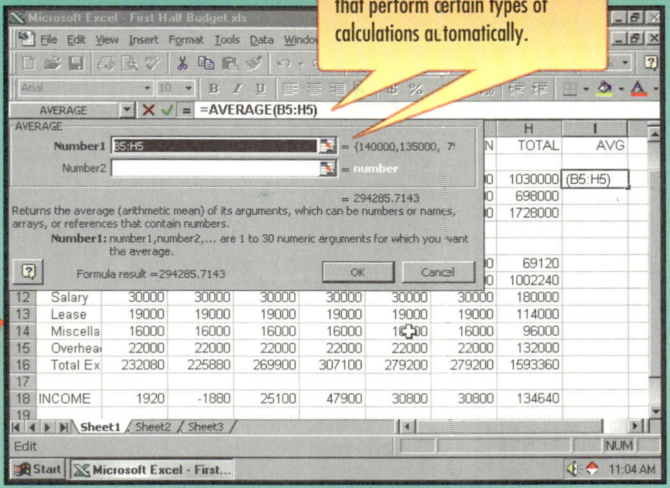

Functions

Functions are prewritten formulas that perform certain types of calculations automatically.

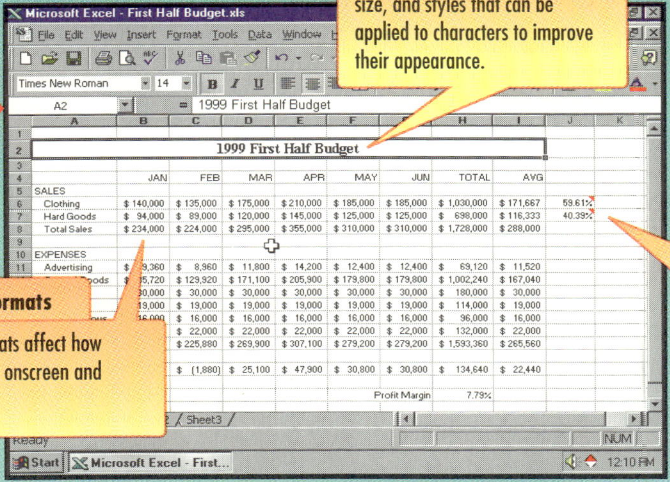

Fonts

Fonts consist of typefaces, point size, and styles that can be applied to characters to improve their appearance.

Styles

A style consists of a combination of formats that have been named and that can be quickly applied to a selection.

Number Formats

Number formats affect how numbers look onscreen and when printed.

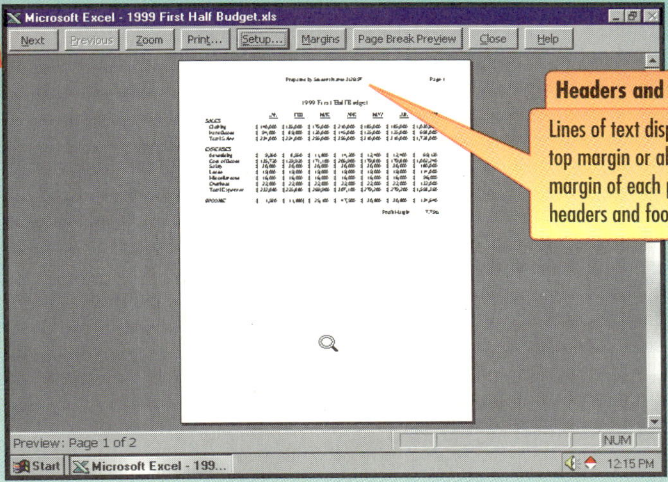

Headers and Footers

Lines of text displayed below the top margin or above the bottom margin of each page are called headers and footers.

3 Managing and Analyzing a Complex Workbook

COMPETENCIES

After completing this lab, you will know how to:

1. **Copy and name sheets.**
2. **Use AutoFill.**
3. **Link worksheets and workbooks.**
4. **Split windows.**
5. **Freeze panes.**
6. **Use what-if analysis.**
7. **Use Solver and Goal Seek.**
8. **Move sheets.**
9. **Open a second workbook.**
10. **Spell-check a worksheet.**
11. **Add color and borders.**
12. **Align a sheet on a page.**
13. **Create custom headers and footers.**

CASE STUDY

After looking at the first-half budget for 1999, the store manager expressed some concern that the profit margin is so low and wants you to look at how this value can be adjusted to be closer to the industry standard of 10 percent for the first six-month time period. You have also been asked to create a worksheet for the data for the second half of the year, in which the profit margin should reflect the industry standard of 13.5 percent.

Additionally, you are to create another worksheet (shown here) for the annual budget that displays the profit margin for each month and for the year. The annual profit margin should be between 12 and 13 percent. Finally, the manager wants you to create a summary worksheet showing only the total values for the year and the projected values for the year 2000.

As you develop the budget workbook and it grows in size and complexity, you will learn about many of the Excel features that help you efficiently manage a large workbook. In addition, you will learn to use several of the built-in tools designed to help you analyze data and to make future projections.

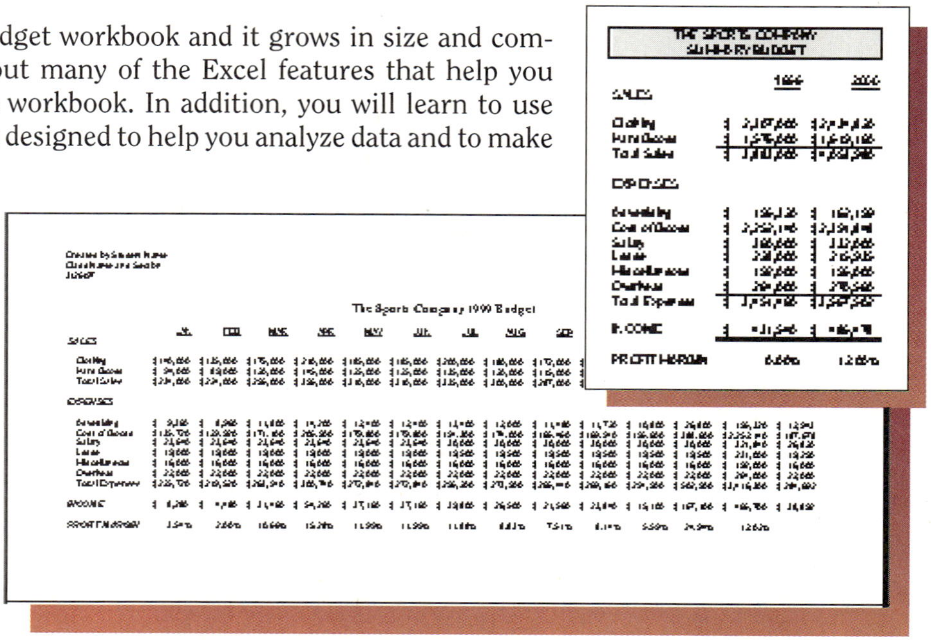

Concept Overview

The following concepts will be introduced in this lab:

1. Sheet Names	Each sheet in a workbook can be assigned a descriptive name to identify the contents of the sheet.
2. AutoFill	The AutoFill feature makes entering long or complicated headings easier by logically repeating and extending the series.
3. Referencing Sheets	A formula reference to cells in different worksheets in a workbook allows you to use data from other worksheets and to calculate new values based on this data.
4. Split Windows	A sheet window can be split into sections called panes to make it easier to view different parts of the sheet at the same time.
5. Freeze Panes	Freezing panes prevents the data in the pane from scrolling as you move to different areas in the worksheet.
6. What-If Analysis	What-if analysis is a technique used to evaluate the effects of changing selected factors in a worksheet.
7. Solver	Solver is an Excel tool that answers what-if problems by determining the value of a cell by changing values in one or more cells in the worksheet.
8. Spelling Checker	A spelling checker feature locates misspelled words, duplicate words, and capitalization irregularities and proposes the correct spelling.
9. Link Workbooks	A link creates a connection between files that updates the linked data automatically in one file whenever the data changes in the other file.
10. Goal Seek	Goal Seek is an Excel tool that is used to find the value needed in one cell to attain a result you want in another cell.

Part 1

Copying a Sheet

First you want to add the budget data to the workbook for the second half of 1999. You want this data in a separate sheet in the same workbook file.

- Load Excel 97 for Windows 95.
- Place your data disk in drive A (or the appropriate drive for your computer system).
- Open the file Six Month 1999 Budget.

Your screen should be similar to Figure 3-1.

FIGURE 3-1

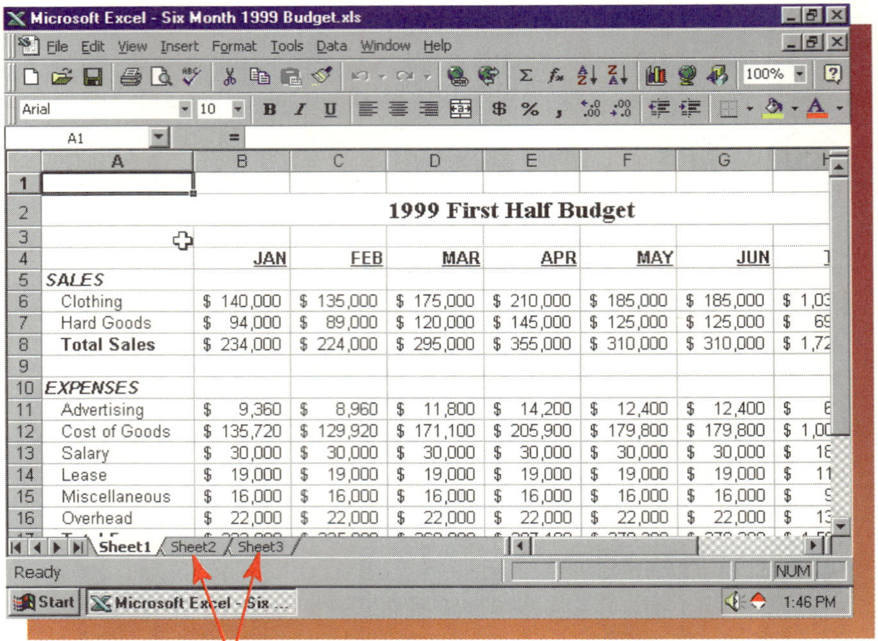

blank sheets

to the next sheet, press Ctrl + Page Up; to move to the previous sheet, press Ctrl + Page Down.

By default new Excel workbook files include three blank sheets. You used the first sheet to hold the first half budget data. To move to the next blank sheet,

- Click Sheet2 tab.

Your worksheet should be similar to Figure 3-2.

blank second sheet in workbook

FIGURE 3-2

cell selector is in active sheet

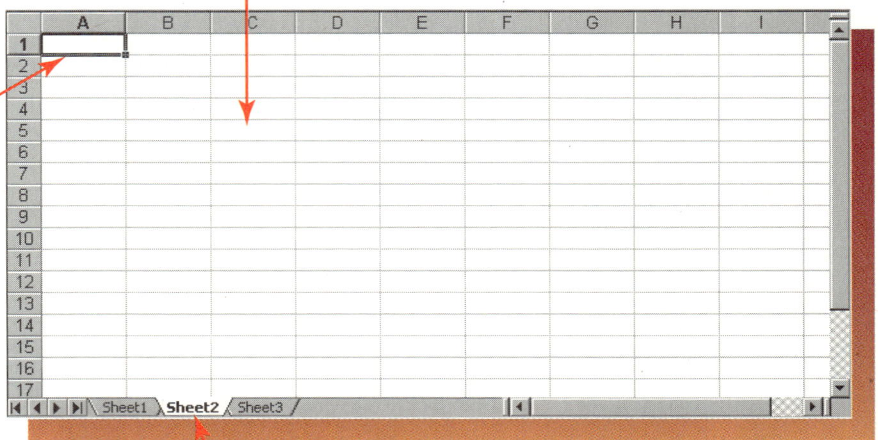

bold name indicates active sheet

The blank worksheet, Sheet 2, is the active sheet because it contains the cell selector and is the sheet that will be affected by any actions. The name of the active sheet is always bold in the sheet tab. Sheet1, containing the budget for the first six months, is behind Sheet2.

To make it easier to enter the budget for the next six months, you want to copy the contents of the first half budget in Sheet1 into another sheet in the workbook. Then you will change the month headings, the title, and the number data. Although the workbook already includes two extra blank sheets, if you pasted the data into an existing sheet, the column width settings would not be copied and you would need to reset the widths. Instead, to duplicate an existing sheet with all its formats, you need to create a new sheet.

To copy the active sheet into a new sheet, you hold down Ctrl while dragging the sheet tab to where you want the new sheet inserted. The mouse pointer changes to a ⍐ as you drag the mouse from one tab to another. The + indicates that the sheet is being copied. A black triangle ▼ also appears, indicating where the sheet will be inserted.

To move a sheet, drag the sheet tab without holding down Ctrl. The mouse pointer appears as ⍐ when the sheet is being moved.

- Click on the Sheet1 tab.
- Hold down Ctrl.
- Drag the Sheet1 tab to the Sheet2 tab. (The ▼ appears between the Sheet1 and Sheet2 tabs.)
- Release the mouse button and then Ctrl.

The menu equivalent is **E**dit/**M**ove or Copy Sheet.

Your worksheet should be similar to Figure 3-3.

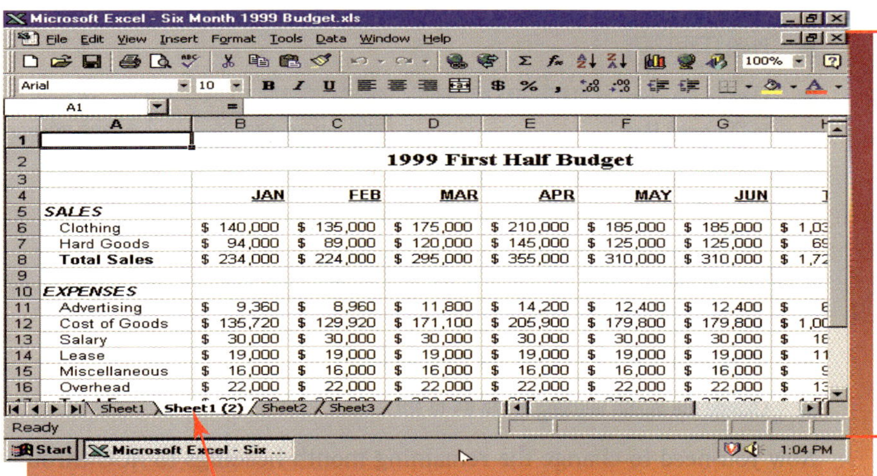

FIGURE 3-3

copied sheet

new sheet tab

Excel names the copy of the sheet Sheet1 (2) and inserts it before Sheet2. The new sheet is the active sheet and contains a duplicate of the first half budget in Sheet1.

To create a new blank sheet, use **I**nsert/**W**orksheet.

- Finally, to update the budget for July through December clothing and hard goods sales, enter the new numbers as shown in the table below.

Clothing		Hard Goods	
Cell	**Number**	**Cell**	**Number**
B6	**200000**	B7	**135000**
C6	**180000**	C7	**120000**
D6	**172000**	D7	**114000**
E6	**175000**	E7	**118000**
F6	**160000**	F7	**110000**
G6	**390000**	G7	**280000**

The worksheet has been recalculated and now contains the data for the second half.

- To see more worksheet data in the window, set the zoom to 75%.

Your screen should be similar to Figure 3-5.

FIGURE 3-5

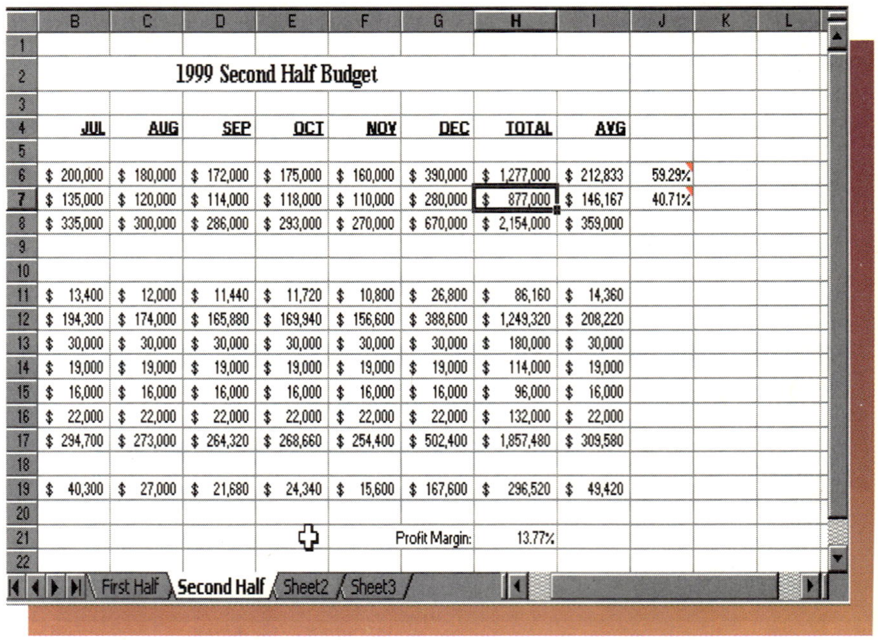

As you can see, the profit margin of 13.77 percent for this half is above the industry standard of 13.5 percent for that period.

Referencing Multiple Sheets

You also want to display a year-to-date income total in cell H22. The formula to make this calculation will sum the total income numbers from First Half cell E19 and Second Half cell E19. To reference data in another sheet in the same workbook, you enter a formula that references cells in other worksheets.

Concept 3: Referencing Sheets

A formula reference to cells in different worksheets of the same workbook allows you to use data from multiple sheets and to calculate new values based on this data. The formula contains a sheet reference as well as a cell reference. The sheet reference consists of the name of the sheet enclosed in quotes. It is separated from the cell reference by an exclamation point. For example, ="Sheet2"!B17 would display the entry in cell B17 of Sheet2 in the active cell of the current sheet. A formula can be created using references on multiple sheets; for example, =Sheet1!A1+Sheet2!B2.

The link can also be created by entering a 3-D reference in a formula. A **3-D reference** is a reference to the same cell or range on multiple sheets in the same workbook. A 3-D reference consists of the names of the beginning and ending sheets enclosed in quotes and separated by a colon. This is followed by an exclamation point and the cell or range reference. The cell or range reference is the same on each sheet in the specified sheet range. For example the formula =SUM("Sheet1:Sheet4"!H6:K6) sums the values in cell H6 of sheets 1 through 4. The formula =SUM ("Sheet1:Sheet4"!H6:K6) sums the values in the range H6 through K6 of sheets 1 through 4. Any sheets stored between the starting and ending names of the reference are included. If a sheet is inserted or deleted, the range is automatically updated. 3-D references make it easy to analyze data in the same cell or range of cells on multiple worksheets.

Just like a formula that references cells within a sheet, a formula that references cells in multiple sheets is automatically recalculated when data in a referenced cell changes.

You will enter a 3-D reference formula in cell H22 and a descriptive text entry in cell G22.

- In cell G22 enter and right-align the entry, **Year-To-Date**.
- Move to H22.
- Click Σ AutoSum.

The SUM function argument will consist of a 3-D reference to cell H19 in the First and Second Half sheets. Although a 3-D reference can be entered by typing it using the proper syntax, it is much easier to enter it by pointing to the cells on the sheets. To enter a 3-D reference, select the cell or range in the beginning sheet and then hold down ⇧Shift and click on the sheet tab of the last sheet in the range. This will include the indicated cell range on all sheets between and including the first and last sheet specified.

- Click H19.
- Hold down ⇧Shift and click the First Half tab.
- Release ⇧Shift.
- Press ←Enter.
- Move to H22.

To reference a cell or range in another sheet, begin the formula or function, hold down ⇧Shift, switch to the other sheet, and select the cell(s).

Keyboard users must enter the 3-D reference by typing it.

Your screen should be similar to Figure 3-6.

FIGURE 3-6

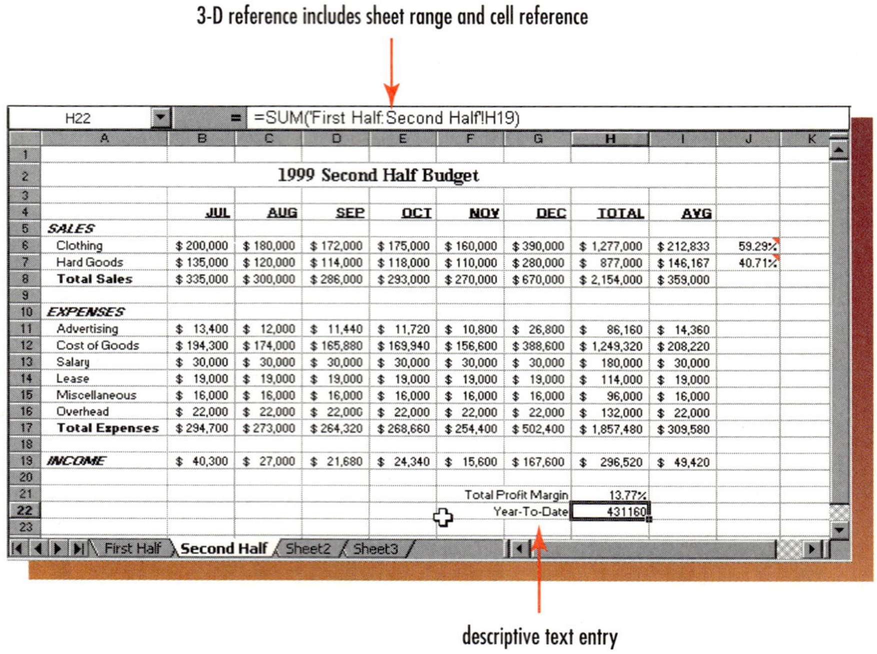

The calculated number 431,160 appears in cell H22, and the function containing a 3-D reference appears in the formula bar. The number does not display in Accounting format because it is outside the range you selected when setting the cell format.

- Change the format of cell H22 to Accounting with zero decimal places.
- Return the zoom to 100%.
- Move to cell A1 of both sheets.
- Update the workbook summary properties.
- Save the workbook file as 1999 Budget.
- Close the workbook file.

Splitting Windows

You presented the completed first and second half worksheets of the estimated operating budget for 1999 to the regional manager. The manager wants you to create another worksheet showing the entire annual budget and to include a row to calculate the monthly profit margin. Several of the changes requested by the manager have already been made and saved on your data disk in the workbook file Annual Budget.

- To see the revised and expanded budget, open the workbook file Annual Budget.xls.

Your screen should be similar to Figure 3-7.

linking formula that references first half sheet

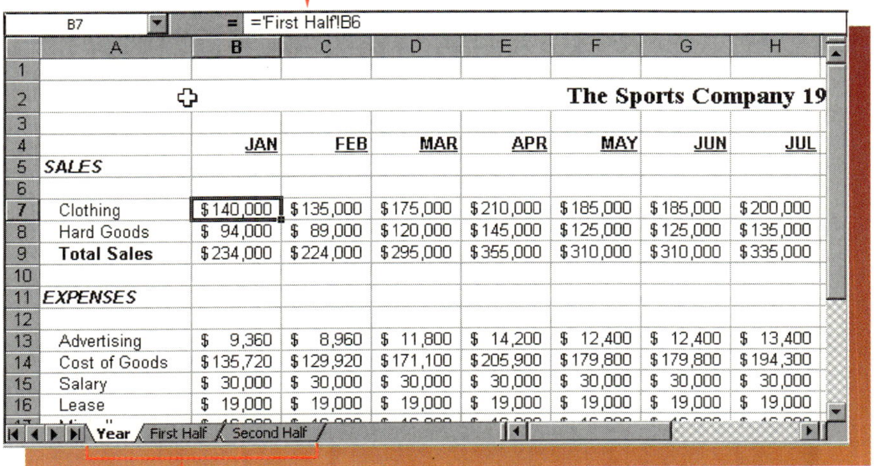

workbook file contains three sheets

FIGURE 3-7

The workbook file now contains three sheets: Year, First Half, and Second Half. The Year sheet contains the numbers for 12 months. Most of the monthly values in the Year sheet, such as cell B7, contain linking formulas that reference the appropriate cells in the First Half or Second Half sheets. Others, such as the total formulas and the formula to calculate the income, do not reference cells outside the Year worksheet.

Note: Although there are quicker ways to move to cells in the worksheet, use the arrow keys when directed. Your screen will then show the same rows and columns as the figures in the text.

To view the rest of the worksheet below row 16 and to the right of column H, using the directional keys,

- Move to B23.
- Move to O23.

If row 23 is already visible in your window, move to B28 and then to O28.

Your screen should be similar to Figure 3-8.

when row and column headings are not visible, it is difficult to know what the data represents

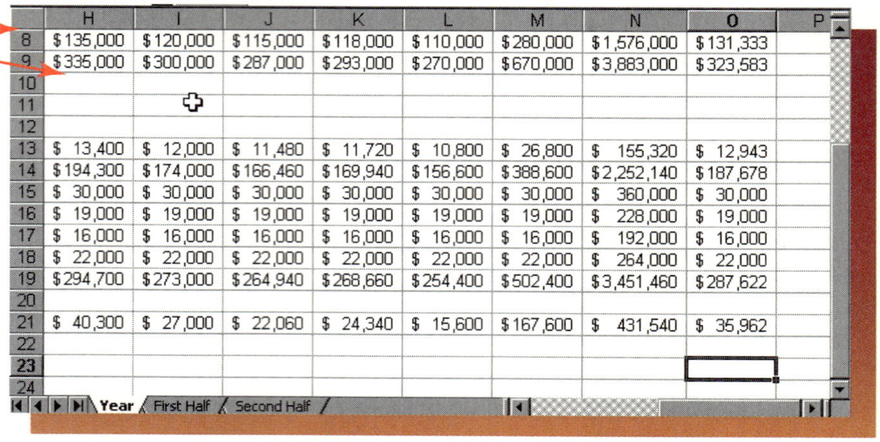

FIGURE 3-8

The row (23) where you need to enter the formula to calculate the profit margin is now visible, as are the Total and Average columns and the numbers for the remaining months. However, it is difficult to know what the numbers represent because the row and column headings are not visible. For example, the number in cell J17 is $16,000. Is this number a lease expense, an advertising expense, or a miscellaneous expense? Which month do the numbers in column J refer to? Without seeing the row and column headings, it is difficult for you to know.

Whenever you scroll a large worksheet, you will find that information you may need to view in one area scrolls out of view as you move to another area. Although you could reduce the zoom percent to view more of the worksheet in the window, you still could not see the entire worksheet because it is too large. To view different areas of the same sheet at the same time, you can split the window into panes.

Concept 4: Split Windows

A sheet window can be split into sections called **panes** to make it easier to view different parts of the sheet at the same time. The panes can consist of any number of columns or rows along the top or left edge of the window. You can divide the sheet into two panes either horizontally or vertically, or four panes if you split the window both vertically and horizontally.

Each pane can be scrolled independently to display different areas of the sheet. When split vertically, the panes scroll together when you scroll vertically, but scroll independently when you scroll horizontally. Horizontal panes scroll together when you scroll horizontally, but independently when you scroll vertically.

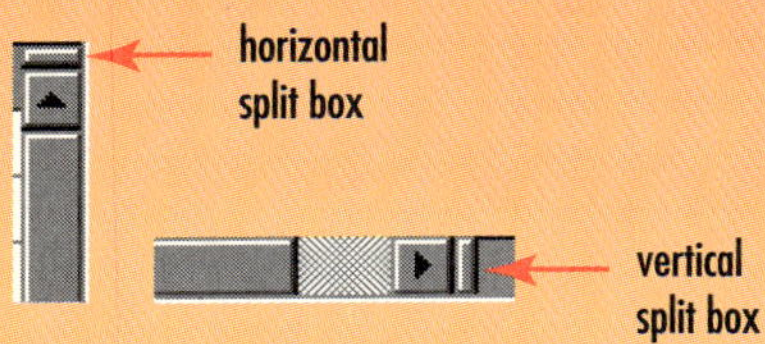

Horizontal Split

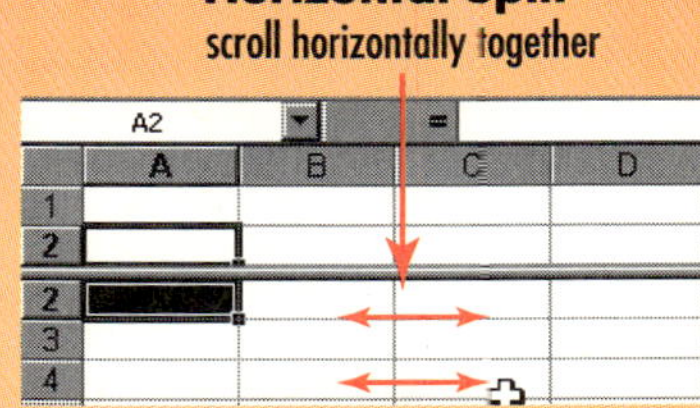

Vertical Split

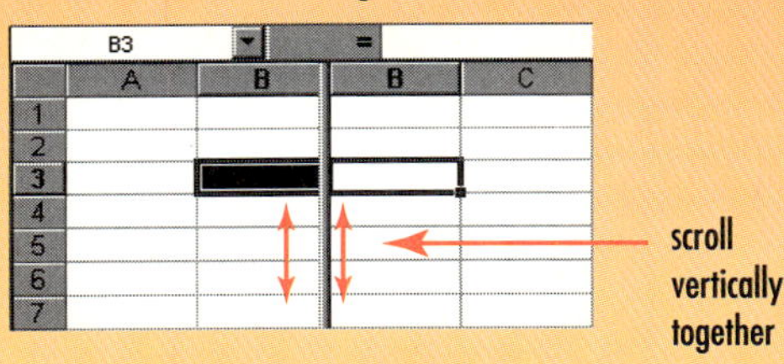

Four-Way Split

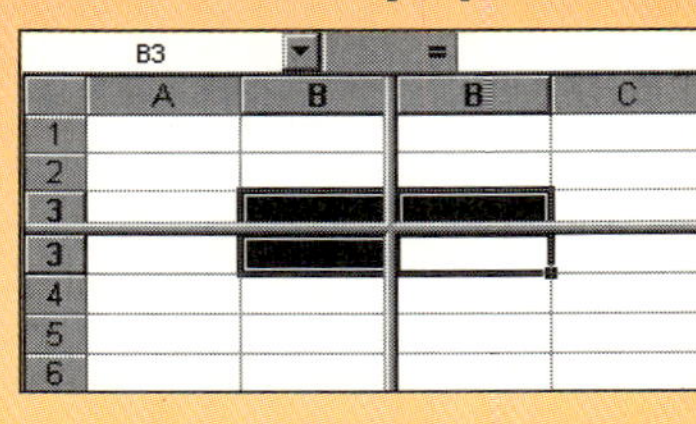

Dragging the split box at the top of the vertical scroll bar downward creates a horizontal split, and dragging the split box at the right end of the horizontal scroll bar leftward creates a vertical split. The Window/Split command can be used to quickly create a four-way split at the active cell.

Panes are most useful for viewing a worksheet that consists of different areas or sections. Creating panes allows you to display the different sections of the worksheet in separate panes and then to quickly switch between panes to access the data in the different sections without having to repeatedly scroll to the areas.

To display the column headings in the window at the same time as you are viewing data in cell J17, you will divide the window into two horizontal panes. Pointing to the vertical split box and dragging the split bar to the left creates a vertical pane.

- Point to the split box in the vertical scroll bar.
- Drag down and position the bar at row 10.

> The mouse pointer changes to ÷ when you can drag to create a split.

Your screen should be similar to Figure 3-9.

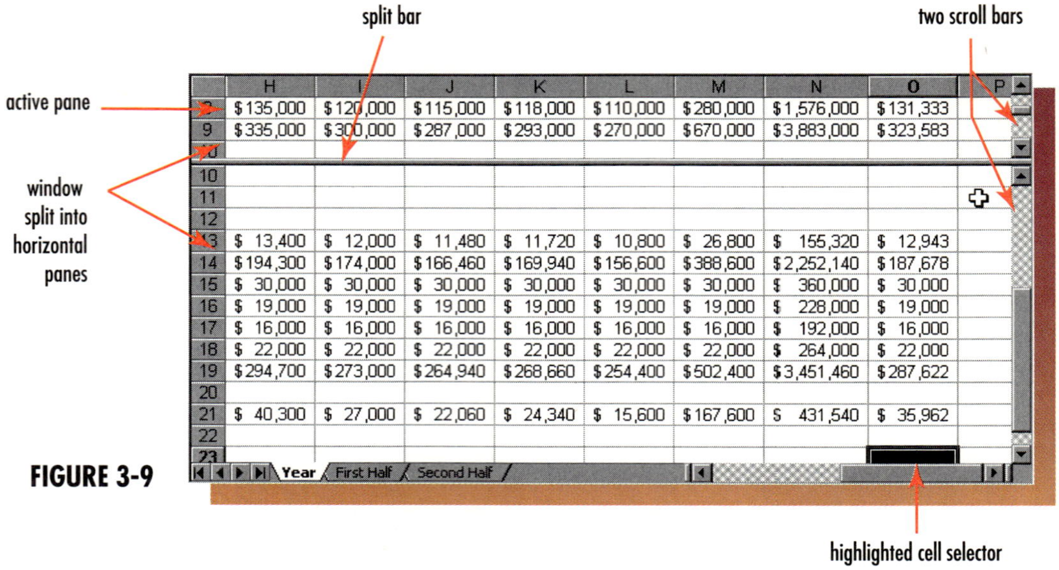

FIGURE 3-9

There are now two horizontal panes with two separate scroll bars. The highlighted cell selector is visible in the lower pane. The top pane also has a cell selector in cell O23, but it is not visible because that area of the worksheet is not displayed in the upper pane. When the same area of a worksheet is visible in multiple panes, the cell selector in the panes that are not active is highlighted whereas the cell selector in the **active pane** is clear. The active pane will be affected by your movement vertically. The cell selector moves in both panes, but only the active pane scrolls.

You will scroll the top pane vertically to display the month headings and then scroll horizontally to display the row headings.

- Click J10 in the upper pane to display the active cell selector in the pane.
- Press ↑ (6 times).
- Press Home.

Your worksheet should be similar to Figure 3-10.

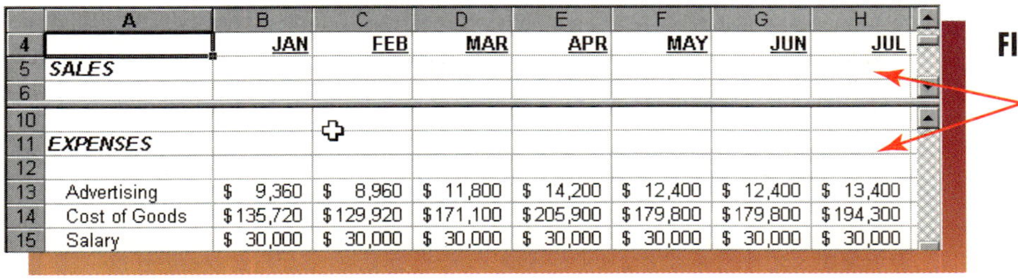

	A	B	C	D	E	F	G	H
4		JAN	FEB	MAR	APR	MAY	JUN	JUL
5	*SALES*							
6								
10								
11	*EXPENSES*							
12								
13	Advertising	$ 9,360	$ 8,960	$ 11,800	$ 14,200	$ 12,400	$ 12,400	$ 13,400
14	Cost of Goods	$135,720	$129,920	$171,100	$205,900	$179,800	$179,800	$194,300
15	Salary	$ 30,000	$ 30,000	$ 30,000	$ 30,000	$ 30,000	$ 30,000	$ 30,000

FIGURE 3-10

The lower pane did not scroll when you moved vertically through the upper pane to display the month headings. However, both panes scrolled together when you moved horizontally. The cell selector in the lower pane is in the same cell location as in the upper pane (A4), although it is not visible.

Creating panes is helpful when you want to display and access distant areas of a worksheet quickly. After scrolling the data in the panes to display the appropriate worksheet area, you can then quickly switch between panes to make changes to the data that is visible in the pane. This saves you the time of scrolling to the area each time you want to view or make changes to it. To clear the horizontal split from the window,

- Double-click anywhere on the split bar.

The menu equivalent is Window/Remove Split.

Freezing Panes

Next you need to enter the formula to calculate the profit margin in row 23. To make it easier to enter the formula, you will first split the window into frozen panes.

Concept 5: Freeze Panes

Freezing panes prevents the data in the pane from scrolling as you move to different areas in a worksheet. You can freeze the information in the top and left panes of a window only.

The Freeze command on the Window menu is used to freeze panes. To create two horizontal panes with the upper pane frozen, move the cell selector in the leftmost column in the window to the row below where you want the split to appear before choosing the command.

To create two vertical panes with the left pane frozen, move the cell selector in the top row of the window and select the column to the right of where you want the split to appear.

To create four panes, click the cell below and to the right of where you want the split.

This feature is most useful when your worksheet is organized using row and column headings. It allows you to keep the titles on the top and left edge of your worksheet in view as you scroll horizontally and vertically through the worksheet data.

Top Pane Frozen

	A	B	C
9	**Total Sales**	$234,000	$224,000
10			
19	**Total Expenses**	$232,080	$225,880
20			
21	*INCOME*	$ 1,920	$ (1,880)
22			

Left Pane Frozen

	A	M	N
9	**Total Sales**	$670,000	$3,883,000
10			
11	*EXPENSES*		
12			
13	Advertising	$ 26,800	$ 155,320
14	Cost of Goods	$388,600	$2,252,140

Top and Left Panes Frozen

	A	M	N
3			
4		**DEC**	**TOTAL**
11	*EXPENSES*		
12			
13	Advertising	$ 26,800	$ 155,320
14	Cost of Goods	$388,600	$2,252,140

You want to keep the month headings in row 4 and the row headings in column A visible in the window at all times while entering the formula to calculate the profit margin in row 23. To do this, you will create four panes and freeze the headings in the upper and left panes. When creating frozen panes, first position the sheet in the window to display the information you want to appear in the top and left panes. This is because data in the frozen panes cannot be scrolled like data in regular panes. The worksheet is already positioned appropriately in the window.

- Move to B5
- Choose Window/Freeze Panes

Your worksheet should be similar to Figure 3-11.

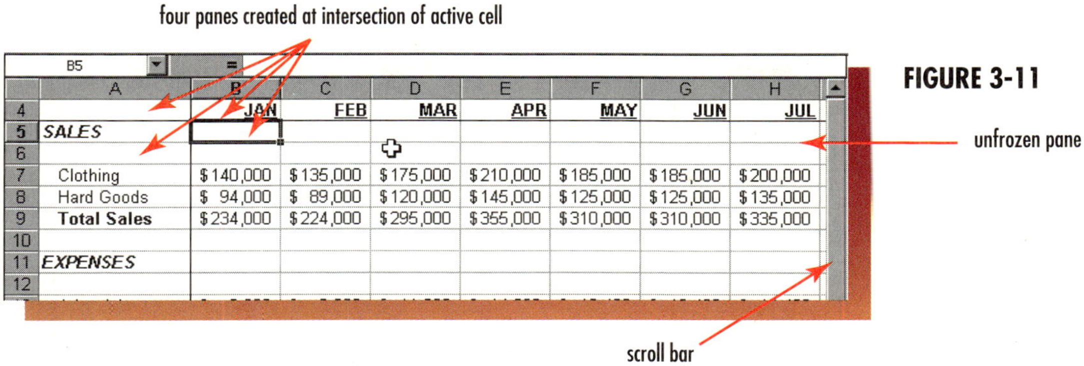

FIGURE 3-11

Only one scroll bar is displayed because the only pane that can be scrolled is the larger lower right pane.

Now, to verify that the rows and columns in the top and left panes are frozen,

- Press ↑ (3 times).
- Press ←.
- Press ↓ (3 times).
- Press →.

Look at the Name box to check the location of the cell selector as you move within the frozen panes.

The cell selector moved through the top and left panes, but the data in the panes did not scroll because the panes are frozen. Also, there is only one cell selector that moves from one pane to another over the pane divider, making it unnecessary to click on the pane to make it active before moving the cell selector in it.

Now, while the panes are frozen, you will enter the formula to calculate the profit margin in cell B23. The formula to calculate the monthly profit margin divides the monthly income by the monthly total sales.

- Move to B23.
- Enter the formula **=B21/B9 in cell B23**.
- Change the display of this number to a percent with two decimal places.

Use [%] to set the format to percent and [.00] to increase the decimal places.

The profit margin for January is .82%. Next you need to copy the formula across the row through the Total column. Because the column headings are frozen in the upper pane, it will be easy to see which column is the Total column while you are specifying the paste range.

- Copy the formula in cell B23 across the row through the Total column (N23).

Your screen should be similar to Figure 3-12.

FIGURE 3-12

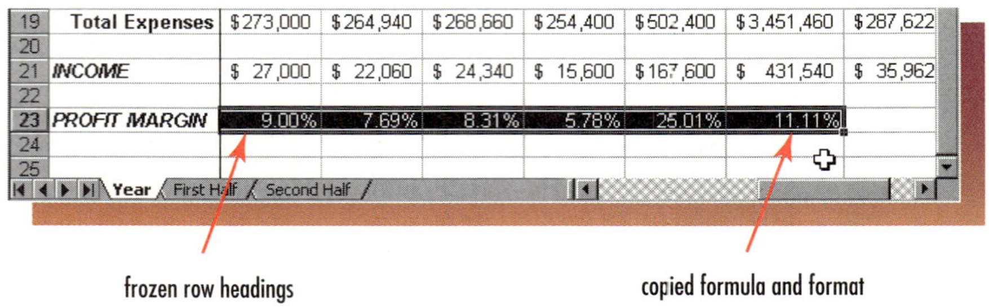

19	Total Expenses	$273,000	$264,940	$268,660	$254,400	$502,400	$3,451,460	$287,622
20								
21	*INCOME*	$ 27,000	$ 22,060	$ 24,340	$ 15,600	$167,600	$ 431,540	$ 35,962
22								
23	*PROFIT MARGIN*	9.00%	7.69%	8.31%	5.78%	25.01%	11.11%	
24								
25								

The total profit margin for the year displayed in cell N23 is 11.11%. As you can see, freezing panes makes it much easier to navigate in and use a large worksheet.

Using What-If Analysis

The manager wants the store to show an annual profit margin of between 12 and 13 percent. Using the figures as budgeted for the year, the total profit margin of 11.11 percent is below this objective. In addition, the manager wants the first half profit margin to meet the industry standard of 100% for that period. After some consideration, you decide to reduce monthly salary expenses by scheduling fewer employees to work during the slow period of January to June to increase the first half profit margin. This change will also increase the profit margin for the year.

You want to see the effect on the first half profit margin as you substitute different salary expense values for the six months. The process of evaluating what effect reducing the salary expenses will have on the profit margin is called what-if analysis.

Concept 6: What-If Analysis

What-if analysis is a technique used to evaluate the effects of changing selected factors in a worksheet. This technique is a common accounting function that has been made much easier with the introduction of spreadsheet programs. By substituting different values in cells that are referenced by formulas, you can quickly see the effect of the changes when the formulas are recalculated.

You want to see the effect on the total profit margin of reducing salary expenses a set amount each month. First you want to see the effect of reducing the salary expenses to $28,000 per month.

- Switch to the First Half sheet.
- Scroll the window so that the month headings are displayed in the top row in the window.
- Freeze the window at cell B5.
- Enter 28000 in cell B13 and copy this value to cells C13 through G13.
- Move to H21.

Your screen should be similar to Figure 3-13.

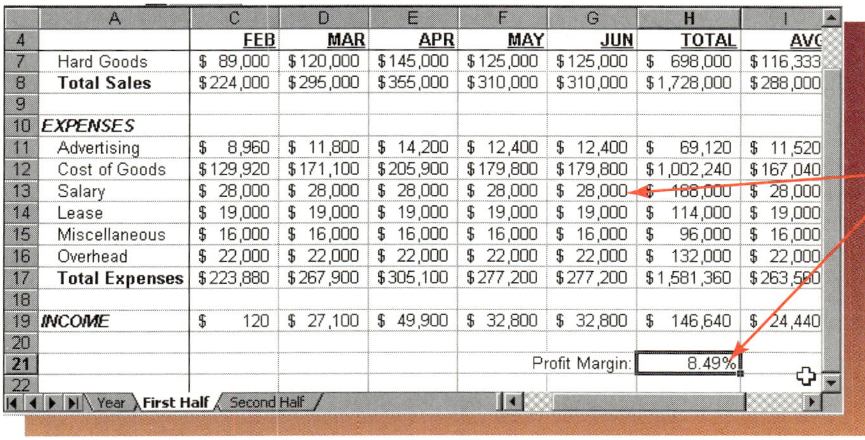

	A	C	D	E	F	G	H	I
4		FEB	MAR	APR	MAY	JUN	TOTAL	AVG
7	Hard Goods	$ 89,000	$120,000	$145,000	$125,000	$125,000	$ 698,000	$116,333
8	**Total Sales**	$224,000	$295,000	$355,000	$310,000	$310,000	$1,728,000	$288,000
9								
10	*EXPENSES*							
11	Advertising	$ 8,960	$ 11,800	$ 14,200	$ 12,400	$ 12,400	$ 69,120	$ 11,520
12	Cost of Goods	$129,920	$171,100	$205,900	$179,800	$179,800	$1,002,240	$167,040
13	Salary	$ 28,000	$ 28,000	$ 28,000	$ 28,000	$ 28,000	$ 168,000	$ 28,000
14	Lease	$ 19,000	$ 19,000	$ 19,000	$ 19,000	$ 19,000	$ 114,000	$ 19,000
15	Miscellaneous	$ 16,000	$ 16,000	$ 16,000	$ 16,000	$ 16,000	$ 96,000	$ 16,000
16	Overhead	$ 22,000	$ 22,000	$ 22,000	$ 22,000	$ 22,000	$ 132,000	$ 22,000
17	**Total Expenses**	$223,880	$267,900	$305,100	$277,200	$277,200	$1,581,360	$263,560
18								
19	*INCOME*	$ 120	$ 27,100	$ 49,900	$ 32,800	$ 32,800	$ 146,640	$ 24,440
20								
21						Profit Margin:	8.49%	
22								

FIGURE 3-13

Now by looking in cell H21 you can see that decreasing the salary expenses has increased the profit margin for the first half to 8.49 percent. This is still below the industry standard of 10 percent for the period.

Using Solver

Solver is an Excel add-on program that must be installed. If it is not on your system, skip this section and enter the value 23604 in B13 through G13 to attain a 10 percent total profit margin.

As you can see, it may take several guesses before you find the salary expense number that will increase the first half profit margin to 10 percent. A quicker way to find the salary expense value is to use the Solver tool.

Concept 7: Solver

Solver is an Excel tool that answers what-if problems by determining the value of a cell by changing values in one or more cells in the worksheet. Solver calculates a formula to achieve a given value by changing one of the variables that affect the formula. To do this Solver works backward from the result of a formula to find the numbers. The cells you select must be related through formulas on the worksheet. If not related, changing one will not change the other.

You will use Solver to find the salary numbers that will make the solution to the formula in cell H21 10 percent.

- Choose Tools/Solver.

The dialog box on your screen should be similar to Figure 3-14.

FIGURE 3-14

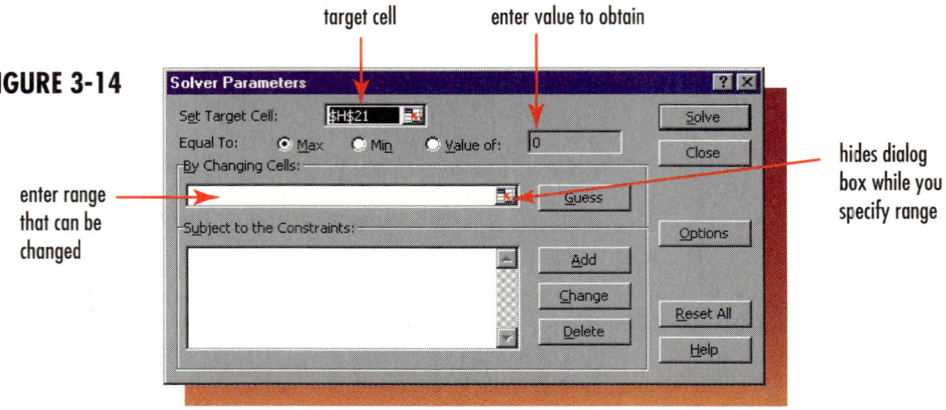

In the Solver Parameters dialog box, you need to supply three items of information. The cell reference of the cell containing the formula you want to solve is entered in the Set Target Cell text box. The cell reference of the active cell, H21, is already correctly entered in this box.

The number you want as the result of the formula is entered in the Equal To text box. You can set the number to be a maximum, minimum, or an exact number. The maximum option sets the target cell to the highest possible number, while the minimum option sets the target cell for the lowest possible number. In this case, however, you are looking for a specific number. To specify an exact number of 10 percent,

- Select Value of.
- Type **.10**.

The final item needed is the cells whose contents can be changed when the formula is computed. These are the adjustable cells. This range is entered in the By Changing Cells text box. Specifying this range is the same as specifying a range when using the Paste Function feature. In this case, the cells to change are the range of cells B13 through G13. To enter the range and have Solver find the values to meet the parameters,

- Click [icon].
- Select the range B13 through G13.
- Click [icon].
- Click Solve.

The status bar briefly displays the message "Setting Up Problem" while Solver finds the solution.

Your screen should be similar to Figure 3-15.

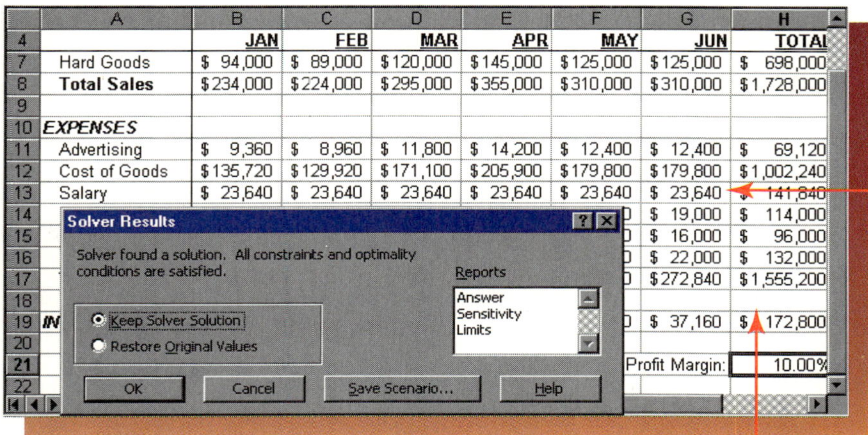

FIGURE 3-15

If necessary, move the Solver Results dialog box to see the salary values in row 13.

The Solver Results dialog box is displayed indicating Solver found a solution. The new salary numbers are entered in the worksheet range and the worksheet is automatically recalculated. The profit margin is 10 percent if salary expenses are reduced to $23,640 per month. This was a lot quicker than making multiple guesses as to the correct value and changing it manually each time.

The Solver Results dialog box allows you to keep the Solver solution, restore original values, or create a report of the results. The default selection to keep the Solver results is acceptable. In addition, you can create several different reports of the Solver results: Answer, Sensitivity, and Limits. These reports are used to help you analyze how the new numbers affect the worksheet. To create a report of the Solver solution,

- Select Answer from the Reports list box.
- Choose OK.

The message "Forming Answer Report" is briefly displayed in the status bar as the Answer report is created. A new sheet tab named Answer Report 1 has been inserted before the First Half sheet.

- Make the Answer Report 1 sheet active.

Your screen should be similar to Figure 3-16.

FIGURE 3-16

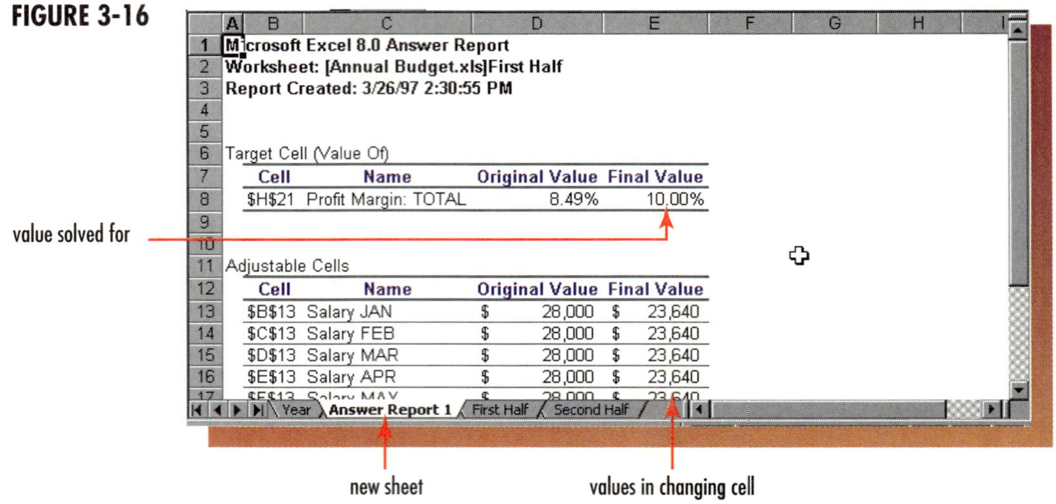

The target cell section of the report shows the original profit margin value of 8.49 percent and the final value of 10 percent. The Adjustable Cells area shows the original and final values for each cell that was changed to achieve the profit margin of 10 percent. The final value entered in each adjustable cell will be the same number even if the original values were different in each cell.

Now you want to see what effect changing the salary values in the first half had on the annual profit margin.

- Make the Year sheet active.

The total profit margin in cell N23 is now 12.10 percent and falls within the range of the industry standard. The total profit margin for the year increased because reducing the salary expense in the first six-month sheet changed the values in the annual sheet, which in turn affected the annual profit margin.

Moving a Sheet

Next you want to move the Answer Report 1 sheet after the Second Half sheet. You can quickly rearrange sheets in a workbook by dragging the sheet tab to the new location. Just as when copying a sheet, the ▾ symbol indicates where the sheet will appear.

- Drag the Answer Report 1 tab to the right end of the Second Half tab.

- Unfreeze the panes in the First Half and Year sheets

The Window/Unfreeze command is used to unfreeze panes.

Note: If you are exiting Excel at the end of Part 1, enter your name in cell A4 of the Answer Report and print the Answer Report only. Save the workbook as 1999 Annual Budget. When you begin Part 2, load Excel, open the 1999 Annual Budget workbook, and display the Year sheet.

Part 2

Opening a Second Workbook

Next you want to create a summary of the annual budget in a separate workbook file. The summary will contain the worksheet headings and the total numbers only. The headings for the summary worksheet budget have already been entered and saved for you in a workbook file.

- To see this workbook, open the file Summary Budget.xls.

Excel displays the Summary Budget workbook file in a second window on top of the Annual Budget workbook window. There are now two active workbook files. To view both files side by side, you will tile the windows.

- Choose Window/Arrange/Tiled/ OK .

Your screen should be similar to Figure 3-17.

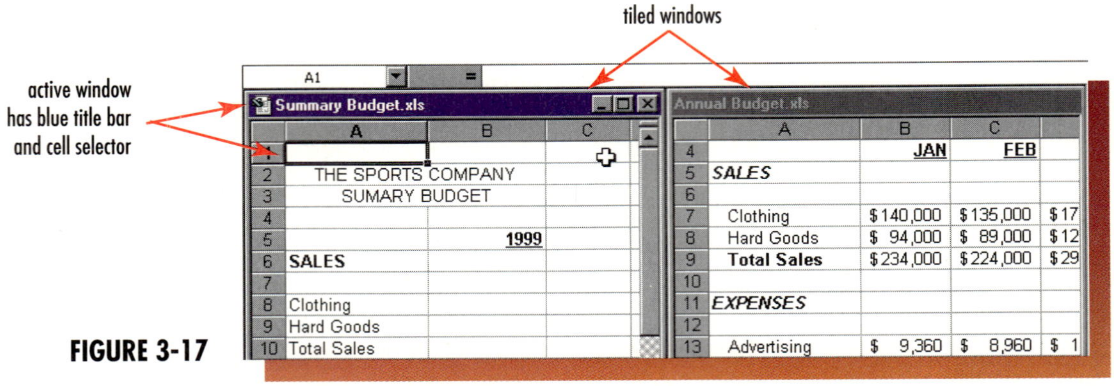

FIGURE 3-17

The two open workbook windows are displayed side by side in the workspace. The title bars display the file names. The window displaying the Summary Budget workbook file is the active window. The file in the active window will be affected by your changes. You can tell it is the active window because it contains the cell selector and the title bar is blue. Simply clicking on the window makes it the active window.

You can also press Ctrl+F6 to switch to the workbook window, or Ctrl+⇧Shift+F6 to switch to the previous window.

- Click on the Annual Budget workbook window.
- Scroll the window to display cell N23.

The cell selector is in the same location it was last in when using that window. If a range was selected, it is still active. You can also display different parts of a sheet or different sheets in a workbook in separate windows. As you will see, using multiple windows makes it easier to enter, edit, and compare data within and between workbooks.

Spell-Checking a Sheet

You notice that the word "Summary" in the title of the Summary Budget worksheet is spelled incorrectly. Just to make sure there are no other spelling errors, you will check the spelling of all text entries in this worksheet.

Concept 8: Spelling Checker

Excel includes a Spelling Checker tool that locates misspelled words, duplicate words, and capitalization irregularities and proposes the correct spelling. The Spelling Checker compares each word to a dictionary of words. If the word does not appear in the main dictionary or in a custom dictionary, it is identified as misspelled. The **main dictionary** is part of the Word program; a **custom dictionary** is one you can create to hold words you commonly use but that are not included in the main dictionary.

Excel also includes an AutoCorrect feature that corrects typing errors automatically as you type by comparing each completed word to a list of commonly mistyped words and phrases. You can also add words and phrases you commonly mistype to the list and they will be corrected automatically as you type.

If you have Microsoft Office, the same spelling dictionary and listing of AutoCorrect entries is shared with the other Office applications.

Excel begins checking all worksheet entries from the active cell forward. To check the spelling in the Summary sheet,

- Make the Summary Budget window active.
- Click Spelling.

The menu equivalent is Tools/Spelling or F7.

Your screen should be similar to Figure 3-18.

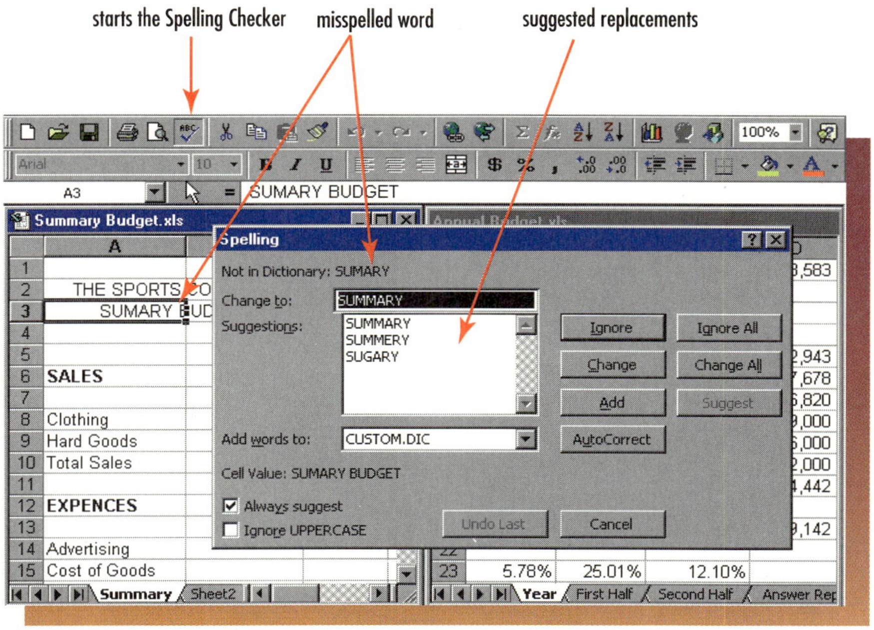

FIGURE 3-18

The Spelling Checker operates the same way in all Office 97 programs.

Immediately Excel begins checking the worksheet for words that it cannot locate in its main dictionary. The cell selector moves to the first cell containing a misspelled word, and the Spelling dialog box is displayed. The word it cannot locate in the dictionary is displayed in the first line of the dialog box. The Change To text box displays the suggested replacement. A list of other possible replacements is displayed in the Suggestions list box. If the Change To replacement is not correct, you could select from the suggestions list or type in the correct word in the Change To text box.

The option buttons shown in the table below have the following effects:

Option	Effect
Ignore	Leaves selected word unchanged
Ignore All	Leaves this and all identical words in worksheet unchanged
Change	Changes selected word to word displayed in Change To text box
Change All	Changes this and all identical words in worksheet to word displayed in Change To text box
Add	Adds selected word to a custom dictionary so Excel will not question word during subsequent spell checks

To accept the suggested replacement,

- Click Change.

The correction is made in the worksheet, and the program continues checking the worksheet and locates the second error, Expenses.

- Correct the word.

The program continues checking the worksheet and does not locate any other errors. A dialog box is displayed, indicating that the entire worksheet has been checked. When it reaches the end of the sheet, if the cell selector was not at the beginning of the sheet when checking started, the program will ask if you want to continue checking at the beginning of the sheet. To end spell-checking,

- Click OK.

Linking Workbooks

You need to copy the numbers from the Total column in the Year sheet of the Annual Budget workbook file into the Summary sheet of the Summary Budget workbook file. However, because you are concerned that more changes may be made to the annual budget, you want to create a link between cells in the two workbook files. Linking the workbooks will ensure that the Summary Budget file will be automatically updated if changes are made in the Annual Budget workbook.

Concept 9: Link Workbooks

A link creates a connection between files that updates the linked data automatically in one file whenever the data changes in the other file. The link between the workbook files is formed by entering an **external reference formula** in one workbook that refers to a cell in another workbook. When data in a linked cell changes, the workbook that is affected by this change is automatically updated whenever it is opened.

The formula is entered in the workbook that receives the data. This workbook file is called the **dependent workbook**. The workbook that supplies the data is called the **source workbook**. The cell containing the external reference formula (the dependent cell) refers to the cell (the source cell) in the source file that contains the data to be copied.

An external reference formula uses the following format:

=[workbook]file reference!cell reference

The file reference consists of the file name of the source file followed by the name of the sheet. The cell reference of the cell or range of cells containing the number to be copied into the dependent workbook follows the file reference. The two parts of the formula are separated by an exclamation point.

You will create a link between the Summary Budget and Annual Budget workbooks by entering external reference formulas in the Summary worksheet that references the cells containing the total numbers in the Year worksheet. The Annual Budget workbook is the source workbook, and the Summary Budget workbook is the dependent workbook.

The first external reference formula you will enter will link the total clothing sales numbers. To create an external reference formula, you copy the contents of the source cell to the Clipboard, switch to the dependent workbook, and then use the Edit/Paste Link command to create the external reference formula in the specified cell of the dependent workbook. The source cell is cell N7 of the Year sheet in the Annual Budget workbook.

- Move to cell N7 of the Year sheet in the Annual Budget workbook.
- Click [Copy button] Copy.
- Move to cell B8 of the Summary worksheet.
- Choose Edit/Paste Special/[Paste Link].

Your screen should be similar to Figure 3-19.

FIGURE 3-19

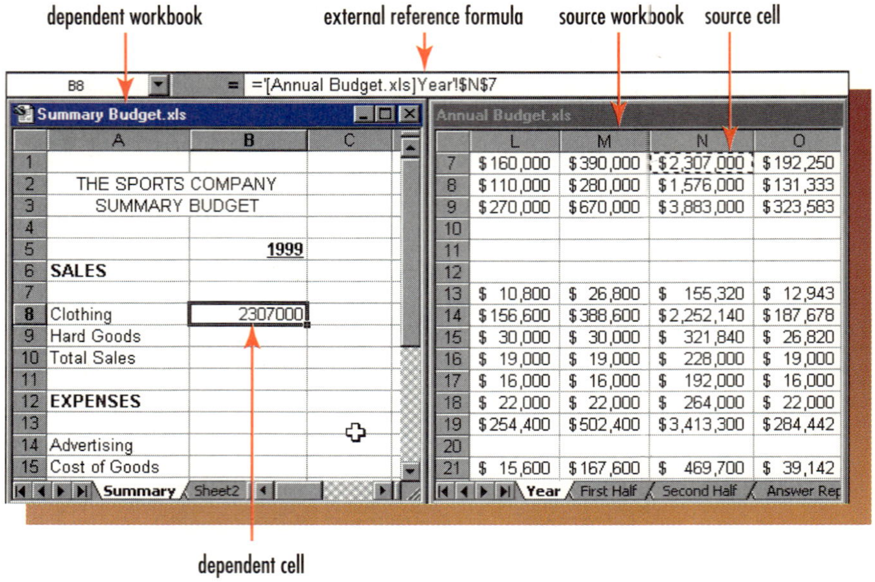

The link is created by entering an external reference formula in the selected cell of the dependent workbook. The formula is displayed in the formula bar, and the number in cell N7 of the source workbook is copied into the dependent workbook and displayed in cell B8. Notice that Excel uses absolute references in the external reference formula. Also notice that the cell format was not copied.

Next you want to create a link between the other total numbers in the source workbook. To do this quickly, you can copy the external reference formula down the column. However, you must first change the cell reference in the external reference formula to relative.

Double-click cell B8 to change to Edit mode.

- Display the formula in cell B8 in Edit mode.
- Position the insertion point on the N7 cell reference in the formula.
- Press F4 (3 times).
- Press ←Enter.

The cell reference (N7) is now a relative cell reference and will adjust appropriately as the formula is copied. You also want to change the cell format to Accounting before copying, so that the format and formula can be copied at the same time.

- Format cell B8 to Accounting format with dollar signs and zero decimal places.
- Copy the external reference formula in B8 down column B through row 24.
- Clear the formula from any blank cells.
- Change the format of the profit margin in cell B24 to Percent style with two decimal places.

Your screen should be similar to Figure 3-20.

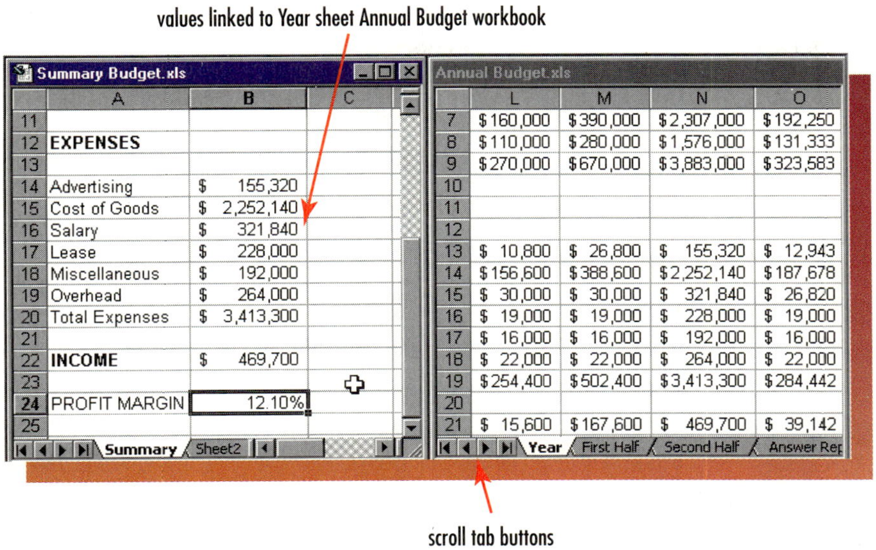

FIGURE 3-20

You showed the Summary Budget and Annual Budget workbook files to the store manager. As you expected, you need to make some changes to the data in the Annual Budget workbook. The manager advises you that the lease for the store will increase to $19,500 a month beginning in July of 1999.

- Change the lease expenses for July through December in the Second Half worksheet to 19500.

All affected formulas are recalculated. You can easily see the effect on the annual profit margin in the Summary Budget workbook window. It has decreased to 12.02 percent. However, this value is still acceptable because it is within the industry standard.

Once an external reference formula is entered in a worksheet, whenever the number(s) in the cell referenced in the source file changes, the dependent file is automatically updated if it is open. However, if the dependent file is not open, it is not updated. To ensure that a dependent file gets updated whenever the source file is opened, an alert message is displayed asking if you want to update references to unopened documents. If you respond Yes, Excel checks the source documents and updates all references to them so that you will have the latest values from the source worksheet.

Use the tab scroll buttons to display tabs that may not be visible.

Using Goal Seek

In addition, the manager has asked you to include a projected budget for the year 2000 in the Summary Budget worksheet. This data has already been entered for you and saved in a separate file named Future. You will open this file in another workbook window and copy the data to column C of the Summary workbook.

- Maximize the Summary Budget window.
- Open the file Future from your data disk.
- Move to B23.

Your screen should be similar to Figure 3-21.

FIGURE 3-21

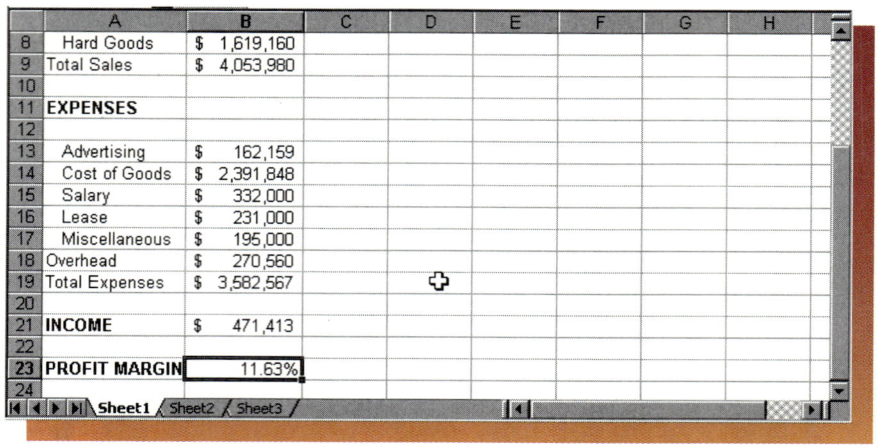

	A	B	C	D	E	F	G	H
8	Hard Goods	$ 1,619,160						
9	Total Sales	$ 4,053,980						
10								
11	**EXPENSES**							
12								
13	Advertising	$ 162,159						
14	Cost of Goods	$ 2,391,848						
15	Salary	$ 332,000						
16	Lease	$ 231,000						
17	Miscellaneous	$ 195,000						
18	Overhead	$ 270,560						
19	Total Expenses	$ 3,582,567						
20								
21	**INCOME**	$ 471,413						
22								
23	**PROFIT MARGIN**	11.63%						
24								

You see that the profit margin for 2000 is 11.63 percent. The first change you need to make to the 2000 budget is to adjust the salary expenses so the profit margin is at least 12 percent for the year. To find this number quickly, you will use the Goal Seek tool.

Concept 10: Goal Seek

The Goal Seek tool is similar to Solver in that it is used to find the value needed in one cell to attain a result you want in another cell. The difference is that the value of only one cell can be changed. Goal Seek varies the value in the cell you specify until a formula that is dependent on that cell returns the desired result.

- Choose Tools/Goal Seek.

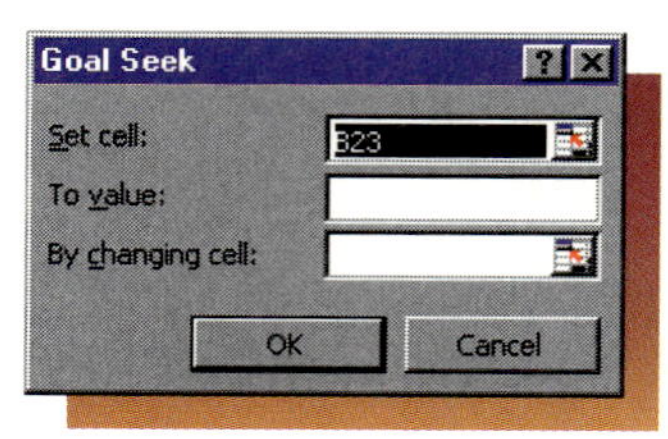

In the Goal Seek dialog box you need to specify the location of the cell containing the formula to be solved, the desired calculated value, and the cell containing the number that can be adjusted to achieve the result. You want the formula in cell B23 to calculate a result of .12 by changing the salary number in cell B15. The Set Cell text box correctly displays the current cell as the correct location of the formula to be solved.

- To complete the settings, enter **.12** in the To Value text box and cell B15 in the By Changing Cell text box.
- Click OK.

The dialog box on your screen should be similar to Figure 3-22.

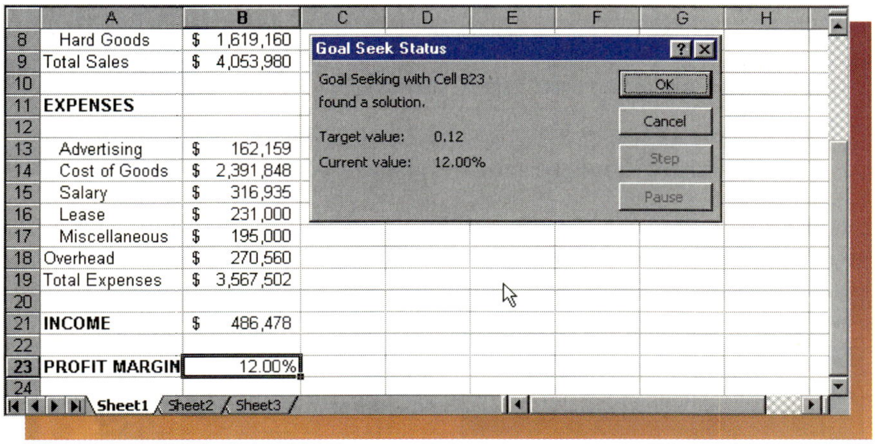

FIGURE 3-22

Goal Seek found the value of 316,935 for salary expense, making the profit margin 12 percent. To close the message box,

- Click OK.

Next you want to copy the data in cells B4 through B23 of the Future file to cells C5 through C24 in the Summary Budget file.

- Select B4 through B23 of the Future workbook.
- Click (Copy).
- Choose Window/Summary Budget.
- Move to C5.
- Click (Paste).
- Increase the column width of column C to 12 to fully display the numbers.
- Press Ctrl + Home.

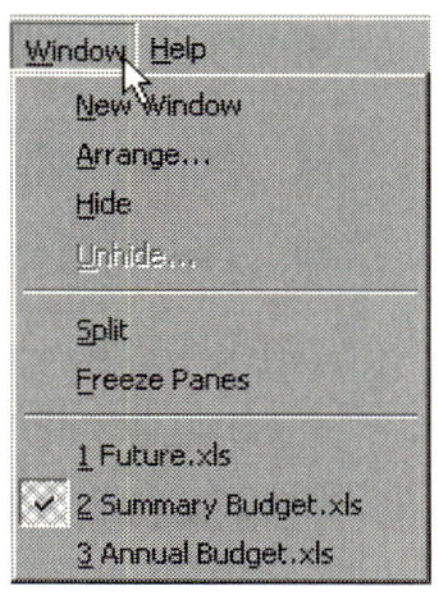

The Window menu displays the file names of all open workbooks at the bottom of the menu.

Adding Color and Borders

Before sending the Summary Budget worksheet to the store manager, you want to enhance its appearance.

- Realign the worksheet titles in cells A2 and A3 so they are centered across columns A through C.

You can align both titles simultaneously using the Format/Cells/Alignment command. If you use (Center Across Columns) each cell must be aligned independently.

The keyboard equivalent is Ctrl+Y.

- Select B19 through C19.
- Choose Edit/Repeat Borders.

The same solid border line is added below the selected range of cells.

- Finally, add a double-line style bottom border below the Income row of data in cells B22 through C22.

Aligning a Sheet on a Page

The Summary Budget workbook is complete.

Click Setup... to access the Header/Footer tab.

- Update the workbook summary properties documentation to display your name and a title.
- Preview the worksheet.
- Add a footer that displays your name, date, and page number.

The changes you made to the header and footer are reflected in the Preview screen (see Figure 3-26).

You would also like to center the worksheet horizontally on the page. To make this change,

- Click Setup....
- Choose Margins/Horizontally.
- Click OK.

Your screen should be similar to Figure 3-26.

FIGURE 3-26

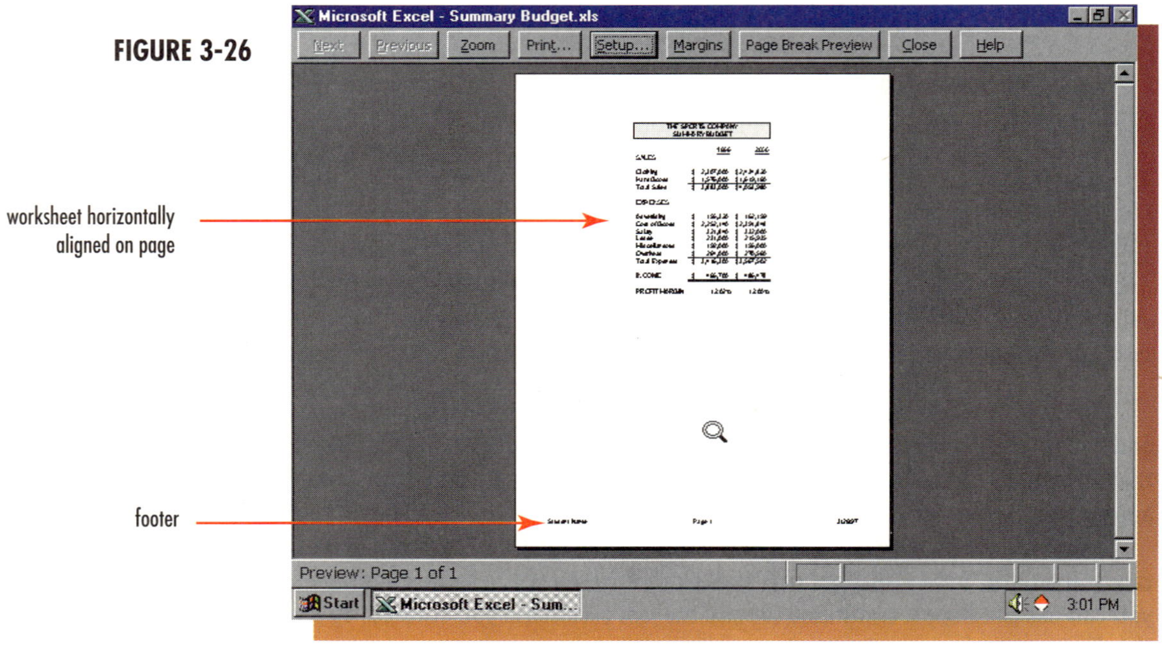

The worksheet appears the way you want it to appear when printed.

- Print the worksheet.
- Save the Summary Budget workbook as 1999-2000 Summary Budget.
- Close the file.
- Save the Future workbook file as Future Revised.
- Close the file.

The colored text and fill will appear shaded if you have a black and white printer.

Previewing a Workbook

The Annual Budget workbook window is displayed. To preview all sheets in the workbook,

- Choose File/Print/Entire Workbook/ Preview .

The first page of the Year worksheet is displayed in the Preview window.

- Use the Next button to view the other sheets in the workbook.
- Change the orientation of the Second Half sheet to Landscape.

Now you like the way the First Half and Second Half budgets are displayed, but you would like to change the Year sheet to display a custom header and fit on one page.

- Display the first page of the Year sheet and change the orientation to Landscape.

Creating Custom Headers and Footers

You would like to add a custom header to this sheet.

- Choose Setup... /Header/Footer.
- Choose Custom Header.

The Header dialog box on your screen should be similar to Figure 3-27.

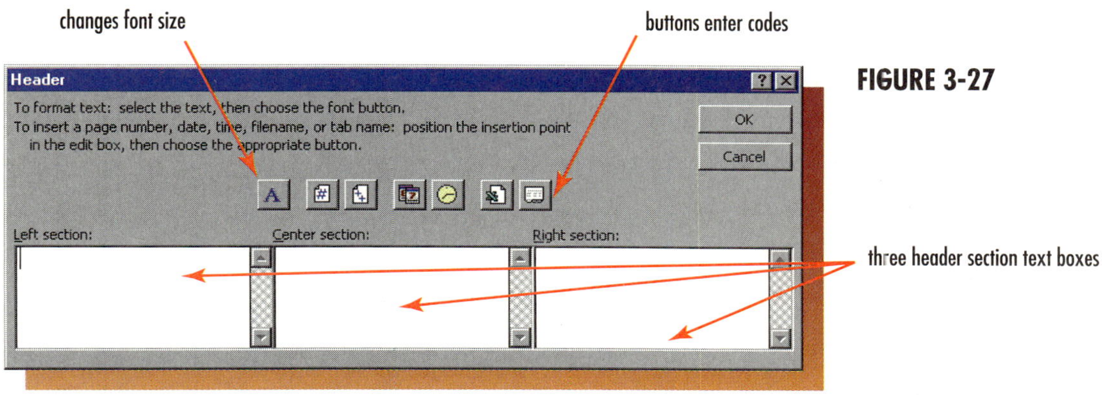

FIGURE 3-27

The Left Section text box will display the header text you entered aligned with the left margin, the Center Section will center the text, and the Right Section will right-align the text. The insertion point is currently positioned in the Left Section text box. You want to enter your name, class, and the date in this box.

- Type **Created by [your name]**.
- Press ←Enter.
- Enter the name of your class and the section or time.
- Press ←Enter.

Next you will enter the date. However, instead of typing today's date, you will enter a code that will automatically insert the current date whenever the worksheet is printed. The buttons above the section boxes are used to enter the codes for common header and footer information.

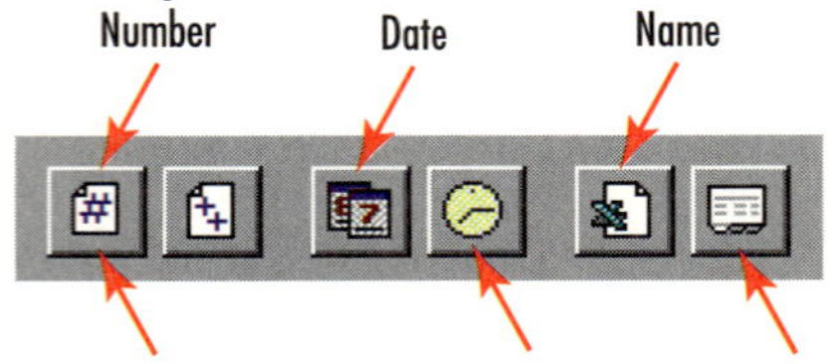

- Click Date.
- Click OK.

The header as you entered it appears in the sample header area of the dialog box.

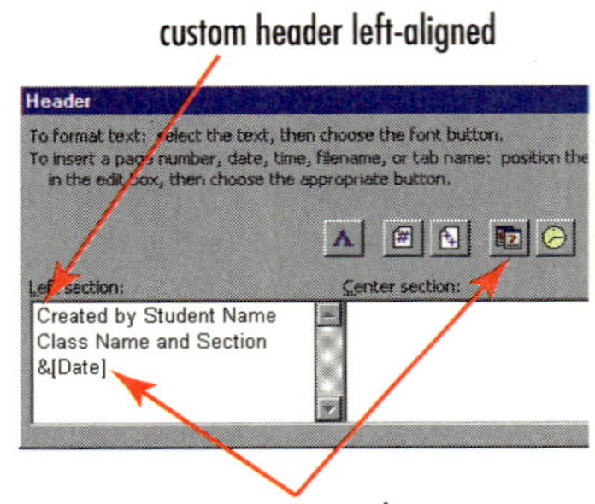

- Click OK.

You would also like the worksheet printed on one page. To do this,

- Click Setup....
- Open the Page tab.
- Choose Fit to.
- Click OK.

By default Excel fits the worksheet to one page wide and one page tall.

Your screen should be similar to Figure 3-28.

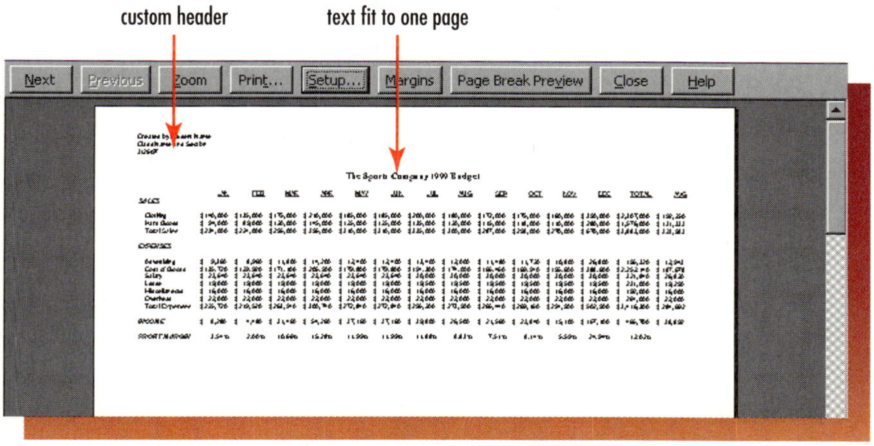

FIGURE 3-28

To print the Year worksheet only, you need to close the preview of the entire workbook and then print the Year sheet. To do this,

- Click Close.

Because the Year sheet is displayed, you can use the button to print the active sheet.

- Click Print.
- Save the file as 1999 Annual Budget, then close the workbook and exit Excel.

If you need to specify a different printer, use the Print command on the File menu to print the worksheet.

LAB REVIEW

Key Terms

3-D reference (SS95)
active pane (SS100)
custom dictionary (SS111)
dependent workbook (SS113)
external reference formula (SS113)
freeze (SS102)
main dictionary (SS111)
pane (SS99)
source workbook (SS113)
what-if analysis (SS104)

Command Summary

Command	Shortcut	Toolbar	Action
File/Print/Entire Workbook			Prints all sheets in workbook
Edit/Repeat	Ctrl + Y		Repeats last-used command
Edit/Paste Special/Paste Link			Creates a link to source document
Edit/Move or Copy Sheet			Moves or copies selected sheet
Insert/Worksheet			Creates an additional worksheet in active workbook
Format/Cells/Font/Color			Adds color to text
Format/Cells/Border/Outline			Adds border around selection
Format/Cells/Border/Bottom			Adds border to bottom edge of selection
Format/Cells/Patterns			Adds shading to selection
Format/Sheet/Rename			Renames sheet
Tools/Spelling	F7		Spell-checks worksheet
Tools/Goal Seek			Adjusts value in specified cell until a formula dependent on that cell reaches specified result
Tools/Solver			Calculates a formula to achieve a given value by changing one of variables that affects formula
Window/Arrange/Tiled			Arranges open windows side by side
Window/Unfreeze			Unfreezes window panes
Window/Freeze Panes			Freezes top and/or leftmost panes
Window/Split			Divides window into four panes at active cell
Window/Remove Split			Removes split bar from active worksheet

Matching

1. =[ANNUAL.XLS] YEAR!B12	______	**a.** prevents scrolling of information in upper and left panes of a window
2. pane	______	**b.** spell-checks worksheet
3. freeze	______	**c.** finds a specific value for a cell by adjusting value of only one other cell
4. 	______	**d.** the sections of a divided window
5. 	______	**e.** an external reference formula
6. dependent workbook	______	**f.** worksheet that supplies data in a linking formula
7. current workbook	______	**g.** worksheet that receives data in a linking formula
8. 	______	**h.** a workbook that is open and available for use
9. Goal Seek	______	**i.** adds text color
10. source workbook	______	**j.** applies bottom border

Fill-In Questions

1. Complete the following statements by filling in the blanks with the correct terms.

a. Excel checks spelling by comparing text entries to words in a(n) ____________________.

b. When a column or row is ____________, it is visible in the window all the time.

c. A worksheet window can be divided into four ________.

d. ______________ is a what-if tool that changes values in a specified range to attain a result in another cell.

e. The ________________ calculates a formula to achieve a given value by changing one of the variables that affect the formula.

f. To view two windows side by side, the Window/ ____________ command is used.

g. The link between workbook files is formed by entering a(n) ________________ in one file that refers to a cell in another file.

h. The workbook file that receives the data from a link is called the ______________________ workbook.

i. A(n) ___________ is a line of text that appears at the top of each printed page.

j. Use ________________ to find the value in a single cell to achieve the result you want in another cell.

Discussion Questions

1. Discuss the differences between splitting a window and freezing a window. When would it be appropriate to split a window? When would it be appropriate to freeze a window?

2. Discuss what happens to formulas that are linked to another workbook when the original workbook is updated. When would it be appropriate to link data between workbooks?

3. Discuss how the features on the Format menu can be used to enhance a worksheet. What should you consider when adding style changes to a worksheet?

4. Discuss how what-if analysis is used in a worksheet. How can Goal Seek and Solver help with the analysis of data in a worksheet?

Hands-On Practice Exercises

Step by Step

Rating System
☆ Easy
☆☆ Moderate
☆☆☆ Difficult

☆

1. To complete this problem, you must have completed Practice Exercise 3 in Lab 2. Open the file Fat Grams from your data disk. In this exercise you will continue to modify the worksheet.

a. Remove the underlines from the column headings. Draw a bottom border across that row.

b. Enclose the worksheet title in a box. Add text color to the title and a background color. Add a background color to the % Fat column of data.

c. Name the sheet tab.

d. Preview the worksheet. Add a custom footer that displays the file name and the sheet name. Center the worksheet horizontally. Print the worksheet. Save and replace the workbook Fat Grams.

☆☆☆

2. To complete this problem, you must have completed Practice Exercise 5 in Lab 2. In this exercise you will continue to modify the income statement for Custom Manufacturing. The sales representatives have recently completed an intensive sales seminar. The results seem positive, and the sales manager is confident that a net income of $85,000 is an attainable goal for the first six months.

a. Open the workbook file Income Statement on your data disk. Appropriately name the sheet tab. Freeze the worksheet panes below the column headings and to the right of the row headings.

b. Use Solver to determine what monthly sales will be required to reach the new net income goal. Keep the Solver solution.

c. Preview the worksheet and add a header that displays the sheet name centered. Print the worksheet centered horizontally on the page and use landscape orientation. Update the documentation to reflect the new sales goal. Save and replace the workbook file.

Next you will link Income Statement to the file Custom Sales on your data disk. This file contains the actual sales for the first six-month period.

d. Open the Custom Sales file and sum the columns and rows. Format the values to display commas and two decimal places. Center the title over the columns. Draw a single bottom border under the column headings and under the Region 4 values. Draw a double-line border under the Total row. Make any other formatting changes you wish.

e. Tile the windows. Make the Income Statement file active. Enter an external reference formula to copy the January total sales number from the Custom Sales file into the corresponding cell of the Income Statement file. Adjust the formula so it can be copied across the row. Maximize the Income Statement file window. Copy the formula. What is the total net income?

f. Unfreeze the panes. Add a note to the Sales heading in column A that informs the users that the sales numbers are linked to the total sales numbers in the Custom Sales workbook.

g. Save and replace the workbook file Income Statement. Print the worksheet using the previously defined settings. Close the file.

h. Preview the Custom Sales worksheet. Add a header that includes your name and the date. Print the worksheet centered horizontally using landscape orientation. Save and replace the workbook file Custom Sales. Close the file.

☆☆☆

3. Kevin O'Neal is a student at Metro Community College. He has just completed his final semester and will graduate with an associate's degree in Information Systems Technology. In this exercise you will calculate semester and cumulative totals and GPA for each semester.

a. Open the file Grade Report on your data disk. Rename the first four sheet tabs Fall 97, Spring 98, Fall 98, and Spring 99.

b. You can edit several sheets at once by selecting the sheets you want to change and modifying the first sheet in the group. In this portion of the exercise, you will draw an outline border around the first four rows of information on the Fall 97 through Spring 99 sheets.

- Make the Fall 97 sheet active.
- Hold down ⇧Shift as you click the Spring 99 sheet. All four sheets should be selected.
- Select cells A1 through G4 of the Fall 97 sheet.
- Draw an outline border around those cells.
- Change the color of the text and the background.
- Click A1 to clear the highlight.
- Right-click the Fall 97 sheet tab and choose the command Ungroup Sheets. Look at each sheet to see that the formatting was copied.

c. Following the above procedure, draw a bottom border across cells A7 to H7 of the four sheets. While the sheets are still selected, bold the column headings in rows 6 and 7 and bold the Semester Total and Cumulative Total headings in rows 14 and 15. Remember to ungroup the sheets when you are done.

d. In the Fall 97 sheet, multiply the Grade by the Credits Earned to calculate Total Points for Intro to Business. Copy that formula down the column. Sum the Credits Attempted, Credits Earned, and Total Points columns and display the results in the Semester Total row.

e. In cell H14, divide the Semester Total's Total Points by the Semester Total's Credits Earned to calculate the GPA for the semester. Use what-if analysis to see what Kevin's GPA would be if he had earned a 3 instead of a 2 in Western Civ. Change the grade back to a 2.

f. Go to the Spring 98 sheet. Select the Spring 98 through Spring 99 sheets and follow the above procedure to calculate Total Points, Semester Total, and GPA on three sheets at once. When you are finished, click the Fall 97 sheet. Clicking a sheet that is not selected is another way of ungrouping the sheets. Look at each sheet to see that the calculations were performed.

g. Go to cell E15 in the Fall 97 sheet. Enter the reference formula =E14 to copy the Semester Total Credits Attempted number to the Cumulative Total row. Copy the formula to cells F15 and G15 to calculate Credits Earned and Total Points.

h. Go to the Spring 98 sheet and calculate a Cumulative Total for Credits Attempted by summing the Spring 98 Semester Total and the Fall 97 Cumulative Total. (Hint: You can use pointing to enter the Cumulative Totals formula.)

i. Copy that formula to the adjacent cells to calculate Cumulative Totals for Credits Earned and Total Points. Repeat this procedure on the Fall 98 and Spring 99 sheets.

j. Go to the Fall 97 sheet. Select all four sheets. In cell H15, calculate the GPA for the Cumulative Total. Format the Semester Total GPA and the Cumulative Total GPA to display two decimals. Look at each sheet to see the GPA for each semester. (Hint: Kevin's GPA at the end of the Spring 99 semester is 3.15.) Display the Sheet tab Shortcut menu and ungroup the Sheets.

k. Go to the Fall 97 sheet and preview the workbook. Enter your name in the left footer position and the current date in the right footer position.

l. Document the workbook. Save and replace the workbook file Grade Report. Print all of the sheets.

You will continue this exercise as Practice Exercise 7 in this lab.

☆☆☆

4. Marion manages a computer lab at a community college. She has four work-study students to assist her. The students are allowed to earn no more than $900 per semester at $4.75 an hour. Marion has created a worksheet that calculates the amount of money the students have left at the end of each week. By monitoring this amount, she can budget their time so that each student earns enough without exceeding the allotted amount.

a. Open the file Work Study Balance on your data disk. The starting amount ($900.00) and hourly rate ($4.75) have been entered in cells B4 and B5 respectively. In cell B10, enter a reference formula that will copy the starting amount for Ed. Keep in mind that you will need to copy that formula to obtain the same starting amount ($900.00) for Carrie Ann, Molly, and Jason. What formula did you use? Copy that formula to cells B11 through B13.

b. There are 15 weeks in a semester. Week 1 has been entered for you in cell C9. Use AutoFill to create the weekly headings in cells C9 through Q9.

c. Open the file Work Study Hours on your data disk. This is a report of the number of hours the students have worked each week from the beginning of the semester through the last full week of classes.

d. Use the logic in step b to enter the column headings Week 1 through Week 15 in cells B5 through P5.

e. Tile the windows. In this portion of the exercise, you will enter an external reference formula that will calculate the amount of money each student has left at the end of each week. (Hint: Since both sheets are visible, you can use pointing to enter the cell references in the formula.) Make the Work Study Balance file active, and go to cell C10. To calculate the amount of money Ed has left after the first week, subtract his Hours Worked*Rate from his Starting Amount. What is the result? Note: It is important that you use cell references and not the numbers they represent in all parts of the formula. Also pay attention to which references should be relative, and which should be absolute.

f. Copy that formula down the column to see how much each student has left at the end of the first week. Maximize the Work Study Balance window.

g. Change the numeric format of the new numbers to match the starting amount. Then copy the Week 1 balances to Week 2 through Week 14, the last week before final exams. Who will be ineligible to work finals week?

h. To keep the row headings in view as you scroll the worksheet, go to column A so you can see all the headings, and then freeze panes at cell C10.

i. What if the students earned $5.00 an hour? Change the rate in cell B5 to $5.00, and scroll to column P. Who will be ineligible to work at the end of the semester? What if the students were allotted $1,000 per semester? Change the starting amount in cell B4 to $1,000. Will everybody be able work the week of final exams? Do you think they will want to?

j. Molly has a lot of money left over. Use Goal Seek to calculate what the hourly rate would have to be before Molly would run out of money by Week 14 if she worked the same number of hours. What is the result? Use The Undo command to reset the values.

k. Unfreeze the panes. Rename the Sheet1 tab Fall 1998.

l. Center the title across the columns. Select a different font, and increase the font size to 16 pt. Draw a bottom border under the column headings in row 9. Draw an outline border around the what-if values and their row labels in cells A4 through B5. Add color to the text and the background within the border. Make whatever other formatting changes you wish using techniques you have learned.

m. Preview the worksheet. Add your name and date to the header. Print the worksheet on one page using landscape orientation. Document the workbook. Save and replace the workbook file Work Study Balance with the new print settings.

n. Close the workbook. The Work Study Hours worksheet should be active. Rename the Sheet1 tab Fall 1998. Use whatever formatting techniques you wish to improve the appearance of the worksheet.

o. Preview the worksheet. Add your name and the date to the header. Remove the page number footer. Print the worksheet on one page using landscape orientation. Document the workbook. Save and replace the workbook file Work Study Hours with the new print settings.

On Your Own

☆☆☆

5. To complete this problem, you must have completed Practice Exercise 2 in Lab 2. Open the workbook file Cookie Jar on your data disk. In this exercise you will continue to modify the quarterly sales worksheet for the gourmet cookie shop, The Cookie Jar.

a. Copy Sheet1 as Sheet1 (2) and insert it before Sheet2. Rename the Sheet1 tab 1st Quarter Sales and rename Sheet1 (2) 2nd Quarter Sales.

b. Use the AutoFill feature to replace the months Jan through Mar with Apr through Jun on the 2nd Quarter Sales sheet.

c. Enter the new April sales numbers as follows:

Type	Number
Chocolate Chip	1900
Chocolate Chip w/ Nuts	1425
White Chocolate Macadamia	1300
Butterscotch	750
Peanut Butter	1000
Oatmeal Raisin	350
Gingerbread	525

d. Aggressive advertising should account for a monthly 10 percent increase in sales. Enter formulas to calculate a 10 percent increase over the previous month's sales for May and June (April Sales*1.10 and May Sales*1.10). Copy those formulas down the column.

e. Enter the heading "Projected Sales" over the May month heading. Bold the heading, and center it over the May and June columns.

f. Enter a heading "Projected Sales to Date Total" in cell B14 of the 2nd Quarter Sales sheet. Bold and italicize the entry. In cell E14, calculate a total for the first six months by summing cells E12 on both sheets. Format the new entry to match the rest of the numbers in the workbook.

g. Add a custom header that contains your name and the date right-aligned in both sheets.

h. Preview the workbook. Save and replace the workbook file Cookie Jar. Print the workbook.

You will complete this exercise as Practice Exercise 3 in Lab 4.

6. To complete this problem, you must have completed Practice Exercise 6 in Lab 2. Open the workbook file Time Sheets on your data disk. In this exercise you will continue to modify the time sheet for Ilsa.

Create a second time sheet in a new worksheet. Use last Friday's date as the Sheet1 name, and use this Friday's date as the Sheet1 (2) name. Enter different Total Hours and Regular Hours (8 is the maximum number for regular hours) in the new time sheet. Enter this Monday's date as the Starting Date in B2. Two rows below the Weekly Total amount, enter a formula to calculate the biweekly total as the sum of both weekly totals. Include an appropriate heading.

Add a custom footer that includes your name left-aligned, the date center-aligned, and your class time right-aligned in both worksheets. Document and save the workbook file as Time Sheets. Preview and print both worksheets.

You will complete this exercise as Practice Exercise 1 in Lab 5.

7. To complete this exercise, you must have completed Practice Exercise 3 in this lab. Open the file Grade Report from your disk. Modify this workbook to match your situation. Add or delete sheets as needed. Rename sheet tabs with appropriate semester labels. Save the workbook file as My Grade Report. Print the workbook.

8. To complete this problem, you must have completed Practice Exercise 6 in this lab. Ilsa also wants to create a worksheet to track her earnings using data from the time sheets she maintains each week.

In a new workbook, create the worksheet to track earnings as shown below. Save the workbook file as Earnings Statement.

	A	B	C	D
1				
2	Earnings Statement Of:	[Student's Name]		
3	Period Ending:	[Date]		
4				
5	**Earnings:**			
6	**Rate**	**Hours**		**Gross Pay**
7	7.5			
8	**Deductions**	**Statutory**		
9		Federal Income Tax		
10		State Income Tax		
11		Local Income Tax		
12		Medicare Tax		
13		Social Security Tax		
14		**Voluntary**		
15		Union Dues		
16		Holiday Club		
17		Total Deductions		
18		**Net Pay**		

Create a link to calculate the gross pay in the Earnings Statement workbook to the total biweekly hours worked from the Time Sheet workbook. Calculate the gross pay as Rate*Hours.

The statutory deductions will be calculated as follows:

Federal Income Tax = Gross Pay*15%
State Income Tax = Gross Pay*3%
Local Income Tax = Gross Pay*1%
Medicare Tax = Gross Pay*1.5%
Social Security Tax = Gross Pay*7%

The voluntary deductions are:

Union Dues = $10
Holiday Club = $25

Total the deductions and calculate Net Pay (total deductions – Gross Pay).

Apply appropriate number formats and styles to enhance the appearance of the worksheet. Print the Earnings Statement with a custom header and centered horizontally on the page.

You will continue this exercise as Practice Exercise 1 in Lab 5.

Concept Summary

Managing and Analyzing a Complex Workbook

3

AutoFill

The AutoFill feature makes entering long or complicated headings easier by logically repeating and extending the series.

Referencing Sheets

A formula reference to cells in different worksheets in a workbook allows you to use data from other worksheets and to calculate new values based on this data.

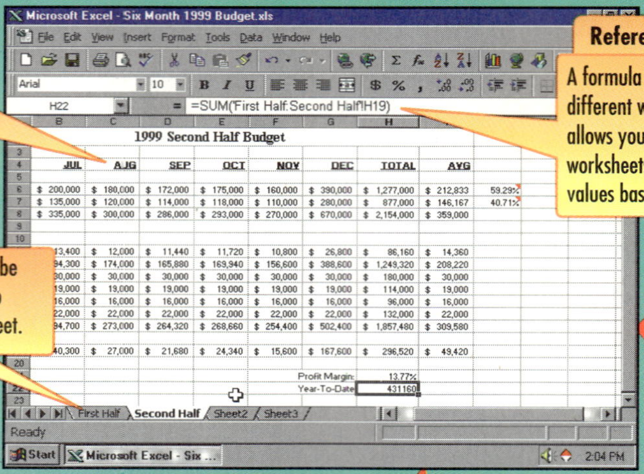

Sheet Names

Each sheet in a workbook can be assigned a descriptive name to identify the contents of the sheet.

Split Windows

A sheet window can be split into sections called panes to make it easier to view different parts of the sheet at the same time.

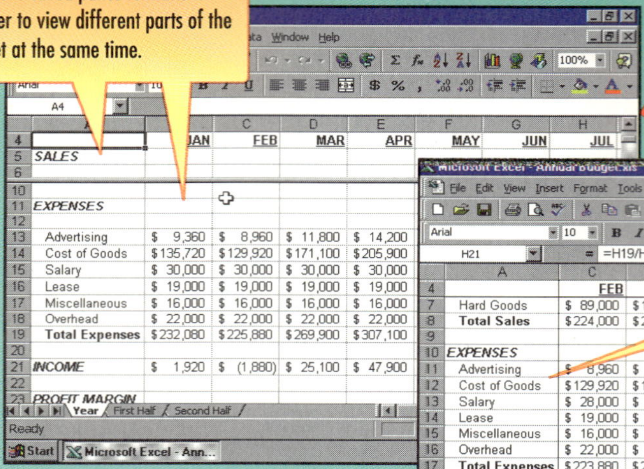

Freeze Panes

Freezing panes prevents the data in the pane from scrolling as you move to different areas in the worksheet.

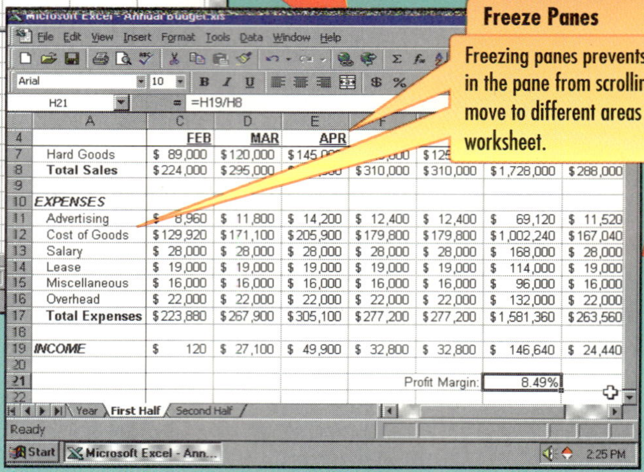

Goal Seek

Goal Seek is an Excel tool that is used to find the value needed in one cell to attain a result you want in another cell.

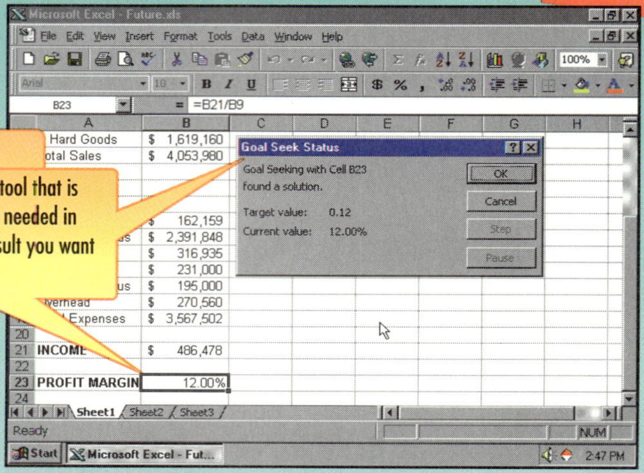

Concepts

- Sheet Names
  AutoFill
  Referencing Sheets
- Split Windows
  Freeze Panes
- What-If-Analysis
  Solver
- Spelling Checker
- Goal Seek
- Link Workbooks

Solver

Solver is an Excel tool that answers what-if problems by determining the value of a cell by changing values in one or more cells in the worksheet.

What-If Analysis

What-if analysis is a technique used to evaluate the effects of changing selected factors in a worksheet.

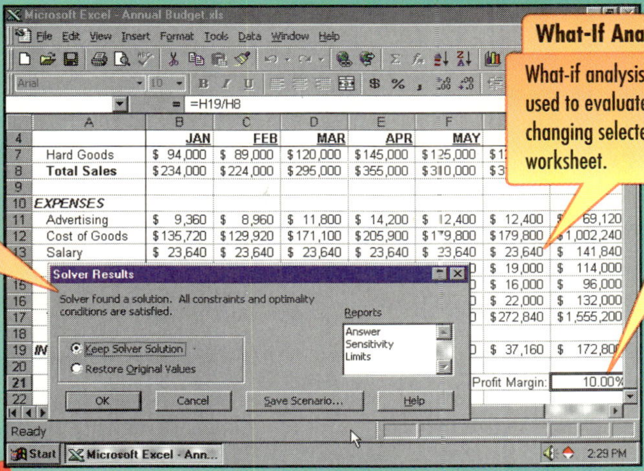

Spelling Checker

A spelling checker feature locates misspelled words, duplicate words, and capitalization irregularities and proposes the correct spelling.

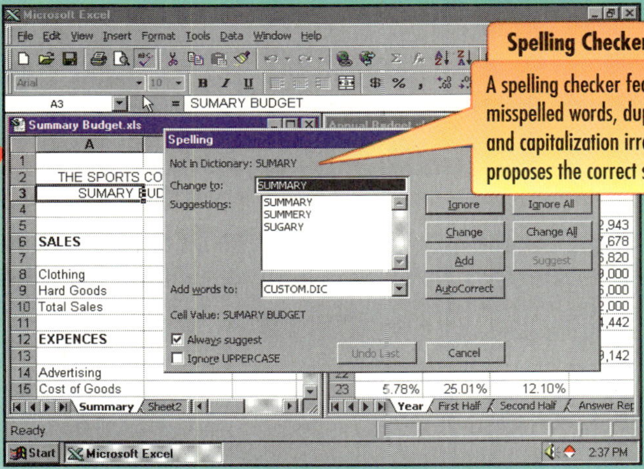

Link Workbooks

A link creates a connection between files that updates the linked data automatically in one file whenever the data changes in the other file.

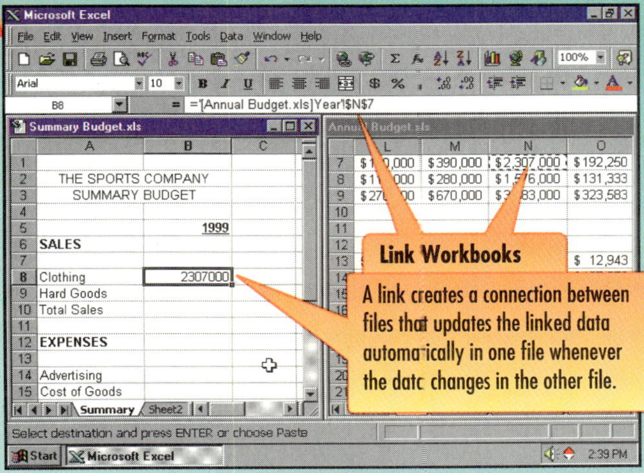

Creating Charts

4

COMPETENCIES

After completing this lab, you will know how to:

1. **Use Autoformats.**
2. **Create several different kinds of charts.**
3. **Select the data to chart.**
4. **Move and size a chart.**
5. **Change the type of chart.**
6. **Move the legend.**
7. **Add patterns, text boxes, and arrows.**
8. **Add data labels.**
9. **Print a chart.**

CASE STUDY

You have noticed over the past few months while working at The Sports Company that sales are increasing in some sports and declining in others. While looking through the store sales records, you have found sales data by sport for the past several years. You want to create several charts of this data to make it easier to see the trends and growth patterns over the years.

Excel has the capability to create many types of charts from data in a worksheet. The different chart types emphasize data in various ways. You will create several different charts of the sales data, as shown below.

Concept Overview

The following concepts will be introduced in this lab:

1. **Autoformat** An autoformat is a built-in combination of formats that can be applied to a range.
2. **Types of Charts** Excel 97 can produce 14 basic types of charts with many different formats for each type.
3. **Chart Elements** A chart consists of a number of parts or elements that are used to graphically display the worksheet data.
4. **Objects** Objects are items that can be added to a worksheet and that can be sized and moved.

Part 1

Using Autoformats

You have created a worksheet of the sales data by sport and will use Excel 97 to create several charts to visually show the sales trends.

- Load Excel 97.
- Put your data disk in drive A (or the appropriate drive for your system).
- Open the workbook file Sales. If necessary, maximize the worksheet window.

Your screen should be similar to Figure 4-1.

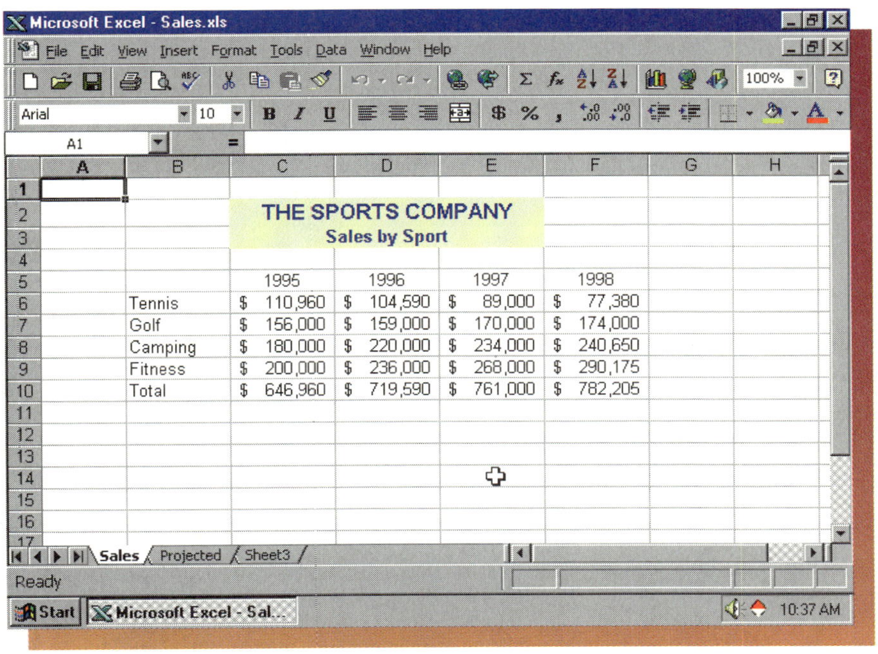

FIGURE 4-1

The Sales sheet displays the sales for the years 1995 through 1998. The worksheet lists four sports categories and a total as row labels in column B. The total is the sum of the sales for the four sports categories for each year. The headings for the four years are displayed in row 5.

You also created a worksheet for the projected sales for 1999.

- To see this worksheet, make the Projected sheet active.

The data for 1999 projected sales for the four categories is displayed. You will use this worksheet later in this lab.

- Make the Sales sheet active again.

Before creating the charts, you would like to improve the appearance of the worksheets by applying an autoformat to the worksheet data.

Concept 1: Autoformat

An **autoformat** is a built-in combination of formats that can be applied to a range of cells. There are 16 autoformats from which you can select. The autoformats consist of a combination of number formats, fonts and styles, colors, patterns, borders, and alignment settings.

To use an autoformat, you first specify the range you want affected by the formatting. In this case, you want to apply an autoformat to cells B5 through F10. You can select the range or you can let Excel select the range for you. To have Excel automatically select the range, move the cell selector to any cell in the range. Excel determines that the range you want to apply the autoformat to is the range of cells that includes the active cell and is surrounded by blank cells.

- Move to B5.
- Choose Format/AutoFormat.

Your screen should be similar to Figure 4-2.

FIGURE 4-2

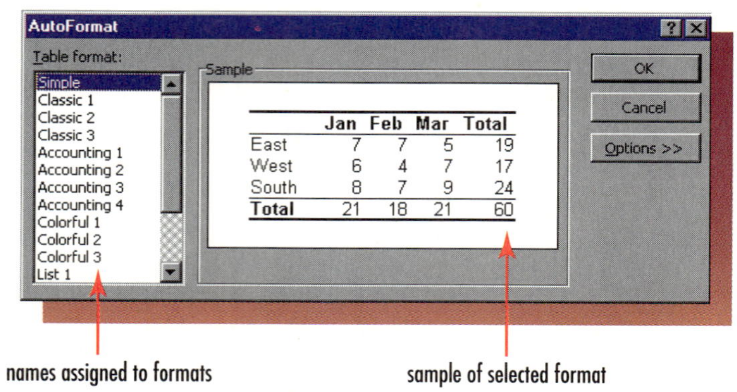

The AutoFormat dialog box displays the names Excel has assigned each of the 16 different formats in the Table Format list box. The Sample box shows how the selected format will look.

- To preview the autoformats, highlight each name in the Table Format list and look at the table layout in the Sample box.

The None autoformat option removes an existing autoformat.

You think the Accounting 2 format would be appropriate for the data in the Sales sheet. To format the worksheet using this layout,

- Select Accounting 2.
- Click OK.

Your worksheet should be similar to Figure 4-3.

Accounting 2 autoformat applied to selected range

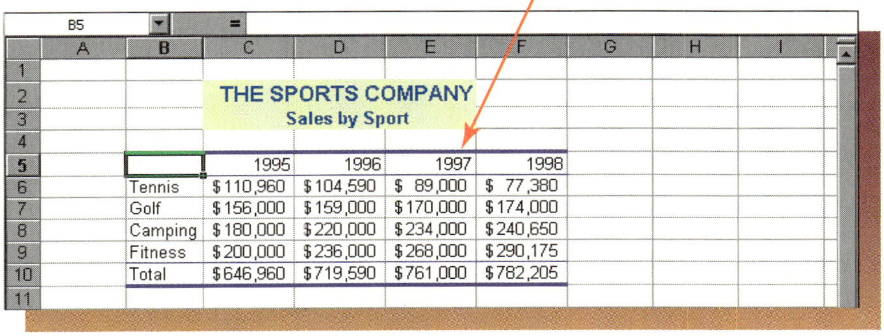

FIGURE 4-3

The Accounting 2 autoformat includes border lines of different weights, color, and accounting number format with no decimal places. You would like to apply this same format to the Projected worksheet.

You can use Edit/Repeat AutoFormat to quickly apply the same autoformat.

- Make the Projected sheet active and apply the Accounting 2 autoformat to cells B5 through C10.
- Make the Sales sheet active again.

About Charts

Although the worksheet shows the sales numbers for each sports category, it is hard to see how the different categories have changed over time. A visual representation of data in the form of a **chart** would convey that information in an easy-to-understand and attractive manner.

Concept 2: Types of Charts

Excel 97 can produce 14 basic types of graphs or charts, with many different formats for each type. The basic chart types are:

Type	Description
	Area charts show the magnitude of change over time by emphasizing the area under the curve created by each data series.
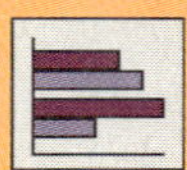	Bar charts display data as evenly spaced bars. The categories are displayed along the Y axis and the values are displayed horizontally, placing more emphasis on comparisons and less on time.
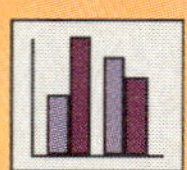	Column charts display data as evenly spaced bars. They are similar to bar charts, except the categories are organized horizontally and values vertically to emphasize variation over time.
	Line charts display data along a line. They are used to show changes in data over time, emphasizing time and rate of change rather than the amount of change.
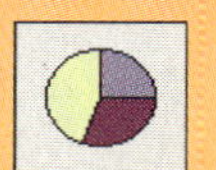	Pie charts display data as slices of a circle or "pie." They show the relationship of each value in a data series to the series as a whole. Each slice of the pie represents a single value in the series.
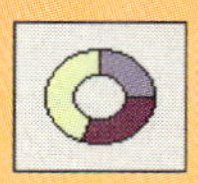	Doughnut charts are similar to pie charts except they can show more than one data series.
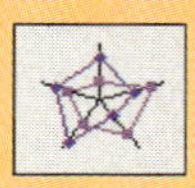	Radar charts display a line or area chart wrapped around a central point. Each axis represents a set of data points.
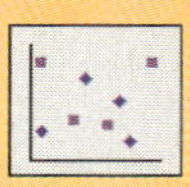	XY (scatter) charts are used to show the relationship between two ranges of numeric data.
	Surface charts display values as what appears to be a rubber sheet stretched over a 3-D column chart. These are useful for finding the best combination between sets of data.
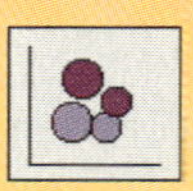	Bubble charts compare sets of three values. It is like a scatter chart with the third value displayed as the size of bubble markers.
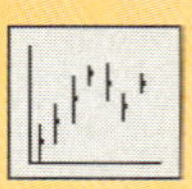	A stock chart is a high-low-close chart. It requires three series of values in this order.
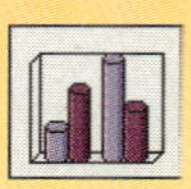	Cylinder charts display values with a cylindrical shape.
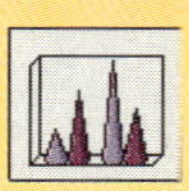	Cone charts display values with a conical shape.
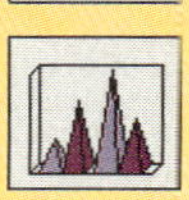	Pyramid charts display values with a pyramid shape.

Selecting the Data to Chart

The first chart you want to create will show the total sales pattern over the four years. All charts are drawn from data contained in a worksheet. To create a new chart, you select the worksheet range containing the data you want displayed as a chart plus any row or column headings you want used in the chart. Excel then translates the selected data into a chart based upon the shape and contents of the worksheet selection.

A chart consists of a number of parts or elements, which are important to understand so that you can identify the appropriate data to select in the worksheet. These elements are described in the concept box below and on page SS138.

Concept 3: Chart Elements

The basic elements of a two-dimensional chart are shown in the figure below.

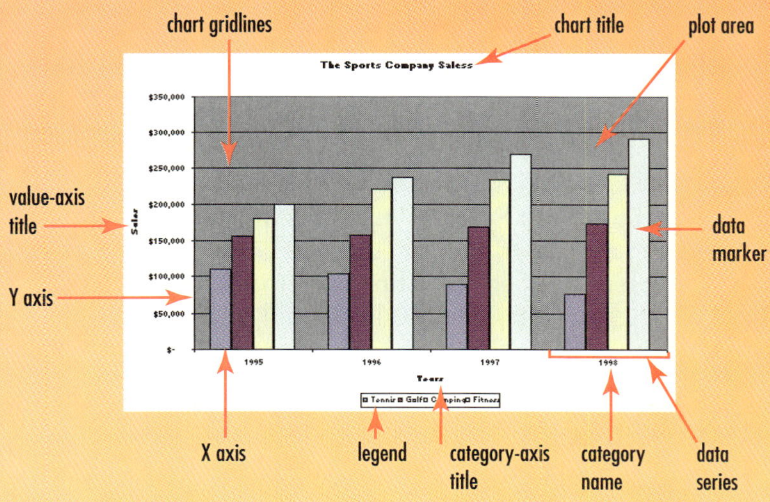

The bottom boundary line of the chart is the **X axis**. It is used to label the data being charted, such as a point in time or a category. The **category names** displayed along the X axis correspond to the headings for the worksheet data that is plotted along the X axis. The left boundary line of the chart is the **Y axis**. This axis is a numbered scale whose numbers are determined by the data used in the chart. Typically the X-axis line is the horizontal line and the Y-axis line is the vertical line.

The selected worksheet data is visually displayed within the X- and Y-axis boundaries. This is called the **plot area**. Each group of related data, such as the numbers in a row or column of the selected area of the worksheet, is called a **data series**. Each number represented in a data series is identified by a **data marker**. A data marker can be a symbol, color, or pattern. To distinguish one data series from another, different data markers are used. In addition, **chart gridlines** are commonly displayed to make it easier to read the chart data. Chart gridlines extend from the Y-axis line across the plot area. A **legend** identifies the chart data series names and data markers that correspond to each data series.

A chart can also contain descriptive **titles** that explain the contents of the chart. The chart title is displayed centered above the charted data. Titles can also be used to describe the X and Y axes. The X-axis title line is called the **category-axis title**, and the Y-axis title is called the **value-axis title**.

In pie charts there are no axes. Instead the worksheet data that is charted is displayed as slices in a circle or pie. Each slice is labeled. In 3-D charts there can also be an additional axis, called the Z axis, which allows you to compare data within a series more easily. This axis is the vertical axis. The X and Y axes delineate the horizontal surface of the chart.

Pie Chart

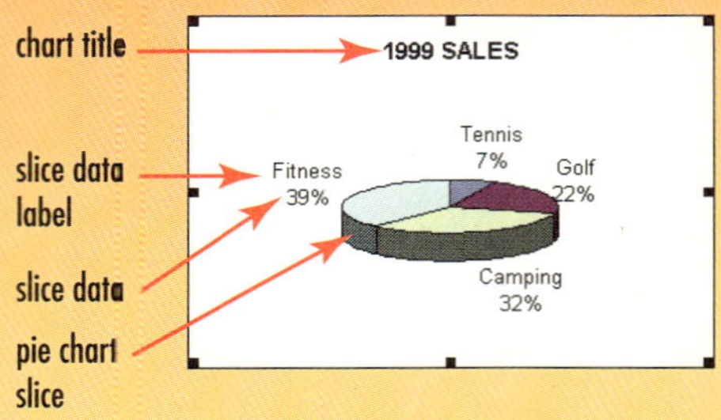

3-D Chart

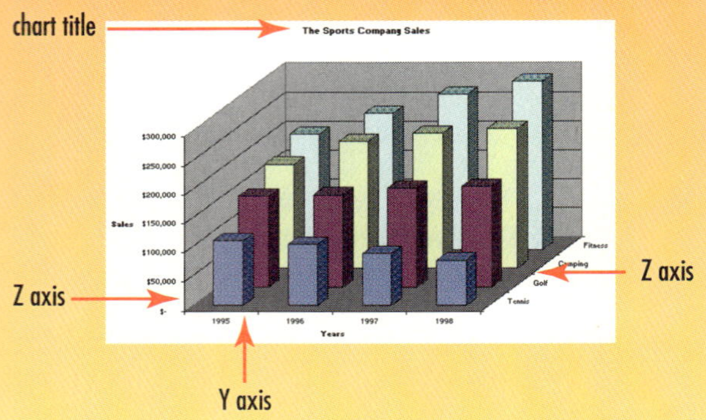

The first chart you will create of the worksheet data will use the year labels in cells C5 through F5 to label the X axis. The numbers to be charted are in cells C10 through F10. In addition, the label "Total" in cell B10 will be used as the chart legend, making the entire range B10 through F10. Notice that the two ranges, C5 through F5 and B10 through F10, are not adjacent and are not the same size. When plotting nonadjacent ranges in a chart, the selections must form a rectangular shape. To do this, the blank cell B5 will be included in the selection. To specify the range and create the chart,

- Select B5 through F5.
- Hold down Ctrl.
- Select B10 through F10.

Refer to Lab 1 for a discussion of nonadjacent selections.

Your worksheet should be similar to Figure 4-4.

FIGURE 4-4

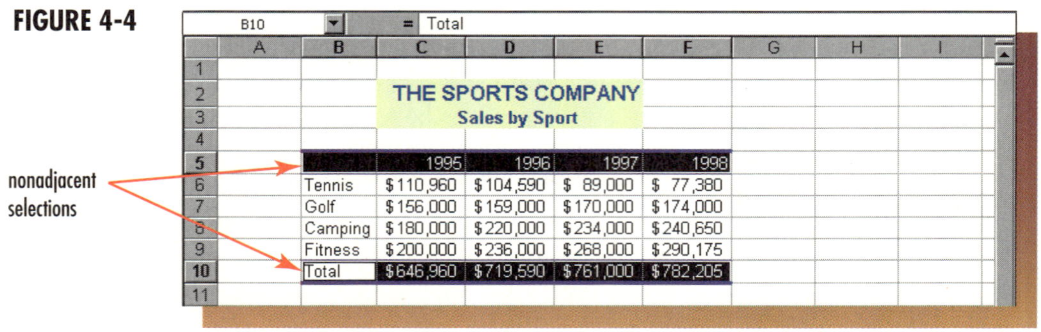

	A	B	C	D	E	F
5			1995	1996	1997	1998
6		Tennis	$110,960	$104,590	$ 89,000	$ 77,380
7		Golf	$156,000	$159,000	$170,000	$174,000
8		Camping	$180,000	$220,000	$234,000	$240,650
9		Fitness	$200,000	$236,000	$268,000	$290,175
10		Total	$646,960	$719,590	$761,000	$782,205

■ Click [Chart Wizard button] Chart Wizard.

You can choose Insert/Chart to create the chart.

The dialog box on your screen should be similar to Figure 4-5.

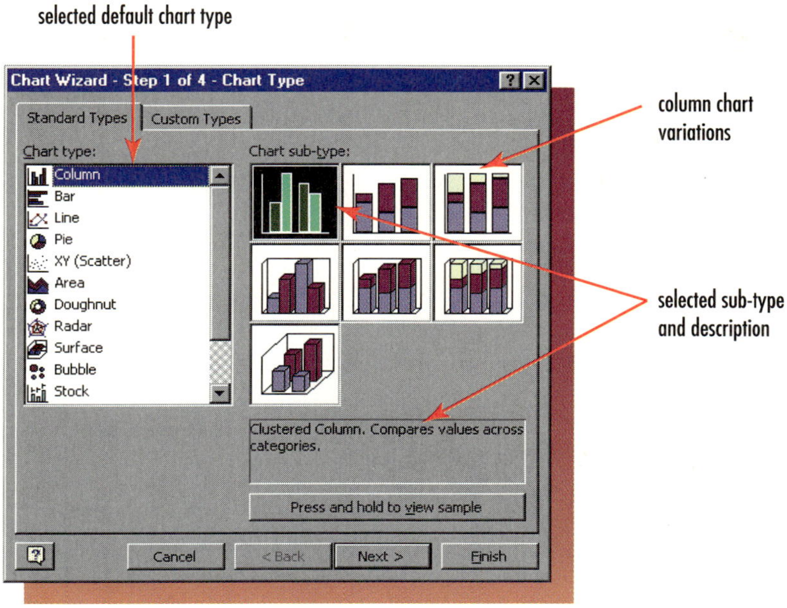

FIGURE 4-5

Chart Wizard is an interactive program that guides you through the steps to create a chart. The first step is to select the chart type from the Chart Type list box. The default chart type is a **column chart**. Each type of chart includes many variations. The variations associated with the column chart type are displayed as buttons in the Chart Sub-type section of the dialog box. The default column sub-type is a clustered column. A description of the selected sub-type is displayed in the area below the sub-type buttons. To accept the default settings and move to the next step,

If the Office Assistant is displayed, you are asked if you want help with this feature.

■ Click [Next >].

Your screen should be similar to Figure 4-6.

FIGURE 4-6

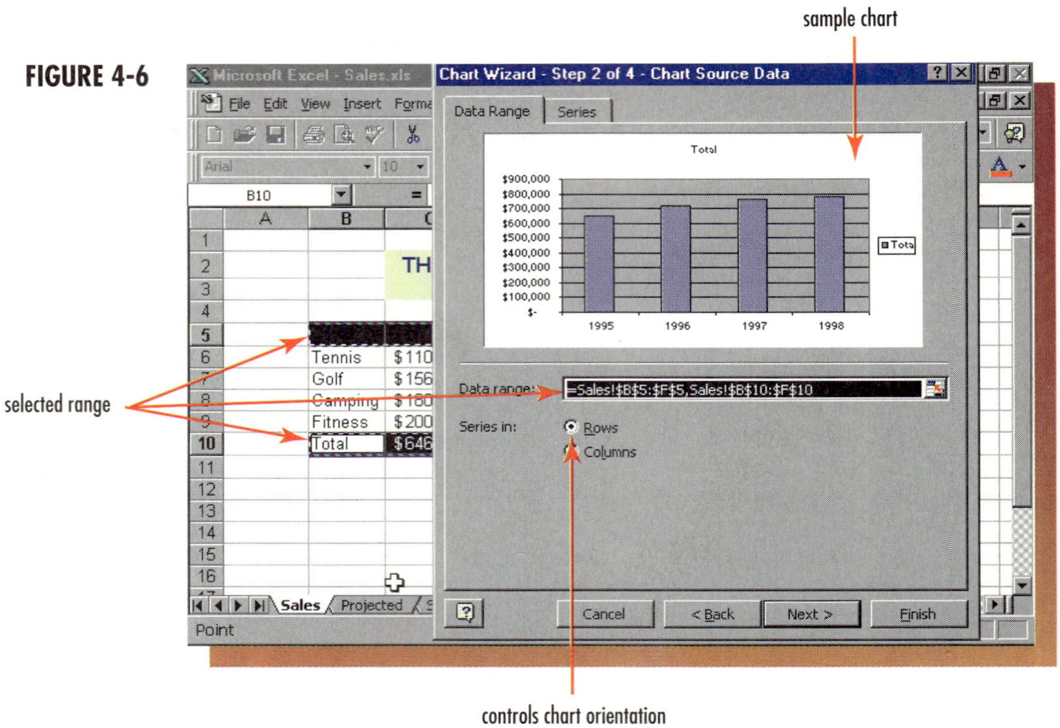

The Chart Wizard Step 2 of 4 dialog box displays a sample of the chart that will be created using the current chart settings and data. The selected range appears in the Data Range text box. You can specify another range in the text box or accept the displayed range.

The two Series In options control how Excel interprets the data series. The interpretation varies depending upon the type of chart selected. In a column chart, the default setting is Rows. In this setting Excel uses the first row as the X-axis category labels and the leftmost column as the legend text. Changing the setting to Columns reverses this, placing the first column of the range along the X axis and the first row of the range as the legend text. To accept the default settings,

- Click Next >.
- If necessary, open the Titles tab.

The dialog box on your screen should be similar to Figure 4-7.

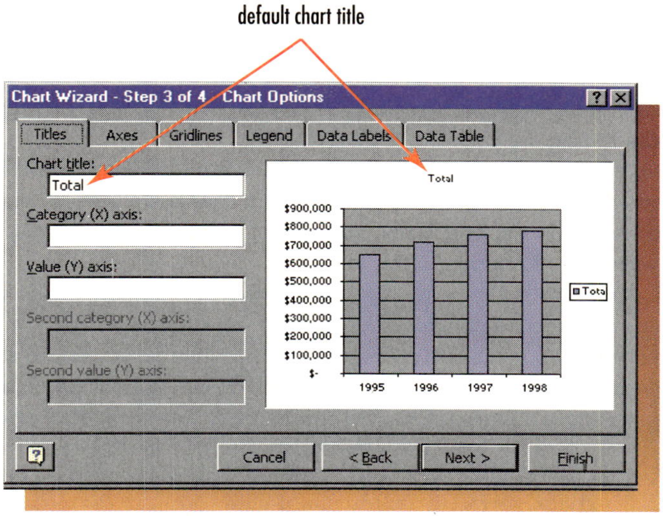

FIGURE 4-7

In the Step 3 dialog box you can change the appearance of chart elements such as a legend and titles. To clarify the chart, you will add a chart title as well as titles along the X and Y axes. As you add the titles, the sample chart will update to display the new settings.

- Replace the default title in the Chart Title text box with **THE SPORTS COMPANY SALES**.
- In the Category (X) Axis text box enter **Years** and in the Value (Y) Axis text box enter **Sales**.
- Click [Next >].

Use [Tab], not [←Enter], after typing the title text. Pressing [←Enter] is the same as clicking [Next >].

The dialog box on your screen should be similar to Figure 4-8.

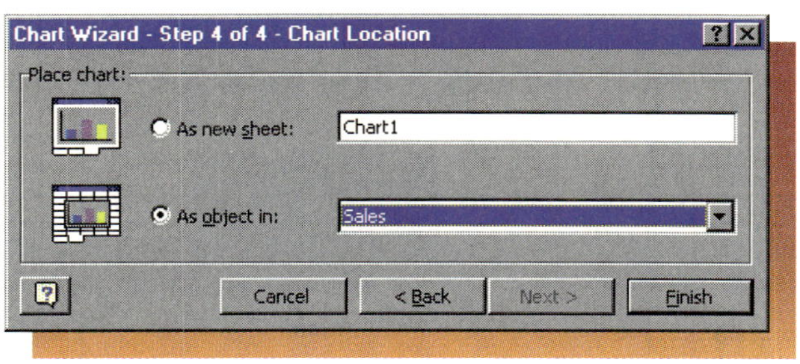

FIGURE 4-8

In the last step you specify where you want the chart displayed in the worksheet. A chart can be displayed in a separate chart sheet or as an object in an existing sheet.

Changing the Type of Chart

Next you would like to see how the same data displayed in the column chart would look as a line chart. A **line chart** displays data as a line and is used to show trends. This is easily done by changing the chart type using the Chart Type button on the Chart toolbar.

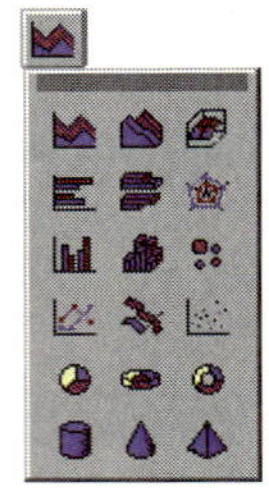

The button initially displays an area chart. Subsequently it will display the last-selected chart type.

- Open the Chart Type drop-down list.
- Click Line Chart.

Your chart should be similar to Figure 4-11.

FIGURE 4-11

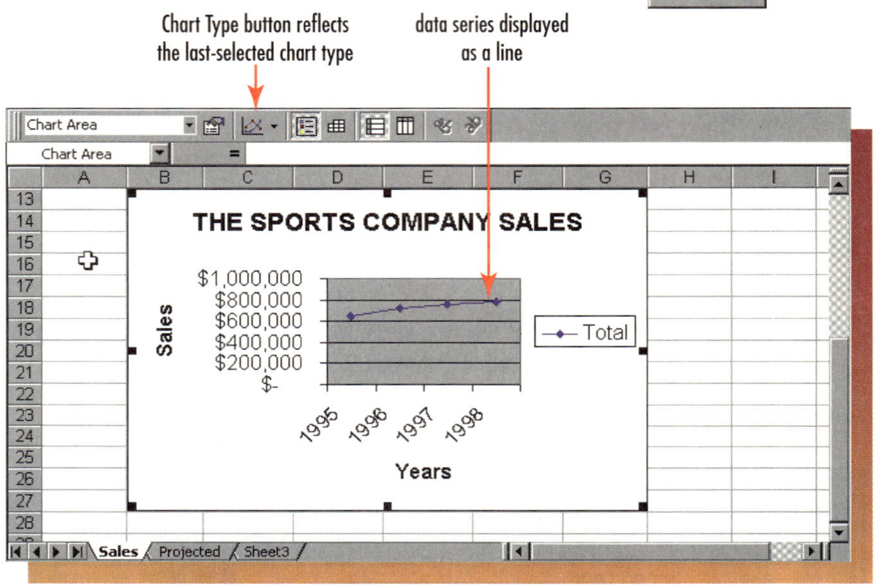

The data for the total sales for each year is now displayed as a line. Although the line chart shows the trend in sales over time, because it contains only one data series, it is not as interesting as the column chart.

You could also click Undo to change the chart type back to the previous type.

- Change the chart type back to Column Chart.

Creating a Chart with Multiple Data Series

Now you are ready to continue your analysis of sales trends. You want to create a second chart to display the sales data for each sports category for the four years. You could create a separate chart for each category and then compare the charts; however, to make the comparisons between the categories easier, you will display all the categories on a single chart.

The data for the four years for the four categories is in cells C6 through F9. The year headings (X-axis data series) are in cells C5 through F5, and the legend text is in the range B6 through B9. To specify the chart data series,

- Select B5 through F9.
- Click Chart Wizard.

The Chart Wizard - Step 1 dialog box is displayed. You think a line chart would be an appropriate chart type. From the Chart Type options list,

- Select Line.

To preview how this default line chart sub-type will look using the selected data series,

- Click and hold Press and hold to view sample.

The dialog box on your screen should be similar to Figure 4-12.

FIGURE 4-12

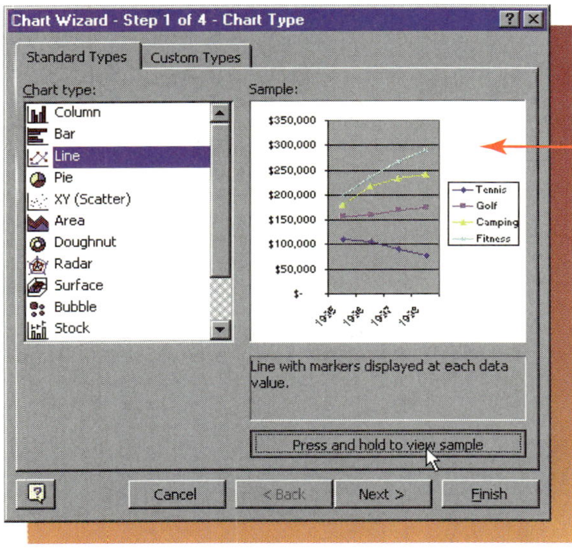

sample of default line chart

You like how it looks.

- Release the Press and hold to view sample button.
- Click Next >.

Again Excel selects Rows as the default orientation. To confirm the data series range and move to the next box,

- Click Next >.

- Enter the following titles:

Title	Entry
Chart title	**The Sports Company Sales**
Category-axis title	**Years**
Value-axis title	**Sales**

- Click Next >.

You would also like this chart embedded in the Sales worksheet.

- Choose Finish.
- Move and size the chart until it covers cells B29 through G44.

Your screen should be similar to Figure 4-13.

FIGURE 4-13

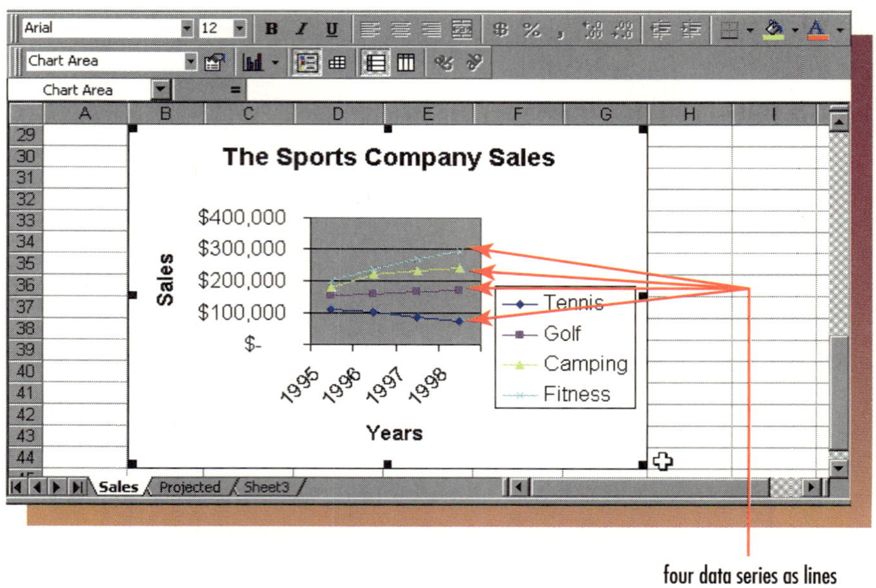

The line chart clearly shows that sales in fitness and camping are increasing, sales in tennis are decreasing, and golf sales are steady.

Although the line chart shows the sales trends for the four years for the four sports categories, it does not give you a feeling for the magnitude of the change. You feel that a stacked-column chart or an area chart may better represent the data. First you will change the type to a stacked-column chart. In a **stacked-column chart** the columns are stacked upon each other rather than displayed side by side. Unfortunately, this type of chart is not an option in the Chart Type palette. It is, however, available from the Chart menu.

When a chart is selected, the Data menu changes to the Chart menu. In addition, many of the commands under the other menus have changed to commands that apply to charts only. The Chart menu contains commands that can be used to modify the chart.

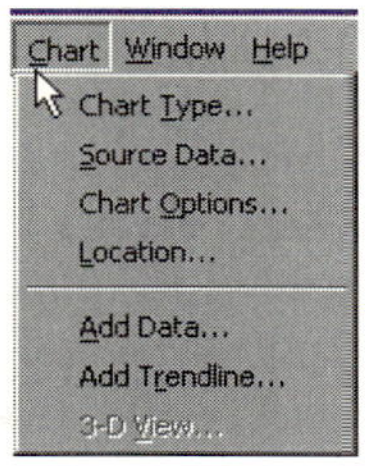

- Choose Chart/Chart Type.

The Chart Type dialog box contains the same options as the Chart Wizard - Step 1 dialog box. The current chart type, line, is the preselected option. To select a column chart,

- Select Column.
- Select Stacked column with 3-D visual effect.
- Click and hold Press and hold to view sample.

The sample chart is redrawn. A stacked-column chart shows the proportion of each type of sport to the total sport sales in each year. The stacked-column chart shows the amount of change better, but it is still difficult to see trends.

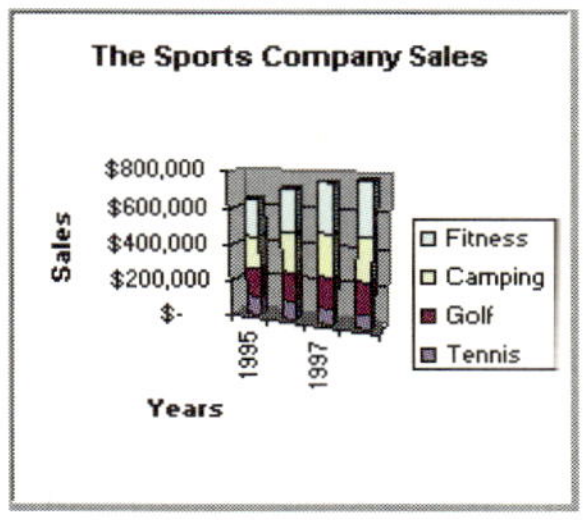

- Release the mouse button.

Next you would like to see the data represented as an area chart. An **area chart** represents data the same as a line chart, but in addition it shades the area below each line to emphasize the degree of change.

- Select Area.
- Click and hold Press and hold to view sample.

The area chart shows the magnitude of change and the trend from year to year better than the other types of charts. To apply this chart type,

- Click OK.

Your chart should be similar to Figure 4-14.

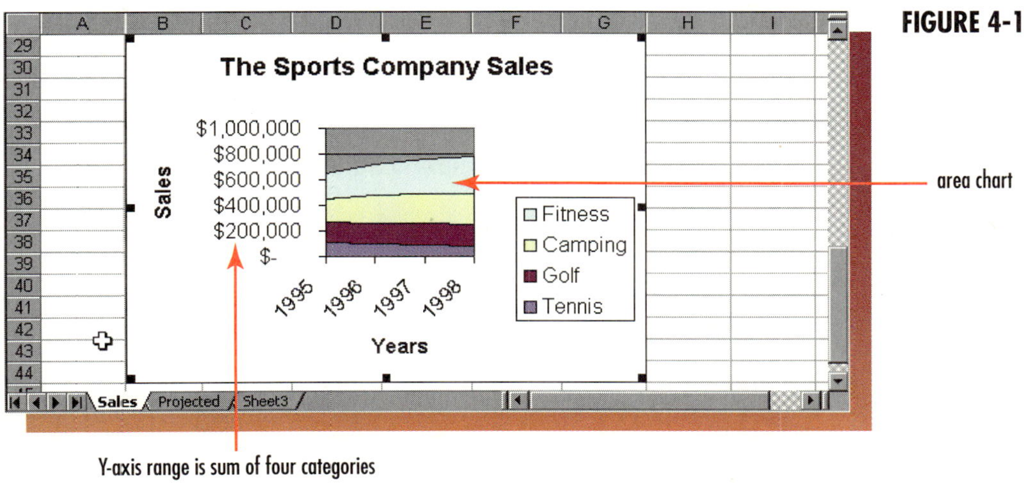

FIGURE 4-14

The Y-axis scale has changed to reflect the new range of data. The new Y-axis range is the sum of the four categories, or the same as the total number in the worksheet. It is now easy to see the magnitude of change each category contributes to the total sales in each year.

As you can see, it is very easy to change the chart type and format once the data series are specified. The same data can be displayed in many different ways. Depending upon the emphasis you want the chart to make, a different chart style can be selected.

Note: If you are ending your lab session now, add your name as a header and print the Sales sheet. Save the file as Sales Charts. When you begin Part 2, load Excel, open Sales Charts, and select the area chart.

Part 2

Moving the Legend

After looking at the area chart, you decide to modify several other chart features. First you want to move the legend below the X axis.

A chart is a grouped object made up of many separate elements. Each object in the group can be individually selected and then formatted or edited. Some of the objects in a chart are also groups that consist of other objects. For example, the legend is a group object. Each item in the legend is a separate object that can be manipulated. Other chart objects are the axis lines, a data series, a data marker, the entire plot area, or the entire chart. You can also select chart objects from the Chart Objects button drop-down list or click on the object to select it.

If the wrong item is selected, reposition the mouse pointer and click again.

- Click on the legend to select it.

Your screen should be similar to Figure 4-15.

FIGURE 4-15

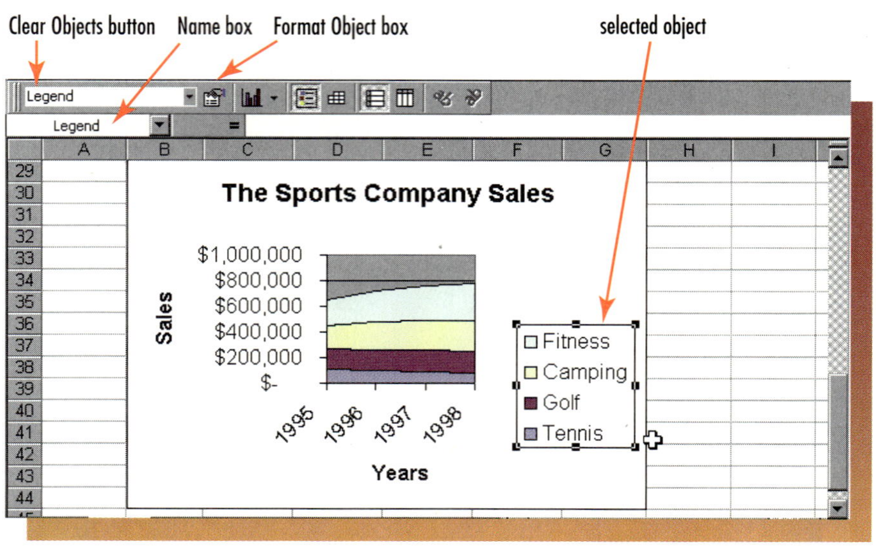

The legend box is surrounded by selection handles, indicating that it is the selected object and will be affected by any changes you make. In addition, the Name box and Chart Objects button display "Legend" as the selected chart object.

- To identify the objects within the Legend group, point to each line in the legend to see the Screen Tip.

As different objects in the chart are selected, the commands on the Format menu change to commands that can be used on the selected object. In addition, the Format Object button to the right of the Legend Chart Object button can be used to format the selected object.

- Click Format Legend.

The menu equivalent is Format/Selected Legend, and the shortcut key is Ctrl + 1.

The dialog box on your screen should be similar to Figure 4-16.

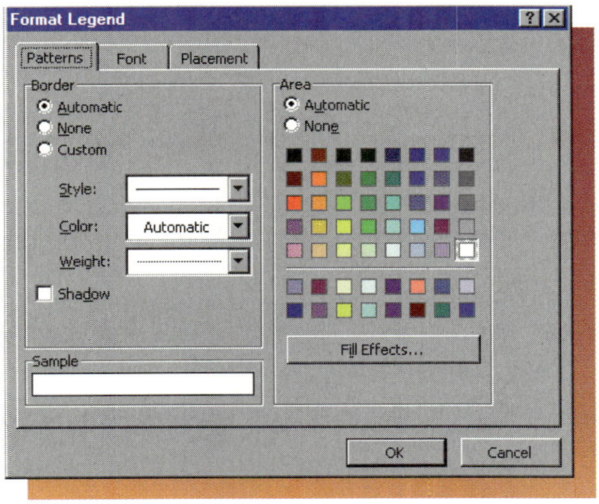

FIGURE 4-16

The Format Legend tab dialog box is used to change the patterns, font, and placement of the legend. To change the legend placement to below the plot area,

- Open the Placement tab.
- Choose Bottom.
- Click OK.

You can also move the legend by dragging it, and then you can resize it to fit the new location.

Your chart should be similar to Figure 4-17.

FIGURE 4-17

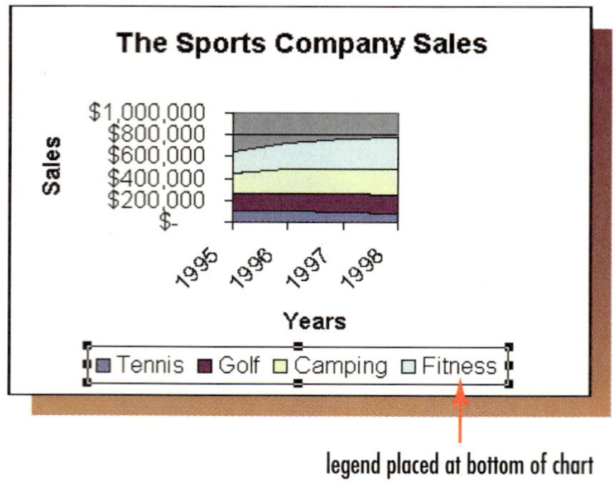

The legend object is centered below the chart and resized to fit below the axis title.

Adding Patterns

The next change you would like to make is to add patterns to the chart data series. If you have a color monitor, the data series are automatically displayed in different colors. If you have a monochrome monitor, they are displayed as varying shades of gray. You want to change the default display to black-and-white patterns to make it easier to distinguish one series from the other. Adding black-and-white patterns is particularly important if you do not have a color printer. Without black-and-white patterns, the colors are printed as shades of gray and may be difficult to distinguish.

To add black-and-white patterns, you need to select each data series object and use the Format command to change the color and pattern settings. The Shortcut menu also contains a Format option. You can quickly select a chart object and open the related Shortcut menu by right-clicking directly on the object.

- Right-click the Fitness series chart object.

Your screen should be similar to Figure 4-18.

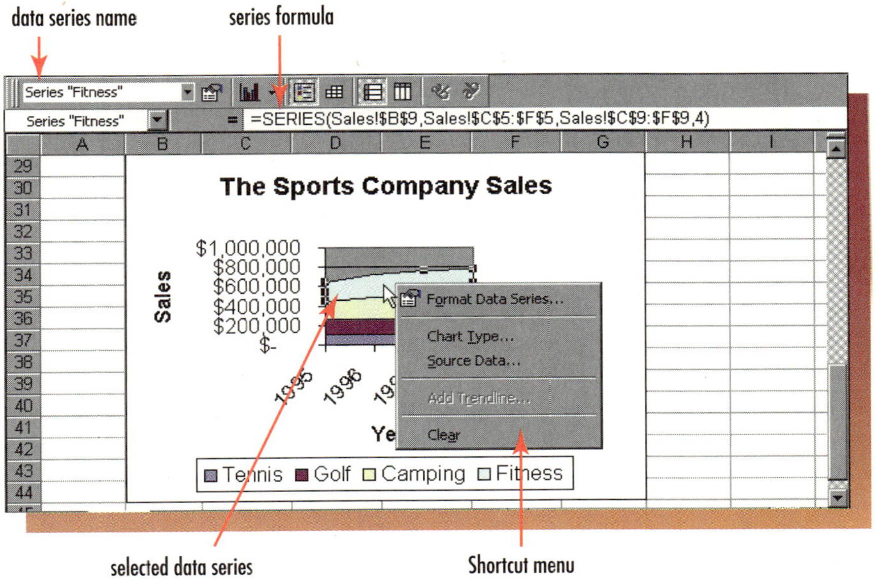

FIGURE 4-18

The Shortcut menu is displayed, and handles appear around the selected series only. Also notice that the formula bar displays a **series formula**. This formula links the chart object to the source worksheet, Sales. The formula contains four arguments: a reference to the cell that includes the data series name (used in the legend), references to the cells that contain the categories (X-axis numbers), references to the numbers plotted, and an integer that specifies the number of data series plotted.

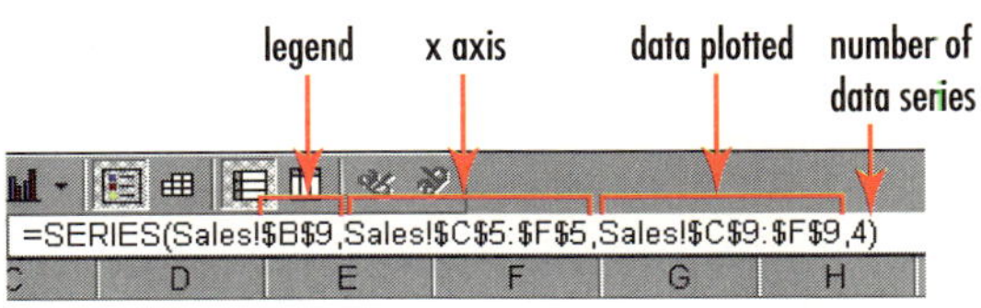

Now you can use the Format menu to change the pattern used in the selected series. From the Shortcut menu,

- Choose Format Data Series.
- If necessary, open the Patterns tab.

The menu equivalent is Format/Selected Data Series, and the shortcut key is Ctrl + 1.

The dialog box on your screen should be similar to Figure 4-19.

FIGURE 4-19

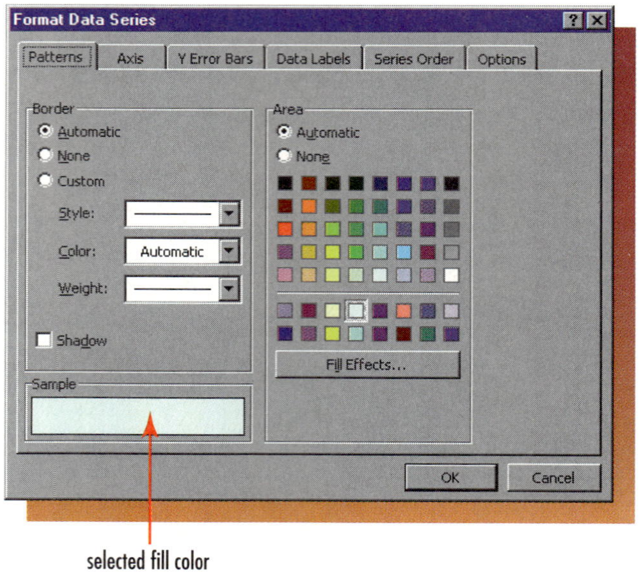

The options available in the Patterns tab vary depending upon the type of data marker that is selected. In this case, because an area data marker is selected, the options let you change the border and the background area of the selected series. The current setting for the selected series is displayed in the sample area. To change the area color to black, and to add a pattern,

- Click Fill Effects... .

The Fill Effects tab dialog box is displayed.

- Choose Pattern.
- Change the foreground color to black.
- From the Pattern palette, select a pattern of your choice.
- Click OK (twice).

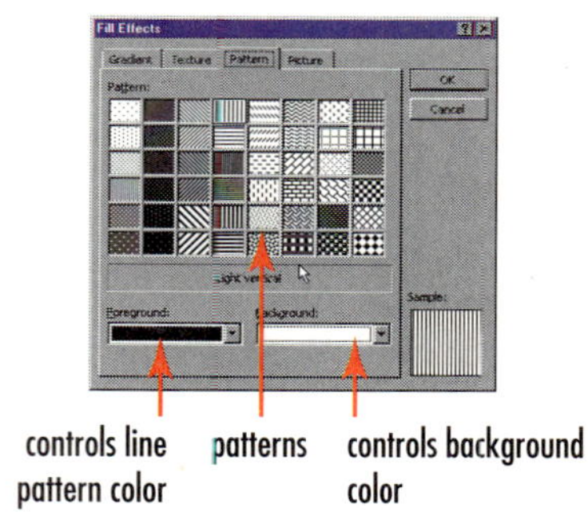

The chart is redrawn with the Fitness area of the chart displaying the black-and-white pattern. The legend has also been updated to reflect the new pattern and color selection.

- In the same manner, select the other three data series and apply a different black-and-white pattern to each.

You can double-click the data series to both select it and open the Format dialog box.

Your chart should be similar to Figure 4-20.

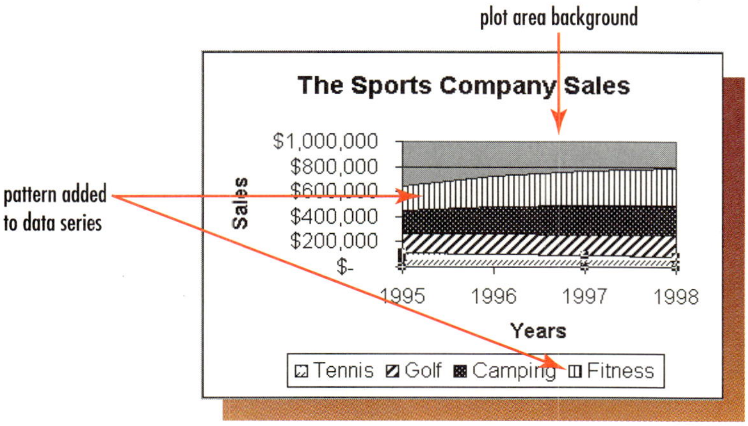

FIGURE 4-20

The chart displays the selected black-and-white patterns for the four data series.

The last change you would like to make is to remove the shading from the plot area background. The only background visible is above the Fitness data area.

- Double-click the plot area.
- Click None (in the Area section).
- Click OK.

Adding a Text Box

The last item you want to add to the area chart is a text box. A **text box** is a rectangular object in which you type text. Text boxes can be added to a sheet or a chart. You will add a text box containing the text "Increasing Sales" to the worksheet to draw attention to the Fitness area of the chart. A text box is created using the Text Box button on the Drawing toolbar. To display the Drawing toolbar,

- Click Drawing.
- Click Text Box.
- Move the mouse pointer to the blank area to the right of the chart and drag to create a text box that is approximately 1/4 inch by 2 inches.

The mouse pointer appears as ↓, indicating a text box will be created as you drag the mouse.

If a chart is selected when you create a text box, it is added to the chart object.

Your screen should be similar to Figure 4-21.

FIGURE 4-21

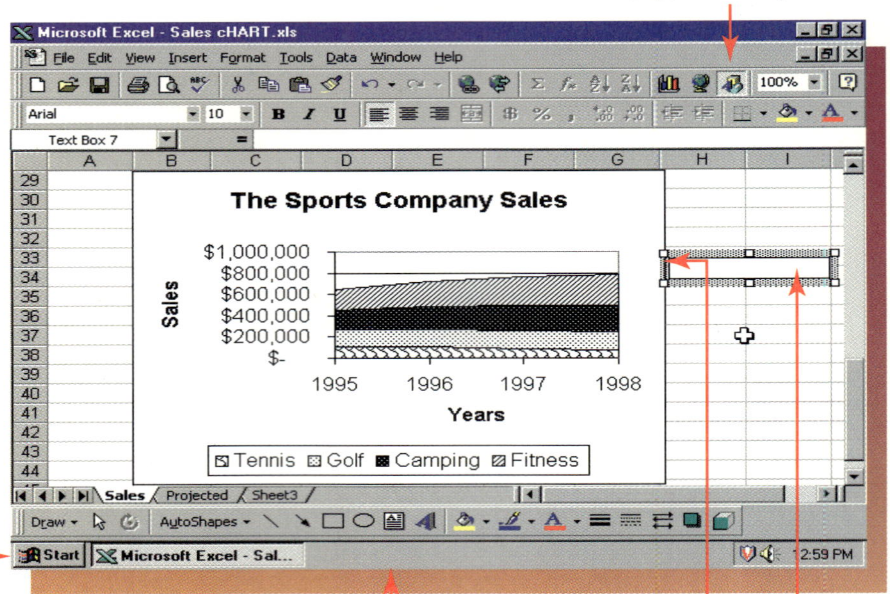

The text box displays an insertion point and is waiting for you to enter the text. As you type the text below, do not be concerned if all the text is not visible within the text box. As you type, the text will automatically begin on the next line when the right edge of the text box is reached. This feature is called **word wrap**. You should not press ←Enter to move to the next line.

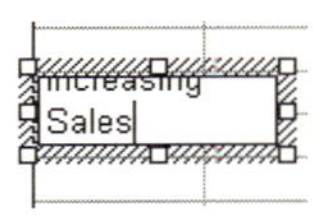

- Type **Increasing Sales**.
- If necessary, adjust the size of the text box until it is just large enough to fully display the text on one line.

You want to make the text font smaller and bold.

You can also choose Format/Text Box to modify the format settings.

- Select the text by highlighting it and choose 8 pt from the 10 Font Size button drop-down list.
- Click **B** Bold.
- Readjust the size of the text box and move it to the position displayed in Figure 4-22.

Your screen should be similar to Figure 4-22.

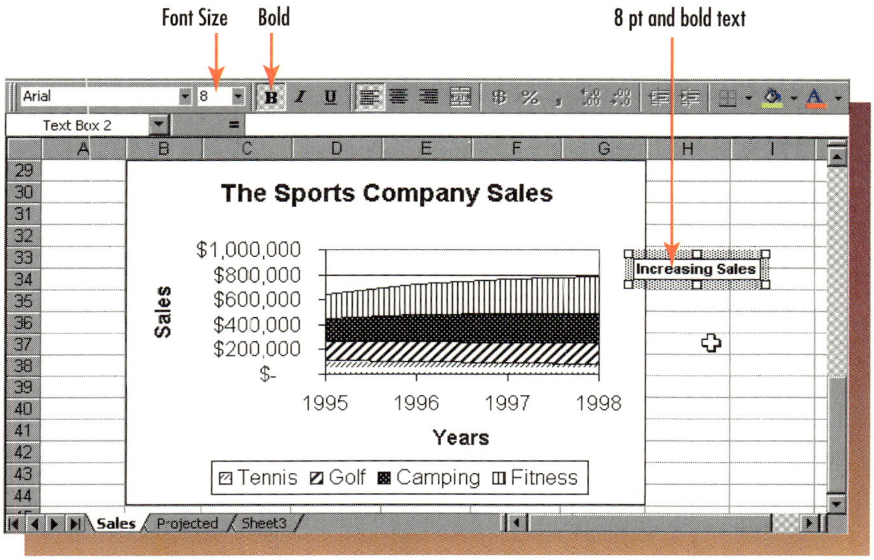

FIGURE 4-22

Adding Arrows

Next you want to draw an arrow from the text box to the Fitness area of the chart.

> The mouse pointer appears as a +.

> If you hold down Shift while dragging, a straight horizontal line is drawn.

- Click Arrow.
- To draw the arrow, click on the left edge of the text box and drag to the Fitness area.

A line with an arrowhead at the end is displayed in the worksheet. The arrow is automatically a selected object. The handles at both ends of the arrow let you adjust its size and location.

- If necessary, move and size the arrow to adjust its position as in Figure 4-23. Deselect the arrow.
- In the same manner, add a text box with the text "**Decreasing Sales**" and an arrow pointing to the Tennis area of data.
- Close the Drawing toolbar.

Your screen should be similar to Figure 4-23.

FIGURE 4-23

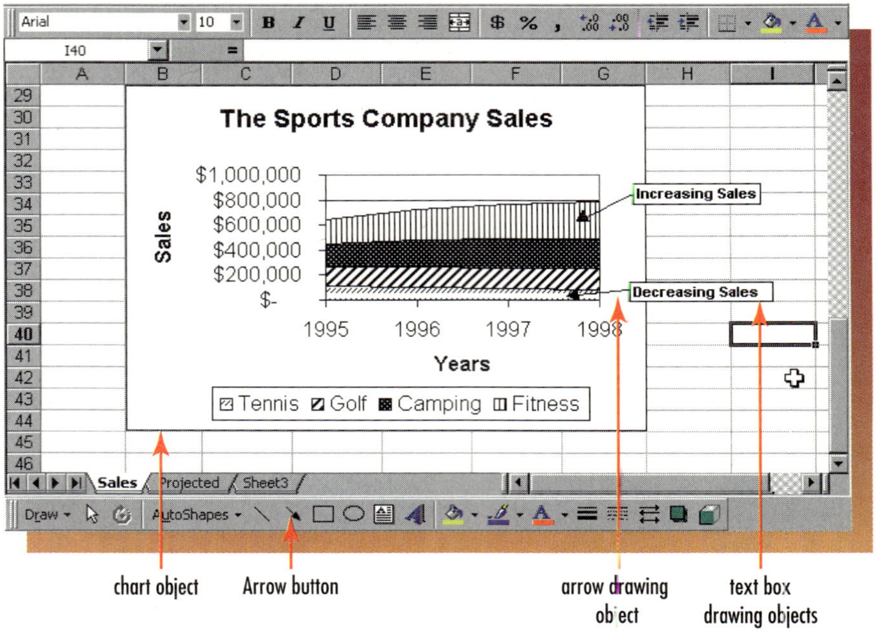

Creating a Combination Chart

The next chart you want to create will show data from both the Sales and Projected sheets. You want to display the past four years' sales numbers as columns and the 1999 projected sales as a line. This type of chart is called a **combination chart**. It uses two or more chart types to emphasize that the chart contains different kinds of information. First you will create a column chart of the sales data for the four years. Then you will add the projected sales data as a line. You want to create this chart in its own sheet.

- Select B5 through F9.
- Click Chart Wizard.
- Click Next >.
- Choose Columns.
- Click Next >.
- Add the chart title **Annual vs Projected Sales**. Enter **Category** as the category-axis title and **Sales** as the value-axis title.
- Click Next >.
- Choose As new sheet.
- Click Finish.

Your screen should be similar to Figure 4-24.

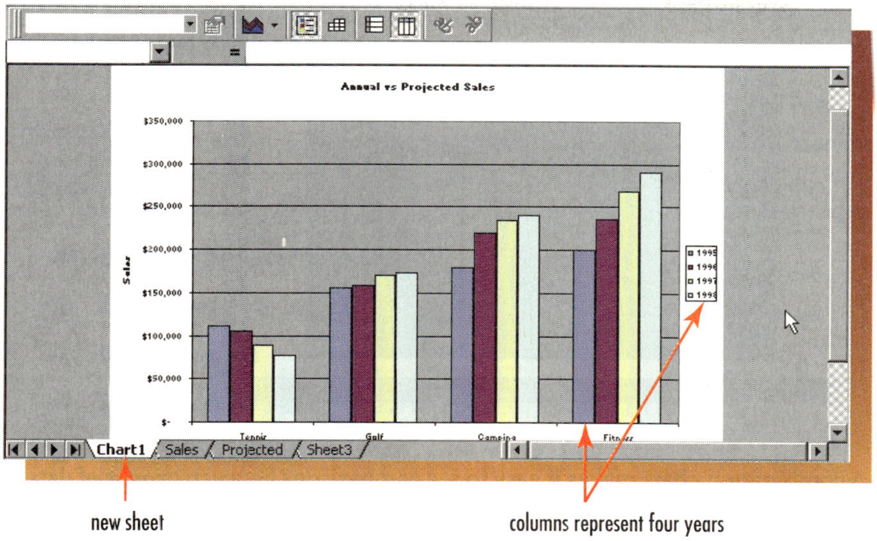

FIGURE 4-24

The column chart is displayed in a new sheet named Chart1. The sheet is inserted to the left of the active sheet. A chart that is not embedded in a worksheet as an object is displayed in a chart sheet. Generally, you display a chart in a chart sheet when you want the chart displayed separately from the associated worksheet data. The chart is still automatically linked to the worksheet data from which it was created.

If the chart was embedded in the worksheet, you could use "drag and plot" to drag data from the worksheet to add a data series to a chart.

Next you need to add the projected sales data series to the chart. To add a data series,

- Select Chart/Add Data.
- Click the Projected sheet tab.
- Select C5 through C9.
- Click OK.

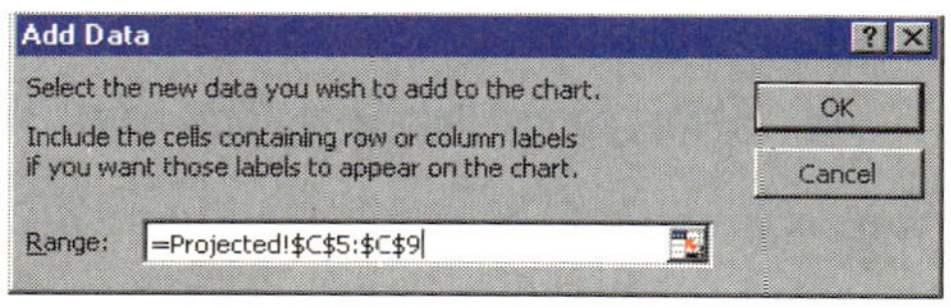

When a chart is displayed in a chart sheet, the chart does not need to be selected before it is modified.

The Add Data dialog box automatically shrinks while you select the worksheet data.

The Paste Special dialog box is displayed. By default Excel appropriately applies the same orientation, Column, as in the existing chart. To identify the first row of data in the range to be used as the legend label,

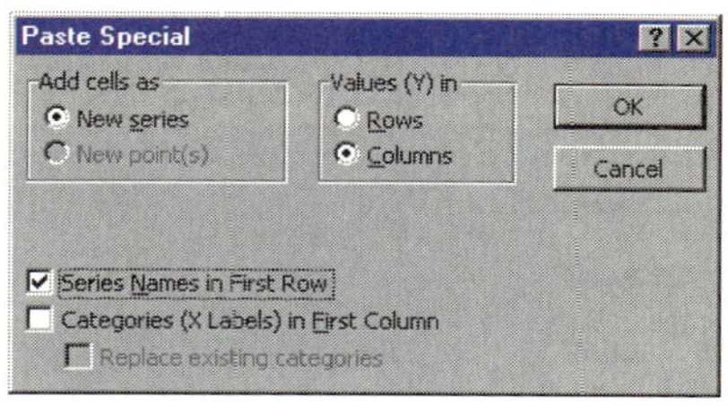

- Select Series Names in First Row.
- Click OK.

The new data series is added to the chart as a column. To change it to a line,

- Select 1999 data series.
- Open the Chart Type drop-down list.
- Choose Line.

SPREADSHEET

SPREADSHEET

A basic pie chart is drawn in the worksheet. It does not include a chart title or labels to clarify the slices of the pie.

- Move and expand the chart to be displayed over cells E4 through I16.

Your screen should be similar to Figure 4-27.

d. Update the summary properties and save the workbook as Top 5 Advertisers. Print the worksheet with the chart centered horizontally on the page.

3. To complete this exercise, you must have completed Practice Exercise 2 in Lab 2. Open the file Cookie Jar on your data disk.

a. Use the column A row headings and the corresponding first-quarter total numbers to create an embedded 3-D pie chart. Add an appropriate title. Remove the legend and add to the slices of the pie data labels that display the different types of cookies and the percents. Size the chart so all labels can be displayed. If necessary, reduce the font size of the labels. Explode the chocolate chip cookie wedge, and add patterns to the slices. Add a text box and an arrow that draws attention to the two wedges that represent the lowest sales.

b. The chart you just created shows a part-to-whole relationship between each cookie type and the total cookie sales for the first quarter. On a new sheet, create a chart that shows a part-to-whole relationship between each cookie type and each monthly value. (Hint: The data will be in rows, not columns.)

c. Add appropriate titles and add patterns to each data series. Size the chart so the legend information can be displayed. Add patterns to each data series, and display the legend below the chart.

d. Update the summary properties for the workbook. Preview the workbook and add headers to both sheets that display your name, the date, and the page number. Print the worksheet. Save and replace the workbook file.

4. As part of a freshman orientation survey, Luzerne University students were asked how many hours a day they expected to spend on school work. The choices were: Less than 1 hour, 1–2 hours, 2–3 hours, and More than 3 hours. Below is a table of the results.

Choice	# Responses
Less than 1 hour	87
1–2 hours	404
2–3 hours	475
More than 3 hours	123

a. Use the table information to create a worksheet, and make any formatting changes you wish.

b. Create an embedded chart that will show a part-to-whole relationship for the four categories of responses. Format the chart as desired.

c. Create a header that displays your name and the current date.

d. Update the summary properties for the workbook. Save the workbook file as Student Survey. Print the worksheet with the chart centered horizontally on the page.

e. At the end of the first semester, the students were again surveyed. This time they were asked how many hours a day they actually spent on school work. The table below shows the results from those who responded.

Choice	# Responses
Less than 1 hour	15
1–2 hours	101
2–3 hours	592
More than 3 hours	246

f. Replace the original values with the new values. Save and replace the workbook Student Survey. Print the worksheet with the chart. Can you relate to the differences in the results?

On Your Own

☆☆

5. Sadie Jacobs, owner of Jacobs Furniture Galleries, likes to have her sales staff close a sale with at least 35 percent of the customers with whom they come in contact. The worksheet below displays this month's results.

	A	B	C	D	E	F	G
1	Jacobs Furniture Galleries						
2	Monthly Sales Report						
3							
4		Ron	Charmaine	Michael	Polly	Al	Mary Claire
5	*Contacts*	113	127	95	129	113	135
6	*Sales*	26	49	42	19	43	54
7	*% of Closings*						
8							

Create the worksheet shown above and calculate the percent of Closings. Create an embedded chart that best compares customer contacts to sales for each employee. Add appropriate titles, and format as desired.

Create a header and footer that displays your name and the current date. Print the worksheet with the chart. Update the summary properties for the workbook. Save the workbook file as Sales Report.

Use Goal Seek to determine how many sales would be needed to increase the percent of Closings to 35 percent for those who do not meet that goal. Save and replace the workbook file Sales Report. Print the worksheet with the chart.

☆☆☆

6. According to "The College Savings Bank," the 1995 cost of a four-year education was approximately $35,000 and $72,000 respectively for public and private colleges.

	A	B	C	D	E	F	G
1	College Costs						
2							
3		**1995**	**1996**	**1997**	**1998**	**1999**	**2000**
4	***Public***	35,000					
5	***Private***	72,000					
6							

Create the worksheet shown above and, using an annual inflation rate of 7.5 percent, complete the worksheet to calculate the cost of a college education for each type of school from 1995 to the year 2000. Add the following comment in a text box below the worksheet:

***Note:* The above costs include tuition, room, board, books, and other expenses and fees.**

Create an embedded chart that will compare private and public school costs annually. Add appropriate titles, and format as desired. Rename the sheet tab.

Create a chart as a new sheet that will show the change in cost from 1995 to 2000. Add appropriate titles, and format as desired. Rename the chart sheet tab.

Create a header to display your name and the current date. Print the workbook.

Update the summary properties for the workbook. Save the workbook as College Costs.

☆☆☆

7. Create a worksheet that tracks your grades. It can be a record of the test scores you received this semester, or it can be a record of your GPA each semester. Create an embedded chart that best represents your grade trends. Use the formatting techniques you have learned to change the appearance of the worksheet and the chart. Save the workbook as Grades. Print the worksheet with the chart.

☆☆☆

8. Create a worksheet that displays a list of your monthly expenses (rent, car payment, food, day care, utilities, insurance, credit cards, etc.). Total the expenses. Create a chart that best shows a part-to-whole relationship between each expense and total expenses. Using the formatting techniques you have learned, change the appearance of the worksheet and the chart. Save the workbook as Expenses. Include your name and the date in a header. Print the worksheet and the chart.

4 Creating Charts

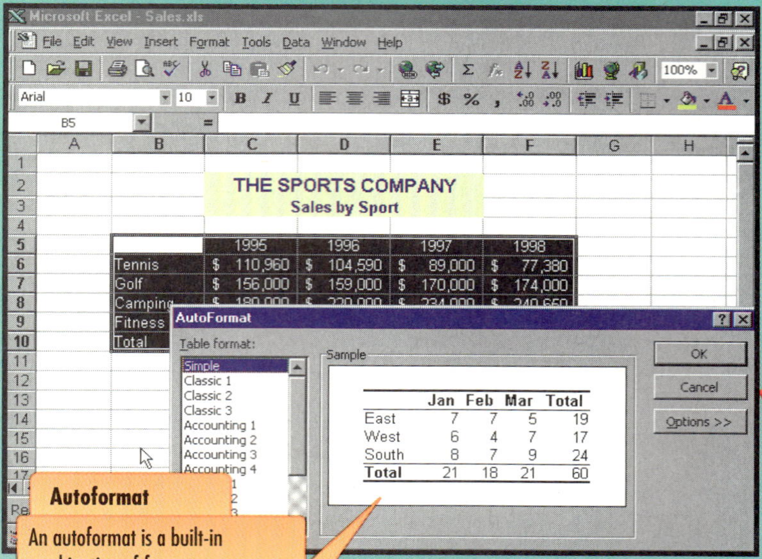

Autoformat

An autoformat is a built-in combination of formats that can be applied to a range.

Concepts

- Autoformat
- Types of Charts
- Chart Elements
- Objects

Chart Elements

A chart consists of a number of parts or elements that are used to graphically display the worksheet data.

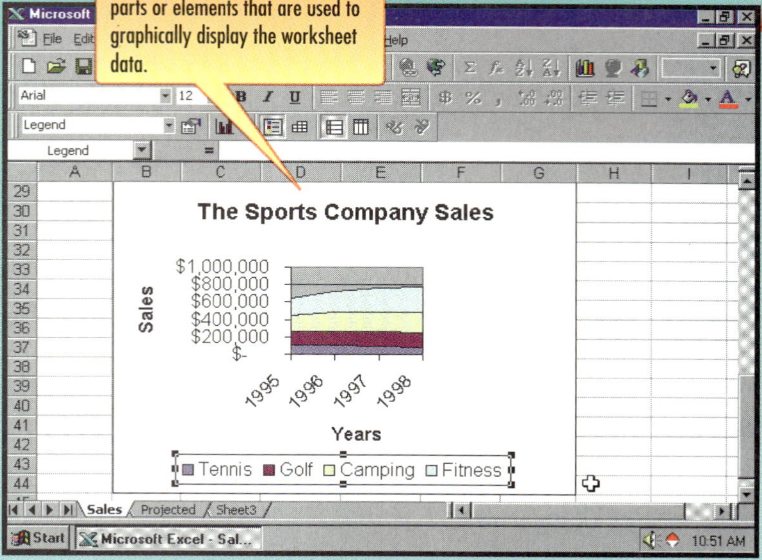

Types of Charts

Excel 97 can produce 14 basic types of charts with many different formats for each type.

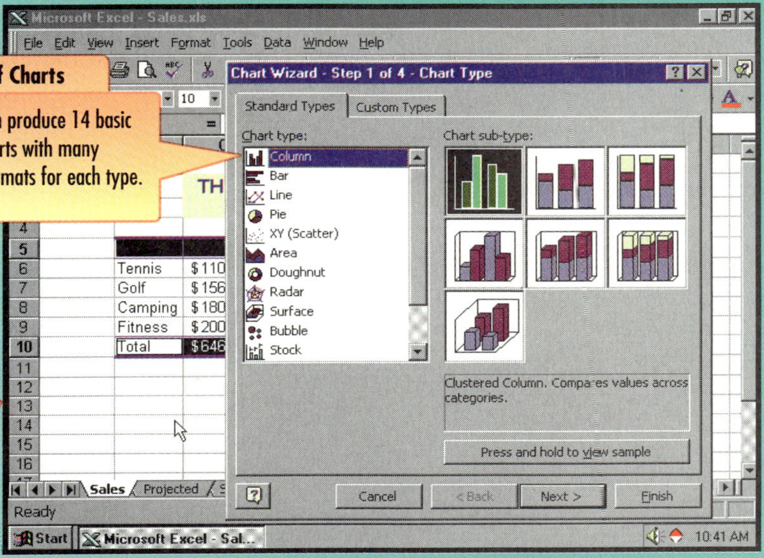

Objects

Objects are items that can be added to a worksheet and that can be sized and moved.

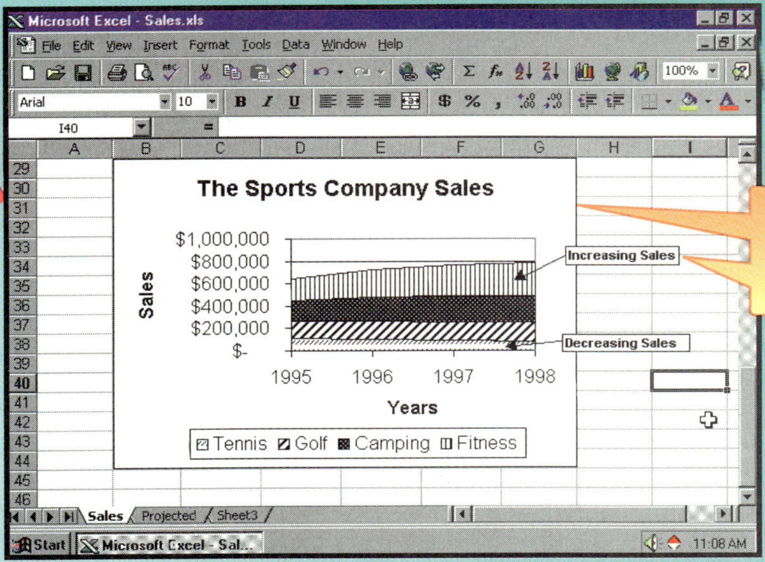

Creating a Form Template

5

COMPETENCIES

After completing this lab, you will know how to:

1. Name a range.
2. Use the IF function.
3. Add controls.
4. Improve the appearance of the form.
5. Hide rows and window elements.
6. Document a form.
7. Protect a worksheet.
8. Create a template file.

CASE STUDY

As you have used Excel to create more complex worksheets and workbooks for The Sports Company, you have seen how the program makes it easier and faster to produce an accurate, attractive, and useful worksheet. Your next project with The Sports Company is to create a form to be used to track the monthly new charge card enrollments and to calculate the employee bonuses. While using Excel to create the form (shown below), you will use many advanced features.

Among the many features are the hundreds of functions included with Excel that are designed to perform complex financial and statistical analysis of data. Specifically you will learn about the IF function, which is used to perform conditional tests on data. In addition, you will learn how to create forms and templates, to add controls, and to protect your worksheets so that their contents cannot be changed.

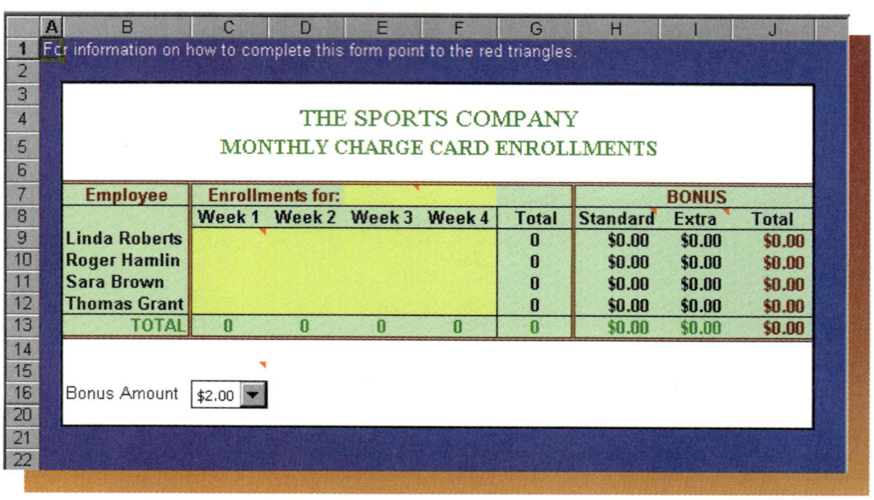

Concept Overview

The following concepts will be introduced in this lab:

1. Range Name	Adding a descriptive range name to a cell or range of cells makes formulas easier to read and understand.
2. IF Function	The IF function checks to see if certain conditions are met and then takes action based upon the results of the check.
3. Controls	Controls are graphic objects that are designed to automate the process of filling out the form. Controls include property settings that affect how they behave and work.
4. Worksheet Protection	To prevent others from changing a sheet's contents, you can protect the entire worksheet or specified areas of the worksheet. When you protect a sheet, all cells and graphic objects on the sheet are locked.
5. Workbook Template	A workbook template is a workbook file that contains predesigned sheets that can be used as a pattern for creating other similar worksheets in new workbooks.

Naming a Range

The Sports Company has decided to offer its own charge card. As an incentive to apply for a card, customers receive 15 percent off any purchases made using the card for the first time. As an incentive to employees to promote the charge card, they earn a bonus for each credit card application they process. The store manager has asked you to create a form to track the enrollments and bonuses each month.

A **form** is a formatted worksheet that is designed to be completed by filling in data in the blank spaces. Forms can be used online on an individual computer or on a network, or can be printed to be completed on paper. The steps in creating a form are the same for both purposes. However, the different elements are more appropriate for one than the other. For example, color and shading are more effective on online forms, while simplicity of design and layout are very important in printed forms. In addition, online forms can contain formulas that immediately calculate results such as totals, whereas printed forms would need to include blank spaces where the calculations would be entered manually.

The first step when creating a form is to decide what information is to be entered on the form and what questions need to be asked. You also need to decide if the form will be computerized or printed. The form to monitor employee bonuses will be used online. You have already started designing the form by entering much of the text, many of the formulas, some formatting to improve the appearance, and some sample data.

- To see what has been done so far, load Excel and open the workbook file Enrollment Bonus. If necessary, maximize the worksheet.

Your worksheet should be similar to Figure 5-1.

FIGURE 5-1

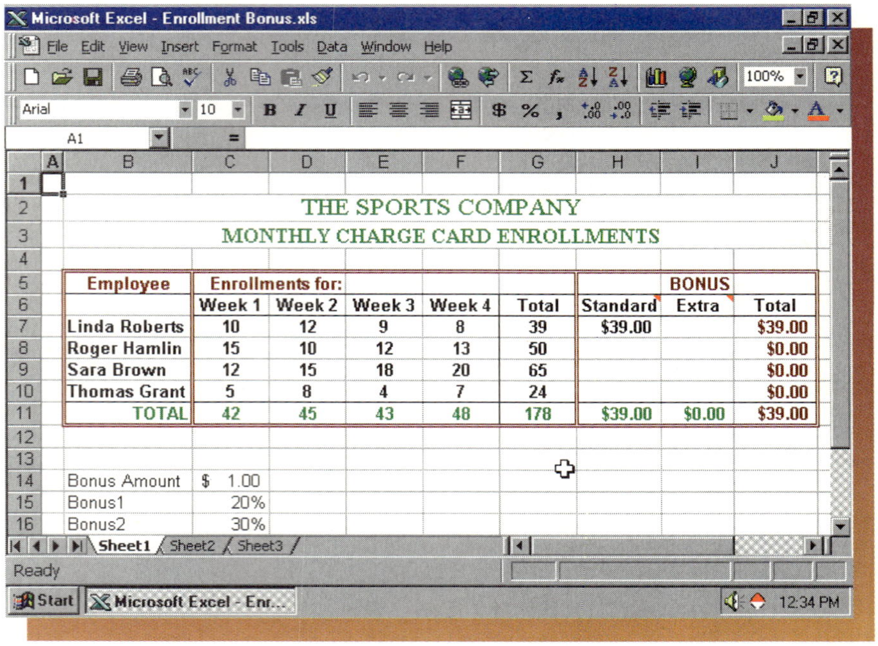

This worksheet displays the names of four salespeople as row headings in column B. The enrollments for each week of the month are entered in columns C through F for each salesperson. The monthly enrollment total is displayed in column G. The worksheet contains some sample enrollment data for each salesperson. The sample data for Linda shows that she enrolled ten charge card applicants in week 1, twelve in week 2, nine in week 3, and eight in week 4, for a monthly total of 39 enrollments.

The three columns to the right of the enrollment data are where the bonus will be calculated. The Sports Company is awarding a standard bonus of $1.00 for each credit card application signed up. Additionally, if a salesperson files 25 applications or more, an extra bonus equal to 20 percent of the standard bonus is awarded. If they file more than 50 applications, the extra bonus amount is increased to 30 percent. The formulas that will be used to calculate the bonus are described below:

Standard	The total number of enrollments times $1.00
Extra	The Standard bonus times 20 percent if total enrollments are 25 or more, or times 30 percent if the total is 50 or more
Total	The sum of the Standard and Extra bonuses

Notice that cells H6 and I6 indicate they contain cell comments.

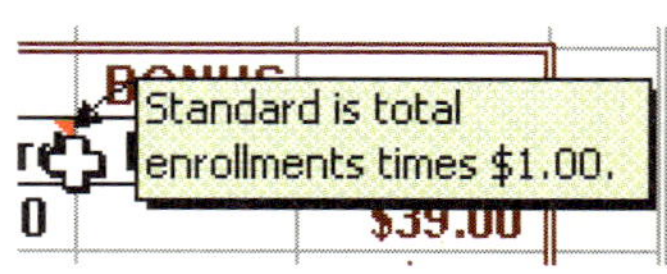

- Display the cell comments for cells H6 and I6.

The comments help clarify the meaning of the data that will be entered in these columns.

The formula to calculate the Standard bonus for Linda Roberts has already been entered.

- Move to H7.

Your worksheet should be similar to Figure 5-2.

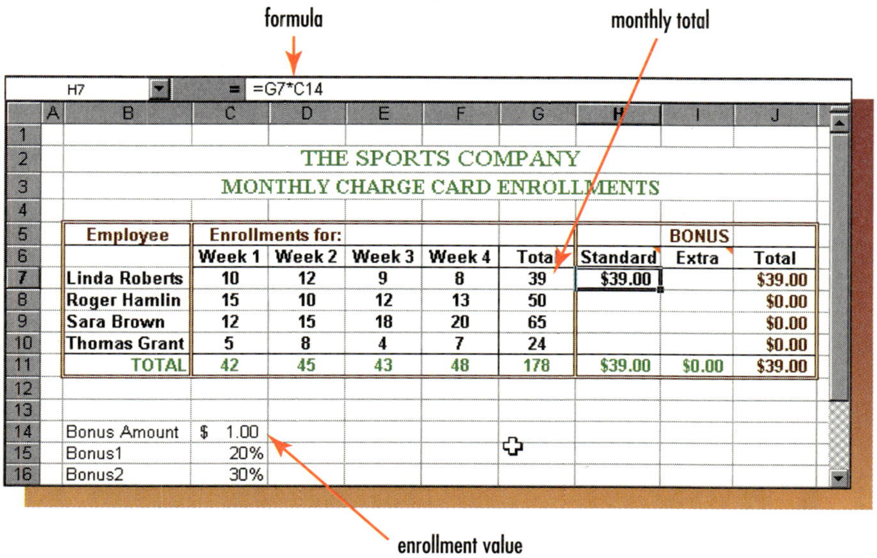

FIGURE 5-2

The formula references cell C14. This cell contains the bonus amount of $1.00. To make the formula easier to read and understand, you will assign a descriptive name to this cell reference.

Concept 1: Range Name

A descriptive **range name** can be assigned to a cell or range of cells and used in place of cell references. The name can be used any time a cell or range is requested as part of a command or in a formula or function.

Excel automatically proposes a name for the cell or range using the contents of the active cell if it contains text, or the cell above or to the left of the active cell if the active cell does not contain text. If the active cell or the cells above or to the left of the active cell do not contain text, or if you do not want to use the proposed name, you can type in a name of your choice. The name can be up to 255 characters. It can include letters, numbers, underlines, periods, backslashes, and question marks. It cannot contain spaces. The first character must be a letter, underline, or backslash. A name that resembles a cell reference is not allowed.

To see how this works, you will assign the name "Bonus Amount" to cell C14.

- Move to C14.
- Choose Insert/Name/Define.

Your screen should be similar to Figure 5-3.

FIGURE 5-3

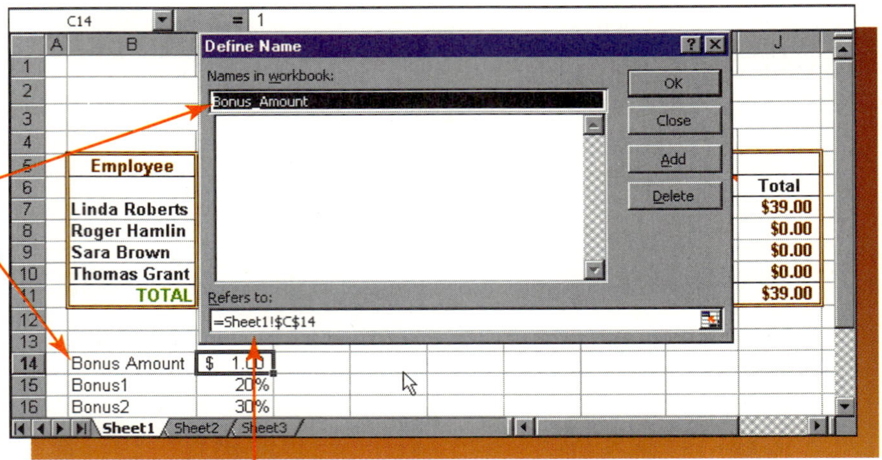

In the Names in Workbook text box, Excel has proposed the name Bonus_Amount. The proposed name is the contents of the cell to the left of the active cell. Excel replaced the blank space between the words with an underline character because a name cannot contain spaces.

You can also name a range by selecting the range and typing the name into the Name box.

The Refers To text box displays the reference for the active cell. The reference includes the sheet name and cell reference. By default Excel makes named cell references absolute. The Names in Workbook list box is empty because this worksheet does not contain any names yet. Since both the name and the cell reference are acceptable, to complete the command,

- Click OK.

You can toggle between displaying the cell reference and the name by clicking on the cell.

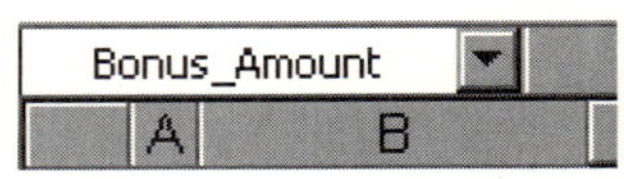

In place of the cell reference in the Name box of the formula bar, the name is displayed. Now you can replace the cell reference in the formula in cell H7 with the name. To do this,

Notice that Range Finder has highlighted the cells in the formula.

- Move to H7.
- Change to Edit mode and select (highlight) the cell reference C14 in the formula.
- Choose Insert/Name/Paste.
- Select Bonus_Amount.
- Click OK.

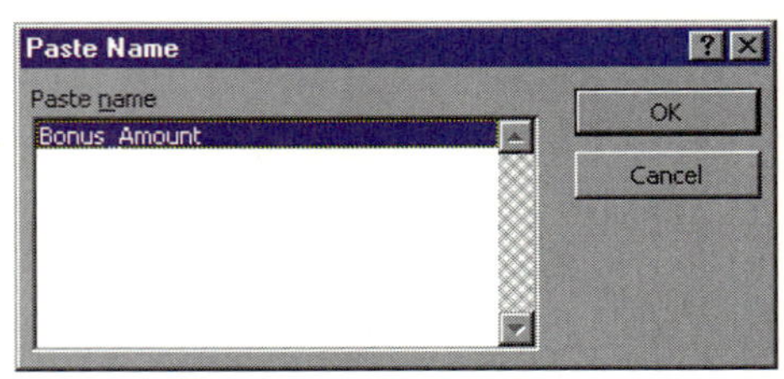

Your worksheet should be similar to Figure 5-4.

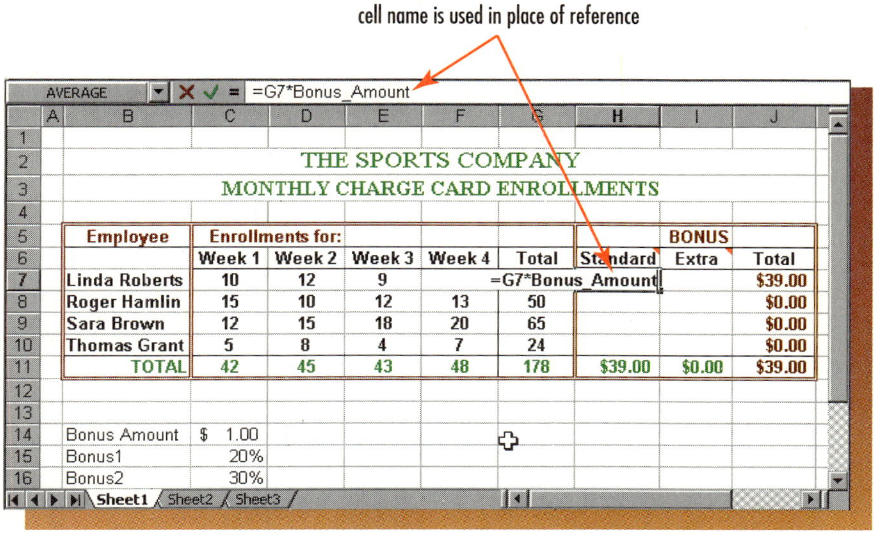

FIGURE 5-4

The name Bonus_Amount has replaced the reference to cell C14 in the formula. Using a name makes the formula easier to understand. To complete the edit,

- Press ←Enter.

Next you will name the bonus percent values in cells C15 and C16 that will be used in the formula to calculate the bonus. You will name both cells at the same time using the headings in B15 and B16 as the names. To create names using headings in a selected range, you specify the location of the headings in relation to the cells to be named. In this case the headings are located in the column to the left of the cells to be named.

- Select B15 through C16.
- Choose Insert/Name/Create.
- Click OK.
- Move to C15.

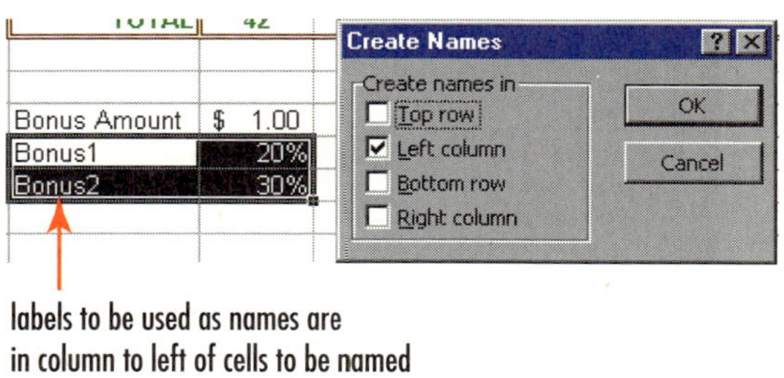

The name assigned to this cell, Bonus1, is displayed in the Name box.

Using the IF Function

Now you are ready to enter a formula in cell I7 to calculate the extra bonus earned. The store awards an extra bonus equal to 30 percent of the Standard bonus if total enrollments are 50 or more, and a 20 percent extra bonus if total enrollments are 25 or more. To calculate this value, you will use the IF function.

Concept 2: IF Function

The IF function checks to see if certain conditions are met and then takes action based upon the results of the check. The syntax for this function is:

IF(logical_test,value_if_true,value_if_false)

This function contains three arguments: logical_test, value_if_true, and value_if_false. The logical_test argument is an expression that makes a comparison using logical operators. **Logical operators** are used in formulas and functions that compare numbers in two or more cells or to a constant. The result of the comparison is either true (the conditions are met) or false (the conditions are not met).

The logical operators are:

Symbol	Meaning	Symbol	Meaning
=	Equal to	<>	Not equal to
<	Less than	NOT	Logical NOT
>	Greater than	AND	Logical AND
<=	Less than or equal to	OR	Logical OR
>=	Greater than or equal to		

The logical test argument asks the question, Does the entry in this cell meet the stated conditions? The answer is either True (Yes) or False (No). The second argument, value_if_true, provides directions for the function to follow if the logical test result is true. The third argument, value_if_false, provides directions for the function to follow if the logical test result is false.

First you will enter the formula to calculate the bonus earned for enrollments of 50 or more. Then you will modify the function to include the other conditions. You will enter the IF function using the Paste Function feature.

The menu equivalent is Insert/Function.

If the IF function name is not listed in the Most Recently Used category, switch to the Logical category to select it.

- Move to I7.
- Click Paste Function.
- Select IF.
- Click OK.

Your screen should be similar to Figure 5-5.

text boxes

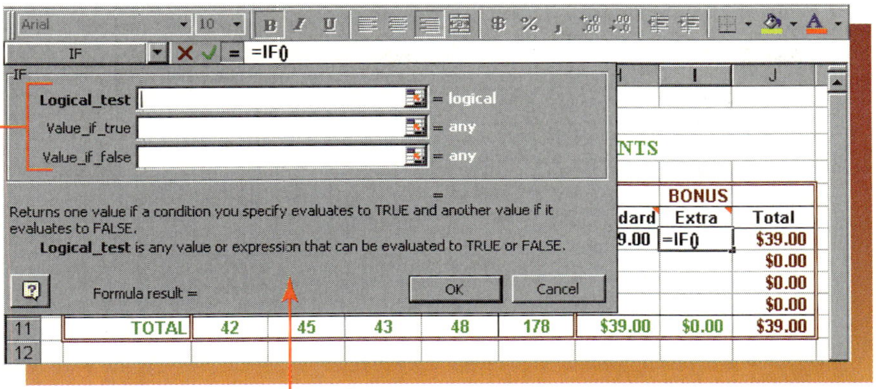

IF formula palette

FIGURE 5-5

The IF formula palette contains three text boxes, one for each IF statement argument. The logical test is whether the total monthly enrollment (G7) is greater than (>) or equal to (=) 50. The logical_test argument will be G7>=50. In the logical_test text box,

- Type **G7>=50**
- Press Tab.

The function in the formula bar displays the logical test argument you specified.

The value_if_true argument contains the instructions that are executed if the condition is true. In this case if the number in cell G7 is greater than or equal to 50 (true), then H7 is multiplied by 30 percent (H7*30%). Instead of entering the bonus amount (30%) to complete the argument, you will reference the named cell, B16, that contains the bonus number. This way, if the bonus changes, the function will not need to be changed. The value_if_true argument then will be: G7*Bonus2. To enter the value_if_true argument,

- Type **G7***
- Choose Insert/Name/Paste.
- Select Bonus2.
- Click OK.

The value_if_false argument contains instructions that are executed if the condition is not true, or false. If the number in cell G7 is less than 50 (false), then the bonus is 0. To enter the last argument,

- Click the dialog box to make it active again.
- Press Tab.
- Type **0**.
- Click OK.

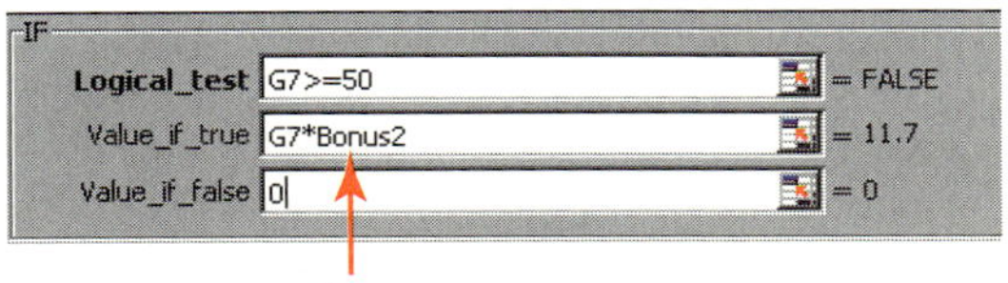

cell name

Your worksheet should be similar to Figure 5-6.

FIGURE 5-6

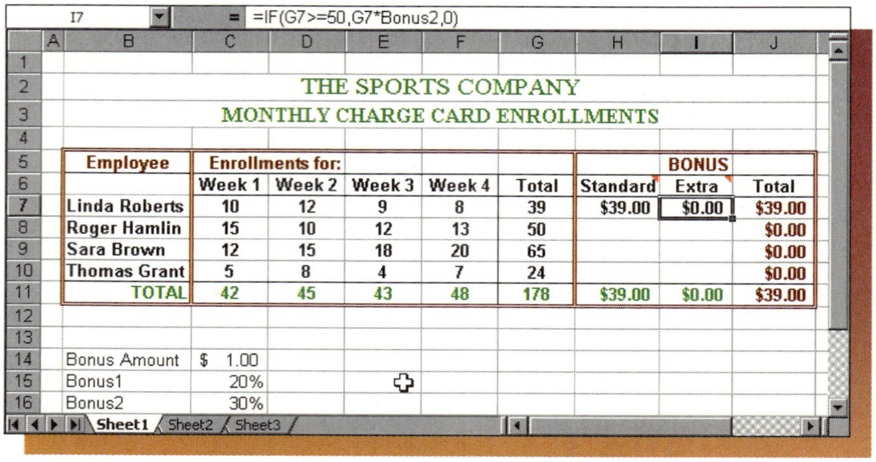

The Extra bonus is calculated for Linda using the sample data. The Extra bonus is $0.00 because the number in cell G7 is less than 50.

Now you need to modify this function to include a second IF statement that will apply the bonus of 20 percent to total enrollments that are greater than or equal to 25. The new IF statement will be IF(G7>=25,G7*Bonus1,0). The arguments for the second IF statement are enclosed in their own set of parentheses within the existing formula. This is called a **nested function**. The new function will be:

IF(G7>=50,G7*Bonus2,IF(G7>=25,G7*Bonus1,0))

second IF statement

To edit the formula using the Paste Function feature,

> You can also add the second IF function directly by editing it in the cell or formula bar.

- Click [=] Edit Formula.
- In the value_if-false text box enter **IF (G7>=25,G7*Bonus1,0)**
- Click [OK].

Your worksheet should be similar to Figure 5-7.

FIGURE 5-7

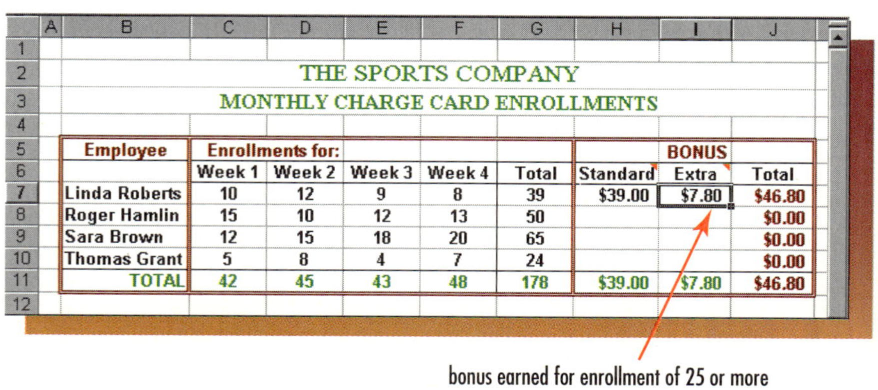

The Extra bonus for Linda is now $7.80. The formula determined that the number in cell G7 was 25 or more and calculated a 20 percent bonus on the number in cell G7.

- Copy the formulas in cells H7 and I7 to cells H8 through I10 to complete the columns.
- Move to I8.

Your worksheet should be similar to Figure 5-8.

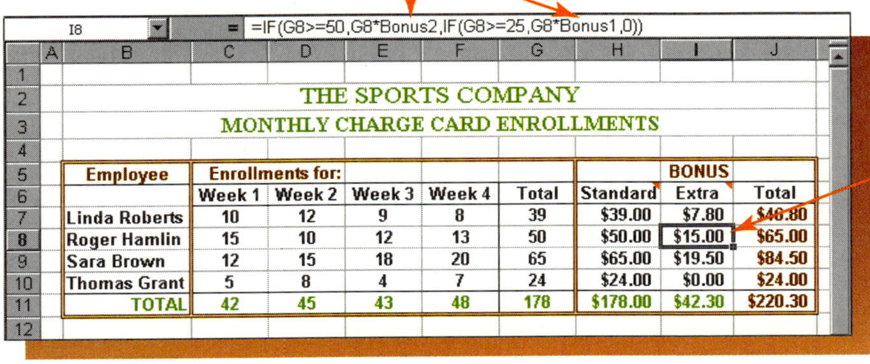

Employee	Enrollments for: Week 1	Week 2	Week 3	Week 4	Total	BONUS Standard	Extra	Total
Linda Roberts	10	12	9	8	39	$39.00	$7.80	$46.80
Roger Hamlin	15	10	12	13	50	$50.00	$15.00	$65.00
Sara Brown	12	15	18	20	65	$65.00	$19.50	$84.50
Thomas Grant	5	8	4	7	24	$24.00	$0.00	$24.00
TOTAL	42	45	43	48	178	$178.00	$42.30	$220.30

FIGURE 5-8

The cell names in the copied formula appear exactly as they did in the formula in cell I7. You did not need to change the names to absolute because named cell references can only be absolute.

The Extra bonus in cell I8 is $15.00. The function calculated the 30 percent bonus because the number in G8 is equal to 50. The bonus in cell I9 is $19.50 because the number in cell G9 is greater than 50. Finally, the function calculated the bonus of $0.00 in cell I10 because the number in G10 is less than 25. The IF function is operating correctly.

Adding Controls

Your manager really likes the layout of the form. One change that needs to be made, however, is to the bonus amount. During some months the bonus amount may be raised to $2.00 or $3.00. The formulas to calculate the bonus will need to be adjusted to use the other two bonus amounts during those months. You could create two additional forms that would each have a different bonus amount in cell C14. This would require that the correct form be used for that month's input based on the bonus award for that month. A simpler way to deal with this problem is to add a control element to the form.

Concept 3: Controls

Controls are graphic objects that are designed to automate the process of filling out the form. Controls include property settings that affect how they behave and work. The properties associated with many controls can be changed to customize the control for your own use. Examples of controls include text boxes, list buttons, scroll bars, and option buttons.

Check box Combo box List box Option box

Using controls makes it easier to fill out a form and increases the accuracy of the information entered in it. This is because many of the controls can include a list of options from which the user selects.

Although controls are most effectively used in online forms, they can also be used in printed forms. For example, controls such as buttons and check boxes can be printed blank and then filled in by the user.

The Forms toolbar is used to add controls. The procedure is similar to adding a text box.

- Display the Forms toolbar.
- If necessary, move the toolbar to the right side of your screen.
- Display the Tooltips.

You will add a combo box control to the form. This control creates a text box and button that will display a drop-down list with the three bonus amounts as options that can be selected. Then the selected option is displayed in the combo text box, which can then be linked to cell C14 to be used in the computation of the bonus.

First you need to enter the three bonus amount values in a columnar range.

- In cells E15 through E17 enter the numbers **1**, **2** and **3**.

The mouse pointer appears as a + to indicate you can drag to create the control.

- Format the range to currency with two decimal places.
- Click  Combo Box.
- Move the mouse pointer into the worksheet and drag to create a combo box the approximate size of a single cell.

Your screen should be similar to Figure 5-9.

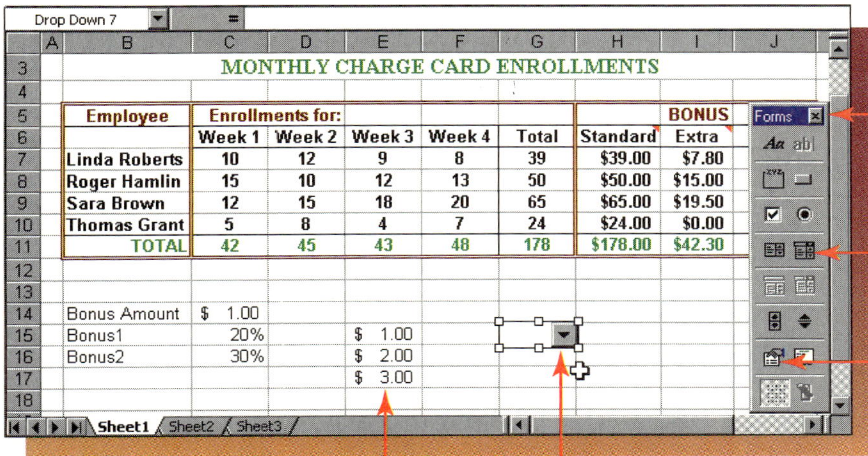

FIGURE 5-9

The combo box is a selected object that can be sized or moved like any other object. Next, you need to specify the information to be displayed in the drop-down list and the location of the cell to link the selection to. Modifying the control's properties makes these changes.

You can also select Format Control from the object's Shortcut menu to modify the properties.

- Click Control Properties.
- If necessary, open the Control tab.
- Specify cells E15 through E17 as the Input Range.
- Specify cell C14 as the Cell Link.
- Click OK.
- Click outside the control to deselect it.

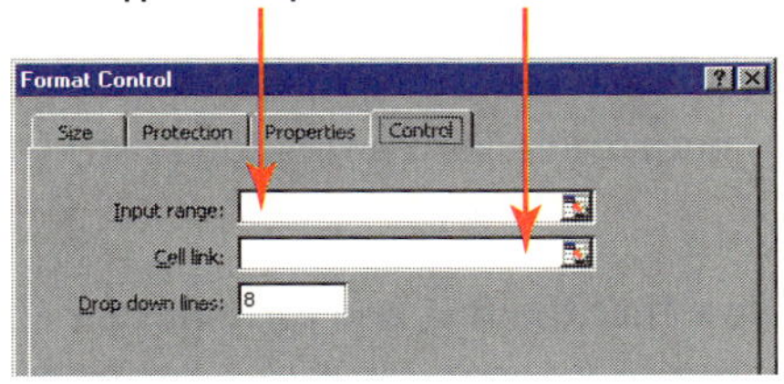

Notice that the bonus amount in cell C14 is empty and the standard bonus formulas have been recalculated. This is because the combo box is blank. You need to select a bonus amount from the combo box drop-down list.

- Open the combo box drop-down list and select $2.00.

The mouse pointer changes to a hand pointer when pointing to a control.

Hiding Window Elements

Now you will turn off the display of several other window elements to simplify the appearance of the online form.

- Choose: Tools/Options/View.

The dialog box on your screen should be similar to Figure 5-13.

FIGURE 5-13

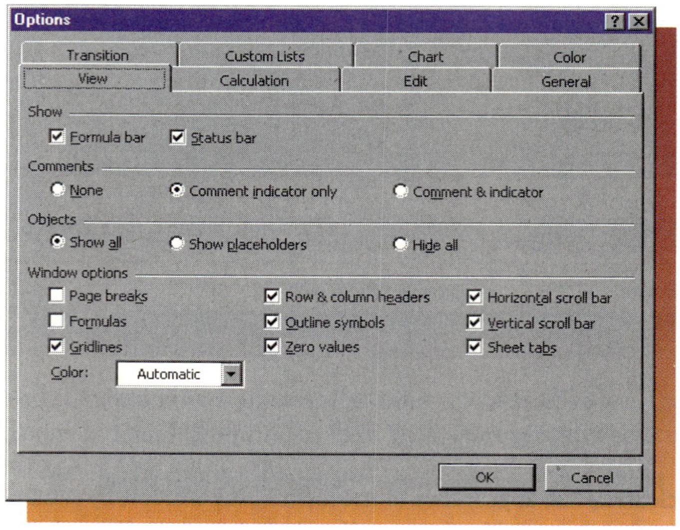

- Clear the following settings: Formula bar, Status bar, Gridlines, Horizontal scroll bar, Vertical scroll bar, and Sheet tabs.
- Click OK.
- Press Ctrl + Home.

Although the screen is much simplified, it looks very plain. To define the edge of the form area, you will add an outline border around the form and a dark color of your choice around the entire edge of the form that is visible in the window space.

- Add two additional blank rows above the title to better center the form in the window.
- Add an outline border around cells B3 through J20.
- Highlight the appropriate rows and columns on your screen and select a fill color of your choice to surround the form.

Your screen should be similar to Figure 5-14.

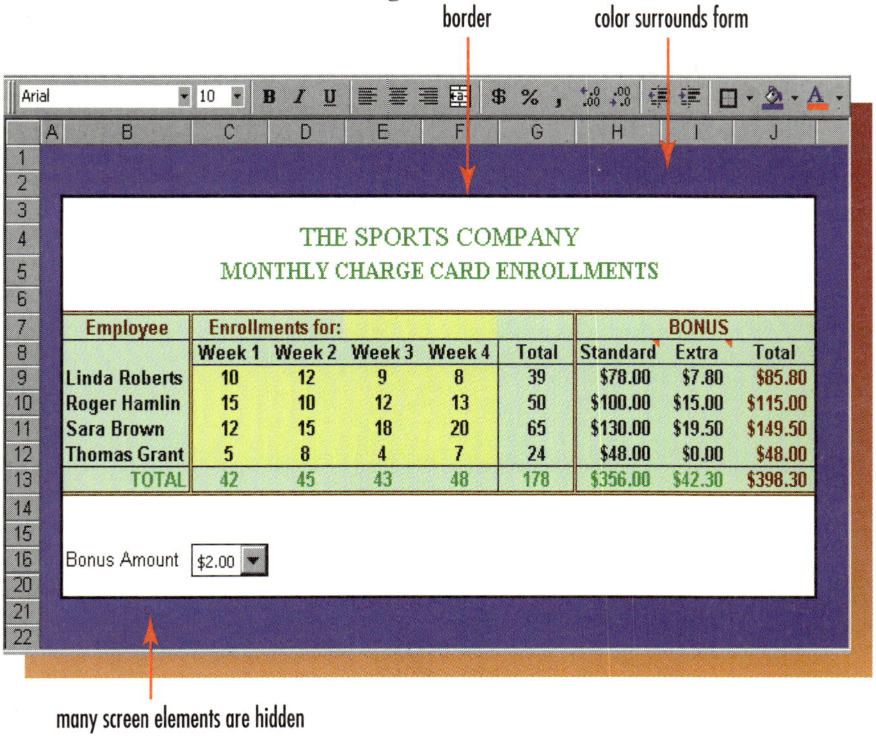

FIGURE 5-14

Documenting a Form

Finally, it is good procedure when creating a form for others to use to include documentation within the form. The documentation should be brief and may include the following:

Purpose	Briefly describes what information is needed to complete the form and what output is generated from the form.
Instructions	Discusses the steps for completing the form.
Procedures	Explains how to move to different areas of the form, enter data, and how to name and save the form.

Some documentation needs to be entered in the form as text entries. Others can be entered as cell comments. Using cell comments is a good method of adding documentation that does not interfere with the appearance of the form. You will add one text entry and several cell comments that will provide the documentation for this form. To make it easier to see your location in the sheet, you will first turn on the display of the row and column headings again.

- In cell A1 enter the following text in white letters and bold: **For information on how to complete this form point to the red triangles.**

Since you will be inserting several cell comments next, you will display the Reviewing toolbar (shown at right) to make it easier to work with comments.

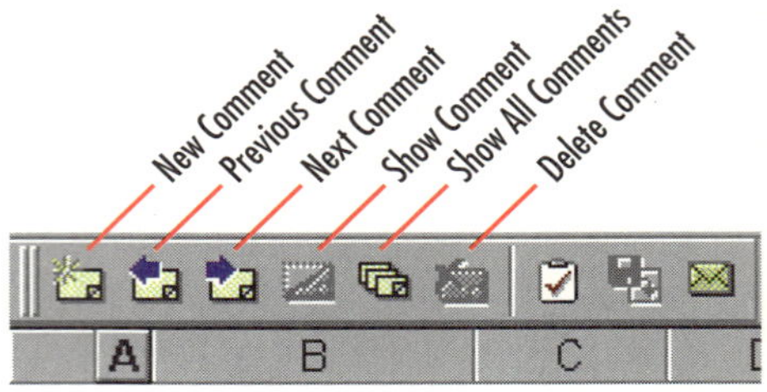

- Display the Reviewing toolbar.
- Using the appropriate Reviewing toolbar buttons, enter or edit the comments shown in the table below in the cells indicated.
- Adjust the size of the comment boxes appropriately.

Cell	Comment
E7	**Type the month here. Use Tab to move to the next space or click on the location.**
C9	**Enter the enrollment values here.**
C15	**Click the button to select a bonus amount for the month.**
H8	**Standard is total enrollments times the Bonus Amount.**

To see all the comments at once to check them,

- Click Show All Comments.

Your screen should be similar to Figure 5-15.

FIGURE 5-15

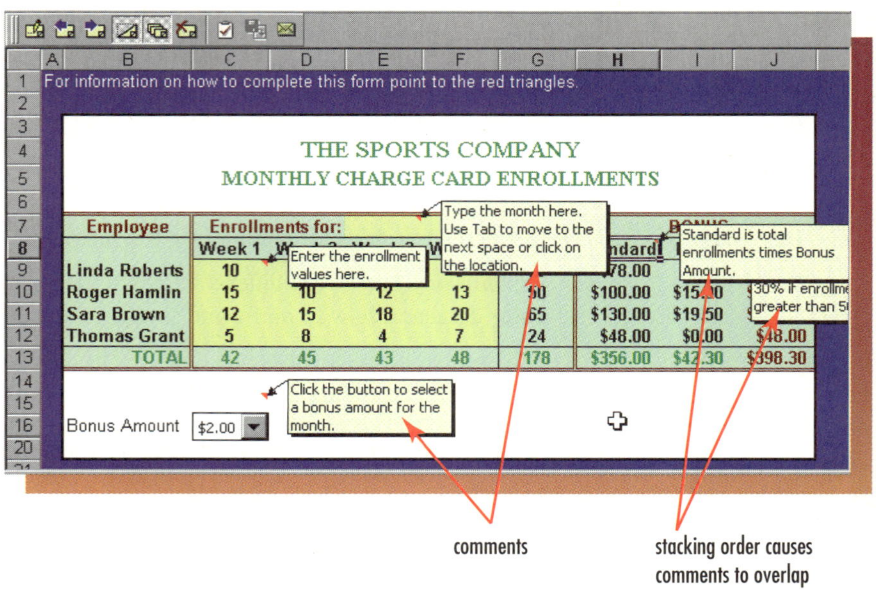

Comments are also graphic objects and may overlap each other.

- Move and resize the comments so they do not overlap.
- Edit any comments as needed.
- Click Hide All Comments.
- Close the Reviewing toolbar.

Protecting a Worksheet

Now that the form is complete, you want to prevent changes to the worksheet that would cause headings and formulas in the worksheet to be altered or cleared. To do this, you can protect the worksheet.

Concept 4: Worksheet Protection

To prevent others from changing a sheet's contents, you can **protect** the entire worksheet or specified areas of the worksheet. When you protect a sheet, all cells and graphic objects on the sheet are locked. The contents of a **locked** cell cannot be changed. If you want to leave some cells unlocked for editing, such as in a worksheet you use as an entry form, you can lock cells containing labels and formulas but unlock the entry fields so that others can fill them in. This type of protection prevents you from entering or changing an entry in any locked cells.

An entire workbook can also be protected from unauthorized changes in two ways. The structure of a workbook can be protected so that sheets cannot be moved or deleted or new sheets inserted. A workbook's windows can also be protected. This prevents changes to the size and position of windows and ensures they appear the same way each time the workbook is opened.

In addition, you can include a **password** that prevents any unauthorized person from turning off protection and changing the worksheet. If you use a password, you must remember the password in order to turn protection off in the future.

Initially all cells in a worksheet are locked. However, you can enter data in the cells because the worksheet protection feature is not on. When protection is turned on, all locked cells are protected. Therefore, before protecting this sheet, you need to unlock the range of cells where the data will be entered.

- Select C9 through F12.
- Choose Format/Cells.
- Open the Protection tab in the Format Cells dialog box.

Format Cells is also on the Shortcut menu.

The dialog box on your screen should be similar to Figure 5-16.

FIGURE 5-16

cells are locked by default

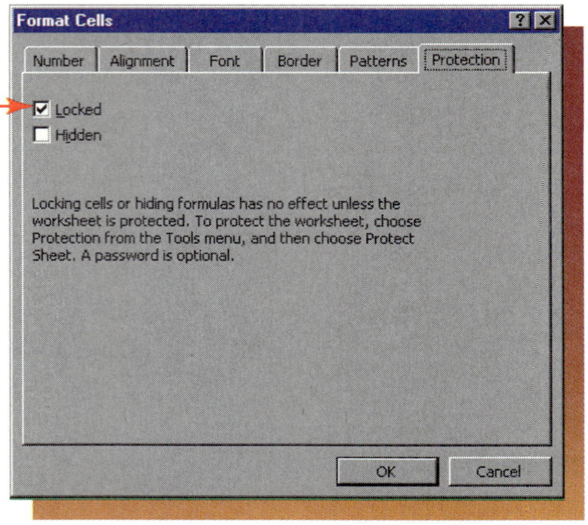

- To allow changes to the selected range of cells, clear the Locked option box.
- Click OK.
- In a similar manner, unlock cell C16 where the selected Bonus Amount is entered.

> Use the arrow keys to move to cell C16.

Now you are ready to turn on worksheet protection. To prevent unauthorized users from removing the sheet protection, you will require a password. A password can be a maximum of 15 characters and can contain any combination of letters, numbers, and symbols. It is also case sensitive, so you must remember the exact combination of uppercase and lowercase letters you used in your password.

- Choose Tools/Protection/Protect Sheet.
- Type **secret**.

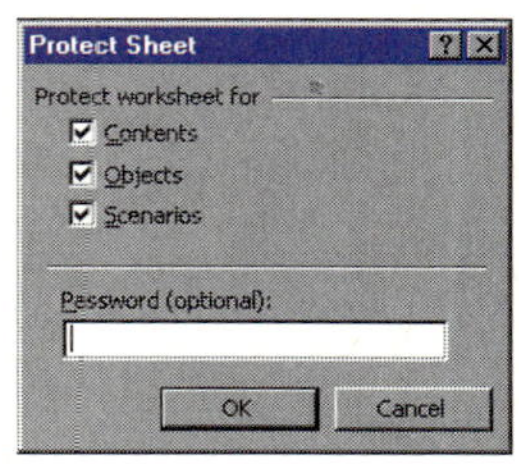

As you enter the password, asterisks are displayed in place of the characters you type to prevent anyone from seeing the password as it is entered.

- Click OK.

Next, you are asked to verify the password by reentering it.

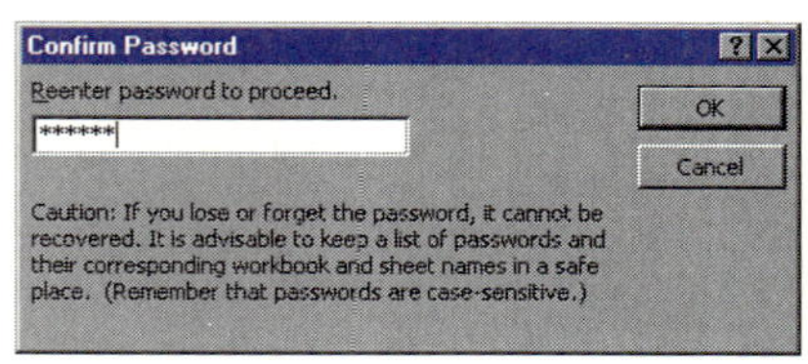

- Type **secret**.
- Read the Caution in this box.
- Click OK.

> If the entry you type does not exactly match the original password entry, a warning appears. Click OK and try again.

Now all locked cells in the worksheet are protected. Any cells you unlocked prior to turning protection on can be changed. To show the effect of trying to enter data into a protected cell, you will try to enter the month in cell E7.

- Move to cell E7 and type any character.

A warning dialog box is displayed, informing you that you cannot change entries in locked cells. To clear the message,

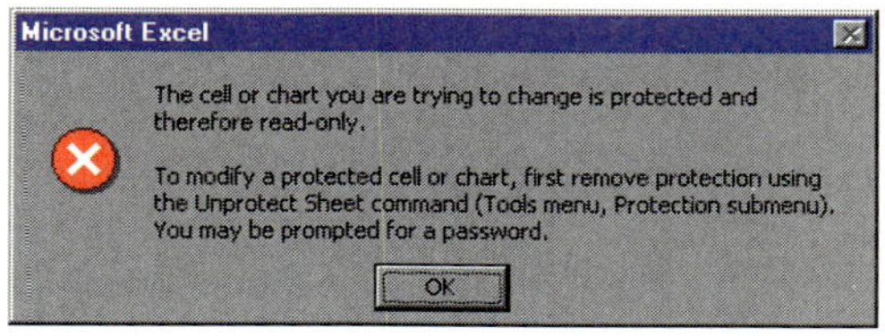

- Click OK.

You need to change this cell to unprotected so you can edit it to display the month. To do this, you first need to turn off worksheet protection and then unlock the cell and turn on protection again.

- Choose Tools/Protection/Unprotect Sheet.
- Type **secret**.
- Click OK.
- Choose Format/Cells.
- Clear the Locked option in the Protection folder.
- Click OK.
- Choose Tools/Protection/Protect Sheet.
- Enter and verify the password "secret."
- To verify that cell E7 can now accept data, enter **October** in the cell.

Reminder: Passwords are case sensitive.

Likewise you will be able to enter the data in cells C9 through F12 because they were unlocked before protecting the worksheet.

Creating a Template File

Each time you use this form, you will be entering data for a new month. Therefore, you want to clear the sample data from the form before saving it.

- Clear the data in cell E7 and in cells C9 through F12.

- Update the file's property summary information with the following documentation:

Title:	**Monthly Charge Card Enrollment**
Subject:	**Monthly report of charge card enrollments and employee bonuses.**
Author:	**[your name]**
Comments:	**Point to the red triangles for information on how to use this form. Enter the report month in cell E7. Enter the enrollment values in cells C9 through F12. Use the print button to print the form. Save the workbook as XXX Bonus, replacing XXX with the month.**

You also want to specify the area to print and to add a header to the printed output before saving the form. Then these settings will be saved with the workbook also.

When the form is printed, you only want the information in cells B4 through J20 to print. To specify this range as the area to print,

The dotted line surrounding the form identifies the print area.

- Select B3 through J20.
- Choose: File/Print Area/Set Print Area.
- Preview the workbook.
- Add a header to the worksheet that displays your name and date only.
- If you have a black-and-white printer and do not want the colored areas of your form to print in shades of gray, select Black and White from the Sheet tab of the Page Setup dialog box.
- Center the form horizontally on the page.

Your screen should be similar to Figure 5-17.

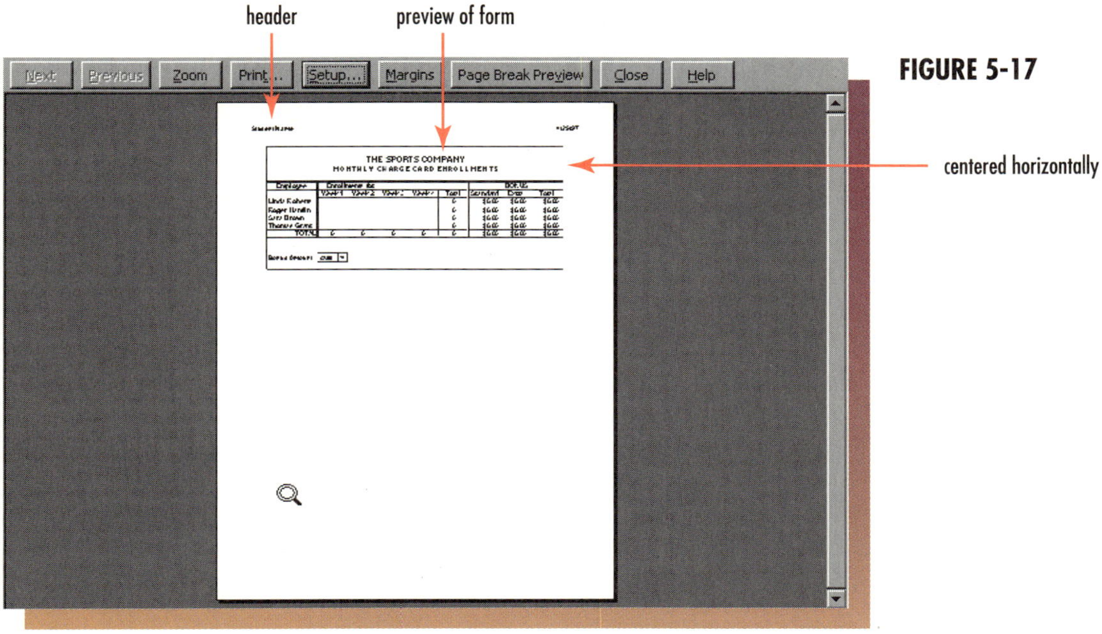

FIGURE 5-17

- Print the form.
- To hide the dotted lines showing the print area, use Tools/Options to turn off the display of page breaks.
- Move to E7.

Because this information will be entered in a different workbook file for each month's data, you will save it as a workbook template.

Concept 5: Workbook Template

A workbook **template** is a workbook file that contains predesigned sheets that can be used as a pattern for creating other similar sheets in new workbooks. Templates are useful in any application where input and output are required using the same format. The template saves the user time by not having to redesign the same worksheet form each time the report is needed. The original design can be used repeatedly by saving the workbook containing the data using a different file name than the file name used to save the workbook template.

Excel saves a workbook template using a special file format with the file extension .xlt. Workbook templates are also stored in a special Templates folder. To use a workbook template, you select the template file name from the General tab of the New File dialog box. When you save the workbook after entering data in the template, Excel automatically displays the Save As dialog box so you can specify the new file name. It also changes the file type to an Excel workbook file (.xls). This ensures that you do not save over the template file unintentionally.

- Choose File/Save As.
- Enter the new file name, **Bonus Form**, in the File Name text box.
- Open the Save As Type list box.

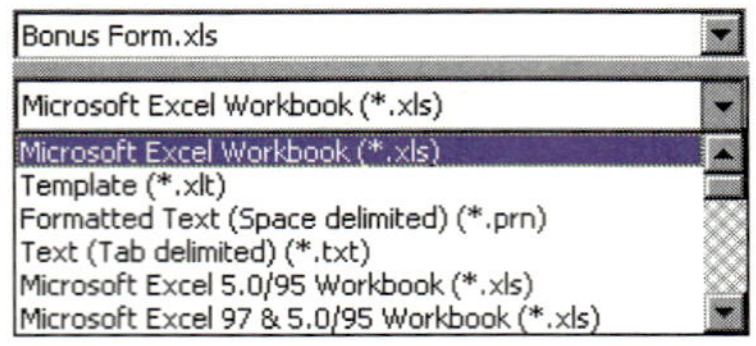

To set the file format to template, you need to specify the type of file from the Save As Type drop-down list box. Your selection from this list determines the way information in a document is stored in a file. Many of the file formats make it easier to use Excel documents with other applications. You need to save the workbook as an Excel template file.

- Select Template.

Notice that the Save In box now displays the Templates folder as the location where the file will be saved.

If you are prompted to replace a file with the same file name, select Yes.

- Click Save.
- Close the Bonus Form template file.

Now you want to create a new workbook file to record the enrollment data for the month of November using the Bonus Form template.

If you save a workbook template to a location other than the Templates folder, the file icon will not appear in the General tab.

- Choose File/New.
- If necessary, display the General tab of the New dialog box.

The Bonus Form template file appears in the General tab as an icon.

- Select Bonus Form.xlt.
- Click OK.

The workbook template is opened and appears just as it did when you saved it.

Use Tab to quickly move from one unlocked cell to another.

- Enter **November** as the month.
- Then enter the following data for each salesperson:

	Week 1	Week 2	Week 3	Week 4
Linda Roberts	**23**	**15**	**22**	**20**
Roger Hamlin	**12**	**11**	**10**	**13**
Sara Brown	**14**	**12**	**10**	**10**
Thomas Grant	**18**	**25**	**18**	**14**

■ Select $3.00 as the Bonus Amount.

When you are done, your screen should be similar to Figure 5-18.

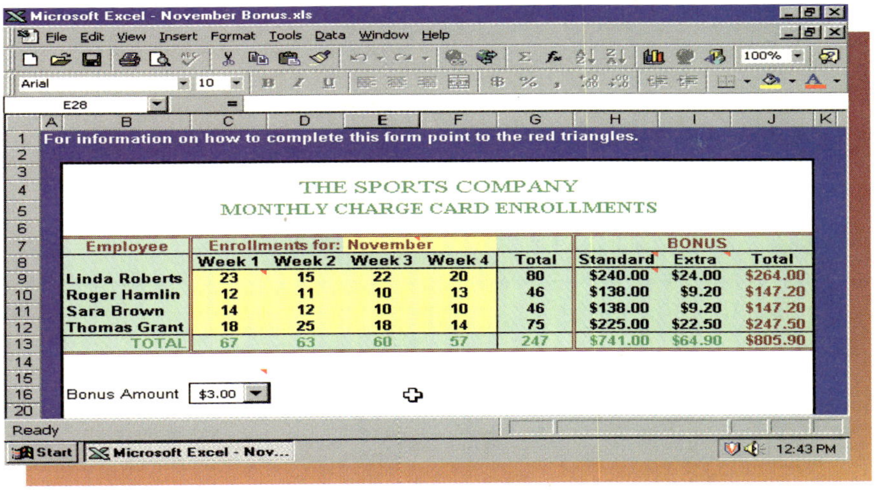

FIGURE 5-18

Now you are ready to save the workbook. You want to use a file name that reflects the month the data represents.

Click Save.

The Save As dialog box is displayed whenever you use a template file. This prevents you from accidentally overwriting the template file with the changes you have made. Excel proposes a file name of Bonus Form1. Notice that the Save As Type text box automatically displays "Microsoft Excel Workbook [*.xls]" as the type of file. Again, this prevents you from accidentally creating another template file.

■ Specify the drive containing your data disk as the location to save the file.

■ Change the proposed file name to **November Bonus**.

■ Click Save.

■ Close the November Bonus file.

■ Use the View menu to turn on the display of the formula bar and status bar again.

■ Exit Excel.

LAB REVIEW

Key Terms

control (SS180)
form (SS171)
lock (SS187)
logical operator (SS176)
nested function (SS178)
password (SS187)
protect (SS187)
range name (SS173)
template (SS191)

Command Summary

Command	Action
File/Save As/Save As Type	Sets file format for document
File/Print Area/Set print area	Sets a range as area to print
Edit/Delete Sheet	Removes sheet from workbook
Insert/Name/Define	Assigns a name you specify to a cell or range of cells
Insert/Name/Paste	Places name in formula bar or lists names in worksheet
Insert/Name/Create	Creates range name using text in cells
Format/Cells/Protection	Changes protection of selected cells to locked or unlocked
Format/Row/Hide	Hides selected rows in worksheet
Tools/Protection/Protect Sheet	Turns on protection for all locked cells
Tools/Protection/Unprotect Sheet	Turns off protection for all locked cells
Tools/Options/View	Turns on/off display of window elements

Matching

1. template ____ **a.** information supplied to a function for calculation

2. < ____ **b.** workbook that contains predesigned sheets to be used as patterns

3. IF ____ **c.** keeps worksheet data from being altered

4. protection ____ **d.** logical operator

5. arguments ____ **e.** evaluates condition and takes one of two actions

6. nested function ____ **f.** function within another function

Fill-In Questions

1. Complete the following statements by filling in the blanks with the correct terms.

a. ______________________ are used in formulas and functions that compare values in two or more cells.

b. A(n) ______________ is a workbook that contains predesigned sheets.

c. A range ________________ can consist of any combination of 255 characters.

d. The ________________ feature is used to keep parts of the worksheet from being accidentally altered or erased.

e. ______________ is important when creating a template so that others will know how the worksheet functions.

Discussion Questions

1. Discuss range names and when it is appropriate to use them. Give some examples.

2. What are logical operators used for? Describe five logical operators and give examples of their use.

3. Discuss why you would want to save a workbook as a template and give several examples of where a template would be useful. Why would you want to protect the cells of a template?

Hands-On Practice Exercises

Step by Step

Rating System

☆ Easy
☆☆ Moderate
☆☆☆ Difficult

☆☆☆

1. To complete this problem, you must have completed Practice Exercises 6 and 8 in Lab 3.

a. Open the workbook files Earnings Statement and Time Sheets (in that order) from your data disk. Close both files without saving. Now, open the same files in the reverse order (Time Sheets first). Is there a difference between the two procedures? What might that be? In this exercise you will use an IF function to calculate Regular Hours on the time sheet, and you will protect the worksheets.

b. In the Time Sheets file rename the sheet tabs Week 1 and Week 2 so they will apply to any biweekly period.

c. The Regular Hours column will be calculated by a formula, so all you have to do is enter the Total Hours, and the remaining columns will be calculated for you. Enter an IF function in the cell that displays Monday's Regular Hours in the Week 1 sheet. The IF function will determine if Monday's Total Hours are greater than or equal to 8 and will enter the number 8, otherwise it will enter Monday's Total Hours. What was the function you used?

d. Copy the IF function down the column and to the corresponding cells in column C of the Week 2 sheet. What was the function you used?

e. Unlock the Total Hours and cells that display the "Week of" information on both sheets. Protect both sheets.

f. In the Earnings Statement file notice that the formula in B7 has adjusted so that it now refers to the Biweekly Total in the Week 2 sheet of the Time Sheets file. Erase and unlock the period-ending date and protect the worksheet.

g. In the Time Sheets file, erase the starting dates and total hours from both sheets. Update the documentation and save the file.

h. In the Earnings Statement file notice the hours are zero, and the statutory deductions are blank. The only values displayed are the rate and the fixed voluntary deductions. Document the worksheet and save the file.

i. Enter new starting dates and total hours of your choosing in both worksheets of the Time Sheets file. Save the file as Current Time Sheet and print the worksheets.

j. In the Earnings Statement file notice that the hours have changed, and the file is linked to the Current Time Sheet file. Modify the period-ending date appropriately. Save the file as Current Earnings Statement and print the worksheet.

From now on, if you remember to save the original files with new names when the variable information changes, you can use the originals over and over again. Using templates with linked files is difficult because the dependent worksheet is always looking for the original source template (.xlt file), and you must redefine the link to the temporary copy that the template has loaded.

☆☆☆

2. To complete this problem, you must have completed Practice Exercise 4 in Lab 2. Open the workbook file Invoice on your data disk. In this exercise you will continue to modify the worksheet.

a. Draw an outline border around the invoice number and date information. Add color to the text and background. Remove the underlines from the column headings and replace them with a bottom border. Enhance the appearance of the worksheet by adding lines and/or color in other locations.

b. A 15 percent discount is given to customers who purchase more than 12 items. Insert a column after the Price column and enter the column heading Discount. In the cell below the heading, enter an IF function that will calculate a 15 percent discount if the quantity for Pentium Computers exceeds 12. Otherwise the cell will display zero. Copy the function down the column. Note: When this formula is copied, cells with a zero in them will display "$-" or "-" if the cells are formatted with the Currency or Comma format.

c. Modify the formula in the Total column so the total will be calculated as Quantity times the difference between the Price and the Discount. Copy the new Total formula down the column.

d. Save and replace the workbook file Invoice. Print the workbook.

e. You want to use this invoice over again. Erase and unlock the entries in the Qty, Description, and Price columns. Erase and unlock the invoice number and the date. Erase and unlock the cells that contain the customer's name and address. Protect the worksheet.

f. Update the documentation. Save the workbook as a template file named Invoice Template. If necessary, respond yes to the prompt to replace existing file. Close the template file.

g. Use the template to enter the following information:

Heading	Entry
Invoice #	**12345**
Date	**current date**
Customer	**your name and address**
Qty	**20**
Description	**Highlighters**
Price	**.99**

h. Unprotect the worksheet and delete the blank rows above the Subtotal. Delete your address information at the top of the worksheet.

i. Save the file as an Excel workbook file named My Invoice. Print the worksheet.

On Your Own

☆☆☆

3. In this lab you learned to create templates that can be the basis of future workbooks. Excel comes with several workbook templates called Spreadsheet Solutions. Included are an invoice, a loan manager, and a purchase order.

To access the Excel templates, open the Spreadsheet Solutions tab of the New dialog box. The invoice and loan manager operate in much the same way as the templates you created. The purchase order is very similar to the invoice. Select one of these templates.

Once the template you selected is loaded, click the Customize sheet tab once. You can now enter personalized information such as the name of the company, your tax rate, and so on in the form. Add information to complete the template. If you use the invoice or purchase order, you can enter information from the invoice exercise (Practice Exercise 2). If you need help, each template displays a toolbar that contains a Help button.

Note: Once you have customized your template and have returned to the worksheet, the Customize tab will no longer be displayed. However, you can click the Customize button in the upper right corner if you need to return. Update the summary properties for the workbook. Save the file and print the worksheet.

☆☆☆

4. Colin Call enjoys keeping track of game statistics for his favorite baseball team. If necessary, refer to your local paper for baseball game statistics. Use the concepts presented in the lab to create a template to keep track of a baseball team.

Your template should contain the team name as a heading, the opponent, and date played. Create a drop-down button that contains all the teams in your team's league. The body of the template should contain the names of the players, number of at bats (AB), runs scored (R), hits (H), runs batted in (RBI), base on balls (BB), and strike outs (SO). Total the columns to produce team statistics.

Protect the appropriate parts of your template. Save the template using the team name. Close the template. Open the template and enter statistics for a game. Print and save the worksheet.

☆☆☆

5. Use the concepts presented in the lab to create a template to keep track of your monthly expenses. Format the worksheet appropriately and protect it. Include your name and the date in a header. Print and save the blank template. Use the template to add data for the current month. Save and print the worksheet containing your monthly expenses.

Concept Summary

5 Creating a Form Template

Range Name

Adding a descriptive range name to a cell or range of cells makes formulas easier to read and understand.

IF Function

The IF function checks to see if certain conditions are met and then takes action based upon the results of the check.

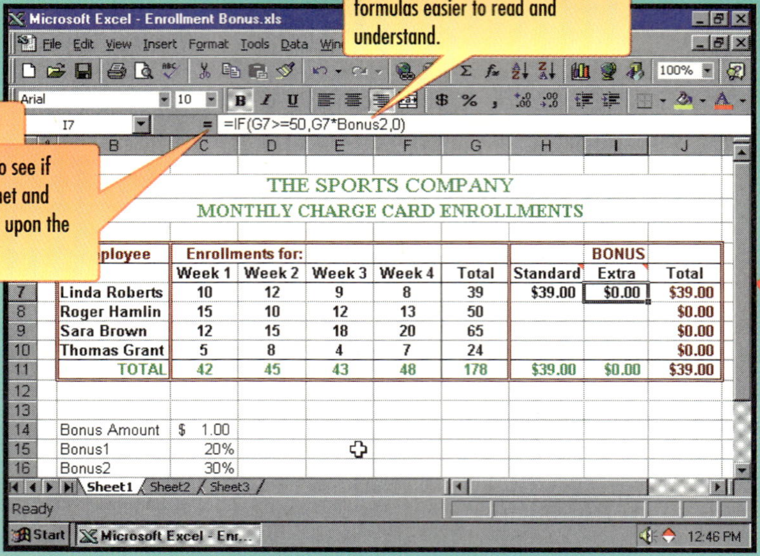

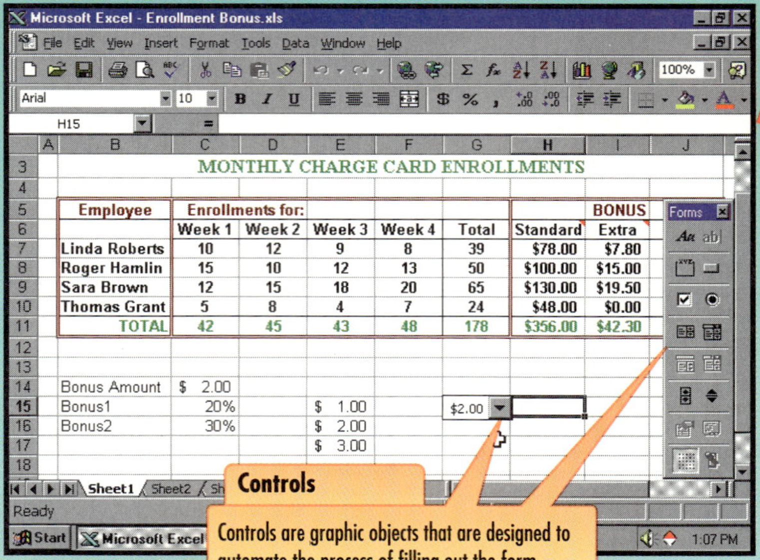

Controls

Controls are graphic objects that are designed to automate the process of filling out the form. Controls include property settings that affect how they behave and work.

Concepts

- Range Name
- IF Function
- Controls
- Worksheet Protection
- Workbook Template

Worksheet Protection

To prevent others from changing a sheet's contents, you can protect the entire worksheet or specified areas of the worksheet. When you protect a sheet, all cells and graphic objects on the sheet are locked.

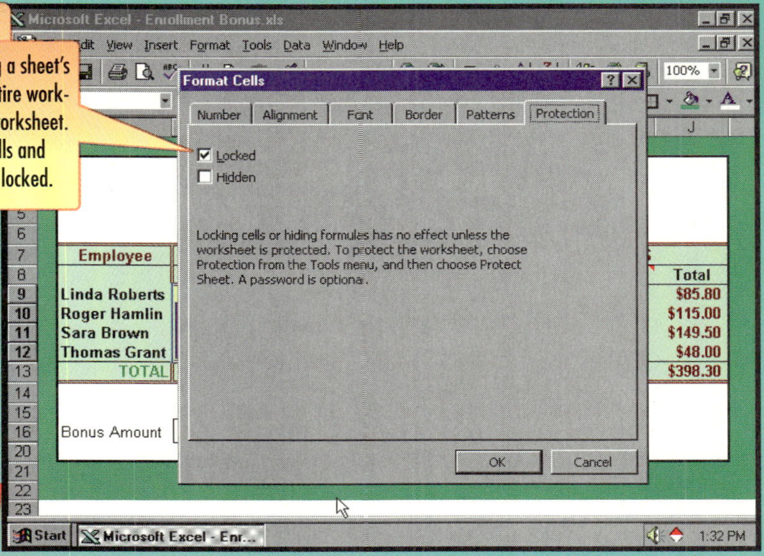

Workbook Template

A workbook template is a workbook file that contains predesigned sheets that can be used as a pattern for creating other similar worksheets in new workbooks.

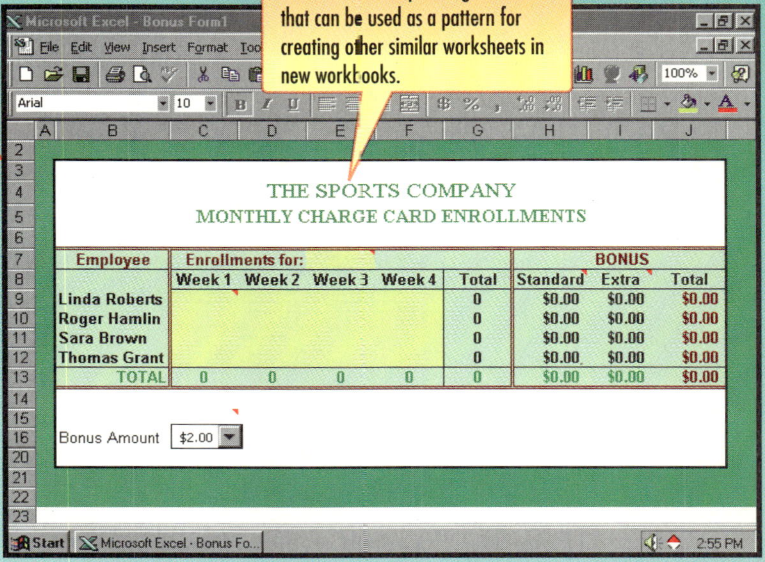

Sharing Data Between Applications

6

COMPETENCIES

After completing this lab, you will know how to:

1. **Copy between applications.**
2. **Link objects.**
3. **Embed objects.**
4. **Update linked and embedded objects.**
5. **Decide when to use linking or embedding.**

CASE STUDY

Your analysis of sales data for the past four years has shown a steady increase in total sales. However, the analysis of sales in four main categories of sporting goods has shown that sales in fitness and camping are increasing, sales in tennis are decreasing, and golf sales remain steady. You would like to send a memo of these findings to the manager of The Sports Company. In addition, you want to include the worksheet and chart of the sales analysis in the memo.

You have probably noticed while using Microsoft Word, Excel, Access, and PowerPoint that the applications have a common user interface such as similar commands and menu structures. In addition to these obvious features, they have been designed to work together, making it easy to share and exchange information between applications.

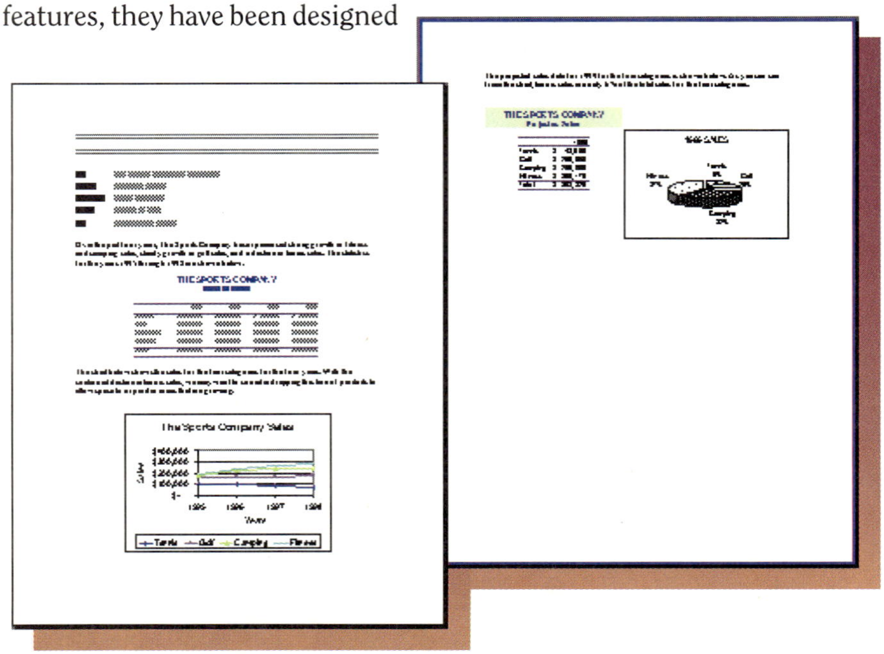

Note: This lab assumes that you have completed Lab 2 of Word and Lab 4 of Excel. You will need the data file Sales Charts you created in Lab 4 of Excel.

Concept Overview

The following concepts will be introduced in this lab:

1. Copy Between Applications Information can be copied between applications and, if possible, inserted in the document in a format the document can edit.

2. Linked Object Information that is copied from one file to another as a linked object maintains a connection between the two files, allowing the linked object to automatically update when the source file changes.

3. Embedded Object Information that is copied as an embedded object to a file created by a different application becomes part of the file and can be updated using the server application from within the document in which it is inserted.

Copying Between Applications

The memo to the manager about the analysis of the sales data has already been created using Word 97. However, you still need to add the Excel worksheet data and charts to the memo.

- Start Word and open the file Sales Analysis Memo on your data disk.
- In the memo header, replace the Student Name with your name and the Professor's Name with your instructor's name.
- Scroll the window to view the three paragraphs in the body of the memo.

Your screen should be similar to Figure 6-1.

FIGURE 6-1

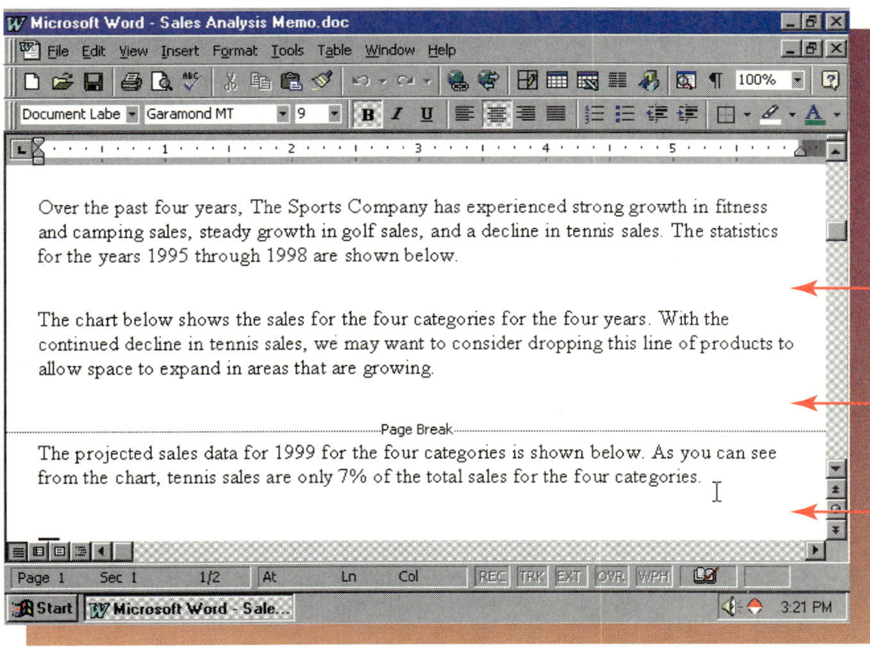

You will insert the data from the Sales sheet of the Sales Charts workbook below the first paragraph. Below the second paragraph, you will display a chart of The Sports Company sales. The second page of the memo will display a chart of the projected sales data for 1999 below the paragraph.

Now you are ready to insert the information from the Excel workbook file into the Word memo.

- Load Excel and open the workbook file Sales Charts on your data disk.
- If necessary, move the cell selector to cell A1 of the Sales sheet.

Your screen should be similar to Figure 6-2.

FIGURE 6-2

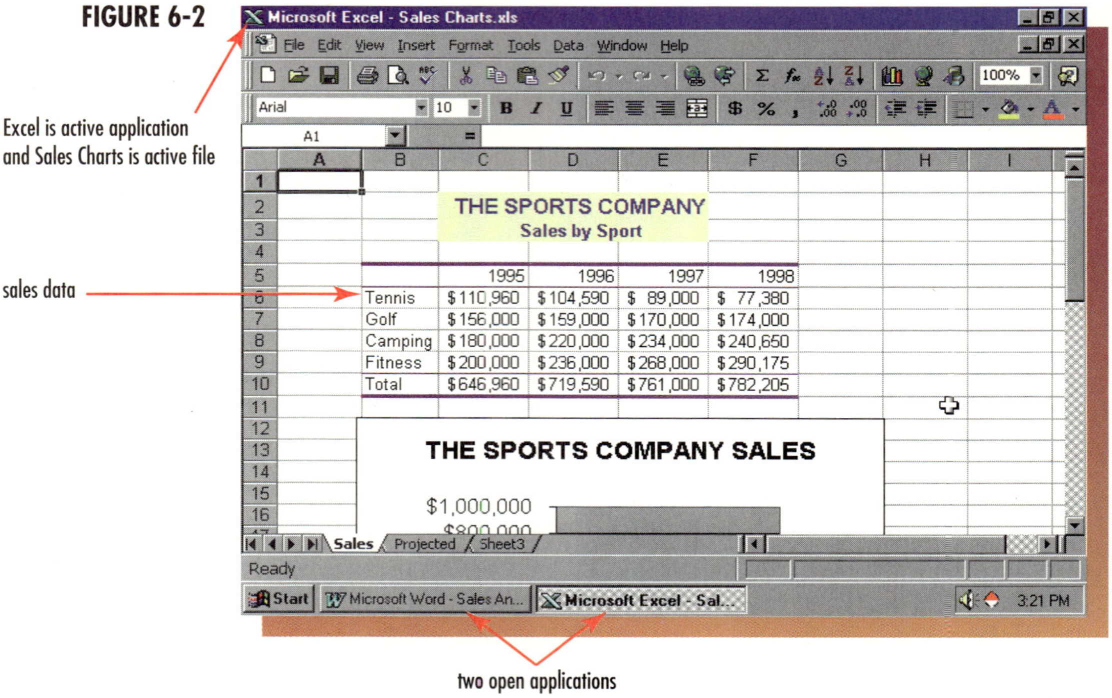

There are now two open applications, Word and Excel. Word is open in a window behind the Excel application window. Both application buttons are displayed in the taskbar. There are also two open files, Sales Charts in Excel and Sales Analysis Memo in Word. Excel is the active application, and Sales Charts is the active file.

First you will copy the worksheet data in the Sales sheet and paste it into the Word memo.

Concept 1: Copy Between Applications

While using the Excel application, you have learned how to use cut, copy, and paste to move or copy information within the same document and between documents in the same application. You can also perform these same operations between applications. For example, you can copy information from a Word document and paste it into an Excel worksheet. The information is pasted in a format that the application can edit, if possible.

- Select and copy the contents of cells B2 through F10.
- Click [Microsoft Word - Sales An...] in the taskbar.
- Move to the second blank line below the first paragraph of the memo.
- Paste the contents of the Clipboard into the memo.

If both program windows are displayed on the screen, you can drag data between applications using the right mouse button. Then select Move Here or Copy Here from the Shortcut menu.

Your screen should be similar to Figure 6-3.

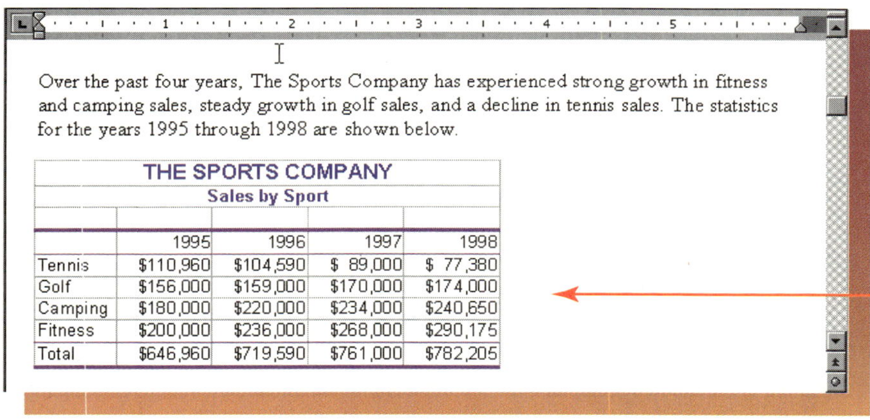

FIGURE 6-3

Excel worksheet inserted into Word document as a table

The worksheet data has been copied into the Word document as a table that can be edited and manipulated within Word. Much of the formatting associated with the copied information is also pasted into the document. However, you think the memo would look better if the table was centered between the margins.

- Select the entire table.
- Click [≡] Center.
- Clear the selection.

To select the table, drag or use Table/Select Table.

Linking an Object to Another Application

Next you want to display the area chart of sales trends for the four categories below the second paragraph in the memo.

Click on the chart to select it.

- Switch to the Excel application and select the area chart.
- Copy the selected chart object to the Clipboard.
- Switch to the Word application and move to the second blank line below the second paragraph of the memo.

You will insert the chart object into the memo as a linked object

Concept 2: Linked Object

Information created in one application can also be inserted as a **linked object** into a document created by another application. When an object is linked, the data is stored in the **source file** (the document it was created in). A graphic representation or picture of the data is displayed in the **destination file** (the document in which the object is inserted). A connection between the information in the destination file to the source file is established by the creation of a link. The link contains references to the location of the source file and the selection within the document that is linked to the destination file.

When changes are made in the source file that affect the linked object, the changes are automatically reflected in the destination file when it is opened. This is called a **live link**. When you create linked objects, the date and time on your machine should be accurate. This is because the program refers to the date of the source file to determine whether updates are needed when you open the destination file.

By making the chart a linked object, it will be automatically updated if the source file is edited. To create a linked object,

To link an entire file, use Insert/Object.

- Choose Edit/Paste Special.
- Select Paste Link.

The Paste Special dialog box on your screen should be similar to Figure 6-4.

FIGURE 6-4

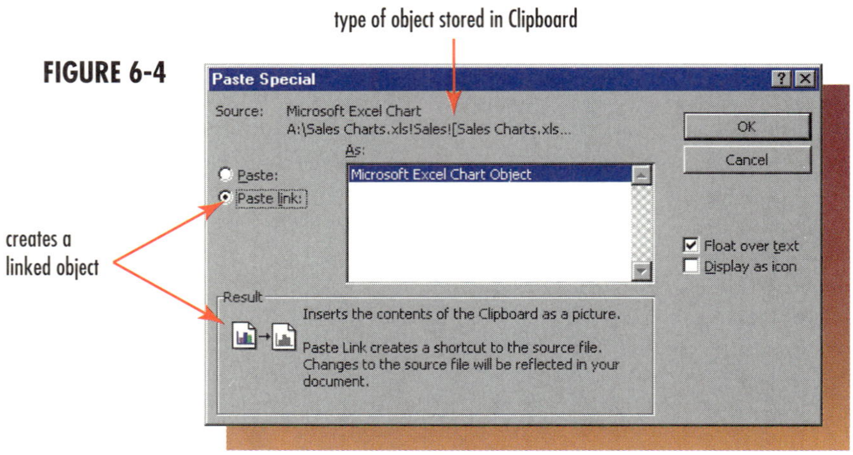

The Source area displays the type of object contained in the Clipboard and its location. From the As list box you select the type of format in which you want the object inserted into the destination file. The only available option for this object is as a Microsoft Excel Chart Object. The Result area describes the effect of your selections. In this case, the object will be inserted as a picture and a link will be created to the chart in the source file.

The last two options in this dialog box allow you to control how the object is inserted and displayed. Float Over Text adds the object to the drawing layer. It can then be positioned anywhere in the document and manipulated using the Draw menu. If this option is cleared, the object is inserted in-line where it behaves like regular text. Selecting the Display as Icon option changes the display of the object from a picture to an icon. Double-clicking the icon displays the object picture. The default selection for both options is appropriate.

If both program windows are displayed on the screen, you can drag data between applications using the right mouse button. Then select Insert Object Here from the Shortcut menu to create a linked object.

- Click OK.

Word changes to Page Layout view and displays the picture of the area chart.

- Set the Zoom to 50%.
- Scroll the window so you can see both the worksheet and the chart on the page.

Your screen should be similar to Figure 6-5.

FIGURE 6-5

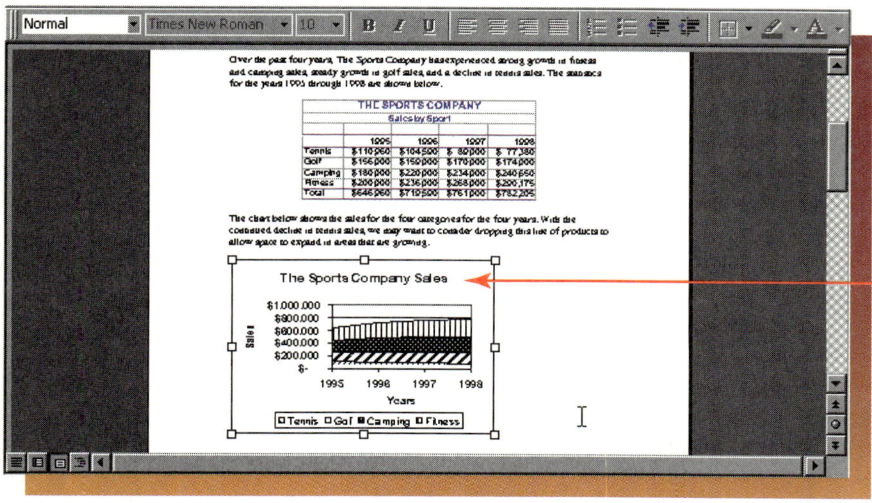

picture of area chart is linked to Excel Sales Charts file

The chart object is displayed at the location of the insertion point aligned with the left margin. The object has been scaled to fit in the document.

- Move the chart object so it is centered horizontally on the page.

Updating a Linked Object

> The menu equivalent is **E**dit/Linked Worksheet **O**bject/**E**dit Link.

> If necessary, open the Chart toolbar.

While reading the text and looking at the chart, you decide to change the chart type from an area chart to a line chart. You feel a line chart will show the sales trends more clearly. To change the type of chart, you need to switch back to Excel. Double-clicking on a linked object quickly switches to the open source file. If the source file is not open, it opens the file for you. If the application is not loaded, it will both load the application and open the source file.

- Double-click the chart object.
- Click [Chart Type button] Chart Type.
- Click [Line button] Line.
- Adjust the placement of the text box and arrows.

You will also make another change while in Excel. You will change data in the worksheet to verify that the worksheet data that is pasted into the memo is not linked to Excel.

- Edit the value in cell F6 to 177380.
- View the line chart to verify that the chart was automatically updated to reflect this change in data.
- To see the changes made in the memo, switch to Word.

Your screen should be similar to Figure 6-6.

FIGURE 6-6

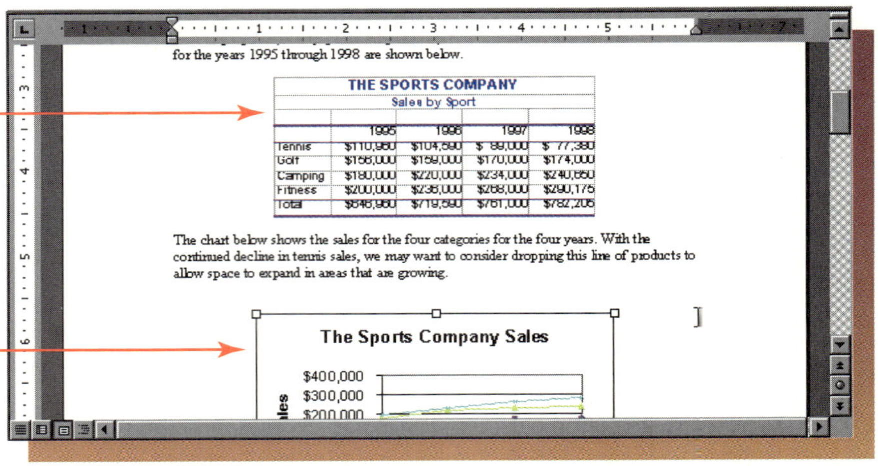

The chart in the memo reflects the change in both chart type and the change in data for the tennis sales. This is because any changes you make in the chart in Excel will be automatically reflected in the linked chart in the Word document.

Because the table is not a linked object, it does not reflect the change in data made in Excel. However, normally you would want to link both the worksheet and the related chart so both would reflect the changes made to the data.

Whenever a document is opened that contains links, the application looks for the source file and automatically updates the linked objects. If there are many links, updating can take a lot of time. Additionally, if you move the source file to another location, or perform other operations that may interfere with the link, your link will not work. To help with situations like these, you can edit the settings associated with links. To see how you do this,

- Choose Edit/Links.

The dialog box on your screen should be similar to Figure 6-7.

FIGURE 6-7

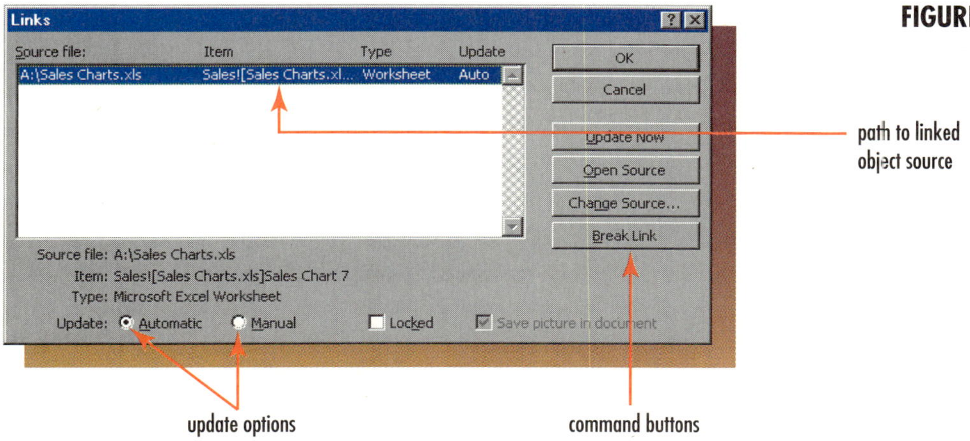

The Links dialog box displays the object path for all links in the document in the list box. The field code specifies the path and name of the source file, the range of linked cells or object name, the type of file, and the update status. Below the list box the details for the selected link are displayed. The two update option buttons, Automatic and Manual, are used to change how the object is updated. The default option, Automatic, updates the linked object whenever the destination document is opened or the source file changes. If you change to Manual, the destination document is not automatically updated and you must use the Update Now command button to update the link. The Open Source command button will open the source document for the selected link, and the Change Source button allows you to modify the path to the source document.

To return to Excel and change the value in cell F6 back to its original value,

> Because the workbook and Excel application were already open, using the Open Source command button simply switched to the application window.

- Click Open Source.
- Change the value in cell F6 back to 77380.
- Switch to Word and view the chart object to verify that it updated automatically and reflects the change in data.
- Return the zoom to Page Width.

Embedding an Object in Another Application

On the second page of the memo, you want to show the projected sales data for 1999 and the pie chart.

- Move to the second blank line immediately below the paragraph on the second page of the memo.
- Switch to Excel and make the Projected sheet active.
- Copy the range A1 through I20.
- Switch to Word.

This time you will embed this selection in the memo.

Concept 3: Embedded Object

Information can also be inserted into another application document as an embedded object. An object that is embedded is stored in the destination file and becomes part of the document. The entire file, not just the selection that is displayed in the destination file, becomes part of the document. This makes a document containing an embedded object much larger than a document containing the same object using linking.

If the user has access to the application that created the embedded document, called the **server**, the embedded object can be edited or updated from within the destination document. The connection to the server is established through the use of a field code that identifies the server associated with the object. Double-clicking on an embedded object starts the server application within the destination document. Any changes you make to the embedded object are not reflected in the original source file, however.

Object Linking and Embedding, or **OLE**, is the program-integration technology that makes it possible to share data between applications. All Office 97 programs support OLE.

A document that contains a linked or embedded object is called a **container file** or **compound document**.

> To embed an entire file use Insert/Object.

- Choose Edit/Paste Special.

The dialog box on your screen should be similar to Figure 6-8.

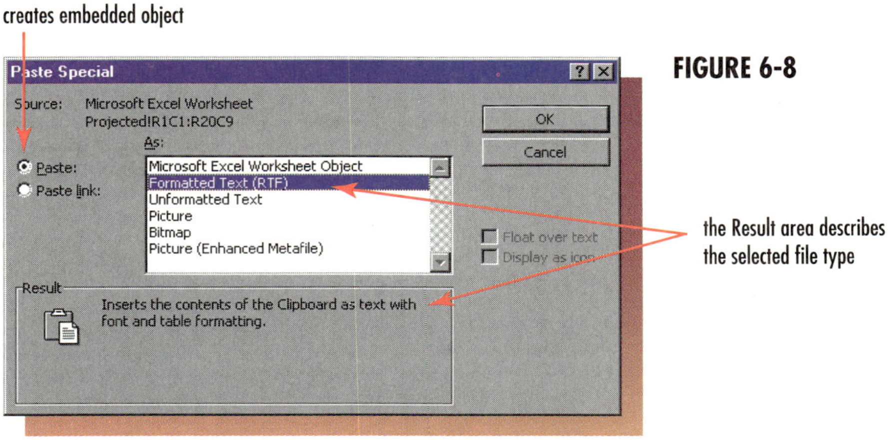

FIGURE 6-8

The Paste option creates an embedded object. This is the preselected option. The As list box displays six file format types that can be used to embed the object. To embed the contents of the Clipboard into a document so it can be edited using the server application, select the option that displays the server name.

- Select Microsoft Excel Worksheet Object.
- Click OK.

Your screen should be similar to Figure 6-9.

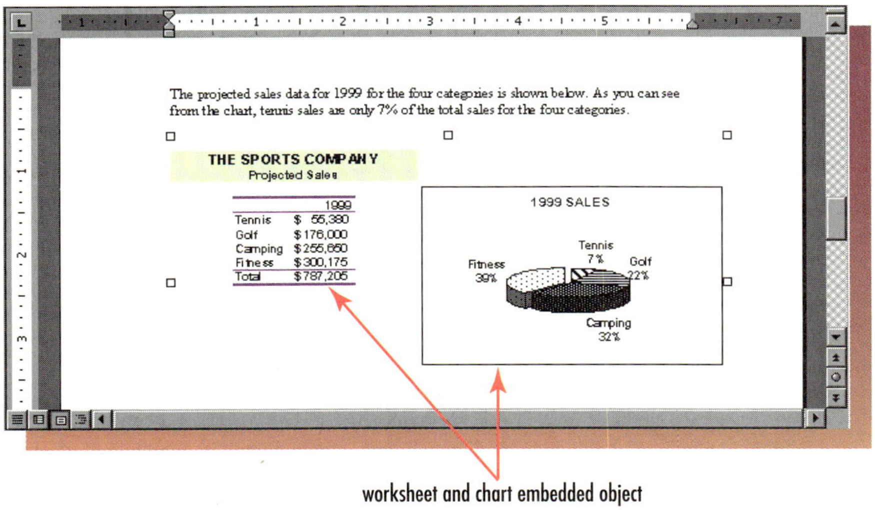

FIGURE 6-9

The entire worksheet selection including the chart is displayed in the memo at the location of the insertion point. When an object is embedded, the entire selection is pasted and displayed in the destination document as a single object.

If you linked this selection, only the worksheet data would appear and be linked in the destination. The chart would not be included in the link. To link the chart, you would need to select the chart object separately and establish a separate link and a separate object.

Updating an Embedded Object

To demonstrate how an embedded object works, you will close the source file and application and edit the worksheet from within the Word document.

- Switch to Excel and move to cell A1 in both sheets.
- Save the workbook file as 1995-1999 Sales Charts.
- Exit the program. If Excel asks if you want to save the Clipboard contents to a file, choose No.

The server application is used to edit data in an embedded object. To open the server, simply double-click on the embedded object.

- Double-click the embedded object.

Your screen should be similar to Figure 6-10.

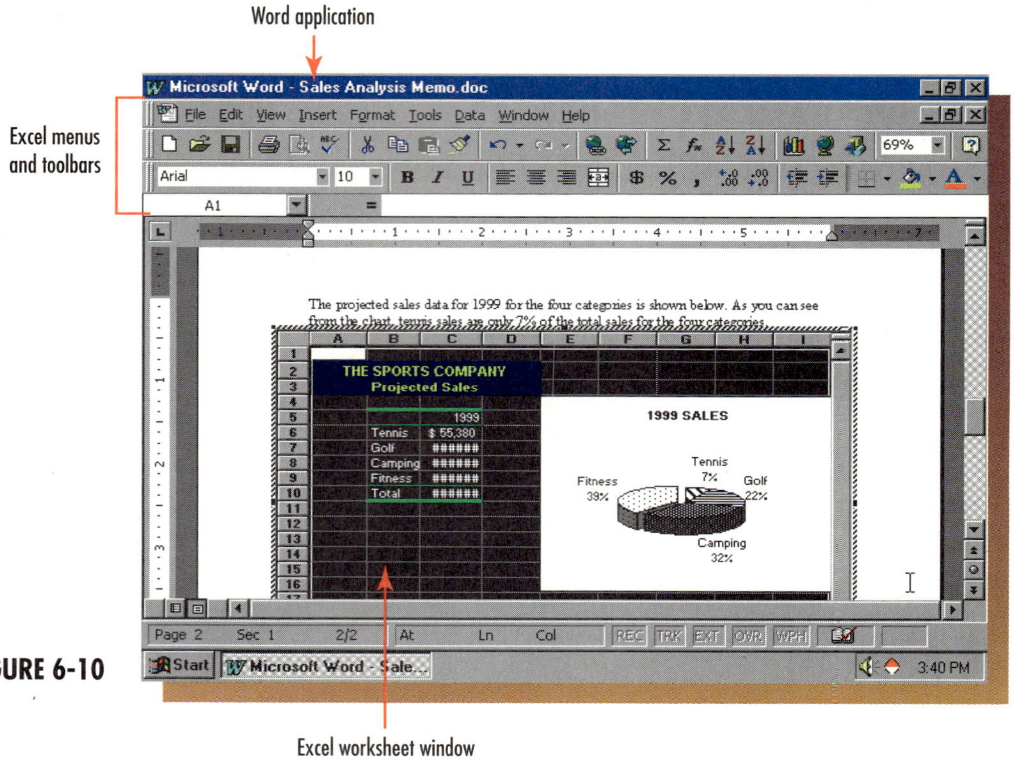

FIGURE 6-10

The server application, in this case Excel, is opened. The Excel menus and toolbars replace some of the menus and toolbars in the Word application window. The selected embedded object is displayed in an editing worksheet window. Now you can use the server commands to edit the object.

- If necessary, expand the column width of column C to fully display the values.
- Reduce the tennis projection value to 48,000 and increase the golf projection to 200,000.

The chart is updated to reflect the change in data. The new projection has decreased the tennis percentage to 6 percent and increased golf to 25 percent. The original Excel file, 1995–1999 Sales Charts, has not been affected by these changes.

- After editing is complete, close the server application by clicking anywhere outside the object.

The embedded object in the memo is updated to reflect the changes you made. It now also displays gridlines. To turn off the display of the cell gridlines,

- Open the server application.
- Choose Tools/Options/View/Gridlines/ OK .
- Close the Server application.
- Edit the lead-in sentence in the memo to reflect the new tennis value (6%).
- Save the memo as 1995-1999 Sales Analysis.
- Preview both pages of the memo in the Preview screen.

Use the Multiple Pages button to view both pages of the document.

Your screen should be similar to Figure 6-11.

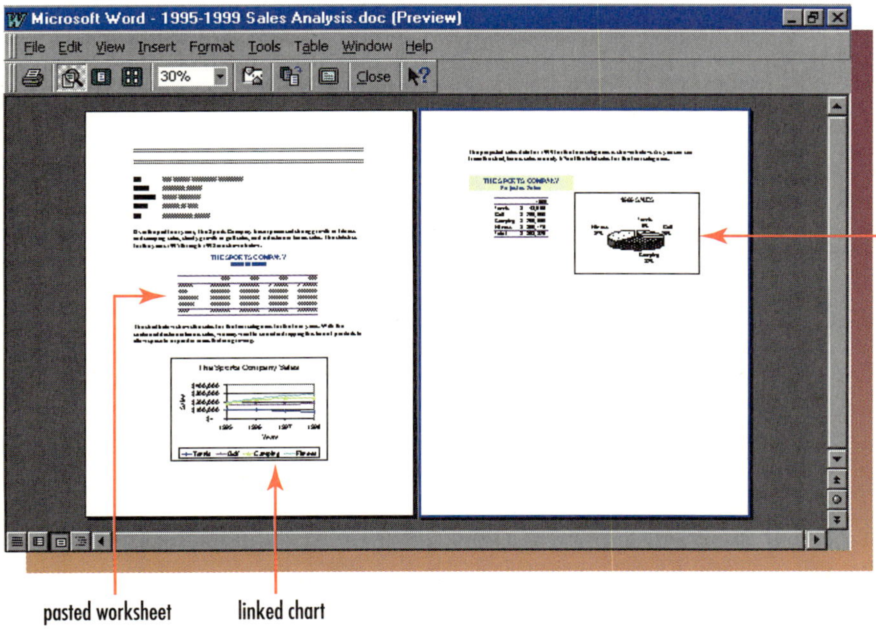

FIGURE 6-11

- Print the memo.

Note: Do not set the printer to draft quality. If you do, the charts will not print.

- Exit Word.

Deciding When to Link or Embed Objects

Most documents would not include both linked and embedded objects. This is because the reasons for using each are different.

Use linking when:	Use embedding when:
File size is important	File size is not important
Users have access to the source file and application	Users have access to the application but not to the source file
The information is updated frequently	The data changes infrequently

LAB REVIEW

Key Terms

compound document (SS208)
container file (SS208)
destination file (SS204)
linked object (SS204)
live link (SS204)
Object Linking and Embedding (OLE) (SS208)
server (SS208)
source file (SS204)

Command Summary

Command	Action
Edit/Paste Special/Paste Link	Links a selection
Edit/Linked Worksheet Object/Edit Link	Allows you to modify path for a link
Edit/Paste Special/Paste	Embeds a selection
Edit/Links	Edits settings associated with a link

Matching

1. destination file	______	**a.** a link that automatically updates when the document is opened
2. live link	______	**b.** file in which object is inserted
3. source file	______	**c.** application that created embedded document
4. server	______	**d.** the document in which the linked or embedded object was created
5. OLE	______	**e.** the program integration technology that makes linking and embedding possible

Discussion Questions

1. Describe how a linked object is created and edited.
2. Describe how an embedded object is created and edited.
3. Explain when you would use linking rather than embedding.

Hands-On Practice Exercises

Step by Step

Rating System
☆ Easy
☆☆ Moderate
☆☆☆ Difficult

☆

1. Karen works for a large hotel chain in the marketing department. She has recently researched hotel occupancy rates for the Phoenix area and has created a worksheet and stacked-column chart of the data. Now Karen wants to send a memo containing the chart to her supervisor.

a. Open a new Word document using the Professional template.

b. Delete the Company Name Here text box. In the header, replace the placeholder information in brackets with the following:

TO:	**Brad Wise**
FROM:	**Karen Howard**
CC:	**[your name]**
RE:	**Hotel Occupancy**

c. Replace the body placeholder text with the following:

Below is a column chart showing the percent of hotel occupancy rates in the Phoenix area for the years 1994 to 1999.

d. Enter two blank lines below the paragraph.

e. Load Excel and open the workbook file Hotel. Link the stacked-column chart to below the paragraph in the Word memo. Center the chart in the memo.

f. Change the stacked-column chart to a side-by-side column chart.

g. You would like to add another sentence to the memo. Enter the following sentence below the chart:

The chart shows that the resort occupancy rate is consistently slightly higher than the overall occupancy rate.

h. Save the Word document as Hotel Occupancy. Preview and print the document. Resave the Excel file.

☆☆

2. Sean Rees has a summer internship with a local car dealership. He has researched changes in new and used car prices and created a worksheet and line chart of the data. Now Sean wants to send a memo containing the worksheet and chart to his supervisor.

a. Open a new Word document using the Contemporary Memo template. Select and remove the faint gray circle element below and to the left of the How to Use the Memo Template information.

b. Replace the placeholder information in the memo heading with the following information:

TO:	**Supervisor**
CC:	**[your name]**
FROM:	**Sean Rees**
DATE:	**[current date]**
RE:	**Changes in Car Prices**

c. Replace the body placeholder text with the following two paragraphs. Separate the paragraphs with two blank lines.

Below is the data you requested showing the percent change in new vs used car prices. I have embedded the Excel worksheet in this Word document file so you can make changes to it if necessary.

d. Enter two blank lines below the last paragraph.

e. Load Excel and open the workbook file Car Analysis. Below the first paragraph of the Word memo, embed the worksheet and line chart from the workbook Car Analysis. Add a border around the entire embedded object. If necessary, adjust the placement of the object so it appears centered under the paragraph.

f. Exit Excel. Do not resave the workbook.

g. The supervisor wants to change the chart to a column chart. Change the embedded line chart to a column chart.

h. Using Word add a text box and arrow identifying the increasing car sales.

i. Save the Word document as New and Used Car Comparison. Preview and print the document.

☆☆☆

3. After completing the first and second half budget for The Sports Company, you want to give the manager the Excel file. You would like to include a memo on a separate sheet of this file to briefly explain the worksheet contents.

a. Open the workbook file 1999 Budget that you created at the end of Lab 3. Insert a new sheet before the Annual sheet and change the sheet tab name to Memo.

b. Open Word and create the following memo to the store manager.

TO:	**Sports Company Store Manager**
FROM:	**[your name]**
DATE:	**[current date]**

The 1999 Annual budget data is contained on the following three sheets. To view the budget worksheets click on the appropriate tab.

If you have any changes or suggestions about the budget, I have scheduled time to work on the budget again next week.

c. Save the memo as Budget Memo. Link the memo to the Memo sheet in the Excel file.

d. After inserting the memo, you decide to add a sentence about the year-to-date income total. Switch back to Word and add the following after the first sentence:

Please note that the profit margin in all three worksheets reflect the industry standard's profit margins for the same time periods.

e. Resave the memo and switch to Excel. Save the Excel file as Sports Company Budget.

f. Print the Word memo document and the Excel Memo sheet only.

On Your Own

☆☆

4. Dave Robson has gathered population statistics on several Native American tribes for a report and has created a worksheet and pie chart of this data. Now Dave wants to include the worksheet and chart as a separate page in his report. Create a new Word document using the Elegant Report template. Replace the Company Name placeholder with your name. Replace the other placeholder text with an appropriate title and subtitle.

Below the titles, copy and paste the worksheet data from the Excel workbook file Tribe Populations. Center the table and remove the gridlines. Copy and link the chart to the document below the table. Center, and size the pie chart. Unexplode the Apache slice. Resave the workbook file. Delete pages 2 and 3 of the template. Save the Word document as Tribal Populations. Preview and print the document.

☆☆☆

5. Each week you see tables of data in publications such as newspapers and magazines. Find a table of interest to you and create a worksheet and chart of the data. Use Word to create a brief report summarizing the data. Embed the chart and worksheet into the Word document. Change the type of chart in the Word document. Include your name and the date as a header in both documents. Print both the Word and Excel documents.

Concept Summary

Sharing Data Between Applications

Concepts

- Copy Between Applications
- Linked Object
- Embedded Object

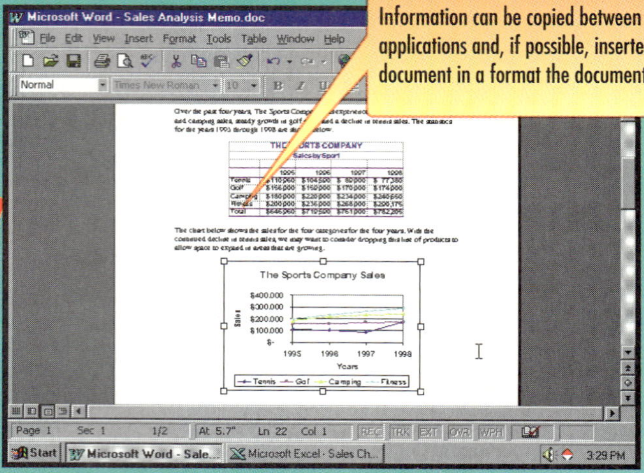

Copy Between Applications

Information can be copied between applications and, if possible, inserted in the document in a format the document can edit.

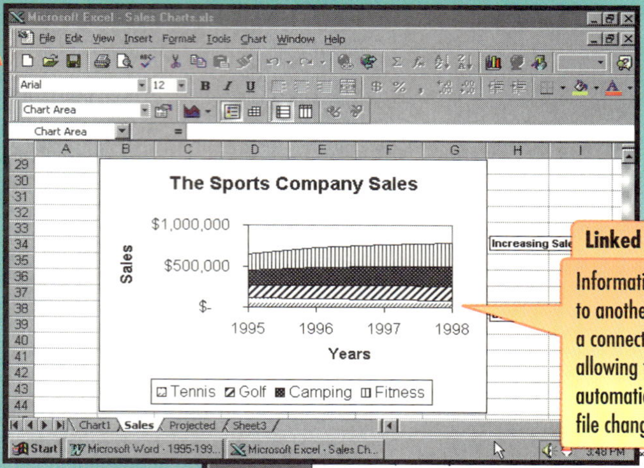

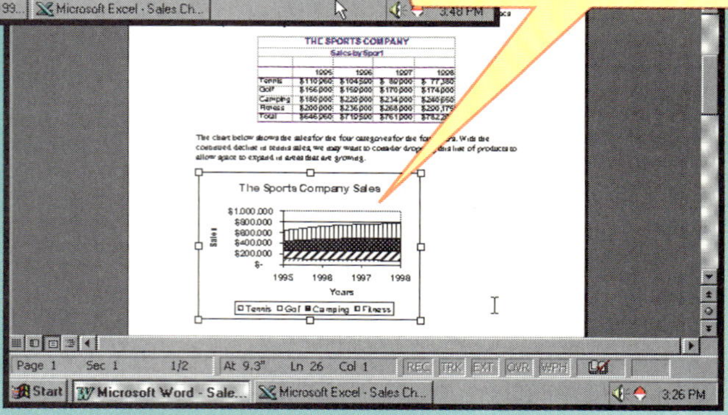

Linked Object

Information that is copied from one file to another as a linked object maintains a connection between the two files, allowing the linked object to automatically update when the source file changes.

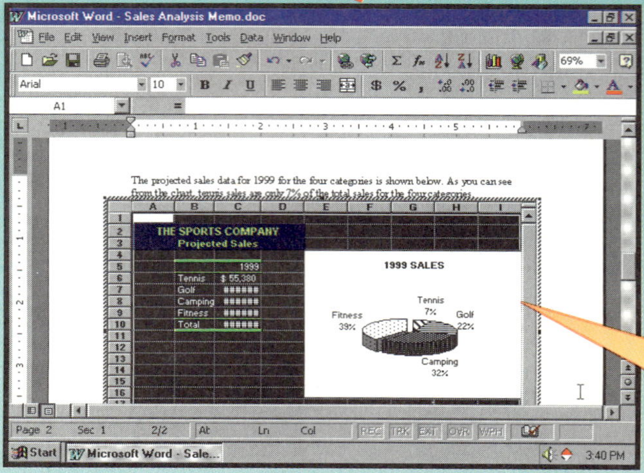

Embedded Object

Information that is copied as an embedded object to a file created by a different application becomes part of the file and can be updated using the server application from within the document in which it is inserted.

Case Project

Introduction

This project is designed to reinforce your knowledge of the worksheet features used in the Excel labs. You will also be expected to use the Help feature to learn more about advanced features available in Excel.

Case

Marianne Virgili is the Director of the Glenwood Springs Chamber Resort Association. Each quarter the Chamber sends a newsletter called *Trends* to all Chamber members. The Director has asked you to create the end-of-year balance sheet, tables, and graphs to be included in the first-quarter issue of *Trends*. The first-quarter issue will contain the end-of-year balance sheet for the previous year.

Part 1

Open the file Glenwood Springs 1999 Balance. This file contains the Glenwood Springs Chamber Resort Association's 1999 balance sheet.

a. Change the width of columns A and B to fully display the headings. Change the width of column C to 4. Delete column D.

b. Enter the formulas and functions in column D needed to complete the totals for the balance sheet. The Total Assets number should equal the Total Liabilities plus Capital numbers.

c. Format the numbers to be displayed with commas and two decimal places. Format the first number in each group and all totals as currency with two decimal places.

d. Delete all blank rows above each subtotal and grand total.

e. Add a bottom-line border under the last number in each group above a subtotal and under subtotals immediately above the grand total. Add a double-line border under the grand total of each group.

f. Change the size of the main title to be displayed larger than the rest of the text. Italicize and bold the headings in cells A4 and A25.

g. Insert three blank rows above the main title. Enter your name and the date in a header. Save and replace the workbook.

h. Preview the worksheet before printing. Print the worksheet.

Part 2

This issue of *Trends* will contain two tables. The first table will provide employment information for 1998 to 1999 for Garfield county. The second table will provide information on gross sales.

a. The employment information is shown below. Create a worksheet from this data.

Job Category	1998	1999
Agr., For., Fish.	174	197
Mining	813	920
Construction	1171	1593
Manufacturing	327	652
Trans., Comm., Util.	504	551
Wholesale Trade	410	466
Retail Trade	2859	3170
Fin., Ins., Real Est.	601	684
Services	2767	2841
Non-classified	15	18
Government	2328	2521

b. Format the two columns of data to display commas with no decimal places. Add an appropriate title to the worksheet.

c. Add a third column of data to show the percent change from 1998 to 1999. Enter the column heading % Change above the new column. Enter the formula to calculate the percent change from 1998 to 1999. Format the column as percent with two decimal places.

d. Add a row to show the total for the two columns of data and the percent change. Enter a row heading and the formulas to make these calculations. Format the data appropriately.

e. Enhance the appearance of the worksheet by adding such features as bold, bottom borders, different fonts, colors, and so on.

f. Put your name and the date in a header. Save and print the worksheet.

The second table will display the percent of gross sales for the second half of 1998 for the five major cities in the county.

g. Open a new worksheet file. Create a worksheet from the following data.

City	Sales	% of Total
Glenwood Springs	172.3	
Silt	4.1	
Rifle	39.7	
Carbondale	22.3	
Parachute	3.0	
Remainder of County	47.2	

h. Add a row to show the total sales. Enter a row heading and formula to make this calculation.

i. Enter the following worksheet title: TOTAL GROSS SALES for JUNE-SEPT. 1999 (in millions of dollars).

j. Enter formulas to calculate the percent of total sales for each city. Display the numbers as percents with one decimal place. Include an appropriate column heading.

k. Enhance the appearance of the worksheet using such features as bottom borders, bold, colors, and font changes.

l. Enter your name and the current date in the worksheet.

m. Save and print the worksheet.

Part 3

This issue of *Trends* will also include two charts. The first chart will be a visual representation of the gross sales table you created in Part 2.

a. Open the file you created containing the gross sales data. Create a 3-D pie chart of the gross sales data below the worksheet.

b. Add an appropriate title to the chart. Increase the font size of the title. Display the legend labels next to the percent values.

c. Add patterns and explode the Carbondale wedge of the pie.

d. Save and replace the worksheet. Print the worksheet.

The second chart included in this issue of *Trends* will display the gross sales for each quarter of 1999 and the last two quarters of 1998 for Garfield county and the two surrounding counties, Eagle and Pitkin.

e. Open the file County Gross Sales.xls. Enter your name in cell A1 and the date in cell A2.

f. Create a 3-D column chart of the data displayed in the worksheet in a new sheet.

g. Enter an appropriate title. Add X-axis and Y-axis titles.

h. Add patterns to the columns.

i. Create a header that contains your name and the current date centered over the chart.

j. Save and replace the worksheet. Print the chart only.

Glossary of Key Terms

3-D reference: A reference to the same cell or range on multiple sheets in the same workbook.

Absolute reference: A cell or range reference in a formula whose location remains the same (absolute) when copied. Indicated by a $ character entered before the column letter or row number or both.

Active cell: The cell displaying the cell selector and which will be affected by the next entry or procedure.

Active pane: The pane that contains the cell selector.

Active sheet: A sheet that contains the cell selector and that will be affected by the next action.

Adjacent range: A rectangular block of adjoining cells.

Alignment: The vertical or horizontal placement and orientation of an entry in a cell.

Area chart: A chart that shows trends by emphasizing the area under the curve.

Argument: The data the function uses to perform a calculation. It can be a number, a cell address, a range of cells, or a formula.

Autoformat: A built-in combination of formats that can be applied to a range.

Automatic recalculation: The recalculation of a formula within the worksheet whenever a value in a referenced cell in the formula changes.

Category-axis title: A label that describes the X axis.

Category name: Labels displayed along the X axis in a chart to identify the data being plotted.

Cell: The space created by the intersection of a vertical column and a horizontal row.

Cell selector: The heavy border surrounding a cell in the worksheet that identifies the active cell.

Chart: A visual representation of data in a worksheet.

Chart gridlines: Lines extending from the axis lines across the plot area that make it easier to read and evaluate the chart data.

Column: A vertical block of cells one cell wide in the worksheet.

Column chart: A chart that displays data as vertical columns.

Column letters: The border of letters across the top of the worksheet that identifies the columns in the worksheet.

Combination chart: A chart type that includes mixed data markers, such as both columns and lines.

Compound document: A document that contains a linked or embedded object.

Constant: A value that does not change unless you change it directly by typing in another entry.

Container file: A file that contains a linked or embedded object.

Control: A graphic object designed to automate the process of filling out a form.

Copy area: The cell or cells containing the data to be copied.

Custom dictionary: An additional dictionary you create to supplement the main dictionary.

Data labels: Labels for data points or bars that show the values being plotted on a chart.

Data marker: Represents a data series on a chart. It can be a symbol, color, or pattern, depending upon the type of chart.

Data series: The numbers to be charted.

Date numbers: The integers assigned to the days from January 1, 1900 through December 31, 2099 that allow dates to be used in calculations.

Dependent workbook: The workbook file that receives linked data.

Destination: The cell or range of cells that receives the data from the copy area or source.

Destination file: A document in which a linked object is inserted.

Docked: A toolbar or menu bar that is fixed to the edge of the window.

Embedded chart: A chart that is inserted into another file.

Embedded object: Information inserted into a destination file of another application that becomes part of this file but can be edited within the destination file using the server application.

Explode: To separate a wedge of a pie chart slightly from the other wedges in the pie.

External reference formula: A formula that creates a link between workbooks.

Fill handle: A small black square located in the lower right corner of the selection that is used to create a series or copy to adjacent cells with a mouse.

Floating: A toolbar or menu bar that appears in its own window.

Font: The typeface, type size, and style associated with a worksheet entry that can be selected to improve the appearance of the worksheet.

Footer: A line of text printed just above the bottom margin on each page.

Form: A formatted worksheet that is designed to be completed by filling in data in the blank spaces.

Format: Formats are settings that affect the display of entries in a worksheet.

Formatting toolbar: A toolbar that contains buttons used to change the format of a worksheet.

Formula: An entry that performs a calculation.

Formula bar: The bar near the top of the Excel window that displays the cell contents.

Freeze: To fix in place on the screen specified rows or columns or both when scrolling.

Function: A prewritten formula that performs certain types of calculations automatically.

Group: An object that contains other objects.

Header: A line of text printed just below the top margin on each page.

Heading: Row and column entries that are used to create the structure of the worksheet and describe other worksheet entries.

Landscape: The orientation of the printed document so it prints sideways across the length of the page.

Legend: A brief description of the symbols used in a chart that represent the data ranges.

Line chart: A chart that represents data as a set of points along a line.

Link: A relationship created between files that allows data in the destination file to be updated automatically when changes occur in the source file.

Linked object: Information created in a source file from one application and inserted into a destination file of another application while maintaining a link between files.

Live link: A linked object that automatically reflects in the destination document any changes made in the source document when the destination document is opened.

Lock: Cells whose contents cannot be changed when a worksheet is protected.

Logical operators: Symbols used in formulas that compare values in two or more cells.

Main dictionary: The dictionary included with Office 97.

Merged cell: A cell made up of several selected cells combined into one.

Minimal recalculation: The recalculation of only the formulas in a worksheet that are affected by a change of data.

Mixed reference: A cell address that is part absolute and part relative.

Name box: The area located on the left side of the formula bar that provides information about the selected item such as the reference of the active cell.

Nested function: A second argument in a function that is enclosed within its own set of parentheses.

Nonadjacent range: Cells or ranges that are not adjacent but are included in the same selection.

Number: A cell entry that contains any of the digits 0 to 9, and any of the special characters + = ( ) , . / $ % E e.

Object: An element such as a text box that can be added to a workbook and that can be selected, sized, and moved.

Office Assistant: A feature that is used to get Help on features specific to the Office application you are using.

OLE: Object Linking and Embedding is the program integretion technology that makes it possible to share data between applications.

Operand: A value on which a numeric formula performs a calculation.

Pane: A division of the worksheet window, either horizontal or vertical, through which different areas of the worksheet can be viewed at the same time.

Password: Prevents unauthorized users from turning off protection.

Paste area: The cells or range of cells that receives the data from the copy area or source.

Pie chart: A chart that compares parts to the whole. Each value in the data range is a wedge of the pie (circle).

Plot area: The area of the chart bounded by the axes.

Portrait: The orientation of the printed document so it prints across the width of a page.

Protection: A worksheet feature that prevents changes to data and formats.

Range: A selection consisting of two or more cells in a worksheet.

Range name: A descriptive name assigned to a cell or range of cells.

Reference: The column letter and row number of a cell.

Relative reference: A cell or range reference that automatically adjusts to the new location in the worksheet when the formula is copied.

Row: A horizontal block of cells one cell high in the worksheet.

Row numbers: The border of numbers along the left side of the worksheet that identifies the rows in the worksheet.

Selection handles: Small boxes surrounding a selected object that are used to size the object.

Series formula: A formula that links a chart object to the source worksheet.

Server: The application in which an embedded object is created.

Sheet: A division of a workbook that is used to display different types of information in Excel.

Sheet tab: On the bottom of the workbook window, the tabs where the sheet names appear.

Source: The cell or range of cells containing the data you want to copy.

Source file: The document that stores the data for the linked object.

Source workbook: The workbook file that supplies linked data.

Spreadsheet: A rectangular grid of rows and columns used to enter data.

Stack: The order in which objects are added in layers to the worksheet.

Stacked-column chart: A chart that displays the data values as columns stacked upon each other.

Standard toolbar: A toolbar that contains buttons used to complete the most frequently used menu commands.

Style: A named combination of formats that can be applied to a selection.

Syntax: Rules of structure for entering all functions.

Tab scroll buttons: Located to the left of the sheet tabs, they are used to scroll sheet tabs right or left.

Template: A workbook file that contains predesigned worksheets that can be used as a pattern for creating other similar sheets in new workbooks.

Text: A cell entry that contains text, numbers, or any other special characters.

Text box: A rectangular object in which you type text.

Title: In a chart, descriptive text that explains the contents of the chart.

Typeface: The appearance and shape of characters. Some common typefaces are Roman and Courier.

Value-axis title: A label that describes the values on the Y axis.

Variable: The resulting value of a formula that changes if the data it depends on changes.

What-if analysis: A technique used to evaluate what effect changing one or more values in formulas has on other values in the worksheet.

Word wrap: Feature that automatically determines when to begin the next line of text.

Workbook: The file in which you work and store sheets created in Excel.

Workbook window: A window that displays an open workbook file.

Worksheet: Similar to a financial spreadsheet in that it is a rectangular grid of rows and columns used to enter data.

Workspace: The area of the Excel application window where workbook windows are displayed.

X axis: The bottom boundary line of a chart.

Y axis: The left boundary line of a chart.

Command Summary

Command	Shortcut	Toolbar	Action
File/**O**pen <file name>	Ctrl + O		Opens an existing workbook file
File/**C**lose			Closes open workbook file
File/**S**ave <file name>	Ctrl + S		Saves current file on disk using same file name
File/Save **A**s <file name>			Saves current file on disk using a new file name
File/Save **A**s/Save As **T**ype			Sets file format for document
File/Propert**i**es			Displays information about a file
File/**P**rint	Ctrl + P		Prints a sheet
File/Page Set**u**p/Header/Footer			Adds header and/or footer
File/Page Set**u**p/**L**andscape			Prints worksheet across length of paper
File/Prin**t** Area/**S**et Print Area			Sets a range as area to print
File/Print Pre**v**iew			Previews worksheet as it will be printed
File/E**x**it			Exits Excel
Edit/**U**ndo	Ctrl + Z		Undoes last editing or formatting change
Edit/**R**epeat	Ctrl + Y		Repeats last-used command
Edit/**C**opy	Ctrl + C		Copies selected data to Clipboard
Edit/**P**aste	Ctrl + V		Pastes selected data from Clipboard
Edit/Paste **S**pecial/Paste **L**ink			Creates a link to the source document
Edit/Paste **S**pecial/Paste			Embeds a selection
Edit/F**i**ll			Fills selected cells with contents of source cell
Edit/Cle**a**r/**C**ontents	Delete		Clears cell contents
Edit/Cle**a**r/Co**m**ments			Removes comment from cell
Edit/**D**elete/Entire **R**ow			Deletes selected rows
Edit/**D**elete/Entire **C**olumn			Deletes selected columns

Command	Shortcut	Toolbar	Action
Edit/Delete Sheet			Removes sheed from workbook
Edit/Move or Copy Sheet			Moves or copies current sheet
Edit/Links			Edits settings associated with a link
View/Toolbars			Displays/hides selected toolbars
View/Formula Bar			Displays/hides formula bar
View/Status Bar			Display/hides status bar
View/Zoom		100%	Changes magnification of window
Insert/Rows			Inserts a blank row
Insert/Columns			Inserts a blank column
Insert/Worksheet			Inserts a new blank worksheet in workbook
Insert/Chart			Inserts chart into worksheet
Insert/Function	Shift + F3		Inserts a function
Insert/Name/Define			Assigns a name you specify to a cell or range of cells
Insert/Name/Paste			Places name in formula bar or lists names in worksheet
Insert/Name/Create			Creates names using text in cells
Insert/Comment			Inserts a comment to a cell
Format/Cells	Ctrl + 1		Applies formats to selected cells
Format/Cells/Protection			Changes protection of selected cells to locked or unlocked
Format/Cells/Number/Currency			Applies Currency format to selection
Format/Cells/Number/Accounting			Applies Accounting format to selection
Format/Cells/Font			Changes font and attributes of cell contents
Format/Cells/Font/Color			Adds color to text
Format/Cells/Alignment/Horizontal/Left, Center, or Right			Aligns data left, center, or right in cell space
Format/Cells/Alignment/Center Across Selection			Centers cell contents across selected cells
Format/Cells/Alignment/Horizontal/Left/Indent 1			Indents cell entry one space
Format/Cells/Border/Outline			Adds border around selection
Format/Cells/Border			Adds border to selected edge of selection
Format/Cells/Patterns			Adds shading to selection
Format/Row/Hide			Hides selected rows
Format/Row/Unhide			Displays hidden rows
Format/Column/Width			Changes width of columns

Command	Shortcut	Toolbar	Action
Format/Column/Autofit Selection			Changes column width to match widest cell entry
Format/AutoFormat			Applies one of 16 built-in table formats to the worksheet range
Format/Style			Applies selected style to selection
Format/Sheet/Rename			Renames sheet
Tools/Spelling	F7		Spell-checks worksheet
Tools/Protection/Protect Sheet			Turns on protection for all locked cells
Tools/Protection/Unprotect Sheet			Turns off protection for all locked cells
Tools/Goal Seek			Adjusts value in specified cell until a formula dependent on that cell reaches specified result
Tools/Solver			Calculates a formula to achieve a given value by changing one of variables that affects formula
Tools/Options/View			Changes worksheet view options
Tools/Options/View/Gridlines			Turns on/off display of cell gridlines
Window/Arrange/Tiled			Arranges open windows side by side
Window/Split			Divides window into four panes at active cell
Window/Remove Split			Removes split bar from active worksheet
Window/Freeze Panes			Freezes top and/or leftmost panes
Window/Unfreeze			Unfreezes window panes
Charts			
Format/Selected Data Series/ Data Labels	Ctrl + 1		Inserts data labels into chart
Format/Selected Legend	Ctrl + 1		Changes legend
Format/Selected Data Labels	Ctrl + 1		Changes format of data labels
Format/Selected Data Series/ Patterns	Ctrl + 1		Applies color and patterns to selected data series
Format/Text Box			Changes format of text box
Chart/Chart Type			Changes type of chart
Chart/Chart Options			Adds or modifies chart elements
Chart/ Add Data			Inserts new data into chart

Index

Notes

Appendix A

Additional Microsoft Excel 97 User Specialist Certification Topics

- Sort Data
- Clear Formats
- Save Spreadsheets as HTML Documents
- Create and Modify 3D Shapes
- Delete Worksheets

Sorting Data

Often the data in a worksheet consists of rows that contain related data. For example, in the worksheet shown below of a grade book for an introductory computer class each row in column A contains the last name of each student in the class. Data organized in this fashion can be rearranged or sorted to make it easier to locate information. In this case, the instructor wants the information in alphabetical order by name for his/her own use when entering the grades.

This file can also be downloaded from www.mhhe.com/cit/apps/oleary.

- Create the worksheet of student grades shown in Figure A-1 below.
- Save it as Grades.

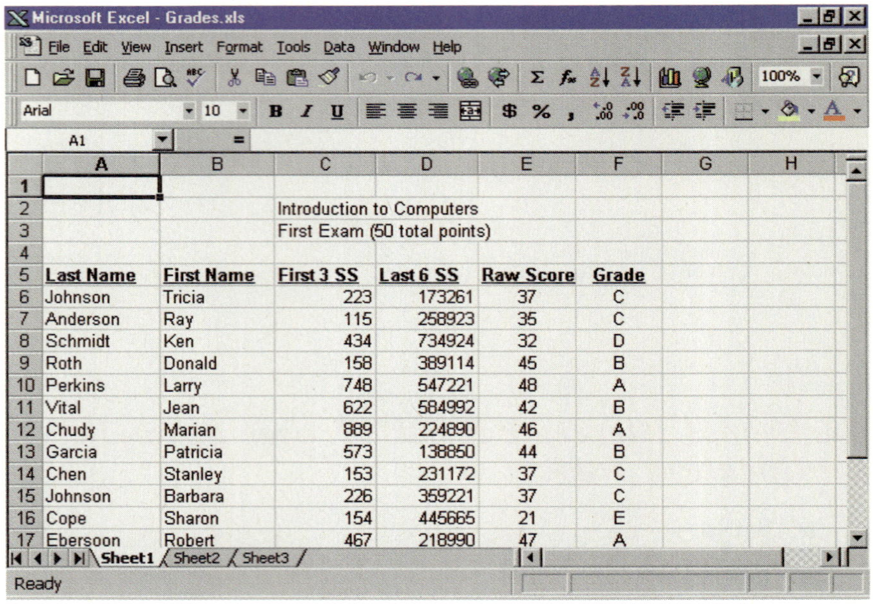

FIGURE A-1

You can also sort data by date. Excel sorts lists alphabetically by default.

The data in a worksheet can be rearranged by sorting the information into ascending (1 to 9, A to Z) or descending (9 to 1, Z to A) sort order. When you sort, Excel rearranges the rows, columns, or individual cells according to the sort order you specify.

You want the worksheet to appear in ascending alphabetical order by last name. To indicate which column to sort on you first position the cell pointer in any cell of the column to be sorted.

The menu equivalent is Data/Sort.

- Move to any cell that contains a name in column A.
- Click .

Your screen should be similar to Figure A-2.

FIGURE A-2

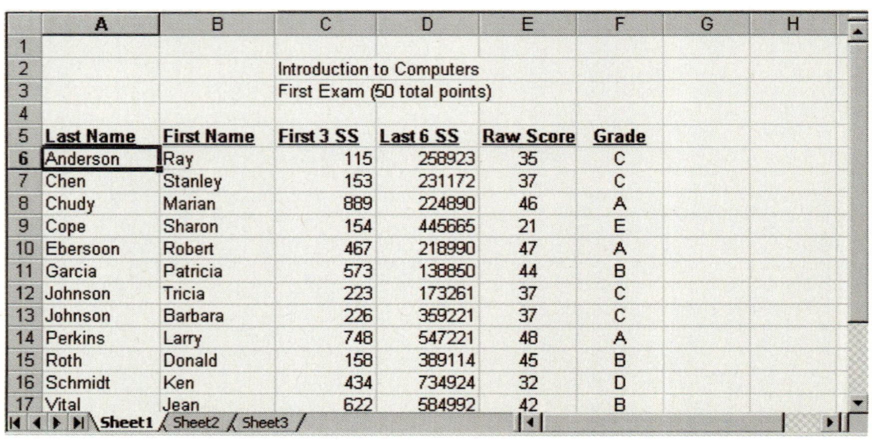

The worksheet data is rearranged to display in ascending alphabetical order by last name. However, notice that although the records for Tricia and Barbara Johnson are sorted correctly by last name, they are not by first name. You want the records that have the same last name to be further sorted by first name. To do this, you will perform a sort on the contents of more than one column. This is called a **multilevel sort**.

- Choose Data/Sort.

The Sort dialog box on your screen should be similar to Figure A-3.

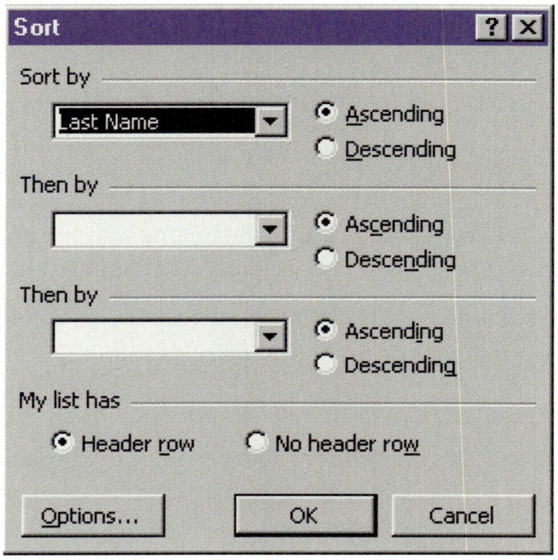

FIGURE A-3

The Sort by text box correctly displays the column header of the column containing the cell pointer on which the sort will be performed. Additionally, because the default setting is ascending sort order, this option does not need to be changed. A multilevel sort uses the first column selected in Sort by as the primary sort column; all other sort columns are sorted in order after the primary sort is performed. You need to specify the second column, First Name, in the first Then by box, as the second column to be sorted.

- Select First Name from the first Then by drop down list.

When a sort is performed, Excel assumes that you want all data except the uppermost row contained in contiguous rows and columns surrounding the selected cell to be sorted. The first row is not included in the sort range because the default setting assumes that the first row contains headers that you do not want included in the sort. If your data did not include a header row as the first row in the range, you would need to choose the No Header Row option to change the setting to include this row in the sort. Since this worksheet includes a header row as the first row, the Header row option is correctly specified already.

- Click OK.

Your screen should be similar to Figure A-4.

FIGURE A-4

	A	B	C	D	E	F	G	H
1								
2			Introduction to Computers					
3			First Exam (50 total points)					
4								
5	Last Name	First Name	First 3 SS	Last 6 SS	Raw Score	Grade		
6	Anderson	Ray	115	258923	35	C		
7	Chen	Stanley	153	231172	37	C		
8	Chudy	Marian	889	224890	46	A		
9	Cope	Sharon	154	445665	21	E		
10	Ebersoon	Robert	467	218990	47	A		
11	Garcia	Patricia	573	138850	44	B		
12	Johnson	Barbara	226	359221	37	C		
13	Johnson	Tricia	223	173261	37	C		
14	Perkins	Larry	748	547221	48	A		
15	Roth	Donald	158	389114	45	B		
16	Schmidt	Ken	434	734924	32	D		
17	Vital	Jean	622	584992	42	B		

Sheet1 / Sheet2 / Sheet3

The worksheet has been sorted first by last name and second by first name wherever a duplicate occurred in the primary sort column.

- Add a header that displays your name and the current date to the worksheet.
- Print the worksheet.
- Save the worksheet as Sorted Grades to your data disk.

Clearing Formats and Saving Spreadsheets as HTML Documents

All Office 97 programs include the capability to convert documents to HTML format.

Excel worksheet data can also be saved in HTML (Hypertext Markup Language) format so it can be posted on the World Wide Web (WWW). The WWW is a part of the Internet that consists of information containing text and graphic images and hypertext links. The information must be written using the HTML programming language so that a browser program, such as Internet Explorer, can display it. To demonstrate this feature, you will use the Sorted Grades file you created in the previous section.

- If necessary, open Sorted Grades.

Many instructors post their grades to a Web site for students to access. To insure privacy, grades are posted by the last six digits of the social security number. To make it easier for students to locate their grade in the list you want the numbers sorted in ascending numerical order and to add formatting to the data to make it read across the row.

- Sort the worksheet by the Last 6 SS column in ascending order.
- Apply the Colorful 1 Autoformat to the worksheet data.
- Click outside the selection to see the formatting.

You decide that you do not like how this formatting looks and want to try a different autoformat. To remove the formats applied to this range without effecting the data,

- Select the worksheet range.
- Choose Edit/Clear/Formats.

All formats are removed and the normal text style is applied to all cells in the range.

- Apply the List 1 Autoformat to the data range.
- Center the data in the Raw Score and Grade columns.

This format will make it easier for students to scroll across the row to see their grade. Now you want to save the worksheet data as an HTML document so you can post it to the class Web site.

- Choose File/Save as HTML.

Your screen should be similar to Figure A-5.

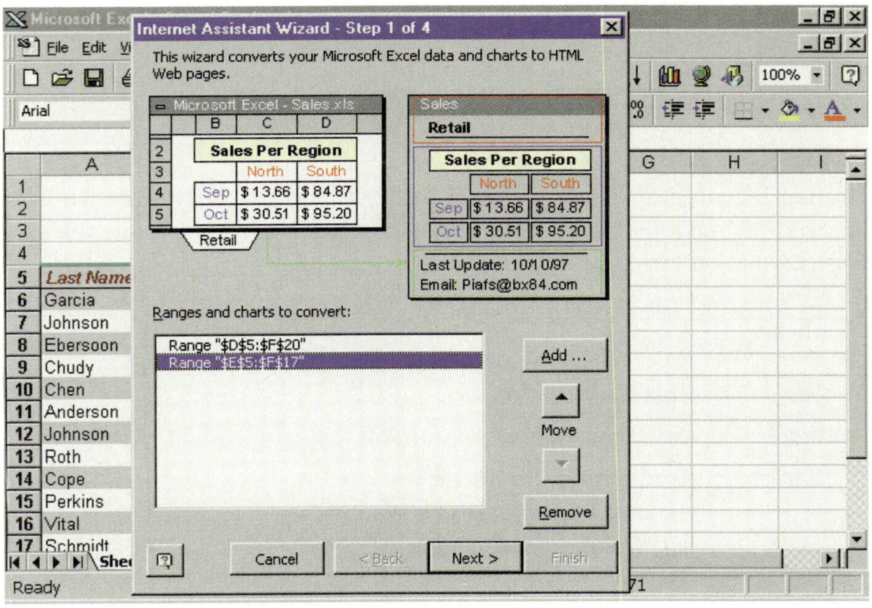

FIGURE A-5

The Internet Assistant Wizard dialog box is used to guide you through the steps to convert the worksheet to an HTML document. The first step is to specify the range of data you want to be included in the HTML document. In this case, the only information you want is the data in columns D, E, and F.

- Click Add ... .
- Select the data range including the headers in columns D, E and F.
- Click OK .

The selected range appears at the top of the list in the list box. If there are other ranges in the list box that were specified by a previous user, you need to remove them.

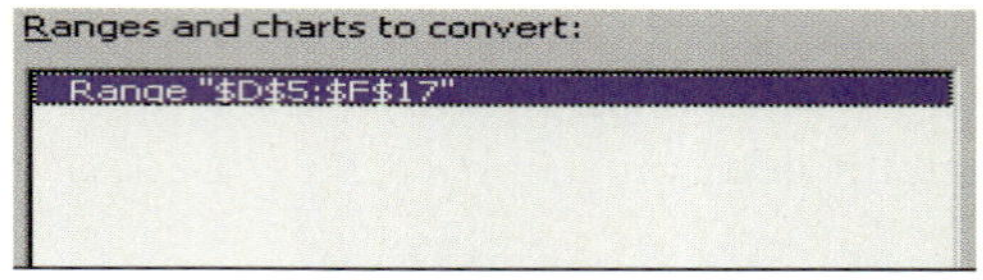

- If necessary, select any other ranges in the list and click Remove.
- Click Next >.

The selected default in the next step to create a new Web page is the correct selection. To continue,

- Click Next >.

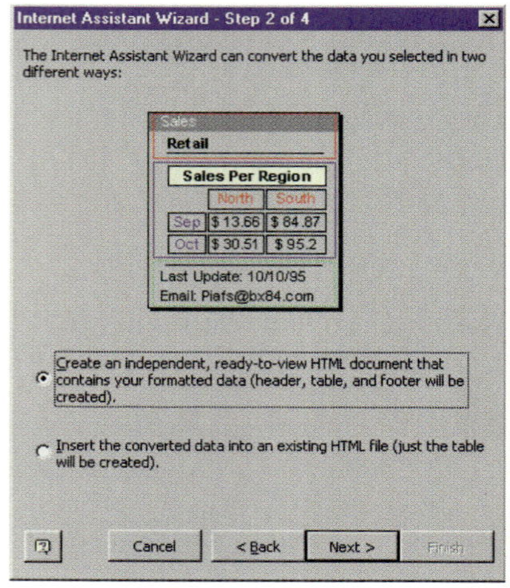

The Step 3 dialog box is used to specify a title to appear in the title bar, a header to appear at the top of the document, descriptive text to accompany the data and information to appear in a footer.

- Enter the following information in the appropriate text boxes.

Title:	**First Exam Grades**
Header:	**First Exam Grades**
Description:	**Grades appear in ascending numerical order by the last 6 digits of your Social Security number.**
By:	**Your Name**

- Turn on the two options to include horizontal lines above and below the data.
- Click Next >.

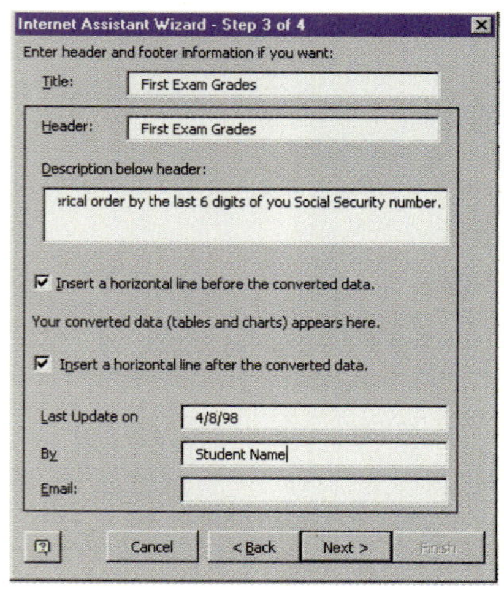

The only setting you need to change in the last dialog box is to specify drive A containing your data disk as the location to save the file and a file name.

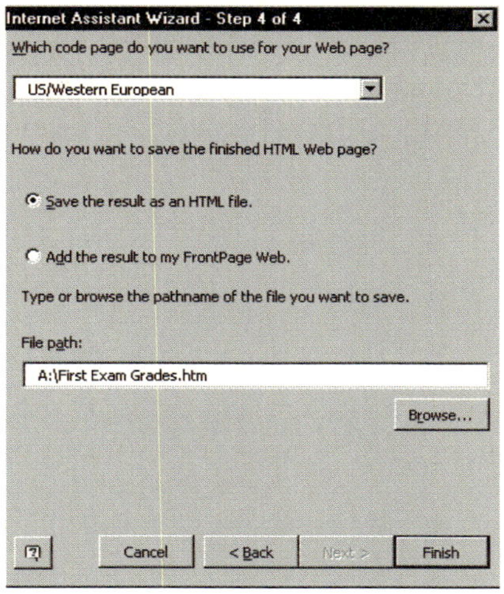

- Type **A:\ First Exam Grades.htm** in the File Path text box.
- Click Finish.

If you have a Web browser program such as Internet Explorer, you can open the First Exam Grades.htm document to view the Web page as it would appear on the WWW. Alternatively, you can open the document in Excel and preview it.

- Close without saving the Sorted Grades file.
- Open First Exam Grades.html (change the file type to All Files).

Your screen should be similar to Figure A-6.

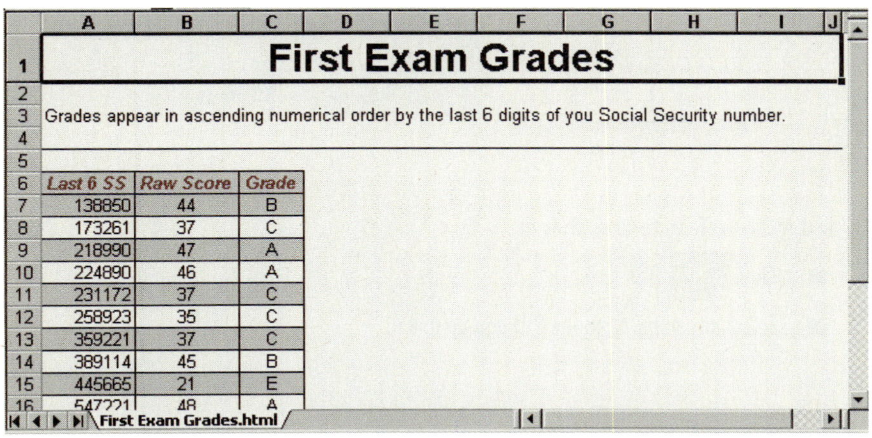

FIGURE A-6

The header, horizontal lines, data range, and footer information you specified appear similar to how they will appear if displayed in a Web browser.

- Preview, then print the document.
- Close the file.

Creating 3-D Shapes and Deleting Worksheets

In addition to the drawing features you learned about in Lab 4 you can create 3 dimensional (3-D) shapes using the Drawing toolbar. To learn about this feature, you will further enhance the Sales Chart worksheet you created in Lab 4.

- Open the worksheet file Sales Charts from your data disk.
- Make the Sales sheet active.
- Copy the Increasing Sales drawing object to Sheet 3.

You will apply several different 3-D features to this object to learn about how this feature works.

- If necessary select the object.
- Increase the size of the object until it is approximately 4 cells high and two cells wide.
- Display the Drawing toolbar.

Your screen should be similar to Figure A-7.

FIGURE A-7

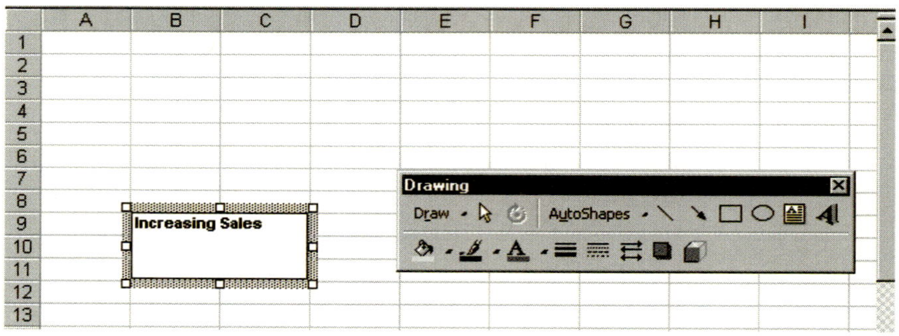

To add a 3-D effect to the shape,

- Click 3-D
- Select any shape from the 3-D pop-up menu.

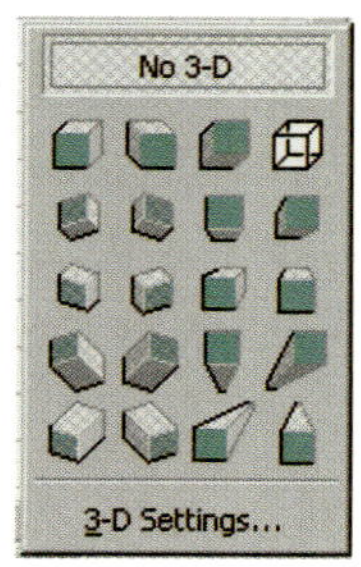

Your screen should be similar to Figure A-8.

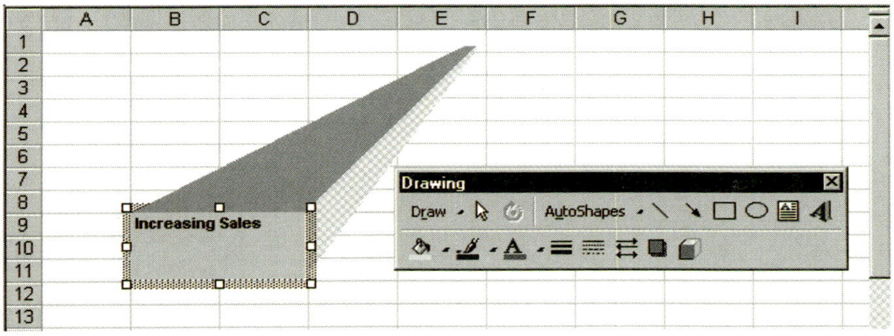

FIGURE A-8

Figure A-8 shows the 3-D Style 19 shape.

- Select several other 3-D shapes to see how they look when applied to the object.

In addition, you can modify the 3-D settings using the 3-D Settings toolbar. To open this toolbar,

- Click  and choose 3-D Settings.

The buttons in this toolbar are used to modify the depth (the extrusion) of the object and its color, rotation, angle, direction of lighting, and surface texture.

- Use each of the 3-D settings to modify your shape.
- Select a 3-D design that you think would look good in place of the original Increasing Sales text box in the Sales sheet.
- Resize the object until it is just large enough to display the text on a single line.
- Copy the object to the Clipboard.
- Make the Sales sheet active.
- Delete the Increasing Sales text box (and arrow if necessary, depending upon the 3-D shape you created).
- Paste the new 3-D object in the worksheet and position it appropriately to point to the increasing sales section of the chart. Adjust the object as needed.
- Apply the same 3-D effect to the Decreasing Sales object.
- Preview the worksheet. Adjust the location of the charts and 3-D objects as needed so that it prints on a single page.

Your screen should be similar to Figure A-9.

FIGURE A-9

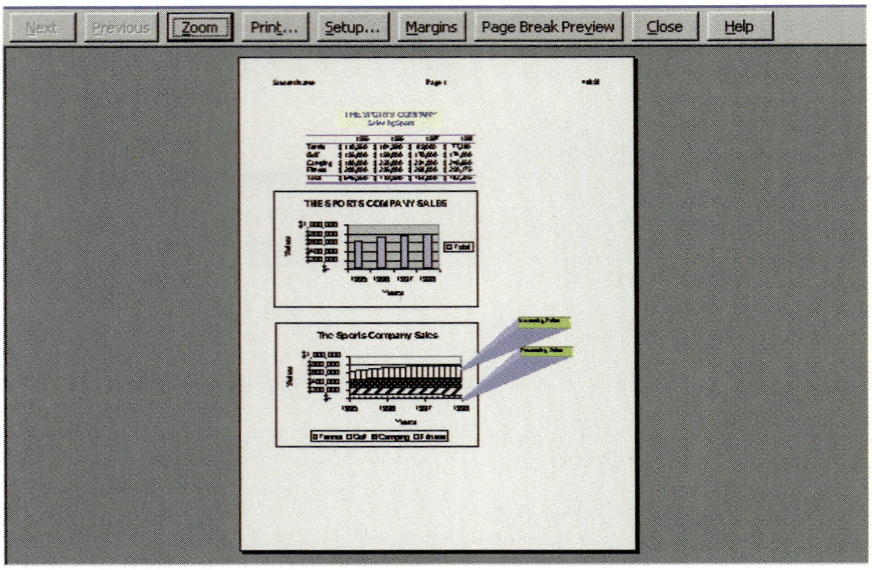

- Print the Sales worksheet.
- Close the 3-D Settings toolbar and the Drawing toolbar.

Since you do not need Sheet3, you will remove it.

- Select Sheet3.
- Choose Edit/Delete Sheet/ OK.
- Save the revised workbook as 3-D Effects to your data disk.

Practice Exercises

1. Open Sorted Grades. Change the sort order to descending order by Raw Score. Sort the worksheet data again by three columns: Raw Score as the primary sort, Last Name as the second, and First Name as the third. Add a 3-D text object containing text that describes the effect this sort had on the data. Print the worksheet. Save it to your data disk as Sorted Grades 3.

2. Open the 1998-1998 Summary Budget worksheet you created at the end of Lab 3. Replace the worksheet title with a 3-D colored text box containing the same information. Print the worksheet. Save the worksheet as Summary Budget Revised on your data disk.

   Save the worksheet a second time as an HTML file named Summary.HTM on your data disk. Because the drawing object cannot be saved in the HTML document, set the range to include the worksheet data only. Add horizontal lines. Include the following information in the HTML document:

Header:	Sports Company Budget
Description:	Below is the proposed budget for 1998 and the projected budget for 1999.
By:	Your Name

   Preview and print the first page of the HTML document.

McGRAW-HILL

Microsoft Access 97

Timothy J. O'Leary
Arizona State University

Linda I. O'Leary

Irwin McGraw-Hill

Boston, Massachusetts Burr Ridge, Illinois Dubuque, Iowa
Madison, Wisconsin New York, New York San Francisco, California St. Louis, Missouri

Irwin/McGraw-Hill

A Division of The ***McGraw-Hill*** *Companies*

Microsoft Access 97

This book is printed on acid-free paper.

domestic 5 6 7 8 9 0 BAN BAN 9 0 0 9
international 6 7 8 9 0 BAN BAN 9 0 0 9 8 7

ISBN 0-07-012594-5

The Sponsoring Editor was Rhonda Sands.
The Deve.opmental Editor was Kristin Hepburn.
The Editorial Assistant was Kyle Thomes.
The Marketing Manager was James Rogers.
The Production Supervisor was Richard DeVitto.
The cover was designed by Lorna Lo.
Project management was by Elaine Brett, Fritz/Brett Associates.
Composition was by Pat Rogondino, Rogondino & Associates.
The typeface was ITC Clearface.
Banta Co. was the printer and binder.

Library of Congress Cataloging Card Number 97-72180

When ordering this title, use ISBN 0-07-115473-6

http://www.mhhe.com

Contents

Database Overview

A database is an organized collection of related data. Before computers, most data was kept on paper. Paper records organized in a filing cabinet by name or department are a database. The information in a telephone book, organized alphabetically, is a database. A school's records of teachers, classes, and students are a database.

With computers, the same type of information can be entered and stored electronically using a database application program. The big difference is that an electronic database can manipulate—sort, analyze, and display—the data quickly and efficiently. What took hours of time to pull from the paper files can be extracted in a matter of seconds using a computerized database.

Relational Database Programs

Most microcomputer database programs are relational. These programs organize data into tables consisting of columns (called fields) and rows (called records). For example, a state's motor vehicle department database may have a table consisting of personal information on each vehicle owner, such as their name and address. Each vehicle owner's personal information forms a record. Each record may consist of the following fields of data: first name, last name, street, city, state, zip code, Social Security number, and license number.

The tables in a relational database are related or linked to one another by a common field. For example, the motor vehicle department may have a second database table containing data for each vehicle owned and a third on outstanding citations. The data in one table can then be linked to the data in another table by using a common field, such as the owner's Social Security number or driver's license number. The ability to link database tables creates a relational database (see example below). Relational databases allow you to create smaller and more manageable database tables, since you can combine and extract data between tables.

Address Table

SS#	License #	First Name	Last Name	Street	City	State	Zip Code
777-77-7777	FJ1987	Linda	Aaron	——	——	——	——
999-99-9999	LK3457	Jack	Abel	——	——	——	——
555-55-5555	VT9482	Thomas	Abrams	——	——	——	——
⋮	⋮	⋮	⋮	⋮	⋮	⋮	⋮

link on common field

link on common field

Owner's Table

SS#	Plate #
777-77-7777	ABK 241
999-99-9999	LMJ 198
555-55-5555	PTY 042
⋮	⋮

Outstanding Citation Table

License #	Citation Code	Violation
VT9482	00031	Speed
SJ1971	19001	Park
KB8423	84100	Speed
⋮	⋮	⋮

Advantages of Using a Database Program

One of the main advantages of using a computerized database program is the ability to quickly locate specific records. Once you enter data into the database table, you can quickly search the table to locate a specific record based on the data in a field. In a manual system, you can usually locate a record by knowing one key piece of information. For example, if the records are stored in a file cabinet alphabetically by last name, to quickly find a record you must know the last name. In a computerized database, even if the records are sorted or organized by last name, you can still quickly locate a record using information in another field.

A computerized database also makes it easy to add and delete records from the table. Once you locate a record, you can edit the contents of the fields to update the record or delete the record entirely from the table. You can also add new records to a table. When you enter a new record, it is automatically placed in the correct organizational location within the table.

Another advantage of using a computerized database system is its ability to arrange or sort the records in the table according to different fields of data. You can organize records by name, department, pay, class, or any other category you need at a particular time. This ability to produce multiple table arrangements helps provide more meaningful information. The same records can provide information to different departments for different purposes.

A fourth advantage is the ability to analyze the data in a table and perform calculations on different fields of data. Instead of pulling each record from a filing cabinet, recording the piece of data you want to use, and then performing the calculation on the recorded data, you can simply have the database program perform the calculation on all the values in the specified field. Additionally, you can ask questions or query the table to find only certain records that meet specific conditions to be used in the analysis. Information that was once costly and time-consuming to get is now quickly and readily available.

Another advantage of database programs is the ability to quickly produce reports ranging from simple listings to complex, professional-looking reports. You can create a simple report by asking for a listing of specified fields of data and restricting the listing to records meeting designated conditions. You can create a more complex professional report using the same restrictions or conditions as the simple report, but you can display the data in different layout styles, or with titles, headings, subtotals, or totals.

In manual systems, there are often several file cabinets in different departments containing some of the same data. With a computerized database system, more than one department can access the same data. Common updating of the data can be done by any department. The elimination of duplicate information saves both space and time.

Database Terminology

Database: An organized collection of related data that is commonly stored as a table in a file.

Delete: To remove a record from the database file.

Edit: To change or update the data in a field.

Field: The smallest item of information about a record, such as last name.

Query: To ask questions of the database, which then displays only those records meeting specified conditions.

Record: A collection of related fields, such as Social Security number, first name, and last name.

Report: A printed and formatted presentation of specified fields of data for specified records in the file.

Search: To locate a specific record in a file.

Sort: To arrange the records in a file in a specified order.

Table: A collection of data that is organized into columns (fields) and rows (records).

Case Study for Labs 1–5

As a recent college graduate, you have accepted your first job as a management trainee with The Sports Company. This company consists of a chain of sporting goods stores located in large metropolitan areas across the United States. The stores are warehouse oriented, discounting the retail price of most items 15 percent. They stock sporting goods products for all the major sports; basketball, football, tennis, aerobics, and so on.

Your training program emphasis is on computer applications related to retail management. You have been assigned to the Southwest regional office as an assistant to the regional manager and have been asked to suggest how to make the current recordkeeping system of maintaining employee information more efficient.

The company has recently purchased Microsoft Office 97, and you will use the Access 97 database program to computerize the employee records.

In Lab 1 you will learn how to design and create the structure for a computerized database and how to enter and edit records in the database. You will also print a simple report of the records you enter in the database file.

In Lab 2 you will continue to build, modify, and use the employee database of records. You will learn how to sort the records in a database file to make it easier to locate records. Additionally, you will create a customized form to make it easier to enter and edit data in the database file.

In Lab 3 you will learn how to query the database to locate specific information. You will also learn how to use and link multiple tables and create calculated fields.

In Lab 4 you will learn how to use Access 97 to create weekly and monthly employee status reports and mailing labels. The reports will display selected fields of data for the records in the database. They will also include a report title, subgroupings of data, group calculations, and descriptive text to clarify the meaning of the data in the report.

Lab 5 demonstrates the sharing of data between Access and Word. You will learn to import an Access table into a Word document and an Excel spreadsheet, and to perform a mail merge using a Word letter document and an Access table as the data source.

Before You Begin

To the Student

The following assumptions have been made:

- Microsoft Access 97 has been properly installed on the hard disk of your computer system.
- The data disk contains the data files needed to complete the series of labs and practice exercises. These files are supplied by your instructor.
- You have completed the Windows 95 labs or you are already familiar with how to use a mouse and with basic Windows 95 terminology and procedures.

To the Instructor

The following assumptions have been made:

- Microsoft Access 97 has been installed using the default program settings. These settings are in effect each time the program is loaded.

- When the table window is maximized, the number of rows and columns that are displayed varies with the computer system display settings established in Windows. These labs assume a standard VGA display setting (640 x 480), which displays 18 rows. The text and figures reflect this setup.
- The Tip of the Day is not displayed at startup.
- The Office Assistant is on.
- The Advanced Wizards have been installed so that the Input Mask Wizard is available.

Office Shortcut Bar

The Microsoft Office Shortcut Bar (shown below) may be displayed automatically on the Windows 95 desktop. Commonly, it appears in the upper right section of the desktop; however, it may appear in other locations, depending upon your setup. Because the Shortcut Bar can be customized, it may display different buttons than shown below.

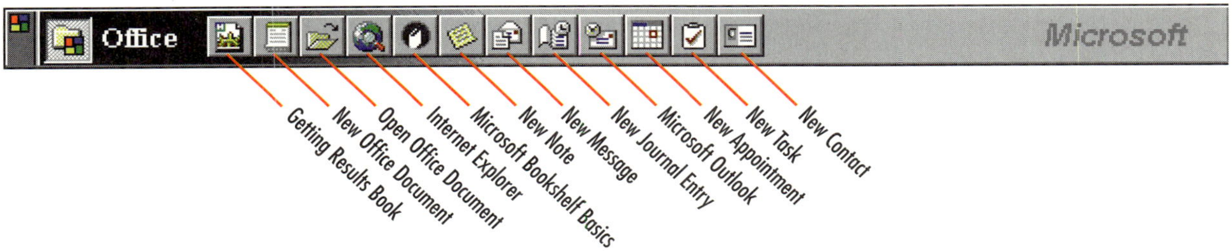

The Office Shortcut Bar makes it easy to open existing documents or to create new documents using one of the Microsoft Office applications. It can also be used to send e-mail, add a task to a to-do list, schedule appointments using Outlook, or add contacts or notes.

Instructional Conventions

This text uses the following instructional conventions:

- Steps that you are to perform are preceded with a bullet (■) and are in blue type. Anything you are to type appears in bold blue type.
- Command sequences you are to issue appear following the word "Choose." Each menu command selection is separated by a /. If the command can be selected by typing a letter of the command, the letter will appear bold and underlined.
- Commands that can be initiated using a button and the mouse appear following the word "Click." The menu equivalent and keyboard shortcut appear in a margin note when the action is first introduced.
- Anything you are to type appears in bold text.

1 Creating a Database

COMPETENCIES

After completing this lab, you will know how to:

1. **Load Access 97.**
2. **Plan and create a database.**
3. **Use the Office Assistant.**
4. **Create a table.**
5. **Save the table structure.**
6. **Switch views.**
7. **Enter and edit data.**
8. **Adjust column widths.**
9. **Add records in Data Entry.**
10. **Preview and print a table.**
11. **Close and open a database.**
12. **Exit Access.**

CASE STUDY

Currently The Sports Company employee information is maintained on paper forms and stored in file cabinets organized alphabetically by last name. Although the information is well organized, it still takes time to manually leaf through the folders to locate the information you need and to compile reports from this data.

Your current assignment in the management trainee program is to update the employee recordkeeping system to an electronic database management system. A computerized database will not only store and organize the data to make access to the information it contains quick and easy, but allows you to manipulate and present information in a variety of ways.

You will begin by creating an employee database and a table (shown below) of basic employee information.

Employee ID	Date Hired	Last Name	First Name	Street	City	State	Zip Code	Phone Number	Birth Date
0234	4/12/91	Bergstrom	Drew	8943 W. Southern Ave	Mesa	AZ	84101-8475	(602) 555-8201	8/7/61
0434	6/4/91	Long	William	947 S. Forest St.	Tempe	AZ	86301-1268	(602) 555-4494	4/20/70
0728	7/15/91	Toroyan	Lucy	2348 S. Bala Dr.	Tempe	AZ	85301-7985	(602) 555-9870	3/15/61
0839	8/14/91	Artis	Jose	358 Maple Dr.	Scottsd	AZ	85205-6911	(602) 555-0091	12/10/63
1151	10/14/90	Anderson	Susan	4389 S. Hayden Rd.	Mesa	AZ	85205-0346	(602) 555-1950	6/14/65
9999	10/5/98	Student	Name	89 Any Street	Mesa	AZ	85202-9999	(602) 555-5555	8/30/70

Concept Overview

The following concepts will be introduced in this lab:

1. Database Development	The development of a database follows several steps: plan, create, enter data, edit, form design, data analysis, report design, and preview and print.
2. Objects	A database file is made up of many different types of objects, such as tables, forms, and reports.
3. Fields	A field, the smallest unit of information about a record, is identified by a field name.
4. Data Types	The data type defines the type of data the field will contain.
5. Field Properties	Field properties are a set of characteristics that are associated with each field.
6. Primary Key	A primary key is a field that uniquely identifies each record.
7. Views	Access allows you to view objects in your database in several different window formats, called views.
8. Edit and Navigation Modes	The Edit and Navigation modes control how you can move through and make changes to the data in a table.
9. Column Width	Column width refers to the size of each field column in Datasheet view. It controls the amount of data you can see in the column.

Part 1

Loading Access 97

The Sports Company recently purchased the Office 97 application software suite and will use the Access 97 database management program to create several different computerized databases of information. A computerized **database** is an organized collection of information that typically stores the information in tables. A **table** contains data about a specific topic that is organized into vertical columns and horizontal rows. Each row contains a **record**, which is all the information about one person, thing, or place.

You will begin by creating a table using Access 97 to hold the employee data.

Refer to the overview for a complete description of a database.

- If necessary, turn on your computer and put your data disk in drive A (or the appropriate drive for your system).

If a Shortcut to Access 97 button is displayed on your desktop, you can double-click on the button to start the program.

- Click Start.
- Choose Programs/Microsoft Access.

If the Microsoft Office suite is on your system and the Office Shortcut Bar is displayed, you can click the New Office Document button, select Blank Database, and click OK to load Access.

Your screen should be similar to Figure 1-1.

FIGURE 1-1

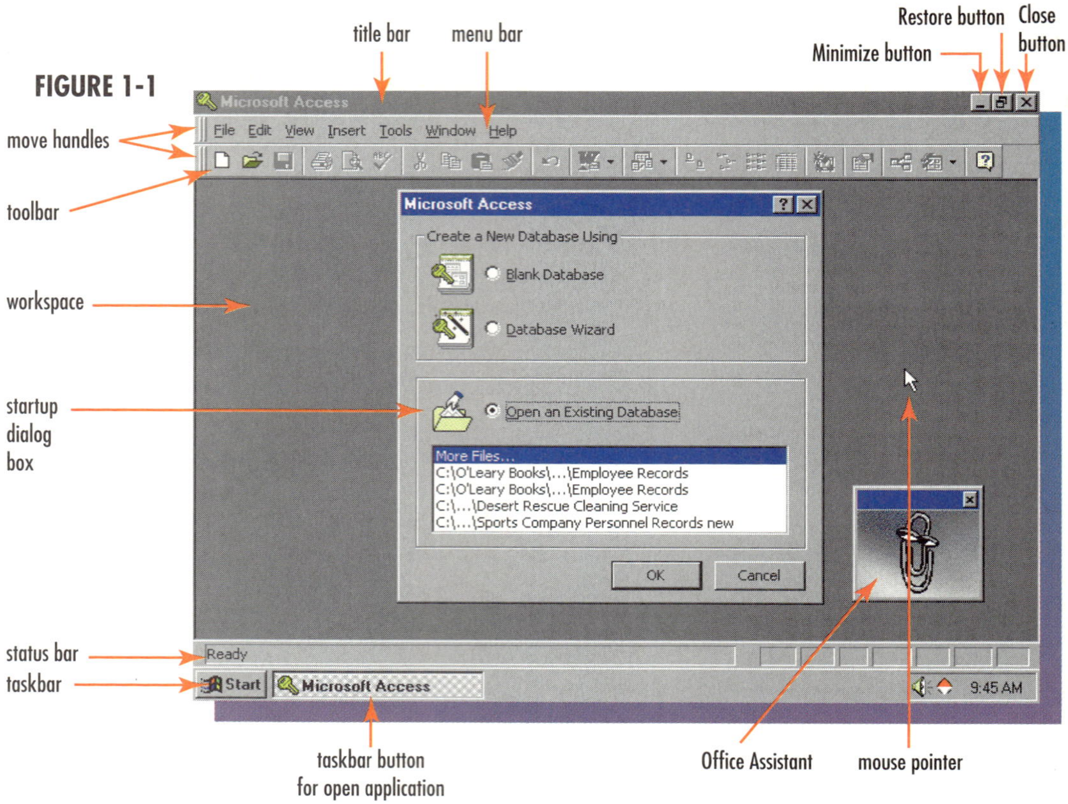

Your Office Assistant may display a different character than in Figure 1-1. Do not be concerned if the Assistant is not displayed; you will learn how to display it shortly.

If necessary, maximize the Access window.

The Microsoft Access application window with the startup dialog box open should be displayed. The startup dialog box allows you to create a new database or open an existing database. In addition, a small dialog box called the Office Assistant may also be displayed on your screen. The Assistant provides help on any command or window element. You will learn about this feature shortly.

The Access application window includes the same features that are common to the Windows 95 environment: a title bar, menu bar, toolbar, Minimize, Restore, and Close buttons, icons, and mouse compatibility. You can move and size Access windows, select commands, use Help, and switch between files and programs just like in Windows 95. Your knowledge of how to use Windows 95 makes learning about and using Access much easier. The taskbar at the bottom of the screen displays the button for the open application.

The menu bar contains seven menus. The menus and commands that are available at any time vary with the task you are performing.

Pointing to the toolbar buttons displays the button names in a toolbar screen tip.

The toolbar contains buttons that are mouse shortcuts for many menu commands. Many of the buttons are the same as you have seen in toolbars in other Windows 95 applications. Many, however, are specific to Access. Only the first two buttons, New Database and Open Database, and the last one, Office Assistant, are currently available for use. All the other buttons are dimmed, indicating they are unavailable. There are 19 toolbars in Access. Most toolbars appear automatically as you perform different tasks and open different windows. The left end of the menu and toolbar displays a **move handle** that when dragged moves the menu or toolbar to another location. Both menus and toolbars can be docked (as they are now) or floating. When **docked** they are fixed to an edge of the window and display the move handle. When **floating** they appear in a separate window that can be moved by dragging the title bar.

The center area of the window is the **workspace** where different Access windows are displayed as you are using the program. Just below the workspace, the status bar provides information about the task you are working on and the current Access operation. In addition, the status bar displays messages such as button and command descriptions to help you use the program more efficiently.

The mouse pointer appears as an arrow and operates as in Windows. It also changes shape depending on the task you are performing or its location in the window.

Planning a Database

The Sports Company plans to use Access 97 to maintain several different types of databases. The database you will create will contain information about each Sports Company employee. Other plans for using Access include keeping track of preferred customers and inventory. To keep the different types of information separate, the company plans to create a database for each group. Creating a new database follows several basic steps.

Concept 1: Database Development

The development of a database follows several steps: plan, create, enter data, edit, form design, data analysis, report design, and preview and print.

Plan: The first step in the development of a database is to understand the purpose of the database and to plan what information your database should hold and the output you need from the database.

Create: After planning the database, you create tables to hold data by defining the table structure.

Enter Data: Once a table has been set up, you enter the data to complete each record.

Edit: While entering data, you may make typing and spelling errors that need to be corrected. This is one type of editing. Another is to revise the structure of the tables by adding, deleting, or redefining information in the table.

Form Design: After you create a table, you can create a form for easier data entry. Forms also make editing easier.

Data Analysis: To analyze the data stored in your tables, you ask questions, called queries, of the table data. The results of queries allow you to look at only selected data or to view data in a specific format. For example, you can examine data to determine the largest sales, monthly birthdays, or to make projections.

Report Design: To be able to print your data in a professional and attractive format, you create reports. Reports allow you to customize the appearance of the data.

Preview and Print: The last step is to print a hard copy of the database or report. This step includes previewing the document onscreen as it will appear when printed. Previewing allows you to check the document's overall appearance and to make any final changes needed before printing.

You will find that you will generally follow these steps in order as you create your database. However, you will probably retrace steps as the final database is developed.

Your first step is to plan the design of your database tables: how many tables, what data they will contain, and how they will be related. You need to decide what information each table in the employee database should contain and how it should be structured or laid out.

You can obtain this information by analyzing the current recordkeeping procedures used throughout the company. You need to understand the existing procedures so your database tables will reflect the information that is maintained by different departments. You should be aware of the forms that are the basis for the data entered into the department records, and of the information that is taken from the records to produce periodic reports. You also need to find out what information the department heads would like to be able to obtain from the database that may be too difficult to generate using their current procedures.

After looking over the existing recordkeeping procedures and the reports that are created from the information, you decide to create several separate tables of data in the database file. Creating several smaller tables of related data rather than one large table makes it easier to use the tables and faster to process data. This is because you can join several tables together as needed. The main table will include the employee's basic information, such as employee number, name, and address. Another table will contain job-related information, such as department and job title. A third will contain data on pay rate and hours worked.

Creating a Database

Now that you have decided on the information you want to include in the tables, you are ready to create a new database to hold the table information. From the startup dialog box,

- Select Blank Database.
- Click OK.

The File New Database dialog box is displayed. The first step is to specify a name for the database file and the location where you want the file saved. By default Access uses the name db1. You want the program to store the database on your data disk using the name Employee Data.

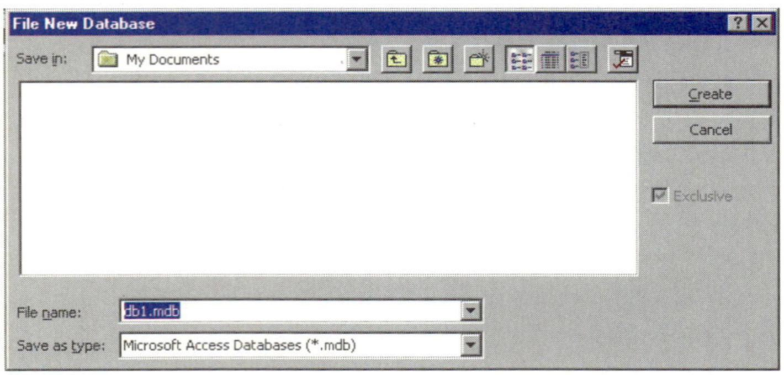

The number in the default file name on your screen may be different.

- If necessary, change the Save In location to the drive containing your data disk.
- Replace the default database file name with Employee Data.
- Click Create.

The file name can be entered in either uppercase or lowercase letters, but the name will be stored and displayed the way you type it.

After a few seconds, your screen should be similar to Figure 1-2.

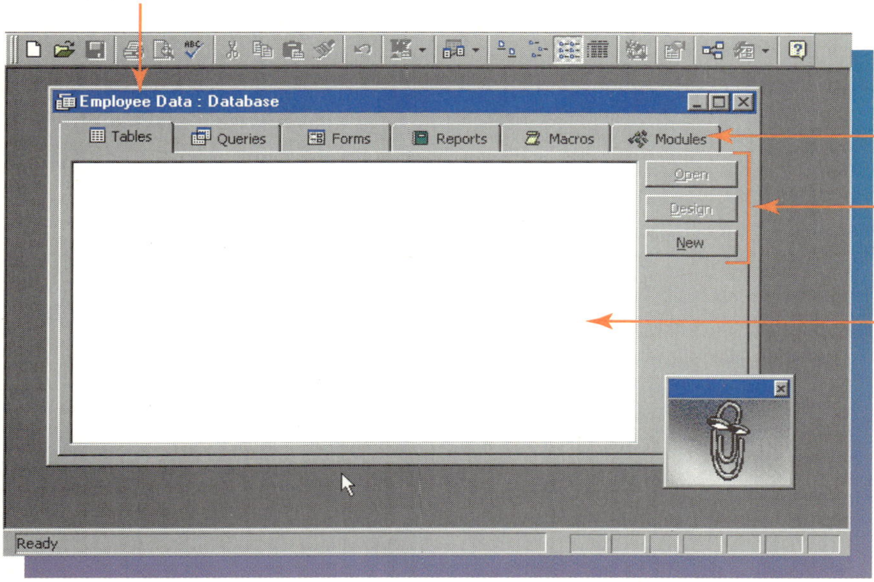

FIGURE 1-2

The Database window displays the name of the database, Employee Data, followed by the name of the window in the window title bar. From the Database window you can create and use any database object.

Concept 2: Objects

An **object** is an item, such as a table or report, that is made up of many elements, and that can be created, selected, and manipulated as a unit. The **object tabs** at the top of the Database window are used to select the type of object you want to use. The currently selected object tab is Tables. The table object is the basic unit of a database and must be created first, before any other types of objects are created. The object list box under the object tabs normally displays a list of objects associated with the selected object tab. The Tables object list box is empty because you have not created any tables for this database yet.

Access displays each different type of object in its own window. You can display multiple object windows in the workspace; however, you cannot open more than one database file at a time.

Using the Office Assistant

If the Office Assistant is not displayed, click [?] or press F1.

To find out more about tables, you will use the Office Assistant. The **Office Assistant** is used to get Help on features that are specific to the Office application you are using. The Assistant display tips that point out how to use the features or keyboard shortcuts in the program more effectively. A tip is available when a yellow light bulb appears in the Assistant; click the light bulb to see the tip. It can also automatically display Help suggestions relevant to the specific task you are performing. In addition, you can activate the Assistant at any time to ask for help on any topic. To activate it,

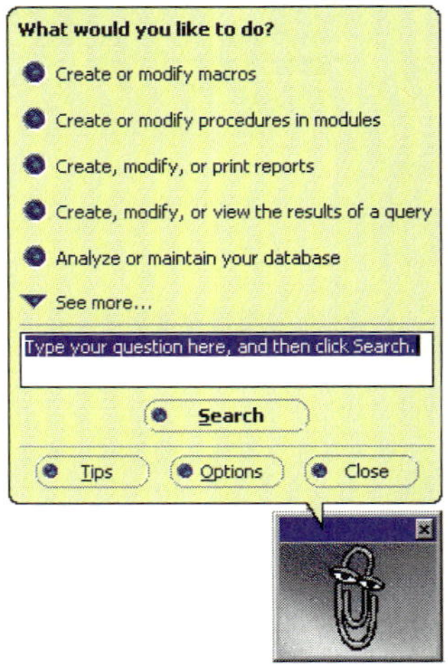

You can also access Help using the Help menu.

- Click Office Assistant.

A yellow balloon displays a prompt and a text box in which you can type a question and the Assistant will display a list of topics related to your request. Selecting a topic then will display the Help information on the topic. For Help information about tables,

- Type **What are tables**
- Click Search.
- Choose Tables: What they are and how they work.

Your screen should be similar to Figure 1-3.

FIGURE 1-3

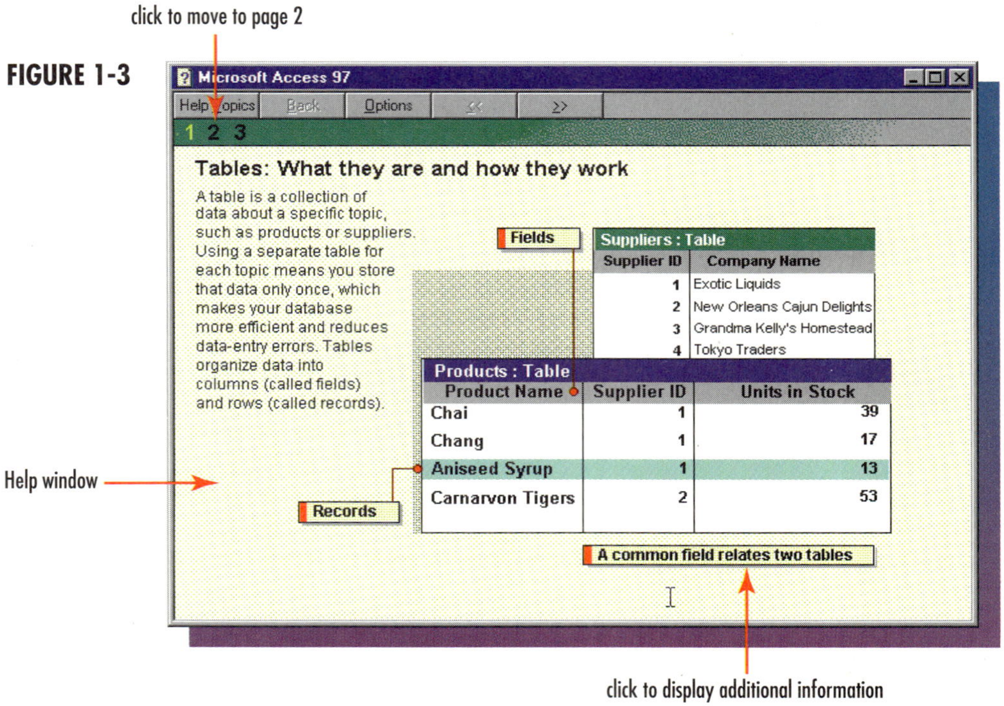

Page 1 of three pages of information about tables is displayed. Clicking on the yellow boxes in the window will display additional information about the feature.

- Read the information in the three pages of Help on tables.
- Click X.

Click on the number to move to the next page.

You can leave the Office Assistant open or you can close it and activate it when needed.

The illustrations in this text will not display the Assistant open.

- If you want to hide the Assistant, click X in the Assistant's window.

Creating a Table

After naming the database, your next step is to create the new table to hold the employee data by defining the structure of the table.

- Click New.

The New Table dialog box provides five different ways to create a table. The first three, Datasheet View, Design View, and Table Wizard, are the most commonly used. The Table Wizard option starts the Table Wizard feature, which lets you select from 45 predesigned database tables. The Wizard then creates a table for you based upon your selections. The Datasheet and Design View options open different view windows in which you can create a new custom table from scratch.

Access includes 19 different Wizards that can be used to create different Access objects.

You will use the Design View option to create the table.

You will learn more about views later in the lab.

- Select Design View.
- Click OK.

Your screen should be similar to Figure 1-4.

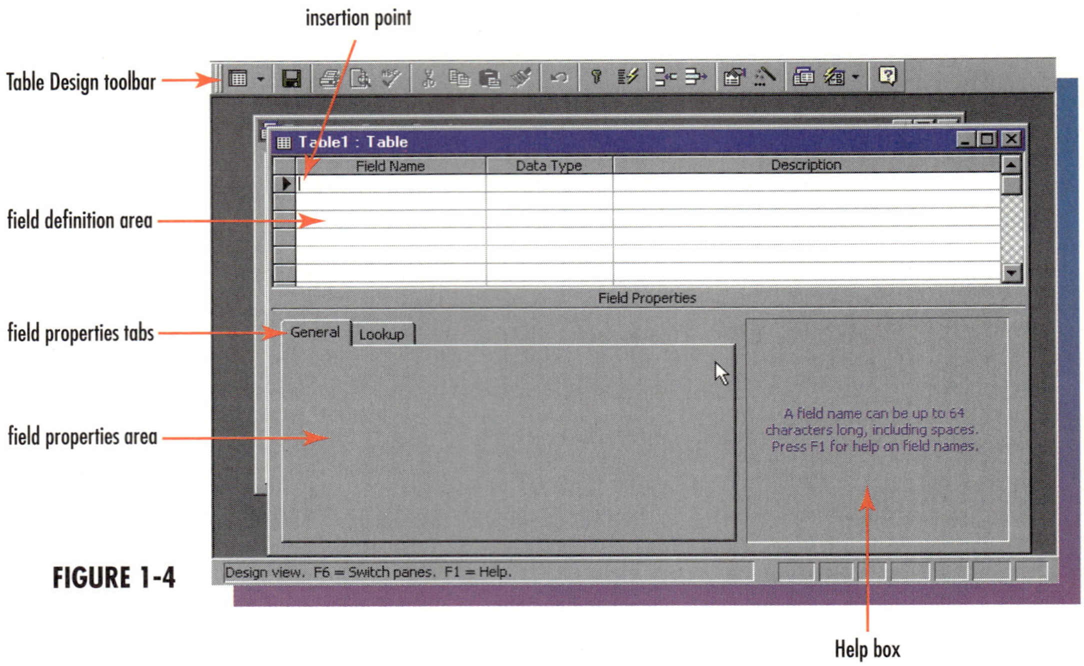

FIGURE 1-4

The Table Design window is opened and displayed over the Database window in the workspace. The Table Design toolbar is also displayed. This toolbar contains the standard buttons as well as buttons (identified below) that are specific to this window.

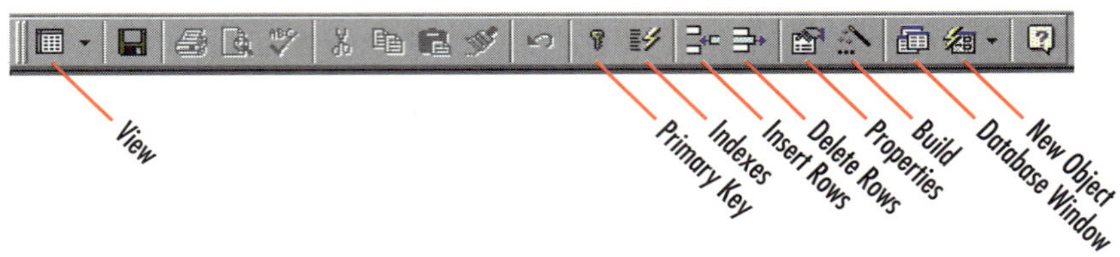

The upper section of the Table Design window consists of a grid where you define each field to include in the table.

Concept 3: Fields

A **field** is the smallest unit of information about a record. A **field name** is used to identify the data stored in the field. A field name should be descriptive of the contents of the data to be entered in the field. It can be up to 64 characters long and can consist of letters, numbers, spaces, and special characters, except a period, an exclamation point, an accent grave (`), and brackets ([]). You also cannot start a field name with a space. Examples of field names are: Last Name, First Name, Address, Phone Number, Department, Hire Date, or other words that describe the data. It is best to use short field names to make the tables easier to manage.

Each row in the grid is where a field is defined by entering the required information in each of the columns. You decide to include the data currently maintained in the personnel folder on each employee in one table using the following 10 fields: Employee ID, Date Hired, Last Name, First Name, Street, City, State, Zip Code, Phone Number, and Birth Date.

In the lower right section of the dialog box, a Help box provides information on the task you are performing in the window. Since the insertion point is positioned in the Field Name text box, the Help box displays a brief description of the rules for entering a valid field name.

The first field of data you will enter in the table is the employee number, which is assigned to each employee when hired. Each new employee is given the next consecutive number, so no two employees can have the same number. It is a maximum of four digits.

> The ▶ to the left of the first row indicates the current field.

> The field name can be typed in uppercase or lowercase letters, and will be displayed exactly as entered.

- Type **Employee Number**

Since the data you will enter in this field is a maximum of four characters, you decide to change the field name to Employee ID, so the field name is closer in size to the data that will be entered in the field. To edit the entry,

> The (Backspace) key will delete the characters to the left of the insertion point, and the (Delete) key will delete characters to the right.

- Press (Backspace) (6 times).
- Type **ID**
- Press (←Enter).

The window on your screen should be similar to Figure 1-5.

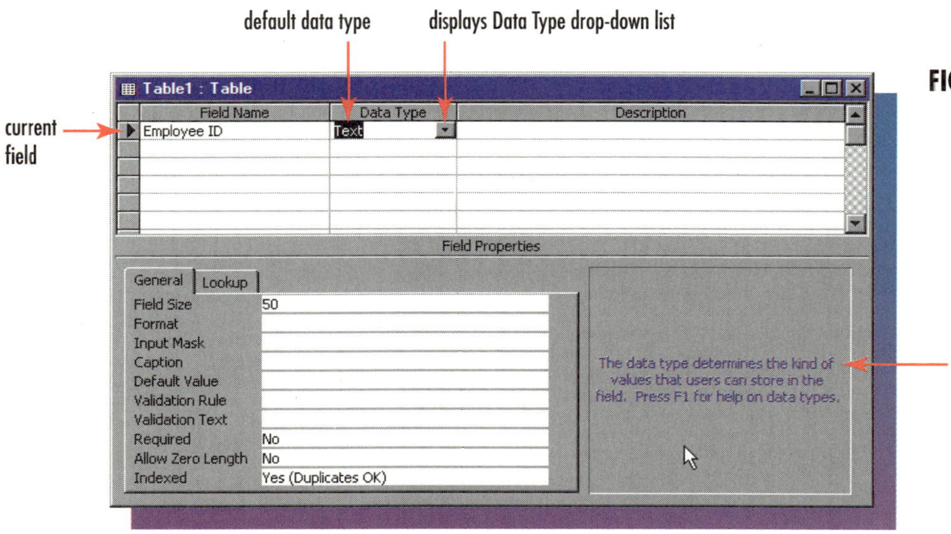

FIGURE 1-5

The insertion point has moved to the Data Type column where the default data type of "Text" is automatically entered.

- Display the Data Type drop-down list.

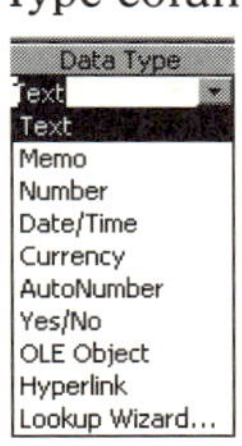

Concept 4: Data Types

The **data type** defines the type of data the field will contain. Access uses the data type to ensure that the right kind of data is entered in a field. It is important to choose the right data type for a field before you start entering data in the table. You can change a data type after the field contains data, but if the data types are not compatible, such as a text entry in a field whose data type accepts numbers only, you may lose data. Nine data types are described below.

Data Type	Description
Text	Text entries (words, combinations of words and numbers, numbers that are not used in calculations) up to 255 characters in length (this is the default). Names and phone numbers are examples of Text field entries. Text is the default data type.
Memo	Text that is variable in length and usually too long to be stored in a Text field. A maximum of 65,535 characters can be entered in a Memo field.
Number	Digits only. Number fields are used when you want to perform calculations on the values in the field. Number of Units Ordered is an example of a Number field entry.
Date/Time	Any valid date. Access allows dates from January 1, 100 to December 31, 9999. Access correctly handles leap years and checks all dates for validity.
Currency	Exactly like Number fields, but formatted to display decimal places and a currency symbol.
AutoNumber	A unique, sequential number that is automatically incremented by one whenever a new record is added to a table.
Yes/No	Accepts only Yes/No, True/False, or On/Off entries.
OLE Object	An object, such as a graphic (picture), sound, document, or spreadsheet, that is linked to or embedded in a table.
Hyperlink	Accepts hyperlink entries that are a path to an object, document, Web page, or other destinations.
Lookup Wizard	Displays a list of options you choose from another table in the database. Choosing this data type starts the Lookup Wizard.

A hyperlink is a connection to another document that when clicked on jumps to the referenced location.

Even though a field such as the Employee ID field may contain numeric entries, unless the numbers are used in calculations the field should be assigned the Text data type. This allows other characters, such as the parentheses or hyphens in a telephone number, to be included in the entry. Also, by specifying the type as Text, any leading zeros (for example, in the zip code 07739) will be preserved, whereas leading zeros in a Number type field are dropped (which would make this zip code incorrectly 7739).

To close the Data Type list and accept Text as the data type,

- Press Esc.

Also notice in the Field Properties area of the dialog box that the General tab now displays the default field property settings associated with a Text data type.

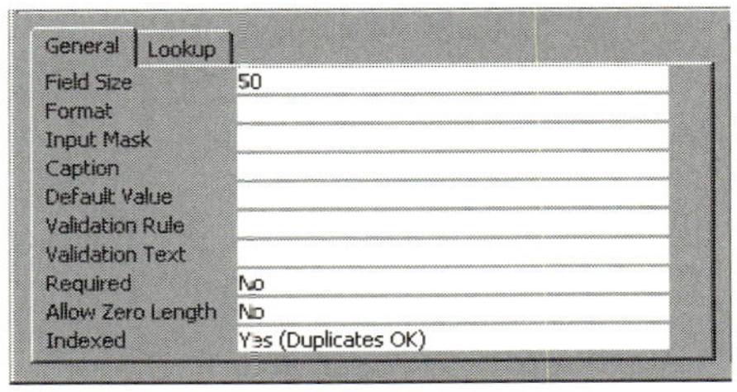

Concept 5: Field Properties

Field properties are a set of characteristics that are associated with each field. Each data type has a different set of field properties. Setting field properties enhances the way your table works. Some of the more commonly used properties and their functions are described below.

Property	Function
Field Size	Sets the maximum number of characters that can be entered in the field.
Format	Specifies how data displays in a table and prints.
Input Mask	Simplifies data entry by controlling what data is required in a field and how the data is to be displayed.
Caption	Specifies a field label other than the field name.
Default Value	Automatically fills in a certain value for this field in new records as you add to the table. You can override a default value by typing a new value into the field.
Validation Rule	Limits data entered in a field to values that meet certain requirements.
Validation Text	Specifies the message to be displayed when the associated Validation Rule is not satisfied.
Required	Specifies whether or not a value must be entered in a field.
Allow Zero Length	Specifies whether or not an entry containing no characters is valid.
Indexed	Sets a field as an index field (a field that controls the order of records). Speeds up searches on fields that are searched frequently.

You need to set the **field size** for the Employee ID field. By default Access sets a Text field size to 50. Although Access uses only the amount of storage space necessary for the text you actually store in a Text field, setting the field size to the smallest possible size can decrease the processing time required by the program. Additionally, if the field data to be entered is a specific size, setting the field size to that number restricts the entry to the maximum number. Since the Employee ID field will contain a maximum of four characters, you want to change the field size from the default of 50 to 4.

- Click the Field Size property text box.
- Replace the default entry with the number 4.

This is the only field property that you want to change. To continue defining the Employee ID field, you will enter a description of the field in the Description text box. Although it is optional, a field description makes the table easier to under-

You can also press F6 to switch between the upper and lower areas of the dialog box.

Clicking on the left edge of the field or property text box when the mouse pointer is a ⇗ will select the entire entry in the box.

stand and update because the description displays in the status bar when you enter data into the table.

Text in the Description box scrolls horizontally as needed.

- Click the Description text box for the Employee ID field.
- Type **A unique 4-digit number assigned to each employee as hired**

Next you want to make this field a primary key field.

Concept 6: Primary Key

A **primary key** is a field that uniquely identifies each record. Most tables have at least one field that is selected as the primary key. The data in the primary key field must be unique for each record. For example, a Social Security number field could be selected as the primary key because the data in that field is unique for each employee. Other examples of a primary key field are parts numbers or catalog numbers.

A primary key prevents duplicate records from being entered in the table and is used to control the order in which records display in the table. This makes it faster for databases to locate records in the table and to process other operations. The primary key is also used to create a link between tables in a database.

Although any field can be the primary key, traditionally the first field or group of fields in the table is the primary key field.

To define the field as a primary key,

The menu equivalent is Edit/Primary Key.

- Click Primary Key.

Your screen should be similar to Figure 1-6.

FIGURE 1-6

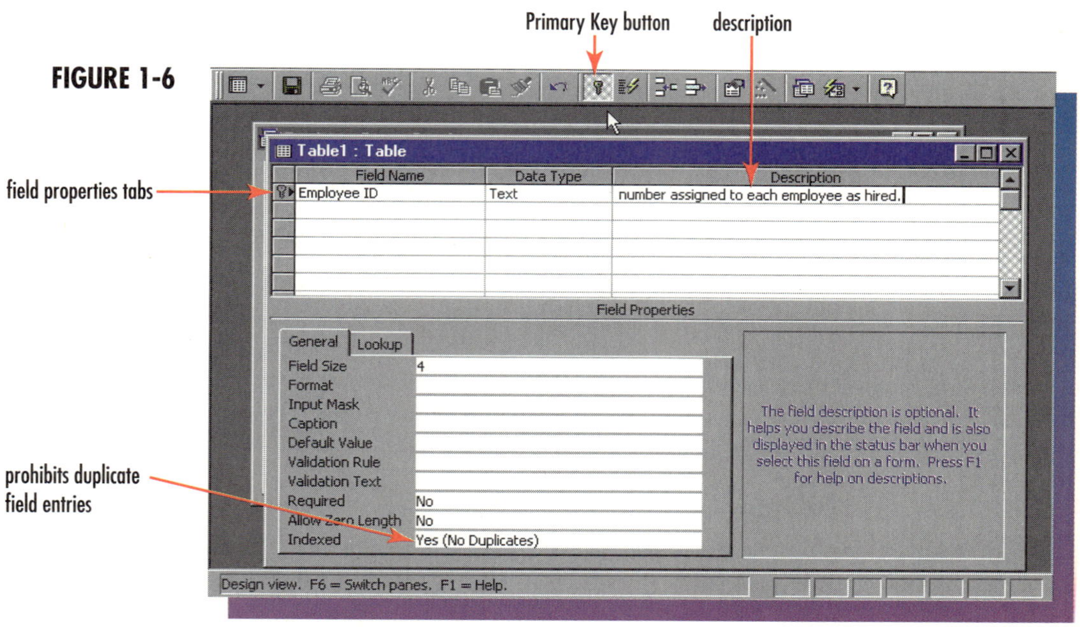

The icon appears in the column to the left of the field name, showing that this field is a primary key field. Now that this is the primary key field, the Indexed property setting has changed to Yes (No Duplicates). This setting prohibits duplicate values in a field.

The second field will display the date the employee started working at The Sports Company in the form of month/day/year. To enter the second field name,

- Press ←Enter.
- Type **Date Hired**
- Press Tab or →.
- Select the Date/Time data type.

The default field properties for the selected data type are displayed. This time you want to change the format of the field so that the date will display as mm/dd/yy, regardless of how it is entered.

- Select the Format property box.
- Open the drop-down list of Format options.
- Choose Short Date.
- In the Description text box of the Date Hired field, enter the description: **Acceptable entry formats are 4/4/99, Apr 4, 1999, or April 4, 1999**

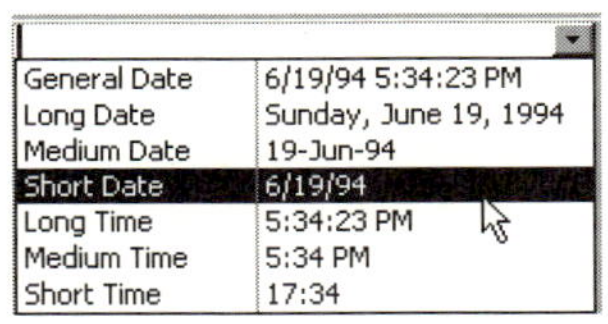

- Press ←Enter.

The third field is a Text field type that will contain the employee's last name. Because the field name is descriptive of the field contents, a description is not needed.

- Type **Last Name**
- Press ←Enter (3 times).

Using Tab or → has the same effect as pressing ←Enter; it moves the insertion point to the next column to the right. Shift + Tab or ← moves the insertion point to the left one column.

You can also enter the data type by typing the first character of the data type option. For example, you can enter "d" for Date/Time.

You cannot set the field size in Date/Time fields.

- In the same manner, enter the information shown below for the next seven fields. If you make a typing mistake, use Backspace and Delete to correct errors.

Field Name	Data Type	Description	Field Size/Format
First Name	Text		50
Street	Text		50
City	Text		50
State	Text	A 2-character abbreviation entered in all capital letters.	2
Zip Code	Text	Use the 9-digit zip code if available.	10
Phone Number	Text	Enter using the format (555) 555-5555.	15
Birth Date	Date/Time	Acceptable entry formats are 4/4/99, Apr 4, 1999, or April 4, 1999.	Short Date

You can copy the description from the Date Hired field to the Birth Date field.

When you have completed the seven additional fields, your field definition grid should be similar to Figure 1-7.

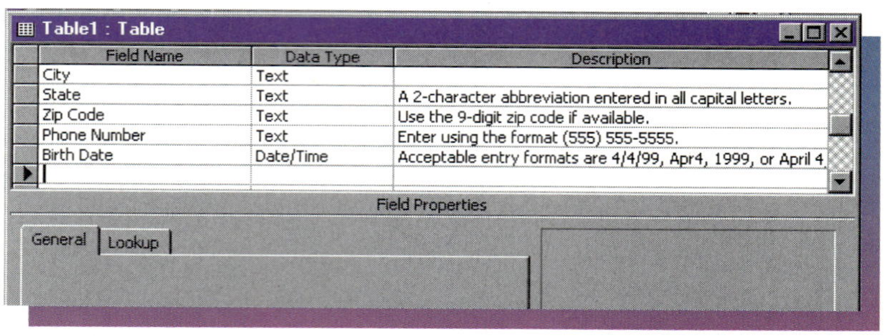

FIGURE 1-7

After looking over the fields, you decide to change the field sizes of the Last Name, First Name, and City fields to 20-character entries. Positioning the insertion point in any column of a field will display the properties for that field.

You may need to scroll the field name grid to see the Last Name field.

- Move to any column in the Last Name field.
- Change the field size to 20.
- In a similar manner, change the field size for the First Name and City fields to 20.
- Carefully check your screen to ensure that each field name and field type was entered accurately and make any necessary corrections.

To delete an entire field, move to the field and choose Edit/Delete Rows.

Saving the Table Structure

Once you are satisfied that your field definitions are correct, you can save the table design by naming it.

> The menu equivalent Is File/Save, and the keyboard shortcut is Ctrl + S.

- Click Save.

In the Save As dialog box, you want to replace the default name, Table 1, with a more descriptive name. A table name follows the same set of standard naming conventions or rules that you use when naming fields. It is acceptable to use the same name for both a table and the database, although each table in a database must have a unique name. You will save the table using the table name Employees.

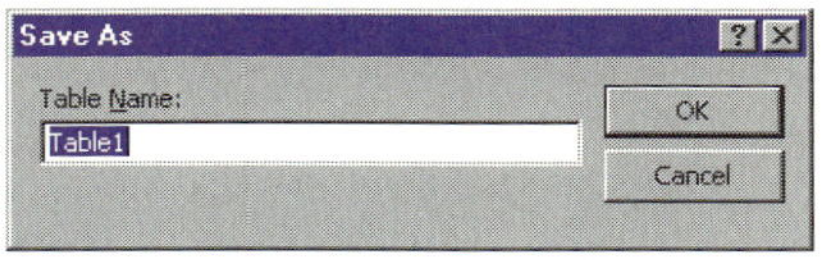

- Type **Employees**
- Click OK.

The table structure is saved with the database file. You have created a table named Employees in the Employee Data database file.

Note: If you are ending your lab session now, follow the directions beginning on page DB37 to close and open a database and exit Access. When you begin Part 2, load Access, select Open an Existing Database from the startup dialog box, and open the file Employee Data from your data disk. Then choose Design from the Tables tab of the Database window.

Part 2

Switching Views

Now that the table structure is defined and saved, you can enter the employee data into the new table. You enter and display data in the table in Datasheet view.

Concept 7: Views

Access allows you to view the objects in your database in several different window formats, called **views**. The basic views are described in the table below.

View	Use
Design view	Used to create a table, form, query, or report.
Datasheet view	Provides a row-and-column view of the data in tables, forms, and queries.
Form view	Displays the records in a form.
Preview	Displays a form, report, or datasheet as it will appear when printed.

Each view includes it own menu and toolbar designed to work with the object in the window. The views that are available change depending on the type of object you are working with.

> Clicking the ▾ next to the Table View button displays a drop-down list of available views.

> The menu equivalent is View/Datasheet.

The Table View button is a toggle button that switches between the different available views. The graphic in the button changes to indicate the view that will be displayed when selected. The Table View button appears as for Design view and for Datasheet view.

■ Click Datasheet View.

Your screen should be similar to Figure 1-8.

FIGURE 1-8

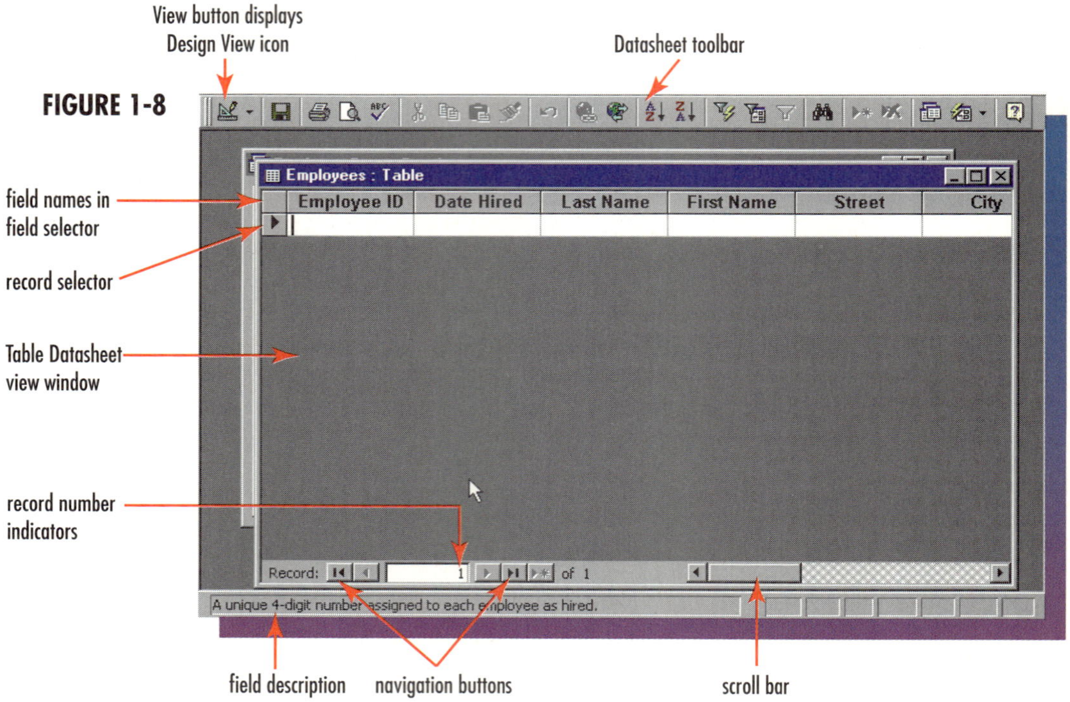

In Table Datasheet view you can enter and delete records and edit field data in existing records. In addition, this view automatically displays a Table Datasheet toolbar containing the standard buttons as well as buttons (identified below) that are specific to the Table Datasheet view window.

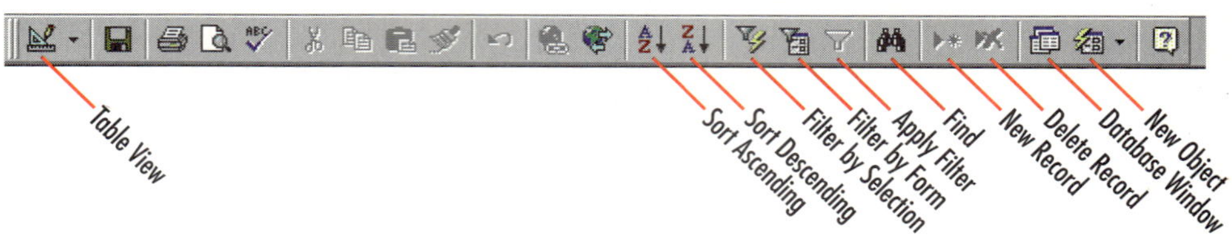

Datasheet view displays the table data in a row-and-column format. Each field is a column of the table. The field names you entered in Design view are displayed as column headings. The column heading area is called the **field selector** for each column. Below the field selector is a blank row where you will enter the data for a record. To the left of the row is the **record selector** symbol ▶, which indicates which record is the **current record**.

The bottom of the window displays a horizontal scroll bar, navigation buttons, and a record number indicator. The **record number indicator** shows the number of the current record as well as the total number of records in the table. Because the table does not yet contain records, the indicator displays "Record: 1 of 1" in anticipation of your first entry. On both sides of the record number are the **navigation buttons**. You use these buttons to move through records with a mouse.

Only the first few field names are visible because there is not enough space in the Employees table window to display all the fields.

You will learn about using the navigation buttons in Lab 2.

- To see more information in the window, maximize the window.

Now that you can see several more field columns, you notice that the column widths are all the same, even though you set different field sizes in the Table Design window. This is because the Table Datasheet view window has its own default column width setting. You will learn how to change the column width later in this lab.

Entering Data

The insertion point is positioned in the Employee ID field, indicating the program is ready to accept data in this field. The description in the status bar provides the user with information about the data that should be entered in the field. The data you will enter for the first record is as follows:

Field Name	Data
Employee ID	1151
Date Hired	October 14, 1990
Last Name	Anderson
First Name	Susan
Street	4389 S. Hayden Rd.
City	Mesa
State	AZ
Zip Code	85205-0346
Phone Number	(602) 555-1950
Birth Date	June 14, 1965

When you enter data in a record, it should be entered accurately and consistently. The data you enter in a field should be typed exactly as you want it to appear. This is important because any printouts of the data will display the information exactly as entered. It is also important to enter data in a consistent form. For example, if you decide to abbreviate the word "Street" as "St." in the Street field, then it should be abbreviated the same way in every record where it appears. Also be careful not to enter a blank space before or after a field entry. This can cause problems when using the table to locate information.

You will try to enter an Employee ID number that is larger than the field size of 4 that you defined in Table Design view.

- Type **11510**.
- Press ←Enter.

Your screen should be similar to Figure 1-9.

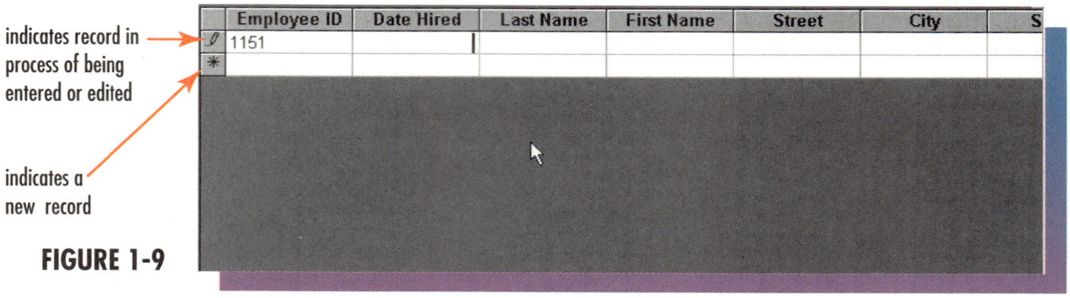

FIGURE 1-9

The program accepted only the first four digits you typed. The field size restriction helps control the accuracy of data by not allowing an entry larger than specified. Also notice that a second row has appeared in the table. The * symbol in the record selector column indicates the end of the table or where a new record can be entered. In addition, the current record symbol has changed to a ✎. This symbol means the record is in the process of being entered or edited and has not yet been saved.

To enter the date hired (it is intentionally incorrect) for this record,

- Type **10/41/90**
- Press ←Enter.

An informational message box is displayed. Access automatically performs some basic checks on the data as it is entered based upon the field type specified in the table design. This is another way Access helps you control data entry to ensure the accuracy of the data. In this case the date entered (10/41/90) could not be correct because there cannot be 41 days in a month. To close the message box,

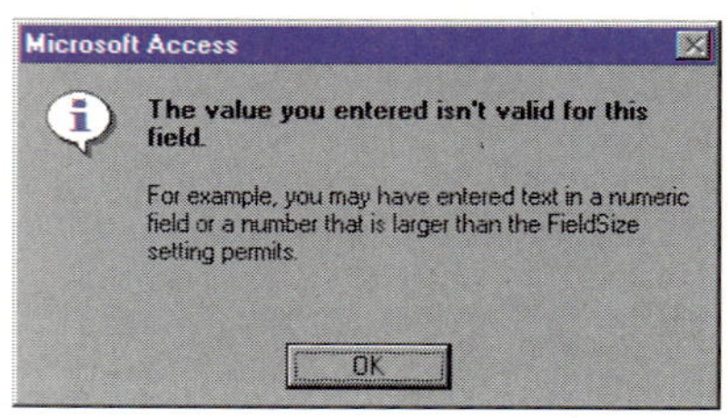

- Click OK.

Editing Data

Next you need to edit the entry to correct it. How you edit data in Access depends on which mode of operation is active.

Concept 8: Edit and Navigation Modes

The Edit and Navigation modes control how you can move through and make changes to data in a table. **Edit mode** is used to enter or edit data in a field. In Edit mode the insertion point is displayed in the field so you can edit existing data or enter new data. To position the insertion point in the field entry, click at the location where you want it to appear. The keyboard keys shown in the table below can also be used to move the insertion point in Edit mode and to make changes to individual characters in the entry.

Navigation mode is used to move from field to field and to delete an entire field entry. In Navigation mode the entire field entry is selected (highlighted), and the insertion point is not displayed. You move from field to field using the keyboard keys shown in the table below.

Key	Edit Mode
← or →	Moves insertion point left or right one character.
Ctrl + ← or →	Moves insertion point left or right one word.
↓	Move insertion point to current field in next record.
Home or End	Moves insertion point to beginning or end of field in single-line field.
Ctrl + Home or End	Moves insertion point to beginning or end of field in multiple-line field.
Delete	Deletes character to right of insertion point.
Backspace	Deletes character to left of insertion point.
Tab or ⇧Shift + Tab	Ends Edit mode and highlights next or previous field.

Key	Navigation Mode
→ or Tab	Moves highlight to next field.
← or ⇧Shift + Tab	Moves highlight to previous field.
↓	Move highlight to current field in next record.
Home or End	Moves highlight to first or last field in current record.
Delete or Backspace	Deletes highlighted field contents.

To activate Navigation mode, point to the left edge of a field and click when the pointer is a ✥. To activate Edit mode click on the field when the mouse pointer is an I-beam. To switch between modes using the keyboard, press F2.

> If you want to cancel your changes in the current field, press Esc.

Because you are entering data in a new record, Edit mode is automatically active.

- Edit the entry to be 10/14/90.
- Press ←Enter.

> You can also press Tab to move to the next field. → will move to the next field if the insertion point is at the end of the entry or you are in Navigation mode.

> The fields will scroll on the screen as you move to the right.

The corrected date is accepted, and the insertion point moves to the Last Name field. Because no description was entered for this field, the status bar displays the name of the current view, Datasheet View, instead of a field description.

- Enter the data shown below for the remaining fields, typing the information exactly as it appears.

Field Name	Data
Last Name	**Anderson**
First Name	**Susan**
Street	**4389 S. Hayden Rd.**
City	**Mesa**
State	**AZ**
Zip Code	**85205-0346**
Phone Number	**(602) 555-1950**
Birth Date	**6/14/65**

To complete the record,

- Press ←Enter.

Your screen should be similar to Figure 1-10.

first record

second record

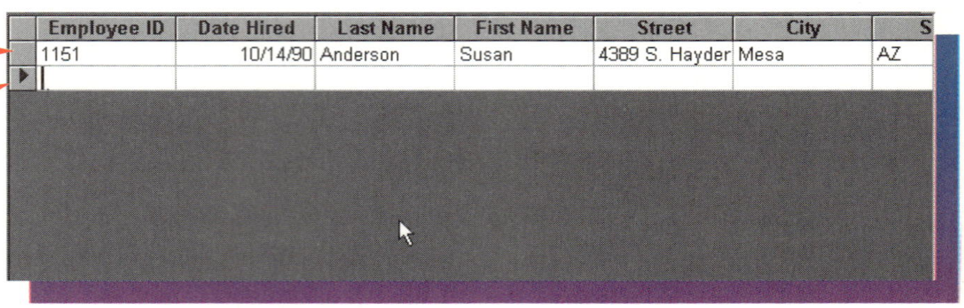

FIGURE 1-10

The data for the first record is complete. The insertion point moves to the first field on the next row and waits for input of the employee number for the next record. As soon as the insertion point moves to another record, the data is saved on the disk and the number of the new record appears in the status bar. The second record was automatically assigned the record number 2.

Next you will check the first record for accuracy.

> You could also press ↑ to move up one record and change to Navigation mode.

- Point to the left end of the Employee ID field for the first record. When the mouse pointer appears as ✚, click the mouse button.

The entire field is selected (highlighted), and you have activated Navigation mode. If you type, the entire selection will be replaced with the new text. To select the Street field to check the field contents,

- Press [→] (4 times).
- Click the Street field with the mouse pointer shape as an I-beam.

The insertion point is positioned in the field, and you have activated the Edit mode. Now you can edit the field contents if necessary. To move the insertion point to the end of the address so that you can check the rest of the entry,

- Press [End].

The text scrolled in the field, and the insertion point is positioned at the end of the entry. However, now you cannot see the beginning of the entry. To expand the field box to view the entire entry in the field,

You can also expand a text box in the same way to make it easier to edit.

- Press [⇧Shift] + [F2].

The entry is fully displayed in a separate zoom window. You can edit in the window just as you would in the field box.

- If the entry contains an error, correct it.
- Click [OK].
- Press [Tab].
- Continue to check the first record for accuracy and edit as needed.

- Enter the following data for the second record.

You can also use the horizontal scroll bar to scroll the window to check fields that are not visible.

Notice that the date format changed automatically to the format set in the date property field.

Field Name	Data
Employee ID	**0434**
Date Hired	**June 4, 1991**
Last Name	**Long**
First Name	**William**
Street	**947 S. Forest St.**
City	**Tempe**
State	**AZ**
Zip Code	**86301-1268**
Phone Number	**(602) 555-4494**
Birth Date	**April 20, 1970**

- Press [↵Enter].
- Check the second record for accuracy and edit it if necessary.

Your screen should be similar to Figure 1-11.

FIGURE 1-11

second record

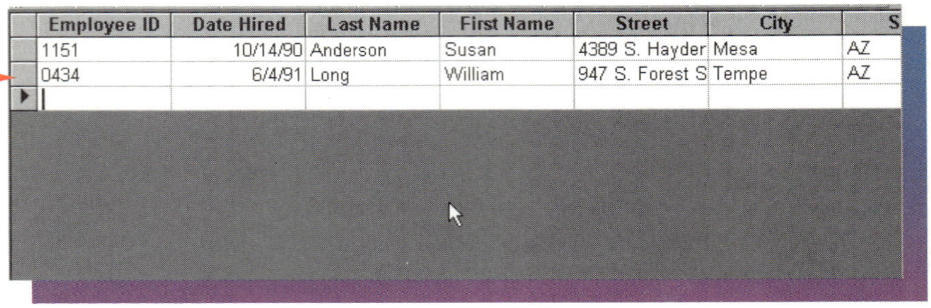

Adjusting Column Widths

As you have noticed, some of the fields (such as the Street field) do not display the entire entry, while other fields (such as the State field) are much larger than the field's column heading or contents. This is because the default column width in Datasheet view is not the same size as the field sizes you specified in Design view.

Concept 9: Column Width

Column width refers to the size of each field column in Datasheet view. The column width does not affect the amount of data you can enter into a field, but does affect the data that you can see on the screen. The default column width in Datasheet view is set to display 15.6667 characters. You can adjust the column width to change the appearance of the datasheet. It is usually best to adjust the column width so the column is slightly larger than the column heading or longest field contents, whichever is longer. Do not confuse column width with field size. Field size is a property associated with each field; it controls the maximum number of characters that you can enter in the field. If you shorten the field size, you can lose data already entered in the field.

To quickly modify the column width, simply drag the right column border line in either direction to increase or decrease the column width when the mouse pointer shape is ↔. As you drag, a column line appears to show you the new column border. When you release the mouse button, the column width will be set. First you will increase the width of the Street field so the entire address will be visible.

- Point to the right border line of the column heading of the Street field name.
- Drag the border to the right until you think it will be large enough to display the field contents.
- Adjust it again if it is too wide or not wide enough.

You can also adjust the column width to a specific number of characters using Format/Column Width.

Your screen should be similar to Figure 1-12.

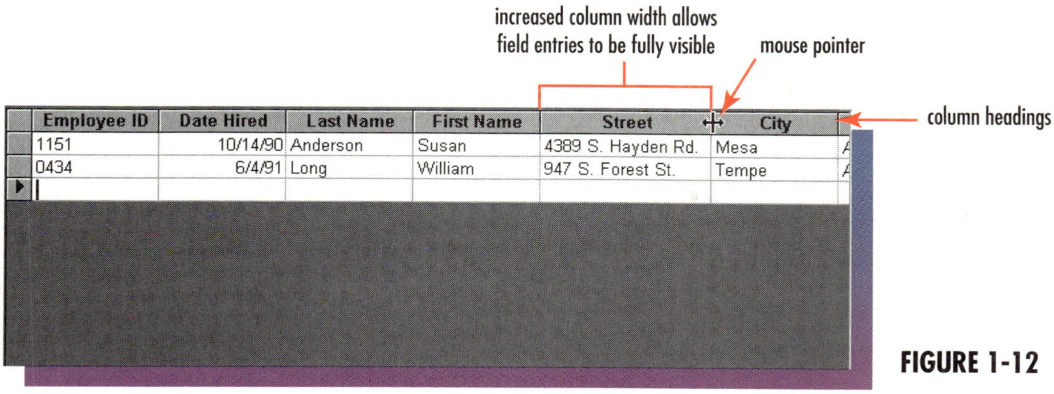

FIGURE 1-12

Rather than change the widths of all the other columns individually, you can select all columns and change their widths at the same time. To select multiple columns, point to the column heading in the field selector area of the first or last column you want to select. Then, when the mouse pointer changes to ⬇, click and without releasing the mouse button drag in either direction across the column headings.

> To clear a selection, click anywhere in the table.

> The fields will scroll horizontally in the window as you drag to select the columns.

- Point to the Employee ID field name.
- When the mouse pointer is ⬇, drag to the right across all column headings.
- Use the horizontal scroll bar to bring the first field column back into view in the window.

Your screen should be similar to Figure 1-13.

> The keyboard equivalent for selecting columns is to select a field entry in the first column, press Ctrl + Spacebar, then press ⇧Shift + the appropriate arrow key to select multiple columns.

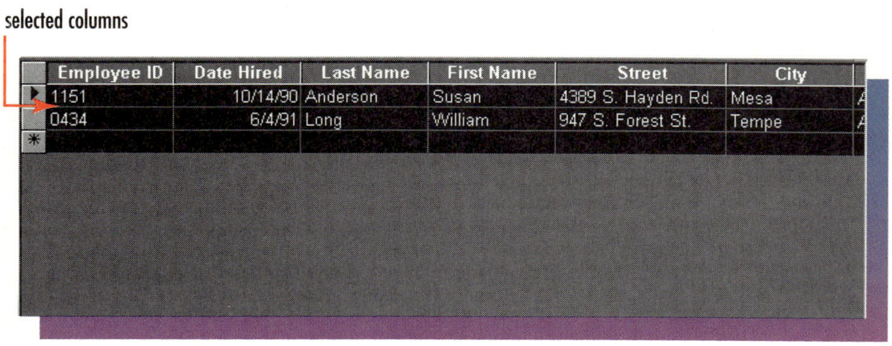

FIGURE 1-13

Multiple columns are highlighted. Now, if you were to drag the column border of any selected column, all the selected columns would change to the same size. However, you want the column widths to be adjusted appropriately to fit the data in each column. To do this you can double-click the column border to activate the Best Fit feature. The **Best Fit** feature automatically adjusts the column widths

> The menu equivalent is Format/Column Width/Best Fit. The Column Width command is also on the shortcut menu when an entire column is selected.

Clicking the box to the left of the first field name will select the entire table; however, you cannot use Best Fit when the entire table is selected in this manner.

of all selected columns to accommodate the longest entry or column heading in each of the selected columns.

- Double-click any selected column border with the mouse pointer as ↔.

Your screen should be similar to Figure 1-14.

column widths adjusted using Best Fit

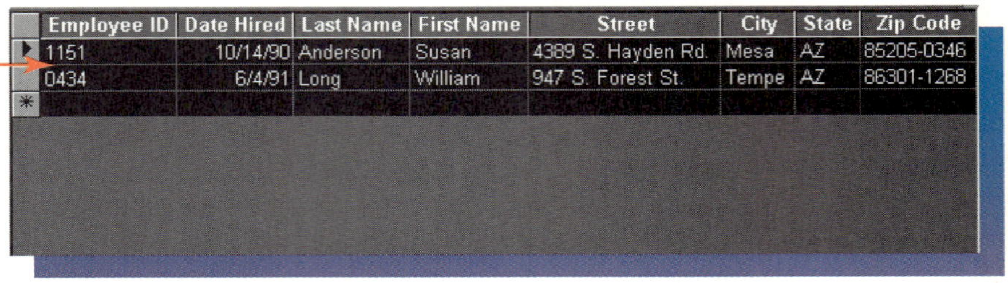

FIGURE 1-14

- Now that you can see the complete contents of each field, check each of the records again and edit any entries that are incorrect.
- Add the following record to the table as record 3.

Field	Date
Employee ID	**0434**
Date Hired	**April 12, 1991**
Last Name	**Bergstrom**
First Name	**Drew**
Street	**8943 W. Southern Ave.**
City	**Mesa**
State	**AZ**
Zip Code	**84101-8475**
Phone Number	**(602) 555-8201**
Birth Date	**August 7, 1961**

- Press ←Enter.

As soon as you complete the record, an error message dialog box appears indicating that Access has located a duplicate value in a key field. The key field is Employee ID. You realize you were looking at the employee number from the previous record when you entered the employee number for this record. To clear the message and enter the correct number,

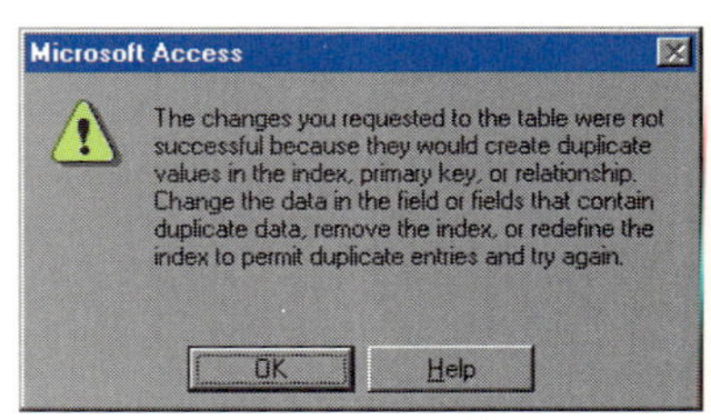

- Click [OK].
- Change the Employee ID for record 3 to 0234.
- Press ↓.

The record is accepted with the new employee number. Notice that the address for this record does not fully display in the Street field. It has a longer address than either of the other two records.

- To fully display the Street field data, best fit the field again.

Double-click the right border of a field to best fit a single column.

When you add new records in Datasheet view, the records are displayed in the order you enter them. However, they are stored on disk in order by the primary key field. You can change the display on the screen to reflect the correct order by using the ⇧Shift + F9 key combination.

- Press ⇧Shift + F9.

Your screen should be similar to Figure 1-15.

FIGURE 1-15

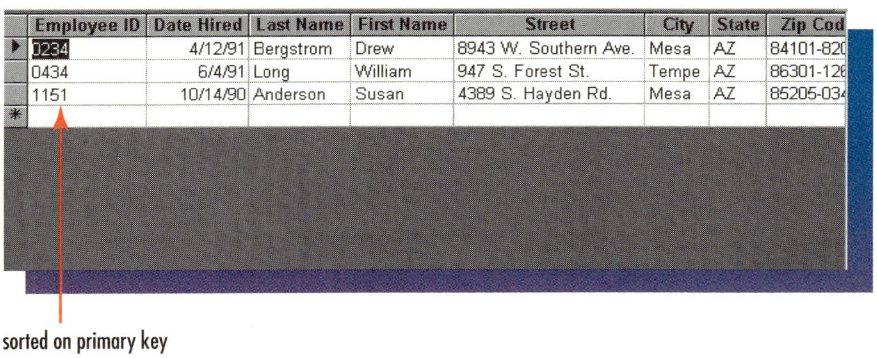

The records are now in order by employee number. This is the order determined by the primary key field.

The table order is also updated when you close and then reopen the table.

Adding Records in Data Entry

Next you want to add several more employee records to the table. Another way to add records is to use the Data Entry command on the Records menu. This command does not display existing records, which prevents accidental changes to the table data.

- Choose Records/Data Entry.

Your screen should be similar to Figure 1-16.

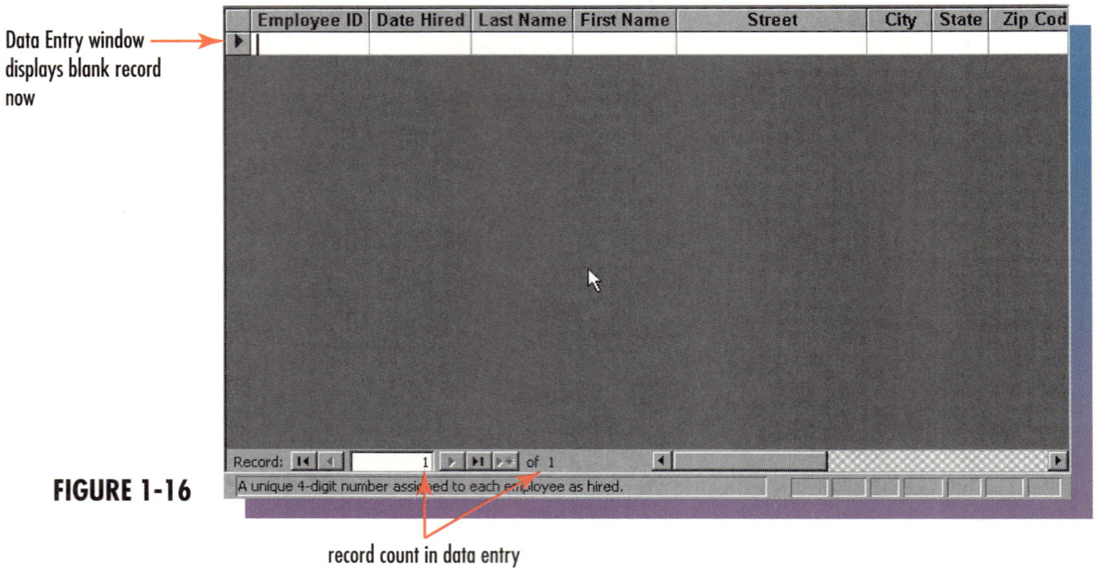

FIGURE 1-16

The existing records are hidden and the only row displayed is a blank row where you can enter a new record. The status bar displays "1 of 1." This number reflects the number of new records as they are added in Data Entry rather than all records in the table.

- Enter the data for the two records shown below.

Field	Record 1	Record 2
Employee ID	**0839**	**0728**
Date Hired	**August 14, 1991**	**July 15, 1991**
Last Name	**Artis**	**Toroyan**
First Name	**Jose**	**Lucy**
Street	**358 Maple Dr.**	**2348 S. Bala Dr.**
City	**Scottsdale**	**Tempe**
State	**AZ**	**AZ**
Zip Code	**85205-6911**	**85301-7985**
Phone Number	**(602) 555-0091**	**(602) 555-9870**
Birth Date	**December 10, 1963**	**March 15, 1961**

- Enter a final record using your first and last name. Enter 9999 as your employee number and the current date as your date hired. The information you enter in all other fields can be fictitious.

- Best fit the City column and any other columns that do not fully display the field contents.
- Check each of the records and correct any entry errors.

Now that you have entered the new records, you can redisplay all the records in the table. To do this,

- Choose Records/Remove Filter/Sort.

Your screen should be similar to Figure 1-17.

records in sorted order by employee ID

Employee ID	Date Hired	Last Name	First Name	Street	City	State	Zip
0234	4/12/91	Bergstrom	Drew	8943 W. Southern Ave.	Mesa	AZ	84101
0434	6/4/91	Long	William	947 S. Forest St.	Tempe	AZ	86301
0728	7/15/91	Toroyan	Lucy	2348 S. Bala Dr.	Tempe	AZ	85301
0839	8/14/91	Artis	Jose	358 Maple Dr.	Scottsdale	AZ	85205
1151	10/14/90	Anderson	Susan	4389 S. Hayden Rd.	Mesa	AZ	85205
9999	10/5/98	Student	Name	89 Any Street	Mesa	AZ	85202
*							

FIGURE 1-17

The new records are added to the table in order by employee number. If you had added these records in Datasheet view, they would not appear in primary key field order until you updated the table display. This is another advantage of using Data Entry.

Previewing and Printing the Table

If you have printer capability, you can print a copy of the records in this table. Before printing the table, you will preview how it will look when printed using the Print Preview view. Previewing the document displays each page of your document in a reduced size so you can see the layout. Then, if necessary, you can make changes to the layout before printing, to both save time and avoid wasting paper.

To preview the Employee table,

- Click Print Preview.

The menu equivalent is File/Print Preview.

Your screen should be similar to Figure 1-18.

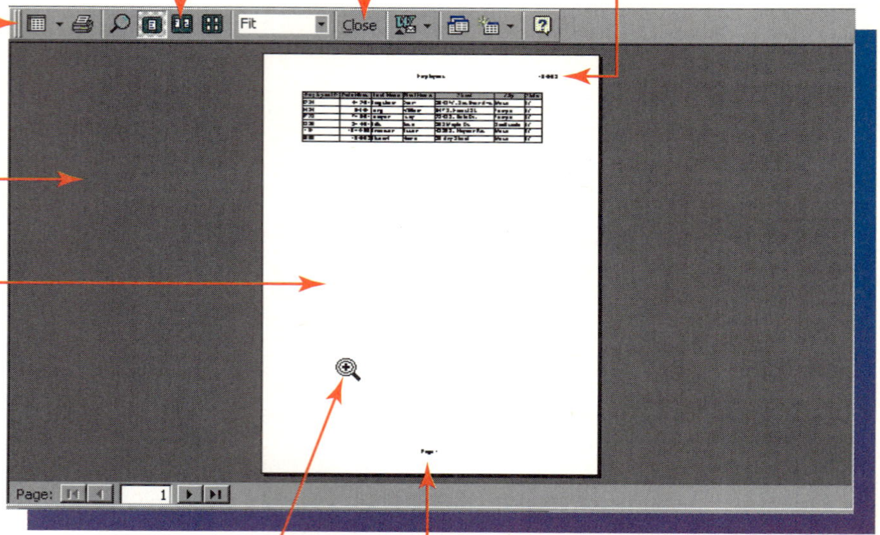

FIGURE 1-18

The Print Preview window displays a reduced view of how the table will appear when printed. The window also includes its own toolbar.

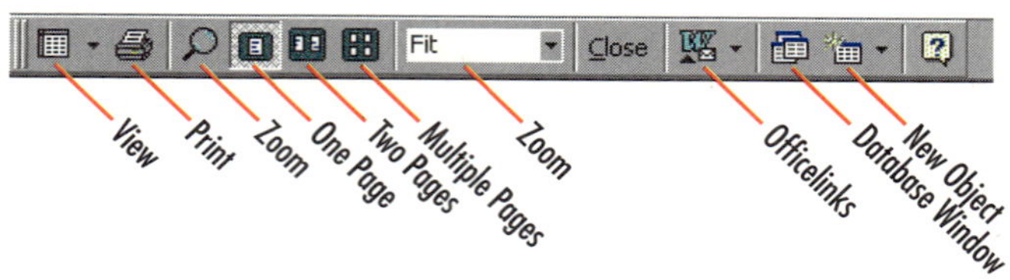

The document will be printed using the default report and page layout settings, which include such items as 1-inch margins, the table name and date displayed in a header, and the page number in a footer. Notice, however, that because the table is too wide to fit across the width of a page, only the first seven fields are displayed on the page. The rest of the table will be printed on a second page. To see both pages,

- Click Two Pages.

The last three field columns are displayed on the second page. You would like to print the table on a single page. One way to do this is to change the page orientation. **Orientation** refers to the direction text prints on a page. Normal orientation is to print across the width of an 8 1/2-inch page. This is called **portrait** orientation. You can change the orientation to print across the length of the paper. This is called **landscape** orientation. Using landscape orientation lets more information appear on the page because you are printing across the 11-inch length of the paper. To change the orientation to landscape,

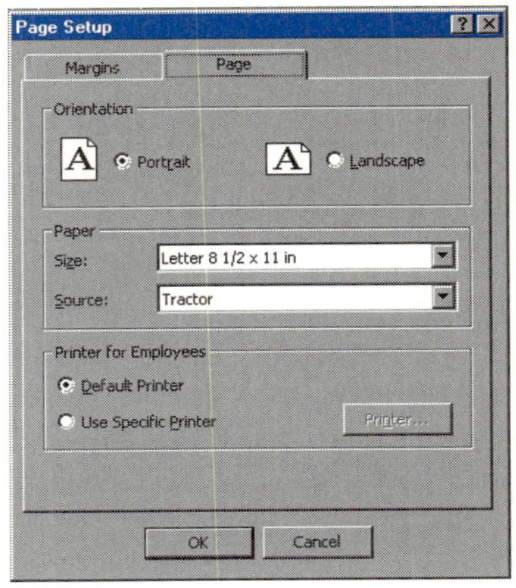

- Choose File/Page Setup.
- If necessary, open the Page tab.
- Select Landscape.
- Click OK.

Your screen should be similar to Figure 1-19.

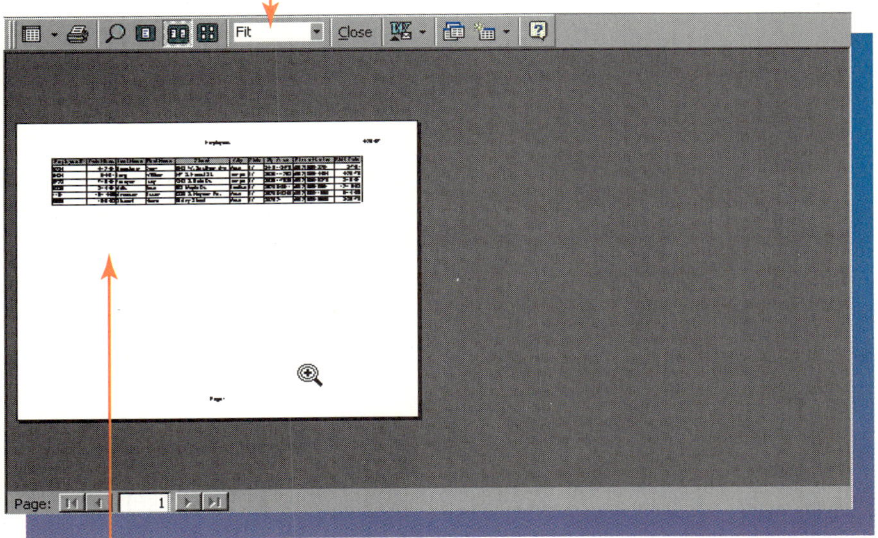

FIGURE 1-19

Using landscape orientation, the entire table easily fits across the length of the page. To better see the information in the table, you can change the magnification level of the Preview window. The current magnification level is Fit as displayed in the Fit button in the toolbar. This setting adjusts the magnification of the page to best fit in the size of the window. Notice that the mouse pointer is a magnifying glass when it is positioned on the page. This indicates that you can click on the page to switch between the Fit magnification level and the last used level.

- Click on the center of the table.

Use the Fit Zoom button on the Print Preview toolbar to select a magnification percentage or type.

Clicking the Zoom button in the toolbar will also toggle between the magnification levels.

Your screen should be similar to Figure 1-20.

current magnification percent displayed in Zoom button

FIGURE 1-20

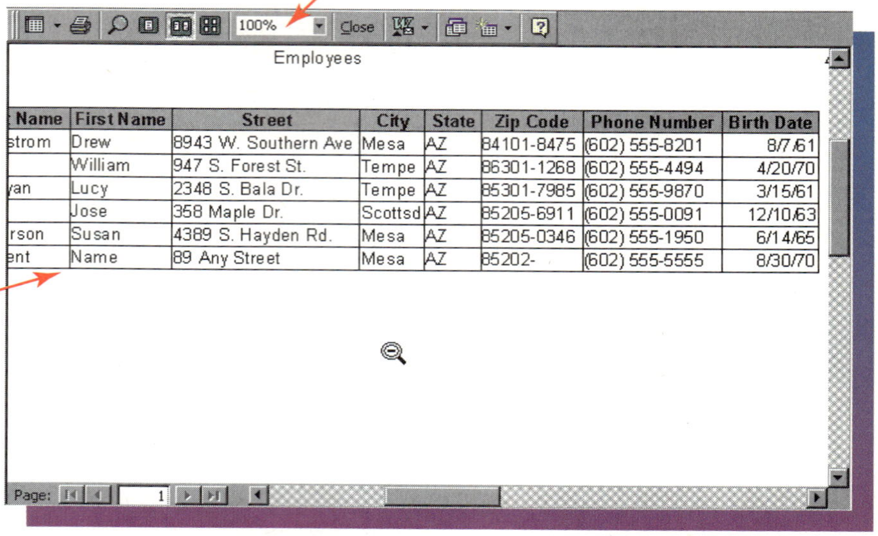

table displayed in 100% magnification

Because Access remembers the last zoom percentage, your zoom percentage may be different. Use the Zoom button to change your percentage to 100%.

The table appears in 100% magnification. This is the size it will appear when printed.

- Click on the table again to return to the Fit magnification level.

Now you are ready to print the table. The Print button on the toolbar will immediately start printing the report using the default print settings. To check the print settings first, you need to use the Print command on the File menu.

The keyboard shortcut for the Print command is Ctrl + P.

- If necessary, make sure your printer is on and ready to print.
- Choose File/Print.

Note: Please consult your instructor for printing procedures that may differ from the directions below.

The Print dialog box on your screen should be similar to Figure 1-21.

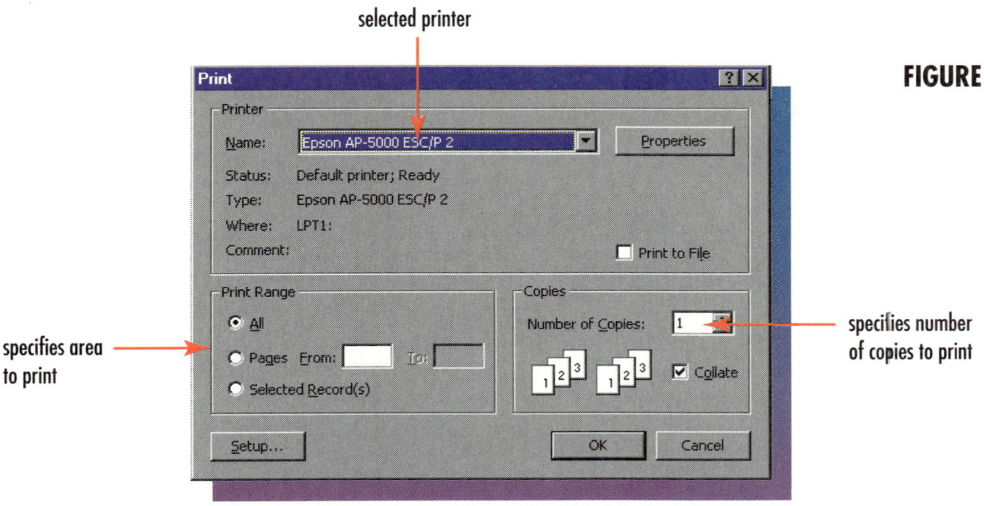

FIGURE 1-21

From this dialog box you need to specify the printer you will be using and the print settings. The Print Range options are used to specify how much of the document you want printed. The Copies area of the dialog box is used to specify the number of copies you want printed. The default settings to print one copy of the entire document are appropriate.

- If you need to change the selected printer to another printer, open the Name drop-down list box and select the appropriate printer (your instructor will tell you which printer to select).
- Click OK.

The printed copy should be the same as displayed in the Print Preview window. To close the Print Preview window and return to the Datasheet view,

- Click Close.

The menu equivalent is View/Datasheet View.

Closing and Opening a Database

To close the table,

- Click ☒ Close (in the Table window).

The menu equivalent is File/Close or Ctrl + W.

Because you changed the column widths of the table in Datasheet view, you are prompted to save the layout changes you made before the table is closed. If you do not save the table, your column width settings will be lost.

- Click Yes.

The Database window is displayed again. The name of the table you created appears in the Table object list. Now the Open and Design command buttons can be used to modify the selected table in the list box. To close the database file,

- Click Close (on the menu bar).

The menu equivalent is **F**ile/**O**pen Database, and the keyboard shortcut is Ctrl + O.

Then to open and redisplay the table of employee records,

- Click Open Database.
- If necessary, display the Look-in drop-down list and select the location of your data disk.

Selecting Open an Existing Database from the startup dialog box will also display the Open dialog box.

The Open dialog box on your screen should be similar to Figure 1-22.

database file name

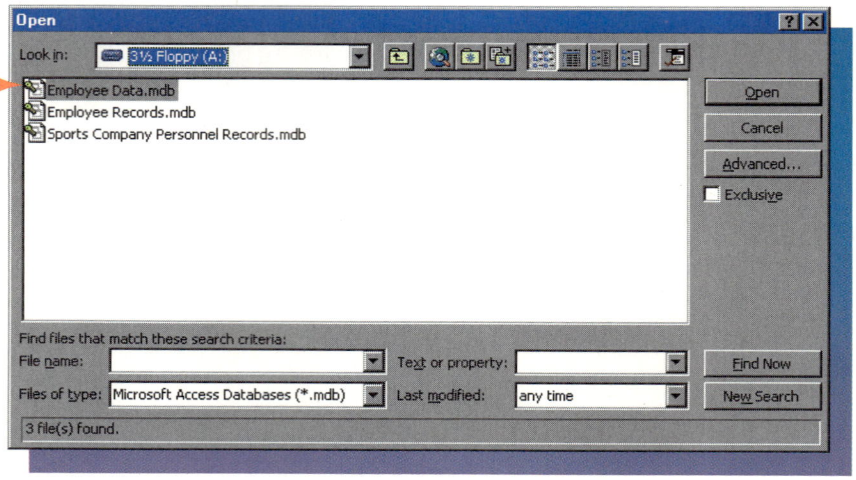

FIGURE 1-22

Now the name of the database file you just created, as well as others you will use in the labs, is displayed in the list box.

You can also double-click the file name to open the database.

- Select Employee Data.
- Click Open.

Then, to open the table of employee records,

- Click Open.

The table of employee records is displayed in Datasheet view again, just as it was before you saved and closed the table.

- Close the table again.

Notice that this time you were not prompted to save the table because you did not make any changes.

Exiting Access

You will continue to build and use the table of employee records in the next lab. To exit Access and return to the Windows 95 desktop,

Click [X] Close (in the Access window title bar).

The menu equivalent is File/Exit, and the keyboard shortcut is Alt + F4.

WARNING!

Do not remove your data disk from the drive until you close the Access application window.

LAB REVIEW

Key Terms

Best Fit (DB29)
column width (DB28)
current record (DB22)
data type (DB16)
database (DB7)
docked (DB9)
Edit mode (DB25)
field (DB14)
field name (DB14)
field property (DB17)
field selector (DB22)
field size (DB17)
floating (DB9)
landscape (DB34)
move handle (DB8)
navigation buttons (DB23)
Navigation mode (DB25)
object (DB11)
object tab (DB11)
Office Assistant (DB12)
orientation (DB34)
portrait (DB34)
primary key (DB18)
record (DB7)
record number indicator (DB23)
record selector (DB22)
table (DB7)
view (DB21)
workspace (DB9)

Command Summary

Command	Shortcut	Toolbar	Action
File/Open Database	Ctrl + O		Opens an existing database
File/New Database	Ctrl + N		Creates a new database
File/Close	Ctrl + W		Closes open window
File/Save	Ctrl + S		Saves table
File/Page Setup/Landscape			Changes page orientation to landscape
File/Print Preview			Displays file as it will appear when printed
File/Print	Ctrl + P		Prints contents of file
File/Exit	Alt + F4		Closes Access and returns to Windows 95 desktop
Edit/Delete Rows			Deletes selected field in Design view
Edit/Primary Key			Defines a field as a primary key field
View/Datasheet			Displays table in Datasheet view
Format/Column Width			Changes width of table columns in Datasheet view
Format/Column Width/Best Fit			Sizes selected columns to accommodate longest entry or column header
Records/Remove Filter/Sort			Displays all records in table
Records/Data Entry			Hides existing records and displays Data Entry window mode

Matching

1. Best Fit	________	**a.**	attributes of a field that affect its appearance or behavior
2. database	________	**b.**	controls the type of data a field can contain
3. field property	________	**c.**	an organized collection of related information
4. primary key	________	**d.**	used to define the table structure
5. record	________	**e.**	feature used to adjust column width to largest entry
6. field size	________	**f.**	collection of related fields
7. field	________	**g.**	field used to order records
8. Design view	________	**h.**	displays table in row and column format
9. Datasheet view	________	**i.**	specific item of information contained in a record
10. data type	________	**j.**	controls the maximum number of characters that can be entered in a field

Fill-In Questions

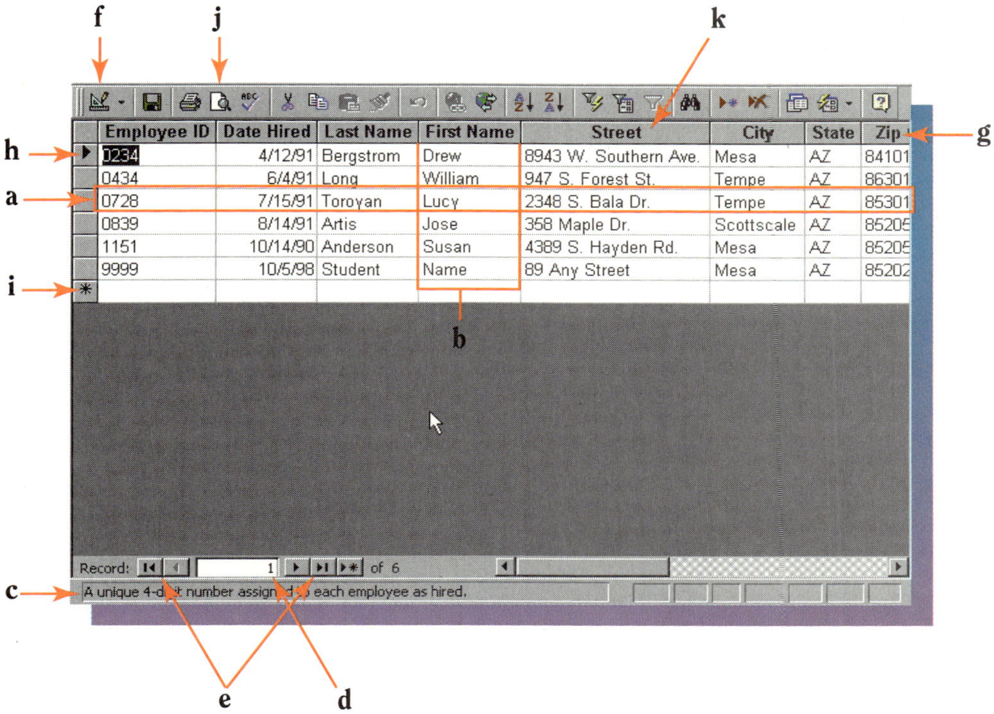

1. Identify the parts of the Access screen by entering the correct term for each item.

a. ______________________ **g.** ______________________

b. ______________________ **h.** ______________________

c. ______________________ **i.** ______________________

d. ______________________ **j.** ______________________

e. ______________________ **k.** ______________________

f. ______________________

2. Complete the following statements by filling in the blanks with the correct terms.

a. A(n) ____________________ is a collection of organized information. The information is stored in ______________.

b. Relational databases define __________________ between tables by having common data in the tables.

c. The first step in developing a database is ______________________.

d. The ____________________ defines the type of data that can be entered in a field.

e. A(n) ___________________________ is an item made up of different elements.

f. The set of characteristics associated with a field are the ________________.

g. A descriptive label called a(n) __________________ is used to identify the data stored in a field.

h. The ____________________ data type is used to format numbers with dollar signs and decimal places.

i. A(n) ____________________ is a field that uniquely identifies each record in a table.

j. ______________________ view allows the user to enter, edit, and delete records in a table.

Discussion Questions

1. Discuss several uses you may have for a relational database. Then explain the steps you would follow to create the first table.

2. Discuss why it is important to plan a database before creating it. How can proper planning save you time later?

3. Discuss the difference between Edit mode and Navigation mode.

4. Design view and Datasheet view are two of the Access views. Discuss when it would be appropriate to use each of these views.

5. Discuss why it is important to choose the correct data type for a field. What may happen to the data if you change the data type?

Hands-On Practice Exercises

Step by Step

Rating System

☆ Easy
☆☆ Moderate
☆☆☆ Difficult

☆

1. There are many ways to customize the tables you create using Access. In this exercise you will use the Office Assistant to search for information on the ways you can customize Access tables.

a. Open the Access Office Assistant.

b. Request Help information on customizing tables.

c. Based on the Help information you find, list four ways you can customize a table in Design view.

☆☆

2. Debbie started a commercial cleaning business while she was in college. Her business has now grown to a full-service company with four other employees, and she wants to computerize her business records. Debbie wants to start by transferring her client records to Access.

a. Help Debbie create a database named Cleaning Service Records. Design a table using the field information defined below.

Field Data	Type	Field Size	Description
Client #	Text	5	5-digit unique number
Company	Text	50	
Contact	Text	50	First & Last Name of contact person
Address	Text	50	
City	Text	50	
State	Text	2	2-letter abbreviation entered in all capital letters
Zip Code	Text	10	Include the 4-digit extension number if possible
Phone	Text	15	Include the area code in parentheses: (999) 123-4567
Cleaning Day	Text	3	3-letter day code: MON, TUE, WED, THU, FRI, SAT, or SUN
Square Ft	Number		
Rate	Currency		

b. Make the Client # field the primary key field.

c. Change the City field size to 25 and the Contact field size to 40.

d. Save the table as Clients.

e. Enter the following records into the table:

Record 1
95037
St. John & Associates Law Offices
Kelley St. John
13271 N. Central Ave.
Phoenix
AZ
84137-7214
(602) 555-7991
FRI
5000
$150

Record 2
94103
The Sports Company
[your name]
8915 E. Hayden Rd.
Scottsdale
AZ
85254-8211
(602) 555-1294
WED
20000
$500

Record 3

96052
TechnoBabble Electronics
Eddie Fitzpatrick
9860 E. Chandler Blvd.
Chandler
AZ
85601-3144
(602) 555-9876
MON
10000
$250

Record 4

95836
Home Office Supply Co.
Paul Miller
1892 S. Olive Dr.
Phoenix
AZ
89472-8141
(602) 555-1781
TUE
15875
$410

f. Adjust the column widths appropriately.

g. Display the records in primary key order.

h. Preview the table. Change the orientation to landscape. Print, save, and close the table.

☆☆

3. Michael is the human resources manager for a small working dude ranch resort in Colorado. One of Michael's responsibilities is to maintain employee records. To help him keep track of the employee information, Michael wants to create an Access database.

a. Create a database named Resort Records. Design a table using the field definitions shown below.

Field Name	Data Type	Field Size	Description
Social Security #	Text	11	include hyphens
Last Name	Text	50	
First Name	Text	50	
Middle Initial	Text	1	1 character only
Address	Text	50	Complete street address
City		15	
State		2	
Zip Code		10	complete zip code
Date Hired	Date	Short Date	
Department	Text	50	

b. Make the Social Security # the primary key field.

c. Change the two Name fields sizes to 20, the Address to 30, and Department to 15.

d. Save the table as Staff Records.

e. Enter the following records into the table:

Record 1

015-11-4141
[your last name]
[your first name]
W
34 Maple Dr.
Durango, CO 81301-1131
[current date]
Administration

Record 2

131-31-4199
Johnson
Samantha
T
984 Mountainside Way
Cortez, CO 81205-7100
5/31/95
Housekeeping

Record 3

216-11-2141
Wesley
William
P
9742 S. Gifford Lane
Durango, CO 81301-4141
October 12, 1994
Administration

Record 4

139-99-9891
Feldman
Annie
K
8217 E. Country Rd.
Cortez, CO 81205-7100
2/7/96
Reservations

f. Adjust the column widths appropriately.

g. Display the records in primary key order.

h. Preview and print the table using landscape orientation. Save and close the table.

On Your Own

☆☆

4. James works at a small office supply store. He needs to create a database to keep track of the store inventory.

Help James create a database named Office Supplies to track item numbers (5-digit unique numbers), item names, quantity on hand, and item cost. The database table, named Inventory, should have a primary key. Enter five sample inventory items into the database. Enter your name in the sixth record item name field. Print the table with the records in primary key order using the appropriate orientation.

☆☆

5. Michelle owns a small catering business servicing business clients. She has a list of regular clients, and wants to use her computer and Microsoft Access to maintain her client records.

Help Michelle create a database named Catering Business to keep track of her clients. The table, named Customers, should include each customer's identification number, company name, contact person, address, phone number, preferred theme, and favorite dish. Include a primary key field and appropriately size the fields. Enter five records in the table using fictitious data. The last record should include your name. Print the table in primary key order using the appropriate orientation.

☆☆☆

6. Create a new database named Lab1PE6 using the Blank Database template. Use the Table Wizard to help you create a table by selecting one of the table samples of your choice from the Personal category. Follow the directions in each step of the Table Wizard and make appropriate selections to create your table. Modify the table design to suit your needs. Add five records to the table. Adjust column widths as needed. Preview, then print your table using the appropriate orientation.

Concept Summary

Creating a Database

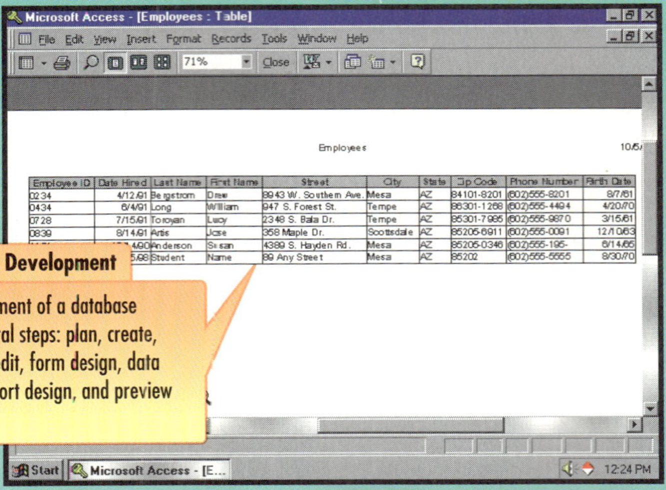

Database Development

The development of a database follows several steps: plan, create, enter data, edit, form design, data analysis, report design, and preview and print.

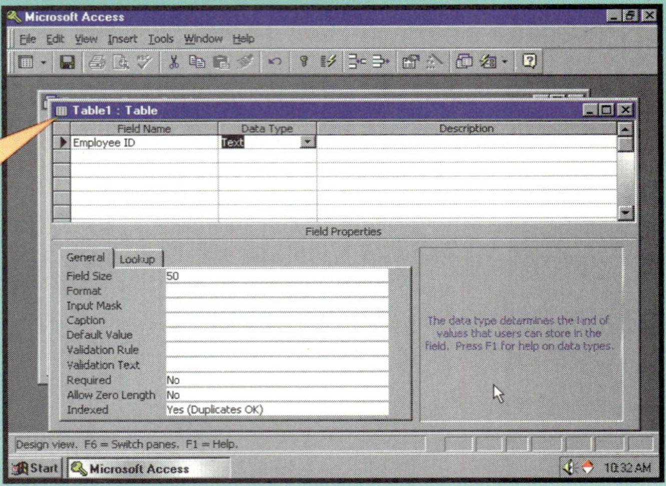

Objects

A database file is made up of many different types of objects, such as tables, forms, and reports.

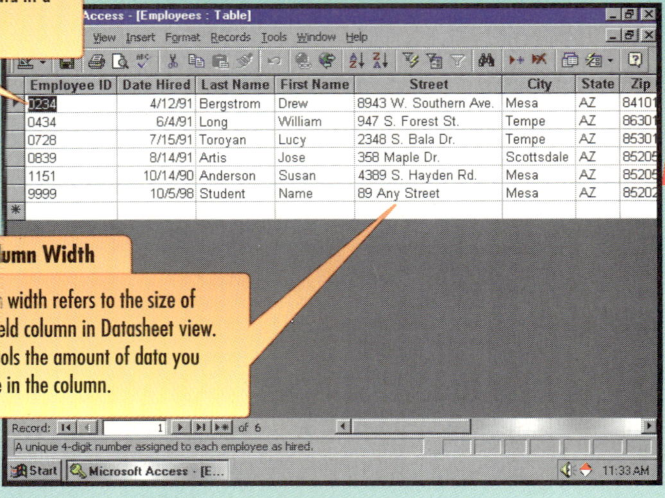

Edit and Navigation Modes

The Edit and Navigation modes control how you can move through and make changes to the data in a table.

Column Width

Column width refers to the size of each field column in Datasheet view. It controls the amount of data you can see in the column.

Concepts

- Database Development
- Objects
- Fields
  Data Types
  Field Properties
  Primary Key
- Views
- Edit and Navigation Modes
  Column Width

Primary Key

A primary key is a field that uniquely identifies each record.

Fields

A field, the smallest unit of information about a record, is identified by a field name.

Data Types

The data type defines the type of data the field will contain.

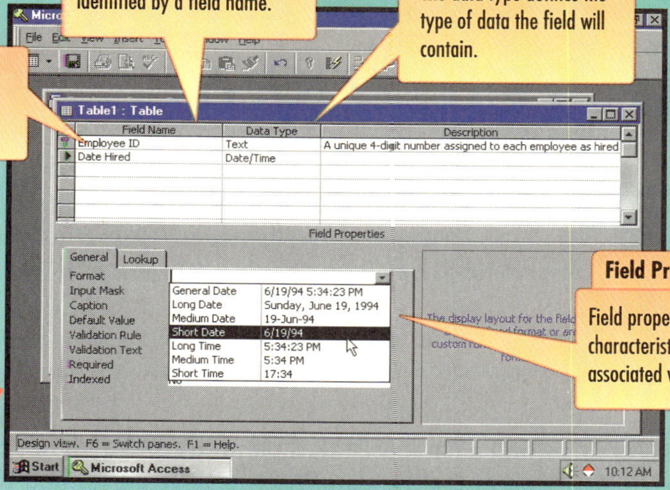

Field Properties

Field properties are a set of characteristics that are associated with each field.

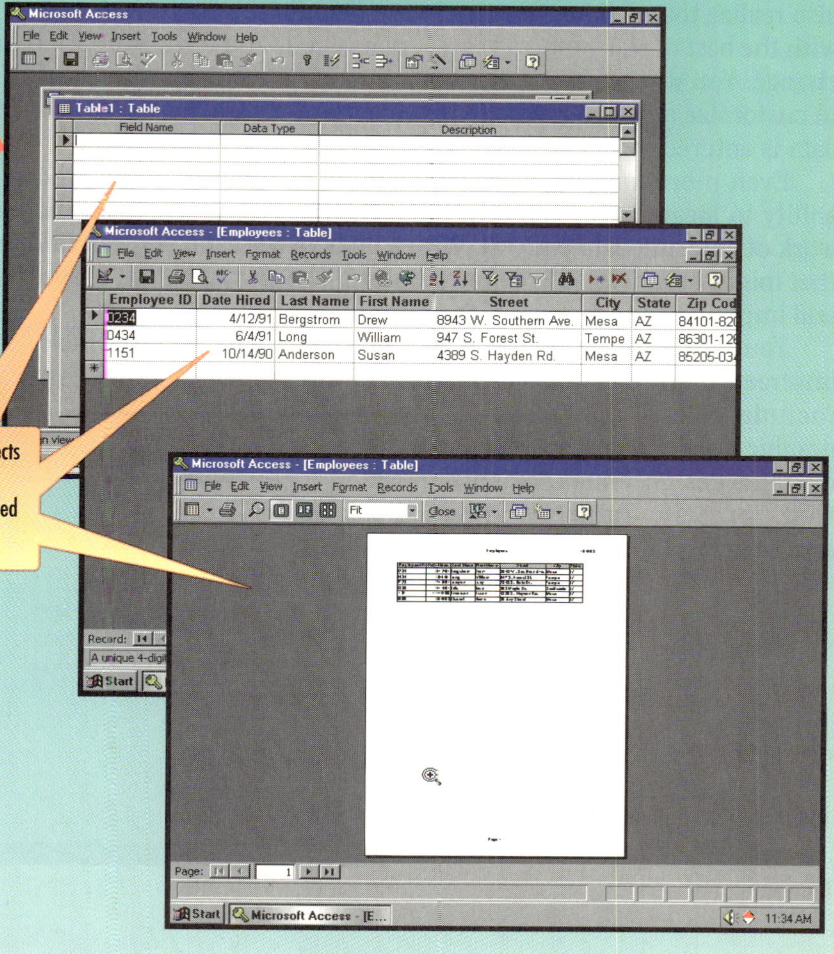

Views

Access allows you to view objects in your database in several different window formats, called views.

The Database window for the Employee Records file is displayed. To open the table with the additional employee records, Sports Company Employees,

- Click Open.
- Maximize the Datasheet window.

Your screen should be similar to Figure 2-1.

FIGURE 2-1

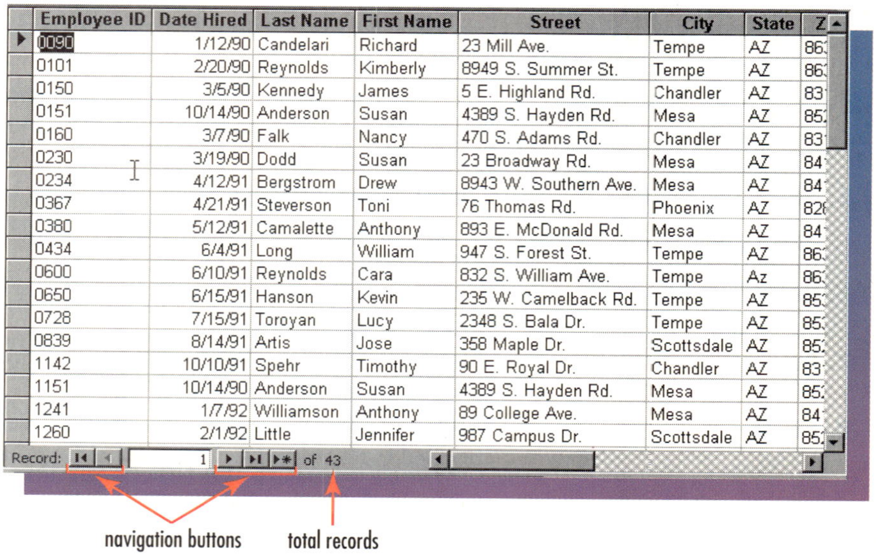

Employee ID	Date Hired	Last Name	First Name	Street	City	State	Z
0090	1/12/90	Candelari	Richard	23 Mill Ave.	Tempe	AZ	86
0101	2/20/90	Reynolds	Kimberly	8949 S. Summer St.	Tempe	AZ	86
0150	3/5/90	Kennedy	James	5 E. Highland Rd.	Chandler	AZ	83
0151	10/14/90	Anderson	Susan	4389 S. Hayden Rd.	Mesa	AZ	85
0160	3/7/90	Falk	Nancy	470 S. Adams Rd.	Chandler	AZ	83
0230	3/19/90	Dodd	Susan	23 Broadway Rd.	Mesa	AZ	84
0234	4/12/91	Bergstrom	Drew	8943 W. Southern Ave.	Mesa	AZ	84
0367	4/21/91	Steverson	Toni	76 Thomas Rd.	Phoenix	AZ	82
0380	5/12/91	Camalette	Anthony	893 E. McDonald Rd.	Mesa	AZ	84
0434	6/4/91	Long	William	947 S. Forest St.	Tempe	AZ	86
0600	6/10/91	Reynolds	Cara	832 S. William Ave.	Tempe	Az	86
0650	6/15/91	Hanson	Kevin	235 W. Camelback Rd.	Tempe	AZ	85
0728	7/15/91	Toroyan	Lucy	2348 S. Bala Dr.	Tempe	AZ	85
0839	8/14/91	Artis	Jose	358 Maple Dr.	Scottsdale	AZ	85
1142	10/10/91	Spehr	Timothy	90 E. Royal Dr.	Chandler	AZ	83
1151	10/14/90	Anderson	Susan	4389 S. Hayden Rd.	Mesa	AZ	85
1241	1/7/92	Williamson	Anthony	89 College Ave.	Mesa	AZ	84
1260	2/1/92	Little	Jennifer	987 Campus Dr.	Scottsdale	AZ	85

Record: 1 of 43

By default, the Datasheet view of the Table window is displayed. As you can see from the record number indicator, there are now 43 records in the table.

In a large table, there are many methods you can use to quickly navigate, or move, through records in Datasheet view. You can always use the mouse to move from one field or record to another. However, if the information is not visible in the window, you must scroll the window first. The table below presents several keyboard methods that make moving around a table faster in Navigation mode.

Keys	Effect
Page Down	Down one page
Page Up	Up one page
Ctrl + Page Up	Left one window
Ctrl + Page Down	Right one window
End	Last field in record
Home	First field in record
Ctrl + End	Last field of last record
Ctrl + Home	First field of first record
Ctrl + ↑	Current field of first record
Ctrl + ↓	Current field of last record

The Navigation buttons in the status bar also provide navigation shortcuts. These buttons also move in Navigation mode and are described below.

Button	Effect
	First record, same field
	Previous record, same field
	Next record, same field
	Last record, same field
	New (blank) record

You can also type the record number you want to move to in the record indicator box of the status bar.

Currently, records 1 through 18 are displayed in the window. To see the next full window of records,

- Press Page Down.

Your window may display more records, depending on your monitor settings.

Now records 19 through 36 are displayed in the window. The first record in the window is now the current record.

Due to the number and width of the fields, not all fields can be displayed in the window at the same time. Rather than scrolling the window horizontally to see the additional fields, you can quickly move to the right a window at a time.

- Press Ctrl+Page Down.

Your screen should be similar to Figure 2-2.

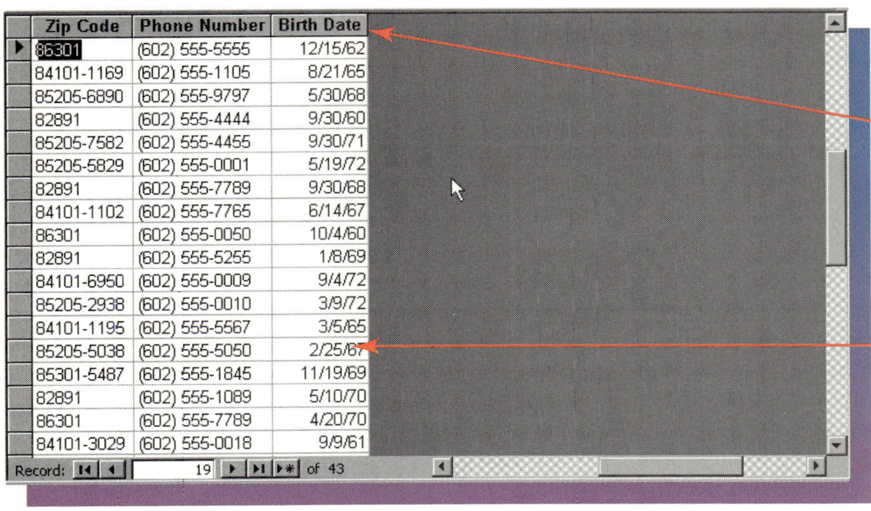

Zip Code	Phone Number	Birth Date
86301	(602) 555-5555	12/15/62
84101-1169	(602) 555-1105	8/21/65
85205-6890	(602) 555-9797	5/30/68
82891	(602) 555-4444	9/30/60
85205-7582	(602) 555-4455	9/30/71
85205-5829	(602) 555-0001	5/19/72
82891	(602) 555-7789	9/30/68
84101-1102	(602) 555-7765	6/14/67
86301	(602) 555-0050	10/4/60
82891	(602) 555-5255	1/8/69
84101-6950	(602) 555-0009	9/4/72
85205-2938	(602) 555-0010	3/9/72
84101-1195	(602) 555-5567	3/5/65
85205-5038	(602) 555-5050	2/25/67
85301-5487	(602) 555-1845	11/19/69
82891	(602) 555-1089	5/10/70
86301	(602) 555-7789	4/20/70
84101-3029	(602) 555-0018	9/9/61

FIGURE 2-2

one window right displays last 3 fields

one window down displays records 19 through 36

The contents of the first field in the window to the right are selected. To quickly move to the same field of the last record and then back to the first field of the first record,

- Click .
- Press Ctrl+Home.

Changing Field Properties

As you viewed the records in the database, you may have noticed that records 11, 22, and 25 have mixed-case entries in the State field. You would like all the state field entries to be in all uppercase letters. Also, rather than having to enter the same state for each record, you want the field to display the state AZ automatically. This will make data entry faster because all the stores are located in Arizona and it is unlikely that the employees will live in another state.

In Lab 1 you set the field properties of several fields. For example, you set the Employee ID field size to 4 so that a larger number could not be entered into the field. In addition, you set the format of the Date Hired field to display a date using the Short Date style. You can also set a field's property to automatically change the entry to uppercase characters. To change the properties of a field, you use Design view.

- Click Design View.
- Make the State field the current field.

The properties associated with the State field are displayed in the General tab. The Format property is used to customize the way an entry is displayed.

Concept 1: Format Property

You can use the Format property to create custom formats that change the way numbers, dates, times, and text display and print. Format properties do not change the way Access stores data, only how the data is displayed.

To change the format of a field, different symbols are entered in the Format text box. Text and Memo Data Types can use any of these four symbols:

Symbol	Description	Example
@	A required text character or space.	@@@-@@-@@@@ would display 123456789 as 123-45-6789. Nine characters or spaces are required.
>	Forces all characters to uppercase.	> would display SMITH whether you entered SMITH, smith, or Smith.
<	Forces all characters to lowercase.	< would display smith whether you entered SMITH, smith, or Smith.
&	An optional text character.	@@-@@& would display 12345 as 12-345 and 12.34 as 12-34. Four out of five characters are required and a fifth is optional.

To enter the symbol to change all entries in the field to uppercase,

- Move to the Format field property text box.
- Type >

Next you want to change the State field property to automatically display the default value of AZ.

Concept 2: Default Value Property

The Default Value property is used to specify a value that is automatically entered in a field when a new record is created. This property is commonly used when most of the entries in a field will be the same for the entire table. That default value is then displayed automatically in the field. When users add a record to the table, they can either accept this value or enter another value. This saves time while entering data.

- Move to the Default Value field property text box.
- Type **AZ**
- Press ←Enter.

Your screen should be similar to Figure 2-3.

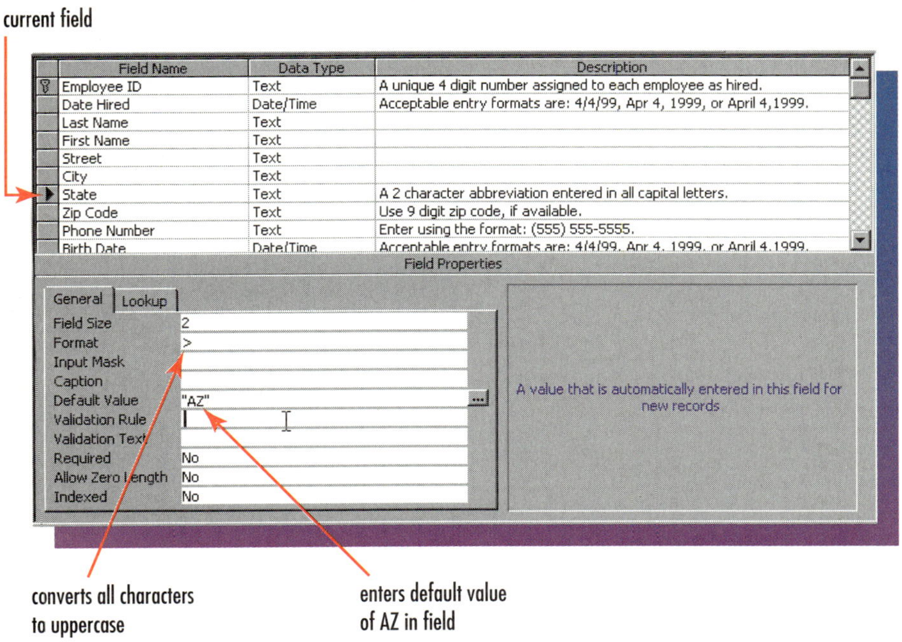

FIGURE 2-3

The default value is automatically enclosed in quotes to identify the entry as a group of characters called a **character string**.

Creating an Input Mask

While making this change, you decide to change the properties of the Zip Code field to make data entry easier. You want the Zip Code field to display the hyphen and restrict the entry to numbers only. Creating an input mask will set up the field in the desired manner.

Concept 3: Input Mask Property

An **input mask** is a pattern that controls the data that can be entered in a field. It consists of literal characters, which are displayed in the field, and mask characters, which are not. **Literal characters** are characters such as the parentheses surrounding the area code of a telephone number, or a hyphen used to separate the parts of a telephone number. **Mask characters** are symbols that control where the data is entered in the field, the type of data that can be entered, whether the data is required or optional, and the number of characters. They are not displayed in the field and are replaced by the entry as it is typed into the table.

Many of the most common mask characters are described below.

Character	Description
0	A required number entry 0 to 9 (plus (+) and minus (-) signs not allowed)
9	An optional number or space entry (plus and minus signs not allowed)
#	An optional number or space (spaces are displayed as blanks while in Edit mode, but blanks are removed when data is saved; plus and minus signs allowed)
L	A required letter entry (A to Z)
?	An optional letter entry (A to Z)
A	A required letter or digit entry
a	An optional letter or digit entry
&	A required entry of any character or a space
C	An optional entry of any character or a space
.,:;-/	Decimal placeholders and thousands, date, and time separators.
<	Converts all characters to lowercase
>	Converts all characters to uppercase
!	Causes the completed entry in a field to display from right to left, rather than from left to right in the input mask. Characters as you type still fill the input mask from left to right. Use when characters in the input mask are optional. The exclamation point can be entered anywhere in the input mask.
\	Enter before any of the mask characters listed above to have the mask character interpreted as a literal character.

An input mast can have up to three parts, with each part separated by a semicolon. For example, the input mask for a zip code field may be 00000-9999;0;_. The first part, 00000-9999, specifies the input mask itself. The second part, 0, specifies whether the literal display characters are stored in the table when you enter data. If you enter 0 for this section, all literal display characters (for example, the hyphen in a zip code input mask) are stored with the value; if you enter 1 or leave this section blank, only characters you type are stored. The third part specifies the placeholder character that is displayed while entering data to show the space where you should type a character in the input mask. You can specify any character; if this section is left blank, the default displays an underscore. To indicate a blank space, type " " (quote, space, quote).

- Make the Zip Code field current.
- Move to the Input Mask field property text box.

Notice that the [...] Build button appears to the right of the text box. This button starts the Input Mask Wizard that helps you enter many common input masks as well as create and store your own custom masks.

- Click [...] Build.
- Click Yes.

You can also type an input mask directly in the Input Mask text box.

If the Build [...] button is not displayed, the Input Mask Wizard is not installed on your system. Skip to Figure 2.5 and enter the mask shown in the Input Mask text box.

The Input Mask Wizard dialog box on your screen should be similar to Figure 2-4.

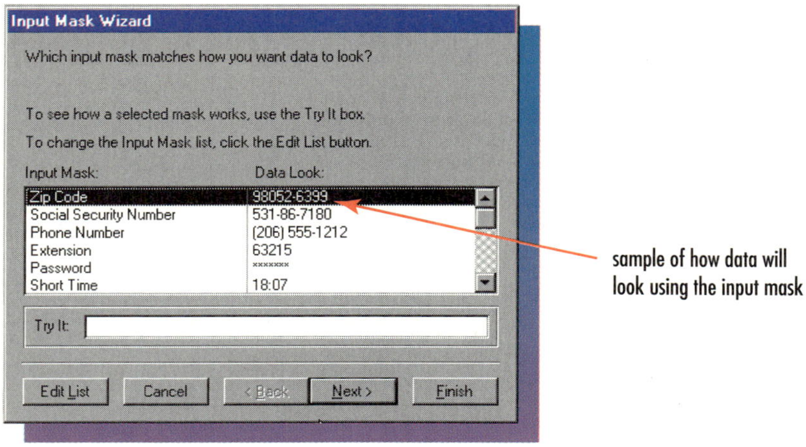

FIGURE 2-4

The first Wizard dialog box asks you to select an input mask from the list. The Zip Code input mask is already selected. A sample of how data will appear in the mask is displayed to the right. This looks like how you want the field to appear. To try out this mask,

- Press Tab.
- Enter your full zip code in the Try It text box (do not include the hyphen).
- Click Next >.

If you do not know your full zip code, enter a ficticious number.

The second Wizard dialog box asks if you want to change the proposed input mask of 00000-9999, and to select the placeholder symbol to display in the mask. The proposed input mask uses zeros to restrict data entry to required numbers for the first five digits of the zip code entry. The last four numbers are optional, therefore 9s are used as the character mask. The hyphen will automatically be entered between the two parts of the zip code. Both the default mask and placeholder of an underscore are acceptable.

- Click Next >.

The third Wizard dialog box asks if you want to store the literal (hyphen) as part of the value. This is generally not recommended, because in a large database the extra space consumed by these symbols may become significant. Therefore the proposed response is correct.

- Click [Next >].
- Click [Finish].
- Press [←Enter].

Your screen should be similar to Figure 2-5.

FIGURE 2-5

current field

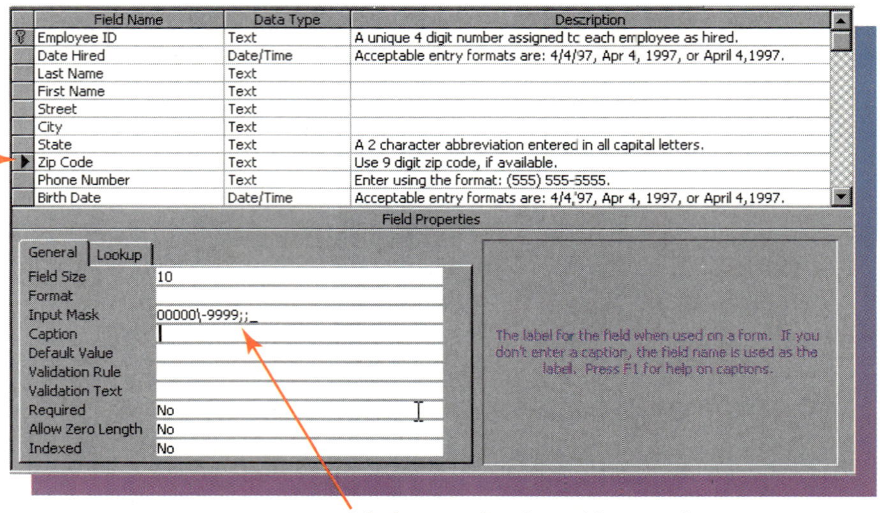

input mask for five required numbers and four optional

Notice the \ character preceding the hyphen. The program enters the symbol for you to indicate that the hyphen is a literal character to display in the field.

You also decide to make a similar adjustment to the Phone Number field property. Rather than having to type the parentheses and hyphen, you want these characters to automatically display in the field. In addition, you want the field to accept numeric entries only.

If the Input Mask Wizard is not available, enter the phone number mask directly in the text box.

- Use the Input Mask Wizard to enter the input mask for the Phone Number field.
- Press [←Enter].

When you are done the input mask in this field property should be: !\(999") "000\-0000;;_.

To see how the new field property settings have changed the table,

- Click [Datasheet View icon] Datasheet View.
- Click [Yes].
- Move to the Phone Number field of record 1.

Your screen should be similar to Figure 2-6.

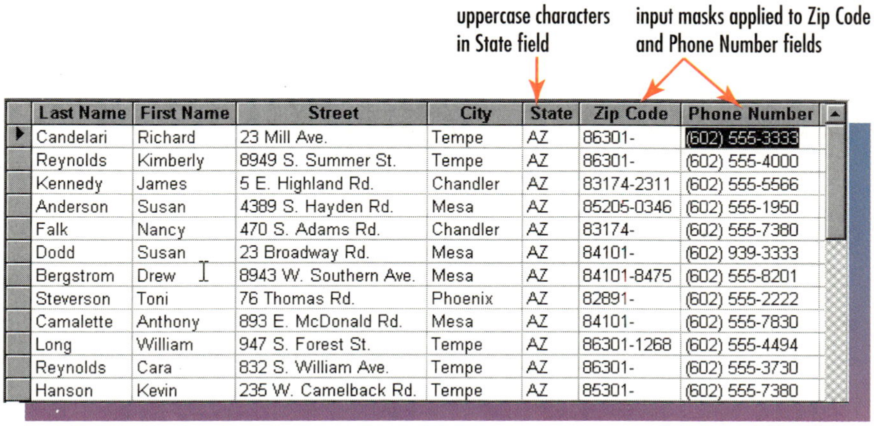

Last Name	First Name	Street	City	State	Zip Code	Phone Number
Candelari	Richard	23 Mill Ave.	Tempe	AZ	86301-	(602) 555-3333
Reynolds	Kimberly	8949 S. Summer St.	Tempe	AZ	86301-	(602) 555-4000
Kennedy	James	5 E. Highland Rd.	Chandler	AZ	83174-2311	(602) 555-5566
Anderson	Susan	4389 S. Hayden Rd.	Mesa	AZ	85205-0346	(602) 555-1950
Falk	Nancy	470 S. Adams Rd.	Chandler	AZ	83174-	(602) 555-7380
Dodd	Susan	23 Broadway Rd.	Mesa	AZ	84101-	(602) 939-3333
Bergstrom	Drew	8943 W. Southern Ave.	Mesa	AZ	84101-8475	(602) 555-8201
Steverson	Toni	76 Thomas Rd.	Phoenix	AZ	82891-	(602) 555-2222
Camalette	Anthony	893 E. McDonald Rd.	Mesa	AZ	84101-	(602) 555-7830
Long	William	947 S. Forest St.	Tempe	AZ	86301-1268	(602) 555-4494
Reynolds	Cara	832 S. William Ave.	Tempe	AZ	86301-	(602) 555-3730
Hanson	Kevin	235 W. Camelback Rd.	Tempe	AZ	85301-	(602) 555-7380

FIGURE 2-6

First, notice that the entry in the State field for record 11, Cara Reynolds, which had lowercase characters, has been converted to uppercase characters. This change is a result of the format property setting you entered for the State field. The Zip Code field displays the existing five-digit zip codes followed by the hyphen character as specified by the input mask for that field.

Because the entries in the Phone Number field already include the parentheses and hyphen, it is not possible to see the effect of the input mask on the field. However, when you enter a new record, you will see how this mask helps data entry.

- Move to a new blank record.

You can click ▶* to quickly move to a new blank record.

Notice that the new record displays "AZ" as the default value in the State field.

- To see how the new format and input mask settings affect data input, enter the following new record:

Field	Data
Employee ID	**1388**
Date Hired	**5/17/92**
Last Name	**Nelson**
First Name	**Linda**
Address	**422 Candy Ln.**
City	**Phoenix**

Because the state for this record is AZ, you can accept the default field value and skip this field. If the state were other than AZ, you could edit the entry.

- Press ←Enter.

Next, in the Zip Code and Phone Number fields, you do not type the hyphens or parentheses, as they are supplied by the input mask. If you enter any characters except numbers in these fields, they will be rejected. Complete the record by entering the data shown below.

You must enter three blank spaces if you do not want to include the area code in the phone number.

Field	Data
Zip Code	**828911605**
Phone Number	**6025557268**
Birth Date	**9/14/45**

To complete this record and return to the first record,

- Press ←Enter.
- Click ⏮.

Finding and Replacing Data

Next you want to update the Zip Code field for the existing records. You have checked with the U.S. Postal Service and found that all zip codes of 82891 have a four-digit extension of 1605. To locate all the records with this zip code, you could look at the Zip Code field for each record to find the match and then edit the field to add the extension. If the table is small, this method would be acceptable. For large tables, however, this method could be quite time consuming and more prone to errors. A more efficient way is to search the table to find specific values in records and then replace the entry with another.

Concept 4: Find and Replace

The Find command will locate all specified values in a field, and the Replace command will both find a value and automatically replace it with another. For example, in a table containing supplier and item prices, you may need to increase the price of all items supplied by one manufacturer. To quickly locate these items, you would use the Find command to locate all records with the name of the manufacturer and then update the price appropriately. Alternatively, you could use the Replace command if you knew that all items priced at $9.95 were increasing to $11.89. This command would locate all values matching the original price and replace them with the new price. Finding and replacing data is fast and accurate, but you need to be careful when replacing not to replace unintended matches.

The Replace command will search the current field to find the specified data and replace it with other data.

The keyboard shortcut is Ctrl+H.

- Move to the Zip Code field of record 1.
- Choose **E**dit/Repl**a**ce.

The Replace in Field dialog box shows the name of the field it will search (the current field) in the title bar. In the Find What text box you enter the text you want to locate, and in the Replace With text box you enter the replacement text exactly as you want it to appear in your document. You do not include input mask literal characters such as hyphens that are entered by the input mask in the replacement text. In the search drop-down list box, you can select All to search all records, or Down or Up to search down or up from the insertion point in the selected field. The other search options you can use to modify how the search is conducted are discussed below.

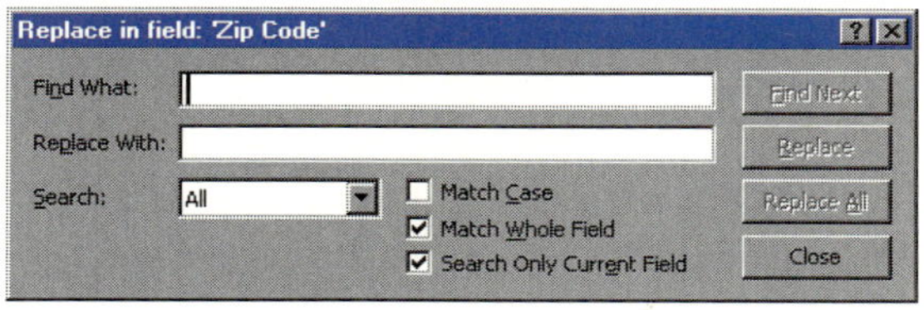

Option	Effect on Text	Example
Match Case	Finds only those text entries that have the same use of uppercase and lowercase text as the entry in the Find What text box. This option is off by default.	Enter "Southwest" in the Find What text box, turn on Match Case. You would not Locate "southwest."
Match Whole Field	Finds only whole words, not the same text inside longer words. This option is on by default.	Enter "cat" in the Find What text box, turn on Match Whole Field. You would not locate "catastrophe" or "indicate."
Search Only Current Field	Searches only the field in which the pointer is currently located, ignoring other fields in the table. When not selected, this option searches all fields for each record in the table. This option is on by default.	If you Search Only the Last Name field for "Smith," you would locate only those individuals whose last names are Smith. You would not locate anyone living in the town of Smith or on Smith Road.

To enter the zip code to find and the replacement zip code, and to search using the default options,

- Type **82891-**
- Press Tab.
- Type **828911605**
- Click Find Next.

If necessary, move the dialog box so you can see the located entry.

Your screen should be similar to Figure 2-7.

FIGURE 2-7

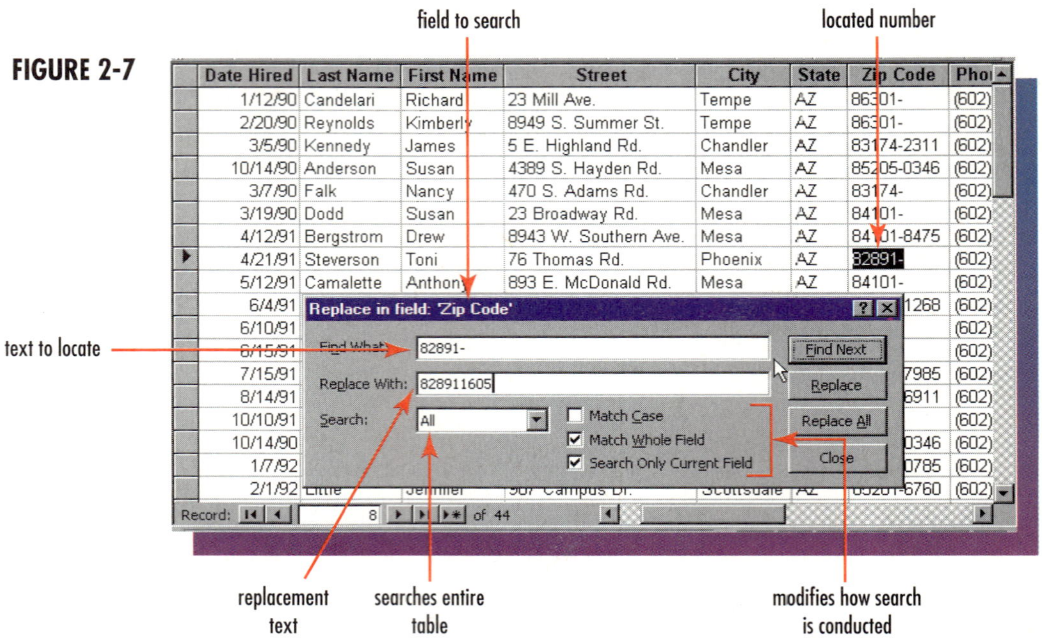

Immediately the highlight moves to the first occurrence of text in the document that matches the Find What text and highlights it. To replace the highlighted text,

- Click Replace.

Access immediately continues searching and locates a second occurrence of the entry. You decide the program is locating the values accurately, and it will be safe to replace all finds with the replacement value. To do this,

- Click Replace All.

When Access completes the search, the message "You won't be able to undo this Replace operation" is displayed. To approve the changes,

- Click Yes.

It is much faster to use Replace All than to confirm each match separately. However, exercise care when using Replace All, because the search text you specify might be part of another word and you may accidentally replace text you want to keep.

- In the same manner, update the zip code for 86301 to include the extension 1268.
- Close the Replace in Field dialog box.

Over the past few days you have received several change request forms to update the employee records. The first change request is for Carman Artis, who recently married and has both a name and address change. To quickly locate this record you will use the Find command. This command works just like the Find and Replace command, except it does not enter a replacement.

- Move to the Last Name field of record 1.
- Click Find.
- Type **artis**
- Click Find First.

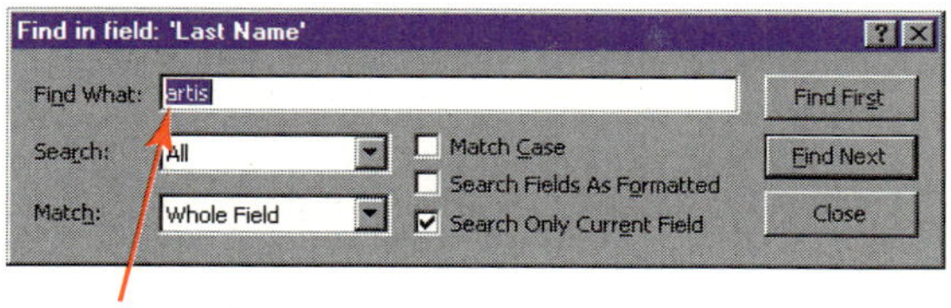

enter text to locate

> The menu equivalent is Edit/Find, and the keyboard shortcut is Ctrl + F.

> Because the Match Case option is not selected, Find will look for an exact match regardless of uppercase or lowercase characters.

Access searches the table and moves to the first occurrence of the entry. The Last Name field is highlighted in record 14. To change the last name to Richards,

- Close the dialog box.
- Type **Richards**
- Press ←Enter.

Note: If the Find command did not locate this record, reissue the command and make sure you enter the name Artis exactly as shown and are searching the Last Name field.

Using Undo

Now that the highlight is on the First Name field, you notice this is the record for Jose Artis, not Carman. You changed the wrong record. You can use the Undo command to quickly undo this change.

You can use Undo to cancel your last action as long as you do not make any other changes to the table. Even if you save the record or the table, you can undo changes to the last edited record by using the Undo Saved Record command on the Edit menu or by clicking the Undo button. Once you have changed another record or moved to another window, the earlier change cannot be undone. To quickly undo the change made to this record,

- Click Undo.

> You can also press Esc before leaving the field you are editing to cancel changes you have made.

> The menu equivalent is Edit/Undo, and the keyboard shortcut is Ctrl + Z.

Your screen should be similar to Figure 2-8.

FIGURE 2-8

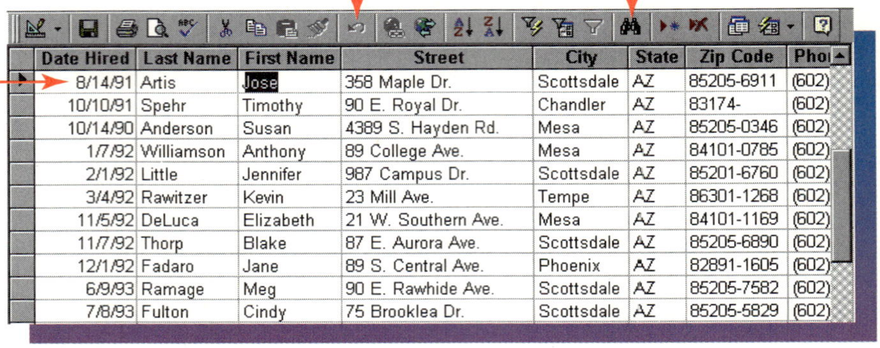

	Date Hired	Last Name	First Name	Street	City	State	Zip Code	Phon
▸	8/14/91	Artis	Jose	358 Maple Dr.	Scottsdale	AZ	85205-6911	(602)
	10/10/91	Spehr	Timothy	90 E. Royal Dr.	Chandler	AZ	83174-	(602)
	10/14/90	Anderson	Susan	4389 S. Hayden Rd.	Mesa	AZ	85205-0346	(602)
	1/7/92	Williamson	Anthony	89 College Ave.	Mesa	AZ	84101-0785	(602)
	2/1/92	Little	Jennifer	987 Campus Dr.	Scottsdale	AZ	85201-6760	(602)
	3/4/92	Rawitzer	Kevin	23 Mill Ave.	Tempe	AZ	86301-1268	(602)
	11/5/92	DeLuca	Elizabeth	21 W. Southern Ave.	Mesa	AZ	84101-1169	(602)
	11/7/92	Thorp	Blake	87 E. Aurora Ave.	Scottsdale	AZ	85205-6890	(602)
	12/1/92	Fadaro	Jane	89 S. Central Ave.	Phoenix	AZ	82891-1605	(602)
	6/9/93	Ramage	Meg	90 E. Rawhide Ave.	Scottsdale	AZ	85205-7582	(602)
	7/8/93	Fulton	Cindy	75 Brooklea Dr.	Scottsdale	AZ	85205-5829	(602)

The original field value of "Artis" replaces "Richards."

- To continue the search to locate the next record with the last name of Artis, move back to the Last Name field of this record.
- Click Find.
- Click Find Next.
- Close the Find in Field dialog box.
- Change the last name to **Richards** and the street to **5401 E. Thomas Rd.**
- Use the Find command to search the table for the following records and correct the entries.

Reminder: The insertion point must be on the field you want to search before clicking Find.

Employee Name	Field	Correction
Adam Robson	Street	**4290 E. Alameda Dr.**
Kevin Hanson	City, Zip Code	**Scottsdale, 85205-3211**
Meg Ramage	Last Name	**Miller**

- When you are done, return to the first field of record 1.

Inserting a Field

While continuing to use the table, you have realized that you need to include a field of information to hold each employee's gender. Although it is better to include all the necessary fields when creating the table structure, it is possible to add or remove fields from a table at a later time. After looking at the order of the fields, you decide to add the new field, Gender, between the Phone Number and Birth Date fields. To insert the new field in the table and define its properties,

- Click Design View.
- Make the Birth Date field current.
- Click Insert Rows.
- Enter the new field information as follows:

Field Name:	**Gender**
Data Type:	**Text**
Description:	**Enter M for male or F for female.**
Field Size:	**1**
Format:	**>**

Your screen should be similar to Figure 2-9.

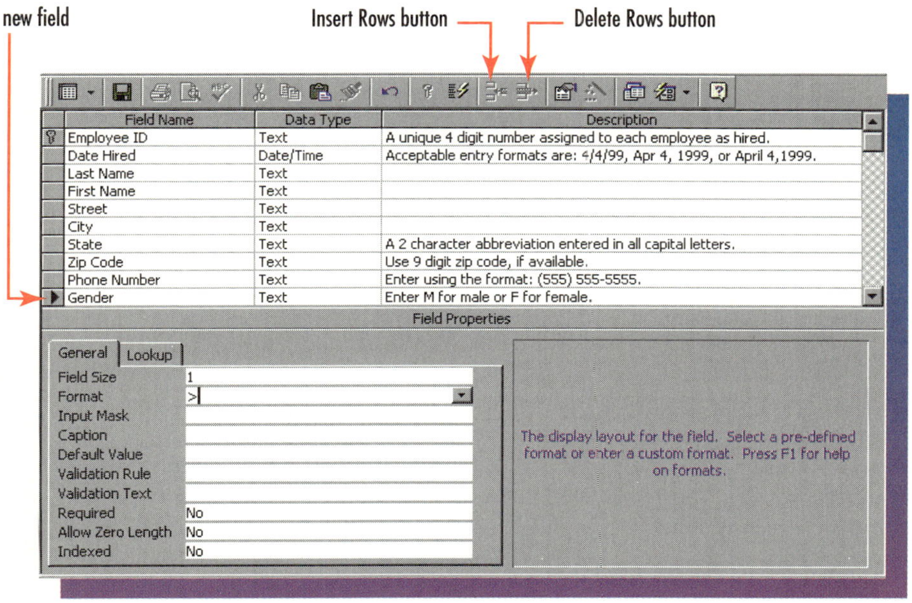

FIGURE 2-9

If you remove a field, Access permanently deletes the field definition and any data in the field. or Edit/Delete Row removes a field.

You can also add or delete fields in Datasheet view.

The menu equivalent is Insert/Field. You can also use the Insert Field command on the Shortcut menu.

Adding Validity Checks

The only two characters you want the Gender field to accept are M for male and F for female. To specify that these two characters are the only entries acceptable in the field, you will include a validity check.

Concept 5: Validity Checks

Access automatically performs certain checks, called **validity checks**, on values entered in a field to make sure that the values are valid for the field type. A Text field type has few restrictions, but you can create your own validity checks for a field, which Access will apply during data entry.

A validity check is set by entering an expression to describe acceptable values. **Expressions** are combinations of symbols that produce specific results. Expressions are used throughout Access to create validity checks, queries, forms, and reports. These are examples of possible expressions:

Expression	Result
=[Sales Amount] + [Sales Tax]	Sums value in two fields
="M" OR "F"	Includes M or F entries only
>=#1/1/95# AND <=#12/31/95#	Includes entries greater than or equal to 1/1/95, and less than or equal to 12/31/95
="Tennis Rackets"	Includes Tennis Rackets entries only

You create an expression by combining identifiers, operators, and values to produce the desired result. An **identifier** is an element that refers to the value of a field, a graphical object, or property. In the expression =[Sales Amount] + [Sales Tax], [Sales Amount] and [Sales Tax] are identifiers that refer to the values in the Sales Amount and Sales Tax fields.

An **operator** is a symbol or word that indicates that an operation is to be performed. The Access operators include = (equal to), <> (not equal to), >= (greater than or equal to), <= (less than or equal to), LIKE, OR, and AND. In the expression ="M" OR "F", the = sign and OR are operators. The = operator is assumed if no other operator is specified.

Values are numbers, dates, or groups of characters. Character strings such as "M", "F", or "Tennis Rackets"are enclosed in quotation marks. Dates are enclosed in pound signs (#), as in >=#1/1/95# AND <=#12/31/95#.

When you add a validity check, you can also add validation text in the Validation Text property box. **Validation text** appears in a message box if you attempt to enter invalid information in a text field for which there is a validity check. For example, if you added a validity check to a field to only allow the numbers 1 through 10, you might create validation text that would display the message, "The only valid entries for this field are numbers 1 through 10." If you do not specify a message, Access displays a default error message, which will not clearly describe the reason for the error.

You want to add a validity check to allow only M or F to be entered in the field. You also want to include a Validation Text message that will be displayed if the wrong character is entered in the Gender field.

- Move to the Validation Rule field property text box.
- Type **=M or F**
- Press ⏎Enter.
- Type **The only valid entries are M or F**

Your screen should be similar to Figure 2-10.

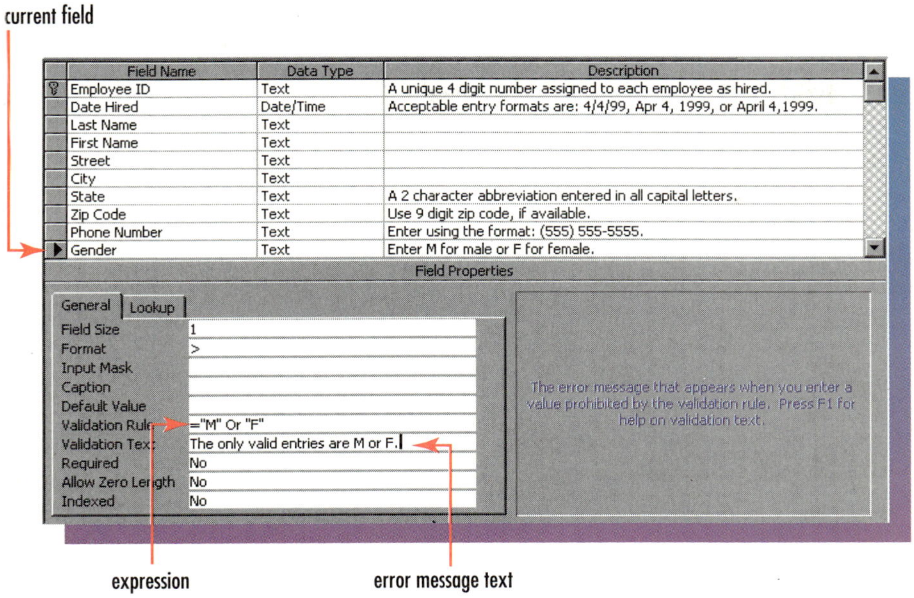

FIGURE 2-10

The expression states that the acceptable values can only be equal to an M or an F. Notice that Access automatically added quotation marks around the two character strings and changed the "o" in "or" to uppercase.

Next you want to add the data for the Gender field to the table.

Because the Format property has been set to convert all entries to uppercase, an entry of m or f is also acceptable.

- Click Datasheet.
- Click Yes.

A message box appears advising you that data integrity rules have been changed. When you restructure a table, you often make changes that could result in a loss of data. Changes such as shortening field sizes, creating validity checks, or changing field types can cause existing data to become invalid. Because the field is new, there are no data values to verify, and a validation check is unnecessary. To continue,

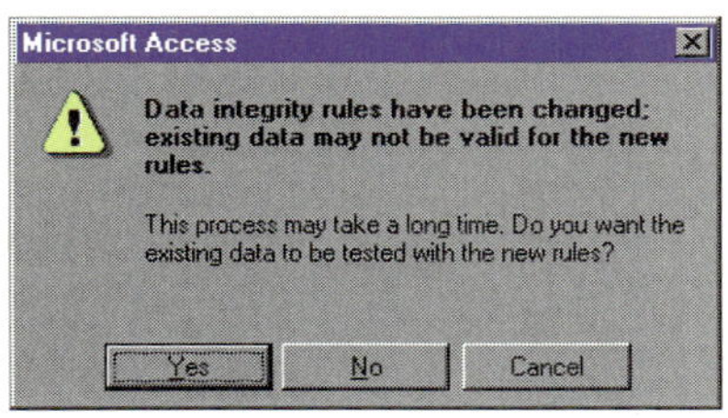

- Choose No.
- Move to the Gender field for record 1.

Your screen should be similar to Figure 2-11.

FIGURE 2-11

The new field was added to the table between the Phone Number and Birth Date fields.

Hiding and Redisplaying Fields

You can most likely tell the gender for each record by looking at the employee's first name. Unfortunately, you cannot see the First Name field at the same time you are entering data in the Gender field. A quick way to view the fields side by side is to hide the fields that are in between.

Drag in the column heads to select the fields.

- Select the Street field through the Phone Number field.
- Choose **F**ormat/**H**ide Columns.

Now both the First Name and Gender columns are next to each other, and you can see the first name for record 1 is Richard. Therefore the Gender field for record 1 should be M. To verify that the validity check works, you will enter an invalid field value in the Gender field for this record.

- Type **g**
- Press ←Enter.

Your screen should be similar to Figure 2-12.

FIGURE 2-12

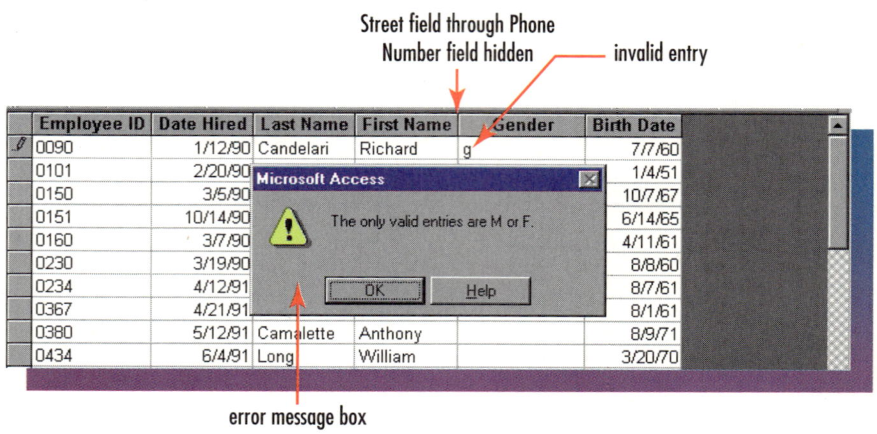

Access displays the error message you entered in the Validation Text box of the Design view. To clear the error message and correct the entry,

- Click OK.
- Press ←Backspace.
- Type **m**
- Press ↓.

The entry for the first record is displayed as an uppercase M. Next you will enter the gender for each record and then redisplay the hidden fields.

- Enter the Gender field values for the remaining records by looking at the First Name field to determine whether the employee is male or female.
- Reduce the size of the Gender field using the Best Fit command.
- Choose F**o**rmat/**U**nhide Columns.
- Select the five fields that do not display checkmarks.
- Click Close.
- Move to the first field of record 1.

hidden fields are not selected

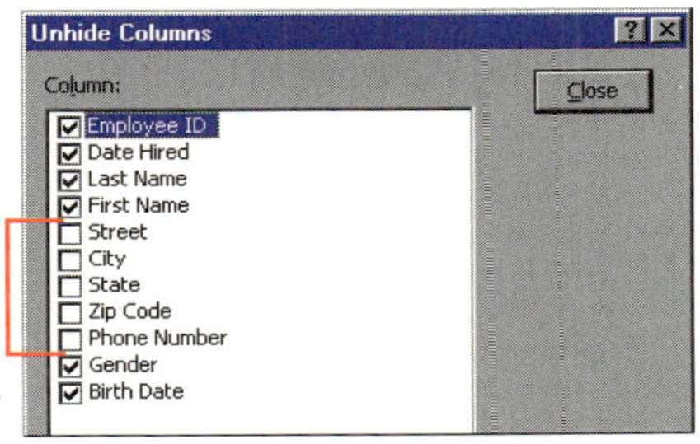

Sorting on a Single Field

As you may recall from Lab 1, the records are ordered by the primary key field, Employee ID. The Accounting department manager, however, has asked you for an alphabetical list of all employees. To do this you can sort the records in the table.

Concept 6: Sort

You can quickly reorder records in a table by **sorting** a table to display in a different record order. Sorting data often helps you find specific information quickly. In Access you can sort data in ascending order (A to Z or 0 to 9) or descending order (Z to A or 9 to 0).

You can sort all records in a table by a single field, such as State, or you can select adjacent columns and sort by more than one field, such as State and then City. When you select multiple columns to sort, Access sorts records starting with the column farthest left, then moves to the right across the columns. For example, if you want to quickly sort by State, then by City, the State field must be to the left of the City field.

Access saves the new sort order with your table data and reapplies it automatically each time you open the table. To return to the primary key sort order, you must remove the temporary sort.

For the first sort, you want the records arranged in ascending alphabetical order by last name.

The menu equivalent is **R**ecords/**S**ort/**A**scending.

- Move to the Last Name field of any record.
- Click Sort Ascending.

Your screen should be similar to Figure 2-13.

FIGURE 2-13

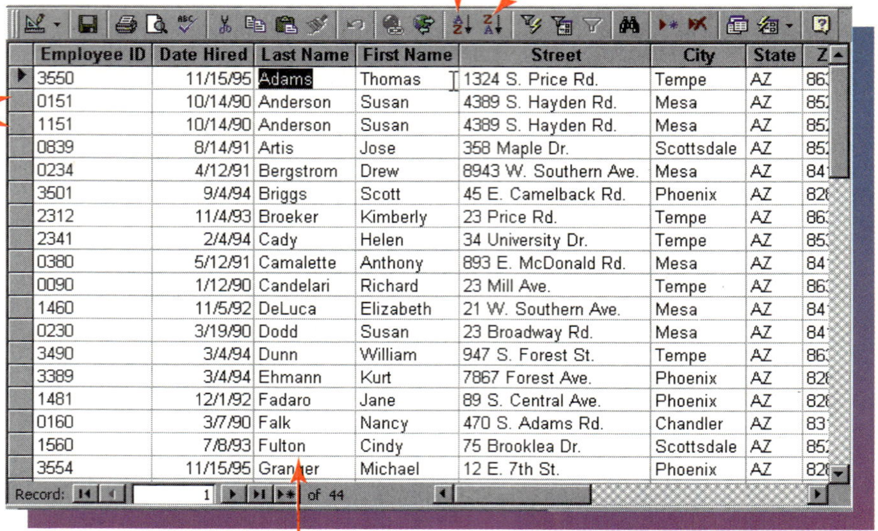

The employee records are displayed in alphabetical order by last name.

Deleting Records

Now that the records are alphabetically arranged, you immediately notice that Susan Anderson's record has been entered into the table twice. The records contain identical information in all the fields except for the Employee ID field. By checking the employee card, you determine that the record with the employee number of 1151 is incorrect. You need to delete the duplicate record.

> You cannot use Undo to restore deleted records.

Records can be removed from a table by selecting the entire record and pressing (Delete) or clicking Cut. This method is useful when you have multiple records to be deleted that you can select and delete as a group. It is quicker, however, to use the Delete Record button when you want to remove records individually. This is because the record is both selected and deleted at the same time.

> Records are selected using Edit/Select Record or by clicking in the row selector when the mouse pointer shape is ➡. In Navigation mode (⇧Shift)+(Spacebar) selects the current record.

- Move to any field in record 3.
- Click Delete Record.

> The menu equivalent is Edit/Cut, and the keyboard shortcut is (Ctrl) + X. The Cut command is also on the Shortcut menu when a record is selected.

As a precaution against accidentally deleting records, Access displays a confirmation dialog box. To indicate you want to permanently delete the record,

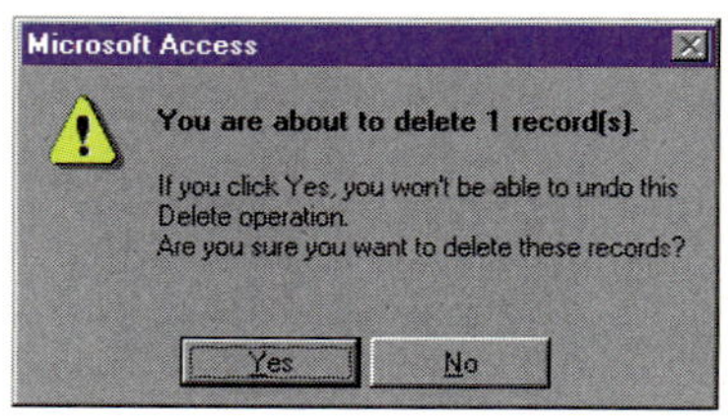

- Click Yes.

Your screen should be similar to Figure 2-14.

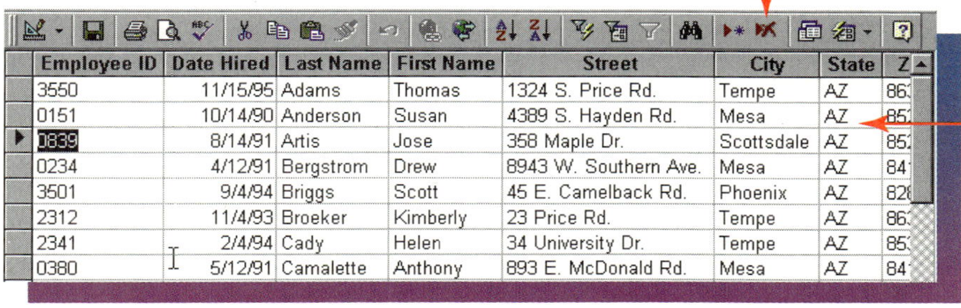

Employee ID	Date Hired	Last Name	First Name	Street	City	State	Z
3550	11/15/95	Adams	Thomas	1324 S. Price Rd.	Tempe	AZ	86
0151	10/14/90	Anderson	Susan	4389 S. Hayden Rd.	Mesa	AZ	85
0839	8/14/91	Artis	Jose	358 Maple Dr.	Scottsdale	AZ	85
0234	4/12/91	Bergstrom	Drew	8943 W. Southern Ave.	Mesa	AZ	84
3501	9/4/94	Briggs	Scott	45 E. Camelback Rd.	Phoenix	AZ	82
2312	11/4/93	Broeker	Kimberly	23 Price Rd.	Tempe	AZ	86
2341	2/4/94	Cady	Helen	34 University Dr.	Tempe	AZ	85
0380	5/12/91	Camalette	Anthony	893 E. McDonald Rd.	Mesa	AZ	84

FIGURE 2-14

Sorting on Multiple Fields

- Use the scroll box to scroll down to record 27.

As you drag the scroll box, the record location is displayed in the scroll tips box.

Record: 27 of 43

Notice that the records for Patty and Carman Richards are sorted by last name but not by first name. You want the records that have the same last name to be further sorted by first name. To do this, you specify multiple sort fields. When sorting on multiple fields, the fields must be adjacent to each other, and the most important field in the sort must be to the left of the secondary field. The Last Name and First Name fields are already in the correct locations for the sort you want to perform. To specify the fields to sort on, both columns must be selected.

If the columns are not adjacent, you can hide the columns that are in between. If they are not in the correct order, you can move the columns. You will learn how to do this in Lab 3.

- Select the Last Name and First Name field columns.
- Click Sort Ascending.
- Scroll down to record 27 again.

Your screen should be similar to Figure 2-15.

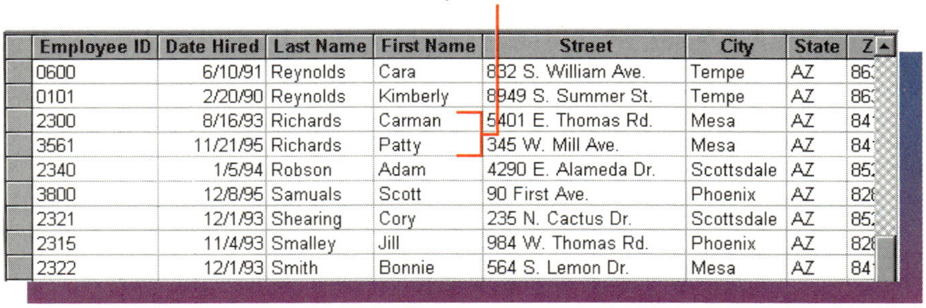

Employee ID	Date Hired	Last Name	First Name	Street	City	State	Z
0600	6/10/91	Reynolds	Cara	832 S. William Ave.	Tempe	AZ	86
0101	2/20/90	Reynolds	Kimberly	8949 S. Summer St.	Tempe	AZ	86
2300	8/16/93	Richards	Carman	5401 E. Thomas Rd.	Mesa	AZ	84
3561	11/21/95	Richards	Patty	345 W. Mill Ave.	Mesa	AZ	84
2340	1/5/94	Robson	Adam	4290 E. Alameda Dr.	Scottsdale	AZ	85
3800	12/8/95	Samuals	Scott	90 First Ave.	Phoenix	AZ	82
2321	12/1/93	Shearing	Cory	235 N. Cactus Dr.	Scottsdale	AZ	85
2315	11/4/93	Smalley	Jill	984 W. Thomas Rd.	Phoenix	AZ	82
2322	12/1/93	Smith	Bonnie	564 S. Lemon Dr.	Mesa	AZ	84

FIGURE 2-15

As you can see, sorting is a fast, useful tool. The sort order remains in effect until you remove the sort or replace it with a new sort order. Although Access remembers your sort order even when you exit the program, it does not actually change the table records. You can remove the sort at any time to restore the records to the primary key sort order. To do this,

- Choose **R**ecords/**R**emove Filter/Sort.
- Close the table and save your design changes.

Note: If you are ending your session now, close the database file and exit Access. When you begin Part 2, load Access and open the Employee Records file.

Part 2

Creating a Form

One of your responsibilities is to make the database easy to use. You know from experience that long hours of viewing large tables can be tiring. Therefore you want to create an onscreen form to make this table easier to view and use.

Concept 7: Forms

Forms are database objects used primarily to display records onscreen to make it easier to enter new records and to make changes to existing records. Forms are based on an underlying table and include design elements such as descriptive text, titles, labels, lines, boxes, and pictures. Forms often use calculations as well, to summarize data that is not listed on the actual table, such as a sales total. Forms make working with long lists of data easier. They enable people to use the data in the tables without having to sift through many lines of data to find the exact record.

Forms are linked to the underlying table by using controls. **Controls** are graphical objects that can be selected and modified. Once a control is selected, it can be sized, moved, or enhanced in other ways. The most common type of control is a text box. A **text box control** creates a link to the underlying source, usually a field from a table, and displays the field entry in the form. This type of control is called a **bound control** because it is tied to a field in an underlying table. The form usually also includes a label with each text box control. A **label control** initially displays the field name from the underlying table associated with the text box control. Label controls can also display custom names you want to display instead of the field name or other descriptive text entries such as a title or instructions for the user. These controls are **unbound controls** because they are not connected to a field. Other unbound controls contain elements that enhance the appearance of the form such as lines, boxes, and pictures. A third type of control is a **calculated control** that displays the results of a calculation in the form. It uses an expression that uses data from the underlying table or another control as its source of data.

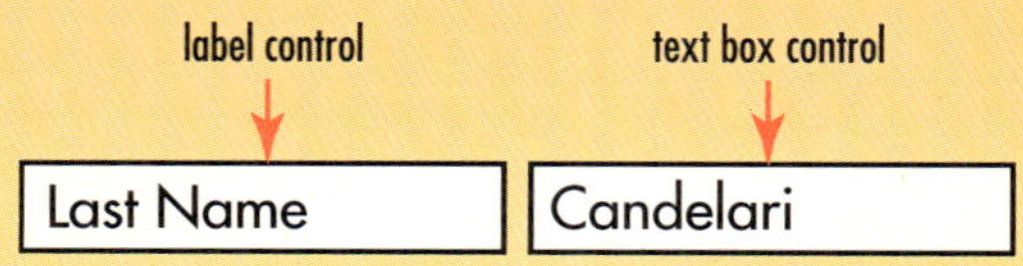

You will create a form to be used by the Personnel department to add new employee records and to update existing employee records in the Sports Company Employees table. The input for the table comes from the paper Employee Data form that each employee fills out when hired. The paper form looks like this:

EMPLOYEE DATA

First Name: ____________ Last Name: ____________

Street: ________________________________

City: ____________ State: ______ Zip Code: ______

Phone Number: ____________

Gender: ____________ Birth Date: ____________

For Personnel Use Only:

Employee ID: ____________

Date Hired: ____________

The order of information in the Employee Data form is different than the order that the data is entered into the table. To make the job of data entry easier, you want the table form to reflect the order of the paper form used by employees. As when creating a table, there are several different methods that can be used to create a form. You will use the Form Wizard to guide you through the steps to create a form.

- To create a form, open the Forms tab.
- Click New.
- Select Form Wizard.
- Click OK.

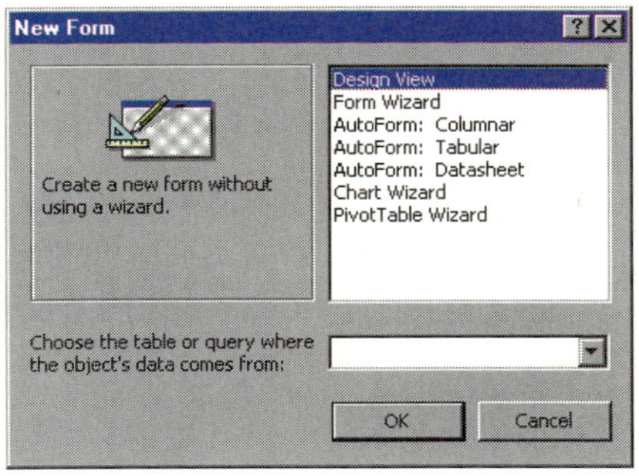

The first Form Wizard dialog box on your screen should be similar to Figure 2-16.

FIGURE 2-16

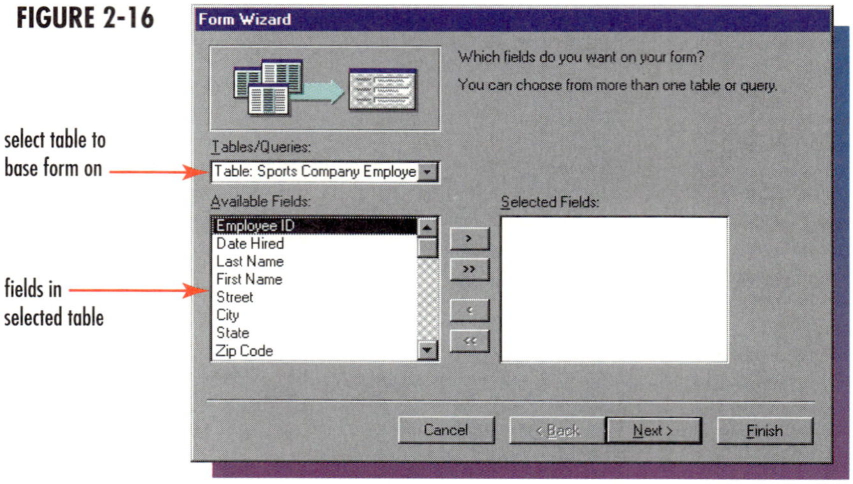

The dialog box displays the name of the current table, Sports Company Employees, in the Tables/Queries list box. This is the table that Access will use when creating the form. If your database contained multiple tables, you would display the Tables/Queries drop-down list to select a different table.

After selecting the table, you select the fields to include in the form. The fields from the selected table will appear in the Available Fields list box. The order in which you select the fields is the **tab order**, or the order in which the highlight will move through the fields on the form during data entry. You would like the order to be the same as the order on the paper form. To add the First Name field to the form first, from the Available Fields list box,

You can also double-click on each field name in the Available Fields list box to move the field name to the Selected Fields list box.

The [>>] button adds all available fields to the Selected Fields list.

- Select First Name.
- Click [>].

The First Name field is removed from the Available Fields list and added to the top of the Selected Fields list box.

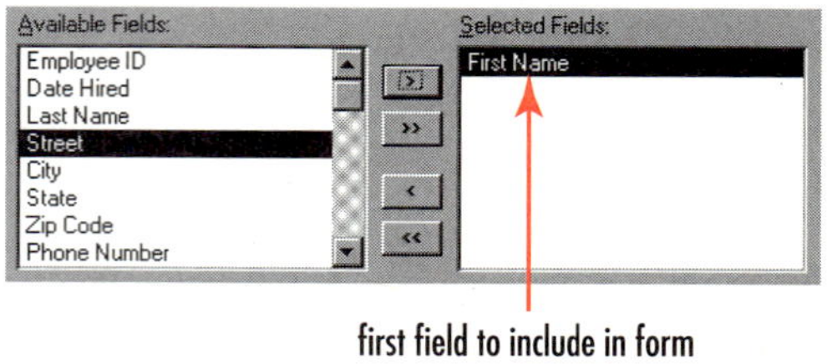

- In the same manner, select the fields in the order shown below and add them to the Selected Fields list.

Last Name
Street
City
State
Zip Code
Phone Number
Gender
Birth Date
Employee ID
Date Hired

When you are done, the Available Fields list box should be empty, and the Selected Fields list box should list the fields in the selected order. To move to the next Form Wizard screen,

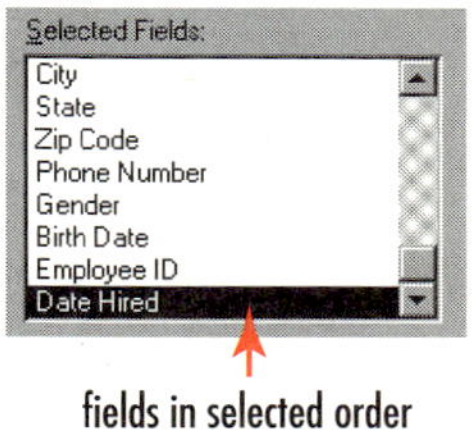

- Click Next >.

The second Form Wizard dialog box on your screen should be similar to Figure 2-17.

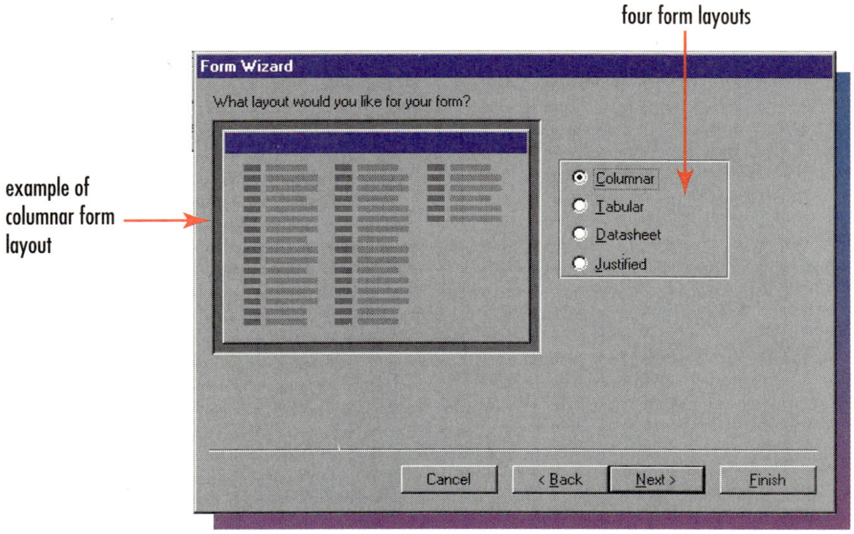

FIGURE 2-17

In this dialog box you are asked to select the layout for the form. Four form layouts are available: Columnar, Tabular, Datasheet and Justified. They are described in the table below.

Form Layout	Description
Columnar 	Presents data for the selected fields in columns. The field names display down the left side of the page with the data for each field just to the right of each field name. A single record is displayed in each form window.
Tabular 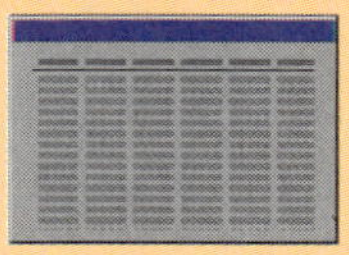	Presents data in a table layout with field names across the top of the page and the corresponding data in rows and columns under each heading. Multiple records are displayed in form view, each on a single row.
Datasheet 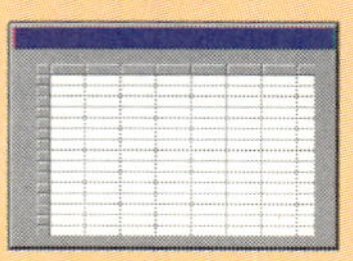	Displays data in rows and columns similar to the Table Datasheet view, but only selected fields display in the order chosen during form design. Displays multiple records, one per row in the form window.
Justified 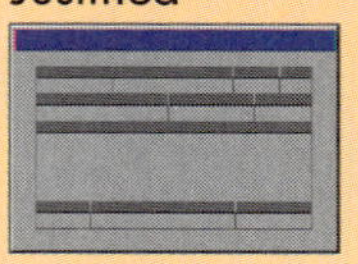	Displays data in rows with field names across the top of the row and the corresponding field data below it. A single record may appear in multiple rows in the form window in order to fully display the field name and data.

The columnar layout would appear most similar to the paper form currently in use by the personnel department.

- If necessary, select Columnar.
- Click Next >.

From the next dialog box you select from ten different styles for your form. A sample of each style as it is selected is displayed on the left side of the dialog box. You will create the form using the Clouds style.

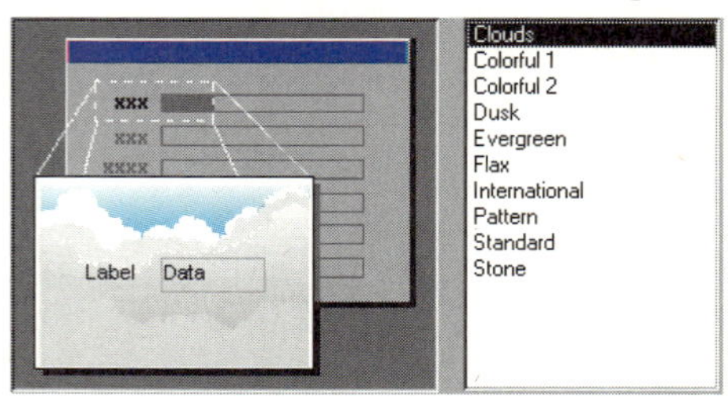

- Select Clouds.
- Click Next >.

Finally, you need to enter a form title to be used as the name of the form and to specify whether the form should open with data displayed in it. You want the form to display data, but you want to change the form's title. To do this,

- Type **Employee Data Form**
- Click Finish.

The Wizard uses the name of the table as the default form title.

The completed form is displayed in the Form view window. This view typically displays one record at a time in the form for data entry or editing purposes.

- If necessary, maximize the Form window.

Your screen should be similar to Figure 2-18.

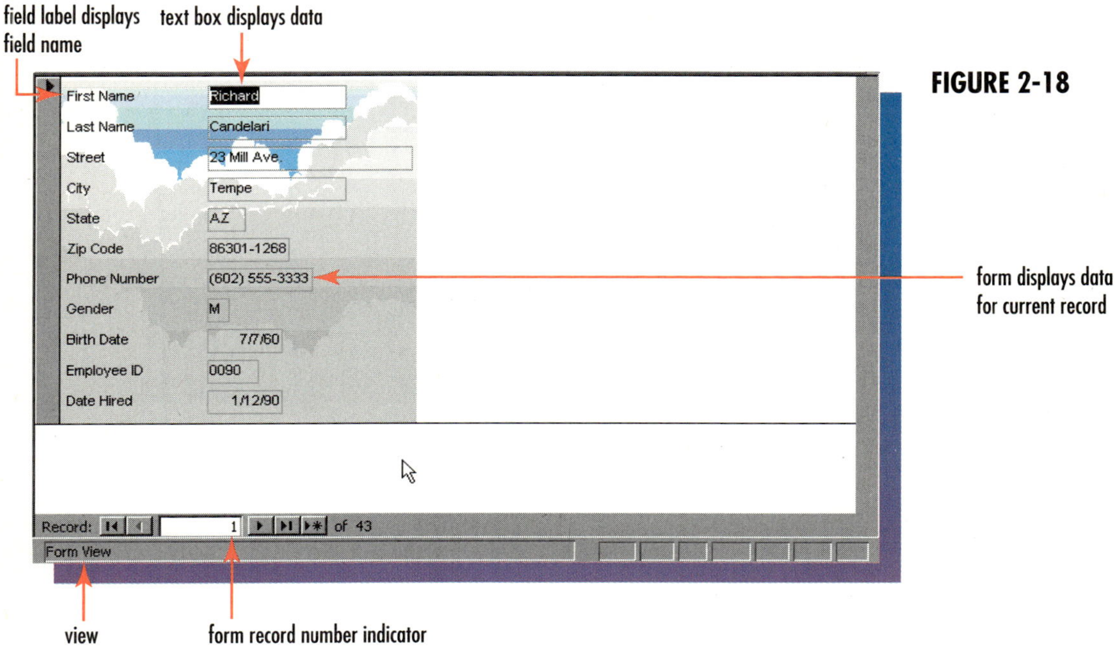

FIGURE 2-18

The form displays the selected fields in columnar layout using the Clouds style. The field name labels are in a column along the left margin, and the field text boxes are in an adjacent column to the right. The employee information for Richard Candelari, record number 1, is displayed in the text boxes.

You use the same navigation keys in Form view that you used in Datasheet view. You can move between fields in the form by using the navigation buttons at the bottom of the form, or the Tab, ←Enter, ⇧Shift + Tab, and directional arrow keys on the keyboard. In addition, the Page Up and Page Down keys allow you to move between records in Form view.

- Move to record 2.

Kimberly Reynolds' record is displayed in the form.

Now that you have looked at the first two records, you want to change the layout of the form to more closely resemble the paper entry form used in the Personnel department. Form Design view is used to design a new form or to change the layout of an existing form.

The menu equivalent is **View/Design View.**

- Click Design View.

Your screen should be similar to Figure 2-19.

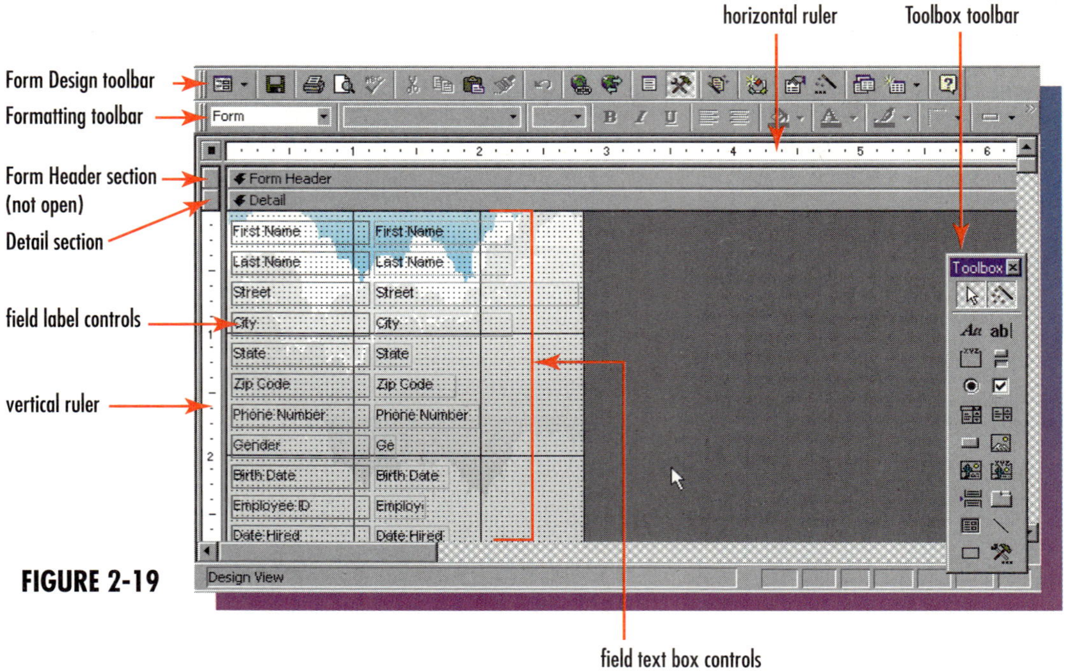

FIGURE 2-19

Form Design view displays the form in a window that is bordered along the top by a horizontal ruler and along the left by a vertical ruler. The rulers help you correctly place items in the Form Design window.

The Form Design view automatically displays three toolbars: Form Design, Formatting, and Toolbox. The Form Design toolbar contains the standard buttons as well as buttons that are specific to the Form Design view window. These buttons are identified below.

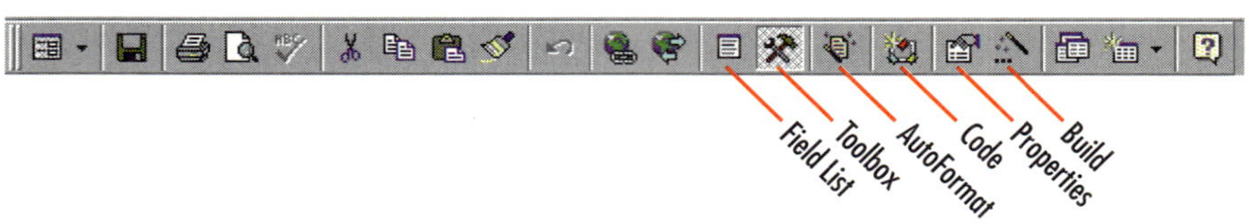

The Formatting toolbar contains buttons that allow you to make text enhancements. The buttons on the Formatting toolbar are identified below.

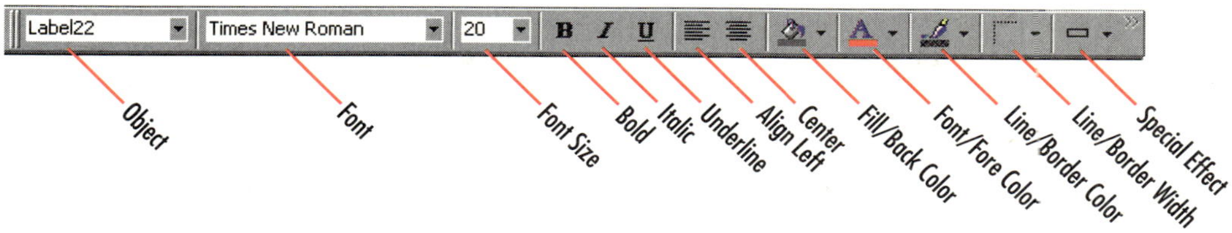

The Toolbox toolbar contains buttons that are used to add and modify controls. The Toolbox buttons are identified below.

If the Toolbox is not displayed, click Toolbox on the Form Design toolbar.

The Toolbox on your screen may be in a different location than in Figure 2-19. If necessary, move the Toolbox to the bottom right corner of the window.

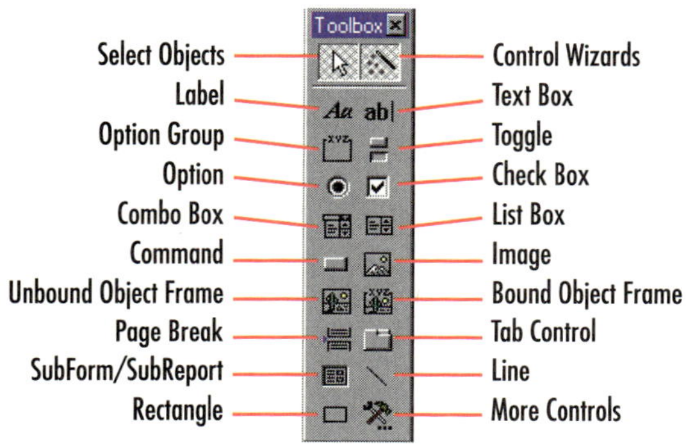

The Form Design window is divided into three areas, Form Header, Detail, and Form Footer (see Figure 2-19). The contents of each section appear below the horizontal bar containing the name. The sections are described in the table below.

Section	Description
Form Header	An optional section that you can include to display information such as the form title, instructions, or graphics. The contents of a Form Header appear at the top of the screen or, if you print the form, at the top of the first page. Form Headers are not visible in Datasheet view, and do not scroll as you scroll through records. The Form Header currently contains no data.
Detail	The area where the table data displays. The Detail section currently displays the controls for the Sports Company Employees table.
Form Footer	Another optional section that can include notes, instructions, or grand totals. Form Footers appear at the bottom of the screen or, if printed, at the end of the last page. Like Form Headers, Form Footers do not display in Datasheet view. The Form Footer section currently contains no data.

If necessary, scroll down to view the Form Footer section.

Selecting Controls

Remember that the label controls are on the left in each set of controls.

The mouse pointer must be when selecting controls.

Every object in a form is contained in a control. In this form design, the label controls are to the left of the text box controls. You need to select controls in the form to modify them. To select the First Name control,

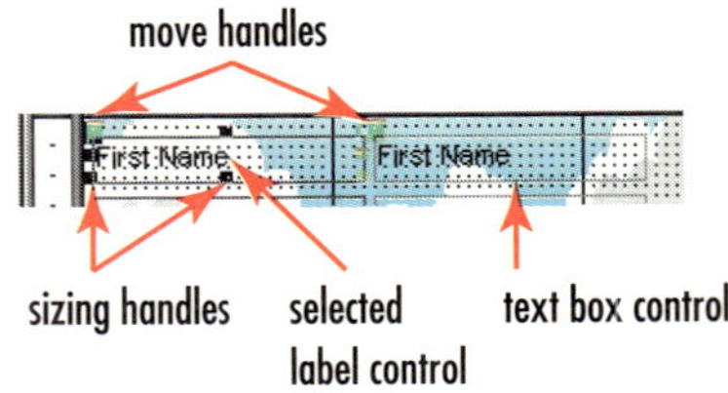

- Click First Name label control.

The First Name label control is surrounded by eight small boxes, called **sizing handles**, that indicate the label control is selected. The sizing handles are used to size the control. In addition a large box in the upper left corner is displayed. This is a **move handle** that is used to move the selected control. Notice the text box control also displays a move handle. This indicates that the two controls will act as one when manipulated. This type of control is called a **compound control**.

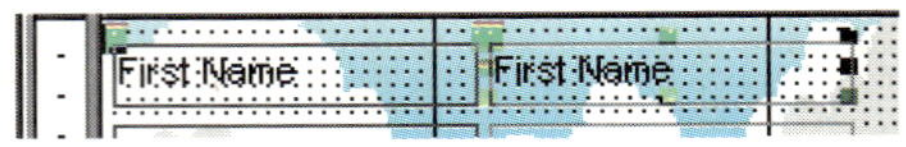

You can also press Tab to select the next control. Shift + Tab selects the previous control.

- Click First Name text box control.

Now the text box control is surrounded by eight sizing handles, indicating that it is the selected control. The move handle still appears on both parts of the compound control.

Moving and Sizing Controls

Once you select a control, you can change its location and size. The grid of dots helps you position the controls on the form. It not only provides a visual guide to positioning and sizing controls, but controls are "snapped" to the grid, or automatically positioned on the nearest grid line. You will rearrange the controls in the form as shown in Figure 2-20 on the next page.

You will begin by moving the Last Name label and text box controls to begin at the 2.5-inch position on the same line. When you can move a selected control, the mouse pointer shape appears as . You can then drag the control to any location in the form. As you move the controls, the right edge of the form will expand to accommodate the new width of the design.

You can also delete controls by selecting them, then pressing Delete.

When you first click on a control, the shape appears and will display as long as you hold down the mouse button.

Do not point to a sizing or move handle.

The move handle is used to move just the text box or label control independently in a compound control.

You can also move controls using Ctrl + the directional arrow keys.

- Select either part of the Last Name compound control.
- Point to the top or bottom border of the control.
- When the mouse pointer is a , drag the control to the right until the left edge of the outline aligns with the 2.5-inch ruler position.
- Next, drag the First Name controls down the left margin of the form to the same line as the Last Name.
- In a similar manner, move the other controls to the positions shown in Figure 2-20.

Do not be concerned if your controls are not evenly aligned with the left edge of the form or on the lines. You will learn how to adjust the spacing next.

Your screen should be similar to Figure 2-20.

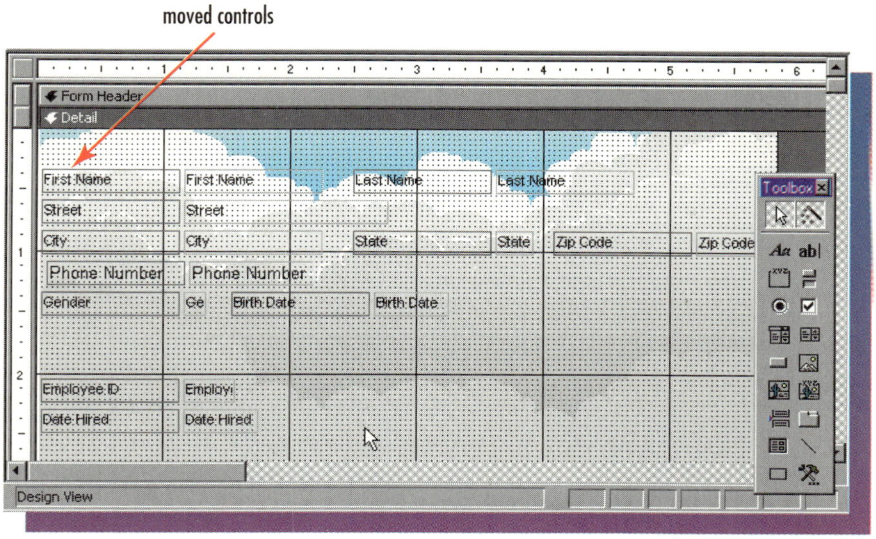

FIGURE 2-20

Next you will increase the size of the Street text box control. When you position the mouse pointer on a sizing handle, it changes to a ⟷. The direction of the arrow indicates in which direction dragging the mouse will alter the shape of the object. This is similar to sizing a window.

- Select the Street text box control.
- Point to the middle handle on the right end of the Street text box control.
- When the mouse pointer appears as ⟷, drag the control to the right until it aligns with the end of the Last Name text box control on the line above it.

Aligning Controls

Next you need to align the First Name, Street, City, Phone Number, and Gender controls to ensure that they are even along the left edge. Rather than selecting each control individually and moving it, you can select several controls at the same time. When you select multiple controls, you can move all the selected controls as a group, align the selected controls so they are evenly spaced or in line one below the other, or make other changes to the entire group of controls. To select multiple controls hold down ⇧Shift while clicking on each control. To select, then align these controls as a group,

- Hold down ⇧Shift.
- Click the First Name, Street, City, Phone Number, and Gender controls.
- Release ⇧Shift.
- Choose **F**ormat/**A**lign/**L**eft.
- Deselect the controls by clicking any blank area of the form.

When aligning controls, select only controls that are in the same row or column.

Your screen should be similar to Figure 2-21.

FIGURE 2-21

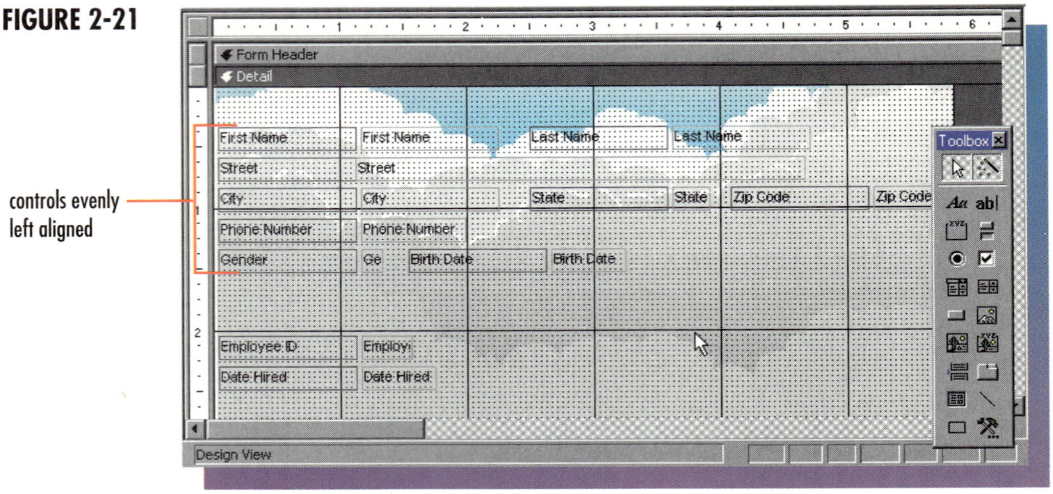

The controls all shifted to the left and are aligned with the control that was farthest left. You now want to adjust the spacing between all the controls in the upper section of this form to ensure that there is an even amount of vertical space between each control. This vertical spacing can be adjusted between any group of selected controls.

Another way to select controls is to drag a selection box around the controls. To select the controls using this method, point to a blank area above the first control and drag until the box surrounds the controls you want to select. When you release the mouse button, all the controls inside the box will be selected. To make the vertical spacing equal between these controls,

- Select all the controls (excluding the Employee ID and Date Hired controls) on the form by dragging a selection box around them.
- Choose **F**ormat/**V**ertical Spacing/Make **E**qual.
- Deselect the controls.

You can fine-tune placement by selecting a control and using Ctrl + directional keys to move it in increments.

At least three controls must be selected, and if they are compound controls, the text box part of the control must be selected.

The vertical space between controls is adjusted to make the vertical spacing between the selected controls equal. The top and bottom controls do not change locations; only the middle controls in the selection are adjusted to equalize the spacing.

Adding Text to a Form

Next you will add a label control in the form header to display the form title. In addition, you want to add two subheads within the form to identify the personal data and company data areas. The Toolbox buttons let you add text, arrows, boxes, and other design elements to a form. To add the control to the form header, you first need to add a space in the Form Header area.

- Point to the top of the Detail section bar.
- When the mouse pointer is a ✝, drag the Detail section bar down approximately 1/2-inch on the vertical ruler.

Your screen should be similar to Figure 2-22.

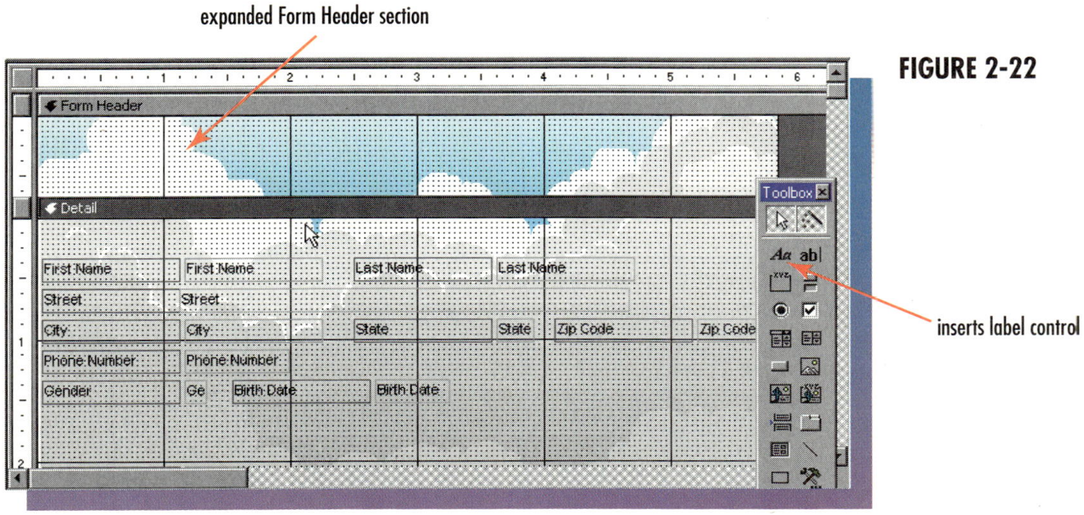

FIGURE 2-22

The [Aa] on the Toolbox is used to add a label control to a form. The mouse pointer changes to $^{+}$A when this feature is in use. You indicate where you want the control to appear by clicking on the location in the window. Then an insertion point is displayed indicating that you can begin typing the descriptive label.

- Click [Aa] Label
- Click in the Form Header area.
- Type **The Sports Company Employee Record**
- Press ←Enter.

You can edit text in label controls just as you edit other text.

The text entry feature is turned off. The form title appears in a label control box and can be sized and moved like any other control. Now you will add two more label controls for the subheads in the Detail section.

- Click [Aa] Label.
- Click in the space above the First Name control in the Detail section.
- Type **Personal Data:**
- Press ←Enter.
- In a similar manner, enter the subhead **Company Data:** in the space above the Employee ID control.

Your screen should be similar to Figure 2-23.

FIGURE 2-23

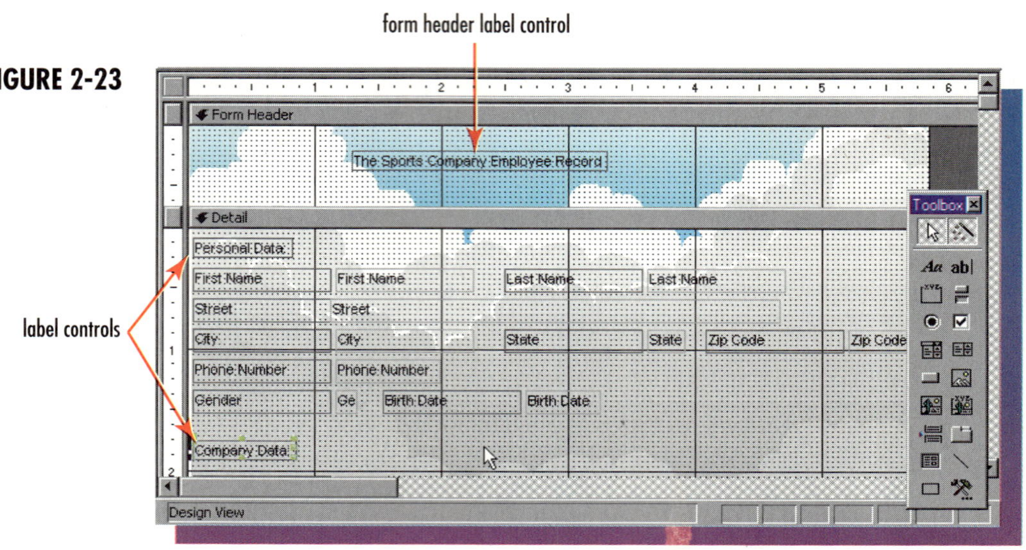

- Align the two subhead label controls along the left edge and adjust their vertical spacing appropriately.

Changing Fonts

You can further change the way a form appears by changing the font settings of the text in the controls.

Concept 8: Fonts

Fonts consist of three elements: typeface, size, and style that can be applied to characters to improve their appearance. A **typeface** is the design and shape of characters. Two common typefaces are Times New Roman and Courier. Type size refers to the size of the printed characters and is commonly measured in **points**. A 72-point character is 1 inch tall. The most common type size for text is 10 or 12 points.

Type style refers to the special attributes you assign to characters, such as bold or italic. You can also add special effects such as underlines and color to the characters.

Several common fonts in different sizes and styles are shown in the table below.

Font Name	Font Size	Font Style
Arial	This is 12 pt. This is 18 pt.	**Bold 18 pt.**
Courier New	This is 12 pt. This is 18 pt.	**Bold 18 pt.**
Times New Roman	This is 12 pt. This is 18 pt.	**Bold 18 pt.**

Although you must apply font changes to entire controls rather than changing individual characters or words, you can apply multiple font changes to a table, form, or report by selecting and changing fonts for individual controls. You should be careful, however, not to combine too many different fonts and colors or to use fancy fonts that might make it difficult to read the screen or are distracting to use for long periods of time.

The first text enhancement you want to make is to increase the font size of the text in all controls of the form. Larger fonts make it easier to read the data that is displayed in the form.

- Choose **Edit/Select All**.

The keyboard shortcut in Ctrl+A.

The Formatting toolbar buttons are used to make text enhancements, such as changing the font, font size, font style, or adding color. Notice that the Font

Size button displays "8" as the point size of all text in the selected controls. You want to increase the font size to 10 points.

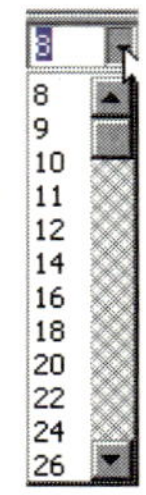

- Open the Font Size drop-down list and select 10.

The point size of all text in the selected controls changes to 10 points and is now much easier to read. Next you want to make the form title an even larger font size. You also want to change the title typeface from the default typeface of Arial to Times New Roman.

- Select the form header label control.
- Open the Font drop-down list and select Times New Roman as the typeface.
- Change the form header font size to 20.

Now the title is too large to be fully displayed in the control box. You can size the control to fully display the label by dragging on the selection handles as you did earlier, or you can allow Access to automatically size the control to fit the contents. To automatically resize the control,

- Choose **F**ormat/**S**ize/To **F**it.
- Move the form header label control to center it in the Form Header section.

Your screen should be similar to Figure 2-24.

FIGURE 2-24

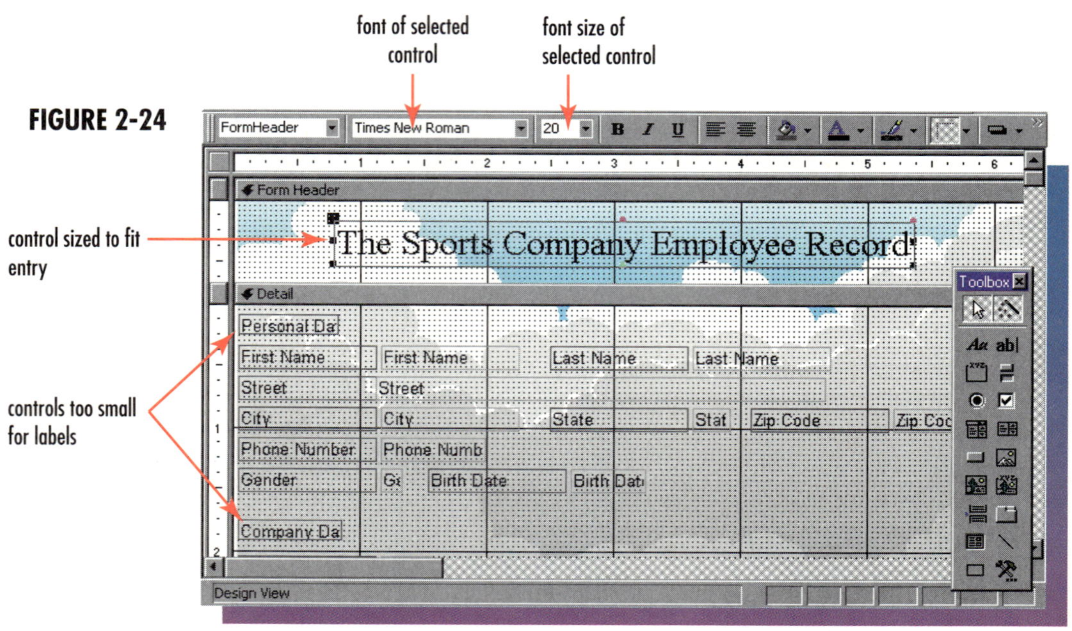

You also want to size the controls of the subheads and change their labels to bold to make them stand out from the rest of the text.

- Select the Personal Data label control.
- Click **B** Bold.
- Choose Format/Size/To Fit.
- In a similar manner, bold and size the Company Data label control.
- If necessary, adjust the vertical spacing of the two label controls.

Adding Text Color

You can also make controls more noticeable by adding color to their background, text, or borders. In addition, you can use special effects such as shadows to enhance the control border. You will make the text in the form header label red and add a shadow box to the control.

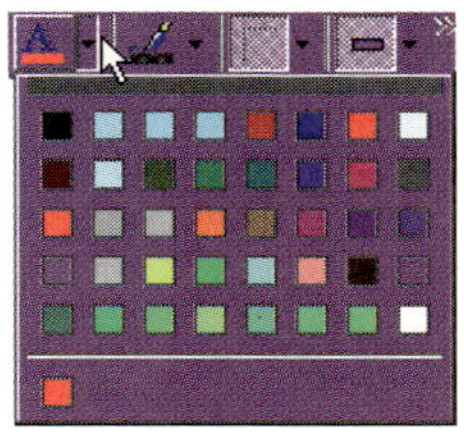

- Select the form header label control.
- Open the Font/Fore Color drop-down list.
- Click (red).
- Open the Special Effects drop-down list.

- Click Shadowed.
- Clear the selection.

The color and shadow settings have been applied to the form title. To see how the form will look onscreen, you will switch to Form view.

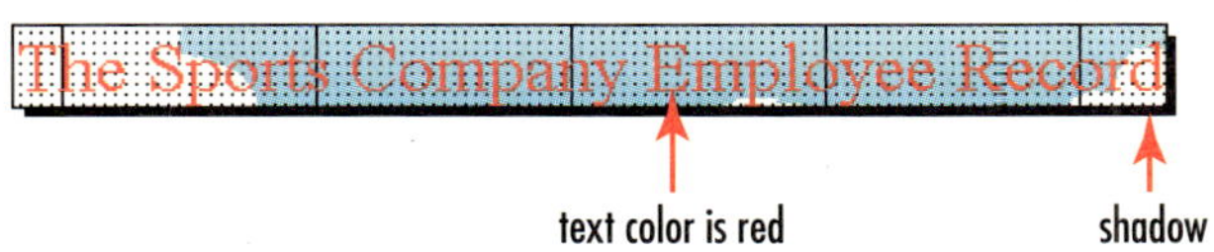

- Click Form View.

The menu equivalent is View/Form View.

Your screen should be similar to Figure 2-25.

FIGURE 2-25

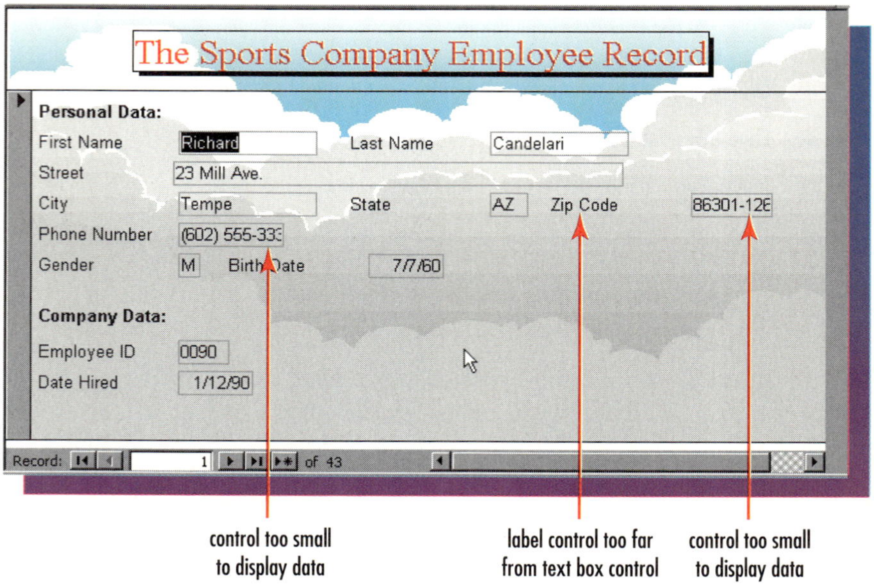

The layout and design changes greatly enhance the appearance of the form. However, now you can also see that the Zip Code and Phone Number text box controls are not wide enough to display the data in the fields. You also notice that some of the text box controls are separated by too much space from the label controls. You will increase the size of the label controls and move the text box controls closer to their labels to decrease the space between the label and data.

Depending on your screen display, other controls may not be wide enough. Make the necessary adjustments as you did for the Zip Code and Phone Number fields.

- Switch back to Form Design view.
- Increase the size of the Zip Code and Phone Number text box controls.
- Reduce the size of the State, Zip Code, and Birth Date label controls.
- Select the State text box control.
- Point to the move handle of the State text box control.
- When the mouse pointer is a , drag the control closer to the State label control.
- In a similar manner, adjust the Zip Code and Birth Date text box controls.
- Return to Form view.

Your screen should be similar to Figure 2-26.

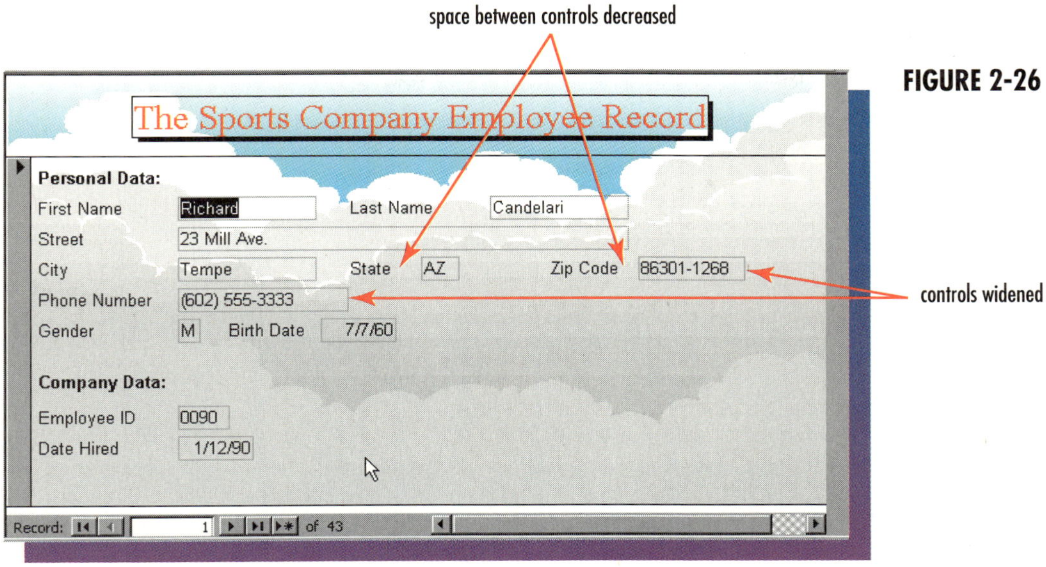

FIGURE 2-26

Entering Records in Form View

Now that the custom form is complete, you can use it to enter new records.

- Move to a new blank entry form and enter the following data for a new record.

> Use New Record in the Form toolbar or the navigation button to display a blank form.

> Press Tab to move to the next control.

> The input masks will appear in the form as you type in the field's control.

EMPLOYEE DATA

First Name: **Brent** Last Name: **Smith**

Street: **89 E. Southern Dr.**

City: **Tempe** State: **AZ** Zip Code: **85301-2316**

Phone Number: **(606) 555-1234**

Gender: **M** Birth Date: **April 13, 1971**

For Personnel Use Only:

Employee ID: **1027**
Date Hired: **September 12, 1995**

Using the form makes entering the new employee data much faster because the fields are in the same order as the information in the paper Employee Data form used by the Personnel department.

- Enter another record using your special Employee ID 9999 and your first and last name. The data in all other fields can be fictitious, except enter the current date as your date hired.

The menu equivalent is **View/Datasheet View**.

- To see the records you entered in Form Datasheet view, open the View button drop-down list and click Datasheet view.
- Scroll up a few rows to display both new records.

Your screen should be similar to Figure 2-27.

FIGURE 2-27

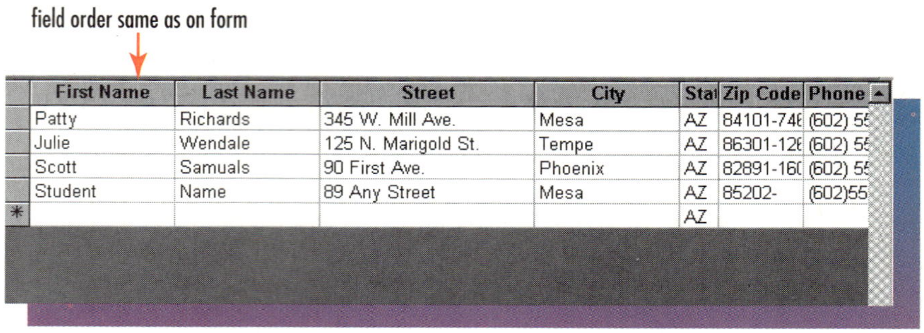

Form Datasheet view provides a datasheet view of the form data. Although it appears similar to Table Datasheet view, Form Datasheet view includes all fields from the form, including calculated fields.

Notice that the field columns are in the same order as in the form. Form Datasheet view also reflects the same field order as in the form. The Table Datasheet view, however, has not been affected by the changes you made in the form layout. Also notice that the new records are not in primary key order by employee number. When you open the table in Datasheet view, the new records will appear in primary key order.

Previewing and Printing a Form

You want to preview, then print just the form displaying your record.

You can also click in the vertical bar at the left edge of the Form window to select the record.

- Switch back to Form view.
- Check Print Preview.

Your screen should be similar to Figure 2-28.

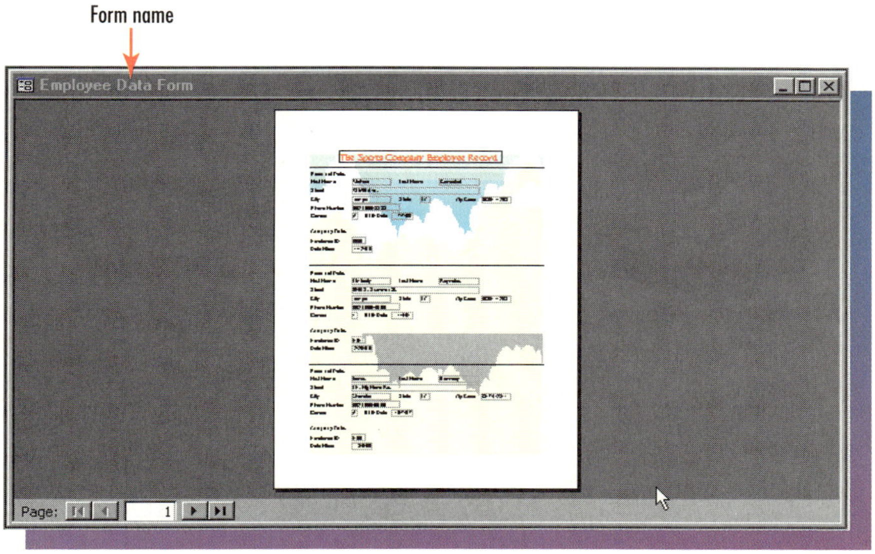

FIGURE 2-28

Form Print Preview displays whatever view of the form you were just looking at in the preview window. In this case, because you were last in Form view, the form is displayed in the preview window. The form header appears at the top of the page and three records appear below the header. You want to print only the form displaying your record. To do this,

- Return to Form view and display your record in the form.
- Choose **E**dit/Select **R**ecord.
- Choose **F**ile/**P**rint.
- Select Selected **R**ecord(s).
- Click OK.

Closing and Saving a Form

Next you will close and save the form.

- Close the Form window.
- Click Yes.

The Database window is displayed, showing the new form object name in the Forms tab object list.

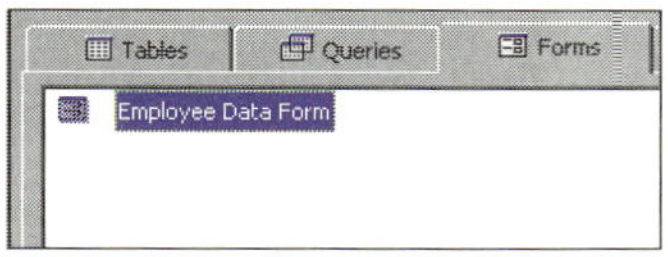

- Exit Access.

WARNING!

Do not remove your data disk from the drive until you exit Access.

LAB REVIEW

Key Terms

bound control (DB70)
calculated control (DB70)
character string (DB53)
compound control (DB78)
control (DB70)
expression (DB64)
font (DB83)
form (DB70)
identifier (DB64)
input mask (DB54)
label control (DB70)
literal character (DB54)
mask character (DB54)
move handle (DB78)
operator (DB64)
points (DB83)
sizing handles (DB78)
sort (DB67)
tab order (DB72)
text box control (DB70)
typeface (DB83)
unbound control (DB70)
validation text (DB64)
validity check (DB64)
value (DB64)

Command Summary

Command	Shortcut	Toolbar	Action
Edit/Undo	Ctrl + Z		Cancels last action
Edit/Cut	Ctrl + X or Delete	or	Deletes selected record
Edit/Select Record	⇧Shift + Spacebar		Selects current record
Edit/Select All	Ctrl + A		Selects all controls on a form in Form Design view
Edit/Find	Ctrl + F		Locates specified data
Edit/Replace	Ctrl + H		Locates and replaces specified data
View/Design View			Display a form in Design view
View/Form View			Display a form in Form view
View/Datasheet View			Display a form in Datasheet view
Insert/Field			Inserts a new field in table in Design view
Format/Hide Columns			Hides columns in Datasheet view
Format/Unhide Columns			Redisplays hidden columns in Datasheet view
Format/Align/Left			Aligns selected controls to left
Format/Size/To Fit			Automatically resizes a control to fit contents
Format/Vertical Spacing/Make Equal			Equalizes vertical space between selected multiple controls
Records/Sort/Ascending			Reorders records in ascending alphabetical order

Matching

1. operator ______ a. links a form to the underlying table
2. sizing handles ______ b. used to check that value entered in a field is valid for field type
3.  ______ c. database object used primarily for onscreen display
4. ="Accounting" or "Finance" ______ d. adds a text label control to form
5. control ______ e. symbol, such as = or AND, that indicates operation to be performed
6. > ______ f. example of an expression that would limit data that could be entered in a field
7. sort ______ g. toolbar button to locate specified data
8. validity check ______ h. small boxes that surround a selected control
9.  ______ i. changes display order of a table
10. form ______ j. format character that forces all data in field to uppercase

Fill-In Questions

1. Complete the following statements by filling in the blanks with the correct terms.

a. A(n) ____________________ is a combination of symbols that produces specific results.

b. The ____________________ property is used to specify a value that is automatically entered in a field when a new record is created.

c. When ____________________ are performed, Access makes sure that the entry is acceptable in the field.

d. Records can be temporarily displayed in a different order by using the ____________________ feature.

e. Forms are primarily used for ____________________ and making changes to existing records.

f. The ____________________ property changes the way data appears in a field.

g. The four form layouts are ____________________, ____________________, ____________________, and ____________________.

h. A(n) ____________________ is a pattern that controls the data that can be entered in a field.

i. When a form control in selected, it is surrounded by ____________________.

j. A(n) ____________________ is the design and shape of characters.

Discussion Questions

1. Discuss several different format properties and how they are used in a database.

2. Discuss why you would use input masks in a database. Give several examples of input masks and describe how they would affect the entry of data in a field.

3. Describe the three types of controls and give examples of each.

4. Discuss how validity checks work. What are some advantages of adding validity checks to a field? Include several examples.

5. Discuss the different ways records can be sorted. What are some advantages of sorting records?

Hands-On Practice Exercises

Step by Step

Rating System
☆ Easy
☆☆ Moderate
☆☆☆ Difficult

☆

1. James O'Dell at Valley of the Sun Office Supplies has created a database to track inventory.

a. Open the Valley of the Sun Office Supplies database and the Inventory table. Make the following changes to the records indicated:

Item #78564	should read "clips," not "blips"
Item #28765	should indicate 10 Rolls/Box
Item #18719	has 8 pens in stock, not 863
Item #25743	price is $18.50 not $185.00

b. Using the Find command, find item #53410 and enter the correct item number, 54301.

c. Add a field property to the Item Name field to force the data in the field to display in all capital letters.

d. Enter the item number 99999 in the Item # field and your name in the Item Name field of a new record. Resize the Item Name column. Sort the table by Item Name, then print the table.

e. Return the table to the primary key sort order.

f. Close the table, saving any changes.

☆☆

2. Michelle owns Food for Thought Catering. As her catering business continues to grow, she has established a reputation for excellent gourmet health foods. Nevertheless, she continues to serve whatever kinds of food her customers request. She wants your assistance to help her customize her database of client records.

a. Open the Food for Thought Catering database and the Customers table.

b. To help Michelle track which customers prefer healthy foods, in Table Design view, add a field after the Preferred Theme field. Use the following guidelines to define the new field:

Field name:	Healthy Foods
Data type:	Text
Description:	Does client prefer health-conscious foods?
Field size:	8
Format:	Display in all capital letters
Validation rule:	"Always" or "Never" or "Optional"
Validation text:	"Selection must be either Always, Never, or Optional"

c. Update the table by entering an option in the Healthy Foods field for each record.

d. Using the Form Wizard, create a columnar form. Use the Colorful 2 style. Title the new form "Customer Information Form." In Design view, move the controls to make the computerized form look similar to Michelle's current paper form shown below. Also add the label for the title and a subhead for the Customer Preferences section of the form as shown in the paper form.

Customer Information Form

Customer #:		
Company:		
Contact:		Phone:
Address:		
City:	State:	Zipcode:

Customer Preferences

Healthy Food?
Preferred Theme?
Favorite Dish?

e. In Form Design view, make these enhancements to the form:

- Increase the font size for all controls to 12 points.

- Change the font for the Customer Information Form label control to a typeface of your choice and to 20 points, then size the control to fit.
- Change the font for the Customer Preferences label control to 14-point italic, then size the control to fit and underline the text.

f. Add these new customers to the table using the new form:

Customer Information Form

Customer #: 27691
Company: Desert Rescue Cleaning Service
Contact: Debbie Harrington Phone: 212-3999
Address: 6730 E. Ray Rd.
City: Chandler
State: AZ
Zipcode: 85601

Customer Preferences

Healthy Food? Always
Preferred Theme? Merry Maids
Favorite Dish? Souffle

Customer Information Form

Customer #: 41476
Company: Sunset Publishing
Contact: Jessica Herrera Phone: 999-6110
Address: 3276 S. Rural Rd.
City: Tempe
State: AZ
Zipcode: 89562

Customer Preferences

Healthy Food? Always
Preferred Theme? Library
Favorite Dish? Spinach Salad

g. Adjust the size of any controls as needed to display the data appropriately. Adjust the alignment and vertical spacing of controls as needed.

h. Display the record for The Sports Company in the form. Change the contact name to your name. Print the record.

☆☆☆

3. Eddie Fitzpatrick of TechnoBabble Electronics heard from Michelle at Food for Thought Catering that you are great with Access databases. Eddie needs you to help him customize the database that his cousin Teddy helped him set up. He has been putting in records, but doesn't know how to edit the data or to create a data entry form.

a. Open the TechnoBabble Electronics database and the Inventory table. Make these changes to the records:

Item #7195: change 100 to 133 in the Description field

Item #8031: change sEcurty to Security in the Description field

In all records where MPS is the supplier, change MPS to CTC.

b. Teddy created sample entries for the table while Eddie was learning how to use the database. You now need to delete those records. Delete records for items #5640, #5926, and #6832.

c. Find item #8205 and change the cost from $200 to $150.

d. In Table Design view, add a field for the purchase price between Cost and Quantity on Hand, with these specifications:

Field name:	Purchase Price
Data type:	Currency
Description:	Cost to Customer

e. Add a field between Shelf Location and Supplier for the status of each item, indicating whether it is a regularly stocked item or a special order item. Use these specifications:

Field name:	Status
Data type:	Text
Description:	What is the stocking status of this item?
Field size:	9
Format:	Display in all capital letters
Default value:	STOCK
Validation rule:	Stock or SpecOrder
Validation text:	Stocking status must be either Stock or SpecOrder

f. Change the Quantity on Hand field name to # On Hand, and the Shelf Location field name to Shelf. Change the supplies description to "3-character supplier code."

g. Add customer prices and stocking status to the existing data in the table.

h. Sort the table on the Description field, resize the columns, then print the table.

i. Return the table to the primary key sort order.

j. Create a columnar form for Eddie using the Form Wizard. Use the Evergreen background and name the form TechnoBabble Electronics Inventory List.

k. In Form Design view, move the controls so the form layout looks similar to Eddie's existing data entry form shown below. Add the label controls to display the form title and the Confidential subhead. Adjust the alignment and vertical spacing of controls as reached.

TechnoBabble Electronics Inventory List

Item #: ______________
Description: ______________________
Shelf: ________ # On Hand: ________
Purchase Price: ___________

Confidential
Supplier: ______________________
Status: ________ Cost: ____________

l. In Form Design view, enhance the form by making these changes:

- Change the form title text to yellow.
- Bold all controls in the form.
- Change all controls to 10-point Times New Roman.
- Change the text in the title control to a typeface of your choice and 18 points, then size the control to fit.
- Change the text in the Confidential control to 14-point Arial italic, then size the control to fit.
- Enlarge the Status text box control.

m. Using the form, enter the following two new records:

TechnoBabble Electronics Inventory List

Item #: 2317
Description: Pager
Shelf: B-21 # On Hand: 4
Purchase Price: $74.50

Confidential
Supplier: CTC
Status: STOCK Cost: $32.95

TechnoBabble Electronics Inventory List

Item #: 9611
Description: Keyboard, Electronic Music
Shelf: H-01 # On Hand: 1
Purchase Price: $324.35

Confidential
Supplier: MEE
Status: SPECORDER Cost: $178.50

n. While looking at the form, you notice several controls are not sized appropriately for the data they display. Return to Design view and adjust the textbox controls as needed.

o. Use the Find command to locate the record for Item #3910. Add your name in the Description field. Select, then print the record. Close the form, saving any changes.

On Your Own

☆☆

4. Debbie owns Desert Rescue Cleaning Service. Her commercial cleaning business is prospering, and she has asked you to help her by entering some new data and customizing her database of client records.

Open the Desert Rescue Cleaning Service database and the Clients table, then add five new records with either real or fictitious data. Change the contact in The Sports Company record to your name. Adjust the column widths as necessary.

Make any changes to the field properties that would make data entry easier, such as adding format properties or validation rules.

Use the Form Wizard to create a columnar form for data entry, named Desert Rescue Cleaning Service Client Data Form, arranging the controls to make data entry easy. Remember to add a title and any other helpful information on the form as a label.

Find the record for The Sports Company and print that form.

☆☆

5. Michael has just contacted you from Go West Dude Ranch. The database you helped Michael create is working well, but he needs to make some changes. He is adding clients daily. Most of the clients are medium-sized companies who rent the Dude Ranch for special company functions, meetings, or other corporate events. Michael would like to track these customers. Help him with the database by making the following changes:

Open the Go West Dude Ranch database. Add a phone number field and data to the Staff table. Create a new table named Business Clients to track clients. Include an identification field and a contact person for each company. Remember to create a primary key field. Use appropriate field properties to make data entry easier.

Add three new business clients to the table. Adjust the display so that all information is displayed in each column. Sort the data by company name, then print the table. Return the order to primary key order. Remember to save any layout changes to the table.

Create a columnar form based on the Business Clients table for entering new clients into the table, and name it Go West Dude Ranch New Client Information. Enter three more new clients, including The Sports Company, making yourself the contact person for the company. Print that record form.

Create a columnar form named Go West Dude Ranch Employees, based on the Staff Records table, for the employees table that you helped Michael create earlier. You have agreed to take on another part-time job helping Michael out at the Dude Ranch in the Data Processing department, so enter a record for yourself using the new form, then print your record.

☆☆☆

6. You are looking for a new job. To keep track of all the companies you have contacted, you decide to create a database file of this information.

Name the database file My Contacts. Create a table named Contacts that includes fields such as the company name, address, phone number, name of the contact person, and type of company. Include a field that is a unique number that you can assign each record. Make this field the primary key. Include other fields that you can use to track your status with the company, for example, fields that indicate the date a resume was sent, a phone contact was made, or the date of an interview.

Add appropriate field properties, such as formats, validation rules, and input masks. Enter at least five records. Print the table.

Create a columnar form named [Your Name] Employment Contacts. Use the form to add five additional records. Print one record.

2 Modifying a Table and Creating a Form

Concepts

- Format Property
- Default Value Property
- Input Mask Property
- Find and Replace
- Validity Checks
- Sort
- Forms
- Fonts

Format Property

You can use the Format property to create custom formats that change the way numbers, dates, times, and text display and print.

Default Value Property

The Default Value property is used to specify a value to be automatically entered in a field when a new record is created.

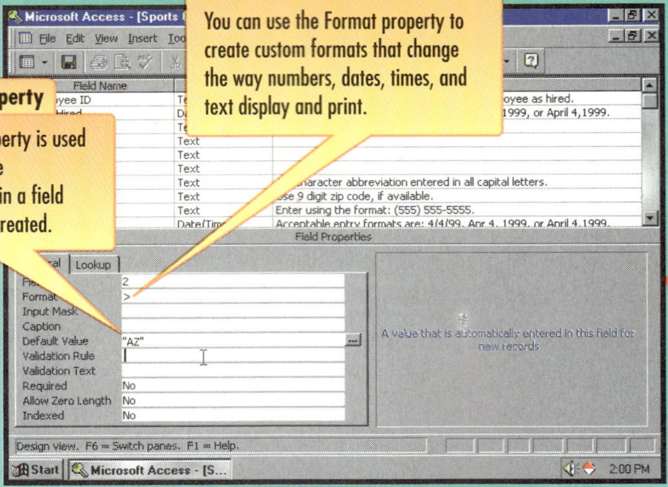

Input Mask Property

An input mask is a pattern that controls the data that can be entered in a field.

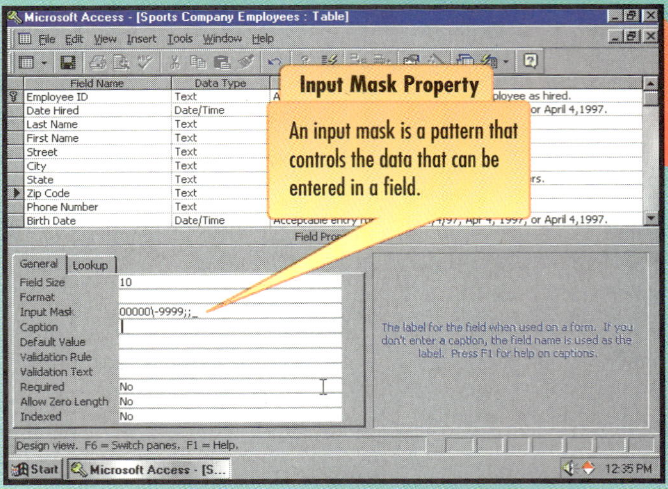

Sort

You can quickly reorder records in a table by sorting a table to display in a different record order.

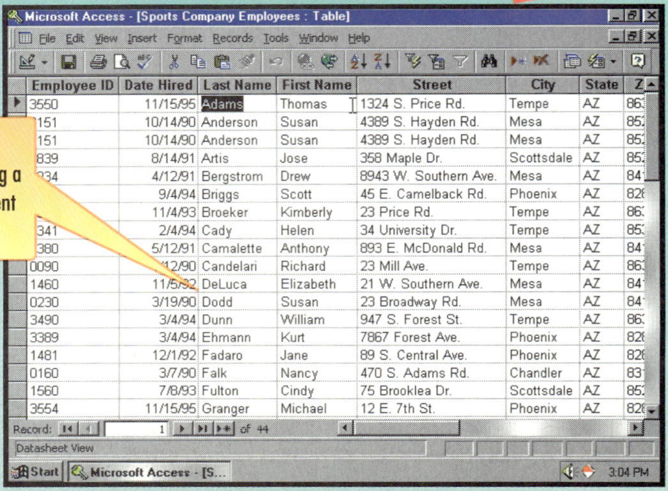

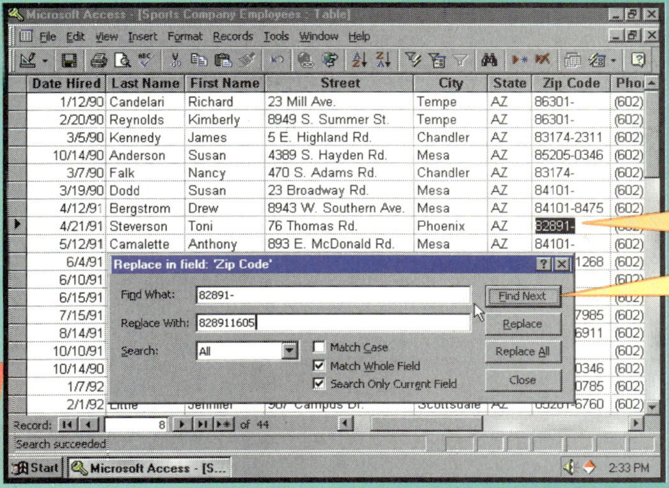

Find and Replace

The ability to quickly find specific information and automatically replace it with new information is one of the main advantages of a computerized database.

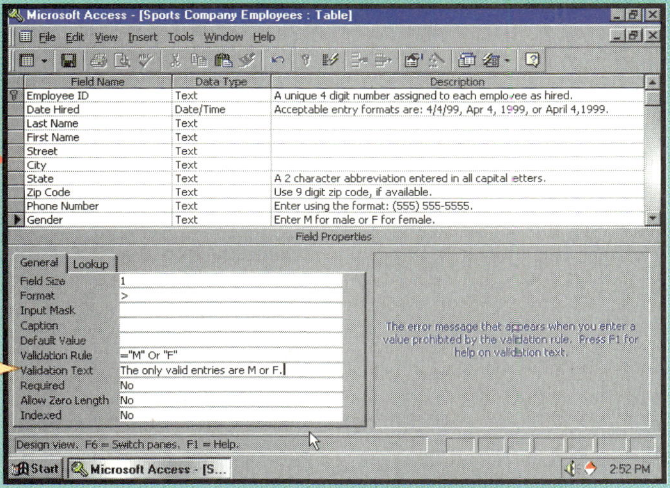

Validity Checks

Access automatically performs certain checks, called validity checks, on values entered in a field to make sure that the values are valid for the field type.

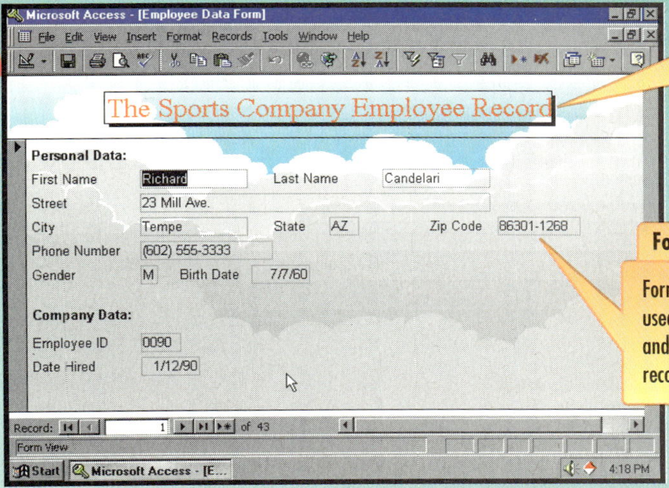

Fonts

Fonts consist of three elements: typeface, size, and style that can be applied to characters to improve their appearance.

Forms

Forms are database objects used primarily for data entry and making changes to existing records.

3 Filtering and Querying Tables

COMPETENCIES

After completing this lab, you will know how to:

1. **Filter table records.**
2. **Create a query.**
3. **Move columns.**
4. **Query with comparison operators.**
5. **Query multiple tables.**
6. **Save a query.**
7. **Create a calculated field.**
8. **Create a multiple-table form.**

CASE STUDY

You are satisfied with the structure of the table of employee records and have entered many more records. You have also created several other tables that contain employee data such as pay rates and job titles. However, compiling, storing, and updating information in your database is useful only if you can find the information you need quickly, and can manipulate it and analyze it to answer specific questions.

You will use the information in the tables to provide the answers to several inquiries about The Sports Company employees. As you learn about the analytical features, think what it would be like to do the same task by hand. How long would it take? Would it be as accurate or as well presented? Your appreciation grows as you learn more about what the application can do for you. The output from one of your inquiries is shown here.

Department	Last Name	First Name	Hourly Rate	New Rate
Clothing	Fisher	Sarah	$5.00	$5.38
Sports Equipment	Lawson	Tamara	$5.00	$5.38
Sports Equipment	Moran	Jeannie	$5.00	$5.38
Sports Equipment	Lye	Hin	$5.00	$5.38
Warehouse	Castillo	Blas	$4.50	$4.84
Warehouse	Lockwood	Craig	$5.25	$5.64
Warehouse	Hayes	Carol	$5.00	$5.38
Warehouse	Granger	Michael	$4.50	$4.84
Warehouse	Jessup	Hart	$5.00	$5.38
Warehouse	Fulton	Cindy	$5.00	$5.38

In addition, you will create another form (shown on the right) to be used to update information in several tables simultaneously.

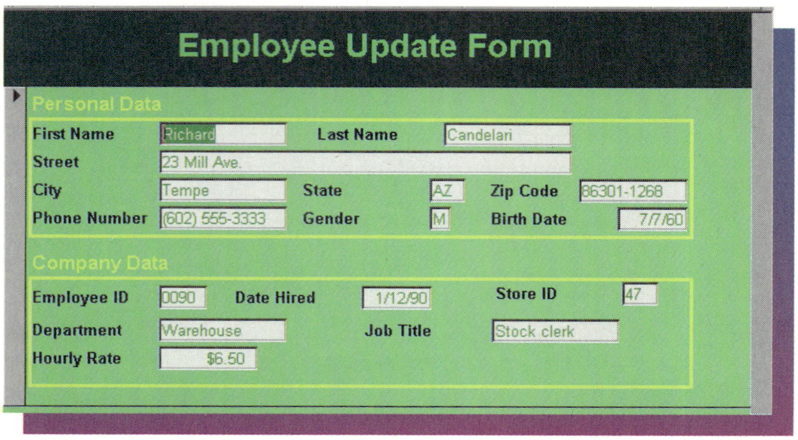

Concept Overview

The following concepts will be introduced in this lab:

1. Filter	A filter is a restriction you place on records in the open datasheet or form to temporarily isolate and display a subset of records.
2. AND and OR Operators	The AND and OR operators are used to specify multiple conditions that must be met for the records to display in the datasheet.
3. Wildcard Characters	Wildcard characters are placeholders that represent any series of characters or any single character.
4. Query	A query is a question you ask of a database that allows you to view data in different ways, to analyze data, and even to change existing data.
5. Joins and Relationships	You can bring information from different tables in your database together by defining a relationship to join the tables.
6. Calculated Field	A calculated field displays the result of a calculation in a query.

Part 1

Using Filter by Selection

You have continued to enter employee records into the Employees table. The updated table has been saved for you as Sports Company Employees in the Sports Company Personnel Records database on your data disk.

- Start Access 97. Put your data disk in the appropriate drive for your system.
- Open the Sports Company Personnel Records database file.

The Tables list box of the Database window displays the names of four tables in this database: Sports Company Employees, Weekly Hours Worked, Employee Pay Rates, and Employees by Department and Position. These tables will be used throughout the lab.

- Open the Sports Company Employees table.
- If necessary, maximize the table Datasheet window.
- Add your information as record number 73 using your special ID number 9999 and the current date as your hire date.

While you are using the table, the manager asks you for two items of information. The first is a request from an employee who wants to form a carpool. The employee wants to know the names of other employees who live in her town. The second is to help figure out the name of the employee who recently sent the manager a memo. The memo suggested how the warehouse could save time and money by changing one of the reporting procedures it uses. Although the first name in the memo is legible, the last name is not. The manager can only make out the first letter of the last name, C.

To answer both questions, you could sort the table and then write down the needed information. However, this could be time consuming if you had hundreds of employees in the table. A faster way is to apply a filter to the table records to locate this information.

Concept 1: Filter

A **filter** is a restriction you place on records in the open datasheet or form to quickly isolate and display a subset of records. A filter is created by specifying a set of limiting conditions, or **criteria**, you want records to meet in order to be displayed. A filter is ideal when you only want to display the subset for a brief time, then return immediately to the full set of records. You can print the filtered records as you would any form or table. A filter is only temporary and all records are redisplayed when you remove the filter or close and reopen the table or form. The filter results cannot be saved. However, the last filter criteria you specify are saved with the table and the results can be quickly redisplayed.

To find only those employees in the city of Chandler, you can quickly filter out all the other records using the Filter by Selection method. **Filter by Selection** is used when you can easily find and select an instance of the value in the table that you want the filter to use as the criterion to meet.

If the selected part of a value starts with the first character in the field, the subset displays all records whose values begin with the same selected characters.

How the value is selected determines what results will be displayed. Placing the insertion point in a field selects the entire field contents. The filtered subset will include all records containing an exact match. Selecting part of a value in a field (by highlighting it) displays all records containing the selection. For example, in a table for a book collection, you could position the mouse pointer anywhere in a field containing the name of the author Stephen King, choose the Filter by Selection command, and only records for books whose author matches the selected name, "Stephen King," would be displayed. Selecting the last name "King" would include all records for authors Stephen King, Martin Luther King, and Barbara Kingsolver.

You want to filter the table to display only those records with a City field entry of Chandler. To specify the city to locate, you need to select an example of the data in the table.

The menu equivalent is Records/Filter/Filter by Selection.

- Move to the City field of record 3.
- Click Filter by Selection.

Your screen should be similar to Figure 3-1.

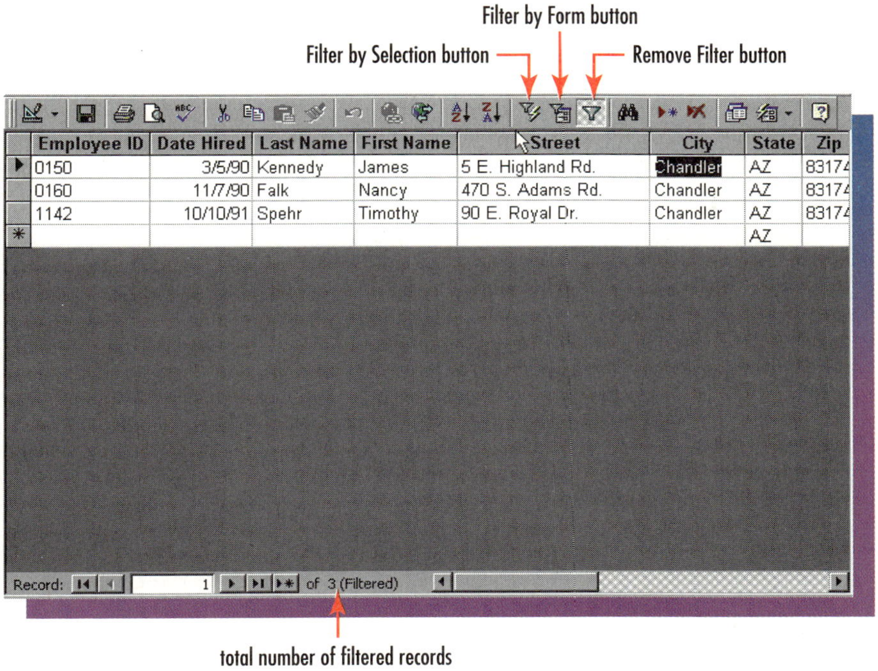

FIGURE 3-1

The datasheet displays only those records that contain the selected city. All other records are temporarily hidden. The status bar indicates the total number of filtered records and shows that the datasheet is filtered. To remove the filter,

- Click Remove Filter.

You can print the filtered datasheet like any other datasheet.

The menu equivalent is Records/Remove Filter/Sort.

Using Filter by Form

After seeing how easy it was to locate this information, the manager asks you to also locate employees who live in the city of Mesa. This information may help in setting up the carpool, since the people traveling from the city of Chandler pass through Mesa on the way to the store. To find out this additional information, you need to use the **Filter by Form** method. This method allows you to perform filters on multiple criteria.

- Click Filter by Form.

The menu equivalent is Records/Filter/Filter By Form.

Your screen should be similar to Figure 3-2.

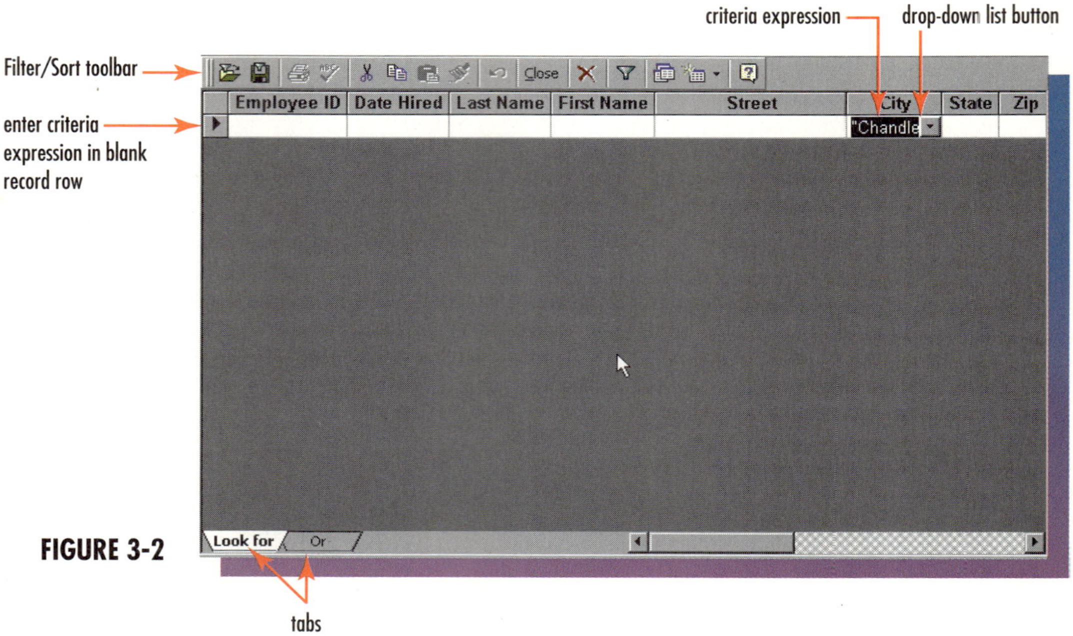

FIGURE 3-2

The Filter by Form window displays a blank version of the current datasheet with empty fields in which you specify the criteria. This window automatically displays a Filter/Sort toolbar that contains the standard buttons as well as buttons (identified below) that are specific to the Filter by Form window.

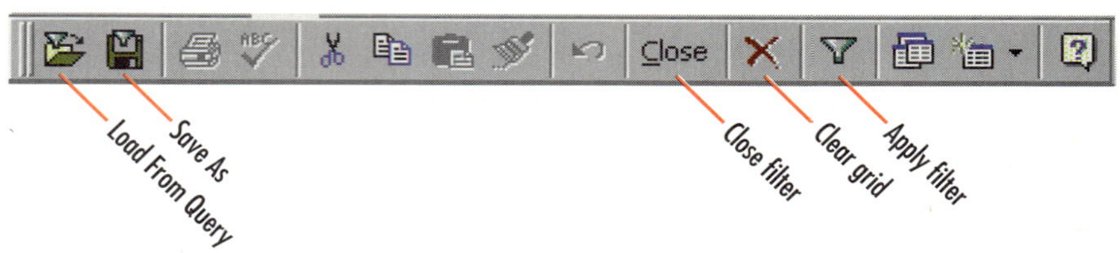

Refer to Concept 6: Validity Checks in Lab 2 to review expressions.

The window also includes two tabs, Look For and Or, where you enter the filter criteria. The criteria are entered in the blank field space of the record row as an expression. A **criteria expression** specifies the criteria for the filter to use. You can either type values or choose values from a drop-down list in the desired field to create the criteria expression.

Currently the City field displays the criterion you last specified using Filter by Selection as the criteria expression. Notice that the field displays a drop-down list button. Each field will display a drop-down button when the field is selected. Clicking the button displays a list of values that are available in that field from which you can select to help you enter the criteria expression.

Since the City field already contains the correct criterion, you do not need to enter a different criterion. Next, you need to add the second criterion to the filter to include all records with a City field value of Mesa. To instruct the filter to locate records meeting multiple criteria, you use the AND or OR operators.

Concept 2: AND and OR Operators

The AND and OR operators are used to specify multiple conditions that must be met for the records to display in the filter datasheet. The AND operator narrows the search, because a record must meet both conditions to be included. The OR operator broadens the search, because any record meeting either condition is included in the output.

The AND operator is assumed when you enter criteria in multiple fields. Within a field, typing the word "AND" between criteria in the same field establishes the AND condition. For example, in the book table you could enter "Stephen King" in the author name field, then you could enter "Horror" in the category field to display records where the author's name is Stephen King and the category is Horror.

The OR operator is established by entering the criterion in the Or tab, or by typing "OR" between criteria in the same field. For example, you could enter "Stephen King" in the author name field, select the Or tab, then enter "Horror" in the category field. This filter would display those records where the author's name is Stephen King or where the category is Horror.

In this filter you will use an OR operator so that records meeting either city criterion will be included in the output. To include the city as an OR criterion, you enter the criterion in the Or tab.

A value must be entered in the Look For tab before the Or tab is available.

- Click Or.

The Or tab is opened and a new blank row is displayed. You will enter the expression specifying the criterion by selecting the criterion from the City drop-down list.

You could also have entered the expression "Chandler" or "Mesa" in the City field of the Look For tab.

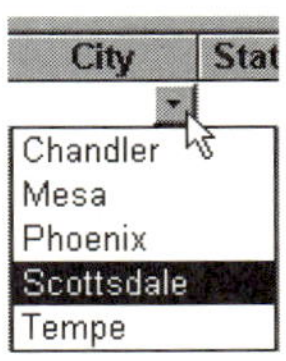

- Click (in the City field).
- Choose Mesa.

Your screen should be similar to Figure 3-3.

FIGURE 3-3

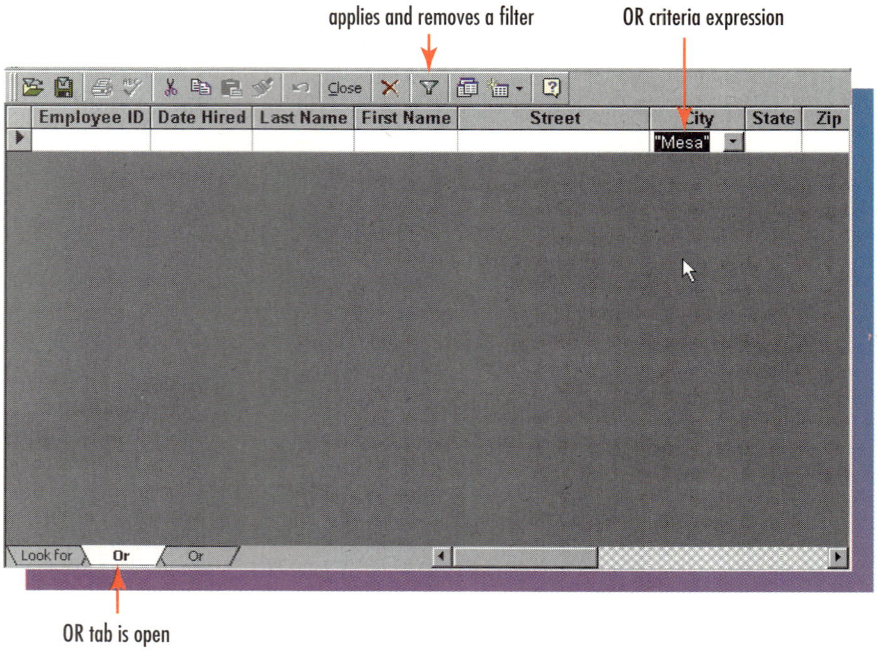

The selected criterion is displayed in the City field. It is surrounded by quotes, as required of all text entries used in an expression. The Look For tab still contains the criteria for city of Chandler. To apply the filter,

> [Apply filter button] is a toggle button that applies and removes a filter.

> The menu equivalent is Filter/Apply Filter/Sort.

- Click [Apply filter button] Apply filter.

The filtered datasheet displays the records for all 21 employees who live in the city of Chandler or Mesa.

Your screen should be similar to Figure 3-4.

FIGURE 3-4

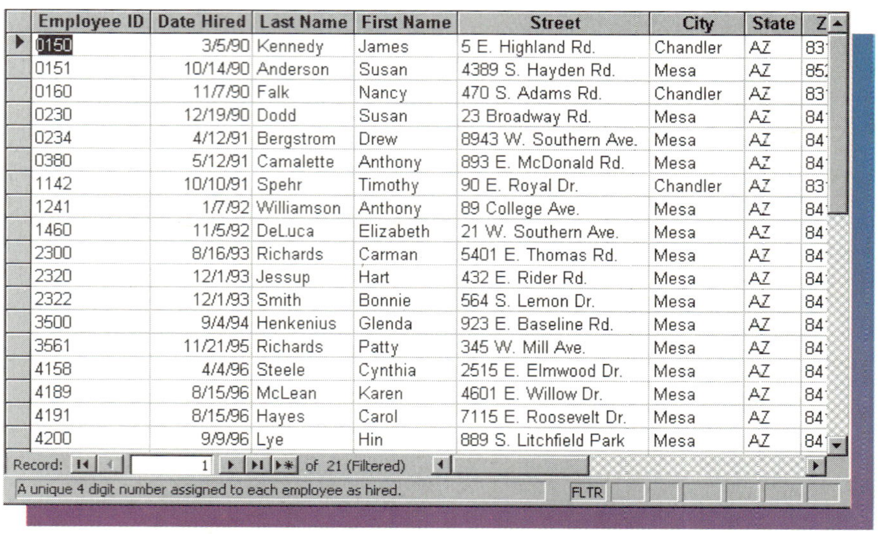

Employee ID	Date Hired	Last Name	First Name	Street	City	State	Z
0150	3/5/90	Kennedy	James	5 E. Highland Rd.	Chandler	AZ	83
0151	10/14/90	Anderson	Susan	4389 S. Hayden Rd.	Mesa	AZ	85
0160	11/7/90	Falk	Nancy	470 S. Adams Rd.	Chandler	AZ	83
0230	12/19/90	Dodd	Susan	23 Broadway Rd.	Mesa	AZ	84
0234	4/12/91	Bergstrom	Drew	8943 W. Southern Ave.	Mesa	AZ	84
0380	5/12/91	Camalette	Anthony	893 E. McDonald Rd.	Mesa	AZ	84
1142	10/10/91	Spehr	Timothy	90 E. Royal Dr.	Chandler	AZ	83
1241	1/7/92	Williamson	Anthony	89 College Ave.	Mesa	AZ	84
1460	11/5/92	DeLuca	Elizabeth	21 W. Southern Ave.	Mesa	AZ	84
2300	8/16/93	Richards	Carman	5401 E. Thomas Rd.	Mesa	AZ	84
2320	12/1/93	Jessup	Hart	432 E. Rider Rd.	Mesa	AZ	84
2322	12/1/93	Smith	Bonnie	564 S. Lemon Dr.	Mesa	AZ	84
3500	9/4/94	Henkenius	Glenda	923 E. Baseline Rd.	Mesa	AZ	84
3561	11/21/95	Richards	Patty	345 W. Mill Ave.	Mesa	AZ	84
4158	4/4/96	Steele	Cynthia	2515 E. Elmwood Dr.	Mesa	AZ	84
4189	8/15/96	McLean	Karen	4601 E. Willow Dr.	Mesa	AZ	84
4191	8/15/96	Hayes	Carol	7115 E. Roosevelt Dr.	Mesa	AZ	84
4200	9/9/96	Lye	Hin	889 S. Litchfield Park	Mesa	AZ	84

Record: 1 of 21 (Filtered)

A unique 4 digit number assigned to each employee as hired. FLTR

The manager's second request is to locate the employee whose last name begins with the letter C. This filter requires that you enter an expression in the Last Name field. To clear all existing expressions from the Filter Form window,

- Click Filter by Form.
- Click Clear Grid.
- Move to the Last Name field.

You do not need to remove a filter before applying another.

The menu equivalent is Edit/Clear Grid.

To specify the criteria to find this employee, you will use a wildcard character in the expression.

Concept 3: Wildcard Characters

Wildcard characters are placeholders in an expression that represent any series of characters or any single character. They specify a value you want to find when you either know only part of the value or want to find all values that begin with a certain letter or match a specific pattern.

The six wildcard characters are described below.

Character	Use	Example
*	Matches any number of characters.	"Smit*" locates Smitt, Smith, Smithers. "*ing" locates all occurrences of values ending in "ing."
?	Matches any single character.	"Smit?" locates Smitt and Smith, but not Smithers. "b?t" locates bet, bit, but, or Bat, but not beat.
[]	Matches any single character within the brackets.	"b[iu]t" locates bit and but, but not bet or bat.
!	Matches any character not in the brackets.	"b[!iu]t" locates bet and bat, but not bit or but.
-	Matches any one of a range of characters that you specify.	"[a-h]eat" locates beat, feat, and heat, but not meat, neat, or seat.
#	Matches any single numeric character.	"1#3" locates 153 or 163, but not 1453 or 19653.

The expression C* will find any series of characters that follows the letter C.

- Type **c***
- Press ←Enter.

The letter can be entered in either upper- or lowercase, because Access is not case sensitive.

Access automatically converts the entry you typed to "Like 'c*'." Access gives you flexibility in the way you enter expressions, but it will convert what you type into expressions displaying the correct rules or syntax for the expression. In this case Access added the LIKE operator to the expression and enclosed the expression in double quotation marks. If you do not include an operator when using wildcard characters, Access automatically enters the appropriate operator for you.

criteria expression with wildcard character

- Click Apply Filter.

Your screen should be similar to Figure 3-5.

FIGURE 3-5

Employee ID	Date Hired	Last Name	First Name	Street	City	State	Zip
0090	1/12/90	Candelari	Richard	23 Mill Ave.	Tempe	AZ	86301
0380	5/12/91	Camalette	Anthony	893 E. McDonald Rd.	Mesa	AZ	84101
2341	2/4/94	Cady	Helen	34 University Dr.	Tempe	AZ	85301
4255	3/2/97	Carrier	Kirk	932 E. Parkway Dr.	Mesa	AZ	84101
4269	5/3/97	Castillo	Blas	382 E. Meadow Ave.	Phoenix	AZ	82891
*						AZ	

The filtered datasheet displays the records for all employees (five) whose last names begin with the letter C. Now the manager can determine which employee sent the memo.

To redisplay all records in the table and continue working.

- Click Remove Filter.
- Close the Sports Company Employees table (save your changes).

The filter criteria you last specified are saved with the table, and the results can be redisplayed simply by applying the filter.

Creating a Query

Your next request for information is for a list of all employees and their hire dates. Although you could use a filter to get the information, a filter displays the entire record. You want the list to display only the employees' names and hire dates. To create this list, you need to use a query.

Concept 4: Query

A **query** is a question you ask of the data contained in your database. You use queries to view data in different ways, to analyze data, and even to change existing data. Since queries are based on tables, you can also use a query as the source for forms and reports. The five types of queries are described in the table below.

Query Type	Description
Select query	Retrieves the specific data you request from one or more tables, then displays the data in a query datasheet in the order you specify. This is the most common type of query.
Crosstab query	Summarizes large amounts of data in an easy-to-read, row-and-column format.
Parameter query	Displays a dialog box prompting you for information, such as criteria for locating data. For example, a parameter query might request the beginning and ending dates, then display all records matching dates between the two specified values.
Action query	Makes changes to many records in one operation. There are four types of action queries: a make-table query creates a new table from selected data in one or more tables; an update query makes update changes to records, such as when you need to raise salaries of all sales staff by 7 percent; an append query adds records from one or more tables to the end of other tables; and a delete query deletes records from a table or tables.
SQL query	Created using SQL (Structured Query Language), an advanced programming language used in Access.

To create a new query,

- Open the Queries tab.
- Click New.

The New Query dialog box contains five options for creating queries. You can create a query from scratch in Query Design view or by using one of the four Query Wizards. The table on the next page explains the type of query each of the four wizards creates.

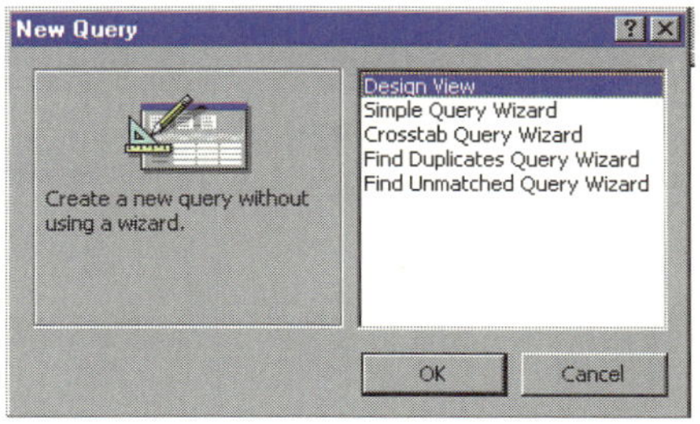

Query Wizard	Type of Query Created
Simple	Select query
Crosstab	Crosstab query
Find Duplicates	Locates all records that contain duplicate values in one or more fields in the specified tables
Find Unmatched	Locates records in one table that do not have records in another. For example, you could locate all employees in one table who have no hours worked in another table.

To create a select query using the Simple Query Wizard,

- Select Simple Query Wizard.
- Click OK.

In the first Simple Query Wizard window (shown in Figure 3-6), you specify the table and the fields from the table that will give you the desired query result. You need a list of employees and hire dates from the Sports Company Employees table.

- Open the Table/Queries drop-down list.
- Select Table: Sports Company Employees.
- Add the Date Hired, Last Name and First Name fields to the Selected Fields list.

Double-click the field name in the Available Fields list to add it to the Selected Fields list.

The dialog box on your screen should be similar to Figure 3-6.

FIGURE 3-6

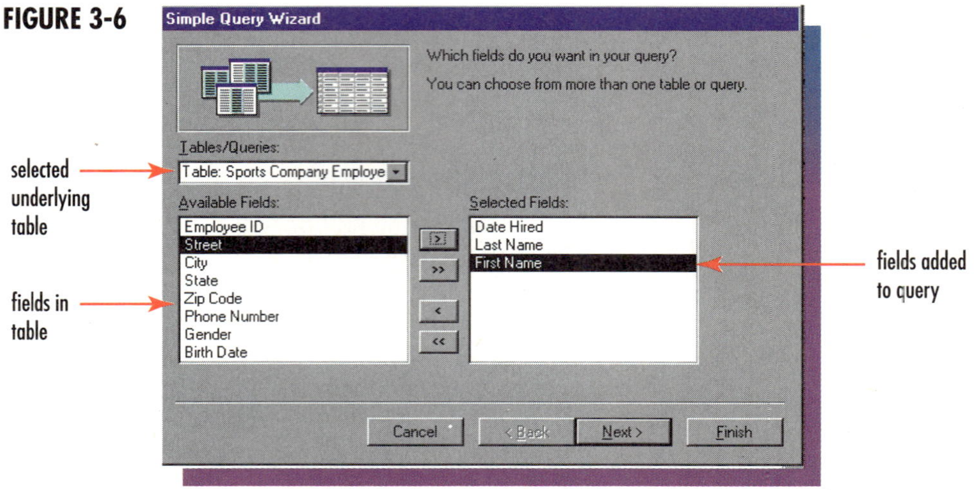

- Click [Next >].
- Replace the suggested title in the text box with "Hire Date."
- Click [Finish].

After a few moments, your screen should be similar to Figure 3-7.

Query Datasheet view displays query results

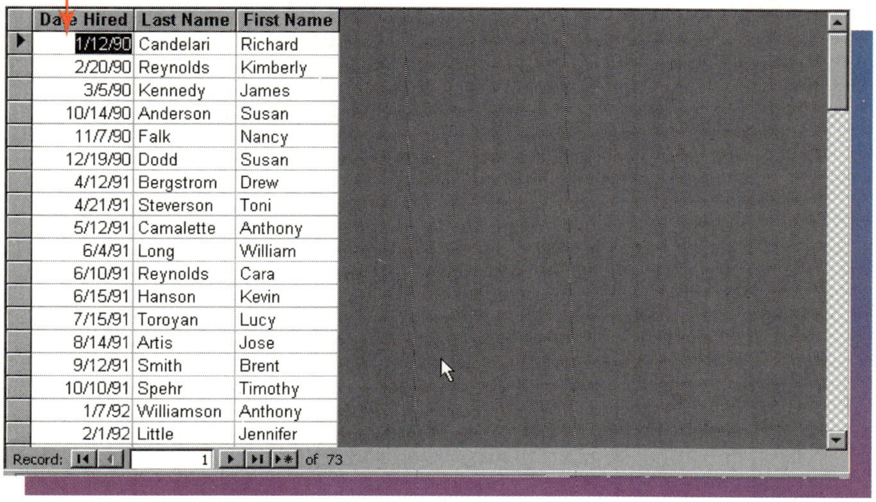

Date Hired	Last Name	First Name
1/12/90	Candelari	Richard
2/20/90	Reynolds	Kimberly
3/5/90	Kennedy	James
10/14/90	Anderson	Susan
11/7/90	Falk	Nancy
12/19/90	Dodd	Susan
4/12/91	Bergstrom	Drew
4/21/91	Steverson	Toni
5/12/91	Camalette	Anthony
6/4/91	Long	William
6/10/91	Reynolds	Cara
6/15/91	Hanson	Kevin
7/15/91	Toroyan	Lucy
8/14/91	Artis	Jose
9/12/91	Smith	Brent
10/10/91	Spehr	Timothy
1/7/92	Williamson	Anthony
2/1/92	Little	Jennifer

Record: 1 of 73

FIGURE 3-7

The result or answer to the query is displayed in a **query datasheet**. The query datasheet displays only the three specified fields for all records in the table. Query Datasheet view includes the same menus and toolbar buttons as in Table Datasheet view.

Moving Columns

The order of the fields in the query datasheet reflects the order they were placed in the Selected Fields list. However, the manager wants the list of names to be organized with the first name before the last name. You can change the display order of the fields by moving the columns. To reorder columns, first select the column you want to move and then drag the selection to its new location. You want to move the First Name column to the left of the Last Name column.

- Select the First Name column.
- Click and hold the mouse button on the First Name column heading.
- Drag the First Name column to the left until a thick black line is displayed between the Date Hired and Last Name columns. Release the mouse button.
- Clear the selection.

Reminder: Click on the First Name column heading when the mouse pointer is a ⬇ to select it.

When the mouse pointer is a [move pointer], it indicates you can drag to move the selection.

The keyboard equivalent is [Ctrl] + [F8] to turn on Move mode. Then press [←] or [→] to move the column in the desired direction, then press [Esc].

Your screen should be similar to Figure 3-8.

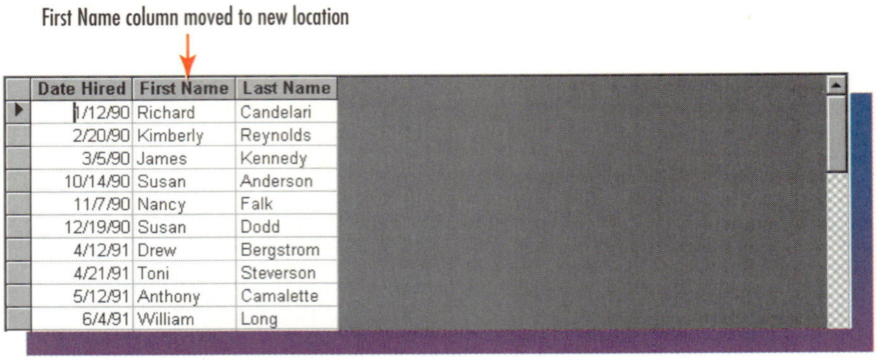

Date Hired	First Name	Last Name
1/12/90	Richard	Candelari
2/20/90	Kimberly	Reynolds
3/5/90	James	Kennedy
10/14/90	Susan	Anderson
11/7/90	Nancy	Falk
12/19/90	Susan	Dodd
4/12/91	Drew	Bergstrom
4/21/91	Toni	Steverson
5/12/91	Anthony	Camalette
6/4/91	William	Long

FIGURE 3-8

You can move fields in Table Datasheet view in the same manner.

Now the query datasheet is displayed in the order requested by the manager. Changing the column order in the query datasheet does not affect the field order in the table, which is controlled by the table design.

Querying Using Comparison Operators

The manager would like to recognize the employees who have worked with The Sports Company for at least five years. To help the manager locate these employees, you can modify the Hire Date query to create a list of all employees who were hired before January of 1992.

The query datasheet is based on settings that were entered in the Query Design window by the Wizard. To see the Query Design view,

- Click Design View.

Your screen should be similar to Figure 3-9.

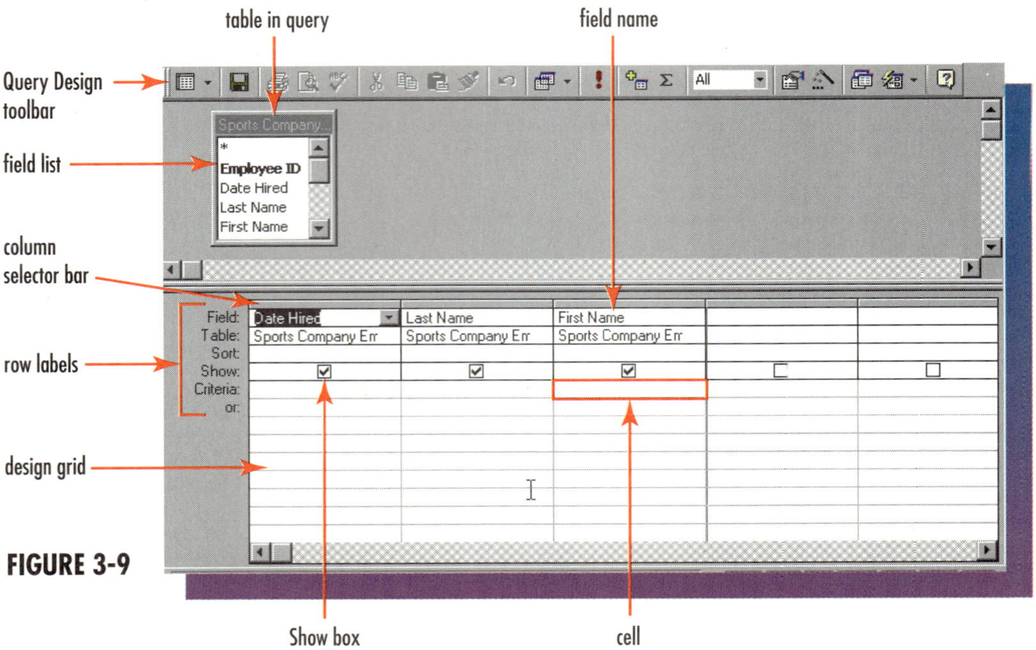

FIGURE 3-9

The Query Design view is used to create and modify the structure of the query. This view automatically displays a Query Design toolbar that contains the standard buttons as well as buttons (identified below) that are specific to the Query Design view window.

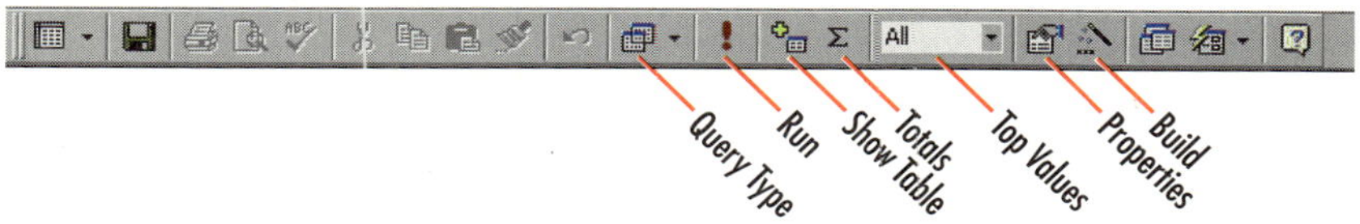

The Query Design window is divided into two areas. The upper area displays a list box of all the fields in the selected table. This is called the **field list**. The lower portion of the window displays the **design grid**, where the settings that are used to define the query are displayed. Each column in the grid holds the information about each field to be included in the query datasheet. The design grid currently displays the Date Hired, Last Name, and First Name fields. Above the field names is a narrow bar called the **column selector bar**. It is used to select an entire column. Each row label identifies the type of information that can be entered. The intersection of a column and row creates a **cell**. This is where you enter expressions to obtain the query results you need. Notice the boxes, called Show boxes, in the Show row. The Show box is checked for each field. This indicates that the query result will display the field column.

In the Criteria row of the Date Hired column, you need to enter a criteria expression to locate only those records where the date hired is prior to January 1992. To specify the criterion, you will enter an expression that contains a comparison operator. A **comparison operator** is used to compare two values. The comparison operators are = (equal to) <> (not equal to), < (less than), > (greater than), <= (less than or equal to), and >= (greater than or equal to). You will use the < comparison operator to locate all records with a date less than 1/1/92. To specify the criterion,

- Move to the Date Hired Criteria cell.
- Type **<1/1/92**
- Press ←Enter.

Your screen should be similar to Figure 3-10.

FIGURE 3-10

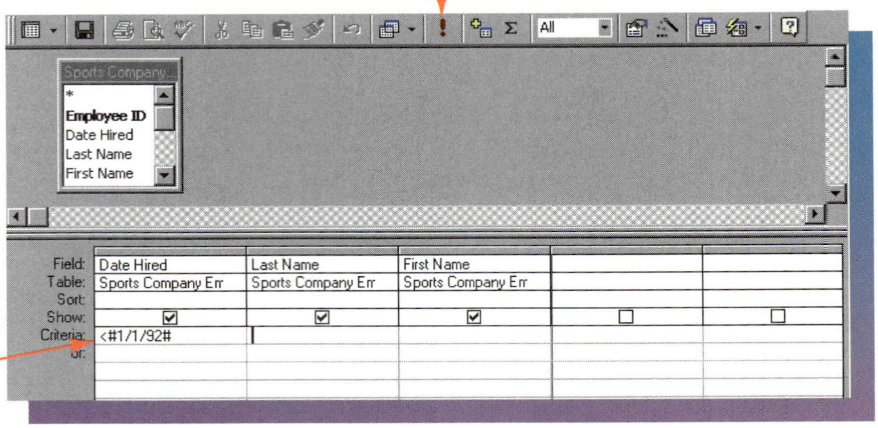

The expression appears in the cell as <#1/1/92#. Access adds # signs around the date to identify the values in the expression as a date.

To display the query results, you run the query.

- Click Run.

Your screen should be similar to Figure 3-11.

FIGURE 3-11

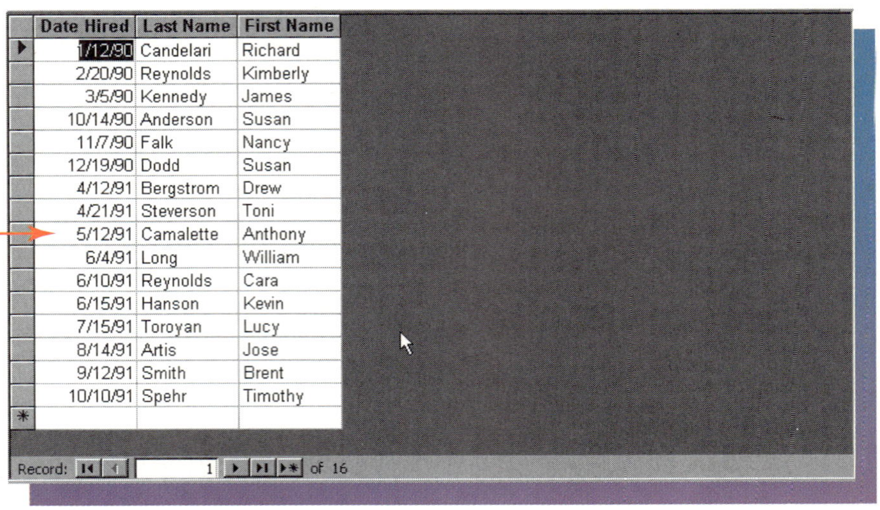

Date Hired	Last Name	First Name
1/12/90	Candelari	Richard
2/20/90	Reynolds	Kimberly
3/5/90	Kennedy	James
10/14/90	Anderson	Susan
11/7/90	Falk	Nancy
12/19/90	Dodd	Susan
4/12/91	Bergstrom	Drew
4/21/91	Steverson	Toni
5/12/91	Camalette	Anthony
6/4/91	Long	William
6/10/91	Reynolds	Cara
6/15/91	Hanson	Kevin
7/15/91	Toroyan	Lucy
8/14/91	Artis	Jose
9/12/91	Smith	Brent
10/10/91	Spehr	Timothy

The menu equivalent is Query/Run. You can also click Datasheet View to run the query and display the query datasheet.

Click , or use File/Print if you need to specify printer settings.

The query datasheet displays only those records meeting the date criterion. The record number indicator of the query datasheet shows that 16 employees were hired before January 1992. Notice that the fields are again in the order in which they appear in the Design grid.

- Move the First Name column before the Last Name column.
- Print a copy of the query datasheet for the manager.

Specifying Multiple Criteria in a Query

Because many of the requests you get for information ask you to locate records using more than one criterion, you decide to practice creating queries using multiple criteria. As in a filter, the AND and OR operators are used to specify several criteria in a query.

First you will query the table to find all employees who have a date hired <1/1/92 *and* have a first name that starts with S. When you enter criteria in separate fields on the same row of the grid, an AND operation is established.

- Switch to the Query Design view.
- Enter **s*** in the First Name Criteria cell.

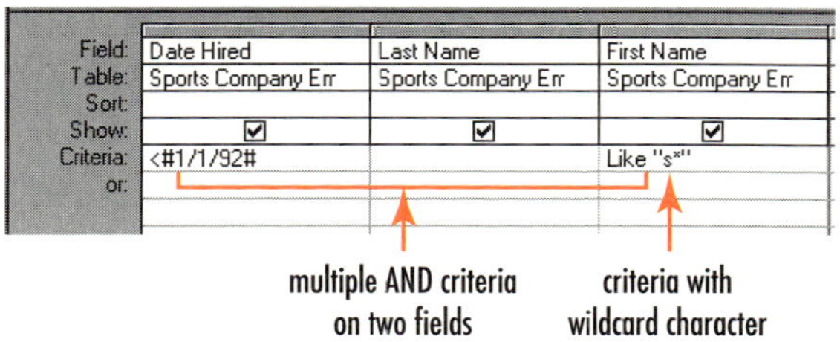

- Run the query.

Date Hired	First Name	Last Name
10/14/90	Susan	Anderson
12/19/90	Susan	Dodd

The query datasheet shows that two employees were hired before January 1992 and have a first name that starts with S.

Next you want to see how many employees have a hire date prior to 1/1/92 *or* have a first name that starts with S. When you enter criteria in separate fields on separate rows, an OR operation is established.

- Switch to the Query Design view.
- Remove the criterion from the Criteria cell of the First Name column.
- Enter **s*** in the Or cell of the First Name column.

To clear cell contents, highlight the entry and press Delete.

You can use Cut and Paste to move the criterion.

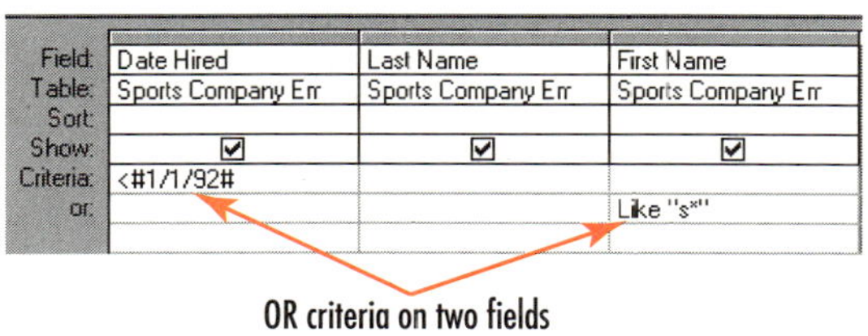

- Run the query.

Your screen should be similar to Figure 3-12.

FIGURE 3-12

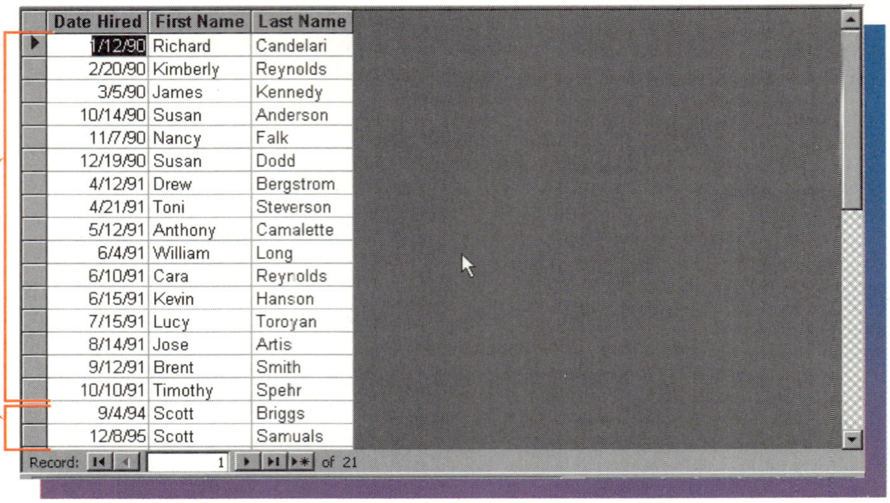

query result shows records whose date hired is prior to 1/1/92
or
first name begins with 'S'

The query datasheet displays all records that meet either criterion.

You can also specify multiple criteria in a single field by using the AND and OR operators. The AND condition is established by typing the AND operator in the cell as part of the expression. An OR condition in a single field is established by entering the second criterion in the Or row cell of the same field. To see how this works, you will find out how many employees have a hire date between 1/1/92 and 12/31/93.

- Switch to Query Design view.
- Clear the criteria from the Criteria cell in the Date Hired column and from the Or cell in the First Name column.
- Enter **>=1/1/92 and <=12/31/93** in the Criteria cell of the Date Hired column.
- Widen the Date Hired column to fully display the criteria.
- Run the query.

multiple AND criteria on a single field

Drag the column line to adjust the column width.

You can also specify the OR operator in a single field in the same manner.

If an expression is entered incorrectly, an information box is displayed indicating the source of the error.

Your screen should be similar to Figure 3-13.

query result shows records whose
Date of Hire is between 1/1/92 and 2/31/93

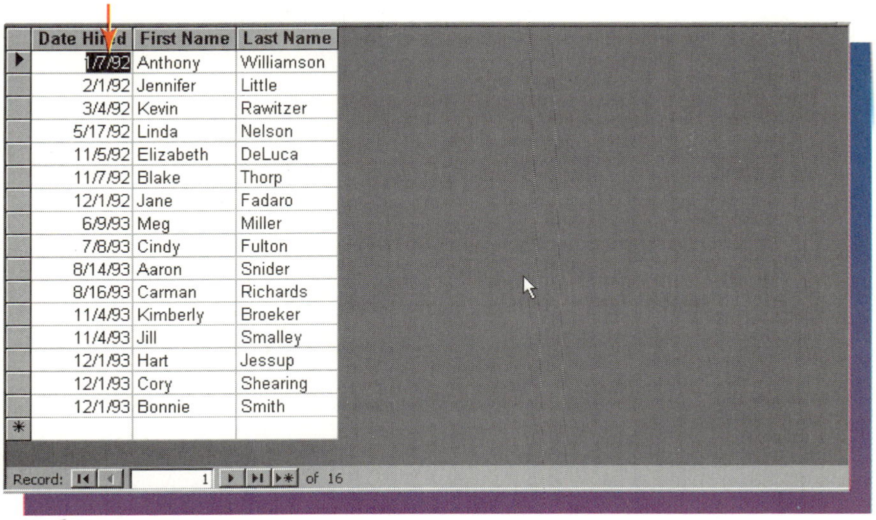

FIGURE 3-13

Sixteen records were located in which the hire date met the specified criteria.

- Close the Query Datasheet window.
- Save the changes to the query.

The Database window is displayed, and the query name is displayed in the Queries object list.

Note: If you are ending your session now, exit Access. When you begin Part 2, open the Sports Company Personnel Records database file.

Part 2

Querying Two Tables

The manager looked at the list of employees hired before January 1992 and suggested that the query would be more helpful if it included the employee's department. Unfortunately the Sports Company Employees table does not contain this information. This information, however, is available in another table named Employees by Department and Position.

- From the Tables tab, open the Employees by Department and Position table.

Your screen should be similar to Figure 3-14.

FIGURE 3-14

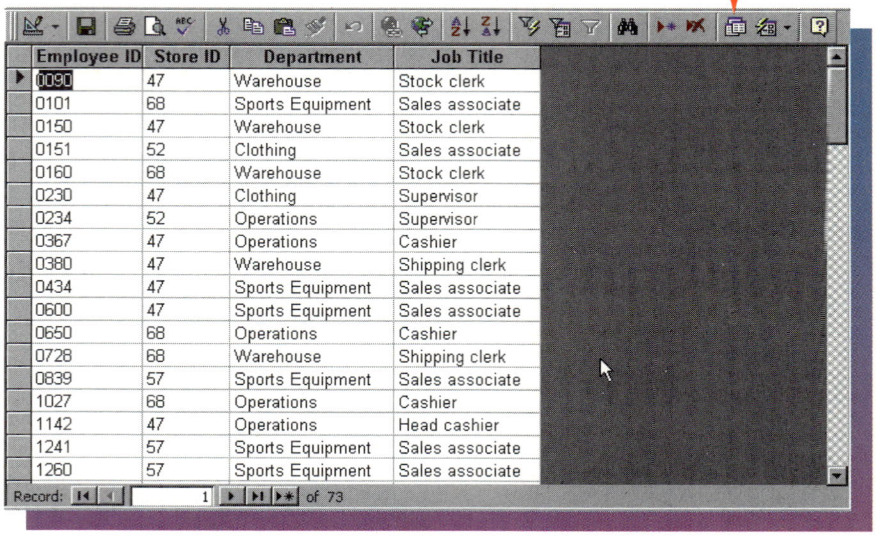

Employee ID	Store ID	Department	Job Title
0090	47	Warehouse	Stock clerk
0101	68	Sports Equipment	Sales associate
0150	47	Warehouse	Stock clerk
0151	52	Clothing	Sales associate
0160	68	Warehouse	Stock clerk
0230	47	Clothing	Supervisor
0234	52	Operations	Supervisor
0367	47	Operations	Cashier
0380	47	Warehouse	Shipping clerk
0434	47	Sports Equipment	Sales associate
0600	47	Sports Equipment	Sales associate
0650	68	Operations	Cashier
0728	68	Warehouse	Shipping clerk
0839	57	Sports Equipment	Sales associate
1027	68	Operations	Cashier
1142	47	Operations	Head cashier
1241	57	Sports Equipment	Sales associate
1260	57	Sports Equipment	Sales associate

The Employees by Department and Position table contains four fields of data: Employee ID, Store ID, Department, and Job Title. To display the information the manager wants, you need to create a query using information from this table and from the Sports Company Employee table. A query that uses more than one table is called a **multitable query**.

The menu equivalent is Window/1 Sports Company Personnel Records: Database.

To switch back to the Database window and create the query from scratch,

You can also click on any visible part of the Database window or press F11 to switch to it.

- Click Database Window.
- Open the Queries tab.
- Choose New/Design View/OK.

The Query Design window is open with the Show Table dialog box open on top of it. The dialog box is used to add tables to the query design. The three tabs—Tables, Queries, and Both—contain the names of the existing tables and queries that can be used as the information source for the query. You need to add the Sports Company Employees and the Employees by Department and Position tables to the query design.

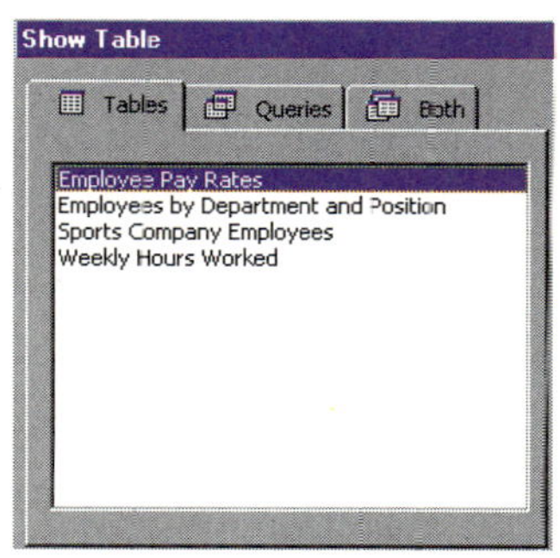

- If necessary, open the Tables tab.
- Select Sports Company Employees.

- Click Add.
- Select Employees by Department and Position.
- Click Add.

> You can also double-click the table name to add it to the query design.

Your screen should be similar to Figure 3-15.

two field lists for selected tables added to Query Design window

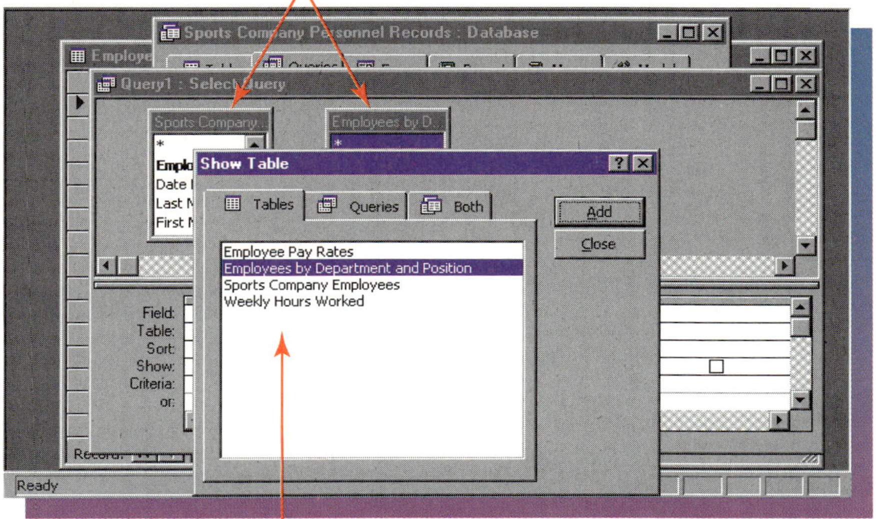

available tables

FIGURE 3-15

Field lists for the two selected tables are added to the Query Design window.

- Close the Show Table dialog box.
- If necessary, maximize the Query Design window.

The line between the two field lists indicates that the two tables have been temporarily joined.

join line

Concept 5: Joins and Relationships

You can bring information from different tables in your database together if you join the tables. A **join** is an association that tells Access how data between tables is related. A **relationship** is established between tables usually through at least one common field. The common fields must be of the same data type and contain the same kind of information, but can have different field names. When you add multiple tables to a query, Access automatically joins tables based on the common fields if one of the common fields is a primary key. This is called the default join or **inner join**. If the common fields have different names, Access does not automatically insert the line and create the join. You can create the join manually by dragging from one common field to the other. The default join instructs the query to check for matching values in the joined fields. When matches are found, the matching data is added to the query datasheet as a single record.

The three types of relationships, one-to-many, many-to-many, and one-to-one, are described in the table below. The most common type is a one-to-many relationship.

More information and examples of relationships are available through the Office Assistant.

Use Tools/Relationships to define permanent relationships between tables.

Relationship Type	Description
One-to-many	A record in table A can have many matching records in table B, but a record in table B, has only one matching record in table A.
Many-to-many	A record in table A can have many matching records in table B, and a record in table B can have many matching records in table A. This requires a third table in the relationship, known as a junction table, that serves as a bridge between the two tables.
One-to-one	A record in table A has only one matching record in table B, and a record in table B has only one matching record in table A.

In a one-to-many relationship there is a primary table and a related or foreign table. The primary table is usually the "one" side of two related tables in a one-to-many relationship, and the related table is usually on the "many" side of a one-to-many relationship.

Using Tools/Relationships, you can also define permanent relationships between tables that will enforce the rules of **referential integrity**. These rules help ensure that the database always contains accurate and complete data. When these rules are enforced, you cannot add records to a related table when there is no associated record in the primary table. You also cannot change values in the primary table that would result in records that do not have a match in a related table, or delete records from the primary table when there are matching related records in a related table.

The diagram below shows that when the Employee ID fields of the two tables are joined, a query can be created using data from both tables to provide the requested information.

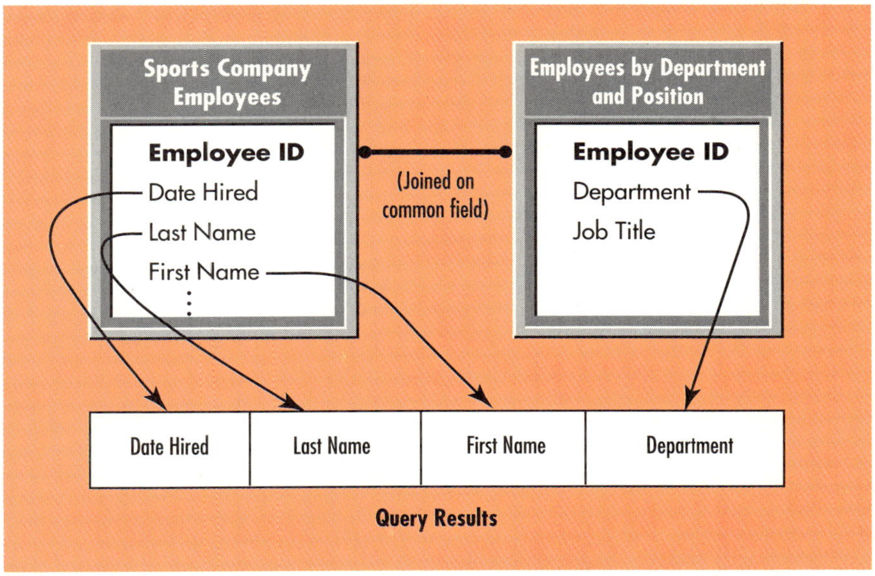

The type of relationship created using these two tables is a one-to-one relationship. This is because each record in the first table has one matching record in the second table.

Next you need to add the fields to the grid that you want to use in the query. The methods you can use to add fields to the design grid are described below.

- Drag the field name from the field list to the grid. You can add several fields at once by pressing ⇧Shift and clicking to select adjacent fields, or by pressing Ctrl and clicking to select nonadjacent fields. When you drag multiple fields at a time, Access places each field in a separate column.
- Double-click on the field name. The field is added to the next available column in the grid.
- Select the Field cell drop-down arrow in the grid, then choose the field name.

To select all fields, double-click the field list title bar.

In addition, if you select the asterisk in the field list and add it to the grid, Access displays the table or query name in the field row followed by a period and asterisk. All fields in the table are included in the query results. Using this feature also will automatically include any new fields that may later be added to the table and exclude deleted fields. However, you cannot sort records or specify criteria for fields unless you also add those fields individually to the design grid.

- Add the Date Hired, Last Name, First Name, and Department fields, in that order, to the design grid.
- To specify the date hired criterion, enter the expression **<1/1/92** in the Date Hired Criteria cell.
- Run the query.

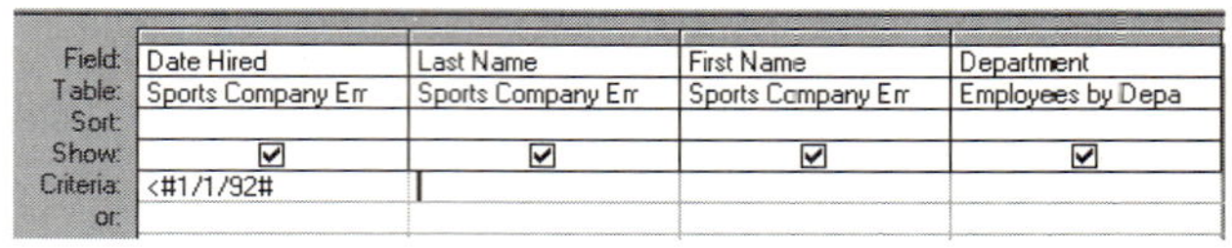

Field:	Date Hired	Last Name	First Name	Department
Table:	Sports Company Em	Sports Company Em	Sports Company Em	Employees by Depa
Sort:				
Show:	☑	☑	☑	☑
Criteria:	<#1/1/92#			
or:				

Your screen should be similar to Figure 3-16.

FIGURE 3-16

query results consist of information from two tables

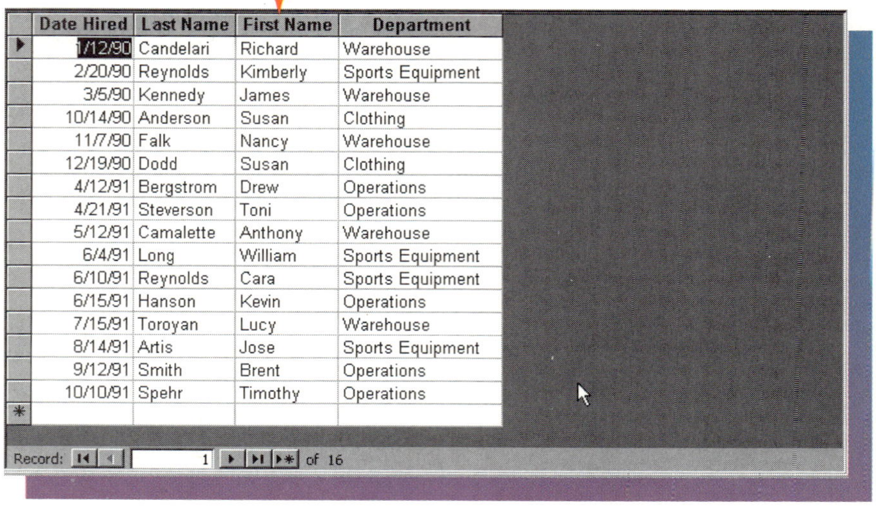

Date Hired	Last Name	First Name	Department
1/12/90	Candelari	Richard	Warehouse
2/20/90	Reynolds	Kimberly	Sports Equipment
3/5/90	Kennedy	James	Warehouse
10/14/90	Anderson	Susan	Clothing
11/7/90	Falk	Nancy	Warehouse
12/19/90	Dodd	Susan	Clothing
4/12/91	Bergstrom	Drew	Operations
4/21/91	Steverson	Toni	Operations
5/12/91	Camalette	Anthony	Warehouse
6/4/91	Long	William	Sports Equipment
6/10/91	Reynolds	Cara	Sports Equipment
6/15/91	Hanson	Kevin	Operations
7/15/91	Toroyan	Lucy	Warehouse
8/14/91	Artis	Jose	Sports Equipment
9/12/91	Smith	Brent	Operations
10/10/91	Spehr	Timothy	Operations

Record: 1 of 16

The query datasheet displays the same 16 records as in the original query, and in addition displays the Department field. Each record consists of information from both tables. Both tables must contain matching records in order for a record to appear in the query's result.

Next you want to change the order of the columns and sort the query datasheet by Department and Last Name.

- Change the column order to Department, Last Name, First Name, and Date Hired.
- Select the Department and Last Name columns.
- Click Sort Ascending.

Your screen should be similar to Figure 3-17.

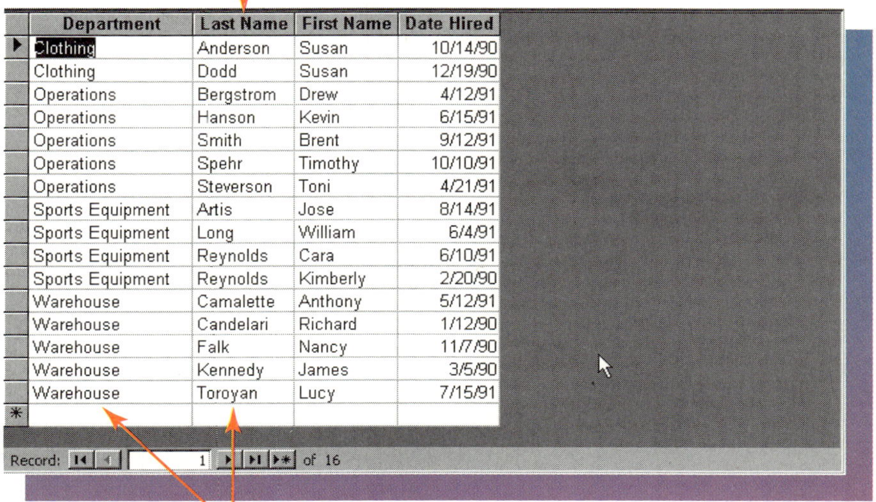

Department	Last Name	First Name	Date Hired
Clothing	Anderson	Susan	10/14/90
Clothing	Dodd	Susan	12/19/90
Operations	Bergstrom	Drew	4/12/91
Operations	Hanson	Kevin	6/15/91
Operations	Smith	Brent	9/12/91
Operations	Spehr	Timothy	10/10/91
Operations	Steverson	Toni	4/21/91
Sports Equipment	Artis	Jose	8/14/91
Sports Equipment	Long	William	6/4/91
Sports Equipment	Reynolds	Cara	6/10/91
Sports Equipment	Reynolds	Kimberly	2/20/90
Warehouse	Camalette	Anthony	5/12/91
Warehouse	Candelari	Richard	1/12/90
Warehouse	Falk	Nancy	11/7/90
Warehouse	Kennedy	James	3/5/90
Warehouse	Toroyan	Lucy	7/15/91

FIGURE 3-17

Saving a Query

You would like to save this query for the manager. You can save a query as an object, then you can run the query whenever needed. To do this,

- Choose File/Save As/Export.
- Type **Pre 1992 Hire Date**
- If necessary, select "Within the current database as."
- Click OK.

You now have two named queries in the database: Hire Date and Pre 1992 Hire Date.

Querying Three Tables

Next the manager would like you to create some queries that will help in the analysis of the employee payroll information. The payroll information is in a table named Employee Pay Rates. This table contains the Employee ID and hourly pay rate.

You will create a query that will locate all employees hired after 11/15/93 and who work in the Clothing department. The manager would like the query to also display the employees' hourly rates. To create this query, you can modify the existing query by adding the Employee Pay Rates table to the query design and by changing the criteria.

The menu equivalent is **Query/Show Table**.

- Return to the Query Design.
- Click Show Table.
- Add the Employee Pay Rates table to the Query Design window.
- Close the Show Table dialog box.

Access automatically links the Employee ID field of the Employee Pay Rates table to the Employees by Department and Position table.

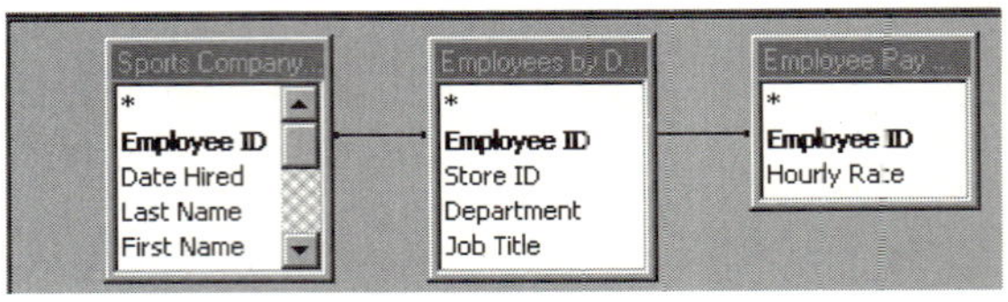

Next you need to set up the criteria to display the requested information.

- Add the Hourly Rate field to the design grid.
- Replace the existing criterion in the Data Hired Criteria cell with **>11/15/93**.
- Enter **"clothing"** as the criterion in the Department Criteria cell.

Field:	Date Hired	Last Name	First Name	Department	Hourly Rate
Table:	Sports Company Em	Sports Company Em	Sports Company Em	Employees by Depa	Employee Pay Ra
Sort:					
Show:	☑	☑	☑	☑	☑
Criteria:	>#11/15/93#			"clothing"	
or:					

Finally, you also want the query datasheet to display the records in alphabetical order by last name. Another way to set the sort order is to specify the sort direction in the Sort cell of the grid.

- Move to the Sort cell of the Last Name field and open the drop-down list.
- Select Ascending.
- Run the query.

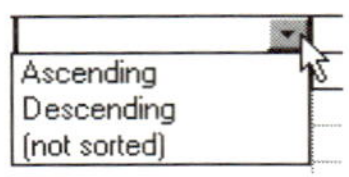

The query datasheet should be similar to Figure 3-18.

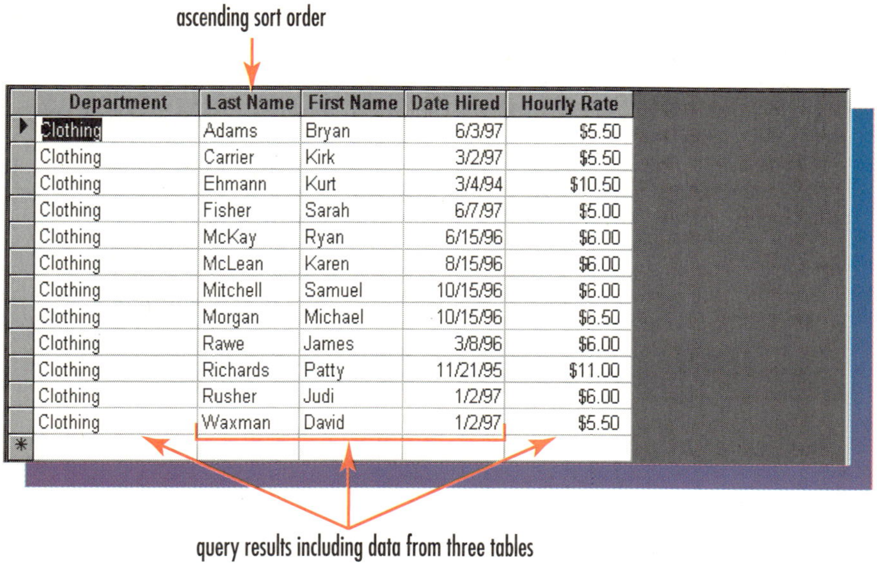

Department	Last Name	First Name	Date Hired	Hourly Rate
Clothing	Adams	Bryan	6/3/97	$5.50
Clothing	Carrier	Kirk	3/2/97	$5.50
Clothing	Ehmann	Kurt	3/4/94	$10.50
Clothing	Fisher	Sarah	6/7/97	$5.00
Clothing	McKay	Ryan	6/15/96	$6.00
Clothing	McLean	Karen	8/15/96	$6.00
Clothing	Mitchell	Samuel	10/15/96	$6.00
Clothing	Morgan	Michael	10/15/96	$6.50
Clothing	Rawe	James	3/8/96	$6.00
Clothing	Richards	Patty	11/21/95	$11.00
Clothing	Rusher	Judi	1/2/97	$6.00
Clothing	Waxman	David	1/2/97	$5.50

FIGURE 3-18

The query result shows, in alphabetical order by last name, the employees who were hired after 11/15/93 and work in the Clothing department. It also displays their hourly rate of pay.

The manager has also requested another list, sorted by Department, of all employees who earn less than $5.50 per hour. You will modify the query to display this information. In addition, since you no longer need the Date Hired field, you will remove it from the design grid.

Select a column by clicking on the column selector bar above the field name in the grid when the mouse pointer is ⬇.

- Return to Query Design view.
- Select the Date Hired column.
- Press Delete.

The menu equivalent is Edit/Delete Columns.

- Clear the criterion from the Department field.
- Enter the expression **<5.50** in the Hourly Rate Criteria cell.
- Set the Department sort order to Ascending
- Set the Last Name sort order to not sorted.

Deleting a column from the design grid does not change the underlying table.

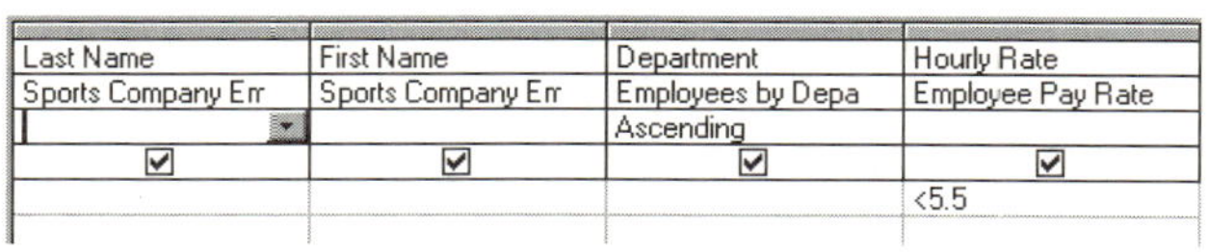

Last Name	First Name	Department	Hourly Rate
Sports Company Em	Sports Company Em	Employees by Depa	Employee Pay Rate
		Ascending	
☑	☑	☑	☑
			<5.5

- Run the query.

Your screen should be similar to Figure 3-19.

query results show employees earning less than $5.50 per hour

FIGURE 3-19

Department	Last Name	First Name	Hourly Rate
Clothing	Fisher	Sarah	$5.00
Sports Equipment	Lawson	Tamara	$5.00
Sports Equipment	Moran	Jeannie	$5.00
Sports Equipment	Lye	Hin	$5.00
Warehouse	Castillo	Blas	$4.50
Warehouse	Lockwood	Craig	$5.25
Warehouse	Hayes	Carol	$5.00
Warehouse	Granger	Michael	$4.50
Warehouse	Jessup	Hart	$5.00
Warehouse	Fulton	Cindy	$5.00

The query datasheet shows that 10 employees earn less than $5.50.

Creating a Calculated Field

The manager reviewed the list of employees and has decided it is time to give these employees a raise. You have been asked to create a query that will calculate a 5 percent increase for these employees.

When creating queries you are not limited to just the fields in the database tables. You can also create fields based on information contained in other fields used in the query. This type of field is called a calculated field.

Concept 6: Calculated Field

A **calculated field** displays the result of a calculation in a query. You can perform a variety of calculations in queries. For example, you can calculate the sum of all inventory, the average salary for a department, or the highest sales figures among all sales personnel in the company. You can create your own calculation or use one of Access's seven predefined calculations shown below.

Predefined Calculation	What It Calculates
Sum	Totals values in a field for all records
Average	Averages values in a field for all records
Count	Counts number of values, excluding empty cells, in a field for all records
Minimum	Finds lowest value in a field for all records
Maximum	Finds highest value in a field for all records
Standard Deviation	A measure of the dispersion of a frequency distribution
Variance	Square of the standard deviation

To create a calculated field, you enter an expression in the design grid that instructs Access to perform a calculation using the current field values. Then the calculated result is displayed in the calculated field column of the datasheet.

To create a calculated field, you will enter the expression to perform the calculation in the Field row of a blank column

- Return to the Query Design window.
- Move to the Field row of a blank column.

You will need to enter a custom calculation to calculate the new pay rate for the records in the query. The first part of the expression will name the new calculated field. The second part of the expression does the actual calculation. In this case, to calculate the raise, the expression will multiply the value in the Hourly Rate field by 1.05 to calculate the 5 percent increase for each employee.

- Type **New Rate:**
- Press [Spacebar].
- Type **[Hourly Rate]*1.05**
- Press [←Enter].
- Increase the column width to fully display the expression.

Field names are enclosed in square brackets in an expression.

If you made an entry error, a message box will appear advising you of the error. Clear the box and correct the expression.

Before running the query, you would like to change the new field's properties so it will display the calculated values as currency with two decimal places.

- Select the New Rate column.
- Click [Properties button] Properties.
- Select Currency from the Format drop-down list.
- Close the Field Properties dialog box.
- Run the query.

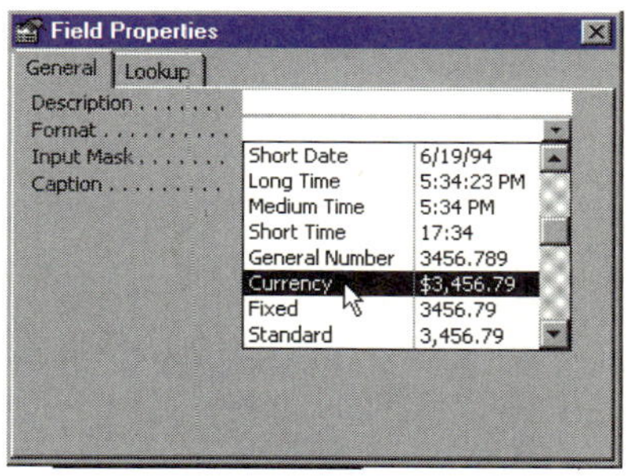

Your screen should be similar to Figure 3-20.

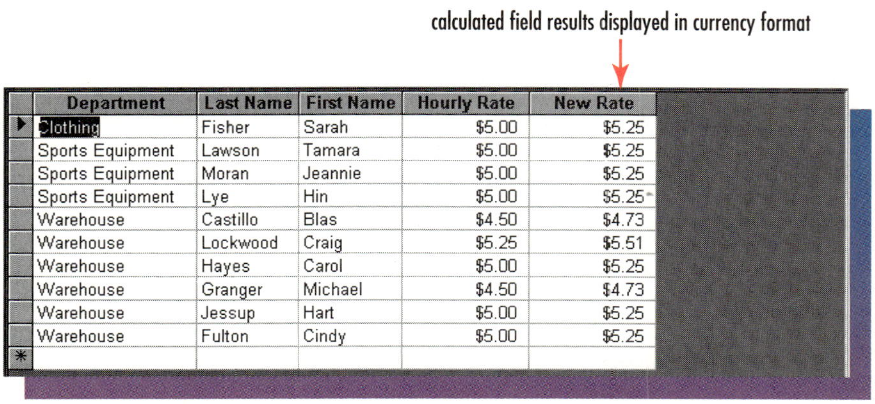

Department	Last Name	First Name	Hourly Rate	New Rate
Clothing	Fisher	Sarah	$5.00	$5.25
Sports Equipment	Lawson	Tamara	$5.00	$5.25
Sports Equipment	Moran	Jeannie	$5.00	$5.25
Sports Equipment	Lye	Hin	$5.00	$5.25
Warehouse	Castillo	Blas	$4.50	$4.73
Warehouse	Lockwood	Craig	$5.25	$5.51
Warehouse	Hayes	Carol	$5.00	$5.25
Warehouse	Granger	Michael	$4.50	$4.73
Warehouse	Jessup	Hart	$5.00	$5.25
Warehouse	Fulton	Cindy	$5.00	$5.25

FIGURE 3-20

The query datasheet displays the 10 employees and shows their new pay rates in the last column. The New Rate column of values appears in the currency format you selected. You would like to save this query in case the manager wants to try different percent increases.

- Save the query as Pay Rate Increase.

Finally, the manager has asked you to figure out what the average hourly rate is for all employees. Access can automatically make this calculation for you.

- Switch to Query Design view.
- Choose **E**dit/Cle**a**r Grid.
- Add the Hourly Rate field back to the grid.

To calculate the average hourly rate, you need to display a new row called the Total row in the Design grid. The Total row is used to perform calculations such as a sum or average on values in one or more fields for all the records or a group of records in the query. The Total row is hidden by default. The Σ Totals button toggles between hiding and displaying the row in the grid.

The menu equivalent is **V**iew/**T**otals.

- Click Σ Totals.

When calculating a total value, only one field, the field on which the calculation will be made, is displayed in the grid.

The Total row is displayed as the third row in the design grid. Every field in the grid must have a setting entered in the Total row. By default Access enters "Group By" as the setting. This setting is used to group data in the query. You need to change the setting to calculate the average of the Hourly Rate field.

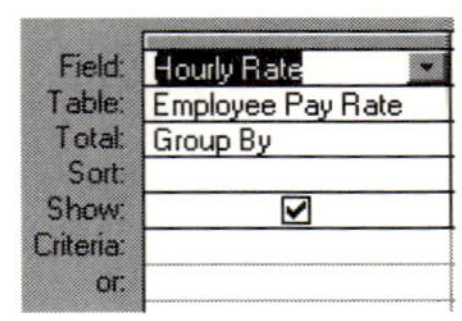

- Move to the Total cell of the Hourly Rate column.
- Select Avg from the Total drop-down list.
- Run the query.

Your screen should be similar to Figure 3-21.

query result displays calculated average pay rate

FIGURE 3-21

When summary calculations are performed, the query result displays one record with a calculated value. In this case Access calculates $7.09 as the average rate of pay. You can now send this information along with the printout to the manager.

Querying Four Tables

The last query the manager requested will display the weekly gross pay for all employees sorted by department. To calculate the weekly gross pay, you will need to use the Weekly Hours Worked table, which contains the employee numbers along with the hours worked in the past weeks.

- Switch to the Query Design window.
- If necessary, maximize the window.
- Clear the grid.
- Hide the Total row.
- Add the Weekly Hours Worked table to the Query Design.

Click [Σ] to hide the Total row.

This field list displays the fields Employee ID, Week Ending, and Hours. The table has been joined to the Employee Pay Rates table on the common field. Notice that Employee ID in this field list is not bold. When a field is bold, it indicates that it is a primary key field. Employee ID in this table is not a primary key field because there are multiple entries with the same numbers.

Next you will add the fields to be included in the query to the grid and create a calculated field to calculate the gross pay for the week ending 10/16/98.

- Add the Last Name, First Name, Department, and Week Ending fields to the design grid in that order.
- Sort the Department field in ascending order.
- Move to the field cell of a blank column.
- Type **Gross Pay: [Hourly Rate]*[Hours]**
- Press [←Enter].
- Set the Format property for the calculated field to display as currency.
- Enter the expression **=10/16/98** into the Week Ending Criteria cell.
- Clear the Show box for the Week Ending field so the date will not display in the query datasheet.

Click on the Show box to clear the check box.

Your screen should be similar to Figure 3-22.

four tables joined on Employee ID field

FIGURE 3-22

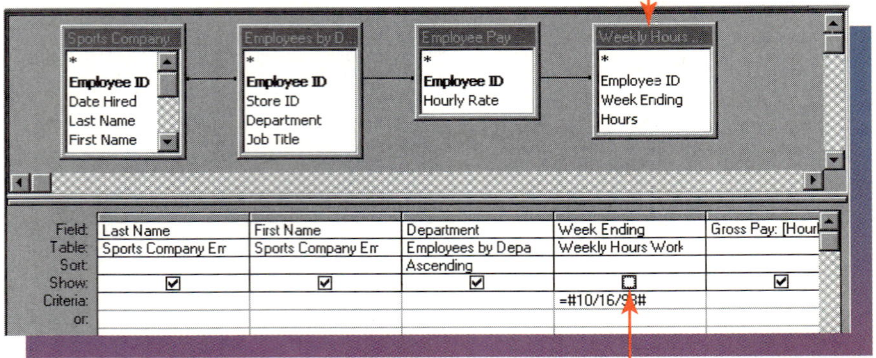

clear Show box so field does not display in query result

- Run the query.

Your screen should be similar to Figure 3-23.

gross pay for week of 10/16/98

FIGURE 3-23

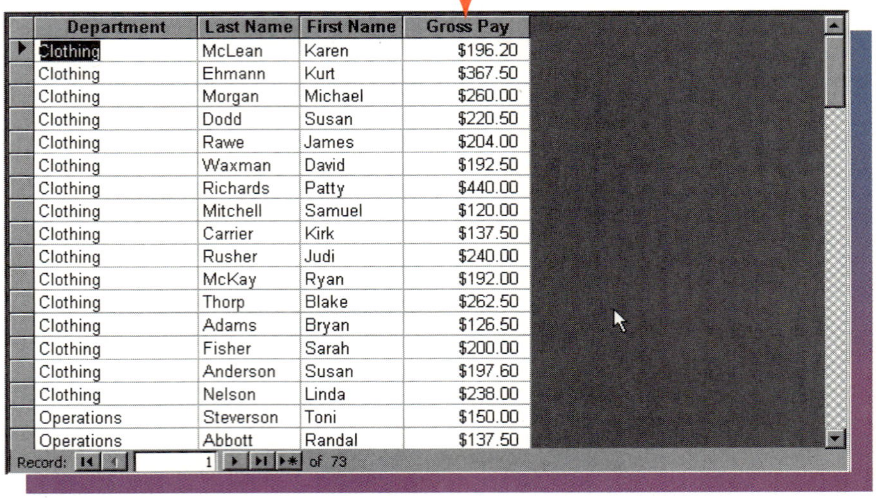

Department	Last Name	First Name	Gross Pay
Clothing	McLean	Karen	$196.20
Clothing	Ehmann	Kurt	$367.50
Clothing	Morgan	Michael	$260.00
Clothing	Dodd	Susan	$220.50
Clothing	Rawe	James	$204.00
Clothing	Waxman	David	$192.50
Clothing	Richards	Patty	$440.00
Clothing	Mitchell	Samuel	$120.00
Clothing	Carrier	Kirk	$137.50
Clothing	Rusher	Judi	$240.00
Clothing	McKay	Ryan	$192.00
Clothing	Thorp	Blake	$262.50
Clothing	Adams	Bryan	$126.50
Clothing	Fisher	Sarah	$200.00
Clothing	Anderson	Susan	$197.60
Clothing	Nelson	Linda	$238.00
Operations	Steverson	Toni	$150.00
Operations	Abbott	Randal	$137.50

Record: 1 of 73

The query datasheet displays the gross pay for each employee sorted by department for the week ending 10/16/98.

- Print a copy of the query datasheet for the manager.
- Save this query as **Gross Pay for 10/16/98**.
- Close the Query Datasheet window.
- Close the Employees by Department and Position table.

Creating a Multiple-Table Form

You have been using several tables of employee information that need to be updated each time information changes in an existing record. The form you created to use with the Sports Company Employees table can only update the records in that table. You want to create a form that will update the Sports Company Employees, Employee Pay Rates, and Employees by Department and Position tables. First you must create a query that will combine all the information you need, then you add the fields to the query that you want to display in the new form.

- If necessary, open the Queries tab.
- Choose New/Design View/OK.
- Add the Sports Company Employees, Employees by Department and Position, and Employee Pay Rates tables to the Query Design window.
- Close the Show Table dialog box.
- If necessary, maximize the Design View window.
- From the Sports Company Employees table field list, add the following fields to the design grid in the order indicated (this will be the tab order on the form):

  First Name
  Last Name
  Street
  City
  State
  Zip Code
  Phone Number
  Gender
  Birth Date
  Employee ID
  Date Hired

The fields continue to be added to the grid even though they are not all visible onscreen. Use the scroll bar to move to the other fields.

- From the Employees by Department and Position table, add the following fields to the query design grid:

  Store ID
  Department
  Job Title

- From the Employee Pay Rates table, add the Hourly Rate field to the design grid.

Your screen should be similar to Figure 3-24.

FIGURE 3-24

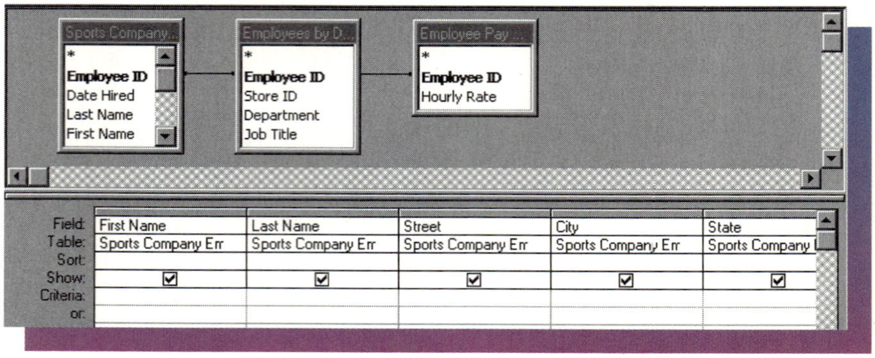

- Save the query as **Comprehensive Employee Query**.
- Close the Query Design window.

You are now ready to create the new form based on the Comprehensive Employee Query you just created. The form will include all fields in the query. You will use a columnar form style.

> Although you can create a form from scratch using Design view, it is much easier to create the form using a Wizard and then modify it in Form Design view.

- Open the Forms tab.
- Choose New/Form Wizard.
- Click OK.
- Select Comprehensive Employee Query from the Table/Queries drop-down list.
- Click >>.
- Click Next >.
- Click Next >.
- Select a style of your choice.
- Click Next >.
- Enter the form title **Employee Update Form**.
- Click Finish.

> This text will use Evergreen.

After a few moments, the Form window displays the form in the selected style and layout. Next you want to modify the layout of the Form.

- Click Design.
- If necessary, maximize the window.
- Rearrange the controls as in Figure 3-25.
- Enter the form title and section headings shown in Figure 3-25.

- Set the font size of all controls to 10 and size the controls as appropriate.
- Set the title font to 20, size the control to fit, and add color.
- Set the Personal Data and Company Data font size to 12, size the controls to fit, and add color.
- Adjust the spacing and alignment of controls appropriately.

Your screen should be similar to Figure 3-25.

FIGURE 3-25

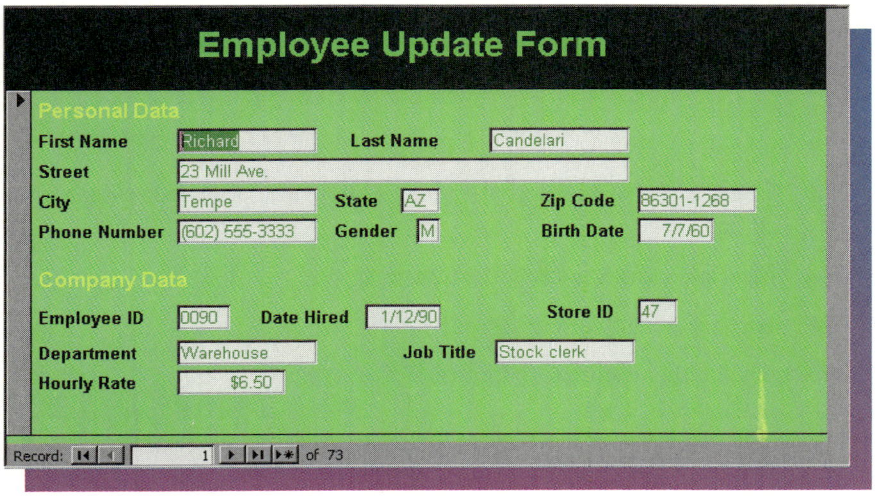

Next you want to add transparent rectangles around the controls in the Personal Data and Company Data sections of the form. To create the rectangle around the Personal Data section of the form first,

- Click Rectangle.
- Drag to create a box around the controls as you did to select multiple controls.
- Click Fill/Back Color.
- Select Transparent.
- Click Line/Border Width.
- Click .
- Click Line Border Color.
- Select the same color as the titles.

Your screen should be similar to Figure 3-26.

FIGURE 3-26

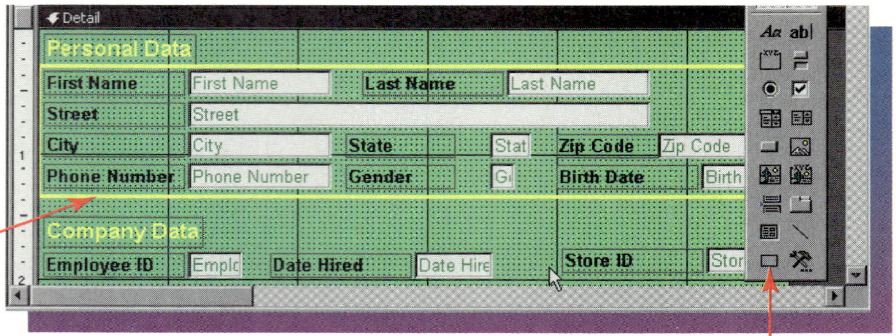

rectangle with color border line

creates rectangle

- Create a second rectangle around the Company Data section of the form using the same settings.
- Adjust the rectangles so they are the same width.
- When you are done, view the form in Form view.

Your screen should be similar to Figure 3-27.

FIGURE 3-27

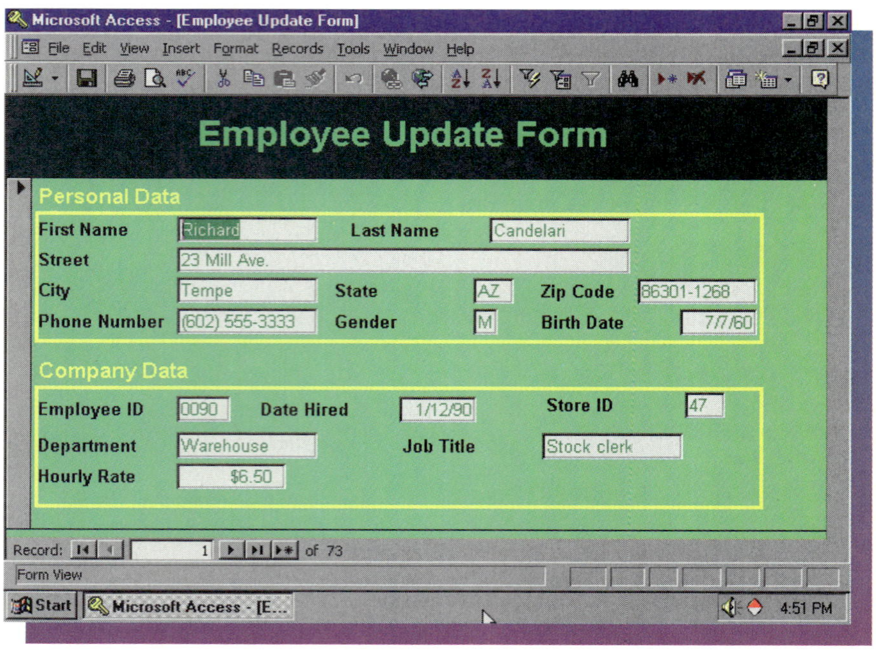

To see how quickly the form can be used to update all three files, you will make several changes in the data to your record.

- Use the Find Records command to quickly display the record containing your information.

- Change the data in the following fields:

Field	Data
Zip Code	85000-0000
Store ID	68
Hourly Rate	9.75

Use Tab to move between fields in the form.

- Select your record and print the form with your record information displayed.
- Close the form, saving your layout changes.
- To verify that the changes were made to the tables, open each of the tables, locate your record, and note the changes.

As you can see, using a single customized form to update records in all three tables simultaneously is a great time-saving feature.

- Close the open tables, saving any changes.
- Exit Access, responding Yes to any prompt to save.

LAB REVIEW

Key Terms

calculated field (DB124)
cell (DB111)
column selector bar (DB111)
comparison operator (DB111)
criteria (DB100)
criteria expression (DB102)
design grid (DB111)
field list (DB111)
filter (DB100)
Filter by Form (DB101)
Filter by Selection (DB100)
inner join (DB118)
join (DB118)
many-to-many relationship (DB118)
multitable query (DB116)
one-to-many relationship (DB118)
one-to-one relationship (DB118)
query (DB107)
query datasheet (DB109)
referential integrity (DB118)
relationship (DB118)
wildcard character (DB105)

Command Summary

Command	Shortcut	Toolbar	Action
File/SaveAs/Export			Saves a database object with a new name
Edit/Delete Columns	Delete		Removes selected column from design grid
Edit/Clear Grid			Clears all fields from filter form or query design grid
View/Totals			Displays/hides Total row in query design grid
Records/Filter/Filter by Selection			Displays only records that contain a specific value
Records/Filter/Filter by Form			Displays blank datasheet for entering values to be displayed
Tools/Relationships			Defines permanent relationship between tables
Filter/Apply Filter/Sort			Applies filter to table
Query/Run			Displays query results in Query Datasheet view
Query/Show Table			Displays Show Table dialog box
Window/1 <name>			Displays selected window
			Displays Database window

Matching

1.  _____ **a.** intersection of a column and row
2. query _____ **b.** matches any single character
3. multitable query _____ **c.** temporary restriction placed on displayed data to isolate specific records
4. criteria _____ **d.** includes any records containing either condition
5.  _____ **e.** symbols used to represent unknown characters in expressions
6. filter _____ **f.** runs a query and displays query datasheet
7. OR operator _____ **g.** used to ask questions about database tables
8. wildcard operator _____ **h.** query that uses data from more than one table
9. ? _____ **i.** set of limiting conditions
10. cell _____ **j.** accesses Filter By Form feature

Fill-In Questions

1. A(n) ____________________ is used to isolate and display a specific group of records.
2. The ________________ operator narrows the search for records that meet both conditions.
3. Placeholders called ________________________ are used to specify a value when you want to find all values that begin with a specific character.
4. __________________ is an association that shows how data between tables is related.
5. A(n) _____________________ retrieves specific data from one or more tables and displays the results in a query datasheet.
6. The ______________________ of the Query window is where the fields to be displayed in the query datasheet are placed.
7. Tables are joined by defining a(n) ____________________ between the tables.
8. A(n) ______________________ relationship is only possible if there is a junction table between the two tables.
9. The ________________________ row is used to perform calculations on all the values in a field.
10. In expressions field names are enclosed in ____________________.

Discussion Questions

1. Discuss what filters are and how they can be used in a database. When would it be appropriate to use a filter?

2. Discuss the differences between the AND and OR filter conditions.

3. Describe the six wildcard characters that are available in Access. Give an example of each.

4. Discuss what a query can do and some advantages of using queries.

5. Discuss the three types of relationships. Give an example of how an inner join could be created in a database.

Hands-On Practice Exercises

Step by Step

Rating System
☆ Easy
☆☆ Moderate
☆☆☆ Difficult

☆

1. This problem is a continuation of Practice Exercise 4 in Lab 2. Debbie from Desert Rescue Cleaning Service wants you to help her use her database to make management decisions concerning her growing business. She needs to be able to compare rates by square feet among all of her clients, wants to identify her largest clients, and wants you to create a query that she can refer back to as her business grows to track total square feet cleaned and total income.

a. Open the Desert Rescue Cleaning Service database. Filter the Clients table to display only those clients with 10,000 square feet or more. Print the filtered datasheet. Remove the filter.

b. Next, help Debbie create a new query based on the Clients table. Add the Company, Square Feet, and Rate fields to the design grid. Run the query, then print the query datasheet.

c. Debbie is pleased with the data you were able to extract for her. Now she wants to know which clients have at least 10,000 square feet of space. Return to Query Design view, then add the expression >=10000 in the Square Ft Criteria cell. Run the query, then print the query datasheet.

d. Debbie now wants a query, which she plans to use repeatedly, that will give her a summary of the size of her jobs and her expected income. Return to Query Design view, remove the criterion in the Square Ft column, then remove the Company field. Display the Total row in the design grid. Display the Total drop-down list and replace Group By with Sum in both fields in the grid. Run the query, then print the query datasheet. Save the query as Square Feet and Rates Totals.

☆☆

2. This problem is a continuation of Practice Exercise 3 in Lab 2. Eddie Fitzpatrick of TechnoBabble Electronics wants you to help him check his inventory and print a list of inventory supplied by his favorite supplier. Eddie is also working with his local bank to secure a small business loan and wants you to help him find the total value of each item in inventory.

a. Open the TechnoBabble Electronics database and the Inventory table. Filter the table to display only those records where the number on hand is less than 5. Print the filtered datasheet. Remove the filter. Close the Inventory table.

b. Open the TechnoBabble Electronics Inventory List form and add the following new records to the inventory:

	Record 1	Record 2
Item #:	5396	5837
Description:	Calculator, Desktop	Projector, Computer Display
Shelf:	L-10	P-17
# On Hand:	10	2
Purchase Price:	$24.60	$1123.25
Supplier:	BTO	BTO
Status:	STOCK	SPECORDER
Cost:	$15.00	$797.15

c. Next you will query the table to display a list of inventory items from his favorite supplier, Business Technology Originators, with the supplier code BTO. Create a new query based on the Inventory table, then add the Item #, Description, and Supplier fields to the design grid. Enter the criteria to display all records that have BTO as the supplier. Clear the Show box of the Supplier field. Run the query. Print the query datasheet.

d. Now you will help Eddie get the inventory totals for his bank loan officer. You will need to know the number on hand of each item and the item's cost to TechnoBabble to calculate the total value of each item. Delete the Supplier column from the design grid, then add the # On Hand and Cost fields to the grid. To calculate the total value of each item, enter the expression Total Value: [Cost]*[# On Hand]. Set the format of the calculated field to currency. Run the query, then print the query datasheet.

e. So that Eddie can track the total value of his inventory as he buys and sells items, save the query as Inventory Value.

☆☆☆

3. This problem is a continuation of Practice Exercise 2 in Lab 2. Michelle at Food for Thought has been updating her database, and has added a table that tracks billing by client number. Michelle recently spoke with Debbie at Desert Rescue Cleaning Service about the queries you helped Debbie create. Michelle needs the same kind of analysis of her own clients and wants you to help her find clients who had at least one party that cost more than $1000 during 1995.

a. Open Updated Catering Records, the database that contains Michelle's updated records for Food for Thought. Create a new query based on the Billing table, then add the Customer #, Amount, and Invoice Date fields to the design grid. To indicate invoices of more than $1000 for 1995, enter >1000 in the Criteria cell of the Amount column and >=1/1/95 AND <=12/31/95 in the Invoice Date column. Run the query.

b. Michelle realizes that the query datasheet is not really useful without the customer names. Return to Query Design view and add the Customers table to the Query window. Add the Company field to the design grid, then run the query.

c. Michelle now has the information she needs in the query datasheet, but would prefer that the company name be displayed between the Customer # and Amount columns. Move the Company column to the new location, then print the query datasheet and close the Query window without saving the query.

d. You are about to leave when Michelle remembers that she got a good buy on beans and wants to find out which customers like baked beans. Use a filter to display only those customers who prefer baked beans. Print the filtered datasheet. Then remove the filter and close the table.

On Your Own

☆☆

4. This problem is a continuation of Practice Exercise 1 in Lab 2. James O'Dell needs to gather data about his store inventory. He wants to gather information about a series of item numbers that he fears may be overstocked. In addition, he would like to see the value of each item in stock.

Open the Valley of the Sun Office Supplies database, then create a new query to display all records where the item numbers begin with either a 2 or a 3. Include appropriate fields in the query. Run the query and print the query datasheet.

James wants more detailed information about the items you located in the first query. He wants to know which items begin with either a 2 or a 3 and have more than 40 items on hand. Run the query and print the query datasheet.

James has almost all the information he needs, but he would like to see dollar amounts for each item. Calculate the total value of each item in the query datasheet. Run the new query and print the query datasheet.

Save the query as Overstocked Items and close the Query window.

☆☆

5. This problem is a continuation of Practice Exercise 5 in Lab 2. Now that you are on staff at the Go West Dude Ranch, Michael wants you to add some capabilities to his payroll records. You have already created a new table, called Time Card, that tracks weekly hours worked. Next you will add a field to the Staff Records table to track salaries. You will also create a form for the new table you created. Finally, you will create queries for figuring the weekly paychecks for each employee.

Open the Dude Ranch Payroll database with the updated records, then add the Pay Rate field to the Staff Records table. Format the field to display as currency.

Enter the following pay rates for each employee in the Staff Records table:

Employee #	Pay Rate
015	$12.50
131	6.75
139	8.25
216	4.75
275	4.75

Due to a data processing error, your personal information was lost. Reenter your data, including a pay rate for yourself and an employee number.

Your updated database includes a Time Card table that tracks weekly hours worked by each employee. Create a columnar form based on the Time Card table and name the form Weekly Time Card. Use the new Weekly Time Card form to enter data for the current week:

Employee #	Hours Worked
015	40
131	38
139	27.25
216	40
275	20
Your #	Your Hours

Now you need to create a new query that will figure paychecks for all employees. Create a multitable query to display the pay rate and total hours worked for each employee during the current week. You will also need to calculate the gross pay for each employee. Format the gross pay field to currency. Print the query datasheet, then save the query as Weekly Paychecks.

☆☆☆

6. This problem is a continuation of Practice Exercise 6 in Lab 2.

Open the My Contacts database and create a query to display company name, contact, and phone number for all records. Print the query datasheet.

Open the form you created in Lab 2. Change the form colors and fonts to make it easier to read and more attractive. Print one record in the revised form. Save any changes to your form.

Create at least two other queries of the data in your table that you can use to analyze the data. Print the query results.

Concept Summary

Filtering and Querying Tables

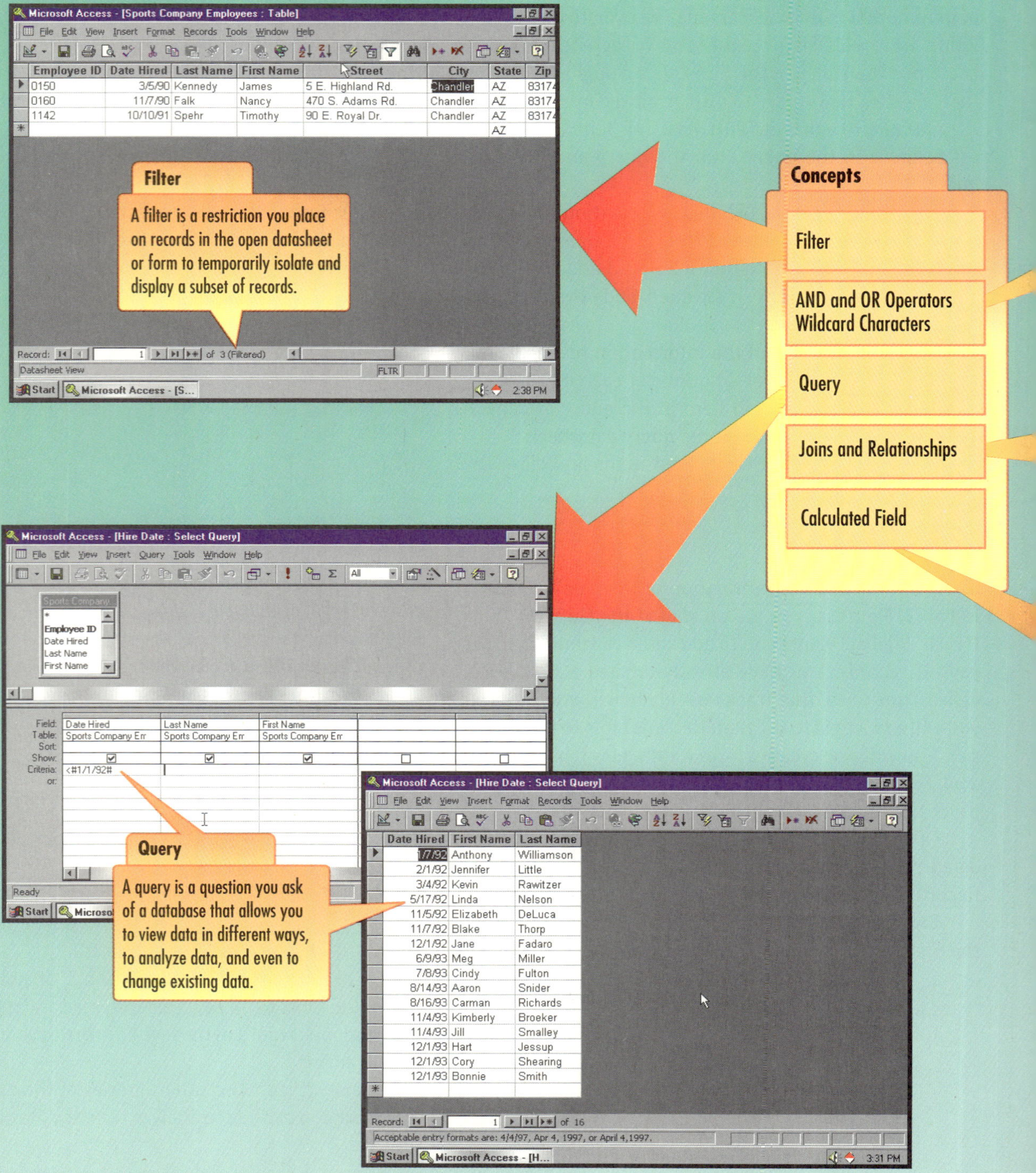

AND and OR Operators

The AND and OR operators are used to specify multiple conditions that must be met for the records to display in the datasheet.

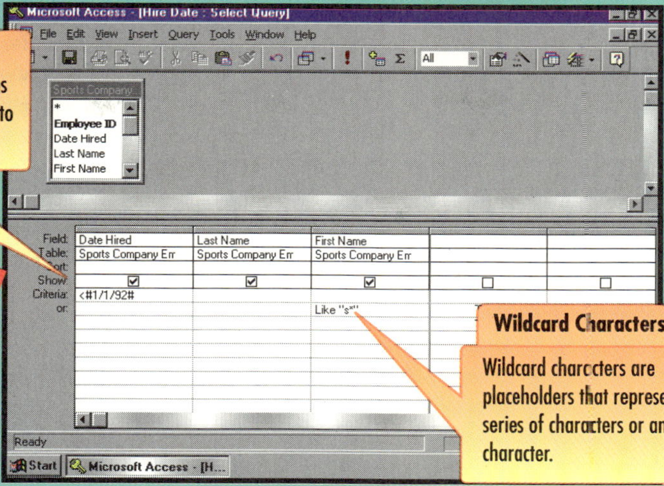

Wildcard Characters

Wildcard characters are placeholders that represent any series of characters or any single character.

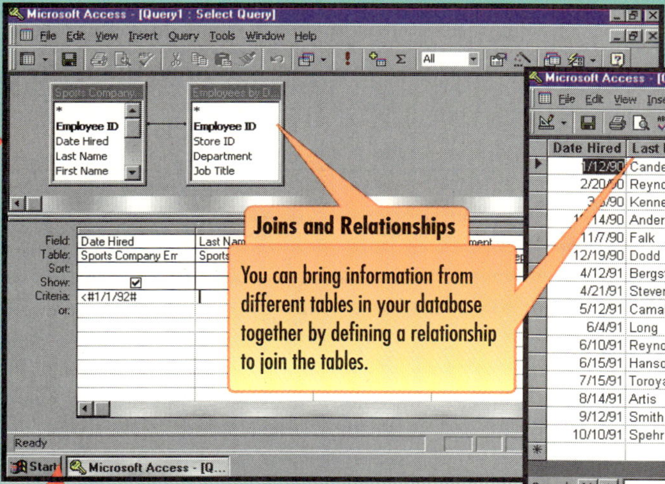

Joins and Relationships

You can bring information from different tables in your database together by defining a relationship to join the tables.

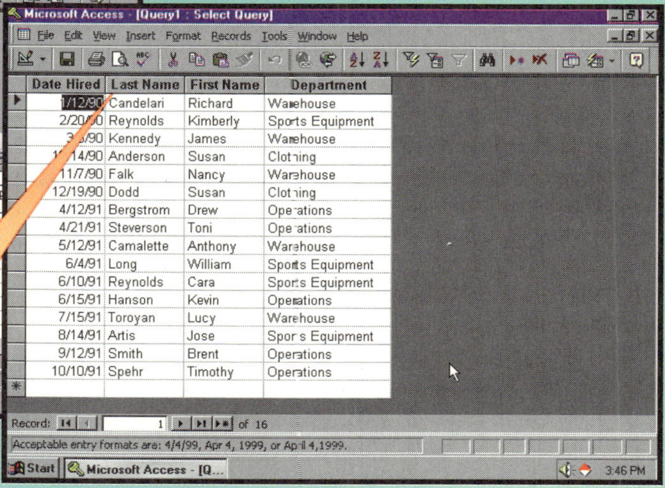

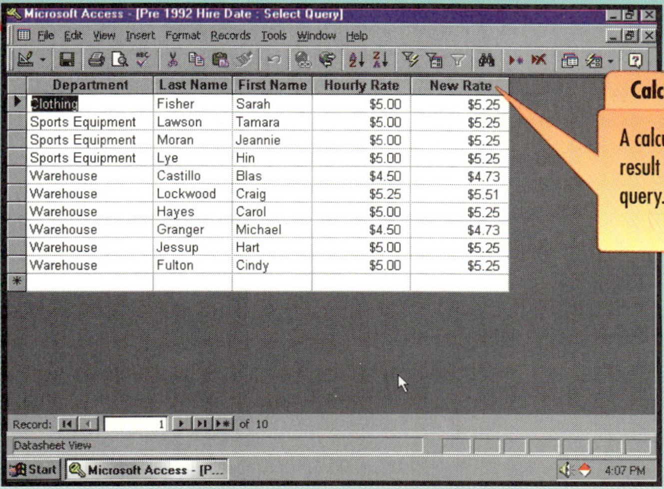

Calculated Field

A calculated field displays the result of a calculation in a query.

Creating Reports and Mailing Labels

COMPETENCIES

After completing this lab, you will know how to:

1. **Use the AutoReport Wizard.**
2. **Zoom a window.**
3. **Use the Report Wizard.**
4. **Create a report from a query.**
5. **Group a report.**
6. **Modify the report design.**
7. **Change control properties.**
8. **Add font, color, and line enhancements.**
9. **Create mailing labels.**

CASE STUDY

The manager is impressed with your ability to use Access to quickly locate and analyze the data in the employee tables. You have used the program to automate the daily updates and changes that occur to the employee tables and to quickly find answers to many different types of queries. The printed output of the query results is a simple report that is acceptable for many informal uses.

Next you have been asked to create weekly and monthly employee status reports. You want these reports to have a more professional appearance suitable for a formal report or presentation. You will create several reports that group and summarize the data in an organized and attractive manner. An example of one of the reports you will create is shown at right.

Finally, you have seen asked to create mailing labels from the employee database. One page of the labels you will create is shown below.

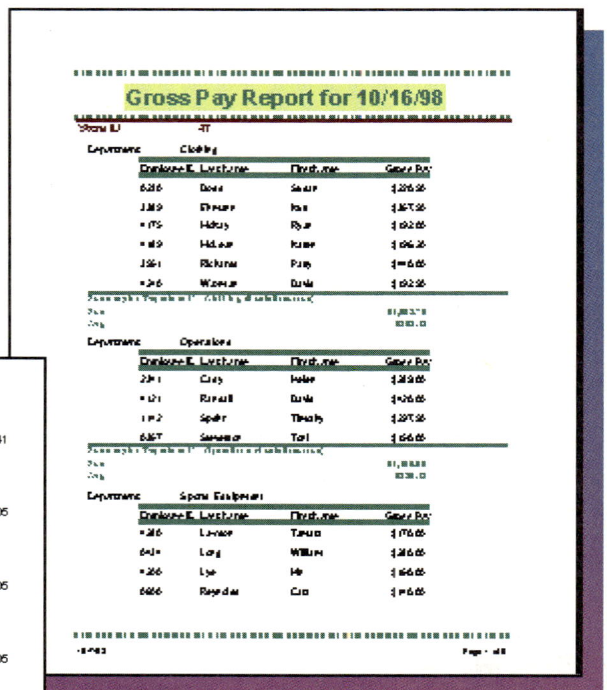

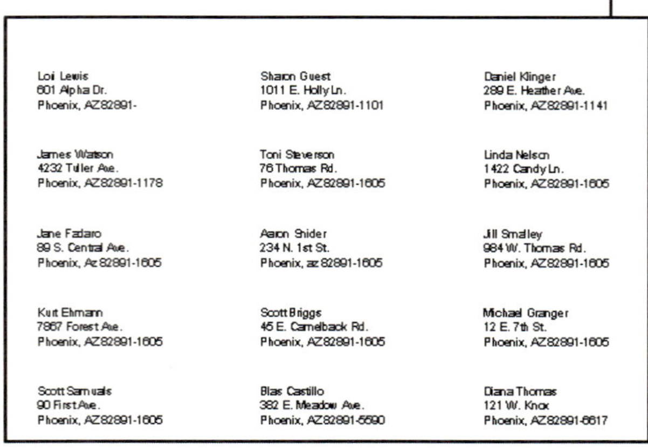

Concept Overview

The following concepts will be introduced in this lab:

1. Reports	Reports are the printed output you generate from tables or queries.
2. Grouping Records	Records in a report can be grouped into categories to allow you to better analyze the data.
3. Group Calculations	If you group data in your report, you can perform calculations on values, such as a group total, an average, a minimum value, and a maximum value.
4. Layout Preview	Layout Preview displays a sample of the data in the report so you can quickly check the report's layout.

Part 1

Using the AutoReport Wizard

The manager would like a report that displays the employees' names and addresses ordered by name. You have already created and printed several simple reports using the Print command on the File menu. This time, however, you want to create a custom report of this information.

Concept 1: Reports

Access **reports** are the printed output you generate from tables or queries. It might be a simple listing of all the fields in a table, or it might be a list of selected fields based on a query.

Access also includes a custom report feature that allows you to create professional-appearing reports. The custom report is a document that includes text formats, styles, and layouts that enhance the display of information. In addition, you can group data in reports to achieve specific results. You can then display summary information, such as totals, by group to allow the reader to further analyze the data. Creating a custom report displays the information from your database in a more attractive and meaningful format.

You will create the address list report using the data in the Sports Company Employees table in the Sports Company Personnel Records database.

> Use the Sports Company Personnel Records database from the end of Lab 3.

> The menu equivalent is Insert/Report.

- Load Access 97. Put your data disk in drive A (or the appropriate drive for your system).
- Open the Sports Company Personnel Records database file.
- Open the Reports tab.
- Click New.

The New Report dialog box on your screen should be similar to Figure 4-1.

FIGURE 4-1

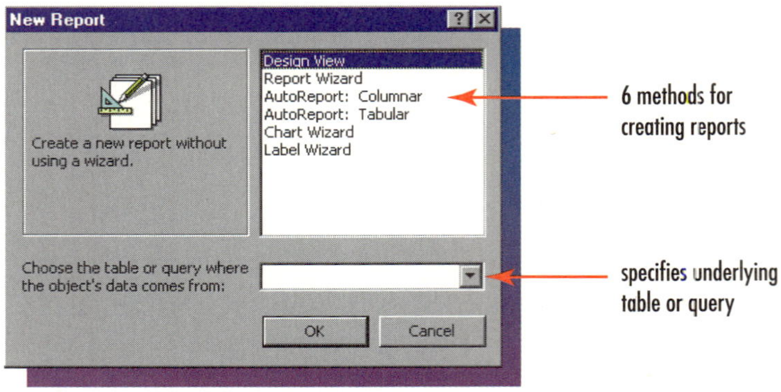

The dialog box presents six ways to create a report. You can create a report from scratch in Design view, or by using the Report Wizard or one of the AutoReport Wizards. The Report Wizard lets you choose the fields to include in the report and it helps you quickly format and lay out the new report. The AutoReport Wizard creates a report that displays all fields and records from the underlying table or query in a predesigned report layout and style.

You decide to use the AutoReport Wizard to create a columnar report using data in the Sports Company Employees table.

- Select AutoReport: Columnar.
- Select Sports Company Employees from the Choose the Table or Query drop-down list.
- Click OK.

After a few moments, the report is created and displayed in the Print Preview window.

- To see more of the report, maximize the window.

Your screen should be similar to Figure 4-2.

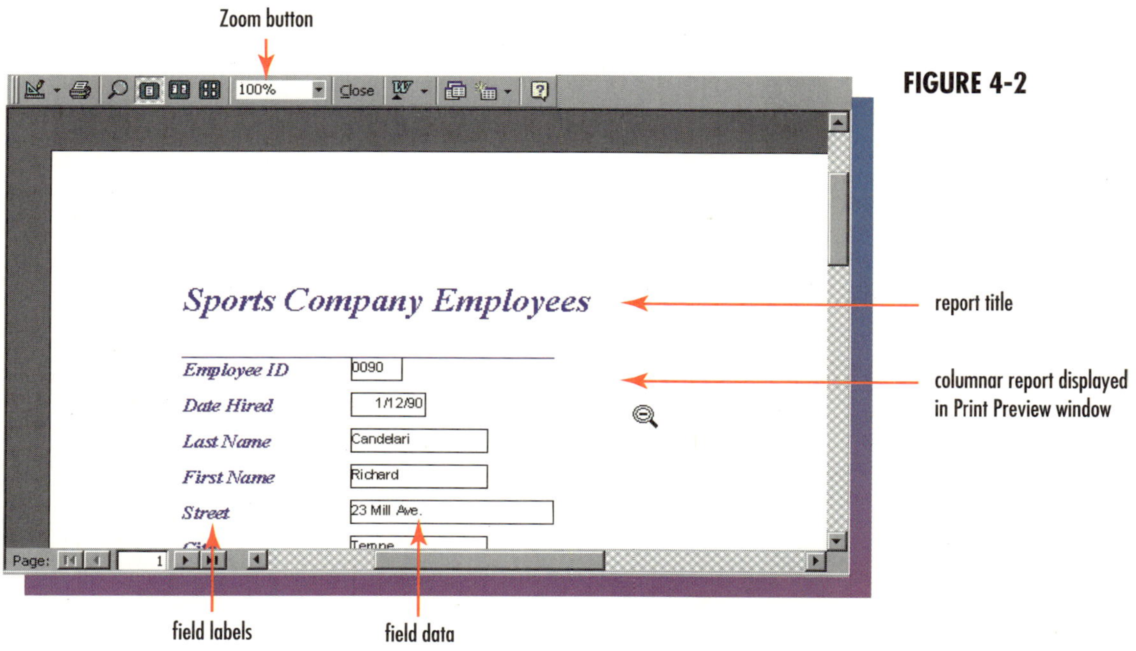

FIGURE 4-2

The AutoReport Wizard creates a columnar report that displays each field on a separate line in a single column for each record. The fields are in the order they appear in the table. The report appears in a predefined report style and layout. The report style shown in Figure 4-2 uses the table name as the report title and includes the use of text colors, typefaces and sizes, and horizontal lines and boxes.

Your report may be displayed with a different style. This is because when creating an AutoReport, Access remembers the last autoformat report style used to create a report, then applies that same style to the new report. If the Autoformat command has not been used, the report will use the basic style. You will learn how to change styles later in this lab.

Zooming the Window

Only the upper part of the first page of the report is visible in the window. To see more of the report in the window at one time, you can decrease the onscreen character size by specifying a smaller magnification percentage using the Zoom command. The default magnification percentage of 100% is displayed in the Zoom toolbar button. This setting shows the characters the same size as they will be when printed. You can increase the character size up to two times normal display (200%) or reduce it to 10%.

- Open the [100%] Zoom Control drop-down list.
- Choose 50%.

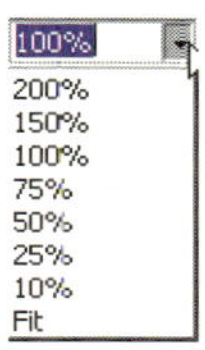

The Zoom feature is available in all Print Preview windows.

The menu equivalent is View/Zoom/50%.

The text is reduced in size by half, allowing you to view more of the page in the window. You can now see three sides of the page. You can further adjust the magnification to display the whole page in the window using the Fit option.

The menu equivalent is **V**iew/**Z**oom/**F**it to Window.

■ Choose Fit from the Zoom drop-down list.

Your screen should be similar to Figure 4-3.

FIGURE 4-3

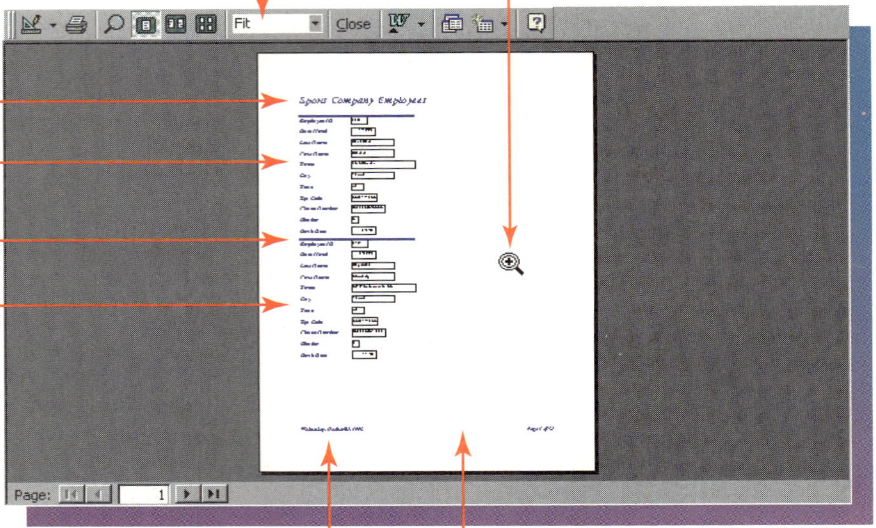

Just as in Table, Form, and Datasheet views, you can use the navigation keys and navigation buttons to move through the pages of the report.

Now the entire page is visible, but most of the text is too small to read. However, you can now see the entire page layout. The report title appears at the top of the page, and each field of information is displayed on a separate line in a single column for each record. Each record is separated from the next by a horizontal line. The current date and page number appear at the bottom of the page in the footer. The first two records from the Sports Company Employees table are displayed on the first page of the report.

Notice that the mouse pointer is a when it is positioned on the page. This indicates that you can you can switch between the last magnification level you set and the Fit magnification by clicking on the report. The location of the pointer on the report when you click indicates the area of the report that will appear in the window.

You can also click Zoom in the toolbar to zoom in and out.

■ With the mouse pointer as , click on the report title.

The page is displayed at 50% magnification again. You can also view multiple report pages at the same time in Print Preview. To view six pages,

The **V**iew/P**a**ges command can be used to display up to 12 pages, and the button can be used to display up to 20 pages of a report in the window.

■ Click Multiple Pages.

■ Drag to select six pages (2x3).

Use to quickly display two pages and to display a single page.

Your screen should be similar to Figure 4-4.

displays multiple pages

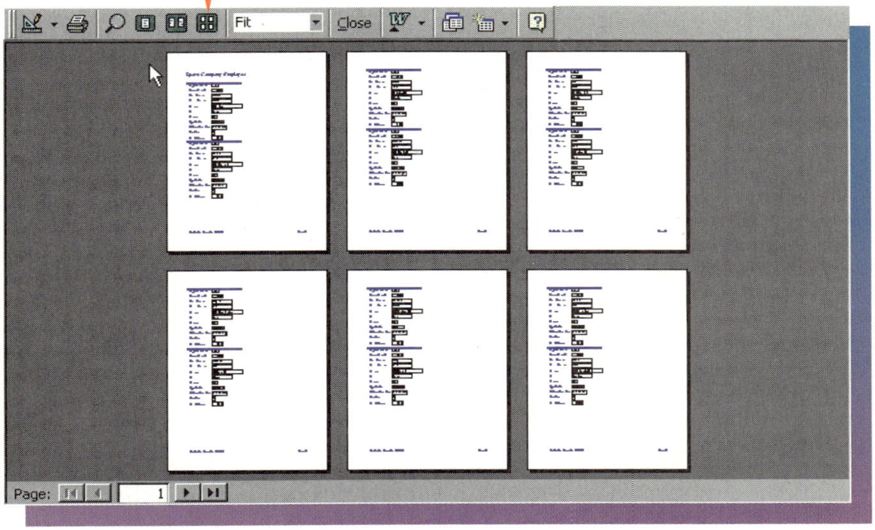

FIGURE 4-4

After looking over the columnar report, you decide the layout is inappropriate for your report because only two records are printed per page, making the report larger than 50 pages. In addition, you do not want the report to include all the fields from the table. To close the report file without saving it,

- Click [X].
- Click [No].

Do not click [Close] on the toolbar. This closes the Print Preview window, but does not close the report file.

Using the Report Wizard

You want the report to display the field contents for each record on a line rather than in a column. You also want to display the employee name and address information only. The Report Wizard will create this type of report. From the Reports tab,

- Choose [New]/Report Wizard/[OK].

The Report Wizard consists of a series of dialog boxes, much like the Form Wizard. In the first dialog box (see Figure 4-5) you specify the table or query to be used in the report and select the fields.

- Select Table: Sports Company Employees from the Tables/Queries drop-down list.

Fields are added just as in Form Wizard.

- Add the fields to the Selected Fields list in the following order:

The fields appear in the report in the order in which you place them in the Selected Fields list.

First Name
Last Name
Street
City
State
Zip Code

You do not have to include all the fields in the table on a report.

The Report Wizard dialog box on your screen should be similar to Figure 4-5.

FIGURE 4-5

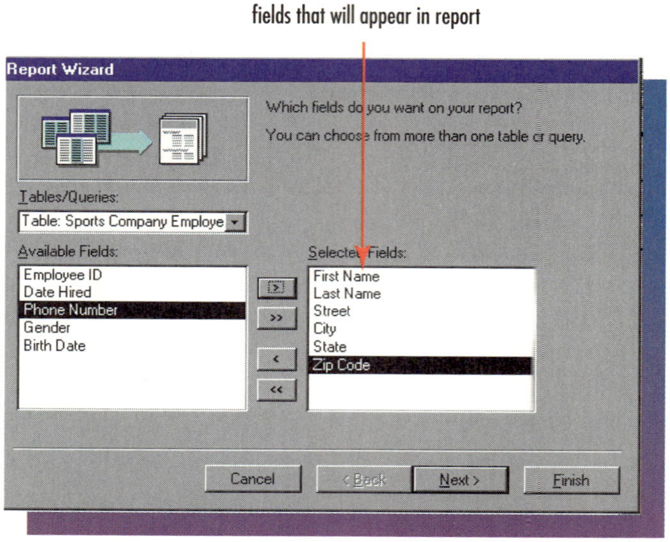

- Click Next >.

You will learn about grouping later in this lab.

In the second Report Wizard dialog box you specify how to group the data in the report. The manager does not want the report grouped by any category. To move to the next dialog box,

- Click Next >.

The next dialog box (see Figure 4-6) is used to specify a sort order for the records. A report can be sorted on up to four fields. The manager would like the report sorted in ascending order by last name and by first name within same last names.

- Select Last Name from the number 1 drop-down list and First Name from the number 2 drop-down list.

Clicking [A↓Z] toggles between ascending and descending sort order.

The default order of ascending for both fields is appropriate.

The dialog box on your screen should be similar to Figure 4-6.

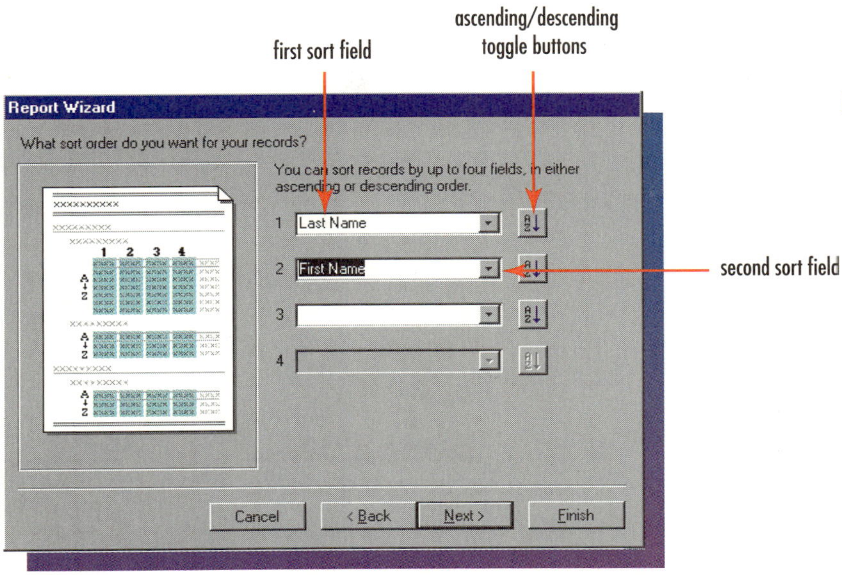

FIGURE 4-6

- Click Next >.

The next dialog box is used to change the report layout and orientation. The default report settings create a tabular layout using portrait orientation. In addition, the option to adjust the field width so all fields fit on one page is selected. Because this report is very wide, the only change you will make is to change the orientation to landscape.

- Select Landscape.
- Click Next >.

From this dialog box you select a style for the report. The preview area displays a sample of each style as it is selected. You believe the Bold style is most appropriate for this report.

- Select each style to preview the style options.
- Select Bold.
- Click Next >.

The last Report Wizard dialog box is used to add a title to the report and to specify how the report should be displayed after it is created. The only change you want to make is to replace the table name with a more descriptive report title.

- Type **Employee Address Report**
- Click Finish.

The program takes a minute to generate the report, during which time Report Design view is briefly displayed. In a few moments, the completed report with the data from the underlying table is displayed in the Print Preview window.

Your screen should be similar to Figure 4-7.

FIGURE 4-7

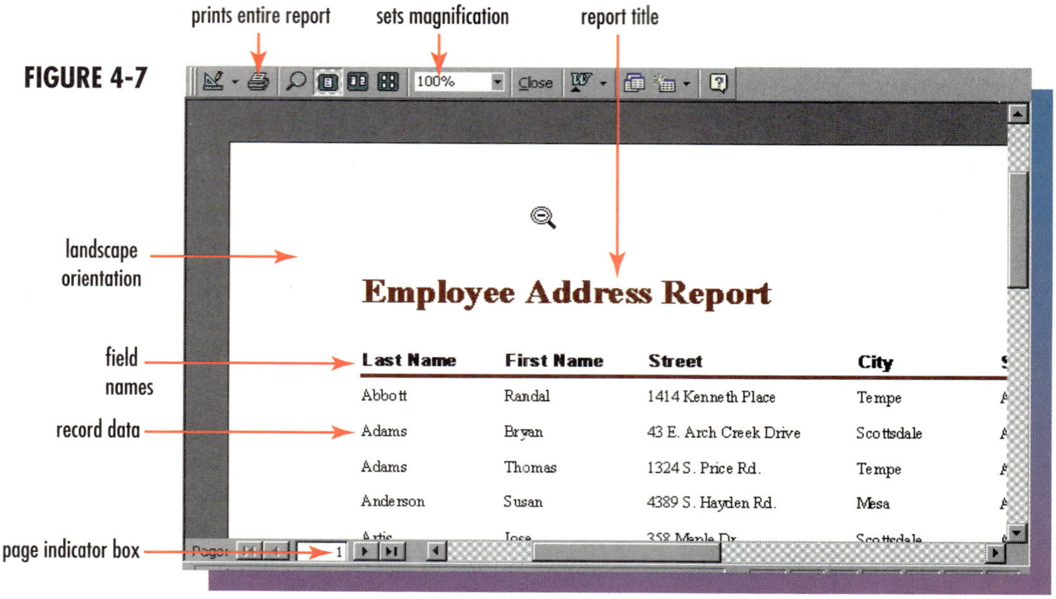

The Print Preview window displays the first page of the report in landscape orientation using the selected Bold report style. The report title reflects the title you specified using the Wizard. The names of the selected fields are displayed on the first line of the report and each record appears on a separate row below the field names. Notice that the Last Name field is the first field, even though you selected it as the second field. This is because the sort order overrides the selected field order.

- Change the magnification to Fit.

You can now see the layout of the report on the entire page. The address information easily fits across the page with the orientation set to landscape. You like the layout of this report and do not need to make any changes to the report design. Next you will print the page containing your record.

> Increase the magnification to locate your record more easily.

> The page number is displayed in the page indicator box.

> The Print button prints the entire report.

- Move to the page of the report that contains your name.
- Choose File/Print.
- If necessary, select the appropriate printer for your system.
- Select Pages.
- Type the page number containing your record in the From and To text boxes.
- Click OK.
- Close the Employee Address Report file.

The Database window is displayed again, and the report object name is listed in the Reports object list. The Report Wizard automatically saves the report using the report title as the object name.

Creating a Report from a Query

The next report you want to create will display the employees' gross pay grouped by store and department. You have sketched out the report to look like the one shown below.

Gross Pay Report for xx/xx/xx

Store ID: XX			
Department:	XXXXXXXX		
Employee ID	Last Name	First Name	Gross Pay
XXXXXXXX	XXXXXXX	XXXXX	$XXXX.XX
XXXXXXXX	XXXXXXX	XXXXX	$XXXX.XX
Sum by Dept.			$XXXXX.XX
Avg by Dept.			$XXXXX.XX
Sum by Store			$XXXXX.XX
Avg by Store			$XXXXX.XX

To create this report, you will use the query you created in Lab 3 and saved as Gross Pay for 10/16/98. It is usually helpful to run the query first to remind you of the data that the query gathers.

If you create a report based on multiple tables, the relationship between tables must be established first using Tools/Relationships.

- From the Queries tab, open the Gross Pay for 10/16/98 query.

The query datasheet displays the Department, Last Name, First Name, and Gross Pay fields. In addition, you need the report to display the Employee ID and the Store ID fields. To include these fields in the report, you need to add them to the query design grid.

- Switch to Query Design view.
- Add the Employee ID and Store ID fields to the design grid.
- Run the query.
- Arrange the field columns so Store ID is the second column and Employee ID is the third column.
- Clear the highlight.

Your screen should be similar to Figure 4-8.

FIGURE 4-8

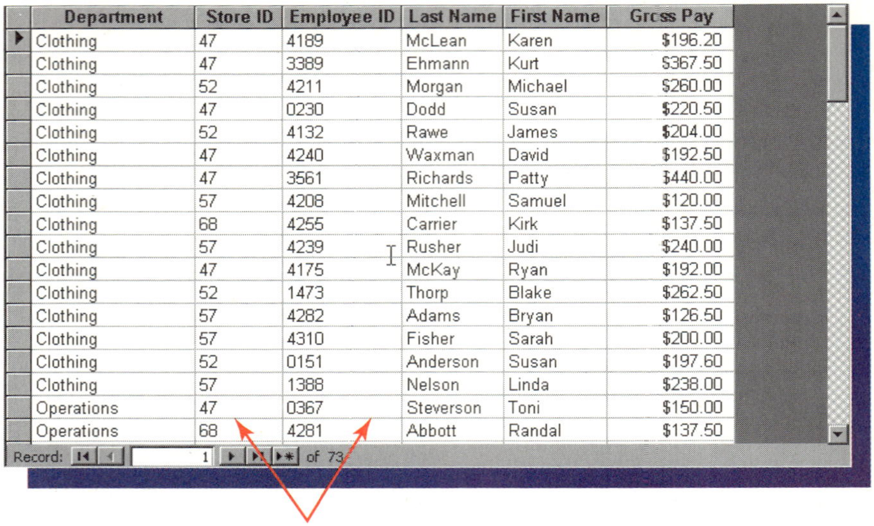

Department	Store ID	Employee ID	Last Name	First Name	Gross Pay
Clothing	47	4189	McLean	Karen	$196.20
Clothing	47	3389	Ehmann	Kurt	$367.50
Clothing	52	4211	Morgan	Michael	$260.00
Clothing	47	0230	Dodd	Susan	$220.50
Clothing	52	4132	Rawe	James	$204.00
Clothing	47	4240	Waxman	David	$192.50
Clothing	47	3561	Richards	Patty	$440.00
Clothing	57	4208	Mitchell	Samuel	$120.00
Clothing	68	4255	Carrier	Kirk	$137.50
Clothing	57	4239	Rusher	Judi	$240.00
Clothing	47	4175	McKay	Ryan	$192.00
Clothing	52	1473	Thorp	Blake	$262.50
Clothing	57	4282	Adams	Bryan	$126.50
Clothing	57	4310	Fisher	Sarah	$200.00
Clothing	52	0151	Anderson	Susan	$197.60
Clothing	57	1388	Nelson	Linda	$238.00
Operations	47	0367	Steverson	Toni	$150.00
Operations	68	4281	Abbott	Randal	$137.50

new fields added to query

Now you are ready to create a report using the data from the query. Rather than switching to the Report tab of the Database window and choosing New, you can use the New Object button to create a new object of any type.

- Open the New Object drop-down list.
- Select Report.
- If you are prompted to save the query, click Yes.

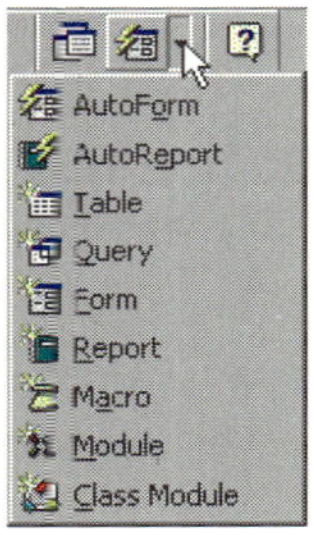

The New Report dialog box correctly displays the name of the selected query as the object on which the report will be based.

- Choose Report Wizard/OK.

The Available Fields list box displays the fields that are included in the design grid in the Gross Pay for 10/16/98 query. You want to include all the fields in the report.

- Click >>.
- Click Next >.

Grouping a Report

In the next dialog box you need to select the fields on which you want to group the report.

Concept 2: Grouping Records

Records in a report can be **grouped** by categories to allow you to better analyze the data. It is often helpful to group records and calculate totals for the entire group. For example, it might be useful for a store manager to group payroll records by department. Then, rather than getting a long list of pay for individual employees, the manager could get a report showing total payroll for each department. A mail order company might group orders by date of purchase, then by item number to see detailed sales information.

In Access you can create a report that will automatically group records based on fields you choose to group by. You can group by up to 10 fields in any one report.

Groups should be created based on priority from the largest to smallest. To group the report by store number and then by department within store number,

The Priority buttons can be used to change the grouping order of priority.

- Select Store ID.
- Click [>].
- Select Department.
- Click [>].

The dialog box on your screen should be similar to Figure 4-9.

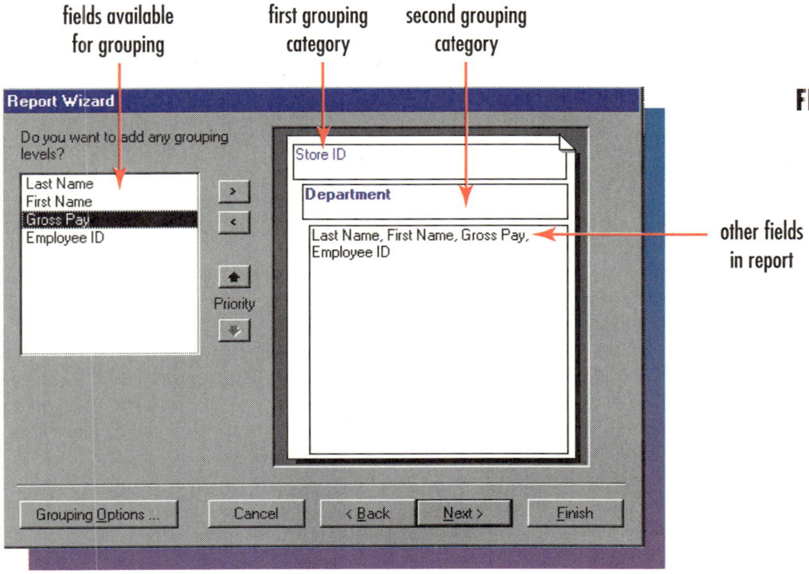

FIGURE 4-9

- Click [Next >].

In this dialog box you specify a sort order for the data grouped within each field. In addition, because you have specified groups, you can also include calculations to summarize the grouped data.

Concept 3: Group Calculations

If you group data in your report, you can perform one or more of the following calculations on values: Sum (adds all values by group), Avg (calculates the average value for the group), Min (calculates the lowest value for the group), and Max (calculates the highest value for the group).

You can select multiple calculations to complete different analyses of the data. For example, a mail order company might calculate the sum of different products sold on each day of the month and the average sale for each day. You can also calculate the percent of total for the sums. For example, the mail order company might want to know what percentage of total sales were made on a specific product for June 15.

You can further customize the report to display both detailed information and the summary information, or just the summary information while hiding the details about the individual items.

You would like the report sorted by last name and then by first name, and to display a total and average for each department and store.

- Select Last Name as the first field to sort on and First Name as the second field to sort on.
- Click Summary Options ... .
- Select Sum.
- Select Avg.
- Click OK.
- Click Next >.

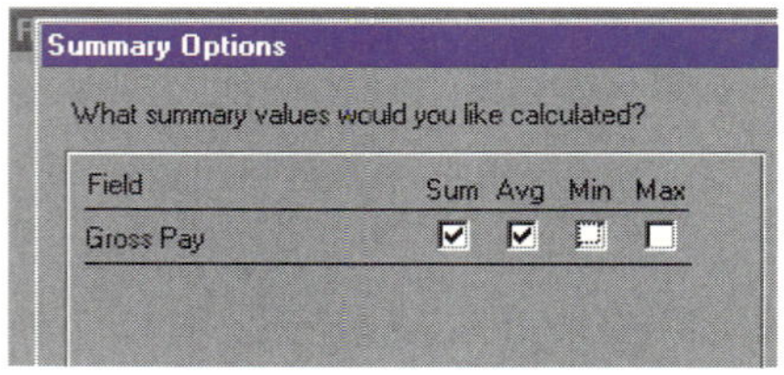

The dialog box on your screen should be similar to Figure 4-10.

FIGURE 4-10

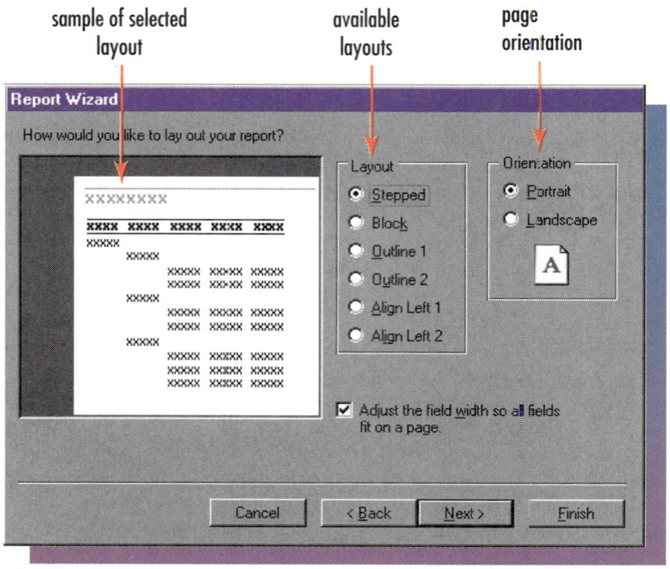

In this dialog box you are asked to select from six different layout options for a grouped report. You will use the Outline 1 layout.

- Select each layout option and look at the sample previews.
- Select Outline 1.
- Click Next >.

From the last two Report Wizard dialog boxes, you will select the report style and enter the title.

- Select Casual.
- Click Next >.
- Edit the report title to be **Gross Pay Report for 10/16/98**.
- Click Finish.
- Set the Print Preview window magnification to 75%.

Your screen should be similar to Figure 4-11.

FIGURE 4-11

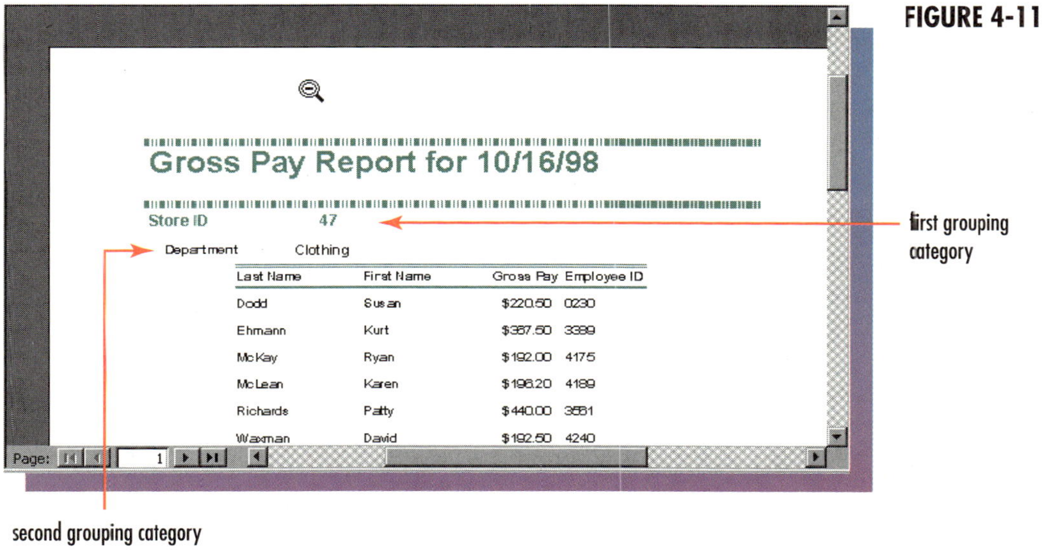

The data in the report is grouped by store and department, and the records are alphabetized by last name within groups. The information for store 47 is the first store group, and the Clothing department is the department group within the store group.

- Scroll the report to see the summary data at the bottom of the Clothing group.

In addition, each department group displays a count of employees and the sum and average values below the Gross Pay data column.

- Display page 2 and, if necessary, scroll the report to see the information at the end of the store 47 group and the beginning of the store 52 group.

Your screen should be similar to Figure 4-12.

FIGURE 4-12

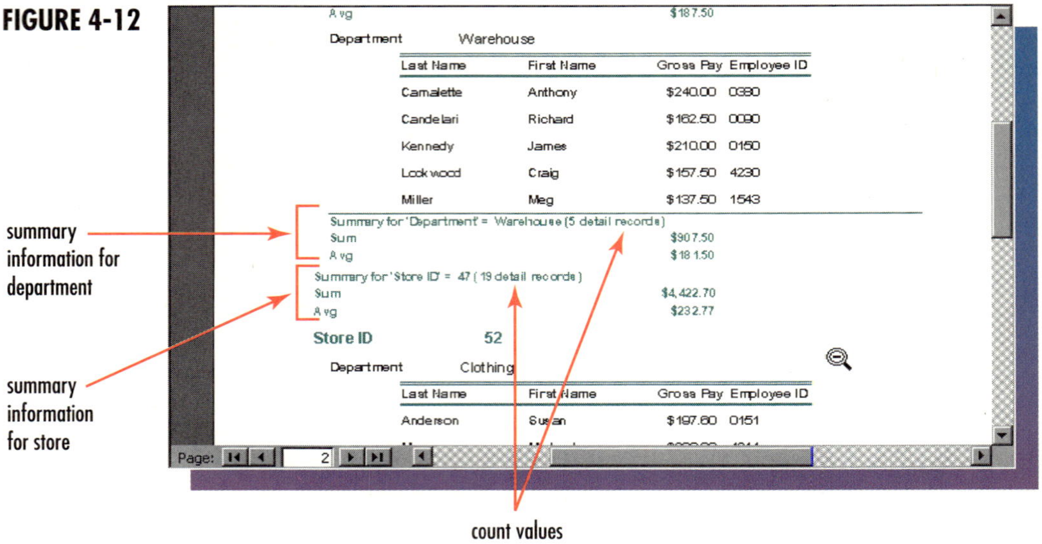

The summary information for store 47 appears above the Store 52 group head. It includes a count value, and total and average gross pay values for the store.

- Display the top of the last page of the report.

A grand total value for all stores appears at the end of the report.

- Display the top of page 1 again.

Note: If you are ending your session now, close the Report file and exit Access. When you begin Part 2, open the Sports Company Personnel Records database file. Then Preview the Gross Pay Report for 10/16/98.

Part 2

Modifying the Report Design

As you looked through the report, you saw several changes you wanted to make. The first change is to rearrange the order of the fields in the report and to size the fields appropriately. In addition, you want to make the store group head more noticeable, to change the display of the date in the footer to exclude the day of the week, and to center the title over the report. Report Design view is used to modify the appearance of the report.

- Click Report Design.
- If necessary, move the Toolbox to the right border of the window.

Your screen should be similar to Figure 4-13.

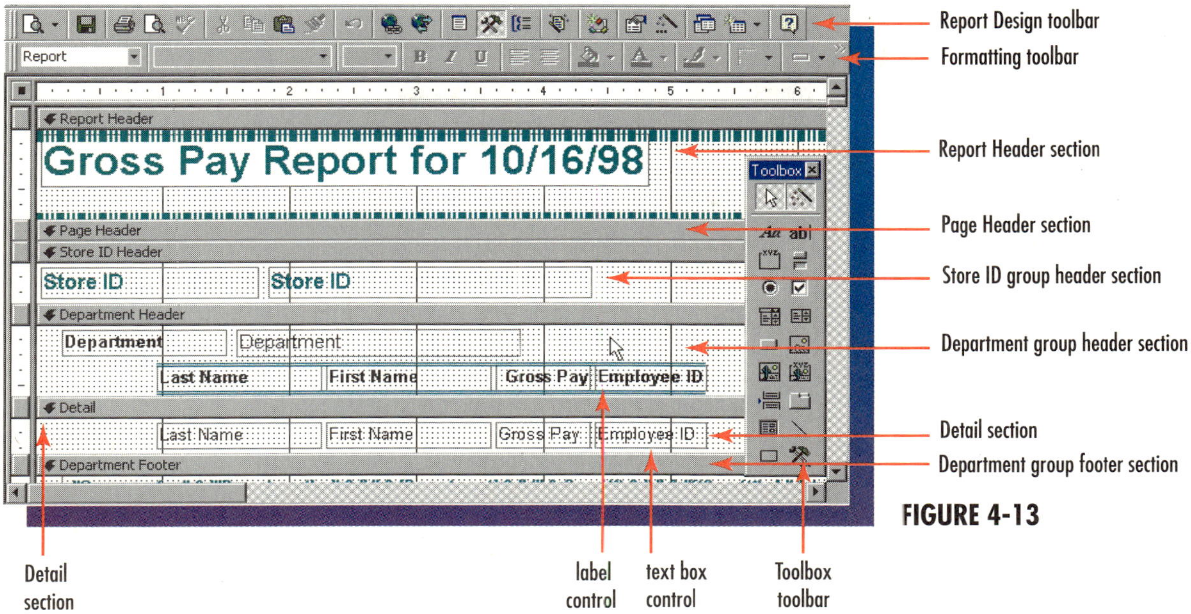

FIGURE 4-13

As you can see, Report Design view is very similar to Form Design view. It displays horizontal and vertical rulers to help with the placement of controls on the grid. It also displays three toolbars: Report Design, Formatting, and Toolbox. The Formatting and Toolbox toolbars are the same as in Form view. The Report Design toolbar contains the standard buttons as well as buttons (identified below) that are specific to the Report Design view window.

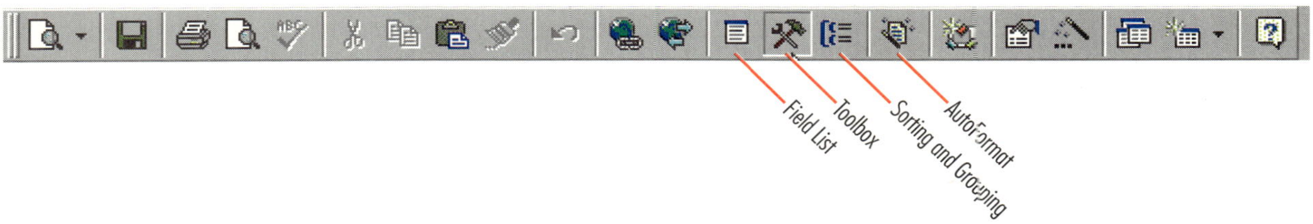

Some sections may not be currently visible in the Report Design window.

The Report Design view window consists of seven report sections, which break the report into distinct areas consisting of one or more lines. Above each section is the section name. (See Figure 4-13.)

Section	Description
Report Header	Contains information to be printed once at the beginning of the report. The report title is displayed in this area.
Page Header	Contains information to be printed at the top of each page. In an ungrouped report, the column headings displaying the field names often are displayed in this area. The Page Header section is empty in the current report.
Group Header	Contains information on groups. This report has two Group Headers: Store ID Header and Department Header. The information in the Group Headers is displayed each time there is a new group.
Detail Section	Contains the records of the table. The field column widths are the same as the column widths set in table design.
Group Footer	There is one Group Footer for each group. The Group Footers often contain formulas that instruct Access to display group totals. In this report, there are totals by Department and by Store ID in the Group Footers.
Page Footer	Contains information to be printed at the bottom of each page, such as the date and page number.
Report Footer	Contains information to be printed once at the end of the report. The current Report Footer includes a grand total for all employees.

You can add fields to a report using View/Field List. Added field controls are inserted as compound controls. Use Cut and Paste to separate the controls to move them into separate report sections.

The first change you will make is to reorganize the display order of the fields in the report. Notice that the Department Header section displays the label control for each field column, while the Detail section contains the text box control. Report controls are selected and manipulated just like Form controls, but unlike Form controls, the text and label controls are not attached. You will select both controls and move them simultaneously.

Hold down ⇧Shift while clicking to select multiple controls.

- Select the Employee ID controls in the Department Header and Detail sections.
- Move the selected controls to the left of the Last Name controls.
- Next, select all eight controls and move them as a group to the right as shown in Figure 4-14.
- Clear the selection.

When you are done, your screen should be similar to Figure 4-14.

FIGURE 4-14

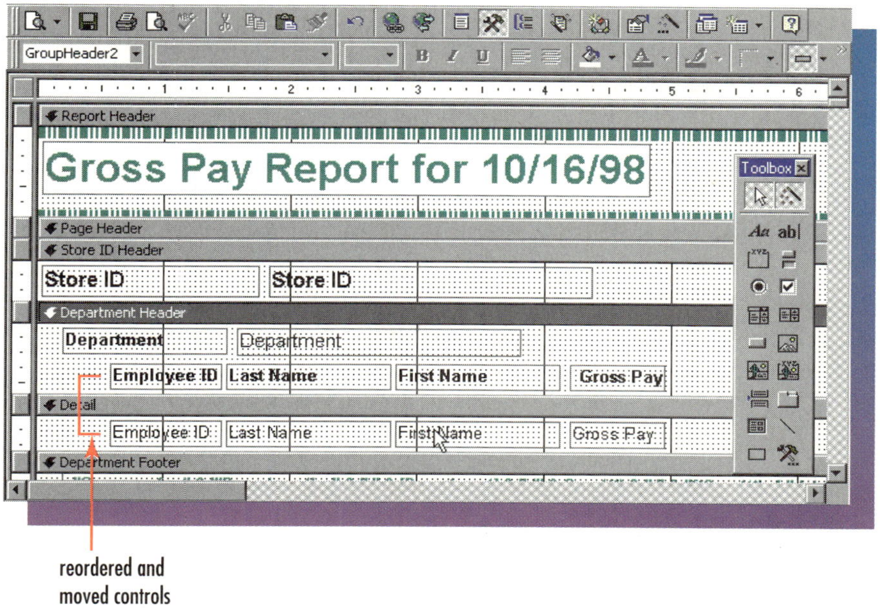

To see how this change has affected the report, you will preview the report using Layout Preview.

Concept 4: Layout Preview

There are two ways to view the report as it will appear when printed. You can use Print Preview to view the entire report page by page. Because this view displays all the data in the report, it takes longer to generate. This is the view you have seen whenever a new report is displayed, and is the view you used when previewing forms.

Another way to view the report is to use Layout Preview to take a quick look at the report. Layout Preview displays just a sample of the data in the report so you can quickly check the report's layout. Because it does not display all the data, it is much quicker to generate.

As a general rule, you should use Print Preview to view the entire report as it will print. Use Layout Preview for quick checks of design layout. When a report is large and you just need to check a layout change you have made, this is the preferred view.

- Select Layout Preview from the View drop-down list.
- If necessary, set the magnification to 75%.

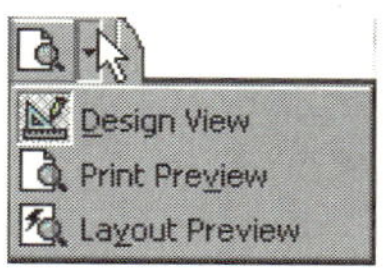

The menu equivalent is **V**iew/La**y**out Preview.

Your screen should be similar to Figure 4-15.

FIGURE 4-15

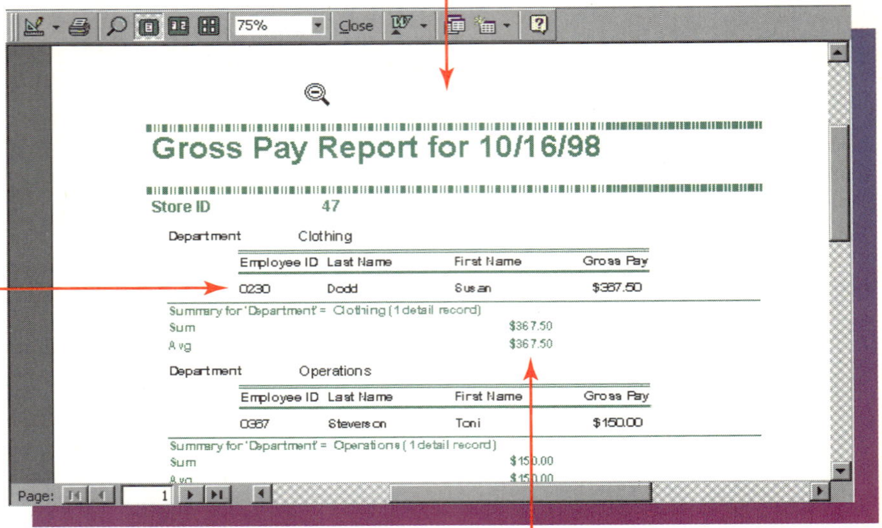

The Layout Preview shows a sample of records in each group as an example of the report layout. The change in the order of the fields improves the organization of the report. However, now you notice that the summary fields for Gross Pay no longer align with the field column. To fix this you will move the controls for the Gross Pay summary fields below the Gross Pay column of data.

- Click Design View.
- Scroll the window to see the Department, Store ID, and Report Footer sections.
- Select the five Gross Pay summary controls and move them to the right to align with the Gross Pay controls in the Detail section (approximately 5.25" position on the ruler).

Align the right border of the controls.

Changing Control Properties

The next change you will make is to change how the date is displayed in the Page Footer. Notice that the date control in the Page Footer is =Now(). This is an expression that directs Access to enter the current date maintained on your computer into the report. Each control has property settings that affect how the control looks and acts. By default the property setting associated with the date control displays the date in the Long Date format. To change the date control properties,

- Select the date control in the Page Footer section.
- Click Properties.

The menu equivalent is View/Properties, or Properties on the Shortcut menu. You can also double-click a control to display its properties.

Your screen should be similar to Figure 4-16.

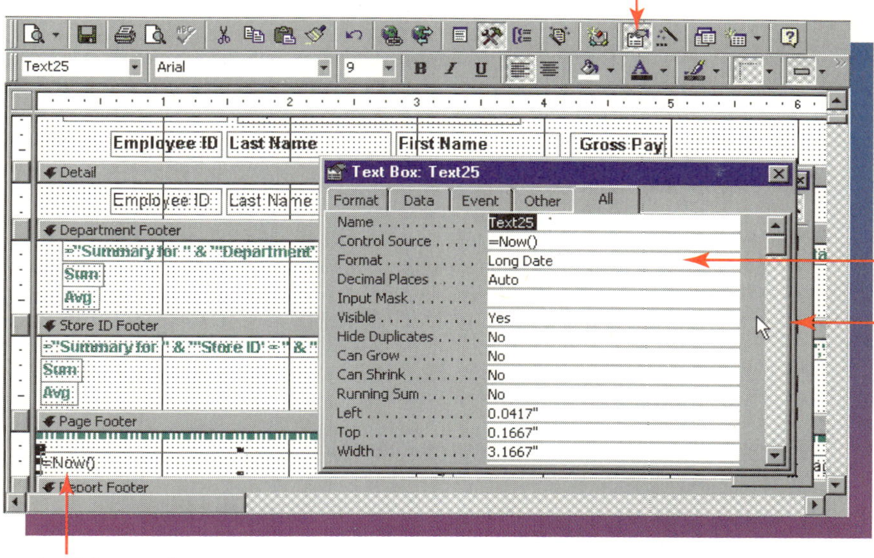

FIGURE 4-16

The property sheet box for the date control is displayed. The All tab displays a list of all properties associated with the selected control. The Format properties contain the same options as in Table Design and vary with the data type of the field. The Format text box displays "Long Date." This date format displays the date as Day, Month xx, 19xx. You want to display the date in the Short Date format of mm/dd/yy.

- Open the Format property drop-down list.
- Select Short Date.
- Close the property sheet.
- Using Layout Preview, preview the changes you have made to the report.
- Scroll to the bottom of page 1.

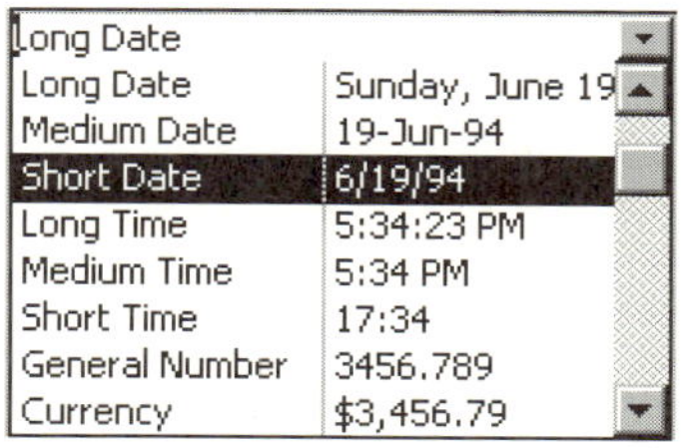

Your screen should be similar to Figure 4-17.

FIGURE 4-17

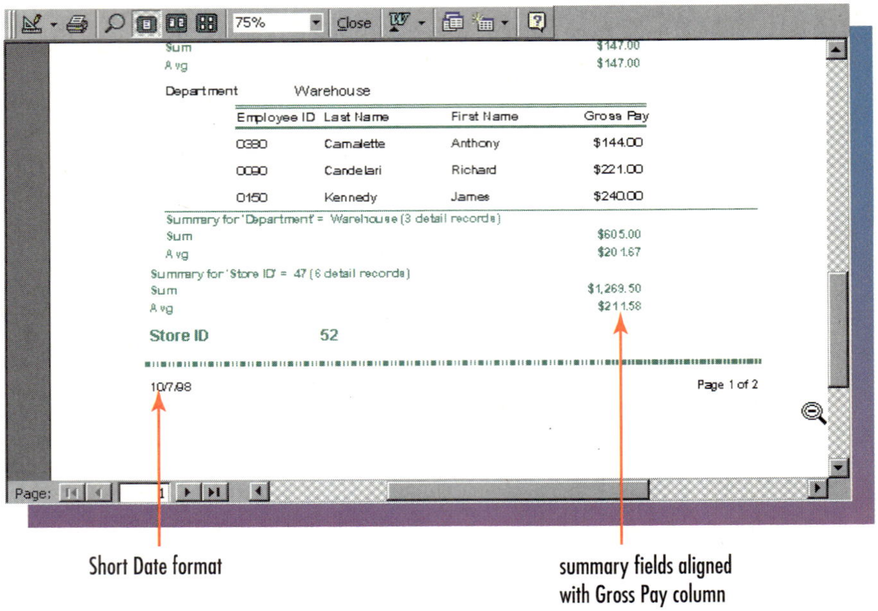

The Gross Pay summary fields are aligned with the Gross Pay column of data, and the date appears in the new Short Date format.

- Return to Design view.

Adding Font, Color, and Line Enhancements

Next, to make the Store ID heading stand out more, you will change the text color and add a heavy colored horizontal line above the controls to help visually separate report areas.

- Select the Store ID label and text box controls in the Store ID Header section.
- Select a color of your choice from the Font/Fore Color palette.
- Click Line.
- Select 3-pt from the Line/Border Width drop-down list.
- Select the same color as the Store ID controls for the line from the Line/Border Color palette.
- Move to the space above the Store ID control and drag from the left margin to the 6.5-inch position on the ruler.

Do not extend the line beyond the 6.5-inch ruler position or the report width will be too wide to fit on a single page.

Your screen should be similar to Figure 4-18.

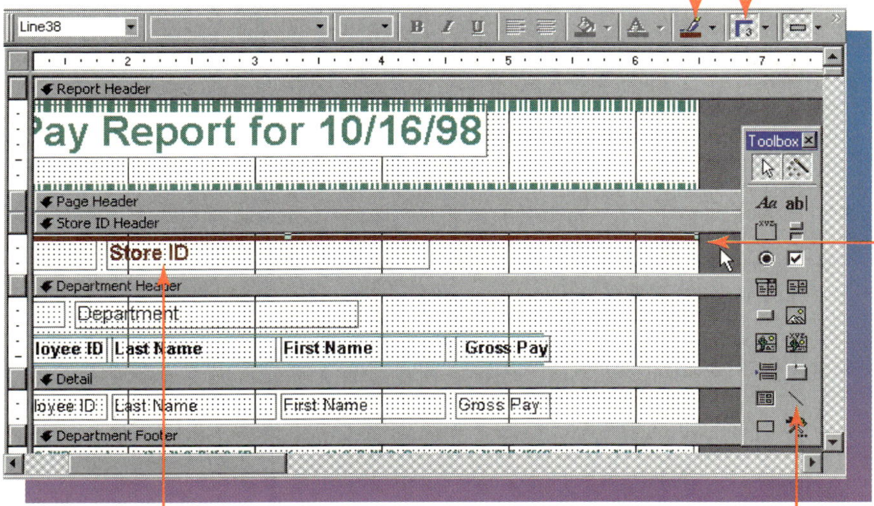

FIGURE 4-18

Finally, you also want to center the title over the report and change the background shading color of the Report Header control.

- Select the report title control (in the Report Header section).
- Drag the title until the left border of the box aligns with the .75-inch ruler mark and the control is centered vertically in the Report Header section (see Figure 4-19).
- Select a color of your choice from the [Fill/Back Color button] Fill/Back Color palette.

Your screen should be similar to Figure 4-19.

FIGURE 4-19

You are now ready to view your report as it will look when you print it.

- View the report using Print Preview.
- Change the display to view two pages.

Your screen should be similar to Figure 4-20.

FIGURE 4-20

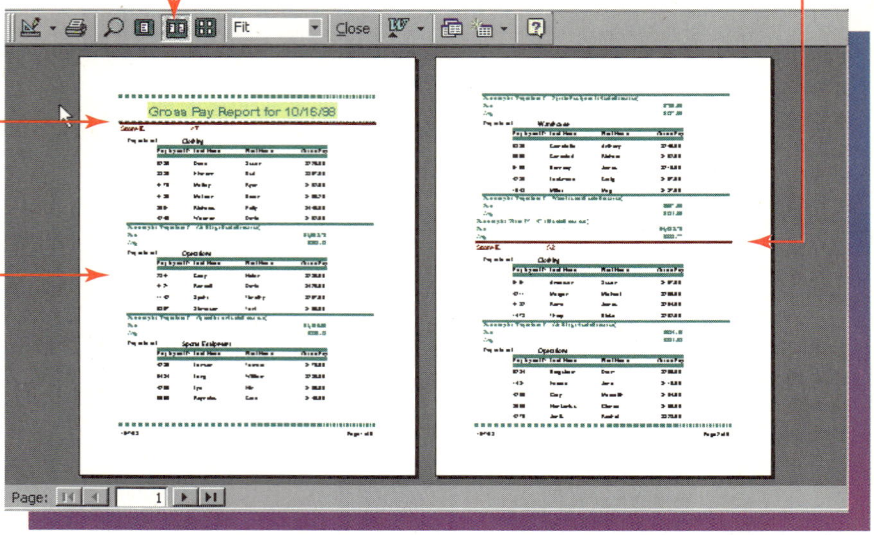

The title appears centered and with the background color you selected. The color change you made to the Store ID controls and the addition of the colored horizontal line make it much easier to locate the beginning of a new section.

- Print the entire report.
- Close the report, saving any layout changes.
- Close the Gross Pay query.
- Open the Database window Reports tab.

The names of the two reports you have created are displayed in the Reports object list.

Creating Mailing Labels

Finally, you want to set up a report to print mailing labels for every employee in the Sports Company Employees table. A sample of a mailing label appears below:

Susan Anderson
4389 S. Hayden Rd.
Mesa, AZ 84101

The Report Wizard includes a Label Wizard that will create mailing labels. To use this feature, from the Reports tab,

- Choose New/Label Wizard.
- Select the Sports Company Employees table from the Table or Query drop-down list.
- Click OK.

The Label Wizard dialog box on your screen should be similar to Figure 4-21.

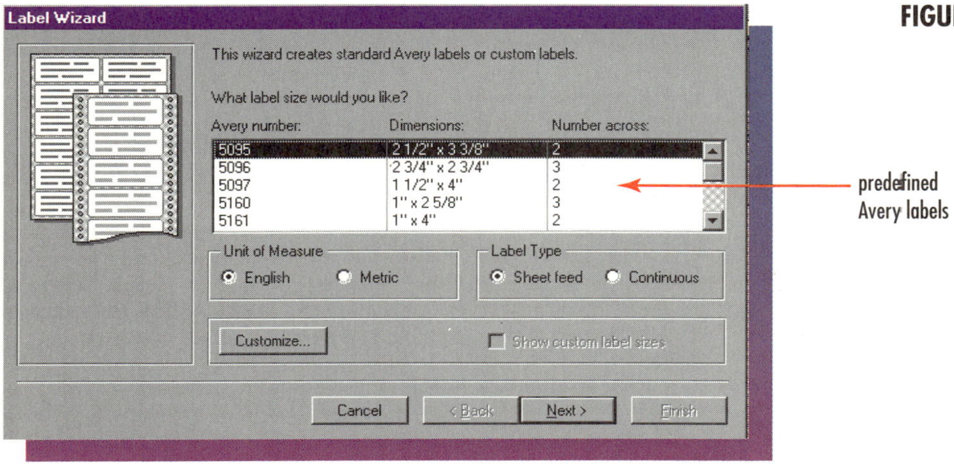

FIGURE 4-21

In the first Label Wizard dialog box, you specify the type of label you want to create. You can either use a predefined label or create a custom label. The Sports Company uses mailing labels made by Avery, number 5160. These labels appear three across the width of the paper.

- Select Avery number 5160.
- Click Next >.

In this dialog box you specify the font and text color settings for the labels. The default font is Arial and the default font size is 8.

The font settings in this dialog box retain the previous settings chosen using the Label Wizard, so other settings may be displayed.

- If necessary, change the font to Arial and the font size to 10 point.
- Click Next >.

Just as with other reports, you select the fields from the table to include in the labels. Unlike other reports, however, as you select the fields, you also design the label layout in the Prototype Label box. You may type any additional text, such as punctuation or a holiday message, directly onto the prototype.

- Add the First Name field to the Prototype Label box.

The dialog box on your screen should be similar to Figure 4-22.

FIGURE 4-22

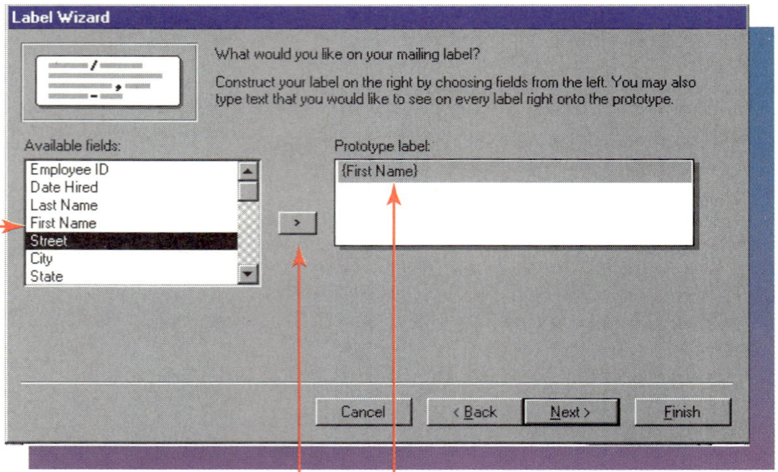

The First Name field is displayed in the Prototype Label box. The last name will be on the same line as the first name, separated from the first name by a space. To enter a space to separate the first and last names,

- Press Spacebar.
- Add the Last Name field to the label prototype.
- Press ←Enter.
- To complete the rest of the label, add the Street, City, State, and Zip Code fields to the prototype using the punctuation and spacing shown here.

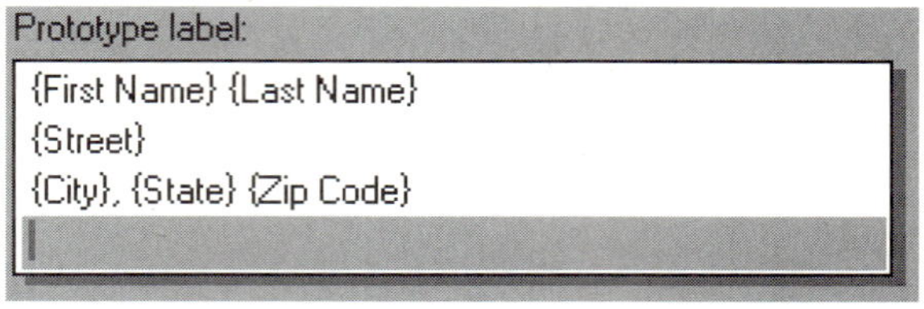

- Click Next >.

In the next dialog box you can specify a field on which to sort the labels. You want to take of advantage of postal discounts resulting from mailings that are sorted by zip code.

- Add the Zip Code field to the Sort By list box.
- Click: Next >.

- Finally enter **Employee Mailing Labels** as the label report name.
- Click Finish.
- Maximize the Print Preview window.
- Zoom the window to 75% to see all three columns of labels.

Your screen should be similar to Figure 4-23.

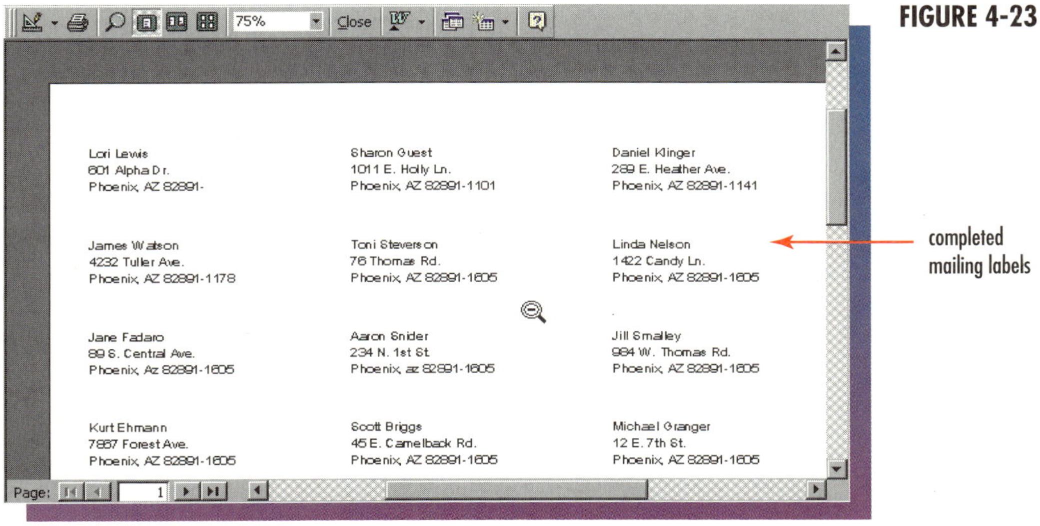

FIGURE 4-23

Three columns of mailing labels appear across the width of the page. The placement of the labels on the page corresponds to the 5160 Avery labels you selected using the Label Wizard. The labels are also sorted by zip code, from left to right across the rows, then down the page from top to bottom.

- Print the page of labels that displays your name.
- Close the mailing labels report.
- If you are ready, exit Access.

LAB REVIEW

Key Terms

Detail Section (DB156)
group (DB151)
Group Footer (DB156)
Group Header (DB156)
Page Footer (DB156)
Page Header (DB156)
report (DB141)
Report Footer (DB156)
Report Header (DB156)

Command Summary

Command	Toolbar	Action
View/Layout Preview		Displays report layout as it will appear when printed
View/Properties		Displays properties for selected control
View/Field List		Adds fields to a report
View/Zoom		Changes magnification of Preview window
View/Pages		Changes number of previewed pages
Insert/Report		Creates new report

Matching

1. Summary Options ...	______	**a.** creates a simple report using all fields in table
2. grouping	______	**b.** displays a sample of how report will appear when printed
3. Page Footer section	______	**c.** allows predefined calculations to be performed in grouped reports
4. Layout Preview	______	**d.** displays entire page in Preview window
5. Report Footer section	______	**e.** contains information that prints at top of first page of report
6. Detail section	______	**f.** part of report that contains table data
7. AutoReport Wizard	______	**g.** contains information that is printed at end of report
8. label prototype	______	**h.** contains information that prints at bottom of each report page
9. Report Header section	______	**i.** used to design the label layout
10. View/Zoom/Fit to Window	______	**j.** arranges data by major categories for clarity and ease of understanding

Fill-In Questions

1. Printed output generated from tables or queries is called a(n) ________________.

2. The ____________________ creates a report that displays all the fields and records from the underlying table or query.

3. The ________________ allows you to choose the fields to include in the report.

4. The ________________ window displays the report on the screen as it will appear when it is printed.

5. You can display the whole page in the window by adjusting the magnification to ________________.

6. Records ________________ by categories to allow better analysis of data.

7. Reports that are grouped can contain ____________________ fields.

8. The calculation that computes the average value for a group is ______________________.

9. The ____________________ section of Report Design view contains information to be printed at the top of each page.

10. __________________ and __________________ can be added to the design of a report to enhance the report's appearance.

Discussion Questions

1. Discuss the advantages of creating reports.

2. Discuss how grouping records in a report makes the report more meaningful.

3. Discuss how queries can be used to create reports. What are the advantages of creating a report from a query?

4. Discuss how group calculations can be used in a report. Give examples of the kinds of information that could benefit from summary data.

Hands-On Practice Exercises

Step by Step

Rating System
☆ Easy
☆☆ Moderate
☆☆☆ Difficult

☆

1. This problem is a continuation of Practice Exercise 4 in Lab 3. James O'Dell at Valley of the Sun Office Supplies is still worried about his inventory and his suppliers. He wants to print a report of all overstocked items so he can encourage his sales staff to push those items.

   a. To review James' query that locates the overstocked items, and to help him create a report based on the query, open the Valley of the Sun Office Supplies database you updated in Lab 3, then open the Queries tab and run the Overstocked Items query. Examine the data in the datasheet, then close the Query window.

   b. To create James' new report, open the Reports tab, then create a tabular AutoReport based on the Overstocked Items query.

   c. Print the report, then close the Report window and save the report as Overstocked Items.

☆☆

2. This problem is a continuation of Practice Exercise 3 in Lab 3. Michelle at Food for Thought Catering wants to know the sum of all the purchases made by each of her customers. She needs you to help her create a query to find the information and then a report to print it out.

   a. Open the Updated Catering Records database you updated in Lab 3. Create a new query and add the Billing and Customers tables to the design grid. Add the Company and the Amount fields to the grid, then save the query as Billing History. Run the query and review the data.

Michelle likes the data, but it does not explain exactly what she wanted to know. The query shows each invoice amount for every customer, but does not give a total of all invoices for every customer. You assure Michelle that you can best retrieve that information by creating a report that groups invoices by company then gives a sum for each company.

b. Close the query datasheet. Create a new report using the Report Wizard. Base the query on the Billing History query you just created, then add all fields in the query to the report.

c. Group the data by company and add a summary option to calculate the sum of the Amount field for each company. You think Michelle could also benefit from knowing what percentage of her business goes to each client, so check the Calculate Percent of Total for Sums box.

d. Select a layout, use portrait orientation, and choose an appropriate style. Name the report Income by Company, then preview the report.

e. As you look through the report, you notice that some company names do not display completely in the text box controls. Modify the report design by adjusting the text box controls and making changes to improve the report appearance, such as lines, text color, boxes, and font changes.

f. Preview, then print the report.

g. Close the Report window, saving any layout changes.

☆☆

3. This is a continuation of Practice Exercise 5 in Lab 3. Michael at Go West Dude Ranch wants to know how he is spending his money. It seems to disappear quickly every time he does payroll. He also needs to know the total gross payroll per week so he can better budget his money. You assure Michael that you can get all the information he needs by creating a query and a report.

a. Open the Dude Ranch Payroll database you updated in Lab 3, then open the Weekly Paychecks query in Design view. You determine that this query will work well for the report you need, but you need to remove the criteria from the Pay Date column. Remove the criteria, save the query using the same name, and close the Query window.

b. Create a new report using the Report Wizard and base it on the Weekly Paychecks query you just updated. Add the Pay Date, Employee #, First Name, Last Name, and Gross Pay fields to the Selected Fields list box.

c. Group the report by Pay Date (Access will then group the Pay Date by month), then sort it by Pay Date (to divide the weeks within the months).

d. You decide that in addition to knowing the sum of his payroll, Michael might be better able to see how his money is being spent if he knows the average pay of his employees. Add Summary Options to calculate a sum and an average of the pay.

e. Select an appropriate layout, use landscape orientation so all the data will fit, and select a style. Name the report Payroll Summary, then preview the report.

f. Make any changes to adjust the size of controls, and improve the appearance of the report by adding such features as lines, color, and font changes. Then preview the report again. Print the report.

On Your Own

☆☆

4. This problem is a continuation of Practice Exercise 1 in Lab 3. Debbie at Desert Rescue Cleaning Service wants to do some target marketing, sending flyers to all customers who have at least 10,000 square feet of space. She also wants to know what her average client in Arizona is like. She wants to determine this by examining the average rate and the average square feet of all her Arizona customers. Debbie calls you to help her out.

Open the Desert Rescue Cleaning Service database you updated in Lab 3, then create a new query, named Big Clients, that will select clients with at least 10,000 square feet of space.

After creating the query, you tell Debbie she can use it for many different reports. All she needs right now is mailing labels for those select few big clients. Create mailing labels for Debbie, then print the labels and save the report as Big Clients Labels.

To help Debbie with her other request, you need to create a new report based on the Clients table that will tell Debbie what the average rate and square footage are for all of her Arizona clients. (Hint: You should group the report by state, and format the Square Footage field to standard or fixed.) Make the report look attractive so Debbie can take the report to her next staff meeting. Name the report Average Arizona Clients, then print the report.

☆☆☆

5. This problem is a continuation of Practice Exercise 2 in Lab 3. Eddie at TechnoBabble needs his database updated again. Eddie needs a new table that lists his suppliers by code, name, and phone number, and he wants a form to use for data entry.

Using the TechnoBabble Electronics database you updated in Lab 3, create a table of suppliers to hold the information below and make the Supplier field the primary key field. Then create a form, Suppliers, to enter the information.

Supplier	Supplier Name	Phone Number
AMS	American Memory Service	(602) 555-7896
BOC	Balanced Output Company	(303) 555-3426
BTO	Better Tech Offerings	(970) 555-8620
CCR	Crystal Clear Radios	(619) 555-1762
CTC	Cellular Telephone Co.	(202) 555-4139
HSC	Home Security Corp.	(602) 555-8760
LLM	Laser Light Management	(602) 555-5700
MEE	Musical Electronic Engineering	(303) 555-1999

Now that the new information is in the database, Eddie wants to see a report showing the total value of both regular stock items and special order items that are currently on hand, grouped by supplier name and by status. Create a query, named Inventory Status, then a new report, named On Hand Inventory Status Report, to help Eddie find the data he needs. Print the report.

☆☆☆

6. This problem is a continuation of Practice Exercise 6 in Lab 3. Open the My Contacts database file you have been working on and last updated in Lab 3.

Create mailing labels for all the contacts in your table. Print the mailing labels.

Create a query and a report of your choice using the data in your database. Print the report.

Concept Summary

Creating Reports and Mailing Labels

4

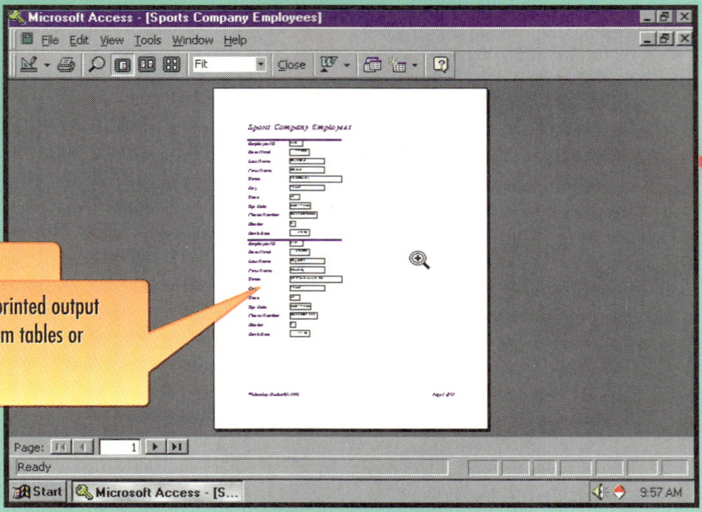

Reports

Reports are the printed output you generate from tables or queries.

Group Calculations

If you group data in your report, you can perform calculations on values, such as a group total, an average, a minimum value, and a maximum value.

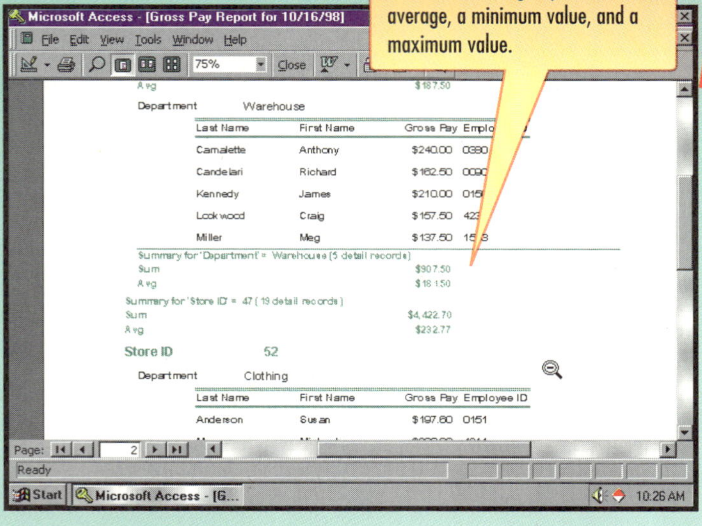

Concepts

- Reports
- Grouping Records
- Group Calculations
- Layout Preview

Grouping Records

Records in a report can be grouped into categories to allow you to better analyze the data.

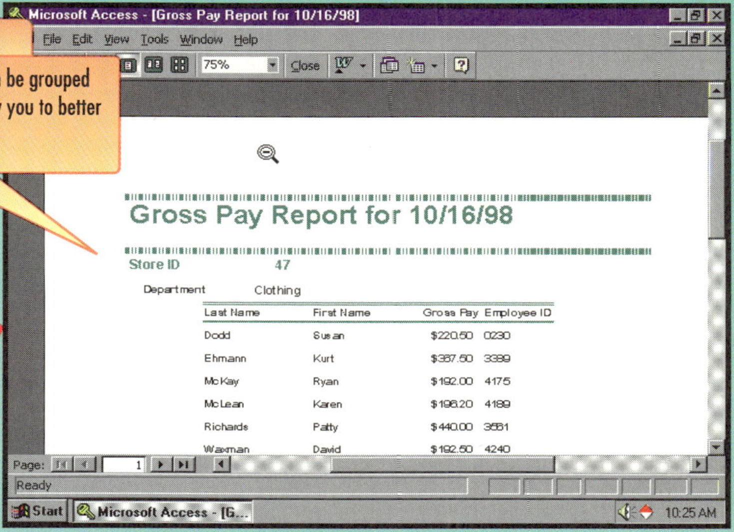

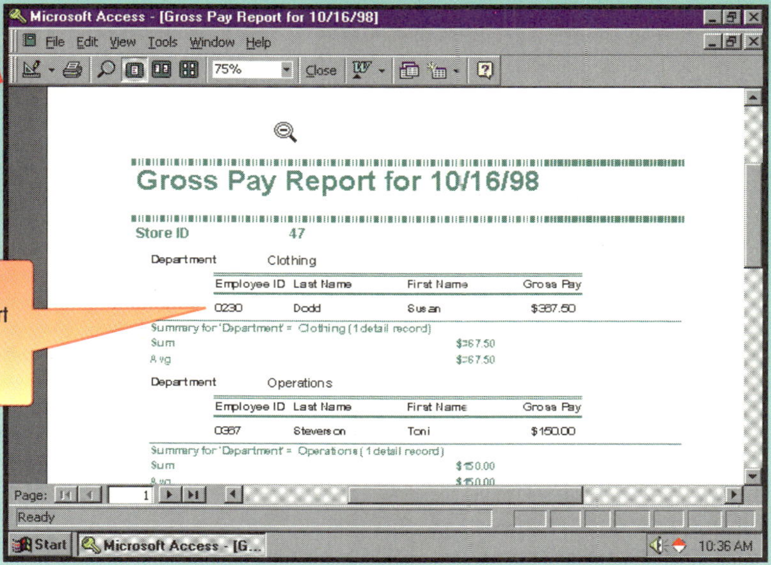

Layout Preview

Layout Preview displays a sample of the data in the report so you can quickly check the report's layout.

5 Sharing Information Between Applications

COMPETENCIES

After completing this lab, you will know how to:

1. **Copy between applications.**
2. **Link an Access object to another application.**
3. **Export Access data to Excel.**
4. **Create a mail merge using Word and Access.**

CASE STUDY

You have used Access to obtain information from the Employee database that was requested by the manager. Now you want to include the query results with a brief memo to the manager. To do this you will learn how files created using Access that have their own unique format can be translated into a format that can be used by other applications. Your memo containing the query results generated by Access will look like that shown here.

You have also been asked to create a letter to all employees, offering them a special employee credit card. You have created the letter and will perform a mail merge with data from the Sports Company Employees database to supply the inside address information for the letter. Your completed letter will be similar to that shown here.

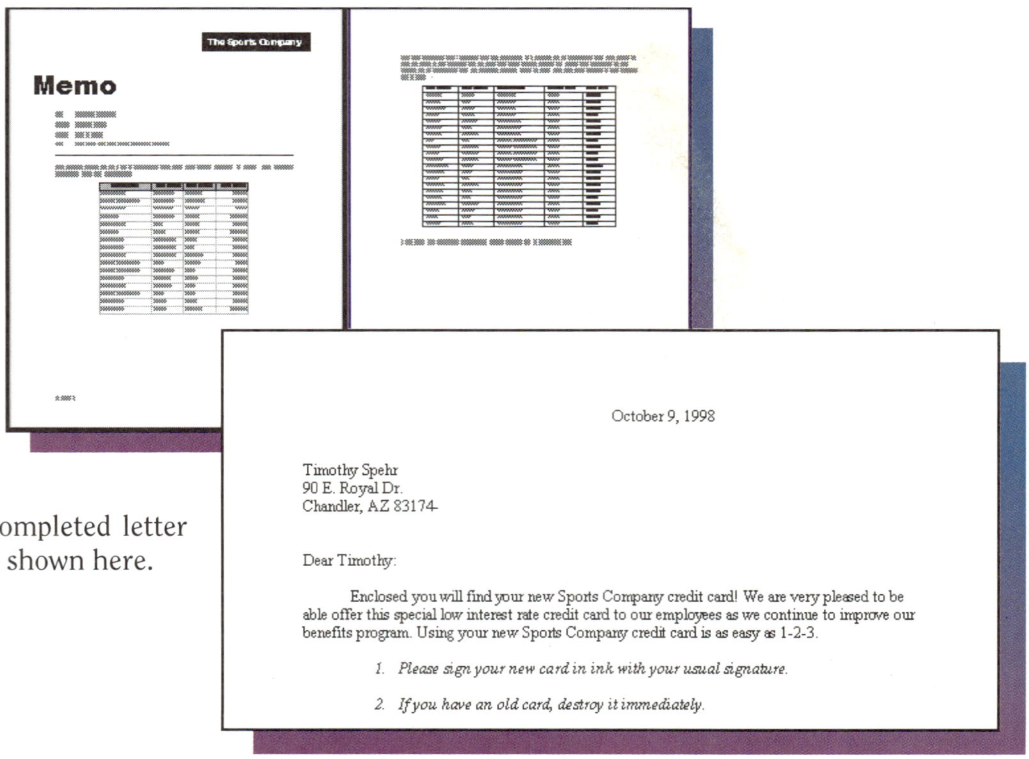

Concept Overview

The following concepts will be introduced in this lab:

1. Copy Between Applications	Information can be copied between applications and if possible is inserted in a format the document can edit.
2. Linked Object	Information that is copied from one file to another as a linked object maintains a connection between the files, allowing the linked object to automatically update when the source file changes.
3. Exporting and Importing	Exporting saves data created using Access in another format, and importing retrieves data that has been saved in another format into an Access table.

Note: This lab assumes that you have completed Lab 3 of Access. You need the database file Sports Company Personnel Records that you saved at the end of Lab 3.

Part 1

Copying Between Applications

The first project you will work on is to create a memo to the manager that contains the list of employees who were hired before 1/1/92.

- Start Access 97.
- Open the Sports Company Personnel Records database from your data disk.
- Open the Pre 1992 Hire Date query.

Note: If an Enter Parameter Value dialog box is displayed, click OK twice to reset the sort order of the Department and Last Name fields in the query datasheet.

- If necessary, maximize the window.

Your screen should be similar to Figure 5-1.

FIGURE 5-1

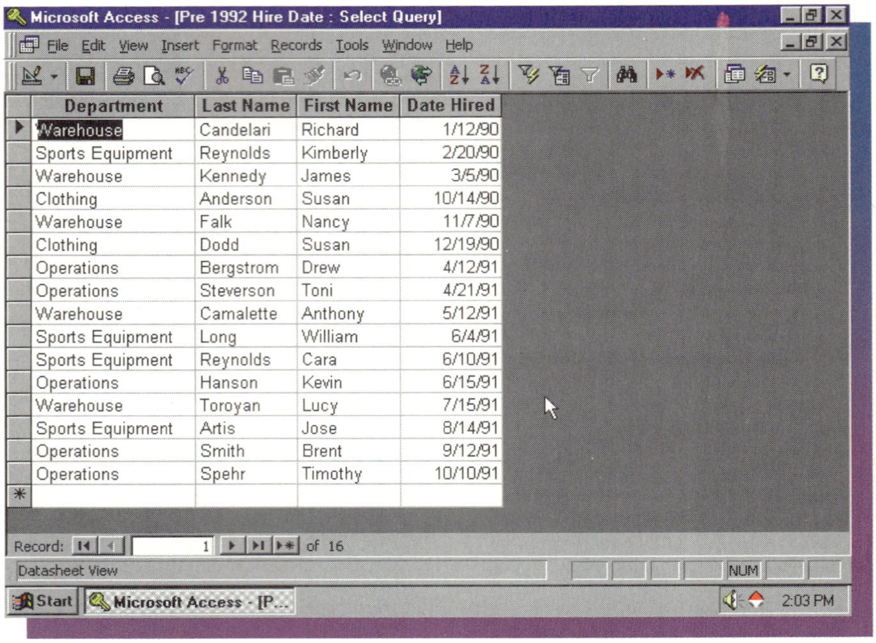

The 16 employees who were hired before January 1, 1992, are listed in the query datasheet. You want to copy the output from the query into a memo to the manager.

Access uses exporting and importing of data to assist in the data transfer between applications.

Concept 1: Copy Between Applications

As with all Office applications, you can cut, copy, and paste selections within and between tables and objects in an Access database. You can also perform these operations between Access databases and other applications. For example, you can copy a database object or selection into a word processing document. The information is inserted in a format the application can edit, if possible.

To do this, you can use Copy and Paste or drag and drop between applications to copy the database object. To use drag and drop, both applications must be open and visible in the window. The memo to the manager has already been created using Word.

- Load Word and open the document Query Results from your data disk.

Your screen should be similar to Figure 5-2.

FIGURE 5-2

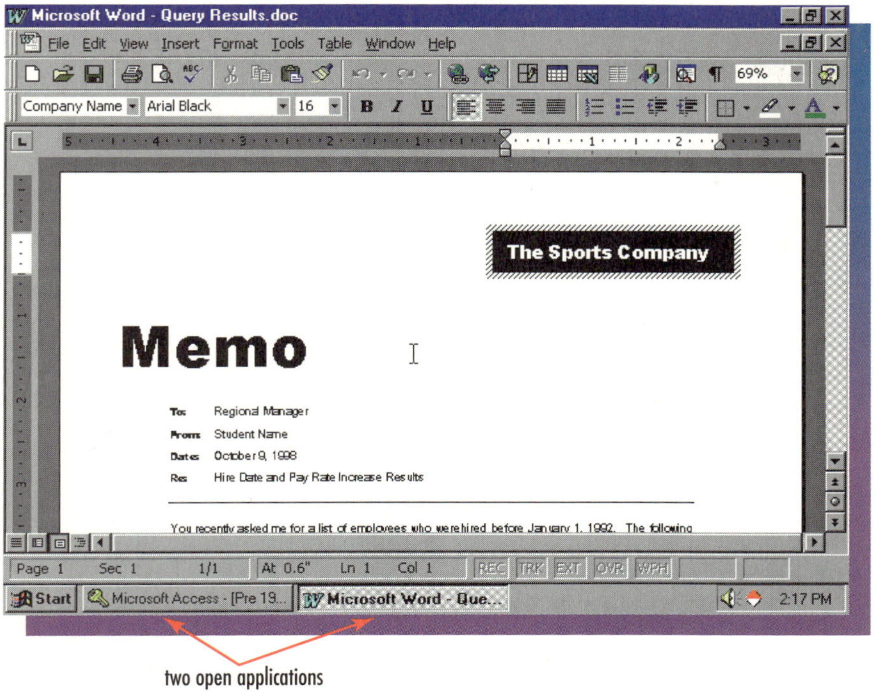

This document contains the text of the memo to the manager.

- Replace "Student Name" in the memo header with your name.
- Scroll the memo to read the memo text.

The memo consists of three paragraphs. It also includes blank space between paragraphs where you will enter the information from Access related to the topic discussed in the paragraph.

- To display both applications at the same time on the desktop, tile the two open applications vertically in the window.
- Switch to the Access application window and use Edit/Select All Records to select the query datasheet table.
- Drag the selected table to the space below the first paragraph of the memo in the document.

Right-click the taskbar and choose Tile Vertically.

The mouse pointer must be a ↖ when you drag the selection to copy it.

You could also drag the query object in the Queries tab of the Database window to copy it into the document.

Your screen should be similar to Figure 5-3.

FIGURE 5-3

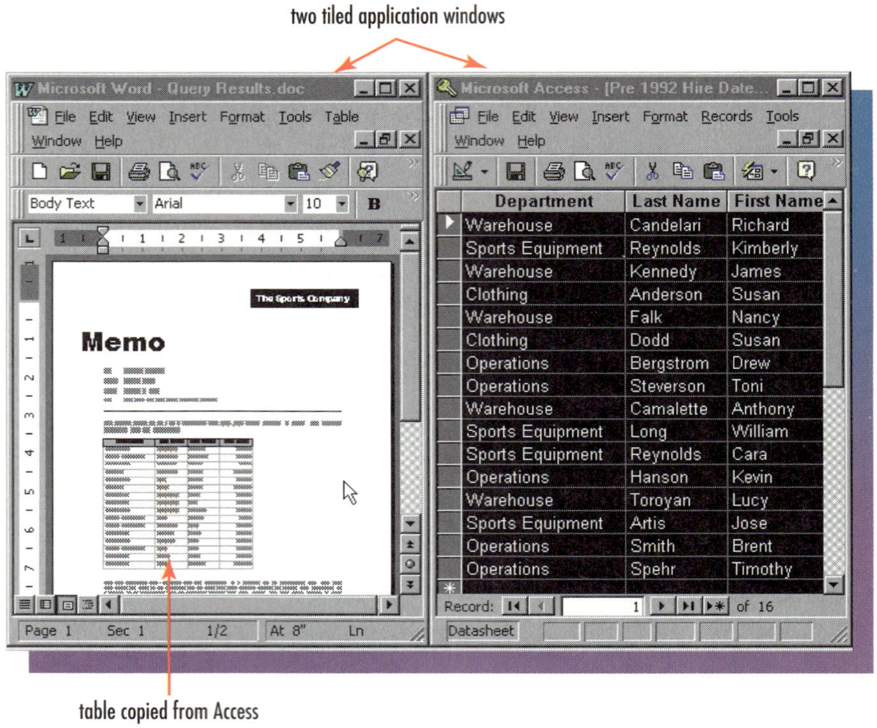

The query results are copied into the memo document. It is inserted as a formatted table, having retained the format settings that it had in Access. The table can now be manipulated like any other Word table.

- Undo the vertical window tile.
- Switch to Word and scroll the memo to view the table.
- Select the entire table and center it on the page.
- Create a page break below the table.

> To select the table, drag or use Table/Select Table, then click [center] to center it.

> Right-click the taskbar and select Undo Tile.

> Press Ctrl + ←Enter to create a manual page break.

Linking an Access Object to Another Application

Next you need to insert the query results that calculate the new pay rate for all employees who earn less than $5.50 an hour below the second paragraph of the memo. As you consider the memo, you are concerned that the manager may ask you to modify the query to provide a different analysis of the pay rate increase. If this request is made, you want the memo to be automatically updated when you modify the query. To do this you will link the query object to the memo.

Concept 2: Linked Object

Information created in one application can also be copied into another application as a **linked object**. When an object is linked, the data is stored in the **source file** (the document it was created in). A graphic representation of the data is displayed in the **destination file** (the document in which the object is inserted). A connection between the information in the source file is established by the creation of a link. The link contains references to the location of the source document and to the object within the source document that is linked to the destination document.

When changes are made in the source file that affect the linked object, the changes are automatically reflected in the destination file when it is opened. This is called a **live link**.

When you create linked objects, the date and time on your machine should be accurate. This is because the program refers to the date of the source file to determine whether updates are needed when you open the destination file.

To create a link to the query, you use the Insert Database button on the Database toolbar.

- Display the Database toolbar.

The Database toolbar buttons are identified below.

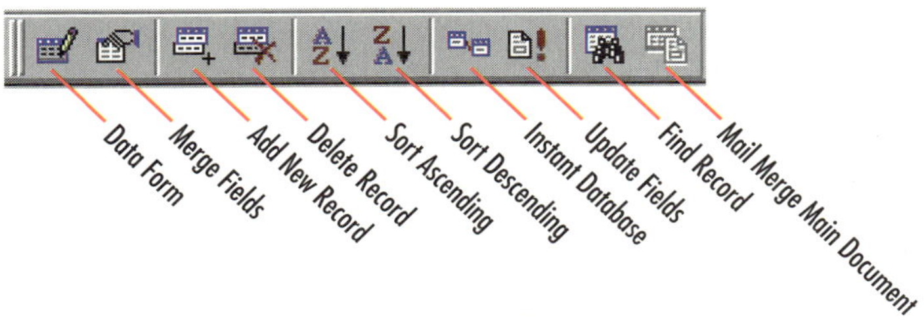

- Move to below the second paragraph of the memo (located on the second page).
- Click Insert Database.

The Database dialog box on your screen should be similar to Figure 5-4.

FIGURE 5-4

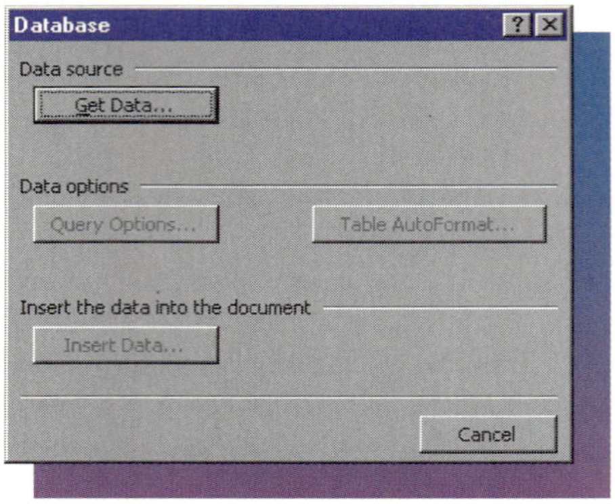

First you need to specify the database file to be inserted into the memo.

- Click [Get Data...].
- If necessary, select the drive containing your data disk from the Look In drop-down list.
- To display Microsoft Access file types, select MS Access Databases from the Files of Type drop-down list.
- Open the file Sports Company Personnel Records.

In the Microsoft Access dialog box, you select the table or query you want to insert in the Word document.

- Open the Queries tab and select Pay Rate Increase.

Notice that the Link to Query option is preselected. This option establishes the link between the query object and the Word document.

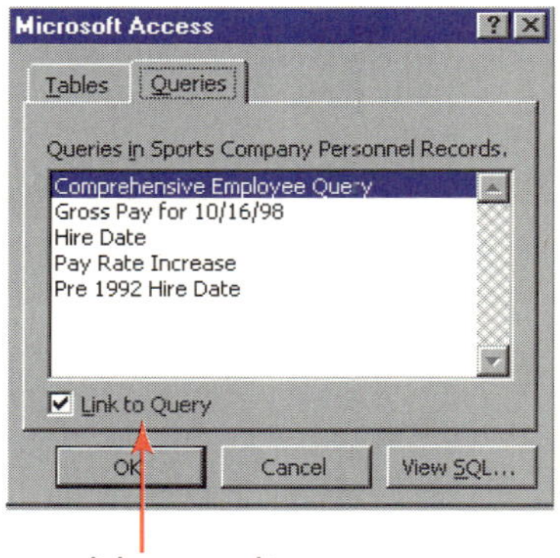

creates link to query object

- Click [OK].

The Database dialog box is displayed again. The Query Options button allows you to modify the query settings. Since you want it to appear as it is, you do not need to use this option. The AutoFormat button lets you select a format to apply to the table. If you do not select a format style, the datasheet is copied into the document as an unformatted table.

> You could also apply a format to the table after it is inserted into the document.

- Click [Table AutoFormat...].

The Table Autoformat dialog box on your screen should be similar to Figure 5-5.

FIGURE 5-5

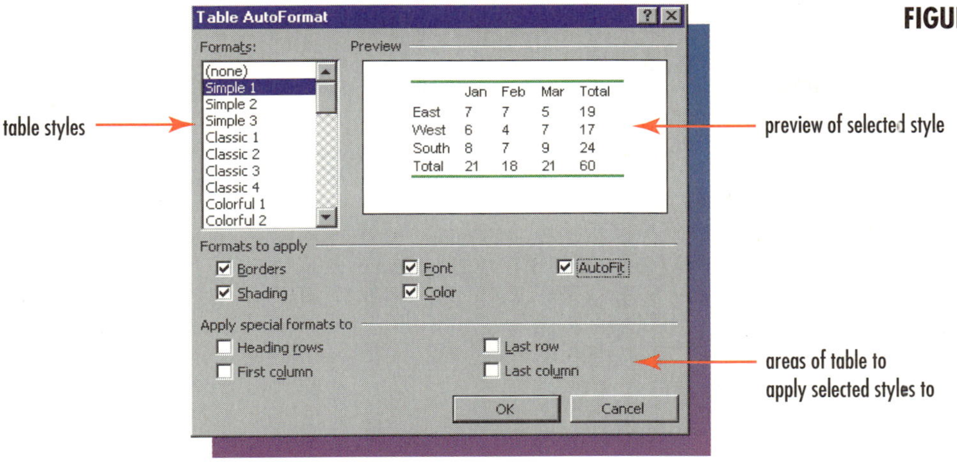

From this dialog box you select the style you want to use and the parts of the table you want to apply it to.

- Select Heading rows and Last column as the two areas to apply special formats.
- Select a style of your choice.
- Click OK.

This text uses the Simple 2 AutoFormat style.

The Database dialog box is displayed again. Finally, to insert the data into the document,

- Click Insert Data... .

From the Insert Data dialog box, you specify what records to include in the inserted table and whether to insert the data as a field. Inserting it as a field allows the data to be updated whenever the source changes.

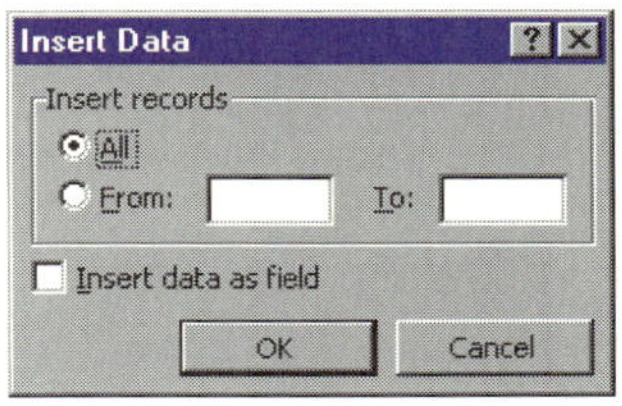

- If necessary, select **All**.
- Select **Insert Data as Field**.
- Click OK.
- Select the table and center it on the page.
- Clear the selection and if necessary scroll the document window to see the entire table.
- If necessary, insert a blank line between the paragraph and the table.

Your screen should be similar to Figure 5-6.

FIGURE 5-6

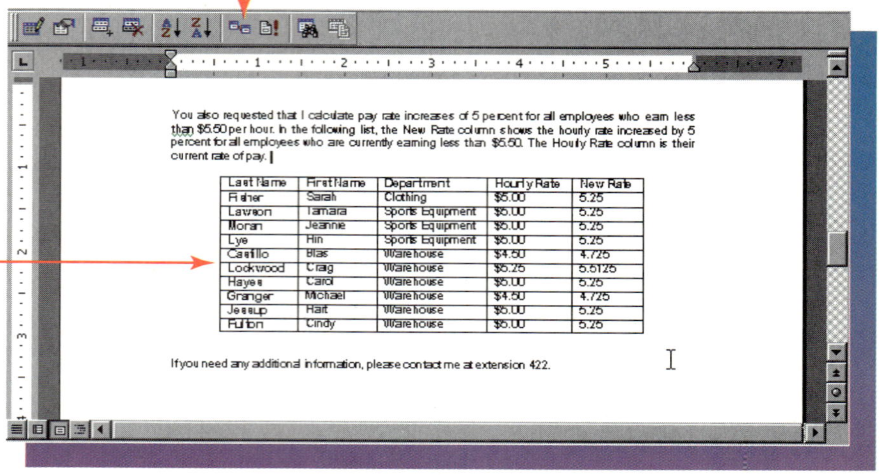

> The currency format set in query design for the calculated field is not copied to the Word document.

The link to the database file and to the query object is established, and the database table is inserted into the document in the selected format style. The table lists the 10 employees who earn less than $5.50 and their new rates of pay.

You dropped off a copy of the memo to the manager, and after a short time, you receive a call asking you to include employees who are earning $5.50 and to increase the pay rate percentage from 5 percent to 7.5 percent. To make these changes, you need to modify the query design.

- Switch to Access.
- Open the Pay Rate Increase query in Design view.
- Change the Hourly Rate criterion to <=5.50.
- Change the New Rate formula to calculate the increase at 7.5 percent.
- Run the query.

The query datasheet now lists 21 employees who earn $5.50 or less, and also lists their new pay rate based on a 7.5 percent increase.

> If you were opening the Word document, the changes would be automatically updated.

- Save the query using the same name.
- Switch to Word.

The Word table has not changed to reflect the changes made in the source file. To update data in the fields,

- Click anywhere in the table to select it.
- Click [Update Fields icon] Update Fields (in the Database toolbar).
- Select the entire table and center it on the page.
- Clear the selection.

You can also press F9 or choose Update Field on the Shortcut menu. The object must be selected when you update it.

Your screen should be similar to Figure 5-7.

Update Fields button

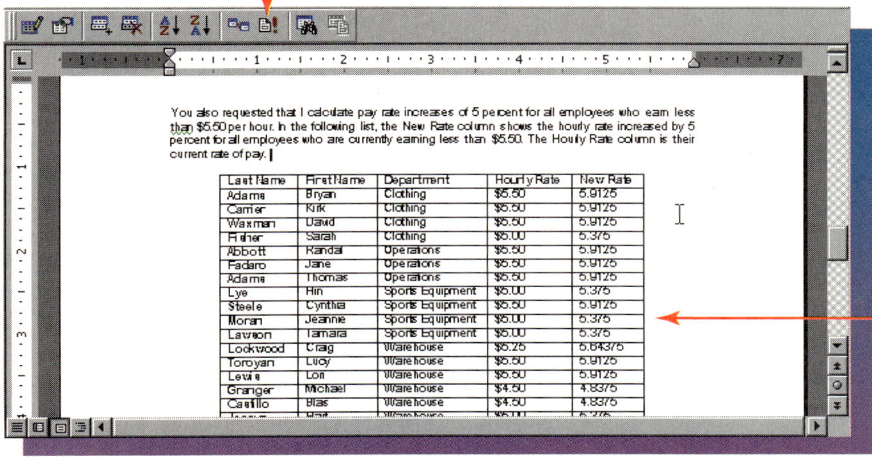

FIGURE 5-7

updated Access query in Word document

The table is redrawn to include the new records and now reflects the data in the revised query.

- Update the memo text in the paragraph above the table to reflect the change in data shown in the table.
- Save the memo using the file name Revised Query Results.
- Print the document.
- Close the Database toolbar.
- Exit Word.
- Close the Pay Rate Increase query.

The Database window should be displayed.

Your screen should be similar to Figure 5-9.

FIGURE 5-9

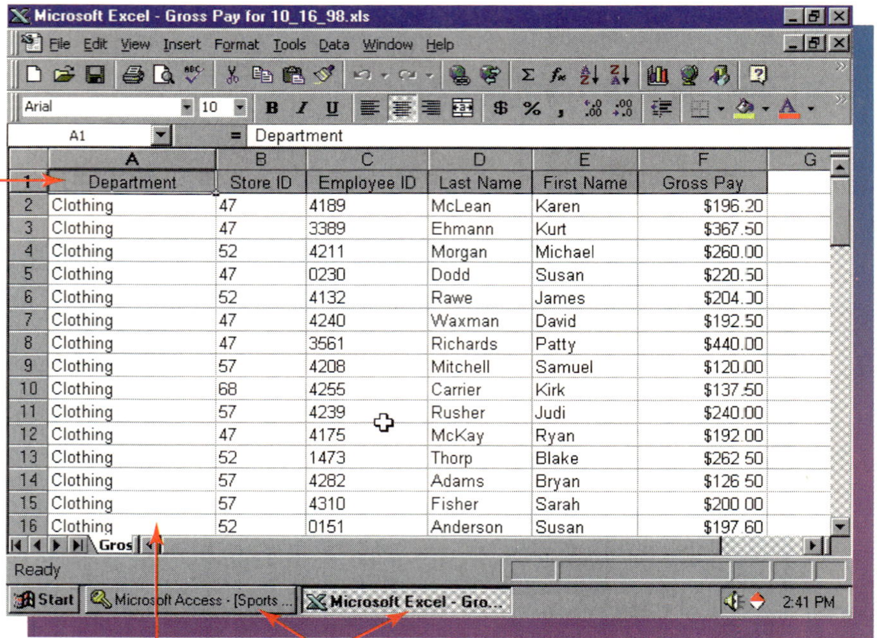

The new workbook file is open with the information from the query displayed in it. The field names are placed in the first row of the spreadsheet, and the data begins in row 2. The column heads and column widths are formatted as they appeared in the query datasheet. Now the data can be manipulated using Excel commands and features. For example, it would be easy to calculate total and average values by departments.

Click [Σ] to sum the Gross Pay column.

- Display a grand total of the Gross Pay column in cell F75.

The changes you have made to the worksheet do not affect the Access table from which the data was obtained.

- Print the worksheet.
- Save the worksheet using the same file name.
- Exit Excel.

Part 2

Creating a Mail Merge Using Word and Access

Note: It is helpful if you have completed the Merge section of Lab 4 of Word 97. If you have not, read the information in that section to become familiar with the procedure before completing the following section.

The Sports Company has also decided to send all its employees a Sports Company credit card. The body of the letter to accompany the credit cards has already been created and saved as Employee Credit Card Letter on your data disk. You want the letter to display each employee's name and address information as an inside address and to include the first name in the salutation.

This data is maintained in the Sports Company Employees table. To include this information for each employee in the letter, you will perform a mail merge between Word and Access.

First you will need to create a query to include all fields needed in the inside address.

- Using the Sports Company Employees table, create a query named Employee Address that will display each employee's first name, last name, street, city, state, and zip code (in that order).

To help in sorting the mail, you want the merged letters to appear in sorted order by zip code. Because you also want to test the merge with a small amount of records, you will also limit the scope of the query to employees in the city of Chandler.

- Set the sort order of the Zip Code field to ascending.
- Enter Chandler in the City criteria field.
- Then, to include your record in the query output, in the OR row of the grid enter your first and last name in the appropriate criteria fields.

Your screen should be similar to Figure 5-10.

FIGURE 5-10

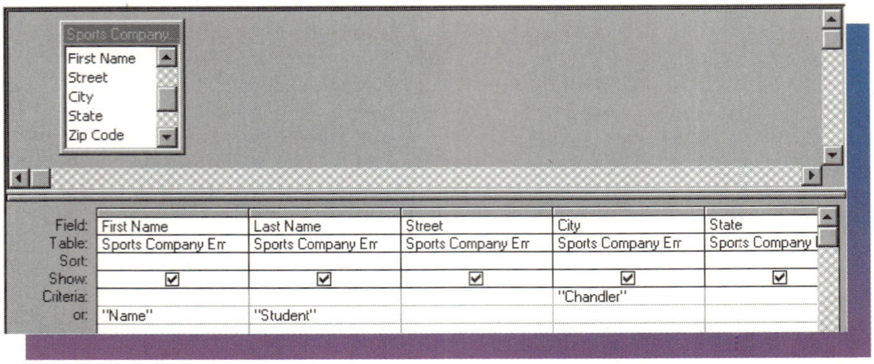

- Run the Query.
- If the query output does not display three records with a city of Chandler and your record, fix the query grid criteria to achieve the correct results.
- Save the query as Employee Address.
- Close the Query window.

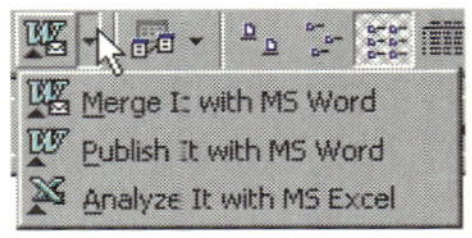

The Mail Merge feature is used to insert field data from an Access table into a Word document. Performing a mail merge between Access and Word is part of the automated Office Links feature. The Office Links drop-down list button includes three choices:

Merge It is the default Office Links button.

Option	Effect
Merge It with MS Word	Starts the Mail Merge Wizard, which merges Access data with a Word document.
Publish It with MS Word	Outputs to an .rtf file format, loads Word, and opens the file in a new document window.
Analyze It with MS Excel	Outputs the object to an Excel file format, loads Excel, and opens the file in a new workbook.

To merge the address data in the query with a Word document,

The menu equivalent is Tools/Office Links/Merge It.

You can also begin a mail merge from within Word.

- Select the Employee Address query object, if necessary.
- Click Merge It with MS Word/ OK .

The Microsoft Word Mail Merge Wizard dialog box is displayed. Your first step is to indicate whether you will use an existing document (the default) or whether you will need a new doccument. To accept the default,

- Click OK.

The Select Microsoft Word Document dialog box appears next.

- If necessary, select the drive containing your data disk as the location.
- Select Employee Credit Card Letter.
- Click Open.
- If necessary, maximize the application window.

Your screen should be similar to Figure 5-11.

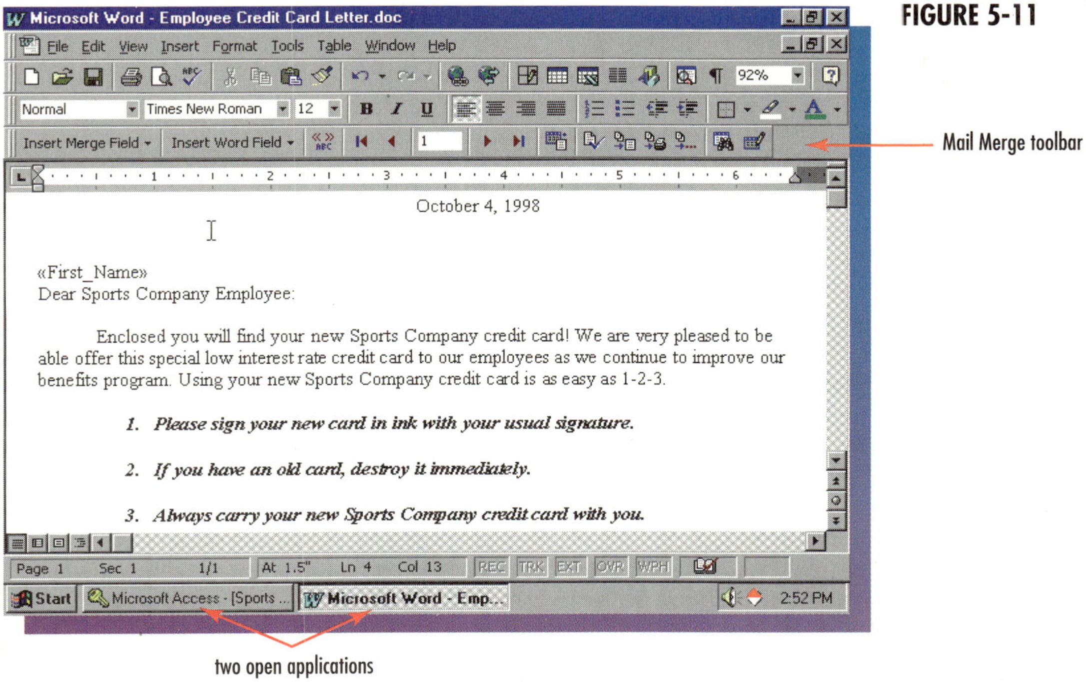

FIGURE 5-11

Word is loaded, and the Employee Credit Card Letter document is opened. In addition, the Mail Merge toolbar is displayed. These buttons are identified below.

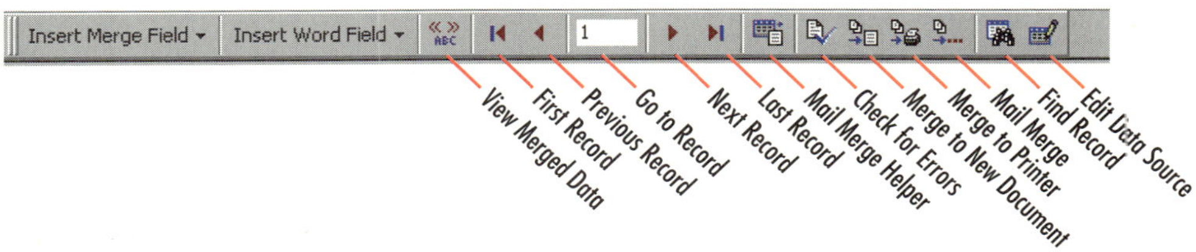

- If necessary, dock the Mail Merge toolbar below the Formatting toolbar.

Next you need to enter the merge fields in the letter to create the inside address. This is similar to creating a mailing label prototype. The first merge field you will specify will display the employee's first name in the inside address.

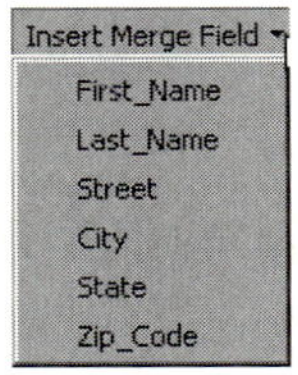

- Move to the line above the salutation (Ln 4).
- Click Insert Merge Field.
- Select First_Name.

Your screen should be similar to Figure 5-12.

FIGURE 5-12

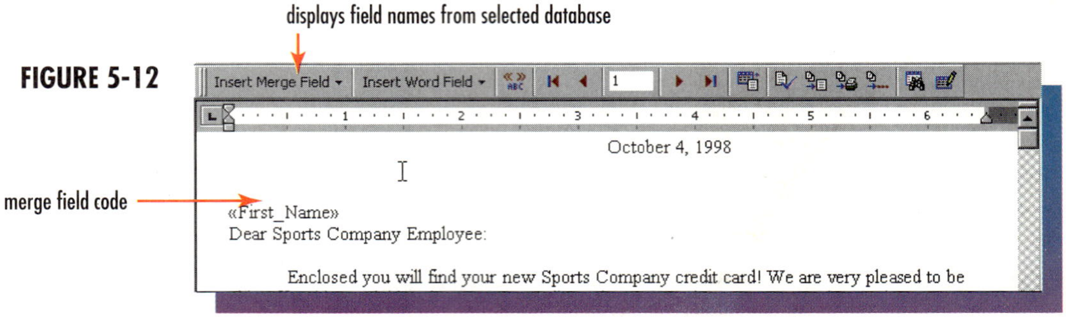

- Continue to select the field names to add the merge fields to the letter using the punctuation and spacing shown in Figure 5-13.
- Insert two blank lines above the salutation.

The last change you need to make to the document is to insert each employee's first name in place of "Sports Company Employee" in the salutation.

- Replace the text "Sports Company Employee" with the First Name merge field.

Your screen should be similar to Figure 5-13.

FIGURE 5-13

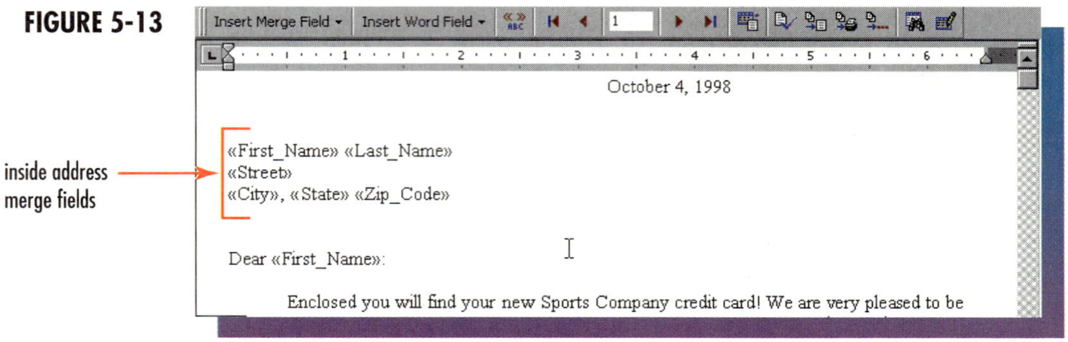

You are now ready to merge the addresses from Access into the Word document.

- Click [button] Merge to New Document.

The menu equivalent is Tools/Mail Merge/Merge/Merge.

Your screen should be similar to Figure 5-14.

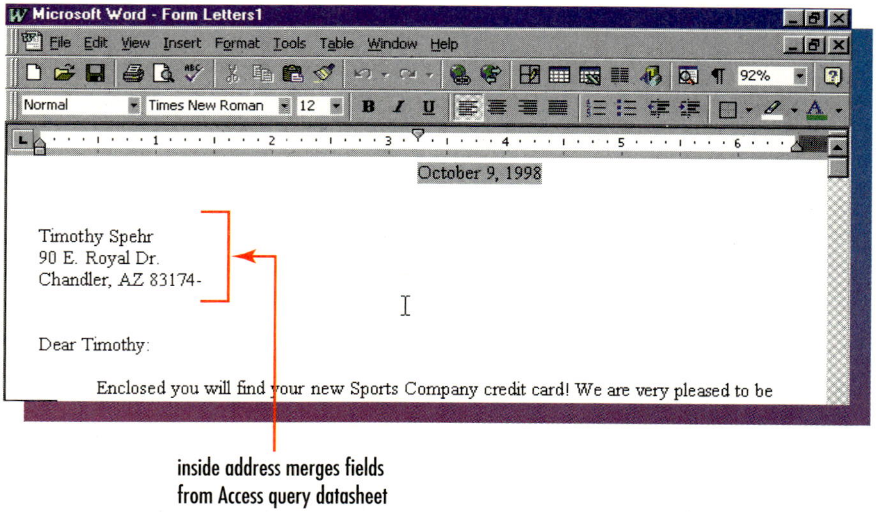

FIGURE 5-14

After a few seconds, Word displays the first personalized letter. The field information from the first record in the query replaces the appropriate merge field codes. The merge fields create a link to the Access database and query. Whenever needed, you can reopen the Word document to print a batch of letters using the current data in the Access table.

- Scroll the file to view the other letters.
- Print the letter displaying your information only.
- Close the merge document without saving it.
- Save the merge form letter document as Employee Credit Card Letter Merge.
- Exit Word and Access.

LAB REVIEW

Key Terms

destination file (DB177)
export (DB182)
import (DB182)
linked object (DB177)
live link (DB177)
source file (DB177)

Command Summary

Command	Button	Action
Tools/OfficeLinks/Merge It		Starts the Word Mail Merge

Fill-In Questions

1. Data that is ____________________ has been saved in another format into an Access table.

2. ________________ saves data created using Access in another format.

3. Text that is ________________________ contains values separated by commas.

4. When an object is ________________________, the data is stored in the source document.

5. When a document has a(n) ________________, changes are automatically reflected in the destination document.

Discussion Questions

1. Discuss the difference between importing and exporting data. Give examples of how each could be used.

2. Discuss the types of formats in which Access can save data. What feature is used to save data in a different format?

3. Discuss the differences between fixed-width and delimited text. Give examples of how data would be displayed with each type.

4. Discuss how an object can be linked from Access to another application. Discuss how a live link works.

Hands-On Practice Exercises

Step by Step

Rating System
☆ Easy
☆☆ Moderate
☆☆☆ Difficult

☆

1. This problem is a continuation of Practice Exercise 4 in Lab 3. James O'Dell, the manager of the Valley of the Sun Office Supplies company, has asked you for an inventory report on all supplies whose cost is over $3.00 and quantity is more than 50.

a. Open the Valley of the Sun Office Supplies database and create a query that displays the item number, item name, and price of all products that have a quantity on hand greater than 50 and are priced over $3.00.

b. Save the query as Stock with Quantities over 50.

c. Open Word and enter the following text.

TO: **James Green**
FROM: **[your name]**
DATE: **[current date]**

Below is the information you requested on inventory.

d. Copy the query results into the Word document.

e. Save the memo as Stock On Hand. Print the document.

☆☆

2. To complete this problem, you will use the Sports Company Personnel Records database. The Sports Company wants to invite all employees who have worked for the company since before 1992 to a special recognition luncheon. You have been asked to write invitations to these employees.

a. Open the Sports Company Personnel Records database file and select the Pre 1992 Hire Date query object.

b. Load Word and create the following memo.

To: **Sports Company Employee**
From: **[your name]**
Date: **[current date]**

You are cordially invited to a luncheon in honor of all employees who have worked for The Sports Company since before 1992. The luncheon will be held at the Corporate Center on May 25. Please RSVP to your department manager by May 20.

c. Save the memo as Employee Luncheon.

d. Merge the first and last names of the employees from the query in place of the "Sports Company Employee" text in the memo.

e. Print one of the merged letters. Do not save the merged document. Resave the memo.

☆☆

3. This problem is a continuation of Practice Exercise 5 in Lab 3. The Dude Ranch Payroll Service Company has recently introduced several new services. You have been asked to write a letter to all Phoenix customers announcing the new services.

a. Open the database and create a query that contains the name and address information of all customers whose city is Phoenix.

b. Open Word and create the following letter:

[current date]

Dear Customer:

The Dude Ranch Payroll Company is offering several new services described in the enclosed brochure. In appreciation for your business and as an incentive to try one of our new services, enclosed you will find a voucher for a 5 percent discount on the cost of our new services.

We hope to hear from you soon.

Sincerely,

[your name]

c. Save the letter as Dude Ranch New Services.

d. Enter merge fields in appropriate locations in the Word document. Merge the addresses from the Access query into the Word document. Print one letter from the merged document.

e. Do not save the merged document.

On Your Own

★★★

4. Debbie of Desert Rescue Cleaning Service would like you to create a letter to be sent to all her customers. Use the Desert Rescue Cleaning Service database for the names and addresses to be included in the letter. The letter should thank the customers for their loyalty and offer them a 10% discount for recommending another customer to Desert Rescue Cleaning Service. Merge the addresses from the database into the letter you create. Save and print the letters.

★★★

5. Using the Sports Company Personnel Records database, export the Pay Rate Increase query to Excel. In Excel, calculate the average Hourly Rate and New Rate by department and for all employees. Add a worksheet title. Include your name and the current date in a subtitle. Print the worksheet.

Concept Summary

Sharing Information Between Applications

Copy Between Applications

Information can be copied between applications and if possible is inserted in a format the document can edit.

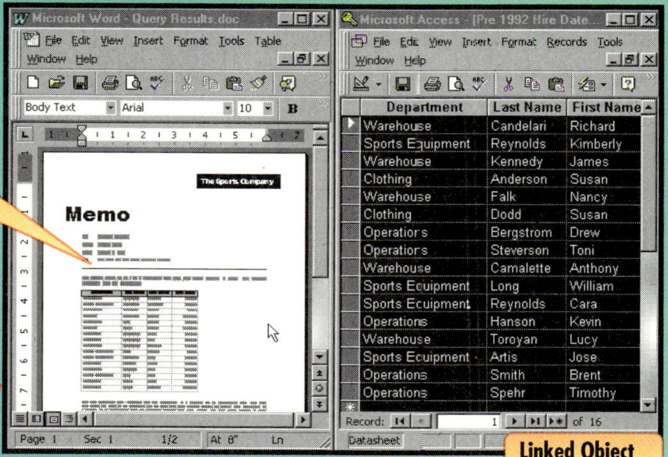

Concepts

- Copy Between Applications
- Linked Object
- Exporting and Importing

Linked Object

Information that is copied from one file to another as a linked object maintains a connection between the files, allowing the linked object to automatically update when the source file changes.

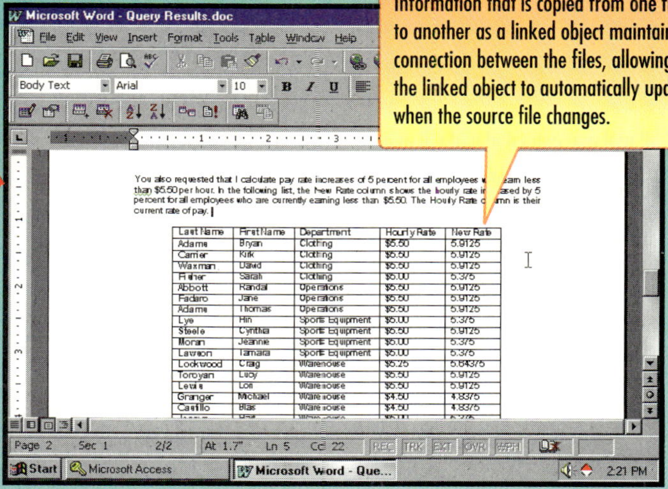

Exporting and Importing

Exporting saves data created using Access in another format, and importing retrieves data that has been saved in another format into an Access table.

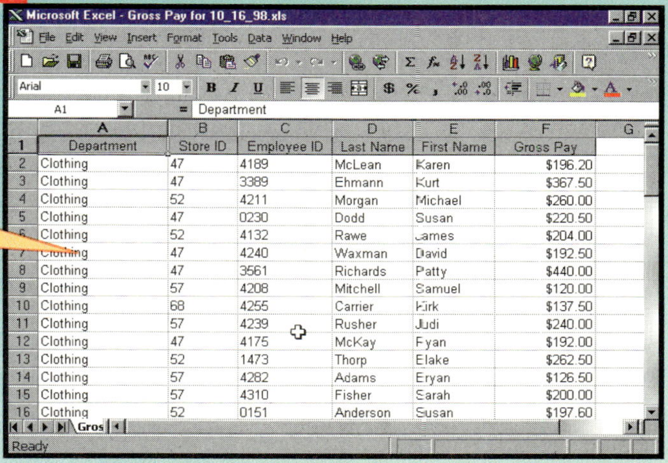

Case Project

Introduction

This project is designed to reinforce your knowledge of the database features used in the Access labs. You will also be expected to use the Office Assistant to learn more about advanced features available in Access.

Case

Marianne Virgili is the Director of the Glenwood Springs Chamber Resort Association. She has asked you to create a database file of the Chamber members.

Part I

In this section you will create the tables that will make up your database.

a. On paper, design a table to hold information about the Chamber members. The table should include a membership number, the business name, address (including street, city, state, and zip code), a telephone number, and contact name.

b. On paper, design a table to hold the types of businesses that belong to the Chamber Resort Association. This table should include the membership number, type of business, and the number of employees the business employs. (Hint: Companies employ a single number of employees, for example, "1" or "50", not "1 to 50.")

c. On paper, design a table to hold the dues payments for the Chamber members. This table should include the membership number, the date the payment is due, and the amount of the payment. The amount of payment is based on the number of employees the company employs. The companies are divided into three categories: small (1 to 20 employees), medium (21 to 60 employees), and large (61 or more employees). Small companies' dues are $200, medium are $300, and large are $500.

d. In Access create a database to hold the three tables.

e. From your paper designs, create the three tables. Add descriptions to fields that do not have field names that fully describe how the data should be entered. Change the field widths and properties as necessary. Create primary key fields. Save the tables using appropriate names.

f. Create a customized form for each of the tables.

g. Use the customized forms to enter 25 members into the tables. (Add yourself as one of the company names.) Be sure to enter the same membership number for each individual member so the records can be joined in queries and reports. Also remember that the number of employees determines the payment amount due.

Part II

You will use the tables you created in Part I to create queries on the data.

a. Create a query that shows the membership number, member name, and the city. Sort the query by city.

b. Print the query datasheet.

c. Create a query that shows the types of businesses that belong to the Chamber Resort Association, along with the name, membership number, and number of employees they employ.

d. Sort the query by type of business and membership number.

e. Save the query as Member Type.

f. Print the query datasheet.

g. Create a query to display the members that employ more than 50 employees. Display any fields you feel would be appropriate in a report that contains this data.

h. Print the query datasheet.

Part III

In this section you will create reports from the data in your tables.

a. Create a customized report that shows the due date for all members whose dues are due from the current date to two months from now. Include any fields you feel would be appropriate for this report. Use groups if necessary and add an appropriate title.

b. Print the report.

c. Open the saved query Member Type. Create a customized report from the query. Group the report by type of business.

d. Print the report.

e. Create a customized report that groups the companies by categories (small, medium, and large). Total the dues payments for each group and display the percentage for each group. Include the members' names and any other fields that you feel are appropriate.

f. Print the report.

Glossary of Key Terms

Best Fit: A feature that automatically adjusts column width to fit the longest entry.

Bound control: A control that is tied to a field in an underlying table.

Calculated control: A control on a form or report that displays the result of a calculation.

Calculated field: A field that displays the result of a calculation in a query.

Character string: A group of characters.

Cell: The space created by the intersection of a vertical column and a horizontal row.

Column selector bar: In Query Design view, the thin gray bar just above the field name in the grid.

Column width: The number of characters that are displayed in a field column in Datasheet view.

Comparison operator: A symbol used in expressions that allows you to make comparisons. The > (greater than) and < (less than) symbols are examples of comparison operators.

Compound control: Two related controls, such as a text box control and its associated label control.

Control: In Form and Report Design views, a graphical object that can be selected and modified.

Criteria: Specific set of limiting conditions that you want records to meet in order to be displayed in a query, form, or report.

Criteria expression: An expression that will select only the records that meet certain limiting criteria.

Current record: The record, containing the insertion point, that will be affected by the next action.

Data type: Attribute for a field that determines what type of data it can contain.

Database: An organized collection of related information.

Design grid: The lower part of the Query Design window, which displays settings that are used to define the query.

Destination file: The document in which a linked object is inserted.

Detail section: Section of Form and Report Design that contains the records of the table.

Docked: A toolbar or menu bar that appears in a separate window that is fixed to an edge of the Access window.

Edit mode: In Datasheet view, when an insertion point is displayed.

Export: To save data created using Access in another format.

Expression: Description of acceptable values in a validity check, which can contain any combination of the following elements: operators, identifiers, and values.

Field: A single category of data in a table, the values of which appear in a column of a datasheet.

Field list: A small window that lists all fields in an underlying table.

Field name: Label used to identify the data stored in a field.

Field property: An attribute of a field that affects its appearance or behavior.

Field selector: A small gray box or bar in datasheets and queries that can be clicked to select the entire column. The field selector usually contains the field names.

Field size: Field property that limits a text data type to a certain size or limits numeric data to values within a specific range.

Filter: A restriction placed on records in an open form or datasheet to temporarily isolate a subset of records.

Filter by Form: This feature provides a blank version of the current form or datasheet. Values are typed into the blank form or selected from a pull-down list. Records are filtered based on the values entered into the blank form.

Filter by Selection: A type of filter that displays only records containing a specific value.

Floating: A toolbar or menu bar that appears in a separate window that can be moved by dragging.

Font: The typeface, size, and style of printed characters.

Form: A database object used primarily for data entry and making changes to existing records.

Form Footer: Section of Form and Report design that may display information such as instructions, notes, or grand totals.

Form Header: Section of Form and Report design that may display information such as a title, instructions, or graphics.

Group: A way of organizing data on a common attribute. When data is grouped, calculations can be performed on all data in each group.

Group Footer: Section of Report Design that contains information such as group totals to be printed below each group.

Group Header: Section of Report Design that contains information to be printed at the beginning of each group.

Identifier: A part of an expression that refers to the value of a field, control, or property.

Import: To retrieve data that has been saved in another format into an Access table.

Inner join: The default join between tables; based on common fields if one of the common fields is a primary key.

Input mask: Used in fields and text boxes to format data and provide control over what values can be entered into a field.

Join: An association between tables that tells Access how data between tables is related.

Label control: A control found on a form or report that displays descriptive titles, instructions, or notes.

Landscape: Printing orientation that prints a report across the length of the page.

Linked object: An object that is pasted into another application. The data is stored in the source document, and a graphic representation of the data is displayed in the destination document.

Literal character: In an input mask, a character such as the parentheses surrounding the area code of a telephone number, or a hyphen used to separate the parts of a telephone number.

Live link: When the source document is edited, the changes are automatically reflected in the destination document.

Many-to-many relationship: Records in both tables can have many matching records in the other table.

Mask character: In an input mask, a symbol that controls where and what type of data is entered in a field.

Move handle: Used to move menu bars and toolbars to a new location.

Multitable query: A query that uses more than one table.

Navigation buttons: Used to move through records in Datasheet and Form views. Also available in the Print Preview window.

Navigation mode: In Datasheet view, when the entire field is highlighted.

Object: A table, form, or report that can be selected and manipulated as a unit.

Object tab: In the Database window, used to select the type of object.

Office Assistant: Used to get help on features specific to the Office application you are using.

One-to-many relationship: Records in one table can have many matching records in a second table, but the second table can have only one match in the first table.

One-to-one relationship: Records in both tables have only one matching record.

Operator: A symbol or word that indicates that an operation is to be performed.

Orientation: The direction the paper prints, either landscape or portrait.

Page Footer: Section of Report Design that contains information to be printed at the bottom of each page.

Page Header: Section of Report Design that contains information to be printed at the top of each page. The column headings displaying the field names are displayed in this area.

Point: A measurement of the height of characters. One point equals approximately 1/72 inch.

Portrait: Printing orientation that prints the report across the width of a page.

Primary key: One or more fields in a table that uniquely identify a record.

Query: Used to view data in different ways, to analyze data, and to change data.

Query datasheet: Where the result or answer to a query is displayed.

Record: A row of a table, consisting of a group of related fields.

Record number indicator: A small box that displays the current record number in the lower left corner of most views. The record number indicator is surrounded by the navigation buttons.

Record selector: Displayed to the left of the first column; it can be used to select an entire record in Datasheet view.

Referential integrity: Rules that are used to preserve the defined relationships between tables when you enter or delete records in tables that are joined.

Relationship: A link made between tables, usually through at least one common field.

Report: Printed output generated from queries or tables.

Report Footer: Section of Report Design that contains information to be printed once at the end of the report.

Report Header: Section of Report Design that contains information to be printed once at the beginning of the report. By default, the report title and date are displayed in this area.

Sizing handles: Boxes that surround a selected object that can be used to adjust the size of the object.

Sort: A temporary record order in the Datasheet that reorders records in a table.

Source file: The document in which a linked object is created.

Tab order: The order in which Access moves through a form or table when the Tab key is pressed.

Table: Consists of vertical columns and horizontal rows of information about a particular category of things.

Text box control: A control on a form or report that displays data from a table or query.

Typeface: The appearance and shape of characters, such as Times Roman and Courier.

Unbound control: A control that is not tied to a field in an underlying table.

Validation text: Text that is displayed when a validation rule is violated.

Validity check: A check that Access performs to see whether data meets certain criteria.

Value: A part of an expression that is a number, date, or character.

View: An Access window format for viewing objects in a database.

Wildcard character: Placeholder for other characters when using Find and Replace, queries, filters, and expressions.

Workspace: The center area of the window where different Access windows display as you are using the program.

Command Summary

Command	Shortcut	Toolbar	Action
File/New Database	Ctrl + N		Creates a new database
File/Open Database	Ctrl + O		Opens existing database
File/Close	Ctrl + W		Closes open window
File/Save	Ctrl + S		Saves table
File/Save As/Export			Saves a database object with a new name
File/Page Setup/Landscape			Changes page orientation to Landscape
File/Print Preview			Displays file as it will appear when printed
File/Print	Ctrl + P		Prints contents of file
File/Exit	Alt + F4		Closes Access and returns to Windows 95 desktop
Edit/Undo	Ctrl + Z		Cancels last action
Edit/Cut	Ctrl + X or Delete		Deletes selected record
Edit/Select Record	Shift + Spacebar		Selects current record
Edit/Select All	Ctrl + A		Selects all controls on a form in Form Design view
Edit/Find	Ctrl + F		Locates specified data
Edit/Replace	Ctrl + H		Locates and replaces specified data
Edit/Delete Columns	Delete		Removes selected column from design grid
Edit/Delete Rows			Deletes selected field from table in Design view
Edit/Primary Key			Defines a field as a primary key field
Edit/Clear Grid			Clears all fields from design grid

Command	Shortcut	Toolbar	Action
View/**D**esign View			Displays the Design view window
View/**F**orm View			Displays the Form view window
View/Data**s**heet View			Displays the Datasheet view window
View/La**y**out Preview			Displays sample report layout as it will appear when printed
View/Print Pre**v**iew			Displays table, form, query, or report as it will appear when printed
View/**Z**oom			Changes magnification of Preview window
View/P**a**ges			Changes number of previewed pages
View/**P**roperties			Displays properties for selected control
View/Field **L**ist			Adds fields to a report
View/**T**otals			Displays Total row in Query design grid
Insert/**F**ield			Inserts a new field in table in Design view
Insert/**R**eport			Creates new report
Filte**r**/Appl**y** Filter/Sort			Applies filter to table
Query/**R**un			Displays query results in Query Datasheet view
Query/Show T**a**ble			Displays Show Table dialog box
F**o**rmat/**C**olumn Width			Changes width of table columns in Datasheet view
F**o**rmat/**C**olumn Width/**B**est Fit			Sizes selected columns to accommodate longest entry or column heading
F**o**rmat/**H**ide Columns			Hides columns in Datasheet view
F**o**rmat/**U**nhide Columns			Redisplays hidden columns in Datasheet view
F**o**rmat/A**l**ign/**L**eft			Aligns selected controls to left
F**o**rmat/**S**ize/To **F**it			Automatically resizes a control to fit contents
F**o**rmat/**V**ertical Spacing/Make **E**qual			Equalizes vertical space between selected multiple controls
Records/**F**ilter/**F**ilter by Form			Displays blank datasheet for entering values to be displayed
Records/**F**ilter/Filter by **S**election			Displays only records that contain a specific value

Command	Shortcut	Toolbar	Action
Records/**S**ort/**A**scending			Reorders records in ascending alphabetical order
Records/**R**emove Filter/Sort			Removes sort order or filter and redisplays original records and order
Records/**D**ata Entry			Hides existing records and displays the Data Entry window
Tools/**R**elationships			Defines a permanent relationship between tables
Tools/Office**L**inks/**M**erge It			Starts the Word Mail Merge
Window/**1** <name>			Displays selected window

Index

Notes

McGRAW-HILL

Microsoft PowerPoint 97

Timothy J. O'Leary
Arizona State University

Linda I. O'Leary

Irwin McGraw-Hill

Boston, Massachusetts Burr Ridge, Illinois Dubuque, Iowa
Madison, Wisconsin New York, New York San Francisco, California St. Louis, Missouri

Irwin/McGraw-Hill

A Division of The ***McGraw-Hill*** *Companies*

Microsoft PowerPoint 97

This book is printed on acid-free paper.

domestic 4 5 6 7 8 9 0 BAN BAN 9 0 0 9
international 1 2 3 4 5 6 7 8 9 0 BAN BAN 9 0 0 9 8 7

ISBN 0-07-231669-1

The Sponsoring Editor was Rhonda Sands.
The Developmental Editor was Kristin Hepburn.
The Editorial Assistant was Kyle Thomes.
The Marketing Manager was James Rogers.
The Production Supervisor was Richard DeVitto.
The cover was designed by Lorna Lo.
Project management was by Elaine Brett, Fritz/Brett Associates.
Composition was by Pat Rogondino, Rogondino & Associates.
The typeface was ITC Clearface.
Banta Co. was the printer and binder.

Library of Congress Cataloging Card Number 97-72179

International Edition

When ordering this title, use ISBN 0-07-115476-0

http://www.mhhe.com

Contents

Graphics Presentation Program Overview

You are in a panic! Tomorrow you are to make a presentation and you want it to be good. To the rescue comes a new and powerful tool: graphics presentation programs. These programs are designed to help you create an effective presentation, whether to the board of directors of your company or to your fellow classmates. An effective presentation gets your point across clearly and in an interesting manner.

The use of graphics presentation software has been increasing dramatically in the past few years. Three of the most popular graphics presentation programs today are Lotus' Freelance Graphics, Corel Presentations, and Microsoft's PowerPoint.

Definition of Graphics Presentation Programs

Graphics presentation programs are designed to help you produce a high-quality presentation that is both interesting to the audience and effective in its ability to convey your message. A presentation can be as simple as overhead transparencies or as sophisticated as an on-screen electronic display. Graphics presentation programs can produce black-and-white or color overhead transparencies, 35mm slides, on-screen electronic presentations called screen shows, and support materials for both the speaker and the audience.

The graphics presentation program includes features such as text handling, outlining, graphing, drawing, animations, clip art and multimedia support. With a few keystrokes the user can quickly change, correct, and update the presentation. In addition, graphics presentation programs suggest layouts for different types of presentations and offer professionally designed templates to help you produce a presentation that is sure to keep your audience's attention.

Features of Graphics Presentation Programs

Creating an effective presentation is a complicated process. Graphics presentation programs help simplify this process by providing assistance in the content development phase, as well as the layout and design phase. In addition, these programs produce the support materials you can use when making a presentation to an audience.

The content development phase includes deciding on the topic of your presentation, the organization of the content, and the ultimate message you want to convey to the audience. As an aid in this phase, some graphics presentation programs help you organize your thoughts based on the type of presentation you are making. Several common types of presentations sell a product or idea, suggest a strategy, or report on the progress of a program. Based on the type of presentation, the program suggests ideas and organization tips. For example, if you are making a presentation on the progress of a sales campaign, the program would suggest that you enter text on the background of the sales campaign as the first page, called a slide; the current status of the campaign as the next slide; and accomplishments, schedule, issues and problems, and where you are heading on subsequent slides.

The layout for each slide is the next important decision. Some graphics presentation programs help you by suggesting text layout features such as title placement, bullets, and columns. You can also incorporate graphs of data, tables, organizational charts, clip art, and other special text effects in the slides.

Most programs also include professionally designed templates to further enhance the appearance of your slides. These templates include features that standardize the appearance of all the slides in your presentation. Professionally selected combinations of text and background colors, common typefaces and sizes, borders, and other art designs take the worry out of much of the design layout.

Once you have written and designed the slides, you can then have the slides made into black-and-white or color overhead transparencies or 35mm slides. Alternatively, you can use the slides in an on-screen electronic presentation. An electronic presentation uses the computer to display the slides on an overhead projection screen. When using this type of presentation, many programs also include a rehearsal feature. This feature lets you practice and time your presentation. The length of time to display each slide can be set and your entire presentation can be completed within the allotted time.

Finally, these programs also allow you to produce printouts of the materials you have created. You can print an outline of the text showing the titles of the slides and main text but not the art. The outline allows you to check the organizational logic of your presentation. You can also print speaker notes that you can refer to while making your presentation. These notes generally consist of a small printout of each slide with any notes on topics you want to discuss while the slides are displayed. Finally, you can create printed handouts of the slides for the audience. The audience can refer to the slide and make notes on the page as you speak.

Graphics Presentation Terminology

The following terms are generic in nature and are associated with most graphic presentation programs.

Handout: Small printed version of slides for audience use during the presentation.

Layout: The styles, such as colors and fonts, applied to a slide that control how entries in the slide are displayed.

Outline: Displays the titles and text in each slide without the art.

Presentation: A collection of slides, handouts, notes, and outline, all in one file.

Rehearsal feature: Allows you to practice and time your presentation.

Screen show: An on-screen electronic presentation.

Slide: Individual "page" of the presentation, which can include text, art, graphs, and so on.

Speaker notes: Small printed version of each slide plus any notes the speaker has entered to refer to while making the presentation.

Case Study for Labs 1–3

As a recent college graduate, you have accepted your first job as a management trainee for The Sports Company. The Sports Company is a chain of discount sporting goods stores located in large metropolitan areas throughout the United States. The management trainee program emphasis is on computer applications in the area of retail management and requires that you work in several areas of the company.

In this series of labs, you are working in the marketing department. You have recently completed a project analyzing past, present, and future sales. The marketing manager has asked you to prepare a presentation for the weekly sales meeting about your findings. The company has recently purchased the graphics presentation program Microsoft PowerPoint 97. You will use this package to create the presentation.

In Lab 1 you use PowerPoint to enter and edit the text for your presentation. You also learn how to delete and move slides and to run a slide show.

In Lab 2 you enhance the appearance of your slides by adding clip art and graphs. You also learn how to add transitional effects to make the presentation more interesting. Finally, you create speaker notes to help you keep your cool during the presentation.

Lab 3 demonstrates the sharing of information between applications. First you learn how to link a chart created in Excel to a PowerPoint slide. Then you learn how to embed a PowerPoint slide presentation in a Word document.

Before You Begin

To the Student

The following assumptions have been made:

- The Microsoft PowerPoint 97 program has been properly installed on the hard disk of your computer system. A mouse is also installed.
- Your student data disk contains the files needed to complete the series of labs. These files are supplied by your instructor.
- You have completed the McGraw-Hill Windows 95 lab module or you are already familiar with how to use Windows 95 and a mouse.

To the Instructor

Please be aware that the following settings are assumed to be in effect for PowerPoint 97. These assumptions are necessary so that the screens and directions in the manual are accurate.

- Microsoft PowerPoint 97 has been installed using the default program settings.
- The Screen Tips feature is active (Use Tools/Options/View).
- The Clip Art gallery is installed.
- The Office Assistant is on.
- The Common Tasks toolbar is not on.
- The Additional Content templates have been installed.
- In addition, all figures in the manual reflect the use of a standard VGA display setting (640 x 480) and an Epson AP5000 printer. If another monitor type is used, there may be more lines of text displayed in the windows than in the figures. This setting can be changed using Windows setup. The selected printer also affects how text appears onscreen. If possible, select a printer and monitor type that will match the figures in the manual.

Microsoft Office Shortcut Bar

The Microsoft Office Shortcut Bar (shown below) may be displayed automatically on the Windows desktop. Commonly, it appears in the upper right section of the desktop; however, it may appear in other locations, depending upon your setup. Because the Shortcut Bar can be customized, it may display different buttons than shown below.

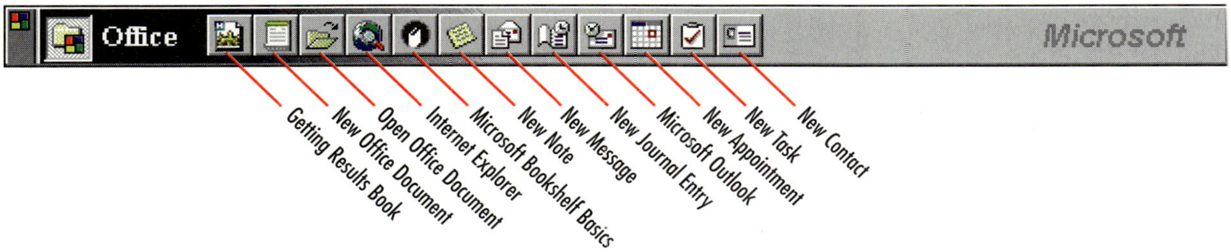

The Office Shortcut Bar makes it easy to open existing documents or to create new documents using one of the Microsoft Office applications. It can also be used to send e-mail, add a task to a to-do list, schedule appointments using Outlook, or add contacts or notes.

Instructional Conventions

This text uses the following instructional conventions:

- Steps that you are to perform are preceded with a bullet (■) and are in blue type.
- Command sequences you are to issue appear following the word "Choose." Each menu command selection is separated by a /. If the command can be selected by typing a letter of the command, the letter will appear bold and underlined.
- Commands that can be initiated using a button and the mouse appear following the word "Click." The menu equivalent and keyboard shortcut appear in a margin note when the action is first introduced.
- Anything you are to type appears in bold text.

1 Creating a Presentation

COMPETENCIES

After completing this lab, you will know how to:

1. Load PowerPoint.
2. Use the Office Assistant.
3. Plan a presentation.
4. Use the AutoContent Wizard.
5. View and edit a presentation.
6. Save a presentation.
7. Open a presentation.
8. Use the Spelling Checker.
9. Delete and move slides.
10. Run a slide show.
11. Add a slide footer.
12. Change font size.
13. Size and move a placeholder.
14. Preview and print a presentation.
15. Document a file.
16. Exit the PowerPoint program.

CASE STUDY

As a recent college graduate, you have accepted your first job as a management trainee for The Sports Company, a chain of discount sporting goods stores located in large metropolitan areas throughout the United States. Your present position is in the marketing department of The Sports Company. You have recently completed a project that analyzed the past, present, and future sales for the firm.

The marketing department manager has just informed you that you will present your findings tomorrow at the weekly sales meeting. To help you create the presentation, you will use PowerPoint 97, a graphics presentation application that is designed to create high-quality and interesting presentation materials that will dazzle your audience. Several screens of your presentation are shown here.

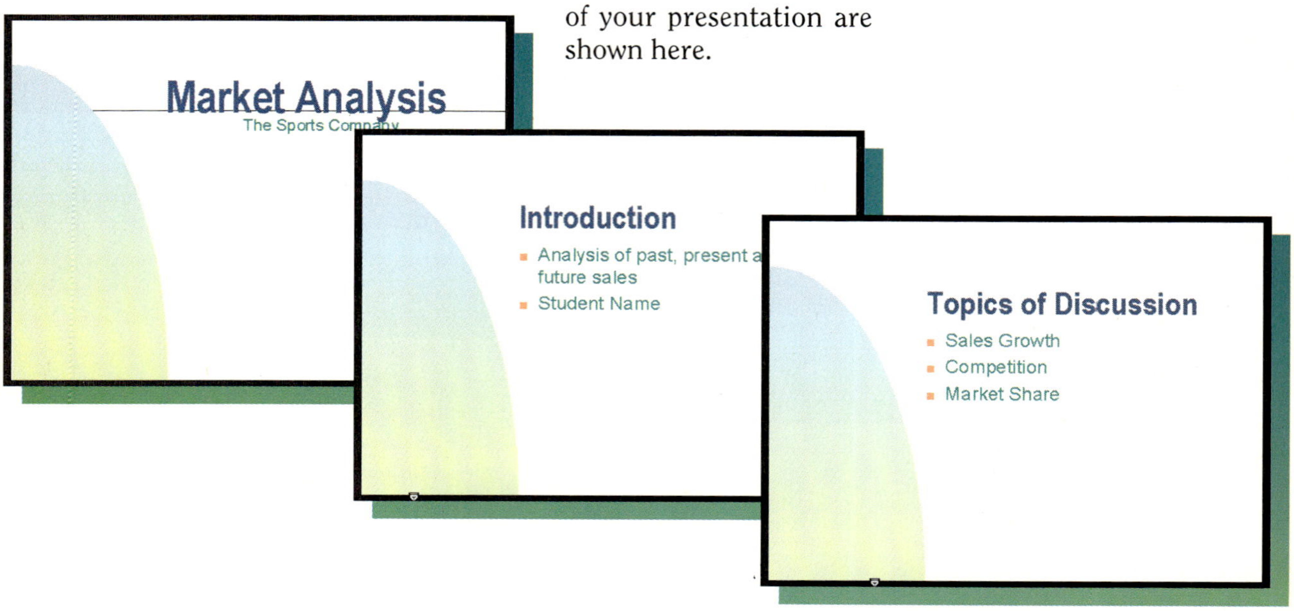

Concept Overview

The following concepts will be introduced in this lab:

1. Presentation Development The development of a presentation follows several steps: plan, create, edit, enhance, and rehearse.

2. Types of Presentations You can use PowerPoint to create on-screen presentations, black-and-white or color overhead transparencies, and 35mm slides.

3. Slides A slide is an individual "page" of your presentation. The first slide of a presentation is the title slide. Additional slides are used to support each main point in your presentation.

4. Presentation Views PowerPoint provides five different views that are used to look at and modify your presentation.

5. Spelling Checker PowerPoint automatically checks the spelling of each word as you type by checking the word against the main and custom dictionaries.

6. Fonts A font is a set of characters with a specific design. Using fonts as a design element can add interest to your presentation.

Part 1

Loading PowerPoint

The Sports Company has just purchased the graphics presentation program, Microsoft PowerPoint 97. Using this program you should have no problem creating a presentation for tomorrow's meeting.

- If necessary, turn on your computer and put your data disk in drive A (or the appropriate drive for your system).
- Click Start.
- Choose Programs/Microsoft PowerPoint.

If a Shortcut to Microsoft PowerPoint PowerPoint button is displayed on your desktop, you can double-click the button to start the program.

After a few moments, the PowerPoint application window with the startup dialog box open in it as shown in Figure 1-1 is displayed.

FIGURE 1-1

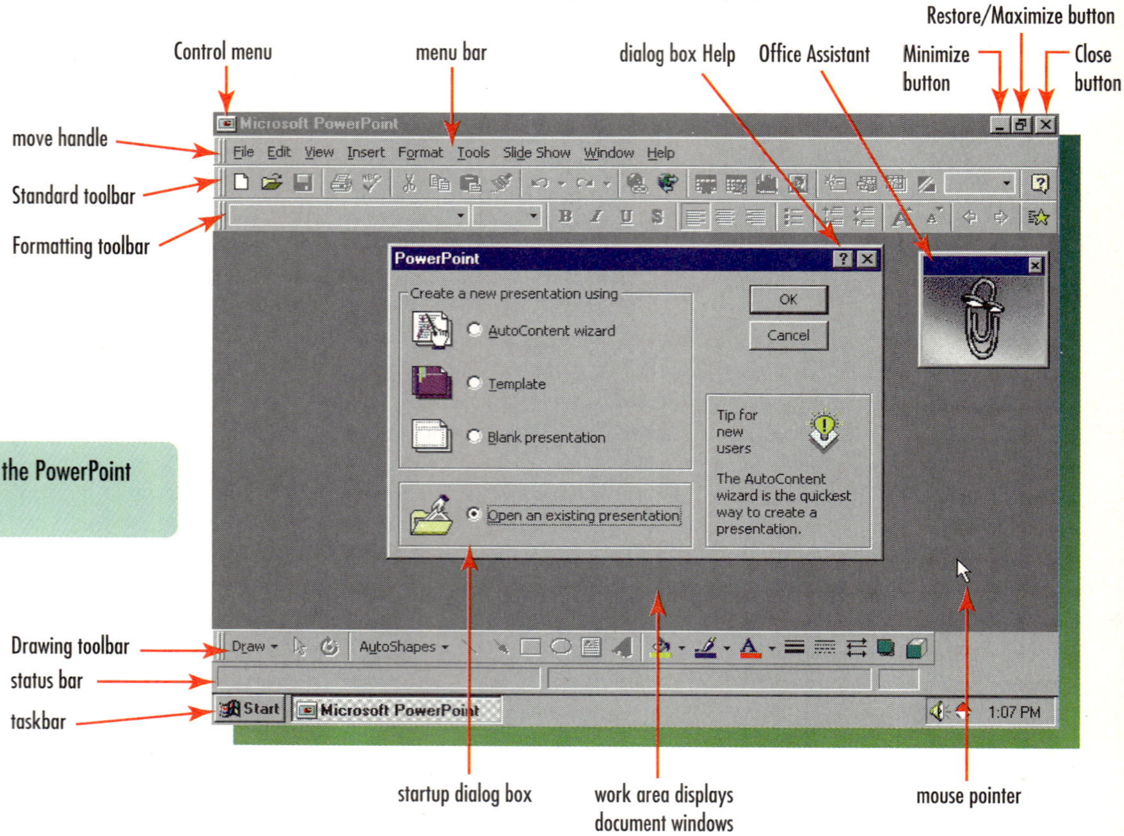

If necessary, maximize the PowerPoint application window.

The PowerPoint application window has many of the same features as in Windows 95 and other Microsoft products. Among those features are a title bar, menu bar, toolbars, document window, Minimize, Restore/Maximize, and Close buttons, and mouse capability. You can move and size PowerPoint windows, select commands, and use Help, just as in other Windows 95 applications. The taskbar at the bottom of your screen allows you to switch between other open applications and to access the Windows 95 desktop. Your knowledge of Windows 95 makes learning and using PowerPoint much easier.

The initial PowerPoint window that is displayed is called the main window. The menu bar below the title bar displays the PowerPoint program menu, which consists of nine menus. The left end of the menu bar displays the document window Control-menu icon, and the right end displays the document window Minimize, Restore, and Close buttons.

The window also includes three toolbars. As in other Office 97 applications, the Standard and Formatting toolbars appear below the menu bar. The **Standard toolbar** contains buttons that are shortcuts for many of the most frequently used menu commands. The **Formatting toolbar** contains buttons that are used to change the format or design of the text in the presentation. The **Drawing toolbar** is displayed along the bottom edge of the window. It contains buttons that are used to enhance text and create shapes. Most toolbars appear automatically as you perform different tasks and open different windows.

The left end of both the menu and the toolbars displays a **move handle** that when dragged moves the menu or toolbar to another location. Both menu and toolbars can be **docked** (as they are now) or **floating**. When docked they are fixed to an edge of the window and display the move handle. When floating they appear in a separate window that can be moved by dragging the title bar.

There are 11 different PowerPoint toolbars.

The large area containing the startup dialog box is the **work area**. It is where your presentations are displayed as you create and edit them. The status bar at the bottom of the PowerPoint window displays messages and information about various PowerPoint settings. Currently the status bar is empty.

In addition, your screen may display the Office Assistant. This feature is discussed next.

Using the Office Assistant

As in all Microsoft applications, there are several ways to get onscreen help. For brief information about different screen elements, you can display a Screen Tip. Pointing to a toolbar button displays the button name in a Screen Tip box. For information on other window elements, you can use the What's This option on the Help menu and click on an element to display a brief description. To see a Screen Tip for a dialog box option, click the ? button in the title bar and then click the option. For example, using this feature in the Startup dialog box displays the Screen Tip about the AutoContent Wizard at the right.

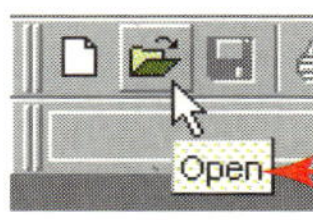

toolbar Screen Tip

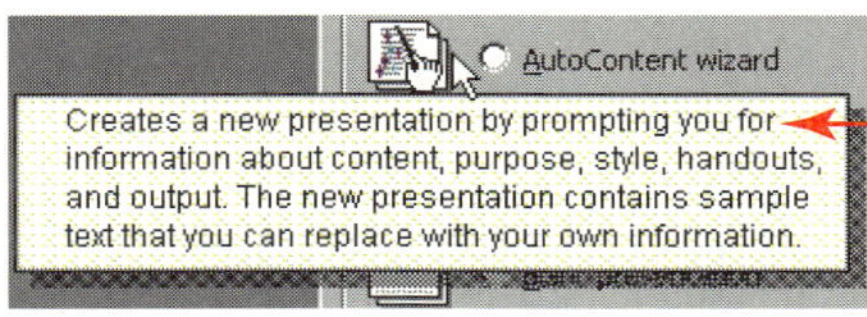

dialog box Screen Tip

If the dialog box does not have a ? button, select the option and then press ⇧Shift + F1.

Another method of getting Help in all Office 97 programs is through the **Office Assistant**. The Office Assistant is used to get help on features that are specific to the Office application you are using. The Assistant can display tips that point out how to use the features or keyboard shortcuts more effectively. A tip is available when a yellow light bulb appears in the Assistant; click the light bulb to see the tip. It can also automatically display help suggestions based on your actions. In addition, you can activate the Assistant at any time to ask for help on any topic. To activate it,

The Office Assistant feature is common to all Office 97 programs.

- Click Office Assistant.

If your Office Assistant is not displayed, press F1 to display the Office Assistant. The ? button is not available while the Startup dialog box is open.

A yellow balloon displays a prompt and a text box in which you can type the topic on which you want help. In addition, the Tips option button displays the most recent tip and lets you scroll through tips that the Office Assistant has recently displayed. The Options button is used to change Office Assistant so it provides different levels of help.

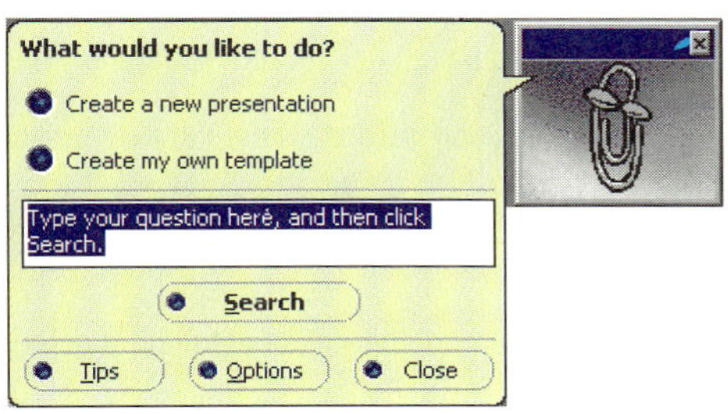

Your Assistant character may be different from the one displayed in this text.

You can also access Help using the Help menu.

Your tip may be different than displayed here.

- Click [Tips] and read the tip that appears in the box.
- To clear the tip, click [Close].

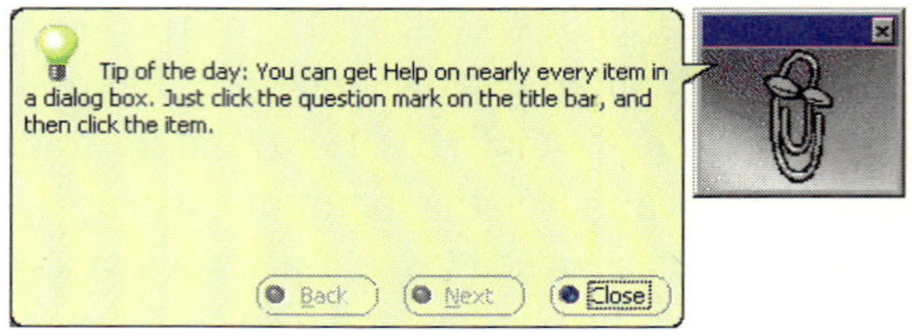

Next you will use the Assistant to find out what types of items you can create using PowerPoint.

- Click Office Assistant.
- Type **What does PowerPoint make**
- Click [Search].
- Select What you can create with PowerPoint.

Your screen should be similar to Figure 1-2.

FIGURE 1-2

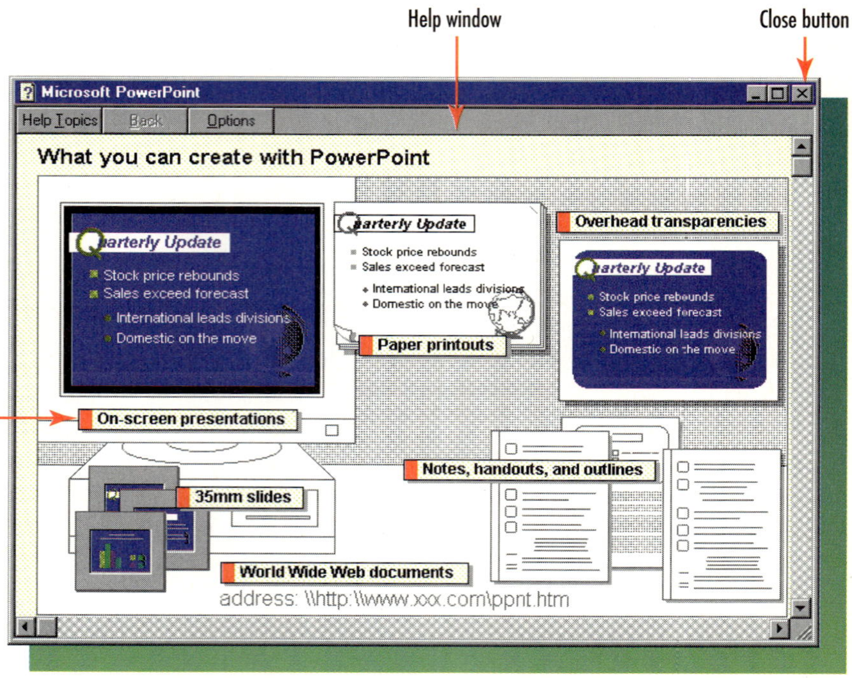

The Office Assistant displays a Help window with several topic boxes that you can click on to get more information.

The mouse pointer changes to a 👆 when pointing to a box.

- Click on each box to learn about the different items that can be created using PowerPoint.
- When you are done, close the Help window.

You can leave the Office Assistant open or you can close it and activate it when needed. This text will not display the Assistant open.

- If you want to hide the Assistant, click [X] in the Assistant's window.

Planning a Presentation

During your presentation you will present findings from a project you recently completed. This project analyzed the company's past, present, and future sales. As you prepare to create a new presentation, you should follow several basic steps.

Concept 1: Presentation Development

The development of a presentation follows several steps: plan, create, edit, enhance, and rehearse.

Plan: The first step in planning a presentation is to understand its purpose. You also need to find out the length of time you have to speak, who the audience is, what type of room you will be in, and what kind of audiovisual equipment is available. These factors have an impact on the type of presentation you will create.

Create: To begin creating your presentation, develop the content by typing your thoughts or notes into an outline. Each main idea in your presentation should have a supporting slide with a title and bulleted points.

Edit: While typing you are bound to make typing and spelling errors that need to be corrected. This is one type of editing. Another is to revise the content of what you have entered to make it clearer, or to add or delete information. To do this you might insert a slide, add or delete bulleted items, or move text to another location.

Enhance: You want to develop a presentation that grabs and holds the audience's attention. Choose a design that gives your presentation some dazzle. Wherever possible add graphics to replace or enhance text. Add slide transitions, which control how a slide appears and disappears, and build slides, which reveal text in a bulleted list one bullet at a time.

Rehearse: Finally, you should rehearse the delivery of your presentation. For a professional presentation, your delivery should be as polished as your materials. Use the same equipment that you will use when you give the presentation. Practice advancing from slide to slide and then back in case someone asks a question. If you have a mouse available, practice pointing or drawing on the slide to call attention to key points.

After rehearsing your presentation, you may find that you want to go back to the editing phase. You may change text, move bullets, or insert a new slide. Each time you make a change, rehearse the entire presentation again. By the day of the presentation, you will be confident about your message and at ease with the materials.

The purpose of your presentation is to summarize the company's sales activity. In addition, you want to impress the marketing department manager by creating a professional presentation.

Using the AutoContent Wizard

The startup dialog box is used to specify how you want to start using the PowerPoint program. It includes three options that provide access to different methods you can use to create a new presentation. The preselected option, AutoContent Wizard, is a guided approach that helps you determine the content and organization of your presentation through a series of questions. Then it creates a presentation that contains suggested content and design based on the answers you provide.

You can also create a new presentation beginning with a design template, which is a file containing predefined settings that determine the presentation's color scheme, fonts, and other design features. Finally, you can create a new presentation beginning with a blank presentation, with the color scheme, fonts, and other design features set to default values. As suggested in the startup dialog box tip, you will use the AutoContent Wizard.

You will learn more about design templates in Lab 2.

If the Microsoft Office Suite is on your system and the Office Shortcut Bar is displayed, you can click Start a New Document and select the method you want to use to create a new presentation while loading the PowerPoint program.

- Select AutoContent Wizard.
- Click OK.

The first AutoContent Wizard dialog box on your screen should be similar to Figure 1-3.

FIGURE 1-3

green indicates current steps

outline of steps to create a presentation

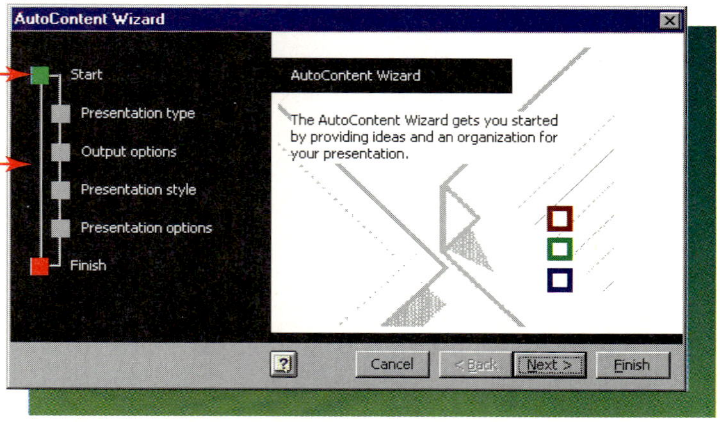

As the AutoContent Wizard guides you through creating the presentation, it shows you which step you are on in the outline on the left side of the window. The green box identifies the current step. To move on to the next step,

The menu equivalent is File/New/Presentation/AutoContent Wizard.

You can also click the outline box on the left side to move directly to any step.

- Choose Next >.

Your screen should be similar to Figure 1-4.

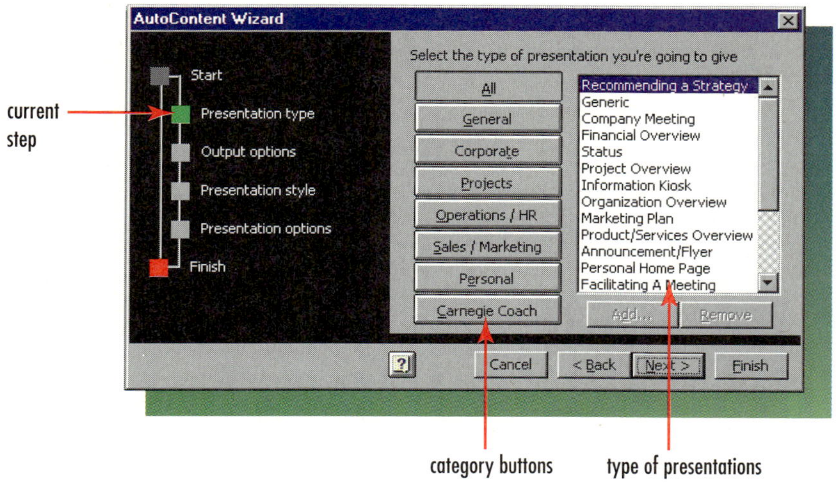

FIGURE 1-4

In the second AutoContent Wizard dialog box, you are asked to select the type of presentation you are creating. You can select one of 20 different types of presentations. Each type has a different recommended content and design. Currently, all the presentation types are listed. Each type is also indexed under a category.

- Click on each category button to see how the presentation types are organized.

The presentation you are creating is a report of the firm's market analysis. You will use the Generic presentation option.

- Click All.
- Select Generic.
- Click Next >.

The Generic option is also available under the General category.

From the third AutoContent Wizard dialog box, you can select how the presentation will be made; in person in a meeting, or online (such as on the Internet) to be viewed without your being present. Your presentation will be presented in person.

- If necessary, select Presentations, informal meetings, handouts.
- Click Next >.

The fourth AutoContent Wizard dialog box on your screen should be similar to Figure 1-5.

FIGURE 1-5

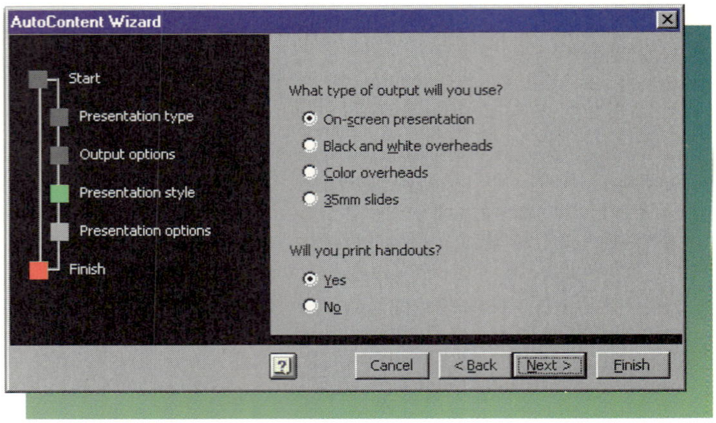

In this dialog box, you select the type of output your presentation will use.

Concept 2: Types of Presentations

You can use PowerPoint to create on-screen presentations, black-and-white or color overhead transparencies, and 35mm slides. The type of equipment that is available to you will have an impact on the type of presentation you create.

If you have computer projection equipment, which displays the current monitor image on a screen, you should create a full-color on-screen presentation. Often you will have access only to an overhead projector, in which case you can create color or black-and-white overhead transparencies. Most laser printers will print your overheads directly on plastic transparencies, or you can print your slides and have transparencies made at a copy center. If you have access to a slide projector, you may want to use 35mm slides. You can send your presentation to a service bureau that will create the slides for you.

Because the room you will be using to make your presentation is equipped with computer projection equipment, you will create an on-screen presentation. The Wizard selects the color scheme best suited to the type of output you select. In addition, you also plan to provide handouts. **Handouts** are small printed copies of each page of your presentation that can be used by the audience while listening to your presentation. Since these are the default selections, to accept them and move to the next step,

- Click Next >.

Your screen should be similar to Figure 1-6.

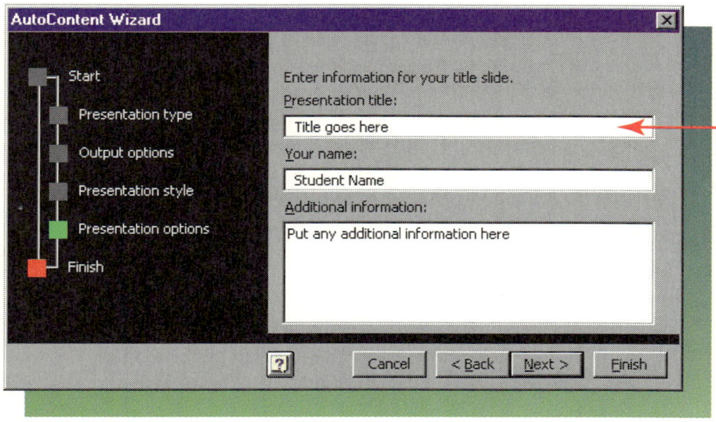

FIGURE 1-6

The default information in the dialog box displayed on your screen may be different from the information displayed in Figure 1-6.

In the fifth AutoContent Wizard dialog box, you are asked to enter some basic information that will appear on the first slide of the presentation.

Concept 3: Slides

A **slide** is an individual "page" of your presentation. The first slide of a presentation is the title slide. It is used to introduce your presentation. Additional slides are used to support each main point in your presentation. The slides give the audience a visual summary of the words you speak, which helps them understand the content and keeps them entertained. The slides also help you, the speaker, organize your thoughts, and prompt you during the presentation.

- Replace the default information in the Presentation title text box with **Market Analysis.**
- Enter your name as the author.
- Enter **The Sports Company** in the Additional Information text box.
- Click Next >.

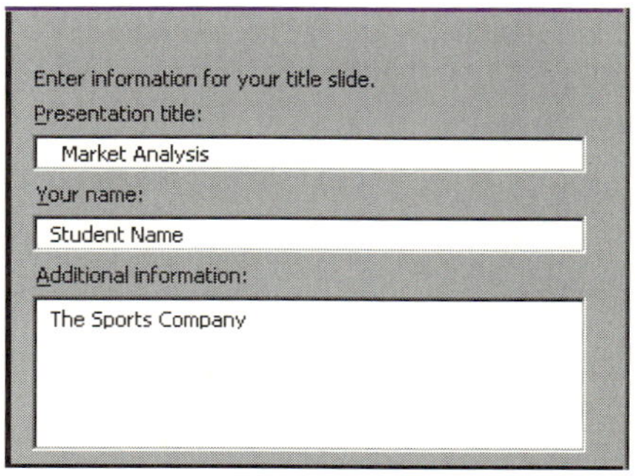

Click on the text box to move to it, and select the text by dragging. Use Tab to move to the next text box and also automatically select the entry.

If you make a typing error, use the Backspace key to delete the characters to the left of the insertion point and then retype the correct text.

You have entered all the information PowerPoint needs to create your presentation.

- Click Finish.

Viewing the Presentation

Based on your selections and entries, the AutoContent Wizard creates a presentation and displays it in a document window in the work area.

Your screen should be similar to Figure 1-7.

FIGURE 1-7

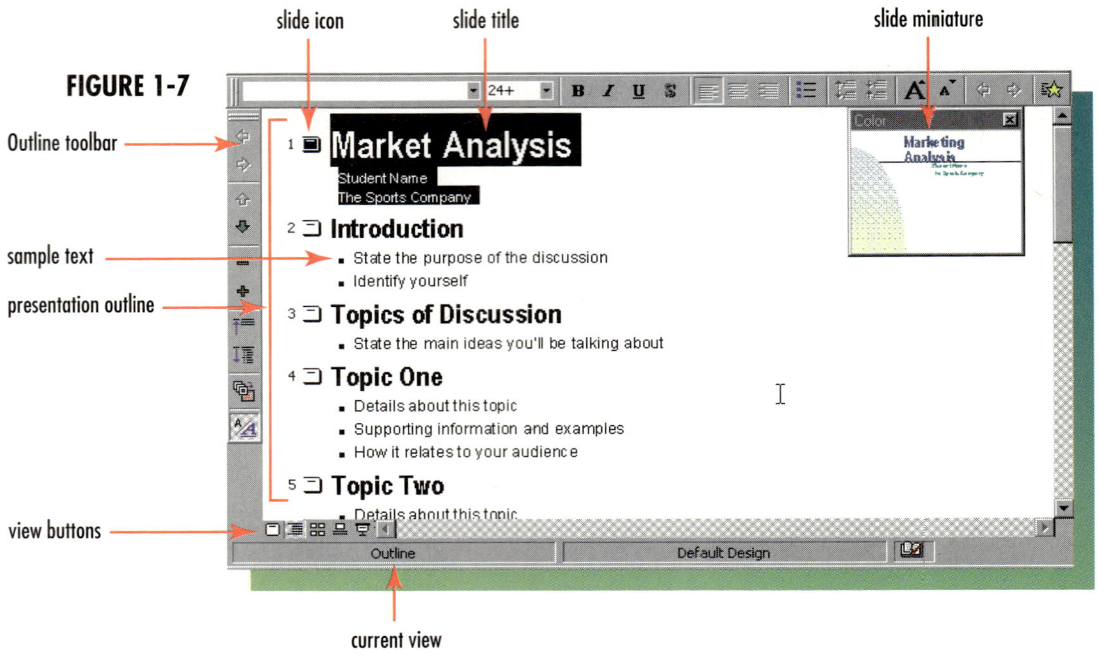

- If necessary, maximize the document window.

The status bar displays the name of the current view.

The presentation is displayed in Outline view. This is one of five views available in PowerPoint.

Concept 4: Presentation Views

PowerPoint provides five different **views** you can use to look at and modify your presentation. Depending on what you are doing, one view may be preferable to another. The commands to change views are located in the View menu. In addition, to the left of the horizontal scroll bar are five view buttons that are used to quickly switch from one view to another. The buttons and views are described below.

Button	View	Description
	Slide	Each presentation slide is shown in its final form. This view is typically used to enter and edit the content and appearance of the presentation.
	Outline	Presents the content of the presentation in a standard outline format. It is typically used to enter and edit the presentation's content. A miniature of the slide is also displayed.
	Slide Sorter	A miniature of each slide is presented. It is typically used to reorder slides, add special effects such as transitions, and set timing between slides.
	Note Pages	Like Slide view, each slide is shown in its final form. The size of the slide is much smaller, however, and space is available to insert speaker notes.
	Slide Show	Used to practice or to present the presentation. It displays each slide in final form.

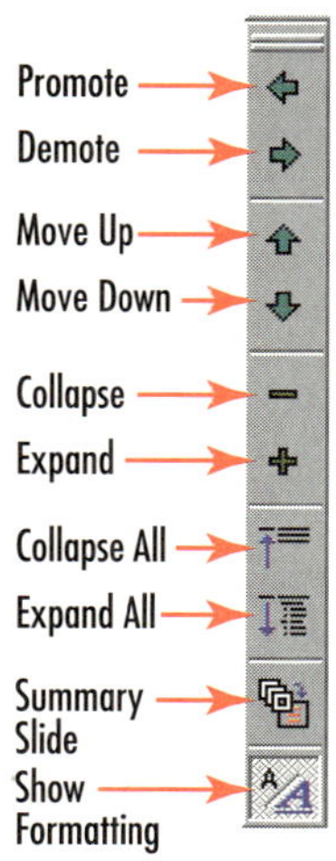

Outline view displays in outline format the title and text for each slide in the presentation. This view is used to organize and develop the content for your presentation. In Outline view the Drawing toolbar has been replaced with the **Outline toolbar.** This toolbar contains buttons (identified on the right) that make it easier to modify the outline.

To the left of each slide title is a slide icon and number that identifies each slide (see Figure 1-7). The text for the first slide, consisting of the title and text you specified when using the AutoContent Wizard, is selected. A miniature of this slide is also displayed.

The other slides in the outline contain sample text that was included by the Wizard based upon the type of presentation you selected. The sample text suggests the content for each slide to help you organize your presentation's content. For example, the second slide recommends an opening statement to explain the purpose of the discussion and to introduce yourself.

- Click "Introduction."

The slide miniature now displays the second slide.

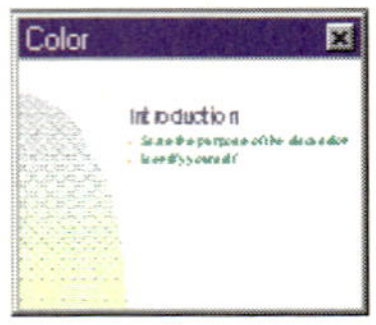

Editing a Presentation in Outline View

> In Outline view the mouse pointer appears as an arrow, an I-beam, or a four-arrow pointer.

> The selection and editing procedures used in PowerPoint are the same as in Word or most other word processors.

> If you accidentally drag selected text, it will move. To return it to its original location, use the Undo command on the Edit menu or the Undo toolbar button.

> As you make changes to the outline, the slide miniature updates immediately.

You need to replace the sample text with the appropriate information for your presentation. In addition to the usual methods of selecting text, such as dragging, in Outline view you can quickly select an entire paragraph and all subparagraphs by triple clicking on a line or by pointing to the left of the line and clicking when the mouse pointer is a four-arrow pointer. In addition, you can click the slide icon to the right of the slide number to select all text on the slide.

- Using one of these methods, select the sample text, "State the purpose of the discussion."

To enter the purpose for your presentation (this word is intentionally misspelled),

- Type **Analsis**

Your screen should be similar to Figure 1-8.

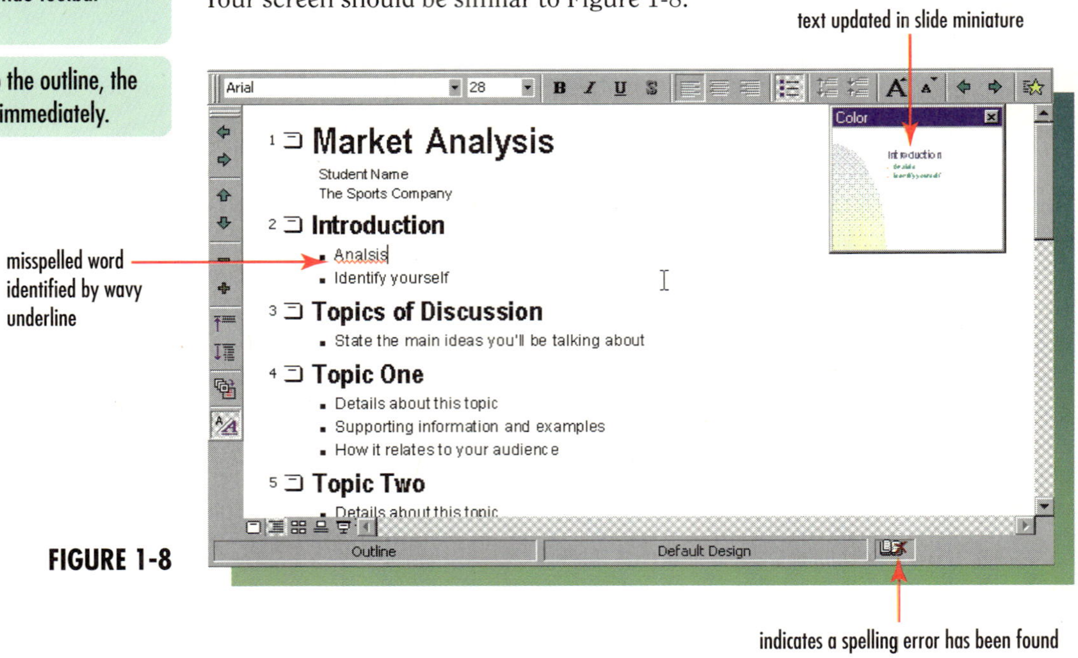

FIGURE 1-8

As you enter text, the program checks the word for accuracy. PowerPoint has identified the word as a misspelled word by underlining it with a wavy red line. In addition, the spelling indicator in the status bar appears as [icon], indicating a spelling error has been found.

> The [icon] indicator means no spelling errors have been found.

Concept 5: Spelling Checker

PowerPoint includes a Spelling Checker tool that automatically checks the spelling of each word as you type against words in a **main dictionary** that is included with the PowerPoint program. If the word does not appear in the main dictionary, the program checks a **custom dictionary**, which you can create to hold words you commonly use but that are not included in the main dictionary.

If the word does not appear in either dictionary, the program identifies it as misspelled by displaying a wavy red line below the word. You can then correct the misspelled word by editing it. Alternatively, you can display a list of suggested spelling corrections for that word and select the correct spelling from the list to replace the misspelled word in the document.

> The Spelling Checker works just as in the other Microsoft Office applications.

Because you have discovered this error very soon after typing it, and you know that the correct spelling of this word is "analysis," you can quickly correct it using Backspace. The Backspace key removes the character or space to the left of the insertion point; therefore, it is particularly useful when you are moving from right to left (backward) along a line of text. To correct this word, and continue entering the text for this slide,

- Press Backspace 3 times.
- Type **ysis**
- Press Spacebar.
- Type **of past, prsent**

> As you type, an animated pen appears over the spelling indicator while the Spelling Checker is in the process of checking for errors.

Again, the program has identified a word as misspelled. Another way to quickly correct a misspelled word is to select the correct spelling from a list of suggested spelling corrections displayed on the Spelling Shortcut menu.

- Right-click on the word to display the Spelling shortcut menu.

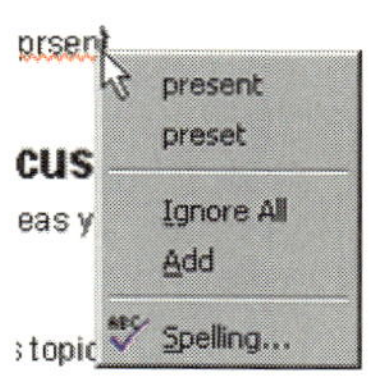

This menu displays two suggested correct spellings. The menu also includes several related menu options. Ignore All instructs PowerPoint to ignore the misspelling of this word throughout the rest of this session, and Add adds the word to the custom dictionary list. When a word is added to the custom dictionary, PowerPoint will always accept that spelling as correct. The last option, Spelling, starts the Spelling Checker tool to check the entire document. You will learn about this feature later in this lab.

Sometimes there are no suggested replacements because PowerPoint cannot locate any words in its dictionary that are similar in spelling or the suggestions are not correct. If this happens, you need to edit the word manually. To replace the word with the correct spelling and complete the outline entry,

- Click "present."
- Clear the highlight.
- Type **, and future sales**

To enter your name on this slide,

- Select "Identify yourself."
- Type **[your name]**

Your screen should be similar to Figure 1-9.

FIGURE 1-9

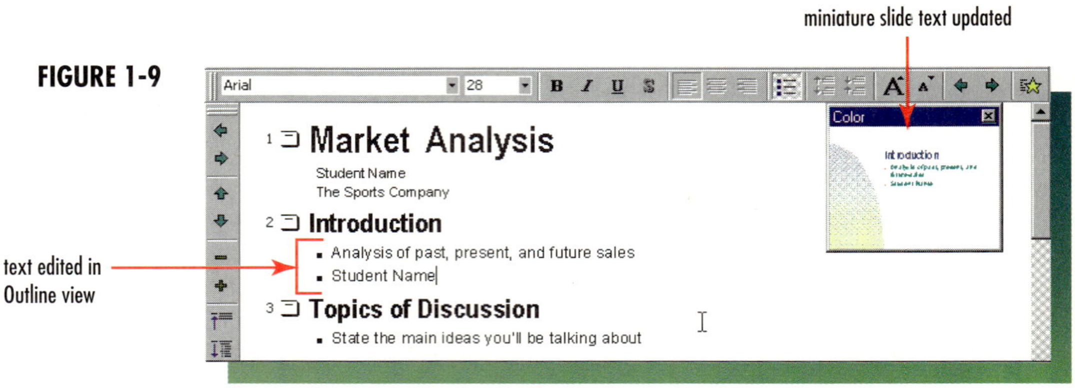

You realize that you now have your name on both the first and second slides of the presentation. You would like to remove your name from the first slide. To do this,

- Select your name on slide 1.
- Press Delete.

You are now ready to update the third slide in your presentation. You will be discussing three main topics: sales growth, competition, and market share. To enter these into the Topics of Discussion slide,

- Select "State the main ideas you'll be talking about."
- Type **Sales Growth**
- Press ←Enter.
- Type **Market Share**
- Press ←Enter.
- Type **Competition** (do not press ←Enter).

Pressing ←Enter creates a blank line and a bullet.

If a fourth bullet is displayed, press Backspace to delete it.

You realize that you entered the topics in the wrong order. You want to change the order of the second and third items in the list. A bulleted point can be moved easily by selecting it and dragging it to a new location or by using the Move Up or Move Down buttons in the Outline toolbar. To move the bulleted item on the current line up one line,

- Click Move up.

Your screen should be similar to Figure 1-10.

Move Up button

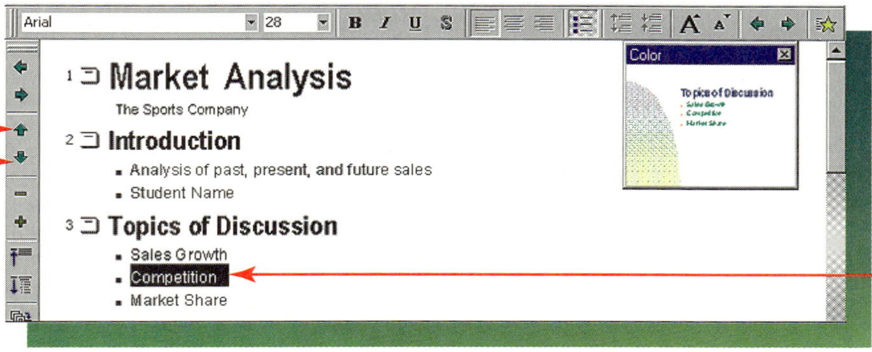

Move Down button

topic moved up one line

FIGURE 1-10

Although you can see the changes in the slide miniature, it is difficult to see because it is so small. To see an enlarged view of it, you will switch to Slide view.

- Click Slide View.

Your screen should be similar to Figure 1-11.

Pointing to a view button displays its name in a Screen Tip.

The menu equivalent is View/Slide.

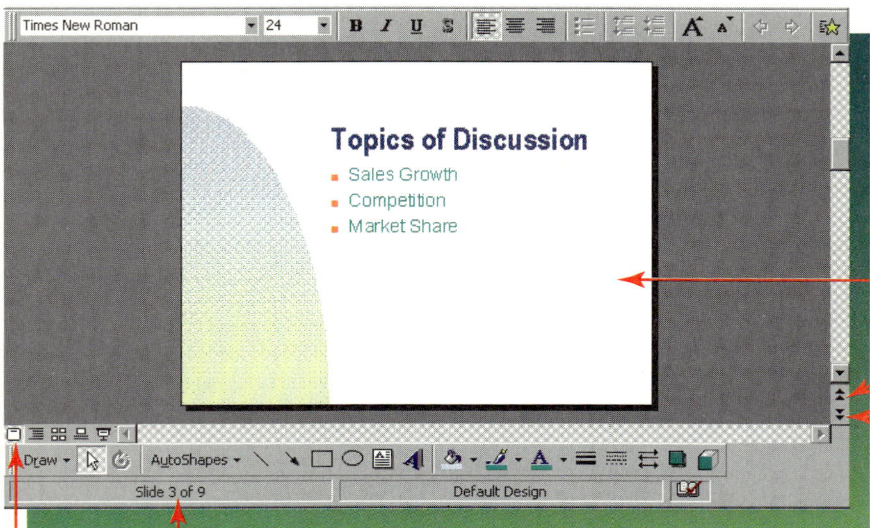

slide

Previous Slide button

Next Slide button

Slide View button

slide number

FIGURE 1-11

The slide you are on in Outline view is the slide that is displayed in Slide view.

The third slide is displayed in Slide view, and the status bar shows the current slide number and the total number of slides in the presentation. It is now much easier to see how the text appears in the slide as well as the slide design and colors. All the slides in the presentation use the same design style, associated with a generic presentation. The design style sets the background design and color, as well as the text style, color, and layout.

The following features can be used to move within Slide view:

The Previous Slide and Next Slide buttons are located at the bottom of the vertical scroll bar.

Action	Result
Click [Previous Slide button] or Click above scroll box or Press Page Up	Displays previous slide
Click [Next Slide button] or Click below scroll box or Press Page Down	Displays next slide
Drag scroll box	Displays slide indicated in slide indicator box 

■ Using any of the methods presented above, view the first two slides in Slide view.

Editing in Slide View

Now you want to continue to update the information in the presentation. You can also edit the slide content in Slide view.

■ Display slide 4.

The fourth slide contains the title "Topic One" and a list of three bulleted items. The title and the bulleted list are two separate elements or **placeholders** on the slide. Placeholders are boxes that are designed to contain specific types of items or **objects** such as the slide title, bulleted text, charts, tables, and pictures. Each slide can have several different types of placeholders. To indicate which placeholder to work with, you must first select it. You want to change the sample text in the title placeholder.

■ Click anywhere on the sample title text.

Your screen should be similar to Figure 1-12.

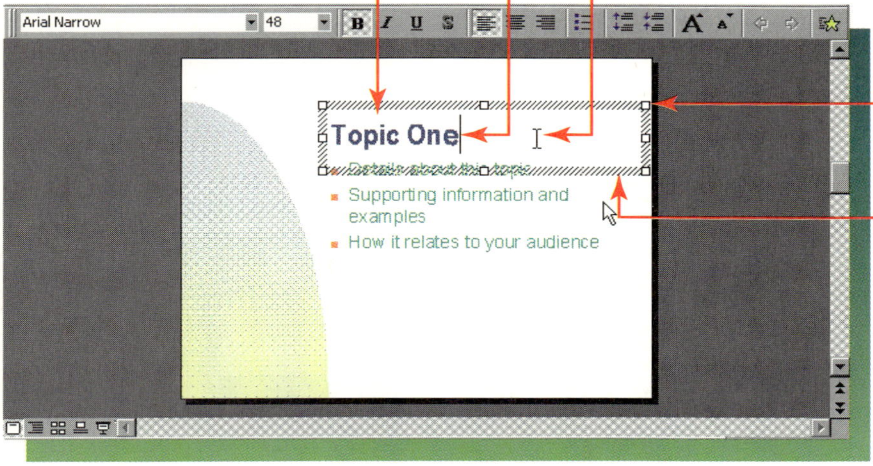

FIGURE 1-12

The title placeholder is surrounded with **sizing handles** (eight boxes) and a **selection rectangle**. Dragging on the sizing handles changes the size of the placeholder. Because the title placeholder contains text, an insertion point also appears to show your location in the text and to allow you to select and edit the text. The mouse pointer appears as an I-beam to be used to position the insertion point. To enter the new title for this slide,

> To deselect a placeholder, click anywhere outside the selected placeholder.

- Select the title text.
- Type **Sales Growth**

> Drag to select a portion of the text or triple-click to select a line.

Next you need to replace the sample text in the bulleted list placeholder with the sales data.

- Click on any of the bulleted items.
- Select all three items in the placeholder.
- Type **1995 sales $5,100,000**
- Press ←Enter.
- Type **1996 sales $5,900,000**
- Press ←Enter.
- Type **1997 sales $7,400,000**
- Press ←Enter.
- Type **1998 sales $10,200,000** (do not press ←Enter).

> Drag to select multiple lines of text.

> If you accidentally press ←Enter and a fifth bullet is displayed, press Backspace to delete it.

Your screen should be similar to Figure 1-13.

FIGURE 1-13

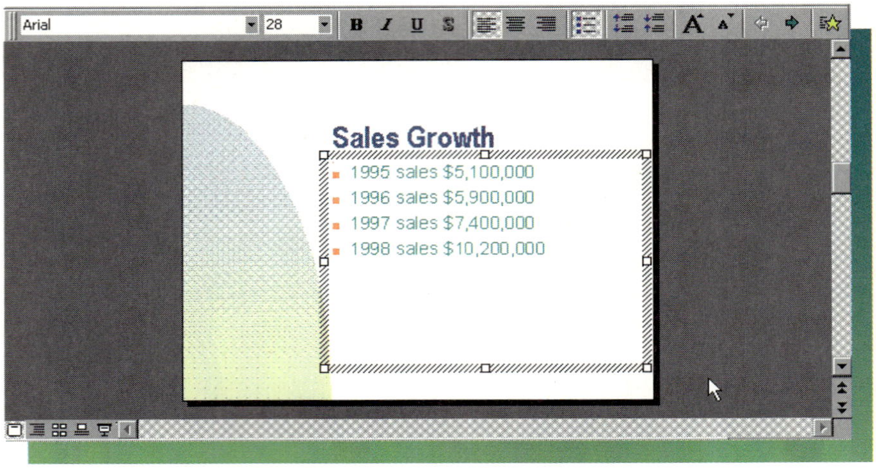

- Display the fifth slide.

You want this slide to display the names of the companies that are competitors of The Sports Company, the year they opened, and their home office location.

- In place of the sample title text, type **Competition**
- Click on any bulleted item.

You can select the bulleted items by dragging the mouse over them as you did in the previous slide, or you can use the Edit/Select All command shortcut key, Ctrl + A. To do this,

> The menu equivalent is Edit/Select All.

- Press Ctrl + A.

All three bulleted items inside the selected placeholder are selected. To enter the replacement text for the first bulleted item,

- Type **Action Corporation**
- Press ←Enter.

You want the next bulleted item to be indented below the first bulleted item. Indenting a bulleted item to the right **demotes** it, or makes it a lower or subordinate topic in the outline hierarchy.

> The Demote button is on the Formatting toolbar.

- Click Demote (Indent more).

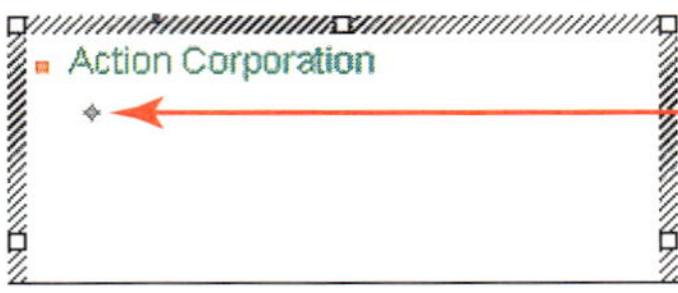

demoted item appears as indented bullet

The bullet style of the demoted line has changed to a ◆. To enter the next two lines of text,

> When you demote a bulleted item, PowerPoint continues to indent to the same level until you cancel the indent.

- Type **established in 1986**
- Press ←Enter.

- Type **located in Union, Oregon**
- Press ←Enter.

You are ready to enter the information for the second competitor. Before entering the company name, you want to remove the indentation, or **promote** the line. Promoting a line moves it to the left, or up a level in the outline hierarchy.

You can also demote and promote bulleted items in Outline view using the and buttons.

- Click Promote (Indent less).
- Type **Teams Unlimited**
- Press ←Enter.
- Type **established in 1989**
- Click Demote (Indent more).
- Press ←Enter.
- Type **located in Spring, Maine**
- To clear the selection, click outside the selection.

The insertion point can be anywhere on the line to be promoted or demoted.

You can also press Tab or ⇧Shift + Tab to demote or promote it.

Your screen should be similar to Figure 1-14.

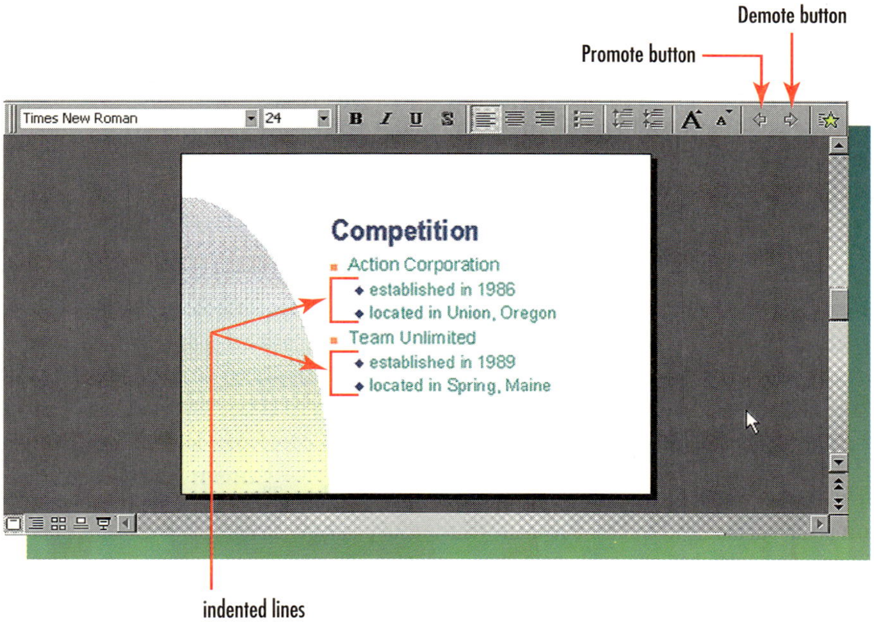

FIGURE 1-14

Saving a Presentation

You have just been notified of an important meeting that is to begin in just a few minutes. Before leaving for the meeting you want to save the presentation as a file on your data disk. You can use the Save or Save As command on the File menu. The Save command or the Save button will save the current document to disk using the same file name. The Save As command allows you to save the

Your screen should be similar to Figure 1-16.

FIGURE 1-16

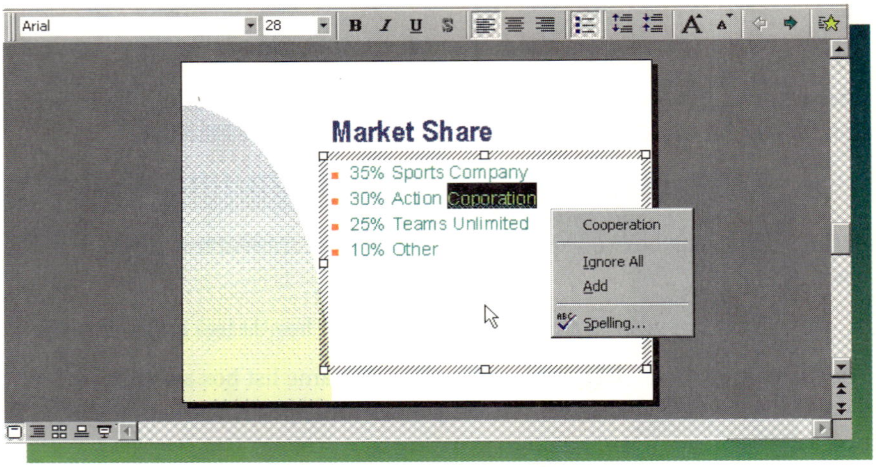

The program jumps to slide 6, which shows the market share percentage of The Sports Company and its competitors. The misspelled word "Coporation" is identified, and the Spelling Shortcut menu is open. However, the suggested replacement is not the correct word. You will use the Spelling dialog box to correct the spelling error.

- Choose **S**pelling.

The Spelling dialog box on your screen should be similar to Figure 1-17.

FIGURE 1-17

misspelled word

suggested word

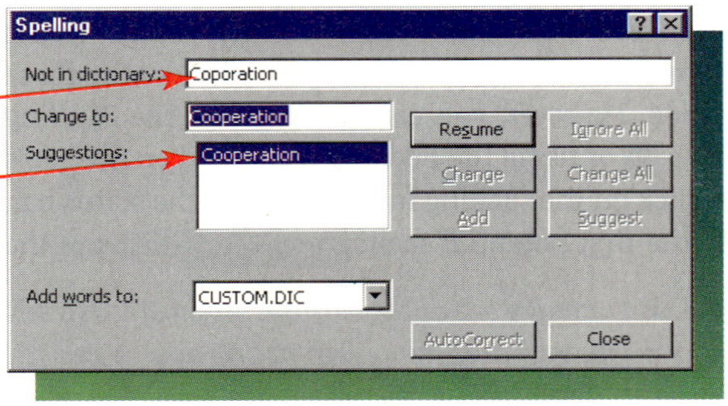

The misspelled word "Coporation" is identified in the dialog box as not being in the dictionary and the Suggestions box lists the possible replacement. Since the suggested replacement is incorrect, you need to correct this misspelling manually.

- Type **Corporation** in the Change To text box.

To proceed, you need to choose one of the option buttons described below.

Option	Action
Ignore	Accepts the highlighted word in the document as correct for this occurrence only.
Ignore All	Accepts the highlighted word in the document as correct throughout the spell-check of this document.
Change	Enters the word displayed in the Change To text box in place of the highlighted word in the document.
Change All	Enters the word displayed in the Change To text box in place of the highlighted word throughout the spell-check of this document.
Add	Adds the word to the custom dictionary. When a word is added to the custom dictionary, the Spelling tool will always accept the added word as correct.
Suggest	Suggests replacement words if the Suggestions check box is turned off.

- Click Change.

Once the Spelling dialog box is open, the Spelling Checker tool continues to check the entire document for spelling errors. The next misspelled word, "Stremgths," is identified. In this case the suggested replacement is correct.

If necessary, move the dialog box to see the located misspelled word.

- Click Change.

The next misspelled word is identified, and "Weaknesses" is the correct replacement.

- Click Change.

There should be no other misspelled words. However, if the spelling tool encounters others in your file, correct them as needed. When no others are located, PowerPoint will display a message box telling you that spell-check has finished. To close the message box,

- Click OK.

Deleting Slides

To get a better overall view of the slides in the presentation, you can switch to Slide Sorter view.

- Click Slide Sorter View.

The menu equivalent is View/Slide Sorter.

Your screen should be similar to Figure 1-18.

FIGURE 1-18

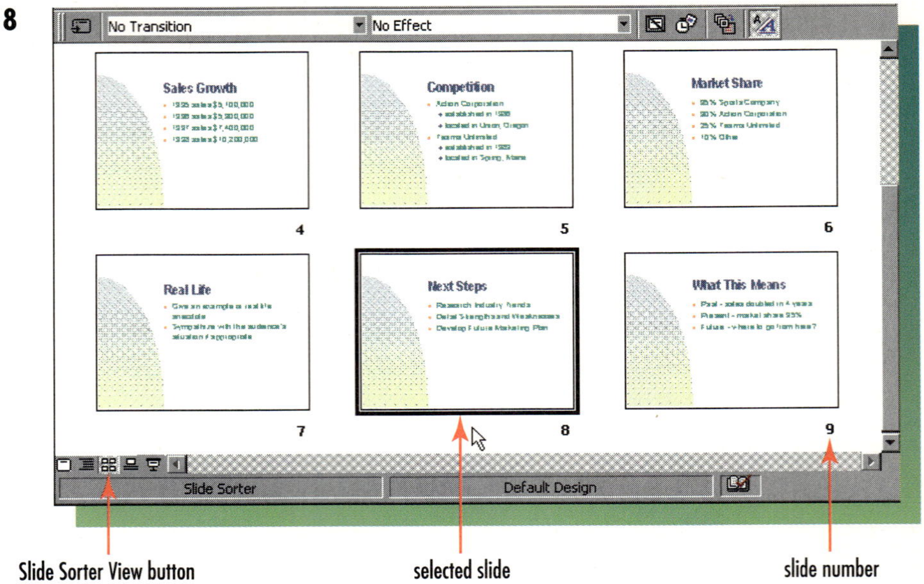

> Additional slides can be viewed by scrolling the window.

> This view also has its own toolbar that is used to add enhancements to your presentation. You will learn about these features in Lab 2.

> Clicking on a slide selects it.

> The menu equivalent is Edit/Delete Slide.

> You can also delete slides in Slide view using the same procedure.

This view displays a miniature of each slide in the presentation in the window. Viewing the slides side by side helps you see how your presentation flows. Now you can see that you need to delete slide 7 since you do not have any real-life examples that you want to add to your presentation. The slide number appears below each slide. Notice slide 8, the slide you were last viewing in Slide view, is displayed with a dark border around it. This indicates that the slide is selected. To select slide 7 and delete it,

- Select slide 7.
- Press Delete.

The Real Life slide has been deleted, and slides 8 and 9 have been appropriately renumbered. There are now eight slides in the presentation.

Moving Slides

Next you decide to switch the order of slide 8, What This Means, with slide 7, Next Steps. To reorder slides in Slide Sorter view, drag a slide to its new location using drag and drop. As you drag the mouse pointer, an indicator line appears to show you where the slide will appear in the presentation. When the indicator line is located where you want the slide to be placed, release the mouse button.

- Select slide 7.
- Drag the mouse pointer to after slide 8.

You can also use the Cut and Paste commands on the Edit menu to move slides in Slide Sorter view.

Your screen should be similar to Figure 1-19.

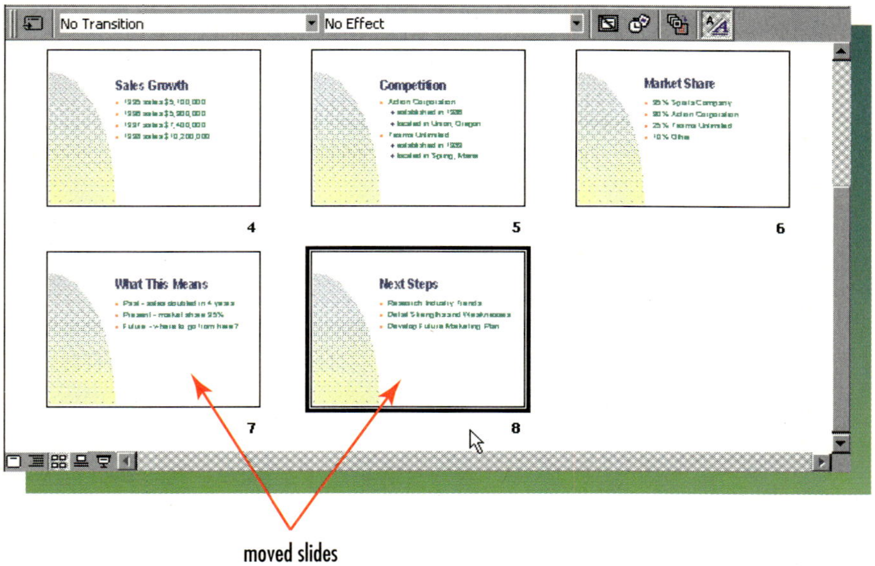

FIGURE 1-19

Running a Slide Show

Now that the slides are in the order you want, you would like to display the presentation electronically as a slide show. A **slide show** is an on-screen display of your presentation. Each slide fills the screen, hiding the PowerPoint application window, so you can view the slides as your audience would. To begin the slide show starting with the first slide,

- Select slide 1.
- Click Slide Show.

Use the scroll bar to scroll the Slide Sorter view window.

The menu equivalent is View/Slide Show.

Your screen should be similar to Figure 1-20.

FIGURE 1-20

Pressing F1 while in Slide Show opens a Help window of features you can use in this view.

Moving the mouse pointer in Slide Show displays [button] in the lower left corner of the window. Clicking [button] also opens the Shortcut menu.

To return to a previous slide, press Page Up.

The presentation title slide is displayed full screen as it will appear when projected on a screen using computer projection equipment. The easiest way to see the next slide is to click the mouse button. You could also press Spacebar or Page Down or select Next from the Shortcut menu.

- Click to display the next slide.
- Using each of the methods described, slowly display the rest of the presentation.

After the last slide is displayed, the program returns to the view you were last using, in this case Slide Sorter view.

Adding a Slide Footer

You would also like the company name, date of the presentation, and slide numbers displayed on the bottom of each slide in a footer. A **footer** is text or graphics that appears at the bottom of each slide.

- Choose View/Header and Footer.
- Open the Slide tab, if necessary.

The Header and Footer dialog box on your screen should be similar to Figure 1-21.

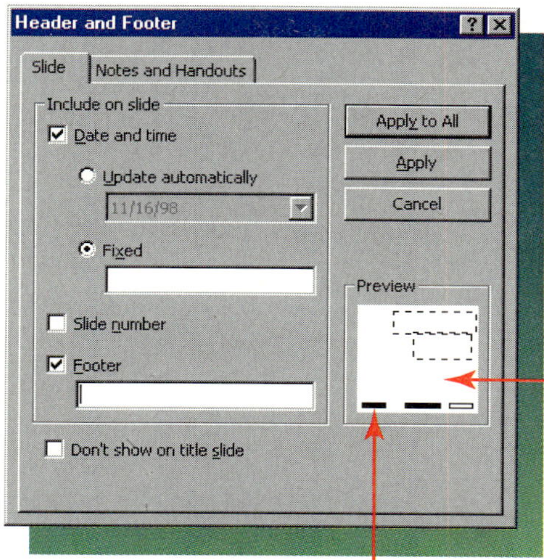

FIGURE 1-21

The Date and Time option is already selected. The two date and time options allow you to update the date automatically using the current system date and time or to enter a fixed date that will not change. Fixed is the selected default, but because the text box is empty, this information does not appear on your slides. To specify the date of the presentation, you will enter a permanent date.

If the Date and Time option and the Fixed option are not the default selections on your screen, select them.

- Enter the current date in the Fixed text box.

You also want to include the slide number and the company name. To add this information to the footer,

- Select Slide Number.
- Type **The Sports Company** in the Footer text box.

Notice that the Preview area of the dialog box displays three solid boxes where the footer information will appear on the slide. The date appears aligned with the left margin, the slide number at the right margin, and the footer text is centered. You do not, however, want this information displayed on the title slide.

- Select Don't show on title slide.
- Click Apply to All.

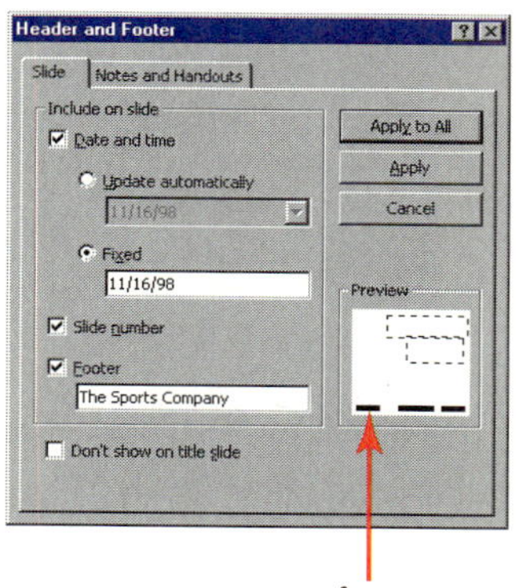

The Apply command button applies the footer settings to the current slide only.

Your screen should be similar to Figure 1-22.

FIGURE 1-22

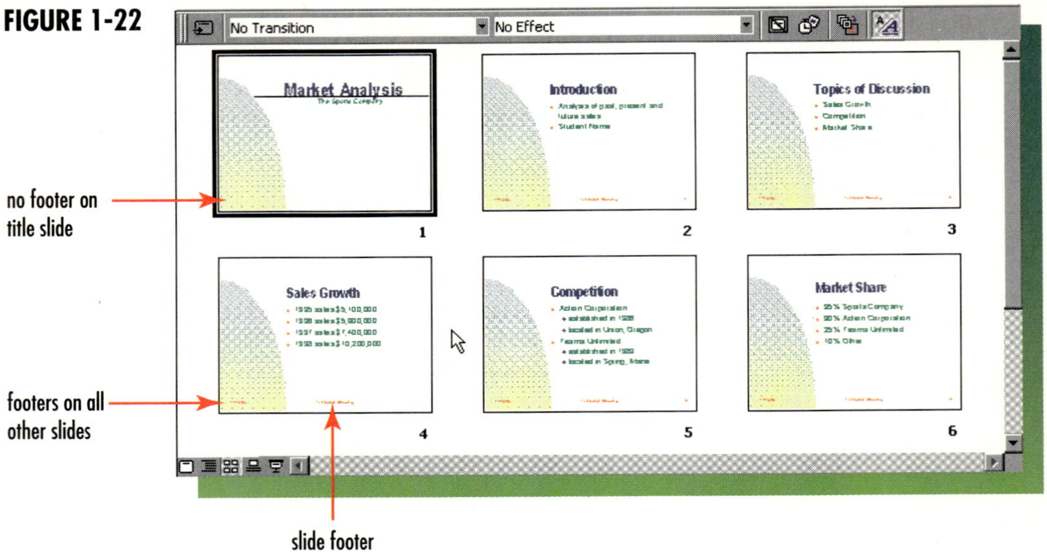

To see make the footer easier to see,

- Select slide 2.
- Switch to Slide view.

Changing Font Size

- Display slide 1.

While looking at the title slide, you decide its appearance could be improved by changing the font design and increasing the size of the subtitle text.

Concept 6: Fonts

A **font** is a set of characters with a specific design. The designs have names such as Times New Roman and Arial. Using fonts as a design element can add interest to your presentation. There are two basic types of fonts, serif and sans serif. **Serif fonts** have a flair at the base of each letter that visually leads the reader to the next letter. Serif fonts generally are for the main part of your presentation as they are easy to read. **Sans serif fonts** do not have a flair at the base of each letter. Because sans serif fonts have a clean look, they generally are used for headings to grab the audience's attention. Try not to use more than three different fonts in your presentation.

Each font has one or more sizes. **Font size** is the height of the character and is commonly measured in **points**, abbreviated "pt." One point equals about 1/72 inch, and text in most presentations starts at 24 points. For headings on your slides, you should use 48 to 60 points. Some common fonts in different sizes are shown below.

This is Arial 12 pt.

This is Arial 24 pt.

This is Arial 36 pt.

This is Times New Roman 12 pt.

This is Times New Roman 24 pt.

This is Times New Roman 36 pt.

To change the font for existing text, you must first select the text you want to change. You will change the font of the subtitle to Times New Roman with a size of 44 points.

- Select the subtitle text "The Sports Company."
- Open the Arial Font drop-down list.
- Choose Times New Roman.
- Open the 24 Font Size drop-down list.
- Choose 44.

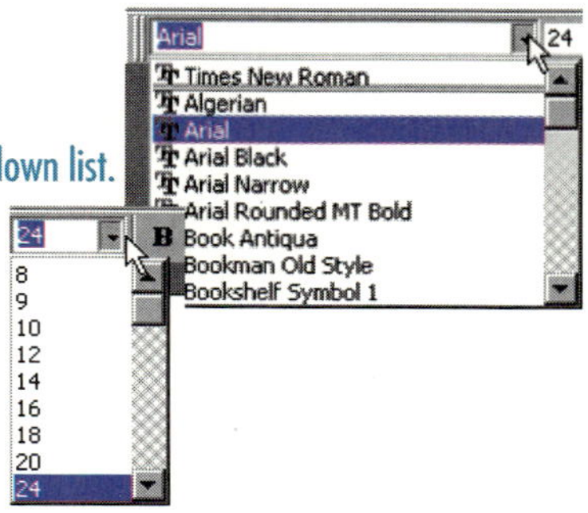

To change font settings before typing the text, use the command and then type. All text will appear in the specified font and font size until another is selected.

The menu equivalent is Format/Font.

If the selection included text in several different sizes, the smallest size would appear followed by a + sign in the Font Size text box.

Your screen should be similar to Figure 1-23.

FIGURE 1-23

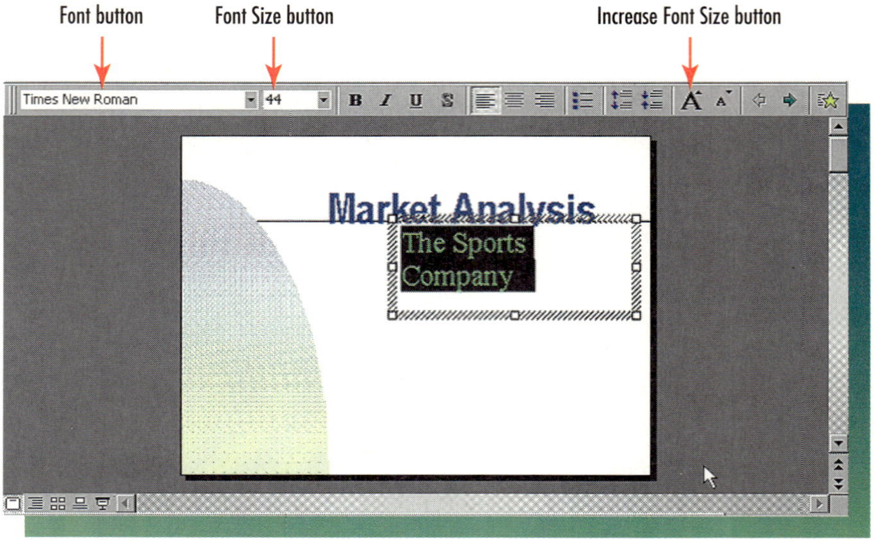

The selected text is displayed in a different font and a larger type size. The Font button displays the selected font, and Font Size button displays the point size of the selection.

> The Increase Font Size button will incrementally increase the point size of selected text.

Sizing and Moving a Placeholder

Now, however, the subtitle text wraps to a second line in the placeholder because it is larger than the width of the placeholder. To fix this you will increase the placeholder size. You also want to move the subtitle down slightly to separate it more from the main title.

To adjust the placeholder size, drag the sizing handles. The corner handles will adjust both the height and width at the same time, whereas the center handles adjust the side borders to which they are associated. The placeholder needs to be longer only.

> The mouse pointer appears as ↔, indicating the direction you can drag to adjust the size.

- Point to the left center handle and drag to the left.

When the placeholder is large enough, the subtitle will display on a single line. Next you want to move the placeholder down slightly. A placeholder is moved by dragging the selection rectangle. A dotted outline is displayed as you drag to move the placeholder to show you the new location.

> The mouse pointer appears as ✥ when you can move a placeholder.

> You can also move a selected placeholder by holding down Ctrl and pressing the directional keys.

- Point to the selection rectangle (not a handle) and drag the subtitle to its new location (use Figure 1-24 as a reference).

- Clear the selection.

Your screen should be similar to Figure 1-24.

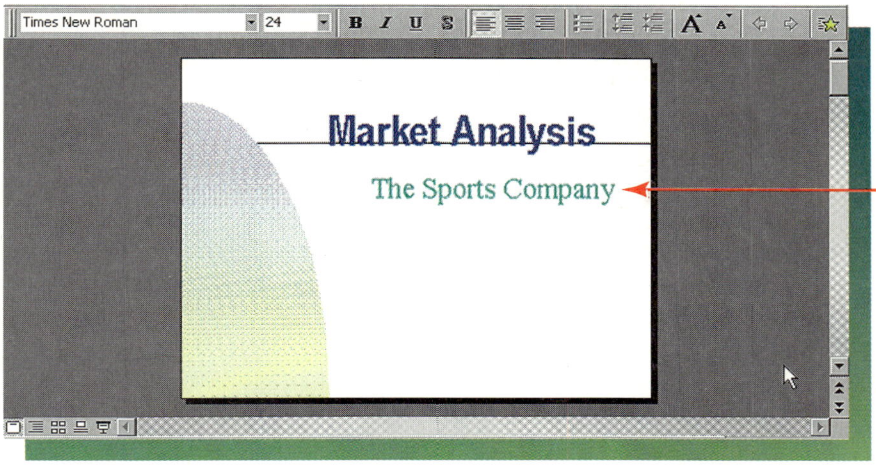

FIGURE 1-24

In the next lab you will learn more about enhancing the look of your presentation.

Previewing a Presentation in Black and White

Although your presentation is in color, you want to print a black-and-white copy of the slides for the marketing department manager to review. Because shaded fills, patterns, and backgrounds that look good on the screen can make printed handouts unreadable, you want to preview how the printout will look in black and white first.

The menu equivalent is **V**iew/**B**lack and White.

- Click Black-and-White View.

Your screen should be similar to Figure 1-25.

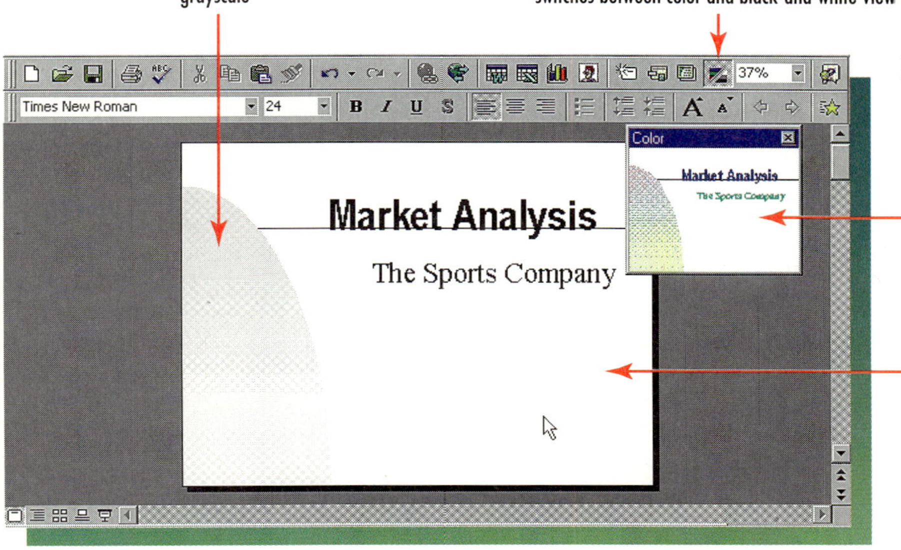

FIGURE 1-25

You can close the slide miniature window by clicking Close or choosing View/Slide Miniature.

The slide is displayed using the default black-and-white options, and a miniature slide window displays the slide in color. The default settings display the background white, text black, and patterns in grayscale. Grayscale displays shades of gray to represent colors and shadings. The default settings can be changed to improve the appearance of the printed slides.

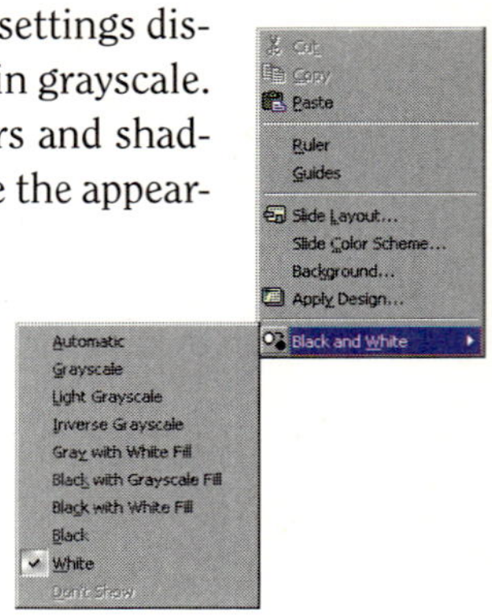

- To see these options, display the slide shortcut menu and point to Black and White.

The Black-and-White submenu options are used to select different variations of the black-and-white slide. The default setting, White, creates a black-and-white slide using shades of gray and black on a white background. You like how the black-and-white version of your presentation looks.

- Click anywhere in the work area to cancel the menu.
- Click Black-and-White View.

The slide is displayed in color again.

Printing a Presentation

You can use the Print button to print a presentation if you do not need to make any changes to the default print settings.

The keyboard shortcut is Ctrl + P.

You are now ready to print the slides, outline, and handouts. To print the presentation,

- Choose File/Print.

The Print dialog box on your screen should be similar to Figure 1-26.

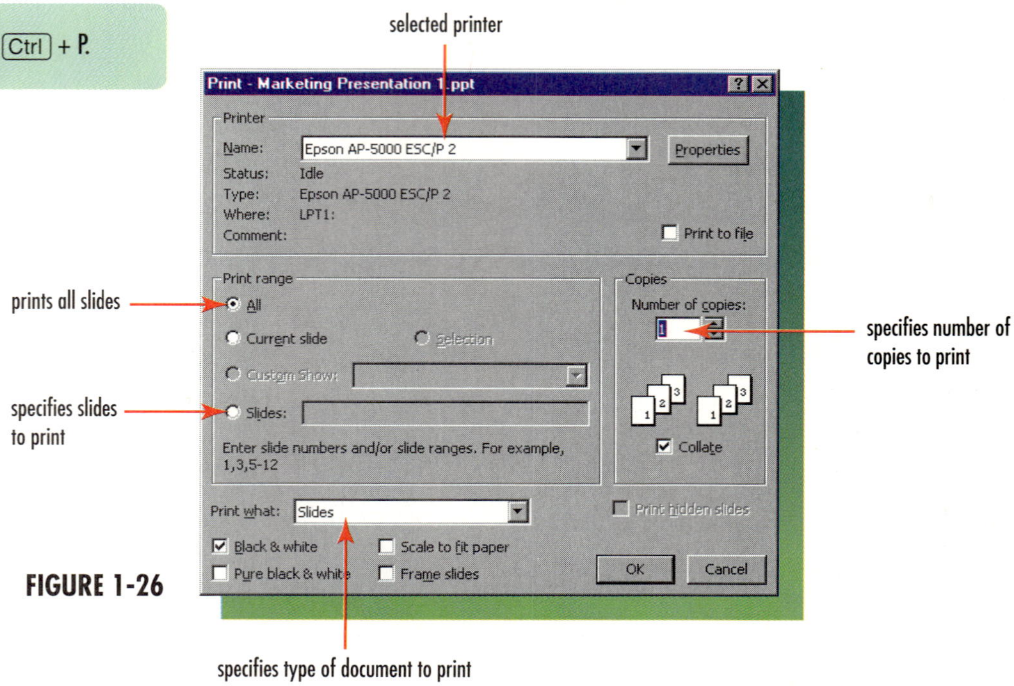

FIGURE 1-26

The Name text box in the Printer section displays the name of the selected printer. You may need to specify the printer you will be using. (Your instructor will provide the printer to select).

- If you need to select a different printer, open the Name drop-down list and select the appropriate printer.

The Print Range settings specify which slides to print. The default setting, All, prints all the slides and Current Slide only prints the slide you are viewing. The Slides option is used to specify specific slides or a range of slides to print by entering the slide numbers in the text box.

The Copies section is used to specify the number of copies of the specified print range. The default is to print one copy. The Print What option is used to specify the type of presentation document you want to print: slides, handouts, outlines, or note pages. PowerPoint can print only one document type at a time. The default prints the slides in a presentation.

At the bottom of the dialog box, PowerPoint displays options that allow you to print color slides as black-and-white slides, to make the slide images fill the paper, and to add a frame around the slide. Black-and-white printed slides is the default. Because your manager can review the content of the presentation from the outline, you choose to print only two slides for review of the design. To print the first two slides in black and white,

> The Pure Black and White option prints your presentation in pure black and white, which hides all shades of gray.

- Select Slides.
- In the Slides text box, type **1,2**
- Click OK.

The Printer icon appears in the status bar, indicating that the program is sending data to the Print Manager.

> If you begin printing the second item before the printer icon is cleared, a dialog box appears advising you that another item is currently printing. The Print Status dialog box is displayed until the print job is complete.

As soon as the slides are sent to the Print Manager program, you can tell PowerPoint to print the outline for the presentation.

- Choose File/Print.
- Select All.
- Select Print What.
- Select Outline View.
- Click OK.

Your presentation outline should be printing.

As soon as the outline is sent to the Print Manager program, you can tell PowerPoint to print the handouts for the presentation. Handouts are small printouts of each slide that can be used by the audience to follow the presentation and make notes. You can print two, three, or six slides per page. You want to print three slides per page.

- Choose File/Print.
- From the Print What drop-down list, select Handouts (3 slides per page).
- Click OK.

Documenting a File

You will save the completed presentation in a new file named Marketing Presentation 2. The original file, Marketing Presentation 1, will remain unchanged on your disk in case you want to repeat this lab later. In addition, you want to include file documentation with the file when it is saved. To do this,

- Choose File/Properties.
- Open the Summary tab if necessary.

The Summary tab text boxes are used for the following:

Option	Action
Title	Enter the presentation title. This title can be longer and more descriptive than the presentation file name.
Subject	Enter a description of the presentation's content.
Author	Enter the name of the presentation's author. By default this is the name entered when PowerPoint was installed.
Manager	Enter the name of your manager.
Company	Enter the name of your company.
Category	Enter the name of a higher level category under which you can group similar types of presentations.
Keywords	Enter words that you associate with the presentation so the Find File command can be used.
Comments	Enter any comments you feel are appropriate for the presentation.

If you press ←Enter, the OK button will be selected and the dialog box will close. To reopen the Summary Info dialog box, choose File/Properties.

- In the Subject text box, enter **Analysis of company sales and competition**
- In the Author text box, enter your name.

To close the dialog box and save the presentation using a new file name,

- Click OK.
- Choose File/Save As.
- In the File name text box, enter **Marketing Presentation 2**
- Click Save.

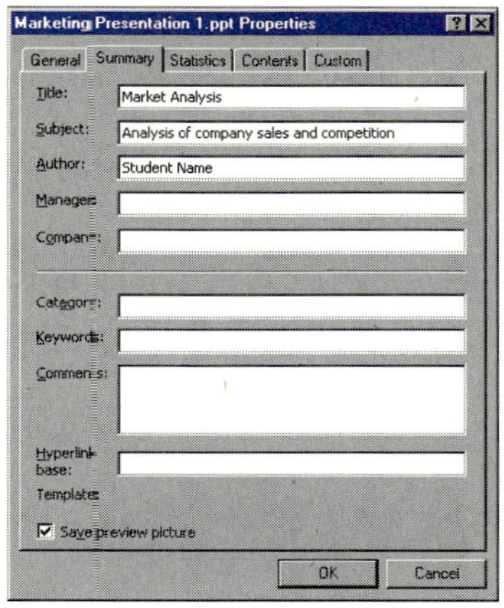

Exiting PowerPoint

You will continue to work on the presentation in the next lab. If you are ready to exit the PowerPoint program,

- Choose File/Exit.

LAB REVIEW

Key Terms

custom dictionary (PR19)
demote (PR24)
docked (PR9)
Drawing toolbar (PR8)
floating (PR9)
font (PR35)
font size (PR35)
footer (PR32)
Formatting toolbar (PR8)
handouts (PR14)
main dictionary (PR19)
move handle (PR9)
object (PR22)
Office Assistant (PR9)
Outline toolbar (PR17)
placeholder (PR22)
point (PR35)
promote (PR25)
sans serif font (PR35)
selection rectangle (PR23)
serif font (PR35)
sizing handles (PR23)
slide (PR15)
slide show (PR31)
Standard toolbar (PR8)
view (PR17)
work area (PR9)

Command Summary

Command	Shortcut	Button	Action
File/New	Ctrl + N		Creates a new presentation
File/Open	Ctrl + O		Opens selected presentation
File/Close			Closes presentation
File/Save	Ctrl + S		Saves presentation
File/Save As			Saves presentation using new file name
File/Print	Ctrl + P		Prints presentation using default print settings
File/Properties			Displays information about a file
File/Exit			Exits PowerPoint program

Command	Shortcut	Button	Action
Edit/Select All	Ctrl + A		Selects all slides in presentation, all text and graphics in active window, or all text in selected object
Edit/Delete Slide	Delete		Deletes selected slide
View/Slides			Switches to Slide view
View/Outline			Switches to Outline view
View/Slide Sorter			Switches to Slide Sorter view
View/Slide Show			Runs slide show
View/Black and White			Displays slides in black and white
View/Slide Miniature			Displays or hides a slide miniature of current slide
View/Header and Footer			Specifies information that appears as headers and footers on slides, notes, outlines, and handout pages
Format/Font		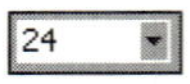	Changes font and font size
Tools/Spelling	F7		Spell-checks presentation

Matching

1. Match the following words with their definition or function.

1. AutoContent Wizard	______	**a.** displays text content of presentation only
2. Outline view	______	**b.** displays miniatures of all slides in presentation
3. placeholder	______	**c.** guides you through steps to create a presentation
4. selection rectangle	______	**d.** small printed copies of slides used by the audience
5. demote	______	**e.** indents bulleted item
6. .ppt	______	**f.** an electronic on-screen display of a presentation
7. Slide Sorter view	______	**g.** used to move and size a placeholder
8. slide show	______	**h.** slide elements that contain objects
9. handle	______	**i.** PowerPoint file name extension
10. handouts	______	**j.** hashed line surrounding a selected object

2. Match the following icons with their menu equivalent.

1. 	______	**a.** Outline command on View menu
2. 	______	**b.** Slide Sorter command on View menu
3. 	______	**c.** Print command on File menu

4.  ______ d. Spelling command on Tools menu

5.  ______ e. Font/Size command on Format menu

6.  ______ f. Slide command on View menu

7.  ______ g. Save command on File menu

8.  ______ h. Open command on File menu

9.  ______ i. Black and White command on View menu

10.  ______ j. Slide Show command on View menu

Fill-In Questions

1. In the following PowerPoint screen, several items are identified by letters. Enter the correct term for each item in the space provided.

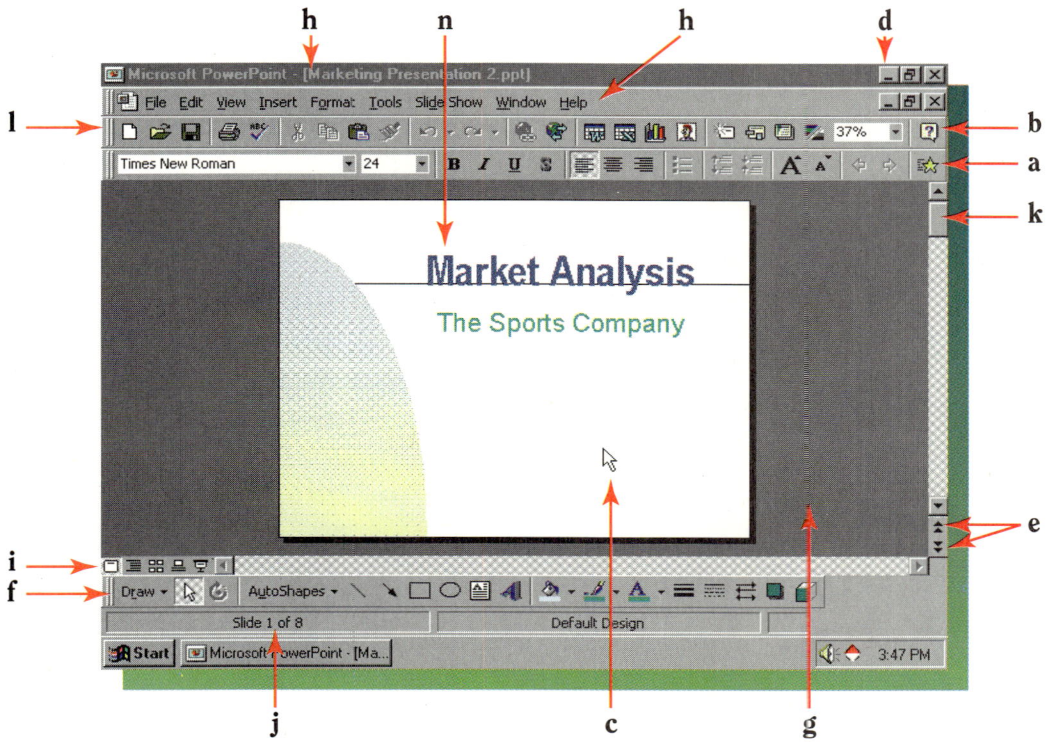

a. ______________	f. ______________	k. ______________
b. ______________	g. ______________	l. ______________
c. ______________	h. ______________	m. ______________
d. ______________	i. ______________	n. ______________
e. ______________	j. ______________	

Hands-On Practice Exercises

Step by Step

Rating System
☆ Easy
☆☆ Moderate
☆☆☆ Difficult

Note: All the presentations created in the following exercises will be used as a basis for the presentations created in the practice exercises in Lab 2.

☆

1. Damion Kolb, manager of the University Recreation Center, is planning a presentation on how to prepare for a workout. To begin the presentation, complete the steps below.

a. Using the AutoContent Wizard, select Generic as the type of presentation, select Presentations as how it will be used, and select Color Overheads as the type of output for the presentation. Enter "Preparing for a Workout" in the Presentation Title text box and "University Recreation Center" in the Your name text box. Clear the Additional Information text box if necessary.

b. In Outline view, replace the sample bulleted text on slide 2 with the following:

Bullet 1: **How to have an injury-free workout**

Bullet 2: **[Your Name]**

c. Change the title of slide 3 to "Steps to Follow" and replace the sample bulleted text with the following:

Bullet 1: **Warm up**

Bullet 2: **Stretch**

Bullet 3: **Cool down**

d. Switch to Slide view. Change the title of slide 4 to "Stretch" and replace the sample bulleted text with the following:

Bullet 1: **Stretch all major muscle groups**

Demoted Bullet 1: **Stretch and hold 10-20 seconds**

Demoted Bullet 2: **Move slowly and smoothly**

Demoted Bullet 3: **Do not bounce**

Bullet 2: **Benefits**

Demoted Bullet 1: **Increases flexibility**

Demoted Bullet 2: **Helps prevent pulls and strains**

e. Change the title of slide 5 to "Warm Up" and replace the sample bulleted text with the following:

Bullet 1: **Minimum of 5-10 minutes**

Demoted Bullet 1: **Low-level aerobic activity**

Demoted Bullet 2: **Slow stretches**

Bullet 2: **Benefits**

Demoted Bullet 1: **Increases body temperature**

Demoted Bullet 2: **Warms up muscles**

Demoted Bullet 3: **Increases blood flow**

f. Change the title of slide 6 to "Cool Down" and replace the sample text with the following bulleted items:

Bullet 1: **Slow stretching helps prevent muscle soreness**

Bullet 2: **Minimum of 5-10 minutes slow jogging or walking**

g. Switch to Slide Sorter view and delete the Real Life and What This Means slides (slides 7 and 8).

h. Switch to Slide view and change the title of slide 7 to "On Your Mark, Get Set, Go!" Size the title placeholder so the title appears on one line. Replace the sample bulleted text with the following:

Bullet 1: **The better you prepare, the more you can get out of your workout**

Bullet 2: **Come to our next presentation for your personal fat analysis**

i. Include the current date, the name of your school, and the slide number as a footer on all slides of the presentation.

j. Reduce the title on the title slide to 60 pt. Increase the subtitle to 40 pt and change the font to Times

New Roman. Appropriately size and move the subtitle placeholder.

k. Run the slide show.

l. Switch to Outline view. Change the order of the two bulleted items on slide 6.

m. Switch to Slide Sorter view. Switch the order of slides 4 and 5.

n. Add file summary information and save the presentation as Workout. Print the slides in black and white as handouts (three per page). Close the presentation.

You will complete this presentation in Practice Exercise 1 of Lab 2.

☆☆

2. Jason Ruskey is the promotions manager for Back-Road Bikes. His job is to promote the use of off-road bikes. He is planning a presentation for a group of outdoor clubs. To begin the presentation, complete the steps below.

a. Using the AutoContent Wizard, select Generic as the type of presentation, select Presentations as how it will be used, and select on-screen presentation as the medium for the presentation. Enter "Back-Road Biking Adventures" in the Presentation Title text box and enter your name in the Your Name text box. Clear any information from the Additional Information text box.

b. In Outline view, replace the sample bulleted text on slide 2 with the following:

Bullet 1: **What's new in off-road biking**

c. Replace the sample bulleted text in slide 3 with the following:

Bullet 1: **Mountain bikes**

Bullet 2: **Rental locations**

Bullet 3: **Trails**

d. Switch to Slide view. Change the title of slide 4 to "Mountain Bikes" and replace the sample bulleted text with the following:

Bullet 1: **What are they?**

Bullet 2: **Why would you want to ride one?**

e. Change the title of slide 5 to "Rental Locations" and replace the sample bulleted text with the following:

Bullet 1: **American Sport**

Demoted Bullet 1: **903 Route 66**

Demoted Bullet 2: **$14.99 per half day**

Bullet 2: **Mountain Sports**

Demoted Bullet 1: **54 S. Mountain St.**

Demoted Bullet 2: **$15.95 per half day**

Bullet 3: **Western Cycles**

Demoted Bullet 1: **721 E. Maple Ave.**

Demoted Bullet 2: **$20.00 per half day**

f. Change the title of slide 6 to "Trails" and replace the sample bulleted text with the following:

Bullet 1: **Informational books**

Bullet 2: **Maps**

g. Change the title of slide 7 to "Real Life Adventure" and replace the sample bulleted text with the following:

Bullet 1: **Mud and Muck**

Bullet 2: **Trail Dogs**

h. Replace the sample bulleted text on slide 8 with the following:

Bullet 1: **Increased interest in the sport**

Bullet 2: **Fund-raising possibilities**

Bullet 3: **Group discounts**

i. Change the title of Slide 9 to "Special Events." Replace the sample bulleted text on slide 9 with the following:

Bullet 1: **Day tours**

Bullet 2: **Races**

Bullet 3: **Overnight trips**

j. Change the font and size of the title and subtitle on the title slide to improve its appearance.

k. Include the current date in the format mm/dd/yy on a footer of all slides.

l. Display slide 1 and run the slide show.

m. Switch to Outline view. Change the order of the second and third bulleted items on slides 5 and 9.

n. Switch to Slide Sorter view. Move slide 5 to follow slide 6.

o. Add file documentation and save the presentation as Back Road Biking. Print slide handouts (three per page) in black and white and the outline. Close the presentation.

You will complete this presentation in Practice Exercise 2 of Lab 2.

☆☆

3. In 1999 the Parks and Recreation Department plans to build three new swimming pools. The total cost of this project is $1.2 million. However, the department does not have enough money to build the new pools. You have been asked to create a presentation that will be used to inform people about the benefits and costs of the project.

a. Using the AutoContent Wizard, select Marketing Plan as the type of presentation, select Presentations, informal meetings, handouts, as how it will be used, and select on-screen presentation as the medium for the presentation. Enter "Westwood Parks and Recreation" in the Presentation Title text box and enter your name in the Your Name text box. Clear the Additional Information text box.

b. In Outline view change the title of slide 2 to "New Pools" and replace the sample bulleted text with the following:

Bullet 1: **Why do we need three?**

Demoted Bullet 1: **Population growth**

Demoted Bullet 2: **School programs**

Demoted Bullet 3: **Summer programs**

c. Change the title of slide 3 to "Presentation Overview" and replace the sample bulleted text with the following:

Bullet 1: **Where they will be built**

Bullet 2: **Benefits we can expect**

Bullet 3: **Cost of the pools**

d. Change the title of slide 4 to "Locations" and replace the sample bulleted text with the following:

Bullet 1: **Lake Side School**

Demoted Bullet 1: **984 S. Lake Side**

Bullet 2: **Westwood Park**

Demoted Bullet 1: **832 N. Plaza Place**

Bullet 3: **Baseline Park**

Demoted Bullet 1: **743 E. Thunderbird Rd.**

e. Change the title of slide 5 to "Benefits" and replace the sample bulleted text with the following:

Bullet 1: **Increased pool usage**

Bullet 2: **Increased revenue**

Bullet 3: **Community service jobs**

f. Switch to Slide view. Change the title of slide 6 to "Cost" and replace the sample bulleted text with the following:

Bullet 1: **Total needed: $1.2 million**

Demoted Bullet 1: **guarantee from city: $500,000**

Demoted Bullet 2: **pledged from fund-raising: $400,000**

Bullet 2: **Need to raise $300,000**

Demoted Bullet 1: **Telephone fund-raiser**

Next Demoted Bullet 1: **Expected amount: $100,000**

Demoted Bullet 2: **10K Fun Run**

Next Demoted Bullet 1: **Expected amount: $85,000**

g. Change the title of slide 7 to "How you can help" and replace the text placeholder with the following bulleted items:

Bullet 1: **Donate money**

Bullet 2: **Volunteer time with 10K Fun Run**

h. Switch to Slide Sorter view and delete slides 8 through 17.

i. Increase the size of your name on slide 1.

j. Add the current date and slide number to all slides except the title slide. Run the slide show.

k. Add file documentation and save the presentation as Pool Project. Print the slides as handouts (three per page) and the outline. Close the presentation.

You will complete this presentation in Practice Exercise 3 of Lab 2.

☆☆☆

4. Karen Miller is vice president of the Future Workers of America Association. She plans to do a presentation for college seniors on the outlook for jobs after college. To begin the presentation, complete the steps below.

Note: If the Business Plan template is not available, use Generic.

a. Using the AutoContent Wizard, select Business Plan as the type of presentation, select Presentations as how it will be used, select Color Overheads as the medium for the presentation, and enter "Degree-Rich Job-Poor" in the "Presentation Title" text box and enter your name in the "Your name" text box. Include your school name in the Additional Information text box.

b. Delete slide 2, Mission Statement.

c. Make the following changes to the slides indicated:

Slide 2 Title: **Outlook**
- Bullet 1: **Campus recruiting**
- Bullet 2: **New hires**
- Bullet 3: **Salary increases**

Slide 3 Title: **Campus Recruiting**
- Bullet 1: **Campus visits declining**
- Bullet 2: **Number of interviews**

Slide 4 Title: **New Hires**
- Bullet 1: **New hires obtained through on-campus recruiting**
- Bullet 2: **Growth in professional positions**

Slide 5 Title: **Salary Increases**
- Bullet 1: **Changes in starting salaries**

Slide 6 Title: **Steps You Can Take**
- Bullet 1: **Be an early bird**
- Bullet 2: **Get involved and get experience**
- Bullet 3: **Go to employers**
- Bullet 4: **Do your homework**
- Bullet 5: **Be creative**
- Bullet 6: **Don't give up**

Slide 7 Title: **Suggestions**
- Bullet 1: **Consider taking a job that does not require a degree to get a foot in the door**
- Bullet 2: **Network with people who hold jobs you would like to have**
- Bullet 3: **Take an internship to gain experience**
- Bullet 4: **Volunteer—the more people you meet, the more likely you will find a job**

d. Delete slides 8 through 11.

e. Increase the font size of the title on slide 1.

f. Run the slide show.

g. Add file documentation and save the presentation as Job Outlook. Print the slides as handouts (three per page) and the outline.

You will complete this presentation in Practice Exercise 4 of Lab 2.

On Your Own

☆☆☆

5. As sales manager for American Cruise Incorporated, Sean Tyler is preparing a presentation to his sales associates on cruise packages around Hawaii. The company is trying to increase sales of travel packages for the third quarter.

To create this presentation, use the AutoContent Wizard and select Product/Services Overview for the type of presentation. Sean wants the presentation to include audience handouts. The presentation will be made using an on-screen presentation. Enter an appropriate title.

If necessary, improve the appearance of the title slide. Include your name on the slide. Then use the information below for the content of each slide.

Slide 2 Title: **Cruise Hawaii**
- Bullet 1: **Target audiences**
- Bullet 2: **Destinations**

Slide 3 Title: Destinations

Bullet 1: Historical

Demoted Bullet 1: Ancient war god Ku

Demoted Bullet 2: Oahu's Iolani Palace

Bullet 2: Scenic

Demoted Bullet 1: Kauai's Kalalau Valley

Demoted Bullet 2: Mt. Mauna Kea volcano

Slide 4 Title: Target Audiences

Bullet 1: Singles

Bullet 2: Families

Bullet 3: Groups

Slide 5 Title: Benefits

Bullet 1: Year-round travel dates available

Bullet 2: Reduced rates for cruise departures in July and August

Bullet 3: Find exotic destinations without leaving the country

Slide 6 Title: Action Plan

Bullet 1: Create brochures for travel agents

Bullet 2: Advertise in travel magazines

Bullet 3: Make group presentations

Delete slide 7. Run the slide show. Change the order of the first and third bulleted items on slide 5. Move slide 3 to follow slide 4. Add "Unbeatable Combination of Service and Great Prices" as bullet 4 on slide 5. Run the slide show again. Add file documentation and save the presentation as Cruise Promotion. Print the slides as handouts (three per page) and the outline.

You will complete this presentation in Practice Exercise 5 of Lab 2.

★★★

6. You work in an HMO's regional offices in the Patient Relations Department. One of your responsibilities is to prepare presentations to be given at the local HMO offices. Your current project is to prepare a presentation on weight control. After researching the recent literature and consulting with several experts on the topic, you have compiled the following information for managing your weight.

The experts all agree that the only way to maintain a healthy weight is by eating a healthy diet and getting regular exercise.

The following tips will help you attain a well-balanced, healthy diet:

Eat more low-fat, low-cholesterol foods, such as fruits, vegetables, rice, and pasta. These foods are high in fiber and complex carbohydrates and are filling without being high in fat.

Bake, broil, or steam your food instead of frying.

Use oil for cooking instead of butter or margarine. Canola, safflower, and olive oils are good choices.

Trim the fat from meat, remove the skin from chicken, and add more fish to your diet.

Choose low-fat products. Milk, cheese, mayonnaise, and salad dressing are all available in low-fat or fat-free varieties.

Eat smaller portions at a slower pace to avoid overeating.

Try not to eat after 7 P.M., so your body has time to digest your food before you go to sleep.

Regular exercise is just as important as watching what you eat. Exercise burns fat and develops muscles. It also increase the metabolism. Here are some tips about adding physical activity to your daily routine.

- **Take stairs instead of the elevator.**
- **Get off the bus at an earlier stop and walk the rest of the way.**
- **Walk your dog.**
- **Start out slowly and increase the level of exercise gradually.**
- **Choose an activity you enjoy.**
- **Consult your physician before you begin an exercise routine.**
- **Attend an aerobics class.**
- **Work out with a friend.**

Use the information presented above and any other knowledge you may have on this topic to create an on-screen presentation using the AutoContent Wizard and selecting the Project Overview presentation type. Include your name on the title slide. Print the first slide and the presentation outline. Save the presentation as Weight Control.

★★★

7. Create a presentation based on a lecture that could be or has been given in one of your classes. Use the AutoContent Wizard to create the presentation. Select the Generic presentation type. Add titles and bullets to the slides. Save the presentation and print the outline and slides.

You will complete this presentation in Practice Exercise 5 of Lab 3.

Concept Summary

1 Creating a Presentation

Types of Presentations

You can use PowerPoint to create on-screen presentations, black-and-white or color overhead transparencies, and 35mm slides.

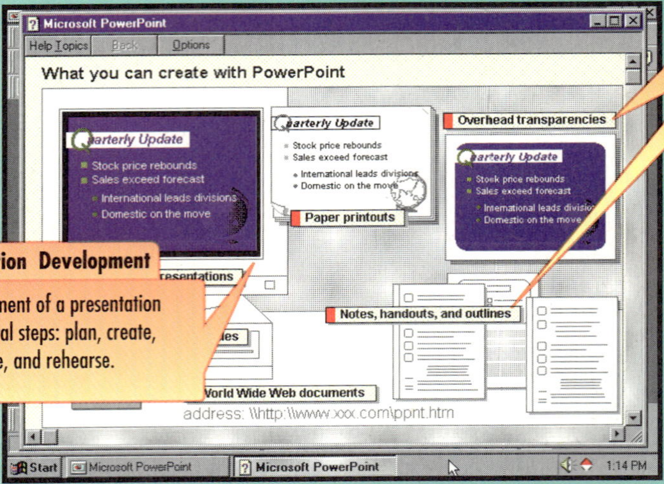

Presentation Development

The development of a presentation follows several steps: plan, create, edit, enhance, and rehearse.

Spelling Checker

PowerPoint automatically checks the spelling of each word as you type by checking the word against the main and custom dictionaries.

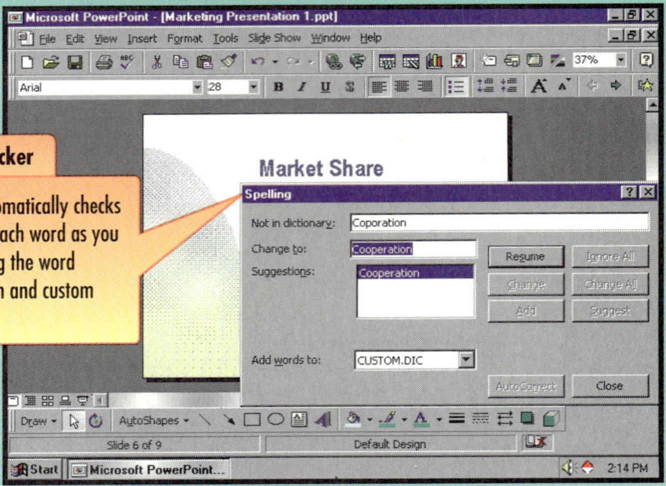

Fonts

A font is a set of characters with a specific design. Using fonts as a design element can add interest to your presentation.

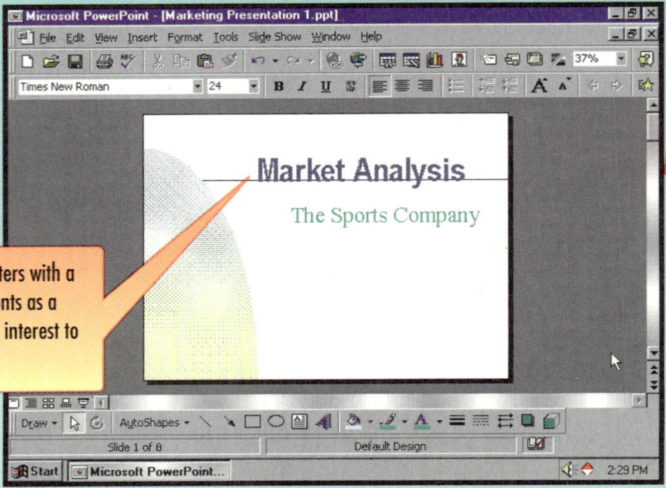

Concepts

- Presentation Development
  Types of Presentations
- Slides
  Presentation Views
- Spelling Checker
- Fonts

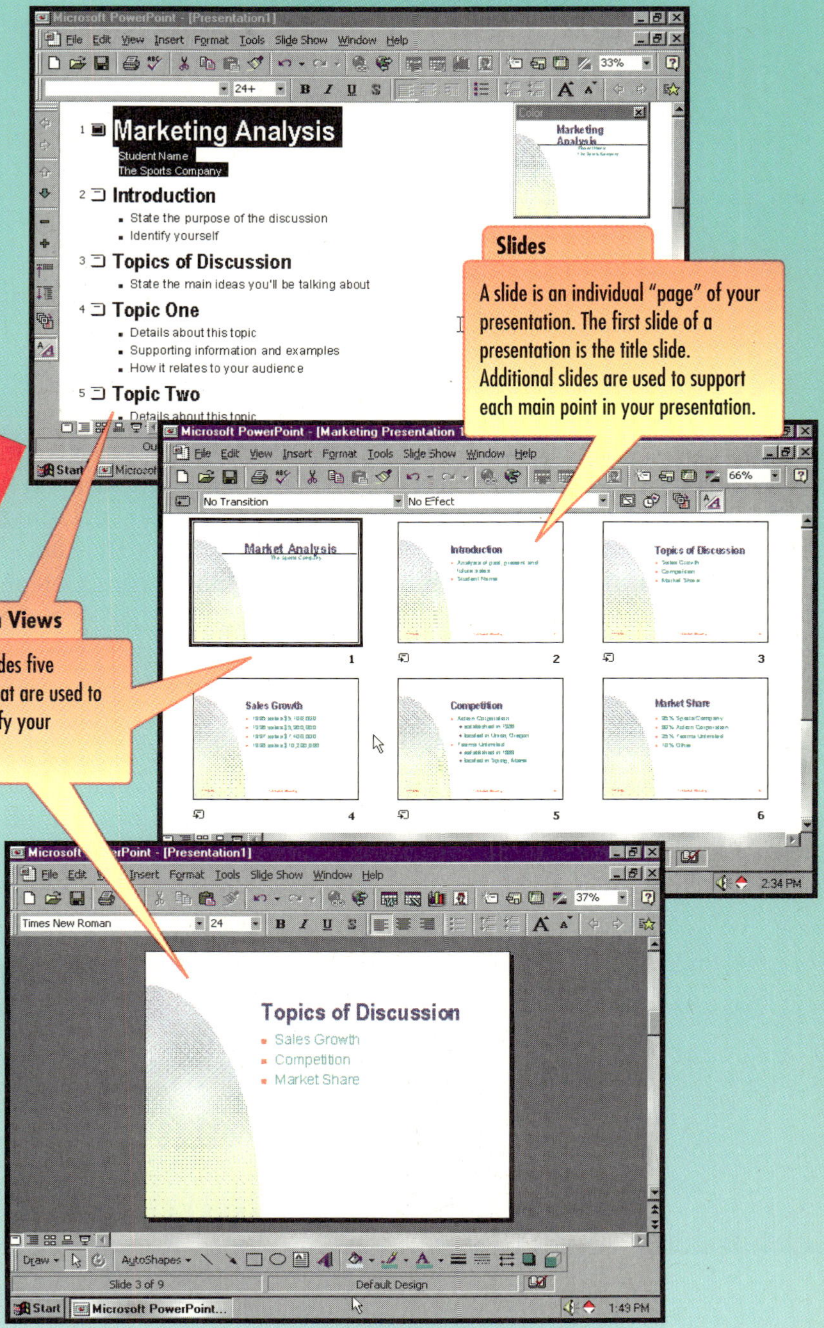

Slides

A slide is an individual "page" of your presentation. The first slide of a presentation is the title slide. Additional slides are used to support each main point in your presentation.

Presentation Views

PowerPoint provides five different views that are used to look at and modify your presentation.

2

Enhancing a Presentation

COMPETENCIES

After completing this lab, you will know how to:

1. **Change the presentation design.**
2. **Change the color scheme.**
3. **Expand slides.**
4. **Modify attributes.**
5. **Insert clip art.**
6. **Change the slide layout.**
7. **Insert a new slide.**
8. **Create a chart.**
9. **Draw a box.**
10. **Hide slides.**
11. **Add transition and build effects.**
12. **Control a slide show.**
13. **Add freehand annotations.**
14. **Create speaker notes.**
15. **Check the presentation.**
16. **Print selected slides and handouts.**

CASE STUDY

You have discussed the presentation with the marketing department manager, who suggests that you include graphs to illustrate the data on sales and market share. It was also suggested that you consider including art and other graphic features to enhance the appearance of the slides. Finally, you have been asked to include some additional information about the competition.

PowerPoint 97 gives you the design and production capabilities to create a first-class on-screen presentation. These features include artist-designed layouts and color schemes that give your presentation a professional appearance. In addition, you can add your own personal touches by modifying text attributes, incorporating art or graphics, and including animation to add impact, interest, and excitement to your presentation.

Several slides from your completed presentation are shown below.

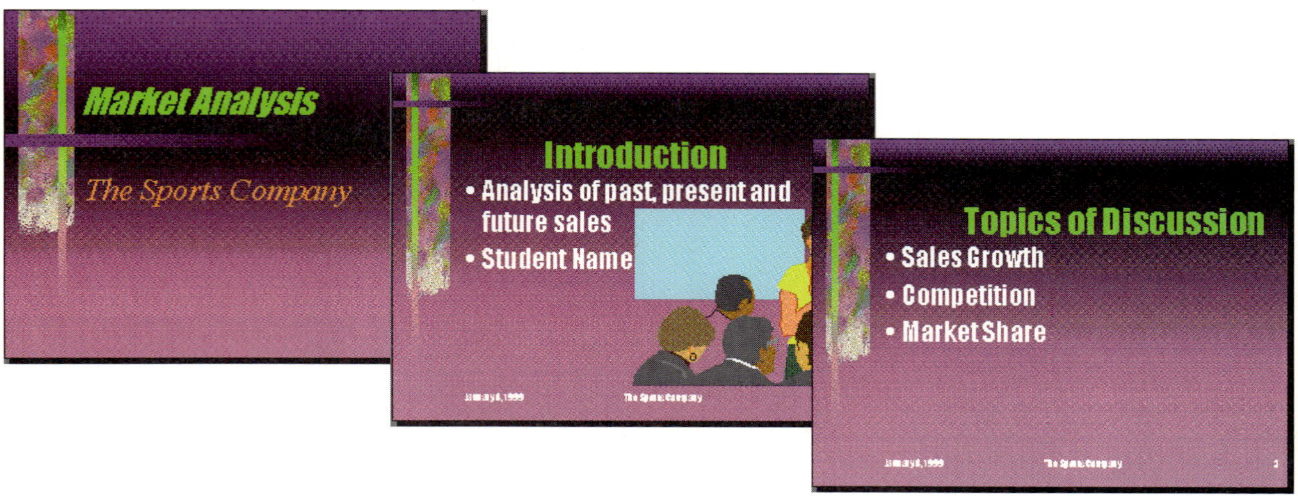

Concept Overview

The following concepts will be introduced in this lab:

1. Design Templates	Design templates are professionally created slide designs that can be applied to a presentation.
2. Attributes	An attribute is a feature associated with an object or text that can be enhanced using drawing tools and menu commands.
3. Master	A master is a special slide or page on which the formatting for all slides or pages in your presentation is defined.
4. Graphics	Graphics are objects such as charts, drawings, and pictures that you can add to a presentation to provide visual interest or clarify data.
5. AutoLayout	PowerPoint includes 24 predefined slide layouts, called AutoLayouts, that are used to control the placement of objects on a slide.
6. Charts	Charts, visual representations of numeric data, are used to help an audience grasp the impact of your data more quickly.
7. Special Effects	Special effects such as slide transitions and builds are used to enhance the on-screen presentation.

Part 1

Changing the Presentation Design

You have updated the content to include the additional information on the competition and are now ready to make several changes to improve the overall appearance of the presentation.

- Load PowerPoint 97.
- Put your data disk in drive A (or the appropriate drive for your system).
- Open the file Marketing Presentation 3 from your data disk.
- Replace Student Name on slide 2 with your name.
- Switch to Slide Sorter view.

Slide 6 contains the additional information on the competition.

You will be using many PowerPoint features to enhance the presentation. To make it easier to access these features, you will use the Common Tasks toolbar.

- Display the Common Tasks toolbar.
- Move it to a corner of the work area.

Select the Common Tasks toolbar from the toolbar Shortcut menu.

Your screen should be similar to Figure 2-1.

FIGURE 2-1

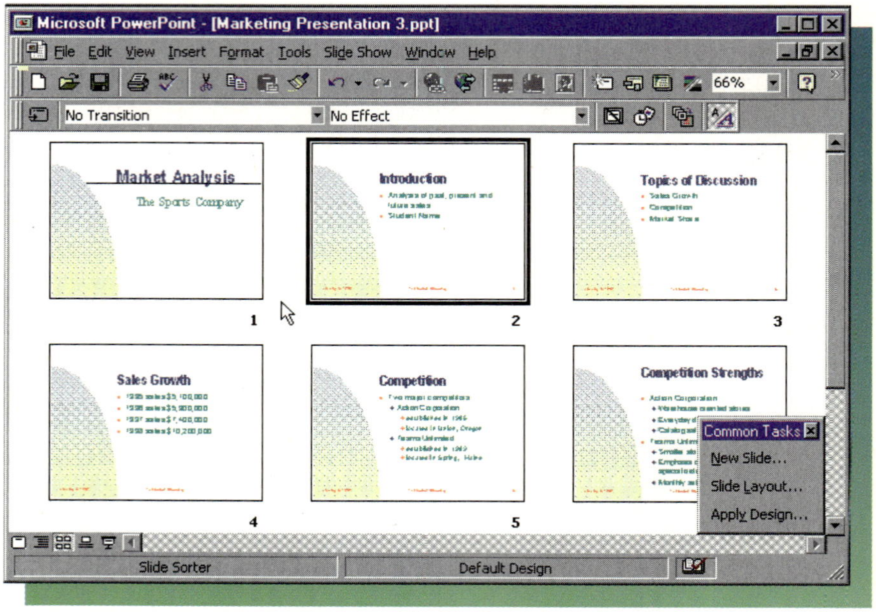

This toolbar consists of three buttons that are frequently used to modify a presentation.

Although you are satisfied with the presentation's basic content and organization, you want to change its style and appearance by applying a different design template.

Concept 1: Design Templates

Design templates are professionally created slide designs that can be applied to your presentation. They contain color schemes, custom formatting, background designs, styled fonts, and other layout and design elements that have been created by artists. There are more than 100 design templates from which you can select to quickly give your presentations a professional appearance. Selecting a design template changes all slides in your presentation to match the selected template design. This ensures that your presentation has a consistent look throughout.

To change the design template,

The menu equivalent is Format/Apply Design.

- Click Apply Design... .

The Apply Design dialog box on your screen should be similar to Figure 2-2.

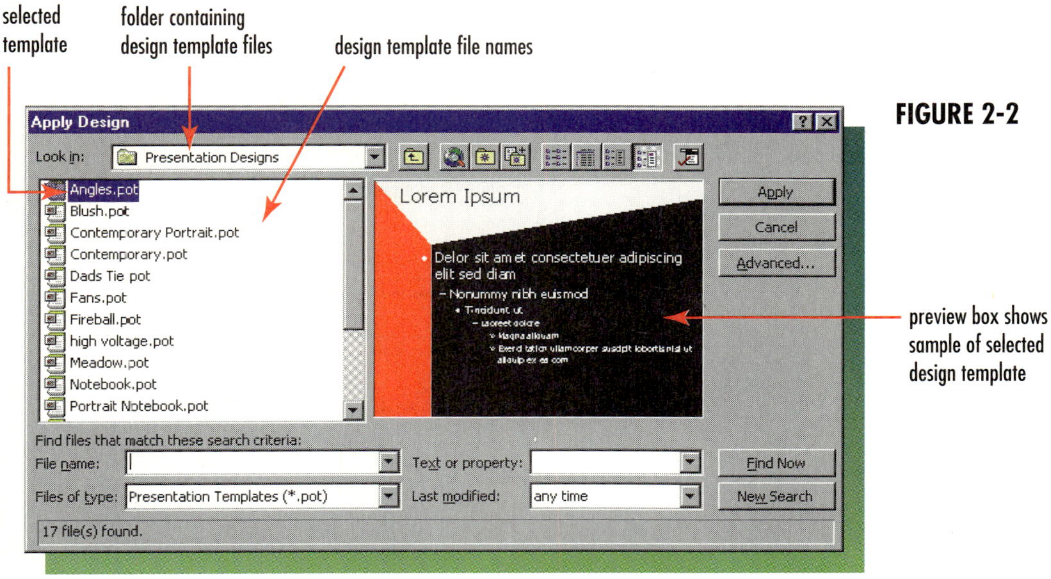

FIGURE 2-2

The large list box on the left displays the names of the design templates located in the Presentation Designs folder. When a design template file name is selected, the preview box displays a sample of the colors, fonts, and designs for the selected design. The first design template in the list, Angles, is the selected and displayed design template.

The file extension for PowerPoint design templates is .pot.

- Select several design templates and view the samples in the preview box.

Click on the design file name to select it.

After previewing the templates, you decide to use the Blush template for your presentation.

- Double-click Blush.

Your screen should be similar to Figure 2-3.

FIGURE 2-3

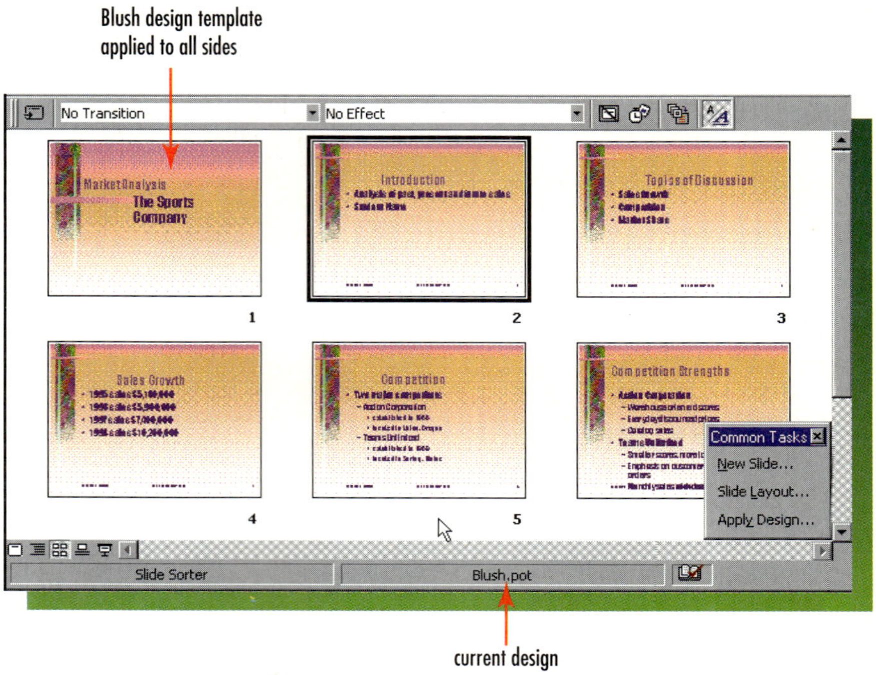

The design has been applied all slides in the presentation. The status bar displays the name of the current design.

Changing the Color Scheme

As you look at the new design style, you feel the color is not very powerful. To make your presentation more lively, you decide to try a different color scheme. Each design template has several alternative color schemes from which you can choose. To see the color schemes that are available for the Blush template,

- Choose Format/Slide Color Scheme.
- If necessary, open the Standard tab.

The Color Scheme dialog box on your screen should be similar to Figure 2-4.

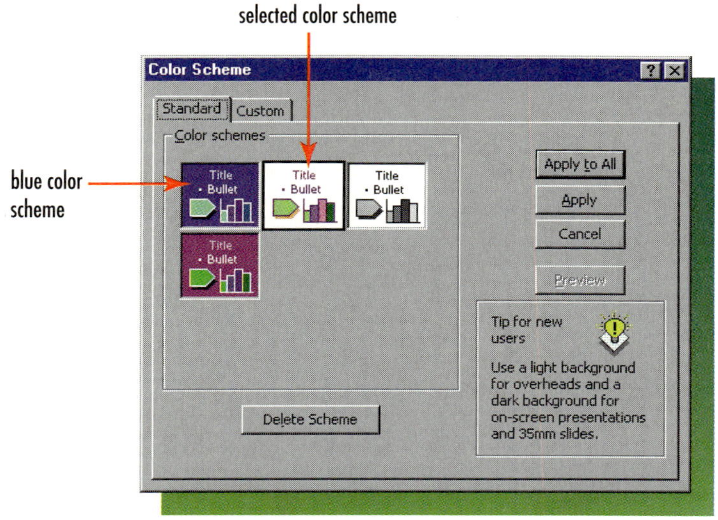

FIGURE 2-4

The four color schemes for the Blush design template are displayed. The color scheme with the white background is selected. Each color scheme consists of eight coordinated colors that are applied to different slide elements. Using predefined color schemes gives your presentation a professional and consistent look. To see how the pink color scheme would look,

- Select the pink color scheme option (first design, second row).
- Click Preview.
- Move the dialog box so you can see the upper row of slides in the work area.

Your screen should be similar to Figure 2-5.

FIGURE 2-5

The current slide is displayed in the selected color scheme. Although you like this color scheme, you think the background is too dark, and you want to change the standard colors of the template design.

- Open the Custom tab.

The Color Scheme dialog box on your screen should be similar to Figure 2-6.

FIGURE 2-6

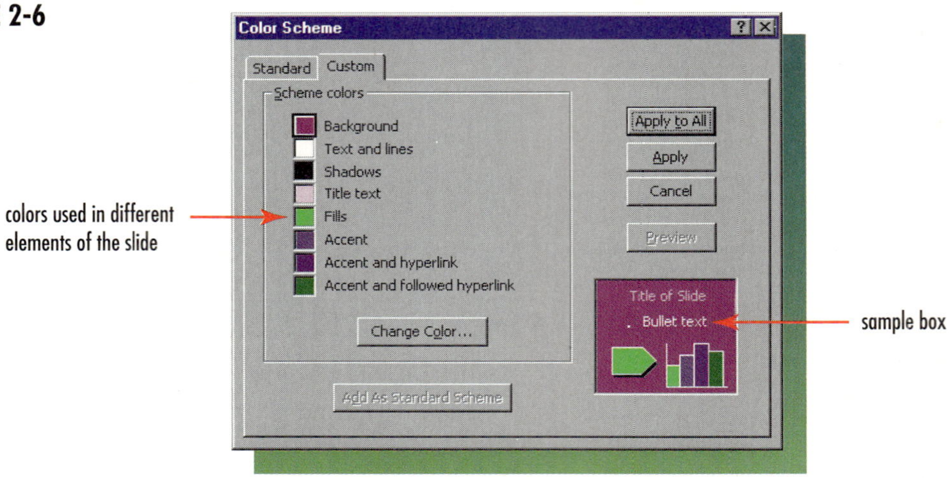

The Scheme Colors area of the dialog box shows you the eight colors that are applied to different elements of the template design. The sample box shows how the selected colors are used in a slide. The option to change the background color is selected by default. To select a different color for the background,

- Click Change Color... .

The Background Color dialog box on your screen should be similar to Figure 2-7.

FIGURE 2-7

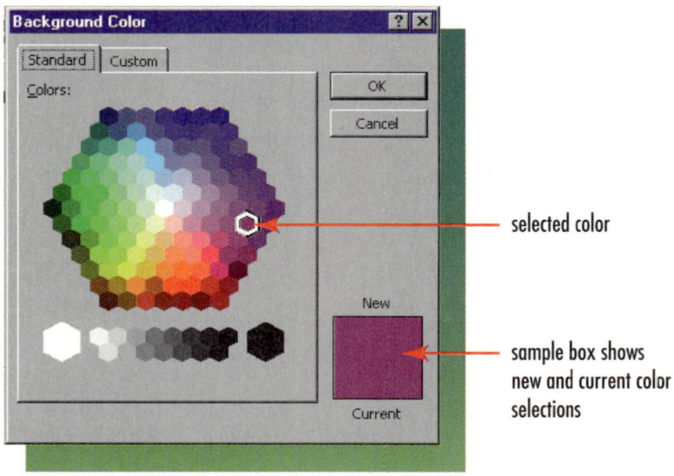

The dialog box displays a palette of standard colors. The current color of the background is selected. The sample box shows the new color in the upper half and the current color in the lower half. Because you have not yet selected a new color, only one color is displayed. To see how the lighter shade of the same color will look,

- Select the color two to the left of the current selected color.

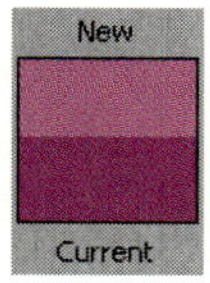

As you can see in the New and Current sample boxes, the new color is much brighter and gives the slide the look you want. You can apply the different color scheme to just one slide in your presentation or to all the slides. To apply the new color to all the slides,

- Click OK.
- Click Apply to All.
- To see how the changes you have made look when the slide is full screen, run the slide show.

> The same procedure is used to change the colors of any other elements on the template.

Expanding Slides

As you looked at the slides, you noticed that slide 6 with the new information on the competition contains too much information. You want to break the information into separate slides. You could do this in Outline view by changing the levels of heads to create two separate slides. Another way is to use the Expand Slide feature to create separate slides for each paragraph on the slide. To use this feature,

- Select slide 6.
- Choose Tools/Expand slide.
- If necessary, scroll the window to see slides 7 and 8.

Your screen should be similar to Figure 2-8.

FIGURE 2-8

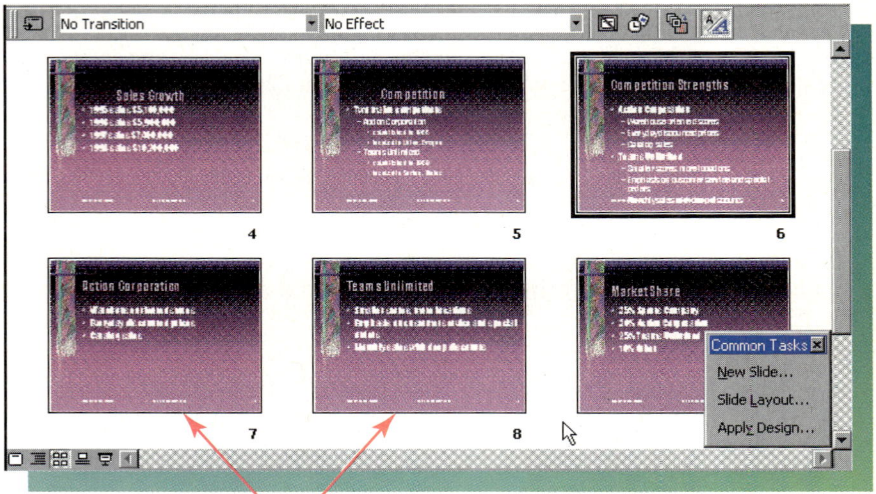

expanded slides

Two new slides, 7 and 8, have been created, one for each paragraph in slide 6. Slide 6 is unchanged.

- Since you no longer need slide 6, delete it.

Modifying Attributes

Also while viewing the slide show, you noticed many slides had a lot of blank space. You want to reduce the amount of blank space by increasing the font size on all the slides. You also think the slide appearance could be improved by using different effects to enhance the text attributes.

Concept 2: Attributes

An **attribute** is a feature associated with an object or text that can be enhanced using drawing tools and menu commands. Text attributes can be enhanced by applying different styles and effects to the text to add impact or interest. Fonts and font size are two basic text attributes. Other text attributes are text color and style. **Style** refers to text attributes such as bold and italics. You can also apply special effects such as shadows and embossed text effects to text. Object attributes that can be manipulated are the object's line style, fill, shadow, color, and shape. Examples of text attributes and object attributes that have been enhanced are shown below.

Text

Object

In a well-designed presentation, the use of different attributes enhances the presentation. However, too many different attributes may clutter and detract from the content rather than enhance the presentation.

First you will eliminate some of the blank space on the slides by increasing the font size. Although you can change each slide individually as you did in Lab 1, you can make the change much faster to all the slides by changing the slide master.

Concept 3: Master

A **master** is a special slide or page on which the formatting for all slides or pages in your presentation is defined. Each component of a presentation—title slide, slides, note pages, and handout pages—has a corresponding master. The master contains formatted placeholders for the titles, main text, footnotes, background elements, and so on that appear on each associated slide or page. Any changes you make to a master affect all slides or pages associated with that master. The four masters are described below.

Master	Function
Slide Master	Defines the format and placement for the title and body text as well as the background art for each slide in a presentation.
Title Master	Defines the format and placement of titles and text for slides that use the title layout.
Handout Master	Defines the format and placement of the slide image, text, headers and footers, and other elements that are to appear on every audience handout.
Notes Master	Defines the format and placement of the slide image, note text, headers and footers, and other elements that are to appear on all speaker notes.

If you modify the text color, font style, or size for slide titles on the slide master, all slides in the presentation will change accordingly. Likewise, if you add a graphic such as a company logo to the slide master, it appears on every slide. However, if you modify the format or layout of the title master, only those slides you have designated as title slides in your presentation will change. When you apply a new design template to a presentation, all slides and masters are updated to those of the new design template.

You can create slides that differ from the master by changing the format and placement of elements in the individual slide rather than on the master. For example, when you change the font of a title on a single slide, the slide master is not affected. Only the individual slide reflects the change, making it unique. If you have created a unique slide, the elements you changed on that slide retain their uniqueness even if you later make changes to the slide master, including changing the design template.

Using the master to modify or add elements to a presentation ensures consistency and saves time.

Each master is displayed in its own view. To display the slide master,

- Choose View/Master/Slide Master.

You also can hold down Shift and click the Slide View button to display the slide master.

Your slide master should be similar to Figure 2-9.

FIGURE 2-9

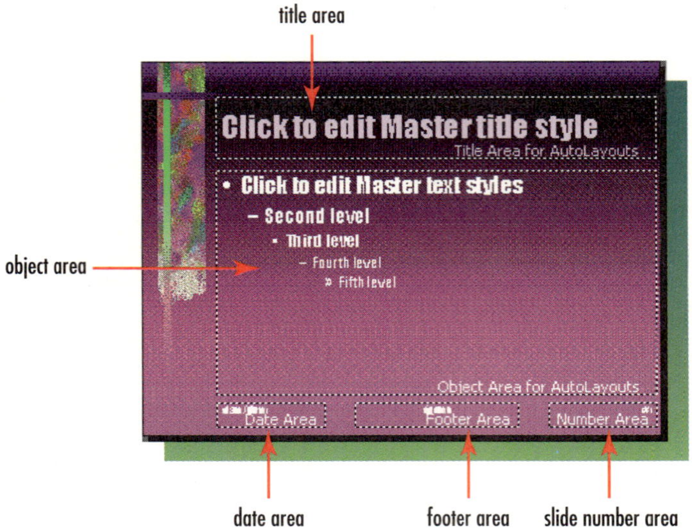

The Master toolbar may also be displayed.

The slide master consists of five placeholders that control the appearance of all slides. Each placeholder displays sample text to show you how changes you make in these areas will appear. First you will increase the size of the title text from 44 to 54 points.

- Click on the title area.
- Use the 44 Font Size button to increase the font size to 54.

Next you want to change the title text color. Color is one of many attributes that can be modified to enhance the appearance of text or objects.

- Click A Font Color.

The More Font Colors option opens the standard color palette.

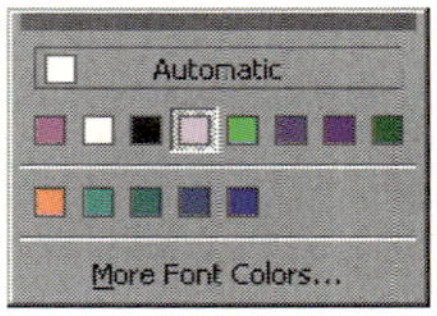

Thirteen colors that are coordinated with your selected color scheme are displayed in the drop-down list.

- Select lime green.

Your slide should be similar to Figure 2-10.

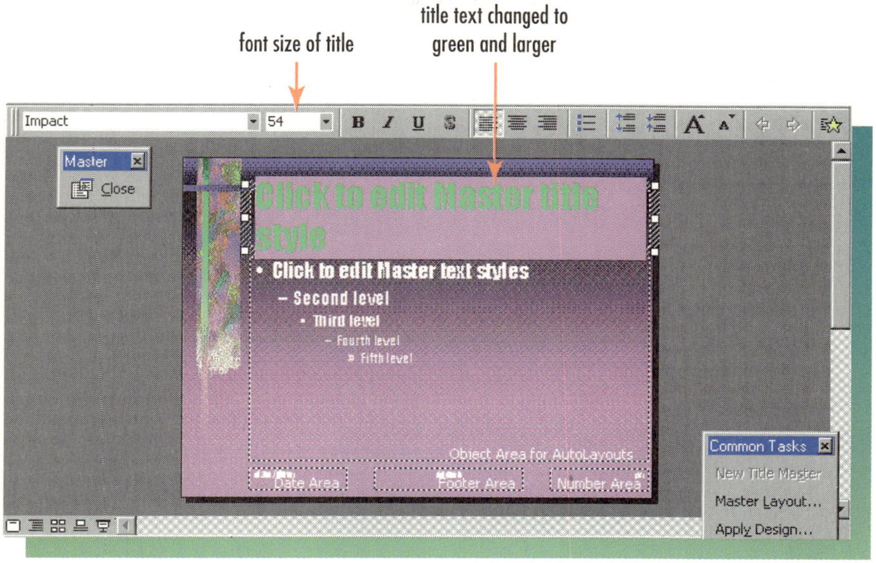

FIGURE 2-10

Next you want to increase the size of the bulleted text in the object area.

- Click the first-level head in the object area and increase the font size from 32 to 40.
- In a similar manner, increase the font size of the second-level bulleted text from 28 to 32.

Your slide master should be similar to Figure 2-11.

FIGURE 2-11

To see how the changes you have made to the slide master affected the slides,

- Click Slide Sorter View.

The point size and color changes to the title appear in all slides. The changes to the two levels of bulleted text are reflected in all slides containing those level heads.

You think the Competition slide (slide 5), which contains a lot of text, would look better if the font of the first- and second-level bulleted text was a smaller size.

- Display slide 5 in Slide view.
- Select the first-level bulleted text.

> The Increase Font Size button will increase the point size by 10 percent.

You will decrease the font size to 36 points using the Decrease Font Size button. This button will decrease the point size of the selected text in 10 percent increments.

> The menu equivalent is Format/Font/Size/32.

- Click Decrease Font Size.

Your screen should be similar to Figure 2-12.

FIGURE 2-12

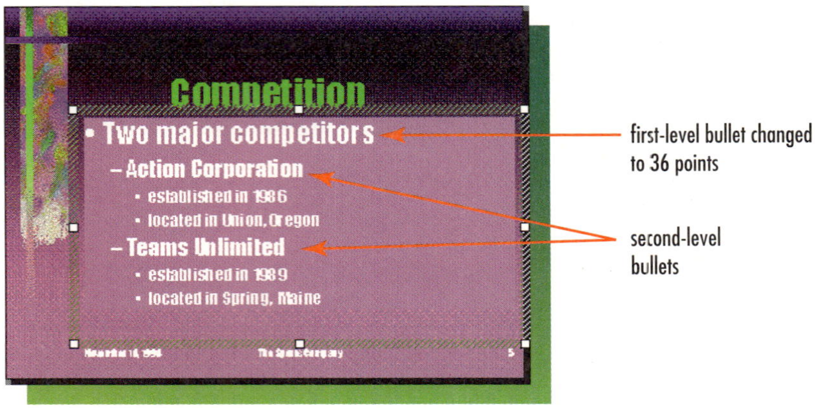

- In a similar manner, reduce the size of the two second-level bulleted items to 28 points.

The changes you have made to this slide affect the current slide only, making it a unique slide in the presentation. The slide master is not changed. If you now changed the second-level bulleted text on the slide master, the second-level text on this slide would not be affected, because changes made to an individual slide override the master slide.

Next you want to enhance the appearance of the title slide by adding a shadow and italics to the title and changing the subtitle text to a different color with a shadow using the title master.

- Display slide 1.

> The menu equivalent is View/Master/Title Master.

- Hold down ⇧Shift and click Slide View.
- Click the master title text placeholder.

Your screen should be similar to Figure 2-13.

title font style

title font size

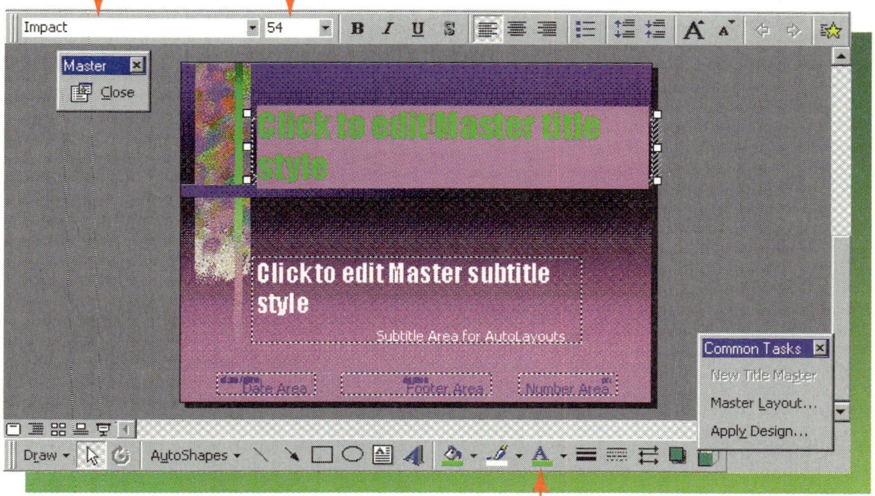

title text color

FIGURE 2-13

Notice that the title master has a slightly different appearance from the title slide in your presentation. This is because you modified the title slide in the previous lab, making it a unique slide. The unique changes you made to that slide (the font, style, point size, and location of the subtitle) were not changed to those in the title master of the Blush design template. The attributes that are applied to the title text are Impact, 54 points, with a text color of lime green. The toolbar buttons indicate these settings are in use.

A depressed button means the feature is on.

- Click Italic.
- Click Shadow.

The menu equivalent is Format/Font/Font Style/Italic/Shadow.

- In a similar manner, apply italics and a shadow to the subtitle text and change the text color to orange (first color, second row).

To see how the title slide looks with the changes you have made,

- Click Slide View.

You feel the subtitle is too large and close to the title.

- Select the subtitle text and reduce the font size to 48.
- Increase the size of the placeholder so the subtitle is displayed on a single line.
- Move the subtitle to the location shown in Figure 2-14.
- Clear the selection.

Your screen should be similar to Figure 2-14.

title text with shadow and italics

FIGURE 2-14

subtitle text with shadow and in new color

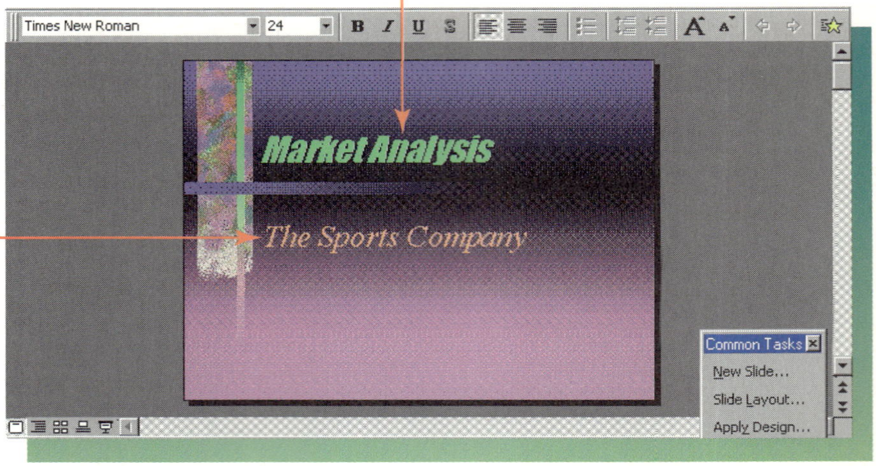

Inserting Clip Art

As suggested by the marketing department manager, you decide to add several graphic elements to the slides.

Concept 4: Graphics

Graphics are objects such as charts, drawings, pictures, and scanned photographs you can add to a presentation to provide visual interest or clarify data. Drawing objects, pictures, and clip art are all types of graphic objects.

A **drawing object** consists of shapes such as lines and boxes that can be created using the Drawing toolbar. A **picture** is an illustration created by combining lines, arcs, circles, and other shapes. It is commonly created using a graphic application such as Paint. You can also draw a picture using the features on the Drawing toolbar. Pictures created using other applications are stored as graphic files. **Clip art** refers to a collection of graphics that usually is bundled with a software application. You also can purchase clip art packages to add to your collection.

As you add objects to a document, they automatically stack in layers. When objects overlap in the layer, the top object covers a portion of objects beneath it, creating an overlapping stack. Many times this is the effect you want to achieve. Other times, however you do not want the layers to overlap. You can move and size graphic objects and change their stacking order to suit your needs. Once graphic files are inserted into a presentation, they are saved with the presentation.

Graphics files commonly have file extensions such as .wmf, .bmp, .tif, .pcx, .wpg, .pic, and .cgm.

The menu equivalent is Insert/Picture/Clip Art.

First you will add a clip art drawing to the second slide.

- Move to slide 2.
- Click Insert Clip Art.

The Microsoft Clip Gallery 3.0 dialog box on your screen should be similar to Figure 2-15.

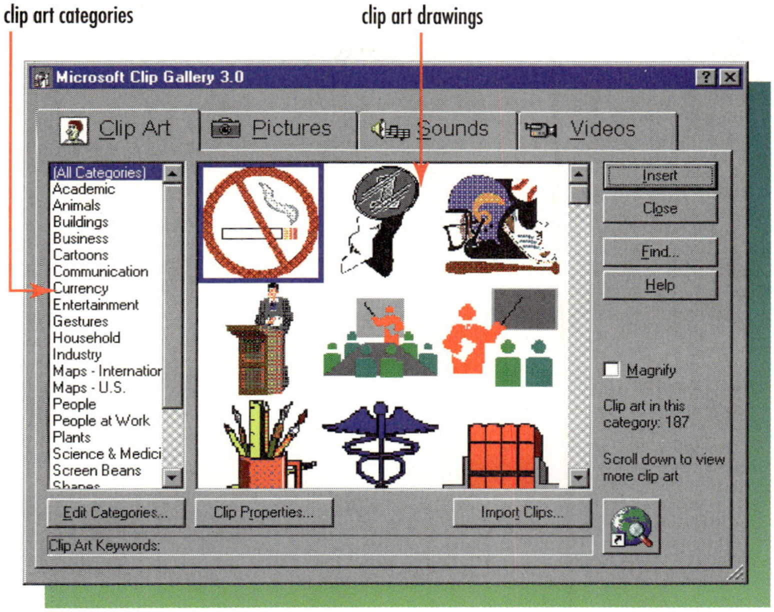

FIGURE 2-15

The categories and images in your dialog box may be different from those in Figure 2-15.

The Categories list box lists all categories of clip art images. Because the selected category is All Categories, the gallery displays images of all the clip art drawings that are available. You want to add an image to slide 2 showing leadership. To help find an image that might reflect this characteristic,

- Click Find... .

The Find Clip dialog box on your screen should be similar to Figure 2-16.

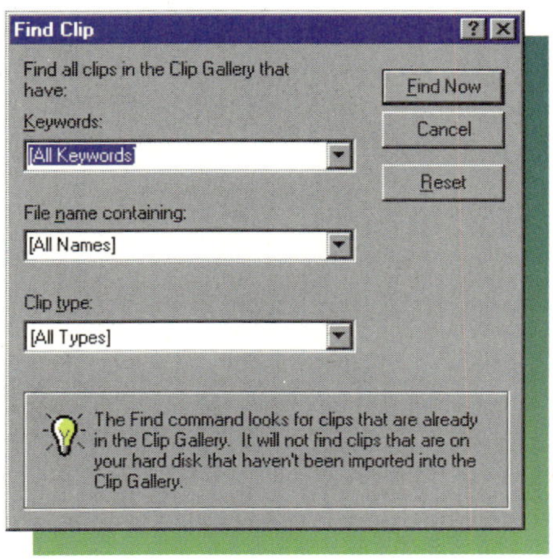

FIGURE 2-16

Each clip art image has been named and assigned several keywords that describe the content of the image. You can search for clip art by entering a keyword, or by the file name or file type. To search using a keyword,

- In the Keywords text box, type **Leadership**
- Click Find Now.

After a few moments, all clip art images that have "leadership" in their description are displayed.

Refer to Figure 2-17 to help you find the correct clip art image.

- Select .
- Click Insert.

Your slide should be similar to Figure 2-17.

FIGURE 2-17

Your image may come in a different size than shown here.

The selected clip art image is displayed on the slide, but it is not the size you want and overlaps the bulleted text. Notice that the image is displayed with handles, indicating that it is a selected object. The Picture toolbar is also automatically displayed whenever a graphic object is selected. Its buttons (identified below) are used to modify and enhance the picture object.

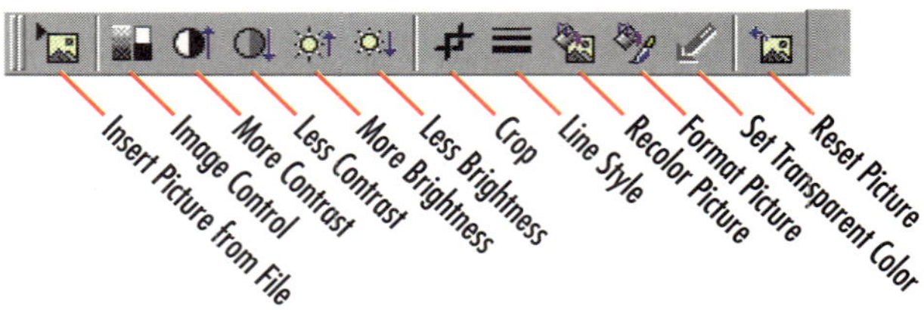

You move and size objects just like selected placeholders.

- Move and size the image until your slide is similar to Figure 2-18.
- Clear the selection.

Your slide should be similar to Figure 2-18.

moved and sized clip art image

FIGURE 2-18

Changing Slide Layout

You would also like to add a clip art drawing to slide 10. Before inserting the clip art, you would like to change the layout of this slide to make space for the clip art object. To do this,

- Display slide 10.
- Click Slide Layout... .

The menu equivalent is Format/Slide Layout.

The Slide Layout dialog box on your screen should be similar to Figure 2-19.

selected layout

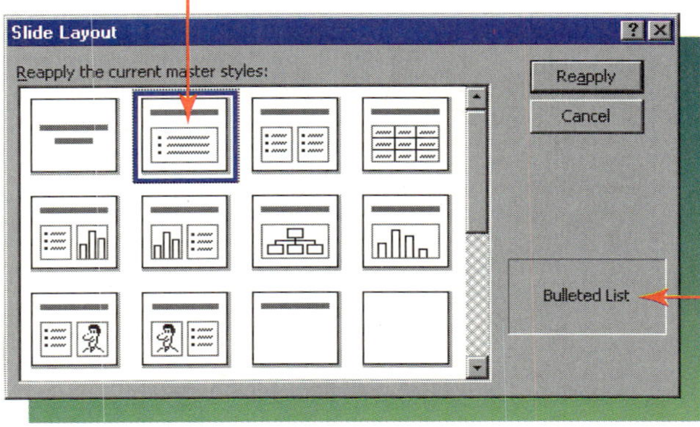

layout name

FIGURE 2-19

The current layout, Bulleted List, is selected. You want to change the layout to a style that is designed to accommodate both text and clip art.

Concept 5: AutoLayout

PowerPoint includes 24 predefined slide layouts called **AutoLayouts** that are used to control the placement of objects on a slide. For example, there is a layout that includes placeholders for a title and bulleted text, and another with placeholders for a title, text, and clip art. The title and text placeholders follow the formatting of the slide master for your presentation. You can move, resize, or reformat the layouts so they vary from the slide master.

You also can change the layout of an existing slide. If the new layout does not include placeholders for objects that are already on your slide (for example, if you created a chart and the new layout does not include a chart placeholder), you do not lose the information. All objects remain on the slide, and you can rearrange them to fit the new layout.

To make creating slides easy, use the predefined layouts. The layouts help you keep your presentation format consistent and, therefore, more professional.

To apply a new layout to the current slide,

- Select Text & Clip Art (first slide in third row).
- Choose Apply.

Your slide should be similar to Figure 2-20.

FIGURE 2-20

All the text has moved into the bullet placeholder on the left side of the slide, and a clip art placeholder has been inserted on the right. You are ready to add a new clip art image.

Refer to Figure 2-21 to help you locate the correct clip art image.

- Double-click the clip art placeholder.
- From the Categories list box, select Shapes.
- Double-click [arrow clip art].

Your screen should be similar to Figure 2-21.

clip art image inserted in place of clip art placeholder

FIGURE 2-21

By changing the slide layout before inserting the clip art, you do not need to adjust the size of the clip art and the image does not overlap any text on the slide.

Now you want to change the color of the graphic to coordinate with the other slide colors.

- Click Recolor Picture.

Recolor Picture is located on the Picture toolbar.

The Recolor Picture dialog box on your screen should be similar to Figure 2-22.

maroon shadow

red fill color

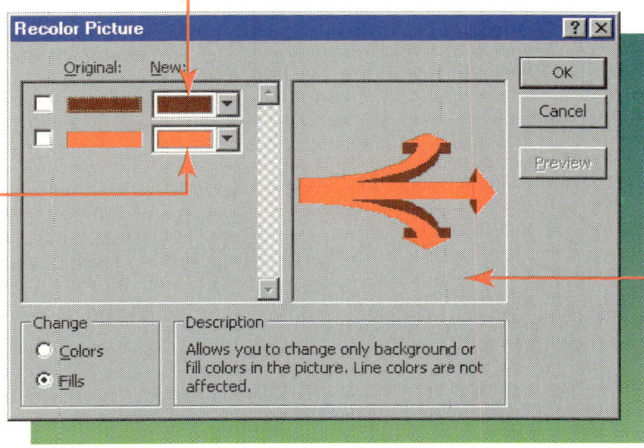

preview area

FIGURE 2-22

- Change the maroon shadow to dark green and the red fill color to lime green.

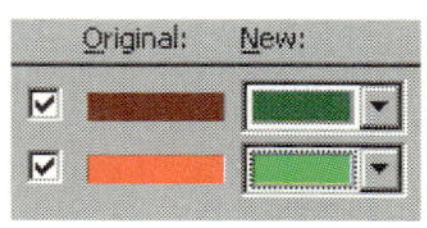

The preview area changes to match your selection. To see how the new colors look on your slide,

- Click Preview.
- Move the Recolor Picture dialog box out of the way to see the graphic on the slide.
- Click OK.
- Deselect the picture.

Note: If you are ending your session now, save the presentation as Final Marketing Presentation and exit PowerPoint. When you begin Part 2, open this file.

Part 2

Inserting a New Slide

During your discussion with the marketing department manager, it was suggested that you graphically illustrate the data on sales and market share shown in slide 4 and 9. To include this information in the presentation for the sales data, first you will insert a new slide after slide 4.

- Display slide 4.
- Click New Slide... .

The menu equivalent is **I**nsert/**N**ew Slide, and the keyboard shortcut is Ctrl + M.

The slide AutoLayout options are displayed in the New Slide dialog box. You want the slide to include a bulleted item above a graph of the sales data. Although there are layouts that include both text and graphs, these layouts place the text and graph side by side on the slide. Because you want the bulleted text to appear above the graph, you will select the Bulleted List AutoLayout and then add the graphed data to the slide.

- Double-click Bulleted List.

A new slide, 5, with title and bullet placeholders is inserted after slide 4. The new slide has the same design settings as the master slide.

- Replace the sample title text with **Sales Growth**
- Replace the bulleted item sample text with **Sales doubled in 4 years**

Your slide should be similar to Figure 2-23.

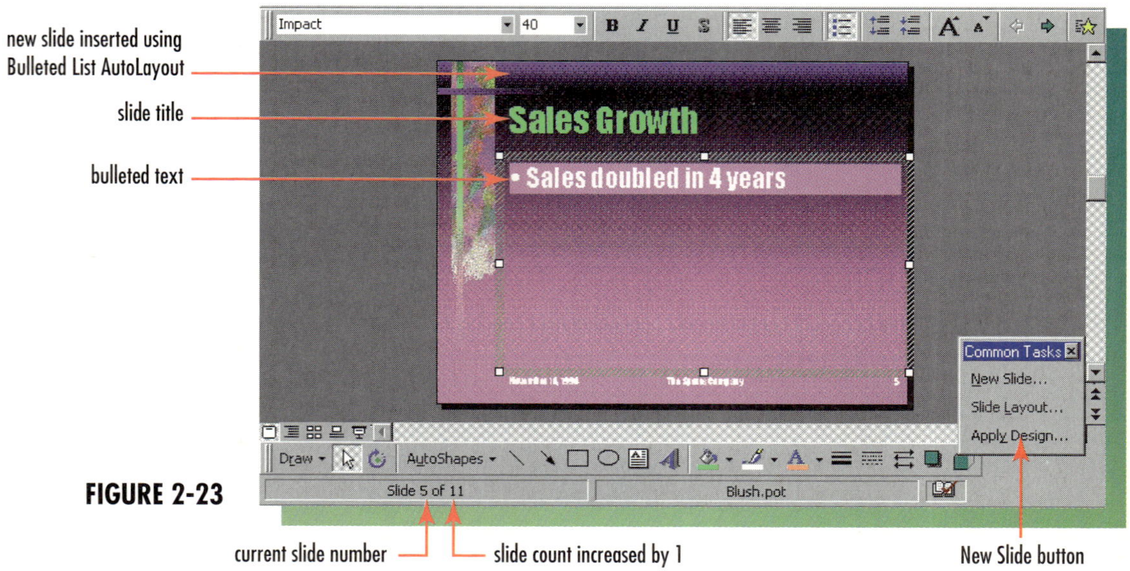

FIGURE 2-23

Creating a Chart

The new slide will visually display the data from slide 4 in the form of a chart.

Concept 6: Charts

A **chart**, also called a **graph**, is a visual representation of numeric data. When you are presenting data to an audience, they will grasp the impact of your data more quickly if you present it as a chart. PowerPoint can produce 14 types of charts with many different formats for each type. Each type of chart represents the data differently and has a different purpose. It is important to select the type of chart that will provide the right emphasis to support your presentations. The basic chart types are shown below.

Type of Chart	Description
Area chart	Shows the relative importance of a value over time by emphasizing the area under the curve created by each data series.
Bar chart	Displays the categories vertically and the values horizontally, placing more emphasis on comparisons and less on time. Stacked-bar charts are often used to compare values and totals by stacking bars on top of one another.
Column chart	Similar to a bar chart, except categories are organized horizontally and values vertically.
Line chart	Shows changes in data over time, emphasizing time and rate of change rather than the amount of change.
Pie chart	Shows the relationship of each value in a data series to the series as a whole. Each slice of the pie represents a single value in the series.

Most charts are made up of several basic parts.

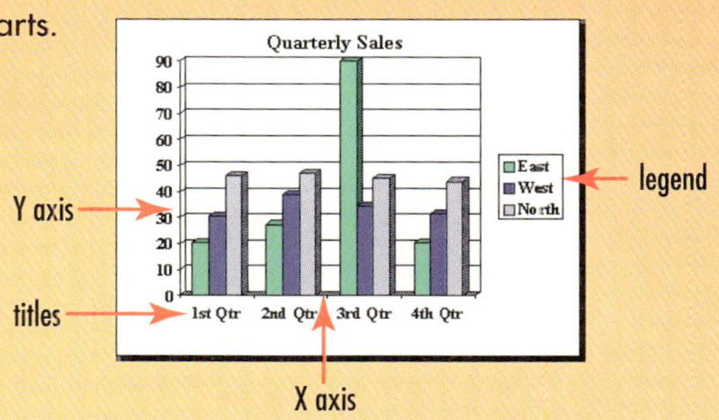

Part	Description
X axis	The bottom boundary of the chart, also called the category axis, is used to label the data being charted; the label may be, for example, a point in time or a category.
Y axis	The left boundary of the chart, also called the value axis, is a numbered scale whose numbers are determined by the data used in the chart. Each bar in the chart represents a data value. In pie charts there are no axes. Instead, the data that is charted is displayed as slices in a circle or pie.
Legend	A brief description of the symbols used in a chart.
Titles	Descriptive text used to explain the content of the chart.

> The menu equivalent is Insert/Chart.

> You can also insert a chart created in Excel.

To insert a chart, the Graph application within PowerPoint is used.

- Click Insert Chart.

Your screen should be similar to Figure 2-24.

FIGURE 2-24

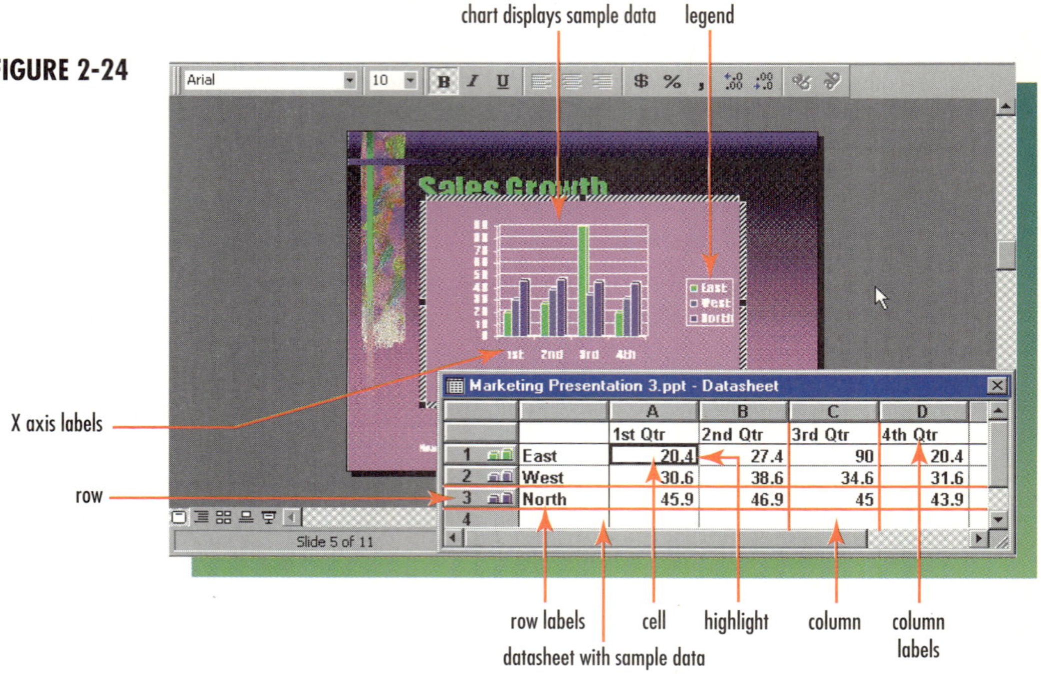

A datasheet containing sample data is displayed in the Datasheet window, and a bar chart using the sample data from the datasheet is displayed in the slide. The **datasheet** is a table consisting of rows and columns. The intersection of a row and column creates a **cell** in which text or data is entered. The cell that is surrounded by the border, called the **highlight**, is the selected cell. The selected cell is the cell you can work in.

> Drag the Datasheet window title bar to move the window.

- If necessary, move the Datasheet window to the bottom of the work area.

> The sample entries are automatically replaced when you enter new data.

To create a chart that displays the sales growth for the four years, you need to replace the sample data in the datasheet with the actual sales data. In addition to displaying sample data, the datasheet also contains placeholders for the row labels, which are used as the legend in the chart, and for the column labels, which are used as X-axis labels. First you will replace the Qtr labels with the years from slide 4. To do this you need to select the cell you want to change by moving the highlight. To move the highlight, click on the cell you want to move to or use the directional keys.

- Select the cell containing 1st Qtr.

- Type **1995**
- Press (→).
- Type **1996**
- Press (→).
- In a similar manner, change 3rd Qtr and 4th Qtr to 1997 and 1998, respectively.

Pressing any directional key completes the entry and moves the selector one cell in the direction indicated.

The chart is updated to reflect the changes as they are made to the datasheet. The years appear along the X axis. Next you will replace the East label with Sales and enter the sales data. The amounts will be entered in millions of dollars. For example, $5,100,000 will be entered as 5.1.

- Move to the cell containing East.
- Type **Sales**
- Press (→).
- Type **5.1**
- Press (→).

Notice that the datasheet displays the column letters A through D and row numbers 1 through 4. Each cell has a unique name consisting of a column letter followed by a row number. For example, cell A1 is the intersection of column A and row 1.

- Enter the rest of the data in the following cells of the datasheet:

Cell	Entry
B1	**5.9**
C1	**7.4**
D1	**10.2**

The chart reflects the change in sales data. Finally, you need to remove the remaining two rows of sample data.

- Click the row heading to the left of the West label and drag down to select row 3.
- Press (Delete).

Your screen should be similar to Figure 2-25.

FIGURE 2-25

new chart menus

Graph toolbar

chart shows sales for each year as a bar

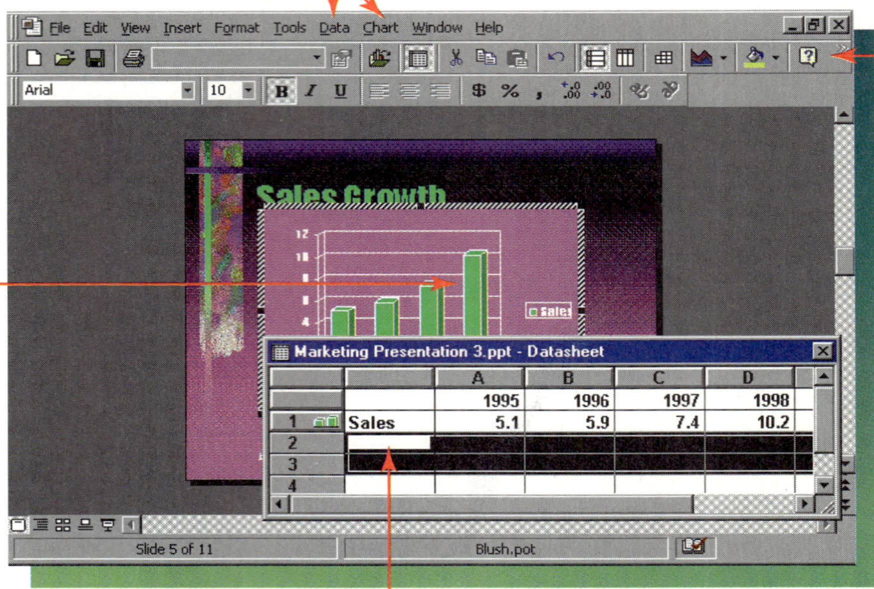

datasheet containing sales data

The sample data in rows 2 and 3 are erased, and the bar chart now displays the single set of sales data. After considering the bar chart, you feel this type of chart will not represent the sales data very well. You want to show the importance of sales over time from 1995 to 1998. You feel that an area chart would show this best. The Graph application also includes its own menus and toolbar buttons (identified below) designed to modify charts.

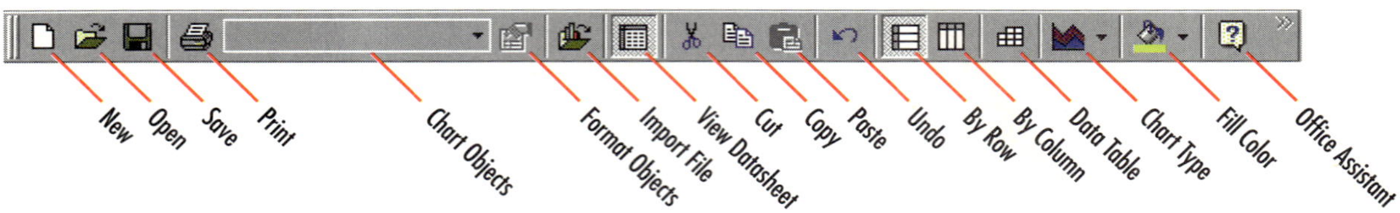

The menu equivalent is Chart/Chart Type.

You can redisplay the Datasheet window using the View menu.

- Open the Chart Type drop-down list.
- Select Area Chart.
- Close the Datasheet window.

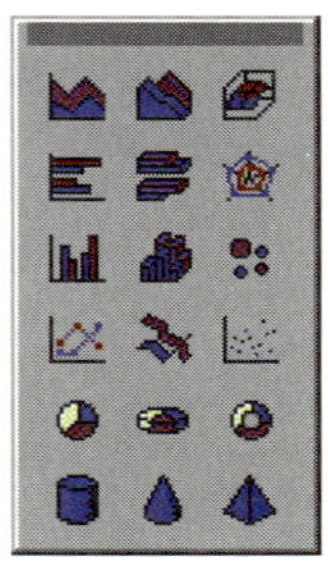

Your slide should be similar to Figure 2-26.

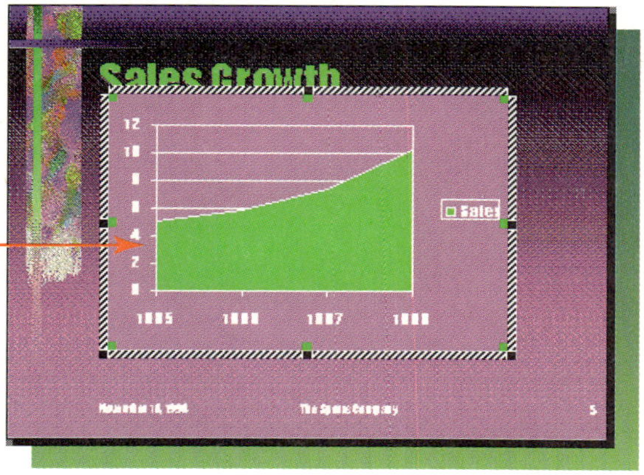

FIGURE 2-26

The Graph application is still active and the Graph menu and toolbar are still displayed, so you can continue to edit the graph. Because the chart contains only one set of data, you do not need a legend. To delete the legend from the chart,

- Click on the legend.
- Press Delete.

The Chart/Chart Options/Legend/Show Legend command hides and displays a chart legend.

The chart clearly shows how sales have increased over the last four years. However, it overlaps and conceals the bulleted text.

- Size and move the chart until it fits below the bulleted item.
- Clear the selection.

Your slide should be similar to Figure 2-27.

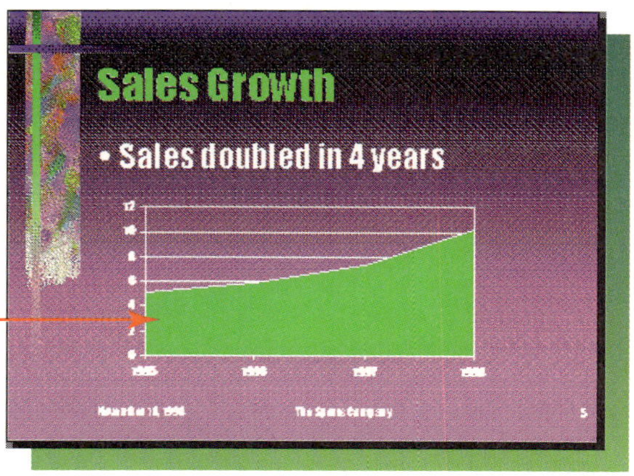

FIGURE 2-27

The Graph application is closed and you are returned to PowerPoint.

Double-clicking on the chart will open the Graph application again.

Drawing a Box

To help define the chart space, you decide to draw a box around it using the Rectangle Tool on the Drawing toolbar.

- Click Rectangle.

> If your border line is not displayed, click and select Automatic.

- Position the mouse pointer at the top left corner of the chart, and drag to create an outline box around the chart.

The graph is covered by the default fill color of the box you created. To remove the fill color,

- Open the Fill Color drop-down list.

> The menu equivalent is Format/Colors and Lines/Color/No Fill.

- Click No Fill.
- Clear the selection.

Your slide should be similar to Figure 2-28.

FIGURE 2-28

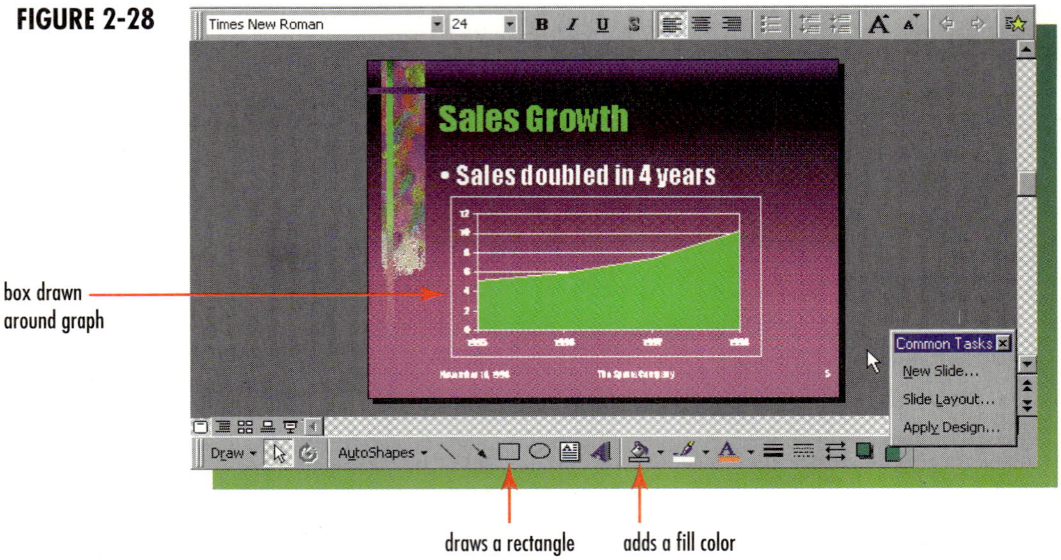

Inserting a Pie Chart

Next you want to add a chart on a new slide following slide 9 to represent the data on market share.

- Insert a new slide after slide 9 using the Text and Chart AutoLayout.
- Replace the sample title text with **Market Share**.

- Add the following two bulleted items:

  Two major competitors

  The Sports Company share is 35%

You want the graph to show the relative size of each company's market share to the total market. To do this, you will use a pie chart.

- Double-click the chart placeholder.
- Change the chart type to a pie chart.
- Update the datasheet with the data shown in the datasheet below.
- Delete the East label.
- Delete rows 2 and 3.

Marketing Presentation 3.ppt - Datasheet

		A	B	C	D
		Sports	Action	Teams	Other
1	Pie 1	35	30	25	10
2					
3					
4					

The datasheet now contains all the information for the pie chart.

- Close the Datasheet window and clear the selection.

The default label Pie 1 will appear in the datasheet window.

Your slide should be similar to Figure 2-29.

FIGURE 2-29

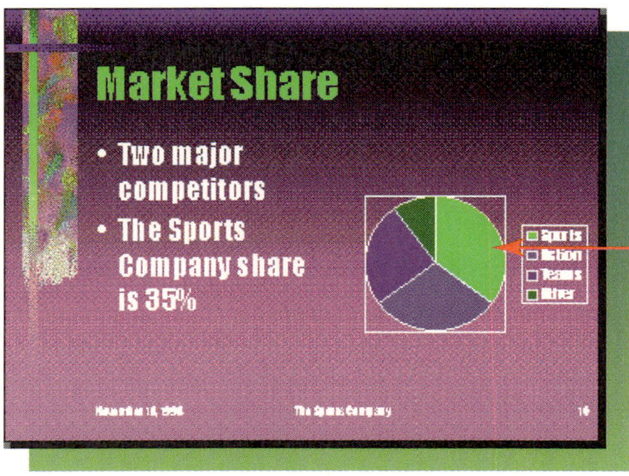

The pie chart is inserted into the slide. Now that you have completed the slide, you would like to run the slide show.

- Display slide 1, run the slide show, and view all the slides in the presentation.

Hiding Slides

Now that you have created the charts of sales growth and market share, you feel that the original slides showing the data are unnecessary. You decide to show only the charts during the presentation and to show the corresponding data slides only if requested. To do this you will hide the slides containing the data. You can hide slides in several views, but the procedure is easiest in Slide Sorter view.

- Switch to Slide Sorter View.

> If the Slide Sorter toolbar is not displayed, select it from the toolbar Shortcut menu.

Slide Sorter view also has its own toolbar, replacing the Formatting toolbar. While using this view, the buttons in the toolbar (identified below) help you perform many tasks.

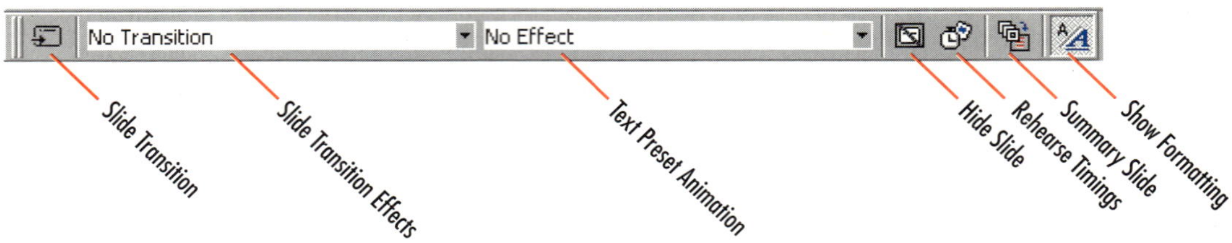

First you want to move slide 4 (with the data) to follow slide 5 (with the chart). Then you will hide the slide that contains the data.

> Drag the slide to move it.

> The menu equivalent is Sli**d**e Show/**H**ide Slide.

- Move slide 4 to follow slide 5.
- Click Hide Slide.

Notice that the slide number for slide 5 is surrounded by a box with a slash drawn through it. This indicates that the slide is hidden.

- In a similar manner, reverse the order of slides 9 and 10 and hide slide 10.

You will run the slide show next to see how the hidden slides work.

- Select slide 1 and run the slide show until the fourth slide (Sales Growth with area chart) is displayed.

Because the next slide, 5, is the hidden slide, it will not be displayed when you continue the slide show.

- Display the next slide.
- Continue the slide show until slide 9 (Market Share with chart) is displayed.

> The command to display a hidden slide is Go/Hidden Slide on the Shortcut menu. H is the keyboard shortcut.

The next slide is the hidden slide of Market Share data. To see the hidden slide,

- Press H.
- Continue the slide show until you are returned to Slide Sorter view.

Adding Transition Effects

Now that all the slides are created, you would like to use some of PowerPoint's special effects to enhance the on-screen presentation.

Concept 7: Special Effects

There are several special effects you can add to an on-screen presentation. Slide transitions, build slides, and animation are three commonly used special effects.

Transitions control how one slide moves off the screen and the next one appears. There are many different transition choices from which you can select. You may choose Dissolve for your title slide to give it an added flair. After that, you could use Wipe Right for all the slides until the next to the last and then use Dissolve again to end the show. As with any special effect, use slide transitions carefully.

Builds are used to display each bullet point, text, paragraph, or graphic independently of the other text or objects on the slide. You set up the way you want each element to appear (to fly in from the left, for instance) and whether you want the other elements already on the slide to dim or shimmer when a new element is added. For example, if your audience is used to reading from left to right, you could design your build slides so the bullet points fly in from the left. Then, when you want to emphasize a point, bring a bullet point in from the right. That change grabs the audience's attention.

Animation adds action to text and graphics so they move around on the screen. You can assign sounds to further enhance the effect.

When you present a slide show, the content of your presentation should take center stage. You want the special effects you use, such as builds, transitions, and animation, to help emphasize the main points in your presentation—not draw the audience's attention to the special effects.

The first enhancement you would like to make is to add a transition effect to the slides.

- If necessary, select slide 1.
- Click Slide Transition.

The menu equivalent is Slide Show/Slide Transition.

The Slide Transition dialog box on your screen should be similar to Figure 2-30.

FIGURE 2-30

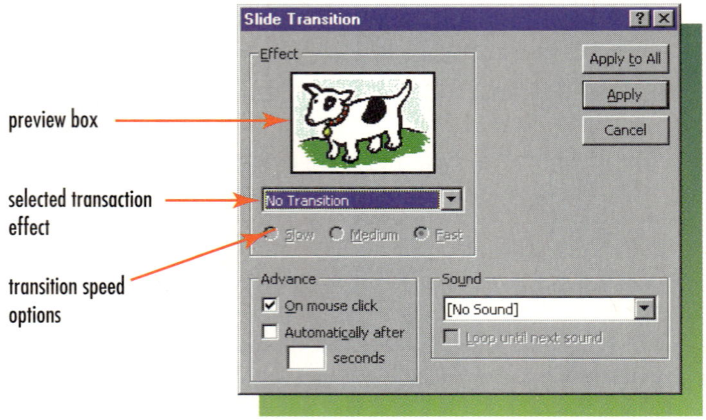

> You can vary the speed of each transition using the three-speed option.

- Open the Effect drop-down list.

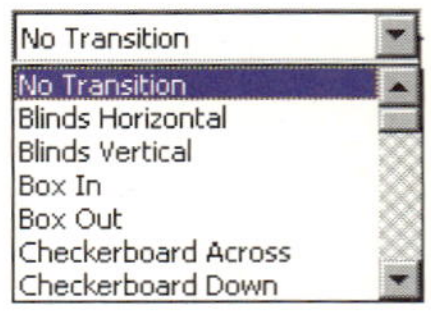

The Effect drop-down list box displays the names of the transition effects that can be used on the slides. Currently No Transition is selected. To see how a transition works, watch the preview box as you select the first effect, Blinds Horizontal.

> Using ↑ and ↓ to move the highlight in the list box selects the effect and leaves the list open so you can preview others.

- Press ↓.
- Select a few of the other transition effects to see how they work.

You decide to try the Wipe Right transition effect on this slide.

> You can click the Preview box to watch the selected transition effect again when the Effect list is closed.

- Select Wipe Right.
- Click Apply.

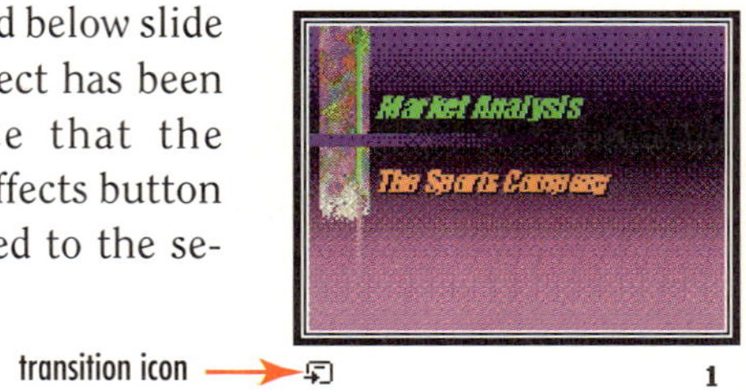

Notice the transition icon displayed below slide 1. This indicates that a transition effect has been applied to the slide. Also notice that the Wipe Right Slide Transition Effects button displays the name of the effect applied to the selected slide.

You feel this transition was not very noticeable, and instead decide to use the Random Transition effect, which will randomly select different transition effects to use. To select and change all the slides at once,

- Choose Edit/Select All.

> The keyboard shortcut is Ctrl + A.

- Click [Wipe Right] Slide Transition Effects.

> Using the Slide Transition Effects button does not display the Slide Transition dialog box and it cannot be used to preview the effects.

- Choose Random Transition (last option in drop-down list).

The transition icon now appears below each slide, indicating that a transition effect has been applied to all slides.

Adding Build Effects

The next effect you want to add to the slides is a build to progressively display each bullet on a slide. When a build is applied to a slide, the slide initially shows only the title. The bulleted text appears as the presentation proceeds. A build slide can also include different build transition effects, which are similar to slide transition effects. The effect is applied to the bulleted text as it is displayed on the slide.

> You cannot preview build effects.

You would like to add a build to all slides in the presentation except slides 1, 4, and 9. Because all slides are still selected, you need to deselect the three slides only. To do this, hold down ⇧Shift while clicking on the slide.

> You can select and deselect multiple slides by holding down ⇧Shift while making your selection.

- Deselect slides 1, 4, and 9.

Now, to add a build to all the selected slides and use the Fly From Left build transition effect,

- Click [No Effect] Text Preset Animation.
- Choose Fly From Left.

The Build icon is displayed below the selected slides, indicating they are build slides. The Text Build Effects button shows the selected build effect.

> You can also use the Preset Animation and Custom Animation options on the Slide Show menu to add sound build effects. To use this option, you must be in Slide view.

Now that you have added the transition and build, you would like to see how they affect the slide show.

- Select slide 1 and run the slide show.

The first slide is displayed using a randomly selected transition effect.

- Move to the next slide.

The second slide is displayed without the bulleted items. When a build is applied to a slide, the bulleted items are displayed only when you click or press Spacebar. This allows the presenter to focus the audience's attention and to control the pace of the presentation. The build effect displays the bulleted text using any one of the build transition effects. As you continue to display bulleted items, different build effects will be used.

- To display the first bulleted item, click or press Spacebar.

Your screen should be similar to Figure 2-31.

FIGURE 2-31

first bulleted item

- Click or press Spacebar until you have viewed the entire presentation.

You are returned to Slide Sorter view.

The last change you would like to make to the presentation is to add a final slide to mark the end.

- Select slide 12 and insert a new slide using the Title Slide AutoLayout.
- Switch to Slide view.
- Enter the slide title **The Sports Company Market Analysis**
- Reduce the point size of Market Analysis to 48.
- Click Center.
- Enter the slide subtitle text **The End**
- Click Center.
- Clear the selection.

Your screen should be similar to Figure 2-32.

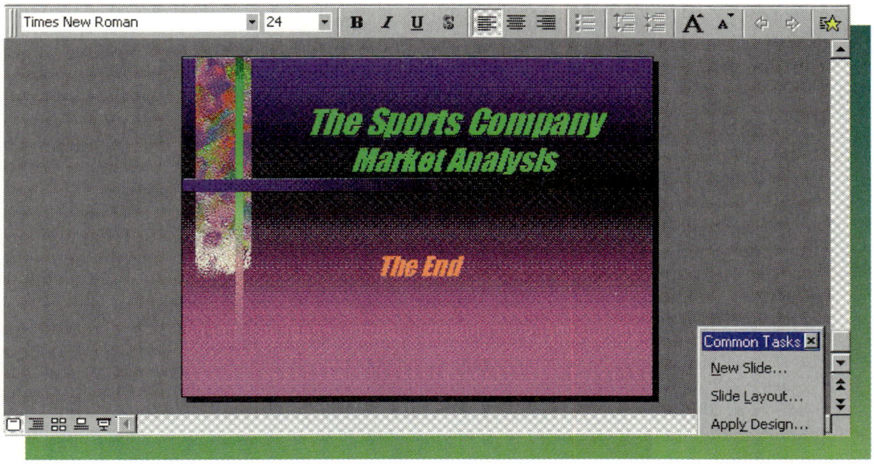

FIGURE 2-32

The changes you made to the title master slide are reflected in the new title slide. The changes you made to this slide however, do not change the master.

Controlling the Slide Show

Now that you have made the layout changes to the presentation, you decide to run the slide show again from the beginning. If you were rehearsing the presentation, you could use the Rehearse Timings option on the Slide Show menu. It records the time you spend on each slide as you practice your narration. If your computer is set up with a microphone, you could even record your narration with the Record Narration option.

- Move to slide 1 and start the slide show. View the first three slides.

Slide 4 should be displayed. As much as you would like to control a presentation, the presence of an audience usually causes the presentation to change course. PowerPoint has several ways you can control a slide show during the presentation. If someone has a question about a previous slide, you can go backward. For example,

- Press Backspace.

You also can select Previous from the shortcut menu or type P to go back a slide.

You return the on-screen presentation to slide 3. But now, because the audience already viewed slide 4, you want to advance to slide 5. To go to a specific slide number, you type the slide number and press ←Enter.

You also can choose Go/Slide Navigator from the Shortcut menu to select a slide to move to.

- Type **5**
- Press ←Enter.

Slide 5 is displayed.

- Display the four bulleted items.

Sometimes an audience member may get the entire presentation off track. If you find yourself on another topic altogether, you can black out the screen. To do this,

You can also choose Screen/Black Screen from the Shortcut menu.

- Press B.

The screen goes to black while you address the topic. When you are ready to proceed with the presentation, to bring the slide back,

- Press B.

Adding Freehand Annotations

During your presentation, you may want to point to an important word, underline an important point, or draw checkmarks next to items that you have covered. To do this you can use the mouse pointer during the presentation.

- To display the mouse pointer, move the mouse pointer on the screen.

In its current shape, you can use the mouse pointer to point to items on the slide. You can also use it to draw on the screen by changing the pointer to a pen, which activates the freehand annotations feature.

You can also click the button that appears in the lower left corner of the slide when you move the mouse to open the Shortcut menu.

- Right-click to display the Shortcut menu.
- Choose Pen.

The keyboard shortcut is Ctrl + P.

The mouse pointer changes to a 🖉. To see how the freehand annotation feature works, you will underline the 1998 sales value. To draw, you drag the pen pointer in the direction you want to draw.

To draw a straight line, hold down ⇧Shift while dragging.

- Move the mouse pointer under the $ in $10,200,000.
- Drag the pen pointer until an underline is drawn.

Your screen should be similar to Figure 2-33.

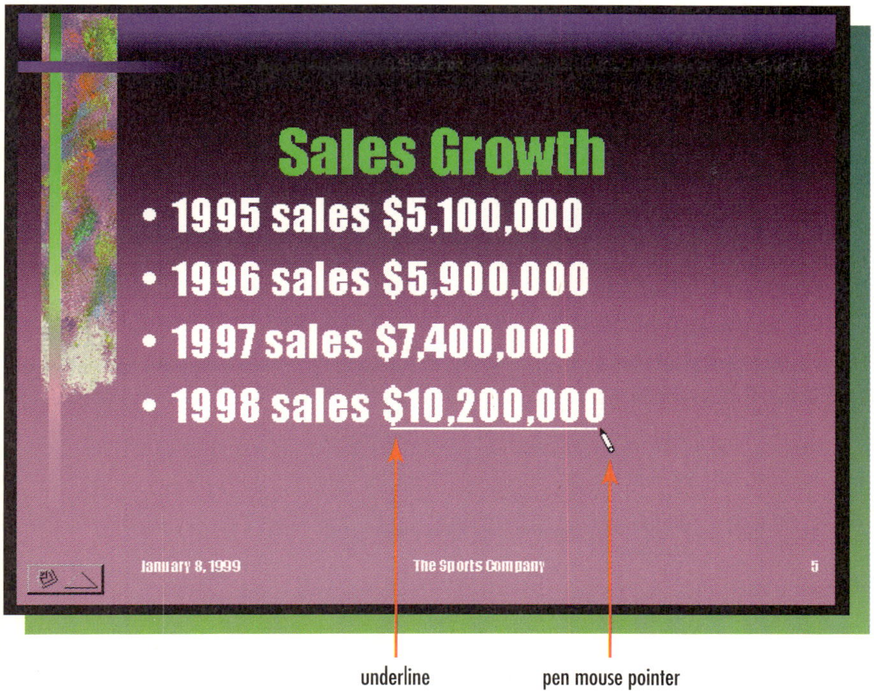

FIGURE 2-33

- Practice using the freehand annotator to draw any shapes you want on the slide.

You can also erase annotations by selecting Screen/Erase Pen from the Shortcut menu. The keyboard shortcut is E.

You do not have to be concerned about cluttering your slides with freehand annotations because any freehand drawings are erased when you continue the presentation.

- To turn off the freehand annotation feature, select Arrow from the Shortcut menu.

The keyboard shortcut is Ctrl + A.

The mouse pointer shape returns to the arrow pointer.

- Continue running the slide show to view the rest of the presentation until you are returned to slide 1 in Slide view.

Creating Speaker Notes

When making your presentation, there are some critical points you want to be sure to discuss. To help you remember the important points, you can use speaker **notes pages**. These pages show a miniature of the slide and provide an area to enter notes. You can create notes pages for some or all of the slides in a presentation. Notes pages can also be used to remind you of hidden slides. You decide to create speaker notes for the charts in slides 4 and 9.

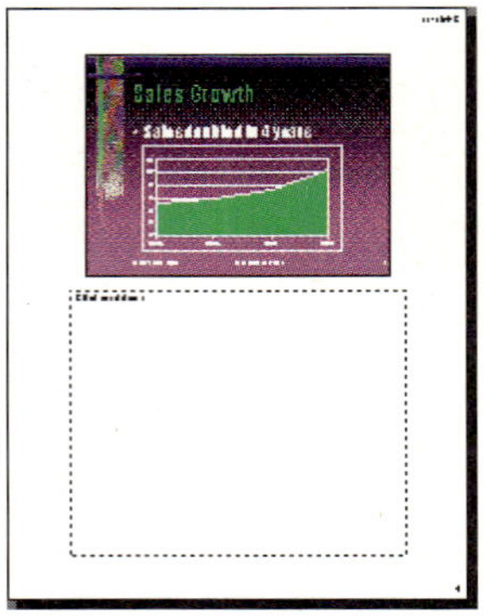

- Display slide 4.
- Click Notes Page View.

> The menu equivalent is View/Notes Page.

The top of the page displays the slide, and the lower part is a text box that is used to enter speaker notes.

- Click in the Notes text box.

Notice that the Font Size button shows the current font size is 12 points. To make the speaker notes easy to read in a dimly lit room while you are making the presentation, you would like to use a larger type size. While entering the text, you will also increase the screen magnification to make it easier to see the text as you type.

- Increase the font size to 24.
- Open the 28% Zoom control drop-down list.
- Select 75%.

> The menu equivalent is View/Zoom.

- Type **1. The chart shows the growth in sales in millions of dollars.**
- Press ←Enter.
- Type **2. Sales increased from $5,100,000 in 1995 to $10,200,000 in 1998.**
- Press ←Enter.
- Type **3. Show the hidden slide next to see the sales data.**

Your screen should be similar to Figure 2-34.

FIGURE 2-34

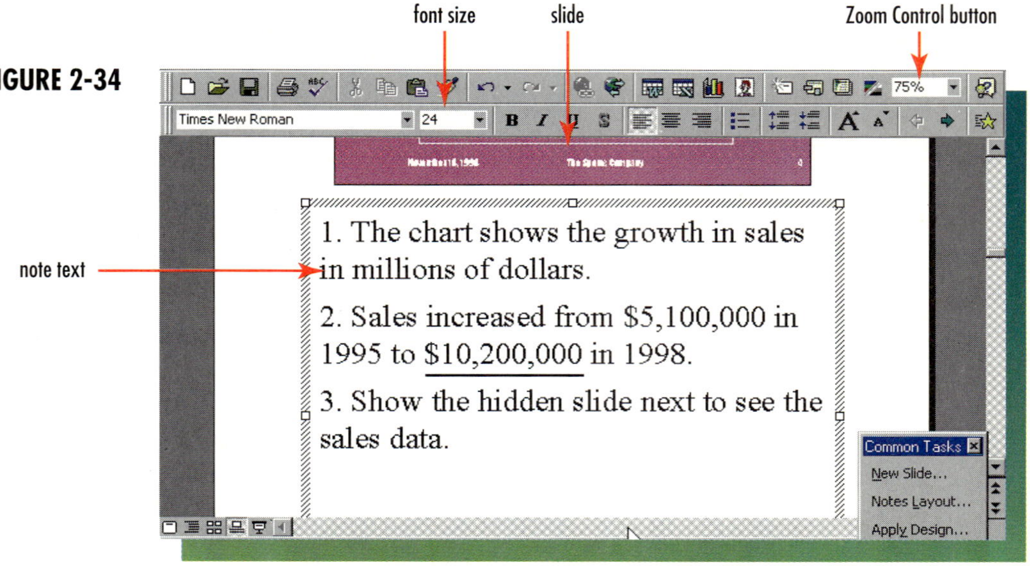

You would also like to add speaker notes for slide 9.

- Move to Notes: 9 Market Share.
- Select the notes text box and set the font size to 24.
- Enter the following text for this notes page:

  1. **Show the hidden slide next to see the data.**
  2. **The Sports Company has been increasing steadily: 29% in 1995, 30% in 1996, 32% in 1997, and 35% in 1998.**

- Set the zoom control to Fit and switch to Slide Sorter view.

You move in Notes Page view just as in Slide view.

Checking the Presentation

Before printing the presentation, you want to use the Style Checker to make a final check for typing errors and for visual clarity.

- Choose Tools/Style Checker.

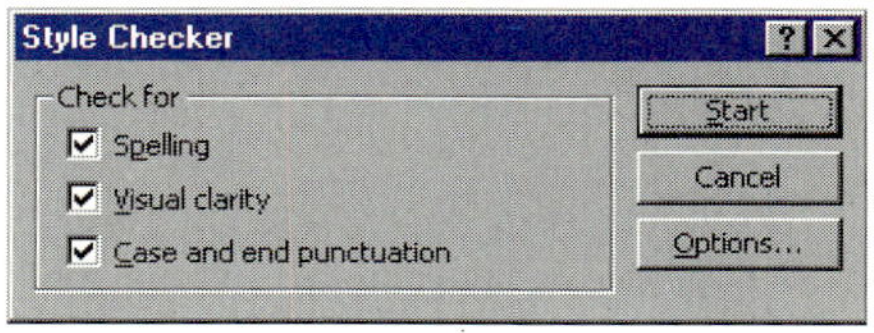

To see more details on what the Style Checker looks for,

- Click Options....

To return all the options to their original default settings,

- Click Defaults.

The Style Checker Options dialog box on your screen should be similar to Figure 2-35.

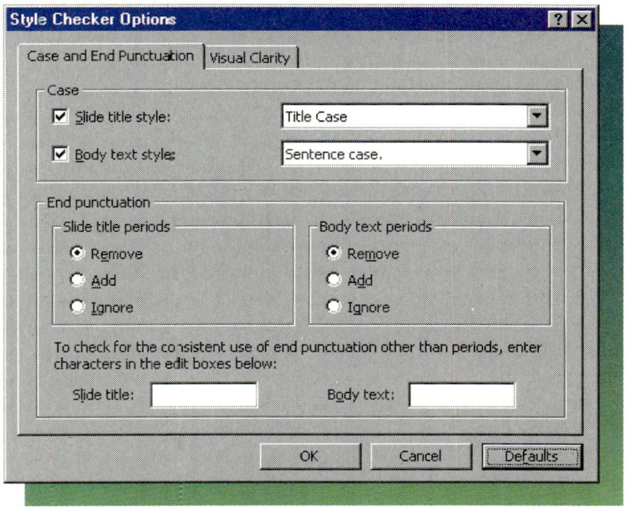

FIGURE 2-35

Notice that the default slide design uses Title Case (first letter of each word is capitalized) for slide titles and Sentence case (first letter of sentence is capitalized) for body text. No end punctuation is used. However, leaving the body text style option selected will change proper names to lowercase. To turn off this option,

- Select Body text style.
- Open the Visual Clarity tab.

Examine the Visual Clarity settings. The default settings use guidelines for proper slide design. The font size is large, the number of fonts used is small, and the amount of text on a slide is limited. All these settings help you adhere to good slide design. To run the style-check,

- Click OK.
- Click Start.

The Style Checker checks each slide in your presentation. If any words are misspelled, it stops so you can make the corrections.

- Correct any words that are spelled incorrectly.

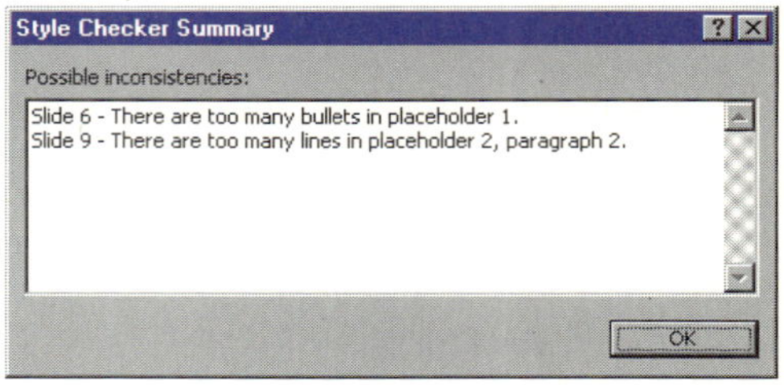

The Style Checker Summary dialog box shows that slide 6 exceeds the number of recommended bullets and slide 9 exceeds the recommended number of lines.

- Click OK.
- Switch to Slide view and display slide 6.

This slide did not meet the visual clarity standards because there are seven bulleted items and the recommended maximum is six. The Visual Clarity settings are guidelines for good design. You can use your own judgment in deciding whether to change a slide or not. You feel this slide is acceptable.

- View slide 9.

The last bullet in this slide contains three lines of text and the recommended maximum is two. Again, you feel this slide looks good.

The view you are in when saving the file is the view that will be displayed when the file is opened.

- Save the completed presentation file as Final Marketing Presentation.

Printing Selected Slides and Handouts

You have created both slides and notes pages for the presentation. To print the notes pages on which you entered text,

If necessary, select the appropriate printer for your system.

- Choose File/Print/Print what/Notes Pages.
- From the Print Range area, select Slides.
- Type **4,9**

The comma is used to identify individual page numbers. If you wanted to print notes pages 4 through 9, you would use a hyphen to separate the page numbers.

- Click OK.

The notes pages should be printing. Next you will print a few selected slides to be used as handouts.

- Choose File/Print/Print what/Handouts (three slides per page).
- Select Slides.
- Type **1,2,4**

To scale the slides to fit the paper in your printer, and to add a thin border around the slides as a frame,

- Select Scale to Fit Paper.
- If necessary, select Frame Slides.
- Click OK.
- If you are done working for the day, close the Common Tasks toolbar and exit PowerPoint.

The Black & White print option is used to print colored slides on a black-and-white printer and is on by default.

LAB REVIEW

Key Terms

animation (PR81)
attribute (PR60)
AutoLayout (PR70)
build (PR81)
cell (PR74)
chart (PR73)
clip art (PR66)
datasheet (PR74)
design template (PR54)
drawing object (PR66)
graph (PR73)
graphics (PR66)
highlight (PR74)
legend (PR73)
master (PR61)
notes page (PR87)
picture (PR66)
style (PR60)
title (PR73)
transition (PR81)
X axis (PR73)
Y axis (PR73)

Command Summary

Command	Shortcut	Button	Action
View/Notes Page			Displays notes pages
View/Master/Slide Master	⇧Shift +		Displays slide master for current presentation
View/Master/Title Master			Displays title master for current presentation
View/Zoom		28%	Changes magnification of screen
Insert/New Slide	Ctrl + M	New Slide...	Inserts new slide
Insert/Picture/Clip Art			Inserts selected clip art on slide
Insert/Chart			Inserts chart
Format/Font/Font Style			Changes font style
Format/Slide Layout		Slide Layout...	Changes or creates a slide layout
Format/Slide Color Scheme			Changes color scheme of one or all slides in presentation
Format/Apply Design		Apply Design...	Changes appearance of slide by applying a different design template
Format/Colors and Lines			Sets the line and fill color of selected object
Tools/Style Checker			Checks spelling and slide design
Tools/Expand Slide			Creates two slides out of one
Slide Show/Preset Animation		No Effect	Adds build and animation effects
Slide Show/Slide Transition			Adds transition effects
Slide Show/Hide Slide			Hides selected slide
Chart/Chart Type			Changes chart type
Chart/Chart Options/Legend/Show Legend			Turns on/off display of legend

Matching

1. transitions	_____	**a.**	shortcut for Select All command
2. Tools/Hide Slide	_____	**b.**	the progressive display of one bulleted item at a time in a slide show
3. notes pages	_____	**c.**	datasheet intersection of column and row
4. clip art	_____	**d.**	hides selected slide
5. builds	_____	**e.**	shortcut for Insert Slide command
6. Ctrl + A	_____	**f.**	visual effects you see when you go from one slide to the next in a slide show
7. chart	_____	**g.**	professionally drawn pictures
8. Ctrl + M	_____	**h.**	predefined design settings for layout and colors
9. cell	_____	**i.**	graphic representation of data
10. design template	_____	**j.**	provides picture of slide and area for speaker notes

Hands-On Practice Exercises

Step by Step

Rating System
☆ Easy
☆☆ Moderate
☆☆☆ Difficult

☆

1. Damion is still working on his presentation on the proper way to prepare for a workout. He has had a larger sign-up for the presentation than expected and has scheduled a larger meeting room that is equipped with an on-screen projector system. He wants to make several changes to the presentation to take advantage of the new setup.

a. Open the presentation Workout created as Practice Exercise 1 in Lab 1. If necessary, switch to Slide view.

b. Change the design template to High Voltage. Select a color scheme and custom color for the background.

c. Use the title master to change the main title to Times New Roman, bold, 54 points. Change the subtitle to a point size of 40.

d. Clear the header and footer information from all slides. Add your name and the current date to the notes and handouts pages.

e. Add transitions and build effects of your choice to the slides. Run the slide show.

f. Switch to Notes Pages view. Move to note 7 and increase the font size of the note area to 24. Type the following note text:

Topic:	**Fat Analysis**
Date:	**May 16**
Time:	**7:00 PM**
Where:	**Room 327 B**

g. In Slide Sorter view, insert a new title slide at the end of the presentation for a closing slide. Add appropriate text and transition effects.

h. Check the presentation using the Style Checker; make any appropriate changes.

i. Run the slide show. Save the completed presentation as Workout Presentation.

j. Print the notes pages for slides 1 and 7. Close the presentation.

☆

2. Jason Ruskey, the promotions manager for Back-Road Bikes, wants to complete the presentation he will give to the outdoor clubs.

a. Open the presentation Back-Road Biking, created as Practice Exercise 2 in Lab 1. If necessary, switch to Slide view.

b. Change the template to Serene.

c. Change the title slide's subtitle to "Presented by [your name]."

d. Use the title master to change the font of the title slide to Ribbon 131 Bd BT and change the font size to 88. Change the subtitle to the font Ribbon 131 Bd BT, with a point size of 66. Change the text color to a color of your choice.

e. Use the slide master to change the title size to 54 and decrease the size of the second-level bullets to 24.

f. Clear the footer from all slides. Add your name and the current date to the notes and handout pages.

g. Add transitions and build effects of your choice to all the slides. Run the slide show.

h. Switch to Notes Pages view. Move to note 7 and increase the font size of the note area to 24. Type the following note text.

Mud and Muck—Tell funny story about sudden rain and hail storm last summer.

Trail Dogs—Tell funny story about wild dog and partner's reaction.

i. Insert a new title slide to the end of the presentation. Add appropriate text and transition effects.

j. Check the presentation using the Style Checker and make any appropriate changes.

k. Save the completed presentation as Back-Road Biking 2. Print the notes pages for slide 7. Print handouts (three per page) for slides 1, 7, and 10.

☆☆

3. To complete the presentation for the Parks and Recreation Department on the building of three new pools, complete the following steps.

a. Open the presentation Pool Project, created as Practice Exercise 3 in Lab 1. If necessary, switch to Slide view.

b. Change the template to Whirlpool.

c. Change the font of the title on the title master to Caslon Openface BT. Change the text color to a color of your choice.

d. Insert a new slide after slide 6 using the Chart AutoLayout option. Increase the title font to 54. Enter the title "Money for Pools."

e. Create a pie chart using the information shown below. Clear the simple data in column D.

City	Fund Raising	Needed Funds
500000	400000	300000

f. Move the chart legend to the lower right corner of the chart area. Add a box with no fill around the chart.

g. Add a sun clip art image to slide 2 (or other appropriate image of your choice). Size the image and select a fill color.

h. Switch to Notes Pages view for slide 2. Increase the font size of the note text to 20 and enter the following text:

1. **Park Central pool condemned.**
2. **City has experienced a 35% increase in pool usage.**
3. **Swimming program participation has increased by 55%.**

i. Clear the footer information from all slides. Add your name and the current date to the notes and handouts pages.

j. Insert a new title slide to the end of the presentation. Add appropriate text.

k. Check the presentation using the Style Checker and make any appropriate changes.

l. Add transition and build effects of your choice to all the slides except slide 7. Hide slide 4. Run the slide show.

m. Save the completed presentation as New Pool Project. Print the notes pages for slides 2 and 7.

☆☆☆

4. Karen Miller is ready to complete her presentation for the Future Workers of America Association.

a. Open the presentation Job Outlook, created as Practice Exercise 4 in Lab 1. If necessary, switch to Slide view.

b. Change the font of the title master to Wide Latin. Make the subtitle bold.

c. Change the font size of the bulleted items on slide 7 to 28 points.

d. Change the design template to Professional. Change the template colors to colors of your choice. Add the date to the handout pages.

e. On slide 2 insert the clip art titled Confused from the Cartoons category. Move and size the clip art appropriately.

f. On slide 3 insert the clip art Two Men Meeting at Desk from the People category. Move and size the clip art appropriately.

g. Move to slide 4. Insert a new slide using the Chart AutoLayout option. Enter the title "Hires through Recruiting 1996." Add a 3-D pie chart using the data shown below. Clear the sample data in columns C and D. Move the legend to the lower right corner of the chart area.

On-Campus	Off-Campus
73	27

h. Insert a new slide using the Chart AutoLayout option. Enter the title "Hires through Recruiting 1997." Add a 3-D pie chart using the data shown below. Move the legend to the lower right corner of the chart area.

On-Campus	Off-Campus
65	35

i. Insert a new title slide to the end of the presentation. Add appropriate text.

j. Add your name and the current date to the notes and handouts pages.

k. Add transition and build effects of your choice to all the slides except slides 1, 5, and 6. Hide the slides that contain the charts. Run the slide show.

l. Check the presentation using the Style Checker and make any appropriate changes.

m. Save the completed presentation as Job Hires. Print the handouts (three per page) for all the slides.

On Your Own

★★★

5. In this exercise you will complete the presentation for American Cruise Incorporated you started in Practice Exercise 5 of Lab 1.

Open the presentation Cruise Promotion. Enhance the appearance of the title slide. Select another design template. Include the company name American Cruise Inc. on the slides and handout pages. Add a clip art image of your choice to slides 2 and 3.

Insert a new slide as slide 6 using a layout for 60 pt bulleted text and a chart. Change the title of slide 6 to "Packages Sold" and make the font size 54. Enter the following bullets:

Bullet 1: **3rd Qtr sales declining**
Bullet 2: **4th Qtr sales soaring**

Add a chart to this slide using the data shown below.

	1st Qtr	2nd Qtr	3rd Qtr	4th Qtr
3 Day	234	200	78	356
5 Day	432	373	135	564
7 Day	346	290	164	432

Size the chart so the X-axis labels are displayed on two lines. Add a box with no fill around the chart.

Add transitions and build effects of your choice to all slides. Add a sound effect to slide 6. Include text on at least two notes pages. Save the completed presentation as Cruise Promotion 2. Print slide 6 and the two notes pages.

★★

6. To complete this problem, you must have created the presentation in Practice Exercise 6 of Lab 1. You would like to improve the appearance and add interest to your presentation on managing your weight.

Open the presentation Weight Control. Enhance the presentation by changing the slide template, changing font styles and sizes, adding clip art, and applying builds and transitions.

Create notes pages for two of the slides. Add a header to the notes and handout pages that contain your name and the current date.

Print the notes pages. Save the presentation as Weight Control 2.

Concept Summary

Enhancing a Presentation

2

Design Templates

Design templates are professionally created slide designs that can be applied to a presentation.

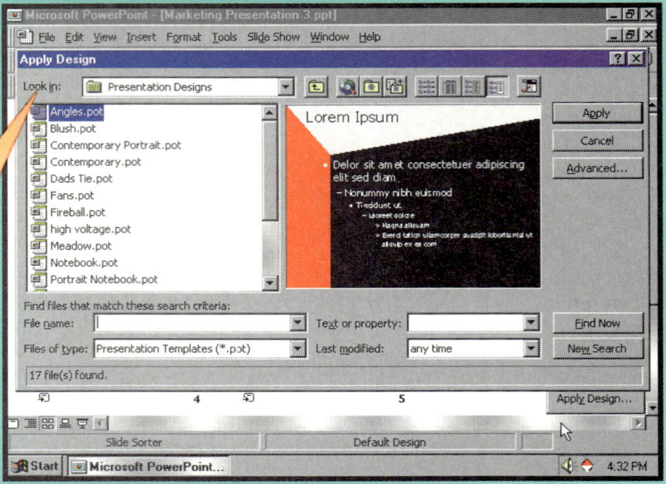

Graphics

Graphics are objects such as charts, drawings, and pictures that you can add to a presentation to provide visual interest or clarify data.

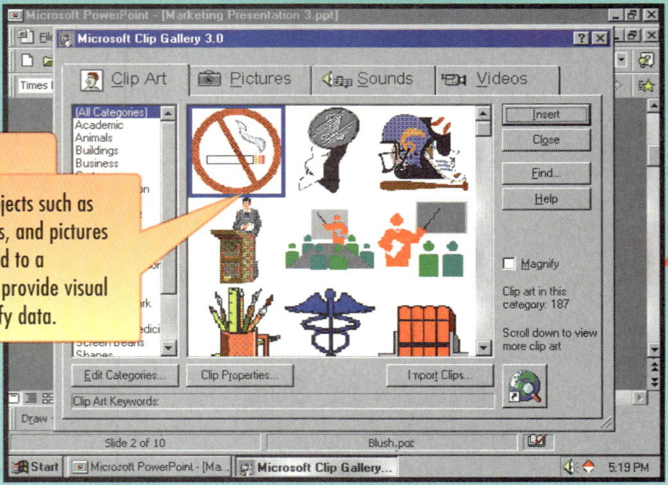

AutoLayout

PowerPoint includes 24 predefined slide layouts, called AutoLayouts, that are used to control the placement of objects on a slide.

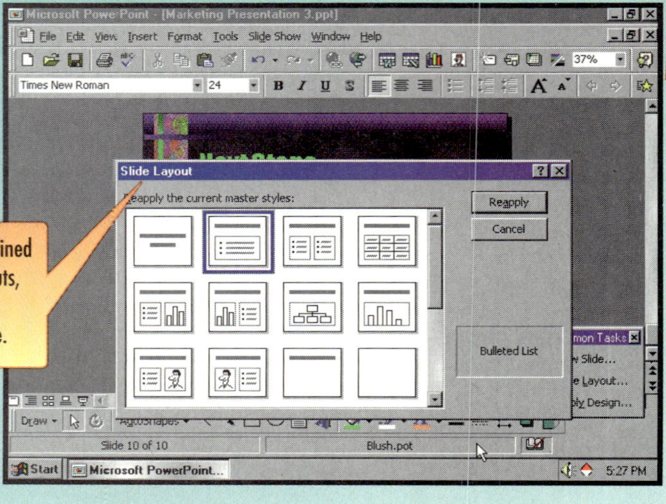

Concepts

- Design Templates
- Attributes
  Master
- Graphics
- AutoLayout
- Charts
- Special Effects

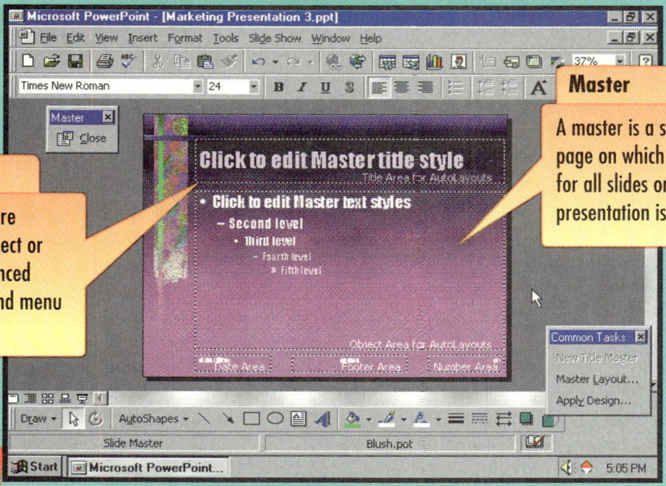

Attributes

An attribute is a feature associated with an object or text that can be enhanced using drawing tools and menu commands.

Master

A master is a special slide or page on which the formatting for all slides or pages in your presentation is defined.

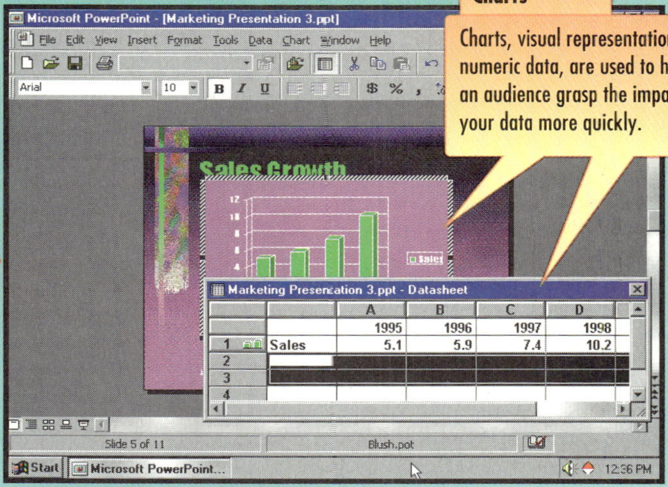

Charts

Charts, visual representations of numeric data, are used to help an audience grasp the impact of your data more quickly.

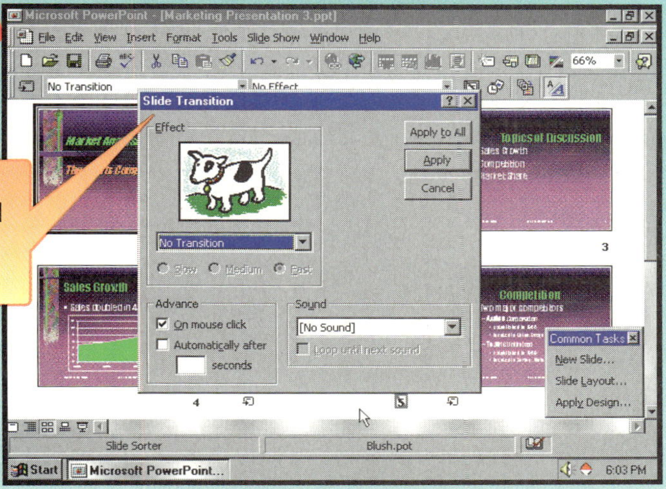

Special Effects

Special effects such as slide transitions and builds are used to enhance the on-screen presentation.

3 Sharing Information Between Applications

COMPETENCIES

After completing this lab, you will know how to:

1. **Copy between applications.**
2. **Link an Excel chart to a PowerPoint presentation.**
3. **Embed a PowerPoint presentation in a Word document.**
4. **Run a slide show from Word.**
5. **Edit an embedded object.**
6. **Break a link.**
7. **Decide when to use linking or embedding.**

CASE STUDY

The Sports Company marketing manager reviewed the PowerPoint presentation you created and has asked you to include a chart created in Excel showing sales growth by product. Frequently you will find that you will want to include information that was created using a word processor, spreadsheet, or database application in your slide show. As you will see, it is easy to share information between applications, saving you both time and effort by eliminating the need to recreate information that is available in another application.

In addition, you are asked to distribute a copy of the PowerPoint presentation on a disk to those managers who are unable to attend the meeting. Because many of the managers are not familiar with PowerPoint, you have decided to embed the presentation in a Word document so you can provide instructions for running the presentation.

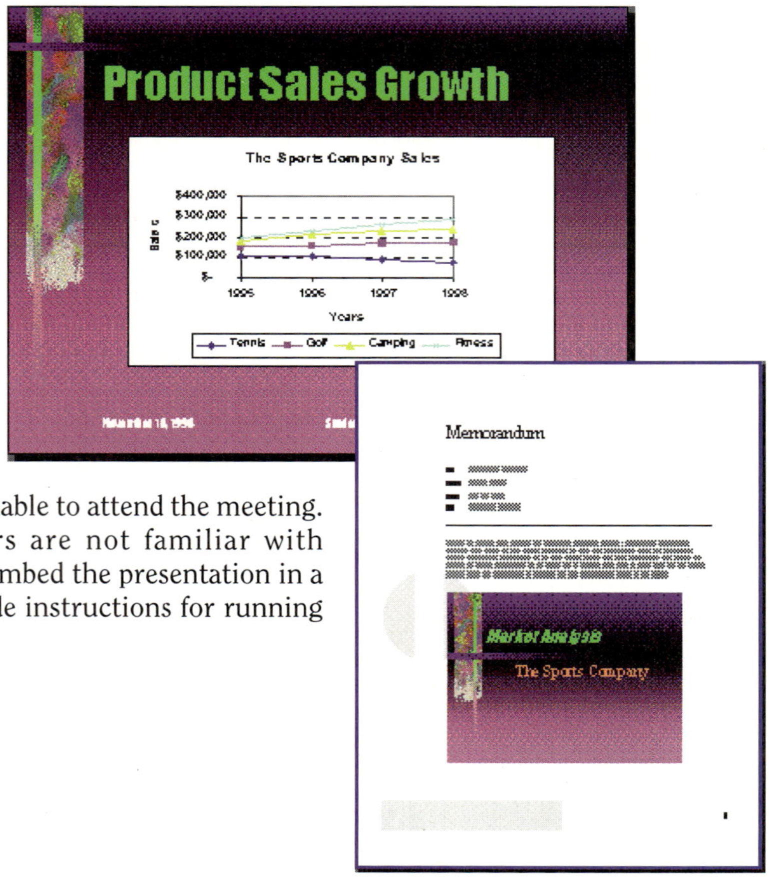

Concept Overview

The following concepts will be introduced in this lab:

1. Copy Between Applications Information can be copied between applications and, if possible, inserted in the document in a format the application can edit.

2. Linked Object Information that is copied from one file to another as a linked object maintains a connection between the two files, allowing the linked object to automatically update when the source file changes.

3. Embedded Object Information that is copied as an embedded object to a destination file created by a different application becomes part of the file and can be updated by opening the object server from within the document in which it is inserted.

Copying Between Applications

First you will modify the PowerPoint presentation to include the graph showing sales by product. You have also decided to include a hidden slide with the actual product sales data. You have revised the presentation to include these new slides.

This lab assumes that you are familiar with the Excel 97 program and how to chart data.

- Load PowerPoint 97.
- Open the file Marketing Presentation 4.
- Scroll the window to see slides 6 and 7.

Your screen should be similar to Figure 3-1.

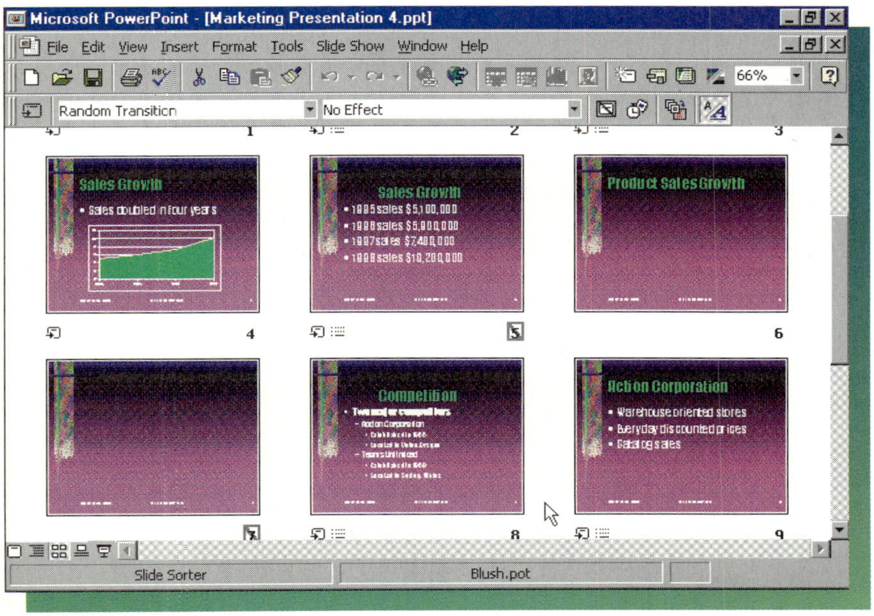

FIGURE 3-1

Slide 6 will display the chart, and slide 7, which is the hidden slide, will display the worksheet data. First you will copy the sales data from the Excel 97 file Product Sales to slide 7.

- Display slide 7 in Slide view.
- Load Excel 97 and open the file Product Sales on your data disk.

Your screen should be similar to Figure 3-2.

FIGURE 3-2

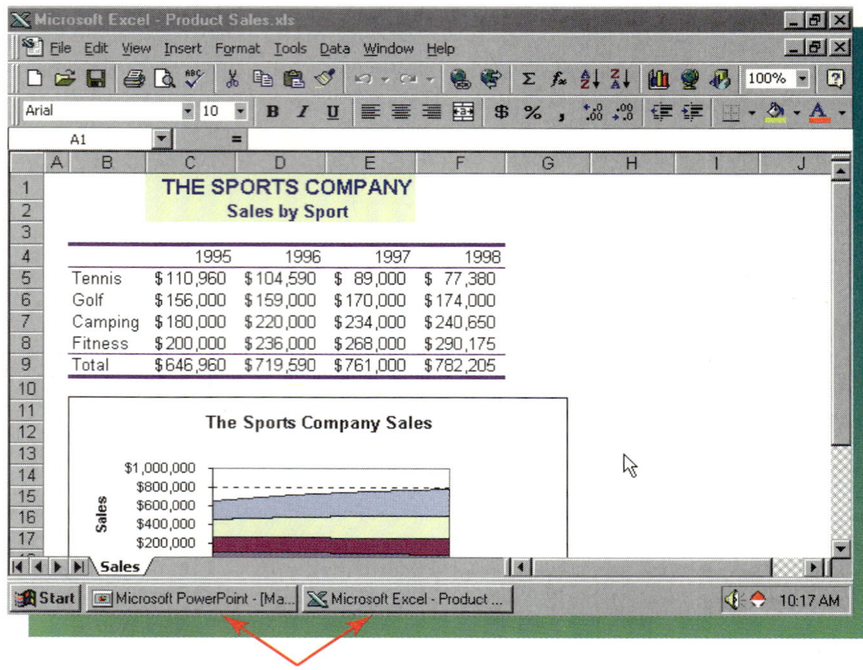

two open applications

The worksheet contains sales data by sport and an area chart of the data. There are now two open applications, PowerPoint and Excel. To make it easier to work with two applications, you will tile the windows to view both on the screen at the same time.

> Right-click the taskbar and select Tile Vertically from the Shortcut menu.

> Click anywhere on the application window to switch between applications.

- Tile the two application windows vertically.
- Select the spreadsheet data in cells B1 through F9.
- Click [Copy button] Copy.
- Switch to the PowerPoint window.
- Choose Edit/Paste Special.

The Paste Special dialog box on your screen should be similar to Figure 3-3.

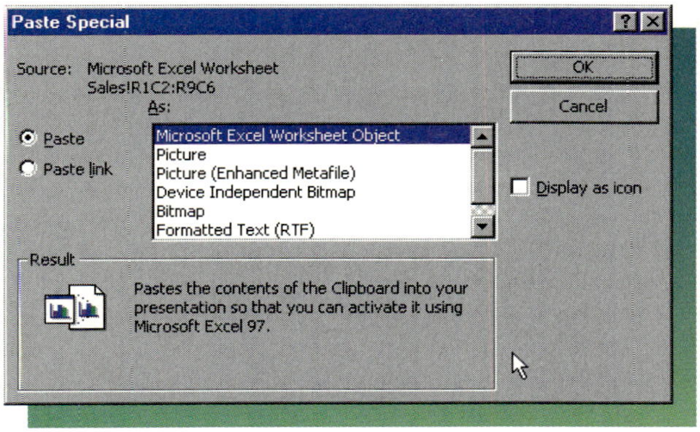

FIGURE 3-3

From the dialog box, you need to specify how you want the selection inserted into the slide. You want to paste the selection as a picture in PowerPoint.

You will use many of these dialog box options throughout this lab.

Concept 1: Copy Between Applications

While using the Microsoft applications, you have learned how to use cut, copy, and paste to move or copy information within the same document and between documents in the same application. You can perform these same operations between applications. For example, you can copy a graph from an Excel worksheet and paste it into a PowerPoint presentation. Likewise, you can copy a PowerPoint presentation, or even a single slide, into a Word document. The information is pasted in a format that the application can edit, if possible.

From the As list box,

- Select Picture.
- Click OK.
- Maximize the PowerPoint application window.
- Size and move the worksheet picture object appropriately.
- Change the background fill of the object to white so the data is easier to see.
- Deselect the object.

Use the Fill Color button to change the background.

Your screen should be similar to Figure 3-4.

FIGURE 3-4

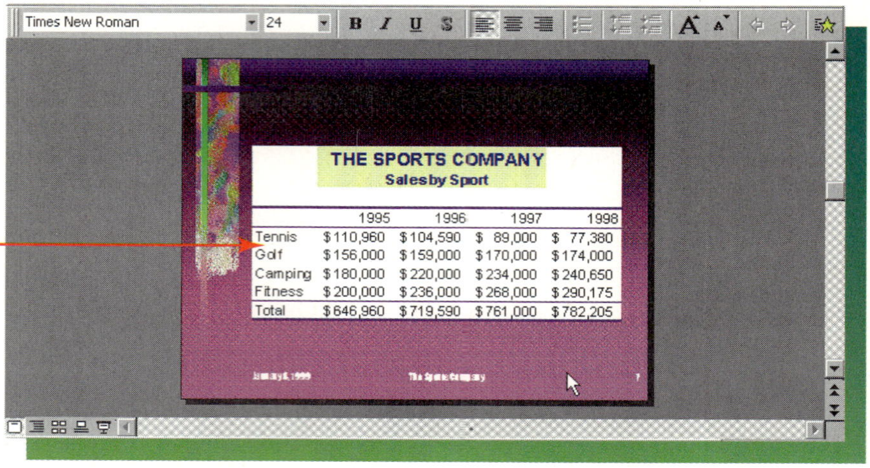

Excel worksheet copied to PowerPoint as a picture object

The worksheet is inserted into the slide as a picture object that can be manipulated from within PowerPoint using the Picture toolbar. Since you do not expect the sales data to change, this is acceptable.

Linking an Excel Chart to a PowerPoint Presentation

Next you will copy the area chart into slide 6 of the PowerPoint presentation.

- Restore the PowerPoint application window to its previous size.
- Display slide 6 in Slide view.
- Select the area chart.
- Switch to the Excel window and select the area chart.
- Click Copy.
- Switch to the PowerPoint window.

Because you anticipate you may want to change the chart type, you will paste the chart object into the presentation as a linked object.

Concept 2: Linked Object

Information created in one application can also be copied into a document created in another application as a **linked object**. When an object is linked, the data is stored in the **source file** (the file it was created in). A graphic representation or picture of the data is displayed in the **destination file** (the document in which the object is inserted). A connection between the information in the source file and the destination file is established by the creation of a link. The link contains references to the location of the source file and to the selection within the document that is linked to the destination file.

When changes are made to the source file that affect the linked object, the changes are reflected automatically in the destination file while it is open. Otherwise the link is updated when the destination file is first opened. This is called a **live link**. When you create linked objects, the date and time on your machine should be accurate so that when you open the destination file, the program refers to the date of the source file to determine whether updates are needed.

- Select Edit/Paste Special/Paste Link/ OK .
- Appropriately size and center the linked object on the slide.
- Deselect the object.

The object type of Microsoft Excel Chart Object is already appropriately selected in the As list box.

Your screen should be similar to Figure 3-5.

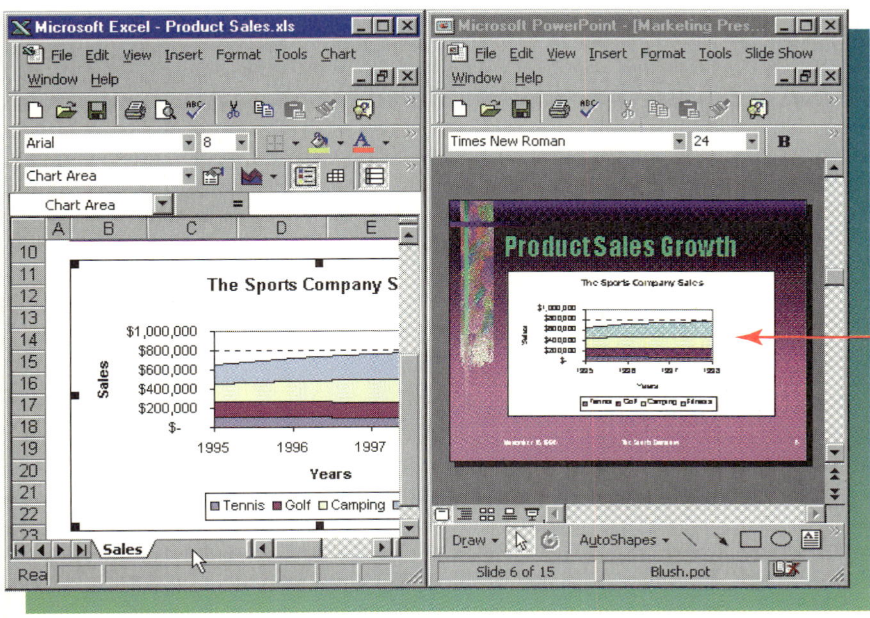

FIGURE 3-5

Because the chart is a linked object, if you change the data upon which this chart is based or make changes to the chart in Excel, the changes will be reflected in the chart in the slide. To see how this works, you will change the chart type to a line chart in Excel.

- Switch to the Excel window and, if necessary, select the chart.
- Open the Chart Type drop-down list.
- Click Line Chart.

Your screen should be similar to Figure 3-6.

FIGURE 3-6

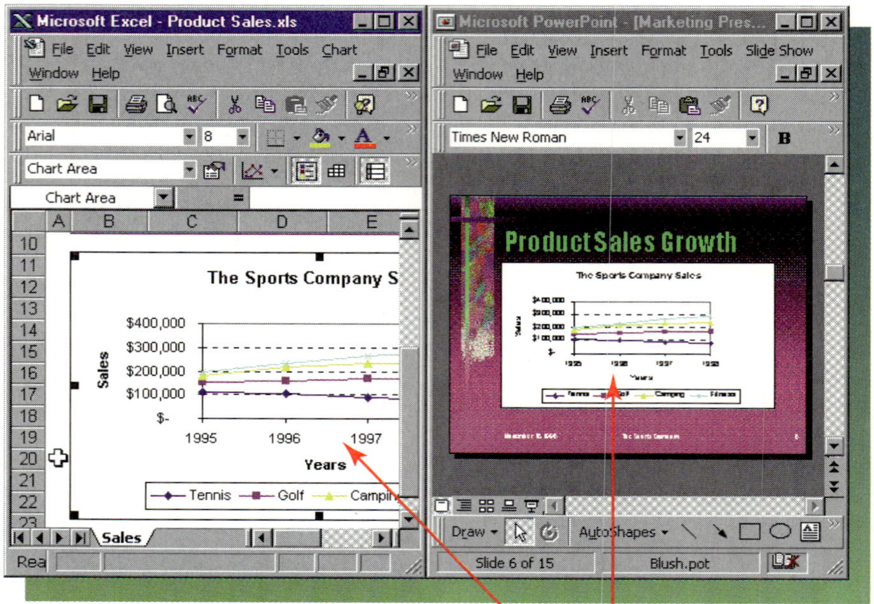

chart type changed in Excel and reflected in PowerPoint

The chart changes to a line chart in Excel, and the change is automatically reflected in the linked chart in PowerPoint.

> If your chart did not update automatically, switch to PowerPoint, choose Edit/Links and select the linked object, click Update Now to update it.

- Untile the application windows.
- Modify the slide footer to display your name and the current date on all slides except the title slide.
- Print the two new slides only.
- Update the file properties, save the PowerPoint presentation as Linked Marketing Presentation, and exit PowerPoint.
- Save the workbook file using the same file name and exit Excel.

Embedding a Presentation in a Word Document

Now that the PowerPoint presentation is complete, you will include a copy of the PowerPoint presentation in a Word memo for those managers who cannot attend the meeting. The memo to the managers has already been created.

- Load Word 97.
- To see the memo, open the file Marketing Presentation Memo.
- If necessary, maximize the application and document windows.

Your screen should be similar to Figure 3-7.

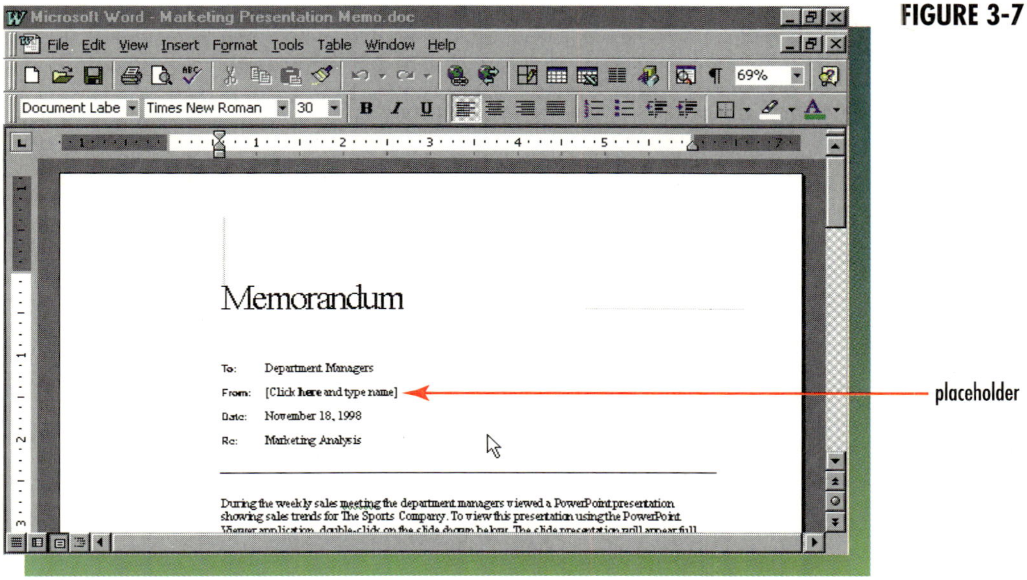

FIGURE 3-7

- Replace the placeholder with your name following "From:" in the memo heading.
- If necessary, select the date and press F9 to update the date to display the current date.

Now you are ready to copy the presentation into the memo. You will copy it as an embedded object.

Concept 3: Embedded Object

Information can also be inserted into another application document as an **embedded object**. An object that is embedded is stored in the destination file and becomes part of the document. The entire file, not just an image of the selection that is displayed in the destination file, is stored. This makes a file containing an embedded object much larger than a file containing the same object using linking.

If the user has access to the application that created the embedded object, called the **server**, the embedded object can be edited or updated from within the destination file. The connection to the server is established through the use of a field code that identifies the server associated with the embedded object. Double-clicking on the embedded object starts the server application within the destination file. Any changes you make to the embedded object are not reflected in the original source file.

Object Linking and Embedding, or **OLE**, is the program integration technology that makes it possible to share data between applications. All Office 97 programs support OLE.

You should include PowerPoint Viewer on the disk with the memo for distribution to the managers.

Use Insert/Object in PowerPoint to link or embed an entire file.

By embedding the presentation, those managers who do not have a full version of PowerPoint can view the presentation using PowerPoint Viewer. PowerPoint Viewer is a separate application included with PowerPoint that can be distributed freely to others. It allows users to view presentations only.

- Move to the blank line below the memo text.
- Choose Insert/Object.

The Object dialog box is displayed. This dialog box is used to insert a new object or existing object into the current document. You will insert the contents of an existing presentation file into the memo.

- Open the Create From File tab.

The Object dialog box on your screen should be similar to Figure 3-8.

FIGURE 3-8

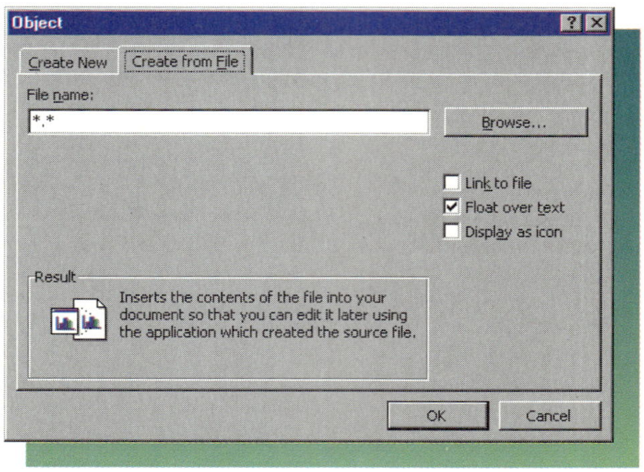

- Click [Browse...].
- From the Look In drop-down list box, select the appropriate drive for your system.
- Select Linked Marketing Presentation.
- Click [OK].

The file name appears in the File Name text box. If you choose [OK], you will embed the object. You can also link the object by selecting the Link To File option or display the embedded object as an icon by selecting the Display As Icon option. Whether you choose to link or embed the object, using this command places the entire contents of the source file into the destination file. If you want to place only selected pieces of text or graphics, use Copy and then Edit/Paste Special/Paste Link to link the selection, or Edit/Paste Special/Paste to embed the selection.

Since you will be distributing the memo on a disk, you cannot link the presentation because the readers will not have access to the source file. Therefore, you want to embed the presentation in the document. You also do not want to embed it as an icon, because you want the title slide to display in the printed copy of the memo to entice the reader to run the onscreen presentation.

You also can open PowerPoint, use Edit/Select All to select all slides, use Edit/Copy or [Copy] to copy the slides to the Clipboard, and then use Edit/Paste Special to embed the selection into the memo.

- Click [OK].

After a few moments, the first slide of the presentation appears in the memo.

It may take a moment for the slide to appear in the document.

- Change the zoom setting to Whole Page.
- Center the slide on the page below the paragraph.
- Clear the selection.

Your screen should be similar to Figure 3-9.

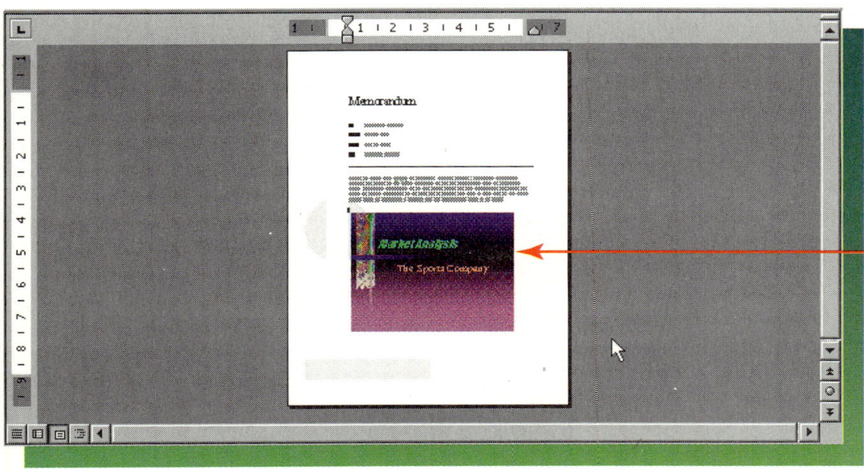

FIGURE 3-9

first slide of presentation embedded in Word document

Running the Slide Show from Word

Now that the presentation is embedded in the memo, you can view it from within Word.

- Double-click on the slide.

PowerPoint is loaded or, if the full version of PowerPoint is not available, the PowerPoint Viewer application is loaded. The first slide of the presentation is displayed.

You can cancel the slide show by pressing Esc.

- Continue running the slide show to view the rest of the slides in the presentation.

After viewing the last slide, you are returned to the Word document.

Editing an Embedded Object

If you are using the full version of PowerPoint to view the presentation in Word, you can also edit the presentation from within Word. As you are running the slide show, you decide to add your work phone number extension to slide 2 in case the managers want to ask a question about the materials. To edit the embedded presentation,

Use Edit/Object/Edit in PowerPoint to edit embedded objects.

- If necessary, select the presentation object.
- Choose Edit/Presentation Object/Edit.

A warning box appears asking you if you want to update the links in the presentation. Since you linked an Excel chart in the presentation, you want to update the link in case any information was changed. To do this,

- Click OK.

After a few moments, the first slide appears in an editing border, and the PowerPoint application menu and toolbars are displayed.

- Increase the Zoom to 50%.

Your screen should be similar to Figure 3-10.

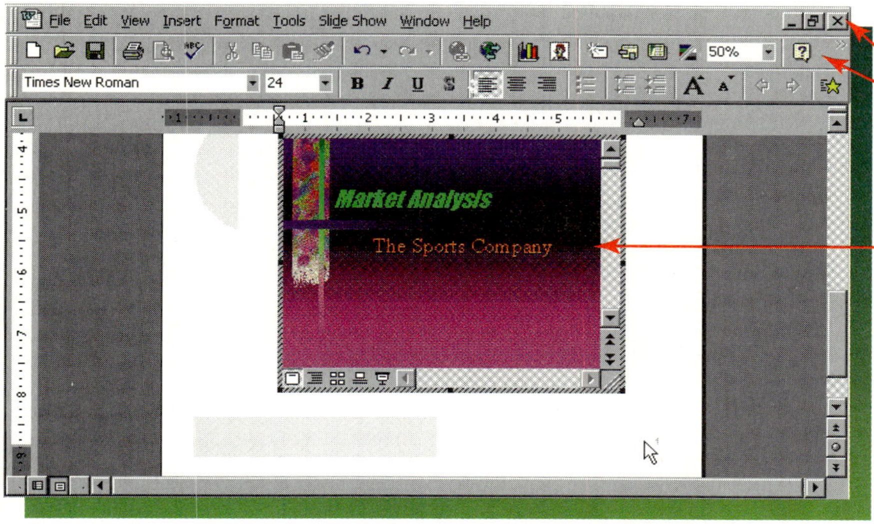

FIGURE 3-10

PowerPoint menu and toolbar

PowerPoint application opens in Word Document

- Display slide 2 and replace Student Name with your name.
- Add a demoted bullet below your name to display "-ext. 5264".

Breaking a Link

You also decide you do not want the presentation to be linked to the Excel file containing the chart, because you do not plan to include a copy of the Excel file with the memo document file that you will be giving to the managers. To break the link between the files,

- Choose Edit/Links.

The dialog box is used to modify settings associated with linked objects. It displays paths and settings for all links in the document in the list box.

- Select the link in the list box.

The Links dialog box on your screen should be similar to Figure 3-11.

FIGURE 3-11

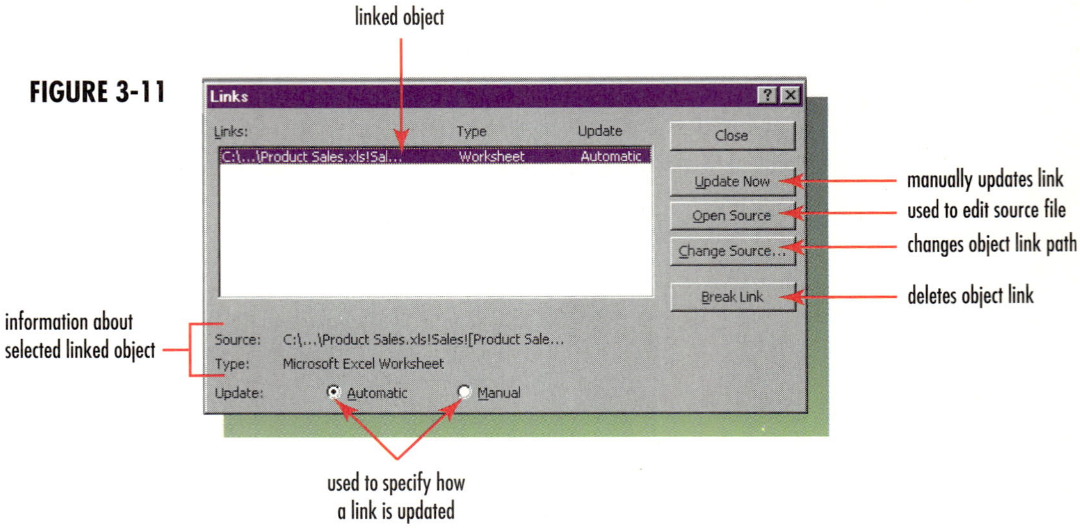

Now, below the list box, file information about the selected link is displayed.

The two update settings, Automatic and Manual, are used to change how a link is updated. Automatic, the default, updates the link whenever the file is opened. However, if a file contains many links, updating can take a lot of time. In a situation like this, you may want to change a link to update only when you specify using the Update Now button. The Open Source button will open the source file for the selected link. The Change Source... button allows you to modify the path to the source file if you move the source file to another location. Finally, the Break Link option deletes the object link field code, thereby breaking the connection between the source and destination files.

- Click Break Link.

The object is removed from the Links list box.

- Click Close.

The chart that you inserted into the presentation as a linked object is no longer linked to the copy of the presentation embedded in the memo. It is simply a pasted object. If any changes are made to the data or chart in Excel, the slide in this version of the presentation will not be updated. The chart is just a picture in the embedded presentation. However, the link still exists between the original presentation and Excel.

- Clear the selection.

Before you save the file and copy it for distribution to the managers, you need to set the view as you want it to appear when the managers open the file.

- Change the zoom to 75%. Move to the top of the document.
- Update the file properties and save the document as Embedded Marketing Presentation Memo.
- Exit Word.

Deciding When to Use Linking or Embedding

Most documents will not include both linked and embedded objects because the reasons for using each are different.

Use linking when:	Use embedding when:
File size is important.	File size is not important.
Users have access to the source file and application.	Users have access to the application, but not to the source files.
The information is updated frequently.	The data changes infrequently.

LAB REVIEW

Key Terms

destination file (PR103)
embedded object (PR106)
linked object (PR103)
live link (PR103)
Object Linking and Embedding (OLE) (PR106)
server (PR106)
source file (PR103)

On Your Own

★★★

4. To complete this problem, you must have completed Practice Exercise 5 in Lab 2 and created the file Cruise Promotion 2. You want to create a one-page brochure about the cruise packages.

In a new Word document, enter:

> **American Cruises, Inc.**
> **Plan your vacation today.**

Format the text appropriately for the brochure. Link the Cruise Promotion 2 presentation you created below the text. Change the link to a Manual update. Return to the original presentation and add the bullet "Track increased requests for information" to slide 7. Manually update the brochure.

Save the Word document as Cruises On-screen Brochure. Print the document. Close the file.

★★★

5. In this problem you will complete the presentation you started in Practice Exercise 7 of Lab 1 for a class you are taking. Add transitions, builds, charts, and clip art that is appropriate for the presentation. Select a new template for the presentation. Add notes pages to slides that need reminders.

Create a link in your presentation to an Excel worksheet or chart. Embed the presentation you completed in a memo that introduces the presentation. Save the presentation and print the slides, notes pages, and handouts.

Save and print the memo.

Concept Summary

3 Sharing Information Between Applications

Copy Between Applications

Information can be copied between applications and, if possible, inserted in the document in a format the application can edit.

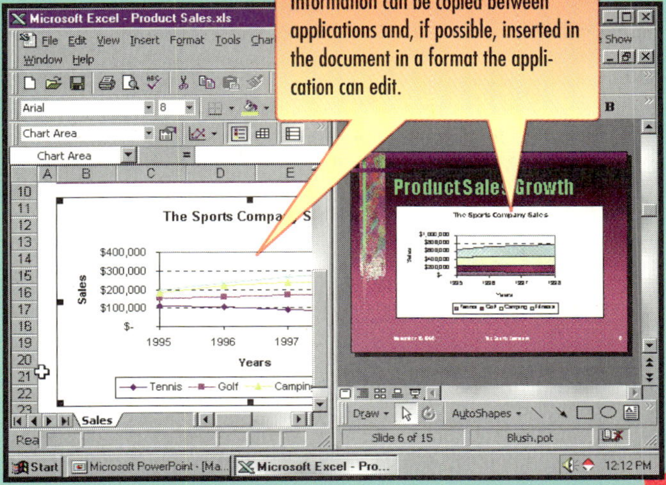

Concepts

- Copy Between Applications
- Linked Object
- Embedded Object

Linked Object

Information that is copied from one file to another as a linked object maintains a connection between the two files, allowing the linked object to automatically update when the source file changes.

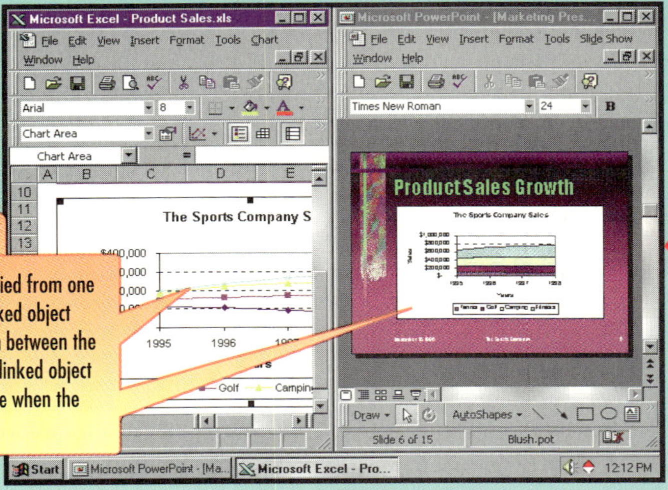

Embedded Object

Information that is copied as an embedded object to a destination file created by a different application becomes part of the file and can be updated by opening the object server from within the document in which it is inserted.

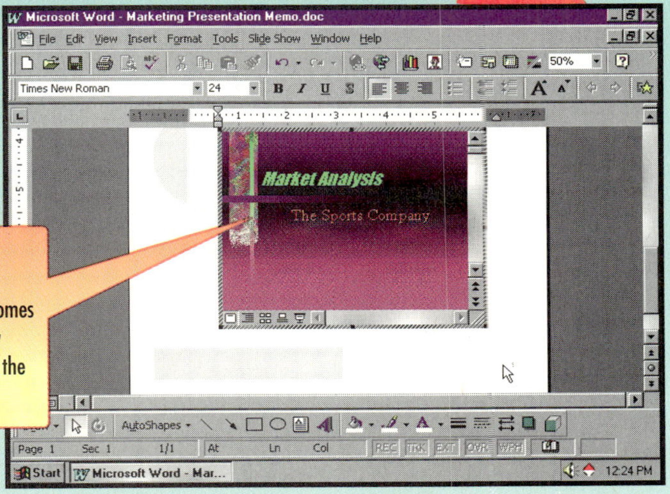

Glossary of Key Terms

Animation: Effect that adds action to text and graphics so they move around on the screen.

Attribute: A feature associated with an object or text that can be enhanced using drawing tools and menu commands.

AutoLayout: A predefined slide layout that is used to control the placement of elements on a slide.

Builds: An effect that progressively displays the bulleted items as the presentation proceeds.

Cell: The space on a datasheet created by the intersection of a vertical column and a horizontal row.

Chart: A visual representation of data.

Clip art: Professionally drawn images.

Custom dictionary: A dictionary you can create to hold words you commonly use but that are not included in the dictionary that is supplied with the program.

Datasheet: Table consisting of rows and columns holding data used to enter data to graph.

Demote: To move a topic down one level in the outline hierarchy.

Design template: Professionally created slide design that can be applied to your presentation.

Destination file: The document receiving the linked or embedded object.

Docked: A toolbar or menu bar that is fixed to an edge of the window.

Drawing object: An object consisting of shapes such as lines and boxes that can be created using the Drawing toolbar.

Drawing toolbar: A toolbar that is used to add objects such as lines, circles, and boxes.

Embedded object: An object created in one application and copied into another. It is stored in the destination file and edited using the screen.

Floating: A toolbar or menu bar that appears in a separate window that can be moved by dragging.

Font: A set of characters with a specific design.

Font size: Height of a character measured in points.
Footer: Text or graphics that appear on the bottom of each slide.
Formatting toolbar: A toolbar that contains buttons used to modify text.
Graph: *See* Chart.
Graphics: Non-text elements, such as charts, drawings, pictures, and scanned photographs, in a slide.
Handouts: Printed output that displays two or more slides on a page with space for audience members to make notes.
Highlight: Border surrounding the selected cell in a datasheet.
Legend: A brief description of the symbols used in a chart.
Linked object: An object that is created in a source file and linked to a destination file. Edits made to the source file are automatically reflected in the destination file.
Live link: A link that automatically updates the linked object whenever changes are made to it in the source file.
Main dictionary: Dictionary that comes with the PowerPoint 97 program.
Master: A special slide on which the formatting of all slides in a presentation is defined.
Move handle: Used to move menu bars and toolbars to a new location.
Notes page: Printed output that shows a miniature of the slide and provides an area for speaker notes.
Object: An item on a slide that can be selected and modified.
Object Linking and Embedding (OLE): The program integration technology that makes it possible to share data between applications.
Office Assistant: Used to get help on features specific to the Office application you are using.
Outline toolbar: Displayed in Outline view, it is used to modify the presentation outline.
Picture: An illustration created by combining lines, arcs, circles, and other shapes.
Placeholder: Box that is designed to contain objects such as the slide title, bulleted text, charts, tables, and pictures.
Point: A unit of type measurement. One point equals about 1/72 inch.
Promote: To move a topic up one level in the outline hierarchy.
Sans serif font: A font that does not have a flair at the base of each letter, such as Arial or Helvetica.
Selection rectangle: Hashed border that surrounds a selected placeholder.
Serif font: A font that has a flair at the base of each letter, such as Roman or Times New Roman.
Server: The application used to modify an embedded object.
Sizing handles: Small boxes surrounding selected objects that are used to change the size of the object.
Slide: An individual page of the presentation.
Slide show: Used to practice or to present the presentation. It displays each slide in final form.
Source file: The document in which the linked object was created.
Standard toolbar: A toolbar that contains buttons that give quick access to the most frequently used program features.

Style: Refers to the attributes, such as bold and italics, that can be applied to text.

Title: Text added to a chart to describe the data.

Transition: An effect that controls how a slide moves off the screen and the next one appears.

View: A way of looking at the presentation. Five views are available in PowerPoint.

Work area: Large area of the window where the presentation is displayed.

X axis: The horizontal axis of a chart.

Y axis: The vertical axis of a chart.

Command Summary

Command	Shortcut	Toolbar	Action
File/New	Ctrl + N		Creates new presentation
File/Open	Ctrl + O		Opens selected presentation
File/Close			Closes presentation
File/Save	Ctrl + S		Saves presentation
File/Save As			Saves presentation using new file name
File/Print	Ctrl + P		Prints presentation using default print settings
File/Properties			Displays statistics and enters information about the presentation
File/Exit			Exits PowerPoint program
Edit/Paste Special/Paste Link/As/<object type>			Links a selection
Edit/Paste Special/Paste/As/<object type>			Embeds a selection
Edit/Delete Slide	Delete		Deletes selected slide
Edit/Select All	Ctrl + A		Selects all slides
Edit/Links/Update Now			Updates selected linked object immediately
Edit/Links/Break Link			Breaks link to an object
Edit/Object/Edit			Edits an embedded object
View/Slide			Switches to Slide view
View/Outline			Switches to Outline view
View/Slide Sorter			Switches to Slide Sorter view
View/Notes Page			Displays notes pages
View/Slide Show			Runs slide show
View/Master/Slide Master	⇧Shift +		Displays slide master for current presentation

Command	Shortcut	Toolbar	Action
View/Master/Title Master			Displays title master for current presentation
View/Black and White			Displays slides in black and white
View/Slide Miniature			Displays or hides a slide miniature of current slide
View/Header and Footer			Specifies information that appears as headers and footers on slides, notes, outlines, and handout pages
View/Zoom		28%	Changes magnification of screen
Insert/New Slide	Ctrl + M	New Slide...	Inserts new slide
Insert/Picture/Clip Art			Inserts selected clip art on slide
Insert/Chart			Inserts graph
Insert/Object			Links or embeds a file
Format/Font/Font		Times New Roman	Changes font typeface
Format/Font/Size		24	Changes size of font
Format/Font/Font Style			Changes font style
Format/Slide Layout			Changes or creates a slide layout
Format/Slide Color Scheme			Changes color scheme of one or all slides in presentation
Format/Apply Design		Apply Design...	Changes appearance of slide by applying a different design template
Format/Colors and Lines			Set the line and fill color of selected object
Chart/Chart Type			Changes chart type
Tools/Spelling	F7		Spell-checks presentation
Tools/Style Checker			Checks spelling and slide design
Tools/Expand Slide			Creates two slides out of one
Slide Show/Preset Animation/ Custom Animation		No Effect	Adds build and animation effects
Slide Show/Slide Transition			Adds transition effects
Slide Show/Hide Slide			Hides selected slide

Index

Appendix A

Additional PowerPoint 97 Features

- Create a presentation from an existing presentation
- Find and replace text
- Import text from Word
- Apply a template from another presentation
- Modify a sequence in Outline view
- Draw, rotate, and fill an object
- Add sound and movies
- Change tabs
- Add scanned images (pictures)
- Create a custom background
- Add an organizational chart
- Add a table
- Add links to other slides within the presentation
- Set automatic slide timing
- Electronically incorporate meeting feedback
- Export to overheads and 35 mm slides
- Present with Presentation Conferencing
- Save for Internet

- Save for use on another computer.
- Export an outline to Word.

Create a Presentation from an Existing Presentation

Many times it is faster to create a new presentation from an existing presentation. You can do this easily by modifying the existing presentation to meet the requirements of the new presentation and then saving the revised presentation using a new file name. You will change the Marketing Presentation to a Sales Presentation.

- Open Marketing Presentation 4.
- In slide sorter view, delete slide 3. Then delete slides 5 through 12.

Your screen should be similar to Figure A-1. The presentation now consists of six slides whose content is directly related to sales.

FIGURE A-1

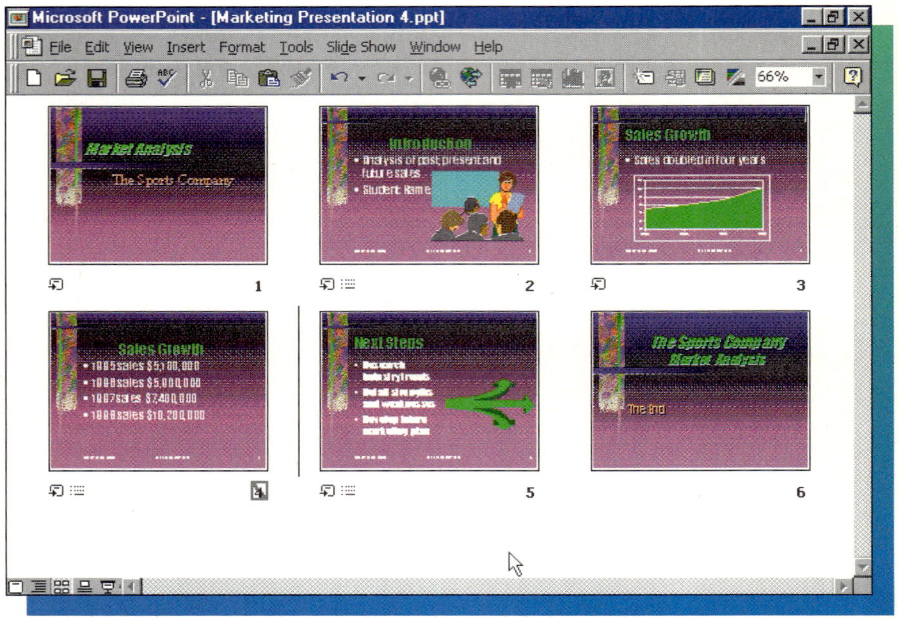

Find and Replace Text

You can also highlight text to restrict the search to the selection.

Next you want to edit the presentation by replacing the title text Market Analysis with the new presentation title, Sales Analysis. To do this quickly, you will use the Find and Replace feature to find the text you specify and automatically replace it with other text.

- Move to slide 1 and switch to Slide view.
- Choose Edit/Replace.

The keyboard shortcut is [Ctrl]+H.

The Edit/Find command locates specified text only.

The Replace dialog box should be similar to Figure A-2.

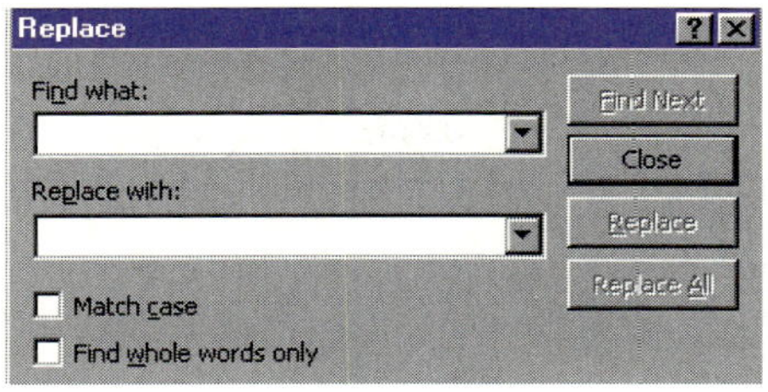

FIGURE A-2

In the Find what text box, you enter the text you want to locate. The two options described in the table below allow you to refine how the search for the text you want to locate is conducted.

Option	Effect on Text
Match Case	Distinguishes between uppercase and lowercase characters. When selected, it finds only those instances in which the capitalization matches the text you typed in the Find what box.
Find Whole Words Only	Distinguishes between whole and partial words. When selected, it locates matches that are whole words and not part of a larger word. Finds cat only and not catastrophe too, for example.

The text you want to replace is entered in the Replace with text box. The replacement text must be entered exactly as you want it to appear in your document. You want to find all occurrences of the complete word "market" and replace them with the word "Sales." To enter the text to find and replace and begin the search,

- Type **market** in the Find what text box.
- Type **Sales** in the Replace with text box.
- Select Find Whole Words Only.
- Click Find Next.
- If necessary, move the dialog box so you can see the located text.

After entering the text to find, do not press ←Enter or this will choose Find Next and the search will begin.

Immediately, the first occurrence of text in the presentation that matches the entry in the Find what text box is located and highlighted.

Your screen should be similar to Figure A-3.

FIGURE A-3

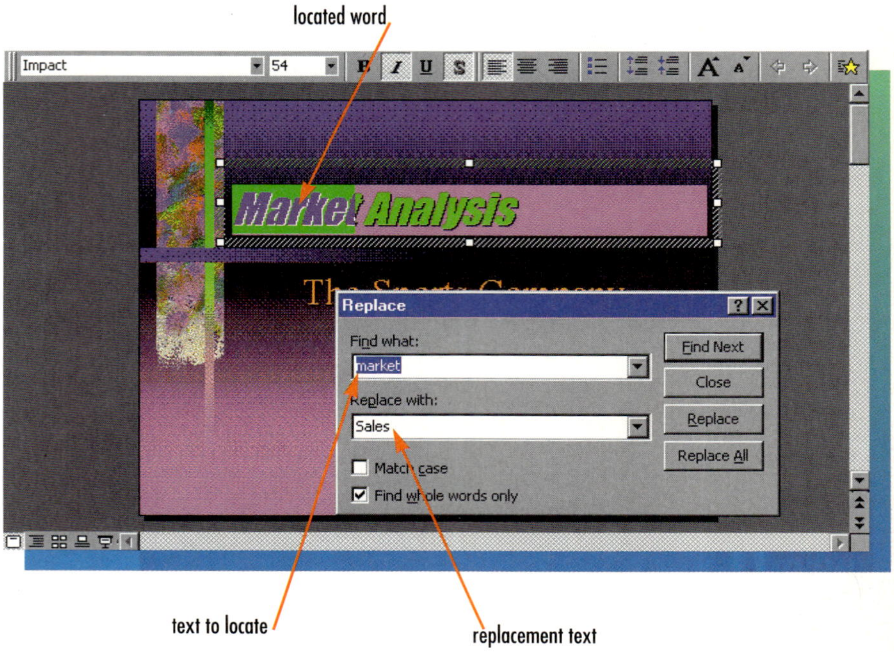

To replace the located word with the replacement text,

- Click Replace.

The highlighted text is replaced and the search immediately continues. The next occurrence of the Find text is located.

- Replace this occurrence.

The third occurrence of matching text is located in the notes pages.

- In a same manner, replace this occurrence.

If you are changing all the occurrences it is much faster to use the Replace All command button. Exercise care when using Replace All, because the search text you specify might be part of another word and you may accidentally replace text you want to keep.

When using the Find command you can close the dialog box and use the ⯭ and ⯯ to find the previous or next occurrence of the text.

A message is displayed advising you that the search is complete. To close the message box,

- Click OK.
- Close the Replace dialog box.
- Switch back to Slide view.
- Fix the title in the closing slide so that "Sales Analysis" is on the second line.
- Replace Student Name in slide 2 with your name.

Now you are ready to save the presentation using a new file name.

- Choose File/Save As.
- Specify the location of your data disk (A:) as the location to save the file.
- Enter the file name **Sales Analysis.**
- Click Save.
- Print handouts (3 slides per page).
- Close the Sales Analysis presentation.

Import Text from Word

The next presentation you are working on is for the new employee orientation meeting that is held each month. You have created a document in Word of topics to be used in this presentation and want to use this document as the basis of your presentation. To do this, you can import text created in other programs into PowerPoint to create a new presentation or to add slides to an existing presentation. PowerPoint determines the outline structure for the presentation from the heading styles in the imported document; Heading 1 style becomes a slide title, Heading 2 style becomes the first level of text, and so on. If the document does not contain heading styles, the paragraph indentations are used to create the outline. In plain text documents, tabs at the beginning of paragraphs define the outline structure. The document you will import has been formatted with Heading 1 and 2 styles.

- Click [Open icon].
- Choose All Outlines from the Files of Type drop-down list box.
- Change the location to your data disk and select Orientation Agenda.rtf.
- Click Open.

You can also use Insert/Slides from Outline to import text into an existing presentation.

Your screen should be similar to Figure A-4.

FIGURE A-4

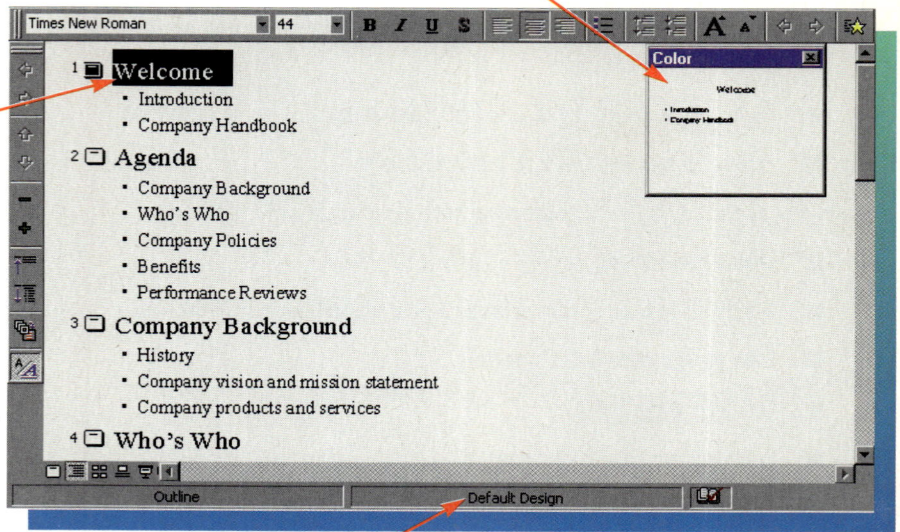

The new presentation created from the text file you imported is displayed in Outline view. Each Heading 1 style is the title for a new slide and each Heading 2 style appears as the text for the slide. The presentation uses the blank design style.

Apply a template from another presentation.

Next, you will apply the design used in the sales presentation to your new presentation.

- Click .
- If necessary, change the location to your data disk.
- Change the file type to Presentations and Shows.
- Select Sales Analysis.ppt.
- Click Apply.

Your screen should be similar to Figure A-5.

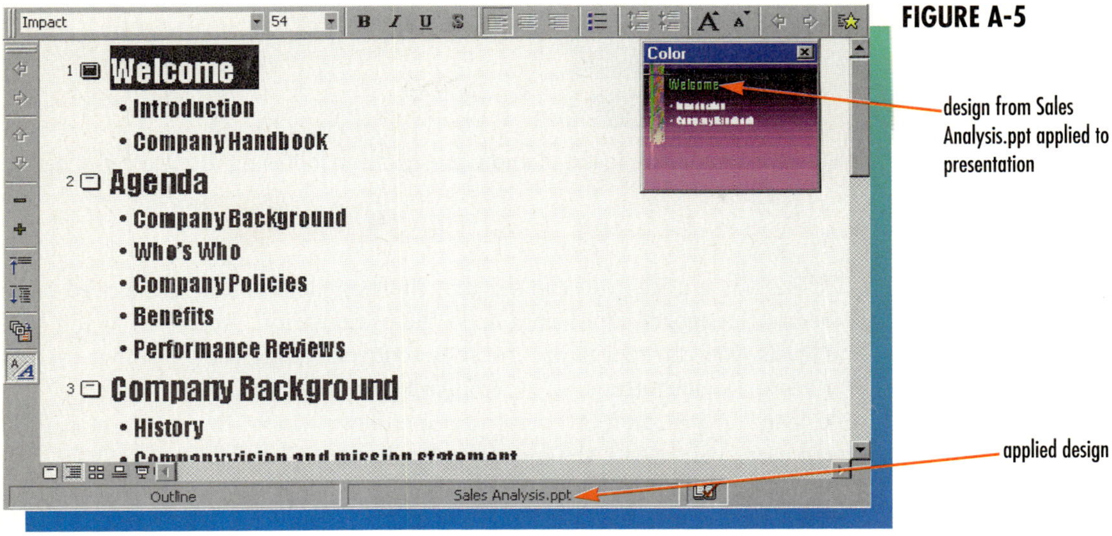

FIGURE A-5

The design is applied to all slides in the presentation.

You also want to copy the title slide and the closing slide from the Sales Analysis presentation to the new employee orientation presentation.

- Choose Insert/Slides From Files.
- Click Browse... .
- Select the Sales Analysis file.
- Click Open .
- Click Display .

The Slide Finder dialog box on your screen should be similar to Figure A-6.

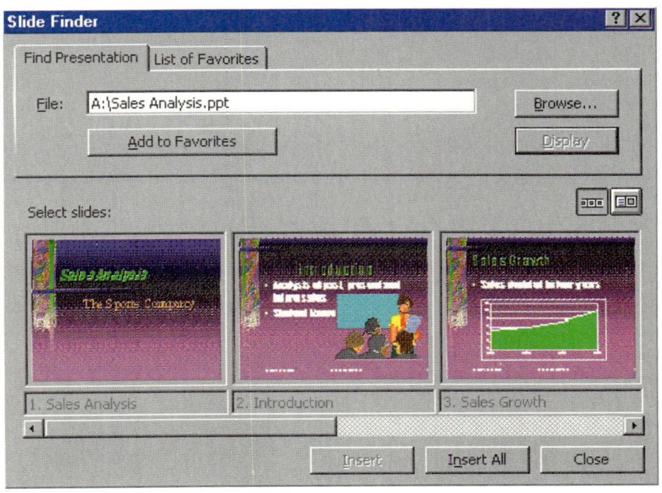

FIGURE A-6

You can now select the slides you want to add to your presentation.

- Select slides 1 and 6 in the presentation by clicking on them.
- Click Insert.
- Click Close.

The two new slides are inserted in the presentation following the selected slide (1).

Modify a Sequence in Outline View

Checking the outline, you can see that the two slides you inserted need to be moved to the appropriate locations in the presentation. Just like moving outline levels, you can reorganize the slide sequence using the Move Up and Move Down buttons or by dragging and dropping the slide icon. As you drag, a horizontal line shows where the selection will be placed when you release the mouse button.

- The third slide icon and text are already selected. Drag the slide selection to the end of the presentation.
- Click on the slide 2 icon to select it and drag it above the first slide icon.

Your screen should be similar to Figure A-7.

FIGURE A-7

slides rearranged in Outline view

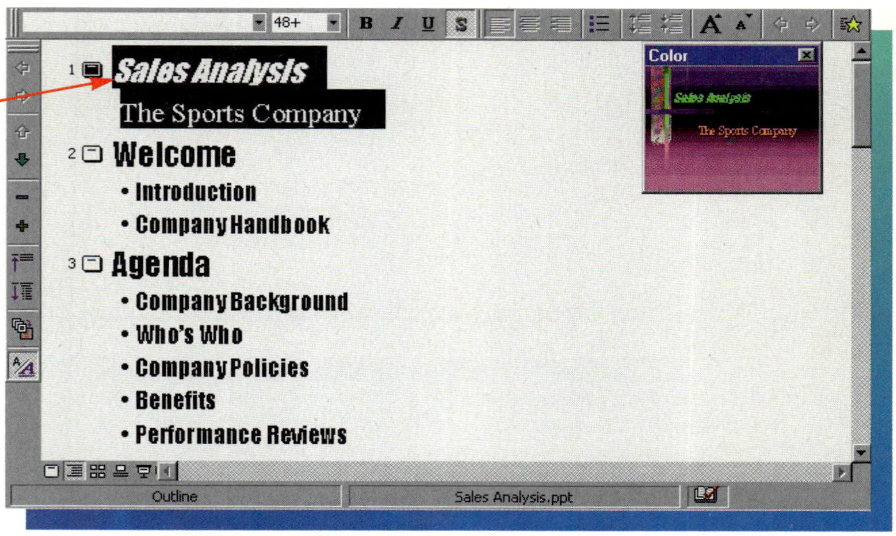

The slides are now in sequence in the correct order.

- Use Find and Replace to change the title on the Title and End slides to New Employee Orientation.
- Close the Replace dialog box.

Draw, Rotate, and Fill an Object

The next change you want to make is to add a drawing to the title slide to make it more interesting. You will include text in the object and enhance its appearance by adding a shadow, rotating the shape and filling it with a pattern.

- Display the title slide in Slide view.
- Display the Drawing toolbar.
- Click AutoShapes and select Stars and Banners.
- Click Down Ribbon.
- Click on the slide below the company name and drag to create the autoshape object.
- If the shape is not visible, click and select Automatic.

Your screen should be similar to Figure A-8.

FIGURE A-8

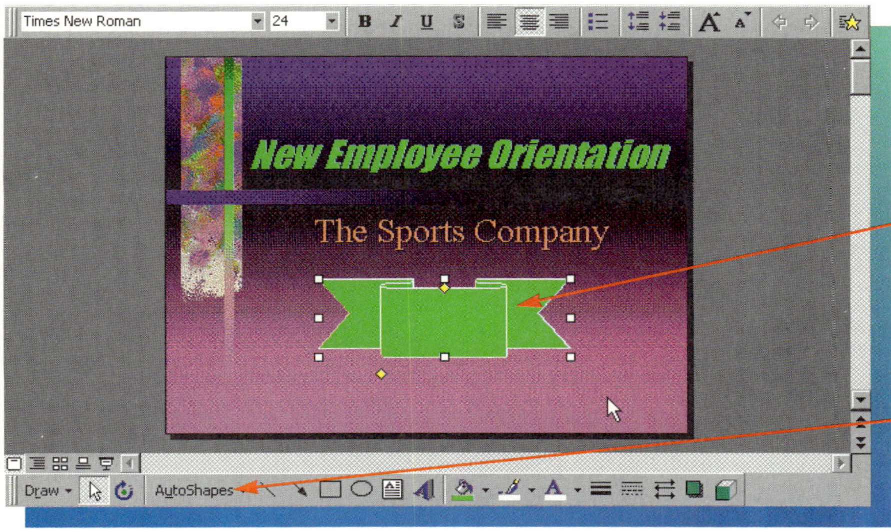

Next you will add text to the object and enhance its appearance using several features on the drawing toolbar.

- Right-click on the autoshape object to open the Shortcut menu and select Add Text.
- Change the font to Arial and bold.
- Type **A Great Place to Work!**

- Click Shadow and select any shadow style from the pop-up menu.
- Click Shadow and select Shadow Settings.
- Use the Shadow Settings toolbar to enhance the appearance of the shadow by changing the shadow color to a color of your choice and nudging the shadow as needed.
- Close the Shadow Settings toolbar.
- Click Rotate.
- Drag the rotate handle to change the angle of the shape.
- Click Rotate again to turn off this feature.
- Click Fill Color and choose Fill Effects.
- Select a color of your choice from the Texture tab of the Fill Effects dialog box.
- Size the shape appropriately.
- If necessary change the font color.

The rotate handles are small circles on each corner of the selected object.

Your screen should be similar to Figure A-9.

FIGURE A-9

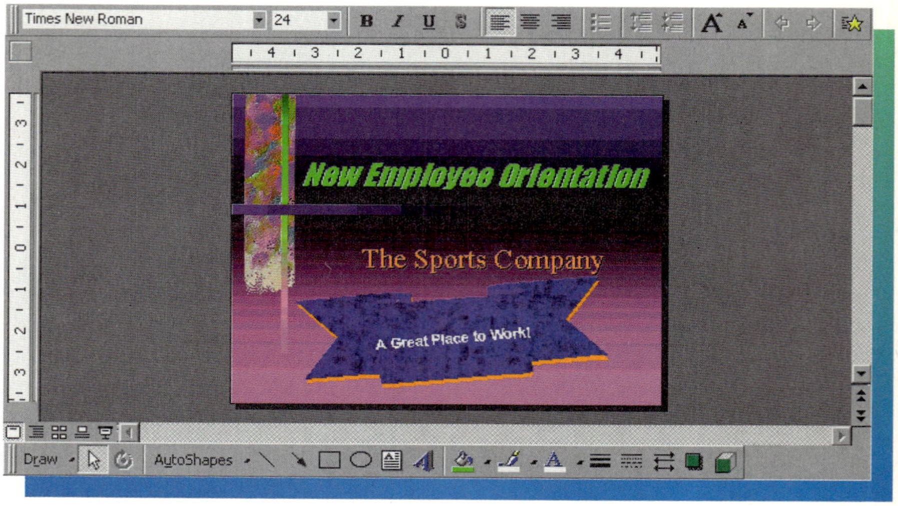

Add Sound and Movies

Sound and movies can be used to draw the audience's attention to a particular point or to liven up a slow presentation. By default, the sound or video starts when you click its icon during a slide show. PowerPoint also allows you to change the play settings to play the sound or video as soon as you move to the slide. You will add the Drum Roll sound clip to the Welcome slide to attract the audience's attention.

- Display slide 2 in Slide view.
- Choose Insert/Movies and Sounds/Sound from File.

The Insert Sound dialog box lists the sound files that are included with Office 97.

- Double click Drumroll.wav.

A sound icon appears on the slide. You can play the sound by clicking the sound icon during a slide show.

- Move the sound icon to the bottom right corner of the slide.
- Click to run the slide show starting with the current slide.
- Click the sound icon.

If you have speakers you will hear the sound. Instead of clicking the sound icon to start a sound, you can change how you start a sound by positioning the mouse over the icon. In addition, you can add custom animation settings to a sound clip. You will change the settings so that the sound plays automatically before any other animation occurs on the slide.

- Press [Esc] to return to Slide view.
- Add a slide transition effect of your choice to this slide.
- Choose Slide Show/Custom Animation.
- From the Play Settings tab, select Play Using Animation Order.
- Select Hide While Not Playing.
- From the Timing tab, select Automatically.
- Click OK.
- Start the slide show again from this slide to see how your changes affect the presentation.

The drum roll plays immediately following the slide transition.

Change Tabs

Next you will add a slide presenting a brief history of the company.

- Insert a new slide after slide 4 using the Bulleted List layout.
- In Slide view, add the slide title History.
- Click in the text placeholder box.
- Click to turn off bullets.
- If necessary, display the ruler.

You will enter the list of dates and events shown on page A-13. To make it easier to align the two columns, you will set tab stops. A **tab stop** is a stopping point along a line to which text will indent when you press Tab. You can select from four different types of tab stops that control how characters are positioned or aligned with the tab stop. The four tab types, the alignment tab mark that appears on the ruler, and the effects on the text are explained in the following table.

Alignment	Tab Mark	How It Affects Text	Example
Left	⌊	Extends text to right from tab stop	left
Center	⊥	Aligns text centered on tab	center
Right	⌋	Extends text to left from tab stop	right
Decimal	⊥.	Aligns text with decimal point	35.78

The default tab type is Left.

Setting different types of tab stops is helpful for aligning text or numeric data vertically in columns. Using tab stops ensures that the text will indent to the same set location. Setting tab stops instead of pressing Tab or Spacebar repeatedly is a more professional way to format a document, and it's faster and more accurate.

You can quickly specify tab stop locations and types using the ruler. To select a tab stop type, click the tab alignment selector box on the left end of the ruler to cycle through the types. Then to specify where to place the selected tab stop type, click on the location in the ruler. Drag any tab marker to a new position or off the ruler to remove it. You will add a left tab stop at the 1 inch and 2.5 inch positions.

- Click the 1 position on the ruler.
- Click the 2.5 position on the ruler.
- Press Tab twice.
- Type **Year**
- Press Tab.
- Type **Event**
- Press ←Enter.

Your screen should be similar to Figure A-10.

FIGURE A-10

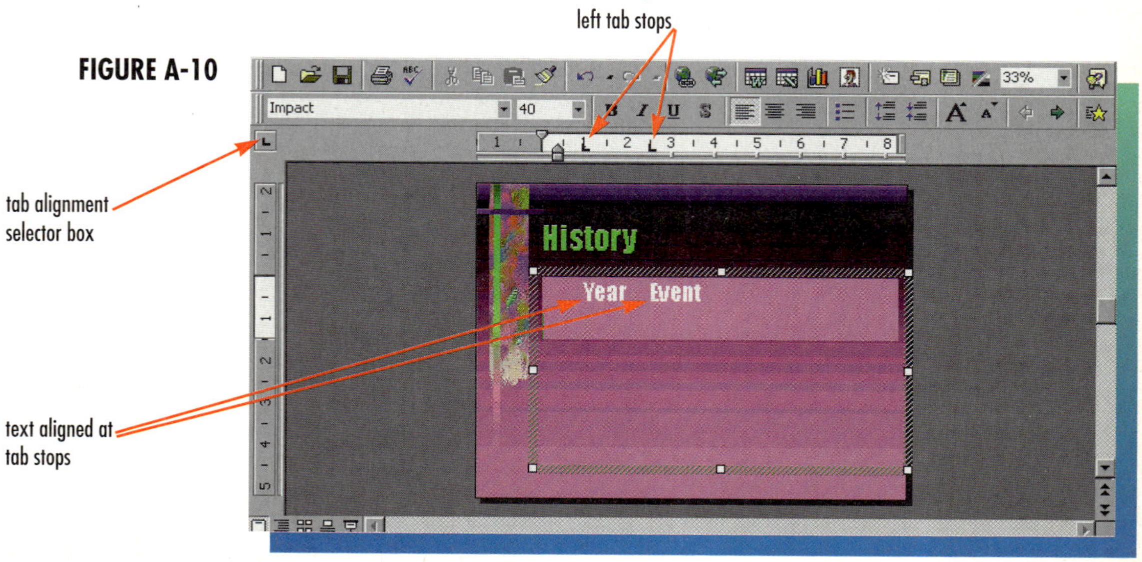

- Set the font size to 32.
- Continue entering the information shown below. Remember to press Tab to create the columns.

1948 Founded by Harvey Wilton
1952 Built first store
1976 Acquired 3 new stores
1985 P. J. McCurdy, President
1993 Expanded to 20 stores

Add Scanned Images

Next, you want to add a picture of Harvey Wilton to the history slide. You can use Insert/Picture/From Scanner to create a digital copy of a photograph using a scanner that is connected to your computer. Then the image can be edited using Microsoft Photo Editor and saved as a picture file. The picture file is then inserted into the slide just like any other graphic.

Microsoft Photo Editor must be installed to edit a scanned image.

- Choose Insert/Picture/From File/Wilton.jpg.
- Click Insert.

After a picture is added to a slide, you can further edit it using features on the Picture toolbar. For example you can crop the picture, add special effects to it, and adjust its brightness, contrast, and color.

- Use the Picture toolbar features to crop and modify the picture as you like.
- Move and position the text and image on the slide as appropriate.
- Clear the selection.

Your screen should be similar to Figure A-11.

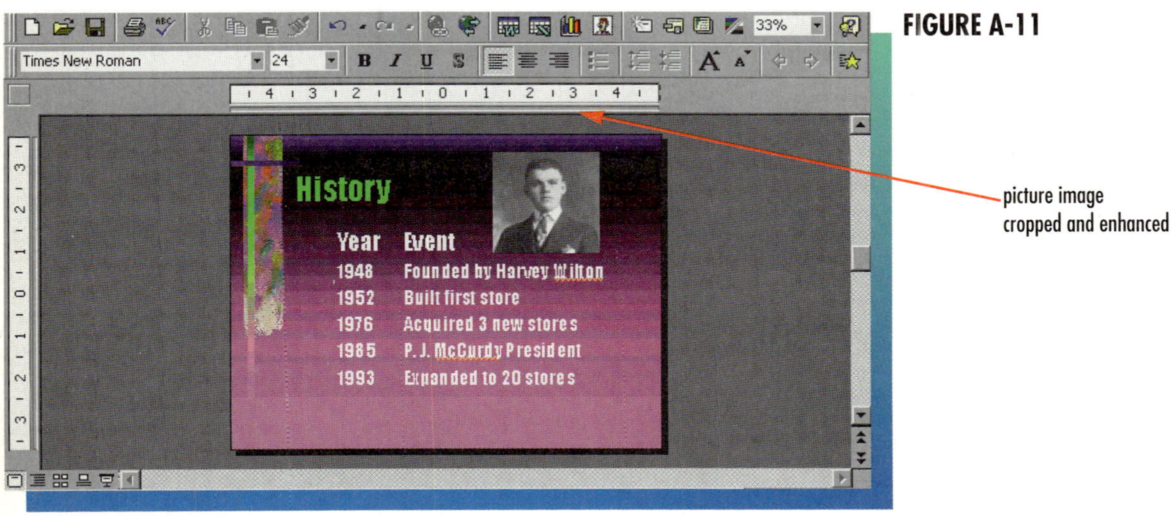

FIGURE A-11

Create a Custom Background

Finally, because this slide contains a lot of information, you want to change the slide background of this slide only to a simple background design.

- Choose Format/Background.
- Open the color drop down list and select Fill Effects.
- Select a background of your choice from the Texture tab.
- Click OK.
- Select Omit background graphics from master.
- Click Preview to see how your selection will appear. If necessary, select a different texture color.
- Click Apply to only change current slide.
- Move and size the text placeholder box until it is centered on the slide.

This text uses the purple mesh texture

Your screen should be similar to Figure A-12.

FIGURE A-12

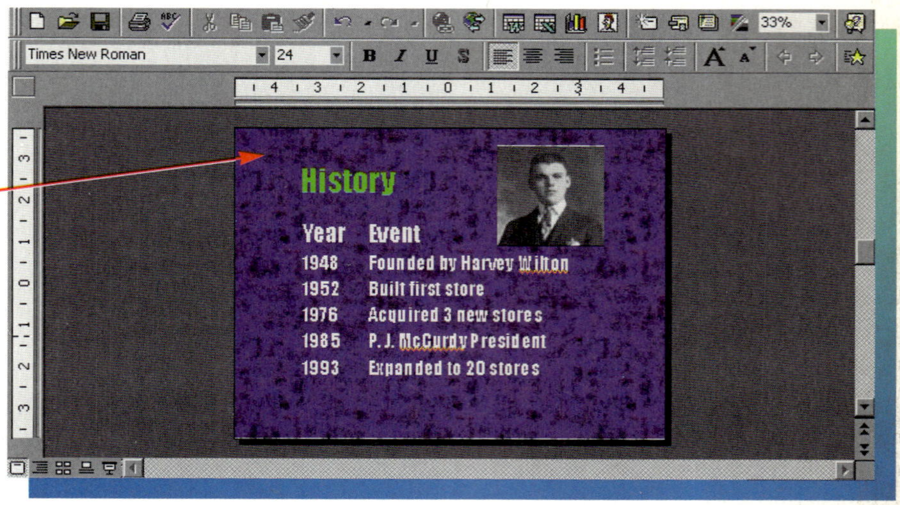

Add an Organizational Chart

The next slide you want to add to the presentation is a graphic representation of the organization of the company called an organizational chart.

You can also use Insert/Picture/Organization Chart to add this element to a slide.

- Insert a slide after slide 6 selecting the Organization Chart layout style.
- If necessary, switch to Slide view.

A placeholder for the organizational chart containing four boxes is displayed in the new slide.

- Add the title **Sports Company Organization** in a font size of 48.
- Double-click the organizational chart to activate it.

The Organization Chart window on your screen should be similar to Figure A-13.

FIGURE A-13

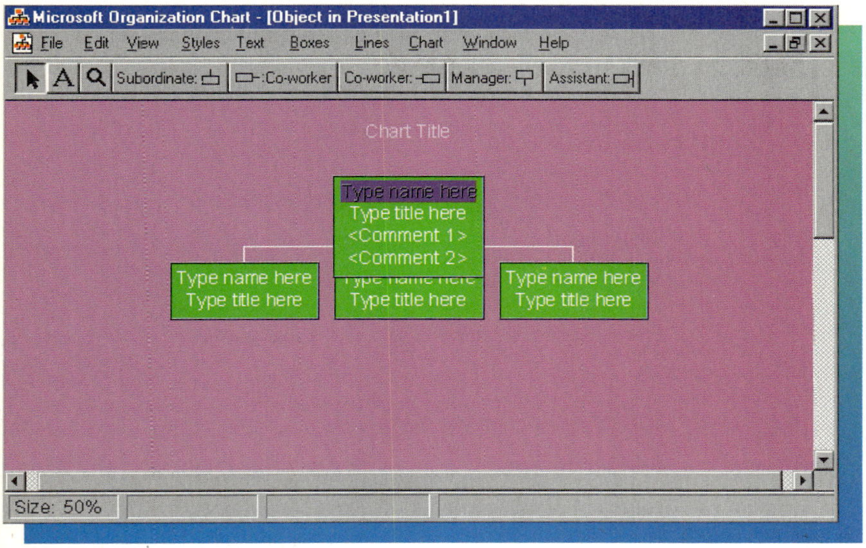

The chart is displayed in the Microsoft Organization Chart program window. The menu and toolbar are used to edit and enhance the appearance of the chart. You need to replace the placeholder labels in each box with the people's names and positions within the company. The top box is activated and ready for you to replace the placeholder text.

Use Help/Index on the Organization Chart menu for further help on this feature.

- Enter the name **P. J. McCurdy** and the title **President.**
- Click in each of the other boxes to activate them and replace the placeholders with the following information:

David Stofka	Marsha Santori	Your Name
Vice President	Vice President	Vice President
Personnel	Finance	Add a title of your choice

- Enhance the appearance of the chart by adding features such as borders and shadows, and changing the color of the boxes and text to colors of your choice.
- Choose File/Exit and Return to Presentation.
- Click Yes to update the chart in the presentation.
- Size and position the organizational chart on the slide.
- Clear the selection.

Your screen should be similar to Figure A-14.

FIGURE A-14

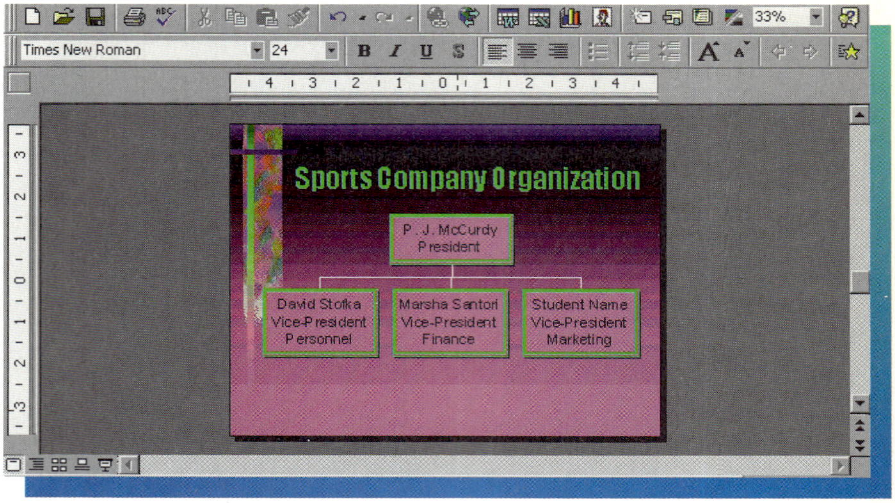

Add a Table

Next, you want to create a table to display information about vacation benefits (shown on page A-17). A table is made up of rows and columns of cells that you can fill with text and graphics. Tables are commonly used to align numbers in columns and then sort and perform calculations on them. They make it easier to read and understand numbers.

- Insert a new slide after slide 9 using the Table layout.
- Remove the title placeholder and drag the table placeholder up to cover the title space.
- Double-click the table placeholder.
- Specify 2 columns and 7 rows.
- Click OK.

Your screen should be similar to Figure A-15.

FIGURE A-15

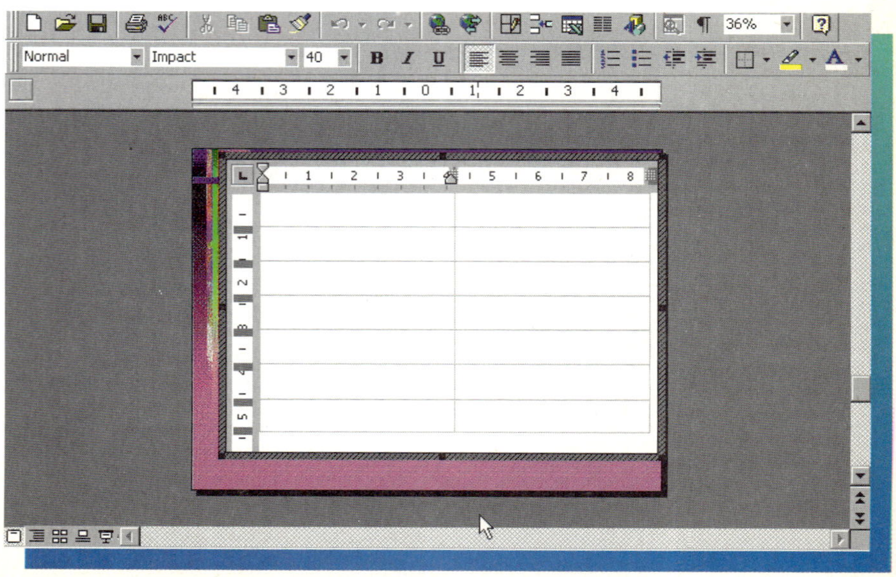

The table placeholder is enlarged so you can add text and modify the table using the menu and toolbar features. To add text, simply click in each cell and type. Use Tab to move to the next cell.

- Drag to select row 1 and set the font size to 36 for the column headings.
- Select rows 2 through 7 and set the font size to 28.
- Add the information shown below to the table (see Figure A-16).

Length of Service	Annual Vacation Days
Less than 1 year	0
1 - 3 years	5
3 - 5 years	10
5 - 10 years	15
10 - 20 years	20
Over 20 years	30

Using the Table menu or Borders and Table toolbar buttons, modify the table as follows:

- Set the Cell Height and Width to Auto (Table/Cell Height and Width/AutoFit).
- Center the text in all columns.
- Change the font color of the table heading to bright green and all other cells to white.
- Click outside the table window to return to the slide and adjust the size and placement of the table.

Your screen should be similar to Figure A-16.

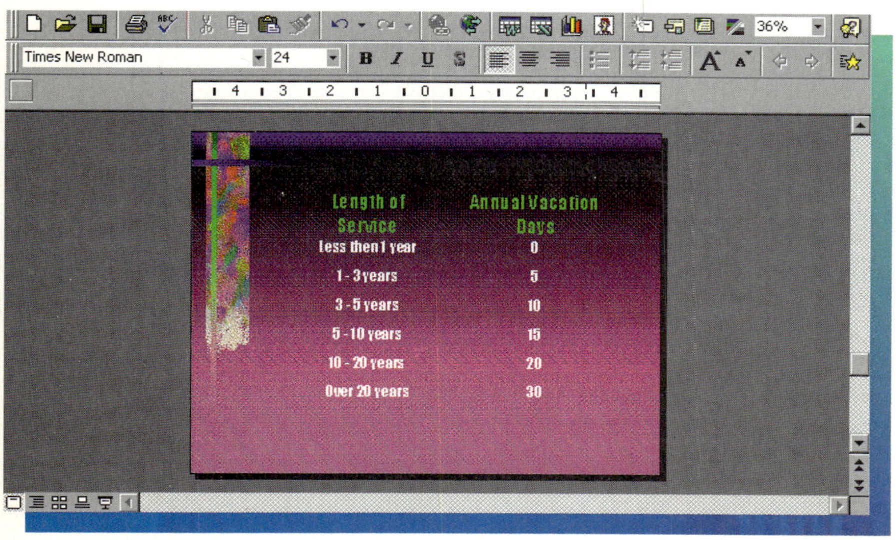

FIGURE A-16

- Save the presentation as New Employee Orientation to your data disk.

Add Hyperlinks

The next addition to the presentation you want to make is to create hyperlinks between slides in the presentation. A **hyperlink,** also called a **hypertext link** or simply a **link,** is a connection to another slide in the presentation, to another presentation, to a Word document, or to an address on the Internet. Clicking on a link quickly displays the location associated with the requested link. You can create a hyperlink from any text or object, including a shape, table, or picture within a presentation. When you use a hyperlink within a presentation, you might want to consider creating a return hyperlink so you can quickly return to the original slide.

First you will create a hyperlink from the Agenda slide to the Company Background slide and then back to the Agenda slide.

- Move to slide 3.
- Highlight the "Company Background" text.
- Click Insert Hyperlink.
- Click Browse... next to the Named Location in File text box.
- Select "4. Company Background" from the Hyperlink to Slide dialog box.
- Click OK.
- Click OK.

The menu equivalent is Insert/Hyperlink and the keyboard shortcut is [Ctrl]+K.

Your screen should be similar to Figure A-17.

FIGURE A-17

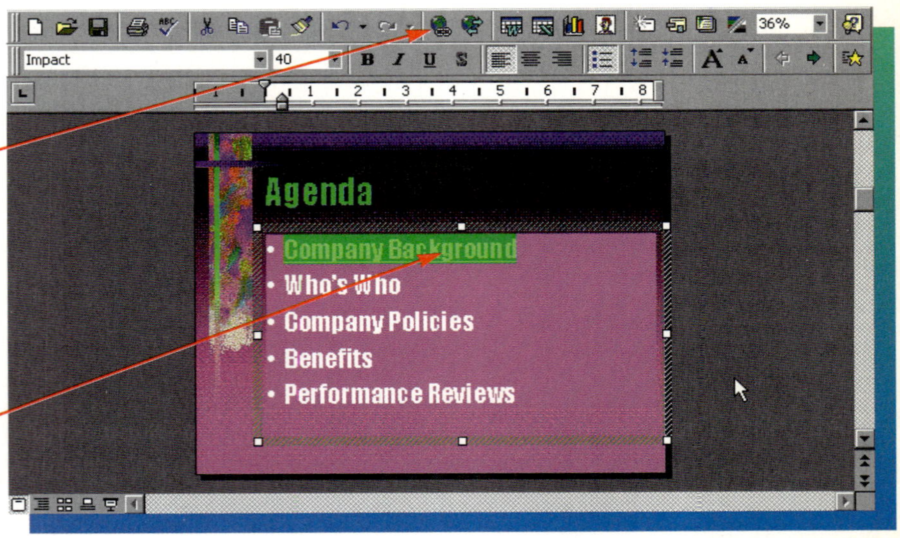

inserts hyperlink

hyperlink

The hyperlink text appears underlined and in a color that coordinates with the color scheme you are using. To see how the hyperlink works,

- Run the slide show from the current slide.
- Click the Company Background hyperlink.

The Company Background slide is displayed. Next you will create a hyperlink back to the Agenda slide. You will add an action button to the slide and associate the hyperlink with the button.

- Display slide 4 in Slide view.
- Click AutoShapes on the Drawing toolbar and select Action Buttons.
- Click Return.
- Drag to create the button shape on the bottom right corner of the slide.

The Action Settings dialog box on your screen should be similar to Figure A-18.

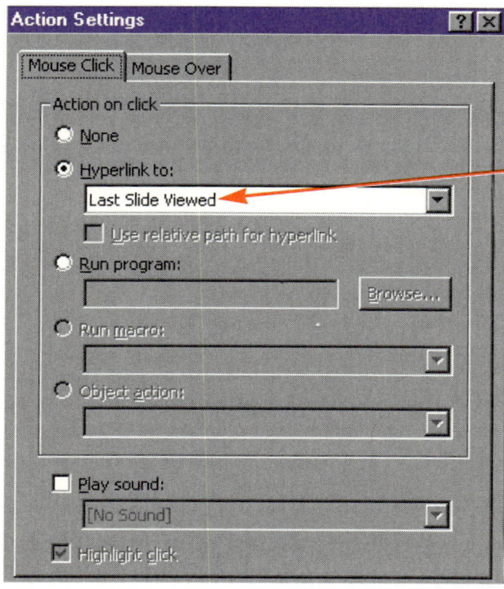

FIGURE A-18

The tabs in this dialog box allow you to associate two actions with the object: clicking the hyperlink or holding the mouse over it to activate it. You can also set a hyperlink to play a sound when the mouse moves over an object and then click the object to jump to another slide. When you set up a hyperlink, it's best to select the mouse-click method. If you select the mouse-over method, it's possible to jump when you really don't want to.

Your next step is to a ssociate the action that you want to occur with the button. In this case, you want to create a hyperlink to another slide in the presentation.

The menu equivalent is Slide Show/Action Buttons.

- From the Hyperlink To drop down list, select Slide.
- From the Hyperlink to Slide dialog box, select 3. Agenda.
- Click OK.
- Click OK.
- If the action button does not display, click Fill Color and select Automatic.

Your screen should be similar to Figure A-19.

FIGURE A-19

To see how the hyperlink works,

- Run the slide show from the current slide.
- Click the Action button.

The Agenda slide is displayed.

You can use copy and paste to quickly copy the Action button from slide 4 to the other slides.

- Return to Slide view and create hyperlinks on the Agenda slide to slides 6, 8, 9, and 11 and add Action button hyperlinks on each of these slides back to the Agenda slide.
- Run the slide show again to test your hyperlinks.

Set Automatic Slide Timing

Use Slide Show/Rehearse Timings to access the rehearsal feature.

In addition to manually moving through a slide show, you can set the length of time a slide appears on the screen. To do this, you can set a time manually for each slide, and then run the slide show and view the timings you set. Another way is to use the rehearsal feature, where you can record timings automatically as you rehearse. You can also adjust the timings you've already set and then rehearse the new ones.

First you will add a transition to all slides. Then you will manually set a length of time to display the first 3 slides.

- Switch to Slide Sorter view and make slide 1 active.
- Click Slide Transition in the Slide Sorter toolbar.
- Apply the Random Transition effect to all slides.
- Select slides 1, 2, and 3.
- Click Slide Transition in the Slide Sorter toolbar.
- In the Advance box, clear the On Mouse Click option and select the Automatically After option.

- Set the time to 5 seconds.
- Click Apply.

Your screen should be similar to Figure A-20.

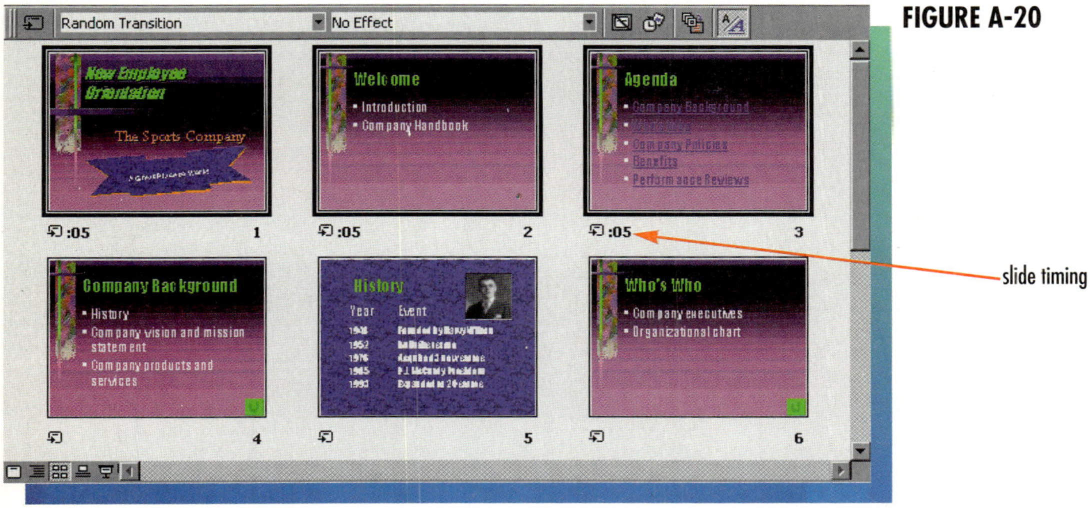

FIGURE A-20

- Run the slide show again to see how the timings work (remember to wait 5 seconds to allow the first 3 slides to advance automatically).

Electronically Incorporate Meeting Feedback

While you are running a presentation, you can take minutes, record action items, and add to notes pages using the Meeting Minder. You want to practice using this feature so you are comfortable using it during the real presentation. You will create a meeting note recording the date of the presentation and an action item to remind yourself to invite the Vice President of Personnel to attend the next new employee orientation.

- Run the slide show from the beginning.
- Right-click on the first slide and from the Shortcut menu select Meeting Minder.
- In the Meeting Minutes text box type **September orientation meeting.**
- In the Action Items tab, type **Invite VP Personnel** in the Description text box.
- Type **your last name** in the Assigned To text box.

The Meeting Minder dialog box on your screen should be similar to Figure A-21.

FIGURE A-21

If you click on the slide you can continue running the presentation and the Meeting Minder dialog box remains open and ready for you to continue to record notes.

- Click Add.
- Click OK.
- End the slide show and make slide 13 active in Slide Sorter view.

Action items appear on a new slide at the end of your slide show. You can also post the action items to Microsoft Outlook, or you can transfer the minutes and action items to a new Word document and then print that document.

- Choose Tools/Meeting Minder.
- Click Export....
- Select Send meeting minutes and action items to Microsoft Word.
- Click Export Now.

Your screen should be similar to Figure A-22.

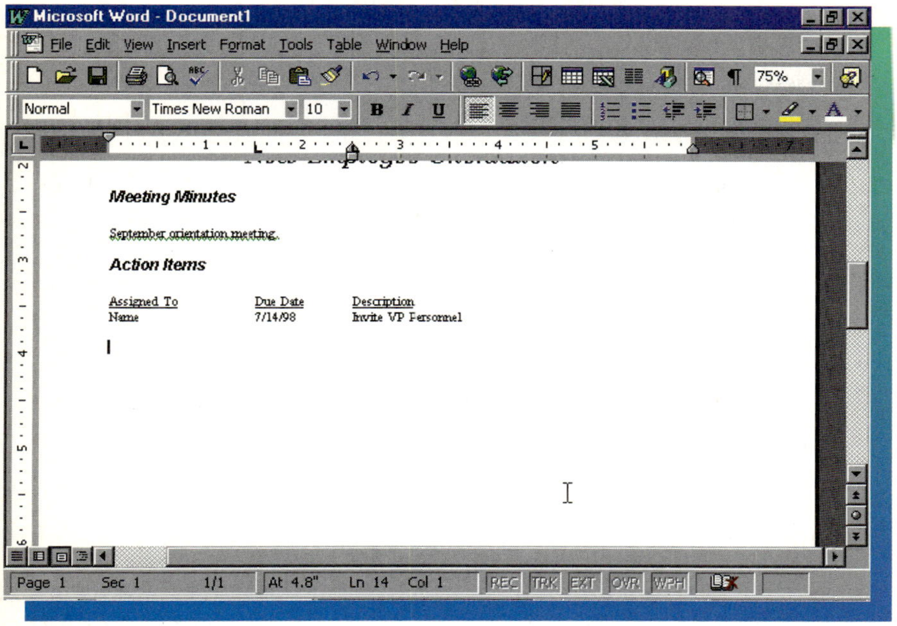

FIGURE A-22

Word opens and the text from the meeting minutes and action items is entered into a new document.

- Print the document.
- Exit Word without saving the document.
- Since you do not want slide 13 to be part of the final presentation, delete the slide.

Export to Overhead and 35mm Slides

As mentioned in Lab 1, you can also create a presentation for use with other types of output, such as overhead transparencies and 35mm slides. When planning a presentation it is always a good idea to choose the correct format for your presentation before you begin creating slides. Otherwise, slide layouts you create may not work with the output you plan to use. This is because the format settings you choose set the frame size for your slides. You want to see how your presentation would look if it were formatted for 35mm slides.

- If necessary, switch to Slide Sorter view.
- Choose File/Page Setup/Slides sized for/35mm Slides.

The Page Setup dialog box should be similar to Figure A-23.

FIGURE A-23

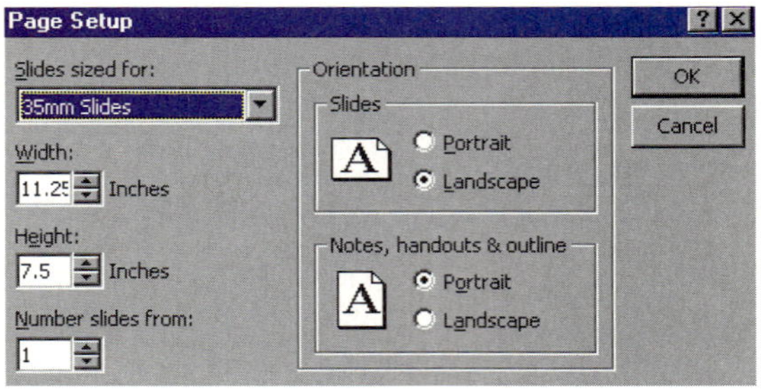

The height and width settings automatically change to reflect the size needed for 35mm slides. To see how this change effects your slides,

- Click OK.

Each slide is reformatted to the new size needed for 35mm slides. If you were to actually have 35mm slides made, you would check the slides to make sure all the information is fully displayed. In addition, you would remove the action buttons and the hypertext links from the slides. Finally, when your presentation is complete you can contact a service bureau that can make 35mm slides from the PowerPoint file. PowerPoint includes access to Genigraphics, a service bureau that can be used to prepare slides and other media from PowerPoint files. If you have installed the Genigraphics wizard, it can be used to help you prepare an electronic order and automatically transmit your file and order to Genigraphics for processing. To see how this feature works,

- Choose File/Send To/Genigraphics.
- Read the information in each step of the Genigraphics Wizard, clicking Next > to move through the steps. Click Cancel when the Shipping Instructions screen appears.
- When you are done, return the format of the presentation to On-screen Show.

If the Genigraphics Wizard is not installed on your system this command will not be available.

Present with Presentation Conferencing

Over a network or the Internet you can make a presentation to participants in different locations at the same time using the Presentation Conference Wizard. If you are preparing a presentation for use with Presentation Conference the following elements of a presentation cannot be viewed or heard by the audience:

- Multimedia objects such as sound or video clips except sound effects applied to transitions and animations if the audience's computers have the necessary hardware.
- Embedded objects, such as a chart from Microsoft Excel.
- Editing of linked or embedded objects.

Before using presentation conference, set up a conference call to exchange information such as the names of computers on which the audience will view the presentation or, if using the Internet, the address of the presentation. Then, both the presenter and participants use the Presentation Conference Wizard to guide them through the setup process.

Although you cannot actually run a presentation conference, you will use the Presentation Conference Wizard to see what questions are asked and what information you would need to provide before giving a presentation conference.

- Choose Tools/Presentation Conference.

The Presentation Conference Wizard dialog box on your screen should be similar to Figure A-24.

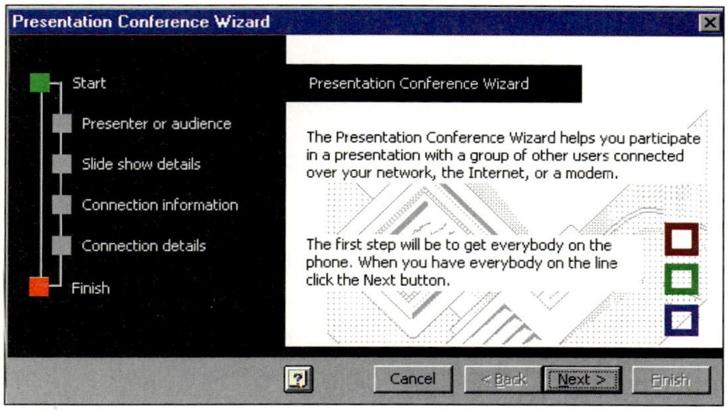

FIGURE A-24

- Read the information in each step of the Presentation Conference Wizard, clicking Next > to move through the steps.
- Click Cancel to end the wizard at the last step.

If you were actually a participant in a presentation conference you would need to click Finish before the presenter does, or you won't be connected. When the conference begins, the presentation appears on the screen.

As the presenter, you have access to all the tools that can normally be used to control a slide show such as the Slide Navigator and Slide Meter. You can also use the Meeting Minder without it appearing on the participants' computers. All conference participants can use the annotation pen to write and draw on the slides.

Save for Use on the Internet

If you want to publish a presentation on the Web, PowerPoint provides several online templates that help you design your presentation for online viewing. You can also save any existing presentation in HTML format for viewing on the Web. You would like to see how the New Employee Orientation presentation would look if it were converted for use on the Web.

- Choose File/Save as HTML.

The Save As HTML Wizard dialog box on your screen should be similar to Figure A-25.

FIGURE A-25

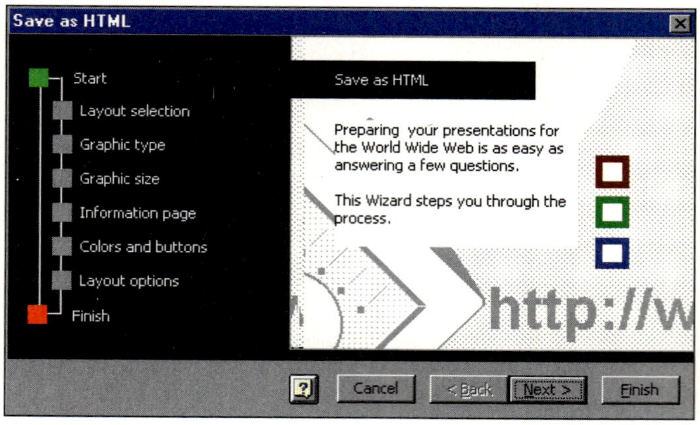

- Read the instructions in the Save As HTML Wizard clicking Next > to move through the Wizard accepting the defaults for all options. When asked to save the file, specify your data disk as the location. When asked if you want to save the final settings, select Don't Save.

The presentation was quickly converted into a series of linked Web pages. To view the presentation on the Web you would need to open a browser program such as Netscape Navigator or Internet Explorer. If you have access to a browser complete the following steps.

- Click to open the Web toolbar.
- In the address text box, enter **a:\Employee Orientation\sld001.htm**

You could also open your browser program and type the file name in the location text box.

Your browser program is opened and the first page of the presentation is displayed in the window.

- Click the Forward button to move through the presentation.
- When you are done, close your browser program.
- Close the Web toolbar.

Save for Use on Another Computer

Often you may give a presentation in another location using a computer at that location. To make it easy to take your presentation with you, PowerPoint includes the Pack and Go Wizard. This wizard is used to compress and save a presentation across multiple disks. It also includes all linked documents and multimedia files that are used in the presentation. If the computer you will be using does not have PowerPoint installed, it also packages the PowerPoint Viewer on the disk. To see how the Pack and Go Wizard works, you will use it to copy the New Employee Orientation presentation.

- Choose File/Pack and Go.
- Follow the instructions in the Pack and Go Wizard. Do not include the viewer.

The files are compressed and saved to a file with a PPZ file extension. When you are ready to use the PowerPoint file on the other machine, you need to unpack the file first by running the Pngsetup.exe file that was created by the Pack and Go Wizard. You will also need to specify the location on the computer where you want to copy the presentation to.

Export an Outline to Word

Now that the text and organization of the New Employee Orientation presentation is nearly complete, you want to copy it to Word. You can then provide the speakers in the presentation with the outline to use as a guide to create the content of the additional support slides to include in the presentation.

- Choose File/Send To/Microsoft Word.

From the Write-Up dialog box you select the layout you want the presentation to appear in Word. The options allow you to position existing notes next to or below the slides, to include blank lines for additional notes, or to export just an outline of the presentation text without slide images. To export the outline only,

- Choose Outline Only.
- Click OK.

Your screen should be similar to Figure A-26.

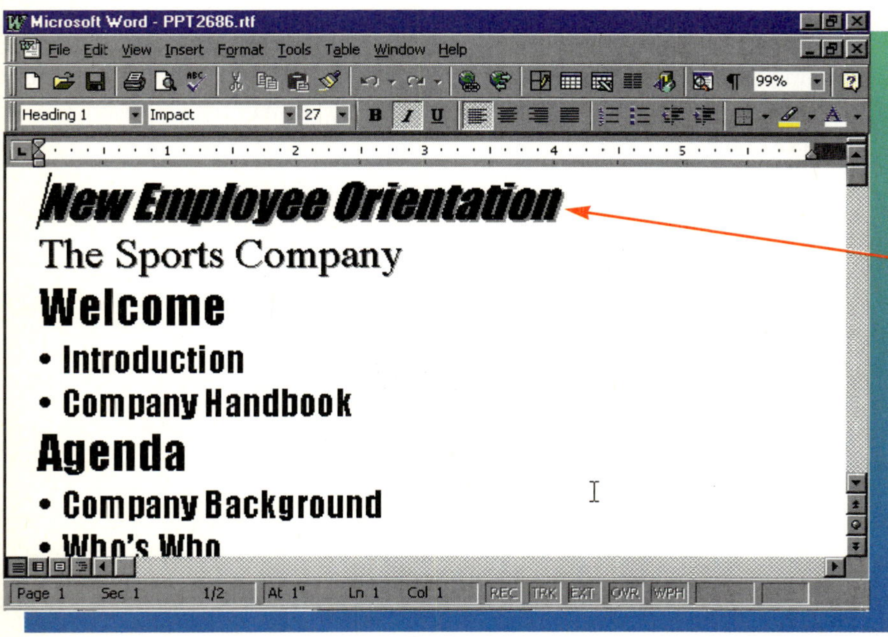

FIGURE A-26

presentation outline exported to Word document

Word is opened and a copy of the outline is exported from PowerPoint and imported into Word as a new document with a temporary file name.

- Save the outline as Orientation Outline with a Word document file type (.doc) to your data disk.
- Print the document.
- Close Word.
- Print handouts (3 slides per page) of the New Employee Orientation presentation.
- Close the presentation.
- Exit PowerPoint.

Key Terms

Hyperlink
Hypertext link
Link
Tab stop

Practice Exercises

★

1. Open the Job Outlook presentation you created in problem 4 of Lab 1. You are planning to write an article for a company newsletter and would like to use the presentation as an outline. Export the presentation to Word. Save the document as Job Outline. Print the outline.

★★

2. To complete this problem you must have completed problem 3 of Lab 2. Now that construction of the swimming pools is almost complete you would like to create a new presentation to honor the staff and fundraisers. Open the Pool Outline.doc file in PowerPoint and apply the slide design from the New Pool Project presentation. Insert the first and last slide from the New Pool Project presentation into the new presentation. Use Find and Replace to change "Expanded" to "Increasing" in the presentation. Create hyperlinks to the slides on the Presentation Overview slide and Action buttons back to the Overview slide. Save the new presentation as Thank you Presentation. Print the slides six per page.

☆☆

3. Open the Back-Road Biking 2 presentation you created in problem 2 of Lab 2. Add the Mountain.jpg picture to slide 2. Use the picture toolbar to modify the picture as necessary. Add a new slide after slide 9. Apply the Table slide layout. Enter the slide title "Attendance Projections." Create a table that contains the following:

Event	Maximum Capacity	Pre-registered
Day tours	50	35
Overnight trips	120	25
Races	300	175

Center the data in the capacity and pre-registered cells. Add a Callouts AutoShapes object of your choice to the Real Life Adventure slide (7). Add the text "Did you hear the one about" to the object. Appropriately size and color the object and text. Use the Rotate Object button to change where the callout points. Print slides 1, 2, 4, 7, and 10 as six per page. Save the presentation to your data disk.

☆☆☆

4. Open the Cruise Promotion 2 presentation you created in problem 5 of Lab 2. You would like to modify the presentation to be given to new sales associates. Delete slide 4. Insert a new slide after slide 3 and apply the organizational chart layout. Add appropriate text to the organizational chart and include your name as one of the vice presidents. Apply a custom background to the organizational chart slide to make it unique. Add a new slide after slide 6 and apply the title slide layout. Create an end-of-presentation slide on the new slide. Add a drawing object of your choice to the slide. Use the features you learned to change the color, size and shape of the object. Use Pack and Go to compress the presentation for use on another machine. On a separate disk, save the presentation for Internet use and preview the presentation in you Internet browser. Print the slides six per page. Save the presentation as Cruise Associates.

☆☆☆

5. Create an outline in Word for a presentation you plan on giving. Import the outline into PowerPoint. Apply the slide design from the Market Analysis Presentation to the outline. Add a sound transition to the second slide to draw the audience's attention. Insert a new slide where appropriate and create a table of data using custom set tabs. Use Meeting Minder to remind yourself of the things you need to do before the presentation. Practice your presentation with Rehearsal timings. Run the presentation and adjust the timings as necessary. Enhance the presentation as necessary and print the slides six per page.